Encyclopedia of

AMERICAN SOCIAL HISTORY

Encyclopedia of

AMERICAN SOCIAL HISTORY

MARY KUPIEC CAYTON
ELLIOTT J. GORN
PETER W. WILLIAMS

EDITORS

Volume I

CHARLES SCRIBNER'S SONS / NEW YORK
MAXWELL MACMILLAN CANADA/TORONTO
MAXWELL MACMILLAN INTERNATIONAL/NEW YORK OXFORD SINGAPORE SYDNEY

Library of Congress Cataloging-in-Publication Data

Encyclopedia of American social history / Mary Kupiec Cayton, Elliott J. Gorn and Peter W. Williams, editors.
p. cm.—
Includes bibliographical references and index.
ISBN 0–684–19246–2
1. United States—Social conditions—Encyclopedias. 2. United States—Social life and customs—Encyclopedias. 3. Social history—Encyclopedias. I. Cayton, Mary Kupiec. II. Gorn, Elliott J., 1951– III. Williams, Peter W. IV. Series.
HN57.E58 1992 92-10577
301′.0973—dc20 CIP
ISBN 0-684-19246-2 Set
ISBN 0-684-19455-4 Volume 1
ISBN 0-684-19456-2 Volume 2
ISBN 0-684-19457-0 Volume 3

Published simultaneously in Canada
by Maxwell Macmillan Canada, Inc.

2 3 4 5 6 7 8 9 10

Printed in the United States of America.

The paper in this book meets the guidelines for permanence and
durability of the Committee on Production Guidelines for Book Longevity
of the Council on Library Resources.

EDITORIAL STAFF

Managing Editor
John Fitzpatrick

Assistant Managing Editor
Richard Fumosa

Copy Editors, Researchers, Bibliographers

Jonathan G. Aretakis   Ted Byfield   Stephen Wagley
Elizabeth I. Wilson

Lesley Ann Beneke   Christopher J. Duffy   Jerilyn Famighetti   David R. Hall
Candace Lyle Hogan   Robert Legault   John E. Little   Leland S. Lowther

Proofreaders
Carol Holmes   Adrian Saich

Editorial Assistants
Jennifer Jenkins   Ann B. Toback

Cartography
Deasy GeoGraphics

Picture Research
Barbara Schultz   Wendy Wills

Index
Astor Indexers

Manufacturing

Terri Dieli, *Director*

Blake Logan, *Designer*
Benjamin Barros, *Production Assistant*

Publisher
Karen Day

CONTENTS

Volume I

CONTENTS

CONTENTS

CONTENTS

CONTENTS

CONTENTS

Volume III

CONTENTS

CONTENTS

CONTENTS

PREFACE

The Encyclopedia of American Social History, the sixth entry in the Scribner American Civilization Series, includes essays on the major issues that have dominated historical writing during the past generation. Social history has been variously defined: as history "from the bottom up"; as the history of everyday life; or, as the history of groups and the power relationships between them. History from the bottom up immediately brings to mind images of the working class, black slaves, the poor. The history of everyday life chronicles change over time in the fabric of ordinary existence—sometimes minute and subtle, occasionally rapid and momentous. Family and the home, labor and the workplace, popular thought and recreation are among its subjects. Concerning the interaction between groups, social history prods us to ask questions about the identities that unite and divide us according to such overlapping categories as gender, race, ethnicity, religion, social class, and sexual and political orientation. Social historians explore the relationships between diverse groups, but they also examine how people develop the cultures and ideologies that bind them together or set them at odds.

In 1960 this *Encyclopedia* would have been inconceivable. The term "social history" was not unknown at that time, nor were many of the topics it subsumes unstudied. Beginning in the 1960s, however, American historians started to focus less of their attention on battles, presidential administrations, and treaties, and more on ethnic groups, women, working people, and the relationships of those groups to the American social structure. For the past generation, social history has been the predominant form of historical discourse. Even those who study topics beyond social history proper—politics, economics, diplomacy, religion, thought—have been deeply affected by the relationships between social structures and their particular subject matter.

An academic revolution does not take place in a vacuum; social history has its own social history. Before the current generation of scholars, an avant-garde wrote a more socially based history than was common in the profession. During the Great Depression, Progressive historians like Charles Beard and Carl Becker sought the popular origins of American democracy. In the 1950s, "consensus" historians like Richard Hofstadter and Oscar Handlin wrote of mass movements such as populism and grand dramas like the immigration of millions of people to these shores. Scholars in other countries also offered models for American historians. For decades the French *Annales* school had explored relationships between economy, social structure, and worldview. English Marxist historians wrote of the creation of modern class structure and of the rise of the working class as an active agent in history. The Italian scholar Antonio Gramsci described with great sophistication the relationship between ruling elites and those whom they proposed to lead.

In the 1960s, even as a generation of graduate students was discovering these earlier scholars, social movements of monumental force dominated the news, starting with the civil rights struggles that had begun in the Deep South during the previous decade. The college youth throughout the country who joined the masses of black protesters helped win some important victories. Many then turned their energies toward other causes, most particularly the war in Southeast Asia in which the United States was becoming more deeply mired. Meanwhile, historians, once predominantly white males of northwestern European stock, now exhibited a growing diversity of social backgrounds. Universities expanded rapidly beginning in the late 1950s, partly in response to the perceived Soviet threat as dramatized by the launching of *Sputnik* in 1957, and even more in response to the needs of a growing technocratic economy. More than ever, people from middle- and even working-class backgrounds found themselves enrolled in college. *Their* American heritage was likely to be a struggle to hold onto a midwestern farm, or the fear of the small businessman before an engulfing corporation, or the efforts of trade unionists to organize their fellow workers. Some of those students stayed in school, took advanced degrees, and entered the professoriat. The new cohort was more diverse than the previous ones. Through the eyes of women, blacks, Jews, Asian Americans, Italian Americans and others, the nation's history took on a different cast.

The impact of this transformation was not simply a pluralization of the ranks of the profession but also a new questioning about the aims and assumptions of the historical enterprise. For example, the rise of gay and lesbian consciousness coincided with various poststructuralist currents of contemporary European thought; together they spurred many historians to confront the notion that sexuality as we know it is not inexorably given. But if people construct their own social reality—including a whole range of historical attitudes toward sexuality—it followed that the basic premises as to what should and should not be taken for granted about society came in for some fundamental challenges.

The essays that constitute this *Encyclopedia* attempt to capture the results of the generation-long paradigm shift that has led to a radical rethinking of the historian's craft. Since social history is still highly effervescent—debates rage, methods come and go, issues have brief lives—we have attempted to make the most of this creative flux by drawing boundaries as broadly as possible. Thus we have chosen to err on the side of inclusiveness in our choice of topics. Other editors might have emphasized different areas of social history, or they might have produced a different arrangement of topics. A few essays we had hoped to include simply never came in from the authors commissioned to write them. For any given topic, no two historians would have produced the same essay; history is interpretive. These essays offer not *the* solutions to historical questions, but stimulating, thoughtful, contingent answers. Indeed, while most of the writers here are professional historians, we have sometimes turned to scholars from such disciplines as American studies, ethnology, geography, literature, religion, anthropology, and sociology in order to enlarge the perspective. The authors had considerable leeway in defining their subjects; we have sought interpretive essays, not mechanical coverage of subjects.

Critics often remark that social historians dissipate their creative energies into narrow and fragmented topics, that they produce a series of disjointed case studies, that social history offers no synthesis. This is partly true. There can be no single governing narrative—the peopling of a continent, the spread of democracy, the rise of technological progress—for a nation with such a diversity of groups and struggles. But if there is no one grand narrative line, there are common themes in American social history, and it has been our goal to begin the work of synthesis, to invite authors to draw together the scholarship of their specializations.

The *Encyclopedia*'s first section consists of thirteen lengthy essays, each dealing with a distinct period in the development of American society. The boundaries of these periods are defined, in part by conventional criteria such as major wars, but particularly by changes in fundamental social arrangements. This unit may be read straight through as a self-contained chronological survey, or in conjunction with other essays focusing on matters especially relevant to that particular epoch.

The second major division will be of particular interest to professional historians. Its essays deal with theoretical and methodological issues in the study of social history, such as the roles of Marxism, feminism, and racial ideology in influencing social historical thought; interpretive concepts, such as modernizations and *mentalité*; methods of data collection, such as oral history; and influences from other parts of the world (particularly modern Europe) and other disciplines, such as anthropology and geography. The third section is also somewhat theoretically oriented, and deals with the construction of social identity through such contributing factors as race, ethnicity, social class, gender, sexual orientation, religion, and region.

PREFACE

The fourth cluster of essays concerns the large-scale forces that have shaped American society, such as industrialization, urbanization, and the market revolution. There follow two sections providing synoptic overviews of American society from complementary perspectives: ethnicity and region. The complexity of regional structure and the almost endless multiplicity of ethnic groups in this country make it impossible to cover every conceivable place and type of person; the collective results, however, provide a broad overview of the role of each dimension in American social life. The geographical motif continues in the following section, which deals with types of physical space (for example, farms, small towns, cities, and suburbs) and their impact on social life and structure.

The next units begin to shift the focus toward the ways in which groups of people lead their lives. Section VIII considers patterns of everyday life, centering on topics such as food, clothing, and housing. It is followed by a collection of articles dealing with work and labor, divided according to historical period, types of work, and groups of those who have performed the work. Work then yields to leisure, with a lengthy collection of essays on a wide variety of aspects of recreation and popular culture. The growing importance of leisure in American life has in recent years been met with increasing scholarly interest in the history of popular culture.

Section XI continues to consider aspects of social life, here arranged according to the phases of the life cycle, with a stress on age and gender. It is followed by a section on social deviance and social control. Here we include essays concerned with problematic categories of behavior (such as crime, alcoholism, and prostitution); with their causes; with organized efforts to suppress or reform them; and with the social history of institutions designed to maintain order in various forms, such as urban police forces and the military. The next section considers the impact of science and technology on American life and includes several articles on health and its maintenance. Finally, the concluding group of essays looks at the institutions and classes of people dedicated to the promotion of education and "culture," the latter term here used in its narrower sense of "elite" or "highbrow" culture as opposed to the popular cultural forms dealt with earlier.

We would like to acknowledge at least some of the many people—contributors, scholars, and support staff—who helped make this work possible. Karen Day, the publisher of Charles Scribner's Sons, has been an enthusiastic supporter from the very beginning; the entire enterprise would never have materialized without her efforts on its behalf. John Fitzpatrick served as managing editor for the duration and, with the aid of Ann Toback and Richard Fumosa, patiently helped to unravel endless snags and delays. Lynn Allen, Penny Henry, and Sharon Long provided essential secretarial support throughout the project at the Miami University end of the editorial work. Other Miami colleagues—Robert Atchley, Andrew Cayton, Mary Frederickson, Jack Kirby, Richard Quay, Michael O'Brien, Carl Pletsch, and Allan Winkler prominent among them—provided a number of valuable suggestions, as did the following scholars at other institutions: Bruce Levine and Zane Miller at the University of Cincinnati; Stuart Blumin, Cornell University; Anne Butler, Utah State University; Kenneth Cmiel and Malcolm Rohrbough, University of Iowa; the late Marcus Cunliffe, George Washington University; Lynn Dumenil, Occidental College; Mary Odem, Emory University; Lewis Erenberg, Loyola University (Chicago); Judith Fryer and Kathy Peiss, University of Massachusetts at Amherst; Patricia Hill, Wesleyan University; Daniel Walker Howe, UCLA; John Larson, Purdue University; Ronald Numbers, the University of Wisconsin; Kevin Sweeney, Amherst College; and Richard Guy Wilson, the University of Virginia. Our thanks to them, the contributors, and others who in various ways helped make this eminently collaborative endeavor possible.

These volumes stand as witness to the richness and complexity with which historians today are thinking about the American past and the American peoples. The range of subjects and approaches is daunting. Yet in the end, we do no more for ourselves than historians have done for generations: we tell stories about who we are and where we have been in order to make sense of our lives. As we labor, we harbor the implicit hope that our stories about the past—partial and contingent as they are—will enrich the lives of those who come after us, who will one day tell their own stories of identity and belonging, irony and struggle. These volumes are for the rising generation; most particularly, for us as editors, they are for our children—Elizabeth and Hannah Cayton, Jade Yee-Gorn, and Dana and Jonathan Schneider.

Mary Kupiec Cayton
Elliott J. Gorn
Peter W. Williams

Part I

PERIODS OF SOCIAL CHANGE

NATIVE PEOPLES PRIOR TO EUROPEAN ARRIVAL

Olive Patricia Dickason

THE AMERINDIAN CIVILIZATION revealed to Europe by the Columbian voyages was a kaleidoscope of societies that spread throughout the Americas, each one distinct and individual, yet all more or less sharing a basic cultural pattern. These societies had evolved over thousands of years in directions quite different from those of Europe. Amerindians looked upon the universe as a complex of reciprocating forces, which in order to be kept operating smoothly called for the careful observance of rituals and taboos. These pervaded all walks of life, giving great importance to the roles of shamans, or spiritual leaders, specialists in relationships between the seen and the unseen. Humans, instead of being at the center of the universe as in Judeo-Christian belief, were seen as a part of an intermeshing whole, no single part of which dominated. In their attitude toward land, too, Amerindians differed widely from Europeans. They viewed the Earth as their mother, the resources of which were to be used for the benefit of all, including plants and animals; the European concept of exclusive private ownership of land was outside of their terms of reference. Europeans, unprepared for these and other differences, had difficulties in assessing the societies they had found. They labeled the Americas a "New World," and assumed that Amerindians were in a state of cultural infancy. It was a first impression that has persisted, even as archaeology and anthropology, with the aid of improved techniques, have slowly revealed the antiquity and complexity of Amerindian culture. The process continues, as there is still much to learn about these early peoples and their societies.

It is now established that the Americas, far from being "new," have been inhabited for at least fifteen thousand years, and perhaps for much longer. Neither does the notion that Amerindians were in their cultural infancy equate with the actual evidence for an advanced culture. When Tenochtitlán (Mexico City) fell to Hernán Cortés (1485–1547) in 1521, it had a population that has been estimated at between 250,000 and 500,000; there was no city in Europe of that size at that time. Its monumental architecture, orderliness, and cleanliness, have been well documented. Similarly, Cahokia, on the Mississippi near today's Saint Louis, Missouri, at its peak (A.D. 1050–1250) had been home to an estimated 30,000 to 40,000 people, and had covered 5 square miles (13 square kilometers), bigger than contemporaneous London. Cahokia had the largest single concentration of population north of the Rio Grande in pre-Columbian North America. Unlike Tenochtitlán, built with stone and wood, Cahokia's constructions were massive earth mounds, topped with small buildings.

LAND OF MANY TONGUES

At the time of the arrival of Europeans, Amerindians had spread throughout the length and breadth of the Americas, and had done so for about eleven thousand years, although individual sites have been dated much earlier. Entry into the Americas, believed to have been via the Bering Strait, was probably made by small groups of people, perhaps in waves—three or four are currently seen as most likely. Dense populations clustered in the Pacific coastal regions, particularly California, which not surprisingly had the greatest concentration of languages. In fact, the New World had an extraordinary richness of languages, about twenty-two hundred, almost two-thirds of which were spoken in South America. In North America, the greatest diversification was in California and on the north coast of the Gulf of Mexico. The continent's languages are usually classified into twelve major groups, although there are those who hold that they can be reduced to three: Amerind, the oldest and by far the biggest, spread over all South America and most of North America; Na-dene, in western and northwestern North America; and Eskimo-Aleut, the most recent, across the Arctic from the Pacific to the Atlantic. Cree, an Algonkian language, and Inuktitut (Eskimo-Aleut), were spoken over very large areas, while comparatively small California had a multitude of tongues (sixty-four), many of them only very remotely related to each other. If linguistic diversification can be related to length of human occupation, as some maintain, then the greatest time span for human settlement in the Americas is on the Pacific Coast and the Gulf Coast, and in Central America and South America. Languages tend to be more stable than cultures.

With so many tongues, it is not surprising that multilingualism was common in pre-Columbian America. In a few cases, one group's language could become the lingua franca of a region. In the sixteenth century, this was the case with Huron in the northern Great Lakes region; on the southern plains between the Arkansas River and the Rio Grande early in the eighteenth century, Comanche came into general usage. Trading languages appear to have been widespread; one of the best-known, Chinook, was flourishing on the Northwest Coast when Europeans arrived, and it quickly incorporated English and French words. On the East Coast during the sixteenth century, Amerindians were reported to be speaking Basque, picked up from the whalers who had come to exploit the whale runs of the Strait of Belle Isle. In the western interior sign language was very popular, and in some meetings important matters were discussed without a word being spoken.

HUNTER-FARMERS

Despite the popular image of Amerindians as being essentially hunters, the fact remains that apart from such regions as the Arctic, subarctic, high plains, and some seacoasts, most of the people combined hunting with farming, even in North America. Amerindians began to experiment with domesticating plants about nine thousand years ago, in Central and South America; around seven thousand years ago corn (*Zea mays*) was being cultivated in the Teotihuacán Valley of central Mexico, and its use would eventually spread both north and south to the limits of agriculture. It is believed that corn, one of the world's most efficient crops in terms of yield, needed at least a thousand years of selective breeding to be developed into the many varieties being grown when Europeans arrived, an achievement that has been classed as one of the world's greatest in plant science. Along with potatoes (*Solanum tuberosum*), a Peruvian domesticate, corn is one of the world's four basic food crops today (the other two are wheat [*Triticum vulgare*] and rice [*Oryza sativa*]). In sixteenth-century North America, agriculture was practiced on a regular basis as far north as Maine; in the interior, it had reached Lake Huron, and sporadically beyond. The French missionary Gabriel Sagard, who was in Huronia in 1623, reported that "it was easier to get lost in a cornfield than in a forest." More than one hundred of the crops routinely grown today were developed by Amerindians.

Although sedentary settlements are associated with the rise of agriculture, that was not always the case in the Americas. Archaeology has revealed permanent villages dating to thirteen thousand years ago, long before the domestication of plants; and even afterward, stable communities in rich environments had little or no incentive to take up farming. This was the situation along the Northwest Coast; another well-known example is Koster, in the Upper Mississippi region, which developed into a permanent community about 4000 B.C. and never needed to take up farming as a principal subsistence base. The rich resources of the Ohio Valley supported the Adena culture (ca. 600 B.C.–100 B.C.) and the subsequent Hopewell (ca. 300 B.C.–A.D. 400) with little, if any, assistance from agriculture. These chiefdoms left a legacy of carefully constructed mounds that can still be seen. Their influence spread northward to the Saint Lawrence River, reaching the Canadian Maritimes in the east and Alberta in the west. On the Northwest Coast, nonagricultural sedentary chiefdoms were flourishing at the time of European contact, made possible by the bounty of the sea, but with some help from the land. However, for the development of the social and economic complexities necessary for the rise of cities and city-states, a more bountiful and secure food base was needed, and this was provided by agriculture. In the Americas, agriculture developed in association with hunting.

The combination of farming and hunting arose from the fact that there were few animals in the American wild that could be domesticated as livestock. The Peruvians had domesticated the llama and the guinea pig; the dog, however, was the most widespread domestic animal in North America, although not universally present among the tribes. In North America, the presence of dogs has been dated to 6500 B.C.; they were widely used for work (pulling sleds in the far north, hauling travois on the plains, besides being used as pack animals), as well as for ceremonial food. They were not much used for hunting, although on the Northwest Coast, owning hunting dogs was a privilege of the higher classes among such people as the Tsimshian; in the Great Basin, dogs were used for mountain sheep drives. Also on the West Coast, a breed of dog with white woolly hair was raised to provide fibers for weaving. A variety of fowl and birds, including turkeys, were kept for their eggs, meat, and feathers, as the case might be. The people of the Northwest, as well as the Maya, practiced fish farming. In other words, Amerindians domesticated the animals and birds that were available for a variety of uses.

In general, plants, whether domesticated or wild, provided the principal basis for subsistence, with some regional exceptions, such as the Inuit in the Arctic, the bison hunters of the plains, and the fishermen of the Northwest Coast. The realm of medicine was also the realm of plants; according to the Cherokee, animals brought diseases and plants provided the cures. Europeans soon had occasion to be impressed with Amerindian herbal knowledge; Cortés, for instance, relied upon Amerindian doctors for the care of his men. The Recollect missionary Chrestien Le Clercq (ca. 1641–after 1700), who worked in Acadia between 1675 and 1686, reported that Amerindians were "all by nature physicians, apothecaries, and doctors, by virtue of the knowledge and experience they have of certain herbs, which they use successfully to cure ills that seem to us incurable" (*New Relation,* p. 296). More than five hundred drugs in the medical pharmacopoeia today were originally used by Amerindians.

It is not at all clear what caused hunters and gatherers to turn to farming, particularly as the agricultural way of life, far from being easier, is physically more demanding than hunting. The process appears to have been both gradual and not in the least uniform across the Americas. Those people who relied more upon gathering than they did upon hunting may have been predisposed to experiment with domesticating plants; digging for roots can easily be seen as a precursor of tillage. The line separating the two ways of life is not well defined; nonagriculturalists such as hunters of the northwestern plains moved plant stocks from one location to another, and farming pueblos in the Southwest retained their knowledge of wild foods, so that when disasters such as drought and floods struck, they resorted to gathering what was available naturally. Hunters used fire to control the movements of game, both directly and indirectly through the modification of vegetation. Early agriculturalists also availed themselves of fire, for reasons similar to those of hunters, as well as for clearing land. By the sixteenth century, farmers of the eastern woodlands had modified their environment into a habitat particularly suitable for deer, and nonagriculturalists in California had done the same thing, and for the same reasons.

SOCIETY, TECHNOLOGY, AND TRADE

With permanent settlement, the complexities of social organization increased, and ranked societies emerged in the form of chiefdoms, some of which would become states (the Aztecs of Mexico City, for example). In North America, chiefdoms developed on the Northwest Coast and in California, along the Mississippi River and its tributaries, and in the Southeast. Although these chiefdoms varied considerably, they all shared a concern for rank based on lineage, and accorded more power to their chiefs than did mobile hunters and gatherers; chiefs were also the agents through whom the distributive economies functioned. They all developed high artistic traditions, the Californians in basketry, the northwest coasters in woodwork, the Ohioans and Mississippians in stone sculpture, shell and copperwork, the east coasters in feather work and hide painting. The Adena, Hopewell, and Mississippian chiefdoms were the only ones to produce monumental earthworks. These can still be seen in Ohio, along the Mississippi and eastward to the Atlantic coast, and to the north in some modest manifestations in Ontario.

The Stone Age technology of Amerindians resulted from an accumulated fund of knowledge and was an indicator of how they looked upon the world and their own societies. This technology was highly developed in the Americas, its products ranging from tiny, symmetrically flaked projectile points to the massive constructions of the Aztecs and Incas. The development of stone and bone tools was a tremendous stride forward into technological sophistication, and had the same basic requirements as later technologies—sharp and detailed observation of nature, backed by a social organization that allowed for freedom to experiment. In some respects, stone tools could outdo metal ones; cutting edges, for instances, could be sharper. Metal had the advantage of durability; stone was frangible, so that early tools and weapons had to be constantly replaced. Besides making heavy demands in labor and time, Stone Age technology was also material intensive: its huge structures yielded comparatively little usable space. The question is sometimes asked why the Peruvians, Mexicans, and the coastal peoples in between, did not utilize their well-developed metallurgical skills for the production of tools and weapons, instead of just for ritual and ceremonial purposes. The answer is a cultural and ideological one: in their concentration on the transcendental significance of gold, "the sweat of the sun," and silver, "the tears of the moon," they reserved this technology for the gods and, with isolated exceptions, did not apply it to mundane metals or uses.

As with human societies the world over, social development was far from being consistent in the Americas, even among peoples following a similar way of life under similar circumstances. Some hunting and gathering societies, for example, continued in their traditional ways, while others adopted aspects of agricultural cultures. This could happen even when different peoples lived near each other; for example, California villagers continued in their non-agricultural way although they were familiar with adjacent agricultural communities of the lower Colorado River valley; neither did they adopt the pottery of the latter. Pottery, as a matter of fact, was not found anywhere on the Northwest Coast. There were farming peoples who retained the Archaic mode even as some of their neighbors developed city-states and, in one or two cases, empires. The spectrum of societies in the Americas by the sixteenth century was as varied as that of languages, and greater than that of Europe at the time. Yet fundamentally they were variations on a theme; one can speak of an Amerindian civilization just as one can speak of a European one.

Trade played a major role in developing this rich diversity of cultures. There is clear archaeological evidence for extensive networks dating back at least ten thousand years; for example, large amounts of worked and unworked obsidian from Edziza, British Columbia, have been found as far east as Ohio; the quarries from which it was obtained were in use from 8000 B.C. Copper was also actively traded; a principal source was the surface deposits at the western end of Lake Superior. Cherts and flints (silicas) suitable for arrowheads and other tools were much in demand, and could travel long distances as they passed from hand to hand. Other valuable trade items were plants, prized either for ritual purposes or for their medicinal properties, or perhaps both; often they only grew in restricted regions. Peyote, a cactus native to the Southwest, and tobacco, a South American plant widely cultivated in North America, are two of the best known; both were important for rituals. Barter was the usual means for exchange, but shells and other items were used as currency in some regions. The most famous of these were the shell beads known as wampum in the Northeast; on the Northwest Coast, dentalia shells were used. Wampum was laboriously manufactured from the lining of conch and quahog shells; dentalia was gathered from the ocean bottom, a labor-intensive and slow process. In Mesoamerica, cacao beans provided the standard of value.

RISE OF CITY-STATES

The "mother" of Amerindian civilizations is known as Olmec, after the present-day inhabitants on the Tehuantepec region on the Gulf coast of Mexico, where the civilization developed. Whether or not those ancient people are related to the present-day inhabitants has not been determined; it is not even known what language they spoke. They began to build their monumental ceremonial centers about 1500 B.C. with an architectural skill and high artistry in sculpture that continues to astonish, many centuries later. The oldest evidence for recording time in the New World was found in an Olmec inscription of a Long Count date equivalent to 31 B.C.; the calendar would be perfected later by the Mayas. Lasting until about the time of Christ, although in decline before that, the Olmec civilization spread its influence far and wide, despite the fact that its center (which moved at least three times) was restricted in size and its population apparently small. Teotihuacán (A.D. 150–800, located outside of today's Mexico City), a much larger urban center with a population conservatively estimated at two hundred thousand, was affected by it, as was the Zapotec-Mixtec city of Monte Albán (400 B.C.–A.D. 900), atop a mountain in Oaxaca, and the Mayan city-states of Mesoamerica. Traces of the Olmec style are present as far south as Sechín on the Peruvian coast, and Chavín de Huantar, high in the Andes. This cultural dynamism existed independent of writing, which the Olmecs did not possess until late; a glyphic script was in use at Monte Albán several centuries earlier. Eighteen different writing systems have been identified as existing in Mesoamerica in the sixteenth century.

Following the fall of Teotihuacán, the Toltec city of Tula, north of the Valley of Mexico, came into its own. A much smaller city (population about sixty thousand), Tula gave rise to a powerful warrior class that dominated the region for about a century and a half, until they gave way to the Aztecs. The culture hero of the Toltecs had been Ce Acatl Topiltzin Quetzalcoatl, which translates as "One Reed [birth date], Our Prince of the Precious-Feathered Serpent." A supporter and patron of the arts, Topiltzin had favored peace and the abolition of human sacrifice; losing out to the militarists, he sailed toward the east with a band of followers, promising to return. This tale was incorporated by the Aztecs into their cosmology. Cortés would arrive during the calendrical year One Reed (1519), a coincidence that would cause the fatal hesitation of Moctezuma II to expel Cortés, which would cost him his life and for the Aztecs the end of their period of power.

THE AZTECS

The Nahuatl-speaking Aztecs (who called themselves Mexica) admired the superior culture of the Toltecs, and when they established their ascendancy over Tenochtitlán (Mexico City) and its environs in 1433, they did so as inheritors of the Toltec tradition they had adopted as their own. From there they began their expansion, conquering neighboring city-states and tribes and incorporating them into a loose hegemony that has been called an "empire," but which lacked the strict centralized control put into effect by the Inca in Peru. Still, by the sixteenth century, the Aztecs were the dominant nation of Mexico, without imposing either their religion or their language upon those they conquered. When the Spaniards arrived, their attention was immediately focused on the Aztec emphasis on human sacrifice for keeping the cosmos in order, particularly the sun upon which earth depended. These bloody rituals contrasted with their well-ordered society, their love of the arts and crafts, and especially of poetry and nature—"flower and song." The Aztec word for ruler translates as "he who possesses speech." Their fascination with nature was expressed in their custom of bringing plants, birds, and animals from conquered regions and installing them in Tenochtitlán's botanical gardens, which far surpassed anything comparable in Europe at that time. The garden of Huastepec was also a center for teaching medicine, to which the Spaniards would send one of their own doctors to observe and report.

SOUTHWESTERN KALEIDOSCOPE

The Southwest, geographically a northern extension of Mexico, includes Sonora, Chihuahua, Arizona, New Mexico, and parts of Texas, Utah, and Colorado. It counted four principal groups of people, three of which were hunter-farmers: the Uto-Aztecan Pima and Papago, descendants of the ancient Hohokam, irrigation farmers who had come up from Mexico about 300 B.C.; the Pueblos, (when not capitalized, pueblo means a town) descendants of the Anasazi, "ancient alien ones," dating to about A.D. 700; and the Hokan-Siouan Yuman who practiced an early form of farming on the floodplains of the Colorado River, and who lived on *rancherías* rather than in towns. Agriculture in the region long predated these arrivals, and has been traced back to about 3500 B.C. The recently arrived Navajo and Apaches were hunters and gatherers, who supplemented their bison hunting with raiding and, in some cases, farming. The Navajo and Apache were Athapaskan speakers from the far north who had started their southward migration several centuries earlier, following a volcanic eruption in Alaska; once in the Southwest, those who retained their hunting ways followed the bison herds on the plains, while those who took up agriculture moved onto lands that had been deserted by the Pueblos during the periodic droughts.

The Pueblos are best known for their multistoried dwellings, which have been described as early versions of apartment buildings. During their heyday, from 1100 to 1300, these units contained up to eight hundred rooms, and could house as many as twelve hundred individuals. They were entered through holes in the roof that were reached by ladders, apparently a protective measure, as earlier buildings had doors which were later blocked. The units were built around open plazas in which kivas, ceremonial structures, were sunk. Chaco Canyon, in northwestern New Mexico, at its height counted eight towns in the canyon and four others on nearby mesas, apparently astronomically aligned, and connected by a system of roads that reached outliers as far as 60 miles (100 kilometers) away. Most spectacular of all were the pueblos that were built into canyon cliff faces for protective purposes, such as at Mesa Verde, Colorado, or Canyon de Chelly, Arizona. These cliff-faced towns, as well as those of Chaco Canyon, had all been abandoned by the sixteenth century. The pueblos of the Rio Grande and its tributaries, as well as those to the west, were flourishing, however; Europeans would first hear about them as "the seven cities of Cibola." The largest was Acoma, high on a mesa, with a population of about three thousand; in all, there were nearly seventy, counting a total of about fifty thousand souls.

The Pueblos were autonomous, and displayed marked variation in their social structures, but shared in their religious rituals and concepts. Where the eastern Tanoan Pueblos organized their societies on the moiety system (the division of the village into two for ceremonial purposes), and did not have clans, the western Pueblos, such as Hopis and Zunis, had matrilineal clans that controlled property, such as dwellings, kivas, and ceremonial regalia, through the female line. The Keresan Pueblos were in between, both geographically and socially. They combined both types of organization, but their clans had no powers over property; instead, their concerns were for extended family matters. All the Pueblos had special-purpose associations that recruited members across the board, thus acting as integrative agents for their communities. They looked after community affairs such as rituals, maintained public order, and regulated hunts; they were also responsible for external affairs such as war and trade. Medicine societies were responsible for health matters. Keeping the whole structure in balance were the clown societies, whose members took advantage of public occasions to mercilessly caricature those who did not conform to the Pueblo ideal of modesty and cooperation, or who did not practice moderation. In the west, where water was scarce, rain-calling ceremonies were important; in the east, more exposed to outside human forces, war associations were prominent. In some of the pueblos, men did the weaving.

The Navajo and western Apache came strongly under Pueblo influence, and adopted much of their way of life; the eastern Apache clung to their traditional ways, and once they acquired the horse from the Spaniards, expanded their raiding to become the terror of the plains. Their earlier relationship with the Pueblos had been somewhat more peaceful, and an active trade had developed between some of the groups. Early accounts tell us of the "dog nomads" of the plains bringing in trains of hundreds of dogs burdened with the products of the buffalo hunt to trade for the agricultural products and crafts of the Pueblos. The Navajo and western Apache adopted matrilineal clans, and later added sheepherding to their farming. The Navajo have since become the most populous tribe of the United States.

THE SOUTHEAST

In the Southeast during the sixteenth century, Muskogean, related to Algonkian, was the dominant language group, surrounding an enclave of Iroquoian speakers among whom were the Cherokee and Tuscarora; there were also some Caddoan and Algonkian speakers. The Muskogeans, including the Chickasaws, Choctaws, Creeks, and the now-extinct Timucuans, formed an eastern outpost of the Mississippian mound builders, who had been flourishing since about A.D. 500. They practiced an agriculture centered on corn, beans, and squash, and were socially organized into chiefdoms, some based on class (Natchez), but others on rank (Creeks) acquired primarily through merit and only secondarily through inheritance. They had far-flung trade networks that included at least some of the city-states of Mexico. Underlying cultural similarities were exemplified in the layout of the towns with their central plazas, as well as in their agriculture, ritual ball games, and highly developed feather work. Societies were structured on matrilineal clans, with much attention paid to rank and privilege. Although the degree of social stratification decreased toward the north, the basic cultural pattern still prevailed, in contrast to the more diversified cultures of the Southwest. Ritual highlights were the Green Corn Festival (a major harvest ritual), and the kindling of the fires at New Year; human sacrifice was also practiced, particularly in connection with rain ceremonies.

Stable settlement in the region has been dated to 5500 B.C.; planned towns with monumental earthworks began to appear about 1400 B.C. One of these settlements in the lower Mississippi Valley in Louisiana, Poverty Point, features six rows of man-made ridges set concentrically in a partial circle 1,320 yards (1,200 meters) across. Its scale and complexity, as well as the style of the objects found there, suggests an Olmec connection, perhaps as part of a trade network. Its principal mound, however, is twice the size of the one at the Olmec site at La Venta in southern Mexico. Curiously, pottery shards, usually so abundant on this type of site, here are in short supply; what are found instead are soapstone shards. Another puzzle is the lack of evidence for agricultural activity; a construction of such scope would only have been possible with a larger assured food supply than could have been provided naturally. Poverty Point is a vivid reminder of how little is really known about pre-Columbian America.

A few centuries later, another mound-building society, Adena, appeared in Ohio showing some affinities with Poverty Point in the midst of strong differences. It still displayed a Mesoamerican connection, however, as did the whole mound builders' complex. Adena was followed by Hopewell, which spread into Illinois and western New York; last of all came the agricultural Mississippian mound builders, still flourishing when the Europeans arrived. One of their most spectacular manifestations was Cahokia, the metropolis on the upper Mississippi that was apparently largely abandoned by the middle of the fifteenth century. Thousands of mounds are the legacy of the great outpouring of activity that characterized this entire cultural phenomenon.

CENTRALIZED CHIEFDOMS

It was within this complex that chiefdoms reached their greatest centralization of power north of Mexico. In a narrow coastal strip from Louisiana to Florida, then up the Atlantic coast to Virginia, chiefs were vested with absolute authority over their people, including that of life and death. The two best-known examples of this were the Natchez of Louisiana, who were still building mounds when Europeans arrived, and the Powhatan of Virginia. The supreme chief of the Natchez was also the high priest—the Great Sun, "brother" of his heavenly counterpart; next in authority was the war chief, younger brother to the Sun, called "Tattooed Serpent." Since the Great Sun's feet were never allowed to touch the earth, he was carried about in a litter. Below this level there were three classes, the nobles, the Honored Men, and the lowest, the commoners called Stinkards. The upper echelons had to select spouses from the Stinkards; only the latter were allowed to marry within their own class. The Sun himself had to have a Sun mother and a Stinkard father. When the Great Sun died, his wives and servants were killed to serve him in the afterlife, a practice not unique to the Natchez. It is not known how the ranks of the Stinkards were replenished to meet the demands of this system, but it could have been through the absorption of peoples defeated in war.

The Algonkian matrilineal Powhatans were a rising power early in the seventeenth century, in terms of both internal centralization and external expansion. The paramount chief, who became known to the English as Powhatan although his name was Wahunsonacock, had inherited control over several towns and was in the process of adding others to the list; it is claimed that at his height of power, more than two hundred communities acknowledged his authority and paid tribute to him. His godlike status meant that his least frown caused fear and trembling. As he acquired towns, so he acquired wives, as the custom was for the chief to take one from each. These wives continued to live in their own communities, to be periodically visited by the chief and his retinue. Powhatan collected tribute from his own people as well as from others, and had complete control over its redistribution. In matters relating to war, however, he shared authority with priests and counselors.

PACIFIC COAST

The only other area where chiefdoms developed in North America was on the Pacific Coast, which from Alaska to Baja California shared several cultural features, despite the region's multiplicity of languages. These included reliance upon the resources of the sea instead of upon agriculture, although tobacco was cultivated, and a ranked social order based upon wealth and heredity. From Alaska into northern California, fir and cedar were important for construction of houses and canoes; in California, acorn oaks provided an important subsistence base. Regional variations in cultural patterns emerged between three thousand and twenty-five hundred years ago.

Chiefdoms were more complex toward the north. Tlingit, Haida, Tsimshian, Kwakiutl, and Nuchahnulth (Nootka) not only clearly distinguished between chiefs, nobles, and commoners, they also graded within each class. Slaves were outside this system, usually prisoners of war, but sometimes individuals who had lost status because of debt (gambling could be a factor); one could also be born into slavery, one of the few regions in North America where this happened. Without rights, slaves could be put to death at the will of their masters. Overriding class, and even tribal distinctions, among the more northerly tribes (Tlingit, Haida,

Tsimshian in southern Alaska, northern British Columbia, and the Queen Charlotte Islands) was the division of each group into two exogamous moieties, important in the conduct of the ceremonial life. These in turn were subdivided into matrilineal clans. Further south, the Kwakiutls, Bella Coola, and Nuchahnulth did not have moieties, recognized both the male and female lines of descent, and practiced a ritual life that was dominated by secret societies. Continuing southward to the southern end of Vancouver Island, southern British Columbia, Washington, Oregon, and northern California, these characteristics were less pronounced among the Salish. They favored patrilineal descent, but were not dogmatic about it; and their chiefs did not have the power of their northern counterparts. The Salish word for chief translates best as "leader."

In the northern sector, the elaborate giveaway feasts known as potlatches could be used for various purposes, one of which was to validate claims to title or social position, and another to redistribute wealth. Wealth was measured either in material goods or in rights such as those to certain songs, dances, or rituals. Despite the emphasis on rank and wealth, a fundamental egalitarianism prevailed as far as the basic necessities of life were concerned; a village's hunting, fishing, and gathering territories were divided among its kinship groups, and exploited accordingly. Some fishing sites have been frequented for a very long time, such as the one at Kitselas Canyon on the Skeena River in western British Columbia, in use for at least five thousand years. It was in the north that the distinctive northwest coast art style developed, a style that is known and recognized around the world. Less dramatic, but also highly developed, was the basketry of California. The absence of pottery on the Pacific Coast is something of a puzzle.

The most important and elaborate event in the yearly cycle of the northern Californians (mainly Athapaskan speakers) centered around puberty rites for girls. Lasting for several days, they involved the whole community, as well as invited outsiders. This type of puberty ceremony was peculiar to the western part of the continent, being rare or nonexistent in the east. The Salish also had similar ceremonies, but on a lesser scale; the only other people to mark such an event with their most important ritual of the year were the Athapaskan Apaches of the Southwest. Since the ceremonies in all three areas have a number of similarities, they appear to have had a single origin. The Athapaskans of the boreal forest, however, do not have such ceremonies. Among them, girls at puberty go into seclusion.

Among the more southern Californians, social organization was simplified and consisted mainly of patrilineal extended families. They had a much simpler life-style than the peoples to the north, despite the fact that they lived in an equally fertile environment, with a much more agreeable climate, and had one of the continent's densest populations. Instead of the multifamily plank houses of the north, they lived in small domed, thatched houses or perhaps in bark-covered tepees, and assigned hunting and gathering territories on an individual basis, an unusual feature among Amerindians.

NORTHEASTERN WOODLANDS

Other sedentary peoples were the Iroquoians, such as the Huron and Five Nations (later Six Nations, usually referred to simply as Iroquois) of the Saint Lawrence and Great Lakes region, who became among the best-known of northeastern aboriginal societies. They were all farmer-hunters, practiced slash-and-burn agriculture, and lived in longhouses clustered in palisaded villages that counted up to fifteen hundred inhabitants, and occasionally even more. Villages were moved to new sites when local resources, such as land and firewood, became exhausted, which could happen in anywhere from ten to fifty years. For these people, the fourteenth into the fifteenth centuries was a period of population growth during which some villages expanded and others disappeared, and the "three sisters"—corn, beans, and squash—rose to dominate the regional agricultural scene. Although the Iroquois had earlier experienced intrusions from the burial-mound peoples to the south, their cultures appear to have been indigenous developments, even as they adopted and absorbed traits from others. The southern Iroquoians, such as the Cherokee and Tuscarora, were culturally closer to the southeastern Amerindians than they were to their northern cousins.

Sometime during the sixteenth century, or perhaps earlier, groups of Iroquoians organized into confederacies that were to have powerful impacts on regional politics. These were the League of the Hode'nosaunee (People of the Longhouse), as the Five Nations called themselves, and the League of the Wendat (Islanders or People of the Peninsula), which was the Huron name for themselves. Actually, the term "Wendat" referred not just to the

Huron, but to their confederacy. The Five Nations, situated in the Finger Lakes region south of Lake Ontario, consisted of the Mohawk, Oneida, Onondaga, Cayuga, and Seneca, each speaking its own distinct language. The "Great League of Peace" was governed by a council of fifty sachems, representing the member tribes, but not equally divided among them. Despite this disparity, each tribe had only one vote. The council operated on the principle of consensus; however, centralization was by no means complete, and member tribes maintained a considerable degree of autonomy, especially in internal tribal affairs. Rather than being an overriding authority, the council was a "jural community" charged with maintaining the peace through ceremonial words of condolence and ritual gifts of exchange. The founding of the league has been linked with an eclipse of the sun which was seen in the Finger Lakes region in 1451.

The Wendat, concentrated between Lake Simcoe and the southeastern corner of Georgian Bay, consisted of four nations, with a possible fifth, and was concerned with trade rather than with war and peace. Situated as it was at a crossroads in the trading networks that crisscrossed North America, the confederation at the end of the sixteenth century dominated the region in both trade and politics. More populous, wealthier, and more powerful than the Five Nations, the League of the Wendat held them in check by a system of alliances that extended as far south as the Susquehanna in Virginia. By far their most important ceremony was the Feast of the Dead, held whenever a village had to be relocated. Those who had not died violent deaths were removed from their temporary tombs and reburied with much ceremony and lavish offerings in a common ossuary. The bodies of others from outside the village who were connected in some way were also included; this mingling of the bones from throughout Huronia in a common grave symbolized the unity of Wendat, and encouraged the people to cooperate with each other. The confederation, still expanding when Europeans arrived, would disintegrate within a generation after contact, leaving a power vacuum into which the Five Nations would step.

Other peoples of the northeastern woodlands were mobile hunters and gatherers, although there were several who were at least partly agricultural, and others who had been influenced by farming cultures. The Odawa in certain areas depended quite heavily on their planted crops, and the Chippewa (also called Ojibwa, Anishnabe) on a largely uncultivated one, wild rice (*Zizania aquatica*). Their care of wild-rice stands presaged farming, encouraging more bountiful yields, and extended the range of the plant beyond areas where it was found naturally. While the Chippewa did not depend on wild rice to the extent that the Iroquoians relied upon their crops (up to 80 percent of their food requirements), this is still one more illustration of the large "gray" area between hunting and farming. Both Chippewa and Iroquoians harvested maple sap in the spring to make syrup and sugar. Other peoples of the boreal forests, such as the Montagnais and Nipissings, did some planting, but they were too far north for this to be other than marginal for their subsistence. (In the far northwest, the Athapaskan Kutchin and related Han and Tutchone of the Yukon were among those who "encouraged" the growth of plants near their encampments, particularly those used for medicinal purposes.) In the cultural domain, the Nipissings practiced the Huron custom of the Feast of the Dead, a far more elaborate ceremony than was usually found among northern hunting societies. The Micmac and Maliseet of the Atlantic coast had a tradition that they had descended from an agricultural people who had migrated from the south and west; archaeology has confirmed a connection with Adena and Hopewellian mound builders. Micmac social organization was more complex than that of their northern neighbors; for one thing, they had paramount chiefs. The Algonquians of the Atlantic seaboard were hunter-gatherers in the north and farmers in the south, the transition zone being in southern Maine. North of the Merrimack River the birchbark canoe was the means of transportation; to the south, it was the dugout canoe. All of these coastal people were skilled hunters on sea and land; there are reports that the Penobscot of Maine pursued whales.

THE PLAINS

Settled villages were also found on the eastern edge of the Great Plains, in the parklands and along river valleys. The most northerly of these were the Siouan Mandan and Hidatsa on the Missouri River and its tributaries in North Dakota; and the Algonquian Cheyenne of southern Minnesota; further south were the Caddoan Wichita of central Kansas, and Pawnee of central Nebraska. All of these people built earth lodges, combined bison hunting with farming, and had trade networks that extended to the Pacific coast in the west and the Mississippi in the east. With the introduction of the horse, the Cheyenne would move onto the high plains, leaving their farms behind to join the ranks of the mobile bison hunters, such as the Blackfoot and Comanche. Plains cultures displayed many similarities with those of the eastern woodlands, particularly among the sedentary peoples. Throughout the plains, the most important festival was the Sun Dance, usually lasting four days, an occasion for spiritual renewal and symbolically reaffirming the unity of the universe. It is still performed today.

Although at certain times of the year bison could be stalked by individual hunters, the principal means of harvesting the herds was by means of communal drives and jumps. As these could be very dangerous, particularly before the introduction of the horse, they had to be carefully organized and executed, sometimes on an intertribal basis when the harvests were big enough. An enormous jump site (an escarpment or dry-land cliff over which animals were driven to their deaths) was Head-Smashed-In in southern Alberta, a complex of thirty different mazeways lined with up to twenty thousand cairns that directed the stampeding herds. The type of drive called impounding or corralling (in which animals were driven into a box canyon or a coulee or into a specially built corral) was less spectacular, but more reliable and so more frequently used. It has been described as a precursor, if not an early form, of domestication. Medicine wheels, used in hunting rites, ringed the bison's northern summer range; some were in use for at least five thousand years.

GREAT BASIN AND PLATEAU

Human capacity to wrest a living out of the most unpromising of environments is well illustrated in the Great Basin. Here came the Uto-Aztecan Numa to live—Ute, Paiute, Shoshoni—dispersing into small groups to take advantage of the seasonal rounds of wild foods, but also to practice a stripped-down agriculture. Grasslands were burned to prepare them for chenopod seeds, and canals dug to extend available water to where wild food plants were growing. In some watered valleys, corn, beans, and squash were planted. From time to time the Shoshoni made forays into the plains to hunt bison. The Great Basin people were skilled basket makers, and wove light, warm fabrics from strips of rabbit skins. Their dwellings were called wickiups, conical pole frames covered with reed mats, grass, or brush. Apaches also used this type of shelter.

To the north, on the plateau, salmon was the staple for subsistence, and in dried form was the basis of a thriving trade that centered in the western sector at The Dalles on the Columbia. Turquoise found in the region that came from far to the south attests to the scope of this commerce. Linguistically, the region was shared by the Sahaptin speakers (Nez Percé, Yakima, among others), and Salish speakers (Coeur d'Alene, Shuswap, to name only two). The Kutenai tongue was an isolate, as distinctive to the region as their kayaklike "sturgeon-nose" canoe, whose closest counterpart was a world away on the Amur River in Siberia. Like the Shoshoni, the Kutenai made seasonal trips to the plains to hunt bison and skirmish with the Blackfoot.

ARCTIC AND SUBARCTIC

Three principal language groups prevailed north of the plateau, in the huge sweep of the subarctic and arctic: Eskimo-Aleut of the tundra and icebound coasts, Athapaskan of the western boreal forests, and Algonkian in the eastern and central boreal woodlands. Of all the language and cultural groups in North America, the Eskimo-Aleut is said to have the best match between language and culture area; also, it is the only New World stock to be clearly connected with the Old World. That is due to the fact that the ancestors of the modern Inuit, called Thule, were the most recent arrivals in North America, and so had less time to diversify. Coming across from Siberia, they did not reach the Atlantic until sometime during the fifteenth century. They are the largest ethnic group of the far north. The Inuit, along with the Aleut, were master sea-mammal hunters; their technology for deep-sea whaling during the thirteenth to the seventeenth centuries was the most advanced in the world. It was adopted by the whalers of the Northwest Coast, such as the Nuchahnulth (Nootka) of Vancouver Island and the Makah and Quinault of the Olympic Peninsula.

The Aleuts, like others of the Pacific Coast peoples, had a ranked society, and valued material wealth. This was not the case with their distant relatives, the Yupik-speaking Pacific Inuit of Alaska or the Inupik-speaking Bering Sea Inuit, whose patrilineal societies followed the basic pattern for mobile hunters, although with adaptations to local conditions. While some men, such as whaling captains, might have more and better equipment than others, their society was relatively egalitarian. The captain could have inherited his gear, which indicated he had been selected for the position and then trained for it. His training involved learning complex rituals for success in whaling, rituals that involved the participation of his wife and community.

Caribou was the staple for the various Athapaskans of the Mackenzie River and central subarctic, while further east moose helped sustain the Algonquians.

CONCLUSION

All of the Amerindians of North America, whether mobile or sedentary, whether living in complex societies or in simple bands, lived within cultural frameworks that met social and individual needs by emphasizing the group rather than the self; on the other hand, individuals were taught severe self-discipline to stand alone against an uncertain world, and to acquire as much personal power as possible. Cooperation was necessary for survival, but a person's lot in life was individually determined. The pull between the needs of the group and those of the individual was reflected in social organization, which ranged from egalitarian to totalitarian, with many shadings in between. Humor was highly valued, and Amerindians thoroughly approved of anything that provoked laughter. They all observed the law of hospitality, the violation of which was considered a crime.

The power of the word was universally respected; its centrality was signaled by the importance of keeping one's word. For Amerindians generally, poetry and song were linked to the divine, and so were the means for experiencing the truth. The Amassalik Inuit of eastern Greenland use the same word for "to breathe" and "to make poetry"; its stem means "life force." Among the Salish, the loss of a power song was tantamount to losing one's soul. For Amerindians generally, the material and nonmaterial worlds were a continuum, different aspects of the same reality; the universe was one.

The unity of the universe meant that all living beings were related—indeed, were "people," and all had minds. So did some objects that the Western world considers to be inanimate; for instance, certain stones, under certain conditions, could be inhabited by minds. Equilibrium and harmony were of the utmost importance, not always easy to achieve, as the demands of life could make it necessary to break the rules; hence, the importance of the trickster in many myths. This element of uncertainty meant that the most respected leaders were also shamans (medicine men, sometimes women), individuals who had special abilities for communicating with the nonmaterial world.

Whatever the form of their particular societies, Amerindians led full and satisfying social lives within the framework of complex cosmologies, despite the apparent simplicity of some of their social organizations and material equipment. As Le Clercq wrote (in *New Relation,* p. 69), referring to the Micmac, they lived like "the first kings of the earth," as in biblical times.

BIBLIOGRAPHY

General Works

Driver, Harold E. *Indians of North America.* 2d ed., rev. (1969). A good anthropological survey.

Fitzhugh, William W., ed. *Cultures in Contact.* Anthropological Society of Washington series (1985).

Jennings, Jesse D., ed. *Ancient Native Americans* (1978). An archaeological view of early America.

Kehoe, Alice B. *North American Indians* (1981). Anthropology with a large dose of history.

McMillan, Alan D. *Native Peoples and Cultures of Canada: An Anthropological Overview* (1988).

First Peopling

Bryan, Alan Lyle. *Early Man in America from a Circum-Pacific Perspective* (1978).

Diamond, Jared M. "The Talk of the Americas." *Nature* 344 (1990).

Fiedel, Stuart J. *Prehistory of the Americas* (1987).

Fitzhugh, William W., and Aron Crowell, eds. *Crossroads of Continents: Cultures of Siberia and Alaska* (1988). Aspects of the Bering land bridge.

Greenberg, J. H., C. G. Turner II, and S. L. Zegura. "The Settlement of the Americas: A Comparison of the Linguistic, Dental, and Genetic-Evidence." *Current Anthropology* 27, no. 5 (1986).

Gruhn, Ruth. "Linguistic Evidence in Support of the Coastal Route of Earliest Entry into the New World." *Man* 23, no. 1 (1988).

Heyerdahl, Thor. *Early Man and the Ocean: The Beginning of Navigation and Seaborne Civilizations* (1978).

Riley, Carroll L., et al., eds. *Man Across the Sea: Problems of Pre-Columbian Contacts* (1971).

Sauer, Carl Ortwin. *Land and Life* (1963).

Shutler, Jr., Richard, ed. *Early Man in the New World* (1983).

Settling In

Ames, Kenneth M. "The Evolution of Social Ranking on the Northwest Coast of North America." *American Antiquity* 46, no. 4 (1981).

Chiapelli, Fredi, ed. *First Images of America.* 2 vols. (1976).

Le Clercq, Chrestien. *New Relation of Gaspesia.* Edited and translated by William F. Ganong (1910; repr. 1968). A seventeenth-century missionary's account of the Micmacs.

Needham, Joseph, and Lu Gwei-Djen. *Trans-Pacific Echoes and Resonances: Listening Once Again* (1985). Possible transoceanic intercultural contacts.

Sauer, Carl Ortwin. *Sixteenth Century North America: The Land and People as Seen by the Europeans* (1971).

Tkaczuk, Diana Claire, and Brian C. Vivian, eds. *Cultures and Conflict* (1989).

Vogel, Virgil J. *American Indian Medicine* (1970).

Weatherford, Jack. *Indian Givers: How the Indians of the Americas Transformed the World* (1988). The world's debt to Amerindians.

Topical Works

Bernal, Ignacio. *The Olmec World* (1969; repr. 1976).

Capoeman, Pauline K., ed. *Land of the Quinault* (1990). An Amerindian view of themselves.

Dickason, Olive Patricia. "A Historical Reconstruction for the Northwestern Plains." *Prairie Forum* 5, no. 1 (1980).

Greenberg, Joseph H. *Language in the Americas* (1987).

León-Portilla, Miguel. *Aztec Thought and Culture* (1963).

Sagard, Gabriel. *The Long Journey to the Land of the Hurons.* Translated by H. H. Langton (1939). A seventeenth-century view of Huronia.

Trigger, Bruce G. *Children of Aataentsic: A History of the Huron People to 1660.* 2 vols. (1976). A contemporary view of ancient Huronia.

Vennum, Thomas. *Wild Rice and the Ojibway People* (1988).

Verbicky-Todd, Eleanor. *Communal Buffalo Hunting Among the Plains Indians: An Ethnographic and Historic Review* (1984).

SEE ALSO **American Indians of the East; American Indians of the West.**

NATIVE PEOPLES AND EARLY EUROPEAN CONTACTS

William R. Swagerty

THIS ESSAY OUTLINES broad themes of Native American social systems at around A.D. 1500 and explores the earliest contacts between Native Americans and Europeans in the period now commonly recognized by scholars as the protohistoric era. That period has no precise chronological boundaries applicable to all North America. Typically, it precedes sustained colonization efforts by Europeans but follows direct human interaction between indigenous peoples and European invaders. However, in some cases, the protohistoric begins with the introduction of the Old World's material, biological, and ideological culture into native areas prior to face-to-face meetings between Europeans and Native Americans. The protohistoric thus follows the traditional period of prehistory and precedes the true historic era, during which documented colonization by Europeans takes place. We know a great deal about a select number of European voyages and overland expeditions during the protohistoric era due to the survival of relatively detailed written records.

CROSSROADS OF CONTINENTS

Europeans' accounts of their immediate activities in North America are more reliable than the record they left of the Indian peoples they contacted. Even so, more often than not, Europeans were fascinated with the native societies they encountered and they recorded aspects of what they saw; or, more precisely, what they *thought* they saw. As the historian John H. Elliott has observed, Europeans were prisoners of their own preconditioned mindsets and they "all too often saw what they expected to see" (*The Old World and the New,* p. 21).

Furthermore, what they saw they often did not comprehend; firsthand contacts as reported in letters, journals, and ship logs presented, at best, a clouded view of Native American realities. Once reinterpreted back in Europe for public and private reading audiences by publishers who had never been to the Americas, much was lost or distorted in the process of transposition. In the earliest published literature on the Americas, many positive, paradisiacal images of North America circulated simultaneously with negative reports of the land and its bestial peoples. Both views were based upon the supposed empirical observation of explorers, colonists, and early natural scientists whose words and images were presented as truthful. This early travel literature generated and reinforced many myths about the Americas that are still being refuted in the present.

Even more problematic is the lack of surviving documentation for some early contacts, making the most basic of chronological and thematic reconstructions difficult. For most major expeditions during the protohistoric era, some documentation exists, but it is often too vague or too sparse to answer many important questions. The problem of assessing Native American reaction to European contacts is of paramount importance; although the explorers offered their views of how Indians acted when confronted with outsiders, we do not know precisely what Indians thought or how they interpreted their participation in these initial meetings.

Given the lack of an Indian perspective on this early history, there is wide variance in interpretation of the extant evidence and much speculation. The best reconstructions have relied on ethnohistory, a methodology that employs a creative blend of sources from archaeology, anthropology, and conventional history.

For example, where trade goods, disease, or ideas moved inland in advance of European explorers and colonizers, we must rely exclusively on archaeological finds matched with later reports of face-to-face contacts. This technique, known as "upstreaming," is valid only when cultures in the historic era are similar to those in protohistoric or prehistoric eras. Because cultures change across time, this approach works best for those cultures least affected by outside influences undocumented by firsthand observers. It is quite inadequate as a method for cultures whose fundamental political, social, or religious systems changed between first contact and later observation during the colonial era.

The examples that follow stick closely to the documentary and archaeological evidence and begin, appropriately, in the general area where Native Americans first walked onto North American soil. Described by William Fitzhugh, a leading scholar at the Smithsonian Institution, as the "Crossroads of Continents," peoples of the Arctic and Subarctic, as well as some of their neighbors to the south in the northeastern woodlands, experienced the first waves of European probes that set out to exploit the Western Hemisphere.

NORSE BEGINNINGS

It has been customary since the mid nineteenth century to credit the Norse with sporadic contacts with native peoples of North America in the period preceding the Columbian voyages of the late fifteenth century. But until quite recently, artifactual evidence was lacking to provide a link with oral tradition in Norway of early voyages to the land of the *skraelings,* the term used by Viking explorers to describe the inhabitants of the newly found lands. Lately that has begun to change and we are now forced to push the clock back as we begin surveying earliest contacts between Europeans and Native Americans.

The evidence comes from two small but important archaeological excavations conducted during the 1970s. At a windswept site overlooking the Atlantic coast in present-day Maine, archaeologists unearthed, wedged between layers of stone tools known to have been made by ancestors of modern Eskimo peoples, a Norse penny minted between A.D. 1065 and 1080. What is particularly exciting about the find is its association with exotic trade items from north of the Gulf of Saint Lawrence and the fact that the coin was perforated so that its user could wear it as a pendant.

Patient searching for a true Norse campsite was rewarded at L'Anse aux Meadows, in present-day Newfoundland. There, soapstone oil lamps and other implements obtained through trade by Europeans, were uncovered under the floor of the shop of a Norse blacksmith. Again, what is impressive is the distance that the soapstone lamp had to travel as a trade item to reach the Norwegian campsite. These independent discoveries, coupled with oral tradition, help confirm that Norse voyages to Labrador and other parts of the Northeast from bases in Iceland and Greenland occurred sporadically from the eleventh through the fourteenth centuries, well before the voyages of Columbus.

What is unclear is their purpose and their impact on native peoples. Were these contacts the result of boats blown off course when Vikings colonized Greenland? Or, were Norse pilots looking to establish trading relationships with Indians and Eskimos who possessed many products useful to Europeans? Were these voyages, like one documented in 1347, sent further west with the purpose of collecting wood for building materials in Greenland—a land largely devoid of usable timber?

Historical and archaeological evidence is far too thin to suggest that these infrequent contacts greatly changed native lifeways. Items such as chain mail, bronze objects, and Scandinavian broadcloth have been found in native village sites of Greenland and Canada, but European iron tools have not. Nor is there evidence that native peoples acquired knowledge of the process of smelting of iron from ores readily available in local bogs. However, even today, the Western Eskimo term for iron is *savik,* a word of Greenlandic rather than Siberian origin, indicating that trade and communication networks introduced the concepts if not the hardwares associated with invaders from the eastern lands.

By the late fourteenth and early fifteenth centuries, Norse interaction with peoples of North America declined and the relatively small influences they had wrought on native peoples appear to have diminished or disappeared entirely during the next half century. As one contact era closed with the dawn of the fifteenth century, another era began from southern rather than northern European shores.

FISHERMEN'S SUMMER INTERLUDE IN TERRANOVA

As early as 1480, English fishing vessels out of the port of Bristol may have contacted North America while plying the cod-rich waters beyond Greenland. How long before 1480 these voyages had been occurring remains unresolved. During the first two decades of the sixteenth century, English, French, Portuguese, Spanish, and Basque vessels would find their way to the Grand Banks fisheries off of Newfoundland (known to southern Europeans as Terranova—"new land"), where cod and other fish would be caught, dried, salted, and shipped back to Europe.

This pattern of seasonal exploitation of North American waters was best developed by French and Spanish Basques. Beginning in 1540, Basques began sending larger ships to North America, taking whales in the North Atlantic and establishing stations on Labrador in the Strait of Belle Isle as processing plants. Southern Europeans were eager to acquire whale products for heating, cooking, and lighting, and each summer hundreds of ships would establish a camp for rendering whale blubber into oil. As many as one thousand boatmen joined coopers, smiths, and other craftsmen on shore in final preparations for taking the prized whale oil home in large casks. By 1580, perhaps as many as twenty thousand Europeans had set foot on northeastern shores as part of these seasonal whaling and fishing operations. In 1578 alone, one European estimated that between 350 and 380 ships were involved in the Newfoundland fishery.

At the end of each season, these Basque whaling stations, their cooperages, and their tryworks for boiling whale blubber, were usually plundered of all usable items by local Eskimos (Inuit). Although they did not live on Labrador's coast at the time, the Inuit were drawn from traditional lands further north by the prospects of trade with Europeans during the whaling season, as well as prospective pillage of these stations in late fall or early winter after the Europeans' departure. Europeans were annoyed by the losses caused by the Inuit, Beothuk, and other native peoples who disassembled shallops, shelters, and barrels for their planks, nails, and iron hoops, but they came to accept the practice as part of the cost of whaling. In some cases, local inhabitants were placated with presents. Some were actually employed in helping process the catch.

The main diplomatic link in many areas seems not to have been prospects for work, but prospects for trade, particularly in animal skins. The beginnings of the North American fur trade is thus closely tied with fish, the first major commodity exported in large quantity. Trade with local and distant Inuit (Canadian Eskimos) and Indians was inevitable and desirable to all parties. Once a fur-trade system was established, relations between Basque fishermen and Montagnais hunters were so good that shallops could be left in Labrador over the winter without fear that they would be taken or burned to retrieve the iron hardware.

Unlike their ancestors, who had little access to iron tools from Norse forges, the historic Inuit, Montagnais, and other Indians used and exchanged many items of European manufacture from the coastal whaling and fishing stations in a trading network that extended far inland. This introduced peoples of the interior and the far north to European material culture long before they actually met or viewed the strangely clad boatmen and craftsmen such as those who summered at Belle Isle. Most items—knife blades, axes, awls, and drills—were modified into usable tools or ornaments that retained their native form and symbolic values. Some new gear such as copper cooking kettles, scissors, spindle whorls, and coopered tubs were integrated into a new Inuit domestic economy, making life a bit easier than in former times. Native peoples were especially eager to acquire reusable portable cooking vessels and were interested in European cutting, sewing, and fishing devices that freed them from the time-consuming task of manufacturing stone blades, as well as awls, fishing hooks, and harpoons from ivory, bone, or hardwoods.

Beyond these limited introductions of material, there is little evidence that these sporadic European contacts changed social or religious systems of the peoples within the native-culture areas comprising the eastern Arctic, eastern Subarctic, and the Northeast. Some skirmishing and violence did occur when small groups of native peoples were surprised by small groups of Europeans. Micmac and Beothuk fishermen were especially threatened by European competition for resources. Europeans armed themselves heavily when sailing or working their waters. By mid century, Europeans had alienated both groups and may have been responsible for creating increased competition among these native residents. In the 1580s, the Beothuk began abandoning their southernmost fishing sites and moved north, probably to escape pressure from both the Europeans and the Micmac. During that same decade, Basque whaling off Terranova declined because of overharvesting of whales, early winter freeze-ups that stranded ships and cost many crews their lives, and Spanish requisitions for Basque ships to serve in the Spanish Armada of 1588.

Native distrust of Europeans was not always the result of being pushed out of traditional subsistence areas; some native hostility was in direct response to the common European practice of abducting "exotic" peoples as trophies to provide evidence of new discoveries. These kidnappings soured relations and placed entire regions on guard against future intrusions. For example, in 1502, three Indians fully dressed in native attire were presented by Sebastian Cabot to the court of Henry VII of England. During his reconnaissance of the eastern seaboard in 1524, Giovanni Verrazano kidnapped a small boy and tried unsuccessfully to abduct a young woman. The pattern of selective and random kidnapping continued throughout the sixteenth century. Only a handful of the hundreds (if not thousands) of Indians taken to Europe from the late fifteenth through the sixteenth century returned to their people.

What began as infrequent exploration and seasonal fishing along North Atlantic shores might best be thought of as a century-long interlude, a calm on the eve of a storm of momentous proportions that would change forever traditional native societies in much of the Americas.

NORTH AMERICAN CULTURAL LANDSCAPE IN 1492

A Diversity of Cultures On 12 October 1492, Christopher Columbus ended a long and memorable day with the following entry in his ship's log:

> Soon they saw naked people; and the Admiral went ashore in the armed launch. . . . All of them go around as naked as their mothers bore them; and the women also, although I did not see more than one quite young girl. And all those that I saw were young people, for none did I see more than 30 years of age. They are very well formed, with handsome bodies and good faces. Their hair [is] coarse—almost like the tail of a horse—and short. They wear hair down over their eyebrows except for a little in the back which they wear long and never cut. Some of them paint themselves with black, and they are of the color of the Canarians, neither black nor white; and some of them paint themselves with white, and some of them with red, and some of them with whatever they find. And some of them paint their faces, and some of them the whole body, and some of them only eyes, and some of them only the nose. (*The Diario,* Dunn and Kelly, trans., pp. 65–67)

Thus began the earliest description of a Native American society written in a European language. We know that Columbus had encountered only one of thousands of distinctive Native American communities, all of which were destined to meet transatlantic invaders over the next three centuries. By 1492, these societies were organized linguistically, socially, politically, and religiously into a diverse ethnic mosaic that stretched from the Arctic Ocean to the tip of Tierra del Fuego in South America.

The concept of culture areas has been used by scholars since the turn of the twentieth century and has convenient, meaningful application for dividing this diverse landscape into separate geographic and ethnic zones. Within North America, ten major culture areas are discernible on the Smithsonian Institution's map of Native American cultural areas in the *Handbook of North American Indians,* vol. 4 (see Map 1). Because Mesoamerica and the Caribbean islands influenced the southernmost of these acknowledged culture areas—the Southwest and Southeast, respectively—inclusion of these two additional regions as distinct cultural areas is necessary in any discussion of what would become the territorial limits of the United States.

Demographics Reconsidered Scholars disagree on how many Indians inhabited most parts of the Western Hemisphere around 1500, traditionally presenting low figures of no more than ten million people on the eve of the Columbian voyages. Leading ethnologists attributed one million people or less living in what today is the coterminous United States.

Due to advances in the science of demography, those figures have now been revised upward. Most scholars are comfortable with an approximation of fifty to sixty million people as the size of the total human population for the Western Hemisphere. Of this total, seven to ten million were living in what comprises Canada and the United States. Another eight to twelve million lived on islands in the Caribbean. Present-day Mexico was very highly populated with twenty to thirty million people. As many as twenty-five million people may have resided in the Central Valley of Mexico, the homeland of the Aztecs, making this the densest urbanized population in the Americas at the time of Columbus. When totaled, these numbers are comparable to those for Europe, which is thought to have been home to between sixty and eighty-eight million persons around 1500.

A Plethora of Languages In Europe, societies geographically remote from one another often spoke the same language, shared the same religious convictions, and adopted similar political systems.

Map 1

By contrast, in the Americas, thousands of vastly different societies spoke hundreds of mutually unintelligible languages as different from each other as English and Russian. Diversity, rather than uniformity to a common way of communicating, worshiping, and governing was the norm. Nevertheless, cultures that shared common territory communicated through bilingual interpreters or through a trade language.

Linguists have not reached a consensus on the number of different languages that were spoken in the Americas at the time of Columbus. One school favors lumping language families into between seven and ten major groups, acknowledging diversity within those linguistic stocks. A second approach argues for breaking rather than combining languages into as many distinct tongues as evidence permits. Accordingly, these scholars have identified over two hundred individual languages that were spoken in North America in 1492. When Mesoamerica and South America are added, the number increases to as many as two thousand separate, mutually unintelligible languages (see Map 2).

Both academic camps agree that dominant languages within culture areas influenced the social and political lives of the majority-tongue-speakers as well as those speaking a minority dialect or separate language. They also agree that trade jargons

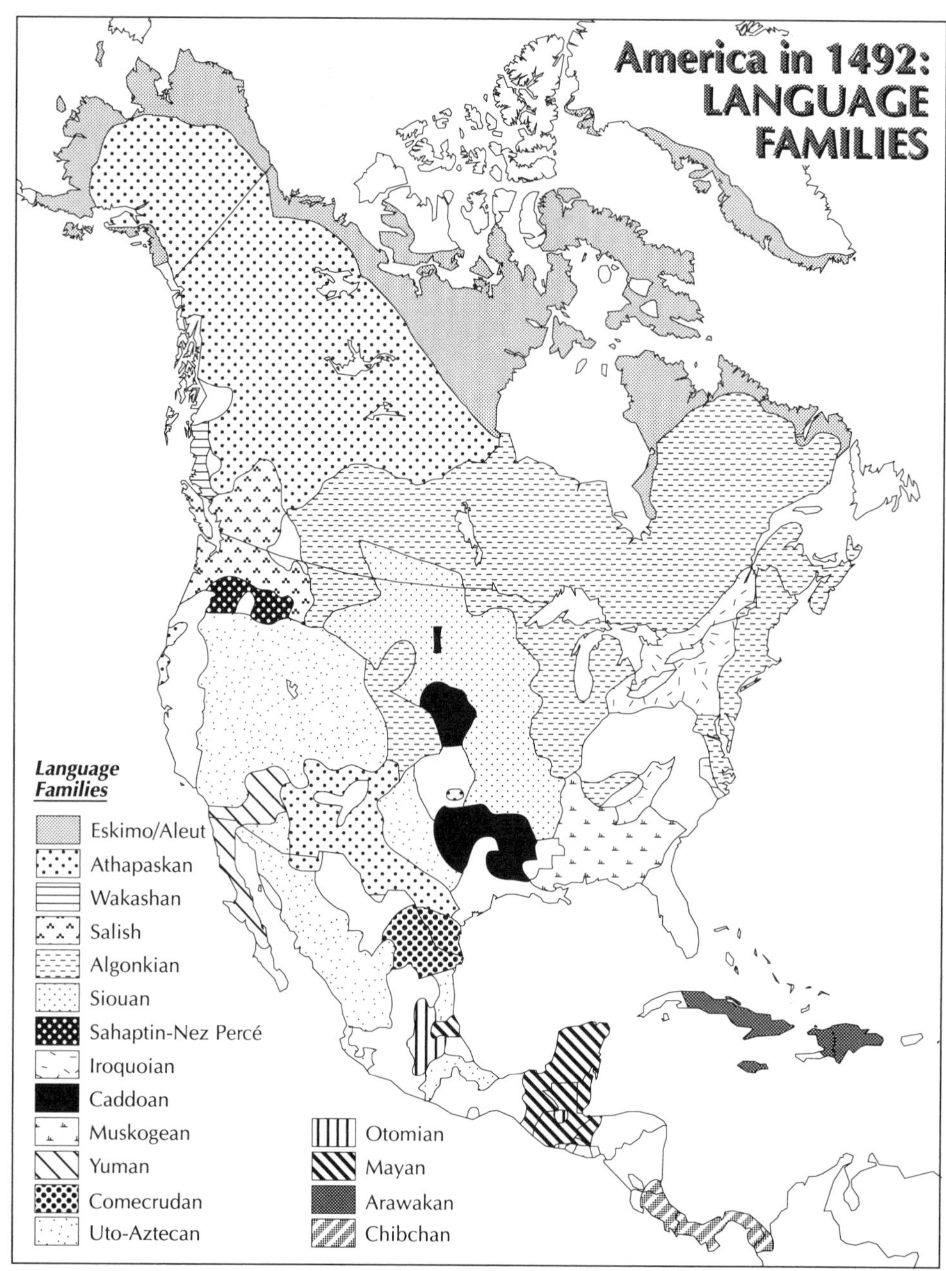

Map 2

Source: Driver and Massey

served as an important bridge connecting otherwise diverse social, economic, and political systems.

Population, language, and culture area studies are useful tools for dividing native peoples into geographic and ethnic components at the onset of European settlement. While generalizations about some aspects of the Native American experience are possible, it must be noted that what applies to one people's experience may be totally invalid for a neighboring or distant group.

SHARED EXPERIENCES OF NATIVE AMERICANS IN 1492

Systems of Identity What similarities do we find among the people generically described as Indians after 1492? First, every native group—large or small—had a familiar name for its members that roughly translates into the "people" or the "real human beings" or the "original ones." Even today, elaborate origin stories are associated with the names that societies used to describe themselves. These stories collectively reminded people of who they were, where they came from, and where they might be going.

The Hopi, a southwestern tribe, took their name from a term that means "gentle people," and the Nez Percé (a French label applied three hundred years after Columbus) called themselves *Nimiipu,* "the Real People." The Powhatan, as the English called one eastern tribe, thought of themselves as "the People of the Great Hare." In other words, what mattered most to these and many other native people throughout the Americas in terms of self-identity were the cosmological associations between man and natural phenomena in the universe and the association with precise place of origin and residence (ethnogeography). A people's identity came from a land ethic that tied emergence stories with a sense of sacred space; this space began at the extended family's central hearth and radiated outward to the village's most sacred areas (especially ceremonial structures, shrines, and burial sites), and the essential landmarks beyond the village that defined the outer world from an internal, often ethnocentric vortex.

Not unlike Europeans, who considered Jerusalem as the center of the world, most North American tribes envisioned a universe with their individual religious shrines and most sacred sites as the beginning point of reference, an earth navel, or a point of emergence. This belief has broad implications for early contacts because many native peoples were forcibly evicted from their villages; others fled to avoid armed confrontation; still others suffered depopulation as waves of disease devastated their towns. In each of these processes, sacred space was profaned; balance was lost in native cosmologies.

Beyond this common sense of place among the many distinct native societies, each individual group shared a comfortable world of common language, common religion, accepted social customs such as kinship, common political organization, and agreement on preferences in foods, housing styles, personal adornment, and aesthetics.

Invariably, however, the space a society called home was surrounded by other cultures, many of which did not share the same language, religion, appearance, social customs, or political succession. This provoked animosity and warfare at times, generosity and sharing on other occasions. Coexistence and co-utilization of the same resources often triumphed. Most societies learned to cope with neighbors, who often became economic allies through trading networks and through intermarriage. Intermarriage served a multiplicity of purposes, extending a society's membership and its influence, while keeping shared territory open for joint use.

Native Rivalries and Conflicts Warfare between native people did occur in America at the time of Columbus. However, unlike Europe and Asia, where large campaigns against adversaries often produced mass mortality, in the Americas, warfare was normally restricted to specific campaigns for specific objects such as the capture of a resource or a person, or to avenge the loss of a loved one. In general, large standing armies did not assemble or meet on the battlefield. Violence and the need to capture, sacrifice, or adopt prisoners of war was an integral part of the cultures of some Indian societies, especially those with highly stratified political systems, such as the Aztecs of Mexico and the Mississippian peoples of the southeastern United States. Both relied on a system of tribute that provided foodstuffs, laborers, and highly prized materials such as obsidian, flint, copper, and shells. Elsewhere, such as among the Iroquois, prisoners were adopted to replace deceased family members or to help with the domestic household. These captives became full members of some societies and were extended most courtesies and privileges available to members born into that society.

Social Systems Class-oriented societies such as the Aztecs of Mexico, the Natchez of the lower Mississippi Valley, and the Tlingit of the Northwest Coast emphasized differences rather than similarities among their own people. As in Europe, if born into a common laboring family, one could not move into the elite by choice or by merit. Leadership was reserved for those born into high office. However, among these societies and others that specialized in crafts, a commoner might well become a skilled artisan, a merchant, or a trader. In short, a middle tier of possibilities existed between the top and the bottom of the social and political ladders.

Most societies respected their elites, who were usually seen as a direct connection between the spirit world and the temporal world of the people. Societies lacking hereditary chiefdomships and priesthoods tended to spread authority and wealth more evenly among all members. Where leadership was by example and not by inheritance or by command, more egalitarian societies could be found. Examples include hunter-gatherers who organized into kindreds or bands consisting of several families, and some agriculturalists such as the village-dwelling Pueblos of the Southwest.

Where several bands or kindreds came together, more complex societies often organized as tribes or as confederacies. Some scholars feel that some societies in the Americas, especially the Aztecs, Incas, and the Natchez, actually developed into formalized "states" similar to those in Europe. These might better be described as "theocracies" wherein political and religious functions were inseparable and not unlike similar developments in the Christian and Islamic worlds. The key to the maintenance of all societies in the Americas as elsewhere was not the power of leaders but the bonds of kinship between those who identified with that society and the strength of families within the community. Among communities with small populations, kinship usually recognized both parents equally and the division of labor reflected obligations to both the husband and the wife's respective lineages.

Many cultures had formal "clans," often linked by song, story, and ceremonial custom to a common ancestor who might or might not be human. Clan initiates acknowledged spiritual and biological ties with the animal, reptile, and insect worlds, in particular. The parrot, bear, spider, and turtle are four of many examples of important clan totems linking several generations of families sharing common lineages.

Marriage customs, inheritance, naming, and responsibilities for the training of youth were not uniform throughout North America. Some cultures practiced matrilineage, passing inheritance of names from mothers to daughters, who retain their maiden surnames at marriage and continue passing the family name on to their children. Examples include the Iroquois of the Northeast, the Creek of the Southeast, the Crow of the Plains, and the Tlingit of the Northwest Coast. Those with male-dominated inheritance of names formed patrilineages, the system endorsed by most Europeans, and a pattern found among coastal Californian societies such as the Chumash, as well as among most Algonkian-speakers of the Great Lakes region such as the Ojibwa. Some societies, such as the Pueblos of the Southwest divided inheritance. Children inherited clan names and social obligations through the mother's side. If male, the child inherited religious obligations through eligibility to membership in a kiva society through his father's lineage (see Map 3).

In all of North America, the nuclear family was important, but the extended family provided a bond beyond household and hearth. Unlike Europe, where the immediate family's bond was paramount, in the Americas relations with the extended family had equal weight in a person's identity, obligations, and prospects in life. Among elites, marriages were arranged, but most commoners wed by choice, not by force. Residence after marriage reflected the social structure of that society. If matrilineal, the husband usually moved into the house of his wife's people (matrilocality) and had little say, even in the education of his own children; if patrilineal, the wife usually moved in with her husband's relatives (patrilocality), becoming subject to the authority of her mother-in-law (see Map 4). All societies had a high regard for children and for the rites of passage associated with aging. These included blessings at birth, naming ceremonies, and puberty rites. Children often were cared for by the extended family, not necessarily by their parents. Although divorce was uncommon among elites, whose vows were to the deities, separations among ordinary people were an acceptable alternative to marital strife.

Daily Life The rhythms of daily life, of feeding and raising families, performing clan or lineage obligations, and participating in social and political events consumed most of the time of native North Americans around 1492. Contrary to age-old stereotypes, most Indian men did not spend all their time hunting and fishing. Nor were their wives and female in-laws the domestic drudges so often depicted in the early travel literature by Europeans. Both male and female worked very hard, and a long and healthy life in most culture areas depended upon good fortune as well as good planning. In agricultural societies, especially in the Southwest, the Southeast, and the Northeast, men often prepared the fields for planting and, where required, participated in the irrigation of crops. Women worked and protected the fields from predators during the growing season and shared equally in the harvest, taking the leading role in storage and food preparation.

In nonagricultural societies such as those of

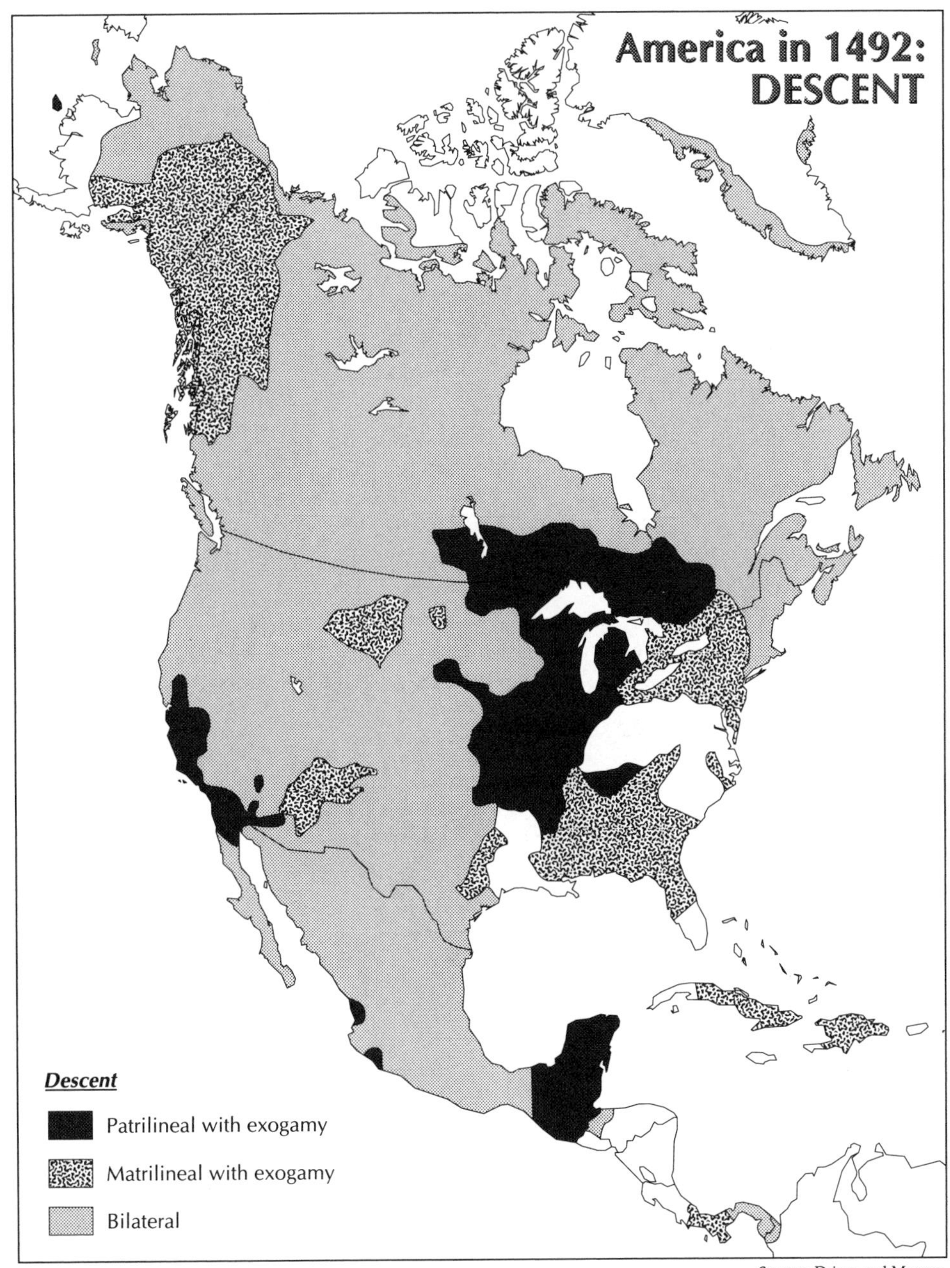

Source: Driver and Massey

Map 3

the Paiutes of the Great Basin and the tribes of California, men hunted or fished a great deal, but both sexes labored in gathering roots, grasses, and other wild foodstuffs, which formed the basis of their diet throughout much of the year. Even in arid sections of North America such as the Great Basin, food was often abundant and surplus economies enabled resource-poor tribes to trade with neighbors for items unavailable in home territories.

Because of the availability of edible goods through trade and because of the widespread dispersion of very successful and nutritious cultigens (especially corn, beans, and squash), most native North American diets included a substantial percentage of garden vegetables. Coastal peoples of California, the Northwest Coast, the Subarctic, and the Arctic often lacked this produce. Diets primarily dependent upon the sea and the annual spawning runs of anadromous fish, especially salmon, gave many nonfarming cultures of the Pacific Coast re-

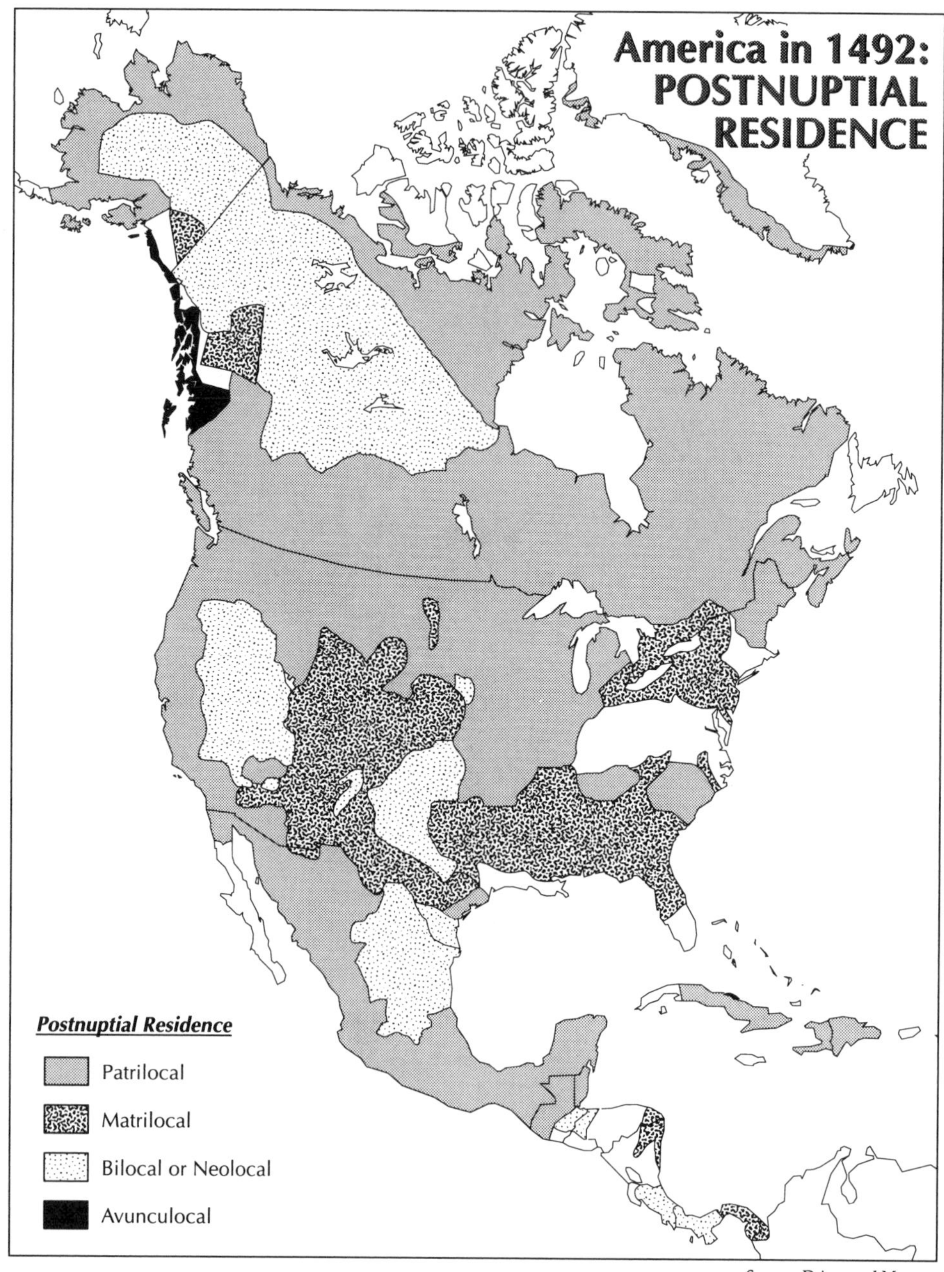

Map 4

Source: Driver and Massey

gion a flexibility in subsistence strategies not found in most parts of the world. These coastal peoples' economies were often described by Europeans as "primitive"; yet, even the harshest of critics marveled at the abundance of food in Nootka, Makah, and Miwok households.

This is not to suggest that Indians did not go hungry. Even on the Northwest Coast, stormy weather, high seas, or other natural or man-induced phenomena could interrupt subsistence patterns. Elsewhere, many Indians expected a time of great scarcity during the cold winter months. They harvested and stored as much food as possible, but this was often insufficient, forcing many villages and societies to disperse into family units until early summer, when fishing, hunting, and planting could resume.

Beyond the food quest, there was time for personal adornment, craftsmanship—objects made for both ceremonial and daily use—and recreation. Every society had its preferred hairstyles and ornamental attachments. Many societies, such as the Arawaks first described by Columbus, excelled in the art of body painting. Others such as the Mohaves of

California and the Timucuas of Florida tattooed their skins with elaborate designs. Other societies such as the Ojibwa and Siouan speakers of the Great Lakes region spent much time adorning birchbark and hide containers, and robes for lodge coverings as well as for personal wear. Still others wove elaborate textiles, reed mats, or highly stylized baskets and hats. In the Caribbean and in the tropical areas of the Americas, many Indians wore very little clothing, but beyond subtropical Florida most native North Americans wore hide clothing and many had garments woven from cotton, yucca, cedar, and other domesticated or wild fibers.

Finally, sports were another common element throughout Indian society; the widespread use of the rubber-ball game in the Caribbean, Mexico, and the Southwest, the use of stick and hoop throughout the Plains, and of racquetball games (such as lacrosse) in the eastern woodlands represent only some of the leisure activities enjoyed by native people on the eve of European invasion.

Domesticated draft animals did not exist in North America at the dawn of the sixteenth century. Although llamas and alpacas had been domesticated in South America, only the dog, the turkey, the parrot, and the muscovy duck had been integrated into economies north of Peru, and only the dog appeared universally in culture areas. Dogs pulled people on toboggans and sleds as well as lodges packed onto carriers, called travois by the French. Dogs were also a source of food for many tribes and served the useful purpose of guarding villages from predators and enemies. Undoubtedly they were also household pets.

Native North Americans knew how to count and how to calculate time through astronomical observation and mathematical prediction and depended on this knowledge for planting and harvesting. In Europe, where astronomy was the basis for astrology, the earth, not the sun, was the center of the universe. Astronomers worked at night and observed events overhead in the zenith sky as the stars became visible. By contrast, in the Americas astronomers worked by day and used the horizon as the main reference point for observing celestial events. Observation devices were constructed so that solstices and other markers of time could be verified.

The technologies that had revolutionized Europe, Asia, and Africa were unevenly distributed or found not at all in North America. Many cultures had limited metallurgical knowledge but none had developed iron smelting or forged iron technology. Also absent were the stepped sail and the axled wheel. Of the five devices that Europeans had mastered since their invention in ancient Greece—the wedge, the inclined plane, the level, the pulley, and the screw—North American Indians found only limited application: wedges in felling and processing huge trees and inclined planes, levers, and pulleys for lifting, hoisting, and moving items. There is no evidence for the use of the screw by native peoples in North America.

European and Native American cultures also differed in their thinking about land use, with most native societies placing a premium on the land associated with their emergence and development. Sacred space such as shrines, cemeteries, and religious lodges was guarded and was not open to use by outsiders. Nor were farming, hunting, and fishing areas unless agreed upon in council or through diplomacy. Nevertheless, Indians did not claim ownership of land; one could lose a garden plot to another family simply by not working the land. By this same principle, usufructuary rights were recognized for hunting and fishing territories whereby families could use a resource as long as they did not damage or permanently alter it. Many tribes thus shared hunting territories and fishing holes. This concept ran contrary to the European notion of property—areas not immediately occupied or worked by Indians often became subject to seizure as "vacant lands." Native usufructuary rights were replaced with European proprietary rights, often claimed in the name of religion, nation-state, or corporation. Lands were charted, platted, and bounded using fences, natural features, and corner markers. This difference in land ethics would bring two worlds into collision.

A WORLD OUT OF BALANCE: BEYOND THE SPANISH MAIN

Columbus was the first to entrap, enslave, and sell Native Americans in Europe. But that was not his main purpose or his desire for the future of the islands he claimed in the name of Spain. His voyages were supported financially and technically by merchants in Spanish and Italian cities whose prosperity was being threatened by growing Turkish control of the eastern Mediterranean. Early Portuguese success in tapping into the trans-Saharan gold trade and in reaching the spice- and textile-rich Orient by way of the Indian Ocean prompted Genoese, Florentine, and Sevillian bankers to open their purses in expectations of immediate profits.

The land of the Arawaks and their enemy-neighbors, the Caribs, did not meet European bankers' expectations but these areas did have enough potential to keep investments alive. Taíno speakers throughout the Caribbean bore the brunt of Europe's insistence on making money out of any newly discovered lands. Earliest Spanish efforts concentrated on Hispaniola (modern Haiti and the Dominican Republic). In the short span of a decade, that large island had been plundered for its placer deposits of gold, its people had been killed through disease, overwork in mining, and despondency, or they had been enslaved by Spanish conquerors. The "handsome, timorous" peoples Columbus described in his first published letter of 1493 would never recover from the devastation that followed this initial encounter.

Nor would their immediate neighbors. The Lucayans of the Bahamas suffered the same fate between 1509 and 1514 as more Indians were needed for work in Spanish mines and on Spanish plantations. By 1519, the Lesser Antilles were literally emptied of their native inhabitants for work on Hispaniola, Puerto Rico, Jamaica, and Cuba. As geographer Carl Ortwin Sauer has noted, in a quarter of a century, the Spanish Main, the strategic corridor of ocean and islands in the Caribbean region, had become "a sorry shell" of its former self.

The arc of that shell had been expanding north since 1513 when Juan Ponce de León, a veteran of Columbus's second voyage, briefly set foot on the Florida peninsula looking for slaves. The prospects on the mainland for repeating Spanish successes on the islands, of rounding up entire villages, were not good but this did not deter Ponce de León and many other Europeans in search of "red gold," the name given to Indians forced into servitude. Rebuffed by the local Calusa, a well-organized, non-agricultural chiefdom situated near present-day Tampa Bay, Ponce de León left without slaves and without locating the "fountain of youth" rumored to lie beyond Bimini Island off the east coast of Florida. A year or so after Ponce de León's Gulf Coast expedition, Pedro de Salazar captured five hundred natives along the south Atlantic seaboard and sold them on Hispaniola. Enslavement continued elsewhere under legal and illegal systems.

In the aftermath of the conquest of Mexico, and following extensive juridical and ecclesiastical debates on the morality of the Spanish conquest in the Americas, the papacy and the crown took slow, independent actions in an effort to curb abuses of Indian peoples at the hands of Spanish masters. Through the determined and persistent efforts of concerned priests, especially Bartolomé de Las Casas, in 1537 Indians were declared by the Catholic church as "truly men." As people deserving humane treatment, Indians were from this point forward eligible for salvation and for incorporation into the Catholic social order. Furthermore, even those native peoples outside the Christian faith were not to be deprived of their liberty or their property. This was followed with several royal ordinances outlawing the worst practices tolerated for the first fifty years of Spanish contact. In 1550 the crown ordered that all conquests be suspended in the Americas until Spain's most distinguished theologians should decide on a "just" method of conducting them. The *encomienda* system, a heinous labor-tribute institution forced upon Indians by Spaniards who were given the labor and the produce of native villages as a reward for faithful service to the crown, was by that time being phased out throughout the Spanish American empire. It would persist well into the North American colonization era disguised or legalized under different names.

Probes Along the Saint Lawrence The development of trade and French beginnings in North America are part of a formula that eventually led to successful colonization of the Saint Lawrence River valley, the Great Lakes region, and the Mississippi River valley. As early as 1524, while sailing for France, Giovanni Verrazano distributed blue beads, bells, and copper ornaments to the Narraganset Indians in what today is southern New England. Years earlier Gaspar Corte-Real, a Portuguese navigator, was amazed when one group of unidentified Indians along the Atlantic coast greeted him with a broken gilt sword and two silver rings that had been manufactured in Venice. That was in 1501, less than a decade after Columbus's first landfall. By the time Jacques Cartier entered the Gulf of Saint Lawrence in 1534 the Iroquois of the Gaspé Peninsula were reluctant to treat with the strangers, but as he moved up the river, Cartier distributed knives, hatchets, beads, and tin trinkets, thus establishing some goodwill and a pattern of protocol that would be repeated thousands of times in as many different places across the next three centuries by French traders. Cartier jeopardized that goodwill among the Laurentian Iroquois later that year by seizing two nephews of the leading chief. In 1535, he destroyed any remaining potential for further French-Iroquois trade and alliance by capturing the Saint Lawrence's leading headman and a large party of his attendants, nearly all of whom died in captivity. When Cartier returned on his third and final voyage in 1541, the Iroquois would have nothing to do with him. By 1603, when Samuel de Champlain explored the river, the Iroquois were no longer in their old villages, having moved south where they must have felt safer. For the rest of the seventeenth century, the Iroquois resisted and warred against the French and their allies—especially the Hurons—in a vicious series of wars over trade spheres, access to trade goods, and habitat.

THE PACE QUICKENS: CONTACTS LEADING TO COLONIZATION

Most contacts in protohistoric North America occurred along the coastal plain or on rivers and bays within sight of the mainland. From the mid 1520s through first successful European colonization in the 1560s, at least six types of contact experience can be distinguished. The first type involved face-to-face meetings between Indians and European exploratory parties, itinerant traders, and crews from ships putting in for provisions or taking refuge from privateers and storms. This pattern typified most mapping and reconnaissance voyages including the expeditions by Corte-Real, Verrazano, and Cartier.

In the Spanish theater of exploration, an expedition up the Gulf of California led by Melchior Díaz in 1539 resulted in some contact with the Cocopa and Yuman (Quechan) of the lower stretches of the Colorado River. Interestingly, peaceful relations were established and maintained for some time to come. A second effort along the Pacific coast by Juan Rodríguez Cabrillo (1542–1543) had the opposite effect on Indian-white relations. Tacking up the Pacific coast, Cabrillo discovered San Diego Bay where the resident Ipai (Digueño) residents indicated "by signs" that they were familiar with Spaniards who carried crossbows and who rode horses for the purpose of killing Indians. Elsewhere Cabrillo found most villagers cautious but receptive to trade and diplomacy. Frustrated from bad weather and not finding metallic wealth, Cabrillo zigzagged through the Channel Islands off California where he anchored for the winter. On San Miguel Island, skirmishes with the local Island Chumash produced casualties on both sides. While the Chumash seem to have come out ahead in the final tally, they paid a heavy price and lost six boys, abducted for use as interpreters, in the final hours of the Spaniards' unwelcomed stay.

A second type of experience was new and involved direct meetings between native peoples of the interior of North America with European explorers. Europeans who had obtained charters or instructions from their governments to establish permanent colonies in the interior were often poorly equipped or ill-prepared to sustain themselves, and they prevailed upon native peoples across a winter or more. In the Spanish sphere, the most important "wintering" expeditions were the ill-fated Narváez expedition (1528–1536), best remembered for the peregrinations of the four survivors across Texas and the account written by Álvar Núñez Cabeza de Vaca; the Hernando de Soto expedition into the heartland of the Southeast and beyond into Texas (1539–1543); the Francisco Vásquez de Coronado expedition (1540–1542) into the Southwest, making some contact with Caddoan groups on the southern Plains; and, the Tristán de Luna expedition to Florida (1559–1561).

In the Coronado narratives, transfers of barter articles such as glass beads, glassware, jingle bells, and other items of small value are noted. Other Spanish expeditions had saddlebags full of similar trade items, but no artifacts directly associated with any of the southwestern reconnaissance expeditions have been identified in Indian sites. Throughout North America, wherever European vessels were lost during storms or through poor navigation, Indians combed beaches and used their best divers to recover utilitarian and ornamental items that soon became incorporated into native daily life. Most of these wrecks occurred along the shores of Florida, the Carolinas, and the Texas Gulf Coast. The Calusa, Ais, and Tequesta of southern Florida gained an early reputation for ship salvage and were especially adept at finding gold and silver objects, as well as European survivors, who were often held for ransom.

In the French sphere, the second and third Cartier expeditions (1535–1536 and 1541–1543) involved wintering. After realizing that the Saint Lawrence is not an inland sea passage to the Orient, Cartier began a regional search for some commodity to justify his discovery and prospects for colonization. The kidnappings mentioned earlier were part of a plan to locate the fabled "Kingdom of Saguenay," reported by some local Iroquois as a land rich in gold and silver, where the people wore woolen clothing. In 1541 and again in 1542, probes sponsored by Cartier failed to penetrate west of the

Lachine Rapids at Montreal. The Iroquois succeeded in thwarting Cartier and French colonization, which would not be realized until 1608.

A third type of contact involved native-to-native contacts between the various Mesoamerican and Caribbean Indians, who accompanied Europeans on their expeditions, and resident North American Indians. During inland *entradas* (the entrance of conquistadors into an area to be explored or settled) such as those of Coronado and de Soto, these "foreign" Indians served as foot servants who performed a variety of essential tasks, from bearing burdens and cooking to translation and communication by signs. Often listed in the documents as "allies," they feared for their lives as accomplices in European designs and were generally quite faithful to the European cause. It appears that they were not treated any differently by local Indians than were European soldiers and officers. By mid century, many were undoubtedly mestizos, the result of the intermarriage of Spanish fathers with Indian mothers. As such, many had been Hispanicized, but others must have maintained identities as Aztec, Tlaxcalan, Tarascan, and other distant peoples.

A fourth type of contact experience was with missionaries. Priests accompanied or led several important expeditions. Franciscans were particularly active in the Southwest from 1539 on. In that year, Marcos de Niza was sent north to confirm rumors of a well-peopled and wealthy province known as Cíbola, a Zuñi Pueblo complex in present-day New Mexico. Niza returned to the province in 1540 as one of six priests accompanying Coronado into the Southwest, two of whom decided to remain behind for mission work. Both are believed to have been martyred. Once colonized after 1598, New Mexico would become a Franciscan province and large mission churches would be built within Indian villages such as Zuñi, Pecos, and Acoma to serve as places of refuge for Indian and white alike during attack by hostile Apache and Navajo raiders, as well as places of worship.

Dominicans were part of the initial unsuccessful colonization attempts by Lucas Vásquez de Ayllón along the South Carolina coast (1526) and Tristán de Luna along the Florida Gulf Coast (1559–1561). Lay priests served Mass for Soto's Expedition (1539–1543) and a few individual Indians were declared "Christians" by the Soto chroniclers, but no large-scale conversions are reported.

In fact, throughout North America during the sixteenth century, European religious personnel attended more to the needs of those born Christians than to those resident peoples forced or persuaded to live with Christians. The Lutheran ministers of Florida, who briefly established a colony on Florida's Atlantic seaboard, were an exception—they were well liked by the local Indians because they did not try to change their traditional customs. Once these Protestants were evicted from Florida, Jesuits took over, but had little success with Indians who had become wary of Spanish intentions. Jesuits gave up by 1573 and were replaced with Franciscans, who built an elaborate chain of missions across northern Florida and Georgia during the next century, congregating surviving Indian populations for catechism and training in traditional European vocational arts such as herding, tanning, weaving, and orchard-tending.

The fifth type of contact experience resulted from a more elaborate version of the basic trade and barter by Indians of skins and furs for European hardware and cloth. Many Europeans out of necessity donned native attire in the form of moccasins, buckskin, and fur robes, but there is little evidence that many envisioned the growth of the fur trade until the 1580s. By century's end, western Europe's demand for fancy furs—especially beaver for hats and marten and fox for coats—and leather increased dramatically, while the local supplies declined precipitously due to overharvesting of wildlife and increased population pressure on grazing and timbered areas. During the seventeenth century it became clear that North America could be Europe's chief source of fancy fur and leather. Cattle hides from European plantations in the West Indies would also be supplemented with the hides of deer, caribou, moose, buffalo, and walrus.

The main focus of the professional fur trade became the Saint Lawrence River valley. On the heels of Cartier and in advance of Champlain's establishment of Quebec in 1608, French, Basque, and Breton merchants sent ships up that river periodically and sold the furs they bought there in Europe. By 1600, Tadoussac in central Quebec had replaced the Strait of Belle Isle as the major source from which European goods were reaching Indians living north and west of the Saint Lawrence Valley.

The final type of direct contact was through the colonial venture. Most sixteenth-century colonization efforts failed, but the volume of material culture introduced into native hands and the intensity of these contacts from a native perspective make them especially significant in determining rates of acceptance or rejection of European ways and goods. Only a few of the earliest European camp and village sites have been located, but the documentary record and evidence of artifacts in native use later, or those found in the ground in the general vicinity of these sites, suggest their impact on native societies.

One of the earliest and longest-lived colonies was established by a Portuguese entrepreneur, João Fagundes, in 1520. The first European colony since the Norse settlements and the only example of a permanent base for fishing established in North America in the sixteenth century, his community—probably located on Cape Breton Island—fished, farmed, and made soap. The colonists tried to replicate the way of life found back in their homeland (especially the Azores), but it appears Micmac hostility forced abandonment of the settlement after several years. Between 1520 and the end of the century, several other towns were built. Spain's first settlement north of Mexico was established at San Miguel de Gualdape, probably on the South Carolina coast, in 1526. Due to disease, storms, and poor choice of location, the colony lasted only a year, leaving behind much of the hardware intended to sustain some six hundred farmers, fishermen, craftsmen and their families as well as a number of Black slaves. Fourteen years later, Spanish expeditionaries noted in their journals the presence of Biscayan axes, Spanish daggers, and many trade beads among Indians of the region.

Further south, the French constructed a substantial post in 1564 and named it Fort Caroline. By the time the fort was captured by the Spanish in 1565, it was clear that the French had greatly influenced the region by sending traders to live among some native groups. The French had also become political brokers in inter-Indian diplomacy and had aided one powerful chieftain in his war against a neighboring rival. This pattern would be repeated by the Spanish in Florida after 1566 in a series of wars of "fire and blood" in which European soldiers, arms, and fighting techniques were integrated by one native community for use against another. No native society won in the long run.

After 1609 the French used a "divide-and-conquer" military strategy in New France (present-day eastern Canada and the Great Lakes region) among the Huron and Montagnais in their wars against the Iroquois, who were supplied by the Dutch and the English. By 1701 a truce was arranged, but the Hurons had been nearly destroyed and much damage and loss of life had occurred on both sides, accelerating clan and family vengeance raids, known as "mourning wars," as well as dependency on European guns and means of repairing arms.

English efforts after 1585 to garrison and eventually to colonize North Carolina's Roanoke Island were on a much smaller scale than any of the examples explored above. Nevertheless, the local Indians were so alienated by the actions of soldiers under the governor, Ralph Lane, who assassinated their leader, Wingina, that they moved away in 1586. By then, the colony was totally dependent on the Indians for food and for protection. With or without resupply from England, given the unpreparedness of the colonists and the aggressiveness of English soldiers of fortune, Roanoke would be a disaster for both the Indians and the white settlers.

In distant New Mexico, Spaniards under Juan de Oñate established San Gabriel del Yunque literally within the village limits of the Tewa-speaking pueblo now called San Juan. Allowed to occupy a large section of the adobe compound, the Europeans and Mexican Indian allies modified it to their own specifications by adding doors, windows, and other European architectural preferences, including outdoor *hornos* or round baking ovens. The original settlement included four hundred women, children, servants, soldiers, and priests, as well as a large number of livestock. Relations were tenuous at best, but local Tewas and Spaniards shared food, technology, and ideas until 1610, when the colony moved south to a better-timbered and more defensible site at Santa Fe. By then, Oñate had been replaced as governor, in part for his violation of Indian rights and for not finding any valuable commodities to justify further colonization.

The only successful permanent colony preceding the founding of the New Mexican capital was Saint Augustine in Florida, which endured sacking at the hands of English privateers under Francis Drake in 1586 and many internal problems from 1565 on. As Kathleen Deagan has written in *Spanish Saint Augustine: The Archaeology of a Colonial Creole Community,* despite all its problems Saint Augustine is an example of successful ethnic fusion, becoming America's first "melting pot." Local Timucuans really had no choice but to accept Spanish domination once the French were ousted. They adapted as best they could, intermarrying with Spaniards, Azoreans, Cape Verde Islanders, and other Europeans as well as some Africans, and sharing their housing styles and preferences in cuisine. What emerged was a uniquely American creole culture—a pattern repeated in other parts of North America, especially in the French and Spanish colonial Southeast, later in the colonial period.

EFFECTS OF CONTACTS IN PROTOHISTORIC NORTH AMERICA

Biological Transfers Disease was not unknown in the Americas at the time of Columbus's landfall. Indians commonly suffered bacillary, amoebic, and endoparasitic disorders and were subject to a wide array of bone and respiratory problems brought on by smoky multifamily, multihearthed dwellings. Dental problems, brought on by attrition to teeth from using stone-grinding devices that invariably left grit in food, very often killed people before old age through apical or periodontal infection. Others died or were crippled from arthritis, tuberculosis, or pneumonia. Some succumbed to bone disorders such as myeloma, while others died of infections from simple lesions or broken limbs. Although heart disease and most forms of cancer appear minimal, dietary imbalances as a result of overreliance on carbohydrates in maize-rich economies affected health adversely, as did an American strain of syphilis. Still, relative to Europe, North America lacked a heavy disease pool, especially numerous "crowd infections" and was a healthier and much more sanitary place for its inhabitants than most of Europe.

Despite these differences, life expectancy in sixteenth-century North America does not appear to have been significantly greater than it was in Europe during this period. According to one study, individuals born into European ruling families during the period 1480 to 1579 could expect to live an average of 33.7 years. Mississippian peoples may have had an average life span of twenty-five years, although the odds of living twice that long increased once the age of fifteen was achieved. Pueblos at Pecos, the largest of the villages in the Southwest during this period, had an average life span of twenty-six. An "elder" probably meant just that, but many adults had lived out their lives by age thirty. Those living in towns may have lived shorter lives than rural Indians owing to the same sanitation and attendant microbial problems that troubled sedentary populations in preindustrial Europe.

After 1492 the thin disease pool of North America thickened rapidly as microbes and parasites from Europe, Africa, and Asia were unintentionally released wherever ships landed. Germs traveled both ways. On their return voyage from America, some of Columbus's men carried back a virulent form of venereal syphilis that was not life-threatening to the Arawaks, but which proved lethal to Europeans and Asians. Within two decades, New World syphilis spread into every corner of Europe and beyond, killing and maiming hundreds of thousands of people.

By 1520 and possibly as early as Columbus's first expedition, the Americas were struck with what Alfred W. Crosby has termed "virgin-soil epidemics," that is, new strains of diseases to which native people had no familiarity or genetic resistance. These included measles, scarlet fever, whooping cough, chicken pox, bubonic plague, tropical malaria, cholera, diphtheria, influenza, and, the greatest killer of all—smallpox. Many Europeans also died from these diseases, but many more who contracted them survived due to acquired immunities from previous generations' exposure.

In the Americas, mortality rates during the first waves of a virgin-soil epidemic such as smallpox or measles could reach 90 percent. Usually between one-third to one-half of a native village would die, leaving a widowed landscape. For survivors, the social effects were as devastating as the medical implications. Entire age-groups within a culture were lost within days of the outbreak of the killer disease. Those who lived were often demoralized, physically scarred, and subject to desperate acts including suicide and infanticide.

From 1518, when the first recorded epidemic of smallpox hit Hispaniola, to the twentieth century, every major American Indian group has had to endure periods of population loss and cultural transformation due to the Old World's silent killers. During the protohistoric era, the Southeast was hardest hit, suffering one or more major epidemic in the 1520s and 1530s, probably originating with sick colonists at South Carolina's Santa Elena settlement. Some scholars agree with Henry Dobyns, who argues that a major "pandemic" began around 1520 and spread as far as the Saint Lawrence River and deep into western North America before the end of the sixteenth century. Seventeen major epidemics are on record for the Americas between 1520 and 1600, but the evidence is not conclusive how far the diseases traveled from germination points in the West Indies and Mexico.

The Northeast's turn came later in the seventeenth century when chicken pox, bubonic plague, and influenza all wiped out sizable portions of the Algonkian- and Iroquoian-speaking peoples of that region between 1616 and 1640. And no hard evidence exists for the spread of the disease horizon into the sixteenth-century Southwest, but Texas was clearly affected. Most Indians living there at the time of first description by Europeans (ca. 1540) had vanished when the region was recontacted decades later. In many areas, Indians fled and thus saved some of their people, but in Texas, it appears the coastal groups in particular were almost totally annihilated.

What should be remembered is not only the power of disease as a biological killer, but also its political and social implications for those affected. The experience both softened and hardened Native Americans, thinned in number and weakened in spirit; the biological holocaust also strengthened commitments to endure adversity and, in some cases, to strike back at the cause of such ill fortune. Europeans, wildlife, the spirit world, and sorcerers within tribal groups were all blamed in due course by various Indian groups. The religious societies of some tribes added new medicines and new ceremonies in order to prevent and cure diseases and thus elaborated on traditional culture; others sought new medicines and invited missionaries or adopted aspects of Christianity to strengthen older, weakened ceremonial ways.

Material Exchanges In protohistoric North America, Europeans doled out more technological hardware to Indians than they received. The weight of evidence tilts markedly in the opposite direction when one considers foodstuffs, shelter, and labor. Archaeological sites show that ancient Native American trade trails carried European goods along with traditional specialized items such as seashells, obsidian, copper, turquoise, mica, exotic feathers, foodstuffs, and prepared hides. The ubiquitous Venetian glass bead, mirrors, hawkbells, bracelets, metal musical tinkle cones, knives, buttons, copper cookware, fishhooks, sewing awls, and varieties of European and Asian cloth, especially satin ribbon, silk scarfs, and broadcloth shirts have all been found hundreds, and in some cases, thousands of miles from the place at which the initial transfers were made.

These items, especially cutting, cooking, and sewing devices, made life more interesting and possibly a bit easier, but none revolutionized Indian daily life—at least not during the protohistoric era. Once European settlements became permanent, in each region, a more complex technological relationship developed, usually involving guns, shot, and powder as well as nonmilitary hardware. By 1622, the Powhatans had guns and knew how to use them. High mortality during the Iroquois Wars of the seventeenth century can be attributed in large part to access to firearms supplied by European rivals. But in the sixteenth century, especially when the cumbersome and often unreliable matchlock or harquebus was standard issue, few Indians acquired firearms or the knowledge of how to use them.

The largest material contributions given by Indians to Europeans were food and shelter. Explorers and early colonists literally slept on Indian beds in Indian lodges from the outset. Small parties were often invited guests; larger ones were unwelcome and therefore usually forced themselves upon Indian hosts. The largest of expeditions—those of Coronado in the Southwest and de Soto in the Southeast—made a habit of evicting Indians from their towns, nevertheless expecting that the Indians would continue to feed the Spanish invaders.

Fortunately for Europeans, Indians in the agricultural hearths of the Southeast and the Southwest had mastered their environments. Those villages that escaped a virgin-soil epidemic had abundant agricultural surplus at the time of these early contacts. Their granaries and larders provided thousands of meals for large and small European armies and travelers long before the Indians were declared "conquered" or "subject" peoples. It is plausible to suggest that without Indian help, the vast majority of Europeans who entered North America before 1630 or so would have starved or died of exposure. During this time of Indian hospitality, Europeans came into contact with a wide variety of new foods and herbs that would eventually revolutionize diets throughout the world.

For western Europeans, especially those from southern Europe, the new diets were far from ideal. Early chroniclers comment consistently on the abundance and the variety found in the typical American Indian pantry, while lamenting the lack of familiar fare. In North America, the new cuisine varied from culture area to culture area, but consistently it included local wild game, especially fish and venison; maize, which Europeans equated with animal fodder or basic cereals known as "corns" in England; and many varieties of highly nutritious beans and squashes. Europeans and their Indian allies also benefited from new foods acquired in Mexico and the Caribbean and introduced some of these into North America, including cacao (chocolate), manioc, tomatoes, potatoes, sweet potatoes, peanuts, melons, and chilis.

The European barnyard complex of cows, sheep, horses, goats, and hogs had little impact during the protohistoric era. Europeans guarded their animals carefully. Even so, some fell into Indian hands and were added to that culture's food supply. Hogs, perhaps the ancestors of the razorback of the Southeast, were lost on most *entradas,* especially that of de Soto. During the seventeenth century, hogs and sheep would become important in native diets in both the Southwest and Southeast, and the horse diffused widely onto the Plains after the founding of Santa Fe in 1610 and San Antonio, Texas, in 1718, more than a century later.

EARLY CONTACTS IN HISTORICAL PERSPECTIVE

This essay has demonstrated the difficulties of generalizing about all Native North Americans' experiences in the poorly documented era of protohistoric America. Looking back from the late twentieth century, this was a period of trial and error for Indian and white alike. While Europeans groped to describe and to comprehend the land and its peoples, Native Americans must have pondered the differences as well as the similarities between the new tribes of peoples so different in manner, appearance, and technology who entered their worlds. Each Indian culture would eventually rationalize the coming of the white man with stories. Some would compose songs; others, such as the Pueblos of the Southwest, would add masked gods *(kachinas)* to their ceremonies to remember the first black and first white people they met in the sixteenth century.

There is little direct connection in the stories that have survived with specific sixteenth-century contacts. At least three major varieties of interpretation have been handed down in legends, prophecies, and narrative poetry. One suggests that many Native Americans regarded European tribes as supernatural beings. Columbus claimed that the Arawaks he first met thought he and his men came from the heavens. The Micmac and Montagnais were reported to have believed the first ships they saw to be floating islands inhabited by spirit beings. So did most New England and Great Lakes tribes, the latter of whom who still held these beliefs in the seventeenth century, a period for which much better documentation exists. The Ojibwa told how visitors from heaven brought red and blue silk and satin to a great medicine lodge and how the people remembered these fine things once trade opened with the white man. Beyond these legends, the fact that many Europeans were allowed to live and to pass freely across Indian linguistic and cultural boundaries adds weight to this view. Fear and curiosity, mixed with respect by Indians for the potential power of the new men helps to explain some responses and lack of resistance.

A second body of literature tells a very different story and is quite ethnocentric. The Great Creator made all men, but in so doing, he made slight mistakes. Whites are the result. According to one Pima story, the Creator did not bake whites enough; he overbaked blacks, but Indians came out perfectly. There are many variations of this rationalization for differences in white and black peoples' appearance and behavior.

A third and rather sizable body of first memories assigns ill motives to whites and recalls the negative effects of the meetings with Europeans. To the Hopi, prophecies of the coming of the white man tell of his intelligence, his many wonderful tools, but also of his selfish interest in finding wealth. In short, whites had strayed from the Great Spirit and would use any means to get what they wanted. Zuñis predicted that drinkers of dark liquids would descend upon the land, speaking filth and nonsense. The Louisiana Choctaw, some of whose people met Soto's pillaging army in 1541, prophecied that the land would become overcrowded with new tribes—some wicked and cruel—and that the land would not be able to sustain them all, causing all people to fight among themselves.

The "average" experience as recorded in documents leads to the conclusion that first contacts can be divided fairly evenly between diplomatic discussion and trade, punctuated with distrust and fear on the part of Indians (as one major response), and overt distrust leading to armed resistance and continued hostility to European designs or trespass (as a second major response). Whether peaceful or hostile at the initial stages, the evolution of those relationships conclusively points toward a failure to maintain mutual respect. The alienation of resident peoples during this period was far more common than was diplomatic success in establishing meaningful economic, political, or social partnerships.

The greatest areas of conflict took place where large European armies, such as those of Soto in the Southeast and Coronado in the Southwest, forced their way into villages, demanded servants, food, and concubines, and often left scorched earth in their paths. In each case where European armies—however large or small—exacted tribute or violated Indian women, those native groups sought vengeance, usually forcing Europeans back to home bases by land and by sea.

The greatest examples of accommodation and reciprocity are the barter and trade networks established very early by itinerant traders, fishermen, and privateers along the Atlantic coast; the experience of the French in Florida with Timucuans in the 1560s; the beginnings of French political and economic alliances with Hurons and Algonkian speakers along the Saint Lawrence after 1630; and, during the early settlement phase, the accommodation by Timucuans of Spaniards in Saint Augustine and by Tewas in New Mexico.

By 1620 or so, European reconnaissance, exploration, and attempts at exploitation of North American resources—whether French, Spanish, or English—had shown that no treasures comparable to those found in South America and Mesoamerica were likely to be found in North America. Furthermore, most Europeans reluctantly concluded that they would have to work for themselves. No longer could Indian hospitality be relied upon to sustain European enterprises. In the generations that followed, within French and Spanish colonization spheres, many Indians would be recognized as sovereign nations and would be treated diplomatically as such. Through intermarriage, some of their people would be incorporated forming *métis* (French-Indian) and *mestizo* (Spanish-Indian) populations. In other parts of North America, especially in the British sector, Indians increasingly were segregated from white society and were pushed off their native lands. While many powerful tribes such as the Iroquois Confederacy, the Cherokees, and the Creeks would retain sovereignty until after the American Revolution, most eastern tribes became marginalized as the number of English settlers overwhelmed them during the seventeenth and early eighteenth centuries.

Elsewhere across North America, the protohistoric continued for decades, and in some cases, centuries beyond the Spanish, French, and English "historic" periods in the Southwest, Southeast, and Northeast. Through trade and communication networks, stories of the new settlers circulated, and evidence of their presence could occasionally be touched when metal, glass, or cloth materials moved deep into remote quarters of the Plains, Great Basin, Plateau and Northwest Coast. Prior to the third quarter of the eighteenth century, however, the Europeans were invisible invaders for most peoples living in the Far West; only their germs, their hardwares, and their occasional appearance by land and by sea interrupted traditional ways of life. When first colonized, some native peoples such as the coastal societies of California, succumbed rapidly to disease, missionization, and colonial enterprises. But most did not, preserving traditional cultures well into the nineteenth century or until changes in resource bases forced confrontation and eventual acceptance of European-American–imposed dependency.

BIBLIOGRAPHY

General Works

Driver, Harold E. *Indians of North America.* (1961, rev. ed. 1969).

Morison, Samuel Eliot. *The European Discovery of America.* 2 vols. (1971–1974).

Quinn, David Beers. *North America from Earliest Discovery to First Settlements: The Norse Voyages to 1612* (1977). The most authoritative general survey.

———, ed. *New American World: A Documentary History of North America to 1612,* 5 vols. (1979–). The most accessible documentary collection.

Sauer, Carl Ortwin. *Sixteenth Century North America: The Land and the People as Seen by the Europeans* (1971). The best survey by a cultural geographer.

Trigger, Bruce G., and William R. Swagerty, "Entertaining Strangers: Sixteenth Century North America." In *Cambridge History of the Native Peoples of the New World, North America,* edited by Bruce G. Trigger and Wilcomb E. Washburn (1992).

PERIODS OF SOCIAL CHANGE

Indian America at 1492

Josephy, Alvin, Jr. *The Indian Heritage of America* (1968).

———, ed. *America in 1492* (1992). Newberry Library Quincentenary Project.

Kopper, Philip. *The Smithsonian Book of North American Indians: Before the Coming of the Europeans* (1986).

Ortiz, Alfonso, ed. *Southwest.* Vol. 9 of *Handbook of North American Indians* (1979).

Trigger, Bruce G., ed. *Northeast.* Vol. 15 of *Handbook of North American Indians* (1978).

Native American Legends

Erdoes, Richard, and Alfonso Ortiz, eds. *American Indian Myths and Legends* (1984).

Nabokov, Peter, ed. *Native American Testimony: An Anthology of Indian and White Relations: First Encounter to Dispossession* (1978).

First Images of America

Chiappelli, Fredi, ed. *First Images of America: The Impact of the New World on the Old,* 2 vols. (1976).

Elliott, John Huxtable. *The Old World and the New, 1492–1650* (1970).

Honour, Hugh. *The New Golden Land: European Images of America from the Discoveries to the Present Time* (1975).

Lorant, Stefan, ed. *The New World: The First Pictures of America* (1946; rev. ed. 1965).

Columbian Exchanges

Crosby, Alfred W., Jr. *The Columbian Exchange: Biological and Cultural Consequences of 1492* (1972).

Dobyns, Henry F. *Their Number Become Thinned: Native American Population Dynamics in Eastern North America* (1983).

Heiser, Charles Bixler, Jr. *Seed to Civilization: The Story of Food* (1973; rev. ed. 1990).

Ramenofsky, Ann F. *Vectors of Death: The Archaeology of European Contact* (1987).

Smith, Marvin T. *Archaeology of Aboriginal Culture Change in the Interior Southeast: Depopulation During the Early Historic Period* (1987).

Thomas, David Hurst, ed. *Columbian Consequences,* 3 vols. (1989–1991).

Thornton, Russell. *American Indian Holocaust and Survival: A Population History Since 1492* (1987).

Weatherford, Jack. *Indian Givers: How Indians of the Americas Transformed the World* (1988).

Norse and Basque Contacts

Fitzhugh, William W., ed. *Cultures in Contact: The Impact of European Contacts on Native American Cultural Institutions, A.D. 1000–1800* (1985).

Laxalt, Robert. "Discovery in Labrador: A 16th-Century Basque Whaling Port and Its Sunken Fleet." *National Geographic* 168, no. 1 (1985).

Spanish Contacts

Bannon, John Francis. *The Spanish Borderlands Frontier, 1513–1821* (1970).

De Vorsey, Louis, Jr., and John Parker, eds. *In the Wake of Columbus: Islands and Controversy* (1985).

Deagan, Kathleen A. *Spanish St. Augustine: The Archaeology of a Colonial Creole Community* (1983).

Dunn, Oliver, and James E. Kelly, Jr., trans. and eds. *The Diario of Christopher Columbus's First Voyage to America, 1492–1493* (1989).

Ellis, Florence Hawley. *San Gabriel del Yungue as Seen by an Archaeologist* (1989).

Hammond George Peter, and Agapito Rey, eds. *Narratives of the Coronado Expedition, 1540–1542* (1940).

———, eds. *Don Juan de Oñate, Colonizer of New Mexico, 1595–1628.* 2 vols. (1953).

Hoffman, Charles A., comp. "On the Trail of Columbus." *American Archaeology* 6, no. 2 (1987). Special Thematic Issue.

Judge, Joseph. "Our Search for the True Columbus Landfall." *National Geographic* 170, no. 5 (1986).

Lowery, Woodbury. *The Spanish Settlements Within the Present Limits of the United States,* 2 vols. (1901, 1911).

Lyon, Eugene. *The Enterprise of Florida: Pedro Menéndez de Avilés and the Spanish Conquest of 1565–1568* (1976).

Milanich, Jerald T., and Susan Milbrath, eds. *First Encounters: Spanish Explorations in the Caribbean and the United States, 1492–1570* (1989).

Sauer, Carl O. *The Early Spanish Main* (1966).

Spicer, Edward Holland. *Cycles of Conquest: The Impact of Spain, Mexico, and the United States on the Indians of the Southwest, 1533–1960* (1962).

Swanton, John R., et al. *Final Report of the United States DeSoto Commission* (1939).

Wagner, Henry Raup, ed. *Spanish Voyages to the Northwest Coast of America in the Sixteenth Century* (1929).

French Contacts

Bennett, Charles E., ed. *Laudonnière and Fort Caroline: History and Documents* (1964).

Biggar, Henry Percival, ed. *Voyages of Jacques Cartier* (1924).

———, ed. *The Works of Samuel de Champlain,* 6 vols. (1922–1936).

Dickason, Olive Patricia. *The Myth of the Savage and the Beginnings of French Colonialism in the Americas* (1984).

Eccles, W. J. *The Canadian Frontier, 1534–1760* (1969, rev. 1983).

Jaenen, Cornelius J. *Friend and Foe: Aspects of French-Amerindian Cultural Contact in the Sixteenth and Seventeenth Centuries* (1976).

Pendergast, James F., and Bruce G. Trigger, *Cartier's Hochelaga and the Dawson Site* (1972).

Trigger, Bruce G. *The Children of Aataentsic: A History of the Huron People to 1660,* 2 vols. (1976).

Trudel, Marcel. *The Beginnings of New France, 1524–1663* (1973).

English Contacts

Andrews, Kenneth R. *Trade, Plunder, and Settlement: Maritime Enterprise and the Genesis of the British Empire, 1480–1630* (1984).

Axtell, James. *After Columbus: Essays in the Ethnohistory of Colonial America* (1988).

Barbour, Philip L., ed. *The Jamestown Voyages Under the First Charter, 1606–1609,* 2 vols. (1969).

Fausz, J. Frederick. "Fighting 'Fire' with Firearms: The Anglo-Powhatan Arms Race in Early Virginia." *American Indian Culture and Research Journal* 3, no. 4: 33–50 (1979).

Kupperman, Karen Ordahl. *Settling with the Indians: The Meeting of English and Indian Cultures in America, 1580–1640* (1980).

Quinn, David B. *England and the Discovery of America, 1481–1620* (1974).

———, ed. *The Roanoke Voyages, 1584–1590,* 2 vols. (1955).

Salisbury, Neal. *Manitou and Providence: Indians, Europeans, and the Making of New England, 1500–1643* (1982).

Von Der Porten, Edward P. "Drake and Cermeño in California: Sixteenth Century Chinese Ceramics." *Historical Archaeology* 6 (1972): 1–22.

Wagner, Henry R. *Sir Francis Drake's Voyage Around the World: Its Aims and Achievements* (1926).

SEE ALSO **Agriculture; American Indians of the East; American Indians of the West; American Social and Cultural Geography; Family Structures; The French and French-Canadians; Iberian Peoples; Labor: Colonial Times Through 1820; Minorities and Work; Public Health; Slavery; Technology and Social Change.**

THE AMERICAN COLONIES THROUGH 1700

Norman S. Cohen

RECIPROCAL DISCOVERY

IN THE EARLY MORNING of 12 October 1492 Rodrigo de Triana, a seaman aboard the *Pinta,* sighted land, an island that Christopher Columbus named San Salvador "in honor of our Blessed Lord." Hauling in all his sails but the mainsail, Columbus lay to until sunrise and then went ashore, where he raised the royal banner and flags that signified his taking possession of these unknown lands in the name of Ferdinand and Isabella of Spain; he and his crew then recited a prayer of thanksgiving. While the Spaniards engaged in their ritual of conquest, the naked inhabitants of the island, "young people, none of whom was over 30 years old," gathered and began to intermingle with these strange intruders into their lands who gave them gifts of "red caps and glass beads."

We have Columbus's description of this fateful encounter, taken from his log with his own hidden agenda: he wanted to convince the Spanish monarchs that the people of the Indies desired to convert to Christianity, "for they seem to have no religion," and that they were peaceable people willing to trade their wealth—gold, precious stones, and spun cotton—for European baubles of little worth. Convinced that he was close to Japan, he navigated his small fleet from island to island observing the "Indians," their golden adornments, and the fertile lands that he constantly described in glowing terms that promised enrichment for himself and his monarchs. What the Amerindians thought of these strange persons and their large ships remains in obscurity.

By contrast to the informative log of Columbus's travels, we have little knowledge of John Cabot's voyage to the Newfoundland region aboard the *Mathew* in 1497 that was the basis for England's claim to North America in the reign of Henry VII (1485–1509). These initial voyages were followed up by the Spanish, English, French, and Portuguese who came to lay claim to the riches of the continent as part of what Samuel Eliot Morison has called "the European discovery of America," but what with greater accuracy Francis Jennings in his *The Invasion of America* has termed "reciprocal discovery."

By 1504—some ethnohistorians say as early as 1480—French fishermen were working the Grand Bank fisheries and mixing with the indigenous Beothuks. In Giovanni da Verrazano's voyages of 1524–1528, his ships and crew sailed along the coast of North America and came upon the Wampanoags whom they found to be friendly and charitable. In Maine, by contrast, they came upon the Abnaki, who apparently had some earlier dealings with European traders, and whom Verrazano found to be "bad people," being both discourteous and warlike. When mooned by the Abnaki braves the French sailors were upset, but they were more uncomfortable when it became clear that it was the Abnaki who controlled the terms of trading. Verrazano also encountered the Amerindians of the Cape Fear region of North Carolina, and in the New York Narrows. In Mexico and Peru the Spanish invaders had begun the conquest of the Aztecs and Incas, and within that first quarter of the sixteenth century, Spanish armies had invaded North America's southwest as well. And as Europe transformed the American continents, Europe was itself transformed by the transculturation that took place when these conflicting cultures came into contact.

The ethnohistorian Calvin Martin illustrates this process in an interesting essay on the Micmac, an Algonkian-speaking people, who occupied the eastern region of present-day Canada just north and east of Maine. Already decimated by European diseases, the Micmacs were further threatened by the introduction of Christianity, which destroyed their cosmology and brought about "the dispiritualization of the material world" ("European Impact," p. 21). In their well-balanced ecosystem, hunting and fishing for beaver, moose, bear, caribou, and salmon was regulated by a belief in manitou, magical supernatural forces that operated subject to interpretation and control by the shaman.

Various rituals and taboos served as a valuable "control mechanism on Micmac land-use, maintaining the environment within an optimum range of conditions" ("European Impact," p. 13). The European invasion undermined this spiritual edifice, which proved insufficient to protect the people from the diseases that decimated their population while having no effect upon the foreign invaders. The European priestly powers appeared superior to those of the shamans. And, as the shamans became discredited, the Micmac began to overkill the wildlife upon which their ecosystem relied. Drawn into a commercial trading network that exploited their natural resources, they "became dependent on the European marketplace, both spiritually and economically" ("Impact," p. 25). The new weapons of European technology obtained in trade gave them a decided competitive advantage over other Amerindians, enabling the Micmac to push beyond their traditional boundaries. In defense, their neighbors, both Algonquian and Iroquois, were obliged to participate in this trading nexus in order to survive.

This pattern of reciprocity of discovery occurred throughout the Americas. Contact initiated by Europeans created epidemics that decimated the Amerindians and undermined native belief systems that gave coherence and identity to their existence. The invaders then seized Amerindian lands and settled on them, using survival skills adapted from native technologies and justifying their behavior by citing Christian theology and European legal statutes on the rights and sanctity of private property. In return, their technology subverted Amerindians, who increasingly became dependent upon the metal tools and weaponry of the Europeans. In order to survive, the Amerindians were dragged into the competitive marketplace based upon production for exchange in place of their customary production for use and, as the Europeans became increasingly self-sufficient and independent in the New World, the Amerindians lost their own independence and control of their ecosystems.

Thus Spain, advancing into the most heavily populated areas of the Americas, created an empire that extended throughout the Caribbean, Mexico, Central America, Peru, and much of the South American continent. Those Amerindians they did not annihilate in the process, such as the Arawaks, they enslaved. Wherever they went, they brought their priests to spread Catholicism and royal agents to administer their acquired lands. And in return, the Spanish brought back to the Old World the wealth of the New, as Spain became the most powerful sixteenth-century nation in all of Christendom.

ENGLAND'S FIRST EFFORTS AT COLONIZATION

Spanish success in America had a tremendous impact upon world economies. As the gold and silver from Mexico and Peru filled the coffers of Ferdinand and Isabella, a European price revolution began that continued throughout the sixteenth and seventeenth centuries. In England wages lagged far behind price increases, and persons with fixed incomes found their living costs growing more rapidly than their incomes. Real wages of agricultural workers in Cambridgeshire, for instance, on the eve of the Puritan migrations to New England, were only 44 percent of their fifteenth-century levels. At the same time, England experienced a population explosion that was in part related to the ending of the pandemic plague period that dated from the fourteenth century. England increased from three million people in 1500 to over five million by the middle of the seventeenth century. Somewhere between a quarter to a half of this population lived below the contemporarily recognized poverty line.

In East Anglia, enclosures for agriculture or the raising of cattle and sheep uprooted many poor persons who depended upon access to open fields and common lands to eke out their marginal existence. And as food prices rose, they frequently resorted to violent protest actions to express what E. P. Thompson terms "the moral economy of the crowd," a generalized belief that traditional rules governing social and economic relations had been violated. When, for instance, agents of Charles I attempted to enclose royal lands in the West Country, large crowds gathered and tore down the offending hedges and fences, eventually forcing the king to return much of the property the people claimed.

Persons forced off the land resorted to begging and thieving to survive. Large numbers of these wandering vagabonds (Hobbes called them "masterless men") clogged the roads, towns, forests, and riverbanks of England in search of some means of existence. Many found their way to London and Bristol and other port cities, helping to account for the phenomenal increase of the urban population and associated social problems that arose during this period.

In addition, England, after its break with the Catholic church in the reign of Henry VIII and the increasing Protestantization of the Anglican church under Elizabeth, wanted to stem the expansion of the "great Anti-christ of Rome." The establishment of English colonies in North America would thus not only be a place of refuge for England's excess population, but would provide a home for missionary activity among the Amerindians as well. Moreover, America was a continent full of natural resources, including naval supplies with tall trees for the building of masts for the Royal Navy, and great harbors for English ships "to spoil Philip's navy, and to deprive him of yearly passage of his treasure to Europe."

It was ideas such as these that captured the imagination of the nation and led to the first English attempts at colonization. Two cousins, both named Richard Hakluyt, became the publicists for settling in America. Every deed of Sir Francis Drake and the other English seadogs appeared in the pages of their edited *Principal Navigations, Voyages, and Discoveries of the English Nation* (1589), along with a wide variety of propaganda promoting the creation of trading companies and colonizing ventures. Their publication of Richard Hakluyt's *A Discourse of Western Planting* (1584) led directly to Queen Elizabeth's backing of Sir Walter Raleigh's attempt to establish an English colony in North America.

Despite three earlier costly voyages by Martin Frobisher that had ended in failure, Sir Humfry Gilbert managed to find financial support for the creation of a company that would undertake the settlement of a colony in North America. However, Gilbert died before his venture got under way, and Elizabeth granted a new charter to one of her favorites, Walter Raleigh. Although he was not to go on the voyage himself, he planned and outfitted the fleet that in 1585 planted a colony in Roanoke along the outer banks of the present-day Carolina coast.

Needing a quick financial return so as not to discourage his investors, Raleigh wanted a colony that could serve both as a port from which he could attack Spanish treasure ships and a place of permanent settlement. Unfortunately, the persons selected for the hard work of colonizing under the leadership of John White and Ralph Lane proved totally inadequate for the task. Most of the settlers for this venture had been impressed from the sturdy beggars and criminals—the masterless men—who populated the mother country and had none of the necessary skills for planting a colony. An idyllic belief in the existence of "good Indians," who would work for the English in return for protection from the Spanish and bad "cannibal Indians" quickly proved to be a delusion.

The Roanokes, originally quite hospitable, grew weary of supporting the English, who seemed totally incapable of providing for themselves. Instead of working and planting their own crops, the English killed the Roanoke king and attempted to establish a puppet allied to their interests in his place. The Roanokes refused to recognize the renegade's authority and withdrew all support to the settlement, which sent John White scurrying off to England for assistance. The exasperated Ralph Lane also gave up and sailed for home, and when relief ships arrived in 1590, delayed by the great sea battle in England that resulted in the destruction of the Spanish Armada, all that remained of the settlement were the mysterious markings "CRO" found on a tree and the word "Croatoan" on a wooden post. The rest of the colony had vanished, including Governor John White's daughter and her infant baby, Virginia Dare, the first English child born in what would become the United States. English America had lost its settlement, but gained the myth of the Lost Colony.

JAMESTOWN

With the failure of the Roanoke settlement, English investors were unwilling to risk any new attempts at colonization for the remainder of the sixteenth century. Then in the beginning of the new century, a series of events occurred that changed these sentiments: in 1603 James I succeeded Queen Elizabeth to the throne of England, and the following year the war with Spain came to an end just as the 1603 voyages of Samuel de Champlain ignited French interest in New World colonies. Believing that they now had the backing of the nation and the proper financial incentives, nineteen London merchants who had acquired Raleigh's charter and a separate group of West Country merchants both applied for a new charter to settle in lands claimed by the English along the Atlantic seaboard. Forming themselves into two trading companies under the direction of Sir John Popham, the two groups were granted a single charter to plant two colonies. The West Country investors, calling themselves the

Plymouth Company, quickly failed in their attempt to settle on the Maine Coast at Sagadahoc.

The second group of English merchants, the London Company, outfitted three ships, the *Susan Constant, Godspeed,* and *Discovery,* which sailed from England in the winter of 1606 with 144 colonists on board. Arriving at the mouth of the Chesapeake Bay on 26 April 1607, they attempted a landing, but were driven back by Chesapeake Indians. For the next two weeks they navigated the region in search of a place for settlement. Then on 14 May they picked a site at the mouth of a river they called the James, and began the building and fortifying of Jamestown, the seat of the first permanent English settlement in America. Unloading the settlers, Captain Christopher Newport reconnoitered the river to make peace with the neighboring Powhatans, who were secure in the belief of their superiority over the invaders. For this reason the Powhatans were willing to form an alliance with the English, seeing in them potential allies in their struggles with the neighboring Monacans.

Prior contact with Europeans and their diseases, had nearly destroyed the Amerindians of the Chesapeake, killing off 90 percent of their population. If this terrible depopulation had not occurred, it is doubtful whether the English could ever have gained a foothold in the New World. Certainly their technology was far inferior to that of the Amerindians in this alien environment, and without Amerindian help they would certainly have perished as had the colonists at Roanoke.

Even with Amerindian help the Virginia settlement fared badly. Overcome with sickness, the English managed to plant some wheat, cut trees for clapboard and pitch, and gather sassafras roots for shipping to England as a supposed cure for syphilis. By September half of the population had died. As more English arrived their numbers increased to over five hundred at the onset of winter in 1609. By spring only sixty remained.

This account of the tribulations of the original Jamestown settlement is succintly told in Edmund Morgan's *American Slavery, American Freedom.* The English who had come to Virginia found a land where game abounded, the ground was fertile, and fish were plentiful. Yet the settlers refused to work. They did not plant sufficient crops, depending upon the Indians to provide for them instead. From fall 1608 through August 1609, John Smith served the colony as president, and though he asked but four to six hours of work per day from the settlers, he was unable to get even that. In the winter of 1610–1611 some of the colonists reverted to cannibalism to survive. Yet when Thomas Dale arrived as marshall in 1611 he found the people "bowling in the streets," with few gardens planted and the fields barren.

This behavior could partly be explained by the poor organization and direction of the company. The president had little real power under the terms of the charter and the council was never able to act as a body without quarreling among themselves. Additionally, the work force proved ill-suited to the task of settlement. In England the laboring classes spent large amounts of time in idleness, enjoying their "Saint Monday" holidays and even while starving, they would spend, said John Smith, "4 hours each day . . . in work, the rest in pastimes and merry exercise" (quoted in Edmund S. Morgan, *American Slavery*). Surprisingly there were very few farmers among the settlers, the company evidently believing that the raising of crops would not be a problem.

To make matters worse, an inordinate number of shareholders in the company were noblemen or wealthy gentry whose only contribution to the settlement was their ability to pay their own way. Of the first 105 settlers, 36 were gentlemen; in the next two ships, 56 out of the 190 men were gentlemen, "about six times as large a proportion of gentlemen as England had" (E. Morgan, *American Slavery,* p. 84). These were persons with no manual skills and who looked with disdain upon common labor. Many of these gentlemen brought personal attendants with them, and they likewise had none of the requisite survival skills.

Faced with an incredibly high death rate, the irrational behavior of the settlers, and the lack of any significant financial return, the council in England reorganized the company in 1612, sending over new leadership with strict instructions that demanded every colonist work five to eight hours in the summer and three to six in the winter. Despite the high death-rate, new settlers arrived and spread out in cleared areas along the James so that by 1616, with a population still under four hundred, they were scattered over some seven settlements.

In London, the Virginia Company under the direction of Sir Thomas Smith and Sir Edwin Sandys introduced a headright system for the distribution of land to attract new settlers. Each person who came over to the colony at his own expense received a headright of 50 acres (20 hectares) and an additional grant for others, including servants, whom they brought with them. These settlers had to pay a quitrent of a shilling per year for every 50 acres. Persons who had settled in Virginia prior to 1616 were given a minimum of 100 acres (40 hectares) also subject to a quitrent. In addition, the company paid to transport poorer individuals who would work as tenants on Virginia Company lands for seven years, giving half of their earnings to the company. Upon completion of their tenancy, they would be given 50 acres of their own. Although tobacco had become the major money crop, Sandys tried to limit its production, to encourage the growing of other crops for survival, and alternative items for export and manufacture.

When the company sent their new governor, Sir George Yeardley, to the colony in 1619, they instructed him to "create a laudable form of government" consisting of an elected general assembly of two burgesses from each corporation and borough to make the laws for the colony (D. Hawke, *Colonial Experience,* p. 101). The first assembly met in Jamestown on 30 July 1619, attended by the governor, his council, and twenty-two representatives, as the first popularly elected legislative body to meet in English America. Ironically in the same year, a Dutch merchant vessel unloaded its cargo of twenty African slaves, purchased by the company as servants.

Somehow the company was able to continue repopulating the colony. Between 1619 and 1622, 3,500 new settlers arrived, 75 percent of whom died within three years. Then in 1622 a Powhatan uprising resulted in the death of 347 Englishmen. In a three-year period, more than 3,000 English settlers had perished, and the English settlement in Virginia was still far from secure. Internal struggles within the company led to further difficulties, and finally in 1624 the Crown dissolved the company making Virginia a royal colony.

ENGLISH COLONIZATION OF NEW ENGLAND

The settlement of Virginia was part of a momentous movement of English people in the seventeenth century. Over 250,000 English men and women left England between 1603 and 1660, 50,000 going to Virginia and Maryland (founded in 1634), most coming after 1624. Others immigrated to Ireland, a small group went to Bermuda and over 100,000 to the Caribbean islands of Barbados, Saint Kitts–Nevis, Antigua, and Montserrat. After 1620, 20,000 to 25,000 went to New England.

The founding of Plymouth, the first of the New England colonies, originated in the town of Scrooby in southern Yorkshire. Following Henry VIII's break with Catholicism in 1531–1534, the English clergy had evolved an Erastian solution to the church question (one that involved crown control of the church) based on the Thirty-nine Articles of Religion (1563; rev. 1571) that stated the tenets and rituals of the church in a manner broad enough to accommodate the Christian majority. Catholics, of course, were outside the pale, as were the more radical Protestants who insisted that the church must rid itself of all papist remnants. These iconoclasts uprooted railings in English churches, broke the heads off the statues of saints, and got rid of priestly garb and ritual. In Cambridge a group of Puritan divines preached and taught a theology that merely aimed at purifying the Anglican church. The Puritans and Anglicans had few differences with regard to doctrine, but they were at great odds over church polity and the role of the clergy in that polity.

While Puritans believed that Christians must struggle against sin and the unregenerate within their midst, a small group of Separatists believed that the true saints must remove themselves from all communion with evildoers, sinners, and the unregenerate. In Scrooby a congregation of like-minded Separatists gathered in the manor of William Brewster, who had attended Peterhouse, Cambridge, to hear John Robinson, a Puritan minister, a graduate of Corpus Christi College, Cambridge, preach to them on the need to break completely from the Church of England. Faced with fines and imprisonment for their recusancy, approximately one hundred twenty-five members of two neighboring congregations uprooted themselves and sailed to Amsterdam, settling there briefly, and then moved to Leyden in order to worship according to their beliefs.

The Netherlands proved to be an unsatisfactory haven for many reasons and the Scrooby group decided to move once again, this time to Virginia. Accordingly, William Brewster opened negotiations with Sir Edwin Sandys and received a patent from the London Company to settle within their grant. About fifty of the Leyden group returned to England. Of these, thirty-five of the original Scrooby church set out for America on the two ships, the *Speedwell* and the *Mayflower.* Only the *Mayflower* proved seaworthy. After many difficulties and a transatlantic crossing of sixty-six days, it arrived off the shores of Cape Cod, hundreds of miles from its intended destination, in November 1620. Deciding upon Plymouth as a place of settlement, the leaders drew up a covenant agreed to and signed by the forty-one free adult males on board, to create "a civil body politic." This Mayflower Compact became the basis for civil government, extending freeman status to all signers in the Plymouth Colony. Throughout most of its existence as an independent colony, a majority of adult males were granted freeman status, given property in the various land divisions, and granted the right to vote.

Under the leadership of William Bradford, who was the governor of the colony from 1621 until his death in 1657, Plymouth survived the illnesses that wiped out almost half of the original settlers. The colonists overcame the problems of never having a charter or even legal rights to their land until 1621 when the Council for New England granted them a patent. And the Pilgrims, as they are known in our history, maintained their settlement despite poor agricultural conditions and economic problems. For a brief period the fur trade provided them with a staple export item, but that soon died out, and the lack of good harbors hindered other enterprises. They were mainly poor people with almost no contacts in the mercantile world of wealthy London merchants. And the colony was as culturally impoverished as it was economically: it lacked both an educated ministry and a public schools system until late in its history. By 1691 when Plymouth was absorbed into Massachusetts, the unassuming colony had grown to twenty-one towns, but its greatest importance was in its contribution to our mythic lore of Plymouth Rock, Samoset and Squanto, Thanksgiving, Miles Standish and Priscilla Mullins. Significantly, according to William Bradford, the Pilgrims were the "instruments to break the ice for others who come after with less difficulty" (quoted in *Colonial Experience,* p. 129).

As William Bradford personifies the founding of Plymouth Plantation, the name of John Winthrop is synonymous with Massachusetts Bay. A Cambridge student, Winthrop was a devout Puritan and a representative member of the Suffolk gentry class. Married four times, he was the father of seven sons and one daughter by 1630, and it was not an easy time to raise a family, even for the wealthy. The Thirty Years' War that erupted in 1618 adversely affected English markets and helped create a deepening depression in the textile industry, accompanied by increasing unemployment. In these circumstances Winthrop had a hard time making ends meet: while prices and expenses continued to rise, the rents on his lands were largely fixed. As his children neared adulthood, their financial needs also increased, and he thought of migrating to Ireland. In addition, England seemed to be sinking in sin; the court that surrounded James I grew increasingly corrupt—surely a sign of God's displeasure with the country. The resulting social pressures helped Winthrop decide to leave England, "this sinful land," and plant in America.

In 1630, English colonies existed in Virginia, Plymouth, Barbados, and Bermuda, and there were fur trading posts and fishing villages scattered along the New England coast. The granting of a charter in 1620 to the Council for New England, which had replaced the defunct Plymouth Company, served as an impetus for continuing colonization. With no settlement plans of its own, the council offered licenses to investors such as the Dorchester Company, which established trading and fishing villages around Massachusetts Bay. Following the collapse of the Dorchester Company, the council granted a new license in 1628 to a group of Puritan merchants organized as the New England Company, which captured the attention of John Winthrop. Just prior to Charles I's proroguing of Parliament in 1629, they obtained a charter and Winthrop and eleven others, meeting in Cambridge, took an oath to move the charter and entire Massachusetts Bay Company to New England.

In October of 1629 the company appointed Winthrop as their governor and he took charge of organizing the expedition. In early spring 1630 his fleet of eleven ships and some seven hundred passengers steered a course toward the North American continent. It was the beginning of the great migration, in which over twenty thousand persons emigrated to New England in the period from 1630 to 1642. Aboard the flagship *Arbella,* Winthrop wrote and delivered a lay sermon, "A Model of Christian Charity," in which he explained his goals for the colony they were erecting in the wilderness. "We shall be as a City upon a Hill," he exclaimed, a beacon light for others to follow; by serving God in a model Christian society they would prosper and by their example England would learn and cleanse itself of its sins.

Winthrop's fleet landed in Massachusetts just as another group of settlers arrived and began planting at Dorchester, several miles south of the Boston Harbor. After a brief stay at Salem, Winthrop explored the region north of Dorchester, and came upon the peninsula that the Amerindians called Shawmut, where he settled along the Charles River while others of his group encamped along the Mystic. Assisted by a small number of English inhabitants already dwelling in the region, the new colony quickly located a good source for water and sites for settlement.

Here on what the English saw as "widowed lands," left by the Pawtucket and Massachusetts Amerindians, who had been nearly destroyed by European diseases (only about two hundred remained in the area), the Puritans began building their colony. Within a year they had erected seven towns, and Winthrop had moved across the Charles to Boston, where in October the first general court met, extending freeman status to all the male settlers who took an oath binding them to the laws of the colony, while restricting future membership to church members only.

THE NEW ENGLAND TOWN

Boston's growth from town to city evolved quite differently than did the inland farming communities. Its soil was poor, land was limited, and even firewood was scarce. Its initial success in the fur trade soon passed. But with its natural harbor, Boston developed as a commercial center, open to outside worldly influences that undermined early Puritan concerns for community. The effect was that capital accumulation and material gain became more important than godly behavior. From the very beginning property distribution was unequal—over half of its land was given originally to just thirty families—and this inequality between rich and poor increased over time. As Darrett Rutman shows, individualism and materialism thwarted Winthrop's "concern for community," as his "ideal of the medieval community was transformed into the reality of modern society" (*Winthrop's Boston,* p. 275). By the last decade of the seventeenth century, Boston, with a population of over seven thousand, was no longer a village. It had become the largest port city and commercial trading center in English North America, open to the worldly influences and sins its Puritan founders had hoped to leave behind in England.

As these first settlers arrived in New England, they had no definite plans of church polity or town government to guide them. They had the charter that defined their powers and a governor, deputy governor, and a body of assistants who had been selected in England to serve as a governing body along with the freemen. Beyond that, they had to adapt to the circumstances they found in the New World while relying upon familiar traditions, institutions, and forms of government brought with them from England, where there existed a tremendous diversity in agricultural structures, land systems, and patterns of leadership. No town in New England could be said to be typical, each had its own particular characteristics largely related to the English background of its founders.

In his study of the processes by which English culture, law, and customs were transported to New England, David Grayson Allen found that the settlers attempted to recreate societies and structures with which they were familiar. In Hingham, England, town government was based upon parish organization; in Hingham, Massachusetts, the people "set up a network of relationships in law, government, economy, and society that duplicated their English background." Where there was a "stable, static agrarian society, characterized by a population steady in size, a traditional open-field system of farming, specializing in grain and cattle, and tightly defined social structure," such as in the East Riding of York, these became the characteristics of the "new society created at Rowley, Massachusetts" (*English Ways,* pp. 55, 21). In the chalk regions of Wiltshire and Hampshire, where large-scale capitalistic agriculture was the rule, the "villages were nucleated, surrounded by common fields and open pastures, and meadow" (p. 83). Settlers from this region replicated such a society, complete with its highly stratified class structure and contentiousness, to Newbury in New England.

The resulting diversity in the five towns he studied reflected the regional differences that existed in the mother country. Similarly the people who came and their reasons for emigrating were quite different. For instance, emigrants from English towns in the north and west tended to be younger and from prominent families. Those from the south and east were usually older and from more obscure backgrounds.

Away from the coast, these almost mythic agricultural New England towns developed. Studies of such towns as Andover, Dedham, Sudbury, and Plymouth describe traditional life in colonial America that has been taken incorrectly to be typical of New England life in general. Here, in well laid-out settlements with their centrally located meetinghouses, Englishmen established Puritan communities based on close-knit nuclear patriarchal family structures with strong, supportive, kinship networks. The people who founded Andover in 1646, for instance, came mainly from Lincolnshire, Wiltshire, and Hampshire in England, and attempted to re-create in rural Massachusetts the traditional open-field village with which they were familiar. They laid out their town along two parallel streets, presided over by the meetinghouse, and assigned house lots to inhabitants accepted as townsmen, recognizing "a hierarchy of rank and wealth," yet with a "relative narrowness of the range of landholdings" (Christine A. Young, *From "Good Order" to "Glorious Revolution"* [1980] p. 1). It was to a large extent a one-class society.

The distribution of farmlands followed a similar pattern. Andover, as Philip J. Greven has demonstrated, was a subsistence agricultural village, inhabited by a homogeneous population, sharing communal values and an abiding faith in Puritan piety. Kinship factors played heavily in populating the town and as long as land was plentiful, large patriarchal families lived long, harmonious lives together in healthy environs. Second-generation women married at an average age of 22.3 years, men at 26.7 and with surprisingly infrequent childbirth deaths raised their five-plus children. Other studies, such as Kenneth Lockridge's *A New England Town* (on Dedham), describe similar "homogeneous, closed, corporate, and cohesive," settlements that were based on subsistence farming. Frequently utopian in their origins, the town's inhabitants covenanted together and erected their churches, established a school system that made for "nearly universal male literacy," and supplied the students for Harvard College (founded in 1636), which in turn provided the learned clergy, teachers, and educated men who led the colony into the evolving capitalist world of the eighteenth century.

The commercialized agricultural towns such as Springfield in the Connecticut Valley, however, were quite different and, until recently, unstudied. Stephen Innes's *Labor in a New Land* traces the growth of Springfield from its beginnings in 1636 as a fur-trading post through its development of a diversified economy encompassing gristmills, sawmills, lead mines, turpentine manufactories, ironworks, and house construction largely dominated by William Pynchon, the town's founder, and his son John. It quickly became the commercial center for trade in the upper valley, with about one-third of the town's male population working as wage laborers, and some forty men employed full time by the Pynchons. The indentured servants and low-paid free laborers who worked for Pynchon had to buy their goods in his general store. Innes says in his *Labor in a New Land* that about half of the town depended "in some fashion—rental of land or animals, employment, or debt—on the resources and good graces of Pynchon" (p. xix).

Unlike Dedham or Andover, land tenancy was commonplace in Springfield. As the Pynchons owned most of the agriculturally productive alluvial and bottomlands, and as the poorer town-dwellers could not support themselves on their meager holdings, about one-third of the adult males were forced to rent land or livestock from the Pynchons. This often meant that the tenants, in addition to paying rent, had to perform feudal-like duties on the leasehold. Laborers even had to rent their tools from the Pynchons. The resulting town structure was far from a harmonious community. Springfield was replete with antisocial behavior: "physical assault, family feuds, slander, witchcraft accusations, and drunkenness" (*Labor in a New Land,* p. xviii).

While the majority of the town dwellers lived in poverty, in humble dwellings, working as wage laborers, William Pynchon lived in an ornate mansion from whence he dominated every aspect of town life: he served the town as magistrate, judge of the county court, permanent moderator of the town meeting, and captain of the militia. In addition and of equal importance, the family was Springfield's mediator to the outside world.

Pynchon came to Springfield as a merchant, not as a Puritan; the townspeople readily accepted his entrepreneurship because they shared a common weltanschauung. The triumph of the market economy in Springfield was the victory of nascent capitalism; it was an acquisitive, materialistic society, competitive, individualistic, and non-egalitarian that accepted the ideal of possessive individualism.

As the English of the great migration settled the towns of New England and the Chesapeake, their Puritan brethren in the mother country became embroiled in a revolution and civil war. On 23 October 1642 the forces of the king and Parliament clashed at Edgehill, the opening battle of the Civil War; seven years later, on 30 January 1649 Charles I was beheaded and parliamentary rule established. In New England, news of these events came in infrequent letters: the people were for the most part supporters of Parliament, and some even felt it necessary to return to England. As governor, John Winthrop subjected the colony to Parliament's protection, he argued from the beginning that governments were based on the consent of the governed and that the Puritans, by migrating to America, and covenanting together, had given their consent to be governed by the Massachusetts Bay Charter. Playing it as cautiously as he could, he was clearly a supporter of Parliament in the Revolution. But the Puritan revolution also turned "the eyes of all people" away from his model of Christian charity, and after 1642 immigration slowed considerably, the great migration was over. Parliament in the interregnum moved toward a Presbyterian solution to the religious question, and on 26 March 1649 John Winthrop died, his dream of a Puritan utopia unfulfilled.

With the coeval development of commercialism and Puritanism in Massachusetts, the increasingly unequal distribution of wealth became disruptive to the original settlers' aspirations, resulting in a turbulent period of social unrest. In its zeal for orthodoxy, Massachusetts drove religious dissenters such as Roger Williams and Anne Hutchinson and their followers from their midst. In the 1650s a small number of English Quakers entered the colony with an even greater impact. The Puritans perceived them as a threat, demanding harsh treatment including imprisonment, whippings, exile, and hangings. Only the direct intervention by Charles II could halt this violence against the Quakers. Significantly, the crown continued its attack upon the colony's privileges for the next quarter century, finally revoking its charter in 1684. Following the Glorious Revolution, William and Mary granted a new charter in 1691, making Massachusetts a royal colony.

This assault upon the old social and political structure had severe repercussions in the colony, including the appearance of witches in Salem—a tragic event rooted, as Paul Boyer and Stephen Nissenbaum wrote, "in the prosaic, everyday lives of obscure and inarticulate men and women." Salem, like Boston and Springfield, was a mercantile center with taverns and other disruptive influences, a place where merchants charged usurious prices, and where backcountry farmers warred against commercial capitalism and its insidious individualism. Salem residents fought over land divisions, families split apart because third-generation sons found their access to town lots blocked by their parents, and churches strained the bounds of the covenant as saints and ministers locked in unseemly battles. The tension and repression, sexual and otherwise, created in this environment was vented in accusations of witchcraft brought by neighbor against neighbor—resulting in the hanging of nineteen convicted witches and the crushing to death of Giles Cory. When the fury finally subsided, over one hundred fifty others were in jail faced with death.

Thus despite its success in establishing its towns, the Puritan commonwealth failed in its mission, its errand into the wilderness. The "beacon light of the City upon a Hill" was dimmed by the English Revolution; communal society broke apart on the reef of New World individualism; outward behavior, and display of wealth became more important than inward godliness; and extended family and kinship relations split apart in internal migrations caused by a combination of large family size and longevity. Puritans became Yankees, the counting house surpassed the meetinghouse in importance, and the one-class society gave way to a new hierarchical order of rich and poor.

COLONIZATION IN THE SEVENTEENTH CENTURY

By mid century the first phase of colonization was completed; the English settlements in North America had a population of approximately fifty-five thousand, two thousand of whom were of African heritage. In the Chesapeake region there were two colonies. Virginia was the largest English colony in North America with a population of almost nineteen thousand. Bordering Virginia to the north, Maryland, founded as a proprietary government, competed with its larger neighbor in the production of tobacco and by 1650 had a population of just under five thousand. The Maryland charter granted Cecil Calvert and his heirs 6.5 million acres (2.6 million hectares) in return for the annual payment of two Indian arrowheads, and was intended both as an economic investment and a haven for Catholics in the New World. No English colonies were yet organized along the Atlantic coast between the Chesapeake and the Spanish settlements in Florida. The Carolinas were not settled until after the Restoration when Charles II granted a proprietary charter to a group of eight influential supporters in 1663. To the north of Maryland lay only the Dutch colony in New Netherland, the New England colonies, and the French in Canada.

The Dutch claim in the region stemmed from Henry Hudson's voyages between 1607 and 1609 for the Dutch East India Company. Other explorers followed, and in 1624 the Dutch West India Company established its first settlement at New Amsterdam, purchasing the land from the Manhattan Amerindians of the region. Originally intended as a trading post and commercial center, New Netherland grew very slowly, and a series of disastrous Indian wars between 1641 and 1645 devastated the colony. In spring 1647 Peter Stuyvesant arrived in New Amsterdam as the director of the company. Under his leadership the population doubled to almost four thousand by 1650. As the colony grew and prospered, the Dutch maritime fleet, which dominated the world carrying trade, came into conflict with the English. In the resulting wars, England conquered New Netherland in 1664 and Charles II granted it as a proprietary grant to his brother, the duke of York, renaming the colony New York.

Pennsylvania, like Maryland, the Carolinas, and New York. came into existence as a proprietary colony. Pennsylvania's founder, William Penn, who was an influential member of the gentry class and a close friend to the duke of York, had joined the Society of Friends in the 1660s. In return for a debt owed his father by Charles II, and most likely because of the king's desire to rid the land of the obstreperous Quakers, Penn received a liberal charter in 1681 to a huge landmass over which he had wide yet limited powers. Here, reminiscent of John Winthrop's model Christian community, he intended to plant a colony "that an example may be set up to the nations: that there may be room there . . . for . . . an holy experiment." But he also wanted to raise a substantial income for himself and his children as well—or as he wrote, "though I desire to extend religious freedom, yet I want some recompense for my trouble."

Penn sold about five hundred thousand acres (two hundred thousand hectares) of Pennsylvania property to merchants in order to raise funds for settling the colony. At the same time he traded large tracts to the Free Society of Traders, a group of London Quakers organized as a joint-stock company to promote settlement in Pennsylvania. They in turn sold individual plots outright, while developing their own estate with two hundred servants transported to the colony for that purpose. As part of his deal with the Free Society of Traders, Penn exempted them from paying the normal quitrents and granted them three seats on the provincial council, which they used to contend against his government. To end the internecine squabbling, Penn separated the three lower counties from Pennsylvania and formed it into a new colony, Delaware, with its own assembly. Then in 1701 Penn wrote a new and more liberal frame of government, the Charter of Privileges. By this date, the rapid pace of immigration had pushed the population of Pennsylvania to twenty-one thousand, and propelled Philadelphia past New York as the second largest city in English North America.

Thus by the end of the seventeenth century, all the original thirteen colonies with the exception of Georgia had been founded. The New England colonies of Rhode Island, Connecticut, and New Hampshire had their beginnings as outgrowths of Massachusetts Bay. Dissenters from Puritan orthodoxy such as Anne Hutchinson, Roger Williams, John Wheelwright, and their followers found refuge in lands removed from but claimed by Massachusetts and built their own colonies. In 1691 Massachusetts, which included the remote Maine district until the nineteenth century, absorbed Plymouth. By that date the English contiguous settlement of the Atlantic seaboard from Maine to South Carolina was completed, the business of clearing the land and populating the colonies well under way. As the colonies grew, five colonial cities developed as centers of trade and commerce: Boston in 1700 was the largest with 6,700, followed by Philadelphia and New York, each with 5,000, Newport, Rhode Island, with 2,600, and Charles Town, South Carolina, with 2,000. Protected by the English navy, operating comfortably within the nation's mercantile system, growing in wealth and population, and providing new markets, the twelve colonies had survived the early stages of colonization and emerged as harbingers of a New World far different than that envisioned by the original settlers.

WORK AND LABOR IN EARLY AMERICA

Richard Hakluyt's sixteenth-century promotional literature argued that "the wandering beggars of England, that grow up idly and hurtful and burdenous to this realm," would find employment and new life in America. As he prepared to sail for New England in 1630, John Winthrop worried that England "grows weary of her inhabitants," and echoed the idea that in the colonies jobs were plentiful. Even as late as 1681, William Penn was promoting his colony as a place where the idle would find work and the industrious find means to uplift themselves. The masterless men who wandered aimlessly in seventeenth-century England were part of what Stephen Innes has called the "worst employment crisis ever experienced by the British Isles." They migrated to the cities in large numbers, seeking employment—London's population grew from about 200,000 in 1600 to 575,000 in 1700. One-quarter of England's population lived on the edge of starvation, and real wages declined dramatically, affecting almost the entire unskilled and semi-skilled working classes. And it was the extent of full employment that economists of the time believed to be the measure of economic well-being for the country. Accordingly, "unemployment," Innes writes, "served as one of the principle rationales for the colonial effort."

Unable to find any means of support in London or Bristol, the working poor readily accepted offers to migrate to the colonies. They were typically nonhouseholders with little property of any kind, persons of small means, representing a wide variety of trades and agricultural work. For the most part, they came as servants; some 80 to 90 percent of the immigrants to the Chesapeake were indentured; very few were of the gentry or professional classes. Those who came to the Chesapeake were overwhelmingly male, with a ratio of about three males to each female. With family life uncertain, only sustained immigration enabled Virginia and Maryland to survive in the seventeenth century. Initially work in the Chesapeake consisted of three related activities: clearing the land, growing tobacco for export, and providing food and livestock for subsistence and sale. There was little specialization or diversity. But with the decline in tobacco prices in the last quarter of the century, the Chesapeake region responded by diversifying its output to wheat and corn. At the same time, the demand for craftsmen of all kinds increased, with greater and greater degrees of specialization becoming the rule. Women's work, too, bolstered the local economy and altered the patterns of their labor.

Another cause for the increased diversity in servant labor and the changing patterns of work was the growing importance of and dependence on slavery in the Chesapeake. Virginia and Maryland were becoming what Philip D. Morgan has distinguished as slave-owning societies, but not yet slave societies where slavery "becomes central to the economic functioning of that society" (*Strangers,* p. 163). Initially, following their arrival in 1619, blacks in the Chesapeake found race relations to be somewhat flexible. The passage from slave to freedman remained open, with the legal status of the slave not yet spelled out. Most blacks worked alongside whites in the tobacco fields, others cared for livestock, some were artisans. Interracial sex may have been frowned upon, but it did take place; and the records show that in some instances free black men married white women and there were a number of cases where white servant women gave birth to mulatto children.

While the status of blacks in the period from 1619 to 1661 remains obscure—some blacks lived as freedmen, some owned property, some were servants, and some, probably the majority, were slaves—after 1661, when Virginia enacted its first slave codes, their condition became quite clear and defined. Coincidentally, their numbers grew: 950 in Virginia and 758 in Maryland in 1660 to more than 16,000 and 3,000, respectively, by 1700. And as slaves began to arrive in significant numbers after 1680, there was a corresponding decrease in the number of new white servants. Darrett and Anita Rutman found in their study of Middlesex County, Virginia, that in the last decade of the sixteenth century, slaves exceeded white servants in the work force, and by the end of the century constituted 22 percent of the total population. A fifth of the male heads of households in Middlesex owned at least one slave.

The reasons for this transformation to slave labor, as expressed by Virginia's governor, were clear: "Blacks can make [tobacco] cheaper than Whites" (*A Place in Time,* p. 165). While most slaves toiled at onerous jobs like clearing the fields and plowing, others worked as skilled laborers with artisanal skills. Women slaves got the more monotonous tasks such as hoeing tobacco. And as black men and women replaced whites in the work force, the white servants and poor farmers viewed the very labor they once performed as debased. Virginia gentlemen built their fortunes upon the backs of this degraded white work force and the rapidly increasing slave class.

In the Carolinas, slavery took hold almost from the beginning. In fact a small population of Africans existed in the region prior to the 1619 date that traditionally marks the entrance of blacks into the English colonies. And from the period of South Carolina's earliest settlement, Africans "seasoned" in the Caribbean arrived in large numbers. Between one-fourth and one-third of the colony's newcomers were blacks, with men outnumbering women by a ratio of three to one, and by the first decade of the eighteenth century blacks outnumbered whites in the overall population. Slave labor was by no means merely unskilled: blacks worked as carpenters, cattle herders, and boatmen. Even more significantly, they brought with them from Africa the experience and technology for the cultivation of rice and indigo that in the eighteenth century became South Carolina's major export commodities.

Additionally, Africans could be maintained more cheaply and worked harder and, after the initial investment, made to produce greater profits. Those who suffered from sickle-cell anemia, ironically, had a genetic resistance to malaria that enabled them to survive in the mosquito-infested low country where rice and indigo were grown. Thus there were few inducements for white servants to migrate to South Carolina, and as they had a choice, they were not a major component of the seventeenth-century Carolina low-country work force. So despite the high original purchase price, and fear that Africans would run away—the Spanish town of Saint Augustine was a place of refuge—Carolinians made a conscious choice to build their society based upon slave labor and, beginning in 1690, enacted stringent slave codes to protect their human chattel.

Pennsylvanians pursued a different path, depending upon white indentured servants instead of slaves to supply their labor. By the end of the seventeenth century there were probably fewer than five hundred slaves out of a population of approximately eighteen thousand. While definite figures are hard to calculate, historians estimate that approximately one-third of early settlers were indentured servants. Originally they were offered liberal headrights as part of their freedom dues, but by the end of the century these seem to have been reduced and in most cases removed altogether. Most of the early servants were male. Having served their terms of indenture, they tended to settle in rural areas as nonlandholding laborers. In comparison to Maryland, where 90 percent of former servants became landowners and where social mobility was a reality, Pennsylvania offered little opportunity to its indentured work force.

What indentured servants were to Pennsylvania, free families were to New England. While servants, tenants, and hired labor were common in commercial centers such as Springfield, Massachusetts, and Bristol, Rhode Island, they did not exceed 4 percent of the population in the agricultural towns, where four-fifths of "the farmers kept no male servants at all" (Stephen Innes, *Work and Labor,* p. 56). Likewise, slaves did not provide an alternative to free labor: in all of New England, slaves accounted for about 1 percent of the population, numbering slightly more than one thousand, and as in England, they were mostly house servants. Day laborers hired in time of necessity were another component of the work force, but they were hard to find and the high wages they could command placed them beyond the means of most farmers.

WOMEN AND THE FAMILY

By the end of the seventeenth century, colonial dwellings, even for the poorest, had come a long way from the sod houses and shacks that once existed in Virginia, New Netherland, and New England. Except for the wealthy, English settlers typically dwelt in small single-room houses, twenty-by-twenty feet (six-by-six meters), which provided little light, air, or privacy. These physical limitations work against the popular image of large extended families dwelling together under one roof. Rather, the typical colonial family tended to be neither extended nor nuclear, but rather a "mixed affair of parents, stepparents, guardians, natural children, stepchildren, and wards," living in a small community in which neighbors were also related (Hawke, *Everyday Life,* p. 62). Families in the Chesapeake differed radically from those in the north, owing in part to the higher mortality rates and imbalanced sex ratio in the South. Infant mortality and childbirth deaths were common. As Darrett and Anita Rutman's study of Middlesex County, Virginia, illustrates, of those children born prior to 1689 who managed to survive beyond infancy, almost half had lost one or both parents by the age of nine, and almost two-thirds were orphaned by their thirteenth birthday. Women, always in short supply, married at an early age and when widowed could and did remarry quickly. In such unstable conditions, the makeup of the family was constantly shifting, and patriarchal control was difficult to sustain.

In New England, where there was a more balanced sex ratio and the ravages of disease were less life-threatening, women tended to marry in their early twenties, men in their middle to late twenties. While there are instances of truly large families—Benjamin Franklin, for instance, was one of seventeen—the more typical number of children was somewhere between five and seven. Death in childbirth was much less frequent than in the southern colonies and longevity not uncommon. As women were therefore less likely to be widowed until late in life, the rate of frequent remarriage was small. This translated into family relationships in which the hierarchical structure subordinated the interests of the wife to those of her husband. In such a family the parents could expect to see their children grow, arrange the marriages of their daughters, and exploit their sons' labor until they should reach adulthood and establish their own families—and sometimes beyond.

While women in the South, because of their scarcity, had the ability to select their husbands from a wider field and to obtain a degree of economic independence through widowhood and profitable marriages, women in the North had the advantage of greater marital stability, longer life spans, and more favorable domestic situations in general. But in both North and South, women lived in rigorous patriarchal societies that supported legal restrictions upon women's rights. In some colonies husbands could sell off their wives' property without their consent, and when husbands died intestate—and more than half of all men did so—their wives could expect only dower rights, usually a third of the estate, meant to maintain them and keep them off the relief roles. Even here the widow's property rights were limited and might revert back to the husband's estate if she remarried. The result of these property laws favored the rights of the eldest son over those of the mother, although in some instances widows successfully challenged unfavorable wills and other property settlements. Again, in some colonies women had *feme sole* rights to operate their own businesses and own property in their own name, but this too was a limited right intended to keep women off of public relief.

Women were expected to be the educators of their children, teaching them how to read—but not to write, for it was not seen as necessary for women to write and they therefore frequently lacked this skill. In the early stages of colonization, women worked alongside their husbands in the fields, but they also raised the families and cared for the household. As summed up by Laurel Thatcher Ulrich, "a married women in early New England was simultaneously a housewife, a deputy husband, a consort, a mother, a mistress, a neighbor, and a Christian." On the war-torn frontier she might also become a heroine" (*Good Wives,* p. 9). Alternatively, she might also be the deviant daughter of Eve, guilty of harlotry, infanticide, witchcraft, and adultery. There is thus little evidence for those who seek to find a golden age for women's rights in the colonial past.

The demographic differences from colony to colony with regard to age of marriage, number of children, and longevity, narrowed by the end of the century as the domestic lives of white women became more similar and, at the same time, more restricted. The major exception to this increasingly narrow sphere for women's freedom was Rhode Island, where their roles were conceived more liberally.

SOCIAL STRUCTURE AND CONFLICT AT THE END OF THE CENTURY

By the end of the seventeenth century, the English inhabitants along the Atlantic seaboard had established twelve colonies bordered on the south by the Spanish in Florida, and on the north by the French in Canada. Their founding, as Karl Marx noted in his *Communist Manifesto,* signaled the opening of a world-market system. No longer weak dependent settlements, they had developed within the mercantile system into important markets and providers of raw materials for English merchants. In the American colonies it was the staple-producing economies in the Carolinas and the Chesapeake based on slave labor, and the commercial colonies in the North that utilized wage labor, not the subsistence-farming communities of New England, that were to be the major forces shaping eighteenth-century society.

As these colonies grew in economic power and size, social conflict became more and more frequent. The Amerindians fought back against the English conquest of their lands: local and limited raids and counter-raids produced large-scale wars. In 1622 the Powhatans launched an attack against Jamestown, killing 347 Virginians. The survivors saw this as a blessing, for it enabled them to kill off the Chesapeake peoples without constraint, and, as one noted, "now their cleared ground in all their villages shall be inhabited by us." At one treaty-signing ceremony, the English offered poisoned wine to the Indians, killing over two hundred outright, and an additional fifty in the fighting that followed. In 1644 the Chesapeake nations tried once more to oust the invaders from their lands, but again they were defeated in battle and forced to sign a humiliating treaty.

In New England the Pequots offered the greatest resistance to English conquest. In 1637 the English, aided by the Narragansetts, almost exterminated the Pequots completely. In just one battle at Mystic, the Puritans, invoking God's name, killed five hundred Pequots, and then placed their captives on ships which they sank "to feed the fishes with 'em." Then the English turned on the Algonquians, already weakened by epidemic diseases, and converted them into "praying Indians," forced to live in fourteen villages where they adopted English clothes, customs, and Christianity. As the ethnohistorian James Merrell has shown, where the English lacked power they met with the Amerindians on the latter's terms, adapting to their rituals and customs. Once the white men gained the upper hand, however, they dispensed with the traditional courtesies, and forced the Native Americans to conform to English ways.

In the most serious of these Indian struggles, King Philip's War of 1675, the Wampanoag leader Metacom organized a league of Indian resistance against the colonists, driving them almost into the sea. But disease and shortages of arms and food brought a halt to Metacom's victories, and by the summer of 1676 the war was over, the Wampanoags defeated. A similar fate befell the Tuscaroras, Yamasees, Saraws, Catawbas, Congarees, Santees, and other lesser tribes in the south. The fate of the Iroquois, Creeks, and Cherokees was bound up in the French and English wars for empire that lasted from 1689 to 1783. Forced to take sides in order to survive, they too were ultimately destroyed. By the time of the American Revolution a mere 100,000 Amerindians remained in English North America. While Europeans had fought for empire, the Amerindians had battled for survival, and lost.

There were few opportunities for blacks to fight their oppressors in the seventeenth century. Their numbers were too few; if they ran away—their most effective form of resistance—they were easily identifiable and had but limited knowledge of their local geography. The first large-scale slave revolt did not occur until 1739 in Stono, South Carolina.

Serious rebellions and conflicts occurred within the white population as well. The most threatening to any established government was Bacon's Rebellion in Virginia (1675–1676). What began as a frontier uprising for Indian lands, led by Nathaniel Bacon, a wealthy member of the Virginia council, against the governor, William Berkeley, became a struggle over unequal tax rates, representation, and governmental favoritism. The 1681 uprisings led by John Coode and Josias Fendall in Maryland, and the even more radical 1688–1691 rebellion led by Jacob Leisler in New York, both involved religious struggles that pitted Protestants against Catholics, but there were even more important underlying issues of class discontent that help explain the ferocity of the conflicts in each colony.

Indeed, by the end of the century increasing social and class stratification created major problems. In the colonial cities where the dwellings and clothes of the rich appeared close to the hovels and rags of the poor, these disparities were most obvious. As early as mid century, taxes had to be raised to care for the numerous poor and unemployed who in times of crisis flocked to the cities where riots were always a threat. In Boston in 1689, a crowd gathered and attacked the newly opened Anglican church, breaking its windows and smearing its walls with dung. Seamen, dockhands, laborers, artisans, thieves, and pirates walked the urban streets, and in their wake came the taverns, brothels, jails, and other social indicators of modernity.

In the same towns and on the same streets one could also find schools and colleges, bookshops and printing presses, open-air markets filled with the products of the hinterlands, carted overland on roads extending into the backcountry. The city harbors bustled with activity, town streets echoed with the sounds of a growing economy. These too were social indicators of modernity ushered in by the social, economic, and political changes of the seventeenth century. As the English inhabitants of North America faced the new century, they were no longer dependent and fragile, they were instead the vibrant harbingers of the commercial and industrial might that would change the entire world.

BIBLIOGRAPHY

General Studies

Bailyn, Bernard, and Philip D. Morgan, eds. *Strangers Within the Realm: Cultural Margins of the First British Empire* (1991).

Bridenbaugh, Carl. *Cities in the Wilderness: The First Century of Urban Life in America, 1625–1742* (1955; 2d ed. 1960).

Greene, Jack P. *Pursuits of Happiness: The Social Development of Early Modern British Colonies and the Formation of American Culture* (1988).

Grevin, Philip J., Jr. *Four Generations: Population, Land, and Family in Colonial Andover, Massachusetts* (1970).

Hawke, David Freeman. *The Colonial Experience* (1966).

———. *Everyday Life in Early America* (1988).

McCusker, John J., and Russell R. Menard. *The Economy of British America, 1607–1789* (1985).

Morgan, Edmund S. *Inventing the People: The Rise of Popular Sovereignty in England and America* (1988).

Nash, Gary B. *Red, White, and Black: The Peoples of Early America* (1974; 2d ed. 1982).

Smith, James Morton, ed. *Seventeenth-Century America: Essays in Colonial History* (1959).

European Background and Reciprocal Discovery

Cressy, David. *Coming Over: Migration and Communication Between England and New England in the Seventeenth Century* (1987).

Fischer, David Hackett. *Albion's Seed: Four British Folkways in America* (1989).

Jennings, Francis. *The Invasion of America: Indians, Colonialism, and the Cant of Conquest* (1975; 2d ed. 1976).

Martin, Calvin. "The European Impact on the Culture of a Northeastern Algonquian Tribe: An Ecological Interpretation." *William and Mary Quarterly* 3d ser., 31 (1974): 3–26.

New England Colonies

Allen, David Grayson. *In English Ways: The Movement of Societies and the Transferral of English Local Law and Custom to Massachusetts Bay in the Seventeenth Century* (1981).

Archer, Richard. "New England Mosaic: A Demographic Analysis for the Seventeenth Century." *William and Mary Quarterly* 3d ser., 47 (1990): 477–502.

Boyer, Paul, and Stephen Nissenbaum. *Salem Possessed: The Social Origins of Witchcraft* (1974).

Breen, Timothy H., and Stephen Foster. "Moving to the New World: The Character of Early Massachusetts Immigration." *William and Mary Quarterly* 3d ser., 30 (1973): 189–222.

Erikson, Kai T. *Wayward Puritans: A Study in the Sociology of Deviance* (1966).

Innes, Stephen. *Labor in a New Land: Economy and Society in Seventeenth-Century Springfield* (1983).

Lockridge, Kenneth A. *A New England Town, the First Hundred Years: Dedham, Massachusetts, 1636–1736* (1970).

———. "Assessing the Little Communities of Early America." *William and Mary Quarterly* 3d ser., 43 (1986): 163–178.

Rutman, Darrett B. *Winthrop's Boston: Portrait of a Puritan Town, 1630–1649* (1965).

Southern Colonies

Morgan, Edmund S. *American Slavery, American Freedom: The Ordeal of Colonial Virginia* (1975).

Rutman, Darrett B., and Anita H. Rutman. *A Place in Time: Middlesex County, Virginia, 1650–1750* (1984).

Wood, Peter H. *Black Majority: Negroes in Colonial South Carolina from 1670 Through the Stono Rebellion* (1974).

Middle Colonies

Ritchie, Robert C. *The Duke's Province: A Study of New York Politics and Society, 1664–1691* (1977).

Salinger, Sharon V. *"To Serve Well and Faithfully": Labor and Indentured Servants in Pennsylvania, 1682–1800* (1987).

Schwartz, Sally. *"A Mixed Multitude": The Struggle for Toleration in Colonial Pennsylvania* (1987).

Work, Women, and the Family

Breen, Timothy H. "A Changing Labor Force and Race Relations in Virginia, 1660–1710." *Journal of Social History* 7 (1973): 3–25.

Henretta, James A. "Families and Farms: *Mentalité* in Pre-Industrial America." *William and Mary Quarterly* 3d ser., 35 (1978): 3–32.

Hoffer, Peter C., and N. E. Hull. *Murdering Mothers: Infanticide in England and New England, 1558–1803* (1981).

Innes, Stephen C., ed. *Work and Labor in Early America* (1988).

Koehler, Lyle. *A Search for Power: The "Weaker Sex" in Seventeenth-Century New England* (1980).

Lockridge, Kenneth A. *Literacy in Colonial New England: An Enquiry into the Social Context of Literacy in the Early Modern West* (1974).

Norton, Mary Beth. "The Evolution of White Women's Experience in Early America." *American Historical Review* 89 (1984): 593–619.

Ulrich, Laurel Thatcher. *Good Wives: Image and Reality in the Lives of Women in Northern New England, 1650–1750* (1982).

SEE ALSO **Community Studies; The Deep South; The Middle Atlantic Region**; and various essays in the sections "**Ethnic and Racial Subcultures,**" "**Periods of Social Change,**" "**Space and Place,**" and "**Work and Labor.**"

THE AMERICAN COLONIES FROM 1700 TO THE SEVEN YEARS' WAR

Christine Leigh Heyrman

BY THE BEGINNING of the eighteenth century, the eastern coast of North America had been forever transformed. The fields and forests, rivers and streams where generations of Indian tribes had farmed, fished, and hunted had become a world owned and ruled by white men, a borderland of the British empire.

A combination of epidemic disease and warfare during the seventeenth century had shattered Native American settlements along the Atlantic coast. Metacomet's War (King Philip's War) of 1675–1676 delivered a deathblow to the resistance of New England tribes. At the same time white Virginians launched their final campaign against the Indians of the Chesapeake. In the 1680s the tribes of the Delaware Valley, their strength sapped by disease, ceded territory to William Penn's new Quaker colony. Finally, in 1715–1716 South Carolina settlers crushed the last major pan-Indian uprising of the colonial period, the Yamasee War. Weakened and demoralized, the remnants of these coastal tribes ceded their ancestral territories, retreated inland, or resigned themselves to resettlement in communities regulated by colonial authorities. White invaders gained, as the prize of victory, the preserve of the vanquished—their cornfields and game preserves, their villages and burial grounds.

THE WORLD OF BRITISH NORTH AMERICA

Their control of the Atlantic perimeter secured, white colonials continued to construct, on the ruins of the coastal Indians' old world, a new world. In fact, during the first half of the eighteenth century, the new world of British North America assumed ever more myriad forms.

New England In the northernmost reaches of Britain's empire, the whole of New England was becoming a network of contiguous villages, each within a few miles of the next, knit together by crude roads, droving trails, and rivers. A common or town green commanded the center of each community, and clustered around that open space were small shops and taverns for trading and socializing, a meetinghouse for religious and civic business, and simple two-story wood houses framed in oak and sheathed or shingled in cedar. Scattered beyond the center of town were fields sown with maize and rye, pastures for cows and sheep, orchards, and salt marshes, as well as mills for grinding corn and sawing lumber and, occasionally, forges for smelting iron ore.

Most eighteenth-century New Englanders followed their ancestors into farming. They engaged in the same struggle to wring a subsistence from the region's stony soil and harsh climate. But commercial pursuits intensified among the inhabitants of some coastal towns with fair harbors—Portsmouth and Newburyport, Gloucester and Marblehead, New London and Salem, Providence and Newport. In these burgeoning "satellite ports" of Boston, wharves sprouted within the sheltered bays, coves, and river inlets. At these docksides, boats were anchored, ships were built and repaired, and catches of fish were dried on crudely constructed wooden shelves called flakes. The flourishing traffic in fishing, shipbuilding, and rum distilling cut into the business of Boston, but that city remained the region's main seaport.

The Middle Colonies In the mid-Atlantic colonies of New York, East and West Jersey, Pennsylvania, and Delaware, settlement was more dispersed, agriculture more commercialized and profitable, and land more costly. The entire region was distinguished by the diverse backgrounds of its inhabitants, which became even more varied during the eighteenth century. The fertile Hudson River valley between New York City and Albany, the first of the area's two premier food-producing districts, supported a number of farming families. Many were of Dutch extraction and, like the vast majority of New England's rural folk, they owned the land that they worked. But unlike most New England farmers, these industrious Dutch cultivators produced a surplus of grain and livestock. They floated their goods down the Hudson to merchants in New York City, that region's main entrepôt, for shipment to the Caribbean. With the profits they maintained substantial brick or stone farmhouses adorned with dormers and double doors, roofed in red tile, and surrounded by broad barns and other outbuildings. Far more imposing than the residences of these prosperous farming families were the extensive manorial estates of Hudson Valley's ruling elite, an intermarried group of English and Dutch patroons (landlords) whose acreage was enlarged by an eighteenth-century influx of Scots, Scotch-Irish, and German tenants.

In the other major agricultural district of the mid-Atlantic, the Delaware River valley of New Jersey and Pennsylvania, a similar patchwork of ethnic groups was spread across the countryside. Towns and hamlets were slow to develop, but farmhouses built of gray-brown fieldstone and topped with slate roofs dotted the landscape, along with a scattering of churches, meetinghouses, taverns, and mills. Most farmers in the Delaware Valley—a mixture of English, Welsh, German, Swedish, Dutch, and Scots families—shared the keen commercial instincts of those along the Hudson. They sowed their rolling hills into a sea of wheat, supplemented by crops of flax and hemp, fruit trees, and livestock, producing the largest surplus yielded by any part of British North America. Grain and animals were transported over a network of roads and waterways linking these agricultural districts to Philadelphia and then shipped to consumers in the West Indies and Europe.

The Chesapeake Colonies To the south, the colonial settlements of the Chesapeake sprawled from the head of Chesapeake Bay in the north to North Carolina's Albemarle Sound in the south and westward into the rolling hill country of the Piedmont. This countryside contrasted sharply with the compact, nucleated villages of New England and the neat, sturdy farmsteads of the mid-Atlantic colonies. Although some Chesapeake planters were diversifying their output to include grains, livestock, timber products, and naval stores, tobacco remained the region's main crop. But tobacco depleted the soil's nutrients, obliging farmers to clear and plant new fields every few years while older ones lay fallow. When planters changed fields, they shifted the site of their barns, sheds, and even dwellings. The result was a landscape littered with rotting tree stumps, ragged stretches of spent soil and straggling weeds, and small, squarish wooden houses and barns in various stages of construction, disrepair, or abandonment. Set against this scarred countryside of ramshackle buildings, the estates of the gentry seemed all the more impressive. Their "great houses," built of vivid red brick with symmetrical facades and hipped roofs, opened onto groves of tall trees and elegant gardens. Beyond these mansions lay bustling complexes of workshops, kitchens, storehouses, stables, and the shacks and shanties that comprised the slave quarters.

The plantations of both yeoman and gentry families, ranging from a few hundred to several thousand acres, lined shores of the Chesapeake's myriad rivers and creeks. That location afforded planters ready access to the several hundred British vessels that came annually to collect consignments of tobacco. Directly linked to European markets, the region's rural population had no need for native merchants to serve as middlemen or seaports to sustain commerce. Neither developed, making the Chesapeake the only coastal region in the colonies without a major city.

The only places in the Chesapeake where large numbers of people gathered regularly were the county seats. These tiny hamlets, located at a central crossroads, included the local courthouse and jail, a tavern, a field for training the militia and racing horses, an Anglican church, and, perhaps, a few shops and law offices. Sabbath worship services and court sessions, sometimes accompanied by the occasional fair, horse race, or cockfight, drew families from every corner of the county. They were almost entirely a mixture of free whites of English ancestry and enslaved blacks, who comprised perhaps 35 to 40 percent of the region's population.

The Lower Southern Colonies South of the Chesapeake, another sort of plantation society took shape over the first half of the eighteenth century. The Cape Fear region of North Carolina and the lowlands of South Carolina and Georgia comprised the southernmost extension of colonial settlement on the North American mainland. Its white population was both smaller and more ethnically diverse than that of the Chesapeake, an amalgam of English immigrants from the parent country and the West Indies, French Calvinists known as Huguenots, and a sprinkling of Germans, Swiss, and Sephardic Jews from Brazil. Its black population, almost entirely enslaved and drawn from West Africa and the West Indies, comprised a majority of the area's population by the beginning of the eighteenth century and over two-thirds by 1750. The bound labor force also included a substantial number of Indian slaves from that region's coastal tribes.

The economy of this entire low-country region depended on the Indian trade in deerskins, the production of indigo, and, most particularly, the cultivation of rice in flooded fields. It is likely that the presence of black slaves from the rice-growing coast of West Africa prompted the emergence of that crop as the staple of commercial agriculture in the Carolinas and Georgia. Ironically, black success in cultivating that crop encouraged the importation of slaves in increasing numbers.

Unlike the Chesapeake, which lacked an urban center of any significance, this southernmost plantation society rapidly developed a hub for its commercial and cultural life in Charleston. That city also became a refuge for affluent planting families, who fled their estates in the swampy, mosquito-infested countryside whenever they had the chance. Carolina boasted many such nabobs, for high demand and favorable prices commanded by rice in Europe made its colonial planters the richest single group on the mainland of British America.

Although diversity characterized its landscapes and economies, societies and cultures, the British American mainland remained, throughout the eighteenth century, overwhelmingly rural. Most colonials continued to make their living from the land, and more than 90 percent lived in towns of less than 2,500 people. The rhythms of daylight and darkness, the patterns of climatic and seasonal changes, continued to shape the basic conditions of everyday life. Comparatively isolated from cosmopolitan influences, most colonial farming families were deeply localistic and parochial in their outlook, their concerns focused on kin, church, and community.

BLACK AMERICANS IN THE SOUTH

Only in the South did rural life change dramatically during the first half of the eighteenth century, as the labor force shifted from white servants to black slaves. Although men and women of African ancestry—slave, servant, and free—had lived and labored in the South during the seventeenth century, their numbers expanded dramatically after 1700. Over the first half of the eighteenth century, a much larger percentage of that swelling population also consisted of blacks who had been born in Africa rather than in the Caribbean or the colonial mainland.

Slave importations rose for a number of reasons. A decline in mortality rates throughout the South made investments in lifelong laborers more cost effective. The prosperity of white planters made slaves more affordable, and an increasing supply made them more accessible. Finally, a falling off in white servant immigration foreclosed an important alternative labor supply. Such were the circumstances that conspired to bring some 250,000 black men, women, and children to the North American mainland between 1700 and the American Revolution. These forced immigrants, who had survived both the horrors of captivity in Africa and the appalling mortality rates of the "Middle Passage" across the Atlantic, now faced the challenge of adapting to lives of hardship, deprivation, and toil in the colonial South. There they joined a native-born black population that was almost entirely enslaved, usually consigned to field labor, and increasingly regulated by severe slave codes.

Whether a slave was auctioned off to the Chesapeake or to the lower South shaped his or her future in important ways. Slaves in the low country of South Carolina and Georgia lived on plantations with as many as fifty other blacks, about half of whom were African born. Slaves residing in large lowland quarters, virtually black villages, had infrequent contact with either their masters or the rest of the sparse white population. "They are as 'twere, a Nation within a Nation, in all Country settlements," Francis Le Jau, an Episcopal clergyman, remarked, "they labour together and converse almost wholly among themselves."

Many Chesapeake slaves, like those in the lower South, were African born, but most lived on smaller plantations with fewer fellow blacks. Throughout the eighteenth century more than half lived on plantations with fewer than twenty slaves. Less densely concentrated than in the Carolinas and Georgia, Chesapeake slaves had more contact with whites. Unlike the absentee owners who lingered in Charleston, leaving white overseers and black drivers to run their plantations, masters in the upper South actively managed their estates and subjected their slaves' performance to closer scrutiny.

In the lower South, by contrast, the density of black settlement afforded slaves the opportunity to cultivate a separate sphere in their quarters. The widespread use of the "task system" rather than gang labor on South Carolina plantations also widened the window of freedom within slavery. When a slave had completed his assigned task for the day, one planter explained, "his master feels no right to call upon him." During such free time blacks tended garden plots, growing vegetables and raising poultry to supplement their diets or to sell.

The plantation culture of the Chesapeake may have fostered greater intimacy between blacks and whites than occurred in the lower South. White masters in the Chesapeake contracted both casual liaisons and longstanding relationships with their black bondswomen and occasionally acknowledged the mulatto children produced through such unions by freeing them or making provisions for their support in wills. Sexual or marital ties between black men and white women were less common, but mistresses of large plantations frequently formed affectionate relationships with the black women who served as their maids and cooks. Black women wet-nursed and nurtured white infants and young children, often forming emotional ties that endured for life. On plantations great and small, young children of both races played together, and adolescent boys, learning the workings of the largest estates, passed some of their free time in the company of black drivers and craftsmen. Planters throughout the Chesapeake used the term "our family" to denote both white and black members of their household.

While the intermingling of races fostered some integration of European and African cultures, the infusion of African-born blacks everywhere in the South made it easier for slaves to retain the ways of their lost homeland. African influence appears in the slaves' distinctive agricultural skills and practices, folktales, music, dances, superstitions, and religious beliefs. Christianity won few converts among eighteenth-century blacks, in part because whites resisted baptizing their slaves, fearing that it might make them less tractable, but also because blacks adhered to traditional African religions.

The new influx of Africans and the concentration of enslaved blacks on the southern coast also generated tension and conflict, both within the slave quarters and between masters and slaves. Many slaveholders made a practice of purchasing Africans from several different tribes, hoping to discourage communication and collective resistance. The diversity of backgrounds, languages, and customs in the quarters made for friction between the new arrivals and more acculturated native-born blacks.

One-quarter of all "outlandish Negroes," those recently imported from Africa, died during their first year on southern plantations, and those who survived were introduced to the harsh and disorienting regimen of field labor. Native-born blacks, by contrast, enjoyed better health, a better command of English, and greater experience in dealing with whites. American-born male slaves were also more likely to establish a family life, for their advantages made them the preferred partners of black women, who were outnumbered two to one by black men during the opening decades of the eighteenth century. Finally, it was from the ranks of native-born blacks that slave owners usually recruited artisans and house servants, jobs that required greater skill than most forms of field labor and entailed greater variety. On the largest plantations, a small number of native-born men served as blacksmiths, coopers, masons, potters, carpenters, miners, shoemakers, millers, and boatmen, while black women acquired skills as cooks, laundresses, dairymaids, nurses, and seamstresses. These distinctions between immigrant and native-born within the slave community could occasion rivalries and resentments.

But divisions within the slave quarters did little to diminish black resistance to white domination, and that defiance took many forms. Despite the precautions of some slaveholders, recently arrived slaves commonly made attempts at collective escape. Groups of runaways fled to the interior and formed Maroon communities that re-created their home villages in West Africa. These efforts were usually unsuccessful because the Maroon settlements were large enough to be easily detected; Carolinians even enlisted the Cherokee Indians to return runaways for a reward.

More acculturated blacks adopted subtler ways of subverting slavery. William Byrd, a Virginia planter, left a record in his diary of the range of resistance tactics deployed by slaves on his estate, but he never recognized the pattern of deliberate obstruction in his slaves' behavior. He regularly cataloged complaints about house servants defying his orders, spoiling his furniture, pilfering his liquor, and engaging him and his wife in elaborate contests of will; he fretted over field hands who broke his tools and dragged out their tasks. Domestics and field hands alike faked illness, feigned stupidity and laziness, stole from storehouses, hid in the woods for weeks at a time, or simply absconded for long visits to other plantations. Other slaves, usually escaping bondage as solitary individuals, found a new life as free artisans, dockworkers, or sailors in the relative anonymity of colonial seaports.

More infrequently black rebellion against bondage took direct and violent forms. Whites in communities with substantial numbers of blacks lived in gnawing dread of arson, poisoning, and insurrection. Four slave conspiracies were reported in Virginia during the first half of the eighteenth century. In South Carolina, more than two decades of abortive uprisings and insurrection scares culminated in the Stono Rebellion of 1739, the largest slave revolt of the colonial period. Nearly one hundred blacks, led by a slave named Jemmy, seized arms from a store in the low-country district of Stono, near Charleston, and killed some twenty-five whites before they were caught and killed by the white militia.

The Stono Rebellion triggered other unsuccessful slave uprisings and rumored slave conspiracies throughout the colonies in 1740 and 1741. But throughout the eighteenth century, such rebellions occurred far less frequently on the mainland of North America than they did in the Caribbean or Brazil. Whites outnumbered blacks in all the colonies except South Carolina, and only in the latter did rebels have a haven for a quick escape—Spanish Florida. Most slaves reasoned that the risks of rebellion outweighed the prospects for success—and sought opportunities for greater personal freedom within the slave system instead.

Although slavery had become the dominant form of bound labor only in the South, wealthier farmers throughout British America made more occasional use of enslaved blacks as field hands. Their labor, along with that of white indentured servants, tenants, and free workers, fostered the increasing productivity of the rural hinterland. The surplus of food produced by colonial farms sustained another important trend after 1700—the growing populations and thriving trade of major colonial cities.

THE COLONIAL CITIES

Boston and New York, Philadelphia and Charleston, little more than overgrown villages in the seventeenth century, mushroomed in size, with populations ranging from eight thousand to twenty-two thousand by 1750. Despite this growth, the scale of city life remained intimate: all of New York City was clustered at the southern tip of Manhattan Island, and Boston could be traversed in a walk of less than half an hour.

All these cities were seaports, their waterfronts fringed with wharves and shipyards and dotted with warehouses and distilleries; their streets crowded with a jumble of shops, taverns, and homes; their skylines studded with the spires of churches and the towers of public buildings. The grandest and most populous was Philadelphia, which boasted straight, neatly paved streets lined with sidewalks of flagstone, evenly spaced trees, and three-story brick buildings. Charleston's urban design also reflected some of these "modern" improvements in city planning: brick sidewalks and broad thoroughfares laid out in a gridlike pattern converged on a central square. Its finest homes, decorated with porticos or piazzas and surrounded by gardens, were secluded from busy streets behind high brick walls or iron spiked fences. Older cities like Boston and New York, founded earlier in the seventeenth century, had a more medieval aspect. Wooden structures still predominated, dwellings and shops with tiny windows and low ceilings rose no higher than two stories to steeply pitched roofs. The streets of Boston and New York also offered fewer amenities to pedestrians, who competed for space on the narrow, winding cobblestone mazes with cattle and sheep being driven to the butcher, roaming herds of swine and packs of dogs, and clattering carts, carriages, and horses.

Commerce, the lifeblood of these seaport economies, was managed by merchants who tapped the wealth of the surrounding hinterland. Traders in New York and Philadelphia shipped the Hudson and Delaware valleys' surplus of corn, wheat, cattle, and horses to feed West Indian planters and to power island sugar mills. Boston's merchants sent fish to the Caribbean and Catholic Europe, masts to Britain, and rum to West Africa. Charleston's dealers exported indigo and rice to Britain, the first for sale to English dyemakers and the second for reshipment to European consumers. With the returns of the export trade, merchants in every colonial city imported the coveted luxuries and finished goods produced in England—fine fabrics, ceramics, and tea—along with large lots of coarser textiles and iron farming implements.

Not all manufactured goods were imported from Britain. Some were produced by artisans who made up the middling classes of colonial cities. These urban craft workers did not produce finished goods in large lots for a mass market. Instead, the households of master craftsmen, which usually included a few younger and less skilled journeymen and very young, unskilled apprentices, made specific items for individual purchasers. Some artisans specialized in the maritime trades, the greater rewards going to master mariners, shipbuilders, and blacksmiths who forged anchors and iron fittings, the lesser returns to ropemakers and sailmakers who fashioned rigging. Master craft workers who processed and packed raw materials for export—butchers, millers, and rum distillers—might realize a substantial profit, as could artisans in the luxury trades—goldsmiths and silversmiths, jewelers, cabinetmakers and carriagemakers. Ranking below the master craft workers in the most lucrative trades were those who served the basic needs of city dwellers, the men and, occasionally, women who baked bread, mended shoes, combed and powdered wigs, sewed simple clothing, cut hair and beards, and tended shops and taverns.

At the bottom of seaport social hierarchies were free and bound workers. The free labor force consisted of mainly young white men and women—journeymen artisans, sailors, and fishermen, domestic workers, seamstresses, and prostitutes. The ranks of unfree workers included boys serving apprenticeships to local master craft workers and indentured servants doing menial labor in shops and on the docks.

Black men and women also made up a substantial part of the bound labor force of colonial seaports, not only in southern Charleston but in northern cities as well. While the vast majority of slaves imported from Africa were destined for a lifetime in tobacco fields and rice swamps, a smaller number were sold to urban merchants and artisans. Working as porters at the docks, assistants in craftshops, or servants in wealthy households, blacks made up almost 20 percent of New York City's population by 1750 and accounted for 10 percent of the inhabitants of Boston and Philadelphia.

People of every class and condition who lived in the major colonial seaports—perhaps one out of every twenty Americans—enjoyed a more stimulating and diverse environment than their rural countrymen. The wealthiest could enjoy an occasional ball or concert; those living in liberal New York or Charleston might even attend a play performed by English actors. The middling classes could choose among weekly newspapers and a varied stock at local bookshops and could converse with other tradespeople at private social clubs and fraternal societies. The lower classes, along with their "betters," found diversion in drinking, horse racing, cockfighting, and bull- and bearbaiting.

For what they gained from this more varied, cosmopolitan culture, city dwellers paid a price. Natural and man-made disasters could send shock waves through the delicate economies of colonial seaports, bankrupting merchants and leaving craft workers and laborers out of work. Four wars involving England and rival European powers between 1700 and 1765 disrupted transatlantic trading patterns and filled the seas with privateering vessels. Even in peacetime, commerce was fraught with risk: the storm-tossed ocean swallowed ships; small markets abroad could easily become glutted. The ups and downs of seaport economies swelled the ranks of the poor in all colonial cities by the middle of the eighteenth century, increasing the burden on the public-relief system. While all the major seaports established workhouses to employ the "able-bodied" poor, city governments continued to aid most of the dependent with small subsidies of money, food, and firewood. Not only economic life but often life itself was more precarious for city dwellers: epidemics of smallpox and yellow fever occurred with greater frequency and produced higher mortality rates in congested seaports than in the countryside. Every city except Boston had a major, catastrophic fire sometime in the eighteenth century, which destroyed large parts of the towns.

Eighteenth-century seaports were more volatile societies than the villages and counties of the surrounding countryside. Sailors and fishermen on shore leave often combined with journeymen and apprentices, servants and slaves to vandalize the property of unpopular merchants, tear down brothels, or battle with the press-gangs that dragooned unwilling colonial recruits into the Royal Navy. Some contested issues, such as the new and controversial technique of smallpox inoculation, galvanized crowds comprising a cross section of seaport society. Religious prejudice also occasioned collective action. Crowds in New York City gathered outside of cemeteries to heckle mourners at Jewish funerals. In Boston, the expression of anti-Catholic sentiment was institutionalized in an annual "Pope's Day" riot. Effigies of the pope were paraded by laboring people from the north and south ends of town, with each side trying to destroy their rivals' creation.

Ethnic diversity contributed to the tensions in eighteenth-century cities. The flood of new immigrants who arrived in British America after 1700 entered through these seaports, and some settled there permanently. By the 1770s, white arrivals included a substantial number of English immigrants, but also some 250,000 Scotch-Irish, perhaps 135,000 Germans, and a sprinkling of Swiss, Swedes, Welsh, Highland Scots, and Sephardic Jews. Often driven from their homelands by famine, warfare, or religious persecution, these immigrants risked shipboard mortality rates that often rivaled those on slave vessels in the Middle Passage. And, as in the seventeenth century, many immigrants were desperate enough to mortgage their freedom to redeem the price of passage, signing indentures to work as servants in the New World. Because of this migration, the streets of every major colonial city except Boston—whose strong Puritan influence made it unattractive to immigrants—resounded with a babel of different languages and English dialects. In Philadelphia business was conducted in German as often as it was in English; in Charleston, the range of tongues was wider still, including Gullah, a pidgin language developed by black slaves.

THE FRONTIER

Although seaports attracted some of these new immigrants, the vast majority settled in a wholly different environment. The first several decades of the eighteenth century brought not only a new concentration of population in colonial cities but also an even more remarkable dispersal of population to the frontier. That region became a magnet not only for many recent immigrants but also for a large contingent of young, native-born colonials. Immigration swelled an American population that was already growing at a runaway rate from natural increase. The birthrate in eighteenth-century America was triple the rate in the late twentieth century. Most women bore between five and eight children, and most children born north or west of the fever-ridden Carolina coast survived to maturity. Young men and women who reached their twenty-first birthday could expect to live another forty years or more, although the prospects for longevity were somewhat less favorable in the coastal South. The relatively low rates of childhood mortality and long life expectancy among the majority of eighteenth-century colonials reflected the basic conditions of most of their lives. An increasingly abundant supply of food fostered resistance to disease; the spread of settlement away from the coast to drier and healthier inland regions reduced the incidence of malaria; the low density of settlement in such areas militated against mass contagion from epidemic diseases.

The brisk rate of population growth from both immigration and natural increase made movement away from the coast more a matter of necessity than of choice. By the beginning of the eighteenth century, many older rural communities could no longer accommodate the children of longtime settlers, let alone newcomers. In some New England towns, three and four generations were putting pressure on a limited supply of land, and wasteful farming practices had sapped the soil of its fertility. Farther south, earlier settlers had already snatched up the choice farmland of Philadelphia's outlying counties, the prime tidewater tobacco property, and the best low-country rice swamps. With older rural communities offering few opportunities to either native-born or newly arrived white families, both groups were forced to create new communities in new places.

Since New England did not beckon most new immigrants, the legion descendants of old Yankee families peopled that region's frontier. Throughout the eighteenth century young men, often brothers or cousins who had grown up in the same coastal village, brought their brides to western Massachusetts, eastern Connecticut, Maine, New Hampshire, and Vermont. There they felled trees, built farmsteads, gathered churches, and named tiny hamlets after their hometowns.

Better opportunities to acquire plentiful land at cheaper prices lay south of New York. By the 1720s recent German and Scotch-Irish immigrants as well as land-hungry native-born Pennsylvanians were pouring into the western portion of that colony. Some settled permanently, but others streamed southward into the back parts of Virginia and North Carolina along the eastern side of the Blue Ridge Mountains. There they encountered native Virginians pressing westward across the Piedmont and pushing through mountain gaps to the west side of the Blue Ridge. Westward settlement met with encouragement both from land speculators seeking profits and from colonial governments hoping to attract new taxpayers and to establish a buffer of settlements between the coast and the powerful Indian tribes of the interior.

Considerations of profit and security prompted South Carolinians along the rice-growing coast to foster both the settlement of their colony's interior and the founding of Georgia in 1732. A variety of ethnic groups responded to the lure of acquiring land on favorable terms, and settlements of Swiss, Germans, Austrians, Scots, Scotch-Irish, Welsh, and Irish spread across the Carolina interior and the new Georgia colony.

Wherever they settled in the backcountry, families dispersed across the landscape. Although people who shared kinship ties or a common ethnic and religious background tended to congregate within the same neighborhood, western settlers still endured greater isolation than did other colonials. From many farmsteads it was a day's ride to the nearest courthouse; taverns and churches were often just as distant. One Scots husband consoled his wife with the assurance that "[W]e would get all these trees cut down . . . [so] that we would see from house to house."

Physical distance impeded the formation of strong social bonds, as did the rapid rate at which people came to and left western communities. Many frontier families roamed restlessly within the backcountry, pulling up stakes three and four times before settling down permanently. It was not uncommon for as many as one-third of the inhabitants of a frontier county to move on after a few years—and to be replaced by an even larger number of newcomers. Houses reflected the transiency of their occupants: most families crowded into one-room shacks built on posts sunk in the ground and walled with mud, turf, or crudely hewn logs.

The search for better opportunities propelled much of this movement, but backcountry economies afforded no chance for quick riches. Large portions of the interior lying on unnavigable rivers above the fall line were cut off from easy access to seaport markets. By 1755 several primitive wagon roads linked the backcountry of Pennsylvania and Virginia to towns farther east, including Philadelphia, but transporting crops and driving livestock overland proved prohibitively expensive. Cut off from outside markets, frontier farmers grew only enough to feed their households, selling whatever small surplus remained to new settlers. Not only poor transportation but also the lack of labor kept frontier farmers from tapping the commercial potential of their rich lands. Most backcountry inhabitants relied entirely on the labor of their families; they lacked the means to increase their output by investing in a slave or even a servant.

COLONIAL ECONOMY AND SOCIETY

The settlement of the frontier helped to offset one of the most striking trends of colonial development during the eighteenth century—an increasingly uneven distribution of wealth. As more farmers produced surplus food for sale in urban markets or export abroad and seaport merchants enlarged their trade, the colonial economy as a whole grew and prospered. In absolute terms the total wealth of British America increased, and standards of living for all classes improved. But the share of total wealth claimed by the richest colonials grew larger while the proportion owned by middling and poorer families dwindled.

The distance between richer and poorer colonials was widening most dramatically in major seaports and the coastal plantation districts of the South. The most successful merchants, who far surpassed other seaport dwellers in wealth, invested their surplus capital in land, rum distilleries, iron foundries, and military contracting. Similarly, southern planters who could afford slaves outproduced their poorer neighbors who could not, and plowed their profits into the purchase of more land and more slaves. In short, those with some capital to invest could amass even more wealth. But for families with limited resources, opportunities diminished as population increased. Land along the seaboard became scarcer and more expensive, and tenancy became more common everywhere outside of New England. Inequality would have become even more pronounced if not for the frontier, which siphoned off large numbers of immigrants and young people from more settled districts and supplied them with land at low prices. In fact, the lack of opportunity to market crops or to buy bound labor made the frontier, more than anywhere else in eighteenth-century America, a society of equals.

Increasing economic inequality everywhere except the frontier tended to reinforce the stratified social order that had characterized the colonies since their initial settlement. To be sure, the divisions of class and status were far less deeply etched in eighteenth-century America than in England. The "middling classes," a minority in English society, still made up a majority among white colonials. Ownership of land, rare among English farmers, remained the rule among white Americans; even men who started out as tenants typically became freehold farmers at some time in their lives. On the other hand, late colonial society was, in some ways, more hierarchical than its antecedents. In every colony small groups of interrelated and intermarried families headed by planters, merchants, and lawyers dominated economic life, monopolized the most important political offices, and commanded the deference and respect of their social "inferiors."

In long-settled rural communities of both North and South, the wealthiest farmers and planters constituted a kind of local gentry. These men at the pinnacle of the local pecking order often supplemented their income from farming and enhanced their influence among their neighbors by keeping stores, milling wheat or logs, or practicing law. Year after year their communities entrusted them—and their male descendants—with the responsibilities of directing civic life and church affairs, and overseeing public order and morality. The most successful merchants enjoyed a similar status in seaports. They dominated the choicest positions in city governments and shared power in colonial assemblies with lawyers and the largest farmers and planters.

Only the backcountry lacked an acknowledged "gentry" to supply local leadership. Only a handful of farmers in each frontier county were distinguished from their neighbors by owning a few extra acres or a single slave. To these politically inexperienced and uneducated men fell the thankless tasks of overseeing community order or serving in public office. It was hard for men who commanded little deference from their neighbors to police sprawling backcountry communities. Not surprisingly, coarse and aggressive behavior dominated life on the frontier.

Women and the Family The principle of hierarchy that set its imprint on society in most regions of America continued to shape relationships between men and women, husbands and wives, parents and children. The subordinate position of women in the early settlements, established in law and confirmed by customary practice, carried over into the eighteenth century. Most women of the late colonial period, like their mothers and grandmothers, were, in the eyes of the law, wards of fathers and husbands.

Most eighteenth-century white women, after marrying in their late teens to mid twenties, became hardworking farm wives. While husbands tended fields and livestock, their spouses supervised the dairy, poultry, orchard, and vegetable garden; the spinning of flax and the sewing of clothes; the preservation of foodstuffs and the cooking of meals; the boiling of soap and the dipping of candles. Added to those duties was the oversight of a household of children, to which a new baby might be added every other year. Even more taxing were the responsibilities of white women on the frontier, who, like the majority of black female slaves, worked as field hands alongside male family members. One traveler from the seaboard expressed his astonishment at seeing German women in western Pennsylvania "at work abroad on the Farm mowing, Hoeing, Loading Dung into a Cart."

The growth of eighteenth-century seaports afforded some white women in those settings more freedom from domestic chores. The wives of well-to-do merchants enjoyed almost complete leisure—occupied with visiting, reading, and doing needlework—because of the availability of female slaves and free and indentured white servants, who worked as maids and cooks. Even those women who could not afford the luxury of household help spent less time and energy doing domestic work because city markets supplied most of the food for urban families. They were also relieved of the laborious chores of spinning and weaving by purchasing their cloth at dry goods stores.

For women who had to support themselves, colonial cities offered a number of employments. The most respectable and lucrative occupations for women, all requiring long apprenticeships and expert skill, included midwifery, millinery, and "mantua making" (the making of fashionable dresses and cloaks). Wives of artisans and retailers sometimes assisted in their husbands' businesses and, as widows, often continued to manage groceries, taverns, and printshops. But even in seaports most women were confined to caring for houses, husbands, and children; fewer than one out of every ten city women worked outside her own home.

Just as wives remained subordinate to the authority of husbands, so parents in the mid eighteenth century—particularly fathers—continued to exercise considerable influence over their children. Most young people still expected to pattern their own lives upon those of their parents, to follow the familiar paths of preceding generations rather than to project alternative destinies. But for an increasing number of these young people in older rural areas, those expectations were imperiled by diminishing reserves of family land within their immediate neighborhoods. Farming fathers whose total acreage was too small to subdivide among male heirs pursued various strategies to assure a future livelihood for their offspring. Most commonly one male child was deeded the family farmstead, and other boys were provided with tracts on the frontier, an apprenticeship in a trade, or a college education; daughters, when they married, received dowries of livestock and household goods.

Such strategies sustained the strength of paternal influence over their children's choice of careers and mates. But everywhere in British America, that authority was attenuated somewhat, in part by economic necessity, in part by a greater range of alternative occupations for young men, and in part by an increasing tendency to consider the individual preferences of young people.

The Black Family Young African Americans learned from infancy to submit to authority, but it was masters, rather than fathers or mothers, who claimed the power to command their lives. Slave owners, not slave parents, usually named the infants born on their plantations. Between the ages of seven and ten, black youngsters were sent to work alongside adult slaves in the fields, and between the ages of ten and fourteen, many either left their parental home to live with other relatives or were sold to neighboring planters.

The increasing population of enslaved African Americans sought stable domestic lives against formidable odds. Whenever possible, slaves lived in family groups, the typical household consisting of husband, wife, and children. Blacks began to develop elaborate kinship networks that extended over several plantations in a single neighborhood, maintaining family ties through visits, with or without their masters' permission. But not all slaves were so fortunate. The smaller size of Chesapeake plantations narrowed opportunities for slaves to find partners. Even in the lower South, where plantation populations were denser, families were hard to form because there, as in the Chesapeake, black men continued to outnumber black women.

By the middle of the eighteenth century, a number of changes enhanced the strength and solidarity of the black family and the slave community. While slave importations began to taper off, the rate of natural increase among blacks started to climb. In the Tidewater and the Virginia Piedmont, the black population grew more rapidly than the white, and even in the lower South, slave communities began to increase because of reproduction rather than importation. As the proportion of new Africans dropped and the number of native-born blacks grew, the ratio of men to women in the slave community became more equal. Those changes and the appearance of more large plantations, even in the Chesapeake, created more opportunities for blacks to form families. Because men still outnumbered women, most black males married later than whites, around the age of thirty; black women generally married in their late teens, at about the age of most white southern brides.

The growing number of family groups brought about changes in where slaves lived. While most earlier slaves had been quartered individually in kitchens, lofts, and sheds, or lived communally in huts, by mid century slave families were more likely to live in small cabins. But many black mothers and children did not share their cabins with husbands and fathers. Unlike southern whites, blacks refused to marry their cousins; that taboo meant that many young men chose mates from neighboring plantations. These husbands and fathers resided in barracks with other men on their home plantation, visiting their wives and children whenever they could.

Black family life remained fragile in other ways. Some planters encouraged permanent unions among their bondspeople, hoping that family ties would foster reproduction and discourage running away. But slave marriages had no legal status, and a slave family was only as stable as a master's health and finances were sound. If a planter fell on hard times, members of black families might be sold off to different buyers to meet his debts. When a master died, black families might be divided among surviving heirs. Even under the best circumstances, fathers were often hired out to other planters for long periods or sent to work in distant quarters.

In the cities, as in the countryside, blacks in bondage struggled to create families. In the two decades after 1730, one-third of all immigrants arriving in New York Harbor were African. But the preference among urban masters for importing male laborers upset what had been an equal balance of black men and women in colonial seaports. Disease also took a heavy toll among the newly arrived Africans, and many did not survive their first northern winter: the mortality rate among urban blacks was almost double that for whites. The frequency of death and the dearth of black women impeded the efforts of seaport blacks to fashion stable domestic lives.

PATTERNS OF BELIEF

Hierarchy remained the salient feature of all social relationships during the eighteenth century—between men and women, parents and children, white and black, richer and poorer. But two cultural currents challenged older patterns of subordination to traditional authorities and received wisdom. The first of these influences was the "new learning," the thought of the Enlightenment; the second was a climate of intense religious enthusiasm ushered in by the first Great Awakening.

The Enlightenment By the middle of the eighteenth century, some of the colonies' more cosmopolitan planters, lawyers, and merchants, and a few seaport artisans, had become conversant with the works of the philosophes, the leading figures of the Enlightenment. This intellectual movement, which began in Europe during the seventeenth century, stressed the power of human reason and experience to promote progress by revealing the laws governing nature, society, and government.

Benjamin Franklin's career epitomized the Enlightenment's impact on the colonies. Like the other Americans who imbibed the "new learning," he was drawn most by its emphasis on useful knowledge and experimentation. He pondered air currents and then invented a stove that heated houses more efficiently. He toyed with electricity and then invented lightning rods that protected buildings during thunderstorms. Other amateur American scientists also hoped to gain a more precise understanding of and greater mastery over the natural world: they constructed simple telescopes to observe the transits of Venus and Mercury; they charted temperatures, the direction of winds, and the flow of the Gulf Stream; they filled botanical gardens with plants and identified and classified animal species native to North America; they sought to explain epidemics in terms of natural causes and supported inoculation, the new medical procedure for immunizing people against smallpox.

Enlightenment ideas were disseminated among young men of affluent families through American colleges, where the new learning was entering the curricula. While many scions of colonial families were still educated in England, four colleges had been established in America between 1700 and 1763: Yale (1701); the College of New Jersey (later Princeton, 1746); King's College (later Columbia, 1754); and the College and Academy of Philadelphia (later the University of Pennsylvania, 1755). Most colleges offered courses in mathematics and the natural sciences that taught students algebra and such advanced theories as Copernican astronomy and Newtonian physics.

Some clergymen educated at American colleges left imbued with ideas of the Enlightenment, a spirit reflected in the more liberal theology, known as "rational Christianity," that they developed and preached to their congregations. By 1740 rational Christianity commanded a small following among Americans, usually the wealthiest and most politically powerful families. In place of the Calvinist religion of mystery and miracle, rationalists asserted the essential reasonableness of Christianity. Their God was not the Calvinists' awesome, inscrutable Jehovah but a benevolent, nearly genial deity who opened salvation to all mankind, not just a narrow, predestined elite. According to the rationalists, God's greatest gift to mankind was natural reason, and a religious life consisted of following the moral teachings of Jesus. They muted the Calvinist emphasis on human sinfulness and dispensed altogether with the Calvinist insistence on a soul-shattering conversion experience.

The religious views of the young Thomas Jefferson typified this new outlook. In his twenties, Jefferson rejected belief in both the Trinity and the miracles recounted in the Bible. He also scorned Christian creeds and dogmas as the devices by which ambitious clergymen had sought power and influence. All these systems of theology, in his view, distorted the simple and reasonable teachings of Jesus, the most "sublime ever preached to man." Jefferson and other Christian rationalists rejected venerable religious hierarchies and authorities, elevating individual reason over the teachings of clergy and a literal understanding of the Bible.

Religion in the Colonies Enlightenment philosophy and rational Christianity did not affect the outlook of most Americans. By the middle of the eighteenth century, over half of all white men (and a smaller percentage of white women) were literate, and most children of every class except slaves received some training in reading, writing, and basic arithmetic at home, in village dame schools run by widows or unmarried women, or in schools set up for apprentices by their masters. But most American readers were not prepared to tackle the learned treatises of the leading Enlightenment philosophes, such as John Locke's *Essay Concerning Human Understanding* (1690), Newton's explanation of the law of gravity, or Voltaire's attacks on traditional Christianity. Isolated rural existences insulated the great majority of Americans from exposure to the new learning.

As a result, the outlook that some wealthier and more urbane colonials adopted contrasted sharply with that of less privileged and less well-educated countrymen. Even among members of the elite, the appeal of the new learning and liberal theology was far from universal. The great majority of colonials still looked to God's revelation in Scripture rather than to human reason for ultimate truth, still explained the workings of the world in terms of divine providence rather than of natural law, and still concerned themselves with survival rather than with the possibility of progress.

Their attachment to traditional Christian religious beliefs was expressed and reinforced by the hundreds of meetinghouses and churches built during the first half of the eighteenth century. By 1750 the mid-Atlantic region had more congregations relative to population than any other part of the colonies, although New England continued to lead in the proportion of clergy to laity. Throughout the New England countryside, at intervals of about five miles, there appeared a squarish, compact Congregational meetinghouse, its steeply pitched roof supporting a central turret. In the Delaware Valley the distinctive meetinghouses of the Quakers predominated: simple rectangular structures with massive stone walls, large windows bordered by white shutters, and separate entrances for men and women. In the South, Anglican churches, of brick construction almost always in the shape of a cross, commanded the crossroads of most coastal counties. Seaports boasted an array of churches and meetinghouses, which were often the largest public buildings. Boston and New York had eighteen churches each; Philadelphia, twenty-two.

A spectrum of religious denominations and sects—far more diverse than that of the seventeenth century—filled these churches and meetinghouses. In New England, Congregationalists remained a majority but encountered increasing competition from Anglicans and Baptists. The mid-Atlantic region was a mosaic of Quakers, Anglicans, Presbyterians, Dutch and German Reformed, Lutherans, and smaller communal sects like the Mennonites, Dunkards, and Moravians. The Chesapeake until the 1740s remained solidly Anglican, except for a scattering of Roman Catholics and Quakers in Maryland. Thereafter, Presbyterians, Methodists, and Baptists began to claim large numbers of converts, especially within the entire backcountry region from Pennsylvania to Georgia. In the coastal regions of the lower South, Anglicans and Huguenots predominated, joined by a few settlements of Lutherans and Moravians. Sephardic Jews established synagogues in Newport, Rhode Island, New York City, and Charleston.

In general, affiliation with various sects and denominations cut across class lines, with no religious group claiming a disproportionate number of rich or poor among its members. But three religious bodies enjoyed political and social preeminence within different parts of the colonies. The Anglicans in the southern colonies and the Congregationalists everywhere in New England except Rhode Island continued to be the established denominations. Colony taxes supported their clergy; colony laws discouraged competition from other denominations; and the wealthiest and most powerful families belonged to their churches. In Pennsylvania and West Jersey, Quakerism, although not the established religion, claimed a similar influence among the leading families.

Church attendance probably ran highest in the northern colonies, where some 80 percent of the population turned out for public worship on eighteenth-century Sabbaths. In the South, perhaps because of the greater distances involved and the chronic shortage of clergymen, about 50 percent of colonials regularly attended Sunday services.

The First Great Awakening Despite the commitment to traditional Christianity displayed by the vast majority of eighteenth-century colonials, many clergymen within Calvinist denominations felt an urgency about promoting "true religion." Presbyterian, Congregationalist, and Baptist ministers decried the inroads of Christian rationalism. The spread of population to the frontier heightened competition for members and fostered a sense of crisis in American church life. The clergy recognized that many inhabitants of the backcountry were deprived of the religious consolation and ordered social life offered by churches. They feared that large numbers of lay people might lapse from the Calvinist faith of their ancestors or abandon Christianity altogether.

Exaggerated as these clerical fears may have been, the consequence was a major religious revival that swept the colonies during the middle decades of the eighteenth century, the first Great Awakening. Conversion of thousands of colonials who formed hundreds of new congregations during these decades of revivalism intensified and extended the sway of Protestant Christianity generally and Calvinism specifically throughout British America. But in some of its manifestations, the first Great Awakening, like the Enlightenment, represented a rupture with the traditional social and religious hierarchies of authority and learning.

The first stirrings of religious excitement appeared in the 1730s among Presbyterians and Congregationalists in the mid-Atlantic colonies and New England, especially in congregations of evangelically inclined ministers who stressed the need for "a new birth" through religious conversion. Among these preachers was William Tennent (1673–1746), a Scotch-Irish immigrant who, with his four sons, all ministers, aroused religious enthusiasm among their fellow Presbyterians throughout the mid Atlantic. In New England, evangelicals among the Congregationalist clergy heightened popular concern for salvation by preaching about local epidemics and earthquakes or the deaths of young people. Most prominent was Jonathan Edwards, the pastor at Northampton, Massachusetts, whose preaching combined lyrical descriptions of God's saving grace with sheer psychological terrorism. "The God that holds you over the pit of hell, much as one holds a spider, or some loathsome insect, over the fire, abhors you, and is dreadfully provoked," Edwards preached to a congregation at Enfield, Connecticut, "... there is no other reason to be given why you have not dropped into hell since you arose in the morning, but that God's hand has held you up."

These local revivals were mere tremors compared to the earthquake of enthusiasm that shook the New England colonies in 1739 with the arrival of George Whitefield. This handsome, cross-eyed "boy preacher" from England electrified congregations from Georgia to New Hampshire during his two-year tour of the colonies. What Whitefield preached in churches and open fields was nothing more than what other Calvinist clergymen had been urging for centuries: men and women were utterly sinful and totally dependent for salvation on the mercy of a pure and all-powerful God. But Whitefield presented the message in novel ways. He and his many eager imitators among colonial ministers turned the church into a theater, enlivening sermons with dramatic gestures, copious tears, and gruesome evocations of the torments of hellfire. The pathos, simplicity, and stark violence of such performances appealed to people of all classes, ethnic groups, and races. By the time he sailed back to England in 1741 (he returned to America several times), thousands of awakened souls were joining older churches or forming new ones.

Whitefield also left in his wake a gathering storm of controversy over the revival. Throughout the colonies conservative and moderate clergymen questioned the unrestrained emotionalism of the Evangelicals and the disorder and discord that attended the revivals. "Our presses are forever teeming with books, and our women with bastards," sighed one antirevivalist. Some members of the awakened laity now openly criticized their old ministers as cold and uninspiring. They turned a willing ear to "exhorters," laymen "and even Women and Common Negroes" with a talent for passionate, extemporaneous sermonizing. Among the clergy some of the most popular pro-revival ministers became "itinerants," traveling, like Whitefield, from one town to another. Battles raged within congregations and whole denominations over the challenge to the authority of learned, settled clergy by lay exhorters and itinerants. Critics of the revival inveighed against these "disorders," as well as the evangelical approach to conversion from "the heart" rather than "the head."

The Great Awakening left Americans sharply polarized along religious lines. The largest single group of churchgoing Americans remained within the Congregational and Presbyterian denominations, but they divided internally between advocates and opponents of revivals. Some conservatives within these denominations defected to the Quakers and Anglicans, who shunned the revival, while the most radical Evangelicals joined forces with the warmest advocates of the awakening, such as the Baptists.

Religious enthusiasm on the seaboard finally smoldered to embers in the mid 1740s, but the revival was just catching fire in the backcountry. Mid-Atlantic Presbyterians and New England Baptists spread their gospel throughout the backcountry of Pennsylvania, Virginia, the Carolinas, and Georgia. There they found a receptive audience among Scotch-Irish families who already adhered to Presbyterianism and settlers from the coast of English extraction, whose ties to the Anglican church had always been tenuous. Along with conversions, their efforts reaped contention. While Presbyterian leaders took pains to conciliate that region's Anglican establishments, the Baptists courted—and encountered—less toleration from local authorities. In some parts of the Chesapeake, county officials, prodded into action by Anglican parsons, tried to intimidate Baptist ministers with fines, imprisonment, and beatings, but the preachers stood their ground. These were only the opening shots in the contest between evangelical Presbyterians and Baptists and the southern Anglican establishment that would endure until after the American Revolution.

Suspicion and, occasionally, repression of Evangelicals by the South's Anglican majority arose from a number of sources. The severe, ascetic moralism of Baptists and Presbyterians sounded a silent reproach to the hard-drinking, high-stepping, horse-racing southern gentry. Even more unsettling to that region's slaveholding elite was the intermingling of whites and blacks within evangelical congregations. These racially mixed groups worshiped together, shared ecstatic conversion experiences, offered each other spiritual consolation and encouragement, and disciplined wayward members of both races. It was not uncommon for black male members to "exhort" an entire congregation or for slaves to bring their masters, if they were also members, before the church for discipline. The intimacy and spiritual egalitarianism of such religious gatherings undercut the racial subordination upon which slavery rested.

Whether on the frontier or in more settled regions, the social and cultural import of the first Great Awakening lay in its challenge to established hierarchies and authorities. Although the revival, unlike the Enlightenment, upheld some forms of traditional belief—the literal truth of the Bible and the Calvinist view of God's dealings with humankind—it called into question entrenched modes of social subordination. At its most radical the awakening shared with the Enlightenment a suspicion of clerical authority, encouraging converts to trust their awakened consciences more than their ministers. It also shared with the Enlightenment a concern to separate church and state, emboldening evangelical minorities to defy religious establishments. In other respects the revival exceeded the egalitarianism of the Enlightenment—by allowing women to advance claims to religious leadership and blacks to assert their spiritual equality to whites.

Despite these leveling impulses, the first Great Awakening produced no lasting democratization of colonial religious life. While it reached a far greater number of colonials than did the Enlightenment, the revival's effects were more evanescent. Although some conservative clerical opponents of the awakening were criticized and even repudiated by some awakened congregations, most lay people continued to defer to their ministers. Popular regard for a learned clergy did not diminish, and the most eloquent preachers gained even greater stature and authority because of their charisma. Although a few women exhorted gatherings of the pious and curious, their preaching careers proved to be short-lived. After the enthusiasm abated, the only colonial women accorded a public religious role were, as they had been before the awakening, the pious matrons of the nonevangelical Quakers, who proselytized as missionaries and enforced discipline within local congregations. Although the first Great Awakening marked the first approach of African Americans to affiliation with Christian denominations, the total number of black converts remained minuscule until the nineteenth century. White Baptists and Presbyterians were to prove less consistent in translating spiritual egalitarianism into antislavery sentiment than were the nonevangelical Quakers. Finally, despite the evangelical challenges to state-supported religious establishments, both southern Anglicanism and New England Congregationalism retained their favored positions until after the American Revolution.

THE FRENCH AND INDIAN CHALLENGE

The Enlightenment and the Great Awakening contributed to the shaping of later colonial society and culture. So, too, did the expansion of slavery, the spread of settlement to the frontier, the growth of commerce and seaports, the dynamic rate of natural increase and the influx of immigrants, and the firmer etching of economic and social distinctions. But the changes that would truly transform Britain's American mainland empire were not those being incubated internally. Far more important in shaping the immediate future of British North America were events unfolding just beyond the borders of those colonial settlements.

The diverse inhabitants of the British empire were not alone in creating new worlds in eighteenth-century North America. Populous, powerful Indian tribes of the American interior spent the fifty years after 1700 consolidating their strength, combining their own peoples with the diaspora of defeated coastal tribes. Along the northwestern borders of the British American mainland, the Saint Lawrence Valley and the territory south of Lake Erie and Lake Ontario, the Iroquois Confederacy loomed more formidable than ever. The Confederacy augmented their original alliance of Mohawks, Cayugas, Senecas, Onondagas, and Oneidas by engrafting the surviving members of coastal tribes like the Tuscaroras and the Susquehannocks. Some of these small client tribes had been conquered by the Iroquois; others had been devastated by warfare with white settlers and European disease. By 1750 they had allied and intermarried with the Iroquois and guarded the southern and western margins of the Confederacy in the interior of the mid-Atlantic region. Farther south the Cherokees and Creeks, Choctaws and Chickasaws defined the borders of British American settlement.

The resistance of coastal Indians to white invaders during the seventeenth century had bought the larger interior tribes time to observe the ways of Europeans and adjust accordingly. What they had witnessed, over the course of almost one hundred and fifty years, made them wary. For it became increasingly clear that British America would never become a pluralistic society incorporating Native Americans on an equal basis. Whenever convenience dictated or land hunger ravened, northern and southern colonials alike had abandoned Indian allies and brushed aside Indian claims to sovereignty and territory. With the notable exception of the Moravians, British colonials had predicated their missionary efforts—perfunctory, fitful, and ineffective—upon the insistence that Native Americans surrender their cultures and adopt European ways. By the middle of the eighteenth century, as white settlers spilled over the Blue Ridge, inland tribes recognized the threat to their way of life.

Native Americans settled on a strategy of forging closer ties with the other group of western Europeans vying for control over North America—the French. In this contest British America enjoyed the advantage of numbers: about one million colonists by 1750, compared to perhaps fifty thousand French farmers, traders, trappers, and clergy. These French settlers were spread along a thin arc of fishing stations, trading posts, missions, and farmsteads that began in Canada, extended through the Illinois Country of the middle Mississippi Valley, and ended at New Orleans.

Near the northernmost extent of French settlement was Quebec (founded 1608), the capital of New France, from 1663, where massive stone buildings—the residence of the governor-general, a Roman Catholic cathedral, seminary, college, and convent—commanded a rocky promontory overlooking the docks, warehouses, and river below. In either direction from Quebec, farms producing grain and livestock lined the length of the Saint Lawrence River; fur trappers traveled westward, tapping the rich forests of the Great Lakes and beyond. Many immigrants to French Canada, mostly poor people from the north and west of France, came not in family or neighborhood groups but individually, as indentured servants, pensioned soldiers, exiled prisoners, or wives for colonists. At the southernmost end of French American settlement was New Orleans, founded in 1718. New Orleans served as the base for securing and exploiting a vast hinterland. But in almost every other way New Orleans was different. Its red-tiled brick houses, graced with generous verandas and raised on pillars, sprouted from a swampy ground luxuriant with tropical flowers and trees. By 1750, Catholic churches, convents, and orphanages competed with ballrooms, cafés, and gambling dens for the patronage of Louisiana's ten thousand inhabitants, an assortment of French colonials from Europe, Canada, and the West Indies, as well as German immigrants, black slaves, and Indians. Their labors yielded a small surplus of cotton, indigo, rice, tobacco, and forest products for export, along with skins and furs.

Lying between and beyond Quebec and New Orleans was a vast wilderness sprinkled with a handful of settlements and sporadically inhabited by French soldiers, traders, trappers, and Catholic missionaries. Of the greatest strategic importance was the region linking the Saint Lawrence Valley with Louisiana: the Illinois Country, a region of grain farmers and fur traders lying to the west and south of Lake Michigan, with a small population at mid century of 1,536 French colonists and 890 black and 147 Indian slaves.

Throughout the seventeenth century both the northern Iroquois and the major tribes of the southern interior had regarded the French as rivals in the fur trade. Allied with the English, they had been willing to attack New France and intimidate French traders in order to maintain control of that highly profitable traffic. But during the first half of the eighteenth century, these tribes started to see the value of the French. Perhaps the best that these native peoples could say about the French was that they were few and far more interested in Indian trade than in Indian territory. It was also acknowledged that the French were bold, for, despite their numerical disadvantage, they were planting a chain of forts along their arc of settlement in the North American interior. Finally, the French had demonstrated a tolerance, even a respect, for Native American cultures far surpassing that exhibited by British colonials. French Catholic missionaries, although dogged in their quest for Indian souls, did not insist that native converts adopt other aspects of European culture. Everywhere in French America trappers, traders, farmers, and soldiers had married native women. British colonials, by contrast, despite their usefulness as trading partners, lacked all of these attributes, fostering the suspicion that they were using their allies and clients among the Iroquois, the Creeks, and the Cherokee merely as "a Pack of Hounds" to hunt the French.

Even more compelling to these interior tribes as they reassessed their role in the rivalry between European powers was the prospect of a North America without the French. Without the French as potential competitors for the Indian harvest of skins and furs, what incentive would spur British Americans to keep their prices competitive, and the cloth and iron implements, liquor and guns that they exchanged of consistently high quality? And without the arc of French settlement neatly encircling the British American colonies, what would halt the spread of white settlement?

A world without the French would be one that would afford far less security to the confederated nations of the Iroquois, the Creek, and the Cherokee alike. Over the first half of the eighteenth century, that logic—and the knowledge that Native Americans might determine the balance of power in North America—prompted interior tribes, although now officially neutral, to incline increasingly toward the French.

Among British Americans the wavering allegiance of these major interior tribes aroused alarm. France meant to make a stand in North America; leading French statesmen, like those in England, regarded control over that continent as the key to hegemony in western Europe and control of the world's trade. During the first half of the eighteenth century, France and England had engaged in two major conflicts—the War of the Spanish Succession (1702–1713) and the War of the Austrian Succession (1740–1748)—with fighting raging across Europe, the Caribbean, and the northern frontiers of the American colonies. These conflicts had terrorized settlers in New England and New York, mobilized young colonials in inconclusive military expeditions against Canada, and disrupted seaport economies. Yet they had not, in any essential way, impeded expansion and development. Even so, British Americans dreaded a final, decisive conflict between England and France in which the colonial theater of the war combined the forces of the French with the strength of the Iroquois or the Cherokees. The outcome of such a confrontation would be uncertain, and for all parties involved its consequences would be portentous.

The war came in 1754. What Europeans later dubbed the Seven Years' War British colonials called the French and Indian War, a label acknowledging that their worst expectations had been fulfilled. When the fighting started, some Native Americans adopted neutrality, but many, including the Iroquois, joined the French. Indian raids set frontier settlements ablaze from New England to Georgia. The fighting raged in North America until 1760, but more than a year earlier, as a massive military commitment turned the tide of battle decisively toward the British, most tribes abandoned their French allies.

The treaty that ended the Seven Years' War, formalized in 1763, ended, for a time, the French presence on the continent of North America. With Britain's victory accomplished, Native Americans now awaited the fulfillment of their worst expectations of white expansion into a new world without the French. Across the Atlantic a few farsighted British statesmen grimly harbored their own expectations of a colonial attempt at independence in a new world without the French. But among British Americans the windfall of a new world without the French aroused only heady optimism and deep pride in belonging to the greatest empire since Rome. A vast stretch of land between the Appalachians and the Mississippi River now came under the British aegis, and American speculators and farmers entertained visions of virtually limitless expansion. And those prospects for the expansion of population, agriculture, and trade, colonial leaders were confident, promised a more prominent and powerful role for their families, and North America as a whole, within the British empire.

BIBLIOGRAPHY

Geography

Meinig, D. W. *The Shaping of America: A Geographical Perspective on 500 Years of History.* Vol. 1, *Atlantic America, 1492–1800* (1986).

Native Americans

Axtell, James. *The Invasion Within: The Contest of Cultures in Colonial North America* (1985).

Merrell, James H. *The Indians' New World: The Catawbas and Their Neighbors from European Contact Through the Era of Removal* (1989).

Richter, Daniel K., and James H. Merrell, eds. *Beyond the Covenant Chain: The Iroquois and Their Neighbors in Indian North America, 1600–1800* (1987).

Regions

Beeman, Richard. *The Evolution of the Southern Backcountry* (1984).

Eccles, William John. *France in America* (1972).

Grant, Charles S. *Democracy in the Connecticut Frontier Town of Kent* (1961).

Isaac, Rhys. *The Transformation of Virginia, 1740–1790* (1984).

Kulikoff, Allan. *Tobacco and Slaves: The Development of Southern Cultures in the Chesapeake, 1680–1800* (1986).

Landsman, Ned. *Scotland and Its First American Colony, 1683–1765* (1985).

Lemon, James T. *The Best Poor Man's Country: A Geographical Study of Early Southeastern Pennsylvania* (1972).

Levy, Barry. *Quakers and the American Family: British Settlement in the Delaware Valley, 1650–1765* (1988).

Lockridge, Kenneth. *A New England Town: The First Hundred Years, Dedham, Massachusetts, 1636–1737* (1970).

Morgan, Edmund S. *American Slavery, American Freedom: The Ordeal of Colonial Virginia* (1975).

Sobel, Mechal. *The World They Made Together: Black and White Values in Eighteenth-Century Virginia* (1987).

Weir, Robert M. *Colonial South Carolina: A History* (1983).

Zuckerman, Michael. *Peaceable Kingdoms: New England Towns in the Eighteenth Century* (1970).

African Americans

Berlin, Ira. "Time, Space, and the Evolution of Afro-American Society in British Mainland America." *American Historical Review* 85, no. 1 (1980): 44–78.

Lee, Jean Butenhoff. "The Problem of Slave Community in the Eighteenth-Century Chesapeake." *William and Mary Quarterly* 3d ser., 43 (July 1986): 333–361.

Wood, Peter H. *Black Majority: Negroes in Colonial South Carolina from 1670 Through the Stono Rebellion* (1974).

———. "'I Did the Best I Could for My Day': The Study of Early Black History During the Second Reconstruction, 1960–1976." *William and Mary Quarterly* 3d ser., 35 (April 1978): 185–225.

Colonial Cities

Bridenbaugh, Carl. *Cities in the Wilderness: The First Century of Urban Life in America, 1625–1742* (1938).

Heyrman, Christine Leigh. *Commerce and Culture: The Maritime Communities of Colonial Massachusetts, 1690–1750* (1984).

Nash, Gary B. *The Urban Crucible: Social Change, Political Consciousness, and the Origins of the American Revolution* (1979).

Economy and Society

Henretta, James A. "Farms and Families: *Mentalité* in Pre-Industrial America." *William and Mary Quarterly* 3d ser., 35 (January 1978): 332.

McClusker, John J., and Russell R. Menard. *The Economy of British America, 1607–1789* (1985).

Norton, Mary Beth. *Liberty's Daughters: The Revolutionary Experience of American Women, 1750–1800* (1980).

Ulrich, Laurel Thatcher. *Good Wives: Image and Reality in the Lives of Women in Northern New England, 1650–1750* (1982).

Religion and Culture

Bonomi, Patricia U. *Under the Cope of Heaven: Religion, Society, and Politics in Colonial America* (1986).

Gaustad, Edwin Scott. *The Great Awakening in New England* (1957).

Greven, Philip. *The Protestant Temperament: Patterns of Child-rearing, Religious Experience, and Self in Early America* (1977).

May, Henry Farnham. *The Enlightenment in America* (1976).

Stout, Harry S. *The New England Soul: Preaching and Religious Cultures in Colonial New England* (1986).

SEE ALSO **African Migration; American Indians of the East; English-speaking Protestants; The French and French-Canadians; The Frontier; Labor: Colonial Times Through 1820; The Middle Atlantic Region; Native Peoples and Early European Contacts; New England; The Plantation; Slavery; The Southern Tidewater and Piedmont; Women and Work.**

THE AMERICAN COLONIES FROM THE SEVEN YEARS' WAR THROUGH THE REVOLUTION

Edward Countryman

MEMBERS OF THE REVOLUTIONARY generation wondered about the relationship between the American Revolution and American society. These included famous men like John Adams (who believed that the Revolution marked the political confirmation of an earlier social and ideological change) and the Pennsylvanian Benjamin Rush (who saw just the opposite, predicting that the completion of the political revolution would let loose a ceaseless process of social change). They included less well-known figures. One was the New Yorker Abraham Yates, who climbed from making shoes in Albany to making laws in the state senate and who worked out an interpretation in terms of class conflict. They included foreign observers as well. The radical Englishman Thomas Paine saw the American Revolution as just the beginning of a much larger world transformation. By contrast, the conservative Prussian Friedrich Gentz distinguished the "good" American Revolution that did not disturb the fabric of society from the "bad" French Revolution that did.

For most nineteenth-century writers on the Revolution, however, the issue of social change was peripheral. That explains the air of intellectual adventure, even danger, when the early-twentieth-century "Progressive" historians began probing the Revolution's internal and social dimensions. The history that such scholars as Carl Becker, Charles A. Beard, and J. Franklin Jameson wrote reflected a larger mood of doubt in American intellectual life, and it is not surprising that they received withering criticism during the conformist years of the mid twentieth century. Some of the criticism was valid. The questions they raised proved durable, however, and came alive again in the 1970s and 1980s.

The writing of the 1970s and 1980s is more than a restatement of older themes. Part of the difference stems from a broadening of the concept of social history. In the earlier formulation the focus remained on major political events: the movement for independence (Becker); the making of the Constitution (Beard). The goal was to enrich understanding of these by reference to internal struggle, as opposed to the simple patriotic unity that pious nineteenth-century writers had posited. But many of the newer writers take discrete social experience as their main subject. They also have borrowed a great deal from the social sciences, including rigorous quantification and the explicit use of models and theory, in order to tease meaning from evidence that otherwise would remain mute.

The result has been a great increase in knowledge about how different kinds of people experienced the Revolution. These people include "lesser" white males, the farmers and urban workingmen, who already figured in the Progressive historians' work. They also include African Americans, Native Americans, immigrants, and white women, who had figured in the earlier work little, if at all. In one spectacularly successful case, the city of Philadelphia, we are close to a complete social history. Every single group that was compounded within its social crucible has now been studied: slaves, free black people, indentured white servants, white laborers, skilled artisans, women, militiamen, Revolutionary committees, merchants, even taverngoers. In larger terms, we have altered our vision of the Revolution itself, both its actual process and its transformative qualities. We have learned that many people had a hand in shaping its events. We have also learned how taking part in those events changed the people themselves.

One casualty of the new scholarship has been any simple scenario that might have posited a sequence leading from stability through revolutionary chaos to a "restoration" of order. Late colonial society was complex and volatile. Not all of its volatility was linked to the strictly political situation of the colonies. But all of it did feed into the Revolution, one way or another. The young republic was volatile as well. But many of the questions that the old order had faced were now resolved, and some of the new issues sprang from the Revolution itself.

Four great themes run through the social history of late colonial and Revolutionary America. One is demographic, stemming from population growth and from the jostling of races and cultures. The second is economic, springing from a three-way tension within the colonial economy. The elements in that tension included some that reflected the economy's subordinate and peripheral place in the larger eighteenth-century world; others that pointed toward the autonomous, self-driving development of the nineteenth century; and still others that it shared with the preindustrial European metropolis.

The third theme is war, violence, and social disruption. The Revolutionary generation lived its childhood and adolescence during the great Anglo-French contest for world mastery. It lived its adulthood during the imperial crisis and the war of independence. It saw internal upheaval in virtually every province/state, from minor riots to guerrilla movements and armed insurrection. The fourth theme of the era, springing from all the others, is the problem of legitimate authority. A society based on human inequality was giving way to one resting at least in principle on Thomas Jefferson's proposition "that all men are created equal." The revolutionaries' attempts to resolve these themes marked the American passing from one social order to another.

DEMOGRAPHY AND POPULATION

From the Native Americans' point of view the human price of establishing colonial society was enormous. Disease, war, captivity, and the destruction of whole cultures and environments were what the invaders brought. At the beginning of the Revolutionary era the First People were still strong beyond the Appalachians. But they could be found only as visitors or captives in most places that the Euro-Americans had seized. That does not mean, however, that the Revolution had no meaning for them or that they had no part in it.

As the Native Americans' numbers diminished, the Europeans and African Americans increased phenomenally. Overall, during the colonial period, their population grew at a compounding annual rate of 3.0 percent, which meant that it was doubling itself every quarter-century. In some places and over some intervals the rate was far higher.

New England's growth stemmed almost wholly from natural increase. Most of its European Americans were descended from the thirteen thousand English Puritans who had migrated between 1630 and 1642. They had established stable families and communities; they had not had to deal with fierce diseases; whatever their crimes of aggressive warfare and slave trading against people of color, they did not build their social order on large-scale direct exploitation. Though New England is not as fertile as regions further south, they fed and housed themselves well. They found ample fuel for their winter fires. For all these reasons, they experienced much lower infant and child mortality and much greater longevity than their contemporaries anywhere else in the American colonies. By the mid eighteenth century, however, the idyll seemed to be ending. With a denser population, infectious diseases like diphtheria gave rise to epidemics, life expectancy fell, infant, child, and maternal mortality rose; land was beginning to be in short supply.

Outside New England the driving force was immigration as much as natural growth, and the long-term rate of increase proved even higher. The most spectacular case was Pennsylvania. Its founding came late, in the last decades of the seventeenth century. But climate and fertility made it immensely attractive. So did the land system that the Penn family instituted. Though they held the province as a feudal fief, they countenanced none of the imitations of feudal society that could be found elsewhere, most notably in New Jersey and New York. As a result Pennsylvania's decennial growth rate over the eighteenth century was 44 percent. By 1770 Philadelphia was Britain's premier American city.

Pennsylvania attracted both Quakers and other white migrants. They came from northern Ireland, continental Europe, and the south of England. Many were young single people migrating as indentured servants. Once freed, the males among them might climb to freehold farming or mastery of a skilled craft. But they might also find themselves condemned by circumstances to spend their lives precariously as tenant farmers or hired laborers. For a woman trained only in "huswifery" the outlook could be even more bleak.

In Pennsylvania and New England the number of black slaves was relatively small, forming about

2 percent of the population. Roughly 7 percent of New Jersey people were slaves, and they comprised more than a tenth of New Yorkers. In New York City they accounted for a fifth. Northern slaves never endured a plantation regimen, but they performed important productive work in both town and country.

Below the northern Chesapeake the beginnings had been more difficult, for both whites and blacks. In tidewater Virginia and lowland South Carolina, the early years saw a disastrous combination of disease, unfree labor, and exploitation. Despite high rates of migration, the population grew slowly. By the mid eighteenth century the worst of it was over demographically. Planters and lesser whites had worked out an accommodation based not just on antiblack racism but also on an elaborate social and cultural code. Both provinces were growing by natural increase, among their black people as well as their whites. Newcomers continued to arrive, as servants or free migrants if they were white and in chains if they were black.

The pattern of white migration was different from that of the middle colonies. There were far fewer from continental Europe. Seventeenth-century white southern indentured servants had been field laborers, working in conditions as bad as Africans would face. Now they were often skilled males, including craftsmen hired by great planters and ironworkers for the forges that dotted the Chesapeake interior.

There were also many from the North of England, Scotland, and northern Ireland, and their story was different again. Most came in families and tended to move straight to the highlands and valleys of the interior. As a result they avoided many of the problems of health that plagued migrants to the warmer, wetter lowlands. They also stepped over the class system of plantation society. Africans went to the lowlands, of course. But by the second half of the eighteenth century even South Carolina was not devouring them, at least not the way it had in the first decades of rice production. Eighteenth-century southern population growth was higher than in New England, reversing the previous century's pattern. By independence Virginia had the largest population of any province.

These places were British. Their governments imitated the "King-in-Parliament" in Westminster. Their official language was English. Their white people revered British customs and believed they enjoyed full British freedom. The gentry copied British fashions and some entered the British elite by marriage, migration, education, or economic partnership.

But the Britishness of the provinces was more apparent than real. The most obvious aspect was their non-British populations, including Native Americans and African Americans, the conquered Dutch of New York, the Germans of Pennsylvania, and scattered Huguenot French, Sephardic Jews, and other European groups. Philadelphia was one of the great British cities in 1770, ranking with Bristol or Liverpool. Like Philadelphians, the people of those English ports would have been used to hearing foreign speech and perhaps to seeing black faces in their streets. But a Native American would have been a great rarity for them. And neither town would have had Philadelphia's German-language press or churches.

Even in areas of almost wholly English background, the colonies were not the same as the metropolis. New England villages were a unique New World formation. Their remaining "Englishness" was more a matter of seventeenth-century memories than of eighteenth-century mimesis. However carefully Chesapeake and Carolina planters modeled themselves on English country gentlemen, their slave-based, staple-crop plantations were likewise uniquely American. During the Revolution both New England villagers and southern planters found that they were not as English as they had thought. Even colonials who chose the British side became aware of that. For the Revolutionaries independence meant abandoning English political identity altogether.

THE LATE COLONIAL ECONOMIES

By the time of the Revolution, these people had created a complex economy. In the lower Chesapeake and the Carolina and Georgia lowlands they produced staple crops for sale far away: tobacco, rice, and indigo. Where there were forests (which initially was everywhere), they made naval stores, including pitch and tar, masts, and planks and beams for hulls. From the northern Chesapeake to the Hudson Valley farmers grew vast quantities of grain. Most of New England was less fertile: as a whole the region could not feed itself. But it shipped fish that it took from its offshore waters and the Grand Banks.

The colonies were producing more than the primary products of the fields, the forests, and the sea. Grain needed milling into flour and baking into biscuit and ship's bread. Rice, tobacco, flour, and bread all required barrels and staves for shipping. From New England to the Chesapeake, colonials built ships: by 1770 about a third of the British merchant fleet was American built. By then Americans also were turning out about a seventh of the world's iron.

Approximately nineteen in every twenty colonials were country people. In the Chesapeake tidewater hardly any people lived in towns; the lay of the shoreline and the material requirements of tobacco culture provided no incentive to do so. Charles Town, South Carolina, was the only important urban center in the entire staple-crop South. But urban life did develop elsewhere. In Virginia and in Maryland it took the form of an enormous horseshoe of towns that arched westward, with Baltimore and Norfolk at its two eastern ends. These towns emerged because of the greater complexities that were involved in the processing and the marketing of grain, which the interior and the northern Chesapeake produced instead of tobacco.

But Baltimore and Frederick, Maryland, and Staunton, Richmond, Fredericksburg, and Norfolk, Virginia, remained small places, little more than villages. By modern standards Boston, New York, and Philadelphia were small, too, "walking cities" with populations in 1770 of between fifteen thousand and thirty thousand. All were ports. They prospered (in the cases of New York and Philadelphia) or got by (in that of Boston) on the products of their agricultural, mining, forested, and fishing hinterlands. None had developed the satellite industrial towns that would accompany their nineteenth-century transformations into great world cities.

Yet each had merchants with extensive transatlantic and intercolonial connections, artisans making all manner of goods, and laborers, indentured servants, and slaves. Each was a political capital, linked directly to the highest British authorities. Each displayed such marks of sophistication as newspapers and a college. At the end of the colonial period Philadelphia and Boston each produced an artist of world importance, Benjamin West (Philadelphia) and John Singleton Copley (Boston).

To the British the primary colonial task was to turn out goods for the metropolis, within the political framework that Parliament established with its Navigation and Trade acts. These were passed piecemeal between 1649 and 1764; only in the loosest sense did they stem from grand policy. The Navigation Acts restricted colonial shipping to British vessels with British crews and required that non-British goods be shipped to the colonies via British ports. The Trade Acts encouraged the production and directed the distribution of colonial staples, including tobacco, rice, indigo, naval stores, and West Indies sugar. Such "enumerated goods" could not be marketed outside the British Empire, except for rice, which could be shipped directly to its Mediterranean market. As early as 1669, Parliament forbade the colonials to export manufactured woolens. During the mid eighteenth century it imposed further restrictions on colonial manufactures and on the colonial currency system. Enforcement of these laws was weak. But they signified British recognition that the colonial economy had the potential to rival Britain's rather than complement it.

But the colonies did gain. Their shipping counted as British and enjoyed the Royal Navy's protection. Parliament guaranteed British markets for colonial staples, in the case of tobacco by forbidding production within Britain. In some cases it provided bounties from the British treasury. This was essential for indigo; when the Revolution ended its bounty, production collapsed. But the British displayed virtually no interest in the grain that the northern Chesapeake and the middle colonies produced, or in New England's fish. These could be sold freely around the Atlantic world.

The main colonial ports developed their own trade rather than depending on British shippers. Their greatest merchants did have close British links, as the case of Oliver DeLancey of New York demonstrates. DeLancey made most of his fortune of more than one hundred thousand pounds sterling not by civilian trade but by supplying military goods during the Seven Years' War. His brother James was close to the archbishop of Canterbury, who had been his tutor at Cambridge. DeLancey's sister Susannah married a British naval officer who became an admiral, a knight and a member of Parliament. Not surprisingly, DeLancey opted for the crown when he had to choose. So did many like him.

Nonetheless, the DeLanceys were colonials with deep roots. So were the loyalist Hutchinsons of Boston. So were the patriot Beekmans of New York, the Hancocks of Boston, and the Browns of Providence. So were Robert Morris of Philadelphia and Henry Laurens of Charles Town. So were lesser merchants who leaped to political and economic prominence during the Revolution: New York's Isaac Sears and Charles Town's Christopher Gadsden. There were "she-merchants" as well. Most were small shopkeepers but a few, such as Elizabeth Murray Smith Inman of Boston, operated independently on a large scale. Collectively these people formed a core of colonial merchant capitalists. The ones among them who chose the Revolution or who managed to survive it would become one core of a group that was both capitalist and national. In many ways that group would succeed in identifying its own interests with those of the American republic itself.

Merchants and planters were not the only figures taking part in overseas commerce. Shipwrights, ropemakers, and sailmakers depended on the prosperity of the long-distance economy. So in good part did the millers who processed grain and the coopers who made barrels for flour. So did the New England fishermen whose salt cod provided protein for slaves in the Caribbean and poor people in the Mediterranean. So did the merchant seamen who manned the ships. The immediate interests of these people might or might not coincide with those of the merchants who organized the trade and who made the biggest gains from it. But in the largest terms what was good for overseas commerce was good for them.

Townspeople also produced for the American market, and to many American artisans this was what counted. These included makers of luxury goods, like the silversmith Paul Revere. They also included makers of humbler products like shoes. The American market could be far-flung: the many cordwainers who dwelled in the Massachusetts town of Lynn turned out cheap, rough shoes in large numbers for use by slaves in the West Indies and Carolina. But it could also be narrow: the Boston cobbler George Robert Twelves Hewes dealt with his own neighbors and townsfolk. But whether they traded widely or narrowly, for house carpenters, coach builders, smiths, leatherworkers, furnituremakers, candlemakers, printers, weavers, tailors, ribbonmakers, and dressmakers (to name only a few colonial occupations), what counted was a prosperous domestic economy.

Colonials did not presume that commerce took primacy over all other social obligations and relationships. In virtually all towns, local trade in necessities operated under severe social and political restriction. New York City had five controlled marketplaces for such goods as meat, farm products, and fuel. Market offenses like "forestalling" (buying provisions on their way to market), "regrating" (buying in the market with intent to sell again), and "engrossing" (buying in bulk before a crop was gathered) were punishable at law. The city regularly published an "assize of bread" establishing the size, quality, and price of the ordinary brown loaf. As in towns all over England and Europe, the aim was to balance off the producer's need for a return on labor and the consumer's need for cheap, reliable supplies.

The same principle held in many parts of the countryside. The world of the great southern planters spanned the Atlantic. Often they were major merchants themselves, trading their own crops and those of lesser neighbors. They understood the importance of their good reputation with distant purchasers. Much the same holds for major northern landholders. The Livingstons of New York enjoyed feudal privileges on their manor. They also ran a prosperous ironworks.

South and North alike, smaller agriculturists lived differently. Even the wheat growers of the middle colonies were mixed farmers, producing nonmarket goods for their own use in addition to their cash crop. Small farmers did buy and sell, of course, both in distant markets and locally. The notion that they were wholly self-sufficient makes no sense at any material level above the most primitive. Moreover, they reckoned their obligations to one another in monetary terms, and they kept careful records of who owed what to whom. But they undertook and honored those obligations within a cultural framework that stressed the well-being of communities and families rather than the self-advancement of individuals. Their equivalent of the urban "assize of bread" was networks of mutual debt that might persist for years, without interest ever being charged.

As a producer of primary staple goods, British America was colonial in the technical economic sense of the term. It was subordinate both in British law and in actual practice. This does not mean that it was poor. In terms of overall wealth it was a favored part of the world. South Carolina and Virginia, the two mainland provinces most tightly bound by the navigation system, were the most favored parts of it. But much of their wealth consisted of slaves. If we regard the slaves as people rather than wealth, we can see that however rich they were, the southern provinces presented a profile much like that of the modern Third World. A privileged few of their people gained a great deal. The vast majority, white or black, gained little. Their systems of production offered considerable prospect for quantitative growth but little for qualitative development. This was the first major aspect of the colonies' economic profile.

The middle and New England colonies were more complex. Their cities were not complements to those of England but rivals. The artisans who served their domestic manufacturing sectors understood that point best, perhaps, for they stood to lose from imports. Northern farmers were likewise rivals to their English counterparts, producing much the same crops. But England's Corn Laws banned colonial grain except in time of shortage and thus kept the two sectors separate. During much of the eighteenth century continental Europe was hungry for what American farmers grew. As Thomas Paine wrote in *Common Sense* (1776), American grain would always have a market "while eating is the custom of Europe." This quality of rivaling rather than complementing metropolitan Europe was the colonies' second great economic aspect. It was what foreshadowed nineteenth-century America's transformation into the world's most dynamic economy.

The primacy that custom and culture gave to the needs of the small community formed the third great feature of the colonial economy. This was hardly unique to America; any English person would have recognized and probably honored colonial market practices. But it did help to define the colonies as still part of an older order, based firmly on private property but not yet on the bundle of practices and beliefs that would underpin full-blown nineteenth-century capitalism. The Revolution would bring all three facets—staple crops for the distant market, domestic production of finished goods, and the economic primacy of small communities—under severe strain.

DISRUPTION, WAR, AND UPHEAVEAL

One central fact runs through Revolutionary American lives: disruption. But the story of that disruption can be told in two different ways. Chronologically it traces the disintegration of the British and colonial power structure and the slow creation and legitimation of American republican authority. Thematically the story shows people working out their relationships of power with one another, with the same questions recurring again and again between different groups and in different places. The approach here will be thematic, but a chronological sketch is in order.

Britain first provoked trouble with its decision to reform imperial administration and finance in the mid 1760s. The Sugar Act of 1764, the Stamp Act of 1765, the Declaratory Act of 1766, the Townshend Taxes of 1767, and the Tea Crisis of 1773 all turned on one issue: the extent of Parliamentary power over colonial economic and political life. The initial direct colonial response was restricted to members of the separate provincial ruling elites, who saw their own power threatened, and to the people of the major ports, who were most directly hit by the reforms.

The crisis became revolutionary between the Boston Tea Party in December 1773, and the outbreak of actual fighting at Lexington and Concord, Massachusetts, in April 1775. This was the period when people in the countryside and the smaller towns involved themselves, initially in New England and then with gathering force elsewhere. They entered the crisis at the urging of an emergent group of American political leaders, but they did so as much for their own reasons as for reasons of high patriotism. The result was that independence provided an opportunity for many sorts of people to express their own ideas about the nature of a good society and the shape of the American future.

Between 1776 and the adoption of the federal Constitution in 1787 the relationship between political authority and society at large was highly problematic. The initial state constitutions varied widely, their differences reflecting the different coalitions that achieved independence in each state. The common purpose of those constitutions was to codify relationships between wielders of political power and the people who felt power's effects. But the boundary between the two was often uncertain. So was the stance that the rulers and the ruled ought to take to one another. These are the most fundamental issues that political society can confront. They lay behind the successful drive to establish and stabilize a new national structure of power that created the enduring institutions of the United States.

The colonials did not choose to enter the independence crisis; British policy forced it upon them. But the Americans responded to Britain's expanding claim of power over them against a background filled with social uncertainty. The actual ways that they faced the claim caused still more. They drew upon traditional forms of protest rooted in their long-standing social identities. But they found that both their forms of protest and the societies that gave those forms a measure of legitimacy had to change.

In every province there was a distinction between men who held power and the rest. In Massachusetts the power wielders were the "river gods" of the Connecticut Valley, the graduates of Harvard College, and the major seacoast merchants.

Merchants counted in New York, too. So did the province's quasi-feudal landholders: the Philipses, the Morrises, the Van Cortlandts, the Livingstons, the Van Rensselaers, the Schuylers, and the Johnsons. Virginia was dominated by "the One Hundred," whose names still resound: Lee, Burwell, Carter, Taylor, Randolph. In every other province similar men could be found, ruling on the whole with the consent of the many lesser white males who had enough property to vote. But they did face problems.

One was their own tendency to division. South Carolina's rulers did celebrate their cohesion; with an enormous slave population surrounding them, they had good reason. Virginia's rulers likewise lived by slave labor and likewise clung together. But in Massachusetts, Pennsylvania, and New York the "better sort" often divided bitterly.

A second problem was their own situation. This plagued the Virginians worst. Their sense of British identity was central to their sense of themselves. But the very institutions that defined it kept bringing it under threat. Colonel George Washington's well-known pique at being outranked by the most junior British captain early in the Seven Years' War provides an excellent example. Washington's personal resentment fits perfectly with the House of Burgesses' vehement response a decade later in 1765, when Parliament challenged the Burgesses' exclusive right to raise taxes within the colony. To the Virginians their House of Burgesses was an analogue of Parliament, giving legitimacy to their position as rulers of their world. But to Parliament, the Burgesses were just a convenient means of colonial administration.

George Washington's injured pride was the least of the problems that the Seven Years' War caused for colonials. Young Massachusetts men who signed up to fight the French on the northern frontier likewise resented being treated as inferiors. They came from close communities; their relations with their officers were neighborly as much as deferential; they joined the army for short terms, to see the world and earn some money. But regular enlisted men came from the lowest levels of a class-divided society; their aristocratic officers imposed rigid discipline; all were professionals serving, effectively, for life. Here was the social and cultural difference between the two sides that would face each other at Lexington and Concord in April 1775.

The Seven Years' War brought prosperity while it lasted. But hard times followed the return of peace in 1763, especially in the major ports. Economic depression looms behind the emergence of the three great ports (Boston, New York, Philadelphia) as the Revolution's "urban crucible" just as the frustrations of men like Washington loom behind the lead given by the Virginia elite.

The ingredients of explosion combined first in Boston, where slack trade was nothing new. The town's population had leveled off in mid century at about fifteen thousand, and poverty was becoming a problem among them. Spending to support the poor rose from £18 per thousand people per year early in the eighteenth century to £158 in 1770. The number of men who had enough property to vote at town meetings was shrinking. The property-owning "middling sort" was likewise finding life precarious. The four-fifths of Bostonians who ranked in neither the top nor the bottom 10 percent of property holders had held more than half of the town's wealth in the late seventeenth century. They had only 36 percent in 1771.

Boston was not desperate. The likes of the Hutchinsons and Hancocks enjoyed real wealth. The town had work for makers of luxury goods, like the silversmith Paul Revere. But wealth did provoke resentment. As early as 1749 bystanders had tried to stop firemen from extinguishing a blaze in Thomas Hutchinson's elegant Beacon Hill house, crying, "Let it burn!" Even before the crisis, Boston was troubled.

Like the rest of New England, Boston was heir to the traditions of the seventeenth-century English Revolution. Yankees kept alive their ancestors' Puritan hostility to High Church Anglicanism and Roman Catholicism. They also kept alive Puritanism's radical social vision, including a pronounced hostility to the whole idea of aristocracy and monarchy.

Every 5 November, Bostonians celebrated Pope's Day, the anniversary of the crushing of the "Popish Plot" of 1605 to blow up the houses of Parliament. Crowds of working people would parade with effigies to represent the pope and the plot's leader, Guy Fawkes. In the evening they would burn them in a great bonfire, after a day when they had ruled the streets. As Guy Fawkes Day or Bonfire Night it is still an English popular festival. New Englanders knew that the members of the court that condemned King Charles I to death (the Regicides) had found shelter in Connecticut and Massachusetts when they fled for their lives after the Restoration in 1660. In 1776 one Massachusetts farmer addressed Washington himself as "Great Cromwell."

Pope's Day was peculiar to Boston and a few other places. But the intensely Protestant culture of the colonies influenced the pattern of disruption everywhere. Congregational ministers in New England and dissenting clergy in most other places favored resistance and eventually Revolution. The most striking example, perhaps, is Boston's Reverend Jonathan Mayhew, whose powerful sermonizing told New Englanders that they were "called unto liberty" in 1765. Anglican ministers, however, provided strong voices on behalf of parliament and crown. Samuel Seabury of New York, William Smith of Philadelphia and Samuel Henley in Virginia all offer instances. What clergymen preached did not always fit with how laymen acted. The contrast between the loyalism of much of Virginia's Anglican clergy and the patriotism of almost all its Anglican gentry offers a striking example. Moreover, commitment to resistance and revolution often meant burying religious differences. The unbeliever Thomas Young cooperated closely with both the Congregationalist Samuel Adams, in Boston, and the Presbyterian Benjamin Rush, in Philadelphia.

The Virginia elite opposed the Stamp Act with strong resolutions. Bostonians opposed it with direct action. The Loyal Nine, a group of artisans and small traders, organized an outdoor theater on 14 August 1765 to demonstrate the act's impact, setting up their impromptu stage beneath a liberty tree from which they hung political effigies. In the evening paraders bore the effigies through the streets and then burned them, as on Pope's Day; at the front marched shoemaker Ebenezer MacIntosh, leader of one of the traditional Pope's Day crowds. The paraders sacked a building that belonged to stamp distributor Andrew Oliver and damaged his dwelling. Oliver understood the message and resigned his post. Twelve days later, on 26 August, another uprising devastated the mansion of Oliver's brother-in-law, Lieutenant Governor Thomas Hutchinson.

Boston's leaders applauded the first event as an act of the purest patriotism. But they condemned the second as "subversive of the glorious Cause." Praised or damned, the Bostonians' example inspired emulation. Men like the original Loyal Nine established a network of Sons of Liberty and became the resistance movement's popular leadership. Crowds rioted. They forced stamp distributors from office; they destroyed ostentatious property that belonged to supporters of the Stamp Act, and sometimes property that did not. When the act went into force on 1 November 1765, only Georgia's distributor was still willing to do his job.

Barring war and the mid-century Great Awakening, it was the first time that colonials had acted together across provincial lines. But tactics and concerns did vary. As the main military port throughout the Seven Years' War, New York had grown rich. But now it, too, was stagnant. Unlike their Boston counterparts, its Sons of Liberty openly invoked the popular belief that in a good community, a time of economic distress demanded public action. They did not condemn the crowd that sacked a newly opened theater in May 1766; they led it. "Are our Circumstances altered?" asked "A Tradesman," writing in the city's most radical paper in 1767. "Is Money grown more Plenty? Have our Tradesmen full Employment? Are we more frugal? Is Grain cheaper? Are our Importations less?" (quoted in *The American Revolution,* p. 93).

The port cities remained the center of direct resistance until 1774. But during the second half of the eighteenth century South Carolina, North Carolina, Maryland, Pennsylvania, New Jersey, New York, and Massachusetts experienced severe rural upheaval. Let us run through the events, not chronologically but rather geographically, from south to north.

The two Carolinas saw Regulator movements during the 1760s. These were followed by sullen "disaffection" during the first years of the war of independence and then by vicious guerrilla conflict between loyalists and patriots from 1780 to 1782. Maryland had enough "disaffected" to make the eastern shore of Chesapeake Bay ungovernable during the late 1770s. The Paxton Boys of backcountry Pennsylvania massacred peaceable Conestoga Indians in 1763 and then marched on Philadelphia. The cause was a combination of simple racism and genuine frustration with frontier danger. But the march also laid bare their antipathy to Philadelphia's Quaker elite. Three decades later (1794) other rural Pennsylvanians rose in arms against the federal government when it tried to tax the whiskey they made from their grain.

Major riots over land titles shook central New Jersey between 1745 and 1755. At the same time, tenant farmers in the Hudson Valley were trying to throw off their landlords. In 1766 they rebelled from Westchester County to Albany. Those same counties saw widespread popular loyalism during the war. New York's western frontier saw worse than loyalism; outright civil war tore it apart between 1775 and 1782. Meanwhile, Connecticut men who had migrated into New York's northeastern counties of Cumberland and Gloucester were turning them into the Republic of Vermont. Massachusetts farmers destroyed the power of their provincial government in 1774. In Shays's Rebellion of 1786–1787 they shook their state government. As in other rioting in the northern countryside the fundamental issue was ownership of the land. But to both these farmers and their opponents the fundamental meaning of the Revolution was at stake as well.

Except for Pennsylvania's Paxton Boys these were enduring, organized movements. Taken together, they seem to betoken a general rural crisis. Unlike town rioters, whom Thomas Hutchinson called "a sort of them at least . . . constitutional," country rebels provoked outright suppression from established authority, often by military force. This was true whether the authority in question was British, colonial, state, or federal. A leader might well find himself sentenced to death. It happened in New York in 1766 (to William Prendergast, a Hudson Valley farmer) and in Massachusetts two decades later (to six leaders of Shays's Rebellion). A New York law of 1774 (the "Bloody Act") named the most prominent of the Vermont Green Mountain Boys and declared their lives forfeit without a trial. It was modeled directly on Parliament's fierce suppression of the Scottish Jacobite insurrection of 1715.

The rural rioters displayed links to one another. Like the Green Mountain Boys, the New Jersey and the Hudson Valley rioters drew many of their supporters from New England migrants. All three movements turned on a fundamental conflict between one social vision based on small freehold farming and another based on tenanted estates. The North Carolina Regulator leader Hermon Husbands turned up in postindependence Pennsylvania during the Whiskey Rebellion. The wandering radical Dr. Thomas Young gave his support to the Hudson Valley tenants, the Vermonters, and urban militants in Albany, Boston, Newport, and Philadelphia. Vermont's Ethan Allen appeared during an abortive rising in central Pennsylvania in 1785.

But if we take each movement separately, it seems to represent a distinct stage in the development of a distinct society. The migrant New Englanders of New Jersey and the Hudson Valley developed widespread loyalism and disaffection during the revolutionary war. But in New England itself there was very little. In the South, the North Carolina Regulators protested against the rapacity of a half-formed ruling elite that had not yet learned to identify its own interests with a larger social good. Their South Carolinian namesakes demanded law and order to protect their emerging plantation society. Though the Massachusetts insurrectionists of 1786 called themselves Regulators as well, they shared little else with either of the preindependence southern movements.

For all their complexity, these movements were what propelled country people into the larger Revolution, and it was those people's involvement that made it a genuine revolution. Townsmen had resisted specific laws and had driven obnoxious officials from their posts. But country people alone had the numbers and the firearms to paralyze the entire colonial governing structure. When enough of them fused their specific grievances with the growing problem of British authority, that authority approached its end.

The uprising of the farmers of Massachusetts during the summer and early autumn of 1774 shows how. Their immediate goal was not social but political: to resist the tough Coercion (Intolerable) Acts (1774) that Parliament passed to punish the province for the Boston Tea Party (1773). To the farmers the most important was the Massachusetts Government Act (1774), which altered the royal charter of 1692 by abolishing the provincial council and requiring courts of law to operate under its new terms.

The farmers responded by forcing the judges to resign, much as colonials had treated stamp distributors nine years earlier. But now the action was more organized: in place after place the judges arrived on the first day of the court session to find themselves facing the county's armed militia. If officers had refused to lead the confrontation, the militiamen had elected new ones. They demanded not just resignations but dramatic submission to their will, forcing the erstwhile judges to parade bareheaded before them. The effect was to shatter royal government everywhere outside occupied Boston. Operating through a committee of correspondence, Boston radicals had been trying to rouse the interior since 1772. Now in the summer and early autumn of 1774, the farmers had roused themselves.

Behind their political rising lay their most fundamental social fear: that they would lose their land and descend to the status of tenants or laborers working for someone else. The county gentry who acted as His Majesty's judges and who often graduated to higher posts seemed to be casting themselves for the role of landlords as well. In immediate terms the fear was misplaced, perhaps. But Massachusetts farmers had a long history of facing external challenges that pointed in that direction.

And in fact the crisis of their small-village societies and economies was at hand.

By the early autumn of 1774, Massachusetts was in thorough political revolution, with two separate structures of authority vying for power. What was left of the colonial government derived its power from the crown. The emerging system of town committees and county and provincial congresses drew its power from the consent and involvement of former subjects who were now becoming citizens.

Over the year that followed, royal authority collapsed in the rest of the thirteen colonies. In some places the transfer of power was easy. Rhode Island and Connecticut already enjoyed royal charters that allowed them to elect all their own officials; institutional revolution meant nothing more than altering a few words. Virginia's elite kept control almost as easily. When Lord Dunmore, the governor, closed the House of Burgesses in 1774 for joining the opposition to the Intolerable Acts, the members reconstituted themselves as a provincial congress and continued to rule.

But if some places experienced continuity, others saw total disruption. In New York, local and county committees appeared during 1774. They started by simply exchanging news. Then they took on the task of enforcing the Continental Association, the boycott of foreign commerce that the First Continental Congress decreed late that year. In the spring of 1775, after Lexington and Concord, they began to seize political power. Their members were men who would never have dreamed of exercising major authority under the old institutions. By early 1776, however, the loyalist-dominated provincial assembly was defunct and the governor had taken refuge on a Royal Navy ship.

The change was most difficult in Pennsylvania, where the old institutions vied with the new until the very moment of independence. The old colonial assembly became the bastion not of outright loyalists, as in New York, but of men who wanted to stave off independence in order to preserve their own positions. Toppling the assembly required the combined efforts of radicals in the Continental Congress who wanted independence, like the cousins John and Samuel Adams, and radicals in Pennsylvania who wanted change in their own province.

Philadelphia was the one major town that had taken no part in the original resistance to the Stamp Act. But it joined in the "nonimportation" boycott of British commerce with which colonials responded to Parliament's second attempt at direct taxation, the Townshend duties of 1767. In 1776 it became the most radical place in America.

Radicalism brought division. When nonimportation collapsed in 1770, Philadelphia's merchants and artisans quarreled over who should have a voice in ending it. This marked the first time that Philadelphia working people intervened in the revolutionary crisis. It was not the last: by the time the old assembly fell, the city's revolutionary committee had seen a new political leadership come to power. Among the most prominent participants were the city's master artisans, such as the carpenters whose meeting house became the site of the First Continental Congress. Others who never reached the inside of the committee chamber were making themselves heard as well. Serious, committed, and popular, Thomas Paine's great pamphlet *Common Sense* became the fullest expression of these men's political voice.

The most radical Philadelphians of all in 1775 and 1776 were the privates of the city's militia. These men carried the emerging principles of the Revolution into military life. As civilians they had been the "lower sort," indentured servants and free laboring men for whom life's prospects were often bleak. In most provinces such men were long habituated to military duty; the drinking rituals of "muster day" were one of the traditional means by which officers maintained both popularity among them and authority over them.

But Quaker Philadelphia had no militia tradition, which may explain why its newly formed units tried to define their own terms of service. The militiamen wanted elected officers, not appointed ones. Formal uniforms were too expensive to buy, and to accept them as charity would be demeaning. So they demanded plain hunting shirts instead, for officers and men alike. They opposed the class privilege that allowed well-off conscientious objectors to buy their way out of service. They formed a "committee of privates" to put their case to the authorities and the public.

Militiamen elsewhere shared some of their ideas. Even in hierarchical Virginia the hunting shirt became an emblem of revolutionary military commitment, for both common people and gentry. New Englanders already were used to electing their own officers, and the social distance between officers and men was narrow. In the first months of the war they displayed little of what the eighteenth century regarded as martial appearance, either in costume or in demeanor.

Militiamen's achievements are not to be slighted. In April 1775 Massachusetts farmers forced British Troops back to Boston after the expedition to Concord; in June New England militiamen showed their full courage and ability at the Battle of Breed's (Bunker) Hill; they continued to pin whole regiments down in Boston until the British evacuated in March 1776. Philadelphia militiamen took a significant part in the Pennsylvania and New Jersey campaigns of 1777 and 1778. Militiamen fought most of the terrible battles in western New York between 1775 and 1782 and in the southern backcountry between 1779 and 1781.

The main military story must be told, however, in terms of the European-style "respectable army" that George Washington set out to form and command. Washington understood that in a revolutionary war the strategic goal was political survival rather than straightforward victory. Among his greatest achievements were his retreat from New York City in the face of overwhelming force in August 1776, and his preservation of the army from then until the French-American triumph at Yorktown in 1781.

Washington rejected any notion that the army ought to become a revolutionary force within American society. The popular enthusiasm of 1775 and 1776 did not last. During what Thomas Paine called "the times that try men's souls," the great bulk of the military burden was borne by ordinary soldiers who more and more resembled their British counterparts rather than the citizen-soldiers of patriotic legend. Like Philadelphia's militia privates, they were the kind of people who had spent their civilian lives loading and unloading ships, going to sea before the mast, or farming for others on land that they would never own. They found in the army a social place that civilian life often denied them. Their full story is still to be told. When it is, it will include their submission to the discipline that Washington and his officers imposed. But it will also include their rate of desertion and refusal to reenlist, the outright mutinies of Pennsylvania and New Jersey regiments in 1781, and their shabby treatment when the war was finally over.

The British and hired German opponents of these soldiers were professionals. Americans who fought against the Revolution were as mixed a group as one might imagine. Loyalist strength varied enormously from region to region. In numerical terms almost all New Englanders and white Virginians chose the American side. But in the Carolinas, Maryland, and New York it was another matter. The very top level of provincial officialdom contributed heavily to loyalism in every province. So did the merchant groups of New York and Philadelphia. But the social roots of loyalism were popular as well as elite. In general, the more strife-ridden a pre-Revolutionary province had been, the worse a problem loyalism posed within it. Estimates of the total proportion of loyalists and "disaffected" vary enormously. But the American Revolution drove five times as many people per thousand of population into exile as its French counterpart was to do two decades later.

Not all who fought were white. For many slaves the route to liberation led through the military. Some served in the American ranks, but the British were more receptive. Despite Dr. Samuel Johnson's well-placed statement about hearing "the loudest yelps for liberty among the drivers of Negroes" (Davis, *Problem of Slavery,* p. 275), the British never made the war into an outright struggle against slavery. But from Lord Dunmore's Virginia proclamation in 1775 of freedom for slaves who rallied to him until the final evacuation in 1783, the British did welcome slaves who wanted to free themselves.

Despite the symbolism of the "Mohawk" disguises used by the men who dumped tea into Boston Harbor at the end of 1773, both the European Americans and the British sought initially to keep Native Americans out of the conflict. It was a family quarrel among "brothers." But once war broke out, they necessarily became involved.

The British must be given credit for trying to protect the Indians against white America's expansive urge. The "Proclamation Line" of 1763 tried to establish a permanent western boundary. The "Mohawk Baronet" Sir William Johnson was one of Britain's two superintendents of Indian affairs, and he planned his enormous Mohawk Valley estate as a social buffer between white New Yorkers and the Iroquois. The Quebec Act of 1774 drastically reduced the power of the colonial governments to grant Native Americans' land. But the net effect was to create just one more white American grievance. When the war came, most Native Americans understood that joining the British was their best course.

They fared best in the South. Carolina speculators and backcountry people wanted the land of groups like the Cherokees, the Catawbas, and the Creeks, and the Indians wanted to keep it. "But Brothers, it is this very land which we stand on which is ours," said a Cherokee at a parley in 1777 (quoted in *An Uncivil War,* p. 240). This was one of the reasons for the viciousness of the southern civil war of 1779 to 1781. The southern Indian nations lost a great deal, but they survived; not until the second quarter of the nineteenth century would they be completely dispossessed.

In the North it was another matter. For the six nations of the Iroquois Confederacy, the Revolution became "the last of the forest wars," and it was a political, social, and military disaster. The Mohawks, Onondagas, Cayugas, Tuscaroras, Oneidas, and Senecas had long played the whites off against one another by an adroit combination of warfare and diplomacy. But now their confederacy cracked. The initial stages of Indian warfare in the Mohawk Valley were by no means as fearful as conventional imagery has held. But they provoked a terrible white response in the form of General John Sullivan's expedition of 1779, which devastated Iroquois crops and villages. Though the Iroquois fought back in the same spirit, their situation was weak and British military defeat in the larger war made it hopeless. When the conflict with Britain began, the Iroquois were the lords of most of the land lying west of Albany. At its end they were reduced to a broken remnant on tiny reservations, impotent both politically and militarily. More than any other group, even loyalist exiles, they were the Revolution's great victims.

"NOVUS ORDO SECLORUM"

Two central themes run through American social history between independence in 1776 and the final formation of the Republic in 1787 and 1788. One is the relationship to one another and to the body politic of different groups that were finding political voices. The other is the emergence of a new national elite to self-consciousness and ultimately to political power. In good part that elite's success sprang from the answers it developed to the problems that the first theme posed.

Like the force that had initially resisted Britain, the group that achieved independence was a coalition. The first cracks in that coalition appeared in 1776, as the separate states began to address the task of organizing their "new order of the ages." Initially the issue was posed politically, turning largely on the relative openness of the new institutions and on the balance of power between executive and legislature. Maryland's frightened planter elite defined one extreme, writing a constitution that severely restricted access to power by means of property requirements for voting and holding office and by means of infrequent elections. The Philadelphia and backcountry radicals who took control in neighboring Pennsylvania defined the other. Their new state constitution represented their best effort to erase the boundary between the rulers and the rest, with annual elections, broad suffrage, direct public consultation about major matters, and enforced turnover in office. But hidden behind the purely political question was the problem of the nature of American society.

The social issue came clear when the inflation of 1777 through 1779 destroyed the value of the Continental dollar. The problem was national in scope, reflecting the fact that the Revolutionary War was America's first national economic venture. The inflation sprang from a combination of actual wartime shortage and unlimited paper money that was backed only by promises and hope. Ultimately the problem's resolution would require action on a national scale. But few people saw it that way. Instead, they turned to their long-standing tradition of small communities defending their economies by closing them to the outside world.

No fewer than five of the new state constitutions (South Carolina, North Carolina, Maryland, Pennsylvania, and Vermont) recognized that tradition explicitly, by clauses that permitted the state governments to impose trade embargoes during a crisis. Where such clauses did not exist, the state authorities acted as if they did, for during the worst of the inflation the pressure for embargoes and for such associated measures as price and wage controls was intense. As early as 1777 crowds were beginning to take direct action against monopolizers and hoarders. In 1779 people from Pennsylvania to New England revived their local revolutionary committees, this time with the aim of bringing the economy under control.

The economic crisis provides a lens through which virtually all the social processes and changes of the Revolution come into focus. One element was the remembrance of an older world that people thought had been both communal and radical. Price-control crowds in Boston were led by a costumed figure called "Joyce, Junior." The reference was to Cornet George Joyce of the seventeenth-century Parliamentary army, who had captured King Charles I. In this symbolic costumed figure the cause of community economics and New Englanders' long memory of antimonarchy were fused.

People drew upon their own experience as well. Writers in almanacs and popular newspapers equated direct action against marketplace "oppression" with the very "spirit of liberty." Between 1777 and 1779 they repeated the half-planned uprisings of the early resistance. They also took the first steps toward repeating the way that popular committees seized power during the independence crisis.

They even had high theory on their side: the classical republican belief that individuals and groups should subordinate their own interests to the larger good of the community. But another theme was appearing, and it did not sit well with the tenet of both small-community political economy and classical republicanism that the interests of the general public came first. Older forms of protest had implicitly recognized existing relationships of power: if the elite responded, a riot would end. But this wave of uprisings and of new committee elections showed how strong was the belief of all sorts of Americans that they had a full right to make their voices heard on questions that mattered to them.

The price control movement failed, for the same reasons that Shays's Rebellion failed in Massachusetts in 1786–1787: the means were simply not up to dealing with the problem. The Shaysite rebels faced essentially the same issue, though in a somewhat different context. They lived under a state government that accepted wholly the primacy of long-distance trading relations over every other form of social obligation. But this meant that when depression struck after the war, Massachusetts farmers faced the real possibility of losing their land to creditors far away. It was the nightmare they had thought they faced from the British in 1774, but now it sprang from the government of their own commonwealth.

Like the price controllers, the farmers sought salvation in a combination of community cohesion and direct political action. They could draw on the model of their own successful overthrow of colonial government in 1774. That had begun with meetings in the towns and had ended with direct action to close the county courts. So did Shays's Rebellion. But in 1774 the farmers had the support of the people of the seaport towns, including the denizens of occupied Boston. In the winter of 1786–1787 they stood alone, and the coastal ports sent the state militia west to crush them.

The failure of price controls and the defeat of Shays's Rebellion demonstrated the terms of the social issue that Americans now confronted. The Revolution created a national economic arena in which older ideas of political economy were outmoded. It also forced people to recognize not only their large American identity but also their own specific interests. It did this within a cultural framework in which expressing particular interests was not wholly legitimate. As public reality changed, so did the public consciousness with which people tried to understand it.

The change was most intense among the free white males who had stood on the edges of politics under the old order, particularly small-propertied farmers and artisans. These were among the first to recognize the ambiguity in the assertion of the Declaration of Independence that "all men are created equal." The best reading of Thomas Jefferson's original meaning would simply be that as a people the Americans were equal to anyone else, whatever inequalities existed among themselves. It was not gentlemen like Jefferson but rather the sort of people for whom Thomas Paine wrote *Common Sense* and *The Crisis* who began the process of expanding Jefferson's words. They gained a great deal. One of the major changes that the Revolution wrought was to open the institutions of power at the state level to men like these.

But others took the promise in Jefferson's language still further. If the Revolution was a sheer disaster for loyalists and Native Americans, it had mixed results for black people and for white women. The Revolution did not end slavery; if anything, it opened the way for its expansion into the Old Southwest. But the era did see slavery change for white people from a fact of life that hardly anyone questioned to a moral problem that a growing number believed they had to confront.

The result was that where slavery was not integral to the productive economy, the victorious revolutionaries put it on the road to extinction. A few places acted immediately. White independent Vermont abolished slavery the moment it separated from New York, and in Massachusetts the institution was gone by 1783. In most northern states gradualism triumphed, however, with the result people were still being held in slavery in these "free" states half a century later. But however long the road to freedom proved to be for northern slaves, however cruel the promise of it proved for men and women who never reached its end, the Revolution did lead to the creation of a zone where to be black was not necessarily to be a slave. That was unprecedented anywhere in the western hemisphere. The Revolution did not end slavery. But it did turn it into the South's "peculiar institution."

Within these changes African Americans began

seizing their own freedom. The task was not easy. They understood that they could apply the rhetoric of American liberty to themselves, and some of them tried. They won important white allies. But even where the whites decided that slavery and the principles of the Revolution were incompatible, African Americans had to face overwhelming racism. Some found that the only route to their own freedom was to leave the country, often with the departing British. They went to Canada, to Britain, and back to Africa. Others decided their only choice was to stay, and they began the slow task of building the churches, the schools, the associations, and the businesses that would be the sinews of an autonomous black American community.

White women likewise began to weave the fabric of a separate consciousness. Groups of Daughters of Liberty had appeared even before independence, but generally these were inspired by men. War and the beginnings of republicanism found women starting to speak for themselves. As early as 1776 a New Jersey woman, Mary Hay Burn, asked her soldier husband, "Why should I not have liberty whilst you strive for liberty?" (quoted in *The American Revolution,* p. 235). Writing as "Constantia" in the 1780s, Judith Sargent Murray posed most of the problems that the Englishwoman Mary Wollstonecraft was to raise in her epochal *Vindication of the Rights of Woman* (1792).

In New Jersey black people and women won the right to vote in 1776. But the gain proved ephemeral. Their loss of it in 1807 can stand as an emblem of what the Revolution meant for each group; it was a beginning, but only a beginning. Forcing white males to honor the promise that some African Americans and some women had found would be a slow and difficult task. It would take generations of struggle.

In the midst of all these changes a new national ruling group emerged, defining the political and social issues that the country had to confront, and finally taking control. We know them as the Federalists, meaning not the political party of the 1790s but rather the group that was responsible for proposing, writing, and implementing the federal Constitution. Many of them had their roots in the old colonial elite, and they drew quiet support from former loyalists who had not departed. But the key to understanding them is the terms on which most of them participated in the Revolution and especially the war.

Their leaders spent it at the top. They were generals trying to keep their commands in existence, commissary officers scrabbling for supplies, and members of the Continental Congress begging the states for money. They were diplomats, like John Adams and Benjamin Franklin, and Continental officials, like the "financier of the Revolution" Robert Morris. Socially they were drawn from northern merchants, landowners, and professionals and from large-scale southern planters. Very few of them had any natural sympathy with the small-community political economy of other Americans, and their Revolutionary experience confirmed their doubts. The embargoes and price controls that expressed unselfish patriotism to many in 1779 seemed to these men to be only selfish foolery.

They won their case, in good part because the best minds among them were not afraid to confront the new questions that the emergent new society was posing. Both classical republican political theory and small-community political economy posited the ideal of unselfish individuals' subordinating their interests to the good of a larger whole. This was what the eighteenth century meant by "virtue." But the Federalists of 1787 saw clearly that as individuals their fellow Americans were not virtuous at all, and that as a society they were divided and factious. In truth, the understanding applied to Federalists themselves. However much they proclaimed that their analysis was disinterested and their patriotism was pure, many of them had their own social agenda. But the insight was powerful enough that it attracted many others to their support, including a fair number of people who had clung to the small-community model for as long as they could.

Like the Sons of Liberty of 1765 and the militants for independence of 1776, the Federalists of 1787 used social materials to put together a political coalition. The three coalitions were not the same. Each had its own basis, its own rhetoric which expressed that basis, and its own lines of internal stress along which it would eventually come apart. By 1787 the Federalist leadership was fully aware of this, seeing clearly that abstract issues of patriotism had to be joined to specific appeals to how Americans were now coming to understand themselves in social terms. They made the fullest use of the insight in their campaign for popular support for the Constitution.

The Revolution did not bring the destruction of an entire social class or a complete social principle. That would not happen in America until African Americans forced the North to add the abolition of slavery to national unity as a fundamental purpose of the Civil War. But the Revolution did see a fundamental reordering of the terms on which the people of the United States dealt with and thought about one another. Some of the changes led to intense deprivation, loss, and suffering. This was most especially so for Native Americans but applied to others as well, including not just loyalists but people who committed themselves wholeheartedly to what they had thought the Revolution was about. Some changes led to new forms of freedom. Some led to mixed results. But taken together, these changes meant that King George III's colonies and President George Washington's republic were very different places, even though they occupied the same geographical space.

BIBLIOGRAPHY

Ammerman, David L., and Philip D. Morgan, comps. *Books About Early America: 2001 Titles* (1989). The most up-to-date bibliography for general readers.

Bailyn, Bernard. *Voyagers to the West: A Passage in the Peopling of America on the Eve of the Revolution* (1986). A sweeping exploration of British migration late in the colonial period.

Berlin, Ira, and Ronald Hoffman, eds. *Slavery and Freedom in the Age of the American Revolution* (1983). An outstanding collection of essays.

Countryman, Edward. *The American Revolution* (1985). A synthesis of modern scholarship with a full bibliography to date of publication.

Davis, David Brion. *The Problem of Slavery in the Age of Revolution, 1770–1823* (1975). An extended argument about the debates on slavery.

Doerflinger, Thomas M. *A Vigorous Spirit of Enterprise: Merchants and Economic Development in Revolutionary Philadelphia* (1986). Sets the standard for modern discussion of the Revolution's economic dimensions.

Greene, Jack P., and J. R. Pole, eds. *Colonial British America: Essays in the New History of the Early Modern Era* (1984). State-of-the-art reflections by scholars in mid career.

Gross, Robert A. *The Minutemen and Their World* (1976). One of many early New England town studies, concentrating on Concord, Massachusetts.

Hoffman, Ronald, Thad W. Tate, and Peter J. Albert, eds. *An Uncivil War: The Southern Backcountry During the American Revolution* (1985). A sophisticated anthology; part of an extended series of volumes on specific aspects of the Revolution.

Isaac, Rhys. *The Transformation of Virginia, 1740–1790* (1982). An outstanding state study.

Jones, Alice Hanson. *Wealth of a Nation to Be: The American Colonies on the Eve of the Revolution* (1980). A summary statement of a major quantitative project.

Kurtz, Stephen G., and James H. Hutson, eds. *Essays on the American Revolution* (1973). An important anthology with contributions by major mid-century scholars.

Maier, Pauline. *From Resistance to Revolution: Colonial Radicals and the Development of American Opposition to Britain, 1765–1776* (1972). A study of the Sons of Liberty and of popular uprisings.

McCusker, John J., and Russell J. Menard. *The Economy of British America, 1607–1789* (1985). An extended statement of needs and opportunities for study.

Morgan, Edmund S. *Inventing the People: The Rise of Popular Sovereignty in England and America* (1988). Explores the cultural transition from monarchy to republicanism.

Nash, Gary B. *The Urban Crucible: Social Change, Political Consciousness, and the Origins of the American Revolution* (1979). An exploration of Boston, New York, and Philadelphia.

Norton, Mary Beth. *Liberty's Daughters: The Revolutionary Experience of American Women, 1750–1800* (1980). The best single book on the subject.

Rosswurm, Steven. *Arms, Country and Class: The Philadelphia Militia and the "Lower Sort" During the American Revolution, 1775–1783* (1987). One of the best accounts of military experience. Like Doerflinger (above), it is part of the total social history of Revolutionary Philadelphia.

Shy, John W. *A People Numerous and Armed: Reflections on the Military Struggle for American Independence* (1976; rev. ed. 1990). A collection of essays on the social history of the revolutionary war.

Wallace, Anthony F. C. *The Death and Rebirth of the Seneca* (1970). Deals historically with the Iroquois collapse during the Revolution and anthropologically with their later recovery.

Wood, Gordon S. *The Creation of the American Republic, 1776–1787* (1969). A long exploration of the relationship between political language and political society.

Young, Alfred F. "George Robert Twelves Hewes (1742–1840): A Boston Shoemaker and the Memory of the American Revolution." *William and Mary Quarterly* 3rd ser., 38, no. 4 (1981). The best single account of an ordinary person's experience of the Revolution.

———, ed. *The American Revolution: Explorations in the History of American Radicalism* (1976). A collection of path-breaking essays, several of which led to major books.

SEE ALSO **Agriculture; Immigration; Industrialization; Labor: Colonial Times Through Reconstruction; Regionalism; Slavery; Social Class; Urbanization.**

THE EARLY NATIONAL PERIOD

Andrew R. L. Cayton

DURING THE FEDERAL and early national periods, an era political historians have often defined as encompassing the decades between the ratification of the Constitution in the late 1780s and the election of Andrew Jackson to the presidency in 1828, the United States remained a loose collection of disparate societies. As much divided Americans as united them: they were separated by cultural origins, race, gender, and economic circumstances. Above all, they were segregated into a number of diverse regions. Not only was there nothing approaching a common national culture, but there was nothing remotely resembling a common white culture, a common black culture, a common male world, a common female world, a common patrician or plebeian culture. Remarkable regional and social diversity characterized the ways in which Americans spoke English, the most pervasive language in the new nation.

The significance of these early periods lies less in the existence of these differences than in the fact that many people became acutely aware of their importance. Individuals and families, realizing what they did not have in common with many of their fellow citizens, began to recognize what they shared with others; and they started to organize across local lines in order to protect and assert their particular interests.

Between 1780 and 1820, Americans came into more frequent contact with each other than had been the case in the colonial era. At least three major, interrelated phenomena lay behind the sudden, intense interaction of Americans in the early republic. These were the creation of a powerful national government in the late 1780s and early 1790s; the remarkable geographic mobility of Americans throughout the era; and the impact of the expansion of the international capitalist market on the structures of Americans' lives. These trends brought people together in unprecedented ways. People of different regions, races, classes, and genders were moving, traveling, settling, and resettling together. They were buying and selling goods on a scale unimaginable just a few decades before. And they were governed, voluntarily or not, by a political structure far more powerful than the one against which Americans had rebelled in the 1760s and 1770s. Although Americans had always been different from each other, they had never had to confront their heterogeneity quite so regularly and persistently.

THE EXPANSION OF THE MARKET

According to the census of 1790, the population of the United States was 3,929,214 people; of these 700,000 were slaves. Divided almost equally between the North and the South, Americans were spread mostly along the Atlantic coast and navigable rivers. About two hundred thousand lived in the trans-Appalachian West, and only 5 percent lived in urban areas (places with a population of twenty-five hundred or more). Committed to the economy of the household, where family needs often took precedence over the demands of the market, most people marked time by the seasonal rhythms of agriculture. The nation's few roads were generally in abysmal shape and there was little regular interchange between the various cities and sections of the new republic, especially among the many people who lived more than a few miles from a navigable waterway.

A Changing Population Little more than a generation later, much of this situation had changed. The population had risen to 9,638,453 people in 1820 (of whom 19 percent were African Americans) and reached 12,866,020 in 1830. The United States averaged population increases of over 30 percent in the first decades of the nineteenth century. Remarkably little of this growth resulted from immigration. As late as the 1820s, only 128,502 people (4 percent of the total increase during the decade) immigrated to the new republic. Just 3 percent of the population in the 1830s had been born outside the United States. In fact, the most significant foreign arrivals in the early national period did not come voluntarily. Between 1791 and 1800, 55,888 Africans arrived in the United States (mainly at the port of Charleston, South Carolina); another 156,300 arrived between 1801 and 1810. Still, the closing of the international slave trade to the United States on 1 January 1808 severely curtailed, if it did not eliminate, this profitable source of foreign-born people. The number of imported slaves fell to ten thousand in the 1810s and two thousand in the 1820s.

What lay behind the dramatic population rise was the high birthrate of Americans. There were approximately fifty-five births for every one thousand people in the early republic (compared with fifteen and a half in the United States in 1984). Not surprisingly, most Americans were young. Throughout the period, there were about thirteen hundred children under five years old for every one thousand women between the ages of twenty and twenty-four. The median age of Americans in 1820 was just under seventeen (compared with thirty in 1980).

The citizens of the United States in the early republic were both young and highly mobile. Historians estimate that in the course of an average year, 5 to 10 percent of the nation's population moved, and half of that group went to another state. Thousands of these people migrated to the trans-Appalachian West. By the 1830s, they had conquered and settled areas that had been virtually uninhabited by Anglo-Americans in the 1770s. Ohio, which had only a few hundred white settlers in 1790, had a population of 938,000 in 1830 and soon became a net exporter of migrants. Its experience was not unique. Between 1790 and 1830, the states of Vermont (1791), Kentucky (1792), Tennessee (1796), Ohio (1803), Louisiana (1812), Indiana (1816), Mississippi (1817), Alabama (1819), Illinois (1818), Maine (1820), and Missouri (1821) joined the Union.

Not all people settled in rural areas. Many chose to move to urban centers such as Baltimore, New York, Philadelphia, and Cincinnati. Cities grew very quickly during the period. On the eve of the American Revolution only five places—Boston; Newport, Rhode Island; New York; Philadelphia; and Charleston—qualified as urban areas; Philadelphia, the biggest of the five, had a population of almost thirty thousand. By 1830, four cities had crossed the fifty thousand threshold; 9 percent of Americans lived in urban areas.

Whether to the trans-Appalachian West or to a city, the massive migration of people was a dominant fact of life in the early republic. It was also unsettling to peoples used to relative stasis. The idea of one million people moving to western New York State by 1820, for example, would have been beyond the comprehension of most colonists in 1750.

Economic Growth Fueling the extraordinary population growth was the enviable economic position of the young republic. During most of the period, more specifically from 1793 to 1815, the great nations of Europe—Great Britain, France, Russia, the Austrian empire—were at war with each other. Although the United States was officially at war only once, with Great Britain from 1812 to 1815, the European conflict spilled over into American lives. The Wars of the French Revolution not only became an important issue in American politics; they financed the capitalist transformation of much of the United States. Demand for American cereals and cotton in Europe sent prices soaring. There was profit to be made in overseas trade and in agriculture. Facilitated by the invention of the cotton gin in 1793, cotton production rose from three million pounds in that year to ninety-three million pounds by 1815. The lure of cotton profits pulled families from Virginia and the Carolinas into Georgia, Mississippi, and western Tennessee. With raw cotton bringing eighteen cents per pound in 1806, the cultivation of four acres could yield as much as two hundred dollars of profit per year (at a time when a family of five in New York City could live on about four hundred dollars a year). Similarly, in the Old Northwest, corn and wheat production promised money to aspiring entrepreneurs. In the East, farmers in the Chesapeake Bay area had long since begun to shift their major crop from tobacco to wheat in order to take advantage of the international market. The embargo of 1807–1809 and the War of 1812 seriously impeded the spectacular economic expansion. Nevertheless, the value of American commodities exported rose from around twenty million dollars per year in the 1790s to approximately seventy million dollars per year in the 1820s.

Accompanying and facilitating this growth were significant improvements in communication. There was suddenly an abundance of information in the new republic. The expansion of the United States postal system from seventy-five offices in 1789 to twenty-eight thousand by 1860 facilitated an increase in correspondence among a mobile people. Subsidized by the postal service, newspapers proliferated as people became interested in information from well beyond their local area. With their lives intertwined in an international market, Americans sought knowledge of weather conditions, price fluctuations, and political developments in distant places. They read avidly about Napoleon's European campaigns because his success or failure would eventually impinge upon their lives. Newspapers and the mails also allowed Americans to advertise their own products for sale. Finally, especially in the North, a revolution in printing techniques permitted the widespread distribution of books, religious tracts, and periodicals.

Strains on the Household Economy The impact of the commercial and communication revolutions was profound. Recent historians have debated the speed and pervasiveness of the capitalist transformation of the United States, but most agree that the decades of the early republic were critical in the overall process. In general, colonial Americans had organized their lives around their households. As the basic economic and social institution, the household traditionally connoted both people and places; it involved all family members and dependents who contributed to the economic well-being of the whole group as well as the spaces in which they lived and worked. In both rural and urban areas, the independence of each household depended on the interdependence of all of its members. Children as well as parents contributed to the household economy; slaves and servants were also part of the matrix.

American households were thoroughly patriarchal in the sense that males had unchallenged legal power over all others and the division of labor was gender-based. Men worked in shops or in the fields; women contributed the preparation of food, clothing, and the bearing and rearing of children. The household was neither completely isolated from larger markets nor self-sufficient. But it usually was locally oriented and rooted in customs of reciprocity and cooperation among neighbors. As such, it contrasted sharply with the economic practices of long-distance trade, which involved the use of paper instruments (such as negotiable notes, bills of exchange, letters of credit) as mediums of exchange, the setting of wages and prices in response to competitive pressures, and the growth of staple crops specifically for market.

In relatively stable parts of the United States, such as the Connecticut River valley, the household remained the central economic and social institution in the early republic. Not surprisingly, these areas also remained the most conservative politically. Support for Federalist candidates in the 1790s and early 1800s was especially strong in areas whose population was not increasing as fast as that of the nation as a whole. In fact, the longer established a man's family was in a given locality, the more likely it was that he would vote for Federalists. Jeffersonian Republicans, with their advocacy of equality, opportunity, and laissez-faire economics, on the other hand, did well in places experiencing rapid population growth. They tended to flourish in areas where the market was significantly rearranging basic human relationships as well as systems of labor and capital exchange.

In Boston, New York, and Philadelphia, merchant families benefited greatly from the expansion of overseas trade. Even when the embargo of 1807 threatened their livelihood, many were able to shift their money into other activities, such as manufacturing outside of Boston or real estate in New York City. For people outside the elite, the impact of economic expansion was mixed. Wage rates went up in the decades after 1790, but at the same time skilled artisans and unskilled workers suffered from intermittent unemployment, increased competition, and vulnerability to disease and accidents. The growth of the market wrought havoc on the urban household economy. Most serious was the reconceptualization of labor as a commodity to be bought and sold. People who worked with their hands were identified less and less by their particular skill or relationship with a particular family than by the number of hours they worked at a competitive rate. For urban residents, the increasing use of cash as a medium of exchange, the proliferation of banks, the growing importance of wages and the simultaneous devaluation of individual skill, and the massive migration into the cities were the most visible signs of the great economic boom of the early republic. Those changes also marked the replacement of traditional face-to-face relationships by more impersonal and distant means of interaction.

A similar process took place in some rapidly growing frontier areas. The early developers of the Old Northwest (Northwest Territory) envisioned the region's future as a showplace of commercial capitalism: land was a commodity from the beginning, Native Americans were driven out relatively quickly, and migration and population growth were spectacular. Most people came to the Old Northwest with ambivalent feelings about the market; in fact, some probably came to escape its impact on their households. But despite the persistence of traditional household arrangements in isolated rural areas, the region became a bastion of the capitalist economy, producing corn, hogs, and cereals for sale in New Orleans and beyond. The small towns of the Old Northwest and its big city, Cincinnati, embodied the new capitalist world. The key to the pervasive spread of the market north of the Ohio River and in other areas, such as western New York State, was their phenomenal population growth, which made it virtually impossible for local reciprocity to flourish; people were strangers to each other, and relatively transient ones at that. Residents of the Old Northwest and the hinterlands of Philadelphia, New York, Boston, and Baltimore were able to specialize in particular staple crops (such as corn, wheat, or cotton) produced in large quantities to be sold in distant markets.

Capitalist Transformation The capitalist transformation of the United States took place largely because thousands of Americans decided to participate in the marketplace. It also occurred, in part, because political leaders created interlocked financial and political structures that facilitated and guided the growth of interstate trade as well as the development of a national market economy.

To be sure, there were striking differences between the Federalists, who controlled the national government in the 1790s, and their Jeffersonian Republican critics. The Federalists put their faith in the ability of a powerful central government to direct the evolution of American society into something grander than ordinary citizens could imagine or desire. They tended to see themselves as a disinterested gentry who were better qualified to lead the United States to the status of imperial Rome or Augustan England than the average rowdy, self-interested American. The Jeffersonians, who seized national power from the Federalists in the election of 1800, on the other hand, generally thought that the United States would be better off if it had no overall, national direction. Ultimately, the Jeffersonian rhetoric of laissez-faire and local sovereignty played well in a nation whose citizens did not know, let alone trust, each other and whose economic development was occurring in different ways in different places.

Still, when they assumed office in 1801, the Jeffersonians, who had been so vehement in their criticism of the Federalists as monarchical and corrupt, accepted and worked within the larger framework the Federalists left. Although they removed the trappings of power with which the Federalists had attempted to dignify the government and reduced the most direct examples of federal authority, such as taxes and the military, they ran a government that continued to have an impact on the lives of its citizens. The expanding postal system facilitated the exchange of information so crucial to the success of a market economy. National land policy provided for the sale of federal lands in small sections and at reasonable terms. Federal and state courts established the legal foundations of capitalism by insisting that the rights of private property and contractual agreements took precedence over traditional community customs. Meanwhile, states such as New York began to construct the roads and canals that would form the backbone of a national transportation network. Without these essentially political actions, the capitalist transformation could not have proceeded at the pace or in the manner that it did.

As far-reaching as these economic and political developments were, they were neither all-encompassing nor universally welcomed. The household remained the center of economic production in many parts of the United States. In northern New England, in the Tidewater regions of the South, and in Delaware and other places where well-established social orders remained relatively undisturbed during the decades following the Revolution, the world of the household economy persisted. In Maine, western Pennsylvania, rural Illinois, and the Georgia up-country, historians have found evidence of people who resisted the imposition of long-range commercial values. Often in the face of strong economic and political pressures, many continued to insist that traditional understandings of family and community obligations should take precedence over the demands of the market.

In many ways, the South epitomized the sometimes ambiguous or haphazard impact of the market. No other region of the nation was more tied into the international economy than the South, and yet no region more successfully resisted its transforming power. In the Carolina low country, the Piedmont, the Mississippi Delta, and the Cotton Belt of Georgia and Alabama, planters and farmers produced staple crops—mainly cotton, but also rice, sugar, and tobacco—for distant markets.

There were plenty of southern entrepreneurs, men on the make in the flush times of the early republic. But they acted in response to what they could get from the soil. And, in the South, climate and topography encouraged the development of monocultures: tobacco in Virginia and North Carolina, rice in the South Carolina low country, sugar in Louisiana, and cotton across a band from the Carolinas to Texas. The South failed to develop the kind of pervasive small-town culture that grew up in the Old Northwest, in part because it was not economically necessary. The southern economies were not diversified; their staple crops did not require much in the way of support services. Regional economic structures were wedded to the plantation and to the farm. Thus, as Frederick F. Siegel has argued in his study of the tobacco culture of Danville, Virginia, and its environs, the natural environment often significantly limited economic development: "The Southern economy, wedded to its regional monocultures, grew not by diversifying but by expanding its geographical domain" (*The Roots of Southern Distinctiveness,* p. 1).

Just as important in impeding the transforming qualities of the market in the South was slavery. Most Southerners continued to see the household as the central institution in their social order. Since relationships within the partriarchal household were always unequal, non-slaveholders as well as planters came to see "slavery as a legitimate extension of the familial relationships that defined production through the household economy as a whole" (Rachel N. Klein, *Unification of a Slave State,* p. 271). Slaves were dependents who contributed, not unlike women and children, to the independence of the household as a whole. In this sense, the geographic expansion of the cotton culture from the mid 1790s on helped to unite Southerners and to preserve the household. Both low-country planters and the backcountry gentry were committed to slavery; and non-slaveholders agreed, largely because the entire notion of independence, so important to southern males, rested on their ability to maintain a household of dependents.

From a national perspective, in sum, the spread of the market was haphazard, imprecise, and idiosyncratic. It did not transform the United States overnight into a consensual bastion of capitalism. Rather, the desires of hundreds of thousands of people to improve the material conditions of themselves and their families produced a startling expansion of commercial capitalism that transformed the social relationships of different groups of Americans in different places to differing degrees. In this sense, the uneven nature of the capitalist transformation reinforced—indeed, heightened—the already deep-seated regionalism of the United States and accentuated the differences among people. As the market brought them together, it made them more aware of how much they did not have in common. By the panic of 1819, the first major national economic depression in American history, the tentacles of the international market had spread throughout the country. In most places, people knew, as many had first discovered with the economic impact of Jefferson's embargo of 1807, that their economic well-being was intimately involved with that of people in London, New Orleans, and Philadelphia. When people in Indiana lost land because of a bank panic in Great Britain, human beings were no longer isolated from each other in quite the same ways they had been before the American Revolution.

At the same time that the capitalist transformation brought unprecedented material benefits to Americans, it also led them to reorganize their lives and to deal with a set of entirely new problems. In the colonial period, the primary focus of social identification had been geography: people made sense of their lives and themselves in daily contact with their neighbors. Most also accepted inequality as a natural and inevitable part of the human condition. In the local worlds of colonial America, some white men were simply more important than everybody else. But in the aftermath of a political revolution dedicated to the proposition that "all men are created equal" and in the midst of a market revolution that was eating away at the boundaries of local communities, the social sources of personal identification—how individuals dealt with each other and how they understood their roles in their society—became confused.

Cut loose from the traditional moorings of colonial cultures, buffeted by the transformation of basic economic structures, invigorated by constant public debate about the nature of their political institutions, many Americans began to think more concretely about who they were. Inevitably, they made connections with other people with whom they shared something in common, be it race, gender, class, or region. To be sure, white males continued to dominate the United States in terms of public politics and commerce. But in the confusion of the early republic other people found the opportunity to develop and assert more positive identities with which all Americans would eventually have to come to terms.

THE POLITICS OF GENDER AND CLASS

Few people more dramatically reconceptualized themselves in the early republic than middle- and upper-class women in the Northeast. In the thoroughly patriarchal societies of colonial America, women had had no well-defined public role, despite their critical contributions to the household economy. Legally, women were virtually nonexistent. They could not own property or sue in courts of law. In New England, only about half the women could sign their own names (compared with an 80 percent literacy rate for men). Given the local character of American societies, of course, significant regional variations existed with regard to legal rights. In New England, where Puritan settlers attempted to reform the English common law and insisted upon the unity of the family under the father, the law granted women almost no protection from their husbands. In the South, on the other hand, where there was little reform of the English legal system in the colonial period, courts tended to protect women's traditional rights to property, especially in the areas of dowry and widowhood. Nowhere did women find a divorce easy to obtain, although it was somewhat easier in the South than in the Northeast.

Changing Roles and Images More generally, men in the colonies tended to associate women with antisocial characteristics. Their supposed ignorance, their love of luxury, their deviousness made women particularly unsuited to be citizens of the republic. Women were not reliable; they were corrupt. In the ideological world of the eighteenth century, with its emphasis on the importance of self-sacrifice for the good of the whole, women were dangerous as well as out of place. Political culture was exclusively male. Whether Whig or Tory, Jeffersonian or Federalist, males in the public sphere valued nobility and courage. Above all, they treasured their honor, their public reputation, their fame. Men such as George Washington and Thomas Jefferson assiduously cultivated their public images. They identified with "noble Romans" in the mold of Cincinnatus. They carefully presented themselves to the world as men who enjoyed the repose and comforts of gentlemen but who were willing to sacrifice the pleasures of family and intellectual enlightenment in order to serve their fellow countrymen. Reluctant public officials, they paradoxically added to their fame by seeming to prefer not to serve. George Washington's reputation, for example, rested as much on his reluctance to assume power, not to mention the fact that he twice gave it up, as it did on any military or political achievement. In this political culture, the virtuous (or self-sacrificing) citizens were exclusively male, proven in the fires of war, statecraft, and the defense of their individual honor.

Most of the thousands of voluntary organizations that began to dot the American social landscape in the early republic reflected this sex-based division of roles. Males came together in a variety of groups to promote the public good, as they defined it. Political factions are only the best-known example. Others included the Masons, the Society of the Cincinnati (whose members had been officers in the Continental army), and various groups committed to enlightened improvement of the world. Through their gender exclusivity, these organizations perpetuated the traditional idea that, even in the theoretically egalitarian republic, public and intellectual affairs were the province of men only. There was no place for the serpent-swayed Eve.

Or so thought many men, if they considered the question at all. Many women thought differently. Beginning in the era of the Revolution, middle- and upper-class white women, especially in New England, asserted themselves by systematically distinguishing themselves from men. In other words, they defined their position in the new republic not by replicating male behavior but by suggesting alternatives to it. They found their strength in their connections with each other and in their redefinition of virtuous behavior. While these women were hardly self-conscious modern feminists, they nonetheless laid the foundations for the emergence of women into the public sphere as people who were every bit as important as men.

A republican role for women, Jan Lewis has suggested, led to greater attention to marriage during and immediately after the Revolution. The relationship of husband and wife was seen by upper-middle-class and upper-class people as embodying the republic in miniature. In the new nation, writers argued, people would be linked together by affection. Since marriage was the institution in which these new social ties would be formed, wives were expected to assume a political role that blended their traditional image with the needs of the republic. The contribution of married women to the nation was the seduction of their husbands into honorable behavior in both the private and the public spheres. They were to use their wiles to keep men from indulging in antisocial behavior. Thus, the negative characteristics of women were turned to good advantage. They became the guardians of male virtue. To accomplish their roles, they had to be educated and they had to redefine virtue from association with manliness (self-sacrifice for the good of the whole) to an identification with womanliness (chastity, purity, self-abnegation). Eventually, though, women's roles as republican wives foundered on the rock of male depravity: some men simply could not be redeemed. So women began to direct their attention to children, who ultimately were more malleable than men.

In other words, women such as Hannah Webster Foster, Judith Sargent Stevens Murray, Susanna Haswell Rowson, and Mercy Otis Warren, along with men such as Charles Brockden Brown and Benjamin Rush, invented their own political character. Women's great value to the republic, they argued, lay in their attention to family and the home. Far from the competitive public business of men, women were likely to embody and advocate a new conception of virtue. As Americans in general rejected the republican (particularly Federalist) emphasis on the importance of the public environment in shaping the social order, they began to look to internal, individual mechanisms to regulate behavior in a potentially anarchic republic. They turned increasingly to the family as the model of society, as the place where males and females would learn as children to be self-disciplined, self-controlled, and internally directed. Evidence of this trend can be found in the changing image of George Washington from the noble, detached, Roman tribune to the thoroughly domesticated youth learning lessons about honesty in Mason Weems's exceedingly popular biography (first published in 1800). Both Washingtons taught Americans how republican citizens should behave. But the new version suggested that anyone could become a good person if he or she learned the proper values as a child. Virtue, in other words, was both democraticized and privatized.

In the early republic, women increasingly became the most obvious guarantors of the stability and coherence of the nation. They took the lead in education, in religion, and in care of children. Now females' traditional household roles took on added significance as American society began to emphasize the importance of childhood in creating good citizens. Women, in short, claimed a position for themselves by emphasizing their difference from men. They were republican mothers who would take the lead in ensuring the survival of the republic by teaching young people self-control. Women defined their position in the republic by turning the existing power structure on its head. Precisely because males were so used to exercising power, they could not be fully trusted with it. White women became not *deputy* citizens but *exemplary* citizens, occupiers of a moral high ground that men, because of their success, could not attain. In the words of Linda Kerber, "Virtue would become for women what honor was for men: a private psychological stance laden with political overtones" ("'History Can Do It No Justice': Women and the Reinterpretation of the American Revolution," p. 39).

Middle-class females defined themselves, in other words, by simultaneously segregating themselves from and integrating themselves into public political culture. The source of their new identity lay in their recognition of the positive nature of their differentness from men. They strengthened this sense through what Nancy Cott has called the "bonds of womanhood." Private correspondence, facilitated by the postal system, allowed white middle-class women in the North to create their own translocal community. Ties of affection and interest linked them together in a defense as well as an assertion of women's important functions in American society, laying the groundwork for the female networks that were extremely powerful in nineteenth-century America.

By the end of the first quarter of the nineteenth century, these developments were coalescing into what historians have called a "cult of domesticity," emphasizing women's distinctive but not inferior role. Mothers were idealized as sources of true virtue; they won recognition for their devotion to the home, to a task-centered rather than a time-centered place, and to their self-abnegation.

Changes in education for women reflected their larger social role. In colonial America, women had few opportunities to acquire useful skills and information. Education for them was considered unnecessary, even dangerous to the larger society: it might "unsex" them. Still, while advocates of female education continued to confront enormous obstacles in the early republic, opportunities for women did increase, at least in the Northeast. Female literacy in New England rose from approximately 50 percent at the time of the Revolution to almost 100 percent by 1840. Early in the period, male teachers usually instructed girls in what amounted to de facto private academies. From the 1790s on, however, women began to open academies intended exclusively for women. Among the best known were Susanna Rowson's in Boston (moved to Medford, Massachusetts, in 1800) and Sarah Pierce's in Litchfield, Connecticut. These schools, and dozens like them, made higher education available to middle- and upper-class women throughout the Northeast. Still, female education offered limited vocational opportunities; women learned to be teachers, mothers, and sisters, not lawyers, merchants, or politicians. As elsewhere, this imposed segregation helped foster, according to Nancy Cott, "women's consciousness of themselves as a group united in purpose, duties, and interests" (*The Bonds of Womanhood,* p. 125).

Similarly, the dominance of women in evangelical religion accentuated their differences from more worldly males while reinforcing their sense of group solidarity. In religion, many women found outlets for self-expression and public activity that were denied them in the larger society. It gave them purpose and identity, a sense of belonging to something larger than themselves. At the turn of the nineteenth century, middle-class women were actively involved in the formation of female voluntary societies for the relief of the indigent and the reform of social ills.

The Autonomy of Women in Marriage While the United States remained a patriarchal society in which men held almost all economic and political power, the redefinition of women's particular place in the society led to a relative increase in female autonomy. Indeed, the growing assertiveness of middle-class women was most evident in their personal relationships with men. Marylynn Salmon has pointed out that the property rights of married women expanded after the Revolution. While regional variations remained, it became easier for women to obtain divorces, although few chose to do so. Most Americans continued to rely on separation as the way to terminate a marriage. In eighteenth-century Massachusetts, there were 229 divorces (most of them at the end of the century) and 3,300 notices of separation; such a disparity continued well into the nineteenth century. As late as 1867, there had been only ten thousand divorces in the United States.

Partly related to the rise in the number of divorces was the growing significance of romantic love to middle-class males and females in the early republic. In a more commercial and egalitarian society, marriage was less an economic or family union than the joining of two people who wanted to be together. Because affection was the crucial link between people, there was greater emphasis on the individual's making his or her own choice. In the early 1800s, middle-class men generally married in their mid twenties; their wives were a few years younger. Indeed, marriage was the most important decision a middle-class woman would make in her life. While the male was still expected to initiate the relationship, the female had the power to continue it or to terminate it before marriage. Since the family was such an important part of society, and since love was so critical to its success, the female had to be sure that a relationship was a healthy one.

For women, marriage usually meant a loss of autonomy. In fact, a woman probably never exercised more power in her life than when she chose a mate and established her wedding date. Afterward, she faced not only the prospect of economic dependence but also the physical dangers of frequent pregnancies and painful childbirth. As late as 1910, one mother died for every 154 live births, compared with one for every 10,000 in 1980. Indeed, it was fear that drove middle-class women to welcome the intrusive presence of male doctors, with their drugs and instruments, during labor. In 1800, Judith Walzer Leavitt has estimated, just over 20 percent of American women had a male physician in attendance when they gave birth, up from virtually none in 1750. Reliance on midwives fell steadily from the revolutionary era, reaching 60 percent of reported births by the time of the Civil War and 50 percent by 1900.

Given the dangers inherent in pregnancy, it is little wonder that women were often less eager than men to get married. Nor is it surprising that middle-class women often delayed marriage as long as they possibly could. Crucial to this process was the perfection of elaborate courtship rituals. Betrothed couples began to shy away from sexual intercourse before marriage, engaging in heavy petting as compensation. Historians believe that the last quarter of the eighteenth century had the highest premarital pregnancy rate in American history;

approximately 30 percent of all brides gave birth within eight and one-half months of their wedding. That rate fell dramatically among white middle-class women in the early nineteenth century.

Once married, middle- and upper-class Americans tended to practice birth control more fully and carefully than previous generations had. In addition to the interest of women in limiting the number of pregnancies, middle-class people now saw children as economic liabilities rather than as assets. In 1800, a married couple had an average of just over seven children; by 1825, they had an average of just over six. By the end of the nineteenth century, the birthrate for white middle-class people was half of what it had been in 1800. Delaying marriage was only partly responsible for this decline in fertility. Just as important was the use of birth control methods, ranging from abstention to coitus interruptus to oiled silk condoms to sponges and douching. For the middle class, abortion was also a growing alternative. Historians estimate that in the first quarter of the nineteenth century, there was one abortion for every twenty-five to thirty live births; by the 1850s, it was one for every five or six.

The New England Model Increasing numbers of women in New England refused to marry at all in the early nineteenth century, following what Lee Chambers-Schiller has labeled "the path of singlehood" or "the cult of single blessedness." Rejecting marriage as too confining, spinsters found happiness and usefulness in service, religion, and sisterhood, reveling in the freedom from conventions and traditional expectations. The growth in the number of unmarried women reflected demographic reality in nineteenth-century New England. There were more women than men. But women's positive reaction to this predicament indicated that they saw value in not being married. In some ways, spinsterhood was the logical outcome of the emphasis on the differences between the sexes in the early American republic. Many women in other parts of the United States also avoided marriage whenever possible. Suzanne Lebsock found in her study of the women of Petersburg, Virginia, that free black women often did not marry, while widows of both races tended to avoid remarriage if they could afford to do so. Lebsock suggests that the reluctance of the latter stemmed from their unwillingness to sacrifice the relative autonomy of widowhood.

Thus, middle-class women in the cities and towns of the North asserted themselves both as individuals and as a group more dramatically in the early nineteenth century. They turned their exclusion from the public sphere into moral superiority in the private realm. Beyond their families, their source of identity lay less in allegiance to the United States or a common American culture than it did in their ties with each other, with their "sisters" in a kind of fictive kinship that transcended geographic boundaries. There was in the early republic, then, the emergence of what Lebsock has called "the outlines of a distinctive women's value system of culture." Simply put, "women at times behaved according to standards of their own" (*The Free Women of Petersburg,* p. xix). They gained very little in the way of public power, but they did attain a sense of shared solidarity and a distinctive identity that would form the basis of their increasingly influential role in the religion-based reform movements of the nineteenth century.

Alternatives to the New England Model It is important to remember that these bonds of womanhood were formed primarily among women of a particular race (white), class (middle), religion (Protestant), and geographic area (the Northeast). Historians have, by and large, concentrated their studies on these women. But studies of rural areas, the South, and working-class women warn that the fallacy of generalizing about a single American culture in the early republic applies to the idea of positing a single female culture. Republican motherhood was not an alternative for everyone. Just as certain white males were able to forge political ties that allowed the creation of a national republic, and thus to achieve a position of power in the new republic, so certain kinds of women were able to define the proper role for women. Others reacted differently, largely because they were in different circumstances.

While the lives of southern women have not been explored as thoroughly as those of their middle-class counterparts in the North, Elizabeth Fox-Genovese believes that the persistence of the household economy and a social system of dependency foreclosed the development of a cult of domesticity in the region. The South remained largely rural, its population less concentrated than in the North, its family structure more rigidly patriarchal, and its society more personal. Thus, even as southern white males continued to insist on a code of personal honor and republican independence long after northern middle-class males had traded such ideas for the dictates of individual conscience and self-discipline, southern white women found it difficult to create a special role for themselves. Southern women, Fox-Genovese points out, had their own story, one that must be understood on its own terms, not those established by historians of middle-class women in the Northeast.

In the South, there were fewer opportunities for the formation of a distinctive women's culture outside of a few genuine urban areas such as Petersburg, Virginia. The region lagged behind in developing public education; there was little demand for teachers. Female education, then, remained more ornamental than useful. Because women were discouraged from forming networks and voluntary associations, because there was no strict separation of the public and the private, the workplace and the home, in the South, there was little chance to develop the role of republican mother. Southern women of both races may have spent a great deal of time together in houses, working together and confiding in each other, but their world did not constitute a distinctive female sphere. Significantly, in the South, where white males clung to the values of republican independence, civic virtue, and public reputation with the greatest intensity, white females made the least progress in developing a public role for themselves.

African American women—with the exception of a few, such as the poet Phillis Wheatley—were even further removed from the world of republican wives and mothers. There was no time for nor encouragement of female purity or the legal confirmation of sexual relations. In a world where they were at the mercy of white males, black women were not afforded the privilege of female virtue. Their rates of premarital sexual intercourse were higher than those of white women, and they began to have intercourse at earlier ages. But once they established a monogamous relationship, they practiced marital fidelity to a greater extent than whites. Family was extremely important to African Americans, and they struggled to maintain ties with real and fictive kin once they were established. There was little effort to limit family size among blacks, even though for slave women, the experience of pregnancy and childbirth was more dangerous than for whites. The infant mortality rate of blacks, for example, was twice that of whites.

One index of the differences between North and South lies in church attendance. Among middle-class people in the Northeast, religion was becoming increasingly feminized; although women were not allowed to serve as ministers, females dominated membership lists in Protestant denominations. They also served as the backbones of reform societies. On the other hand, according to Fox-Genovese, actual church congregations, if not membership rolls, had a higher percentage of men in the South than in the North. Rachel Klein suggests that evangelical churches in the South replicated, even as they sustained, the household model of the social order. Evangelicals in the early nineteenth century could see slaves as parts of a household because the household was already fundamentally unequal in terms of gender.

Southern Evangelicals also adopted a much less rigid attitude toward sin than did the middle class of the urban North. According to Klein, they recognized greed, adultery, drunkenness, laziness, and other failings as inherently human. Congregations could do no more than families: they could help those they loved to control their passions, but they could not eliminate sin. Southern churches rarely demanded internalized mechanisms of self-control. Rather, they relied on the household and churches to help flawed people deal with their inevitable imperfections. Just as the South became increasingly different from the North in terms of its basic economic structures, so it became increasingly different in its social system.

Many women in non-slaveholding rural areas also deviated from the New England bourgeois model. Many found ways to take advantage of commercialization without completely accepting the cult of domesticity. Farm women throughout the North were far too intimately involved in the household economy to have much time for education and moral reform. Their work varied by region but, in addition to caring for their families, usually involved the preparation of food, the production of textiles, and the management of goods. In southeastern Pennsylvania, as Joan Jensen has demonstrated, farm women responded to the expansion of the Philadelphia market by shifting their efforts into dairying. In the late 1700s, Philadelphians consumed approximately thirteen pounds of butter per person per year. Farm women therefore moved butter making to the center of their household economies. Still, they managed to preserve the essential characteristics of the traditional patriarchal household. While their families were smaller by the mid nineteenth century and many Quaker women were active as teachers and reformers, their lives did not become as gender-divided as those of middle-class women in New England.

Working women in the cities often were not so lucky. The doubling of New York City's population from 60,000 to 123,000 between 1800 and 1820 reflected the rapid movement of people in search of better economic opportunities. Most of the migrants were from the Northeast, but a substantial number were from the British Isles, among them English radicals fleeing repression in the wake of the Wars of the French Revolution and Protestant farmers and skilled workers from the north of Ireland. This population explosion helped to precipitate dramatic economic and social transformations. Merchant capitalists shifted from using skilled craftsmen at a customary price to employing hired wage laborers at market price. In a world of intense competition and devaluation of skill, laboring males found that work was increasingly seasonal or intermittent, resulting, as Christine Stansell has shown, in the complete disruption of the household economies that persisted so strongly in rural areas and in the South. Left extremely vulnerable by the capitalist transformation to the vagaries of economic cycles, disease, and accidents, many working-class males were unable to provide for their families on a consistent basis. Since the patriarchal authority of males had always rested on their ability to meet the needs of their families, their economic insecurity contributed to the weakening of their traditional social role as head of the household.

The changing economic circumstances of laboring males meant that women had to go to work outside the home. They needed cash to supplement their husbands' often inconsistent and inadequate earnings. To earn money, they became servants, took in lodgers, did other people's laundry, peddled food, or, if they were lucky, worked as seamstresses and craftswomen. Working women did not have the time to think about becoming republican wives and mothers. Certainly, working-class males continued to caricature them as devious, foolish, and untrustworthy. The increased economic importance of women and the breakdown of the household may even have intensified the misogyny of males. Certainly, many working-class couples lived in a world far removed from the elaborate rituals of courtship and romantic love with which members of the middle class seemed to be obsessed. Relationships between men and women developed within a larger atmosphere of treachery and hostility. While middle-class women took on the role of republican mothers, working-class women lived in a culture that continued to label them as deceptive and dangerous. Stansell believes that misogyny in fact became stronger in post-Revolutionary America, at least in urban areas.

Working-class males reveled in a plebeian culture that prized immediate gratification and that was largely separate from the home. They spent time in saloons, enjoying a masculine milieu free from cares—and from women. They also reacted to the upheaval in their lives more directly—by fighting and rioting. In this world, fights between individual men became intrinsic to the competitive, angry atmosphere of male gatherings.

More generally, crowd activity, which, according to Paul Gilje, had essentially represented the purposeful, limited behavior of a community acting within certain boundaries just a few decades earlier, became increasingly fragmented and less predictable. In the dramatically expanding and ever more impersonal world of the city, groups without the economic competence of artisans banded together as a community defined not by geography but by economic, ethnic, or familial interests. Mobs now seemed to get out of control, to go beyond their limited purposes, with unprecedented fury, as in the Baltimore riot of 1812, when a group of Federalists were badly beaten.

Thus, the values and behaviors of working-class men and women were vastly different from those espoused by middle-class society. The household economy was completely disrupted, men and women were treated as little more than commodities, and attitudes of mutual suspicion seemed firmly entrenched. The bonds of womanhood existed in the streets of New York, but in forms that no middle-class woman would recognize.

THE POLITICS OF RACE

As Americans became more aware of gender in the early republic, they also became increasingly conscious of questions of race. Recent historians have become much more sensitive to the chronology of slavery and the regional variety of the African American population. As Ira Berlin has shown, a wide range of African communities existed in colonial America, from those in northern port cities to those in the coastal regions of the Carolinas. The Revolution disrupted blacks' lives no less than whites' and brought them into much more contact with different kinds of people, both white and black. The Revolution also made the position of African Americans problematic, just as it had the position of women. In a society committed to egalitarianism, why were there slaves?

For whites, the answer was clear: to do the work that would allow whites to enjoy a high degree of personal independence. Racism developed hand in hand with the democratic rhetoric of the Revolution. Since African Americans could not be full citizens, white Americans found it necessary to emphasize their differences. The flourishing of white citizenship rested on the foundation of racial segregation. However ambiguous the status of blacks may have been in colonial America, there was no doubt about their position in the early republic. Yet within the parameters of this intensified racism, African Americans, like middle-class women in the Northeast, began to develop common identities by joining together in distinctive communities.

The Relations of Blacks and Whites As with white Americans, the experiences of African Americans varied greatly, depending on where they lived. In the Chesapeake, the shift from tobacco to wheat farming in the late eighteenth century had undermined the economic demand for slaves. Some were sold in regions to the southwest; Allan Kulikoff's figures show that 222,000 African Americans were forcibly transported from the Chesapeake into Kentucky and, later, the lower South between 1790 and 1820. Others were hired out to work at nonagricultural jobs. Still others either were given or purchased their freedom. The number of free blacks in Maryland rose from eight thousand in 1790 to approximately thirty-four thousand by 1810; in Virginia, the increase was from twelve thousand to over thirty thousand in the same period. According to Ira Berlin, free blacks were the fastest-growing part of the upper South's population in the early republic.

In late-eighteenth-century Virginia, many African Americans, both slaves and freed, were skilled artisans and house servants who were relatively well assimilated into white society. Mechal Sobel has emphasized that blacks and whites lived and worked in close proximity. They shared similar perceptions of time, the vast majority lived in similar, small houses, and poor whites and slaves worshiped together.

Without denying the reality of oppression or the real differences between black and white cultures, Sobel believes that a profound symbiotic relationship existed between the two races. She contends that what contemporaries called "promiscuous" interaction helped to reinforce premodern attitudes and behaviors in colonial Virginia. By the end of the eighteenth century, blacks and most whites (with the exception of the enlightened gentry) tended to keep time by the cyclical rhythms of agricultural labor rather than the regular ticking of a clock, to emphasize a strong sense of place, and to believe strongly in the natural world as mysterious and magical. In Baptist and Methodist congregations, where the races worshiped together, they developed a fervent, highly emotional, and highly expressive style that involved experiencing religion and sharing that experience with others. Most interesting, whites accepted an African vision of death as a reunion with family members instead of a frightening mystery, while blacks rejoiced in a Christian conception of heaven open to everyone. "Almost invariably," Sobel concludes, when the Great Awakening came to Virginia, "*it came when and where whites were in extensive and intensive contact with blacks.* Awakenings in Virginia were a shared black and white phenomenon, in which each worldview stimulated, permeated, and invigorated the other" (*The World They Made Together,* p. 180). Even though, after the Revolution, blacks and whites increasingly went separate ways, the experience of the eighteenth century remained critical in shaping southern culture.

Revivals throughout the South in the late eighteenth and early nineteenth centuries primarily involved blacks and poorer whites. These groups shared more than an emotional, experiential approach to religion. They also found in evangelical Protestantism the confidence to assert their ways of living in opposition to the ways of members of the gentry. But this egalitarian cast also eventually split blacks and whites. For though the mass interactions of the awakenings led some whites to question slavery, those whites were unwilling to follow the logic of their answer. They were not willing to grant blacks equal status in this world, particularly after blacks in the United States and in the Caribbean became more vocal in advocating the rhetoric of the American and French revolutions. Once white Baptists and Methodists had succeeded in rebelling against the colonial gentries and had established themselves in positions of power and respectability, they had no desire to open the system further to slaves.

Thus, successful political and religious revolution among whites led to increasing segregation of blacks. The mark of the rise of the whites was their ability to identify blacks as being less than themselves. In the nineteenth century, slaves replaced the degenerate white gentry as the "other" group against whom southern Evangelicals defined themselves. Whites reinforced the bonds forged in the Great Awakening with periodic revivals that seem designed less to convert others than to "recapture the emotional vitality of the movement's early career" and "to maintain the boundaries between themselves and the world" (Donald G. Mathews, *Religion in the Old South,* p. 245). In the early nineteenth century, some whites broke away from the increasingly refined Methodists and Baptists in order to establish supposedly simpler and purer denominations, such as the Disciples of Christ.

Still, it was African Americans who most fully carried the legacy of eighteenth-century evangelism into the nineteenth century. Shut out of white churches, "black Christians," writes Mathews, "became a movement within a movement, a community within a community, a society within a society." Their institutions became "specifically black institutions" (*Religion in the Old South,* pp. xvii–xviii). Because of their race and because of the strong leadership within their communities, both male and female, they were able to create and maintain a sense of distinctiveness apart from other Evangelicals. For blacks, in short, the early republic was a period of intensifying segregation in which they developed ties that linked them together as black people within the broad parameters of the new republic.

Not all Virginia blacks chose the path of religion. In the summer of 1800, a group of about two hundred Africans led by Gabriel Prosser plotted the overthrow of the Virginia government. Gabriel was a Virginia-born, well-traveled, highly skilled man who was assimilated into white society. The conspiracy failed because of poor planning, betrayals, and bad weather. But it nonetheless represented the actions of autonomous people to improve themselves at the expense of whites. Gabriel's Rebellion was, as Gerald Mullin has shown, the work of revolutionaries who wanted to fight slavery collectively, not a quasi-religious outburst like Nat Turner's three decades later.

More typical of the activities of African Americans in the upper South was their single-minded devotion to the preservation of their families. Jacqueline Jones contends that family life was a source of both strength and vulnerability, for families could be torn asunder so quickly. Devotion to family appeared most remarkably in the persistent efforts of slaves and free blacks to buy the freedom of others. They were more likely to be able to do so in the upper South and the North because of economic conditions.

African American Institutions The growing free black population in the upper South and the North experienced life in the early American republic in ways that were both similar to and different from the lives of slaves. The free black population in the United States was 186,466 by 1810, up from 59,466 in 1790. In the North and the upper South, the lot of African Americans was mixed. Usually they suffered a decline in economic level when freed, and they were subjected to innumerable legal and subtle forms of discrimination. But they also were assertive. They protected their families, they took new surnames such as Justice and Freeman, or they gave up their former master's surname for a common English one like Brown. And they found their greatest source of strength in their ties with others in similar positions. Like middle-class women, free blacks linked themselves together in ways that criticized, even as they echoed, white culture. Excluded by whites from churches and schools (after a brief period of integration and the failure of black luminaries such as Phillis Wheatley and Benjamin Banneker to achieve widespread acceptance in white society), African Americans formed their own institutions and organizations.

Among free blacks in Philadelphia, Gary Nash has shown that an initial period of optimism about race relations gave way in the early republic to efforts to establish an autonomous community built around evangelical religion. Here, separation from whites was paramount. African Americans defined themselves in interaction with the racist white world in which they were necessarily involved. At the heart of this community, as with white middle-class women, was the notion that African Americans were not whites with black skins, but members of a distinctive and powerful separate group. Evangelical ministers preached that blacks were in some ways superior to whites who practiced or condoned such sins as slaveholding. African Americans also formed their own voluntary societies to meet the needs of their particular community. Among the most important of these groups was the African Methodist Episcopal Church, which was founded in 1816. In a racist society, blacks had no choice but to create their own world, one that mirrored white worlds even as it revised them. African Americans forged their identity within the constructs of the larger nation, but they did so less by becoming American than by forming bonds that linked them in a common, distinctive cause.

Similarly, slaves in the Deep South formed communities on the basis of interaction with the culture of the dominant whites. Charles Joyner has argued in his study of language, food, work, and leisure among slaves in coastal South Carolina in the 1850s that African Americans adapted the materials of British culture in the context of the Carolina environment to their own needs. What happened linguistically was a metaphor for what happened in the society as a whole: the creation of Gullah as a distinctive language involved the blending of an English lexicon with an African grammar. So, too, slaves ate New World foods with an "African culinary grammar," they completed their assigned tasks with African skills and work patterns, they worshiped a Christian God with African forms of expression and belief. Within the harsh and brutal system of slavery, they prized family relations and, through frequent visiting with slaves on other plantations, created their own networks, their own distinctive community.

The culture Joyner describes originated largely in the early republic. On first glance, such an achievement would seem to have been extremely difficult. The great number of slaves imported in the 1790s and the early 1800s, along with the expansion of rice and cotton production throughout the period, combined to entrench slavery more firmly in the Carolina low country than it had been in the eighteenth century. Still, Philip Morgan believes that African Americans were able to achieve greater autonomy in this region than in any other area of North America, largely because of their skills and numerical preponderance. Despite a life expectancy that was some fifteen to twenty years shorter than that of whites (twenty-eight to thirty-six, compared with forty to fifty-eight in 1850), an infant mortality rate twice that of whites, poor living conditions, and entry into the work force at the age of six, black slaves found ways to maintain a distinctive presence in the expanding South.

Native Americans Native Americans were not quite so fortunate. In the early republic, the Shawnee Tecumseh and his brother, Tenskawatawa, attempted to unite the Indians of the trans-Appalachian West in resistance to Anglo culture. Like middle-class white women and African Americans, the brothers sought to form translocal ties on the basis of a recognition of their cultural distinctiveness. Tecumseh and Tenskawatawa urged Native Americans to resist white intrusions culturally as well as militarily; they were encouraged to avoid the enticements of the Christian religion, European technology, and white civilization in general. The brothers' point was to assert the values and behaviors of Native American societies. They failed because the diversity of Native American cultures, long-standing animosities between groups, and, most of all, the involvement of most Indians in the economic and social worlds of whites doomed their vision of Indian unity as much as the military defeats at Tippecanoe (1811) and the Thames (1813).

By the early 1800s, most Native Americans east of the Mississippi River found it impossible to withdraw completely from European worlds. Since the beginning of colonization, Indians had formed strong economic, social, and diplomatic ties with whites. In the lower Mississippi Valley, they had been engaged in the long-distance trade of deerskins and other commodities with the Spanish and the English throughout the eighteenth century. Many Native Americans in the Old Northwest were relatively recent arrivals in the region; some, such as the Delawares, had migrated there in order to take advantage of more plentiful supplies of skins and goods for trade. The French and the English had long served as intermediaries for Native American trade with Canada, the eastern colonies, and Europe. In other words, Indians and Europeans had been trading, meeting, fighting, eating, and sleeping together for generations. Several important Native American leaders in the early republic—Alexander McGillivray of the Creeks, for example—were descended from both Europeans and Indians, and moved with equal ease and similar discomfort in both worlds.

These characteristics of Indians made it virtually impossible to unite them in a common cause. As with whites, there were simply too many regional and cultural differences to overcome. Even when Tecumseh briefly achieved political unity, it proved to be a double-edged sword. The tenuously united Indians of the Old Northwest were relatively easier to defeat militarily because they were a focused group. In the South, on the other hand, the lack of unity and the fluidity of cultural boundaries meant that battles there were less decisive. Thus, government policy forced the removal of most Native Americans from the South in the 1830s, long after their counterparts in the Old Northwest had ceased to be a viable presence in that region.

While some Native American leaders urged an assertion of their rights and distinctiveness through political means, others stressed the importance of coming to terms with decades of interaction with Europeans. Among these was a Seneca, Handsome Lake, who between 1799 and 1815, led a cultural renaissance among Indians in western New York State. He preached the virtues of temperance in the use of alcohol, the acceptance of technological innovations that would allow the Senecas to become sedentary farmers, and a reconfiguration of the family from a patrilineal to a matrilineal model. On many levels, the Senecas' renaissance rested on an adaptation of white ways (such as farming) and beliefs (particularly in the acceptance of concepts of divine judgment and an afterlife). But Handsome Lake was not advocating a simple surrender of cultural autonomy; he was not suggesting that the Senecas become white. On the contrary, his revival efforts ensured the survival of much of Iroquois culture. Although the Senecas made peace with the whites, they did not adopt white ways so much as they adapted them to their particular circumstances. Ultimately, their rethinking of their culture helped to strengthen their cultural distinctiveness.

Among the Catawba Indians in the Carolina Piedmont, there was no spectacular revival along the lines of Handsome Lake's. Indeed, travelers and government officials tended to view the Catawbas as they did most native peoples in the early republic; they were in decline and disarray, sinking into poverty and lethargy. But the Catawbas, like the Senecas, did not give up in the face of massive white pressure to do so. Despite the efforts of Christian missionaries, they preserved traditional religious beliefs and customs. The Catawbas, concludes James H. Merrell

> neither held onto some fossilized aboriginal way nor abandoned their culture for another. Instead, they continued to do what they had always done: take ideas, customs, crafts, and objects from beyond their cultural frontier and then make those things their own. This creative response enabled Catawbas to adjust to changing conditions while keeping intact the core of their ancient culture. (*The Indians' New World,* p. 271)

In short, like many other peoples in the early national period, many Native Americans were able to assert a distinctive cultural identity in the midst of rapid change. Their experiences reinforced a sense of cultural separation from others, even as they were integrated into the new world defined by capitalist economic practices and the borders of the nation-state.

CONCLUSION

By the 1820s, the citizens of the republic were acutely aware of how different they were from one another. The formation of a strong national government, the growth of the capitalist market, and the tremendous physical and demographic expansion of the nation were bringing peoples into unprecedented contact with each other. In a remarkable burst of cultural creativity, diverse groups were coming together and defining themselves by asserting their distinctiveness and their importance both against and within the national political structures devised largely by white males.

Very little, however, seems to have been resolved in the early national period. The absence of a dramatic, public climax has always made the era difficult for scholars and teachers to conceptualize. Traditionally, the period has been thought of as a transitional time between the American Revolution and the Age of Jackson. But, if nothing else, the work of recent historians has made it clear that the federal and early national periods merit study as a coherent entity.

The people of the United States were not simply moving consensually from a republican model of society to a liberal one between 1789 and 1829. They were engaged in a series of significant and complex debates about the nature of human relationships, about how people should understand themselves and others in a rapidly changing world. These discussions were piecemeal, often more implicit than explicit. But if they lacked the drama of Jefferson's quarrel with Hamilton, they were no less important in shaping the history of the American peoples.

BIBLIOGRAPHY

Overviews: Political and Intellectual History

Appleby, Joyce. *Capitalism and a New Social Order: The Republican Vision of the 1790s* (1984).

Davis, David Brion. *The Problem of Slavery in the Age of Revolution, 1770–1823* (1975).

McCoy, Drew R. *The Elusive Republic: Political Economy in Jeffersonian America* (1980).

Slaughter, Thomas P. *The Whiskey Rebellion: Frontier Epilogue to the American Revolution* (1986).

Watts, Steven. *The Republican Reborn: War and the Making of Liberal America, 1790–1820* (1987).

Wood, Gordon S. "The Significance of the Early Republic." *Journal of the Early Republic* 8 (1988).

Overviews: Cultural and Social History

Berlin, Ira. "The Revolution in Black Life." In *The American Revolution: Explorations in the History of American Radicalism,* edited by Alfred F. Young (1976).

Grossberg, Michael. *Governing the Hearth: Law and the Family in Nineteenth-Century America* (1985).

Hatch, Nathan O. *The Democratization of American Christianity* (1989). A provocative interpretation of religious life.

Horwitz, Morton J. *The Transformation of American Law, 1780–1860* (1977).

Kerber, Linda K. "'History Can Do It No Justice': Women and the Reinterpretation of the American Revolution." In *Women and the American Revolution,* edited by Ronald Hoffman and Peter J. Albert (1989).

Larkin, Jack. *The Shaping of Everyday Life, 1790–1840* (1988). A fascinating study of daily life.

Leavitt, Judith Walzer. *Brought to Bed: Childbearing in America, 1750 to 1950* (1986).

Lewis, Jan. "The Republican Wife: Virtue and Seduction in the Early Republic." *William and Mary Quarterly* 3rd ser., 44 (1987).

Salmon, Marylynn. "Republican Sentiment, Economic Change, and the Property Rights of Women in American Law." In *Women and the American Revolution,* edited by Ronald Hoffman and Peter J. Albert (1989).

Regional, State, and Local Studies: Collection

Hahn, Steven, and Jonathan Prude, eds. *The Countryside in the Age of Capitalist Transformation: Essays in the Social History of Rural America* (1985).

Regional, State, and Local Studies: New England

Chambers-Schiller, Lee. *Liberty, a Better Husband. Single Women in America: The Generations of 1780–1840* (1984).

Clark, Christopher. *The Roots of Rural Capitalism: Western Massachusetts, 1780–1860* (1990).

Cott, Nancy F. *The Bonds of Womanhood: "Woman's Sphere" in New England, 1780–1835* (1977).

Roth, Randolph A. *The Democratic Dilemma: Religion, Reform, and the Social Order in the Connecticut River Valley of Vermont, 1791–1850* (1987).

Rothman, Ellen K. *Hands and Hearts: A History of Courtship in America* (1984).

Taylor, Alan. *Liberty Men and Great Proprietors: The Revolutionary Settlement on the Maine Frontier, 1760–1820* (1990).

Ulrich, Laurel Thatcher. *A Midwife's Tale: The Life of Martha Ballard, Based on Her Diary, 1785–1812* (1990).

Regional, State, and Local Studies: Middle States

Gilje, Paul A. *The Road to Mobocracy: Popular Disorder in New York City, 1763–1834* (1987).

Jensen, Joan M. *Loosening the Bonds: Mid-Atlantic Farm Women, 1750–1850* (1986).

Nash, Gary B. *Forging Freedom: The Formation of Philadelphia's Black Community, 1720–1840* (1988).

Stansell, Christine. *City of Women: Sex and Class in New York, 1789–1860* (1986).

Steffen, Charles G. *The Mechanics of Baltimore: Workers and Politics in the Age of Revolution, 1763–1812* (1984).

Wallace, Anthony F. C. *The Death and Rebirth of the Seneca* (1969).

Wilentz, Sean. *Chants Democratic: New York City and the Rise of the American Working Class, 1788–1850* (1984).

Regional, State, and Local Studies: Old Northwest

Cayton, Andrew R. L., and Peter S. Onuf. *The Midwest and the Nation: Rethinking the History of an American Region* (1990).

Edmunds, R. David. *Tecumseh and the Quest for Indian Leadership* (1984).

Faragher, John M. *Sugar Creek: Life on the Illinois Prairie* (1986).

Walker, Juliet E. K. *Free Frank: A Black Pioneer on the Antebellum Frontier* (1983).

Regional, State, and Local Studies: The South

Fox-Genovese, Elizabeth. *Within the Plantation Household: Black and White Women of the Old South* (1988).

Jones, Jacqueline. "Race, Sex, and Self-Evident Truths: The Status of Slave Women During the Era of the American Revolution." In *Women and the American Revolution,* edited by Ronald Hoffman and Peter J. Albert (1989).

Joyner, Charles. *Down by the Riverside: A South Carolina Slave Community* (1984).

Klein, Rachel N. *Unification of a Slave State: The Rise of the Planter Class in the South Carolina Backcountry, 1760–1808* (1990).

Kulikoff, Allan. "Uprooted Peoples: Black Migrants in the Age of the American Revolution, 1790–1820." In *Slavery and Freedom in the Age of the American Revolution,* edited by Ira Berlin and Ronald Hoffman (1983).

Lebsock, Suzanne. *The Free Women of Petersburg: Status and Culture in a Southern Town, 1784–1860* (1984).

Mathews, Donald G. *Religion in the Old South* (1977).

Merrell, James H. *The Indians' New World: Catawbas and Their Neighbors from European Contact Through the Era of Removal* (1989).

Morgan, Philip D. "Black Society in the Lowcountry, 1760–1810." In *Slavery and Freedom in the Age of the American Revolution,* edited by Ira Berlin and Ronald Hoffman (1983).

Mullin, Gerald W. *Flight and Rebellion: Slave Resistance in Eighteenth-Century Virginia* (1972).

Siegel, Frederick F. *The Roots of Southern Distinctiveness: Tobacco and Society in Danville, Virginia, 1780–1865* (1987).

Sobel, Mechal. *The World They Made Together: Black and White Values in Eighteenth-Century Virginia* (1987).

SEE ALSO **Family Structures; Household Labor; Labor: Colonial Times Through 1820; Slavery; Women and Work.**

THE ANTEBELLUM ERA

William E. Gienapp

THE YEARS SEPARATING the ratification of peace with Great Britain in 1815 and the outbreak of war with Mexico in 1846 form a distinct era in American history. Propelled by the fundamental changes in the economy subsumed under the label "the market revolution," this was a time of wide-ranging transformation of American society and life. These changes launched the United States on the path of modernity, shaped society and values for generations to come, and determined much of what the nation still is today. The antebellum era constituted the transition from the traditional, community-centered, rather leisurely world of the revolutionary generation to the urban-industrial, individualistic, competitive, fast-paced society we associate with the modern age.

THE CREATION OF A DOMESTIC MARKET

The War of 1812, which has been called the Second War for American Independence, marked the end of the Revolution. For the previous half century the major problem confronting the colonies—and after 1776 the new Republic—had been relations with the Old World, particularly England. Foreign interference with American rights on the high seas, the British, French, and Spanish presence in North America, and the hostility of the western Indian tribes allied with foreign powers severely restrained the United States' development.

Even after the United States won its independence in 1783, it continued to be tied economically to Great Britain. Lacking a substantial domestic market, the new nation depended on the exchange of raw materials for European manufactured goods, and economic growth was halting and slow. In the absence of cheap overland transportation, the commercial economy was confined to the Atlantic seaboard and the port cities. Much like modern third world nations, the United States had a dual economy, with a small commercial sector dependent upon international trade, and a much larger semi-subsistent agricultural sector that had only limited involvement in the market and its accompanying mechanisms.

After 1815, however, the United States entered a period of accelerating economic growth, characterized by a sharp decline in the cost of producing and transporting goods, sustained urbanization, rapid industrialization, the dramatic spread of its population westward, and the dissemination of commercial institutions and attitudes throughout the country. Together, these changes created for the first time an extensive domestic market, an economic reorientation that had powerful reverberations throughout American life.

Several factors contributed to the development of this internal domestic market. Britain, after years of trying to block American expansion, finally accepted American independence and abandoned its alliances with Indian peoples in the Ohio and Mississippi valleys. With the European military threat removed by improved relations with Britain, the ouster of the Spanish from Florida in 1819, and the purchase of Louisiana from the French, the United States turned its attention inward.

Another factor was the more active role the government took in the economy. During the War of 1812 power passed to a new generation of political leaders who were eager to use federal power to promote economic growth. Known as the "new nationalism," their program envisioned linking economically the North, the South, and the West; the resulting prosperity, they argued, would foster national unity. In short order, Congress passed a protective tariff, chartered a new national bank (the Second Bank of the United States), and embarked on a program to aid improvement of transportation facilities, including roads, canals, rivers, and harbors.

At the same time, the judiciary increasingly encouraged risk-taking by propounding an innovative probusiness interpretation of contracts. Most important in this regard was the gradual emergence of the legal concept of the corporation, in which a group of investors pooled their resources in a business venture. The advantage of a corporation over earlier forms of organization was that an investor was liable only to the extent of one's investment. This feature, coupled with the need to raise increasingly large sums of money as the scale of business expanded with the economy, made corporations increasingly common. Acting to release economic energy and encourage investment, the courts actively protected the interests of corporations and other business ventures from close state regulation.

The capital to promote the growth of the domestic market came largely from Europe. The final overthrow of Napoleon in 1815 ushered in a period of peace on the European continent, and capital seeking new investments poured across the Atlantic into the expanding American economy. At the same time, the burgeoning cotton trade spurred American economic expansion until the depression of 1839. As cotton prices boomed on the world market after 1815, southern farmers and planters dramatically increased their cotton production to meet the world demand, and cotton profits helped Americans pay for imports, as well as heightened the domestic demand for western foodstuffs and eastern manufactured goods, which were now protected in the domestic market.

Beyond these other stimuli, this economic expansion was made possible by a dramatic advance in the speed and efficiency of transportation and communication. Prior to 1815, the only inexpensive way to move goods in the interior was by water. The cost of transportation over land was prohibitive—hauling a wagonload of wheat a mere thirty or forty miles doubled its cost—so backcountry farmers had no incentive to produce a surplus for sale in distant markets.

A series of technological advances, however, dramatically cut the cost of transportation: in the period 1815–1850—a generation—the cost of land transportation fell 95 percent, while its speed increased fivefold. Public and private money was invested in improving and extending roads; the most famous was the National Road, which eventually stretched from Baltimore, Maryland, to Vandalia, Illinois. More important was the construction of a canal network. The instant success of the Erie Canal, which the state of New York completed in 1825 from Buffalo to Albany, stimulated a frenzy of canal construction, and by 1840 the nation had 3,300 miles of canals. Although the depression of 1839 prevented states from financing further construction, canals continued to be the cheapest, if not the fastest, mode of interior transportation.

Another major innovation was the steamboat. First used on the Hudson River, it became a major means of transportation on the West's extensive network of often shallow rivers. Steamboats plied the Mississippi River and its tributaries from spring thaw until winter freezes, moving both goods and passengers cheaply and quickly. From 1820 to 1860, which was the golden age of the steamboat, the carrying capacity on the western rivers increased a hundredfold.

The other important transportation innovation was the railroad. The first significant railroads in this country were constructed in the 1830s. By 1840 the United States' total rail mileage was as long as its canal system (and almost twice as long as Europe's). In the next decade, the American rail infrastructure tripled, so that by mid century there were 8,879 miles of track. Railroads were not always the cheapest form of transportation, but they could operate year round, followed more direct routes, were faster, and could penetrate areas remote from waterways. Although the railroad replaced canals and steamboats as the dominant form of transportation in the second half of the nineteenth century, the latter were more important in the creation of a national market.

Accompanying these developments was a revolution in communications, spearheaded by the expansion of publishing. The invention of the steam-powered cylindrical press, which significantly increased the speed of printing, revolutionized the industry: the price of books, magazines, and newspapers dramatically dropped while the supply greatly increased. As mass-produced books were distributed far and wide by booksellers and peddlers, and newspapers circulated extensively subsidized by cheap postage, a mass reading audience developed.

Newspapers, especially in the major cities, became larger and contained much more up-to-date information, relayed by improved transportation and later by the telegraph. The penny press (so named because of its price) offered a unique blend of news, gossip, and scandal to more readers than ever before. Whereas in 1801 there were only two hundred newspapers in the country (only twenty of which were dailies), by 1835 the figure had risen to twelve hundred, and by mid century it stood at over twenty-five hundred (with 254 dailies). In fact, by 1840 the United States had more newspapers than any country in the world, and twice as many as its nearest competitor, Great Britain.

Up-to-date commercial news was especially important for the country's economic development. The availability of prices in various markets to merchants, businessmen, and farmers called attention to opportunities in unseen places, stimulated speculation in anticipation of movement in the market, and allowed for more rational planning and investment. The perfection of the telegraph in the 1840s accelerated the rapid dispersal of commercial information. The first experimental line was erected in 1844 from Washington to Baltimore, and within less than a decade twenty-three thousand miles of wire had been strung. Commercial and financial news dominated this new information-disseminating network.

One consequence of these technological innovations was territorial specialization. Manufacturing became increasingly important in the Northeast, where agriculture was unable to compete with the fresh lands being settled in the West. The South, where cheap slave labor made possible large-scale plantations, continued to develop an economy that specialized in the production of staples for export—cotton, sugar, rice, tobacco, and hemp. Finally, the West produced foodstuffs, shipping grain and livestock to eastern and southern markets. With transportation no longer a barrier, farmers increased their production in order to sell the surplus, which in turn permitted larger cities to develop. Profits from the sale of southern and western agricultural goods were used to purchase eastern manufactured goods. Regional specialization increased market efficiency, tied the country together in complex ways, and, most important of all, significantly increased the standard of living for ordinary citizens.

THE DEVELOPMENT OF COMMERCIAL AGRICULTURE

Four-fifths of American families in 1800 farmed the land, but with the exception of those living near cities or navigable rivers, few were integrated into the market economy. Instead, the typical farmer placed first priority on raising enough food to sustain the family through the coming year. Although the truly self-sufficient farm family, growing or making everything it needed, is a myth, rural residents did produce most of their household goods. They exchanged their small surplus and handicrafts with their neighbors or at the local store for those items they could not themselves make. Most of these transactions were by barter, since money of any kind was scarce. Mutual assistance—swapping tools, assisting in work, and performing various services throughout the year—was deeply ingrained in community life, and farmers kept running accounts of these various exchanges. Periodically, family heads settled up with a small transfer of cash or goods and the process of mutual assistance and exchange began anew.

An ethic of personal freedom stood alongside this sense of community. For these families, republican independence was both a way of life and a virtue. Economically beholden to no one, they managed their affairs and shaped their destiny without outside interference. "I am an independent farmer, don't owe five guineas in the world," boasts one character in William Ioor's play *Independence, or, Which Do You Like Best, the Peer, or the Farmer* (1805). His farm yielded "every necessary comfort for me and mine," and he was always "boasting of, his INDEPENDENCE, and declaring, that an honest farmer knows of no dependence, except on heaven."

In a society with only a limited market, clearing additional land or working longer hours to increase one's crop offered no advantages or rewards. Twenty acres (eight hectares) of cultivated land sufficed to meet a family's needs, tools were little changed from what their ancestors had used, and animal and human muscles provided almost all the power. "It was of no importance to the farmer, that his fields, with careful cultivation, would yield from 50 to 100 bushels of corn per acre," one Ohio pioneer explained, "when a fourth part of the quantity would answer his purpose, there being no market for a surplus" (Malcolm J. Rohrbough, *Trans-Appalachian Frontier,* p. 99).

The market revolution, however, transformed the world of the antebellum yeoman farmer. Agriculture became commercialized, families increasingly purchased goods they previously made for themselves, women no longer performed many of the vital economic functions they once had, speculation in land became endemic, and rural society, like the economy, became much more competitive. Farmers surrendered much of their independence for the chance to pursue the pot at the end of the rainbow.

The ability to market one's produce in distant locations stimulated interest in improved farming techniques and agricultural machinery. Farmers put more land into production, worked longer hours, purchased improved livestock breeds, and began to practice scientific agriculture, especially crop rotation and the use of manures to restore soil fertility. State governments sponsored agricultural fairs to disseminate information. Farm machinery—notably the harvester, which Cyrus McCormick perfected, and the steel plow manufactured by John Deere—increased productivity, as well as the capital needed to start and maintain a successful farm. Countless improvements and innovations greatly lessened the amount of labor required to complete particular tasks, thereby allowing more acreage to be farmed. The 1839 *Farmer's Almanack* noted that "scarcely a tool . . . has not been altered for the better in some way or other." Farmers still depended on animal power, and it was expensive to hire labor, but better tools and machinery increased worker productivity and thus profits.

One effect of this process was that farmers began to specialize in order to maximize their return. Sensitive to market mechanisms, New England farmers, whose rocky soil produced relatively low yields, abandoned wheat production and often shifted to dairy or truck farming and supplied fruits, vegetables, milk, and dairy products to nearby cities; others began to graze sheep in response to the burgeoning textile industry. With western farmers now able economically to ship their crop to eastern markets, the center of wheat production moved steadily westward. By mid century, states such as Illinois and Wisconsin had become major producers.

The rise of commercial agriculture quickly displaced the earlier barter system. Farmers now conducted transactions in cash or on credit and thus were integrated for the first time into the banking system. Rather than hauling their own crops to market, they now dealt with middlemen, often located elsewhere, who bought their crops for sale in the larger market. Farmers gradually became part of a vast impersonal system conveying goods from the producer to the consumer in a national and sometimes world market. Poor harvests in Europe and the opening of the English market to foreign grains in the 1840s created a new market for western American wheat. Wheat shipment to Europe grew apace: by mid century it rivaled even cotton in international trade.

Farmers who sought to compete in this new economy came to depend on credit in order to purchase new land and machinery and to put it in production. They expected to repay these loans with profits from future crops, but there was little margin for error, and several poor harvests could cost a person everything.

Not all farmers welcomed this new competitive system. Many feared losing their independence and the older society of neighborly cooperation, and were uncomfortable with impersonal transactions and unseen, unpredictable forces impinging on their lives. Only backwater areas isolated from larger markets by the absence of transportation remained relatively immune to the market. Even in those areas, ambitious individuals often departed for regions offering greater opportunity. Overall, the agrarian world could not withstand the dazzling promise of the market. Though many rural white Americans did not want to pay the social price the market entailed, few could resist the temptations it offered in terms of an improved standard of living. It is striking how quickly this society of communal cooperation and its antimarket ethos expired. Championing the new capitalist order, agricultural reformers ridiculed old-fashioned farmers "who cannot bear to work alone." It was "very pleasant" to "have our neighbours at work with us," they conceded, but "it tends to lounging and idleness, and neglect of business" (Sellers, *The Market Revolution,* p. 19).

Southern agriculture also was affected by the market revolution. Although planters and slaveholders had long raised staples for sale on the world market, the new opportunities of the market drew increasing numbers of southern rural families into this economy. Slavery and the plantation system penetrated into the upcountry (the region above the fall line) of the eastern seaboard states, previously the domain of yeoman farmers; and southern migrants poured over the Appalachian Mountains to open farms and plantations in the rich soil of the old southwest (Alabama, Mississippi, Louisiana, Tennessee, and eventually Arkansas and Texas).

Cotton replaced tobacco as the major southern staple. The arduous labor required to remove the sticky seeds from short-fiber cotton, a variety that could be grown in higher, drier interior lands, was a major obstacle until Eli Whitney's cotton gin solved this problem. A boom in cotton prices after 1815 stimulated a migration westward, and farmers put the fresh soils of the trans-Appalachian South into cotton production. As cotton pushed into the interior, slavery and the plantation system accompanied it. The number of slave-owning families increased, as southerners sought to compete in the new economy.

Despite the rise of the "cotton kingdom," however, more southern farmers remained outside the commercial economy than was the case in the North. Sugar and rice, two other cash crops that prospered in the southern climate, required enormous investments of capital in labor, machinery, and improvements, so only the wealthiest planters grew these crops. Yeoman farmers were more likely to grow a little tobacco or cotton, but even then their labor costs prevented them from competing economically with slaveholders. Slave-owners had a cheap supply of labor, which allowed them to increase production by planting additional acres; as time went on they tended to monopolize the best agricultural land in a county. Yeoman farmers, in contrast, had only family labor, and hence could not produce these staples as cheaply as planters. (Indeed, nonslaveholders were even at a disadvantage in growing corn, the South's largest crop, for their own subsistence.) Finally, the South was much less densely populated than the North, so many more farm families were isolated from the main avenues of transportation and communication. As a result, many yeoman farmers tried to minimize their connection to the commercial economy by placing first emphasis on providing for their family; with the time and acreage remaining they grew small amounts of cotton or tobacco for local sale in order to buy necessities the family could not produce. In general, southern farmers did not enjoy comforts such as a cookstove, the emerging symbol of domestic improvement, which their northern counterparts took for granted by mid century.

A RESTLESS SOCIETY

Farmers were not the only group affected by the market's heady brew and the pent-up forces it released. There was an explosive energy previously lacking from society, and antebellum Americans were truly a people in motion. Excited by the market's potential and the prospects before them, they embraced the idea of progress, manifested a restless temper, and displayed a basic impatience to get things done. "There is no such thing in America as being contented with one's position," Thomas Low Nichols commented in *Forty Years of American Life*. "Everyone is tugging, trying, scheming to advance—to get ahead." When the famous sculptor Horatio Greenough returned to America in 1836 after a lengthy stay in Europe, he was shocked by the transformation of his native land: "Go ahead! is the order of the day," he observed. "The whole continent presents a scene of *scrambling* and roars with greedy hurry" (Robert Remini, *The Revolutionary Age of Andrew Jackson*, p. 5).

This generation on the move created a high-speed society. Antebellum transportation emphasized speed over safety and comfort, and dreadful railroad and steamboat accidents were often the result of trying to coax the last bit of speed out of a vehicle's boiler. Americans were notoriously fidgety when traveling. The unique American design for railroad passenger cars, with seats on either side of a long center aisle rather than private compartments as in Europe, allowed restive passengers to walk (or pace) back and forth the length of the train. Anxious to get on with their business, Americans gulped their food at breakneck speed—one disgusted European complained that an American "eats his food with the rapidity of a wolf" (Pessen, *Jacksonian America*, p. 22). To meet the soaring housing demand in rapidly growing communities, builders developed a new method of constructing dwellings, known by the derisive term "balloon-frame houses," which consisted of a frame of two-by-fours to which the walls and roof were nailed, and that could be constructed quickly and without great skill.

One gauge of this restless society was the rate of population growth, the highest in the Western world: the population continued to double approximately every twenty-three years. The first census in 1790 found almost four million people in the country, but by 1850 the population stood at twenty-three million. Although the birthrate began to decline after 1800, the first sharp drop did not occur until the 1840s, a period of rapid urbanization, when it fell by 10 percent. As a national average, family size among whites fell from 6.4 children in 1800 to 4.9 in 1850. In the cities, especially among the new middle class, marriage occurred later and families tended to be smaller. In other ways, though, certain basic demographic characteristics did not significantly change in this period: compared to Europe, the median age remained very young (17.2 years in 1830 in contrast to 28.1 in 1970) because of the large number of children, life expectancy did not improve significantly, and especially in rural areas an early marriage and family formation remained the norm.

Prior to 1820, the high birthrate accounted for virtually all the nation's population growth. But peace in Europe unleashed the tide of immigration once again. In the 1830s almost six hundred thousand newcomers entered the United States, more than double the 1790–1815 figure, and this was just the beginning. Immigration surged again in the 1840s, as the potato blight in Ireland and the economic and political upheavals on the continent, particularly in the German states, caused many more to emigrate: an unprecedented 1.7 million immigrants came seeking jobs in the new factories and urban centers or hoping to purchase a farm in the West. The arrival of so many newcomers placed a tremendous strain on social services and institutions (jails, insane asylums, almshouses, and so forth), particularly in cities, and exacerbated tensions with the native-born population. Moreover, unlike the earlier immigrants from Germany and Ireland, those who came in the 1840s were predominantly Catholic. The presence for the first time in American history of large numbers of Catholics precipitated the outbreak of nativism in the period.

This rapidly growing and diverse population evidenced an unprecedented geographic mobility. Eager to exploit the opportunities offered by fresh lands and growing cities in the West, Americans poured across the mountains and rapidly settled the Mississippi and Ohio valleys. In 1817 Morris Birkbeck, an Englishman, observed that "old America seems to be breaking up, and moving westward" (*Notes on a Journey in America,* p. 34). The population beyond the Appalachians doubled in the 1820s, and by 1840 more than one in three Americans lived west of the Mississippi River. By 1850 almost half of the American population lived in areas that had not been states in 1789, and an astonishing two million lived in the trans-Mississippi West. Before 1810 only four new states were added to the Union, but in the next three decades no less than nine were admitted, including Missouri, and Arkansas west of the Mississippi. Five more, including California on the Pacific coast, joined by 1850.

Carrying dreams of a cotton plantation, southerners joined this westward surge. "The *Alabama Feaver* rages here with great violence and has *carried off* vast numbers of our Citizens," a worried North Carolinian wrote in 1817. "I am apprehensive if it continues to spread as it has done, it will almost depopulate the country" (Rohrbough, *Trans-Appalachian Frontier,* p. 156). This migration did not abate with time: in the 1830s an Alabama man reported that people were still "pouring in with a ceaseless tide" and the country was being overrun by "Land Sharks" (p. 244). Even planters at the top of the southern social pyramid were likely to move. Captain Basil Hall encountered one family on the road who had sold their Maryland plantation and, with their slaves, was on their way to Florida. The wife complained: "It was all for the mere love of moving. We have ever been doing so all our lives—just moving—from place to place—never resting—as soon as we git [*sic*] comfortably settled, then, it is time to be off to something new" (Clement Eaton, *The Growth of Southern Civilization,* pp. 33–34).

This westward migration was not confined to whites. It occurred at the expense of the southern Indian peoples, who were forcibly displaced to reservations west of the Mississippi River. It also impinged with particular force on African Americans, for the westward movement of the southern population included large numbers of slaves. Major plantation regions took shape in the "black belt" of central Alabama and Mississippi, the "sugar bowl" of the Mississippi Delta, and the rich, cotton-growing lands of the Mississippi Valley. By the 1840s, the cotton frontier, largely confined to the Atlantic states in 1810, had pushed all the way to Arkansas and the new state of Texas.

The slave population was moving not only westward but southward as well. On the one hand, the dispersal of the slave population was fueled by the growing African American population, which increased as rapidly as did whites (slaves had a higher birth rate but suffered from greater infant mortality). On the other, slaveowners, in the border states and upper South, who often were farming exhausted soil and shifting to less labor-intensive crops such as wheat, needed fewer slaves. As their labor force increased naturally, many sold their surplus slaves to planters in the cotton kingdom. These sales were essential to their profit margin. Thus, in the antebellum years, slaves were systematically sold from the upper South—mainly through New Orleans—to eager buyers in the Deep South. This constituted one of the largest forced migrations in history: between 1790 and 1860, more than one million African Americans were moved in the interstate slave trade, and an estimated six hundred thousand slave families were broken up by sale in the years 1820–1860.

The rapid settlement of the West was aided by federal land policy. Efforts to enact a homestead law granting free land to settlers failed, but western representatives, who led the fight for cheap lands and a policy encouraging rapid settlement, did manage to reduce the minimum tract by half to eighty acres and to lower prices for lands unsold after a specified period of time. In 1841, after a series of more limited acts, Congress finally adopted the policy of "preemption," which allowed squatters to buy public land that they had settled at the minimum price when it was offered for sale. Yet because no law limited how much acreage an individual could buy, most of the desirable land fell into the hands of speculators who had greater capital resources. Nevertheless, farmers and other residents were caught up in the speculative mania. "Speculation in real estate . . . has been the ruling idea and occupation of the Western mind," one visitor reported in the 1850s. "Clerks, labourers, farmers, storekeepers merely followed their callings for a living, while they were speculating for their fortunes" (D. W. Mitchell, *Ten Years in the United States,* pp. 325–328). The sturdy yeoman of the agrarian myth, ruggedly independent and suspicious of the market, vanished in the giddiness of soaring land and commodity prices. Farmers bought land on credit, intending to pay with the profit from their first crops, and thus were forced to grow a cash crop. Semisubsistence was not an option.

Land sales skyrocketed from 1815 on. In 1818 sales from the public domain totaled 3.5 million acres, an area greater than Connecticut. In 1800, by way of contrast, only sixty-eight thousand acres had been sold. The panic of 1819 burst this bubble, ruining many farmers and western landowners. Although sales in the 1820s did not approach the 1818 peak, they exceeded the pre-1815 period. From 1829 sales dramatically increased again, peaking in 1836 at over twenty million acres; but the bubble burst once more in the panic of 1837—land values collapsed, credit contracted, and the country entered a severe depression.

These patterns of sales, both short- and long-term, were evidence of the penetration of the market and its associated values into the countryside. Not surprisingly, land sales rose in prosperous periods such as 1815–1818 and 1824–1836. More important, they followed closely swings in commodity prices in eastern markets. Periods of high wheat and corn prices for western farmers and cotton prices for southern farmers were marked by rising land sales, as farmers borrowed to extend their operations; when prices suddenly swung sharply lower, however, many found themselves overextended and some failed. Such behavior reveals the advancing access to market through improved transportation facilities, and the growing availability of current price information and commercial news through the expanding communications network.

European visitors, who were accustomed to a more traditional and stable rural society, were amazed at Americans' geographic mobility. Indeed, the 1850 census revealed that almost half of all native-born white Americans no longer lived in the state of their birth. In urban areas such as Boston, perhaps one-third of the population moved each year; and at least one-half of the population would have left the city by the end of the decade. Even rural areas displayed low rates of persistence. The general rule in antebellum society was "up or out": people either achieved a measure of economic success and social status or they moved on, hoping once again to succeed in a new environment. A stable core of persisters came to dominate the community. They were wealthier than their neighbors, were more active politically, monopolized public office, and dominated the local institutions of all varieties. Michel Chevalier, a French visitor, observed in *Society, Manners, and Politics in the United States* that unlike European peasants the American "has no root in the soil" but "is always in the mood to move on, always ready to start in the first steamer that comes along from the place where he had just now landed." So mobile were the American people, he thought the national emblem should be a steamboat or locomotive. At the root of this restlessness was acquisitiveness: an American moved, a British observer succinctly remarked, "if by so doing he can make $10 where before he made $8" (Pessen, *Jacksonian America,* p. 19). "There are no bounds among us to the restless desire to be better off," the *American Review* commented in 1845. "No man in America is contented to be poor, or expects to continue so."

An increasing number of Americans headed to the many cities that were beginning to dot the western landscape, or to the established urban centers in the East. The antebellum period witnessed the greatest growth of urbanization relative to the population in American history. In 1820 there were only thirty-five cities with a population of five thousand or more, but by 1850 the number had risen to almost 150. By 1860, 20 percent of the population lived in areas the census defined as urban (towns of more than 2,500). In older agricultural regions such as New England, children of farm families often abandoned farming and sought opportunity in towns. The ratio of farmers to towndwellers steadily dropped from 15 to 1 in 1800 to 5.5 to 1 in 1850. By 1860 the most heavily urbanized region was the Northeast (33 percent) while the least urbanized was the South (10 percent). Older cities such as Boston, New York, and Philadelphia grew rapidly in these years. In 1850 New York, with over a half-million residents (not including Brooklyn), was the largest city in the nation. Equally impressive were the major cities of the West: in 1850 Cincinnati and Saint Louis each had over one hundred thousand residents, and the population of Chicago, which in 1830 had stood at only eight thousand, had jumped to more than fifty thousand people. In fact, no less than 40 percent of the country's urban population in 1850 lived in the West.

All of these changes—the continuing population growth, rapid migration westward, and accelerating urbanization—define a fundamental shift in the country's development. In *Democracy in America,* Alexis de Tocqueville (1805–1859) found it difficult "to describe the avidity with which the American rushes forward to secure this immense booty that fortune offers.... Before him lies a boundless continent, and he urges onward as if time pressed and he was afraid of finding no room for his exertions...." Americans were thrilled by their personal and national prospects, and made expansion in all its facets the hallmark of society.

WORKERS' WORLD

The market revolution brought with it the rise of the factory system. Prior to 1815, manufactured goods had been produced by skilled artisans working in small shops or by the (predominantly female) "putting-out" system, in which merchants supplied raw material to be made into finished articles. Rural families often spent the winter months manufacturing items such as brooms, hats, and fans. After 1815, however, large-scale factories using extensive machinery operated by semi-skilled workers began to displace these earlier forms of production.

The rise of factories depended on technological innovations, cheap transportation, adequate capital and credit, the availability of a suitable labor force, and a growing domestic market. Unlike Europe, the United States had neither a surplus population nor large numbers of skilled workers; consequently, American manufacturers relied whenever possible on mechanization instead of labor, and led the way in adopting the system of interchangeable parts in order to minimize the skill necessary to assemble machinery and manufactured goods. The tendency was toward greater specialization, heavier reliance on technology, increased rates of production, and higher efficiency.

As in England, the first factories in this country produced textiles. Americans copied, then improved on, English textile machinery. Manufacturers also moved toward an integrated system in which every process, from opening the cotton bale to shipping the finished bolt of cloth, occurred at a single location. Because the machines were initially run by waterpower, the first factories began not in cities but along riverbanks in the countryside. And while conducted on a much larger scale than the operations of a master craftsman with a few journeymen and apprentices, most factories in this period remained relatively small by modern standards, with fewer than a hundred employees (the textile mills were a conspicuous exception).

Textile factories initially sprang up in New England, where water power was abundant. A group of merchants, known as the Boston Associates, pioneered the development of factory communities, establishing the first fully integrated mill at Waltham, Massachusetts, and the important textile center at Lowell. Concerned about the miserable poverty produced by the English factory system, which depended heavily on child labor, Lowell's founders intended it to be a model community that would demonstrate the compatibility of republicanism and industrialization. Intending to avoid the creation of a permanent working class, they recruited daughters of New England farm families to work in the mills (making them the first factory workers in America). To ease parents' fears about city life, the women lived in company-owned boardinghouses, where they were closely supervised; in their off hours, they could attend school or lectures, take advantage of libraries, or participate in religious services offered by the company. In Lowell, they even published their own magazine, the *Lowell Offering.* To visitors, Lowell seemed a utopian community with its successful blend of employer paternalism and profits.

In important ways, however, reality diverged from this glowing image. These women were paid three to four times what they could earn in any other occupation, but the factory work was tedious and repetitive, involved long hours, and was done under a strict, time-oriented regimen altogether different from the less structured routine they had known on the farm. The workday was twelve hours long (longer in summer), six days per week. For this work women made $2.40 to $3.20 per week, depending on their skill and position.

The relatively high factory wages and the lure of city life attracted a steady stream of rural daughters. For hard-pressed farm families with too many children for their land, the departure of one or more daughters eased the financial burden (though few sent a significant amount of their earnings home). It probably also improved the marriage prospects of these women, since the flight of young men from rural New England left a shortage of marriageable males. The average millworker was between sixteen and thirty years of age, and few intended to do factory work permanently. Instead, they worked on average less than five years before leaving. Most eventually married and retired from the mills. Many worked erratically, going home periodically, then returning to work: factory managers willingly rehired women who had been good workers and had left in good standing. When her parents asked Sally Rice to return to their Vermont farm, she declined. "I must . . . have something of my own before many more years have passed," she wrote, "and where is that something coming from if I go home and earn nothing? . . . I have but one life to live and I want to enjoy myself as well as I can." Periodic leaves from work, the sisterhood that developed in the boardinghouses, decent wages, and the temporariness of their situation made it easier for these women to adjust to factory life.

Increasing competition, however, soon caused deterioration of these conditions. As profits declined, employers' commitment to paternalism waned. They increased productivity by accelerating work and increasing the number of machines tended by an operative. Wages rose but did not keep up with productivity: the average workers' productivity went up 71 percent in the 1830s and 1840s, but wages increased only 16 percent, and the wage differential between high- and low-skilled positions shrank (Dublin, *Women at Work*). Beginning in the 1840s with the arrival of large numbers of Irish, the mills began to employ immigrants, who were more docile and willing to work for lower wages. For immigrant women, factory work was not temporary; many economically desperate families sent their children to work in the mills as well. As native-born women increasingly left the Lowell factories, a permanent working class developed that by 1860 was more than half Irish and included many men and children. This process of creating a permanent, exploited working class—sometimes referred to as the proletarianization of the labor force—was most visible in the textile mills, but it occurred throughout the industrial sector of the economy.

Industrial work eroded the status and pride of the craft trades, which had been integral to the artisanal system. Previously, apprentices learned a skill, became journeymen, and by living frugally and perfecting their craft, hoped eventually to set up shop as independent master craftsmen. Workers had lived and worked together, and the master was responsible for supervising the behavior of his employees, who were considered part of his family. Drinking, both on the job and after hours, was an important component of craft labor; indeed, one duty of an apprentice was to buy spirits for his shopmates. Blending production with what was now coming to be seen as leisure activities, artisanal work was irregular, with periods of intense labor interspersed with relaxation and celebration. Workers in the shop exerted a measure of control over the work routine. "*Vacation* is capital," commented a tailor who took the day off from work. "It tickles one's fancy with the notion of choice. 'Nothing on compulsion' is my motto" (Bruce Laurie, *Working People of Philadelphia,* p. 53).

Factory work, however, emphasized productivity over craftsmanship, and toil was strictly regulated by the clock. This type of work, with its complicated, often dangerous machinery required laborers to be sober, reliable, punctual, and self-disciplined. Mass-produced goods, while serviceable, were of lower quality than those produced by hand. Even modes of production that did not heavily rely on machinery were reorganized along an assembly-line process. Prior to the adoption of the sewing machine in the 1850s, for example, shoes were still made by hand; but instead of making an entire shoe, cordwainers now performed a single step in the process and passed the piece to another worker.

The reorganization of industrial work along these lines was far from smooth. The first generation of factory workers, in particular, chafed at their loss of status and independence. Members of the trades, for whom owning a shop and becoming a small employer was the emblem of accomplishment, saw themselves transformed into semiskilled workers who were no longer able to manufacture a finished item from raw material. As their status declined, they felt exploited and complained bitterly that "the worth and respectability of *manual labor*" was "sinking in the scale of public estimation" (Arthur M. Schlesinger, Jr., *The Age of Jackson,* p. 133). For them, the factory clock symbolized the new tyranny of routinized work. One millworker, on quitting, cited "obedience to the ding-dong of the bell—just as though we are so many living machines" (Thomas Dublin, ed., *Farm and Factory,* p. 13).

The separation between employer and employee became quite distinct. No longer part of a single household, workers lived away from shop owners, who no longer supervised their off-hour activities or felt responsible for their behavior. Work and home became physically separate, and neighborhoods based on status and occupation took shape with workers and factory owners living in different areas of a town. Newly developing middle-class groups prided themselves on—indeed partly defined themselves by—not having to work with their hands. Moreover, the chances of workers rising to supervisory positions decreased, and the prospect of owning one's shop was even less likely; most faced a lifetime of toil as wage laborers. Even the highly skilled who were paid good wages felt a profound sense of loss.

In response to these developments, a labor movement arose in the 1820s and 1830s, attracting not just factory workers but skilled craftsmen who sought to preserve their rapidly eroding way of life. Indicative of the growing division between workers and employers, they excluded the latter from their organizations. Labor leaders advocated unions and demanded the right to strike. Seeking to enlarge opportunity in society, they called for an end to monopolies, the establishment of free public schools, the abolition of imprisonment for debt, and the prohibition of seizure of mechanics' tools. They also challenged the political parties by organizing separate worker parties; but internal division and ideological confusion prevented workingmen's parties from attracting much support or achieving much politically. The union movement made greater headway than did these parties, but its gains were wiped out by the depression that began in 1837: in hard times few workers were willing to strike or to put the collective interests above their own struggle to survive.

Although the political and legal establishment moved to check the labor movement and to support employers, the major obstacle for a successful labor movement was the lack of a class consciousness among workers. Wages remained high compared to other societies, and workers' standard of living was high enough that they weren't radicalized. With the influx of immigrants after 1840, the working community was divided more deeply than ever by ethnic, religious, and racial animosities. Gender, political affiliation, and occupational differences further divided workers. Efforts by labor historians to document a strong sense of class among antebellum workers have produced strikingly meager results: the American labor force was too transient and too divided. Despite workers' longing for equality and their belief that they were exploited, they were unable to stop the changes in their lives precipitated by the factory system and the spread of the market. However ineffective their protests were, they serve as a poignant reminder that the market did not produce greater opportunity for everyone. Not without reason, many workers believed that they were among the losers in this economic transformation.

Workers' longing for the alleged republican equality of the Revolutionary era was little more than nostalgia; their appeals for mutuality ran headlong into the individualism of American society. Although their belief in permanent social conflict was more realistic than those who saw a fundamental harmony of interests between capital and labor, they were unable to turn this insight to their advantage. In the final analysis, their basic complaint was not over the market revolution. Workers, after all, had long been part of the commercial economy and were every bit as anxious as other Americans to advance and participate in a consumer society. Rather, they clung to the outmoded labor theory of value, which posited that all wealth was created by labor: their basic grievance was that the productive classes did not receive what they considered to be a fair share of the wealth their labor generated. Their outlook was summarized by cotton mill operatives in Philadelphia, who protested that the laborer was "degenerating into a mere machine producing wealth by perpetual exertion, yet living a life of unceasing anxiety and want" (Sellers, *Market Revolution,* p. 334).

THE COMMERCIALIZATION OF SOCIETY

The market revolution made the power of materialism in American life increasingly apparent. The antebellum generation did not invent materialism, but the spread of the market strengthened its hold on the popular imagination and made it much more obvious. In his classic work *Democracy in America,* Alexis de Tocqueville, the most famous European traveler in this era, said, "I know of no country, indeed, where the love of money has taken stronger hold on the affections of men." Along this line, the Rev. Thomas P. Hunt published in 1836 *The Book of Wealth: In Which It Is Proved from the Bible That It Is the Duty of Every Man to Become Rich.* And the famous American author Washington Irving (1783–1859), in his story "The Creole Village" (1836), captured perfectly the spirit of these years when he spoke of "the almighty dollar, that great object of universal devotion throughout the land."

Americans not only wanted the material goods that the market offered but judged fellow citizens by their ability to acquire these goods. In the absence of the traditional institutions of social hierarchy that existed in Europe, Americans rated individuals by their wealth: this, rather than occupation or family name, brought with it social standing and prestige. Thus American materialism was more than a desire for physical comfort in life; it also represented a quest for status and social acceptance. Commented one observer: "Americans boast of their skill in money making, and as it is the only standard of dignity and nobility and worth, they endeavor to obtain it by every possible means" (Douglas T. Miller, *The Birth of Modern America,* p. 122).

In this developing consumer culture, the acquisition of certain goods could set an individual apart from others who were either unable to afford these items or lacked sufficient social grace to adopt them. A good example is homespun versus machine-produced cloth. Farm women preferred the latter, not only because it came in more and brighter colors and was smoother, but because it was socially acceptable where homespun was a sign of social crudity if not poverty. Even families in which women still made cloth often sold it locally to buy machine-made textiles to sew into clothing. Families also laid claim to social acceptability by owning various serving pieces, or a chair, dishes, and eating utensils for each family member.

The commercialization of society upheld the values of entrepreneurial capitalism and the marketplace. Society became intensely individualistic and competitive, a place where individuals scampered to exploit opportunities and become wealthy. The assumption was that a fair playing field, with no advantages conferred by government, would efficiently and fairly distribute the rewards of society. Risk and innovation were rewarded: build a better mousetrap, lectured Ralph Waldo Emerson (1803–1882), the most famous philosopher of this generation, and the world will beat a path to your door.

Anxious to improve their lives and unwedded to the past, Americans displayed a special affinity for technology (a word coined in this era). Commented one European visitor: "Everything new is quickly introduced here, and all the latest inventions. There is no clinging to old ways; the moment an American hears the word 'invention' he pricks up his ears" (Stuart Bruchey, *The Roots of American Economic Growth,* p. 163). Unlike tradition-bound Europeans, American mechanics assumed that ways of doing things could always be improved, and many inveterate tinkerers saw innovation as the way to success. James Nasmyth, an English inventor, declared that "there is not a working boy of average ability in the New England states . . . who has not an idea of some mechanical invention or improvement in manufactures, by which, in good times, he hopes to better his position, or rise to fortune and social distinction" (p. 177).

Commercialization involved a new sensitivity to time. The processes of interchangeable parts and mass production as well as the use of metal instead of hand-cut wooden gears brought the price of a clock within the budget of an ordinary family, and the famous "Connecticut clock" became a standard household item in all but the poorest homes. Previously work had been governed by the passage of the sun; now a mechanical clock, dividing the day into precise segments, regulated activity. Competing in the marketplace involved paying attention to time, and even farmers found clocks addicting. In 1844 one frontier traveler marveled that "in Kentucky, in Indiana, in Illinois, in Missouri, and here in every dale in Arkansas, and in cabins where there was not a chair to sit on, there was sure to be a Connecticut clock" (George W. Featherstone, *Excursion Through the Slave States,* p. 91). Peddlers sometimes left a clock with a farm family on some pretense, confident that when they called to retrieve it the members would suddenly learn (in the words of one itinerant salesman) that "having once indulged in the use of superfluidity [i.e., this superfluous item] how difficult it is to give it up" (David Jaffee, "Peddlers of Progress and the Transformation of the Rural North," pp. 528–529). Owning a clock also became a sign that one was in tune with the new ways. Claiming that he could tell in advance whether the occupants of a farmhouse would purchase one of his clocks, one Yankee peddler explained: "If the house had glass windows, if the man of the house did not wear [a cap] but a hat, if he had boots on—the clock was as good as sold" (p. 528).

This market-oriented society also depended on credit and paper exchanges. The process of moving goods from factory or farm to consumer involved a complex series of transactions, often with unseen individuals. Fees for insurance, interest, and storage became part of day-to-day operation of the market; and the buying and selling of stocks and shares in business ventures was an important form of investing and of raising capital, especially for huge undertakings such as railroads. The nature and stability of the banking and currency system and the availability of credit were as crucial to capitalism as access to market through adequate transportation. The older face-to-face world of business gave way to a commercial system of distant transactions based on the cash nexus. With so many unseen persons and impersonal forces involved, individuals inevitably felt their lives were subject to a certain degree of outside control.

One consequence of this specialization and differentiation in American society was a growing maldistribution of wealth. Everywhere in American society the rich became richer and acquired a greater share of society's wealth. Studies of tax records and property holdings have revealed that the concentration of wealth was greatest in northeastern cities, and that society was most fluid along the western frontier. Rural wealth was most concentrated in the cotton kingdom and large slaveholding regions of the Old South. Four large eastern cities—Boston, New York, Brooklyn, and Philadelphia—exemplify these changes: in 1825 the richest 1 percent of the population owned one-fourth of the total wealth in these communities, but by 1850 this had risen to one-half. Similar though less extreme trends occurred in western cities.

This concentration of wealth occurred at the expense of the lower economic echelons of society. In Connecticut towns, for example, between 1831 and 1851 the number of individuals listed as owning no property increased 33 percent. In Cincinnati, the bottom half of the city's taxpayers owned 10 percent of the wealth in 1817, but by 1860 their share had fallen to less than 3 percent. Likewise, in older areas of the South, planters and slaveowners consolidated holdings in land and slaves by buying out their less prosperous neighbors. By 1840, 10 percent of the nation's families owned over 70 percent of its total wealth, with the richest 1 percent controlling almost 30 percent (Pessen, *Jacksonian America,* pp. 81–89; Jeffrey G. Williamson and Peter H. Lindert, *American Inequality,* pp. 36–102).

This generation celebrated self-made men such as John Jacob Astor (1763–1848) and Cornelius Vanderbilt (1794–1877), who had risen from the bottom to the top of society in their lifetimes. Their success, in the popular mythology, testified to the reality of opportunity. "Ours is a country where men start from an humble origins, and from small beginnings rise gradually in the world as the reward of merit and industry," one minister declared. "One has as good a chance as another, according to his talents, prudence, and personal exertions" (Sellers, *Market Revolution,* p. 238). That the United States was a country of "self-made men" (a term coined at this time) was a central faith of this generation, though most wealthy people in antebellum America had been born into wealthy families. Rags-to-riches stories such as Vanderbilts', while true, were quite rare. Those with capital were in the most favorable position to exploit the market's new opportunities.

However, total wealth was dramatically increasing, so ordinary citizens did not necessarily suffer a decline in income. Indeed, between 1825 and 1860 the average per-capita income among whites almost doubled. Workers and farmers in this country enjoyed a higher standard of living than in Europe. Studies have shown that social mobility occurred but on a more limited scale than contemporaries claimed. Most families normally moved at most only a rung or two up the social ladder in a generation. Unskilled workers or their sons moved into the ranks of the semi-skilled, but few workers, even skilled ones, were able to enter the middle-class ranks of managers and professionals. Instead, social mobility entailed a slightly higher status job, a savings account to cushion the downward swings of the economy, and perhaps owning a house (Pessen, "Social Mobility," *Encyclopedia of American Economic History,* vol. 3, pp. 120–135).

With the market's potential for greater wealth came greater uncertainty: one always worried about falling behind in the scramble for success and being pushed downward. Sudden lurches of the economy intensified this sense of insecurity. With Americans linked in an increasingly complex web of commercial relationships, developments anywhere in the world could suddenly plunge the economy into depression and wipe out everything a person had achieved. In place of steady growth the economy followed a boom-bust cycle in which periods of slow, then wildly accelerating expansion gave way to times of depression and correction. Nothing, not even wealth, seemed permanent. After the country pulled out of the 1819–1823 depression, the moderate growth of the 1820s was followed by frenzied speculation in the 1830s; the crash came in 1837 and more severely in 1839, bringing a major depression until 1843. The second half of the 1840s was another period of moderate growth, followed by overheated expansion in the early 1850s and a contraction in 1857–1861. In such an economic environment, nobody—not even those who had achieved great financial success—could rest on their laurels.

Chauncey Jerome, who had made a fortune marketing his clocks around the world, provided a stark warning to this generation. After a series of unwise investments cost Jerome his wealth, he commented bitterly on the little respect he now commanded among his neighbors, who passed by him in silent scorn. "One of the most trying things to me now is to see how I am looked upon by the community since I lost my property," he wrote in his autobiography. "I never was any better when I owned it than I am now, and never behaved any better. But how different is the feeling towards you, when your neighbors can make nothing more out of you.... It is all money and business, business and money which make the man now-a-days. Success is every thing, and it makes very little difference how, or what means he uses to obtain it." Forced to return to the ranks of the ordinary mechanics from which he had risen, he died in poverty.

DEMOCRACY, POLITICAL CULTURE, AND RACISM

The creation of a new democratic political culture after 1815 was rooted in the social conditions of the market and the problems and consequences that followed in its wake. The program of the new nationalism adopted after the War of 1812 had promised to foster national prosperity, and thus when a depression began in 1819, Americans blamed government policies for the economic downturn. Ordinary citizens began to urge that it was the government's responsibility to promote economic growth and to cushion the blow of hard times.

This connection between economic well-being and government policy was the primary cause of the rising popular interest in politics. Beginning in the 1820s, a political reform movement fundamentally reoriented American politics, establishing democracy as the norm instead of republicanism. White manhood suffrage became the rule, property requirements for voting were abolished, and more offices were made elective, opening them (in theory at least) to ordinary citizens. Elections came to be viewed as referenda on public policy, and politicians were expected to bow to the will of the majority of their constituents rather than exercise independent judgment. Political parties, previously feared as selfish institutions, were now accepted as the most effective way to mobilize the sovereign people. Galvanized by these new attitudes, mass involvement rose to unprecedented levels, so that by the 1840s voter turnouts of 75 percent were routine and in many states exceeded 90 percent. The 1840 presidential election, in which nearly 80 percent of the eligible electorate went to the polls, produced one of the highest turnouts in American history.

Office-seeking politicians quickly learned to practice the politics of the "common man." Political leaders such as Andrew Jackson, who symbolized the new democratic system, praised the wisdom of the ordinary citizen and portrayed themselves as the people's champion. Candidates needed to identify with the common people, and the ability to mix easily with the masses, to swap jokes and drink from a common jug, to shake hands and kiss babies counted heavily on the new democratic playing field. Politics became a form of mass entertainment: parades with bands and floats, balloon raisings, picnics, and massive rallies served to attract crowds and energize voters. Treating voters to drinks became an almost universal campaign practice. The democratic style of this system created an enthusiastic electorate with deep-seated partisan loyalties. Even women, barred by law from voting, participated in these activities in surprising numbers. Election day became a social event that brought most adult males together for spirited competition, sharp debate, and rousing celebration.

More and more, voters came to feel that one of the most important functions of parties was to protect equality and opportunity from the threats of privilege and aristocracy. In its social customs and behavior, the United States seemed to be an egalitarian society. When traveling, Americans rode together, ate together from the same serving plate, and slept together in the same bed. "The rich and the poor, the educated and the ignorant, the polite and the vulgar, all herd on the cabin floor of the steamer, feed at the same table, sit in each others laps, as it were," sniffed one upper-class European (Douglas T. Miller, *Jacksonian Aristocracy,* p. 9). Rather than observing rigid social lines, Americans thought nothing of walking up to a total stranger and initiating a conversation "on terms of perfect equality" (Francis Trollope, *Domestic Manners of the Americans*). Moreover, styles of clothing did not vary predictably according to class: one could no longer tell at a glance by what a person was wearing what class he or she belonged to, especially outside the workplace. Europeans were amazed to see men and women workers parading city streets fashionably dressed in sleek coats, stylish gloves and elegant hats. Proud of their egalitarian heritage, Americans resented individuals who put on airs of being superior. Politicians, whose careers depended on retaining popular support, soon learned to dress in ordinary fashions. "If a Candidate be dressed Farmerlike," one southern congressman noted, "he is well received and kindly remembered by the inmates of the Log Cabin, and there is no sensation among the children or the *chickens*" (Richard Sewell, *A House Divided,* pp. 2–3).

Because public policy affected opportunity, voters demanded that parties and politicians adopt programs to promote economic growth while safeguarding equality. Such a task was impossible, for, as noted, the opportunity of the market inevitably produced inequalities in wealth. The antebellum generation resolved this fundamental tension in the American creed by defining equality to mean not equal wealth or status but equal opportunity. Calls for the redistribution of property, such as that proposed by the radical labor leader Thomas Skidmore, won no support. Tocqueville wrote in *Democracy in America,* "I know of no country where profounder contempt is expressed for the theory of permanent equality of property." Andrew Jackson concurred: "Distinctions in society will always exist under every just government. Equality of talents, or education, or of wealth cannot be produced by human institutions" (Richard Hofstadter, *The American Political Tradition,* p. 60). Government was to dispense its favors equally, to see that every white male, at least, had an equal chance in the race of life.

In the 1820s the Anti-Masonic movement, which quickly became a political party, grew out of an incident in western New York in which zealous Masons kidnapped and allegedly murdered a disgruntled member who threatened to reveal the fraternity's secrets, and then when authorities launched an investigation systematically obstructed the wheels of justice. Angry citizens, protesting that Masonry was aristocratic, launched an egalitarian crusade that attempted, among other things, to bar Masons from public office. The movement quickly became an expression of both the resentment of individuals whose isolation excluded them from the market and the fears of those who were trapped in its web. Anti-Masonry became both a celebration of the potential of the market and a protestation against its consequences.

As most Anti-Masons joined the Whig party opposed to the Democratic party of Andrew Jackson, the movement vanished even as its demands for legal equality and the abolition of special privilege remained central to the new democratic political culture. The issue that defined the party system that crystallized in the 1830s was banking. No institution more clearly symbolized the commercialization of American society than banks, and the two parties offered distinct positions on banking. Jackson entered the presidency hostile to banks and paper money, which he considered a system to cheat honest, hardworking people. When he vetoed the bill to recharter the Second Bank of the United States in 1832, the stage was set for his reelection campaign. He condemned the bank as an agent of privilege and a symbol of aristocracy, and thus a violation of the American principle of equality.

Jackson's supporters were largely farmers and workers either outside the commercial economy or suspicious of its workings. One's attitudes toward the market and its mechanisms, more than wealth or personal success, determined one's attitudes toward Jackson and the Democrats' antibank crusade. Jackson himself, after all, had prospered quite handsomely as a slaveholder and cotton planter; but banking and credit encouraged speculation, which, he believed, threatened the moral fiber of the Republic and rewarded parasites who manipulated the paper system over those who performed productive work. In his rigid worldview, farmers and workers were the real people, whereas bankers, financiers, and stock jobbers were would-be aristocrats.

Whigs considered such attitudes as hopelessly backward. They recognized that the market could not be rolled back, and argued that a sound banking system was essential to the economy, for it would regulate economic ups and downs as well as provide a stable currency (which because of the shortage of gold and silver, or "specie," had to be at least partly paper money). They were much more comfortable with the market and commercialization, and argued that bankers, insurance agents, and other occupations facilitating the exchange of goods and services performed no useful function. Large numbers of farmers and workers, embracing the market and its ethic of self-improvement, rallied to the Whig cause. In their voting, workers displayed little class consciousness; indeed, prior to the arrival of large numbers of immigrants in the 1840s, most city dwellers voted Whig. For Whigs, commerce and economic development were civilizing forces that would elevate humankind and improve society. They insisted that there was a basic congruence of interests between labor and capital and argued that economic growth benefited all by creating more jobs and increasing national wealth.

The parties also differed on the role of government in society and the economy. Whigs, who wanted an active government that regulated the economy and upheld morality, supported the use of governmental power to promote humanitarian reforms. Democrats, on the other hand, wanted to restrict governmental power to the abolition of monopolies and special privilege; once all white men had equal opportunity, free competition and the market would regulate society. And they considered governmental regulation of morality an improper interference with personal liberty.

If Jacksonian democracy extolled the common man, it nevertheless was for whites only. Jackson had gained great fame as an Indian fighter in his earlier years, and as a large and wealthy slaveholder he displayed no concern for the welfare of blacks. Despite the pervasive rhetoric about equality, racism was an important aspect of American life in these years.

As the market expanded, racial attitudes toward the subject races hardened. Where the revolutionary generation had emphasized the role of environment and culture in producing racial "inferiority," later American leaders were impressed by scientific research into racial differences and argued that these alleged differences were inherent and irremediable. Their contention that neither African Americans nor Indians could be "civilized" had important consequences for both racial groups.

As president, Jackson undertook to remove the remaining Indian tribes east of the Mississippi River. He was anxious to open these lands to white settlement and agricultural development, and he believed that Indian tribes could survive only if they were isolated from white society. Indian removal was especially popular in the West and the South, where whites desired tribal lands and held a deep-seated contempt for Indian culture. The southern tribes, in particular, controlled rich cotton-growing lands coveted by ambitious whites.

Indian nations were caught between the desire to preserve their cultural independence and the desire for items whites offered in trade. Tribes were divided between those members who clung to traditional ways and those who advocated accommodation to white culture. Although Indians who participated in commercial relationships with white society were most likely to adopt white ways, the traditionalists, like white semi-subsistence yeoman farmers, were unable to resist the products the market offered. Trade with whites and the intrusion of material goods inevitably altered Indian culture: alcohol disorganized tribal society; manufactured articles (such as blankets, pots, firearms, and decorative beads and ribbons) became signs of status; and the fur trade led to excessive trapping so game became scarce. The resulting cultural stress increased violence and altered family structure and gender roles (R. David Edmonds, *The Shawnee Prophet*). Eventually virtually all the eastern Indians were removed; even partially assimilated tribes such as the Cherokee, which had modeled its institutions on white society, were forcibly ejected. Eastern humanitarians denounced the shameful treatment of these tribes, but Indian removal remained overwhelmingly popular outside the Northeast.

The position of the free black population in the United States also deteriorated with the rise of democracy. The northern states did not have a sizable black population in the antebellum period, yet free blacks' rights steadily eroded. Most northern states had never given blacks the right to vote; several, including Connecticut and Pennsylvania, rescinded the franchise after having granted it earlier. Outside of New England, blacks were legally denied other rights such as serving on juries, holding public office, and sending their children to the public schools their taxes supported. Moreover, African Americans were widely segregated in society. Free blacks were prohibited from most hotels and restaurants, and they were forced to sit in separate sections in churches, theaters, and other public places, and were assigned to special "Jim Crow cars" on public transportation. "The policy and power of the national and state governments are against them," commented one sympathetic observer. "The popular feeling is against them—the interests of our citizens are against them. Their prospects . . . are dreary, and comfortless" (John R. Howe, *From the Revolution to the Age of Jackson,* pp. 166–167).

The black population was also the target of white violence. In a number of cities, white mobs rioted in black neighborhoods, attacking and sometimes killing any black person unfortunate enough to fall into their hands. Philadelphia, the city of brotherly love, was the scene of five major antiblack riots between 1832 and 1849. The prominent black leader Frederick Douglass (1817?–1895) complained following the last of these riots, "No man is safe—his life—his property—and all that he holds dear, are in the hands of a mob, which may come upon him at any moment—at midnight or mid-day, and deprive him of his all" (Leon F. Litwack, *North of Slavery,* p. 102).

Black workers were systematically discriminated against in employment. Racist white workers, fearing competition and racial interaction, resisted allowing blacks to learn trades or join unions. With black males relegated to the lowest-paying jobs—most were unskilled laborers—free black families lived in poverty, and black women had to take a job outside the house to help make ends meet. In the face of white workers' hostility, blacks often became willing strikebreakers, but once a strike ended they invariably were replaced by white workers. Lacking an adequate diet and access to health care, African Americans were more susceptible to disease and in 1850 had a life expectancy eight to ten years shorter than whites. Excluded from white institutions, blacks formed self-help societies of their own to aid the less fortunate; yet it was hard to make any headway in the face of unrelenting prejudice. Fighting against hopeless despair, Charlotte Forten, a talented free black woman from Philadelphia, who became a teacher, wrote in her journal, "None but those who experience it can know what it is—the constant galling sense of cruel injustice and wrong."

The lives and freedom of free blacks in the South were also increasingly constricted. Because of planters' hostility to their presence, many free blacks moved to southern towns and cities, where they enjoyed better employment opportunities and could be part of a larger black community. After Nat Turner's rebellion in 1831, southern legislatures moved to restrict their privileges and tighten white control. They were prohibited from assembling without a white present, could not vote or participate in public life, had to carry their free papers with them at all times, were subject to curfew, and had to be licensed to perform many jobs. When whites' fears over the security of slavery ran high in the wake of rumors of slave revolts or national agitation over slavery, free blacks always came under closer white scrutiny. They performed no vital economic functions in the South, and their very existence gave the lie to the claim that the natural condition of black people was slavery. As a result, white power hedged them in closely.

RELIGION, GENDER, AND FAMILY: THE DOMESTIC IDEAL

In the wake of profound changes, a new form of popular democratic religion developed in the United States. A series of religious revivals, known collectively as the Second Great Awakening, swept the nation in the early nineteenth century, peaking from 1821 until 1837, when the depression brought these outbursts to an end. By the time they had run their course American Protestantism had been fundamentally transformed.

The most important figure of the Second Great Awakening was a minister named Charles Grandison Finney (1792–1875). Originally a lawyer, Finney experienced a soul-shaking conversion in 1821 and immediately devoted his life to the church. He repudiated traditional Calvinism, with its emphasis on predestination, in favor of a more optimistic view of human potential: Finney preached that individuals could save themselves by accepting freely offered divine grace. Like the romantics, he emphasized the importance of emotion rather than the intellect as the source of truth, and his revivals became moving emotional experiences. Moreover, Finney embraced the doctrine of millennialism, asserting that a thousand years of peace and harmony would precede the return of Christ; and that of perfectionism, according to which human beings could overcome sin and become literally perfect. (Finney was careful to insist this was a *goal* for all Christians, not an existing condition, but other revivalists failed to make this distinction.) He was a firm believer in human progress and urged devout Christians to perfect society by attacking sin wherever they found it. "The evils have been exhibited, the call has been made for reform," Finney preached. "Away with the idea, that Christians can remain neutral and keep still, and yet enjoy the approbation and blessing of God" (Robert Remini, *The Jacksonian Era,* p. 77). All in all, Finney's message was relentlessly optimistic.

The Second Great Awakening revitalized American religion. Church membership dramatically increased, especially in the most evangelical denominations, most notably the Methodists, Baptists, Presbyterians, and Congregationalists. Indeed, the Methodist church, which had been a small sect in 1790, was the most prorevival of all the churches and, aided by a tight hierarchical organization, emerged as the largest Protestant church in the country. In 1840 an estimated half of the adult population was at least nominally affiliated with some church, the highest figure in almost two centuries.

Evangelicalism, with its endorsement of individual ability, was in accord with the American belief in individualism. Revivals ignored social (but not racial) distinctions, thereby reinforcing the popular beliefs in white democracy and equality. The emphasis on emotion as the source of truth was consistent with the pragmatic, anti-intellectual nature of American society; and revivalists, like businessmen, were success-oriented and judged methods by their results. Most of all, the revivals were awash in optimism concerning human beings and society.

These revivals were an important way for individuals to adjust to their changing lives. Even along the frontier where evangelical revivalism began, it was strongest not in isolated and commercially backward regions but in communities that were entering the market economy or were already thoroughly commercial. Some of Finney's most spectacular revivals were in cities along the Erie Canal in the 1820s. Moreover, although revivals gained converts from all of society, they were particularly successful among the middle class—managers, clerks, storekeepers, and professionals who played a key role in the new market economy. These upwardly mobile citizens found in religion a means to cope with the pressures and uncertainties in their daily lives. Workingmen who embraced evangelical religion were also eager to improve themselves, and Methodism in particular inculcated middle-class values of diligence, frugality, and self-restraint among the laboring classes. Joining a church was evidence one had the self-discipline and values necessary to succeed in society, and brought with it social respectability. Church membership and social mobility were closely linked. For example, in Rochester, New York, two-thirds of the workingmen who became church members improved their occupational status within a decade, often by becoming a skilled laborer or acquiring their own shop. Workers without church affiliation, in contrast, rarely remained in town more than a few years, and those who stayed were more likely to decline in status.

Intent on ushering in the millennium, Finney and the revivalists without intending to also helped Americans accommodate to the pressures of the commercialized society. The new economic order demanded disciplined and reliable workers; churchgoers embraced hard work and sobriety, and fearing unrestrained passion, they internalized self-control. By these means religion promoted social order and control, and employers preferred whenever possible to hire churchmembers.

No group responded more enthusiastically to this evangelicalism than women. A majority of the converts at revivals were female, and many of the males who joined a church were related to women who had already come forward and accepted Christ. Young women between the ages of twelve and twenty-five were especially prominent in the harvest of new churchmembers. For young women, whose future largely depended on getting married, joining a church offered a sense of initiative and purpose, as well as mutual female support and a badge of respectability; and by widening their social activities, it increased their chances of marriage.

The changing economic roles in the family also put pressure on wives and daughters. As the workplace was increasingly separated physically from the home, the American family underwent fundamental transition. Previously, women had performed vital economic functions in the family by manufacturing many household goods such as cloth, candles, and soap; but families were now much more likely to purchase these items. Horace Bushnell (1802–1876), a prominent Congregational minister, noted that the widespread availability of textiles entailed nothing less than "a complete revolution of domestic life" (Percy W. Bidwell and John I. Falconer, *History of Agriculture in the Northern United States,* p. 252). At the same time, the rise of professionalism and the new requirements for licensing and education closed many occupations to women. While middle-class women no longer worked outside the home, they continued to do domestic work, but in the new commercialized society these tasks were no longer perceived as essential to the family's economic welfare. Household labor was increasingly defined as separate from productive work.

The result was a new conception of the home as a female sphere distinct from the masculine sphere. The ideal of domesticity was the creation of ministers and female authors largely located in the Northeast, but it was accepted well beyond this region. Expounding the values of the middle class, this ideal upheld the home as a repository of love and virtue, headed by the wife and mother. As dispensers of love and comfort, women were to subordinate their desires and talents to other family members' needs, to seek fulfillment not in public life but in the home as wives and mothers. Men, on the other hand, were to provide for the family from a (separate) workplace. Previously many men had worked at home, but with the physical separation of business and the home, they were now absent for much of the day; and child raising, previously a joint endeavor, became primarily the mother's responsibility. The male domain was the tumultuous, competitive, innovative world of business. The female sphere was the stable, loving, traditional world of the home. As one young woman told her suitor, "Love is our life[,] our reality, business yours" (Ellen K. Rothman, *Hands and Hearts,* p. 94).

This idea of separate spheres reflected the new belief that while men were physically stronger, women were morally stronger. Thus it was incumbent upon females to uphold moral values. This sexual double standard demanded that women be sexually "pure"; any improper behavior brought permanent social shame, though men suffered no lasting stigma for being unfaithful. Men were to be aggressive, the movers and doers of society, while women were to be passive and find distinction through their husbands. Foreign visitors were surprised at how sharp the demarcation was in America. "In no country," Tocqueville commented in *Democracy in America,* "has such constant care been taken, as in America, to trace two clearly distinct lines of action for the two sexes, and to make them keep pace with the other, but in two pathways which are always different."

While domesticity could be taken as a rationale for male dominance, most women understood it differently; in fact, female authors played a major role in creating and disseminating this ideal in countless advice manuals, books, articles, and especially romance fiction. Catharine Beecher (1800–1878), daughter of the famous revivalist Lyman Beecher, was a leading publicist of this ideology; her sister, Harriet Beecher Stowe, sanctioned the domestic ideal in her many best-selling novels. Proponents argued that domesticity gave women real power by entrusting them with the crucial responsibility of raising America's next generation of leaders. Advocates such as Catharine Beecher asserted that women, to fulfill this obligation, needed to be trained, and so promoted female education. She also argued that the qualities that made women good mothers also made them effective teachers, and she urged that women be given greater opportunities in this field.

The domestic ideal assumed that the husband's income was enough so that the wife need not find employment and thus enjoyed a certain amount of leisure time. Outside the middle class, few families could live up to this ideal. Even in prosperous farm families women worked long hours and often had to help out in the fields at harvest time. Recalling his childhood in rural Ohio, William Dean Howells, the famous postwar novelist, wrote, "The rule was, that whoever had the strength to work, took hold and helped. If the family was mostly girls, they regularly helped their father in all the lighter farm work" (Walter Nugent, *Structures of American Social History,* p. 58). Working-class women's income from factory or other work brought in badly needed money. Immigrant and free black families were especially dependent on female wages; and, obviously, this ideal was irrelevant to enslaved women.

It is striking, then, how widely the ideal was accepted, in light of how few women could live by its maxims. In this regard the experience of women who headed west in the 1840s on the Overland Trail is revealing. Largely drawn from farm families and small-town residents of the Midwest, these migrants set out intending to maintain "traditional" gender divisions in work. The rigors of the trail, however, soon dictated that women would have to help with male tasks if the wagon train was to complete the journey. Before long women found themselves standing guard, repairing wagons, building bridges, and caring for livestock. Yet most women did not seize these opportunities to redefine gender roles. Instead, women complained bitterly about the breakdown of these traditional roles as a negation of home and civilization. When the migrants reached the West Coast, women moved immediately to restore the sexual spheres they had known. When western women spoke of bringing civilization to their new communities, they meant more than schools and churches and law; they also meant homes, families, and their domestic mission.

Nevertheless, capable middle-class women often found this role confining. Few outlets beyond the home and church existed for their talents, particularly in business and commerce. "A gentleman's happiness is not so entirely confined in the domestic circle as a lady's" one man acknowledged. "If he cannot be happy at home, he can go into the world where in the business and bustle of life, he can forget his troubles" (Rothman, *Hands and Hearts,* pp. 94–95). Ironically, one of the country's most successful businesswomen, Sarah Hale (1788–1879), who edited *Godey's Lady's Book,* constantly sanctioned in her writings the idea of separate spheres while blithely disregarding it in her life. Like Hale, many women turned to literature, one of the few outside activities open to them. Harriet Beecher Stowe was plagued by ill health and suffered an emotional collapse before her husband agreed to let her write, after which her persistent health problems suddenly disappeared. Struggling to live up to domesticity's tenets, one woman complained, "The greatest trial . . . is that I have nothing to do. Here I am with abundant leisure, and capable, I believe, of accomplishing some good, and yet with no object on which to expend my energies" (Barbara J. Berg, *The Remembered Gate,* p. 112).

Religion offered women an emotional outlet for these tensions and a means of exerting moral leadership in society. Sunday became known as ladies' day. Finney, for example, made explicit appeals to women, mobilizing them in proselytizing efforts in the community, and, in a shocking break with tradition, allowing them to lead congregations in prayer. Some men found this a dangerous practice that implied a degree of sexual equality. In a letter signed "Anticlericus," one Rochester husband complained of the effect of Finney's visit to his home: "He *stuffed* my wife with tracts, and alarmed her fears, and nothing short of meetings, day and night, could atone for the many fold sins my poor, simple spouse had committed, and at the same time, she made the miraculous discovery, that she had been 'unevenly yoked.' From this unhappy period, peace, quiet, and happiness have fled from my dwelling, never, I fear, to return" (Paul Johnson, *A Shopkeeper's Millennium,* p. 108). Male church members, who were often community and business leaders, believed that church leadership, as distinct from membership, should rest safely in male hands. In church services, prayer meetings, and benevolent activities linked to churches, women received emotional support and mutual comfort from other women in similar situations.

While they embraced the domestic ideal of motherhood, middle-class women, who had often seen their own mothers' health broken by incessant child bearing, now sought to reduce the number of pregnancies in their lives. They were aided in this regard by the new economic pressures on the family. In adjusting to the realities of the market society, the middle-class family developed a new structure and set of practices—notably smaller family size. A large number of children was not the economic asset it had been on the farm, where from an early age children could help with various tasks. In consumer society, which pegged standard of living to social rank, children were a financial burden; and because they were leaving home at a later age, they had to be supported longer. In order to maximize their children's chances, improve the family's lifestyle, and demonstrate personal responsibility, middle-class families began to practice birth control: in the 1830s for the first time the birth rate sharply dropped among urban middle-class families (it would take several generations before this trend spread throughout society). Whereas in 1800 there had been slightly more than 7 children per family, by mid century it had dropped to 5.4, and it was even lower in urban areas. This development had a significant impact on women's health and the quality of their lives. It also allowed parents to invest more time in each child and probably meant that the children were healthier. Like church membership, fewer children were seen as a sign of middle-class self-restraint and solid respectability.

Middle-class families adopted other strategies to give their children advantages in the race of life, to improve their position, and to keep them from falling into the laboring class. They provided more education for their sons, who often did not leave home until in their twenties; this in turn delayed marriage, providing a more stable financial base for couples. Finally, families equalized inheritances rather than favoring sons over daughters, or the first son over other children: indicative of the spread of commercial values, family estates were converted into monetary shares, with each child receiving the same amount. By and large these practices were successful. Children who were given these advantages tended to maintain if not improve upon their parents' status.

THE SPIRIT OF REFORM

The doctrine of perfectionism preached in the revivals unleashed a powerful reform impulse which ran in many directions and involved different motivations. Seeking to eradicate sin from society, devout men and women joined a series of reform movements, many of which were headed by clergymen. In its early stages, reform was often socially conservative and aimed to preserve traditional institutions and values. Reformers, however, soon undertook to remake the world, and reform became more and more radical in its implications. The tendency toward ultraism, carrying ideas to their logical extreme, was increasingly pronounced. By the time the movement had run its course, virtually every value and institution had come under challenge, prompting Emerson in his essay "Man the Reformer" to observe, "In the history of the world the doctrine of Reform never had such scope as at the present hour."

A founding of utopian communities was one manifestation of reform. A number of experimental communities were established as models for the world to emulate; some were explicitly religious, others were secular in doctrine, but all shared a faith that human potential was unlimited. These groups sought to replace competitive individualism with a sense of community and cooperation. "We are all a little mad here with numberless projects of social reform," Emerson confessed. "Not a reading man but has the draft of a new community in his waistcoat pocket" (Alice Felt Tyler, *Freedom's Ferment,* p. 166).

Among the most famous of the religious societies were the Shakers, based on the teachings of the English mystic Ann Lee (1736–1784), and the Oneida Community, headed by a defrocked Congregational minister, John Humphrey Noyes (1811–1886). Although the Shakers practiced celibacy and Oneida was based on a doctrine of complex marriage, both sought to alter the relationship between the sexes. Through effective leadership and a coherent (if unusual) religious doctrine, both were strikingly proficient at recruiting members.

Less successful were the secular communities, of which the most famous was New Harmony, founded by the Scottish industrialist and thinker Robert Owen (1771–1858) in Indiana in 1825. Owen believed that he could reconcile agriculture and manufacturing, and he sought to create a harmonious society based on both in which members would find contentment. Instead, his community quickly split into factions and fell into bitter wrangling, and after several efforts to reorganize it, Owen finally dissolved the experiment in 1827. His influence in socialist circles was eventually eclipsed by the ideas of a Frenchman, Charles Fourier (1772–1837), who also advocated economic cooperativism. A number of communities were founded in the United States based on his writings, but none succeeded. The failure of these experiments demonstrates that in the face of high wages and cheap land, the American individualist ethic was too strong for many to accept cooperative action.

More lasting in their impact were the humanitarian reform movements. Unlike the utopias, these organizations worked within society by combating specific social problems. Countless social evils were identified in these years, and numerous organizations sprang up to deal with these problems. Indeed, the antebellum era had the greatest number of reform movements with significant membership in America's history.

An important reform movement was temperance, which developed in response to the heavy drinking in American society. By 1830, the annual per-capita consumption of distilled spirits exceeded 5 gallons (19 liters), the highest level in American history and three times recent rates (7.1 gallons [27 liters] of absolute alcohol annually). Drinking was even higher among those over the age of 14. The temperance movement originally focused on drunkenness and did not oppose moderate consumption, but in 1826 the American Temperance Society was founded with total abstinence as its goal; in the next decade over five thousand local temperance societies were organized. The Washington Temperance Society, a unique working-class organization led by reformed alcoholics and aimed at the lower classes, attracted considerable attention: its meetings, featuring personal testimony, emotional catharsis, and taking the pledge, paralleled the format of religious revivals. Large numbers were persuaded to give up drinking, but hard-core drinkers, particularly in the working class, proved immune to such appeals. In response to this continuing resistance, the temperance movement decided to attack the source by outlawing the sale of alcoholic beverages. The efforts of temperance candidates, who entered state politics in the 1840s, to enact statewide prohibition laws usually either failed or were overturned by the courts, but the temperance movement nevertheless had a lasting impact. Levels of drinking sharply dropped after 1830.

Another important reform movement was the common school movement. Reformers urged states to follow the lead of Massachusetts and establish tax-supported public schools. These reformers viewed education as a means of uplift and a way to safeguard opportunity in society. They also argued that education would impart the literacy and mathematical skills that workers needed in the new economy. (Indeed, as noted, educational opportunity was a demand of the era's labor movement.) Though sincere, reformers viewed the world through middle-class glasses: they had little regard for working-class culture and viewed schools as the means to inculcate middle-class values in lower-class children. Advocates promised that schools would impart "early habits of industry, temperance[,] neatness, and regularity" (Sellers, *Market Revolution,* p. 394). As such, schools from their perspective would be a bulwark against social upheaval from the bottom by giving future generations the necessary attitudes to adjust to the market society and fill a proper niche. In this sense, the common school movement, like the drive to establish asylums and institutions for orphans, criminals, the poor, and the insane, constituted a form of social control. For these reformers, however, the goal always remained to elevate the individual. By mid century, the United States had the highest rate of schooling in the world.

The influx of immigrants in the 1840s also was met with an outbreak of nativism among the native-born, particularly in eastern cities that attracted large foreign-born populations. Nativism was both a reform movement and a protest against social change and the political system. Nativists feared the social impact of large-scale immigration. They noted the ensuing rises in crime, pauperism, social disorder, urban decay, and political corruption, and they lacked confidence that American society could assimilate such a large number of aliens. At the same time, nativism also appealed to anti-Catholicism, deeply rooted in the American tradition, gave vent to ethnic and racial bigotry, and catered to native-born workers' fears of job competition. Nativism made its biggest inroads among the native-born working class, rather than the middle class, which was put off by the movement's rowdiness and violence. Workers projected their fears of the decline of the crafts and industrialism onto immigrants, whom they identified with low wages and factories (since factory workers were increasingly foreign-born). Nativism was thus an important expression of worker discontent over the profound changes their lives and work were undergoing. Although nativism in the years before 1850 appealed to many values latent in American society, it failed to develop a significant following outside of large cities and manufacturing areas.

The reform movement that posed the most serious threat to the country was the new, more militant form of antislavery that arose in the 1830s, known as abolitionism. Its goals were enunciated by William Lloyd Garrison (1805–1879) in his newspaper, the *Liberator,* founded in Boston in 1831. Rejecting gradualism and impatient with the country's failure to address slavery, Garrison and other abolitionists called for adoption of immediate emancipation without compensation. They denounced as racist and antiblack the colonization movement, which sought to remove free blacks to Africa, and demanded that America live up to its professed ideals of equality. For abolitionists, slavery was always a moral question. In the words of the *Salem Anti-Slavery Bugle,* an Ohio antislavery paper, "we believe slavery to be sin, always, everywhere, and only, sin—sin, in itself" (Martin B. Duberman, *The Antislavery Vanguard,* p. 36).

Abolitionists launched their movement with dreams of rapidly converting slaveowners and the nation to their cause. Abolitionists generally were deeply religious, many of whom had been converted in the revivals of the Second Great Awakening. Armed with religious zeal and determined to live up to the requirements of Christian precepts, they anticipated a quick end of slavery. Instead, they encountered bitter resistance. In the South slaveholders rejected their appeals, mobs drove opponents of slavery out of the South, and legislatures blocked the circulation of abolitionist propaganda. At the same time, northern communities reacted with scorn, ridicule, and sometimes violence: in the 1830s a number of anti-abolitionist mobs appeared, made up in great part from the lower classes though often led by prominent men who feared the social and economic consequences of abolitionism. Anti-abolitionist sentiment drew upon well-grounded fears for the survival of the Union if slavery became an issue, as well as on antiblack racism and on many communities' fears that alienating southern trading customers would bring hard times.

Abolitionists responded to this crisis in two fundamentally different ways. The more moderate group, led by Lewis Tappan (1788–1873), a wealthy New York merchant and backer of benevolent causes, wanted to work through established institutions, especially churches and political parties. They were convinced that American society was basically healthy and needed only limited reform, and that violence against abolitionists and interference with their civil liberties ultimately aided the cause. The more radical group, led by Garrison, believed that anti-abolitionism was evidence of the American society's fundamental rottenness and that nothing short of total reform could save the country. Garrison developed a comprehensive program of reform that included the abolition of all government, rejection of the political parties and political action, abandonment of the churches, northern secession from the Union, and women's rights.

It was this last idea that finally split the abolitionist movement. Like other reform movements, which offered women an outlet for their talents, it had drawn heavily on them for support. Women performed much of the labor in the abolitionist cause, including fund-raising fairs, circulating (and signing) petitions, writing tracts, and speaking in public. Initially, female orators spoke only to women, but they soon began to address mixed audiences. Endorsing this development, Garrison and his followers took up the demand that women also be allowed to hold office in antislavery societies, and when this proposal prevailed at the 1840 national convention, his opponents walked out and established a separate organization. More important, many of them turned to political action and supported the new antislavery Liberty party. Although the party won little support in its first campaign in 1840, it was the seed from which a larger political antislavery movement would grow. The schism of 1840 brought to a close the opening phase of the abolitionist movement; henceforth the major thrust would be in the political arena rather than through voluntary reform.

Thinking about the problems of slaves led women to focus on social inequities they themselves faced. Female abolitionists found it easy to identify with the slave, for both groups faced legal obstacles to self-fulfillment, since both were in some sense victims of male tyranny. Opposition to the rising role of women in the abolitionist movement produced the first major works on feminism in American history. In 1848, two prominent abolitionists, Elizabeth Cady Stanton (1815–1902) and Lucretia Mott (1793–1880), summoned a convention at Seneca Falls, New York, to organize a women's rights movement. The meeting passed a series of resolutions calling for women to be given greater educational opportunities, the right to control property, legal equality, professional employment opportunities, and the right to vote. The last, though the most controversial, would for the next seventy years form the main principle of the organized women's rights movement, of which the Seneca Falls conference marked the beginning. Like abolitionism, this movement challenged entrenched attitudes and institutions and provoked bitter resistance.

THE CLASH OF CULTURES

By geographically separating employer from employee and work from home, the market revolution drew a sharp line between the middle class and the working class. The economic aspects of this distinction were overshadowed by the ways it was expressed in cultural perspectives. In the competitive world of the market, with Americans especially sensitive to status, the middle class enhanced their standing by erecting economic and cultural barriers to separate themselves from the laboring classes. That a married woman did not have a job became a sign of status and cultural respectability, indicating that her husband's income sufficed to support his family and meet his obligations, and hence he was socially well regarded. It also showed that the wife not only accepted but lived by the code of domesticity.

As the earlier craft-oriented society gave way to factory production, it became increasingly difficult for workers to enter the middle-class world of professionals, businessmen, and managers. These occupations assumed a certain level of education and training, which was difficult for workers to acquire. Moving into the middle class, however, also assumed the acceptance of certain cultural norms and behavior patterns.

If domesticity expressed the cultural ideals of the middle class, the idea of physical manhood was important to the working class, particularly those who clung to traditional values. Urban lower-class culture expected men to be dominant and aggressive; their life centered less on home and family than on male camaraderie on the street or at the tavern, boardinghouse, political meeting, volunteer fire company, or sporting event. Men's reputations depended on their ability to take care of themselves, and feats of physical prowess—fighting, for example—earned widespread respect. In its emphasis on hedonism, self-indulgence, reckless profligacy, and present-mindedness, this male culture mocked the values and assumptions of the middle class.

One of the clearest differences between these two cultures was in attitudes toward alcohol. With the rise of the temperance movement of the 1830s, drinking fell into social disrepute among Evangelicals: it interfered with work, squandered family resources, inflicted pain and suffering on women and children, caused social disorder, and was seen as a sign of lack of self-control. Workers' response to the temperance movement was an indicator of their attitudes toward these competing cultures. Drinking had been an integral part of artisan culture, but workers who maintained these attitudes were now seen as rejecting social advancement: they preferred the conviviality of the local saloon to pursuing a better job and social respectability. Workers who took the pledge, in contrast, signaled their desire to advance by adopting middle-class norms. Temperance demonstrated that they had accepted these standards, even if their current occupation or income did not permit them to adopt every facet of middle-class life.

Middle-class spokesmen directly tied temperance to profit. Asking why one person succeeded while another failed, the *Temperance Recorder* answered, "The enterprise of this country is so great, and competition so eager in every branch of business . . . that profit can only result from . . . *temperance*" (Sellers, *Market Revolution,* p. 265). Joseph Brewster, a New York hatter who promoted temperance among artisans, argued that abstinence resulted in harder work and thus increased profits 25 percent. As the middle class adopted the belief that outward behavior revealed inner qualities, and that economic success reflected moral character, the poor came to be shunned and condemned: "*vice* is almost the sole cause of pauperism," one middle-class commentator insisted (pp. 266–267). By viewing poverty as a choice, in effect voluntary, the middle class conflated conditions with behavior, an attitude that made many of the urban poor hostile to censorious reformers. Workers initially resisted the temperance movement, but it made strong inroads into working-class communities after the panic of 1837. The Methodist church, which enjoyed support among the laboring poor, and the Washingtonians were especially important in spreading this ideal among the working class.

A similar demarcation can be seen in other attitudes. Violence, for example, was an integral part of working-class culture but had no accepted place in the middle-class world of legality and self-restraint. Likewise, church membership was a sign of social respectability, carrying public as well as private connotations. Those outside the bonds of a church who spent the Sabbath in raucous celebration were considered socially disreputable. Revivalists were as interested in saving the souls of working folk as others, and evangelical churches made special efforts to reach out to workers, yet they met with a mixed response, since the behavior they demanded of members constituted a repudiation of traditional workers' culture. Those unwilling to abandon this way of life rejected the churches as well.

Notions of gentility, which were based on these differences, were expressed as cultural attitudes through the possession of consumer goods, made possible by their widespread availability. In a consumer society, physical possessions conveyed status, and which goods a family chose to buy revealed its cultural attitudes: for example, items that made the home a center of socializing were socially significant. Even on the frontier, many women proudly displayed their china or silverware, or dressed in store-bought fabrics, as testimony to their upbringing and aspirations for a more refined lifestyle. Simple things, such as a bonnet or an item of furniture, represented a more basic underlying attitude toward respectability.

Popular entertainment was another important element of this cultural conflict. With the emergence of a mass urban audience, American culture was increasingly divided into highbrow and lowbrow entertainment. Violent sports such as cockfighting or boxing found their audience among the working class, as did the minstrel show, with its caricatures of blacks and its virulent racism. The stage was one arena where these two cultures came together and collided. In theaters, working-class patrons proclaimed their national and class identity by hurling vegetables at British actors championed by the upper class while lustily cheering their less talented American rivals. The repository of middle-class values was melodrama, which became the most popular form of entertainment in the country: rather than dealing with pressing social issues, it almost always involved a triangle consisting of a pure but vulnerable heroine, a seductive villain, and a virtuous hero. Melodrama upheld the power of love and redemption while it endorsed the ideals of middle-class life, both at home and in business. As such, it became a unique cultural embodiment of middle-class life.

THE BEGINNING OF MODERN AMERICA

By mid century, the United States was a much different society than it had been in 1815. The dominant feature of this period, the creation of a domestic national market, touched every segment of American life: it produced profound social and economic dislocation, uprooted generations-old attitudes and institutions, transformed the political system, and altered the roles of race, class, and gender in American life. Efforts to enjoy the market's benefits while avoiding its social and psychological costs were futile: the market was too seductive, its influence too pervasive, its rewards too apparent, to be resisted. There was no going back to the semisubsistence society that had characterized most of the United States in 1815.

The market, of course, was not entirely integrative. Although it held out to white Americans dreams of prosperity, physical comfort, and material goods, its allocation of rewards exacerbated many social tensions. It stunted workers' aspirations and alienated them from their work; and while this did not produce a strong class consciousness among workers, it did engender a deep sense of grievance, and it unmistakably widened the economic and cultural gap between workers and the middle class. The market also produced regional tensions. The different economic development of the North and the South led to periodic conflicts over federal policy and the institution of slavery, although these problems became much more severe after 1845. Moreover, racial attitudes hardened precisely when white democracy triumphed, and African Americans, both free and enslaved, were largely shut out from the privileges and benefits of American society. The adverse impact of the market was manifested in free blacks' encounter with segregation and job discrimination, and in slaves' painful experience of disrupted families, forced migration, and long hours of unrequited toil. Finally, the emerging ideal of domesticity transformed gender into a vital social category; more explicitly than in the past, women's social role and identity depended on questions of gender.

The party system failed to resolve these problems and in most cases failed even to address them. The American party system, as has been frequently noted, has never handled fundamental social differences effectively: it is difficult for the nation's broad-based parties to maintain unity when such issues are incorporated in their platforms. The most serious effort at lessening the effects of the market, Jackson's destruction of the national bank, was misguided action that worsened the very problems it attempted to solve. Banking triumphed in the United States because it was an economic necessity. On questions of race and gender, the political system failed abysmally. Society and the economy developed without any central control or plan, and without any public institutions to mitigate the uneven impact of market mechanisms.

Recently, historians have pushed the roots of modernity, consumerism, and commercialization further into the past. In one sense, this is legitimate, for social and economic change derives from previous trends and developments. But such an exercise can be fundamentally misleading, for it minimizes the abruptness of change in revolutionary eras. The pace of socioeconomic change has not been uniform in American history, and the antebellum era was a time of rapid and pervasive adjustment. In the span of little over a generation, the country was profoundly altered. Taken together, these changes represented the beginning of modernization in this society. Many of the consequences of the development of the antebellum period still had to be worked out, and modernization would take on additional components in later periods, but these years laid the foundation for all that followed.

As he looked back on his life at the end of this period, the literary scholar George Ticknor (1791–1871) felt a deep sense of loss. Long before, in Boston, people had "felt involved in each other's welfare and fate as it is impossible we should now, when our numbers are trebled and our affairs complicated and extended . . . too wide." America's new competitive, individualistic ethos left little place for a sense of community. "The interests of each individual," he noted with concern, "are grown too separate and intense to be bound in by any general sympathy with the whole." The antebellum era felt acutely the birth pains of modern America.

BIBLIOGRAPHY

Atack, Jeremy, and Fred Bateman. *To Their Own Soil: Agriculture in the Antebellum North* (1987).

Berlin, Ira. *Slaves Without Masters: The Free Negro in the Antebellum South* (1974).

Blumin, Stuart. *The Emergence of the Middle Class: Social Experience in the American City, 1760–1900* (1989).

Brown, Richard D. *Modernization: The Transformation of American Life, 1600–1865* (1976).

Bruchey, Stuart. *The Roots of American Economic Growth, 1607–1861* (1965).

Cott, Nancy F. *The Bonds of Womanhood: "Woman's Sphere" in New England, 1780–1835* (1977).

Danhof, Clarence. *Changes in Agriculture: The Northern United States, 1820–1870* (1969).

Dublin, Thomas. *Women at Work: The Transformation of Work and Community in Lowell, Massachusetts, 1826–1860* (1979).

Faler, Paul G. *Mechanics and Manufacturers in the Early Industrial Revolution: Lynn, Massachusetts, 1780–1860* (1981).

Faragher, John Mack. *Women and Men on the Overland Trail* (1979).

———. *Sugar Creek: Life on the Illinois Prairie* (1986).

Feldberg, Michael. *The Turbulent Era: Riot and Disorder in Jacksonian America* (1980).

Genovese, Eugene D. *Roll, Jordan, Roll: The World the Slaves Made* (1974).

Glickstein, Jonathan A. *Concepts of Free Labor in Antebellum America* (1991).

Gorn, Elliott J. *The Manly Art: Bare-Knuckle Prize Fighting in America* (1989).

Hahn, Steven. *The Roots of Southern Populism: Yeoman Farmers and the Transformation of the Georgia Upcountry, 1850–1890* (1983).

Handlin, Oscar. *Boston's Immigrants, 1790–1865: A Study in Acculturation* (1941; rev. 2d ed. 1979).

Horowitz, Morton J. *The Transformation of American Law, 1780–1860* (1977).

Johnson, Paul E. *A Shopkeeper's Millennium: Society and Revivals in Rochester, New York, 1815–1837* (1978).

Joyner, Charles. *Down by the Riverside: A South Carolina Slave Community* (1984).

Kasson, John F. *Rudeness and Civility: Manners in Nineteenth-Century Urban America* (1990).

Larkin, Jack. *The Reshaping of Everyday Life, 1790–1840* (1988).

Laurie, Bruce. *Artisans into Workers: Labor in Nineteenth-Century America* (1989).

Litwack, Leon. *North of Slavery: The Negro in the Free States, 1790–1860* (1961).

McLoughlin, William G. *Modern Revivalism: Charles Grandison Finney to Billy Graham* (1959).

McWhiney, Grady. *Cracker Culture: Celtic Ways in the Old South* (1988).

Miller, Douglas T. *The Birth of Modern America, 1820–1850* (1970).

North, Douglass C. *The Economic Growth of the United States, 1790–1860* (1961).

Nugent, Walter. *Structures of American Social History* (1981).

Oakes, James. *The Ruling Race: A History of American Slaveholders* (1982).

Owsley, Frank L. *Plain Folk of the Old South* (1949).

Pessen, Edward. *Riches, Class, and Power Before the Civil War* (1973).

———. *Jacksonian America: Society, Personality, and Politics* (rev. ed. 1978).

Pred, Allan R. *Urban Growth and the Circulation of Information: The United States System of Cities, 1790–1840* (1973).

Prude, Jonathan. *The Coming of Industrial Order: Town and Factory Life in Rural Massachusetts, 1810–1860* (1983).

Rohrbough, Malcolm J. *The Trans-Appalachian Frontier* (1978).

Rorabough, W. J. *The Alcoholic Republic: An American Tradition* (1979).

———. *The Craft Apprentice: From Franklin to the Machine Age in America* (1986).

Ryan, Mary P. *Cradle of the Middle Class: The Family in Oneida County, New York, 1790–1865* (1981).

Sellers, Charles. *The Market Revolution, 1815–1846* (1991).

Stott, Richard B. *Workers in the Metropolis: Class, Ethnicity, and Youth in Antebellum New York City* (1990).

Taylor, George Rogers. *The Transportation Revolution, 1815–1860* (1951).

Walters, Ronald F. *American Reformers, 1815–1860* (1978).

Watson, Harry L. *Liberty and Power: The Politics of Jacksonian America* (1990).

Wells, Robert V. *Revolutions in Americans' Lives: A Demographic Perspective on the History of Americans, Their Families, and Their Society* (1982).

Wilentz, Sean. *Chants Democratic: New York City and the Rise of the American Working Class, 1788–1850* (1984).

SEE ALSO **Antebellum African American Culture; The Deep South; Peninsular Florida; The Natural Environment: The South; Rural Life in the South; Social Reform Movements;** and various essays in the sections **"The Construction of Social Identity," "Family History," "The Processes of Social Change,"** and **"Work and Labor."**

SECTIONAL CONFLICT, CIVIL WAR, AND RECONSTRUCTION

Orville Vernon Burton

SECTIONAL CONFLICT

CONFLICT BETWEEN SECTIONS expanded as the nation itself expanded. Having shared in the Declaration of Independence, the American Revolution, and the Constitution, both North and South believed that the destiny of the new United States was manifest. But this concept demanded that growth be justified; the nation had to carry along with it the cause of liberty. Just when national loyalties were in the process of being cemented, differences arose as to the very meaning of liberty and the national heritage. Sectionalism developed at the same time as national solidification.

The South came into being as a separate entity because of conflict with the North over slavery. Slavery was the central problem facing American society in the nineteenth century, and Southern life revolved around the subordinate status of black people.

It may be, as Southerners claimed, that the North initiated sectional conflict because of dissatisfaction with Southern control of national power in the early nineteenth century. The North resented the slave-owning dynasty that controlled the presidency. From Polk through Buchanan every president was either a Southerner or pro-Southern. Northern resentment, which had flared during the War of 1812, burned again over governmental machinations protecting slavery.

Demographics At the time of the adoption of the Constitution, Southerners expected their population to outstrip the rest of the nation. The climate was conducive to agriculture and to such staple crops as tobacco, cotton, and rice. Natural rivers carried settlers from the Atlantic into the hinterlands. Because of the initial availability of rich farmland and easy water transportation, geographic mobility in the South was very rapid, as farmers could penetrate the hinterlands and still sell their products to distant markets. Settlements, therefore, were sparsely populated, unlike the concentrated towns in New England.

As the eighteenth century passed into the nineteenth, however, the population did not move south. New European immigrants preferred free labor to slavery, cutting the South off from new, invigorating people and ideas and making Southerners more parochial in their outlook. The South became increasingly isolated from the rest of the nation and from Europe, and just as immigration bypassed the South, so too did economic diversity. Most people continued to farm, creating a rather homogeneous region. Southern society lacked cities and with them a dynamic urban middle class; professional opportunities were in short supply and were not avenues to status and success in the rural South. In the South status depended upon land and slaves.

Social mobility also differed between regions. The South had a much more deferential society than the North. The region had fewer self-made leaders. Upward mobility was still possible but it was more difficult to become a great planter than to become a great merchant in the North. In the South, one needed both land and slaves. Already by the time of the American Revolution, only a tenth of Virginia's great planters were self-made men while a third of all the Boston merchants were self-made, a proportion that increased to 60 or 70 percent after the war. The Revolutionary militia officers in the South were largely from important and powerful landed and slave-owning families, whereas in New England recruitment into the officer corps was more egalitarian.

In the first half of the nineteenth century, national patterns of growth intensified sectional conflict. In 1790, the United States consisted of thirteen states and their territories and had a population of

3.9 million, 18 percent of whom were slaves. Only 3 percent of the total population lived in towns of over eight thousand inhabitants. By 1860, nearly thirty-two million people lived in thirty-three states and numerous territories stretching from the Atlantic to the Pacific. About four million people were African Americans, 11 percent free blacks, of whom half lived in each region. In 1790 most of the American population huddled within a hundred miles of the Atlantic Coast; by 1860 half of the people lived west of the Appalachian Mountains, and nearly a tenth in urban areas.

By 1860 the South had its wealthy land- and slave-owning elite, but 75 percent of Southern whites did not own slaves, and less than 50 percent of all masters owned more than five slaves. Landless whites accounted for between 25 to 40 percent of the white population. The majority of whites were landowning yeoman farmers who may or may not have owned slaves. In contrast to the large planters, non-slave-owning yeomen were more interested in self-sufficiency than in profit.

Although yeomen were for the most part nonslaveholders, slavery permitted them a certain degree of independence. Each white male was the patriarch of his domain. Although plantations consumed much of the best land in the South, the great planters were generally content to let their poorer neighbors live their own lives and manage their own economic and political affairs. Because so much of the power in the South was exercised on the plantation, governmental power and social services were limited and left those whites outside the plantation districts basically untouched. The overwhelmingly agricultural, plantation South fostered an extremely decentralized system. Thus, instead of the conflicting economic and social interests that developed in Northern society, most social conflict in the South occurred in terms of personal ambitions and personalities. Moreover, whites were united in their racism; many up-country feared that freedom for African Americans was an economic threat. Thus, slavery was a powerful symbol of degradation that white yeomen contrasted with their own independence.

Sectional conflict represented a contest between two completely different labor systems and social orders, one slave, one free. Both of these systems were complicated and in flux, changing over time with their own dynamics—yet, overall, increasingly fearful and antagonistic toward one another. Because a system of labor defined one's livelihood and way of life, it affected every person, family, and community. A reflection of community values, the labor system also created its own set of values. It influenced family structure and responsibilities; it determined the money system, the transportation system, the education system.

Because the American dream of success was tied to the frontier with its abundance of land, it was fitting that the issue that provoked sectional conflict and led to secession was whether slavery should extend into the western territories. Territorial expansion drew attention to the underlying issue of differences over slavery. With the addition of Texas, the Southwest, and the West coast, the question of slavery's expansion to the new territories took center stage.

Slavery and the Frontier A comparison of northern and southern frontier development as people moved westward provides clues to the origins of sectional conflict. On the northern frontier there was a need to clear the forest, to build homes, to cooperate to build schools and churches, to band together for defense, to guarantee landownership claims against theft, to build prisons. Settlers needed a government to register land claims and administer political functions. In meeting these needs in the Old Northwest, a highly democratic society and egalitarian pattern of landownership developed. Fairly equal land and tax laws were applied, including laws passed to discourage nonresident absentee holders of large tracts of land. While some were richer than others, no unified landholding elite developed.

With population growth, the frontier receded, and small rural settlements became towns. Real estate speculators promoted growth, which increased land values as well as the speculators' personal fortunes. The model for success in the Old Northwest was primarily moving into a town and starting a profitable business or owning property and benefiting by the influx of people and the resulting growth and value of lands. The prosperous man was the self-made businessman. The definition of success in the Northwest involved commerce and town development, and towns, in turn, required good citizens solving problems together.

This democratic community texture did not exist in the Old Southwest. The population was never dense enough nor the economy complex enough to require innovative problem-solving techniques. The population was less dense with fewer towns—five to six times fewer towns in Alabama, Mississippi, Arkansas, and upper Louisiana than in the three states of Ohio, Illinois, and Indiana. The booster spirit that led to community development in the Old Northwest was also missing. In the South, the lack of a manipulative attitude toward government meant that democratic forms or institutions could be introduced, but community leaders would continue to come from slaveholding classes.

Differences in Class Structure Slavery meant that the landholding elite defined success as wealth in slaves. Some argue that slavery made possible a Southern aristocracy that dominated Southern society and condemned the South to backwardness. A recruited aristocracy, its status was based largely on wealth more than upon kinship and breeding, although those qualities did play a role. A cultural myth of the antebellum South portrays all white males as landowning slaveholders, but most white men were simple farmers.

Why class tensions did not convulse antebellum white society is a subject of much historiographical debate. Although wealth discrepancies among whites pointed to class interests, the overall economy and social structure helped to mute class conflict. Since nearly everyone farmed, rich and poor alike shared similar interests and concerns. They belonged to the same kin networks and the same churches; their homes were interspersed. White Southerners' ideas of liberty also diluted class conflict in the South; freedom meant personal independence and the wherewithal to take care of one's family. Tragically, even non-slaveholding whites believed that their freedom rested on the subjugation of blacks. Declared John C. Calhoun in 1848, "With us the two great divisions of society are not the rich and the poor, but white and black; and all the former, the poor as well as the rich, belong to the upper class, and are respected and treated as equals."

There was little difference, North or South, in citizenship and voting. By about 1824, universal white manhood suffrage had been established in all states except Rhode Island, Virginia, and Louisiana. For white males the South was just as democratic as the North, with 78 percent of those eligible voting in 1840, the same as the Northern average. The political system was healthy in the South; in the latter 1840s the competition between the major parties was just as keen in the South as elsewhere in the nation.

Moreover, planters did not seriously oppose the democratic political style in the South because it never really challenged planter leadership. As was also true in the North, class divisions really do not explain political party conflict in the South from the 1830s through the 1860s. Any anti-aristocratic sentiment was mostly rhetorical, so while the primary demands articulated by the institutional representatives of Southern societies were the social, economic, and political needs of the planter class, non-slaveholders seldom challenged their political dominance.

While the South was slow to change, the North experienced enough change for both sections. Prior to the Civil War, the United States as a whole was an agrarian society, but the North was becoming industrialized and urban. In 1860, 10 percent of Southerners lived in urban areas; as compared with 25 percent of Northerners. The Southern white labor force remained 80 percent agricultural in the first half of the 1800s, but the northern labor force declined significantly from 70 percent agricultural to 40 percent. By 1860 the North had 110,000 factories with 1.3 million industrial workers, while the South had 18,000 factories with 100,000 industrial workers.

The decline in apprenticeship, the shift to factory labor, and the parcelization of tasks was a long process and change occurred at varying speeds in varying trades. Most of Northern industry was small scale, with just a few hands, with exceptions like the textile and shoe industries. Single women worked in early industries, but by the 1850s immigrant women replaced native-born women in the factories, and a new ethnic working-class milieu became associated with women in industrial jobs. Skilled male artisans lost considerable personal autonomy when they had to give up self-employment to find work in factories. And, while the status of many old craftsmen was declining, it was not primarily the result of mechanization. More commonly, the job that a craftsman had accomplished alone was divided up among numerous less-skilled workmen. As labor became specialized, the road to independent ownership grew more difficult. Costs for businesses rose, wages fell, and tensions grew between workers and capitalists.

The two sections diverged in other ways. Industrialization of the North went hand in hand with the expansion of the transportation system, so canals and railroads were built. In 1860 the South had 9,000 miles (14,400 kilometers) of railroad, while the North had 22,000 miles (35,200 kilometers). Industrialization also required a financial network: banks, insurance companies, and corporations. The South needed only cotton factors to represent the interests of the slave-owning planters.

Moreover, expansion was so rapid in the Northern cities that few could handle the problems of growth. People left their refuse in the streets; disease, pollution, and an obnoxious stench were widespread. New York City solved part of the problem in the 1840s by setting up reservoirs to provide fresh water, but few cities had the taxing power to raise money for services. Private companies served well-to-do areas, but the poor were ignored. Crime rose drastically, so Boston in 1837 and New York in 1845 instituted uniformed policemen to replace part-time watchmen.

Compared to the relative stability of the antebellum South, Northern society was rocked and traumatized by change. Observers continuously commented on the vast amounts of Northern spatial and social mobility as urbanization took hold. The population in cities was diverse and becoming more so with the arrival of new immigrant groups.

Anxiety accompanied the rapid economic and social change that engulfed the North. Fear of the emerging market economy and growth of capitalism led many to view bankers, speculators, and lawyers as parasites who took a large share of the economic pie but produced nothing. Immigration also led to serious ethnic tensions, even rioting. Earlier immigration had been mostly British Protestants, who expressed religious intolerance toward the newcomers, primarily Catholics from Ireland and Germany. Furthermore, because the tavern represented a social, cultural, and recreational institution for these immigrants, the stereotype of drunken immigrants controlled by corrupt political bosses emerged.

Cultural Differences North and South continued moving in distinctly different patterns, the North valuing progress, reason, contracts, and law, the South remaining much more influenced by feelings, traditions, personal obligations, and honor. Just as life and success had different meanings in the two sections, education had differing goals for North and South. Religion played an important role in American education, and most colleges and some secondary schools were supported by church denominations. Motivated by a popular ideology of democratic capitalism that legitimized industrialization and modernization, New England upper-class reformers established an educational system, based on moral and religious instruction, to produce good citizens and good laborers.

In the rural South, on the other hand, where docile, reliable factory workers were rarely in demand, public education remained a low priority. People read the Bible, and even some slaves were illegally taught to read, but formal schooling was not encouraged. The planter elite ensured that their own children were privately educated by tutors and enrolled in the best academies and colleges (some in the North), but they either ignored the efforts of poorer whites to initiate public schools or actively opposed them, fearing that education would promote new yearnings for upward mobility and blur the distinction between the cultured elite and the ignorant masses. Literacy rates were higher in the North, where 94 percent of the population could read. In the South, about 58 percent of the population was literate: among freemen 83 percent, among slaves nearly 10 percent.

The culture of the United States has always been diverse, and overdrawing contrasts between the North and South neglects local variations. The agrarian South contained some commercial and mercantile centers such as Charleston and Richmond. Within the North lay areas such as the Midwest Ohio River region, settled by Southerners who shared more of the rural values of the South than of the industrialized Northeast. And despite all these regional differences, the United States was one nation that from its inception had relied on compromise to keep the North and South together.

But as cultural differences grew more distinct, the people in each section of the country came to believe their way of life was threatened by the other. Northerners believed their prosperity depended upon free labor; they insisted the western territories remain free and they feared that the South wanted slavery to spread west, choking off opportunity. No friend of black equality, these whites wanted to keep the lands open for themselves. Thus, despite fears of industrialism's toll in the North, they feared the South more.

In contrast, Southerners, planters, and yeomen alike, thought that their prosperity depended upon the extension of slavery into the western territories. Non-slave owners, more likely to move west, aspired to slave ownership as an avenue to wealth and resented being denied that freedom of choice. Southern planters, to remain in power and preserve slavery in the face of soil exhaustion and inefficiency, needed to expand their markets and seize fresh land. Their livelihood, labor system, and their way of life depended on acquiring access to western land. Preventing Southerners from taking slaves into the territories made them feel that their property rights and therefore their freedom, were in jeopardy. One more factor was of vital importance: fugitive slaves in the lower South, if able to escape west, could easily cross to Mexico. Free lands in the territories would encourage this escape route. Slavery advocates needed to control this territory so they could close that border.

Opposition to Slavery Grows Antislavery sentiments had been part of the American scene since before the American Revolution, in both North and South. The most active antislavery group in the 1820s was the American Colonization Society, led by prominent Southerners with a program of voluntary emancipation, based on a Jeffersonian concept of enlightened humanitarianism. Advocating the colonization of Africa by freed slaves, they emphasized the inferiority of blacks, the inability of blacks and whites to live together harmoniously, and the fear of retribution on the part of recently freed slaves if they remained in America. Northern blacks were active and vocal opponents of colonization. Proud to be Americans, they viewed exportation as exile, and they certainly recognized the racism in the plan. In 1832, the peak year of emigration to Liberia, only about eight hundred blacks left America, most of them not free blacks of the North or South, but slaves freed on the condition of their departure for Africa. Black opposition to colonization impressed many whites, including the abolitionist William Lloyd Garrison (1805–1879), and these whites in turn helped persuade other whites that colonization was a futile gesture.

The 1830s were the critical period of American antislavery activity. Previous antislavery feeling predominantly called for gradual emancipation. During the 1830s, however, the dominant form of antislavery thought shifted to abolitionism or immediate emancipation. The change reflected the general reform spirit in the North, and antislavery activity became exclusively Northern at this time. Churches had been struggling with the concept of slavery for some time, and religious revivals in the early 1800s forced a confrontation with the problem. New England Puritanism had imbibed a social service ethic that emphasized a duty to one's fellow man. In a desire to eradicate sin from the world, many Northern religious leaders believed that the most heinous of all sins was slavery. Southern religious leaders, in contrast, stressed individual piety and redemption. Generally arguing God's acceptance of the institution of slavery, they worked to minimize abuse of slaves, regularize slave marriages, and encourage the spiritual life of blacks. As with other aspects of the culture, religion in the North became more diversified, while in the South it became more rigid. As sectional conflict intensified, the South came to perceive itself as the most pious section of the country.

Southern Defense of Slavery Defense of slavery in the South became increasingly staunch after 1830. Settlement of Alabama and Mississippi opened new cotton-lands with rich soil and provided an outlet for surplus slaves. Fear of slave rebellions, such as Denmark Vesey's in 1822 and Nat Turner's in 1831, led to a tightening of the system. The debates in the Virginia legislature in 1832 were the last open discussion of slavery in the South. Slaveholding districts outvoted non-slaveholding districts to defeat proposals for gradual emancipation.

The Southern defense of slavery shifted from a "necessary evil" to a "positive good" position. Pro-slavery theorists like George Fitzhugh (1806–1881) compared slavery favorably to capitalism and concluded that all societies should practice slavery since paternalistic slave-owners cared for old and infirm workers while capitalists cared only about extracting the labor of the workers for as little money as possible. Soon Northern abolitionism and Southern pro-slavery advocates spurred each other to ever-more rigid positions. In the vehemence of pro-slavery arguments, writers ransacked all branches of knowledge and learning to buttress the defense of slavery, now a Southern obsession.

The target of propaganda was not necessarily the enemy to the North. While the pro-slavery writers did want to induce sympathy from the North, they also wanted to maintain white solidarity at home. Three Southern white groups were most important. The pro-slavery argument was aimed at non-slaveowners, in particular those upper South non-slaveholders who had a history of animosity and friction with the lower South. Second, evangelical groups who, in the eyes of slave-owning Southerners, were not very good security risks because they might read the Bible the "wrong way" and conclude that slavery was evil had to be kept in the fold. Third, and perhaps most of all, the pro-slavery argument aimed at those doubts about the morality of slavery that lurked in the hidden recesses of most Southern consciences.

With regionwide endorsement, even sanctification, of slavery, questioning was no longer allowed; opposition was heresy. Southerners opposed to slavery moved North or kept quiet. Newspapers were suppressed, teachers and ministers were fired, and slave codes grew harsher. By the end of the 1830s the South had erected an "Intellectual Blockade" or "cotton curtain" against antislavery sentiment.

Abolitionism and Free Labor Ideology Southerners were not irrational in wishing to cordon their region from verbal attack. Abolitionists utilized the printed media to spread ideas and mobilize a mass audience. Women especially used evangelical arguments and the sanctity of maternalism to fight against the sexual immorality inherent in the system of slavery. While newspapers like *The Liberator* were influential, books like *Uncle Tom's Cabin* graphically portrayed the abomination of slavery. Begun as a serial in 1851 and published as a book in 1852, Harriet Beecher Stowe's novel sold 300,000 copies in the first year. Moreover, across the North the book was produced on the stage, and, as people were entertained, they also were introduced to the horror of a slave system about which many had given very little thought. As they wept for Eliza and Uncle Tom, and became outraged at the cruelty and lasciviousness of Simon Legree, they were mobilized in their opposition to slavery.

At the same time, the slogan of "Free Soil, Free Labor, Free Men" reflected a political ideology and tapped the image Northerners had of themselves as an energetic and prosperous people. Horse-drawn reapers, mowers, and cultivators allowed Northern farmers to increase output at a greater pace than population growth. They could also bring in the harvest faster and thus were not as susceptible to the vagaries of the weather. In the 1850s, when population increased 35 percent, yield improved by 44 percent. By end of 1850s, Cyrus McCormick (1809–1884) was selling an average of 25,000 reapers annually in the nation, and farm equipment was valued at $18 million, an increase of 159 percent since 1849. Such technology was not developing in the South, where agriculture remained labor intensive, even for the yeomen.

Successful Northern farmers associated their prosperity and progress with the Free Labor ideology; republicanism was equated with the absence of slavery. In the South, republicanism had a totally different emphasis—that all whites in a slave society enjoyed liberty and social equality because blacks were enslaved. According to Southern republicanism, slavery made all white men equals. Democrats in the South appealed to racism, threatening white Southerners that they would be ruled by former slaves. White Southern leaders also argued that the stable, well-ordered South defended constitutional principles while the runaway pace of change in the North threatened to subvert the nation. Republicanism in the South meant keeping government small, thereby securing personal independence.

Possibility of Compromise Wanes The unfavorable images that North and South came to hold of each other during the last three decades before the Civil War removed whatever possibility may have existed for an amicable solution to sectional conflict. The Northern negative image of the South was the first to take shape and receive vehement expression. The abolitionists' stereotype of life in a slave society, held by a handful of radicals in the 1830s, grew until by 1860 it was embraced in whole or in part by most Northerners. The abolitionists pronounced slavery the most horrible of sins and slaveowners the most damnable of Southerners. They portrayed masters as sadists who systematically drove, starved, and sexually abused their slaves. The abolitionist stereotype of Southern white society depicted a handful of super-rich planters living lives of voluptuous ease in great white-columned mansions to the detriment of the majority of poorer whites and of all the slaves. Southern politics was denounced as an exercise in oligarchy and conspiracy; Southern religion was blasphemy; Southern churches were "dens of Satan"; Southern education was a mockery; Southern family life was a sham; Southern character was a morass of barbarism and degradation.

In turn Southerners saw the North as a foul nest of atheism, fanaticism, and hypocrisy. White Southerners pointed to Northern "wage slaves" and claimed wage laborers suffered more hardships and indignities than their plantation slaves. According to white Southerners, the North had no ethics save money making, and one Southerner labeled the North a "monstrous abortion." Uneasiness and distrust on both sides grew to hostility, fear, and loathing.

Popular reactions to political events such as the Dred Scott decision (1857) further exacerbated the sectional conflict. The Supreme Court denied that Congress could bar slavery in the territories, and thus nullified the Missouri Compromise (1820) and the idea of popular sovereignty. The outraged North felt betrayed. Furthermore, Chief Justice Taney also ruled that free African Americans were not citizens of the nation and denied them any hope of equal rights under the law in the United States. Northern and western newspapers, though misleadingly, warned that the Dred Scott decision meant that slavery was legal in all the states.

Abraham Lincoln proclaimed that while Northerners thought that slavery was dying out, that while they believed people in neighboring Missouri were "on the verge of making their State free . . . the Supreme Court has made Illinois a slave State." This was the essence of Lincoln's eloquent "House Divided" speech: "Either the opponents of slavery will arrest the further spread of it . . . or its advocates will push it forward till it shall become alike lawful in all the States." Lincoln and abolitionists who objected to slavery on moral grounds, as well as racist Northerners who feared that slavery jeopardized their own chances for obtaining the rewards of the American dream, were convinced that the slave oligarchy was changing slavery from a Southern to a national institution. As Northern outrage mounted, Southerners increasingly felt that those who lived above the Mason-Dixon line could not be trusted, that most Northerners were abolitionists at heart.

Election of Lincoln The realignment of the political parties in the 1850s was crucial to the coming of the Civil War. The short-lived American party, more commonly known as the "Know-Nothings," played upon nativist prejudices against Catholic immigrants. The American party split into Northern and Southern wings, but eventually the new Republican party picked up these nativist voters in the North. Because of its mildly anti-slavery stance, the party had virtually no Southern support, and the development of the new party system had dire consequences for the stability of the Union. In the North, citizens could choose between Democrat or Republican, blaming one or the other for "Papist conspiracies," alcoholism, and poverty. The South, however, had no place to work out its conflicts and could only look to the North and the Republican party as the enemy. First with the demise of the Whig party, then with the split of the Democratic party into Northern and Southern wings, the last national institution became sectional, and no institutional support existed for compromise.

The situation was already explosive when John Brown added more fuel in 1859. Brown's band, with financial backing from abolitionists, attacked Harpers Ferry, Virginia, in hopes of instigating a slave insurrection. Drawing beliefs of sin and atonement from the Bible, Brown felt the sins of the guilty nation had to be purged in blood. The raid confirmed the South's worst fears, and each section scripted Brown's raid as a melodrama, complete with martyrs, heroes, and villains.

Why did the conflict between the North and the South, however intense, impel Southerners toward the extraordinary step of withdrawing from the Union altogether? The election of Abraham Lincoln in 1860 jeopardized the Southern planters' hopes for gaining a guarantee of security for their property and for their slaves in the territories. His election portended, they felt, the eventual abolition of slavery and of the way of life that slavery represented. The union, they now believed, was destroying their freedom.

And why was the North not willing to let the South go? Because liberty was connected with unity, and union had itself become a value in the Northern mind, secession could not be tolerated by the North. Secession meant anarchy; the conflict was between order and chaos. As the forces of modernization concentrated, the more complex Northern society demanded unity and a strong central government. The North was willing to go to war because the dissolution of the federal government would be a destruction of personal liberty. Should the slave power succeed in destroying the Union, democratic government would perish from the face of the earth.

Although Southern senators were willing to compromise, Lincoln refused any compromise on the issue of slavery in the territories. Lincoln mistakenly thought the South was bluffing, and he also misjudged the strength of Southern Unionists. Southerners understood that Northerners were not taking them seriously and thus thought they had to stand firm. Each section underestimated the other's commitment, and no one guessed what Civil War would mean. On 20 December 1860, South Carolina passed an ordinance of secession.

The South may have blundered in not accepting the verdict of Lincoln's election just as the North may have blundered in not acquiescing to secession. But in the final analysis, while both North and South wanted peace, both preferred war to submission.

CIVIL WAR

A watershed for the social, economic, and political integration of the nation, the Civil War changed American society forever. For more than two decades, Southern agrarian representatives in Congress had blocked legislation that benefited modernization and industrialization; now Congress put through a program to benefit manufacturers, including high protective tariffs. A new national banking system ensured the destruction of state banks. Centered in the Northeast, this new financial network caused a geographically unequal circulation of currency, which planted seeds for later agrarian protest movements of the 1880s and 1890s. By 1866, per capita circulation of national currency was $33.30 in New England, $6.36 in Midwest, and only $1.70 in the South. In 1864 the legitimization of "indenture" contracts gave industrialists the right to import cheap foreign laborers under contracts (including Chinese workers for the railroads). Labor circles railed against this law until it was repealed in 1868, and finally in 1894 contract labor was declared illegal.

Before the Civil War, legislators fought over whether the linking of West and East would take a northern or southern route; with the South out of the way, the great transcontinental railroad system received lavish support from the federal government in the guise of land grants. The government provided railroads with everything they needed so that the war machine never slowed down. Government, lacking the knowledge and ability to meet all the economic needs of the war, relied on private-sector experts in railroads, banking, and factories across the North. Because these individuals' expertise was an essential element in winning the Civil War, the government aided private businessmen without placing restraints on them. What was good for business was seen as good for the war effort and hence America. This new relationship between government and business continued throughout the nineteenth century.

Growth of Northern Business and Industry Business, especially bankers and speculators, also profited from the way the federal government financed the war, primarily through issuing bonds. Most of the cost was not met by taxation, although the nation's first income tax was instituted during the war. This income tax, a very popular measure and a powerful force of nationalism, linked almost everyone to the war effort. From a previously weak government, the United States moved to a much more centralized power that extended more forcefully into the lives of its citizens.

The industrialized North suffered a severe recession during the first winter after secession, but by 1862 an economic upturn brought a business boom. Wartime inflation helped businesses, since prewar debts were paid off in cheaper dollars, 25 to 33 percent cheaper in 1863 than in 1860. Widespread utilization of interchangeable parts fueled mechanization. War materials encouraged concentration in certain industries such as iron and some early steel, and business adopted new equipment necessary for large-scale manufacturing. The integration of the economy through these new tools of finance, mechanization, and transportation opened a new America.

The Civil War accelerated trends already firmly established in Northern agriculture: growing technical efficiency, greater integration of the market, and increased specialization. These trends meant higher land costs and the need for more machines. Although some resented the push into the market economy, the Civil War overwhelmed any discontent. Enlistment took away large numbers of farm laborers and tenants who did not own their own land, and who otherwise might have caused class tensions. With fewer farm laborers available, wages rose for those who stayed home. The Civil War years were the most profitable yet for Northern farmers' lives. The war also increased the integration of rural America with large cities through new markets for farm products and machinery. The needs of soldiers connected farmers to industrialized processing in meat, fruit, and vegetable industries.

Federal aid to agricultural and mechanical colleges had been on the agenda since 1857 when Justin Morrill (1810–1898) of Vermont introduced the Morrill Act, but the South prevented approval. In 1862, with the South absent, Congress passed and Lincoln signed the Morrill Act to create land-grant colleges and stimulate the growth of technological education. Southerners had not been the only opponents; some Northerners and Westerners were hostile to any kind of higher education. Nevertheless, by 1900, forty-two land-grant colleges enriched American educational life. Moreover, the Morrill Act passed only two months after Lincoln created an office of agriculture, and these bills plus the Homestead Act gave a political recognition to the independent farmer on the very eve of his displacement as the characteristic American. Even before the Civil War, but particularly with the great movement of peoples during the war, technological, economic, and social forces were destroying the agrarian orientation of American society. Nonetheless, legislation like the Homestead Act and the

Morrill Act testified to the North's faith, however nostalgic, in the virtuous and independent producer of capitalist legend.

The irony, of course, was that the Civil War helped usher in an urban, industrial, and centralized America. Although the agricultural and technological colleges provided education for many Americans, large businesses and industrialists also benefited from the training and recruitment of technologically trained specialists and managers. The expanding influence of the larger Civil War economy meant that communities could be affected by decisions made by non-resident companies and "outside" banking interests. Such developments would produce protests from smaller cities and towns against decisions made in market, industrial, and financial centers such as New York, Boston, and Philadelphia.

Centralization of Southern Economy The South also grew industrially. The war swelled Confederate cities and forced an expansion of Southern production. A need for housing stimulated construction, and textiles and beginning iron industries in the South earned huge profits. Some men were able to amass fortunes through speculation, particularly in land. A very few wealthy planters even made fortunes during the Civil War by investing in railroads and other Northern enterprises.

Scholars now recognize that the Confederate government was much more a centralizing force than had previously been thought. Starting in the crucial spring months of 1862 and continuing throughout the war, a series of executive directives and national legislation regarding conscription, suspension of habeas corpus, impressment of supplies and slaves, and tithing of agricultural production was implemented to bring about a more efficient and balanced use of resources and to foster a unity of purpose. To a great extent it worked (although some Southerners were more "compatible Confederates" than others), and in spite of the North's overwhelming economic, technological, and demographic advantages, the South was able to sustain its rebellion for four long years. The centralizing tendencies of the Confederacy necessarily reduced the importance of "community individualism," leading people to identify less with their locality and more with their nation. This shift, as necessary as it was to wage the Civil War, robbed many Southerners of that community identification that had sustained them throughout the antebellum period and which had contributed to their initial successes on the field of battle. But as opposed to Northern society, the Southerner's emerging commitment to a broader national society ended in that society's defeat.

Changes in Community Structures and Values Ralph Waldo Emerson saw the war as a test of Northern values, and at least initially, many Southerners also viewed the war as a test of their way of life. John C. Calhoun had claimed that the North was an aggregate of individuals while the South was a land of communities. Lincoln's phrase from Mark 3:25, "a house divided against itself," implied the conflict was over the meaning of community. The rituals of community were played out again and again in North and South as women presented flags to their menfolk with stirring rhetoric that harked back to the tradition of the revolutionary war. Contact with men from all over the country weakened parochialism; young soldiers from small rural areas found their notion of community vastly stretched by the experience of war and a broader view of the world. Away from home for the first time, these young men marveled at the world outside their provincial homes, even as they yearned for home's secure environs. Physical closeness and family togetherness no longer maintained community during the war, so newspapers, letters, fleeting visits, and a vague notion of unified purpose had to take their place.

The Civil War undermined community more in the North than in the South, because the Northern commitment to the nation state—to the Union—was successful. Just as in the South, Northern soldiers believed they were fighting for their families and communities, but their love of home stimulated love of the Union. Even the structure of Northern military units changed during the war as more and more men found themselves in fighting units that mixed Maine troops with New Yorkers, Downstate Hoosiers with Upper Peninsula Michiganders. Moreover, the federal government successfully equipped, mobilized, and directed Union troops, thereby assuming a larger role in the war effort than that of the community. Finally, the face of war weaned men from home. The madness, chaos, and bloodshed were far closer and more real to these men, many of them drafted, than their distant homes. The center of morality shifted for those who survived Gettysburg, the Wilderness, Cold Harbor, Petersburg. The hardened veterans of Ohio, Michigan, and Indiana in Sherman's army did things they would never do at home. Northern soldiers, playing by different rules in the second half of the war, put to the torch civilian society and the

Southern homefront. Although common in fighting Native Americans, this was the first use of "total war" against a white population.

Initially, the Civil War was a local affair for most white Southerners, and their response was an affirmation of community identity. With the first call to support a war for Southern independence, white Southerners interpreted the meaning of the conflict and reacted to its demands from the perspective of their own families, relatives, friends, and local community. Some Southern soldiers refused to leave their home areas, which they understood they had volunteered to defend. For most, the war was not simply a cause to secure slavery or protect the planters' way of life; it was a matter of honor—a fight to protect community values. Even the white plain folk who had no slaves and little or no wealth had stakes in the community. Families and kin had settled near one another and often attended the same church in what was termed their "settlement." That the Confederacy held together for four years is remarkable, and this was only accomplished because yeomen and small farmers, many from upcountry non-slaveholding areas, fought as long as they did.

Because most of the battles were fought there, the people and society of the South were most affected by war. The desire to preserve a way of life that precluded change was strong enough to fight for, but paradoxically the war itself forced change upon the community. Southern ideals of independence and autonomy were only understandable in terms of a local community dominated by a highly complex network of kin and neighborhood relationships within a fairly restrictive, patriarchal hierarchy. This concept of community necessarily stretched to the breaking point during the war. The voluntaristic/individualistic worldview that was dominant throughout the South before the Civil War proved inadequate. The personal commitment and enthusiasm of 1861 flagged as the war agonized along and local relief efforts failed.

Gradually support came more from the state and less from local communities. War shattered each local community's isolation as its hardships overwhelmed local welfare institutions. Southern society lacked an infrastructure for relief such as that Northern women had created in their benevolent associations. The breakdown of the self-sufficiency of local neighborhoods had lasting effects. For welfare relief for needy families, neighborhoods had to look beyond their local church, which could not handle all local needs. Relief efforts became countywide, statewide, and even nationwide. This institutional reaction to the problems of society was decidedly a "modern" way of dealing with poverty.

The Union and Confederate Armies During four years of war, the 600,000 men killed represented one man dead for every six slaves freed. Casualty rates are estimates, and Southern statistics are based upon Union estimates. Still, roughly a quarter of Southern white males of military age died. For years after the war, the South experienced low mother/child ratios due to the reduced number of marriage-aged men.

Ultimately nearly four-fifths of all white Southern men of military age served in the Confederacy or state militia; slightly more than half of Northern men of military age served in the Union army or navy. Nearly all Southern white men were involved, but Northern enlistment patterns reflected the changing social structure and economy of the industrializing North. Because in 1860 most people still farmed, both the Union and Confederate armies had a majority of farmers as soldiers. But Northern farmers also made up a smaller proportion of the armed services than their numbers in the general population. Although Northern farmers seemed less willing to fight than other occupational groups, Northern farm laborers and tenants, generally younger with fewer dependents and smaller resources, were much more likely to enlist in service than farmers. Wartime enlistment bounties could serve as an instant down payment on a farm, and the long-standing tradition of rewarding soldiers with land for service also tempted laborers and tenants. The bounties for fighting encouraged those without funds, and especially immigrants, to join the Union army. Volunteers were most likely to be those artisans such as shoemakers who were being displaced by mechanization. Ironically, for those who saw the conflict as an opportunity to raise a stake, the Civil War ultimately speeded the process of consolidation, affirming the trend toward making America a nation of employees.

Still, most workingmen were staunch advocates of the Union war effort. Some, such as miners, even raised their own companies to fight in the Union army. Aside from professionals, skilled workers provided the highest percentage of Union enlistees and were the next largest occupational group, that is in absolute numbers, exceeded only by farmers.

On the other hand, immigrant Catholics were underrepresented in the Union army. Often Democrats, these immigrants were at the bottom of the white working class. Yet, 170,000 Irish Americans and 216,000 German Americans, as well as Scots, French, Welsh, Dutch, Scandinavians, and Hungarians, in all over 500,000 men, formed identifiable ethnic units in the Northern armies.

Opposition to the War Scholars have misinterpreted such incidents as the Pennsylvania coal fields draft resistance and the notoriously racist 1863 New York City draft riots as proof of Northern working class, and particularly Irish, lack of support for the Civil War. Strikes and draft resistance reflected intense industrial conflicts, deep class divisions, differences among the North's elites, a crisis of authority, and the estrangement of workers from Republican party programs. Although working-class support for the Union was strong, many of the working class believed that conscription was an elite Republican party conspiracy.

Still, New York City's skilled workers were nearly unanimous in their condemnation of the "gutter snipes" who rioted in that city. Irish fire companies, braving bricks and bottles thrown by rioters, put out fires, and New York's 69th Regiment (Irish) came fresh from Gettysburg and helped to rout many of their brethren. The Irish nationalist Fenians viewed the contest as one between the Northern republic and the Southern aristocracy, whom they equated with the English. Fenians stirred Irish support for the war effort. Prior to and during the Civil War, labor and Radical Republicans generally had a close working relationship. It was only in the aftermath of the Civil War that class relations became more important than the commitment both shared to the free labor ideology and opposition to slavery. For workingmen the war seemed an opportunity to demonstrate their loyalty to a system that offered them the best hope of achieving advancement and giving every man an unfettered start in life.

Support for the war was not uniform in either North or South. Peace societies existed throughout the Civil War, and where civilian suffering increased, so did peace sentiments. The peace movement in the North had the legitimacy of the Democratic political party, while Southern peace societies sometimes waged their own war against the Confederacy. Secret societies were organized in 1862 in Alabama, Mississippi, Tennessee, Georgia, and Florida. The Order of Heroes of America took root among the hill folks of Tennessee, Virginia, and North Carolina. Many of these areas were Unionist from the start. Anti-Confederacy feelings were evident as soon as secession became a reality, especially in non-slaveholding portions of the South, and every rebel state except South Carolina had a white unit fighting in the Union army.

The homefront also affected soldiers' morale and mounting desertion rates revealed the weakening of loyalty among Southern whites. In the final throes of the war, the army had trouble raising volunteers, and distress at home often caused desertion. One out of seven Southerners inducted into the Confederate army went AWOL at one time or another. As in the North, conscription laws heightened Southern resistance; in Alabama internecine warfare broke out between conscription groups and resisters, while in parts of Mississippi total anarchy reigned. In what some scholars have interpreted as evidence of class warfare among whites, some areas of the South witnessed guerrilla warfare as Southern deserters battled Confederate and state militia. One Confederate judge in South Carolina expressed his joy when the Union army of occupation arrived, thereby ending "the civil war" between Confederate deserters and South Carolina militia.

The Northern army, with a much larger proportion of foreign-born soldiers, had its own problems with disloyalty and desertion. Furthermore, resistance to conscription became much more widespread in the North than in the South. Over a quarter of 776,829 men called in four drafts between the summer of 1863 and spring of 1865 never reported for service. Although large numbers of these men were from ethnic and urban communities, the majority were farmers. Many draft resisters escaped to Canada or the West. Canada received 90,000 Americans during the war. "Substitute brokers" went to Canada and searched for poor men to take the place of Yankees who could pay for substitutes. Wealthy individuals like Theodore Roosevelt's father bought substitutes, and in the aftermath of the victorious war, men like Theodore Roosevelt might well have felt the need to prove themselves worthy in fighting for their country as their fathers had not. Furthermore, the commutation fee was a major source of complaint for Northern workingmen. To the poor, it seemed like "a rich man's war and a poor man's fight." These feelings were expressed in both North and South.

Changes in Women's Roles With men away at war, the number of women at home relative to the number of men increased, and so did their influence. Waging a war necessarily changed the role of women. Churches and women's religious organizations had already partially empowered women in the antebellum North. Since Northern middle-class women had been actively involved in networking through voluntary organizations, including various reform movements such as temperance, women's rights, and abolitionism, they were better able than Southern women to mobilize efficiently and use their organizational skills to aid the war through relief and sanitation efforts. Still, all women found that the exigencies of the Civil War enabled them to make a more substantial contribution to family and community life than previously. They traveled to the front to attend husbands and retrieve wounded sons; they ran farms, businesses, and community institutions with increasing confidence as the war progressed. In both North and South women formed a spate of aid associations to raise funds for their local militia. A lasting legacy of these societies was the continued church and community organizations such as temperance organizations, missionary societies, library societies, and other voluntary groups, especially on a national level. The Civil War increased women's interest in politics as well as their political acumen, and allowed many to envision a broader, more active role for themselves in social and political life.

In addition to the usual openings as teachers, other opportunities opened to Northern and Southern women during the Civil War, nursing prime among them. Construction of a vast hospital system created new jobs for women, who at first simply opened their homes for the sick and injured. Women became nurses and matrons in charge of hospital wards. Sanitation at this time referred to food, clothing, and bandages rather than to cleanliness or disinfectants. Nevertheless, in hospitals run by Southern women, the mortality rate (5 percent) was half that of hospitals run by men. A severe problem with Southern hospitals was a lack of food and supplies, so in addition to caring for the sick, nurses and matrons scavenged and solicited donations.

In both the North and the South, the Civil War opened vocational opportunities in government agencies as women took over such traditional male jobs as scribes and clerks. Women also assumed a larger role in industry. Textile mills, for example, employed increased numbers of adult women. Above all, with the men off at war, women took a more active role in running plantations and farms.

In a war that was longer and more horrifying than anyone had expected, privations on the home front included food shortages, especially in the South. After the destruction of its railroads, the Confederacy increasingly was unable to distribute farm products, and 250,000 Southern refugees compounded food shortages. Non-slaveholding women suffered crushing hardships; for slaveholders whose food was in short supply, rations for blacks were first to be cut. For some women, food riots were the only answer. When the famed noblesse oblige of the planter class failed to support them, yeoman women begged for government relief. With none forthcoming, and with the survival of their families at stake, many women attempted any means available to get their men home. War-weariness and class antagonism reached a point where large numbers of Southern women came to oppose the war, and with the desperation of the starving, many encouraged their menfolk to desert. Initially supporters of the Confederate cause, Southern white women ultimately undermined Southern nationalism and the war effort.

Late in the war, Union raiders pushed themselves past Southern women to take food or sometimes just to destroy it wantonly. Although Southern women supported patriarchal society before and during the war, they blamed the men for the failure to defend home against invaders or to provide the necessities for the family. Even upper-class Southern women felt betrayed by their husbands, who had exposed them to unfamiliar plantation duties, including the frustrations of managing plantation slaves. Women believed they helped maintain the patriarchal system while men had not.

If the war overturned many assumptions about traditional gender roles in the South, the effect was temporary. After the Civil War the patriarchal system rapidly reestablished itself. Vocational opportunities such as Confederate agencies and hospitals were abandoned. Only teaching remained, but the number of applications for teaching was much greater than the number of positions, and the pay was inadequate. Wartime activities of Southern women focused on survival. Moreover, defeat put a burden on Southern women to subordinate their own needs and desires in deference to their husbands' in order to assuage egos. Also Southern women had no previous history of feminism to draw upon. All this delayed the reordering of gender roles that was occurring more rapidly in the North.

Among middle- and upper-class white families, separate spheres of influence, although never absolute, developed for men and women. Men commanded the impersonal and competitive workplace and public sphere; women assumed responsibility for the private sphere—the home. At the same time, progress in women's education meant that middle-class women, poised to be active in philanthropic work, began to push for entry into the public sphere. These women eventually were able to expand their roles as educators and moral arbiters to the public sphere as well. In the South free black women, unable to perpetuate the immediate postwar patterns, and yeoman white women had to work in the home and in the fields. Upper-class white women, who managed households and did not work outside the home, became symbols of purity and morality as the Southern cavalier ideal placed white women on pedestals while exaggerating the male role of protector.

Class Tensions In neither North nor South did class antagonisms disappear in a gush of patriotism. The working classes paid more dearly than other groups in the North during the Civil War. The tariffs granted to manufacturers to defend against foreign competition caused working men and women to pay more for domestic goods. Inflation engendered by the Legal Tender Bill of 1862 hit the poor the hardest. Annual wages of $363 in 1862 were worth only $261 three years later. In many industries, wages did not keep pace with wartime inflation, and labor-saving devices further fragmented crafts. The moment was prime for organization, and national unions grew enormously during the Civil War. Yet when workers tried to organize for better wages, strikes were put down and antistrike laws passed. In 1863 in La Salle County, Illinois, where the first national miners' union was founded, the infamous Black Laws made union organizing a criminal offense. In Saint Louis in 1864 in response to several strikes, the army issued orders prohibiting strikes, meetings, and picketing. These measures may have been necessary for the war effort, but seemed grossly unfair to working men and women. Workers' demands for recognition of their participation in the war led to the foundation of the National Labor Union in 1866.

Prior to the war, Southern planters had tried to construct a society in which class tensions were diffused through racial categories. Ironically, the war, whose very purpose was to maintain the slaveholders' order, created a situation in which class tensions erupted and undermined slavery itself. When the war came home, when people had to sacrifice, some were more dedicated Confederates than others. In local communities, where the Civil War caused a lower standard of living for all, people soon knew who sacrificed the most. The wealthy sacrificed by giving up some luxuries, but most continued to live well and often did not bear their fair share of the war effort. For yeomen and the poor, sacrifice meant doing without necessities. The disparity of sacrifice galled yeoman families, often impoverished by the war. Class tensions unleashed by the Civil War sapped the will to fight.

In both the North and the South, bitter resentment flared when the wealthy used the legal and political processes to their advantage. Especially in the South, yeomen believed conscription was unfair, a burden that fell most heavily on non-slave owners since they had to work their own farms without the help of slaves. Non-slaveholders also chaffed at such laws as the "Twenty-Negro Law" (1862), which allowed owners of twenty or more slaves to be exempt from fighting. Inflation and shortages hit the poor much harder than slave-owning planters, and measures to fight inflation and price gouging were unsuccessful.

African Americans in the War Peace between North and South did not produce peace within the Southern white cultures; suspicion and ill-feeling persisted into Reconstruction and afterwards. So too did suspicion and ill-feeling of whites toward African Americans. Freedom for slaves started to take hold with the outbreak of war. While masters were away, slaves took advantage of the situation to assert more personal autonomy. They expanded their own garden plots and traditional space around their cabins, and black women spent more time with their own families and in their own homes. A number of blacks refused to submit to punishment, and especially so when administered by women. Slaves sometimes accompanied their masters to the front lines to act as valets and cooks; many remained loyal, but some escaped to the Northern lines and freedom—often a complete surprise to the slaveowner.

On the home front, increasing black resistance undermined a planter's confidence in slave loyalty, and most slaveholders worried about the behavior of slaves. Arson was not uncommon. A few slaves murdered their masters and mistresses, and although such behavior was very rare, it produced great anxiety throughout the Southern home front. Even though a slave insurrection while the white men were away never happened, it remained one of Southern whites' greatest fears during the Civil War.

The myth of slave loyalty and memories of slave personal service grew up quickly after the Civil War as a rationalization to justify the great suffering and loss that had occurred in the name of slavery. Indeed, historians have raised serious questions about the loyalty of the slaves during the Civil War. W. E. B. Du Bois argued that a covert general strike of slaves forced Robert E. Lee to surrender at Appomattox because the Confederate army lacked sufficient supplies to continue. Although no other scholar has confirmed an organized work stoppage in the South, frequent cases of insolence, defiance, and refusal to work occurred, particularly in invaded territory behind Union lines. Worse for the Confederation, African American slaves aided the invading Union army. Grant's success at Jackson and Vicksburg depended upon help from African Americans living in that region.

Slavery as an institution never completely broke down until the South was actually defeated. But as the Northern armies took new territories, blacks made their feelings known. Some slaves emancipated themselves by entering Union lines and thereby forcing the issue of emancipation on the army and government. One-half of all slaves were actually freed and outside the control of masters before the war ended. Some new freedmen released pent-up resentments against the master by burning down the big house, the symbol of control, or the cotton gin, the symbol of bond labor. But former slaves resorted to very little personal violence against whites.

Two-hundred thousand blacks fought for the Union army, a tremendous addition to Union manpower. African American soldiers quickly proved their bravery and earned the respect of Lincoln and the Northern public because they died for the Union and their freedom. The 54th Massachusetts proved its mettle at Fort Wagner, South Carolina, where half of the men were lost in battle. (On the other side, black Confederate soldier John Wilson Buckner, the grandson of wealthy free black slave-owner and gin-maker, William Ellison, was wounded defending Battery Wagner on 12 July 1863, less than a week before the famous assault by the 54th Massachusetts.) Black Union soldiers were treated as traitors, not as prisoners of war by Confederates. Confederate soldiers often gave no quarter when facing black troops. The infamous massacre after the surrender of Fort Pillow (12 April 1864) vividly illustrates the racism and dangers that black soldiers faced. Two-thirds of all its black defenders were killed, some literally crucified and burned.

Social history, the everyday experience of men and women at war and on the home front, casts light on the ways in which warfare transformed lives. Economic self-interest, loss of commitment, declining morale, alienation, class and racial conflict, all affected the war effort. The nature of Southern and Northern society and the relationship of the home front to the battlefield are crucial factors in understanding both the four long years Confederates fought and their ultimate defeat. Union victory ensured the Northern Republican party's vision of America and the fulfillment of the Yankee sense of destiny. Losing the war conversely meant demoralization and humiliation for the white South.

However, defeat for the Confederacy certainly did not mean defeat for all Southerners. States with a majority black population actually won the Civil War. Slaves wanted their freedom and they got it. With the end of the war, the North had achieved at least two of its war aims: the Union was preserved, slavery was abolished. A third war aim, the commitment to racial equality, which was expressed very late in the Civil War and only hesitantly by some Northern political elements, was never accomplished.

RECONSTRUCTION

Over the years, remembrances of the war and Reconstruction melded into a common experience, and white Southerners became more unified in those memories than they had ever been during war or Reconstruction.

Reconstruction varied from place to place, just as devastation from the war varied. Some Southern cities and countryside were left in ruin with destroyed bridges and railroads, and crops laid waste; other areas stood untouched by the war. After the war, some cities, such as railroad hub Atlanta, took off in unprecedented growth, while others like Charleston stagnated, never again to reclaim their antebellum glory. In some areas Radical or Black Reconstruction, as it became known, was neither very black nor very radical. In other locales, African Americans controlled the political process, and former slaves made significant economic gains, that, in turn then influenced their place in society.

These various experiences help explain the different interpretations that historians have placed upon Reconstruction, interpretations that have had a powerful effect on race relations. Modern historians no longer see Reconstruction as a tragedy in which venal Yankee carpetbaggers, vicious turncoat scalawags, and ignorant former slaves made a mockery out of Southern government. Charges of graft among Reconstruction politicians are now considered in the perspective of the widespread tolerance of avarice and peculation that produced the Democratic Tweed Ring in New York City (which completely eclipsed any Southern corruption), the scandals of the Grant administration, the "Great Barbecue" of business greed at public expense, and the massive corruption of the "Gilded Age" that followed Reconstruction. Reconstruction is now seen as a tragic chapter in American history because, despite the pain and suffering, America's failure to follow through on emancipation squandered a chance to achieve real equality for African Americans.

Aftermath of Slavery Slavery had been more than a labor system; it was an all-pervasive system of social control. In the rural antebellum South, physical separation between whites and blacks could not exist; segregation and slavery were mutually exclusive. In the unrest that followed Emancipation, neither race was sure of its role, and Southern whites especially felt anxious, frustrated, and aggressive toward African Americans. Relationships were turned upside down, the social fabric was altered. Turmoil and violence erupted as whites and blacks struggled to define their roles toward each other. A "stable" system of race relations was not established in the American South until segregation was firmly ensconced around the First World War.

After the Civil War, white Southerners, for the most part, thought rights for African Americans should be based on the limited rights for antebellum free blacks. Some Southern states merely took sections of their antebellum slave codes and substituted the word "freedmen" for "slaves." Always a component of Southern society, violence after the Civil War reached new heights as it took on racial, economic, and political overtones. In the first year after the Civil War, major race riots occurred in Southern cities, and police joined in terrorizing freedmen. The Ku Klux Klan and other white paramilitary organizations arose shortly after the war and flourished in the Reconstruction era.

It was this white violence against African Americans, this racist intransigence of the traditional Southern elites, that mobilized the North to implement congressional Reconstruction and give African Americans the vote and citizenship so that they could protect themselves from their former owners. Racial equality was a goal for the old abolitionists in the North, but they were a minority, able to win support for their ideal only by capitalizing on the animosity generated toward the South during the war. Allied with abolitionists in animosity toward the South was the Grand Army of the Republic, the Civil War veterans who had become a dominant institution in most Northern communities and enjoyed a social influence commensurate with church or school.

Many women's groups were no longer the allies of freedmen in their quest for justice. Although some leaders for women's rights continued to stay the course on racial equality, others, who had subordinated their own cause to that of abolitionism, felt betrayed when male former slaves, many of whom were illiterate, received the vote while educated women remained disfranchised. These suffragists ceased calling for racial equality and formed a separate independent women's rights movement.

The Union army of occupation during Reconstruction put many Northern soldiers in the South, as did the Freedmen's Bureau. In addition, Northern teachers and missionaries moved South specifically to work with former slaves. Northern businessmen committed to free labor also saw the South as a land of opportunity, as did adventurers. After the Civil War, many white Southerners also moved. Some headed for Texas, the state least affected by the ravages of the war. Others left the country; a handful even attempted to reestablish their former society in Brazil, a nation that still tolerated slavery.

African Americans' Social Emergence In the South, the revolution to incorporate African Americans into full equality between 1863 and 1877 put blacks at center stage. Those who were literate and educated (some free before the war), skilled artisans, or Civil War veterans emerged as the initial leaders of the freedmen. Later, other black men who had been slave laborers or youngsters during the Civil War rose to prominence. Well-organized, former slaves formed a remarkably cohesive unit, with high-participation rates in associations and Union Clubs and a sophisticated understanding of their interests. With the franchise, they maintained an unflinching devotion to the Party of Emancipation, despite economic intimidation and direct threats of physical violence.

The most dramatic change wrought by the war was in the personal lives of African Americans. No longer slaves, they aggressively sought freedom and economic opportunity while they fought to destroy their image as slaves. Some scholars stress class divisions and differences within the black community between darker-skinned African Americans and lighter-skinned mulattoes, especially the better educated, landowning, antebellum free black elite. Such differences existed mainly in larger cities like New Orleans or Charleston. For the most part, because whites perceived all blacks as alike, African Americans worked together in common interest. Relative homogeneity, strong kinship ties, and developing economic and occupational possibilities fostered a sense of belonging among African Americans. Many had come from cohesive plantation and interplantation communities during slavery and immediately developed independent African American communities in the rural and urban South with thriving voluntary groups such as burial societies, beneficent organizations, fraternal orders, and political clubs.

African Americans expressed their newfound freedom not so much by discarding the values of the institutions they had known under slavery as by setting up independent versions of those social, political, religious, and educational institutions. The first need for many families was to bring together missing members. Men and women reconstituted families broken up during slavery. Adhering to traditional patriarchal households, men remained at the heads of their families, and a pattern of male-headed households and long-term marriage among black families was predominant the first two decades after the Civil War.

Both men and women cherished the newfound ability of wives and mothers to care for their own home and children instead of someone else's. They also retreated from work as domestic servants because of vulnerability to sexual exploitation on the job. Emancipation resulted in a massive, if temporary, withdrawal of black married women from paid employment. This family orientation of the black community, especially the desire for personal autonomy in their homes and livelihoods, conflicted with the social interests of whites, who wanted servants if they could not have slaves. Early in Reconstruction, blacks had to contend with planters who claimed legal guardianship and used apprenticeship laws to hold and control black children and make them work.

Overwhelming historical documentation now shows that in every Southern state in the postwar era, former slaves assumed a variety of social and political roles, asserting themselves by teaching, making money, and gaining political power. These African Americans had internalized a powerful work ethic, as well as a dedication to family members that contributed importantly to the political solidarity of the black community.

The role of the church in the definition and maintenance of antebellum and postbellum African American values cannot be overemphasized. With very few exceptions, the integrated churches from antebellum times, which whites firmly controlled, split into black and white congregations. Independent black churches stressed patriarchal roles, solidified community spirit, and often focused community activity toward social and political ends. A source of strength for black leaders, the church inspired the application of ethics to the political problems of the postwar period. The churches helped black leaders to see that their authority was not dependent upon whites, but derived directly from their religious community and the autonomy of their own families. Thus with church and family as sources of black freedom and dignity, African American leadership blossomed in Reconstruction.

The first federally administered social welfare program with the goal of aiding a minority of the population, the Bureau of Freedmen, Refugees, and Abandoned Lands, in some places supported the freedmen in resisting gang labor and in challenging the working conditions imposed by white landowners. Yet in other places the bureau aided the planters in securing labor, punishing, even whipping and hanging freedmen up by their thumbs as discipline. But even where the bureau was helpful, the impetus for change came from the black community.

Black schools represented a community effort, often organized through the churches. Sometimes the church building was the school, and sometimes the church owned the school building. White schools, which enjoyed the support of individual benefactors, did not have these close ties with churches. Throughout several Southern states, African Americans, individually and collectively, contributed their money and labor to build new schools, hire black teachers, and organize responsible supervisory committees. Institutions of higher education, which developed an infrastructure for leadership within the black community, were founded by Southern black churches and received initial (and sometimes, continued) help from Northern religious organizations.

Despite white opposition that often included violence, African Americans persisted and made progress in educating their children and reducing illiteracy. Although the literacy rate among blacks remained considerably lower than whites even after Reconstruction, the rate of increase among blacks was nothing short of remarkable.

Rise of Tenantry System Adjustments to the Civil War among whites vastly differed from those in the black community. Hundreds of thousands of Southerners had been killed, maimed, or psychologically devastated. Moreover, wealthy whites who invested heavily in Confederate bonds lost their fortunes, as did patriots who accepted payment in Confederate currency. Slaves had been the major source of white status, wealth, and power, but emancipation changed all of that. After the war, landownership replaced slave ownership as the major indicator of wealth.

Reconstruction introduced a new social class in the South, that of tenant and sharecropper. Control of land was the central issue, but closely related was control of labor. With emancipation Southern white planters lost their slave laborers, field-workers, and skilled artisans. Immediately after the Civil War planters tried to hire and work black laborers in gangs as under slavery. Black workers, preferring landownership themselves, rebelled against this gang system. A freedman explained, "Gib us our own land and we take care ourselves . . . but widout land, de ole masses can hire us or starve us."

Freedmen forced white landowners into concessions that resulted in tenantry. Large sections of land were parceled out and rented in small holdings among white and black farmers, fragmenting the antebellum plantation system. Whites owning capital in land adapted rather easily to acquiring tenants. Sharecropping also developed partly because of the widespread lack of cash; rent could be paid with the division of the crop one time a year.

Tenantry took on a new meaning after the Civil War when so many former slaves became tenants. For African Americans coming out of slavery, those who made it into the tenantry system took a step up. Within tenantry, differing gradations and statuses depended upon such factors as ownership of farming tools, equipment, or work animals, and whether the rent was paid in cash or a share of the crop. Even at the lower end of these gradations, tenant farmers were economically and socially better off than day laborers (the majority of former slaves). As farm tenants, black families gained some control of the land and their own lives and could pursue the Jeffersonian ideal of the independent yeoman. Yet going farther to actual ownership remained limited. Despite the Homestead Act, congressional action, and in South Carolina a state land commission, land was not effectively made available to former slaves.

Alternative labor systems developed in some areas. Washington County, North Carolina, and the Sea Islands of Georgia and South Carolina instituted small landowning tracts, remarkably like independent peasant cultures elsewhere. In rice plantation areas along the Atlantic coast, the refusal of former slaves to work in gangs helped end one of the wealthiest plantation societies, and the rice economy died out.

Tenantry reinforced the patriarchal culture of the South; men dealt with men on business matters, including landlord/tenant interactions between white and black men. Landowners rented to men, preferably men with families. Farming was a family operation; everyone worked. Moreover, cultural mores dictated gender divisions in agricultural labor; since plowing was considered a man's job, landlords rarely rented out land to a woman (unless she had older sons). Thus tenantry reinforced the strong black family with a male as the head.

Tenantry as a system affected the ability to organize politically. Whereas during slavery blacks lived together in slave quarters, where they could be policed easily, tenantry scattered black families into the countryside, where tenant houses stood amidst cotton or tobacco fields. Although blacks then lived away from the supervision of whites, dispersion made political organization that much more difficult.

While the tenantry system relied on male-headed families, single black women had to seek employment in town, where they were hired as cooks, laundresses, seamstresses, babysitters, and housekeepers for white families. Single women found it safer to live in town, away from attacks of Ku Klux Klan members and from rapists, black or white. Single white women preferred living in town for the same reasons black women did, and during Reconstruction, black and white women headed households in towns in about the same proportion.

Changes in Southern Political Structure Where blacks were in the majority during Reconstruction, their successes included politics. African Americans were elected to almost all levels of Southern governments, and even to federal positions. Through the Republican party, former slaves also held federal, state, and local government positions. Freedmen became attorneys; blacks and whites became business partners. These jobs, as opposed to farming, provided regular cash. The available money, instead of credit until the next crop, added importance and purchasing power to those who held government jobs.

In areas where Republicans controlled the political process, reform was successful. Laws gave lien rights to the worker, and the tenant was guaranteed certain status. Sheriffs and local officials, often former slaves or political allies of the black community, decided landlord-tenant disputes. To keep white landowners from using land as a bargaining chip by withholding it from production, differential rates of taxes were suggested for land not in production. Homestead exemptions helped the smaller landowners (whose rank included most black property owners) keep taxes low. Blacks conducted successful strikes against streetcar segregation, and most "Jim Crow" legislation did not come about until after the collapse of Reconstruction.

Black Reconstruction was the greatest era of reform in the American South. As a political force in some states, African Americans brought about change in women's rights and divorce laws. They also strove for reform in the penal system, ending inhumane punishments such as disfigurement, and stopping imprisonment for debt. They brought improvements in orphanages and asylums, apprenticeship laws, and the like, and pioneered universal public education for the first time. Public education for all children in the South was a lasting legacy of Reconstruction.

This remarkable record of overall success was ended only by a reign of terror. Reactionary and paramilitary Southern whites, in organizations like the Ku Klux Klan, which often were led by war-hardened ex-Confederate officers, attacked and murdered African American leaders. In some areas open warfare between blacks and whites resembled another Civil War.

End of Reconstruction White Southerners violently overthrew Reconstruction out of desperation because Reconstruction was working, not because it was a failure. Reconstruction in the cotton South created the region's most dramatic proportional shift of wealth; as Southern whites fell in per capita income and landowning whites lost their property, African Americans' landownership increased, as did their per capita income. Black children continued to attend school in such numbers that progressive reformers later called attention to the number of white children laboring in the cotton mills, while black children, excluded from jobs, were receiving an education.

White landowners, desperate because they were losing control of labor, supported illegal means to overthrow Reconstruction. The white Democratic party, through terrorism and fraud, once again took over state and local governments. Though timing varied, this happened throughout the South.

When whites had securely seized power, they excluded blacks from government jobs and, in fact, from almost all jobs in towns. Black males were relegated to the stereotypical agricultural work associated with slavery. Once the Republicans were defeated, Southern white farmers were forced into tenantry and the crop lien system and eventually saw their suffrage curtailed as well. The one-party system that emerged after Reconstruction had little economic or social payoff for poor blacks or most whites.

When "Redeemers" took control, they rewrote laws on tenantry, vagrancy, and debt to favor white landlords and merchants. They also began an enclosure movement (already accomplished in the North) by enacting laws that required livestock to be fenced and thus eliminated the need to fence in cropland. The fence laws hurt former slaves and yeomen and herding whites, who could no longer let their animals graze on public land and in forests. Such laws dramatically altered the nature of Southern society.

The Civil War changed both North and South regarding the powers of government at all levels. One aspect of this transition was the growing role of government in the economic system. Slavery, though it received protection from the state, had basically existed in the private sector. After the Civil War, government in the South took a more direct role in the labor system. Once the Southern conservative elite regained political control, convict lease labor quickly developed and the chain gang replaced the whip as the symbol of punishment for black Southerners. Large plantations, mills, mines, and railroads, all benefited by purchasing convict labor.

The "New South" A subject of continuing controversy is the nature of the postwar social order and the amount of continuity and change between the Old and the New South. Careful analysis and attention to nuance is needed when examining Southern society before and after the trauma of war and Reconstruction. Did the upheaval of the 1860s and 1870s leave the planter class crippled and clear the path for a new breed of businessmen and industrialists who sought to remake the region in the image of the North? Or was there continuity of the old regime in the survival of the planter elite as the dominant class in controlling labor and subordinating or containing an upstart merchant and industrialist class?

During the last half of the nineteenth century, a middle class was developing in the South as the number of Southern towns and cities grew. Urban population, which was less than 7 percent in 1860, rose to about 20 percent by 1910. Cities that used to be depots for cotton grew to include warehouses, banks, insurance companies, and shops. Town- and city-dwellers began to see themselves as separate from rural folks, as well as from the "lintheads" who came to work in the cotton mills. The Civil War inspired Southern entrepreneurs, and the textile industry in the piedmont South spawned self-contained, segregated cotton-mill villages. Some credit an emerging business class, which quickly became a coherent group with a common view of municipal goals and urban boosterism, for giving form to the modern South. Actually several antebellum business leaders survived the war and continued promoting urban schemes after 1865. For the most part, neither ante- nor postbellum businessmen had many ties to the planter class.

Overall, Reconstruction failed to redistribute wealth, and a landholding elite generally stayed on top, but a new social system was born. Change certainly took place in the planters' relations to both black and white tenant farmers and to the new merchant class that challenged the planters' hegemony. The adjustment from a slave society to one based on the marketplace exchange of labor, goods, and cash was often painful. With the growth of an urban-commercial network, white yeomen in various parts of the South moved from subsistence farming into the marketplace, at first with eagerness and later with a revulsion that fed the Populist revolt of the 1890s. Often the patriarchal reciprocity that existed under slavery shifted to patterns of patronage and poverty that defined postbellum tenant-landlord relations. While landownership and distribution of wealth shared continuity, the Civil War and Reconstruction dramatically altered antebellum social and cultural patterns.

During Reconstruction and its aftermath, the nation focused its attention on issues of race and class. Discrimination, of course, did not end in the South, and the North, too, had to deal with racial prejudice. Northern blacks had access to their own newspapers and churches and used these forums to demand the right to education and use of public accommodations and transportation. For the most part discrimination in these areas ended, but prejudice did not cease. In the late 1860s the racism of white Southerners reflected the racism that pervaded America.

The interconnections of race and class were further complicated as former slaves became primarily an agrarian labor class and a white, industrial, labor class developed in the rest of the country. After the Civil War, industrialization marked more and more of the American economy, including the South. Southern railroads were rebuilt and expanded, and some cities developed industry, such as iron and steel in Birmingham, Alabama. The proportion of the population living on farms continued to fall steadily from 1870 into the twentieth century. Increased industrialization meant a labor force whose continued employment was at the discretion of employers.

In antebellum Southern cities white laborers had petitioned for the enslavement of skilled free blacks and the prohibition of slaves hiring out their own time. Generally historians believe this animosity and competition between white and black workers continued after the Civil War and was common in the North as well. In the postbellum North and South, especially in urban areas, laborers began to define themselves in terms of their racial and class identity. Exceptions existed, such as interracial unions of coal miners in the North and South. In New Orleans and Cincinnati, black and white longshoremen cooperated in a series of strikes and struggles over work-rules, hours, and pay. However, discrimination and the exclusion of blacks from trade unions was the rule after the Civil War. North and South, capitalists successfully divided the workplace along racial, gender, craft, and occupational lines. The variety of ethnic and racial, rural and urban backgrounds of industrial workers reinforced this stratification.

Postwar Northern Society In some ways the Civil War solidified the Northern working class. Germans, Irish, English, the native-born, and others fought together in the contest and this in some sense eased ethnic tensions. Many of the new unions spawned during the war cut across ethnic lines. The object of union efforts during Reconstruction was the establishment of an eight-hour day. The eight-hour day carried many meanings for workingmen. On the one hand, it simply accorded them more free time to spend with their families. On the other, it was closely tied to workingmen's critiques of wage-slavery. The eight-hour day was an effort to delineate the time belonging to the employer and that belonging to the employee, an effort to stave off attempts to make workers mere appendages of the machine and slaves to the industrial master's will.

Many workingmen feared that the slaveocracy had been defeated only to raise a new monied and industrial aristocracy. During the war, capitalists earned enormous profits and began moving away from working-class neighborhoods. The wealthy moved to suburbs or erected ostentatious mansions on hills. For working-class citizens, this new spatial segregation threatened the tenets for which they had fought the Civil War. Most strikes, particularly by the less skilled, during the Civil War and after the Panic of 1873 concerned wages. However, from 1865 until 1873, skilled workers went on strike mainly over issues of workers' control. Ironically, as laborers fought in the Civil War for the Free Labor ideology, the very world that made such an ideology attractive was changing radically. While laborers still thought of themselves as citizens, they also began to think of themselves as workers who needed cooperative efforts to secure their rights.

Whereas Reconstruction in the South was imposed from outside by the president and Congress, the North went through a time of Reconstruction also, primarily as an industrial revolution that changed every aspect of society. Some of these changes began before the Civil War, and some accelerated during and because of the war, but the period of Reconstruction itself expanded and solidified change, especially the centralization of the economy and the government.

The population in the nineteenth-century United States was becoming more urban; it was also aging, a consequence of the declining birthrate since 1800. The birthrate fell less in agricultural areas and among urban Catholic workers. As urban dwellers aged, their decreased ability to work caused downward occupational mobility and reduced wages; industrial wage earners had to build up savings or sink into poverty. This situation was very different from that on a family farm. The urban aged could not move in with children or have their adult children reside with them as did farmers. Family-owned homes became important investments in urban areas, for one could always rent to boarders or sell for income. The nonfarm, homeownership rate reached nearly 38 percent in 1870.

Growth of Railroads A major cause of the restructuring of Northern society was the growth of manufacturing and with it a burgeoning upper class of corporate businessmen. A cultural symbol of the industrial revolution, the railroad epitomized this new class. Railroads received from the Republican Civil War government enormous bounties of land that ultimately would provide them nearly half a billion dollars. The Civil War land-grant policy gave railroads much of the wealth of the West.

The railroad industry was the strongest force for transforming the American economy from small-scale local operations to a high-volume, well-integrated mass-production system. Operating a large-scale business involving the safety and money of thousands of passengers, investors, and soldiers, the railroads inspired modern business organizations specializing in management and efficiency.

At first, towns did everything they could to attract the railroad; later people fought its all-encompassing power. With government land grants and direct aid, railroads were given welfare allotments far grander than anything planned to help the newly freed slaves, who received little land. Government condemned property that the railroad needed, and federal troops removed squatters from disputed land and quelled labor trouble. Northern and Western workers and small farmers noticed the discrepancy between the vast wealth available to the rich and the meager amount of money available to the poor, but reformers believed that helping industrial development was the best way to help the nation. Moreover, because the railroads had contributed so much to the Union war victory, the line between public and private interests became blurred. But working people were not often persuaded that their interests coincided with Union Pacific's.

The growth of railroads also affected the agrarian ideal of the self-sufficient family. From the Midwest to California, railroads offered family farms a commercial outlet, thereby encouraging cash crops, raising land values, and contributing to the consolidation of land in fewer hands. Farmers now needed more equipment and more fertilizer, which they bought on credit. All these developments meant that farmers became increasingly dependent on a national market. With the standardization of gauges, local and regional markets became national and even international. Chicago shipped midwestern grain to the East Coast, where it was sent to Europe, and, in turn, the eastern industrial centers shipped farm equipment to the Midwest for commercial farm agriculture. An agricultural monoculture developed, with migrant farm laborers making annual rounds for the harvest.

The 1862 Homestead Act, tangible evidence of the Republican party's advocacy of free labor, encouraged the trend toward specialization and integration of the marketplace. It opened lands whose soil and climate made crop specialization a necessity. Moreover, the railroads followed the homesteaders and brought new farmlands into the national market, which in turn decreased transport costs and raised land values. The Homestead Act was not without its detractors. The number of Northern and western farm laborers and tenants did not decline. The land not open to homesteaders was greater than the land they could acquire. Moreover, the Homestead Act did not eliminate the hold speculators had on the American frontier. Between 1864 and 1869, speculators acquired up to fifty million acres.

Strengthening of Federal Government The consolidation of industry meant the consolidation of wealth, which had ramifications for the Free Labor ideology. Labor councils and labor unions grew in these years, and strikes became part of Northern culture. These unions barred or discouraged women; they were seen as competition for the men because they were compelled to work for lower wages, and interfered with men's right to a "family wage." African Americans were also excluded as unwanted competition. Workers wanted an eight-hour day, but more than that, they wanted a certain degree of fairness in the economic system. This fundamental question of fairness raised the accompanying question of class, race, and gender conflict as society became more pluralistic and more combative.

The Civil War and Reconstruction affected the development of the powerful nation-state, and in turn, a more activist federal government affected the evolution of Reconstruction. The North's economy and class structure began to change with the Civil War, and these changes in the relationship of labor and class to means of production led to the eventual undermining of Reconstruction as well as the reciprocity of Northern and Southern Reconstructions.

Most recently historians have emphasized Free Labor ideology as the principle that guided the Republican party's approach to Reconstruction. This ideology assumed that individuals, assured of equal opportunity, could prosper through their own initiative. Accordingly, the federal government's only responsibility was to provide full civil and political equality to former slaves. Even for Radicals who wanted to extend the power of the federal government, Free Labor ideology dictated that freedmen take care of themselves after enfranchisement and basic citizenship rights were assured. In the North many states withheld suffrage from women, Chinese, illiterates, and those too poor to pay property taxes, all devices the white South would later adopt for disfranchising African Americans, as well as the poor whites.

Over the course of Reconstruction, the Republican party came to identify more with the rights of property than with the needs of black Southerners. This increasing concern for property rights grew out of rising class consciousness. In reform movements, the adoption of class ideology meant less concern for beneficence and more for controlling poor and vagrant troublemakers. President Ulysses S. Grant complained that the press opposed stationing United States troops to help the freedmen but had "no hesitation about exhausting the whole power of the government to suppress a strike." Grant's successor, Rutherford B. Hayes, reluctant to use the federal government to protect the rights of African American citizens, enthusiastically committed federal troops to drive out Native Americans from western lands, protect the property of railroads, and break strikes.

Most historians argue that the social revolution of Reconstruction was doomed to failure. To have succeeded, Reconstruction needed a long-term commitment on the part of the federal government to social activism and to intervention in the Southern society and economy on a massive scale and over a long period of time. But in the mid nineteenth century, the American people were not yet accustomed to government intervention in the economy or society except in a regulatory role at the state level. Furthermore, racial prejudice was pervasive in the North as well as the South. Moreover, business became interested in trade with the South and believed order would be restored most quickly by replacing Reconstruction leaders with the old pre–Civil War ruling class. Perhaps most important, the war coalition of labor, reformers, and business was coming apart. Labor violence and threats in the North frightened businessmen. The Republican party became more the protector of private property than the party committed to equality.

The panic of 1873 and the depression that followed also reoriented political issues. Bankruptcies numbered six thousand in 1874. Hit especially hard were textiles in Massachusetts, where nearly one third of the work force was unemployed. Anthracite coal-mining was also decimated; in Pennsylvania owners hanged twenty Irish miners, members of the radical Molly Maguires. Street fighting broke out in Chicago between police and workers, some fifty people were killed, and observers noted women in the mobs. Many northerners, especially the Liberals, blamed the depression on the unsettled conditions in the South.

The white South, especially pre–Civil War leaders, picked up these signals, and "Redemption," the return of the Southern state governments to the control of the orthodox and conservative white landowning elite, became an irresistible tide. The Republican party gave up its attempt to force on the South a new balance of political power. When it did, the Republican party in effect decided that its political and economic interests were better served through cooperating with the traditional landowning elite, leaving to them the task of finding a solution to the problem of race relations. Sectional reconciliation took place at the expense of the rights of African Americans, an oft-repeated and tragic theme in American history.

BIBLIOGRAPHY

Overviews

Two overviews of the entire period are essential reading. Both have excellent bibliographies:

McPherson, James M. *Ordeal by Fire: The Civil War and Reconstruction* (1982).

Randall, James G., and David Herbert Donald. *The Civil War and Reconstruction.* 2d ed. (1969).

There are two excellent historiographical studies of the American South, and both contain relevant essays:

Link, Arthur S., and Rembert W. Patrick. *Writing Southern History: Essays in Historiography in Honor of Fletcher M. Green* (1965). Literature before 1965.

Boles, John B., and Evelyn Thomas Nolen. *Interpreting Southern History: Historiographical Essays in Honor of Sanford W. Higginbotham* (1987). Literature since 1965 until 1983 or 1985, depending on the essay.

The literature on the sectional conflict, Civil War, and Reconstruction is overwhelming. Almost all literature on nineteenth-century America relates to the social history of the period covered in this essay. Much of social history and labor history has come in the form of local or case studies. The following are only samples of readings that raise important questions of social history.

Sectionalism

Barney, William L. *The Secessionist Impulse: Alabama and Mississippi in 1860* (1974).

Cooper, William J., Jr. *The South and the Politics of Slavery, 1828–1856* (1978).

Foner, Eric. *Free Soil, Free Labor, Free Men: The Ideology of the Republican Party Before the Civil War* (1970).

Ford, Lacy K., Jr. *Origins of Southern Radicalism: The South Carolina Upcountry, 1800–1860* (1988).

Freehling, William W. *The Road to Disunion.* Vol. 1, *Secessionists at Bay, 1776–1854* (1990).

Gienapp, William E. *The Origins of the Republican Party, 1852–1856* (1987).

Holt, Michael. *The Political Crisis of the 1850's* (1978).

Johnson, Michael P. *Toward a Patriarchal Republic: The Secession of Georgia* (1977).

McCardell, John. *The Idea of a Southern Nation: Southern Nationalists and Southern Nationalism, 1830–1860* (1979).

Thornton, J. Mills, III. *Politics and Power in a Slave Society: Alabama, 1800–1860* (1977).

Civil War

Beringer, Richard E., Herman Hattaway, Archer Jones, and William N. Still, Jr. *Why the South Lost the Civil War* (1986). Good historiographical discussion.

Faust, Drew Gilpin. *The Creation of Confederate Nationalism: Ideology and Identity in the Civil War South* (1988). Especially sensitive to religion, women, and society.

Fellman, Michael. *Inside War: The Guerrilla Conflict in Missouri During the American Civil War* (1989).

Jimerson, Randall Clair. *The Private Civil War: Popular Thought During the Sectional Conflict* (1988).

Linderman, Gerald F. *Embattled Courage: The Experience of Combat in the American Civil War* (1987).

McPherson, James M. *Battle Cry of Freedom: The Civil War Era* (1988). The masterpiece of historical writing, with a wonderful bibliographical essay for both sectional conflict and Civil War.

Mitchell, Reid. *Civil War Soldiers: Their Expectations and Their Experiences* (1988).

Mohr, Clarence L. *On the Threshold of Freedom: Masters and Slaves in Civil War Georgia* (1986).

Paludan, Phillip Shaw. *"A People's Contest": The Union and Civil War, 1861–1865* (1988). Thorough examination of Northern society during the Civil War with insightful bibliography.

Owens, Harry P., and James J. Cooke, eds. *The Old South in the Crucible of War* (1983).

Rorabaugh, W. J. "Who Fought for the North in the Civil War? Concord, Massachusetts, Enlistments." *Journal of American History* 73, no. 3 (1986): 695–701.

Thomas, Emory M. *The Confederate Nation, 1861–1865* (1979). Still the best one-volume history of the Confederacy.

Vinovskis, Maris A., ed. *Toward a Social History of the American Civil War: Exploratory Essays* (1990).

Voegeli, Victor Jacque. *Free But Not Equal: The Midwest and the Negro During the Civil War* (1967).

Reconstruction

Anderson, James D. *The Education of Blacks in the South, 1860–1935* (1988).

Berlin, Ira, et al., eds. *Freedom: A Documentary History of Emancipation, 1861–1867*. 2 vols. (1982–).

Burton, Orville Vernon. "Race and Reconstruction: Edgefield County, South Carolina." *Journal of Social History* 12, no. 1 (1978): 31–56.

Foner, Eric. *Reconstruction: America's Unfinished Revolution, 1863–1877* (1988). An interpretative synthesis on Reconstruction.

Gutman, Herbert. *The Black Family in Slavery and Freedom, 1750–1925* (1976).

Litwack, Leon F. *Been in the Storm So Long: The Aftermath of Slavery* (1979).

Ransom, Roger L., and Richard Sutch. *One Kind of Freedom: The Economic Consequences of Emancipation* (1977).

Wayne, Michael. *The Reshaping of Plantation Society: The Natchez District, 1860–1880* (1983).

Weiner, Jonathan M. *Social Origins of the New South: Alabama, 1860–1885* (1978).

Woodward, C. Vann. *Origins of the New South, 1877–1913* (1951).

Wright, Gavin. *Old South: New South. Revolutions in the Southern Economy Since the Civil War* (1986).

Gender

Burton, Orville Vernon. "The Effects of the Civil War and Reconstruction on the Coming of Age of Southern Males, Edgefield County, South Carolina." In *The Web of Southern Relations: Women, Family and Education,* edited by Walter J. Fraser, Jr., R. Frank Saunders, Jr., and Jon L. Wakelyn (1985) pp. 204–223.

DuBois, Ellen Carol. *Feminism and Suffrage: The Emergence of an Independent Women's Movement in America, 1848–1869* (1978).

Faust, Drew Gilpin. "Altars of Sacrifice: Confederate Women and the Narratives of War." *Journal of American History* 76, no. 4 (1990): 1200–1228.

Ginzberg, Lori D. *Women and the Work of Benevolence: Morality, Politics, and Class in the Nineteenth-Century United States* (1990).

Jones, Jacqueline. *Labor of Love, Labor of Sorrow: Black Women, Work, and the Family from Slavery to the Present* (1985).

Rable, George C. *Civil Wars: Women and the Crisis of Southern Nationalism* (1989).

Industrialization, the State, Urbanization

Bensel, Richard. *Yankee Leviathan: The Origins of Central State Authority in America, 1859–1877* (1990).

Doyle, Don H. *New Men, New Cities, New South: Atlanta, Nashville, Charleston, Mobile, 1860–1910* (1990).

Gallman, J. Matthew. *Mastering Wartime: A Social History of Philadelphia During the Civil War* (1990).

Jaher, Frederic Cople. *The Urban Establishment: Upper Strata in Boston, New York, Charleston, Chicago, and Los Angeles* (1982).

Russell, James Michael. *Atlanta, 1847–1890: City Building in the Old South and the New* (1988).

Summers, Mark W. *Railroads, Reconstruction, and the Gospel of Prosperity: Aid Under the Radical Republicans, 1865–1877* (1984).

Wallenstein, Peter. *From Slave South to New South: Public Policy in Nineteenth-Century Georgia* (1987).

Labor

Arnesen, Eric. *Waterfront Workers of New Orleans: Race, Class, and Politics, 1863–1923* (1991). Very sophisticated historical analysis of race and class.

Bernstein, Iver. *New York City Draft Riots: Their Significance for American Society and Politics in the Age of the Civil War* (1990).

McLeod, Jonathan W. *Workers and Workplace Dynamics in Reconstruction-Era Atlanta: A Case Study* (1989).

Montgomery, David. *Beyond Equality: Labor and the Radical Republicans* (1967). The starting point for labor and the Civil War.

Palladino, Grace. *Another Civil War: Labor, Capital, and the State in the Anthracite Regions of Pennsylvania, 1840–68* (1990).

Rosenzwieg, Roy. *Eight Hours for What We Will: Workers and Leisure in an Industrial City, 1870–1920* (1983).

Ross, Steven J. *Workers on the Edge: Work, Leisure, and Politics in Industrializing Cincinnati, 1788–1890* (1985).

Walkowitz, Daniel J. *Worker City, Company Town: Iron and Cotton-Worker Protest in Troy and Cohoes, New York, 1855–84* (1978).

Community, Class, and Society

Most studies of Southern communities, regions, or states relate directly to sectional conflict, Civil War, or Reconstruction; most non-Southern local studies do not.

Burton, Orville Vernon. *In My Father's House Are Many Mansions: Family and Community in Edgefield, South Carolina* (1985).

Burton, Orville Vernon, and Robert C. McMath, Jr. *Class, Conflict, and Consensus: Antebellum Southern Community Studies* (1982). Bibliography of local social history studies of antebellum South.

———. *Toward a New South? Studies in Post–Civil War Southern Communities* (1982). Bibliography of local social history studies of postbellum South.

Doyle, Don H. *The Social Order of a Frontier Community: Jacksonville, Illinois, 1825–70* (1978).

Durrill, Wayne K. *War of Another Kind: A Southern Community in the Great Rebellion* (1990).

Escott, Paul D. *Many Excellent People: Power and Privilege in North Carolina, 1850–1900* (1985).

Fields, Barbara. *Slavery and Freedom on the Middle Ground: Maryland During the Nineteenth Century* (1985).

Hahn, Steven. *The Roots of Southern Populism: Yeomen Farmers and the Transformation of the Georgia Upcountry 1850–1890* (1983).

Hahn, Steven, and Jonathan Prude. *The Countryside in the Age of Capitalist Transformation: Essays in the Social History of Rural America* (1985).

Harris, J. William. *Plain Folk and Gentry in a Slave Society: White Liberty and Black Slavery in Augusta's Hinterlands* (1985).

Kenzer, Robert C. *Kinship and Neighborhood in a Southern Community: Orange County, North Carolina, 1849–1881* (1987).

O'Brien, Gail Williams. *The Legal Fraternity and the Making of a New South Community, 1840–1882* (1983).

Shifflett, Crandall A. *Patronage and Poverty in the Tobacco South: Louisa County, Virginia, 1860–1900* (1982).

Siegel, Frederick F. *The Roots of Southern Distinctiveness: Tobacco and Society in Danville, Virginia, 1780–1865* (1987).

SEE ALSO **African Migration; Agriculture; The Aristocracy of Inherited Wealth; The Deep South; Literacy; The Military; Popular Literature; Race; Racism; Slavery; Technology and Social Change; Women and Work**; and various essays in the section "**Processes of Social Change.**"

THE GILDED AGE, POPULISM, AND THE ERA OF INCORPORATION

Stuart McConnell

THE QUARTER CENTURY of dramatic growth and change in America that is now called the Gilded Age was a time of great anxiety. Between 1876 and 1900, the country was greatly transformed. It changed from a rural to an urban industrial nation; its population, once largely northern European or African in origin, increasingly included people from all corners of the globe; its economy, formerly based on yeoman farmers and small businesses, came to depend on wage laborers and gigantic corporations. Although each of these changes had been under way since at least the 1830s, the late nineteenth century witnessed an unmistakable acceleration of pace, experienced by contemporaries as attacks of "nervousness" and reflected in the names given to the period by historians: the Age of Energy, the Age of Industry, the Age of Excess.

This essay concentrates on four broad themes in the social history of the Gilded Age: (1) the consolidation of the American economy and the ways in which the consolidation affected laborers; (2) the clash between a largely native-born Victorian middle class and the wide variety of groups—Asian and European immigrants, African and American Indian—whom it saw as threatening; (3) the rise of the city as the scene of many of these conflicts but also as the center of new forms of social life, particularly for women; and (4) the succession of reform movements, most notably populism, that attempted to grapple with the age's manifold dislocations.

CAPITAL AND LABOR

Although a few well-publicized speculators made substantial fortunes during the Civil War years, the conflict did little to stimulate American economic growth. In the North, materials and labor were diverted to military uses, while in the South the war destroyed much of the infrastructure of the plantation economy. In 1877, the year the last federal troops were withdrawn from the states of the former Confederacy, southern incomes, industry, and capital stock already lagged far behind those of the North. The gap would widen with every passing year.

The war did leave three legacies to the Gilded Age economy: an inflated currency, a high tariff, and the experience of mass organization. The political conflicts generated by the first two were resolved at a fairly early date. The currency was deflated and the gold standard restored with the Resumption Act of 1875; prices then fell almost continuously for the rest of the century. The high wartime tariffs were never really reduced; in fact, they continued to increase until they reached prohibitive levels (46 percent on some items) in the Dingley Tariff of 1897.

The most important development of the period was, however, the rise of large corporations, mass organizations to which Civil War military service offered only the most approximate of introductions. True, most Americans continued to live outside the cities where these enterprises congregated. But by 1900 it was a rare individual who did not buy the products of such a company, supply it with raw material, feed its workers, compete with it in some way, or work for it.

The new enterprises were bureaucratically managed. Following what Alfred Chandler has called the "managerial revolution," such companies came to be controlled by salaried managers rather than by the people who owned them. By the late 1880s the biggest and most successful firms were relying on line-and-staff managements, under which a hierarchy, separate from the personnel responsible for actually doing the work of the company, generated statistical data on production and insisted on cost accounting. At Andrew Carnegie's steel plants, for example, the motto was, "Scoop the market, cut costs, and run the mills full," but in order to do this someone had to have a good idea of what the costs were. Carnegie's tight cost accounting system made this possible, and between 1873 and 1901 he built a giant corporation that drove competitors from the field by undercutting them on price. By 1900, Carnegie was making one-fourth of the nation's steel.

Carnegie was fortunate to have begun his career with the Pennsylvania Railroad, for it was in the railroad industry that the first revolutions in management and business organization took place. The need to coordinate crews, fuel, repairs, ticket receipts and, most important, schedules (an inexact schedule was an invitation to delays and wrecks) over large geographic areas drove railroad managers to systematic management even before the Civil War. After the war, as the various lines vied with each other for control of the new western traffic, coordination became even more vital.

Processors of fluids such as distillers and oil refiners followed the railroads in the managerial revolution. Then came mechanical industries such as tobacco processing, where James B. Duke's introduction of the cigarette-rolling machine in 1884 multiplied the industry's productive capacity. In distribution, mass retailers appeared by the 1880s; companies such as Marshall Field in Chicago and Hudson's in Detroit opened elegant downtown stores, employed large sales forces, created their own purchasing agencies, and employed cost accounting to evaluate managers. By the late 1880s and 1890s, department stores in turn would come under pressure from new catalog houses such as Montgomery Ward and Sears, Roebuck.

Both the mass producers and the mass distributors relied on volume, quick stock turnover, low prices, and efficient management to move the goods. Standard Oil, for example, controlled every step of its production and marketing, from the trees that supplied the wood for its oil barrels to the outlets that dispensed its finished products. Formed in 1870, by 1879 it controlled 95 percent of the oil business. After the turn of the century, other megaproducers, including United States Steel, and new retail chain stores, such as Woolworth's, would devastate smaller, localized competitors. But well before 1900, "big businesses" were widely recognized as different not only in size but in structure.

Consolidation also went on between companies. While vertical monopolies such as Standard Oil streamlined the productive process, horizontal mergers, which absorbed three hundred companies every year between 1895 and 1900, cleared away competition. By 1910, a number of major corporations of the twentieth century, including General Electric, Nabisco, and American Telephone and Telegraph, were in place as "trusts." Most of these companies were in technologically advanced industries, where size produced real economies of scale and the cost of entry for competitors was daunting. By contrast, trusts in low-technology, easy-entry industries—for example, National Cordage, American Bicycle, Consolidated Cottonseed Oil—usually failed.

Neither the creation of a new managerial class nor the rise of gigantic trusts meant, however, that the economy as a whole was well coordinated; in fact, it was chaotic. By 1894 more railroad mileage was in bankruptcy than ever before. In part the railroads' financial problems resulted from overbuilding during the boom of the 1880s; in part they occurred because some of the new capital had come from speculators like Jay Gould and Jim Fiske, who expected to make their money from changes in stock values rather than from actually running businesses. In the 1880s such speculators built rail lines as a form of economic blackmail, hoping to be bought out by their competitors in self-defense. Drastic overbuilding inevitably led to rate wars as railroads vied for business; one price war among the five parallel lines bidding for the New York-to-Chicago traffic reduced the passenger fare to the ridiculous sum of one dollar.

Most industries also suffered from chronic overproduction. In the book trade, for example, warehouses full of surplus copies bankrupted many of the cheap "library" publishers of inexpensive, often pirated, English classics who catered to the new mass reading public of the 1880s and 1890s. In the distilling industry, only about 40 percent of capacity was typically in operation. Heavily indebted railroads had trouble finding enough traffic; they were squeezed by large shippers like Standard Oil, which demanded discounts from the rates charged its competitors. In fact, the oil industry itself usually operated at only 75 percent of capacity.

The combination of speculative financing and overproduction resulted in an economy that veered between uncontrolled booms and what were called, with good reason, "panics." The first such crisis, in 1873, precipitated by the collapse of the banking house of Jay Cooke and Company, led to five and a half years of depression, the longest uninterrupted contraction in American economic history. A brief recovery lasting from 1879 to 1882 was followed by three more sluggish years, then a boom in the late 1880s and early 1890s. But then another panic, in 1893, precipitated a deep depression that lasted until 1898.

To the new managers, the solution to these problems—and the logical end point of business consolidation—was for all the companies in one industry to end up in one giant, managed combination. One step in this direction was the system of voluntary price and production quotas attempted by railroad managers in the late 1870s and early 1880s. When these agreements broke down repeatedly, leading railroad executives sought and obtained federal regulation. Although the Interstate Commerce Commission, created in 1887, was initially a response to the complaints of farmers and small shippers about discriminatory railroad rates, it was soon dominated by railroad interests and fenced in by court rulings that emphasized the railroads' right to "reasonable" profits.

The rise of big business affected different groups of urban workers in different ways. For the new class of middle managers, who were white and male almost without exception, success now meant a lifetime crawl up a career ladder, usually within a single organization. They could never hope to own the enterprises for which they worked, but their high salaries allowed them to turn to consumption as compensation.

In addition, the new corporations' reliance on expertise initially opened jobs for specialized professionals in fields such as law and engineering. After 1890, bureaucratization and specialization began to take over everything from municipal governments to symphony orchestras. The boom in professional employment was paralleled by a flood of new or reenergized professional associations, among them the American Historical Association (1884), the American Economic Association (1885), and the American Sociological Association (1905).

Below the managers and professionals, thousands of new "white collar" positions came into existence. Between 1870 and 1880 the number of bookkeepers doubled, the number of salesmen and saleswomen tripled, and the number of office clerks and copyists quadrupled. Together these white-collar workers formed a new middle class, which gradually superseded an older middle class of artisans and small merchants. They tended to identify themselves as middle-class people, with individual "careers" tied to the health of the firm.

Although white-collar work would become gradually proletarianized in the early twentieth century, with secretaries and clerks filling dead-end jobs at minuscule wages, Stuart Blumin points out that before 1900 it still paid better than manual labor. In 1881, for example, the Treasury and Interior departments paid most of their male clerks annual salaries of more than $1,200. Meanwhile, industrial workers in 1880 earned only $345 per year, well below the generally acknowledged poverty line.

The brunt of industrialization was of course reserved for workers in the new mass industries. These workers were predominantly male and, with significant exceptions such as workers in the meatpacking houses of Chicago, white. To them, the chronic overproduction of the period could mean one of three things, each of which was bad in its own way. An employer might decide to shut down excess plants temporarily, which meant layoffs. Many companies did this periodically, but it became an increasingly difficult option for operations that had taken on large debts or invested in costly machinery. Second, a company might engage in vicious price cutting in order to hold its markets, which in turn meant wage cuts. This is what happened in 1877 on the Baltimore and Ohio Railroad, in 1886 on Jay Gould's sprawling southwestern rail system, in 1892 at Carnegie Steel's Homestead works, and in 1894 at the Pullman Palace Car Company in Chicago. In each case the result was a bitter strike. Third, managers could hold wages constant while straining to squeeze every ounce of work from their employees through "scientific management."

The most direct way to resist such employer tactics was to strike, and in fact the Gilded Age probably saw more work stoppages than any comparable period in United States history. Between 1881 and 1890 there were 9,668 strikes and lockouts, more than 1,400 of them in 1886 alone, the year of an organized push for the eight-hour day. Most of these strikes were local job actions, aimed at such things as maintaining a work rule or removing an unjust foreman. The railroad, Homestead, and Pullman walkouts, however, involved thousands of workers and closed down whole industries for months at a time.

Each of these major strikes was lost, however. Their failures point up some of the weaknesses of labor in the Gilded Age. First, workers' organizations were still subject to official or semiofficial suppression that sometimes turned violent. Union organizers were blacklisted, agents from the Pinkerton National Detective Agency were hired to infiltrate union meetings or to guard plants, and as early as 1870 would-be employees in some industries were being forced to sign "yellow dog contracts" in which they promised not to join unions. The Sherman Act of 1890, intended as an antitrust measure, was used instead to obtain injunctions against strikers for "restraint of trade." In the last resort there were always troops, which broke the strikes against the railroads, Carnegie, and Pullman.

A second labor weakness is that ethnic divisions in the labor force, often deliberately fostered by hiring policies, might hinder organization. Irish and Chinese railroad laborers in the West, for example, found solidarity difficult, as did native-born and Slavic steelworkers in Pittsburgh and Jewish and Italian garment workers in New York. Ethnic tensions were further exacerbated, and labor politics hindered, by a two-party political system that until 1896 mobilized voters around such explosive cultural issues as temperance, Bible reading in schools, and immigration restriction.

Finally, large unions such as the Knights of Labor (1869) and the American Federation of Labor (1881) eschewed electoral politics. As Richard Oestreicher has pointed out, the winner-take-all structure of American elections made it hard for labor parties to gain the foothold in office they needed to shield members from injunctions, battle for new laws, or limit the use of police to break strikes. Labor candidates who did gain local office in cities such as Milwaukee, Buffalo, and Brockton, Massachusetts, found themselves hamstrung by state or federal officials or by the courts. It was safer to concentrate on workplace wages and hours. This was the course that the AFL, which gained ascendancy toward the end of the 1890s, followed.

Even in the workplace, however, questions of power and control always simmered just below the surface. When managers introduced strategies to control production, workers fought back, usually through informal means. Under the "piecework" system, for example, wages were paid per item produced rather than per hour or per day. Managers adjusted the piece prices downward if it appeared that (in the words of the Pullman Company's Thomas Wickes in 1894) "the known less competent and less industrious workmen are regularly making an unreasonable day's wage." Workers retaliated by mutually agreeing to restrict their output—a tactic known as the stint.

It was in response to the stint that Frederick Winslow Taylor developed his famous system of "scientific management" at Midvale Steel in Philadelphia in the 1880s and 1890s. Here the key was to break down complex tasks that required highly skilled labor into simple motions that could be performed by unskilled workers or machine tenders—in effect, the "de-skilling" of work. Although Taylorism was not fully implemented anywhere before 1900, its logic was the same as that behind the famous mechanized Ford assembly line of the early twentieth century.

Workers could, and did, resist de-skilling and mechanization. By refusing to divulge the secrets of their trades—in some cases, by insisting on working as subcontractors, away from the factory floor—skilled workers could retain considerable autonomy. Iron puddlers, for example, retained considerable power and commanded high wages into the 1890s by passing down their skills and furnaces from fathers to sons. Even where mechanization was introduced, a strong union could enforce work rules that limited its use.

Resistance to managerial and mechanical control had cultural roots as well. Immigrants often arrived with very different ideas about the pace, discipline, and organization of work. Polish miners in Pennsylvania might take three days off work to attend a wedding; Greeks celebrated eighty religious festivals a year; skilled Jewish workers in the garment industry resisted attempts to break traditional craft jobs into specialized parts. Native-born workers also carried over customs from the prewar days of independent artisanry: irregular hours, a leisurely work pace, drinking on the job, and "blue Mondays" taken off.

The result in most places was a tense standoff broken by frequent strikes. Few Gilded Age industrial shops saw either the survival of preindustrial work practices or the victory of "scientific management." After the turn of the century, however, as more workers came to see themselves as permanent wage laborers and as employers strove for even greater "efficiency," the space for compromise between them would continue to narrow.

NATIVISTS AND NEWCOMERS

If the emergence of the modern industrial state was the first major event of the Gilded Age, surely the shift from a population dominated by native-born whites to what Randolph Bourne would call in 1916 "trans-national America" was the second. By 1910, eight of every ten persons in Chicago was an immigrant or the child of immigrants; other cities, including New York, Buffalo, and Pittsburgh, boasted similar foreign majorities.

During the depression of the late 1870s, immigration was relatively light. From 1875 to 1879, chain migration worked in reverse, as immigrants already in the United States warned family members or co-villagers to stay at home or returned themselves. Returnees in these years numbered 45 percent of arrivals, a figure higher than in any other comparable period until 1895–1899.

Perhaps because net immigration was so low, the bad times of the 1870s prompted little restrictive legislation. A major exception was the treatment of Japanese and especially Chinese immigrants. As early as 1867, the appearance of Chinese laborers on the West Coast and on the track gangs of the transcontinental railroad spurred attempts to halt immigration from Asia. It also led to violence: in Los Angeles in 1871 a white mob lynched eighteen Chinese; in 1885 another in Rock Springs, Wyoming, murdered twenty-eight Chinese.

This hostility had many roots: sheer racism directed against people who were usually portrayed in the popular press as backward and sinister; a linkage of "the coolie trade" with the volatile slavery issue; and resentment on the part of common laborers, many of them Irish, toward low-wage competitors for jobs. In California, working-class "sandlotters" under the leadership of Denis Kearney made Chinese exclusion a major issue in state politics until a federal act of 1882 virtually cut off Chinese immigration to the United States for ten years. This exclusion was extended and finally made permanent in 1902. A wartime law that had permitted American employers to solicit contract labor was repealed in 1885.

Immigration swelled to 4 million for the decade of the 1880s, almost all of it from Europe, though the tiny migrations from Asia and Mexico had disproportionate impacts in California and Texas. In these years men outnumbered women in most immigrant communities, because single men often preceded wives or other family members, sending for them later once they were established. Some, however, remained separated from their families, while others, such as Abraham Cahan's fictional Jake in *Yekl,* sent for their wives, only to discover that time and distance had produced incompatibility. The strain that migration produced in family life was a common theme in immigrant literature.

More than a few of the migrants simply went back. In harsh economic times such as those of 1895–1899, a period when a nativistic backlash also had begun to appear, the United States saw half as many departures as arrivals. But even in good times, immigrants often came with the intention of amassing capital and returning home.

Such "birds of passage" were a source of worry not just to competing native-born workers but to middle-class reformers who inhabited the largely separate, white-collar job market. As they saw it, single young male immigrants lived at the lowest possible level to save money, exported their savings, took little part in the rituals of public life, and inhabited an urban bachelor culture marked by such amusements as drinking, burlesque, and prizefighting. Native-born lawmakers tried to encourage permanent migration (for example, by writing a family exemption into the 1885 law prohibiting contract labor agreements in most fields), but such efforts were largely fruitless.

The newcomers differed from the native-born in many other ways. Liquor, to take the most prominent example, was central to the social life of many immigrant communities. Where members of the Victorian middle class saw drinking as vice, the Irish and the Slovaks saw it as social cement. Roy Rosenzweig's study of Worcester has discovered that there the saloon was more than a place to consume liquor—it was also a place to inquire after job openings, eat an inexpensive lunch, cash a paycheck (which, during hard times, might be company scrip rather than legal tender), or just keep warm. Most important, the saloon sheltered customs such as "treating" and group singing, which built an ethic of camaraderie, egalitarianism, and mutuality. Small wonder that it was often the site of working-class political organizing.

Politics, in fact, was another area of cultural discord. Where members of the genteel elite such as Charles Francis Adams and Horace White favored limited government by "the best men," immigrant leaders tended to see public office as a matter of practical patronage and elections as tests of factional strength. Urban bosses elected with immigrant votes, such as William Marcy Tweed in New York, stole millions from the public treasury, but they also provided thousands of public works jobs and helped ensure rudimentary services for immigrant neighborhoods. Largely for this reason, Gilded Age voter participation hit record highs before the 1890s, when the violent exclusion of southern black voters precipitated a drop in turnout that has continued to the present day. Even losing presidential candidates such as Samuel Tilden (1876),

Winfield S. Hancock (1880), and James G. Blaine (1884) captured larger shares of eligible voters than has any president elected in the twentieth century.

In religion, the existing nation was predominantly Protestant, while the majority of the newcomers were Catholics and Jews. This provoked some anti-Catholic and anti-Semitic incidents, such as a Protestant-Catholic riot in Montana on the Fourth of July 1894, and the harassment of Jewish businessmen by night riders in Louisiana and Mississippi in 1893. More sustained disputes centered around the increasing number of Catholic parochial schools established after the Third Plenary Council of Baltimore in 1884 and the routine exclusion of Jews from fashionable hotels, beaches, and residential neighborhoods.

These simple polarities hide a more complex picture. If the Worcester Irish patronized saloons, they also founded the Father Matthew Total Abstinence Society. If immigrants often voted for bosses, many of the bosses themselves (Tweed, but also Christopher Magee in Pittsburgh and "Doc" Ames in Minneapolis) were native born, while the most outspoken reformer, editor Edwin L. Godkin of *The Nation,* was a native of Ireland. Middle-class German and Irish Catholics found they had more in common with their Protestant neighbors than with the newcomers from southern and eastern Europe.

For immigrants, the confusion of American life usually was framed around "assimilation" or a lack thereof. Such institutions as the singing society among Finns or the *Turnverein* (gymnastic society) among Germans fostered a sense of ethnic distinctiveness, as did the foreign-language press, which grew from 799 newspapers in 1880 to 1,032 in 1900. In Chicago, German-language papers routinely used the term "Americans" to denote a separate ethnic group—that of the native-born whites. In immigrant memoirs and novels such as Thomas Bell's *Out of This Furnace,* towns and neighborhoods are so insular that Yankees and other foreigners rarely appear.

Probably the strongest immigrant institutions were churches and synagogues. By 1880 the Catholic church was already the largest religious body in the United States, with 6,259,000 communicants; that number would more than triple by 1920. The number of American Jews increased from 250,000 in 1880 to more than 2,000,000 by 1910. Most of the newcomers came from southern and eastern Europe, as did virtually all of the smaller migration of Eastern Orthodox communicants. The churches and synagogues serving these immigrants functioned not only as houses of worship but as community centers. They operated not only schools and theological seminaries but orphanages, homes for the elderly, newspapers, cemeteries, settlement houses, hospitals, mutual benefit societies, and literary clubs.

On the other hand, the American environment exerted a steady pressure on imported customs. At Hull House (founded in Chicago in 1889), Jane Addams reported the anger of immigrant parents whose daughters wished to keep or spend money they had earned rather than turn it over to the family. Marriage between individuals from different ethnic backgrounds, while infrequent across class and religious lines, was not uncommon within these limits, especially outside the cities, where potential partners were few and far between. And though the number of foreign-language newspapers increased, their share of the urban reading public remained more or less constant as immigrants learned enough English to read the new illustrated urban dailies.

No such adaptation was visible to most native-born members of the middle class, who viewed the growing heterogeneity of the 1890s as an alarming slippage in their cultural authority. Following the labor riot in Haymarket Square, Chicago, and violent railroad strikes, both in 1886, the good burghers of many American cities began to see themselves as an encircled minority. Frightened citizens in Chicago, Baltimore, and other cities donated money or taxed themselves to build armories. Newspaper editorialists wrote of "incendiarism" or "the volcano under the city." Opponents of birth control, including soon-to-be President Theodore Roosevelt, warned of "race suicide" if immigrants continued to outbreed the native born.

In this anxious climate, nativism and patriotism flourished. The American Protective Association (1887) fulminated against Catholics, while in intellectual circles social Darwinism became popular. Exclusive hereditary societies such as the Sons and Daughters of the American Revolution (1889, 1890) began to sprout. Existing veterans' groups such as the Grand Army of the Republic mounted campaigns to place American flags on schoolhouses, while a number of "patriotic" organizations vied with each other to censor textbooks. The flag itself became the object of an intense cult that would ultimately produce Flag Day and the Pledge of Allegiance. Students in public schools practiced military drilling.

Driving the nativistic fury was continued heavy immigration that by 1890 was beginning to turn strongly toward southern and eastern Europe. Before the Civil War, roughly five hundred northern and western Europeans immigrated to the United States for every newcomer from southern and eastern Europe. By 1890–1894 the ratio was down to two to one; it would reverse itself well before World War I. This was significant because the quasi-scientific racism of the time labeled the "darker" peoples of the new immigration as "inferior." Hungarians, wrote one nativist editor in Washington, D.C., were "half-savage aliens" who brought only "brigandage and trouble."

The new immigration of the 1890s produced the first moves for general restriction of immigration to the United States. A new law in 1891 barred the immigration of polygamists (a provision aimed at Mormon converts), the diseased, and those entering in response to contract labor advertisements. Another measure, in 1894, doubled the head tax from fifty cents to one dollar at entry. The first of many bills to impose a literacy test on immigrants was introduced in Congress in 1896. Such a test, wrote the congressional committee recommending it, "would shut out those classes of immigrants which statistics show contribute most heavily to pauperism and crime and juvenile delinquents."

The racism and nativism of the 1890s also made life for African Americans more difficult than it already was. With white "redeemer" governments installed in every southern state after 1877, southern blacks (90 percent of the black population in the United States even in 1900) saw their rights evaporate. Although some blacks in the upper South and in certain local enclaves could still vote during the 1880s, black officeholders were removed and black majorities in the Deep South disfranchised by poll taxes, literacy tests, and violent intimidation. A series of Supreme Court rulings and administrative decisions between 1882 and 1888 upheld segregation in public transportation and public amusements. And while a few African Americans continued to own land in 1890, many more were convict laborers or agricultural workers tied to landowners by long-term contracts.

The rest of the century was a nightmare for race relations. Between 1885 and 1900, the United States witnessed 2,400 lynchings, mostly of blacks in the Deep South. "Jim Crow" laws mandating separate public facilities for blacks and whites replaced informal segregation. Race riots erupted in New York and New Orleans in 1900, even as black troops were engaged in helping suppress an insurrection in the Philippines. At the World's Columbian Exposition in Chicago in 1893, black Dahomeyans recently subdued by the French were put on display, while a black woman dressed as Aunt Jemima cooked pancakes for visitors.

Unlike European immigrants, African Americans had no place of refuge. Northern industrial jobs (and northern industrial unions) were closed to them. In the South there were few alternatives to agriculture; as late as 1900 only 6 percent of the southern work force was in industry. Perhaps 30,000 blacks migrated to Kansas after 1877, but there they also encountered hostility. A few graduates of new black colleges such as Fisk (1865) and Howard (1867) managed to carve out careers in the segregated business and professional worlds of the 1890s. But for most blacks, south and north, unskilled labor and domestic service remained the only alternatives.

American Indians fared no better. Displayed in Wild West shows and studied by anthropologists as "primitives," they continued to be removed westward by the federal government. General George Custer's "last stand" (1876) was in fact just an early battle in a twenty-five-year war of removal and resistance that ended only with a true last stand—the slaughter of 146 Dakota Sioux at Wounded Knee, South Dakota, in 1890. The Dawes Act of 1887 imposed white ideas about individual landholding and nuclear family structure upon Indians. It broke up tribal landholdings, allotting to each Indian "head of household" the same 160 acres (64 hectares) promised to white settlers under the earlier Homestead Act, and designated "surplus" land for sale. Two years later, the Indian Territory reserved for earlier American Indian deportees was opened to white settlement.

To different degrees, then, European and Asian immigrants and African Americans and American Indians alike suffered in the 1890s from the rigidity of Victorian thinking about race. In Victorian culture, race, like many other things, was conceived of as dualistic. One was either white or black, just as one was either civilized or savage, male or female, Protestant or Catholic, American or un-American. Indeed, the most famous Supreme Court case of the decade, *Plessy* v. *Ferguson* (1896)—the case in which the Court gave sanction to the "separate but equal" doctrine—turned initially on the question of whether the "octaroon" plaintiff Plessy was "really" a white man or a black man. Similarly, burlesque shows featured not black performers but white performers in blackface—a crude artifice that made it clear these were "really" white men.

Individuals who crossed categories were viewed with pity; those who inverted them, with suspicion. The mulatto, for example, was typically a tragic figure in literature and on stage, while the immigrant's struggle with conflicting identities was usually pictured as the prelude to assimilation. But when the Haymarket anarchists reversed the Victorian categories at their perfunctory trial in 1886—claiming that conventional "order" was really disorder and that "law" was lawlessness—they were hastily executed. And when the crusading journalist Jacob Riis was told of the existence of homosexuals during his research for *How the Other Half Lives* (1890), he replied that this was "impossible.... There are no such creatures in this world."

Despite the formal rigidity of Victorianism, however, accommodations were taking place that by the 1920s would subtly alter American society. In politics, shifting ethnic coalitions would come to replace the regional pieties of the Civil War era. In religion, the new Social Gospel of Protestant ministers such as Washington Gladden and of popular religious novels such as Charles Sheldon's *In His Steps* (1896) treated poverty as a social evil, not an individual vice. In recreation, the boisterous Irish Fourth of July eventually fused with the staid Protestant version to produce a holiday that was neither completely raucous nor completely orderly. Newer burlesque shows combined established minstrel and melodramatic conventions with acts and performers from urban immigrant ghettos. In the universities, children of gentility, such as William James, crossed paths with children of immigrants, such as George Santayana and Thorstein Veblen.

One should not exaggerate the extent of this cultural convergence. Asians, American Indians, and especially African Americans remained largely marginal to it until late in the twentieth century. Native-born white Protestants still wrote the laws and controlled access to the universities. Racial violence continued after 1900 and even intensified in the wave of riots and lynchings following World War I. Nonetheless, the period from 1880 to 1900 was one in which some of the distinct cultures that now make up the United States began to encounter and reshape one another.

URBANITES AND REFORMERS

Business consolidation and ethnic diversification both took place primarily in cities, which in the last quarter of the nineteenth century experienced phenomenal growth. In 1870 the nation had only fourteen cities of 100,000 people. By 1900 it would have thirty-eight, with New York, Chicago, and Philadelphia each having over 1,000,000 residents. Chicago in particular was the wonder of the age, doubling in population from 503,125 in 1880 to 1,099,850 in 1890. By 1910 its population would double again.

As Kenneth Jackson points out, the main reasons for the rise of the city were the concentration of the new industries around transportation hubs and, until the 1890s, slow mass transportation. As late as 1890, more than 70 percent of all street-rail systems relied on horses, mules, or mechanical cables for power. Members of all social classes still needed to live relatively close to work, though the migration of affluent families to railroad suburbs such as Lake Forest, north of Chicago, and Bryn Mawr, west of Philadelphia, had begun. Much urban growth also resulted from huge municipal annexations such as those of Baltimore in 1888 or Chicago in 1889.

With the coming of electric interurban trolleys after 1890, cities spread out and neighborhoods became differentiated by class. The low price of outlying land, cheap construction methods such as balloon framing, and the five-cent streetcar fare combined to make suburban living attractive and affordable even to "middling" urbanites. Sam Bass Warner has shown that by 1900 central Boston was inhabited mostly by those for whom even the five-cent fare was an extravagance, with bands of middle-class construction in the "streetcar suburbs" just beyond and wealthier residents living in railroad suburbs five or more miles from downtown. Similar patterns in other cities were accompanied by tax policies that forced city residents to subsidize the extension of roads and sewer lines to the newer sections.

In working-class neighborhoods, the instability of the Gilded Age economy made domestic life very difficult. Workers needed to take whatever hours they could get whenever they could get them, even if it meant twelve- or fourteen-hour days, because they were almost certain to be out of work completely at some point. In bad years like those of the mid 1870s and mid 1890s, unemployment probably averaged about 20 percent of the work force.

Even when they were employed, wage workers barely earned enough to live. Real wages were stagnant or fell for almost a decade, from 1872 to 1881, though they improved steadily after that. Still, the average nonfarm worker in 1890 earned only $475 per year and worked a day that averaged just over ten hours. Out of these earnings had to come rent, food, transportation, and entertainment. Those who had money left after paying the bills might deposit it in one of the new building and loan associations that grew up to serve immigrant communities. In Chicago, for example, the forty such Bohemian associations paid out $4 million between 1885 and 1895.

Some household economies could cut the cost of living. "Entertainment," for example, often meant not much more than a daily newspaper, a picnic once a year on the Fourth of July, and an occasional visit to the park. Workers who lived near their jobs could save streetcar fare by walking to work. But the easiest way to make ends meet was to take in boarders, a common practice that changed the face of the urban family household. Boarders helped to keep the average household's size at about five persons until almost the turn of the century; in 1890 the census found that 23 percent of all households contained seven or more persons. Boarders also exacerbated overcrowding. By 1900 the tenement district of Manhattan's Lower East Side was the most densely populated place in the world.

Women in the city still lived home lives almost as sheltered as those of the antebellum years, though this was slowly starting to change. As late as 1890 they were only 17 percent of the paid labor force, and better than 80 percent of employed women were unmarried. In store clerking, a position women would later come to dominate, 93 percent of the jobholders in 1880 were men, as were 94 percent of all bookkeepers, cashiers, and accountants and 99 percent of all office clerks. Members of the respectable middle class still tended to see employment for women as something to fill the time before marriage; historically, female careers such as school teaching and social work continued to be extremely ill paid.

Outside the white middle class, however, women's work was much more common. Black women worked in much higher proportions than white, both before and after marriage, with domestic service the leading occupation in 1890 (as, indeed, it was for women in general until well into the twentieth century). Among the daughters of immigrants in the sweatshops of New York's Lower East Side, 85 percent earned wages at one time or another in their lives, often in the home as piecework garment workers. Women were often the proprietors of boardinghouses or of the informal Irish barroom kitchens known as "shebeens." They worked as midwives and in certain skilled trades such as typesetting, bookbinding, and millinery. As mass retailers gained ascendancy in the 1890s, women were often hired as clerks.

As in the middle class, however, working-class families viewed women's labor as a necessary evil, to which even child labor was preferable. Among the poorest quarter of Philadelphia's population in 1880, for example, 77 percent of all two-parent families relied partly on the wages of children; only 2 percent reported having a wage-earning wife. Some unions agitated for a "family wage" (one that would allow wives to remain at home) while others, such as Samuel Gompers's Cigarmakers Union, resisted the admission of women to the trades.

Women's emergence from the home during the Gilded Age came primarily in the realm of consumption. Within households, they were usually the directors of everyday purchases, no small position in an economy of excess production. Once mass retailers became alert to this fact, they courted female customers with department store lounges, covered entrances, and nurseries for children. They sponsored women's sections and advice columns in the new metropolitan dailies, which in turn led to the generation of female-oriented copy to fill those sections. At John Wanamaker's lavish downtown Philadelphia store a woman could shop, eat an elegant lunch, and be entertained by a pipe organ concert without leaving the building. The downtown, formerly the preserve of men, was now opened to women as well.

In fact, the city offered a wide variety of commercial amusements that even relatively humble urbanites could afford to patronize. Baseball took off as an urban spectator sport beginning in the late 1870s, with professional players and standardized rules. Variety and vaudeville houses began running continuous shows; soon after 1900 they would be superseded by nickelodeons. Spectacular new amusement parks appeared in many cities, most famously at New York's Coney Island, where in 1895 the first of several parks began offering thrill rides, light shows, and a carnival ambience.

However, as Gunther Barth has pointed out, the real novelty of city life was the city itself. Streetcar companies were surprised to discover their weekend business rising as people hopped onto the car simply for the pleasure of touring other neighborhoods. Department store windows offered spectacles of consumption even to those, such as Theodore Dreiser's fictional Sister Carrie (*Sister Carrie,* 1900), who did not have the money to buy. Metropolitan dailies such as Joseph Pulitzer's New

York *World* (1883) created the "feature story" as a way of humanizing the strangers one met on the street.

The chaotic energy of urban life worried middle-class suburbanites and small-town dwellers, whose own domestic lives continued to stress privacy and self-restraint. Suburban houses were set back from the public street, domestic havens from the hurlyburly of commerce. Inside they featured cluttered parlors full of heavy, ornate furniture, closed floor plans, and scant natural light. The men who lived in such controlled spaces were expected to work hard, save money, and suppress their "lusts" for such things as strong drink and "frivolous" amusement. Women were to cultivate "higher ideals," teach their children the single truth of Christianity, and treat sex as an unpleasant duty. The popular novels of Horatio Alger only echoed contemporary advice manuals in stressing "character" above all other virtues.

In middle-class Victorian social life, the positions of men and women were strictly defined. They filled different jobs (even within the same workplace), took their leisure separately, patronized different types of entertainment, and engaged in elaborately formal courtships. Of the hundreds of new fraternal orders that invaded middle-class life in this period, only the Knights of Labor admitted women into anything other than a separate "auxiliary." In medicine, as Caroll Smith-Rosenberg has observed, men and women were thought to have fundamentally different sexualities.

From the vantage point of the Victorian middle class, the growing cities were targets of suspicion for a number of reasons. They were largely composed of immigrants, whereas the population of the countryside (and, to a lesser degree, that of the suburbs) remained native born. The cities were anonymous; traditional methods of suppressing vice, such as gossip, no longer worked. Their heterogeneity in matters of religion called into question white Protestant moral certitude, already shaken by the Darwinian revolution in intellectual life. They harbored saloons. They fostered trivial entertainments. And in their massive scale and complexity, they represented the eclipse of the individualism and self-sufficiency upon which so much of the worldview of the middle class relied.

Perhaps most important, cities seemed to be blurring the rigid lines of Victorian gender relations. Kathy Peiss has tellingly described how working-class young women allowed young men to "treat" them to the "cheap amusements" of the city. Some sexual intimacy was usually expected in return, and in fact some of the attractions, such as the Tunnel of Love at Coney Island, were designed to facilitate such encounters. Burlesque shows, as Robert C. Allen has recently argued, inverted middle-class norms of "proper" feminine behavior, as female performers parodied masculinity and flaunted their own sexuality. At the same time, male strongmen such as Eugene Sandow were turning the male body into an object of show.

As with the new immigration, the official response to all of these urban disturbances was restriction. Older agencies of moral reform such as the Young Men's Christian Association (founded 1851) doubled their efforts to save wayward young men. They were joined by newer agencies such as the Salvation Army (1880) and Dwight L. Moody's Moody Bible Institute (1889). Between 1860 and 1880 the newly powerful medical profession pushed through the first laws outlawing abortion. In 1886, B. F. Keith launched his family-oriented "variety" theaters, in an attempt to cleanse the stage of the taint of burlesque. In the 1890s, muckrakers such as Jacob Riis and Lincoln Steffens published exposés of tenement squalor and municipal corruption.

Most widespread were movements against the saloon. In the cities, temperance agitation usually took the form of a campaign to limit liquor licenses; outright prohibition was rare. But outside the cities, where immigrants were less numerous and the force of Victorian values still strong, voluntary temperance gradually gave way to legal prohibition. During the 1880s, almost every southern and Great Plains state was rocked by the issue; in 1889, both Dakotas entered the Union as dry states. By the outbreak of World War I, twenty-six states had passed prohibition laws.

Often these urban reform crusades were led either by women or by men who invoked the need to protect "woman's natural sphere," the home. National temperance organizations such as the Women's Christian Temperance Union (1874) and the Anti-Saloon League (1893) were dominated by women, as were many of the new social work agencies that grew up to serve the urban poor. Individual women such as Frances Willard and Susan B. Anthony often were involved in several reform movements at once, and the movements themselves overlapped considerably. Woman suffrage advocates, for example, argued that temperance would not arrive, and the home not be truly safe, until women could use their votes to "clean up" municipal politics. At Hull House, Jane Addams complained that political corruption was behind the filthy and badly paved streets of the neighborhood.

The realization that most urban problems were systematic and interconnected would lead, after 1900, to the broad collection of reform movements known as Progressivism. But even before the turn of the century, a change of social attitudes was visible. In the 1870s and 1880s, middle-class writers commonly assumed that most of the problems of poor people were the sufferers' own fault. For example, an 1882 editorial entitled "Why Some Are Poor," from a small-town paper in Michigan, cited "cream allowed to spoil, vegetables thrown away that would make a good dinner, and pie crust left to sour instead of making tarts for tea." As Daniel Horowitz notes, early social workers and labor statisticians often built into their studies the assumptions that savings were good, debt and liquor were bad, and "luxuries" were unnecessary.

By the late 1890s, reformers were no longer trying to rehabilitate the individual sinner but rather attempted to change the environment in which the sinner lived. From "scientific charity" to the City Beautiful movement in urban planning (spurred by the orderly architecture of Chicago's 1893 Columbian Exposition), the horizon of reform grew larger, its plans more systematic. Undoubtedly, the need for systematic solutions dawned on the middle classes in part because of the severe depression of the 1890s, which idled more than a few white-collar workers. But it was also a continuation of the same bureaucratizing process that had already swept the corporations. And at bottom it was a conservative response to radical calls for more fundamental change, which by 1890 were being made by laborers and farmers alike.

PRODUCERS AND POPULISTS

The processes of incorporation, immigration, and urbanization profoundly unsettled a population that even in 1890 remained 65 percent rural. In some ways the census overstated the nonurban population, for it classified as rural most of the employees of huge extractive industries such as mining and logging, as well as the country merchants of many a small hamlet. Moreover, as William Cronon points out, country and city were locked in an economic embrace: there would have been no Chicago without the farms that fed it, and few viable farms without a Chicago to feed.

Nevertheless, farmers experienced to an even greater degree than urban dwellers the overproduction, loss of personal autonomy, and concentrated power of capital so characteristic of the late nineteenth century. In areas such as the Georgia piedmont, staple farmers became substantially enmeshed in the relations of the market economy for the first time; in other regions, what had been partial economic integration before the Civil War intensified. In the process, many farmers suffered severe economic distress and began to search for alternatives to industrial capitalism.

For a few agriculturalists, the post–Civil War years brought stable profits. Near the booming cities, in areas such as suburban New Jersey or northeastern Illinois, dairy and truck farming proved lucrative. On the plains, technological advances such as barbed wire (first mass produced in 1874) made large-scale farming and ranching profitable for those with sufficient capital to invest.

For farmers of the great staple crops, however, most notably cotton and wheat, a tenuous situation in 1865 had turned into a disaster by 1900. Over that span the price of cotton per bale dropped from 18 cents to 9 cents, while wheat fell from $2.06 per bushel to 62 cents per bushel. In large part this was the result of a glutted world market. But the farmers' situation was not helped by an urban-dominated Congress whose tariffs protected industrial manufacturers better than they protected farm products, by deflation following the panic of 1873 and the Resumption Act of 1875, and by a highly exploitive credit system.

One needed significant amounts of capital to enter farming. The costs of buying horses and machinery, building a house, breaking sod, drilling a well, and stringing barbed wire around even a modest 80-acre (32-hectare) farm in Kansas ran well over $1,000—more than two years' wages for the average nonfarm worker. Until the first crop came in, the farmer needed money for daily expenses, and even in subsequent years he was stretched thin between the spring planting and the fall harvest. Especially in the plains states, transportation and storage costs were high. As a result, many farmers became debtors.

For the western farmer, credit was obtained by mortgaging the land. When disasters such as the grasshopper infestation of 1874–1877 or the crop failures of 1886–1888 struck, many of these farmers were forced into bankruptcy or tenancy; many simply walked away from the farmstead to start over somewhere else. As late as 1910, more than half the farm population occupied land it had not occupied five years earlier.

In the South, where land was less valuable, credit was obtained by mortgaging the crop. Lawrence Goodwyn has accurately described how the "crop lien" system turned cotton farmers into debt peons. From spring to fall, a local furnishing merchant would supply the farmer's wants while carrying him on credit. When the crop came in, the two would settle accounts. But the combination of falling crop prices, high interest rates charged by merchants, and the dependence of the entire credit system on decisions made in faraway New York meant that often the farmer could not "pay out"—that is, produce enough to cover what he had borrowed. The merchant would then agree to carry him for another year, in return for a lien on the crop.

For some groups of farmers, such sharecropping was not necessarily the worst alternative. Eric Foner has suggested that the new class of southern black producers preferred sharecropping to wage work for white owners because it allowed them to retain control over what they grew and how they disposed of it. But as economic conditions worsened in the 1870s and 1880s, more farms, black and white alike, slid into tenancy. By 1900 almost half of southern farms were run by tenants; in the rest of the country, about one-quarter.

The farmers' growing dependence generated resistance as early as the 1870s. At first they focused on "the currency question" itself, assuming that the root of their problems lay in an insufficient money supply. The Greenback party, which held its first national convention in 1876, contended that staple prices could be raised and credit eased if the currency was inflated; it favored leaving the non-gold-based Civil War greenbacks in circulation in order to accomplish this end. On the currency issue, farmers were joined by other borrowers—notably manufacturers in fledgling industries such as steel—who stood to gain from inflation. In the 1878 congressional elections, the party polled over 1 million votes and elected fourteen members to Congress.

At the same time, midwestern farmers banded together in the Patrons of Husbandry (the Grange). The Grange formed buying cooperatives and between 1872 and 1874 persuaded several states to pass "Granger laws" regulating the railroads. Both Grangers and Greenbackers sought to reform the tax system, which was biased in favor of large property holders, especially in the post-Reconstruction South. In 1882, for example, Mississippi gave railroads and manufacturers a ten-year exemption from taxes.

For Henry George and his many followers, taxes were the only issue, and the tax on land was the only one that mattered. George, a San Francisco editor and economist, was appalled by the rampant land speculation in California at mid century. In *Progress and Poverty* (1879) he argued that the farmer's problem was not deflated currency or railroad corruption but the hoarding of land by people who intended only to sell it later. His "single tax" program, calling for heavy taxes on land that was not in productive use, gained many adherents in the 1880s.

Each of these early movements espoused a variant of the ideology historians have identified as "independent producerism." Rooted in the entrepreneurship of yeoman farmers and skilled artisans before the Civil War, independent producerism glorified farmers and manual laborers as the true creators of wealth and dismissed all others as economic parasites. The Greenbackers saw real producers being shortchanged by "the Money Power" and its manipulation of the currency. The Grangers saw railroad extortions robbing honest farmers. The single taxers saw land speculators reaping immense profits while producing nothing but paper.

None of these movements questioned the legitimacy of private property or entrepreneurial capitalism. Each tended to trace the crises of the Gilded Age to a single cause and to assume that once that cause was removed the economic machine would run smoothly again. It is a mistake, however, to assume that farmers were therefore nascent big businessmen themselves—that, if they could, they all would have imitated Carnegie. Instead, they invoked the world of the early nineteenth century, a world of small proprietors in which land and the control of its produce were fundamental. As George put it in *Progress and Poverty,* "the natural order is land, labor, capital; and, instead of starting from capital as our initial point, we should start from land" (p. 163).

One could find the same ideology at work in the Knights of Labor (1869), the massive fraternal order of laborers that made common cause with the fusion Greenback Labor parties of the late 1870s and later with the Populists. To the Knights, the fundamental division was not between labor and capital but between producers and nonproducers. Thus the Knights welcomed a wide variety of workers, and even some small employers, to their "union of all producers"; only bankers, lawyers, gamblers, stockbrokers, saloonkeepers, and (prior to 1881) physicians were excluded. Like the Grangers, the Knights formed producers' cooperatives.

Unlike the agricultural movements, however, the Knights saw worker-run cooperatives as the first step toward the abolition of the wage system ("workingmen's democracy," in Leon Fink's phrase). While their stress on mutuality made them reluctant to strike, they sometimes gained impressive victories when they did. After the Knights led a successful strike against the Gould rail system in 1885, their membership peaked, at 729,000. But weak leadership, failed strikes, and the unremitting hostility of employers led to the order's decline in the 1890s.

Here and there in the 1890s one could find proposals to redress the injustices of the market system through government spending. In the depression year 1894, for example, Jacob S. Coxey led his army of the unemployed in a march on Washington to demand the creation of employment through a $500 million "good roads" program. Although Coxey's Army was turned away, generous outlays of pensions to the politically powerful veterans of another army—the Union army—represented a massive, if selective, foray into social welfare spending. The Dependent Pension Act (1890) in particular poured money into the economy; by 1893, Union army pensions consumed one dollar of every three the federal government took in.

More systematically, the 1890s saw the vogue of Edward Bellamy's utopian novel *Looking Backward* (1888), probably the most influential book published in the Gilded Age. Like the Knights, Bellamy pictured an egalitarian "cooperative commonwealth" from which wages and private property had been eliminated. But his utopian state also relied on a technocratic elite to manage both production and distribution, a vision of the future that ultimately proved more appealing to urban Progressives than to farmers or laborers.

It was in the Farmers Alliance of the late 1880s and the People's party (Populists) of the 1890s that independent producerism was finally combined with a fundamental critique of capitalism. Developing first in Texas under the leadership of William Lamb and Charles Macune, the Alliance swept over the South and Great Plains between 1887 and 1889. It drew on the same ideals of mutual aid and production for use that had animated the earlier Greenback and labor movements. But it also took practical steps to build what members hoped would be a counter-economy of cooperation, bypassing the merchants, commodity speculators, and bankers.

At the local level, suballiances created "trade stores" to furnish goods on favorable terms, bulked their crops for cooperative sale, and used boycotts to pressure suppliers. As Goodwyn notes, such mutualistic tactics achieved some notable victories. In Kansas, Nebraska, and Missouri, for example, the cooperative marketing of cattle was a success, while an interstate boycott aimed at the high price of jute bagging for cotton resulted in the collapse of the jute trust by 1890.

The most ambitious of the cooperative enterprises, the Texas Cotton Exchange, failed, however, in 1889, largely because it could not market its notes in banking circles. In the wake of the collapse, Macune and others were led back to the same questions of credit and money supply that had obsessed the Greenbackers. By the end of 1889, the Southern Alliance had adopted Macune's subtreasury system, which would extend federal credit to farmers on the surety of their crops in storage. This would allow them to escape the crop lien system and to store produce for later sale, rather than being forced to sell at low harvest prices.

In social life, meanwhile, the Alliance fostered what Goodwyn has dubbed a "movement culture," a set of social practices that reinforced the mutualism of Alliance ideology. Organization was carried on in nonhierarchical settings such as the camp meeting, the mass rally, and the Alliance picnic. The gospel of cooperativism was spread to new areas not by corporately owned newspapers but by a system of traveling lecturers. In some localities, disputes between members were submitted to Alliance judiciary committees rather than to the court system.

At the outset, the cooperative vision appealed not only to small farmers but often to large landholders squeezed by high freight and credit rates and to landless whites who had only recently been dispossessed. In the suballiances of Gwinnett and Jackson counties in Georgia, for example, Stephen Hahn has found that 42 percent of the members owned no land, while 11 percent owned three hundred acres or more.

However, Hahn also notes the tensions built into the new organization. The bitter racism of white suballiances kept many black sharecroppers away. Alliance endorsements in 1890 of local Democrats in the South caused partisan rancor and resulted in the election of candidates who were only lukewarm to the farmers' concerns. Regional hatreds inherited from the Civil War continued to divide midwesterners from southerners. Finally, cooperative marketing and the subtreasury idea forced the farmers away from alliances with townspeople and landlords, who did not want to give up the profits of the crop lien.

The subtreasury scheme hastened the Alliance's entry to politics; by 1892 it had evolved into the People's, or Populist, party. The new party endorsed federal control of the currency, nationalization of railroad and telegraph companies, the eight-hour day for labor, the direct election of senators, and a graduated income tax. It also endorsed the free coinage of silver—yet another scheme to inflate the currency.

It was free silver that became Populism's undoing. Silver was a minor issue in the 1892 election, in which Populist presidential candidate James B. Weaver received more than one million votes. But by 1896 it was a mania. Like the Greenbackers of the 1870s, the silverites seemed to offer a way out of the farmers' debt crisis without drastically altering the existing economic system. Unlike the Greenbackers, they had ready-made political allies in the silver producers of the West.

When the Populists fused with silverite Democrats behind the presidential candidacy of William Jennings Bryan, they surrendered the cooperative commonwealth to professional politicians who were not really interested in it. But coming as it did on the heels of the Homestead and Pullman strikes, three years of depression, and an unprecedented wave of immigration, the 1896 Populist-Democratic campaign thoroughly alarmed the respectable middle classes. Bryan was called a "fanatic," a "traitor," and a "murderer," running on a "platform made in hell." Marcus Hanna, the Republican campaign chief, dunned major corporations for donations—Standard Oil alone gave $250,000. Workers in some plants were told not to report the next day if Bryan won.

The combination of Republican money and Populist internal discord made the election an anticlimax, as William McKinley defeated Bryan soundly. Before McKinley's first term was over, the country would witness the great merger wave of 1895–1900, solve part of its overproduction problem by expanding overseas, and abandon tenant farmers and southern blacks to their own resources.

In short, between 1876 and 1900 the same forces were at work on industry and agriculture alike. In each case, a republic of small producers and artisans became a nation of corporate employees. Just as independent oil drillers sold out to Standard and artisan puddlers gave way to unskilled laborers at Carnegie Steel, so southern tenants now worked for landowners and western grain growers for the banks that owned their farms. And just as decisions about industrial production gravitated upward into the hands of managers, so decisions about agricultural production fell increasingly into the hands of the urban bankers. By 1900 the majority of Americans, knowingly or not, worked for someone else.

BIBLIOGRAPHY

General Works

Ginger, Ray. *The Age of Excess: The United States, 1877 to 1914* (1965).

Painter, Nell Irvin. *Standing at Armageddon: The United States, 1877–1919* (1987).

Schlereth, Thomas J. *Victorian America: Transformations in Everyday Life, 1876–1915* (1991).

Wiebe, Robert H. *The Search for Order: 1877–1920* (1967).

Capital and Labor

Chandler, Alfred D. *The Visible Hand: The Managerial Revolution in American Business* (1977).

Fink, Leon. *Workingmen's Democracy: The Knights of Labor and American Politics* (1983).

Gutman, Herbert. *Work, Culture, and Society in Industrializing America: Essays in American Working-Class and Social History* (1976).

Livesay, Harold. *Andrew Carnegie and the Rise of Big Business* (1975).

Montgomery, David. *Workers' Control in America: Studies in the History of Work, Technology, and Labor Struggles* (1979).

Noble, David F. *America by Design: Science, Technology, and the Rise of Corporate Capitalism* (1977).

Oestreicher, Richard. "Urban Working-Class Political Behavior and Theories of American Electoral Politics, 1870–1940." *Journal of American History* 74, no. 4 (1988).

Rodgers, Daniel T. *The Work Ethic in Industrial America, 1850–1920* (1978).

Zuny, Olivier. *Making America Corporate 1870–1920* (1990).

Immigration, Race Relations, and Nativism

Bell, Thomas. *Out of This Furnace: A Novel of Immigrant Labor in America* (1941; reissued 1976).

Bourne, Randolph. "Trans-National America." *Atlantic Monthly* (July 1916), pp. 86–97.

Dinnerstein, Leonard, and David M. Reimers. *Ethnic Americans: A History of Immigration,* 3d ed. (1988).

Foner, Eric. *Reconstruction: America's Unfinished Revolution, 1863–1877* (1988).

Higham, John. *Strangers in the Land: Patterns of American Nativism, 1860–1925,* 2d ed. (1988).

Rosenzweig, Roy. *Eight Hours for What We Will: Workers and Leisure in an Industrial City, 1870–1920* (1983).

Rydell, Robert. W. *All the World's a Fair: Visions of Empire at American International Expositions, 1876–1916* (1987).

Saxton, Alexander. *The Rise and Fall of the White Republic: Class Politics and Mass Culture in Nineteenth-Century America* (1990).

Takaki, Ronald T. *Iron Cages: Race and Culture in Nineteenth-Century America* (1979).

Urban Life; Women

Allen, Robert C. *Horrible Prettiness: Burlesque and American Culture* (1991).

Barth, Gunther. *City People: The Rise of Modern City Culture in Nineteenth-Century America* (1980).

Blumin, Stuart M. *The Emergence of the Middle Class: Social Experience in the American City, 1760–1900* (1989).

Boyer, Paul S. *Urban Masses and Moral Order in America, 1820–1920* (1978).

Horowitz, Daniel. *The Morality of Spending: Attitudes Toward the Consumer Society in America, 1875–1940* (1985).

Jackson, Kenneth. *Crabgrass Frontier: The Suburbanization of the United States* (1985).

Kasson, John F. *Amusing the Million: Coney Island at the Turn of the Century* (1978).

Peiss, Kathy. *Cheap Amusements: Working Women and Leisure in Turn-of-the-Century New York* (1985).

Smith-Rosenberg, Carroll. *Disorderly Conduct: Visions of Gender in Victorian America* (1985).

Sproat, John. *"The Best Men": Liberal Reformers in the Gilded Age* (1968).

Warner, Sam Bass. *Streetcar Suburbs: The Process of Growth in Boston, 1870–1900* (1962).

Agriculture, Reform, and Populism

Cronon, William. *Nature's Metropolis: Chicago and the Great West* (1991).

Goodwyn, Lawrence. *Democratic Promise: The Populist Moment in America* (1976).

Hahn, Stephen. *The Roots of Southern Populism: Yeoman Farmers and the Transformation of the Georgia Upcountry, 1850–1890* (1983).

Thomas, John L. *Alternative America: Henry George, Edward Bellamy, Henry Demarest Lloyd, and the Adversary Tradition* (1983).

Turner, James. "Understanding the Populists." *Journal of American History* 67, no. 2 (1980).

Unger, Irwin. *The Greenback Era: A Social and Political History of American Finance, 1865–1879* (1964).

SEE ALSO **Business Culture; Industrialization; Labor: The Gilded Age Through the 1920s; The Market Revolution; The Rise and Consolidation of Bourgeois Culture; Sectional Conflict, Civil War, and Reconstruction; Urbanization.**

THE PROGRESSIVE ERA THROUGH THE 1920s

Lynn Dumenil

THE YEAR 1900 marked the end of a century, a dramatic occurrence. Certainly from the standpoint of the late twentieth century, the nineteenth and twentieth centuries stand out with sharp differences: one Victorian, one "modern." But despite the drama of entering a new century, American society in the first three decades of the twentieth century was deeply marked by the legacy of the late nineteenth century. Industrialization, urbanization, and immigration continued to transform the United States into a complex, heterogeneous society. Moreover, the corporate sector's increasing integration and nationalization of the economy continued to diminish local and personal autonomy as the growth of the consolidated, bureaucratic structure of business and government accelerated. But mingling with the effects of the past was evidence of the emergence of a new, more distinctly modern society. Although there are a number of topics that could illuminate the key themes of the social history of the early twentieth century, this essay will focus on four: (1) the continued incorporation of America; (2) the emergence of a modern, consumer culture; (3) the changes surrounding women and the family that accompanied the erosion of the Victorian moral order; and (4) the importance of ethnic and racial pluralism.

THE INCORPORATION OF AMERICA

The incorporation of America—its development in the late nineteenth century as a more organized, centralized, and bureaucratic society shaped by the tremendous power of large corporations—continued into the twentieth century. During the Progressive reform era (roughly 1900–1914), many Americans expressed concern about the power of corporations and finance capitalism over the economy, politics, and workers. Progressivism was a complex movement of shifting coalitions with a variety of agendas encompassed under the reform umbrella. For some reformers, the threat of unrestrained power in the private sector was sufficient to justify expanding the public, or state, power. Promoted in part by muckraking, sensational journalism that exposed naked corporate power, reformers passed measures on the state level that would give some protection to factory workers. Political reforms, such as the direct election of senators, referendum, initiative, and recall, were touted as means to restore government to the people. In addition, Congress passed laws such as the Clayton Antitrust Act of 1914 and the Federal Reserve Act of 1913, which were limited efforts to curtail "bigness" and economic concentration.

Despite the celebration of the success of Progressive legislation, many of the laws had either limited impact or results different from those intended. Indeed, some powerful corporate concerns encouraged federal legislation that would help them rationalize their industries. Thus, large meat packers supported and profited from the Pure Food and Drug Act of 1906, which made it difficult for smaller businesses to compete with the larger firms that could more easily meet federal guidelines. Moreover, the Progressive spirit, with its marked antipathy to the power of corporate America and to businessmen in general, was short-lived; it was replaced in the 1920s with enthusiasm for business and businessmen.

World War I was an important factor in bringing about this reversal. The government and popular press celebrated big business and its wartime productivity as a crucial element in the successful military campaign. Equally significant was the enthusiasm for prosperity and the new consumer products that rolled off the assembly lines after the war's end. Although not everyone shared equally in the fruits of industry, it was hard not to marvel at the extraordinary industrial productivity, reflected in a 12 percent increase between 1910 and 1920 and a 64 percent rise in the period from 1920 to 1930.

In contrast with the prewar years, the 1920s was the heyday of the businessman. Presidents like the Republican Calvin Coolidge could pronounce to general agreement that "The man who builds a factory builds a temple. The man who works there, worships there" (quoted in Leuchtenburg, *Perils of Prosperity,* p. 188). Government enthusiasm went beyond presidential rhetoric. Guided by such men as Secretary of Commerce Herbert Hoover, the federal government assisted business at every turn. It helped promote trade associations of manufacturers who by working together could rationalize their industry and help direct the economy. It also assisted corporations in expanding abroad by using the Commerce Department to collect and distribute relevant information about foreign markets. Supreme Court decisions in the 1920s that protected trade associations from antitrust prosecution (for example, the Cement Manufacturers' Protective Association case, 1925), overturned a federal child labor law (for example, *Bailey* v. *Drexel Furniture Company,* 1922), and limited unions' ability to engage in successful strikes (for example, *Dorchy* v. *Kansas,* 1926) further underlined the pro-business climate.

With a sympathetic Republican leadership and Supreme Court, corporations were largely unrestrained. Internationally, monopolistic corporations flourished. Domestically, consolidations and mergers multiplied, and oligopoly reigned. The process extended to the movie industry. In 1912 more than sixty companies made movies, in contrast with the "Big Eight" that produced 90 percent of the films in the early 1920s. These firms controlled not only the making of films, but their distribution as well, by acquiring theater chains. As movie mogul Marcus Loew put it, "Chain store methods in the movies are just like what you had in railroads, telephones, and automobiles" (quoted in May, *Screening Out the Past,* p. 178).

This continued incorporation of America, with its favorable business climate, had a predictable impact on workers. More workers increasingly worked for large, impersonal firms. By 1923 more than half of the industrial labor force worked for companies with more than 250 employees. These firms represented only 4 percent of the manufacturers in the country. For industrial workers the problem continued to be, as it had been in the nineteenth century, one of control over the nature and conditions of work. As more industries were mechanized and electrified, jobs became increasingly specialized. Henry Ford's innovation of the moving assembly line, which was in place by 1914, was an example of the way in which technology and the management of technology and labor transformed the workplace and deemphasized the individual worker's skill and craft pride.

In the twentieth century, corporate efforts to control the worker, which included both the spread of scientific management and determined anti-union campaigns, intensified. The first two decades of the twentieth century were tumultuous ones for labor-management relations. Immediately after the recovery from the depression of the 1890s, unions, especially those of the craft-oriented American Federation of Labor, began to expand. The economic downturns of 1904 and 1907, as well as a carefully organized open-shop campaign, hampered union growth. But the period after 1909 saw a dramatic upsurge in labor unrest and strikes stemming not from the relatively elite, skilled workers who traditionally dominated unions but from unskilled workers, largely immigrants, in the mass industries. Among the most spectacular strikes were the 1909 International Ladies Garment Workers' Union's "uprising of the 20,000" and the Lawrence strike of 1912 against textile manufacturers.

A rise in radicalism accompanied this enthusiasm for industrial militancy and unionism. The Industrial Workers of the World, committed to anarcho-syndicalism, was established in 1905. It was small in numbers but participated in many significant strikes that coalesced labor discontent and radicalism. At the same time, socialists were gaining ground within the unions of the American Federation of Labor, and socialist candidates were making good showings in municipal elections. In 1912, Eugene Debs, the Socialist Party of America candidate, garnered 6 percent of the presidential vote.

The war years somewhat checked this labor militancy, as eagerness to maintain productivity made the federal government willing to offer some support to organized labor in its constant struggle for union recognition and bread-and-butter improvements. The government established the War Labor Board, which gave some protection and benefits to workers, extracting in exchange a no-strike pledge which nonetheless was often broken. Workers experienced hardships, but there was a certain amount of headiness over the progress made. With war's end, the federal government ceased its protective stance. Labor militancy exploded in 1919. More than four million workers—22 percent of the labor force—participated in thirty-six hundred strikes. The most disruptive were the Seattle general strike, the U.S. Steel strike, the police strike in Boston, and the coal strike. The strikes of 1919 stemmed from the desire to sustain the gains made during the war in the face of employer hostility and to resist the significant problem of inflation, which had been mounting since the beginning of the war. Some of these strikes were led or influenced by radicals, but their goals centered on bread-and-butter issues or the fight for union recognition. For the most part the strikes failed in the face of corporate power and government hostility.

The strikes were also part of the "red scare" of 1919–1920. Ostensibly aimed at Bolshevik agents in the United States, the red scare quickly extended to organized labor and immigrants. Raids of foreigners' organizations, witch-hunts for immigrant radicals, and the deportation of 249 aliens were the most extreme manifestations of the hysteria. The red scare not only destroyed radical organizations but also crippled unions, which newspapers and corporate leaders freely associated with the "red menace." Tainted with the stigma of bolshevism, unions were less able to resist the renewed open-shop campaign of the 1920s, appropriately titled the American Plan. For the rest of the decade, the established unions limped along and the mass industries remained unorganized.

Corporation spokesmen insisted that unions were unnecessary. To forestall organizing and to promote a loyal, efficient work force, the larger firms embarked on a scheme called welfare capitalism. Corporations sponsored company unions (with no power) and benefit plans, and improved factory conditions. Welfare capitalism made factories more humane for those who worked in the fewer than 25 percent of companies that experimented with the new techniques of managing workers. Even for workers who did not benefit from welfare capitalism, the increased prosperity of the 1920s, with its higher wages, fewer work hours, and affordability of consumer goods, may have helped to counter the appeal of unions. To some extent workers made a trade-off. They continued to be powerless vis-à-vis the corporation, but their situation was eased by an improved living standard.

But not all shared equally in the rising prosperity of the decade. African Americans and Hispanics, both urban and rural laborers, enjoyed little of it. Whole industries—coal, textiles, farming—were "sick" throughout the decade. For workers in most industries, unemployment and underemployment continued to be problems. Real wages did indeed rise, but hardly as dramatically as profits. Moreover, the distribution of income was highly skewed. In 1929, 5 percent of American families received one-third of all personal income. And although many workers may have enjoyed an improved standard of living, their expectations were rising. A decent standard of living increasingly included improved health care, education, and the consumer goods the advertising industry relentlessly hawked.

Thus, despite improvements, most workers lived a precarious existence. This is quite evident in *Middletown,* the classic 1929 sociological study of Muncie, Indiana. Helen and Robert Lynd painted a bleak picture of working-class life. They examined the process of de-skilling that had dehumanized the workplace, the decline of unions, and the insecurities of income that haunted working-class families. They also noted a trend that would intensify as the twentieth century progressed—workers in Middletown found alternative forms of satisfaction and measures of success through consumption. For Middletown workers, car ownership was a potent symbol of the freedom and enjoyment that they were denied in their work lives.

The Lynds intentionally isolated a small city that contained relatively few immigrants or African Americans, the better to study the modernization of American society without the complicating factors of ethnicity and race. This flawed plan undoubtedly shaped their findings. The bleakness of working-class life that the Lynds described may well have been shaped in part by their concentration on the white native-born which ignored the racial and ethnic communities that flourished in American cities and helped to sustain workers with a sense of family and tradition. Nonetheless, *Middletown* is a significant reminder of the limits on workers' share in the prosperity of the 1920s as well as of the changing conditions of work.

Blue-collar workers were not the only ones to be affected by increasing incorporation. The supercorporations of the twentieth century were, with few exceptions, no longer the family dynasties of the nineteenth century. Stockholders owned them and professional managers, whose responsibilities went beyond mere production and included planning, distributing, and advertising, ran them. This managerial revolution meant an expansion of the white-collar work force, from high-level managers to clerical workers. The "new" middle class, salaried white-collar employees, increased eightfold in the period from 1870 to 1910.

For the high-level managers, staffing the bureaucracy could mean a loss of autonomy, but it had the compensation of salary, status, and power within the corporation. For the lower-level white-collar workers, their corporate world had parallels with that of the working class: they found increasing specialization, discipline, and regimentation. This was particularly true in the clerical field, which was a significant area of expansion for women workers but which yielded limited opportunities for advancement, was repetitive, and was poorly paid. But for many white-collar workers on the lower rungs of the ladder, clerical work meant a significant rise in status from the blue-collar work force.

The transformation of the white-collar work force also led to shifting notions of the meaning of success. The nineteenth-century Horatio Alger ideas, anachronistic even then, linked success to individualistic virtues of hard work, sobriety, temperance, restraint, and piety. In the twentieth century, writers continued to insist that individualism and success worked, even within the corporate world. But the traits for success shifted somewhat. Personality and style became key elements, and the ability to handle people and to sell oneself were stressed. With the help of the burgeoning advertising industry, consumption—the acquisition of appropriate clothes and accoutrements—became part of the method of success in the twentieth century. Thus success was still possible, but it was within the corporate context and required "style" and consumption.

THE CONSUMER CULTURE

This change in the content of the success ethos was part of a broader transformation of American culture into a consumer society. The consumer society contrasted with the Victorian entrepreneurial ethos of the nineteenth century, which emphasized the production of primary industrial goods and an ethic of scarcity, restraint, sacrifice, and frugality. In contrast, the consumer society was characterized by leisure, relative affluence, and an emphasis on consumer goods and personal satisfaction. By the turn of the century, American society already had many hallmarks of a consumer society. Commercialized leisure—amusement parks, professional sports, and nickelodeons (the forerunners of movies) were already part of the urban world. The middle classes were enjoying the convenience of mass-produced goods such as items of interior decoration and indoor plumbing. Moreover, the advertising industry was already booming by 1900, beginning the process of creating wants and promoting an ideology of consumption as a means to self-actualization.

After World War I, the trend accelerated. Higher wages, lower prices, installment buying, and technological innovations spread the delights of consumption to many members of the working class, who aspired to own the new products transforming the home—electric irons, refrigerators, and vacuum cleaners, all of which took advantage of the increased electrification of the American home. Americans were also spending more money on leisure. By 1928, one-fourth of the national income went to leisure pursuits. Athletics was an especially important part of the new leisure, with mass spectator sports as well as participatory activities gaining dramatically in popularity. One observer captured this new emphasis on leisure succinctly: "To call this a land of labor is to impute last century's epithet to it, for now it is a land of leisure" (quoted by Noverr and Ziewacz, in Baydo, *Evolution of Mass Culture,* p. 103).

In *Middletown,* the Lynds recognized the automobile as one of the most crucial "inventions re-making leisure." As one of their informants exclaimed, "Why on earth do you need to study what's changing this country? . . . I can tell you what's happening in just four letters: A-U-T-O!" (p. 251). Increasingly more people were able to take advantage of the cheaper, mass-produced cars that Henry Ford began introducing by 1914. In 1900, eight hundred cars had been produced; by 1912, the figure was over one million; and by 1929, almost twenty-seven million cars were on the highways. The car industry was crucial to the economy. Not only was it a major industry and employer, it also supported many others—component parts, steel, rubber, and road building. Furthermore, because the car promoted the suburban boom, it assisted the construction industry. In addition to its obvious economic impact, the automobile changed the face of the American landscape—the roads built to accommodate it connected city to country and suburbs to the workplace—and made places like Los Angeles, sprawling metropolises with no core urban centers, possible. A mass-produced product, the car helped to minimize regional differences among Americans and to shape more standardized tastes. It changed patterns of leisure as well—vacations, drives in the country, and even courtship were affected by the automobile revolution.

Radio was yet another important arena for leisure time. When it was first developed, its future uses were unclear. Initially radio was a hands-on form of entertainment; listeners often constructed their own equipment and amused themselves by trying to pick up signals from distant radio stations. Because of the nature of their equipment and the low power of most stations in the early days, local stations, many of which were owned by churches, educational institutions, and even labor unions, dominated radio. In Chicago, as Lizabeth Cohen has pointed out, radio initially did not tend toward a standard, mass-produced product. It began to change to its more modern form in the mid 1920s when a New York station accepted the first paid advertisement. In 1926, the first national network, the National Broadcasting System, emerged; a year later, the Radio Act of 1927 rationalized the rather chaotic stations by means of regulations that were conducive to both commercial radio and national networks. By 1930, one-third of the nation's stations were commercial and one-fifth were linked to the networks, a transformation which would make the 1930s the heyday of radio programs that made people like Jack Benny and Amos and Andy nationally known. By then, the radio was clearly a national medium which could mold American tastes and opinions.

The most dramatic "invention re-making leisure" in this period was the movies. In the early years of the century, nickelodeons appealed primarily to working-class audiences. But after 1910, as entrepreneurs targeted the middle classes by opening theaters in more "respectable" districts, and movie producers made their films more sophisticated by introducing theatrical plots, or "photoplays," movies began to appeal to a wider audience. By the 1920s in urban areas films were shown in motion picture "palaces" characterized by exotic buildings, luxurious appointments, and uniformed ushers. The new theaters were part of a self-conscious assumption that films promoted a "democracy of consumption." Movie promoters insisted that in the luxurious theaters, enjoying vicarious splendors in the films, all classes could enjoy themselves equally. This theme was not unique to the film industry—the promise that consumption could erode inequalities in American life appeared frequently in advertising copy as well.

Movies transformed leisure patterns as millions of Americans incorporated moviegoing into their daily lives. Equally significant were the messages that movies embodied. With the powerful impact of visual imagery, enhanced after 1927 with the introduction of sound, they helped to shape mass taste and opinion. Films were showcases for consumer goods, especially clothing, and their plots often addressed themes appropriate to an emerging consumer culture. As Lary May has argued, movie stars like Douglas Fairbanks reflected and indeed promoted the consumer culture. Both in his personal life and in films, Fairbanks extolled the virtues of play: "We read so much of work and success that someone needs to preach the glory of play" (quoted in May, p. 114).

In promoting physical fitness, spontaneity, and youth as conscious ideals, Fairbanks implicitly offered the world of leisure as an alternative to the boring, humdrum world of corporate bureaucracies, and hinted that work was valuable primarily for the leisure and products it could finance. Fairbanks was also one of many stars who were contributing to the rejection of the Victorian moral code. In his early films, he exuded healthy physicality but toned down the potential eroticism by retaining youthful, all-American qualities. By the mid 1920s, however, Fairbanks was playing dark-skinned, more lusty heroes, and was part of a broader trend popularized by Latin lover Rudolph Valentino, who projected a more overtly erotic image.

Films also projected a new version of womanhood. As Mary Ryan has noted, the rising female stars of the 1920s—Madge Bellamy, Clara Bow, and Joan Crawford, with their physical freedom, energy, and independence—represented the modern woman. The new style of vibrant physicality included an emphasis on sexual attractiveness, as many films featured displays of female flesh in lingerie and scenes set in opulent bathrooms. The new sexuality was often expressed through consumption. Indeed, most heroines achieved their attractiveness to the opposite sex not through the body but through the clothes, jewelry, and cosmetics that adorned it. Films such as *Charge It* and *Gimme* underscored the point. In keeping with this theme of sexuality and consumption, many movies employed the "makeover plot," in which a dowdy, restrained matron traded her old-fashioned clothes for flapper attire as a means of regaining her husband. The makeover movies reveal the limits to women's film transformation. Films might feature sexuality, even infidelity, but women's aim throughout most movies was marriage or the maintenance of marriage. Despite the titillation these films offered, they tended to tame sexuality and keep it from threatening the social fabric.

WOMEN AND THE FAMILY

The ambivalent messages about modern women in films paralleled the experiences of women offscreen. As early as the 1890s, there were the beginnings of popular perceptions of the "new woman," a term that referred to the increasing activism of middle-class women in social reform and the suffrage movement, to women's increased college attendance and modest entry into the professions, and to young women's new athleticism and rejection of weighty, restrictive Victorian garments. After World War I, many observers were convinced that women had achieved emancipation—politically, economically, and sexually. There were indeed significant changes for women in the early twentieth century, but just as films indicated the persistence of traditional values about women, so there were significant limits to the degree of freedom or equality modern women experienced.

Beginning in the late nineteenth century, middle-class women reformers had challenged traditional notions of woman's place within the home, and through their voluntary associations they had become political actors by lobbying for reform legislation, such as factory and child labor laws, prohibition, and a wide variety of campaigns to clean up the cities. Women also continued the battle for full political rights through suffrage. Their rhetoric in defense of the vote reflected the influence of the reform ethos. Unlike the women of the antebellum reform era, who in 1848 at Seneca Falls had issued a proclamation based on the Declaration of Independence's insistence upon equal rights, a significant number of twentieth-century suffragists argued that women should be given the vote for the good they could do with it. Women would bring their moral influence into the political arena and enact wide-ranging reforms. The practical uses of the vote attracted both elite and middle-class reformers as well as working-class women to the campaign. Black women, although generally rebuffed by white women's organizations, also supported the campaign, which they viewed as part of the path toward racial progress.

The long battle for suffrage heated up in 1910 as success in the state of Washington brought renewed enthusiasm to the campaign. At about the same time, more radical voices began to be heard within the women's movement. Although elite and middle-class women were in the forefront of the suffrage movement, working-class and socialist women were a growing presence and helped to strengthen the Congressional Union, later called the National Woman's Party. In 1914, led by Alice Paul, the Congressional Union split from the more conservative National American Woman Suffrage Association (NAWSA), which was directed by Carrie Chapman Catt. Paul insisted upon a national amendment campaign and also on partisan political pressure, calling upon women with the vote to use it at the polls to defeat the party in power—in this case, the Democrats. Influenced both by British suffragists and by the experiences of American working-class women with industrial strikes, the Congressional Union members picketed the White House during World War I. Upon being arrested, they went on well-publicized hunger strikes. NAWSA leaders were distressed by the militant tactics, and continued their more moderate campaigns in which they emphasized women's service to the country during wartime. This uneasy alliance of a wide variety of women, pursuing different tactics, finally overcame determined opposition: the Nineteenth Amendment was ratified in 1920.

In the first years after passage, women's groups, including the newly formed League of Women Voters, expected a permanent, influential voting bloc of women. Politicians clearly anticipated that women would be a potent force in politics. The Democratic convention of 1920 incorporated twelve of fifteen League of Women Voters' recommendations in its platform; the Republican party endorsed five. The biggest success of women lobbyists was the 1921 passage of the Sheppard-Towner Act for educational instruction in health care for mothers and babies. Women's groups, primarily through the efforts of the newly formed Women's Joint Congressional Committee, had lobbied intensively for the bill, threatening retaliation at the polls if it was not passed. But after initial successes, women's political influence seemed to fade: the Sheppard-Towner program was eventually phased out, and politicians stopped listening to women lobbyists. While some of this decreasing influence of women voters can be traced to a general lessening of reform enthusiasm in the 1920s, other factors are equally important. For despite women's and politicians' expectations, no female bloc emerged. Women's voter turnout was quite light, and they appeared not to vote along gender lines. Women divided on the basis of class, ethnicity, and race, divisions always evident within the women's movement but more easily submerged before the achievement of suffrage when women activists could come together for a common goal.

Divisions within their ranks damaged the ability of women to organize during the 1920s. African American women in the National Association of Colored Women sought the assistance of the National Woman's Party and the League of Women Voters in their campaign to register black women in the South. Neither offered support, and Alice Paul, speaking for the National Woman's Party, insisted that it was a race problem, not a women's problem. Black women pursued their campaign alone and did accomplish some increase in their registration. Despite little support from white women's organizations, they also tackled other significant issues, including continuing a long-standing battle against lynching through the Women's Anti-Lynching Crusaders.

There were divisions among white women as well. The National Woman's Party, composed of women who called themselves feminists, focused primarily on equal rights for women, and was responsible for introducing the Equal Rights Amendment (ERA) in Congress in 1923. But many former suffragists earnestly opposed the ERA because they feared it would damage social welfare laws that protected women. Thus the League of Women Voters fought the ERA and instead worked for social welfare laws for both women workers and children, achieving a degree of success on the state and local levels. The existence of these activists, despite their differences, is indicative of a small but dedicated cadre of politically committed women. But their inability to galvanize the masses of women to support their efforts suggests that the suffrage amendment had relatively little impact in changing the political consciousness of most women in the 1920s.

Nor was work a source of tremendous liberation. Just as it was popularly believed that suffrage had led to a new spirit of equality among women, so it was assumed that women were becoming economically independent in the early twentieth century, especially after World War I. As Frederick Lewis Allen put it in his popular history *Only Yesterday* (1931), women "poured out of schools and colleges into all manner of occupations." It was this economic independence that Allen and many other observers felt had led to the "slackening of husbandly and parental authority." In turn had come a moral revolution which encouraged both divorce and women's "headlong pursuit of freedom."

This view of women, work, and liberation is distorted and inaccurate. The war had little permanent impact on women working—only 5 percent of women working during the war were new workers. The most significant rise in women in the work force came between 1900 and 1910, when the percentage of women who worked rose from 20.4 to 25.2. Around 1910, an internal change in the female work force also could be noted, as a dramatic increase in clerical jobs opened up new opportunities for middle-class women, who would have found factory work and domestic service incompatible with their class. Although it offered young, single, middle-class women new opportunities for employment and also for interaction with men in the workplace, clerical work was for the most part badly paid and repetitive. Indeed, for the majority of women, the work available continued to be poorly paid and exploitative.

Nowhere was this more evident than in the experience of black women. Besides farm work, in the early twentieth century they had two occupational choices: teaching, for a tiny minority with sufficient education and opportunity, and domestic service. World War I, with its urban migration of southern blacks, brought some increased opportunities for black women in the least desirable factory jobs. After the war, however, most of these jobs reverted to immigrant white women, and black women who had sought northern factory jobs found themselves employed primarily as domestic servants. Pay was low and the hours were long. And, more than any other racial or ethnic group, married black women found it necessary to work to keep their families afloat. In 1920, five times more married black women than women in any other group were in the paid work force. The experience of black women provides the most potent example that the increase in the number of working women did not translate into women's equality or freedom.

For white women, there was a rise in access to the professions, but the professions most open to women continued to be the nurturing ones of nursing, teaching, and social work. And even in these fields, women met with discrimination. In the 1920s, eight out of ten teachers were women, but they constituted only one in sixty-three superintendents. Women earned about 15 percent of doctorates but represented only 4 percent of full professors. Given the limited opportunities and the discrimination women encountered in the work force, it is difficult to see access to the professions as a factor creating a new, liberated woman. Neither voting nor working really accounts for the new woman so touted by the public.

But there *was* a new woman. The change came not primarily in the public arena but in the private, as increasingly women sought more freedom in their social lives. At the forefront of this change were the working-class young women who by the turn of the century were seeking in Kathy Peiss's words, cheap amusements. To escape from parental authority and from the harsh conditions of work, young women took advantage of the new urban amusements—dance halls, amusement parks, theaters. These unchaperoned, relatively anonymous environments inevitably led to sexual experimentation. Relaxing of sexual standards may also have stemmed from the widespread practice of treating. Poorly paid and often contributing what little they did make to family incomes, these women had few resources to allow them to pay for their entertainments. Men could and did treat them, but frequently with the implicit assumption of sexual favors as part of the exchange. These young women, then, experienced more relaxed sexual standards than those of their parents. At the same time, more elite, "bohemian" women in New York's Greenwich Village, influenced by Sigmund Freud and Havelock Ellis, were also promoting a more liberated personal life-style. In addition to challenging sexual standards, the women were resisting traditional notions of female modesty, gentility, and restraint.

By the 1920s, these changes, filtered to large numbers of women, were taken up by the media, and trumpeted. In particular, young women wanted increased equality with men in matters of style and behavior. They insisted upon their rights to drink and smoke in public, to be unrestrained in their behavior, and, in particular, to obtain sexual satisfaction. This new emphasis on sexuality was evident in changed expectations about the marital sexual relationship. Prompted by the media, the popularization of Freud, and the increasing availability and use of birth control, the ideal marriage was more sexual. Moreover, prevailing norms recognized more erotic contact among unmarried men and women. It is easy to overstate the revolution in sexual mores. Despite the liberalization of sexuality, according to the prevailing norms, intercourse was still reserved to committed couples and, moreover, the double standard was still in place, with women protecting their reputations by exercising discretion and restraint in their sexual choices. Many contemporaries viewed the changes for women as liberating, for many did achieve more equality in the personal arena. But enhanced freedom was also accompanied by sexual objectification, clearly evidenced in the movies and advertising of the time, and thus ushered in the modern trend of defining women in terms of their sexual allure.

Despite the limits to the transformation in women's experiences, many observers were alarmed by the changes embodied in the new woman that they correctly viewed as threatening Victorian notions of womanhood. To the native-born, white middle classes, the idea of women as moral guardians of the home gave them very specific roles in maintaining social order and progress. By controlling their men's passions, women could promote men's entrepreneurial success. And as guardians of the home, they ideally maintained the family as a linchpin of social stability. The phenomena of women's sexuality, work, and even voting, then, not only contradicted Victorian assumptions about women but could be viewed as threatening the stability of the home and society. The threat was all the more alarming because of the growing divorce rate. The number of divorces began to accelerate in the late nineteenth century; in 1880 there was one divorce for every twenty-one marriages. By 1890, the figure was one in twelve, and by 1924, one in seven. Not surprisingly, disturbed observers placed the blame on the new woman and her new freedoms.

While changes in women's experiences may have influenced the divorce rates, there are other compelling explanations. One is the growing secularization of American society which was evident in the early twentieth century. Although religious faith certainly persisted, religion was less important in the public arena of American life. Accompanying this trend was a decrease in the number of marriages sanctified by religious authority. In Middletown, the Lynds found that 85 percent of the marriages were religious in 1890, but only 63 percent were religious in 1923. As marriage became viewed as less sacred, it was not surprising to see a rise in marriage dissolutions.

Yet another crucial factor influencing divorce was change in the family. In the twentieth century, family size continued the gradual decline seen in the nineteenth century. In 1900, the average family consisted of 4.7 persons; in 1910, of 4.5 persons; and in 1920, of 4.3 persons. Although family size shrank in the population as a whole, the change was especially noticeable among the urban middle classes, who were likely to limit their families to between one and three children. Beyond changes in size, scholars of the family have noted that, at least for the middle class, the nature of families was changing as well. These smaller families tended to emphasize the individual potential of each child, and were less authoritarian and more democratic.

Family function changed as well. By the twentieth century, not only did families cease to function as productive economic units, but the social and educative activities associated with the family were absorbed by outside agencies. Increasingly privatized, the family's function became the psychological nurture of its members. The rise of the "affectionate" family changed expectations not only for child rearing but also for marriage. As Elaine Tyler May has argued, popular ideals increasingly emphasized marriage as the source of personal satisfaction, in contrast with the Victorian ideal, which had posited marriage as part of public duty. The changing nature of work, with its increasing bureaucracy and regimentation, accelerated this process of placing heavy emotional demands on marriage and the family as a source of personal fulfillment. It is not surprising that many marriages could not meet the great expectations that were imposed upon them.

ETHNIC AND RACIAL PLURALISM

Incorporation, the consumer culture, and changes in women and the family were all hallmarks of an emerging modern society. A final component of modern America that was a source of exceptional social conflict was ethnic and racial pluralism. This pluralism and the conflict it engendered were rooted primarily in America's cities, which in the twentieth century were growing at a rapid pace. In 1900, twenty-eight million people (36.9 percent of the population) crowded the sixty-three major metropolitan areas of the country. By 1930, over fifty-nine million (48.2 percent) lived in cities. This dramatic growth derived in part from immigration, but also from domestic rural-to-urban migration. Both blacks and whites responded to the economic promise the cities seemed to hold. Not surprisingly, as the cities grew, so did the suburbs; and by the 1920s, outlying areas of major cities were growing more rapidly than the cores of the cities. Technology—first the electric streetcar and later the automobile—fostered suburbanization by dramatically simplifying the commute from home to office. The suburban boom stemmed in part from the appeal of the pastoral image, an ideal dear to modern Americans. In embracing the simpler life they were also rejecting the disorder of the city. And in particular, for many the suburbs represented removal from the growing ethnic pluralism of American cities.

At the heart of this pluralism were the immigrant communities that had transformed the face of the cities. A trend evident in the nineteenth century, strong immigrant communities, strengthened by religious and fraternal institutions, newspapers, work patterns, and shared language and culture, persisted into the twentieth century. One significant change from the nineteenth century was a shift in immigrant origins. After 1890, "old" immigrants from northern Europe were joined by the "new" immigrants from southern and eastern Europe, Asia, and Mexico. Although similar conditions encouraged the new immigrants' decision to migrate—the pull of American jobs and the push of hardships in the old country—the new immigrants were more set apart from old stock Americans than the northern Europeans had been. The old immigration consisted largely of Protestants or, in the case of Irish Catholics, English speakers. The new immigrants—with Italians the largest group and Jews from southern and eastern Europe in second place—were predominantly Catholic and Jewish. Mexicans and Asians made the new immigrants racially diverse. The new immigrants, then, added significantly to the heterogeneity of American culture and society, and the ethnic communities that characterized the American cities of the Northeast, Midwest, and West multiplied. By 1920, 13 percent of the American population consisted of first-generation immigrants, and another 21.5 percent were their children.

Whether working in the steel mills of Pennsylvania, the packing plants of Chicago, the garment industries of New York, or the fields of California, or as personal servants in middle-class homes, most immigrants were poor and worked and lived under harsh conditions. The harshness was mitigated to some extent by the strength of ethnic communities and services that kin and voluntary associations provided. Work patterns often reinforced ethnic ties: Jewish workers dominated the clothing industry, Italians often concentrated in the construction industry, and the Japanese in California clustered in agricultural production and distribution. Out of economic necessity, most families depended on a household economy.

Few immigrant cultures countenanced wives' working for wages, but immigrant wives helped to sustain the family through taking in boarders or doing piecework. Families relied heavily on their children. Southern and eastern Europeans sent both male and female children out to work. The family economy often strengthened familial bonds. That daughters turned over their pay packets to their mothers revealed a strong sense of family obligation. The vital contribution of children's wages, however, may also have served to diminish the strong patriarchal nature of the traditional societies from which immigrants had come. This problem of meshing traditional cultures with economic realities was just one of the adjustments the New World necessitated.

Immigrants also had to cope with strong currents of nativism. World War I was an important watershed for European immigrants. It stopped their immigration temporarily, shutting off the infusion of new blood that sustained the vitality of the ethnic communities. At the same time, the war prompted tremendous anxiety about unassimilated immigrants within American society. Nativist fears led to a strong pressure on immigrants to prove their loyalty, a drive reinforced by many ethnic and religious leaders. This wartime commitment to what was called "100 percent Americanism" led to a more extreme expression of the drive for conformity, the 1919 red scare. The fury died down by 1920, but not until it had unleashed deep-seated suspicions about the loyalty of American immigrants.

The war and the red scare, coupled with extensive nativist publicity that reflected anti-Semitism, anti-Catholicism, racism, and fear of radicalism, eventually led to immigration restriction. Congress passed a temporary act in 1921 and followed it in 1924 with the National Origins Act (Johnson-Reed Act). The act established 2 percent immigration quotas that were based on the 1890 census, thereby effectively discriminating against southern and eastern Europeans. Reflecting intense agitation on the west coast, the act excluded Asian immigration altogether. The efforts of western agricultural interests, eager to maintain a cheap pool of labor, blocked the drive to exclude Mexican immigration; in contrast with other groups, Mexican immigration expanded dramatically in the 1920s, with 485,945 entering between 1920 and 1929.

In the long run, the National Origins Act undoubtedly worked to weaken strong European ethnic communities. The vitality of the community depended in part on the constant infusion of newcomers to sustain the separateness of the culture. Over time, the absence of new immigrants softened the edges of ethnic communities. In contrast, Japanese and Mexican immigrants and their children had few options which would permit the integration that would vitiate ethnic identity. Mexican immigrants, unaffected by restriction and subject to virulent racism, continued to build strong ethnic urban communities, for despite the image of Mexicans as agricultural workers, in the 1920s almost half were urban dwellers. Japanese immigration, which had been significantly limited by the 1907 Gentlemen's Agreement, was not substantially affected by the 1924 legislation. But racial segregation, a widespread phenomenon on the west coast, turned the Japanese community inward, and throughout the interwar years, its members sustained a strong sense of their culture and identity.

Even among European immigrants, there is strong evidence for a continuing ethnic identity. The immediate response of many immigrant, Catholic, and Jewish leaders to the extreme nativism they encountered after the war was a militant insistence on immigrant, Catholic, and Jewish rights. They called for a more inclusive sense of Americanism and attempted to demonstrate their own groups' allegiance to and contributions to American culture. Insisting upon their loyalty to America, they nonetheless sought to maintain a sense of ethnic identity and pride, and in doing so, they articulated a version of cultural pluralism that praised diversity.

Ethnic ties also transcended the boundaries of the old ethnic ghettos. The modest economic mobility of second-generation European immigrants led to movement out of the areas of the first settlement. This dispersal did not necessarily mean a merging with mainstream America. Jews, for example, in part because of residential discrimination patterns and in part because of choice, congregated in new suburbs. Although upwardly mobile and ready to cast off the immigrant past, these second-generation immigrants often sought to maintain their ethnic identity, which they reinforced by creating Americanized forms of traditional institutions. For other immigrant groups, relocation often meant shedding the congestion and harsh poverty of the immigrant ghetto, but not the sense of kinship that had characterized ethnic identity.

In the early years of the century, as Lizabeth Cohen's study of Chicago ethnic communities shows, the onset of mass culture—advertising, chain stores, radios, movies, all propagating a national, homogeneous taste—threatened ethnic identity. However, until the late 1920s, at least, ethnic institutions maintained their hold on the community—insurance companies, banks, and small stores held their own against national insurance firms, mainstream banks, and chain stores. Similarly, in the early days of radio, programs were localized and reflected community interests, with some stations broadcasting "nationality hours" and others programming for ethnic audiences. Even movies were viewed in an ethnic setting, with neighborhood theaters including ethnic live entertainment and providing a meeting ground for the community. By the end of the decade, communities' ability to resist the homogenizing nature of national institutions had weakened significantly. This change, as well as the Great Depression, led to a greater degree of class identification that overcame some of the intense ethnic loyalty that had made labor organizing so difficult in earlier years.

As Cohen suggests, unions eventually became one means of integration into the mainstream. Another was through politics. Immigrant support for urban political machines was a long-standing source of grievance for the native born. Indeed, the Progressive era's experiments in urban reform—including redrawing of municipal and school election districts, touted as a way to restore "democracy"—were in fact efforts to minimize immigrant voting strength and restore political and social power to old-stock elites. Reformers met only temporary success in routing urban machines. Moreover, during the 1920s ethnic voters increasingly identified with the Democratic Party, and by the Great Depression years were an important component of the new urban liberalism that underlay Franklin D. Roosevelt's New Deal.

The political activity of immigrants and their leaders' insistence upon cultural pluralism were indications of rising expectations. Rising expectations were evidenced in yet another source of urban growth in the early twentieth century: the migration of southern blacks to the cities of the North. This migration had begun before World War I, but the war years turned the trickle into a flood. The years 1916–1918 were the most intensive, as 500,000 streamed into Chicago, New York, Pittsburgh, and other cities. The migration subsided briefly, then continued in the 1920s, when one million made the trek north. Part of the impetus to migrate stemmed from the desire to leave the South. The years 1914–1915 were particularly bad ones; crops were ruined by boll weevils and floods. These natural disasters exacerbated an already fragile economic situation. African Americans in the South were tenants and sharecroppers easily exploited by white landlords. They were subject to peonage, the chain gang, and the lynch law. In 1918 alone, sixty-three African Americans were lynched.

But southern conditions had always been bad. It was not the push of the South as much as the pull of the North that explains the timing and the volume of the great migration. During the war years, the North held out the promise of jobs. The war had cut into factory employment by shutting off immigration and drawing off employees for military service. A decreasing labor pool at the same time war orders increased gave employers reason to look to a source of domestic labor they had not tapped—southern blacks. Some firms sent labor agents south to promote migration. Potential migrants also found out about opportunities in the North through word of mouth and through northern black newspapers like the *Chicago Defender*. Beyond economic opportunity, African Americans hoped that the North would bring them and their children better education and a more decent life.

With this combination of hopes, they moved north. The process of migration and resettlement was disorienting and disruptive. Migrants had to find jobs and housing, learn to operate in a cash economy, and adapt work patterns to the demands of modern industry. The process was made easier for many by chain migration, in which one member of the family left first, to prepare the way for others. Migration clubs sprang up and led to whole communities' moving together. Like immigrants, these internal migrants attempted to re-create community in cities, forming their own churches—often the storefront variety—buying southern-style barbecue, and patronizing businesses run by their former neighbors.

Despite the optimism that launched the migration, the promise of the North was not met. African Americans were laid off from the better industrial jobs when whites returned from the war. At the bottom of the industrial ladder, blacks' employment was precarious and opportunities limited for the rest of the decade in most cities. The dirtiest, hardest jobs were the ones open to them. Black women were excluded from the industrial work force almost completely and were left with the traditional domestic service jobs. The majority of unions, especially those in the American Federation of Labor, were hostile to African Americans and tolerated their organization only when it helped white workers.

African Americans' economic problems were deepened by the housing crisis. In most cities affected by migration, there was severe housing pressure, which was especially acute for African Americans because they were forced into segregated areas where rents were exorbitant and housing severely overcrowded. Those who attempted to buy in white areas faced harassment and violence. In 1919, black houses in Chicago were routinely bombed. Much of the animosity came from white ethnic groups resentful of encroachment and eager to protect their investments. Escape from Jim Crow proved to be overrated. De facto residential segregation, bolstered by housing covenants, was standard. Schools might be legally integrated, but neighborhood segregation led to their being heavily black. And these schools tended to be in crowded, older buildings where African Americans received inferior education. In the 1920s, northern cities saw other forms of discrimination multiply as restaurants, theaters, and swimming pools erected barriers to exclude and segregate African Americans.

Perhaps the most striking indication of the limits to black hopes for the North were the race riots that shattered cities across the nation. In 1917, East St. Louis, Illinois, was the scene of a bitter and destructive riot that killed almost forty African Americans. In 1919 violence emerged in several cities within a short period of time. Chicago had the major riot, and there were also outbreaks of violence in Knoxville, Tennessee; Omaha, Nebraska; Washington, D.C.; and Longview, Texas. Each riot had its own etiology, but the roots of conflict were in white denial of rising black expectations. In Chicago resentment of job competition, residential encroachment, and political influence fueled the tensions that ignited over the death of a black swimmer who had drifted into the white section of Lake Michigan. Although the riots were usually begun by white mobs that invaded black sections of a city, they were also characterized by black resistance. African Americans took the battle into white sections and fought back. Black resistance was part of a broader trend that observers termed "the New Negro."

These observers attributed the emergence of the "new Negro" both to the migration experience and to African Americans' experience with World War I. When the United States had entered the war, most black leaders viewed it as an opportunity for African Americans to prove their loyalty and establish their claims to equal citizenship. But as the war went on, they found, contrary to their expectations, that they had to fight even for the right to serve. They were frustrated not only by the military's segregation of black and white troops but also by the lack of provision for black officers and by the military's unwillingness to use African Americans in combat. Disillusionment led to strident militancy after the war, as black leaders insisted that black service during the war entitled all African Americans to full citizenship.

The New Negro also emerged in the Harlem Renaissance, an outpouring of literary and artistic endeavors by black artists who felt they represented the potential of black Americans and proof of their contribution to American culture. Another arena for the New Negro was the first mass movement of blacks in the twentieth century, the Universal Negro Improvement Association (UNIA), founded by Marcus Garvey in 1914; it came to the United States in 1916. Garvey brought the message of black pride and black militancy to urban blacks. A separatist who insisted that blacks could expect nothing from white society, he called for the development of separate black economic institutions. In addition, Garvey hoped to establish black control of Africa and, through a strong African nation, to provide protection to blacks everywhere. He attracted thousands of enthusiasts who marched in parades and invested in Garvey's Black Star Line, an all-black steamship company. The movement dissipated with Garvey's imprisonment for mail fraud in 1925, but not before the organization had done an important job in promoting black pride, self-help, and militancy.

As immigrants and African Americans entered the cities, urban areas become contested terrain. The housing crisis and fears of black encroachment made physical space one aspect of the contest. Immigrants and, to a lesser extent, African Americans challenged the old-stock elites' control of politics. The rising expectations of both groups further dismayed old stock Americans. Still another area of confrontation where a blend of class and ethnic issues came to the fore was urban leisure. Victorians had long been disconcerted by the working classes' amusements. They viewed their raucous play, gambling, fighting, and drinking as antithetical to the work ethic and harmful to public order. By the twentieth century, both technology and the rise of commercialized entertainment had led to a variety of urban amusements. Dance halls, penny arcades, amusement parks, and nickelodeons proliferated and symbolized to old-stock Americans the lack of restraint of the immigrant and black working classes.

The old-stock Americans were especially worried about prostitution and the white-slave traffic. In the late nineteenth and early twentieth centuries, elites mounted campaigns to suppress vice which included a watchful eye on commercial entertainments, the gathering places of young men and women. Reformers lobbied for a variety of measures that would regulate the environment of commercial establishments, especially as a means of protecting young women, and also offered alternative "wholesome amusements" such as chaperoned dances at settlement houses. Nickelodeons were especially alarming, with their dark environment and the dubious messages on the screen. Under fear of government intervention, a voluntary movie industry association in 1909 established what eventually became the National Board of Review, which censored films to weed out immorality—with mixed results. All of these efforts were attempts to establish Protestant "respectable" morality among the immigrant working classes as a means of achieving social order.

The most significant effort in this vein was, of course, prohibition. For the prohibitionists, the saloon had become a metaphor for the dislocations accompanying industrialization, urbanization, and immigration. To the anxious, old-stock middle classes, the saloon fostered vice, prostitution, sexual excess, and crime. It robbed the poor of their wages, working a burden on helpless women and children. As centers of ward politics, saloons formed a key part of the matrix of urban political corruption that was a constant concern of reformers. But central to the focus on the saloon was its association with the immigrant culture. The prohibition movement, which was given its greatest thrust by the Anti-Saloon League (founded in 1893), was inseparable from the nativism and anti-Catholicism that characterized mainstream culture. The goal behind prohibition was to bring immigrant culture into line with Protestant behavior and values. Feeling overwhelmed by immigrant masses whose religion, language, and values, especially in the realms of sexual morality, drinking, and leisure, seemed so much at odds with Protestant morality, prohibitionists hoped to use the law to coerce assimilation—to harness, as Norman Clark put it, "chaotic pluralism." After decades of agitation, the Eighteenth Amendment passed in 1919.

Prohibitionists won the first battle, but the issue continued to be an explosive one. Candidates' support for prohibition was a key factor in elections during the 1920s, as politicians with urban immigrant constituencies outspokenly criticized the "noble experiment." Difficulties with enforcement kept the controversy alive. Although prohibition undoubtedly did reduce alcohol consumption, especially among the poor, who could not afford illegal brews, the law was widely flouted. Until its repeal in 1933, a product of the Great Depression, prohibition continued to be an ongoing symbol of cultural conflict.

The Ku Klux Klan was yet another movement designed to impose the old-stock view of law and order on out-groups. The second Ku Klux Klan, as opposed to the post-Reconstruction Klan, emerged in 1915 on Stone Mountain, Georgia, when sixteen men lit a cross to symbolize the new Klan. Its membership increased sharply after 1919, and during its heyday, between 1920 and 1925, it had an estimated five million members. Its membership was limited to white, Protestant, native-born men, although it had women's and children's auxiliaries that helped to make the Klan a family affair. Klansmen saw themselves as representatives of 100 percent Americanism and shared an antipathy to blacks, Jews, immigrants, and Catholics. Although the nativist and racist side of the institution was an important part of its appeal, the Klan also presented itself as the protector of conventional morality and Protestantism.

The Klan attempted to meet its goals through vigilantism, in which it terrorized moral offenders, blacks, Jews, and Catholics, but it also utilized a more conventional channel, politics. It dominated politics in Indiana, Texas, Oklahoma, and Colorado, and was a potent political force in other states. In 1924, Klan forces helped to deadlock the Democratic national convention when representatives fought over whether to condemn the Klan by name, with the Klan forces victorious by one vote. The Klan was also a lobbying organization and was responsible in 1922, along with the anti-Catholic Freemasons, for passing a referendum in Oregon that would eliminate private schools. (The Supreme Court later held this anti-Catholic referendum unconstitutional.) On the national level, the Klan acted as a major lobbyist in support of immigration restriction. Despite its early successes, the order lost most of its strength by mid decade. The success of immigration restriction, which robbed the Klan of an important part of its agenda, was one factor. Excesses and exposure of malfeasance on the part of Klan officials further damaged the organization.

Although its popularity was short-lived, the Klan was nonetheless highly significant. It symbolized the tremendous anxiety old-stock Americans felt about immigrants, Catholics, Jews, and blacks, who were challenging the exclusive rights of white, native-born Protestants to control American society. But although nativism and racism were crucial to the appeal of the Klan, there was more anxiety under the surface. In many ways, the targets of the Klan—the various out-groups—were scapegoats for broader problems that troubled many Americans. The Klan represented a defensive movement against changes that had been transforming American society for decades. Incorporation had led to the spread of the power of corporations, changed the nature of work, and undermined individual autonomy. There were cultural challenges as well. With industrialization, urbanization, and immigration came an increasingly pluralistic society. The influx of immigrants, in addition to mounting secularism, threatened Protestantism's hold over American culture. Conflicting standards concerning women's roles and sexual morality led to anxiety over the "new woman" and the family. The emergence of a consumer culture, with its rejection of the ethos of restraint and its endorsement of such leisure-time pursuits as drinking, mass entertainment, and consumption, was still further evidence of a diversifying culture.

Not all Americans responded to these changes with the defensiveness of the Klansmen. Many embraced them as liberating and "modern." These developments in the early twentieth century were disruptive ones that made the period one of both reform and reaction, optimism and anxiety. The 1929 stock market crash that marked the beginning of the Great Depression helped to push many of these social and cultural themes to the background as economic concerns took center stage. But the issues of the early twentieth century—ethnic and racial conflict, corporate power, the changing nature of work, the role of women, and the implications of a mass, consumer culture—continued to be among the crucial problems with which Americans found themselves grappling at the end of the twentieth century.

BIBLIOGRAPHY

General Works

Carter, Paul A. *Another Part of the Twenties* (1977).

Hawley, Ellis W. *The Great War and the Search for a Modern Order: A History of the American People and Their Institutions, 1917–1933* (1979).

Leuchtenburg, William E. *The Perils of Prosperity, 1914–1932* (1958).

Lynd, Robert S., and Helen Merrell Lynd. *Middletown: A Study in American Culture* (1929).

Wiebe, Robert H. *The Search for Order: 1877–1920* (1967).

Corporate, Industrial World

Brody, David. *Workers in Industrial America: Essays on the Twentieth Century Struggle* (1980).

Chandler, Alfred D. *The Visible Hand: The Managerial Revolution in American Business* (1977).

Edwards, Richard C. *Contested Terrain: The Transformation of the Workplace in the Twentieth Century* (1979).

Green, James R. *The World of the Worker: Labor in Twentieth-Century America* (1980).

Montgomery, David. *The Fall of the House of Labor: The Workplace, the State, and American Labor Activism, 1865–1925* (1987).

Noverr, Douglas A., and Lawrence E. Ziewacz. "Sports in the Twenties." In *The*

Evolution of Mass Culture in America, 1877 to the Present, edited by Gerald R. Baydo (1982).

Zunz, Olivier. *The Changing Face of Inequality: Urbanization, Industrial Development, and Immigrants in Detroit, 1880–1920* (1982).

Consumer Culture

Cohen, Lizabeth. *Making a New Deal: Industrial Workers in Chicago, 1919–1939* (1990).

Marchand, Roland. *Advertising the American Dream: Making Way for Modernity, 1920–1940* (1985).

May, Lary. *Screening Out the Past: The Birth of Mass Culture and the Motion Picture Industry* (1980).

Ryan, Mary. "The Projection of a New Womanhood: The Movie Moderns in the 1920s." In *Our American Sisters: Women in American Life and Thought.* 3d ed., edited by Jean E. Friedman and William G. Shade (1982).

Women and the Family

Cott, Nancy F. *The Grounding of Modern Feminism* (1987).

DuBois, Ellen Carol. "Working Women, Class Relations, and Suffrage Militance: Harriot Stanton Blatch and the New York Women Suffrage Movement, 1894–1909." *Journal of American History* 74, no. 1 (1987): 34–58.

Fass, Paula. *The Damned and the Beautiful: American Youth in the 1920's* (1977).

Giddings, Paula. *When and Where I Enter: The Impact of Black Women on Race and Sex in America* (1984).

Kessler-Harris, Alice. *Out to Work: A History of Wage-earning Women in the United States* (1982).

Lemons, J. Stanley. *The Woman Citizen: Social Feminism in the 1920's* (1973).

May, Elaine Tyler. *Great Expectations: Marriage and Divorce in Post-Victorian America* (1980).

Peiss, Kathy. *Cheap Amusements: Working Women and Leisure in Turn-of-the-Century New York* (1986).

Immigrants

Bodnar, John. *The Transplanted: A History of Immigrants in Urban America* (1985).

Glenn, Susan A. *Daughters of the Shtetl: Life and Labor in the Immigrant Generation* (1990).

Romo, Ricardo. *East Los Angeles: History of a Barrio* (1983).

Takaki, Ronald T. *Strangers from a Different Shore: A History of Asian Americans* (1989).

African Americans

Grossman, James R. *Land of Hope: Chicago, Black Southerners, and the Great Migration* (1989).

Huggins, Nathan Irvin. *Harlem Renaissance* (1971).

Jones, Jacqueline. *Labor of Love, Labor of Sorrow: Black Women, Work, and the Family from Slavery to the Present* (1985).

Stein, Judith. *The World of Marcus Garvey: Race and Class in Modern Society* (1986).

Ethnic Conflict

Burner, David. *The Politics of Provincialism: The Democratic Party in Transition, 1918–1932* (1967).

Clark, Norman H. *Deliver Us from Evil: An Interpretation of American Prohibition* (1976).

Higham, John. *Strangers in the Land: Patterns of American Nativism, 1860–1925* (1955; corr. ed. 1975).

Jackson, Kenneth T. *The Ku Klux Klan in the City, 1915–1930* (1967).

Moore, Leonard J. "Historical Interpretations of the 1920's Klan: The Traditional View and the Populist Revision." *Journal of Social History* 24, no. 2 (1990): 341–357.

Murray, Robert K. *Red Scare: A Study in National Hysteria, 1919–1920* (1955).

SEE ALSO **Immigration; Labor: The Gilded Age Through the 1920s; The Market Revolution; Nativism, Anti-Catholicism, and Anti-Semitism; Radio; The Rise and Consolidation of Bourgeois Culture.**

THE GREAT DEPRESSION AND WORLD WAR II

Lizabeth Cohen

UNDERSTANDING THE SOCIAL HISTORY of a period of such intense change as the Great Depression and World War II necessitates integrating social analysis with more traditional political and economic history. Examining how social groups perceived and experienced the cataclysms of 1929 to 1945 deepens our understanding not only of the lives of ordinary Americans but also of the events themselves, which so often are recorded in history books as being disengaged from the people who made them happen or felt their impact. A social history of a decade and a half of tremendous upheaval must focus closely upon the interrelationship of specific social, economic, and political changes in American society with shifts in personal experience. How people of different social classes, ethnic and racial groups, genders, ages, and from different regions of the United States found their lives changed from 1929 to 1945 is the present concern. That story cannot be separated from the economic and political history of the Great Depression and World War II.

In order to analyze how the social groups just mentioned negotiated an era marked by both the worst economic depression and the greatest war mobilization in the nation's history, their experiences during three periods shall be examined: as the groups first faced the Great Depression from 1929 to 1933; as they encountered the New Deal, the Roosevelt administration's strategy for coping with the Depression, from 1934 to 1940; and as they lived through wartime, from 1941 to 1945. These people of course had multiple social identities—as, for example, a working-class, second-generation Polish female adolescent from Chicago, or a middle-class professional who was native, male, middle-aged, and living in California—and each characteristic contributed in a particular way to how the individuals felt the impact of the Depression and World War II.

ENCOUNTERING THE GREAT DEPRESSION, 1929–1933

Lore about the origin of the Great Depression fixes it to infamous dates such as "Black Thursday" and "Black Tuesday"—24 and 29 October 1929, when the stock market crashed—but in reality the economic downturn began at least a few years earlier; for many Americans, particularly farmers and unskilled workers, the 1920s had never been the so-called prosperity decade. Weaknesses and inequities in the economy had made the 1920s more advantageous for upper-class businessmen and their middle-class salaried employees than for factory workers, coal miners, or southern sharecroppers. The crash directly affected only the 10 percent of Americans who owned stock, and very seriously affected only less than half that number—those who had portfolios large enough to require a stockbroker; nonetheless, it signaled a new level of economic vulnerability, which had broad repercussions in American society.

As panic spread and confidence ebbed, the consumption of consumer goods—which had already been in decline since 1927—fell off sharply. Between 1929 and 1933, for example, annual sales of automobiles declined from $4.5 to $1.1 million, while construction spending plunged from $8.7 to $1.4 billion. This evaporation of markets led employers to lay off large numbers of workers, worsening what had been a periodic and seasonal fact of life throughout the 1920s. By 1932, one-fourth of the nation's work force was unemployed, and many of those with jobs were not working full-time. In many industrial centers joblessness climbed over 50 percent. Moreover, expectations of continued depression discouraged businessmen from parting with remaining dollars, to the point that business investment plummeted 88 percent from 1929 to 1933.

Life on the farm was no better. When agricultural prices and incomes took a sharp dive in 1930 from their already weakened state during the 1920s, farmers all over the country went bankrupt, frequently taking local banks with them. First rural and then urban banks went under, until more than six thousand banks had failed by 1933, due to the cumulative effects of the stock market crash, other banks defaulting on their obligations, and the withdrawal of savings by fearful depositors. Problems in national and international monetary policies also contributed to what became a worldwide economic crisis.

Class and Economic Crisis People's social class status determined to a large extent how they were affected by the Depression, as well as how they coped with the crisis. While some wealthy people went to bed rich, only to wake up paupers, and a few committed suicide rather than live without fortunes, the great majority of upper-class Americans did not experience the Depression in such sensational ways. More often, the business, industrial, and professional elites of America tightened their belts but continued to live comfortable lives—particularly when compared with many around them. Middle-class Americans were more vulnerable than their economic betters; many of the new white-collar jobs of the 1920s—in advertising, sales, insurance, personnel, and so forth—became more precarious in the midst of the Depression. However, there is no doubt that it was the working-class people, both in industrial centers and in agricultural America, who suffered the most: they were the ones most likely to lose jobs, property, and lifetime savings.

Although working-class Americans may have had the hardest time economically, they were in some ways better equipped to cope with the Depression than those with greater financial resources. Losing a job, depending on the collective earnings of the family (husband, wife, children, and even at times extended kin) to survive, sewing clothing, and planting a kitchen garden and canning for winter were all familiar experiences to industrial workers. Perhaps most important, they had learned during the 1920s to live with economic failure without blaming themselves for it. Many manufacturing workers, for example, had come to believe their employers' welfare capitalist ideology—which attributed workers' well-being to their bosses—so that when hard times came and jobs and company welfare programs were cut, workers pointed the finger at industrialists rather than at themselves.

Middle-class Americans, in contrast, had embraced a culture during the 1920s in which a nonworking wife, schoolgoing children, and high household consumption were indicators of success, particularly that of the chief family breadwinner. When a middle-class family suddenly faced unemployment and scarcity, the psychological cost was often high. These individuals were more likely to blame themselves than the system for their newfound dependency and debt. Historians who emphasize that Americans felt shame at financial failure and being on relief during the Depression are often generalizing from the experience of the middle class.

Working people were also more likely than others to express discontent through collective action in the early Depression, a reflection perhaps of their propensity to fix blame on external forces. In the agricultural Midwest, a militant farmers' organization, the Farmers' Holiday Association, barricaded highways to stop underpriced products from going to market and took other actions to protest low prices. In the cities, thousands of workers joined unemployed councils organized by the Communist party and similar organizations founded by socialists to demand more government relief, better treatment at relief stations, and an end to evictions and the cut-off of gas and electricity when rents and bills went unpaid. Although in general the labor movement remained in the dormant state it had been in since its defeat after World War I (union members made up only 12 percent of the industrial work force in 1930), underground locals organized by Communists and rank-and-file shop-floor efforts were beginning to appear in plants during the early 1930s.

Probably the most significant mass political action of the early Depression took place in the summer of 1932. Seventeen thousand unemployed veterans of World War I marched on Washington to demand payment of their veterans' bonuses, which were not due until 1945. When many of them settled into "Bonus City," a shantytown, to keep their plight in the public eye, President Hoover refused to talk to their leaders and called out the U.S. Army to remove them. The violent confrontation between armed soldiers and impoverished Bonus Marchers contributed to the public's growing lack of confidence in how Hoover was managing the Depression.

Although Communists and other committed radicals often created the structures through which working-class people protested in the early 1930s, organizers learned quickly that the average discontented American was seeking not revolutionary change but rather increased attention from the existing authorities, particularly the government. One Communist organizer of the unemployed recalled how he and others had "spent the first few weeks agitating against capitalism" (Nelson et al., *Steve Nelson,* p. 76). In time, however, they learned that what worked best was "to shift way from a narrow, dogmatic approach to what might be called a grievance approach to organizing. We began to raise demands for immediate federal assistance to the unemployed, and a moratorium on mortgages."

In fact, the most prevalent kind of political protest undertaken by Americans of all social classes in the early Depression was not political agitation but traditional political participation. They voted in larger numbers than ever before for the Democratic party, which—excepting the period from 1911 to 1920—had been subordinate at the federal level to the Republican party since the late 1890s. In 1930 voters barely gave the Republicans enough support for them to retain their control of the House and Senate. Then in 1932 they elected Democratic candidate Franklin Delano Roosevelt to the presidency in a landslide victory of 22.8 million against Republican incumbent Herbert Hoover's 15.7 million, and they gave the Democrats big majorities in both houses of Congress as well.

Social class nonetheless shaped the way and extent to which individuals participated in this electoral upheaval. Upper-class voters for the most part stayed loyal to Republican President Hoover and his message that self-reliance, business voluntarism, local government, private charities, and reduced federal spending and involvement would lead to recovery. Middle-class Americans who were suffering increasingly in the Depression tended to vote Democratic, but more as a rejection of Hoover than as an endorsement of Roosevelt. Working-class people, on the other hand—including many first- and second-generation Americans who had only begun to take an interest in national elections with the Democratic candidacy of Alfred E. Smith in 1928 and who rarely voted before the thirties—supported Roosevelt in 1932 in hopes that he would offer some new solutions to the crisis. What these remedies would be was not at all clear to working-class voters, nor was it clear to Roosevelt himself. As will become evident, by 1936 they would vote for FDR with even greater enthusiasm, actively endorsing his New Deal program and convinced that he had the interests of the working people at heart. Thus, much of the political response to the onset of the Depression took place within the traditional structure of the two-party system, not as a radical challenge to it; nevertheless, class tensions were manifest in this response, and they would be all the more evident by 1936. Significantly, an economic cataclysm of this magnitude, which offered Americans some unity in misery, reinforced class divisions already existing in society.

Ethnicity and Economic Crisis People's experiences in the early years of the Great Depression depended not only on their social class but also on their ethnicity and race. For example, Mexicans had entered the United States in increasing numbers after World War I to work in agriculture, on railroads, and in industry, first as strikebreakers and then to compensate for the loss in European immigration with the quota laws of the mid 1920s. Their ethnicity dictated an unfortunate fate: 500,000, half of whom were American born, left the United States during the 1930s, most deported as a result of vicious repatriation campaigns. With their labor now considered unwanted competition, Mexicans found themselves targeted by citizens and authorities alike for being a drain on precious community resources.

For most ethnic Americans, however, their heritage was less a cause for added misfortune than a structure of their lives—like social class or gender—subtly reshaped by the Depression. By the early 1930s, the "old immigrant" groups who had come to the United States during the nineteenth century—notably the English, Irish, Germans, and Scandinavians—had been here long enough to assimilate into America's culture and institutions. In contrast, the "new immigrants" who had come from eastern and southern Europe in the late nineteenth and early twentieth century—Bohemians, Poles, Slovaks, Italians, Jews, and so forth—still depended for survival on ethnic institutions such as charities, mutual benefit societies, building and loan associations, and even their own banks. In good times and bad, they looked to the institutions of their ethnic and religious communities, often managed by ethnic elites. A vertical social structure of the ethnic community persisted through the 1920s, where working-class members remained tied to institutions dominated by their economic superiors.

The Depression provoked a crisis among ethnic peoples by undermining many of their institutions and, thereby, their confidence in the viability of depending on these communities. Despite the commitment of ethnic- and religious-affiliated welfare agencies to serve their own people, these private agencies could not handle the enormous demand for assistance. In search of money, jobs, food, and clothing, needy ethnic Americans called upon sectarian welfare organizations such as the Slovenian Relief Organization, the Polish National Alliance Benevolent Association, the Bohemian Charitable Association, the Jewish Charities, and the Catholic Charities, only to find that the institutional coffers and pantries were bare. Similarly, the mutual benefit and fraternal insurance societies that had served as anchors of ethnic community life through the 1920s encountered rough seas during the Depression. Under economic pressure, many workers began to have trouble keeping up insurance payments, which quickly threatened the stability of fraternal associations. Many of these organizations had invested assets in real estate, and their financial viability became all the more tenuous when that market collapsed.

Ethnic Americans had also invested in community institutions at prosperous moments, and hence when saving money or buying a home they had depended on ethnic-affiliated banks and building and loan associations. In Chicago, for example, small state-chartered ethnic banks had mushroomed in outlying shopping districts with particular ethnic characters during the 1920s—almost every ethnic community had at least one bank where people could transact business in their native language. In the bank failures that swept the city from 1929 to 1933, these outlying, none too stable banks were the first to collapse. By the time of the national bank holiday in March 1933, 163 of the 199 Chicago banks located outside the downtown Loop had closed their doors. Ethnic building and loan associations, like banks, had facilitated workers' economic advances during the 1920s, only to preside over their downfall during the 1930s. When both these financial institutions failed, as when ethnic welfare agencies and benefit societies faltered, ordinary people not only felt deprived of their traditional "safety net" but also felt let down by the elites of their communities.

African Americans and Economic Crisis African Americans experienced a similar abandonment by previous sources of support. The hundreds of thousands of sharecroppers and tenant farmers tilling southern cotton fields for landlords who held them in debt peonage had hardly felt well treated before the Depression, but the devastation of southern agriculture left them even more vulnerable. In some cases they were forced off the land altogether, as one-third of the southern cotton fields were foreclosed. Those blacks who had moved north during the "great migration" of World War I and the 1920s found their political and economic progress undermined by the Depression. And blacks, having struggled to get industrial jobs, first as strikebreakers in 1919 and later as "strike insurance" by employers—who saw them not only as a good source of cheap labor but also as an impediment to workers' continued organization—found their overall presence in industry declining as the job market deteriorated in the late 1920s.

The situation was all the more frustrating to black workers because they had distinguished themselves as loyal employees during the 1920s, only to find themselves singled out for more than their fair share of layoffs in the 1930s. A combination of low-skilled jobs, lack of seniority resulting from frequent layoffs, and employer racism doomed them to "first fired" status. At a large manufacturing company like International Harvester, for instance, when the immediate unionization threat ended by the mid 1920s, managers fretted that blacks were becoming too numerous in employee ranks. The Depression offered them the pretext to reduce black employment—in one typical plant from a high of 18 percent to 10 percent by 1940. The limited but still viable political voice that blacks had found for themselves in northern cities through the Republican party was proving a disappointment as Republican administrations lost power with the Depression.

Furthermore, within African American communities vast numbers of working-class blacks experienced disillusionment with institutions headed by black elites, much as ethnic Americans had. Black churches, dominated by a well-established northern "black bourgeoisie" that had long played an important welfare role in the black community, stumbled under the increasing weight of need in the early Depression. Black banks and insurance companies, often the bellwethers of the African American business community, also faltered, depriving blacks of sources of pride as well as security. Again, as with ethnic Americans, blacks found themselves more aware of class difference in their communities as a result of the Depression. The Communist party made a special effort to attract blacks as members and participants in its unemployed organizations. While only a small proportion of blacks actually joined the Party, its defense of innocent young black men framed by southern authorities in the celebrated Scottsboro case and its more general attack on American racism suggested to many African Americans the possibilities of identifying with class- rather than race-based institutions. For ethnics and blacks, the first four years of the Depression cut them adrift from the intermediary institutions that had supported them in the 1920s—whether employers, community welfare and insurance providers, or banks—forcing them to fall back on the help of their families, or to look to new institutions.

The Family and Economic Crisis The family that many Americans—black and white—"fell back on" during the Depression itself underwent transformations as a result of the crisis however. The gender and age position of individual family members shaped the way people experienced the Depression, much as their social class, ethnicity, and race did. Most basically, the family that struggled with the early years of the Depression confronted a paradox: on the one hand, an economic reality that demanded multiple breadwinners and flexible gender and age roles, on the other an intensifying ideological climate that prescribed for everyone what had been the middle-class model of the 1920s—chief male breadwinner, homemaker wife, and nonworking children. Reality dictated that women and unmarried children seek work when the chief breadwinner lost his job or had his hours and pay cut. And reality made jobs often more available to women than to men, due to the lower pay for what was considered "women's work" and the greater economic recovery in light industry and the service sector where females predominated. Women's participation in the labor force in fact increased over the decade. Most notably, of the 50 percent increase in married women working outside the home, many were middle-class (working-class women long had been employed). Ideology, however, contradicted these developments. Employers, unions, state legislators, and other influential cultural critics continually argued against women taking jobs in the work force, particularly when a man in the family had one. And apparently their message got across: a Gallup poll in 1936 revealed that 82 percent of the sample believed women should not take jobs if their husbands worked.

Similar tension between the ideal and the real plagued the role of children in the family during the Depression. Assessments of what would most effectively remedy the depressed economy encouraged children to stay in school longer rather than go to work, and as they reached majority to fuel consumption by propagating families as soon as possible. Once again, however, reality dictated otherwise. Although many more adolescents did stay in school as the 1930s advanced, financial pressures kept young people in the work force, contributing to the family income. Blacks, for example, complained that they lost even low-paying and unappealing industrial jobs to young whites who previously had displayed no interest in such work. Charities and local relief agencies struggling with inadequate resources early in the Depression often required economic contributions from as many members of the household as possible, and would withhold funds until convinced that the family could earn no additional income on its own. Furthermore, the marked decline in marriage and birthrates between 1929 and 1933 suggests that young people postponed establishing their own families, opting instead to contribute to the economic survival of their parents' households. The middle-class, male breadwinner–dominated, consumer-oriented nuclear family that was to save America from the Depression doldrums was more viable as an ideal than as a reality in the early 1930s.

Regionalism and Economic Crisis One additional social factor warrants consideration in this analysis of how Americans experienced the Great Depression from 1929 to 1933—where people lived. The various regions of the United States were affected in unique ways, from the cotton disaster of the Deep South to the dust storms of the Great Plains to the paralysis of manufacturing plants in the urban, industrial North. More significant than these differences, however, were the population migrations they encouraged, sending more rural blacks to northern cities, at least 350,000 "Okie" refugees from the Oklahoma region to the West Coast, and onetime industrial workers on the road as hoboes or to rural areas where they hoped for a better life. While most people stayed put, greater than normal geographical mobility of the American population contributed to a widespread understanding of the Depression as a national phenomenon. The Depression was not hitting only one sector of the economy or section of the country. It was everywhere.

On the eve of Roosevelt's assumption of the presidency and his implementation of what would become known as the New Deal, Americans recognized that they were in the midst of a national crisis. It affected social classes, ethnic groups, races, genders, ages, and regions differently, but everywhere people found themselves losing jobs, homes, savings, and insurance policies and, most significantly, being unable to count on the institutional structures they had depended on in the 1920s. Faced with this crisis, they turned inward to their families, often in ways that conflicted with prescriptions of ideal gender and family roles, and outward, in search of new institutional supports. Political radicals and their working-class supporters experimented with class-based collective action, and all Americans became increasingly involved in electoral politics, particularly in supporting a national Democratic party that they viewed as a real alternative to the status quo. Radical and more moderate political strategies, however, shared a vision of a new, more engaged role for the federal government.

THE NEW DEAL, 1934–1940

The New Deal reinforced the reorientations of the early Depression: a decline in people's dependence on community-level mediating institutions such as ethnic benefit societies, welfare capitalist employers, and local philanthropic elites, and their growing reliance on both the more private—such as the family—and the more public and national—such as the federal government and the industrial union movement of the Congress of Industrial Organizations (CIO). President Roosevelt intended his New Deal to save capitalism rather than to radically restructure it, and his effort to patch up a broken-down system led to programs that were often improvisational and inconsistent in quality and purpose. Nonetheless, despite FDR's personal ambivalence about building a strong federal government or increasing deficit spending sufficiently to support a full-scale welfare state, the New Deal conveyed to many Americans the possibilities of the state taking over many of the functions previously lodged in the local institutions that had failed them in the Depression. A majority of Americans came to share this vision of a bipolar world of family and federal government, though how they came to endorse it, and their expectations for it—like their experiences of the preceding events—was shaped by their social class, ethnicity, race, gender, age, and region.

Class and the New Deal Social class was probably more important than any other single factor in influencing how individuals responded to the New Deal. Even in a place as traditionally loyal to the Democratic party as the city of Chicago, voters divided along class lines. In 1936, 83 percent of unskilled and semiskilled workers voted for Roosevelt, while only 32 percent of major business executives and 39 percent of a white-collar professional group like engineers did. Working-class neighborhoods were Roosevelt strongholds, while neighborhoods where well-to-do native whites resided conspicuously favored Republican presidential candidate Alfred Landon and others on the ticket. An observer at the upper-class Fourth Presbyterian Church noted on the Sunday before Election Day in 1936 that "it was a sea of yellow. Everybody was decorated with large yellow Landon sunflower buttons. Just the impact of the thing suddenly made me realize there is such a thing as class distinction in America" (Terkel, *Hard Times,* p. 195). While upper-class Americans felt that Roosevelt was a traitor to his class, working people were convinced by FDR's policies—and particularly his rhetoric—that his administration favored the "common" person against "economic royalists" and "privileged enterprise." Although the New Deal did not radically redistribute wealth or restructure society, both upper- and working-class Americans shared a perception of it as promoting America's most democratic and egalitarian impulses. Middle-class Americans who may at first have been suspicious of the New Deal soon came to value the benefits like social security that it brought them.

In reality, the New Deal was more business oriented and less populist inclined than its image. The Roosevelt administration's first New Deal was built around the National Industrial Recovery Act of 1933 (NIRA), which gave businesses incentives to regulate themselves through industry codes of fair competition designed to maximize people's employment and consumption capabilities while holding prices steady. By the time the Supreme Court found the NIRA unconstitutional in May 1935 it had become clear to many critics that the act favored big business—even monopolies—in its approach to recovery. Although Section 7(a) of the NIRA supposedly protected the right of workers to organize and bargain collectively "through representatives of their own choosing," many companies insisted that employer-dominated company unions met this requirement and prohibited more independent organizing efforts. Other New Deal policies and agencies that were intended to steady the Depression economy—such as the Banking Act of 1935 and the Agricultural Adjustment Act of 1938 (AAA)—did so in ways that favored large established economic interests, in these cases big banks and commercial farmers. Beneficent relief and public works programs such as the 1933 Federal Emergency Relief Administration (FERA), the 1933 Civil Works Administration (CWA), and the 1935 Works Progress Administration (WPA), moreover, were always underfunded and more precarious than people needed.

In fact, it took pressure from grass-roots populist movements to get the Roosevelt administration to promote the New Deal's most progressive legislation, such as the Social Security Act of 1935 and the National Labor Relations Act of 1935 (NLRA). Groundswells of popular support for two programs in particular pushed FDR to establish an American version of a welfare state. The first was Dr. Francis E. Townsend's plan for an old-age pension of two hundred dollars per month to every American over age sixty, provided the recipient retired and spent the entire amount each month; the second was Louisiana Senator Huey Long's "Share Our Wealth" proposal, which called for using taxation to redistribute wealth more equitably. However, the system of old-age pensions, unemployment insurance, and aid for disabled and dependent children that FDR launched in 1935 with the Social Security Act fell far short of European provisions in its regressive payroll tax, its method of funding, its exclusion of many kinds of workers, its small benefits, and the inconsistencies resulting from its administration by the states.

The National Labor Relations Act similarly grew out of public pressure. Violent strikes initiated by autoworkers in Toledo, teamsters in Minneapolis, and longshoremen in San Francisco during 1933 and 1934, as well as calmer grass-roots organizing in steel and other industries finally convinced New Dealers that although the NIRA's Section 7(a) did promise workers enough to mobilize them, it was unable to protect fragile organizational efforts. Roosevelt signed the NLRA (also known as the Wagner Act) in the summer of 1935, as he did the Social Security Act, with a sharp eye on the 1936 election. Despite this political motive, however, FDR institutionalized with his signature the federal government's commitment to workers' rights. The act established a National Labor Relations Board (NLRB) and granted it the power to investigate and prohibit any efforts by employers "to interfere with, restrain or coerce employees in the exercise of their right of self-organization." Now workers could not be fired for joining a union, the government would go after employers engaged in illegal, union-busting activities, and a clear mechanism existed for workers to select their bargaining representatives—a majority vote in an election supervised by the NLRB, not the employer.

Herein lies a central paradox of the New Deal. It indeed enacted programs that helped people and allowed the national government to compensate for the inadequacies of employers and community institutions during the Depression. In place of local charities, the FERA gave financial relief to the needy. Picking up the pieces from waves of bank failures, the Federal Deposit Insurance Corporation (FDIC), created by the Banking Act of 1933, protected savings in banks that the federal government certified as solvent. Instead of local banks and building-and-loan associations, the 1933 Home Owners' Loan Corporation (HOLC) offered long-term, low-interest mortgages to eligible homeowners facing loss of property. Providing recourse beyond the private employer, the 1933 Civilian Conservation Corps (CCC), the 1933 Public Works Administration (PWA), the CWA, and the Works Progress Administration (WPA) gave the unemployed jobs. And the Fair Labor Standards Act of 1938 established minimum wages and maximum hours for workers in many occupations. Federal agencies, the 1933 Tennessee Valley Authority (TVA), and the 1936 Rural Electrification Administration (REA), began to bring electricity to the American farms without it (90 percent of which had none in 1935); by 1940, 40 percent had power. These and many other policies testify to how much the New Deal did deliver to Americans. Yet the Roosevelt administration was often ambivalent about making these innovations, and the impact of policies was often less equitable than advocates desired. Many Americans nevertheless became convinced that a stronger federal government was making a difference. During the 1930s, individuals, particularly in the working and middle classes, developed a multitude of new expectations for the state, though many went unfulfilled. In fact, the New Deal may have been more significant for the attitudinal changes it produced in a generation of Americans than for the lasting accomplishments of its reforms.

Social class had its greatest political expression during the New Deal years through the resurgence of the labor movement. At the start of the Depression, a little more than 2.5 million workers belonged to unions, mostly craft unions within the long-established American Federation of Labor (AFL). By the end of the 1930s, more than 7 million workers were union members, slightly more than half of them in an entirely new labor federation, the Congress of Industrial Organizations, founded by onetime AFL unionists committed to organizing the nation's mass-production industries. Under the leadership of United Mine Workers (UMW) President John L. Lewis, they first tried to work within the AFL but, frustrated with the recalcitrance of craft unions to undertake industrial-style organizing—where all workers in a particular industry would be recruited into the same union whatever their job—they set up an independent structure to coordinate and financially support the campaign. From the mid 1930s through World War II, CIO-affiliated unions successfully organized workers in the major mass-production sectors, including automobiles, rubber, steel, textiles, the electrical and metal industries, meat packing, and farm equipment. When CIO unions signed contracts with America's largest industrialists, employees won many important concessions: recognition of their unions, collective bargaining over wages, hours, and working conditions, grievance procedures to protect them against arbitrary firing and discipline, equitable and higher wages; and the protection of seniority rules.

Less successful but still significant organizing took place during the 1930s in rural America among agricultural workers. In the South, the Communist party helped black and white tenant farmers and sharecroppers to organize the Alabama Sharecroppers Union, while the Socialist party in Arkansas assisted in the establishment of the Southern Tenant Farmers' Union, which claimed as many as twenty-five thousand members at its height. Although these organizations encountered violent harassment and repression from landowners, they were important expressions of working people's class consciousness, since both were biracial and broad in the economic and civil rights issues they raised. Mexican American farmworkers in California similarly sought to realize the New Deal's promises as they faced declining wages and increasing mechanization in harvesting the crops of California's fertile valleys. California growers responded with a combination of police arrests and vigilante attacks that destroyed farmworker unions and left supporters with little recourse. The NLRA had excluded agricultural workers from coverage, in recognition of the strength of the farm lobby. In agricultural America the New Deal gave workers the same hope of constructing class-based union organizations as in industrial America, but it offered them less protection in their efforts to achieve their goals.

Ethnicity, Race, and the New Deal As in the early Depression, so during the New Deal, Americans' ethnic and racial experiences changed along with social class ones. The New Deal, however, had opposite impacts on ethnicity and race.

Ethnicity became less significant as a fundamental structure in people's lives as local community institutions provided less of the safety net that ethnic Americans had come to depend on, as classwide and cross-ethnic organizations like unions became more viable, and as pluralistic mainstream organizations like the Democratic party attracted a broader constituency. Nonetheless, ethnic representatives served, at least transitionally, as mediators to these new institutions through such vehicles as ethnic Democratic party clubs, CIO organizing committees, and a growing presence within government agencies. (Where one in twenty-five Hoover appointments had gone to a Catholic or Jew, one in nine Roosevelt appointments did.) With this institutional reconfiguration of people's lives during the Depression ethnicity did not so much disappear as shift from offering a support structure to fostering a cultural sensibility. Identifying with an ethnicity increasingly meant celebrating Old World holidays, preparing distinctive foods, and reifying ethnic customs and traditions as quaint "folkways." Nationality days featuring native costumes, folk dancing, and authentic cuisine at the New York World's Fair in 1939 exemplified this new and increasingly commercialized image of ethnicity.

In contrast to ethnicity, race became a more viable ground upon which to make demands of the establishment over the course of the New Deal. Blacks underwent the same kind of integration into mainstream institutions like the Democratic party and CIO unions as ethnics did. Having strongly endorsed Republican candidates as late as 1932, black voters realigned in 1936 and gave FDR 71 percent of their votes. With unemployment among blacks running at three times the rate for whites, blacks realized how much they depended on New Deal relief and jobs programs. More basically, as blacks increasingly became northern, urban residents who could vote, they came to see their concerns better represented by the Democrats than the Republicans. Blacks also played a key role in the success of the CIO, recognizing that loyalty to bosses during the 1920s had earned them little protection in the Depression. Moreover, unions actively recruited them, aware that interracial cooperation was crucial for success. Employers had defeated workers' union drives many times before by dividing workers by race.

Despite the support that blacks willingly gave to state and union, however, both still subjected them to discrimination. Blacks accused the NRA of being a "Negro Removal Act." They protested unfair assignments of jobs under the WPA. The CCC and TVA isolated them in segregated camps and settlements, and the AAA pushed blacks off the land in the South. One official of the National Association for the Advancement of Colored People (NAACP) commented that social security "looks like a sieve with the holes just large enough for the majority of Negroes to fall through," and FDR refused to support antilynching legislation, so as not to alienate the southern wing of the New Deal coalition. Similarly, although the CIO paid greater attention to blacks than unions ever had previously, glaring inequities remained in the way employers hired, paid, and treated blacks, as well as in how unions incorporated their unique concerns into bargaining agendas and their representatives into union officialdom. Nonetheless, blacks began to feel that now they had recourse within the corridors of Washington and within their union halls. Letters to Eleanor and Franklin Roosevelt, complaints to New Deal agencies, and appeals to the growing number of black government employees had an impact, as did similar initiatives with unions. Although few programs targeted black needs specifically, blacks benefited enormously from the innovations of the 1930s, though perhaps more in terms of legitimizing their feelings of entitlement than in actually delivering benefits. Thus, ethnics and blacks both moved toward more dependence on mainstream, national institutions over the course of the decade, but race seemed less likely than ethnicity to disappear in the process.

The Family and the New Deal The New Deal had a less dramatic impact on the family than it did on ethnicity and race. Rather, it extended the conservative tendencies manifest early in the Depression, sponsoring programs that reinforced the middle-class ideal family and in fact making it more economically viable. The FERA and the WPA supported a family structure of male breadwinner and nonworking wife, and other programs made sure that compensation for women who worked was inferior to men's: the NRA reinforced lower wages for females while social security and labor legislation gave domestic servants, waitresses, and other traditional women workers few protections. New Deal agencies such as the CCC, NIRA, National Youth Administration (NYA), and FLSA also tried to keep children in school and out of the work force.

Unions, moreover, did their part to reinforce the same conservative gender and age hierarchies in the family. Organizers frequently built union solidarity around masculine images of militance. With this emphasis, as well as by focusing union demands more on the workplace and national politics than on community issues, unions demonstrated little interest in recruiting and involving women. Male members were expected to represent the interests of their immediate families, while women ideally would support the union cause through auxiliary groups. When women were themselves the union members, male leaders rarely rewarded them with staff positions and other forms of power. Most seriously, union support for conventional gender ideology meant that union demands fortified rather than challenged employers' gender distinctions in wage determination, occupational classification, and seniority ranking. Although nearly 30 percent of all women were employed by 1940, they were most often found in "women's work"—low-paying manufacturing, clerical, and service jobs. The demand for seniority, moreover, served not only to keep women from competing with men, but also kept young men out of older men's jobs. Thus, the state and the unions cooperated in the 1930s to ensure that the upheavals of the Depression would not upset the gender and age division of labor in the family, at the workplace, and in society more generally.

Regionalism and the New Deal Finally, the trend of the early Depression toward greater nationalization in American culture expanded during the New Deal years. True, a few New Deal programs such as the TVA targeted regions, and programs such as unemployment compensation encouraged regional inequities in benefits by sharing administration with the states. In politics, the South became increasingly powerful in Congress, thwarting many of FDR's most progressive legislative efforts. Nonetheless, the nation was increasingly integrated culturally by a number of developments—among them the growth in the authority of the president and the federal government, new national-level institutions like the CIO, and an explosion in national culture through commercial network radio, the Hollywood studio system, expansion of chain stores, and greater automobile ownership and household electrification. The patriotic campaigns of the homefront during World War II would build on, rather than create, a national community. It should be made clear, however, that this cultural integration promoted awareness of national experience without breaking down other social boundaries, as between classes, races, and genders. By 1940 the New Deal had helped Americans to have more in common while still identifying with particular interest groups.

THE HOME FRONT IN WORLD WAR II, 1941–1945

Historians frequently debate the relationship between the New Deal and the era of World War II that eclipsed it. Was the New Deal or the war, they ask, most responsible for pulling America out of depression or ensuring the success of the CIO? Most basically, they argue over whether the war represented a significant break with the past or an extension of the economic, social, and political reorientations of the 1930s. The last section of this essay will emphasize the ways that Americans' homefront experience grew out of the transformations that had been under way since the early Depression. This is not to deny that the war brought enormous changes, but rather to state that 1930 and not 1940 was the critical watershed in American social history. The Depression upset the game as it was played and rewrote all the rules. World War II helped elaborate the new rules, clarifying how the world that followed the Second World War would differ from the one that followed the First. In the process, many of the ambiguities that had beset the New Deal—concerning the state's relationship to business, business's interaction with labor, the meaning of ethnicity and race, and the role of women and youth in the family—would be resolved.

The Roosevelt administration's confusion over desirable relations between the federal government and private enterprise, which underlay legislation from the NIRA to the FLSA, clarified under the shadow of war. The state would be an equal partner with business, setting economic agendas, preparing the field—both fiscal and regulatory, and providing orders and resources to help business flourish. This transformed the partnership that had emerged before the Depression, during the 1920s, in what historians have called the "voluntarist state." The 1920s version of the partnership made business the senior partner and government a willing assistant.

Business and Government in Wartime The industrial mobilization that accompanied the war effort restructured the interaction between state and business. Massive government spending meant higher employment and more prosperity than Americans had known since the onset of the Depression. A few figures convey the scale of this revving up of the economy. The federal budget grew from $9.4 billion in 1939 to $95.2 billion in 1945, and the national debt expanded sixfold, to $258.6 billion. The American GNP more than doubled from $90.5 billion to $211.9 billion. This explosion of government spending directly increased employment. Government civilian employees mushroomed from less than 1 million to 3.8 million, while 16 million men and women served in the armed forces by the war's end. The New Deal had brought unemployment down from highs of 25 percent to 14 percent, but it took the war to bring it down further. By 1944 unemployment was practically nonexistent and defense industries had turned to new sources of labor, particularly women and southern blacks.

Although the federal government paid for much of this economic expansion, it went out of its way to filter it through private enterprise. As many new plants were built in 1942–1944 as in the preceding fifteen years. The government either built these defense plants and transferred their ownership to private companies or made corporate capital investments extremely profitable by allowing rapid depreciations and huge tax credits. Lucrative cost-plus contracts for urgently needed products also helped pad the pockets of business, particularly the biggest pockets. Faced with the tremendous demand for war production, the largest companies competed best. The one hundred largest firms that in 1940 were responsible for 30 percent of industrial output by 1945 controlled 70 percent. Many of their executives, moreover, were appointed to "dollar a year" posts with wartime oversight agencies, allowing them to help shape a war economy in which the government relaxed antitrust regulations and financed private research and development. Not surprisingly, after-tax corporate profits doubled during the war, while industrial productivity increased almost 100 percent. America's remarkable mobilization to supply the Allies produced not only planes, jeeps, and warships but also a new team relationship between the public and private sectors.

Other aspects of mobilization also reflected this close government-business partnership. In its efforts to win public support for the war effort, for example, the state turned to the private sector. When, a year after American entry into the war, polls showed one-third of the nation lacking a clear understanding of war aims, the Roosevelt administration called on Madison Avenue and Hollywood for assistance in selling the war to American citizens. In no time, advertisements in magazines and on roadside billboards sold patriotism and war needs along with company products. The War Advertising Council, representing private agencies, negotiated with federal agencies such as the War Production Board and the Office of War Information to ensure that Madison Avenue and Washington mutually benefited from wartime advertising. By the war's end, the council had overseen well over a hundred advertising campaigns pushing war bonds, blood drives, food conservation, labor recruitment, and other requirements of mobilization. Hollywood did its part as well, making both propaganda and training films in cooperation with the Office of War Information and regular movies with pro-war messages for general theater distribution. The state may have become more present in people's lives during the war, extending a course set by the New Deal, but faced with the enormous task of mobilizing, it made corporate America its partner.

Business and Labor in Wartime The war also set in motion another partnership of past rivals, this one between business and labor. Although the numbers of union members grew to about 30 percent of the nonagricultural labor force, and rank-and-file workers remained militant in wildcat strikes on the shop floor, at higher levels a new bargain was being struck by business and labor leaders. Companies would accept unions as a permanent presence and meet their demands with good-faith collective bargaining. The subject of those demands, however, would be carefully circumscribed: business would resist any efforts by unions to redistribute power and authority in American industry. Shorter hours, higher wages, and stricter seniority rules were acceptable subjects for negotiation; union participation in managerial decision making was not.

This "business unionism" that was emerging during wartime coincided with a subtle change in workers' attitudes toward social class. The class consciousness of the working class, which had prevailed through the 1930s, even as it was channeled through mainstream institutions like the Democratic party, the New Deal, and the CIO, was increasingly dulled by full employment, job security, and prosperity. This reorientation of working-class identity was a complex, long-term process that would not take full shape until later in the postwar period, but the seeds were sown during wartime. Perhaps most significant, workers benefited economically from the war. Per capita income rose from $691 in 1939 to $1,515 in 1945, and for the first time in the twentieth century workers' income increased at a greater rate than did the income of the affluent. Workers' income from 1939 to 1945 rose by 68 percent, while the well-to-do's grew at only 20 percent. A much expanded, and progressive, federal income tax contributed to this redistribution of wealth. Although the tax base was broadened during the war to include the lower-middle class—36 million filed in 1942, in contrast to 7 million in 1939—corporations and the wealthy paid their fair share. Workers' wages increased 24 percent during the war, mostly in the year or two before FDR created the National War Labor Board to try to control wage inflation. Even though the board's policies slowed the increase in wages, however, incomes continued to rise because wage freezes and agreements did not cover overtime. By the war's end, weekly earnings had increased 70 percent.

These high earnings, furthermore, carried over into the postwar era. Wartime consumer shortages and savings through the purchase of war bonds meant that working people were eager and ready to purchase the home appliances and cars that would fuel postwar recovery. For those who had served in the military, the GI Bill of Rights assisted their economic advancement by providing education, job training, mortgage loans, and pensions.

Ironically, even as American workers faced the postwar era at a new height in union membership, their unions were more accepting of business unionism and the workers themselves were moving toward defining their ambitions more in terms of middle-class consumerism than distinctive working-class values. The war itself gave rise to workers' sense that the gap was declining between social classes. Not only were working-class people making better money, but in factories they labored alongside people, particularly women, of middle-class backgrounds, and in the military they served with people of all classes. Even the elite of the elite did not escape military service during World War II: of the twelve hundred men in Harvard University's class of 1946, for example, 90 percent served in the armed forces, many times the national average.

Ethnicity in Wartime The war encouraged another kind of amalgamation in American society by assisting in and celebrating the assimilation of white ethnics with European backgrounds. This process of ethnic integration, already under way during the New Deal, expanded greatly during wartime. Citizens and government alike feared the ethnic antagonisms of the World War I era and took action to prevent them. Large numbers of aliens became citizens, encouraged by the Alien Registration Act of 1940. During 1943 and 1944, almost a million people were naturalized. By July 1945, the alien population, which had stood at about 5 million in January 1941, had declined nearly 40 percent. The Democrats, fully aware that many of these ethnic populations contributed substantially to their political base, went out of their way to downplay conflict and encourage naturalization and acceptance. On Columbus Day 1942, for example, Roosevelt revoked the alien status of the 600,000 Italian Americans who were not citizens and eased procedures for their swift naturalization. Hollywood movies that functioned, as we have seen, as part of the war machine reinforced the image of a pluralist America by portraying the typical platoon as an amalgam of ethnically diverse Americans. It should be made clear, however, that this vision of pluralism stressed the assimilation of ethnics to an American norm, not the acceptance of multicultural diversity.

Ethnic groups who were not white and European in background did not fare nearly as well during World War II. Mexican Americans who had managed to survive the deportations of the Depression found themselves discriminated against in wartime. Although not as completely segregated in the armed forces as blacks, their options were still limited. When they stayed on the homefront, they benefited from defense-related jobs, but at the lowest ranks and wages and often at the displeasure of unions. The most blatant insult to Mexican Americans took place in July 1943 in Los Angeles. What became known as the "Zoot Suit" riots because of the distinctive dress of Mexican American *pachincos* (youths), a four-day race riot, was initiated by white soldiers who had heard a false rumor that *pachincos* had beaten a sailor.

Even more horrifying than the wartime treatment of Mexican Americans, however, was the forced internment of first- and second-generation Japanese Americans as a threat to American security. When FDR signed Executive Order 9066 in February 1942, 120,000 West Coast residents of Japanese ancestry—two-thirds of whom were American citizens by birth and the other third of whom had been barred from becoming citizens by the Naturalization Act of 1924—were forced to leave their homes, jobs, and possessions for camps in the interior. Racial prejudice and hysterical fear, rather than any evidence that they posed a security risk, led to the virtual imprisonment of Japanese Americans throughout the war. Generalizing about the war's impact on ethnic groups, then, clearly requires consideration of the particular ethnicity involved.

Race and Gender in Wartime Two other social groups—blacks and women—had complex experiences during World War II: their opportunities increased with the war, but not to the extent of their expectations. Blacks and women were the reserve army of the industrial homefront. With a large proportion of white males serving in the armed forces and a new level of demand for labor, northern blacks who had lost industrial jobs in the Depression, new migrants from the rural South, and women who had never before worked in traditional male industries lined up to claim the new, well-paying jobs.

In the case of blacks, it took Roosevelt's signing of Executive Order 8802 in 1941, which outlawed discrimination in hiring and promotion in firms with government contracts and established a Committee on Fair Employment Practices (FEPC) as monitor, to open up these good defense jobs. And that order came about only because black activist A. Philip Randolph threatened FDR with a massive march on Washington to end racial discrimination in defense industries, government employment, and the military. By 1945, blacks made up approximately 8 percent of defense workers, their numbers in government employment had grown from 60,000 in 1941 to 200,000, and nearly a million served in the armed forces. Now, even more so than during the New Deal, state policy facilitated blacks' economic advancement, but not without limitations. Underfunding weakened the FEPC, so that it could act on only a third of the complaints filed. Discrimination thus continued in industry, as it did in the military, which remained segregated until 1948. Racial violence, including full-scale riots in Detroit and Harlem, provoked by white fears of integration, reminded blacks how far they still had to go to achieve equal participation in American society. Nonetheless, the war was crucial in the opportunities that it did offer and in its ideological climate of repudiating Nazi racism, which stimulated blacks to challenge the racial status quo.

The war economy also gave women new opportunities in well-paying jobs previously closed to them. Whereas blacks had to pressure for their share of defense work, women were recruited by government campaigns urging that "longing won't bring him back sooner . . . GET A WAR JOB!" and other appeals to patriotism. Between 1941 and 1945, 6.5 million women entered the labor force. Whereas before the war women made up one-quarter of all workers, by 1945 they were 36 percent. Historians have disputed to what extent women actually took over male jobs—whether they indeed were "Rosie the Riveter" or simply Rosie the Rivet Sorter. Evidence suggests that although women often remained in female departments or job classifications and earned less than men, they still considered these war jobs better than any they had had before. A government survey in 1945 revealed that 75 percent of working women wanted to keep their jobs. That wish, however, was not to be. At the war's end, government propagandists, business leaders, and union officials collaborated to ensure that returning servicemen returned to jobs in America's factories as well. New opportunities without a basic restructuring of society along racial and gender lines left both blacks and women frustrated at the war's end. Although it would take longer for women to demand greater access than it would for blacks, and their situations differed in many ways, the postwar period would eventually see struggles of both groups for social, political, and economic equality through the civil rights movement and the women's liberation movement.

The Family in Wartime When women left the defense plant after the war, they went back to the same conservative family structure that had predominated during the Depression. The male-headed family would be idealized in the postwar era with greater intensity than ever before, and marriage and birthrates would rise to new heights. Nevertheless, economic necessity would keep women in the labor force in low-paying jobs considered "women's work." After a temporary drop after the war, women's employment would continue to grow until it reached 29 percent in 1950 and more than 50 percent by 1980. The contradiction between the ideal and the real that had characterized the family during the Depression persisted into postwar America, but by now the idealization of women's domesticity and male productivity was so developed as to obscure the fact that women had found a permanent place in the work force—or at best to falsely attribute this fact to their desire for "pin money."

The ideal of youth as a separate stage of life more oriented toward consumption than production also received a boost during World War II. Ironically, a need for young people's unique energy and talents in the military and in defense work was responsible for fueling their distinctive peer culture and their consumer power. In the postwar era, however, these cultural attributes would persist while youths' participation in the work force would decline.

Regionalism in Wartime By the end of World War II it was more possible than at its start to assume that these social and cultural trends were taking place on a national level. This nationalizing process had been under way gradually throughout the twentieth century, and had accelerated during the Depression. World War II only intensified that movement of people, ideas, and culture. Soldiers went to training camps at home and then abroad, defense workers and their families went to new plants in the South and the West, fortune seekers went to the boom areas of the Sunbelt—and all contributed to a major redistribution of population and resources in postwar America. About 7 million newcomers flooded the trans-Mississippi West during four years of war, for example, remaking the metropolitan areas of Los Angeles, San Francisco, Portland, Seattle, and Denver into cosmopolitan urban centers. One could also argue that the war not only encouraged American nationalization but also launched American internationalization, as the United States sought to spread its political and cultural influence abroad in the postwar world.

American society changed tremendously between 1929 and 1945 as it weathered a devastating depression and intensive mobilization for war. In some ways, this decade and a half can be divided—into hard and prosperous times, into peace and war, into an era of social and political conflict and one of national unity. Yet it is important to recognize the long-term trends that cut across the whole period: the growth of state authority, the decline in intermediary local and community institutions between the family and the state, the emergence of a class-conscious labor movement whose success would blunt the intensity of its class agenda, the integration of white European ethnics and the exclusion of Mexicans and Asians into American culture and institutions, the rise in expectations among African Americans—particularly of the federal government—the increase in women's work force participation alongside a growing ideological commitment to a paternally supported and dominated family, the tendency to see youth as a time of consuming rather than producing within the family, and the spread of national culture and institutions to new populations and to new areas of the country such as the South and West. As the United States came out of world war, all these social transformations would help to shape the postwar era. The military-industrial complex, business unionism, the civil rights movement, suburban domesticity, the teen culture, and so much else had its roots in the Great Depression and World War II.

BIBLIOGRAPHY

Works Covering Entire Period

Brody, David. *Workers in Industrial America: Essays on the Twentieth Century Struggle* (1980). Contains some pathbreaking analyses of labor from the 1920s until the postwar era.

Faue, Elizabeth. *Community of Suffering and Struggle: Women, Men, and the Labor Movement in Minneapolis, 1915–1945* (1991). Analyzes implications for gender roles of the transformation of the American labor movement from community forms of solidarity to bureaucratic unionism.

Gerstle, Gary. *Working-Class Americanism: The Politics of Labor in a Textile City, 1914–1960* (1989).

Gregory, James N. *American Exodus: The Dust Bowl Migration and Okie Culture in California* (1989).

Henretta, James A., W. Elliott Brownlee, David Brody, and Susan Ware. *America's History: Since 1865* (1987). See chapters 24–26 for an excellent synthesis of events of the Great Depression and World War II.

Nelson, Steve, James R. Barrett, and Rob Ruck. *Steve Nelson: American Radical* (1981). Interesting memoir of Communist activist.

The Great Depression

Argersinger, Jo Ann E. *Toward a New Deal in Baltimore: People and Government in the Great Depression* (1988).

Banks, Ann, ed. *First-Person America* (1980). Fascinating interviews with all kinds of people carried out from 1938 through 1942 by writers working with the New Deal's Federal Writers' Project.

Bergman, Andrew. *We're in the Money: Depression America and Its Films* (1972).

Bernstein, Irving. *The Lean Years: A History of the American Worker, 1920–1933* (1960). Classic work on labor prior to and during the early Depression.

———. *Turbulent Years: A History of the American Worker, 1933–1941* (1970). Classic work on labor during the New Deal.

Brinkley, Alan. *Voices of Protest: Huey Long, Father Coughlin, and the Great Depression* (1982).

Cohen, Lizabeth. *Making a New Deal: Industrial Workers in Chicago, 1919–1939* (1990). Explores how factory workers became invested in the New Deal and the CIO, with special attention to the impact of mass culture.

Klehr, Harvey. *The Heyday of American Communism: The Depression Decade* (1984).

Lynd, Robert S., and Helen Merrell Lynd. *Middletown in Transition: A Study in Cultural Conflicts* (1937). Depression-era follow-up to their classic sociological study of the 1920s, *Middletown: A Study in American Culture* (1929).

McElvaine, Robert S., ed. *Down and Out in the Great Depression: Letters from the "Forgotten Man"* (1983). Letters from ordinary Americans to Eleanor and Franklin Roosevelt, as well as to New Deal administrators.

Sitkoff, Harvard. *A New Deal for Blacks: The Emergence of Civil Rights as a National Issue* (1978).

Terkel, Studs. *Hard Times: An Oral History of the Great Depression* (1970).

Ware, Susan. *Holding Their Own: American Women in the 1930s* (1982).

Weiss, Nancy. *Farewell to the Party of Lincoln: Black Politics in the Age of FDR* (1984).

Worster, Donald. *Dust Bowl: The Southern Plains in the 1930s* (1979).

World War II

Anderson, Karen. *Wartime Women: Sex Roles, Family Relations, and the Status of Women During World War II* (1981).

Berube, Allan. *Coming Out Under Fire: The History of Gay Men and Women in World War II* (1990). An important new area of research in social history.

Blum, John M. *V Was for Victory: Politics and American Culture During World War II* (1976).

Daniel, Pete. "Going Among Strangers: Southern Reactions to World War II." *Journal of American History* 77, no. 3 (1990).

Daniels, Roger. *Concentration Camps USA: Japanese-Americans and World War II* (1971).

Havighurst, Robert J., and H. Gerthon Morgan. *The Social History of a War-Boom Community* (1951). An interesting contemporary study to read along with Robert and Helen Lynd's *Middletown* and *Middletown in Transition.*

Honey, Maureen. *Creating Rosie the Riveter: Class, Gender, and Propaganda During World War II* (1984).

Isserman, Maurice. *Which Side Were You On?: The American Communist Party During the Second World War* (1982).

Koppes, Clayton R., and Gregory D. Black. *Hollywood Goes to War: How Politics, Profits, and Propaganda Shaped World War II Movies* (1987).

Leff, Mark H. "The Politics of Sacrifice on the American Home Front in World War II." *Journal of American History* 77, no. 4 (1991).

Lichtenstein, Nelson. *Labor's War at Home: The CIO in World War II* (1983).

Milkman, Ruth. *Gender at Work: The Dynamics of Job Segregation by Sex During World War II* (1987).

Nash, Gerald D. *The American West Transformed: The Impact of the Second World War* (1985).

Polenberg, Richard. *War and Society: The United States, 1941–1945* (1972).

Terkel, Studs. *"The Good War": An Oral History of World War Two* (1984).

Wynn, Neil A. *The Afro-American and the Second World War* (1976).

SEE ALSO **Business Culture; Geographical Mobility; Labor: The Great Depression Through the 1980s; Minorities and Work; Socialist and Communist Movements; War; Women and Work.**

THE POSTWAR PERIOD THROUGH THE 1950s

Paul Boyer

WHEN JAPAN SURRENDERED on 14 August 1945, ending World War II, Americans celebrated wildly but also looked ahead in uneasiness. What would the postwar era bring? Many feared a return to conditions of the Great Depression as the war-induced economic boom ended. In fact, the postwar economy soared, producing a level of material abundance unequaled in American history. Millions of citizens acquired new homes in the suburbs; purchased new cars, appliances, and television sets; and spent freely on leisure-time activities.

The economic boom affected all aspects of the American experience in these years. Politically, the twenty-year reign of the Democratic Party—the party of Franklin Roosevelt and the New Deal—ended in 1952 as voters gave the Republicans control of Congress and elected the war hero Dwight Eisenhower as president. The return of prosperity had a profound social and cultural impact as well. Some spoke of postwar America as a "consumer culture"—a culture in which the production, marketing, and acquisition of the material symbols of the good life became the central reality shaping society and its values. Conservative social values prevailed as a newly affluent but uneasy middle class resisted real or imagined threats to the status quo.

But the security, happiness, and tranquillity that such abundance promised eluded the nation in these years. Not only did large pockets of poverty and social distress persist amid the general abundance, but the prospering middle class itself—particularly women—experienced stress and tensions as it tried to live up to a social ideal emphasizing domesticity and devotion to family. Cultural critics, intellectuals, and alienated youth probed the flaws and fault lines beneath the smooth facade of Eisenhower prosperity; racial segregation in the South increasingly emerged as a compelling social issue; and anxieties induced by the cold war and the nuclear arms race mocked the era's surface placidity. American society between 1945 and 1960 thus presents a complex and paradoxical picture of dramatic advances in material well-being uneasily coexisting with severe but only half-acknowledged social problems and cultural strains.

DEMOBILIZATION

The war had brought major social changes to the home front. As millions of men (and many women) entered the military, over six million new women workers had poured into the war plants at home. By 1945, 37 percent of all American women were in the labor force. The war also spurred the cityward migration of Americans that had been under way for decades, including the movement of southern rural blacks to the industrial centers of the North. The black population in the South declined by 1.6 million between 1940 and 1950, while that in the urban North increased correspondingly. In addition, over 935,000 blacks donned uniforms in World War II, many for the first time experiencing life outside the communities where they had grown up. These and other wartime social trends affected postwar life in important ways.

The immediate challenge in 1945, however, was the economic transition from war to peace. As military spending plummeted from $75 billion in 1945 to $43 billion in 1946, and as the Truman administration, under intense political pressure, rapidly demobilized the twelve million men and women in uniform, many observers foresaw massive unemployment and a return to the grim conditions of the 1930s. But in fact the burgeoning economy easily absorbed the returning GIs. A short postwar downturn soon ended, and by the end of 1946 the boom was under way. Economic output in the United States, already at an all-time high of $200 billion in 1946, surged to $318 billion by 1950.

War research contributed to the postwar boom, as developments in electronics, pharmaceuticals, chemicals, aeronautics, atomic energy, and other fields not only made postwar America the world's research center but also sent the economy into overdrive. Electronics sales surged to over $11 billion by 1960; plastics and synthetics, little known before the war, proved to have myriad civilian applications.

The industrial know-how that had produced the planes and ships which helped win the war had direct peacetime applications. So, too, did the backlog of savings resulting from the wartime combination of high wages and scarcity of consumer goods. Americans in August 1945 had some $140 billion in bank savings and war bonds, and this accumulated reserve soon surged into the economy, fueling the postwar demand for consumer goods. The devastation abroad that was part of the war's legacy spurred the economy as well, as American factories, unscathed by bombs, produced the goods for export that could not be made elsewhere. For a time in the late 1940s, one-third of all the world's manufactured goods came from the United States.

The Servicemen's Readjustment Act of 1944 (the so-called GI Bill of Rights), providing educational benefits and business loans to veterans, facilitated the demobilization process. Taking advantage of the law's educational provisions, a tide of 2.3 million veterans surged onto the nation's college campuses between 1945 and 1950.

Though employment continued at a high level as factories converted to peacetime production, most women war workers lost their jobs. Some returned voluntarily to domestic life, but many made the transition unwillingly. A 1944 study by the U.S. Women's Bureau showed that 80 percent of the women who had worked throughout the war hoped to remain employed after the war's end. Nevertheless, women workers were fired at a far higher rate than their male counterparts. In the aircraft industry, for example, where women constituted 39 percent of the wartime work force, they made up 89 percent of those laid off with the coming of peace.

Many black veterans chose to remain in the cities of the North, as did many blacks who had come north seeking factory work. Thus the war speeded up the black migration cityward that had been under way for decades, further shaping the social contours of late-twentieth-century American society.

PROSPERITY YEARS

Statistics suggest the magnitude of the postwar boom, though they cannot convey its full social and cultural meaning. The gross national product (GNP) rose from $212 billion in 1945 to $503 billion in 1960. Though the population grew from 140 million to 181 million in this period, the per capita GNP rose even faster. Led by surging automobile sales—fifty-eight million new cars (most of them domestically produced) rolled out of dealer showrooms in the 1950s—production records fell on all sides. Six million refrigerators, fifteen million radios—the list goes on and on. Enticed by a torrent of advertising and by easy credit (the first credit card, Diners' Club, appeared in 1950; by 1960 Sears Roebuck alone had issued ten million plastic cards), Americans snapped up consumer goods at a mind-numbing clip. Despite several short recessions, the worst in 1957–1958, the economy hummed through most of the period. An upsurge in cold war military spending and foreign aid (much of it in the form of credits for acquiring American goods and military hardware) stimulated the economy. From 1945 to 1960 American economic and military aid abroad totaled $78 billion, and by the mid 1950s defense spending represented fully 10 percent of the GNP. The economist John Kenneth Galbraith captured the spirit of the era in the title of his 1958 book, *The Affluent Society.* While lamenting that much of Americans' new prosperity was going for private consumption rather than for society's common needs, Galbraith readily conceded the reality of that unprecedented prosperity.

Though it was not much noted at the time, low energy costs played a critical role in this economic boom. All forms of power, including oil, were cheap and abundant. Domestic oil production increased by nearly 50 percent between 1945 and 1960, and annual oil imports rose from 74 million to 371 million barrels. The typical Detroit car of the 1950s—the gas-guzzling, chrome-laden behemoth with soaring tailfins ridiculed by the critic John Keats in a book called *The Insolent Chariots* (1958)—typified the era's heedless attitude toward energy. At the bright midday of 1950s prosperity, fossil-fuel shortages, soaring oil prices, and dwindling energy resources were no more than small clouds on a distant horizon.

So, too, were the massive trade deficits that would afflict the economy in the 1970s and 1980s. The specter of massive economic competition from recently defeated Japan, as well as from other nations, still lay in the future. The United States in these years consistently exported far more than it imported. In 1960, for example, America enjoyed a favorable trade balance of nearly six billion dollars.

New technologies that increased productivity represented another major pillar of the postwar boom. From 1945 to 1960, for example, the worker-hours required to manufacture an automobile fell by half. Development of the computer, another product of wartime research, moved forward rapidly after 1945. The invention of the transistor in 1948 by Bell Laboratories scientists offered an alternative to the bulky and unreliable vacuum tubes of the wartime computers. Though the era of the ubiquitous home computer still lay ahead, by 1960 some four thousand computers were at work in private industry, and hundreds more were in such government agencies as the Census Bureau, the Internal Revenue Service, and, above all, the Department of Defense.

But with increased reliance on technological innovation and automated production, the work force changed. An industrial order once heavily dependent on manual labor now increasingly relied on college-trained researchers, engineers, managers, and service personnel. While the percentage of blue-collar workers in the labor force dropped slightly from 1940 to 1960, the proportion of white-collar workers increased from 31 to 42 percent. This trend would intensify in the years ahead.

As the blue-collar ranks thinned and workers shared in the general prosperity, the union movement of the 1930s lost momentum. In 1945 some 36 percent of the nonagricultural work force was unionized; by 1960 this figure had dropped to 31 percent. Restrictive federal labor legislation enacted by an increasingly conservative Congress, notably the 1947 Labor-Management Relations Act (the so-called Taft-Hartley Law) exacerbated this erosion of union power.

Increased productivity changed agriculture as well. With less labor required to meet the nation's food needs, the farm population (continuing a long trend) dropped from thirty million in 1940 to sixteen million in 1960. Blacks left the land at a particularly rapid rate. In 1940, 35 percent of blacks lived on farms; by 1960 only 8 percent did. In the same period, the size of the average farm increased from just over 200 acres to 330 acres, as the small family farm long idealized in song and story gave way to large-scale, mechanized agribusinesses. A government crop-subsidy program favoring large commercial producers hastened this consolidation process. The increase in farm output also reflected the growing use of chemicals and pesticides. With the publication of Rachel Carson's *Silent Spring* (1962), documenting the dangerous ecological effects of pesticides like DDT, Americans began to realize some of the long-term costs of surging agricultural productivity. But, as in many other areas, the underside of abundance went largely unrecognized in the 1950s.

Increased productivity and a rising GNP translated into more income for millions of Americans. In constant dollars, the median U.S. family income rose from about $4,300 to nearly $6,000 in the 1950s. The average inflation-adjusted hourly wage for factory workers rose from $1.78 in 1945 to $2.61 in 1965. Overall, the real income of the average worker grew by more than a third from 1945 to 1960. Bigger paychecks meant greater buying power, and this helped keep the boom going.

Statistics like these underlay the middle class's political and social conservatism in these years. Aware of their own improving situation in contrast with the Great Depression of the 1930s and the disrupted war years, millions of Americans seemed determined to uphold the status quo against alien ideologies, domestic critics, or "subversive elements" that in any way challenged a system that was treating them so well.

A NATION ON THE MOVE

Responding to the lure of jobs and eager to enjoy the fruits of prosperity, Americans moved in record numbers in the 1950s. Since the early nineteenth century, of course, acute social observers had commented on Americans' penchant for uprooting themselves and moving on, but in the postwar era this fondness for geographic mobility was especially apparent. California's population grew by five million in the 1950s as Americans from the East poured into the fabled land of sunshine and orange groves. The population of Orange County, south of Los Angeles, doubled in size during the 1940s and tripled in the 1950s. By 1963 California had become the most populous state in the union.

A monumental program of interstate highway construction facilitated this mobility. The Interstate Highway Act of 1956, a major legislative achievement of the Eisenhower era, earmarked some $32 billion for interstate highway construction over the next thirteen years. As ribbons of concrete and as phalt unrolled across the land, bisecting old city neighborhoods and chewing up thousands of acres of farmland and rolling prairie, motels and fast-food chains followed in their wake. In the early 1930s Franklin Roosevelt had promoted national unity by summoning all Americans to join in the struggle against the Depression; during World War II foreign menaces supplied the glue of social cohesion. In the postwar era, together with a new external foe—the Soviet Union—and centralized mass media, the complex web of interstate highways helped sustain a cohesive—and standardized—American national identity.

Millions of Americans in the postwar years, particularly young couples starting families, moved to the suburbs. A severe housing shortage just after the war eased in the late 1940s as builders like Abraham Levitt and Sons of Long Island bulldozed farms and fields on the urban periphery and with lightning speed erected thousands of suburban tract houses, many of cookie-cutter similarity. Utilizing mass-production techniques they had learned building housing for wartime naval workers in Norfolk, Virginia (and employing unskilled, nonunion labor), the Levitts mastered the technique of transforming open land into streets, lots, and inexpensive houses in a few weeks' time. Other builders across the nation emulated their approach, throwing up suburban developments with sylvan names like Oak Hill and Pine Glen. Thirteen million new homes sprang up in the 1950s; 1955 alone saw a record 1.3 million housing starts. From crowded city apartments and rural towns, eighteen million citizens poured into the suburbs in this decade. By 1960 as many Americans lived in suburbs as in cities.

Together with the low cost of mass-produced housing (the Levitts' homes sold for as little as $6,900 including refrigerator, range, and washing machine), federal policy encouraged suburban growth—and the urban decline that it precipitated. While billions in public monies were spent on forty-one thousand miles of interstate highways in these years, for example, a mere pittance went to urban mass transit. While the Federal Housing Agency (established in the New Deal era) and the Veterans Administration subsidized low-cost mortgages on new homes, urban renters or renovators enjoyed no such benefits. Similarly, homeowners could deduct mortgage interest payments for federal income tax purposes, while the urban renter had no such tax break. The rise of the suburb and the decline of the city did not just happen; it resulted from a series of specific public policy choices.

SUBURBIA AND TELEVISION: SYMBOLS OF AN ERA

The burgeoning suburbs placed an indelible stamp on American life in the 1950s. The move to a spanking new suburb was not merely a geographic transition of a few miles; it had social, cultural, and spiritual implications as well. Many who made this move left behind rural communities or big-city immigrant enclaves with strong ties of family, church, and ethnic group to enter the anonymity of bedroom communities where total strangers found themselves next-door neighbors, sharing recipes, lawn mowers, baby-sitters, and opinions. In such a social setting, the premium was on tolerance, adaptability, "fitting in," and avoiding the idiosyncratic or the controversial—traits that some observers denounced as bland and conformist. In books like John Keats's *The Crack in the Picture Window* (1957), cultural critics wrote harshly of the intellectual sterility and tepid social uniformity supposedly fostered by suburban living.

The new suburbanites themselves, however, often spoke enthusiastically about the liberating experience of moving from a cramped city apartment or tenement, often shared with parents or in-laws, to one's own house on a (sometimes) tree-shaded suburban lot. A generation later, as the lure of suburbia palled, a new generation of young "urban pioneers" would return to the city to rehabilitate aging apartments and crumbling row houses, and take advantage of the city's rich mosaic of social, cultural, and culinary diversity. But in the 1950s the prevailing outlook differed markedly. For a generation seared by economic depression and war, and beset by the amorphous threats and alarms of the cold war era, the move to suburbia symbolized one's break with the past; one's hopes for the future; and, above all, one's desire for security. The cultural aridity and narrowing of social vision that suburban living entailed, while real enough, were doubtless exaggerated by some of the more extreme critics; in any event such drawbacks represented a trade-off millions were more than willing to make.

In a closely related phenomenon the level of religious activity surged in the postwar years. Church membership rose from 50 percent of the population in 1940 to 63 percent in 1960. Americans newly settled in suburbia particularly valued the church's role in promoting family togetherness and providing a source of social cohesion. As a slogan of the day put it: "The family that prays together stays together."

In former times religion had been seen as potentially divisive. Indeed, in the antebellum era Catholics and Protestants had battled in the streets of America's cities; as recently as the 1920s religious prejudice had torn the nation. Postwar America, by contrast, celebrated religion as a unifying social force. This meant emphasizing the most generalized themes common to all faiths and playing down sectarian differences. The religiosity of the period, therefore, while broad, was in many cases not very deep. Best-sellers like Norman Vincent Peale's *The Power of Positive Thinking* (1952) touted religion's value for mental health and success in life. Movies like *The Robe* (1953), *The Ten Commandments* (1956), and *The Greatest Story Ever Told* (1965) offered Hollywood stars in Technicolor biblical extravaganzas. Congress joined in the mood of civic piety, adding "under God" to the pledge of allegiance in 1954, and making the phrase "In God We Trust," which had appeared on the nation's currency and coins since 1865, the country's official motto in 1956.

But the more theologically rigorous Evangelicalism of an earlier era was far from dead. The fiery Baptist revivalist Billy Graham, with his traditional message of sin and salvation, attracted thousands to his crusades. On local radio and television programs, and in evangelical churches across the nation, the older faith survived. In the 1970s it would break forth in a surge of growth and political activism. But in the 1950s climate of togetherness and social unity, differences were played down and commonalities were celebrated.

Indeed, what was true of religion was true of society as a whole. In contrast to the passionate and conflict-ridden 1930s, a spirit of moderation and cautious restraint, epitomized by the "Modern Republicanism" of the Eisenhower presidency, characterized the 1950s. Social harmony and cohesion represented high social and political objectives, even at the price of papering over obvious differences and blunting divisive issues.

A series of critics dissected postwar culture and social values. In *The Lonely Crowd* (1950) the sociologist David Riesman contrasted the era's "other directed" style of interpersonal relations, by which the individual modifies his or her behavior according to the feedback he or she gets from others, with the "tradition directed" and "inner directed" character types of earlier generations. In *White Collar* (1951) the radical Columbia University sociologist C. Wright Mills harshly attacked the blandness, conformity, and opportunism of the rapidly growing white-collar class. William H. Whyte's *The Organization Man* (1956), originally serialized in *Fortune* magazine, took a skeptical look at the lives and values of corporate executives and their wives in an affluent Chicago suburb.

If suburbia offered both admirers and critics one central symbol of postwar America, television, the newest of the mass media, provided another. Though the 1939 New York World's Fair introduced Americans to television, World War II interrupted its commercial development, so that as late as 1946 it remained a novelty confined to a few thousand homes in the major cities. In the fifteen years that followed, however, it spread with lightning speed all over the nation. The first coast-to-coast hookup came in 1951. By 1960, 87 percent of all American households had at least one television set. The time the average American spent watching television grew from about four and a half hours a day in 1950 to more than five hours in 1960. In 1954 the Swanson Company introduced frozen "TV dinners," so that mealtime no longer need interfere with viewers' favorite shows. The most successful new magazine of the postwar years was *TV Guide*.

Television both reflected and intensified the suburban values and the obsession with consumer goods characteristic of 1950s culture. The programming that proved most popular symbolized the degree to which white, middle-class America in these years turned away from the unpleasant or the threatening to a realm of fantasy. After a brief period when TV shows like *Kraft Television Theater* (launched in 1947) offered serious dramas dealing with real social issues—an era sometimes called, with considerable hyperbole, television's "golden age"—Gresham's law was confirmed again as the medium increasingly purveyed superficial and escapist fare. Quiz shows offering contestants thousands of dollars or mountains of consumer goods as prizes symbolized the era's materialistic preoccupations. The ever-cheerful middle-class television families of "situation comedies" (sitcoms) like *Father Knows Best, Leave It to Beaver,* and *I Love Lucy* showed millions of suburban viewers, and those who looked to suburbia as the social ideal, a world they longed to believe was—or could be—their own: a world of strong, devoted parents and likable, well-scrubbed, wisecracking children inhabiting sparkling new houses and confronting only problems that could be resolved in thirty minutes. Exploiting suburbia's minor crises, they rarely challenged its underlying values or confronted the America that lay beyond its well-manicured lawns.

Above all, television provided a powerful new medium by which corporations could entice consumers with alluring images of the new, improved automobiles, refrigerators, detergents, cereals, cigarettes, and soaps available to them. American television evolved as a mechanism for delivering the largest possible audience to its business sponsors, and it fulfilled that function with phenomenal success. The share of corporate America's advertising budget spent on television rose from 3 percent in 1950 to 17 percent by 1965.

To be sure, television had its critics. Ray Bradbury in *Fahrenheit 451* (1953) portrayed a nightmarish future in which all books are burned and the masses are anesthetized by the nonstop entertainment and propaganda fed them by the ruling elite on wall-sized television screens. Vance Packard in *The Hidden Persuaders* (1957) warned of advertisers' insidious influence in shaping not only American consumption but also American values. Newton Minow, chairman of the Federal Communications Commission, denounced TV as a "vast wasteland" in 1961 and challenged network executives to watch for twenty-four hours the fare they were foisting on the public. The acerbic comedian Fred Allen called television "chewing gum for the eyes."

But while the critics wrung their hands, television steadily became the most influential medium of both news and entertainment for most Americans. From the late 1940s to 1960, many newspapers ceased publication or lost subscribers; once-influential magazines like *Life, Collier's,* and *The Saturday Evening Post* vanished or fell on hard times; and movie attendance declined from ninety million to forty-five million. But with each passing year television strengthened its hold on the American mass mind.

WOMEN IN THE EARLY POSTWAR YEARS

After fifteen years of crisis and upheaval at home and abroad, Americans of the 1945–1960 era, particularly the young middle-class couples moving to the suburbs, placed a high premium on material well-being, social stability, and family cohesion. The postwar emphasis on domesticity was reflected in the declining age at which women married; the average age for women at first marriage dropped by more than a year between 1940 and 1960, from 21.5 to 20.3. After decades of decline, the birthrate (the number of live births per one thousand women in the population) rose from 80 in 1940 to 106 in 1950 to a 1957 peak of 123, when it again began a long slide downward.

The surging birthrate contributed to the economic prosperity of these years. Young couples moved to larger quarters and bought a wide range of products for their growing families; communities built schools and hired teachers to cope with the onslaught of pupils. The postwar "baby boom" generation would continue to affect American society as its members moved through their college years, young adulthood, and the successive stages of their lives.

All this had important implications for middle-class women and the prevailing view of their appropriate role. The culture extolled domesticity and what one women's magazine called "togetherness." "Rosie the Riveter," the female factory worker celebrated in a popular World War II song, gave way to maternal images of "the happy housewife." In *Woman: The Lost Sex* (1947), two Freudian scholars, Marynia Farnham and Ferdinand Lundberg, blamed most of modern society's problems on women who had left the domestic sphere to compete with men. Dr. Benjamin Spock's best-selling *Baby and Child Care,* first published in 1946, similarly assumed that women's primary, if not only, role should be as homemaker and mother. Television shows deified the American family, amiably presided over by hardworking dad and apron-clad mom. Advertisers cultivated the image of housewives as the ultimate consumers, endlessly preoccupied with deciding among different brands of detergents or vacuum cleaners. Hollywood, which in the 1930s had portrayed stars like Joan Crawford, Joan Bennett, and Katharine Hepburn as feisty and independent (at least until the end of the movie, when they usually succumbed to stars like Cary Grant and Spencer Tracy), now typically celebrated the domestic virtues with saccharine stars like Debbie Reynolds and Doris Day. Even women's fashion reflected the new cultural norm, emphasizing tight waists; full, sharply defined bosoms; and full skirts featuring layer upon layer of crinoline petticoats.

How did women respond to cultural pressures intent on confining them to a narrow, restricted social role? On the one hand, feminist activism was nearly nonexistent. Old-line organizations such as the League of Women Voters continued their work, but at a low ebb. At the same time, other evidence suggests that many women did not placidly adapt to the niche society built for them. Despite the pressures aimed at confining women to the domestic sphere, the ranks of working women grew steadily after ebbing in the late 1940s. The year 1950 found 31 percent of American women in the labor force (up from 30 percent in 1947); by 1960 the figure stood at 35 percent. Even more significantly, the percentage of *married* women working outside the home rose from some 17 percent in 1940 to 32 percent in 1960. And the number of working women with children under age seventeen rose from forty million in 1950 to fifty-eight million in 1960. In a revealing poll of 1962, only 10 percent of the women surveyed wanted their daughters to have the same kind of life they had led.

But in the 1950s women's discontents remained largely unarticulated and did not find collective or ideological expression. Most women appear to have worked from economic necessity, or a desire to enhance their family's standard of living, rather than from an ideological commitment to a career. And the workplace remained highly stratified along gender lines, with women largely confined to such occupations as clerk, nurse, schoolteacher, and secretary, while medicine, law, and business management remained firmly male preserves.

Not until the political and cultural climate shifted in the early 1960s would women begin actively to resist the gender stereotyping so characteristic of 1950s social attitudes. In *The Feminine Mystique* (1963), a work that launched a new wave of feminist activism, Betty Friedan described the frustrations she and other white, middle-class young women had felt in the 1950s, and the narrowness of their lives as young wives and mothers. The pervasive cultural pressures preventing women from fully realizing their abilities, said Friedan, were "the problem that has no name." Certainly in the 1950s, amid the rush to the suburbs and the cultural celebration of domesticity and the family, the problem was rarely identified or discussed.

SOCIAL TENSIONS AND FEARS

While the economy boomed and consumerism pervaded the culture, anxiety and tensions belied the surface placidity of 1950s society. In this cold war era, fear of Communist expansion abroad and subversion at home, as well as of nuclear war, shaped American life in profound ways. As the long conflict with the Soviet Union took shape in 1946–1947, American society became increasingly obsessed with communism, disloyalty, and dissident opinion generally. These concerns intensified as the Soviet Union tightened its grip on Eastern Europe; the West responded with an anti-Soviet military alliance, the North Atlantic Treaty Organization (1949); a Communist government came to power in China (1949); and the United States fought a bloody and politically divisive war in Korea (1950–1953). This preoccupation helped mold the conservative political and social climate of the decade. As early as 1947 President Truman established a Loyalty Review Board to investigate government workers and dismiss any who presented "reasonable ground for belief in disloyalty."

Republican Senator Joseph R. McCarthy of Wisconsin capitalized most spectacularly on the era's anticommunist obsessions. Speaking in West Virginia in February 1950, McCarthy accused the Truman administration of coddling subversives and waved a paper that he said contained a list of Communists in government. Though he never produced proof, McCarthy over the next few years dominated the headlines, wrecked careers with wild charges, and fed the nation's paranoia with a stream of accusations and innuendos. At last in 1954 McCarthy overreached himself with charges that the Eisenhower administration and the U.S. Army were part of the Communist conspiracy. The televised "Army-McCarthy hearings" that spring, giving the American people the chance to see firsthand the senator's bullying tactics, hastened his downfall—and in the process demonstrated television's power. In December 1954 the Senate voted to censure McCarthy. His star fell rapidly thereafter, and he died in 1957 of complications related to alcoholism.

But though the term "McCarthyism" came to be applied to the antiradical political mood of the early 1950s, the paranoid climate was not confined to the actions of any one individual. The House Committee on Un-American Activities (HUAC), for example, conducted a series of highly publicized investigations of alleged Communist subversion in many realms of American life, including the Protestant clergy, university professors, atomic scientists, and Hollywood filmmakers. HUAC's 1948 investigation of journalist Whittaker Chambers's charges against a former State Department official, Alger Hiss, sent Hiss to jail on perjury charges and furthered the political career of an obscure young California congressman, Richard M. Nixon. In another case fraught with political overtones, Julius and Ethel Rosenberg of New York City were convicted and sentenced to death in 1951 for passing atomic secrets to the Soviets. Despite worldwide protests, some orchestrated by the Communist Party, they went to the electric chair in June 1953. These and less well-known cases contributed to a climate of uneasy apprehension in the 1950s, stifled dissent and controversy, and deepened the mood of caution and restraint. Movies like *Invasion of the Body Snatchers* (1956), in which sinister aliens take over the bodies of seemingly ordinary and innocuous citizens in a California town, epitomized the national aura of suspicion and foreboding despite the prevailing prosperity. The more extreme manifestations of the postwar "red scare" abated as the 1950s wore on, but they left a bitter legacy.

Fear of the Russians took many forms. In October 1957, the Soviets launched Sputnik I, the world's first orbiting satellite. Americans long confident of their nation's technological superiority suddenly found that supremacy under challenge. Frustration intensified when Vanguard I, the missile intended to launch a U.S. satellite, exploded on the launching pad that December. The Eisenhower administration responded with massive increases in spending on missile development (which had military as well as space-exploration relevance) and in 1958 created the National Aeronautics and Space Administration (NASA) to oversee the nation's space program.

Sputnik also triggered a wave of concern about the alleged failure of the nation's education system. *The American High School Today,* a 1959 report by James B. Conant, former president of Harvard University, criticized the high schools for substituting undemanding courses for rigorous work in science, mathematics, and foreign languages. To improve performance at the higher educational levels, Congress in 1958 passed the National Defense Education Act (NDEA), allocating some $800 million for loans to undergraduates and graduate students and provided funds for improving instruction in science, mathematics, and foreign languages. Spurred by such measures, enrollments in the nation's colleges and universities soared from 2.5 million in 1955 to 3.6 million in 1960.

The federal government's growing involvement in education, long the preserve of the states and private groups, represented a major new social trend of the period. Washington's total spending on education rose from $113 million in 1945 to $4 billion by 1965. The new technocratic economic order, as well as the cold war struggle, demanded a highly trained citizenry, and Washington's new educational priorities reflected this realization.

The early postwar years were shadowed not only by the reality of conflict in Korea but also by a pervasive fear of atomic war that shaped the culture in many ways. President Truman's decision to drop the atomic bomb on two Japanese cities in August 1945, while welcomed for its apparent role in ending the war, also set off a shock wave of fear that the same weapon might someday be turned against the United States. Politically active atomic scientists played upon such terror in 1945–1947 as part of their campaign to win support for the international control of atomic energy. This initial wave of atomic fear faded as the cold war turned attention from the bomb to the Russian menace, and as Washington reassured a jittery public with civil-defense plans and glowing propaganda about the peacetime uses of atomic energy.

But fear surged to the surface again in 1949–1950 when the Soviets tested their first atomic bomb, and President Truman responded with a go-ahead for the development of the hydrogen bomb, a doomsday weapon a thousand times more destructive than those which had destroyed Hiroshima and Nagasaki. The United States tested its first hydrogen bomb in 1952; Soviet and British tests soon followed.

Eisenhower's secretary of state, John Foster Dulles, exacerbated anxiety in the mid 1950s by proclaiming a policy of "massive retaliation" to any provocation and insisting on the wisdom of going to "the brink of war" to prove the nation's will. Though the Eisenhower administration's foreign policy in fact continued that of the Truman years in focusing on "containment" (rather than destruction) of Soviet power, the belligerence and moralistic fervor with which Dulles proclaimed this policy deepened public uneasiness. So, too, ironically, did civil-defense programs emphasizing fallout shelters in public buildings and suburban backyards. For many schoolchildren, the most vivid memory of the 1950s would be hiding under their desk during nuclear-attack drills and watching films such as *Duck and Cover,* in which Bert the Turtle offered instruction on how to respond to the atomic flash. Cities conducted practice drills and distributed leaflets listing evacuation routes. The citizens of Madison, Wisconsin, for example, were told to drive to nearby rural counties if nuclear war threatened; those without automobiles, civil-defense officials promised, would be transported in freight cars.

Apprehension deepened in 1957–1958 with the advent of intercontinental ballistic missiles (ICBMs) capable of delivering thermonuclear bombs anywhere in the world at supersonic speeds. As the arms race rose to a new level of menace, the prospect of annihilation seemed more real than ever.

These years also brought widespread concern about fallout from nuclear tests. As American and Soviet H-bomb tests in the Pacific pumped radioactive poisons, including deadly strontium-90, into the atmosphere, clouds of radioactive ash spread far and wide. By the late 1950s, fear of fallout pervaded the nation, spawning a political campaign to ban nuclear tests led by groups such as Physicians for Social Responsibility and SANE, the National Committee for Sane Nuclear Policy. In one SANE newspaper ad Benjamin Spock gazed with furrowed brow at a young child under the caption "Dr. Spock Is Worried."

But while the test-ban campaign challenged the prevailing political inertia of the 1950s, the overall effect of nuclear fear was probably to deepen the decade's mood of disengagement. The turning from politics and social issues to domesticity and private concerns represented one response to global dangers that seemed beyond the individual's power to control. Religion, particularly the soothing "positive thinking" of the Norman Vincent Peale variety, offered another means of coping with nuclear fear.

The bomb hovered over American culture in these years. Theologians debated the ethics of nuclear war. Social psychologists pondered the long-term effects of fallout-shelter confinement. *Life* magazine ran a picture story on a newlywed couple who spent their honeymoon in a fallout shelter. Ray Bradbury's *Martian Chronicles* (1950) and Walter Miller, Jr.'s, *A Canticle for Leibowitz* (1959) were only two of many science-fiction works that imagined scenarios of history's approaching end. Poets and artists offered images of nuclear destruction and human extinction, while Tom Lehrer, a songwriter and performer popular on college campuses, and the humor magazine *Mad* employed ridicule and satire against the insanities of the arms race.

A wave of mutant films launched by *Them!* (1954), in which giant ants spawned in the New Mexico atomic test site go on a rampage in their search for sugar, both reflected and exacerbated popular fears of radioactive fallout. So, too, did Stanley Kramer's *On the Beach* (1959), a bittersweet picture of the nuclear end of civilization played out to the strains of "Waltzing Matilda." TV science-fiction series such as *The Outer Limits* and Rod Serling's *The Twilight Zone* often dealt with themes of atomic war, radioactivity, and the social toll of nuclear fear. In one *Twilight Zone* story, for example, the citizens of a typical suburban community, panicked by a nuclear alert, turn upon each other in fury as they struggle to get into a backyard shelter whose owner has barricaded the door against them. Movies and television programs such as this made it clear that the electronic media, for all their capacity to narcotize the public, could heighten public awareness of serious issues.

Overt nuclear fear continued to eddy through the culture until 1963, when the Limited Nuclear Test Ban Treaty (banning atmospheric and underwater tests) for a time pushed it to the deeper recesses of consciousness. But for much of the 1945–1963 period, the specters of nuclear war and nuclear fallout were never far from the public's awareness. This reality, no less than affluence, consumerism, and suburbanization, is central to an understanding of the social history of the period.

A CULTURE OF DISSENT

The conformity and blandness that troubled social critics like Riesman and Mills became the target of a small but influential cadre of 1950s humorists, novelists, and poets who formed the vanguard of a counterculture that in the next decade would become much more influential. Nightclub satirists like Mort Sahl, Lenny Bruce, and Shelley Berman offered a caustic view of Eisenhower's America. J. D. Salinger's *The Catcher in the Rye* (1951) presented middle-class "phoniness" through the eyes of its late-adolescent hero, Holden Caulfield. The Beat writers, notably Allen Ginsberg and Jack Kerouac, celebrated spontaneity, sensual gratification, alcohol and marijuana, and the freedom of the open road as alternatives to suburban conformity and family commitment. Ginsberg's poem *Howl* (1956), portraying capitalist, nuclear-armed America as a monster devouring its young, and Kerouac's *On the Road* (1957), a thinly veiled autobiographical novel of escape through ceaseless movement and a variety of mind-altering substances, attracted the fierce loyalty of young and alienated Americans repelled by what they saw as the blandness and regimentation of 1950s society. Norman Mailer, who had won celebrity with his realistic novel of World War II, *The Naked and the Dead* (1948), in a 1957 essay called "The White Negro" romanticized young street blacks, or "Hipsters," as cultural models for repressed middle-class whites. From Hollywood came Marlon Brando, the motorcycle-gang leader in *The Wild One* (1954), and James Dean as the misunderstood adolescent in *Rebel Without a Cause* (1955).

But the message of such work was often ambiguous at best. The sardonic routines of Lenny Bruce and Mort Sahl and other stand-up comics encouraged ironic detachment more than activism. At the end of *The Catcher in the Rye,* Holden Caulfield suffers a nervous breakdown and is institutionalized. And in *Rebel Without a Cause* James Dean's rebelliousness is effectively neutralized by a therapeutic social worker who probes the Freudian sources of his malaise (a weak father who dons an apron and helps with the housework) and persuades him to accept society's conventions as embodied in Natalie Wood, the girlfriend who is clearly ready to marry and settle down in suburbia.

The cultural wars of the 1950s spilled over into the world of popular music. While the mainstream music of these years celebrated domesticity, somewhat sanctimonious piety, and a rather treacly form of romantic love, at the end of the decade a very different genre, rock and roll, a watered-down version of the driving beat and open sexuality of black rhythm and blues, became vastly popular with the younger generation. Promoted by radio disc jockeys like Alan Freed of New York's WINS, early rock-and-roll hits like "Shake, Rattle, and Roll" (1954) and "Rock Around the Clock" (1955), both performed by Bill Haley and the Comets, proved harbingers of things to come. Church leaders, educators, and other pillars of the establishment protested, but rock and roll had arrived. Its most famous exponent, Elvis Presley from Tupelo, Mississippi, who recorded his first songs as an eighteen-year-old in a Memphis studio in 1953, enjoyed a phenomenal string of fourteen million-seller records from 1956 through 1958, when he was drafted into the army. Like the nightclub comics and the Beat writers, rock and roll challenged the dominant culture in largely nonideological, nonpolitical ways; in a few years that challenge would become much more explicitly ideological and political.

THE OTHER AMERICA

Although the white, middle-class world of the suburbs set the cultural tone of the postwar era, it was only part of the kaleidoscope of American society in these years. Beyond the trees and lawns of suburbia lay a very different world of Americans with lower incomes, less education, bleaker prospects, and, in many cases, darker skins. In 1960, after over a decade of booming prosperity, some one-third of American families lived on less than $4,000 a year.

In Appalachia and other rural byways, small farmers continued to eke out a bare existence. In the Southwest several million Mexican Americans worked as braceros (migrant agricultural laborers) or held low-paying jobs in the cities. Although official statistics recorded 528,000 immigrants from Mexico between 1951 and 1965, the actual number was vastly greater. In "Operation Wetback," launched in 1953, the Eisenhower administration returned many undocumented workers to Mexico, but the flow of migrants northward continued nearly unabated. In 1960 Hispanics made up an estimated 12 percent of the total population of California, Arizona, Colorado, New Mexico, and Texas. Meanwhile, in crowded East Coast communities like New York's East Harlem lived nearly a million Puerto Ricans, most of whom had arrived since World War II. These Spanish-speaking residents were among the poorest Americans, disadvantaged by a lack of education and by difficulty in speaking, reading, and writing English at a time when all but the most menial jobs increasingly required English verbal skills and advanced training. In the 1950s, one-third of all Hispanics lived below the poverty line as defined by the federal government.

The nation's Native American population, victims of centuries of white exploitation and neglect, existed at the lowest income levels and grappled with a wide range of social and medical problems. Government policies made matters worse. In 1953, intent on opening Indian lands to white development, Congress cut off all special services as a means of pressuring Indians to leave their ancestral lands and blend into the general population. The results were predictable: some sixty thousand Indians, tragically unprepared for urban life, drifted to cities, where they led marginal, deracinated lives, often barely surviving.

The nation's black population, which grew from thirteen million in 1940 to nineteen million in 1960, shared only partially in the prosperity of these boom years. In 1960–1961, the average black family had an income of $3,233, compared with $5,835 for white families; 32 percent existed on less than $2,000—three times the percentage of white families in this lowest income group.

As whites moved to the suburbs, they left the cities to blacks and Hispanics, many of whom held low-paying jobs or no job at all. As the factories that had historically provided entry-level work for immigrants closed or moved to outlying areas, urban unemployment inched upward, as did problems of crime, public health, poor schools, and social disorganization. At the same time the middle-class flight eroded the urban tax base needed to address these problems. The social trends of these years, in short, planted seeds that would produce a bitter harvest of almost intractable urban social problems in the decades ahead.

These grim social realities did not begin to penetrate the awareness of middle-class America, for whom prosperity, consumer abundance, suburban life, and the largely escapist fare of television defined the parameters of social experience. Not until the 1960s, under the spur of urban unrest and of books like Michael Harrington's *The Other America* (1962), would this dimension of American life come sharply into focus as the object of cultural scrutiny and concerted political action.

THE CIVIL RIGHTS MOVEMENT

While the problems confronting inner-city blacks were largely ignored, the more blatant manifestations of racism became the focus of political activism in these years, laying the groundwork for a profound and long-overdue transformation in American race relations. For years, the National Association for the Advancement of Colored People (NAACP, founded in 1910) had chipped away in the courts at the vast structure of racial segregation, especially in the South. World War II heightened awareness of the problem, as the incongruity of fighting racism abroad while tolerating it at home struck many Americans. In 1941, to forestall a threatened civil rights march on Washington, President Roosevelt issued an executive order barring racial discrimination in federal agencies and in war plants. In *An American Dilemma* (1944) the Swedish sociologist Gunnar Myrdal documented the extent of American racism and its heavy social toll.

The cause of racial justice moved still higher on the public agenda after the war, reflecting both blacks' growing political power and Washington's desire to win friends among the darker-skinned people of Africa, Asia, and Latin America. In 1946 President Truman created the Committee on Civil Rights, whose subsequent report, *To Secure These Rights,* documented the magnitude of the task ahead.

Early in 1948, facing a tough reelection battle, Truman proposed a panoply of civil rights measures, including federal laws against lynching, the poll tax (which effectively disfranchised most southern blacks), and racial discrimination in employment. Truman's program met fierce opposition from powerful southern Democratic congressmen, but it did provide a rallying point for the growing civil rights movement.

At the Democratic convention that summer, when northern liberals like Minnesota's Hubert Humphrey pushed through a strong civil rights plank, southern segregationists walked out. Forming a third party, the so-called Dixiecrats, they ran J. Strom Thurmond of South Carolina for president. Despite this challenge (and another from the left-leaning Progressive Party headed by Henry Wallace), Truman narrowly won, demonstrating, among other things, the growing political clout of black voters.

The NAACP's long legal struggle against segregation reached a stunning climax on 17 May 1954, when the Supreme Court, in *Brown* v. *Board of Education,* held school segregation unconstitutional. This landmark ruling reversed the *Plessy* v. *Ferguson* decision of 1896, which had upheld the constitutionality of the "separate but equal" doctrine. In a follow-up decision in 1955, the high court ruled that segregated schools must be integrated "with all deliberate speed."

Initially targeted on the South, *Brown* v. *Board of Education* laid the foundation for a civil rights struggle that eventually confronted the whole vast reality of a racially stratified society. Though far from over by 1960, or even by 1990, this struggle set a course for the future and represents the major social legacy of the Eisenhower years.

President Eisenhower initially disapproved of *Brown* v. *Board of Education.* "You cannot change the hearts of people by law," he believed. Reflecting this view, his administration at first did little to enforce the Supreme Court's ruling amid mounting southern opposition led by the Ku Klux Klan and newly formed white citizens' councils.

A showdown came in September 1957, however, when Arkansas governor Orval Faubus proclaimed his state's determination to resist the court-ordered integration of Little Rock's Central High School. Despite his personal reservations, Eisenhower at last made it clear that the law of the land must be obeyed, and that Arkansas's defiance would not be tolerated. In the face of hundreds of white racists who poured into Little Rock, the president sent federal troops from the 101st Airborne Division to assure the safety of black students who entered Central High. Televised images of black boys and girls entering school protected against jeering whites by federal power conveyed to the nation a powerful message not only of the ugly reality of racism but also of American society's gradually stiffening will to resist it. Once again, television demonstrated its potential for dramatizing great social issues as well as providing mindless escape from such issues. But the *Brown* decision and the showdown at Central High, while major landmarks, represented only early faltering steps of a long journey. As late as 1965 only 2 percent of schools in the Deep South were integrated.

Meanwhile, as the accelerating civil rights movement confronted the larger issue of pervasive racial discrimination in the South, blacks took the lead in challenging the visible symbols of second-class citizenship. The focus in this phase of the struggle shifted to Montgomery, Alabama, which, like other southern cities, required blacks to sit at the rear of city buses and yield their seat to any white who demanded it. On 1 December 1955 a black woman of Montgomery, Rosa Parks, tired after a long day's work as a seamstress, refused to give her seat in the white section of the bus to a white man. She was arrested, jailed briefly, and fined ten dollars. From this spark grew a movement that helped topple the vast structure of legalized racial segregation across the Old Confederacy. Led by Martin Luther King, Jr., the young pastor of the city's Dexter Avenue Baptist Church, and veterans of the labor movement like E. D. Nixon, the blacks of Montgomery organized a bus boycott. For nearly a year, as the bus system lost thousands of dollars, blacks walked to work or gave each other rides. The combination of King's pulpit eloquence, the boycott leaders' tactical skills, and the strong-willed endurance of Montgomery's black community gradually prevailed. In November 1956 the Supreme Court upheld a lower court ruling declaring Montgomery's bus segregation illegal. The boycott had succeeded, and long-entrenched patterns of racial segregation began to fall all across the South.

In the Civil Rights Act of 1957, the first since Reconstruction days, Congress forbade attempts to intimidate citizens from voting, created the U.S. Civil Rights Commission, and established a civil rights division within the Department of Justice. That same year, Martin Luther King and others formed the Southern Christian Leadership Committee (SCLC) to spearhead the campaign. The new organization reflected King's commitment to nonviolence as both a practical strategy and a moral principle. Civil rights activists skillfully organized symbolic actions that dramatized the reality of racism and won the nation's attention and admiration. In 1960, for example, black college students in Greensboro, North Carolina, occupied seats at the lunch counter of a local Woolworth's store that, following southern custom, did not serve blacks. This "sit-in" strategy became a major technique not only in the civil rights campaign but also in the anti-Vietnam war movement of the 1960s.

Black writers contributed to the movement as well. Ralph Ellison's *Invisible Man* (1952), a masterpiece of surreal fiction, conveyed the complex psychological experience of living as a black in white America. In *Go Tell It on the Mountain* (1953) James Baldwin told of his boyhood as the son of a Harlem minister. In *Notes of a Native Son* (1955) Baldwin addressed American racism directly in a series of incisive essays.

Though focused on legally enforced segregation in the South rather than on the broader patterns of racism endemic in American society, the civil rights movement of the 1950s nevertheless played an essential role in confronting racism's more blatant manifestations, sensitizing millions of whites to long-ignored realities, and arousing a generation of young blacks to demand full equality.

SUMMING UP

On a wintry morning in January 1961, as seventy-year-old Dwight Eisenhower watched impassively, a vigorous young John Kennedy took the oath as president. Not only a moment of political transition, the inauguration had broader resonances as well. The Eisenhower era was over; so, too, was a cycle of American history that began with the victory celebrations of August 1945.

THE POSTWAR PERIOD THROUGH THE 1950s

This era challenges social historians because of the sharp disparities between the experiences of different social groups. For many it brought good times as a stream of consumer goods poured forth from a powerful engine of production near its peak of efficiency. American capitalism between 1945 and 1960 made possible a standard of living unmatched in human history; from houses and automobiles to ballpoint pens and Levi's, the cornucopia of consumer goods awed the world. From the perspective of a later generation coping with industrial decline, trade deficits, environmental worries, and soaring energy costs, that distant era of seemingly effortless abundance seems almost a mirage.

Yet the darker side of the picture must be recognized as well. The postwar red scare warped the political process and shriveled intellectual and cultural life. Nuclear fear affected the national psyche in profound ways. A narrow conception of women's role held half the population hostage. And millions of citizens found themselves excluded from the banquet of material affluence.

The era challenges historical interpretation, too, because of the sharp contrast between its reality and the myopic and self-congratulatory tone of a politics and mainstream culture that determinedly ignored important aspects of that reality. Fundamental issues sometimes found political expression, as in the civil rights and test-ban movements, but more often they did not. Only later—in some cases much later—would the nation confront in anything like a comprehensive fashion the era's racism, gender exploitation, nuclear and environmental hazards, and vast class disparities. Also largely unacknowledged were the long-range social implications of the emerging computerized, automated technocratic order. Only in the 1960s, in books like *Silent Spring, The Feminine Mystique,* and *The Other America* (and in films like *Dr. Strangelove,* Stanley Kubrick's brilliant 1963 satire on the nuclear arms race) would the harsher contours of the years between 1945 and 1960 even begin to come into focus.

Given this disparity between reality and the nation's readiness to confront that reality, anyone seeking to understand postwar American social history must heed with particular care the voices on the cultural periphery, where issues found expression in sometimes allusive and distorted ways: science-fiction stories of aliens and robots taking over the world, B-grade mutant movies, the cynical monologues of comedians in smoky nightclubs; the at times hysterical and half-crazed rantings of Beat writers and poets; the raw sexuality and raucous self-assertion of rock and roll, the irreverent satires of *Mad* magazine; the hellfire warnings of evangelical revivalists. To grasp the complex texture of American society in these years, one must attend carefully to sources like these. In them one confronts the issues, tensions, and social forces that stirred beneath the deceptively placid surface of postwar America.

BIBLIOGRAPHY

General Histories

Gilbert, James. *Another Chance: Postwar America, 1945–1985.* 2nd ed. (1986).

Hart, Jeffrey. *When the Going Was Good!: American Life in the Fifties* (1982).

O'Neill, William L. *American High: The Years of Confidence, 1945–1960* (1986).

Perrett, Geoffrey. *A Dream of Greatness: The American People, 1945–1963* (1979).

Thought and Culture; Mass Media

Biskind, Peter. *Seeing Is Believing: How Hollywood Taught Us to Stop Worrying and Love the Fifties* (1983).

Boyer, Paul S. *By the Bomb's Early Light: American Thought and Culture at the Dawn of the Atomic Age* (1985).

Cook, Bruce. *The Beat Generation* (1971).

Frith, Simon. *Sound Effects: Youth, Leisure, and the Politics of Rock 'n' Roll* (1981).

Goldman, Albert. *Elvis* (1981).

Marc, David. *Democratic Vistas: Television in American Culture* (1984).

Wilk, Max. *The Golden Age of Television: Notes from the Survivors* (1976).

Suburbs, Women, and Family

Jackson, Kenneth T. *Crabgrass Frontier: The Suburbanization of the United States* (1986).

Jones, Landon Y. *Great Expectations: America and the Baby Boom Generation* (1980).

Kaledin, Eugenia. *Mothers and More: American Women in the 1950s* (1984).

Kessler-Harris, Alice. *Out to Work: A History of Wage-Earning Women in the United States* (1982).

May, Elaine Tyler. *Homeward Bound: American Families in the Cold War Era* (1988).

Wright, Gwendolyn. *Building the Dream: A Social History of Housing in America* (1981).

Farmers, Minorities, Civil Rights Movement

Acuña, Rodolfo. *Occupied America: A History of Chicanos.* 2nd ed. (1981).

Burt, Larry W. *Tribalism in Crisis: Federal Indian Policy, 1953–1961* (1982).

Fite, Gilbert C. *American Farmers: The New Minority* (1981).

Flynt, J. Wayne. *Dixie's Forgotten People: The South's Poor Whites* (1979).

Kluger, Richard. *Simple Justice: The History of "Brown v. Board of Education" and Black America's Struggle for Equality* (1975).

Lewis, David L. *King: A Critical Biography* (1970).

Sitkoff, Harvard. *The Struggle for Black Equality, 1954–1980* (1981).

Cold War Culture

Caute, David. *The Great Fear: The Anti-Communist Purge Under Truman and Eisenhower* (1978).

Clowse, Barbara B. *Brainpower for the Cold War: The Sputnik Crisis and the National Defense Education Act of 1958* (1981).

Lipsitz, George. *Class and Culture in Cold War America* (1982).

May, Lary, ed., *Recasting America: Culture and Politics in the Age of the Cold War* (1989).

SEE ALSO **Business Culture; The Culture of Consumption; Family Structures; Labor: The Great Depression through the 1980s; The Nuclear Age; Popular Music Before 1950; The Rise of Mass Culture; Rock Music; The Suburbs; Television; Women and Work.**

MODERN AMERICA: THE 1960s, 1970s, AND 1980s

Allan M. Winkler

IN THE YEARS between 1960 and 1990, the United States experienced tremendous social upheaval. The nation had emerged from World War II strong and secure, confident that all problems could be solved on its own terms. Over the next decade and a half, Americans consolidated their gains with the sure sense that growth could continue forever, that social conflict could be minimized, and that their aims and aspirations could provide a model for progress overseas. Then, in the early 1960s, that consensus began to erode as minority groups challenged the assumption that American society offered equal rights for all and a foreign war opened deep divisions within the United States. New movements questioned traditional values and long-silent groups—blacks, Hispanics, and Native Americans, among others—demanded access to the benefits of American life. Women pushed to transform the conditions they faced at work and at home. But none of those changes came easily. For the better part of the recent past, the nation has struggled to cope with the problems of social transformation in a continuing effort to redefine the American dream.

In the period after 1960, the nation shifted course dramatically. Most Americans in the early postwar years agreed with publisher Henry Luce that this was the "American century," and they wanted to preserve the democratic structure they had fought for as they shared the material manifestations of the good life. In the 1950s, they lived comfortably and enjoyed greater prosperity than ever before. Not all shared in the affluence, of course, but a basic agreement about American values continued despite the rifts that began to appear.

The design unraveled in the 1960s and 1970s as the nation experienced a crisis in confidence, and old assumptions were questioned and shelved. The cold war consensus that had pitted the nation against the evil Communist threat seemed less compelling. The growth of presidential power that had seemed beneficial now threatened the delicate constitutional balance. The economy faltered, and traditional economic theories failed to explain the disruptions that became a way of life. Social reform that had helped preserve stability seemed to have run its course. In the midst of that void, disfranchised groups demanded—and won—rights that had long been denied. But their success created a backlash that plagued the nation in the years that followed.

In the 1980s, the United States sought to create a new balance. After congressional efforts to limit foreign entanglements, the nation embarked on a massive military buildup in an effort to recapture a lost sense of national purpose. Led by a conservative president, it sought as well to limit the federal bureaucracy at the very time Americans depended more on government to provide basic security and support in an increasingly complex age. Although certain basic reforms were institutionalized, a new political and cultural conservativism became the dominant force in American life.

AMERICAN SOCIETY IN TRANSITION

After the baby boom of the postwar years, which peaked in 1957, the birthrate in the United States began to decline. The population, which had risen by 19 percent in the 1950s, increased by only 13.3 percent in the 1960s and 11.5 percent in the 1970s, and continued at the same level in the 1980s, as the nation experienced the second lowest growth rate in its history—it had been lower only during the bitter years of the Great Depression. The drop was to be expected, as the pressure felt by returning servicemen to make up for lost time ran its course, but it nevertheless had a powerful effect on national patterns. Census figures highlighted significant structural changes in American society. Cities deteriorated as baby boomers bought affordable homes in new suburbs. The urban rate of growth, which had risen sharply in the early years of the twentieth century but had been slowing since 1950, leveled off. In nineteen states, the rural segment of the population actually increased. There were shifts in age distribution as new drugs lengthened the American life span. Between 1960 and 1980, the number of Americans under the age of five decreased by almost 20 percent, while the number over the age of fifty-five increased by 53 percent.

Household composition changed as well, as relationships began to follow new patterns and divorce became more common. By 1980, 26 percent of all households were classified as "nonfamily households," up from 19 percent a decade earlier. In these units, two or more unrelated individuals shared living quarters in a variety of different arrangements. During the same period, the percentage of more traditional "family households" fell from 81 percent to 74 percent.

Meanwhile, another shift involved the entrance of new immigrants into the United States. A fifth of the population growth in the 1970s came from this source, which was spurred by the Immigration Act of 1965. Part of President Lyndon Johnson's Great Society program, the act overruled the national-origins system of the 1920s, which had favored western Europeans, and authorized the acceptance of immigrants from all parts of the world. Between 1977 and 1979, 40 percent of the new arrivals came from Asia and another 40 percent from Latin America.

Some of the immigrants came in search of jobs. Numerous others came as a result of foreign crises. In the years after 1975, with the Vietnam War finally at an end, the United States accepted more than half a million Vietnamese refugees. In 1980 alone, more than 160,000 arrived. That same year, the nation admitted more than 125,000 Cubans and Haitians fleeing from turbulence in their lands. Legal immigration in 1980 was higher than it had been in 60 years.

Millions of other immigrants came illegally. As Latin American countries struggled with huge population increases and deteriorating economic conditions, more and more people looked to the United States for relief. Leonard Chapman, commissioner of the Immigration and Naturalization Service, estimated that the number of illegal immigrants living in the nation might be as high as twelve million in the mid 1970s. While official estimates were lower, Attorney General William French Smith acknowledged the seriousness of the problem in 1983 when he said, "Simply put, we've lost control of our own borders."

In 1986, Congress addressed the problem by passing the Immigration Reform and Control Act, which tried to curb illegal immigration while offering amnesty to aliens who had lived in the United States since 1982. Turnout for the program was less than expected, until the approach of the 1988 deadline, when the number of applications rose fivefold and all-night lines at legalization centers became common.

Once again the United States was a potpourri of people from very different parts of the world. Throughout the country, the languages heard in the schools and on the streets changed, as did the very complexion of the society. In Los Angeles, for example, Samoans, Taiwanese, Koreans, Vietnamese, and Cambodians competed for jobs and apartments with Mexicans, blacks, and Anglos. The Sunbelt in particular, from Florida to California, felt the impact of the Asian and Hispanic immigrants, and changed most dramatically as a result. A movement to implement bilingual education in the schools in order to ease the transition required of immigrant children made some progress in the 1970s, only to encounter resistance from critics who argued that such aid hindered movement into the American mainstream.

As population patterns shifted, economic patterns changed, too. The prosperity of the postwar decades gave way to problems more serious than any encountered since the 1930s. Declining productivity, galloping inflation, serious oil shortages, and high unemployment affected people in society's middle and upper ranks, but hurt working-class Americans most of all.

After being technological leader of the world since the late nineteenth century, the United States began to lose that position in the 1970s. Productivity slowed in most American industries, and economic growth, which had averaged 3.2 percent in the 1950s, fell to an average of 2.3 percent annually in the 1970s and virtually ceased during a recession in the early 1980s. Real gross national product (GNP) dipped by 0.2 percent in 1980, rose by 1.9 percent in 1981, and dropped by 2.5 percent in 1982. The decline stemmed from rising oil prices as well as from government policies aimed at curbing inflation by keeping credit tight. The Vietnam

War had diverted federal funds from research and development at a time when foreign competitors were increasing expenditures in this area. The results of the decline were devastating. In 1978 the United States provided only 16 percent of the world's iron and steel, compared with 60 percent in 1946. By 1980 the automobile industry was in similar trouble, as Japanese manufacturers captured nearly a quarter of the American market.

As productivity dropped and growth declined, the economy underwent a structural shift. Continuing a trend more than half a century old, service jobs became increasingly important. No longer did a majority of American workers produce tangible objects. Most provided service or expertise to others in the work force in jobs that varied widely in levels of skill and pay. By the mid 1980s, three-fourths of the 113 million employees in the United States worked in the service sector—as fast-food restaurant employees, clerks, computer programmers, teachers, doctors, lawyers, bankers, and bureaucrats.

A decline in trade union activity accompanied the shift to a service economy. Although unions had emerged from World War II claiming 35 percent of nonagricultural workers as members, that figure began to decrease steadily in the mid 1950s. In 1956 it stood at 26 percent; in 1983 it was 20.1 percent; in 1986 it was 17.5 percent. Preoccupied with the problems of consumerism rather than with organization, American workers were far less militant than they had been before, and in a time of economic contraction, union members had to make significant concessions to save their jobs.

As the economy underwent adjustment, it suffered a series of troubles. Poverty was one of the most serious economic problems faced. In the 1960s, Americans began to realize that far too many citizens in the "affluent society" were chronically poor. According to Bureau of Labor Statistics at the start of the decade, a yearly subsistence-level income for a family of four was $3,000; for a family of six, $4,000. But 40 million people, nearly a quarter of the population, lived below those levels, and almost as many were only marginally above the line. Two million migrant workers worked at a subsistence wage, and many less mobile Americans were hardly better off.

Socialist author Michael Harrington exposed those conditions in *The Other America* in 1962. Shocking the country and its political leadership, he described the "economic underworld" in New York City, where "Puerto Ricans and Negroes, alcoholics, drifters, and disturbed people" sought positions as "dishwashers and day workers, the fly-by-night jobs," and pictured as well the rural poor living a hand-to-mouth existence in what songwriter Woody Guthrie ironically called the "pastures of plenty."

Despite the Great Society's war on poverty, the problem persisted. The disruptions of the following decades only made matters worse for those at the bottom of the economic ladder. A survey in 1984 noted a "staggering" increase in poverty in the South. Throughout the country, blacks were worse off than whites. In 1981, 34 percent of all black families were classified as poor, compared with 11 percent of white families. Five years later, 42 percent of black families were living in poverty. Many of these were single-parent households headed by black women who had few prospects for improving their lot.

High rates of unemployment hurt even those not designated as poor. A tax cut in 1964 caused the GNP to rise and unemployment to fall over the next several years, but then the social and economic promise of the Great Society fell victim to the Vietnam War. In the administration of President Richard Nixon, the United States risked modest unemployment in an effort to check inflation, but the rate continued to grow throughout the 1970s. In 1975, after Gerald Ford succeeded Nixon, unemployment reached 9 percent, then declined to 7.5 percent when Jimmy Carter took office in early 1977. It hovered between 5.6 and 7.8 percent for the next four years, only to rise during the recession in the early years of Ronald Reagan's presidency. In 1982 it increased to 10.8 percent, with black unemployment over 20 percent.

Blue-collar workers were hurt most of all as industries around the country laid employees off. In Detroit, one of the nation's worst-suffering areas, the Japanese challenge to the automobile industry hit assembly line workers hard; the unemployment rate rose to more than 19 percent. But countless other areas were similarly affected. In Louisville, Kentucky, for example, General Electric released almost 10,000 of 23,000 workers and International Harvester closed a plant employing 6,500 people. White-collar unemployment increased at the same time, and middle-class college graduates who had expected to secure professional positions often found themselves underemployed.

Inflation was another serious problem. It began to increase as a result of spending for the Vietnam War, and quickly moved out of control. In the late 1960s, the economy was already heated up as a result of a tax cut and spending for social reform. With the rapid increase in the defense budget, the nation's system of production simply could not keep up with demand. As more dollars chased limited supplies of goods, prices began to rise. Had Lyndon Johnson cut back on spending or increased taxes, he could have kept control; but in his effort to conceal the cost of the war, he allowed inflation to get out of hand. Richard Nixon attempted to stop inflation with wage and price controls, then shifted his approach and watched inflation continue to rise. The fourfold increase in oil prices, mandated by the Organization of Petroleum Exporting Countries (OPEC), wrought further havoc. High energy prices affected all aspects of American economic life, as manufacturers, farmers, and homeowners were forced to deal with the consequences. Inflation rose from 2.2 percent in 1965 to 11 percent in 1974 and 12.4 percent in 1980. Under President Ronald Reagan, a recession brought the rate to 8.9 percent in 1981, and it stabilized at about 5 percent for the remainder of his first term.

Not all Americans were victims of economic disruption. Increasing numbers of college students abandoned the search for socially relevant courses that had characterized the late 1960s and enrolled instead in business or economics classes to prepare themselves for business careers. Once in the working world, these young urban professionals, or "yuppies," as they came to be called, devoted themselves to upward mobility and material gain.

In the face of economic and demographic change, the government accepted a larger role than ever before in dealing with social and economic problems. The New Deal and World War II had brought tremendous expansion in government's role, and the 1950s had ratified the changes that had occurred. By 1960, the government was a major factor in the lives of ordinary people. Federal expenditures rose from $75 billion in 1953 to more than $150 billion in the 1960s, and continued to increase in succeeding years.

Lyndon Johnson hoped to use federal power to create a society in which the comforts of life would be more widely shared and poverty would be eliminated. His Great Society in the 1960s drew on initiatives begun in John F. Kennedy's brief presidency, but bore his own unmistakable stamp. Johnson wanted to provide something for everyone: civil rights measures for blacks; a tax cut for the middle class; medical assistance for the aged and the poor; educational aid for the young. Drawing on the legacy of Franklin Roosevelt's New Deal and on the example of reformers in the Progressive era, he helped secure passage of the most extensive legislative program in the twentieth century.

Yet the gains proved short-lived, particularly as an emerging Republican majority seized the reins from the Democrats, who had been in power since the time of Roosevelt. While Richard Nixon recognized the need for government's expanded role and accepted the basic contours of the welfare state, he still catered to those with a larger economic stake in society, as did his successor, Gerald Ford. In the 1980s, President Ronald Reagan made a concerted attempt to reverse the notion that the national government should monitor the economy and assist the least fortunate citizens. Government, he charged, intruded into too many segments of American life, and it was time to cut programs the country did not need in an effort to eliminate "waste, fraud, and abuse." As he pushed for implementation of his program, he often faced a recalcitrant Congress that refused to do everything he asked, though it still accepted the main thrust of his approach.

Meanwhile, advances in technology played an increasingly important role in the United States. Television, which had developed into a staple of daily existence in the 1950s, now became an essential part of the political process and often helped to create a national constituency for social change. By 1970, 95 percent of all American households had at least one television set, compared with 9 percent twenty years before.

Television had a powerful impact on the election of 1960. John Kennedy and Richard Nixon squared off in the first televised presidential debates. While Nixon challenged Kennedy's arguments and got the better of the verbal exchange, Kennedy looked beyond his opponent and seemed to be talking directly to the American people. Polls of those listening to the debates on the radio showed Nixon as the winner; surveys of television viewers placed Kennedy in front. Pollster Elmo Roper estimated that 57 percent of the people voting believed that the debates had influenced their choice, and another 6 percent felt their final decision came from the debates alone. Kennedy himself concluded that "it was TV more than anything else that turned the tide."

Television also helped to educate Americans to abuses that demanded change. In 1963, a horrified public watched as Birmingham, Alabama, police used vicious dogs and high-pressure fire hoses on civil rights demonstrators. As newsman Eric Sevareid observed, "A newspaper or television picture of a snarling police dog set upon a human being is recorded in the permanent photo-electric file of every human brain." Similarly, in 1968, American television networks showed General Loan, the chief of the South Vietnamese National Police, looking at a Viet Cong prisoner, lifting his gun, and calmly blowing out the captive's brains. The clip summarized the brutality of the Vietnam War, caused a wave of protest, and forced people to consider whether the struggle was worth the cost.

Popular television shows reflected changes in the nation. While programs like *Father Knows Best* and *Leave It to Beaver* had featured the stable, family-oriented values of the 1950s, different shows became popular in the following decades. In 1969, *All in the Family,* starring Carroll O'Connor as Archie Bunker and Jean Stapleton as his wife, Edith, started a long run as one of the most successful shows on television. Although it followed the situation-comedy formula of depicting a single family at home, this program gave some sense of the conflicts of American life—middle-aged versus young, liberal versus conservative, blue collar versus white collar, authority versus dissent, ethnic prejudice versus a more cosmopolitan view.

The computer had an even greater impact on American society in the years after 1960. Inventors in the United States and Europe had devised electromagnetic calculating machines before World War II, but they were large, clumsy, and difficult to use. The Electronic Numerical Integrator and Calculator (ENIAC), built in 1946, contained eighteen thousand tubes and could perform five thousand additions or three hundred multiplications a second, but it had no memory and could work on only one task at a time. The development of the transistor in 1948 simplified the computer. The creation of the integrated circuit in 1959 was another step forward, and the building of the microprocessor, the "computer on a chip," in 1971 opened the way to putting small computers in homes and offices throughout the country.

Computers affected every phase of American life. They directed spacecraft, routed telephone calls, recorded hotel and airline reservations and financial transactions, and detected diseases. Their impact was reflected best of all in 1983, when *Time* magazine declined to select a "Man" or "Woman of the Year," and chose instead the computer as "Machine of the Year." The computer, *Time* explained, could "send letters at the speed of light, diagnose a sick poodle, custom-tailor an insurance program in minutes, test recipes for beer." In the process, it could also "give you time for dreams."

ACTIVISM AND REFORM

The Civil Rights Movement As the United States struggled with economic and industrial problems, millions of Americans demanded a greater measure of social equality. The civil rights movement launched by black Americans built on the gains of the 1950s, when the Supreme Court's *Brown* v. *Board of Education* decision (1954) had mandated an end to school segregation and the Montgomery, Alabama, bus boycott (1955–1957) had desegregated public transportation and shown the value of nonviolent direct action. Despite those gains, change was slow. Rapid segregation of public accommodations remained the rule in the South, and residential crowding and limited economic opportunities fostered serious discontent in the ghettos of the urban North.

In 1960, black college students in Greensboro, North Carolina, took their places at a segregated Woolworth's lunch counter and asked to be served. Their challenge to southern segregation laws captured media attention, and such sit-ins soon involved thousands of other blacks throughout the South. The next year the sit-ins gave rise to freedom rides, aimed at desegregating transportation facilities. Organized by the Congress of Racial Equality (CORE) and assisted by the Student Nonviolent Coordinating Committee (SNCC), the campaign sent blacks and whites side by side on buses heading south and stopping at terminals along the way. Though the riders were peaceful, they hoped to provoke confrontations that would force the government to come to their aid. They were subjected to verbal abuse—"Kill the nigger-loving son of a bitch"—and counter-demonstrators stoned and even burned the buses.

Such violent encounters sparked a growing consciousness in both the North and the South of the need to combat racial discrimination. More and more people, many of them students, enlisted in the campaign, as did clergy of various denominations. The civil rights movement became the most powerful moral struggle since the abolitionist crusade before the Civil War. Blacks and whites together vowed to destroy racial barriers once and for all. But while many whites of goodwill aided the campaign, the civil rights movement remained black-led and black-inspired.

The next step came in 1962, when James Meredith, a black air force veteran, sought unsuccessfully to enter the all-white University of Mississippi. Even though the Supreme Court affirmed his claim, Governor Ross Barnett, an adamant racist, vowed that Meredith would not be allowed to enroll and personally blocked the way. As in Little Rock, Arkansas, in 1957, the president had to send in federal forces to quell the riot that resulted. With soldiers on hand to ensure that peace prevailed, Meredith entered the university, where he remained until he graduated.

An even more violent confrontation occurred in 1963 in Birmingham, Alabama. Spurred on by local black leaders, Martin Luther King, Jr., launched another attack on segregation. Forty percent black, the city was rigidly segregated along racial and class lines, and King argued that a victory here could "break the back of segregation all over the nation." The fire hoses and police dogs that city officials turned on the black demonstrators horrified the nation, including President Kennedy, who in a nationally televised address termed the quest for equal rights "a moral issue" and said, "We preach freedom around the world, and we mean it . . . ; but are we to say to the world, and much more importantly, to each other that this is a land of the free except for the Negroes?" Later he asserted that "the time has come for this nation to fulfill its promise." Kennedy sent to Congress a strong civil rights bill prohibiting segregation in public places, banning discrimination wherever federal money was involved, and advancing the process of school integration. Despite powerful lobbying, particularly at the massive March on Washington, the bill was bottled up in committee when Kennedy died in 1963.

Lyndon Johnson was more successful than his predecessor in advancing the cause of civil rights. Calling for passage of Kennedy's bill as a memorial to the slain president, he worked with his former colleagues in Congress and finally secured passage of the Civil Rights Act of 1964. It outlawed racial discrimination in all public accommodations and authorized the Justice Department to move with greater authority on school and voting issues. It also prohibited discrimination in hiring on grounds of race, gender, religion, or national origin in firms with more than twenty-five employees. The act was one of the great achievements of the 1960s and destroyed the legal sanctions for the segregation system.

But Johnson was not done. He knew that patent discrimination still existed in American society, particularly in the realm of voting. Freedom Summer, sponsored by SNCC in 1964, sent black and white students to Mississippi to work for black rights. By the end of the summer, eighty workers had been beaten, and three had been killed. As King proposed another march the next year, this time from Selma to Montgomery, Alabama, to dramatize the situation, Johnson responded by addressing a joint session of Congress. "I speak tonight for the dignity of man and the destiny of democracy," he said. At one point he paused and raised his arms, then slowly repeated the words that had become the marching song of the movement: "And . . . we . . . shall . . . overcome." The Voting Rights Act of 1965, perhaps even more important than the 1964 measure, singled out the South for its restrictive practices and authorized the appointment of federal examiners to register black voters where local officials obstructed their registration. In the year after passage, four hundred thousand blacks registered to vote in the deep South; by 1968 the number reached a million.

Those gains created pressure for further reform and shifted the focus of the movement. Leaders like Malcolm X were impatient with moderate civil rights activity. He grew tired of hearing about "all of this nonviolent, begging-the-white-man kind of dying . . . all of this sitting-in, sliding-in, wading-in, eating-in, diving-in, and all the rest." Stokely Carmichael, elected head of SNCC in 1966, was influenced by Malcolm's message. That year, he and his followers challenged Martin Luther King. At one demonstration, he jumped onto a flatbed truck and shouted, "The only way we gonna stop them white men from whippin' us is to take over. We been saying freedom for six years and we ain't got nothing. What we gonna start saying now is Black Power!"

Violence accompanied the militant calls for reform. H. Rap Brown, who followed Carmichael as leader of SNCC, declared, "Violence is as American as cherry pie." In city after city, riots broke out, and cries of "Get Whitey" and "Burn, baby, burn" replaced the peaceful slogans of the earlier civil rights movement. Those who resisted the pace of reform were often violent as well, and King himself fell victim to an assassin in 1968.

As the 1960s drew to an end, the question of busing students to achieve racial balance in schools became increasingly controversial. Though more than eighteen million American students rode buses in 1970, the matter inflamed passions when it became tangled with the issue of integration. Despite a desegregation plan in Charlotte, North Carolina, many blacks still attended segregated schools, and a federal judge determined that the district was not in compliance with the latest Supreme Court decisions. In 1971, the Supreme Court ruled that district courts had broad authority to order the desegregation of local school systems—by busing, if necessary.

Richard Nixon, elected president in 1968 on a platform that sought the support of the white South, opposed such busing. He approached Congress for a moratorium or even a restriction on busing, and he denounced the practice on television. Although Congress refused to accede to his request, the public knew where he stood. As more and more southern cities were forced to draft transportation plans to integrate their schools, resistance grew. Busing became a bitter issue in the North as well as the South, reflecting the volatile nature of the continuing quest for equal rights.

Republican chief executives hoped to slow down the civil rights movement, and to a degree they did. While Nixon insisted "I care" to one black leader, actions spoke louder than words. So it was with his successor, Gerald Ford (1974–1977). At one point in his brief presidency, Ford asked the attorney general to consider supporting antibusing advocates in a Boston court case. Though he dropped that idea and never came out squarely against civil rights, his lukewarm approach demonstrated a weakening of the federal commitment. Similarly, Ronald Reagan, elected in 1980, opposed busing and authorized the attorney general to dismantle affirmative-action programs. Initially reluctant to support extension of the Voting Rights Act of 1965, he relented in the face of severe criticism from members of both political parties. He also launched an assault on the Civil Rights Commission and hampered its effectiveness.

The civil rights movement underscored the democratic values of the nation, but it also reflected the continuing gap between rhetoric and reality. Though it made important gains, it left a great deal undone as a white backlash developed. Given a wavering presidential commitment to reform for much of the 1970s and 1980s, only pressures from reformers kept the movement alive.

The Women's Movement The black struggle for equality sparked a women's movement that soon developed a life of its own. Many white women joining the civil rights struggle discovered that they were second-class citizens despite their efforts. Men, black and white, held the policy positions and relegated women to menial chores when they were not participating in demonstrations or voter registration drives. Women also felt sexually exploited by male leaders and were infuriated by sarcastic, offensive comments. For example, Stokely Carmichael, when he was asked what the position of women in the movement should be, replied, "The only position for women in SNCC is prone." Appropriating the vocabulary of the civil rights movement and its confrontational approach, women pressed for ratification of their rights.

Meanwhile, even women less engaged in the campaign for social reform began to question the values that had prevailed in the postwar years. Millions read Betty Friedan's explosive critique, *The Feminine Mystique* (1963), which challenged the conventional wisdom that women "devote their lives from earliest girlhood to finding a husband and bearing children." Women's roles, Friedan argued, were unnecessarily circumscribed:

> It was unquestioned gospel that women could identify with *nothing* beyond the home—not politics, not art, not science, not events large or small, war or peace, in the United States or the world, unless it could be approached through female experience as a wife or mother or translated into domestic detail.

Other women voiced discontent as they realized that even though they were entering the labor force in increasing numbers, in 1963 they earned only 63 percent of what a man could expect. Ten years later the situation was worse still; the figure fell to 57 percent.

Women used Title VII of the 1964 Civil Rights Act to support their claims to equal treatment. As originally drafted, the provision prohibited discrimination on the grounds of race. During the congressional debate, conservatives opposed to black rights had added an amendment including discrimination on the grounds of gender in an effort to make the measure ridiculous and secure its defeat. But the amendment passed, as did the entire bill, and women now had a legal tool for attacking discrimination. Unfortunately, they soon found that the Equal Employment Opportunity Commission regarded their complaints as less important than those of blacks.

When existing women's groups proved reluctant to pressure the commission to change its policies, a number of women, including Betty Friedan, decided to form their own organization. The National Organization for Women (NOW), established in 1966 "to take action to bring American women into full participation in the mainstream of American society *now,*" aimed at abuses on a number of fronts. It demanded fair pay and equal opportunity, and challenged the "false image of women" in the media. Some members called for a more egalitarian form of marriage. By 1967, one thousand had joined the organization; four years later membership reached fifteen thousand.

In the 1970s, the movement began to show results. One survey showed that over a two-year period the number of college students who believed women were oppressed had doubled. Another survey revealed that while in 1970 men interested in such fields as business, medicine, engineering, and law outnumbered women eight to one, in 1975 the ratio had dropped to three to one. Between 1969 and 1973, the proportion of women entering law school quadrupled. Women gained admission to the military academies and entered senior officer ranks.

Women's working patterns changed dramatically. While only 30 percent of all wives worked outside the home in 1960, the figure rose to 40 percent by 1970 and to over 50 percent by 1980. In 1980, more than half of all women were in the labor force, and that figure was projected to reach 75 percent in the 1990s. Women constituted approximately 40 percent of the working population by 1980. Pressures for income to maintain standards of living propelled some women into the work force, while others found a nonmonetary satisfaction in taking advantage of opportunities that had long been denied.

New publications reflected the energy of the movement. In 1972, Gloria Steinem, author of a regular column in *New York* magazine, helped establish a magazine aimed directly at women with a sense of social change. *Ms.* succeeded beyond the founders' wildest dreams. In the first eight days, the three hundred thousand copies of the preview issue sold out. After a year, there were almost two hundred thousand subscribers. Most were under thirty-five, had graduated from college, worked in professional, managerial, or technical jobs, and were not necessarily members of feminist organizations. *The New Woman's Survival Catalogue* was another source of useful advice to women readers. *Our Bodies, Ourselves,* a handbook published by a women's health collective, encouraged women to understand and control their own bodies, and sold 850,000 copies between 1971 and 1976. These new books and magazines differed from older women's publications like *Good Housekeeping* and *Ladies' Home Journal,* which focused on domestic interests and romantic fantasies. *Ms.* and its counterparts dealt with sexuality, employment, and discrimination, and provided a forum for discussion of feminist issues.

The women's movement in the 1970s was often diffuse, divided, and decentralized. *Time* magazine observed in 1972 that "the aims . . . range from the modest, sensible amelioration of the female condition to extreme and revolutionary visions." Groups like NOW pressed for equal employment opportunities, child care centers, and abortion reform. They also worked for congressional passage, then ratification, of the Equal Rights Amendment (ERA) to the Constitution, which stated that "Equality of rights under the law shall not be denied or abridged by the United States or by any state on account of sex." Other feminist groups were more radical. They sought fundamental changes in sexual identity to end male domination and social exploitation. Shulamith Firestone, for example, explained in *The Dialectic of Sex* (1970) the necessity for a new society in which women were freed "from the tyranny of their reproductive biology by every means available." Still other women resisted the entire movement, with the argument that feminism was contemptuous of women who stayed at home to perform traditional tasks. Black women faced difficulties more complex than those encountered by their white counterparts and often found race a far more compelling problem than gender.

Despite those rifts, the movement continued to make gains in the 1980s. Early in the decade, Betty Friedan summed up the shifts *The Feminine Mystique* had helped bring: "the enormous and mundane, subtle and not so subtle, delightful, painful, immediate, far-reaching, paradoxical, inexorable and probably irreversible changes in women's lives—and in men's." In the tenth anniversary issue of *Ms.* (August 1982), Gloria Steinem likewise noted the difference that had occurred: "Now, we have words like 'sexual harassment' and 'battered women.' . . . Ten years ago, it was just called 'life.'" She also said, "Now, we are becoming the men we wanted to marry. Ten years ago, we were trained to marry a doctor, not be one." Affirmative action made jobs for women more accessible. Legal changes brought still other opportunities. Title IX of the Education Amendments of 1972 broadened the provisions of the Civil Rights Act of 1964 and barred gender bias in federally assisted education programs. The new legislation stimulated colleges to admit far more women to professional schools and also changed the nature of intercollegiate athletics by mandating that more money be spent on women's sports. Though complete equity remained a distant goal, fully 30 percent of the participants in intercollegiate athletics in 1980 were women, compared with 15 percent before Title IX had become law.

Women made important gains in politics as well. They won mayoral races in Chicago, Houston, Honolulu, San Francisco, and many smaller cities. In 1981, President Ronald Reagan appointed Sandra Day O'Connor as the first woman justice of the Supreme Court; and in 1984, Geraldine Ferraro, a Democratic member of Congress, became the first woman vice presidential candidate on a major party ticket. Far more women were elected to state legislatures and to Congress.

Yet women still faced serious problems. Access to new positions did not change their concentration in lower-paying jobs. Even when they moved into positions traditionally held by men, progress often stopped at lower and middle levels. Wage differentials also persisted. In 1985, despite modest improvement, full-time working women earned only 63.6 cents for every dollar men earned. Arguments that women should receive equal pay for equal work now led to demands for equal pay for comparable work. Another worry, particularly for working-class women, was the growing feminization of poverty. In 1980, more than half of the families defined as poor were headed by single women. Left alone by desertion or divorce, they often had no means of subsistence.

Meanwhile, ratification of the ERA, which had been taken for granted after passage by Congress in 1972, ran into trouble. Although thirty-five of the necessary thirty-eight states ratified the measure, supporters were unable to secure the final three. Phyllis Schlafly and others continued a highly successful opposition campaign, directed toward women who felt threatened by changes taking place. By mid 1982, with a number of states rescinding ratification, the ERA was dead. Abortion, too, polarized women's groups and caused dissension in the country at large. Following the Supreme Court's *Roe* v. *Wade* decision legalizing abortion in 1973, "pro-life" forces mobilized a fierce crusade that led the court to chip away at its earlier ruling in the late 1980s and early 1990s.

Although women savored their gains, some worried about complacency in the younger generation. Many young women enjoying the benefits brought by the movement rejected the feminist label and shunned involvement in militant campaigns. Others were active, persuaded that only continued pressure would bring full equality.

The Chicano Movement Hispanics, like women, learned from the lessons of the civil rights movement. As their numbers increased in the postwar years, they, too, developed a heightened sense of solidarity and group pride, and became more vocal and confrontational in pursuit of their rights. In the 1960s, they hoped that Lyndon Johnson's War on Poverty would bring improved opportunities, but were disappointed as they found that most efforts focused on black Americans and that bureaucrats were often insensitive to the needs of equally exploited but less outspoken groups. That disappointment taught them the need for pressure politics in a pluralistic society and, even more important, the need for direct action.

Hispanics became increasingly active in the political arena. In 1961, Henry B. González was elected to Congress from San Antonio; three years later, Elizo ("Kika") de la Garza of Texas won a seat in the House, and Joseph Montoya of New Mexico went to the Senate. Perhaps more important, near the end of the 1960s, many Hispanics became involved in local campaigns. José Angel Gutiérrez and several associates began to organize followers at the grass-roots level in his hometown of Crystal City, Texas. Those efforts gave rise to the La Raza Unida political party, which began to play an important role in the area and successfully promoted Mexican American candidates for political office. During the next decade, it gained strength in the West and Southwest.

Political activism paid off. In 1978, Rudy Ortiz was appointed mayor pro tem in San Antonio; Henry Cisneros was elected mayor in 1982, then reelected the following year with 94.2 percent of the vote. Also in 1982, Colorado state legislator Federico Peña was elected mayor of Denver, and New Mexico Governor Toney Anaya became, in his own words, the nation's highest elected Hispanic. A 1987 survey documented the progress made. The number of Hispanics holding elective offices nationwide increased 3.5 percent between 1986 and 1987. The number of Hispanic women in such positions grew by 20 percent in the same time.

Direct action brought even more visible gains. César Chávez, founder of the United Farm Workers Union, demonstrated what could be done by organizing one of the most exploited groups of laborers in the nation, the migrant farm workers of the West. Concentrating on itinerant Mexican field hands who worked long hours in the fields for meager pay, he conducted a door-to-door and field-to-field campaign. By 1965, his union had recruited seventeen hundred members and began to attract volunteer help. Chávez first took on the grape growers of California. Calling a strike, he demanded better pay and working conditions, and union recognition. When the growers resisted, he launched a nationwide consumer boycott of their products and eventually was victorious. Boycotts of lettuce and other products harvested by the workers also ended in success. In 1975, Chávez's long struggle ended with the passage of a measure in California requiring growers to bargain collectively with elected representatives of the farm workers.

Chávez's example created pressure for reform in other areas. Beginning in 1968, some Mexican American students began to protest conditions in the secondary schools. They complained about overcrowded and deteriorating institutions and about the 50 percent dropout rate that resulted from expulsion, transfer, or failure because students had never been taught to read. Other students demanded Mexican American studies programs, and by 1969, at least fifty such programs were available in California alone. Their efforts helped promote a growing network of Hispanic educators and programs. "Ten years ago, there was no national Chicano academic community," declared Arturo Madrid, president of the National Chicano Council on Higher Education, in 1982. "Now we have a professional presence in higher education." A colleague estimated that there were five thousand Chicano faculty members in 1980, compared with two thousand a decade before.

Despite such progress, Hispanics still faced real difficulties. Their growing numbers created intense pressure on community resources. The Census Bureau predicted in 1986 that the Hispanic population—the nation's fastest growing minority—would more than double by the year 2020 and would account for 19 percent of the nation by 2080. Yet many Hispanics remained poor; their median household income was only 70 percent of that for whites, and many Mexican American families lived in shanties without plumbing or electricity as they tried to survive on $4,000 or $5,000 dollars a year.

The Native American Movement Like Hispanics, Native Americans launched a campaign for equal rights in the 1960s. They, too, learned from the example of blacks in the civil rights movement and accepted the need for an aggressive, confrontational approach to repudiate their second-class status and promote necessary social change.

As the number of Indians more than doubled between 1960 and 1980, they became determined to take control of their own lives. The federal policy of termination in the 1950s had sought to force them to assimilate into mainstream American life, but that effort had only traded reservation poverty for urban poverty. At a conference in Chicago in 1961, several hundred Native Americans asked the Kennedy administration for the right to help make decisions about budgets and programs for tribes. A group of college-educated Indians at the conference organized a National Indian Youth Council to reestablish Indian national pride. Over the next several decades, it helped change attitudes of tribal leaders and made them more willing to resist white demands.

Native Americans successfully promoted their own values and designs. Their fashions became more common, and galleries began to display their art, as the larger culture came to appreciate their work. In 1968, N. Scott Momaday won the Pulitzer Prize for his book *House Made of Dawn.* Vine Deloria's *Custer Died for Your Sins,* published the next year, had an even wider readership. Popular films like *Little Big Man* (1970) provided sympathetic portrayals of Indian history and culture, and opened the way for the Academy Award–winning *Dances with Wolves* two decades later.

In the 1970s, new educational opportunities created an educated elite. Some tribes founded their own colleges; in 1971, the Oglala Sioux established Oglala Lakota College in the Badlands of South Dakota with the motto "Wa Wo Ici Ya" (We can do it ourselves). Between 1976 and 1986, the number of Native Americans in institutions of higher education increased by over 18 percent. At the same time, several tribes developed business skills, assuming that if they were to be self-supporting, they needed to be entrepreneurs.

Meanwhile, Indians became more confrontational. They worked through the courts whenever possible but challenged authority in more contentious ways when necessary. They were most concerned with protecting what was left of their tribal lands after generations of encroachment by state and federal governments. "Everything is tied to our homeland," anthropologist D'Arcy McNickle told other Indians in 1961. A large number of lawsuits charged violations of treaty rights over the past several centuries. In 1967, in the first of many decisions upholding the Indian side, the Supreme Court upheld an Indian Claims Commission verdict that the government had forced the Seminole tribe in Florida to cede their land in 1823 for an unreasonably low price, and directed payment of additional funds. In the 1970s, when New York State tried to condemn a segment of Seneca land to build a superhighway through part of the Allegany reservation, the Seneca fought the issue in court. In 1981, the state finally agreed to exchange other land and to pay a cash settlement in return for an easement through the reservation. That decision encouraged similar tribal efforts in Montana, Wyoming, Utah, New Mexico, and Arizona. Native Americans also protested a new assault on long-abused water rights, and reasserted traditional fishing rights. Cases in those areas again demonstrated that aggressive litigation could make a difference.

At the same time, some Indians began to display a new militancy. The American Indian Movement (AIM), organized in 1968 by George Mitchell and Dennis Banks, Chippewa living in Minneapolis, sought to help neglected Indians in the city. It got federal poverty funds channeled to Native American–controlled organizations, and established patrols to protect drunken Indians from police harassment. Its successes gave rise to chapters in other cities.

Native American militancy was dramatized in late 1969, when a landing party of seventy-eight Indians seized Alcatraz Island in San Francisco Bay. Three years later, other activists launched the Broken Treaties Caravan to Washington, D.C., where they occupied the Bureau of Indian Affairs for six days. The following year, AIM insurgents took over the South Dakota village of Wounded Knee, where in 1890 American soldiers had massacred more than two hundred Sioux.

Indian protest brought results. Great Society resources became available as long as funds lasted. In 1975, Congress passed the Indian Self-determination and Education Assistance Acts. But serious problems—alcoholism, dislocation, and unemployment—remained. For the Indians, as for other disadvantaged groups, progress came only after a self-initiated struggle, and left them aware that they still had a long way to go.

SOCIAL AND CULTURAL PROTEST

As blacks and other groups clamored for greater access to the advantages of American life, middle-class American society found itself in the midst of major upheaval. Young people in particular challenged the affluent patterns of their parents and the norms that had governed since World War II. Some embraced radical political activity; others appropriated new standards of sexual behavior, music, and dress. They, too, adopted the confrontational techniques of the civil rights movement in an effort to make the social and political worlds more responsive than before.

Students attended colleges and universities in ever-increasing numbers in the post–World War II years. Members of the baby boom generation came of age in the 1960s, and continued their education more actively than any previous generation. By the end of the decade, college enrollment was more than four times what it had been in the 1940s. While college became a training ground for corporate and professional life, it also gave students time, if they chose to take it, to experiment and grow before they had to make a living.

The New Left rose out of student disillusionment with the government's professed commitment to civil rights. Some students had become involved in the movement for racial equality, hopeful that they could bring about meaningful change. When that proved difficult, radical activists organized Students for a Democratic Society (SDS) in 1960. Two years later, the new organization issued a manifesto, the Port Huron Statement, written largely by Tom Hayden of the University of Michigan. "We are people of this generation, bred in at least modest comfort, housed now in universities, looking uncomfortably at the world we inherit," it began. It went on to condemn the isolation and estrangement of modern life and called for a system rooted in "self-cultivation, self-direction, self-understanding and creativity" that could promote "a democracy of individual participation."

The first blow of the student rebellion came at the University of California at Berkeley. At the start of the 1964 academic year, university officials refused to allow students involved in the civil rights struggle to distribute protest material outside the main campus gate. Defiantly, the students resolved to fight back in what came to be called the Free Speech Movement. Though the administration eventually compromised, university regents insisted on disciplinary action against the student leaders, who responded by occupying the administration building. One leader, Mario Savio, called the university an impersonal machine: "It becomes odious, so we must put our bodies against the gears, against the wheels . . . and make the machine stop until we're free." When police stormed the building and arrested the students, a strike enjoying faculty support ensued.

Student protest spread. In 1965, students on campuses around the country questioned methods of college discipline, attacked old drinking and visitation rules, and demanded curricular reform. SDS activists, who had earlier sought to organize workers in the nation's cities, shifted their attention to the Vietnam War. That struggle, in which the Vietnamese attempted to extricate themselves from French, then Japanese, then French control again, had been going on for decades but had involved the United States only since the mid 1950s.

In the 1960s, however, America became the dominant power seeking to quash the independence movement of Vietnamese leader Ho Chi Minh. Lyndon Johnson, often frustrated by what he called "piddly little pissant countries," was determined to stand firm. "I am not going to lose Vietnam," he declared soon after he assumed office. As American involvement increased dramatically after the election of 1964, students became involved in a massive protest campaign. The first antiwar teach-in took place in 1965 at the University of Michigan, and others soon followed. Radical activists campaigned against the draft, attacked Reserve Officer Training Corps (ROTC) units on campus, and sought to discredit firms producing the implements of war. "Make love, not war," banners proclaimed as students became involved in political demonstrations. "Hey, hey, LBJ. How many kids did you kill today?" they chanted as they marched. In 1967, some three hundred thousand people marched against the war in New York City. In Washington, D.C., one hundred thousand tried to close down the Pentagon. Between January and June 1968, hundreds of thousands of students staged more than two hundred demonstrations at more than one hundred educational institutions.

Sometimes the rallies became bloody. When Richard Nixon broadened the war with an incursion into Cambodia in 1970, students at Kent State University in Ohio protested his action. After they burned the ROTC building to the ground, the governor called out the National Guard. With most students so far away they could not have threatened the troops, the Guardsmen opened fire on the unarmed activists. When the firing ceased, four students lay dead, and nine were wounded. A similar encounter at Jackson State College in Mississippi left two people dead.

For a time, the New Left was a powerful force. Although activists never made up a majority in American political life, radicals attracted students and other sympathizers to their cause and helped focus opposition to the war. The movement led Lyndon Johnson to state that he would not seek renomination for the presidency and opened the way to the long, slow process of extrication from the overseas struggle. The student protest movement intertwined with the efforts of outsiders to gain greater social equality, and brought significant cultural change as well.

In the 1960s, many Americans, including those who remained politically inactive, lost faith in the sanctity of the American system. Students shared the general feeling, noted by Joseph Heller, irreverent author of the antiwar novel *Catch-22* (1961), that "the platitudes of Americanism were horseshit." As protests exposed the emptiness of some of the old patterns, the young were the first to seek new ways to assert their individuality and independence. The most outspoken often drew on the example of the Beats of the 1950s, literary figures who rejected conventional canons of respectability in the search for new means of self-expression and self-gratification.

The hippies of the 1960s looked different. Men let their hair grow and sprouted beards; men and women both favored jeans, muslin shirts, and other simple garments. Stressing spontaneity above all, some rejected traditional marital customs and formed communes. Their example, at first shocking to some, soon found its way into the culture at large, as men grew long hair and discarded ties and jackets, and women threw off confining articles like girdles and embraced freer fashions—miniskirts, longer dresses, slacks and jeans for casual wear.

Sexual norms changed, too. A generation of young women came of age with access to "the pill," an oral contraceptive that minimized the risk of pregnancy. Following the example of the young, Americans of all social classes became more open to exploring their sexuality. The arts reflected the new patterns, as federal courts ruled that books like D. H. Lawrence's *Lady Chatterley's Lover,* earlier branded obscene, could not be banned. Nudity became common on stage and screen, as in the rock musical *Hair.*

Hallucinogenic drugs were also part of the counterculture. The Beats and others had experimented with drugs, but now their use became more widespread. Timothy Leary and Richard Alpert, Harvard University researchers, promoted the cause of LSD after they were fired for violating a pledge not to use it in experiments with undergraduates. Working through his League for Spiritual Democracy, Leary preached his message: "Tune in, turn on, drop out." Another apostle of drugs was Ken Kesey, author of the successful novel *One Flew Over the Cuckoo's Nest.* In 1964, he and his commune of "Merry Pranksters" headed east in an old school bus painted in psychedelic colors, wired for sound, and stocked with enough orange juice and LSD to last them across the continent. Marijuana became popular throughout the culture, and "joints" grew as common on college campuses as cans of beer in the previous generation.

Music was an integral part of the cultural change. Rock and roll rhythms and the gentle strains of folk music gave way to a new kind of rock that swept the country. The Beatles were the major influence as they took first Britain, then the United States, by storm. Other groups and singers followed their lead. Mick Jagger of the Rolling Stones could be a violent showman on stage; Jim Morrison of The Doors transmitted a raw sexuality in his dialogue with the audience before his early demise; Janis Joplin was a hard-driving, hard-drinking woman who conveyed the intensity of the new rock world until she died from a drug overdose.

Music provided a focus on a summer weekend in 1969 as some four hundred thousand people gathered in a large pasture near Woodstock, New York, for a rock festival. Despite intense heat and torrential rain, the weekend-long concert unfolded in a spirit of affection. Some people paraded in the nude; others made love in public; most shared whatever they had, particularly the ubiquitous marijuana, as major rock groups provided around-the-clock entertainment for the throng. Supporters hailed the festival as an example of the better world that lay ahead.

Four months later, another rock festival exposed the underside of the counterculture. Three hundred thousand people gathered at a stock car raceway at Altamont, California, to attend a concert climaxing an American tour by the Rolling Stones. A band of Hell's Angels, tough motorcyclists fond of terrorizing the open road, was on hand to keep order. The crowd was ugly from the start, and as a fat man jumped on the stage to dance naked to the music, the cyclists beat him to the ground. By the end of the concert, several people were dead from accidents, overdoses, and beatings. Music critic Greil Marcus summed up the contradictions of both the concert and the counterculture: "A young black man murdered in the midst of a white crowd by white thugs as white men played their version of black music—it was too much to kiss off as a mere unpleasantness."

Social and political movements in the 1960s were interconnected. New Left activists often adopted the surface manifestations of the counterculture in their appearance and dress. Many of those who experimented with new patterns of living and loving found themselves drawn into political protest as the antiwar struggle climaxed near the end of the decade. Marijuana—and other drugs—joined all camps.

Within a few years, both counterculture and New Left ran out of steam. As the United States extricated itself from Vietnam, protest activity declined. Some of the most extreme and flamboyant militants like Abbie Hoffman and Jerry Rubin, visible at most gatherings in the late 1960s, drifted from sight. Hoffman went underground to escape a criminal charge; Rubin later surfaced as a stockbroker. Others, like activists Sam Brown and Tom Hayden, sought to change society in more conventional ways. Brown, who had spearheaded an antiwar drive, became head of ACTION, an agency responsible for the Peace Corps and its domestic counterpart, VISTA, as well as other volunteer programs; Hayden moved into reform Democratic politics in California. While hippies no longer congregated in the Haight-Ashbury section of San Francisco and similar parts of other cities, they had left their mark on American society. Sexual customs, musical forms, and styles of dress were all bolder and more open than before. Even as the nation became more conservative politically and socially, those new patterns remained.

The energy from the civil rights movement and from student protest activity sparked a number of other campaigns. An environmental movement emerged in the mid 1960s and became increasingly important. While only 17 percent of the public questioned in a Gallup poll in 1965 considered air and water pollution to be a major government problem, that number rose to 53 percent in 1970. Rachel Carson, one of the first critics, took aim at chemical pesticides, particularly DDT, in her book *Silent Spring* (1962). Lyndon Johnson's vision of the Great Society included a healthy and pleasant environment, and he secured legislation to halt destruction of the country's natural resources. During Richard Nixon's presidency, Congress passed the Clean Air Act, the Water Quality Improvement Act, and the Resource Recovery Act, and authorized the Environmental Protection Agency to lead the effort to control abuses.

Concern about the deterioration of the environment increased in the late 1970s, as Americans learned more about substances they had once taken for granted. Discarded dioxin, a by-product of the manufacture of herbicides, plastics, and wood preservatives, remained active in the Love Canal area of Niagara Falls, New York, and in other locations. Acid rain, resulting from industrial and automobile emissions, contaminated parts of the eastern United States and southeastern Canada, killing fish, corroding building surfaces, and damaging plants and trees. Activists insisted on dealing with those problems and with the additional problem of nuclear power. Once viewed as the solution to America's energy needs, nuclear power appeared dangerous and potentially destructive after serious accidents at the Three Mile Island plant in Pennsylvania and a Soviet plant at Chernobyl.

Related to the environmental movement was a growing consumer movement. In past decades, Congress had established a variety of regulatory efforts to protect citizens from unscrupulous merchants. Such regulation came of age in the 1970s as the consumer movement sought to protect the interests of buyers and to make business more responsible to those procuring goods. Ralph Nader, a lawyer who became concerned with the issue of auto safety, led the way. His book *Unsafe at Any Speed* (1965) suggested that many cars were coffins on wheels. Head-on collisions, even at low speeds, could kill passengers because cosmetic bumpers could not withstand even modest shocks. His efforts led to passage of the National Traffic and Motor Vehicle Safety Act of 1966. Volunteers called "Nader's Raiders" attacked a variety of other issues and turned out critiques and reports that led to legislation mandating consumer protection at all levels of government. Despite Republican efforts in the 1980s to dismantle the regulatory apparatus, the consumer movement continued to protect the purchasing public.

Still other groups were encouraged by the ferment of social reform. Gay men and lesbians sought the same freedom that women and racial minorities claimed, and worked openly to end discrimination. A riot in response to a police raid on the Stonewall Inn, a homosexual bar in Greenwich Village in New York, in 1969 helped spark the movement for gay rights, and in the 1970s, homosexuals made important gains. In 1973, the American Psychiatric Association ruled that homosexuality should no longer be classified as a mental illness. Two years later, the federal Civil Service Commission ended its ban on employment of homosexuals. Women, like men, became more open about their sexual preferences and became involved in a lesbian movement that included women active in the more radical wing of the women's movement.

The discovery of AIDS (acquired immune deficiency syndrome) in 1981 changed the situation dramatically. The deadly disease struck intravenous drug users and male homosexuals with multiple partners in particularly large numbers. As they learned more about the illness, some Americans, always suspicious, became even more hostile to homosexuality. Gays fought for a greater governmental effort to deal with the epidemic and, through the Human Rights Campaign Fund, contributed money to sympathetic candidates in the election of 1988.

The liberalizing tendencies of the 1960s and 1970s infuriated religious fundamentalists and members of the New Right. Fundamentalists were disturbed about the larger numbers of working women and what they perceived as the corresponding erosion of the family. They objected to abortion and gay rights, and complained about an increase in crime and immorality. Many belonged to the so-called Moral Majority, and followed the Reverend Jerry Falwell and other television evangelists whose audiences, and bankrolls, increased dramatically. Near the end of the 1980s, scandal hit the popular evangelists. Jim Bakker confessed to a sexual liaison with a secretary and to irregularities in the financial empire he and his wife had built. Jimmy Swaggart was next, leaving undenied charges of a visit to a prostitute. Despite those difficulties, fundamentalist attitudes remained strong.

The 1980s brought an even broader reaction that ended the turbulence of the 1960s and early 1970s. Reforms were institutionalized, even as groups that had struggled for hard-won gains continued to press for further progress. Yet such consolidation came in the face of a pronounced political and social shift to the right. Conservatives had made their voices heard in 1964, when they captured the Republican party and nominated Barry Goldwater for president. Despite their loss in that election, they continued their campaign in the next decade and a half with increasingly sharp attacks on liberals and their programs. Some adhered to the economic doctrines of the University of Chicago's Milton Friedman; others embraced the reactionary views of North Carolina Senator Jesse Helms. Together, relying on massive direct mail campaigns and other media appeals, they helped elect Ronald Reagan president in 1980 and defined the national agenda for the next eight years.

Reagan assumed office with strong convictions about what the country should do and a fervent belief that any person could make a mark through individual effort. He had played by the system's rules and had won fame and fortune; others could do the same. He disagreed with the consensus, which had held since the New Deal, that the government should monitor the economy and assist the least fortunate citizens. Government, he claimed, was too intrusive. It was time to eliminate "waste, fraud, and abuse" by cutting programs the country did not need. It was also time to rebuild the nation's system of defense and to revive a militant approach toward the Soviet Union. Insisting, in this latest chapter of the cold war, that the nation was unacceptably vulnerable, he called for, and received, huge increases in spending for nuclear and conventional arms.

Reagan enjoyed extraordinarily high approval ratings throughout the 1980s. Despite charges of "sleaze" and claims that he had little understanding of the policies of his administration, he appeared to be what the nation wanted. He capitalized on the support of the Moral Majority, and of countless other Americans who were distressed with the upheavals of the preceding decades. Even the young, so critical a generation earlier, fell into line. They, too, feared the consequences of economic disruption and worried that they might have to settle for a lower standard of living than their parents had known. They hailed the return of prosperity Reagan brought, even though it was a prosperity built on unmanageable budget deficits that came at the expense of the poor.

THE RECENT PAST IN PERSPECTIVE

The years following 1960 were turbulent ones. Radical upheaval in the 1960s brought fundamental change to the social climate in the United States. First blacks, then women and various minority groups, demanded access to the increasingly visible benefits of American society. Using confrontational techniques, they forced the rest of the country to take heed. Meanwhile, a savage Southeast Asian war sparked a protest movement more heated than any in the nation's past. Disruption on all fronts brought the reorientation of familiar patterns but also sparked a reaction on the part of those troubled by the changes taking place. For the better part of the next twenty years, Americans struggled to come to terms with shifting values as they confronted changes at home and abroad. Disfranchised groups gained some of the rights that were their due; they also aroused the hostility of other Americans who felt they had gone too far. The conservative revival of the 1980s was but the culmination of the difficult process of reconfiguring the American dream.

BIBLIOGRAPHY

General Works

Hacker, Andrew, ed. *U/S: A Statistical Portrait of the American People* (1983). A useful compilation of statistics comparing recent decades.

Hodgson, Godfrey. *America in Our Time* (1976).

Leuchtenburg, William E. *A Troubled Feast: American Society Since 1945*. Rev. ed. (1983). A perceptive text focusing on the growth of the consumer culture.

Matusow, Allen J. *The Unraveling of America: A History of Liberalism in the 1960s* (1984).

Nash, Gary B., Julie Roy Jeffrey, John R. Howe, Peter J. Frederick, Allen F. Davis, and Allan M. Winkler, eds. *The American People: Creating a Nation and a Society*. 2d ed. (1990). The best general survey of the American past integrating social history with political events.

Winkler, Allan M. *Modern America: The United States from World War II to the Present* (1985). An overview of the recent period.

———, ed. *The Recent Past: Readings on America Since World War II* (1989). An anthology of essays and documents with a social history focus.

Reform Movements

Acuña, Rodolfo. *Occupied America: A History of Chicanos.* 3d ed. (1988).

Branch, Taylor. *Parting the Waters: America in the King Years, 1954–1963* (1988). A Pulitzer Prize–winning account of the conflicts in the civil rights movement.

Carson, Clayborne. *In Struggle: SNCC and the Black Awakening of the 1960s* (1981).

Chafe, William H. *The American Woman: Her Changing Social, Economic, and Political Roles, 1920–1970* (1972). An excellent survey that is particularly good on the postwar years.

Evans, Sara. *Personal Politics: The Roots of Women's Liberation in the Civil Rights Movement and the New Left* (1979).

Filene, Peter G. *Him/Her/Self: Sex Roles in Modern America.* 2d ed. (1986).

Hoxie, Frederick E., ed. *Indians in American History: An Introduction* (1988). A good collection with several useful essays on the recent period.

Josephy, Alvin M., Jr. *Now That the Buffalo's Gone: A Study of Today's American Indians* (1982).

Kessler-Harris, Alice. *Out to Work: A History of Wage-Earning Women in the United States* (1982).

Kluger, Richard. *Simple Justice* (1975). The complete story of the *Brown* v. *Board of Education* decision.

Moody, Anne. *Coming of Age in Mississippi* (1968). The eloquent autobiography of a young southern black woman involved in the civil rights movement.

Rodriguez, Richard. *Hunger of Memory: The Education of Richard Rodriguez* (1982). An autobiographical account of a Hispanic boy growing up in the United States.

Sitkoff, Harvard. *The Struggle for Black Equality, 1954–1980* (1981).

Social and Cultural Protest

FitzGerald, Frances. *Fire in the Lake: The Vietnamese and the Americans in Vietnam* (1972). A thoughtful assessment of cultural differences.

Gitlin, Todd. *The Sixties: Years of Hope, Days of Rage* (1987).

Herring, George C. *America's Longest War: The United States and Vietnam, 1950–1975* (1979; 2d ed. 1986).

Miller, James. *"Democracy Is in the Streets": From Port Huron to the Siege of Chicago* (1987).

O'Neill, William L. *Coming Apart: An Informal History of America in the 1960's* (1971). An engaging narrative of a pivotal decade.

Roszak, Theodore. *The Making of a Counter Culture* (1969).

Santoli, Al, ed. *Everything We Had: An Oral History of the Vietnam War by Thirty-three American Soldiers Who Fought It* (1981).

Viorst, Milton. *Fire in the Streets: America in the 1960s* (1979).

Wolfe, Tom. *The Electric Kool-Aid Acid Test* (1968). A vivid account of Ken Kesey and the drug culture of the 1960s.

SEE ALSO **Business Culture; The City; The Culture of Consumption; Labor: The Great Depression Through the 1980s; The Nuclear Age; The Rise of Mass Culture; Rock Music; The Suburbs; Technology and Social Change; Television; Urbanization.**

Part II

METHODS AND CONTEXTS

THE OLD SOCIAL HISTORY AND THE NEW

Peter N. Stearns

THE RISE OF SOCIAL history has been one of the foremost developments in historical and social scientific scholarship since the 1960s. Yet precise definitions of the field have been surprisingly elusive, leading some commentators to describe social history more as a mélange of related themes and impulses than a coherent approach to the past. One common approach to a definition, in the absence of elaborate or widely accepted general statements, was to contrast the "new" social history with the "old." But the old social history was hardly a self-conscious branch of the larger discipline—which means that the baseline for understanding recent practices in social history must itself be determined by diffuse examples.

American history that could be described as "social" began to take shape early in the twentieth century, as in Arthur W. Calhoun's *Social History of the American Family from Colonial Times to the Present* (1917). Still-earlier work in the genre, though without using the formal label, included various publications by Alice Morse Earle, such as her *Child Life in Colonial Days* (1899). Such works were not representative of a formal academic field nor were they a widely promoted approach to the past. Social history emerged somewhat haphazardly from varied interests in widening the understanding of history that was expressed in new theories about American historical dynamics, such as Frederick Jackson Turner's frontier thesis, or Charles A. Beard's concern for objective interpretation, causal explanation, and scientific procedure. Clearly, some dissatisfaction had emerged with standard school versions of American history, which relied largely on the accumulation and interpretation of political and biographical data.

Attention to social history increased in the early decades of the twentieth century, reaching something of a high point with the 1927–1931 publication of the initial twelve-volume History of American Life series, edited by Arthur Meier Schlesinger and Dixon Ryan Fox. Books in this series were in no sense strictly sociohistorical—they included a great deal of familiar political narrative—but they did widen the range of inquiry to include consistent attention to women and to city life and they showed recurrent interest in blacks, the family, and other topics beyond conventional historical fare. The introductions to books in the series referred to social history without, however, attempting an explicit definition.

Work in social history trailed off somewhat in succeeding decades, though Marcus Lee Hansen kept alive one key branch, immigration studies. With a growing consciousness of political challenges to American values, culminating in World War II and the cold war, historians' attention in certain respects narrowed. Furthermore, in the 1940s and 1950s, innovation centered on the rising star of intellectual history; its fascination with the evolution and causal role of elite ideas challenged conventional history but moved away from social historical interests as well. Only an emerging American studies movement, dealing with popular culture in addition to formal literature and intellectual life, maintained a wider topical range.

This situation began to change clearly only in the 1960s, though there were several important transitional scholars. Immigration history by Oscar Handlin, whose work on Boston's immigrants had appeared in 1941 but whose more influential *The Uprooted: The Epic Story of the Great Migrations that Made the American People* (1951; rev. ed. 1973) emerged a decade later, served as a partial bridge between old and new forms of social history. Though subsequently widely criticized, *The Uprooted* and other essays by Handlin anticipated the change in social history, particularly through the kinds of questions addressed to the immigrant experience. In urban history, work by Eric Lampard ("The History of Cities in the Economically Advanced Areas," in *Economic Development and Cultural Change* [1955]) prepared some redefinition, while more generally, studies of American political culture by Richard Hofstadter (*The Progressive Movement, 1900–1915* [1963]) and Bernard Bailyn (*The Ideological Origins of the American Revolution* [1967]) moved intellectual and political history toward the kinds of questions new social historians would ask.

What was to be called the "new" social history began to take its clearest shape early in the 1960s, when Harvard University established a Ph.D. field in social and economic history, applied to the major geographical areas. Work by several graduate students in colonial social history—John Demos; Philip J. Greven, Jr.; and Kenneth Lockridge—began to appear in article form, and their subsequent first books—Demos's *A Little Commonwealth: Family Life in Plymouth Colony,* Greven's *Four Generations: Population, Land, and Family in Colonial Andover, Massachusetts;* and Lockridge's *A New England Town: The First Hundred Years, Dedham, Massachusetts*—all published in 1970, served in effect as an announcement of a major new approach. Research by Herbert Gutman, in working-class history (*Work, Culture, and Society in Industrializing America* [1976]), and Eugene D. Genovese, on the history of Southern slavery (*The World the Slaveholders Made* [1969] and *Roll, Jordan, Roll: The World the Slaves Made* [1974]), began redefining and reviving these areas at approximately the same time. The publication in 1964 of Stephan Thernstrom's first book, *Poverty and Progress: Social Mobility in a Nineteenth-Century City,* converted many younger historians to a new vision of urban history and particularly to the richness of evidence provided through quantitative sources when handled by appropriate methodologies. Key journals emerged at this time also: *Comparative Studies in Society and History,* launched in 1958, dealt primarily with non-American topics, so it was left to the *Journal of Social History* and the *Historical Methods Newsletter,* both begun in 1967, to herald the new American social history. These journals, focusing explicitly on new topics and methods, increased social historians' self-awareness, and joined more established outlets such as the *William and Mary Quarterly* in serving this new field.

If only because of the field's novelty, the defining of the new social history spread across a two-decade span. It was during the 1970s that the label "new" was firmly affixed to the field. A key review article by Laurence Veysey ("The 'New' Social History in the Context of American Historical Writing") that discussed the new social history appeared in *Reviews in American History* in 1979; a book edited by James B. Gardner and George R. Adams (*Ordinary People and Everyday Life: Perspectives on the New Social History*) defining the field, directed toward a nonspecialist audience, and employing the "new" tag appeared in 1983. Thereafter, as research and teaching in social history continued to proliferate, some of the unfamiliarity wore off and, with it, the compulsion to modify the field's name with a proud or apologetic indication of novelty.

Definitions of social history's American history, then, must focus successively on the groundwork laid in the first four decades of the twentieth century, the generational hiatus in the twenty years that followed, and the explosion of interest in the 1960s and the attendant demarcation between the old and the new. Although the practitioners of the new social history did not think of themselves primarily in terms of their encounter with older styles, as will be discussed below, they and other users of history were sufficiently aware of precedent that some distinction seemed imperative. Interestingly, the "new" label developed only in American work. Despite the fact that the new social history was part of a larger international current, it was only in the United States that a generational division seemed worthy of comment.

While fairly clearly delineated in time, the gap between old and new social history must not be exaggerated as regards substance and methods. Considerable fuzziness in definitions marks both versions of social history. Undeniably, the new social historians, like self-conscious promoters in any novel venture, did aim periodic blasts at the old social history—notably, in trying to make it clear that their work differed mightily from what they dubbed pots-and-pans antiquarianism. Many such judgments contained a large kernel of truth, but also substantial oversimplification. Although many of the features of the new social history had precedents in earlier work, important definitional distinctions must be drawn. Individual historians who worked during the famine years of social history (between 1940 and 1960) effectively used interests drawn from the old social history to train some of the earliest practitioners of the newer style. Oscar Handlin's studies of immigrants thus raised central issues of adaptation and alienation that still concern social historians today, whether they deal with ethnic groups, women, or the underclass, and his focus on the underprivileged anticipated what would fifteen years later be hailed as "history from the bottom up"—one of the hallmarks of the new social history. Further, Handlin, himself a student of Schlesinger, trained some of the leading advocates of the new social history, including Thernstrom. Again, making too much of the gulf between old and new would be factually misleading and would obscure creative origins of the field's recent developments in the United States.

TRADITIONAL AMERICAN SOCIAL HISTORY

No historian ever explicitly devoted himself to the pursuit of an old social history, but it is true that most of the work done between 1900 and the 1950s shared certain characteristics, and on balance differed from the kind of research that began to gain ground in the 1960s. The easiest kind of traditional social history to define and the one most clearly criticized by social historians of newer vintage involved simple descriptions of "how people lived" in the past, with attention focused on costumes, eating utensils, and housing design. The purpose of this kind of research was to add some human touches to the drier stuff of academic history, without interrelating social history's subject matter with the larger processes of politics or culture. Characteristic titles include most of the works by Alice Morse Earle, such as *Curious Punishments of Bygone Days* (1896) and *Costume of Colonial Times* (1911). The approach could evoke nostalgia or wry disgust at the weirdness of ancestral ways; it had no larger analytical purpose. Cattily, but not perhaps inaccurately, new social historians would label this approach "pots and pans" and would huffily insist on distinguishing their work from that whole genre—to the point that, according to some critics, they actually neglected aspects of material culture that might aid them in their own rather different research agenda.

A pots-and-pans approach carried into serious academic scholarship, marking social historical segments off from other coverage in much of the History of American Life series. Thus, Allan Nevins, in *The Emergence of Modern America, 1865–1878* (1927, volume 8 of the series), sandwiched a social historical chapter—everyday life of Americans—into his account of Reconstruction in the South, industrial growth in the North, and the farmers' revolt. To capture the flavor of American society, his chapter dealt with home interiors and domestic art, dress styles, dietary innovations (including the introduction of oatmeal), the surge of outdoor sports, and Barnum's 1871 circus—all summarized, in a brief concluding epitaph, as illustrating American fondness for "showy results." Nevins hastened then to his next chapter, on high culture and science, as if to wash away the bad taste of popular Americana. Carl Fish's *Rise of the Common Man, 1830–1850* (1927, volume 6 in the series) contained a similar "Manners and Morals" chapter, which, with a bow to universal suffrage, turned quickly to travelers' accounts and foreign dislike of the appearance of American women, tobacco consumption, and spitting habits, and to the development of new kinds of advertisements in newspapers.

Closely related to the how-people-lived focus of traditional social history was a tendency to define social history topically as "history of people with the politics left out." The phrase in this case belongs to the English scholar G. M. Trevelyan, but it readily described a common American impulse as well. The Schlesinger-Fox series, to be sure, embraced a wide range of topics, including social history along with Manifest Destiny, formal religious splits, and other milestones in politics, diplomacy, and culture. The specifically social historical chapters, however, stood largely alone, at best resting on the context established by such developments as new economic prosperity or new voting rights. Politics did not intrude directly on this coverage, nor was it affected by the developments listed under the rubric of social history.

Traditional social history thus consisted of a set of topics relating to manner of life but separate from more formal, structural features of American society, including the organization and functions of the state or the patterns of high culture. It was also a largely descriptive series of vignettes, to be approached without reference to any particular system or theoretical base. In *The Rise of the City* (1933, volume 10 in the History of American Life series), Schlesinger discussed the nature of city life in the United States at the end of the nineteenth century by moving from crowding to street layout, to the development of telephone switchboards and arc lamps, to the establishment of new hotels, to crime statistics. The unifying theme is obviously urban, but why these topics were chosen and not others, or exactly how the topics themselves interrelate, is not established. Traditional social history was bent on conveying impressions, more than on establishing a sense of structured argument. At most, editorial introductions in the History of American Life series evoked such issues as whether colonial immigrants bettered themselves by leaving eighteenth-century Britain (concluding, happily, that most did) and changing their social conditions. But while comparative analysis was urged, it did not in fact inform the ensuing presentation of social data.

Traditional social history, with its emphasis on the nonpolitical facets of the past, could certainly attend to lower-class and otherwise disadvantaged groups—a vital impulse shared with subsequent versions of the field. In the main, however, the lower classes (including urban workers, immigrants, African Americans, farmers, and farm labor) were treated indirectly, through descriptions of their environment rather than through their own experience. In *The Atlantic Migration, 1607–1860* (1940), Marcus Lee Hansen, the pioneer in scholarly immigration study, thus dealt with relevant American laws (like the Sedition Acts, which briefly deterred immigrants) and with foreign legislation insofar as it alternated between promoting and inhibiting emigration; he listed the economic and political conditions that could spur emigrants, including the famines and revolutionary tumult of the mid nineteenth century; he covered the ways immigrants traveled and the agencies that served or exploited them; and he patiently charted the flow of different national groups into the immigrant stream from 1607 to 1860. But he offered almost no materials from immigrants themselves, no sense of their lives or expectations, save as these might be extrapolated from the contexts established. Arthur W. Calhoun's *Social History of the American Family* (1917) included a fascinating attempt to deal with changes in conditions among African Americans. Evidence was drawn from comments of several contemporary white moralists writing in popular magazines and a few middle-class reports on the subject. Calhoun did, to be sure, acknowledge, on the basis of testimony from a few white and black educators, that some groups of blacks in particular institutional settings were more restrained. But even in admitting these qualifications, he evinced not only bias—for example, "At the opening of the twentieth century, the point where the Negro American was furthest behind modern civilization was in his sexual *mores*"—but also a fairly typical readiness to accept outsiders' accounts as an adequate basis for depicting behaviors and motivations of lower-class people. The same penchant informed most comments about women. Preston W. Slosson's American Life volume, *The Great Crusade and After, 1914–1928* (1931), after noting the existence of female suffrage, turned to new work patterns, the decline of domestic help, new furnishings, more available restaurants, and changes in costume and cosmetics, assuming that these descriptive features, derived mainly from upper-class behaviors and accounts, captured the essential features of women's lives. Here, context mingled with external references, but, characteristically, materials from the group under the microscope were absent. Traditional social historians did use statistics—they charted rates of drunkenness, crime, and some demographic materials—but as part of the fascination with the social environment, not as a key to getting more directly at the experiences of the individuals studied. Thus, crime was a topic, but criminals were not.

Traditional social historians covered a considerable range of topics, many of which would be taken up again by the new social historians. They evoked some analytical issues that would be treated later as well, such as the standards by which family adjustments might be assessed, certain basic qualities of the immigrant experience, and the relationship between women's political achievements and developments in styles of life. The analytical issues remained largely buried, however, as traditional social history clung to a somewhat unsystematic descriptive approach with the fundamental purpose of conveying ways people lived through lists of appliances and styles, plus observer comments.

A perceptive review essay by Laurence Veysey amplified the distinctive features of traditional social history by comparing its approach to life in nineteenth-century Philadelphia to the new social historical view. In *Rebels and Gentlemen* (1942), Carl and Jessica Bridenbaugh offered a series of impressions of Philadelphia conditions, with no particular theme or argument: their menu included a few statistics, considerable description of building aesthetics, and praise for the energy of the merchant elite. Two decades later, Sam Bass Warner, a new-social-history breed of urbanist, probed Philadelphia in *The Private City* (1968; rev. ed., 1987). His purpose was to convey what it was like for people to live there; his data included elaborate statistics, and his analytical structure prompted recurrent efforts to fit Philadelphia into a larger urban typology.

Another contrast, this between mentor and student, establishes similar contours. Oscar Handlin's *Boston's Immigrants* (1941) took a partially narrative approach to his topic, listing major groups by date of arrival; he was content to use a quote by Ralph Waldo Emerson to characterize Boston's resident culture. Stephan Thernstrom's later inquiry into lower-class Bostonians, *Poverty and Progress,* based almost entirely on quantitative data, pushed analytical issues to the foreground, as he constantly worried about representatives of data and organized his materials into a series of arguments in response to initial conceptual questions.

Two final characteristics of traditional social history bear comment, though they shift focus from the intrinsic qualities of the field to its larger role. First, American historians did not apply their interest in social history to work done on other geographical areas. While paying considerable attention to European history, American practitioners were content to focus on political and diplomatic currents plus high culture; the minutiae of social history did not apply. The impulse to define European or world history in terms of leadership and formal ideas alone persisted into the 1990s, although only in some history teaching in the United States, not in research.

Most important, historians who did social history were content to maintain a distinctly subordinate place in the discipline as a whole, a result of defining their subject matter as nonpolitical and of failing to address key theoretical structures in their fascination with descriptive sequences. Nevertheless, the limitation of social history's impact on mainstream concepts was notable. An American Historical Association survey on the state of historical scholarship in 1932 noted that race relations and acculturation constituted a neglected historical field, but its authors could not suggest sample topics any more adventuresome than the effects of German immigration on American musical development and the civilizing of the American Indian. For a statement issued in the heyday of the Schlesinger-Fox series, this was notable for its inadequacy. As late as 1968, an essay on social history in the *International Encyclopedia of the Social Sciences* by J. Jean Hecht could note the lack of vigor in social history in the United States and the "fact" that no one seemed to care; Hecht called attention to developments in Europe as virtually alone worthy of note. Traditional social history, despite several merits, made little mark within the United States.

THE TRANSITION FROM OLD TO NEW

During the 1960s, three basic forces prompted renewed attention to social history in the United States and created a considerable redefinition. The forces were quite diverse, prompting very different versions of a "new" social history and ongoing disputes about how the field could be defined. All three forces, however, required some degree of differentiation from what now came to be thought of as the "old" social history.

The European Inspiration One obvious source of the new social history was the belated acquaintance with European historiography. Social history had been gaining ground in France since the 1920s, under the leadership of the magisterial journal *Annales d'histoire économique et sociale* (renamed *Annales: Économies, sociétés, civilisations* in 1947). The *Annales* historians, or Annalists, dealt explicitly with changes and continuities among the lower classes, with particular attention to peasant history. They explored material culture over the long span of time (the *longue durée*). They dealt with festival forms as expressions of popular belief and community cohesion. Leaders like Marc Bloch and Lucien Febvre urged an even wider array of topics than most Annalists had initially probed; they argued, for example, for attention to historical changes in emotional standards and experience. Work of the *Annales* school gradually came to influence American historians dealing with France and other areas where French historians had produced important sociohistorical work, such as Italy and Latin America. By the 1960s, a number of younger American historians were turning to studies of the French working class, patterns of popular protest, and peasant behavior, inspired by the topics and methodologies by then commonplace in French historical scholarship. One survey indicated, for example, that by 1960 well over 80 percent of all French doctoral work in history fell into the category of social history.

Efforts by American historians dealing with France inevitably affected the topical interests of other Europeanists, accustomed to taking some of their cues from research on France, and also the burgeoning area studies programs, in which historians combined with representatives from other disciplines in building up firmer scholarship on East Asia, Latin America, and Africa. Americanists themselves were exposed to frequent references to the *Annales* school by the 1960s, and some, such as Philip Greven, were strongly affected. On the whole, however, they were more directly influenced by the more recent, somewhat more haphazard, rise of social history in Britain. (Thus, despite the French focus on peasants, they only haltingly developed social histories of rural Americans, forerunners of a new rural history.) Particularly influential among English-speaking historians was E. P. Thompson's massive survey *The Making of the English Working Class* (1963), in which he combined a variety of sources to demonstrate that workers, far from being defined simply by forces beyond their control, had active values and behaviors that were historically influential in their own right. Bent on rescuing these groups from "the enormous condescension of posterity," Thompson inspired many like-minded Americans to look for materials emanating directly from the lower classes and to approach their history in a fashion both more comprehensive and more empathic than had been common in the older social historical efforts. The flexible Marxism of many British scholars also echoed across the Atlantic.

In addition to broadening the sense of social history's topics and sources and introducing new sensitivity to its practice, the European inspiration obviously encouraged new American practitioners to claim a different place for their work in the discipline as a whole than their predecessors had done. In France historical research had become research in social history for all intents and purposes. The field's status was not so august in Britain, but scholars like Thompson and Eric Hobsbawm obviously assumed that their work had significance for the practice of history generally, and not simply for some limited area of study. Americans who came to share Thompson's enthusiasm for rescuing various groups for the historical record also shared his belief that their work would logically redefine the mainstream discipline.

History from the Bottom Up The second source of the recrudescence of social history among younger American researchers in the 1960s, overlapping somewhat with the European impulse, was overtly political. The rise of the civil rights movement, followed by a revival of feminism and the emergence of the gay rights movement, had obvious historical implications. If these groups legitimately demanded a new place in the present, attention might also be given to their place in the past, and indeed a sympathetic historical account might not only reflect but also further the current political demands. Marxist theory joined political and historical agendas for some American practitioners as well. The more general climate of the 1960s, in challenging the American establishment on various fronts, encouraged a new, sometimes rather inchoate, radicalism among many younger historians and legitimized a search for a nonestablishment kind of history. Social history served the intellectual interests of scholars seeking alternatives to the existing power structure, by emphasizing diversity and struggle in the past.

The clearest overall result of this set of impulses was the intense desire to define social history as "history from the bottom up," devoted to providing a full and friendly record of the activities of a host of groups excluded from political and social power in the past. In this reading, social historians had a mission to expand the range of people with whom history in general was concerned and to alter the frequently elitist perceptions through which such groups, if noted at all, had been evaluated.

Compared with the old social history, the bottom-up passion encouraged a number of innovations, while building on some of the concerns traditional social historians had more quietly established. The sheer number of groups perceived to be legitimate subjects of historical research increased. Black history, at first through revived interest in the history of slavery and then through wider interests in the African American experience after emancipation, moved front and center. So, after a slight delay, did women's history, as it shifted from attention to cultural attitudes about women, feminist politics, and notable women of the past—the initial historical response to growing feminist presence—to a genuine sociohistorical approach that focused on ordinary women in their normal range of activities. A variety of ethnic groups, age categories (youth and the elderly), and sexual-preference categories joined the list.

Working-class history added a new and more formal social-structural component to the bottom-up effervescence. Labor history was not new, but it had focused on formal institutions for the most part and so fell more into a political than a social historical framework. With its passion for ordinary people themselves, labor history broadened considerably. It dealt with workers' struggles and adjustments, not just formal protest institutions; it treated family life, work experience, leisure, and outlook.

Social history, stirred by the political passions of the 1960s, changed in other ways as well, beyond expanding the range of subjects. Social historians sought out direct source material from the groups involved. They were profoundly suspicious of outsiders' accounts—women described by men, blacks by slave masters, formal literary sources generally—and, by combining statistics with surprisingly rich literary sources, such as worker autobiographies and untapped letters and diaries by relatively ordinary women, plus court materials, family records, and, in some cases, oral-history evidence, they made an array of groups speak for themselves. At first, reflecting perhaps the legacy of traditional social history with regard to sources, social historians were prone to refer to their groups as inarticulate, but in fact most soon came to conclude that while not all sources were as explicit or as representative as might be desired, inarticulateness was a misleading image for the classes, races, and genders who composed society's masses.

History from the bottom up obviously entailed a distinct merger of social and political history. A few groups seemed so resolutely apolitical that the notion of history with the politics left out might still apply, but in the main this kind of social history—one that resonated to the rich past and current struggles of the downtrodden—looked for evidence of political consciousness and political battles, and often found it. Interpreting protest history as revealing careful rationality and, often, sophisticated political awareness among mass protestors became a key feature of this approach; bread rioters changed from frothing, irrational mobs to purposeful crowds bent on enforcing certain demands on the state, and from peripheral to significant political actors in predemocratic—colonial or monarchical—societies.

The new social historians also disputed the causal role of their subjects. Some, inspired in part by political preferences, saw their subjects as active, politically aware, and ready to challenge the status quo even when blocked from formal collective action. Others found both the historical record and political purpose best served by emphasizing the powerlessness—the unjust powerlessness—of their subjects. Women's social history thus tended to divide between historians bent on showing women effective even under patriarchy and those interested in demonstrating the paralyzing power of male dominance. During the 1970s a social control school emerged, eager to show how seemingly benign institutions, like humanitarian insane asylums or public schools, actually forced their clients to submit to a comprehensive moral discipline. On the whole, however, the new social historians have argued that most of the groups they study, even seemingly the most deprived, interact with the people and institutions who control them; they are not merely passive victims. Whereas traditional social historians avoided commenting about the impact of institutions on the groups they studied (and sometimes treated them as essentially passive in a larger context), the new social history tended, not without debate, to assume more active agency. Slaves thus shaped masters, children altered schools, the poor modified the intentions of almshouse administrators. The new view of historical process, in which leaders interact with led and both act as powerful forces in shaping the past, has proved one of the most durable changes in the way history is done.

The Interdisciplinary Contact While the concern with translating the political energies of the 1960s into a historical agenda generated some of the most dramatic potencies of the new social history, even long after the 1960s, the third creative factor in the emergence of the field was perhaps more important, one that could clash with the political inspiration. A variety of younger historians and some sociologists began in the 1960s to develop interest in interdisciplinary cooperation and common theoretical problems. They addressed issues such as the causation of popular protest, examining theories that argued deprivation as a cause against theories that argued the impact of rising expectations. They searched out historical materials that would enrich empirical social research, and they added factors of timing and periodization to the theoretical arsenal. Concerning protest, for example, social historians quickly produced an understanding of patterns of change in which popular reactions characteristic at one time yielded to other goals when the context fundamentally shifted. Charles Tilly's work, *The Vendée* (1964), thus launched a series of inquiries into the basic conditions that allowed some groups to protest but not others, and into patterns of change in protest goals and methods in Europe from the sixteenth century to the present. Concepts of family structure and function were also tested through historical research and redefined in part through the generalizations that emerged from the new social history, an interaction that also included demography, social structure and social mobility, and crime.

Other than begetting the term "social science history," the interdisciplinary contact, though somewhat haphazard from both the history side and the sociology side, resulted in three concerns for historians. The first concern was simply topical. Social historians became interested in tracing historically the social behaviors and institutions that sociologists had staked out, with or without a historical dimension. Here was a key source of the rapid development of family history—especially among

American scholars—and the less durable flowering of studies of social mobility. Slightly later, other topical interests developed. Social histories of old age, for example, employed some of the generalizations produced by gerontologists, while the history of emotions reflected the concomitant revival of the sociology of emotions.

The second concern was methodological. New social historians turned to the quantitative skills and interests that had been developing in many branches of social science. Much early work on family history thus involved quantitative assessments of family structure. Mobility studies became increasingly quantitative, and historians dealing with crime and demography reflected a growing interest in what numerical evidence could say and a growing sophistication in its statistical manipulation. For a time, indeed, the new social history was equated with quantitative history, though this equation was never complete and in fact began to decline after the mid 1970s. Quantification nevertheless remained a vital facet of social history, both because of its connection to social science and because of the importance of numerical data in conveying patterns of the past in instances in which, because of the kind of behavior studied or because of its lower-class, "inarticulate" clientele, conventional textual evidence was hard to come by.

The third concern was analytical. The social science impulse propelled the new social historians to a strong interest in analysis and at least middle-level generalizations (that speaks to general typologies of family structure or of responses to technological change). The "new" urban historians thus sought to build typologies for whole cities; family historians attempted to establish characteristic structures. Whether social historians applied preexisting theory or, as increasingly became the case, added theoretical statements of their own (particularly through the application of periodization to organize fundamental points of change), their interest in moving beyond description to analysis was high. Along with the more formal exploration of quantitative techniques, this interest particularly marked the new social history off from the older versions.

THE "NEW" SOCIAL HISTORY

The three impulses that generated the new social history, and its increasing drawing power, were not entirely congruent. Historians inspired by social science did not necessarily share the political empathies of their colleagues who approached history from the bottom up, even though the topics covered overlapped substantially. Relatively few of the new studies about workers or women were highly quantitative, though statistical evidence was certainly valued. Crucial debates between quantifiers and the more qualitative social historians arose concerning the study of slavery when Robert W. Fogel and Stanley L. Engerman's *Time on the Cross: The Economics of Negro Slavery* (1974) sounded a surprisingly optimistic tone concerning slaves' material conditions—a finding that drew anguished riposte from critics bent on a different kind of approach to the slave experience.

Nevertheless, despite important tensions as well as a host of specific debates, there were some common features to the new social history that distinguished it from many of the attributes of the old. Social historians contended that the evolution of social structures provided the key to other historical particulars. They defined social structures variously, to be sure: some focused on material conditions, others on hierarchies of power and resultant relationships and contentions among groups, still others on shared consciousness and behaviors. They agreed, however, that social conditions and social changes underlay and interacted with other historical processes, as opposed to the conventional historical assumption of the independent operation of formal ideas or political actions.

History, in this vision, must attend to the groupings, activities, and beliefs of all people in the past, and not only of leadership elites. How ordinary people—and not just the "masses," but middle- and even upper-class groups as well—lived, what they believed, and how they interacted with each other and with the rest of society came into the expanding domain of historical research. Social historians, following their analytical bent, used a variety of disciplinary approaches and theoretical frameworks. Finally, they were interested in a variety of methodologies and a diverse array of source materials, well beyond the conventional archival corpus of purely political or diplomatic history. While definitely not all the new social historians were quantifiers, it was true that almost all of them, of necessity, manifested distinctive concerns about sources. They needed to find materials about groups or activities that did not leave intentional written records. When they could not draw conclusions from firm statistics—as in dealing with the functions of family members as opposed to basic family structure—they needed to worry about how representative their sources were (and ideally, how a variety of sources reinforced one another).

The new social history introduced new topics to the essential historical lexicon, or transformed previously antiquarian, how-they-lived subjects—such as the history of sports—into lively analytical domains, where questions about significance and relationship to other social facets moved to center stage. Social history also began to redefine more established historical fields. Urban history, for example, shifted increasingly from urban politics and other structural features, to inquiries into the kinds of people and kinds of popular experience lived within cities. Labor history moved away from primary concentration on formal organizational patterns—the unions and labor politics—to more diverse research on the lives and outlook of working people themselves. A new political history sought contact with social history in adopting quantitative methods—as in voting studies—and in seeking to link political behavior to wider social groupings. Many intellectual historians developed new concern for the dissemination of ideas, rather than their formal philosophical pedigrees.

The new social history also expanded the geographical range of its subjects. While by the late 1960s publications on colonial communities and families and on slavery focused attention on the United States, American social historians and sociologists were also dealing with lower-class groups in European history and building on European interest in the nature of social protest. Several initial studies concentrated on France, but sociohistorical research was soon applied to Britain, Germany, and other parts of Europe. Social historians, initially drawn to modern topics dealing with the industrial revolution and its antecedent social conditions, soon began to probe the medieval and classical periods as well. Questions about Russia's prerevolutionary tensions were the focus of a host of social-history studies, particularly concerning various segments of the working class. Beginning in the 1960s, the burgeoning area-studies programs—dealing especially with Asia, Africa, and Latin America—commingled historians with scholars from other disciplines, such as anthropology, in ways that made a social-history approach even more natural than in fields, like American and European history, where a conventional history framework was more firmly established. Historians involved in area studies increasingly focused on issues of the structure of peasant societies and peasant protest, along with problems of slavery and ethnic conflict. Their approaches obviously differed from the "great traditions" concern for formal culture and from exclusive attention to Western conquests that had previously marked American scholarship on the non-Western parts of the world.

Social historical work on Asia, Africa, and Latin America differed somewhat from efforts on Europe and the United States. It developed a less wide-ranging set of topics, particularly concerning subjects such as women, demography, and family history; even urban areas were long somewhat neglected. On the other hand, the three basic concerns of social history were apparent: ordinary people and fundamental social patterns (such as land tenures), innovative methodologies (that included not only quantitative techniques but also, particularly among African social historians, oral history methods and analysis of material artifacts), and analytical questions (such as those raised by modernization models or the "moral economy" theory of popular protest initially developed in Britain). These concerns linked third-world social history to the new social history more generally. In a few—probably too few—cases specific comparative work developed, as a means of relating the social history of a particular region to wider international patterns; slavery unquestionably headed the list, along with related work on race relations.

Whatever their regional specialty, the new social historians were concerned with distinguishing themselves from the limited images associated, somewhat unfairly, with more traditional social history: hence the pots-and-pans epithet, and the concerted effort to develop analytical and theoretical, rather than purely descriptive, categories. But the real tension raised by the new social history in the wider historical discipline involved relationships to conventional history; there was no need to linger over previous versions of social history itself that, for better or worse, quickly faded from view. Social historians were at pains to differentiate themselves from other practitioners, particularly in political history; and they recurrently drew fire from those who continued to believe that political issues essentially defined the past.

SOCIAL HISTORY AND CONVENTIONAL HISTORY

The new social historians argued, as their self-definition virtually required, that neglect of most people outside elite ranks and of most activities outside political and diplomatic machinations did not provide a complete picture of the past. Their sense of what topics constituted history obviously differed from the staple definitions of the period before 1960. In a few cases, the contrast led social historians to revive older notions that their field was history with the politics left out.

Topical distinctions pushed social historians also to reconsider conventional historical periodization. Initially, many social historians relied on established chronological boundaries even in dealing with new topics such as the working class or women's family roles. Even today, many studies end with familiar markers such as World War I or the American Civil War. In many cases, however, social historians had to consider different time arrangements when key events did not have a shaping effect in their topic area. Nineteenth-century women's history, for example, adopted the notion of a more general "Victorian" period, finding that the Civil War had little impact on the subject. Periodization on the basis of measurable shifts in values, or demographic behavior, or economic relationships could well differ from standard time slots defined by reigns, wars, or presidencies. The new social historians commonly also looked to a decade or more of transition from one social pattern to another, rather than measuring changes by more specific annual dates. In no sense, even by the 1990s, had social historians agreed upon a full periodization for modern American history and some, interested more in setting particular contexts rather than dealing with processes of change, paid little attention to the issue. Overall, however, the relationship between social-history periodization, and its bases, and conventional chronological markers was complex.

Compared with standard political historians, the new social historians were less interested in events than in processes that summed up a large number of individual ideas or behaviors. In some cases, to be sure, a major war or epidemic launched fundamental changes in the way ordinary people behaved or in the definition of the ordinary institutions of life—thus the role of the Black Death in demographic history or the role of World War II in altering women's work patterns. But social historians, like their old-social-history predecessors, rarely explored events for their own sake. Their presentation was less a clear narrative than an analysis of an unfolding process, such as the way Irish immigrants accommodated to the efforts by the American middle class to preach upward mobility (a major topic in Thernstrom's *Poverty and Progress*) or the causes, timing, and impact of the nineteenth-century American reduction of average birth rates. Initially, the new social historians, while implicitly moving away from event-based narratives, did not pay great attention to the nature of these alternative styles, or to the conceptualization of historical change that the styles suggested. Nevertheless, it was clear that their histories read differently from conventional narratives, following from a vision of history that saw the past more in terms of group than of individual dynamics, more in terms of interaction among various sectors of society than of top-down initiatives neatly defining the characteristics of a particular time or place.

Some social historians aspired to a "total" history that would combine distinctively social processes with politics and intellectual life, defined also in terms of basic patterns more than of the ebb and flow of individual events and personalities. The total history impulse derived from French definitions in the field, and many American (as well as European) practitioners remained quite content to deal with individual topics. Nevertheless, from the early years of the new social history onward, a number of American scholars, dealing with particular colonial communities, working-class towns, or even some larger settings such as southern slavery, attempted to treat the interrelationship among a wide variety of forces and institutions. Here, social historians faced something of a dilemma. Community studies could achieve a range and intensity that were difficult to translate to a larger national scale. Studies of particular topics might allow wider geographical coverage, but at the expense of linkage with other facets of the social or political experience. It is revealing that, except at the textbook level, virtually no social historian attempted an overall social history of the United States, and only a few Americans ventured a general European social-history survey. At the same time, while social historians reacted against many of the conventions of nationalist political history, particularly in pointing out far more complexities in the national record than "consensus" American political history had entertained, most in fact worked within a largely national (if not subnational) framework. Indeed, the issue of the geographical range appropriate to the new social history was not explicitly addressed.

Social historians did not, in fact, challenge historical conventions across the board. They were of course concerned with the past, and ultimately with change and causation. But their distinctive conceptualization rested on three major points. They contended that the focus on groups outside the formal power structures reveals much about the past and about change, not only for the groups involved but for society at large—including the state. They believed that serious, analytical attention to the histories of activities not formally intellectual or political, such as family life, serves the same function by revealing important characteristics about society ultimately linked to other expressions, such as politics. And they maintained that history, in dealing with politics, or women, or eating habits, best captures the past by focusing on patterns and on processes of change in patterns, rather than simply on a series of discrete events.

THE MATURATION OF THE NEW SOCIAL HISTORY

By the mid 1980s, relatively few historians or users of history continued to describe social history as "new." By this point, about 35 percent of all practicing historians in the United States claimed to be social historians. Graduate programs, undergraduate curricula, mainstream historical journals, and even most textbooks at least at the college level routinely included social-history materials and topics. A scholarly assessment edited by Michael G. Kammen of major historical fields in the United States, issued in 1980, essentially revolved around social history's impact, as most topical approaches sought a relationship to social history and as even the more standard geographical and chronological areas came to grips with new findings.

By 1980, social historians had evolved a complex relationship with the larger discipline of history. Most history departments included social historians and other historians. Although a few institutions began to emphasize social history primarily, there was no move to create discrete social-history institutes as in Europe. On the other hand, social historians did have an array of specialist publications such as the *Journal of Interdisciplinary History, Social Science History,* and topical ventures such as the *Journal of Family History* as well as the older social history outlets established in the 1960s. Here too, however, there was creative fuzziness, as social historians began by the later 1970s to gain regular access to the standard history journals and area studies publications as well.

Growing maturity and acceptance did not alter a number of key characteristics of the field. In particular, social historians' ability to generate substantial new topics remained considerable. While research on the working class continued—perhaps with fewer fundamental findings than in the 1970s—work on gender gained new ground, with interest in definitions of masculinity adding to an impressive range of studies on women in the past. Age groups, such as youth, received growing attention. Family history remained a major topical staple, but along with initial focus on structure came increasing research on affective relationships and on life-course analysis (phases of the individual-family interaction). The history of leisure became increasingly central, as social historians were attracted to the interpretation of ritual. The social history of health and medicine constituted another vigorous new interest, displacing older definitions of this field as a series of triumphs of medical research and heroic doctors.

The expansion of topics reflected a considerable evolution of methods and interests. Social history's interdisciplinary outreach remained considerable, and ties with historical sociology, though fluctuating, were actually gaining in importance again in the later 1980s. An increasing number of social historians were also drawn to the methods and topics of cultural anthropology. There was interaction as well with social psychology and literary criticism. Efforts at "thick descriptions" of past rituals and texts, based on studies by Clifford Geertz and Victor Turner, showed the methodological impacts of the new outreach. Ethnographic evidence also received growing attention. These changes signaled growing interest in systems of popular beliefs—or mentalities—as a key means of drawing together various facets of the past and dealing with a primary kind of causation or at least motivation for popular behavior. Beliefs about nature, the body, self, and emotion constituted central topics for a growing number of social historians, dealing with various periods. Relationships with cultural and intellectual history, still complex, were recast, as currents such as the Protestant Reformation were restored and reinterpreted as vital phenomena in social history. With all this, social historians' utilization of quantitative methods, though still active, definitely declined as a feature of the field as a whole. Methodologically, social history became even more eclectic than before.

Maturity and expansion of range brought a number of new issues to the fore, though most had been implied when the new social history first emerged. A number of social historians, as well as other historians assessing the field, became concerned about modes of presentation. If social history could not employ the narrative style, how then could its style be defined? Could narrative be restored to social history—for example, in dealing with events involving ordinary people in activities such as popular festivals—with improved effectiveness? A number of social historians began to use individual experiences as exemplifying larger processes, while rendering these processes more vivid and intelligible.

Closely related to the issue of presentation was the question of social history's role in the teaching of history. In a field defined by its exciting research advances, the new social historians had not initially attended much to pedagogy. With maturity, issues of how to present social history in the classroom, how to define its main findings for high school as well as college students, and how to relate it to conventional coverage became pressing. Political pressures to deal with various minority groups with new seriousness aided the translation of certain kinds of social history to mainstream textbooks. On the other hand, attacks on the effectiveness of history teaching plus pressure from American conservatives to reconvert history teaching to an emphasis on hallowed elite values raised questions about how far social historians could go in conveying their approach to the larger discipline as a teaching field. The success of social history could be measured through the widespread belief, among professionals, that efforts to define history teaching in terms of memorization of a series of agreed-upon "facts" constituted a sterile limitation of the discipline. But it remained true that social history had made fewer advances at the classroom level than in research.

Problems of synthesis also involved social history's research mission. The new social history, as generator of novel topics, inevitably raised questions about putting the pieces together as the field matured. Just as social history produced no single methodology, so it yielded no agreement on what were the unifying forces in causing changes. Yet without some efforts in this direction, it was difficult to know how to relate the history of crime to the history of leisure, and both to family history. Pleas for synthesis in social history, for more work on large theories, gained ground during the later 1980s. They were not unheeded. While some earlier unifying frameworks, such as modernization theory, fell into discredit, a number of social historians sought to define "big changes" from which more specific developments could be derived, as a means of marking out periods and of drawing diverse topics together. Other social historians worked on gender theory as a substantial mechanism for synthesis, beyond the specific findings of women's history. New attention to the relationship between ideas and social history, through the mentalities approach, also promised important connections.

A special feature of the issue of synthesis involved returning to the thorny issue of the social history–political history relationship, as a number of sociologists as well as social historians called for "bringing the state back in." The new political history, defined in terms of major patterns in political constituencies, already connected political action to social groups. Growing interest in the impact of state functions—tracing the actual results of social legislation or welfare efforts as they were shaped by diverse social actors, including the intended recipients—formed another vital connection. Social histories of military organizations and experiences formed yet a third link. The social-political equation was hardly solved. Social historians continued to disagree about whether all their topics were ultimately political, or whether some valid subjects, like the history of death, still might be pursued largely independent of connection to the state. But the notion that social and political history were inherently unconnected or incompatible, that one could be consistently researched without the other, had largely faded from view.

The new social history, by its very success and by its distinctive claims as an overall orientation to the past and not simply as a discrete set of topics, inevitably raised fundamental issues. It was not always clear, even as the field moved into its second generation, how or whether some of these issues would be resolved. The challenges to social history's fundamental claim to generate appropriate theory and conceptual analysis were particularly important. At the same time, the field continued to be vital. Its impact not only on historical research but also on research in kindred social sciences was increasing by the 1990s. Initially a pioneering venture, claiming far more than traditional social historians had presumed, the new social history had become a central approach in the discipline as a whole in the United States. At its best, it had expanded not only the definition, but also the relevance and excitement of the past in the process.

THE OLD SOCIAL HISTORY AND THE NEW

BIBLIOGRAPHY

This bibliography lists works that discuss the methodology of social history, comparative works, and works dealing with social history in other countries. Many of the works that exemplify social history in the United States are mentioned in and listed in the bibliographies of other articles in this encyclopedia.

Method and Theory

American Historical Association. *Historical Scholarship in America* (1932).

College Entrance Examination Board. *Academic Preparation in Social Studies: Teaching for Transition from High School to College* (1986).

DePillis, Mario S. "Trends in American Social History and the Possibilities of Behavioral Approaches." *Journal of Social History* 1 (1967).

Evans, Peter B., Dietrich Rueschemeyer, and Theda Skocpol, eds. *Bringing the State Back In* (1985).

Gardner, James B., and George R. Adams, eds. *Ordinary People and Everyday Life: Perspectives on the New Social History* (1983).

Henretta, James A. "Social History as Lived and Written." *American Historical Review* 84, no. 5. (1979).

Himmelfarb, Gertrude. *The New History and the Old* (1987).

Hunt, Lynn A. *Politics, Culture, and Class in the French Revolution* (1984).

Kammen, Michael G., ed. *The Past Before Us: Contemporary Historical Writing in the United States* (1980).

Landes, David S., and Charles Tilly, eds. *History as Social Science* (1971).

Lemisch, Jesse. "The American Revolution Seen from the Bottom Up." In *Towards a New Past: Dissenting Essays in American History,* edited by Barton J. Bernstein (1968).

Scott, Joan W. *Gender and the Politics of History* (1988).

Stearns, Peter N., ed. "Some Comments on Social History." *Journal of Social History* 1 (1967).

———. *Expanding the Past: A Reader in Social History: Essays from the Journal of Social History* (1988).

Stoianovich, Traian. *French Historical Method: The Annales Paradigm* (1976).

Stone, Lawrence. *The Past and the Present* (1981).

Vansina, Jan. *Oral Tradition: A Study in Historical Methodology.* Translated by H. M. Wright (1965).

Veysey, Laurence. "The 'New' Social History in the Context of American Historical Writing." *Reviews in American History* 7 (1979).

Zunz, Olivier, ed. *Reliving the Past: The Worlds of Social History* (1985).

Comparative Works

Davis, David Brion. *Slavery and Human Progress* (1984).

Fredrickson, George M. *White Supremacy: A Comparative Study of American and South African History* (1981).

Katznelson, Ira, and Aristide R. Zolberg, eds. *Working-class Formation: Nineteenth-century Patterns in Western Europe and the United States* (1986).

Kolchin, Peter. *Unfree Labor: American Slavery and Russian Serfdom* (1987).

Patterson, Orlando. *Slavery and Social Death: A Comparative Study* (1982).

Other Countries

Adas, Michael. "Social History and the Revolution in African and Asian Historiography." *Journal of Social History* 19 (1985).

Davis, Natalie Zemon. *Society and Culture in Early Modern France* (1975).

Gillis, John R. *For Better, for Worse: British Marriages, 1600 to the Present* (1985).

Merriman, John M., ed. *Consciousness and Class Experience in Nineteenth-Century Europe* (1979).

Sabean, David W. *Power in the Blood: Popular Culture and Village Discourse in Early Modern German* (1984).

Stearns, Peter N. *European Society in Upheaval* (1967; 3d ed., with Herrick Chapman, 1991).

Tilly, Charles. *The Contentious French* (1986).

Tilly, Louise A., and Joan W. Scott. *Women, Work, and Family* (1978).

Weber, Eugen. *Peasants into Frenchmen: The Modernization of Rural France, 1870–1914* (1976).

Zelnik, Reginald E. *Labor and Society in Tsarist Russia: The Factory Workers of St. Petersburg, 1855–1870* (1971).

SEE ALSO **Feminist Approaches to Social History; Gender Roles and Relations; Immigration; Life Stages; Marxism and Its Critics; *Mentalité* and the Nature of Consciousness; Quantification and Its Critics; Slavery; Urbanization.**

SOCIAL HISTORY IN GREAT BRITAIN AND CONTINENTAL EUROPE

Gay L. Gullickson

IN THE PAST CENTURY, social historians have created a view of the European past that no one before them imagined could or even should be created. They have pursued separate but overlapping questions, each of which has revealed something new about the past and all of which, when viewed together like stereographs through a stereoscope, yield a picture of enormous detail and complexity. Some historians have concentrated on the large, almost immovable structures—the climate, geography, terrain—of Europe. Others have explored more movable, but nevertheless enduring structures—economic, social, cultural, and demographic systems. And still others have analyzed dramatic, watershed developments—the agricultural revolution, industrialization, urbanization. Not all social historians have agreed with each other; not all of their pictures fit together when overlaid. Not all of the detail is filled in; not all of the causal connections have been drawn. But their work has focused attention away from political leaders and events for almost a century, and has changed the way historians view and write about the past, even when it is the political past.

This essay will examine four major schools that emerged in European historiography during the twentieth century—the *Annalistes,* British Marxists, historical demography, and women's history—with a particular emphasis on the work of British and French historians. These four historiographical schools do not encompass all of the research that historians have done in the social history of Europe and England, even in Britain and France. There are French as well as British Marxist historians who write labor history; there are historians who have devoted their attention to peasants and artisans rather than to the working class; there are numerous French historians who have explored the social and economic causes and consequences of the French Revolution from a variety of perspectives; and there are others as well. But the *Annalistes,* British Marxists, demographers, and, to a lesser extent, women's historians have had considerable influence on the thinking and writing of American social historians. In women's history, more than in the other cases, the lines of influence have moved in both directions, with Americans writing much of the most important work on British and European women. Even in this case, though, the influence of the other schools is significant, for the Americans who have written these social histories were trained in the others' questions and methodologies and, in their spirit, have addressed themselves to a new and previously unexamined social group—women.

THE *ANNALISTES*

In the late nineteenth and early twentieth centuries, French intellectuals waged battles against the artistic and academic establishments that might have pleased their revolutionary forebearers of 1789 and 1848. In the world of art, revolt against the rigid control of style and content began with the Salon des Refusés in 1863 when artists whose work had been rejected by the annual Salon organized their own exhibition. For the next ten years, artists whose styles and chosen subjects ran counter to the art establishment's proclivities—an increasing preference for virile and grand works—chafed under a system seemingly mired in the past, and they struggled to acquire the funds to mount their own show. Finally in 1874, the rebellious artists held the first of what quickly came to be known as the Impressionist Exhibitions, and the revolt that had begun in 1863 became a sustained revolution. New visions of truth and reality swept onto the artistic stage and painting entered a creative new era.

Half a century later, young and rebellious historians staged another revolt against intellectual stagnation and control in France. Like the artists who preceded them, these men, later known as the *Annalistes,* ushered in an expansive new vision of history and truth that, combined with the development of new techniques and new questions, broadened, deepened, and complicated historians' understandings of the past. Seventy years later, their influence is so pervasive it is impossible to imagine what the study of European or American history would be like if they had not pursued their vision of interdisciplinary social history.

By the early twentieth century, the academic world in France was as severely controlled as the art world had been in the nineteenth. The University of Paris (the Sorbonne), the premier educational institution in France, was in the hands of historians who devoted themselves to writing political histories extolling the accomplishments of the great men of France, and divided the past into strict time periods. By the twentieth century, these practices had resulted in the production of "very large tomes on very small matters" (Hexter, "Fernand Braudel and the *Monde Braudellien,*" p. 482) and in the rejection of any historian whose work challenged the accepted orthodoxies.

Historians who crossed the lines between the approved historical time periods or between scholarly disciplines, or whose historical research focused on nonpolitical events, were repeatedly exiled to the provinces. The rejection of some of the most brilliant and creative scholars in France from its leading educational institutions (including the Sorbonne and the Collège de France) was not only personally galling; it also prevented its best students from working with the country's best scholars. It did not, however, prevent these scholars from challenging what they saw as the "satisfied and widespread mediocrity" that existed in the writing of French history (Braudel, "Personal Testimony," p. 461) and eventually from ending the traditionalists' hegemony.

The revolt that would come to be associated with the journal commonly referred to as the *Annales* had deep roots. Lucien Febvre and Marc Bloch, who founded the journal, and the other scholars who wrote for it were profoundly influenced by the ideas of the sociologist Émile Durkheim (1858–1917), the economic historian Henri Pirenne (1862–1935), and the linguist Antoine Meillet (1866–1936), among others. Their most important mentor, however, was the philosopher Henri Berr (1863–1954). Berr provided both a forum for discussion in his *Revue de synthèse historique,* which he founded in 1900 (in 1931 the title was changed to *Revue de synthèse*), and an intellectual model for the younger historians who worked on the journal. As a philosopher, Berr was interested in the theory of history and in ending what he saw as the arbitrary division of historical research into separate categories (political history, social history, economic history, history of science, of art, and so on).

The fateful year for the history of French social history was 1919 when Lucien Febvre and Marc Bloch were appointed to the University of Strasbourg. Both were followers of Berr. Indeed, Febvre credited the *Revue* with "rekindling his enthusiasm for history after he had become disillusioned with the 'banality' of his training" (Fink, *Marc Bloch,* p. 35). Within a decade, Febvre and Bloch had created the journal that was to become the focal point of social history research in France, the *Annales d'histoire économique et sociale.*

The *Annales* was both combative and visionary in its approach to history. In its first issues, Febvre denounced isolated research by historians who paid no attention to the present, and by social scientists who paid no attention to the past. He criticized historians who treated their own fields as though they were "enclosed by high walls," and sociologists who studied either "civilized" or "primitive" peoples and paid no attention to each other. The critics of the *Annales* approach to history were myriad, and for years the editors waged battles in print against their opponents who believed the subject of history should be great men and great events. Far from deterring the *Annalistes,* the constant criticism forced them to hone their theories and arguments with care and made them better and more persuasive historians.

The *Annales* was far more than a forum for criticisms of political history, however. Like Berr, both Febvre and Bloch believed historians should incorporate the insights of all of the human sciences (geography, sociology, economics, demography, law, philosophy, linguistics, and so on) into the study of the past. Their goal was to see and to recreate the totality of the past, to embrace the whole of human activity, to write a "wider and more human history" (Bloch, *The Historian's Craft,* p. v).

Febvre had studied early modern European history, and his interests ranged from rural history to the history of collective consciousness. His doctoral thesis on Philip II and the France Comté, published in 1911, explored many of the ideas that he and others would champion in the future—collective and individual states of mind, economic and social structures, and the effects of geography on human history. In later studies of Rabelais and Martin Luther, he focused on questions of *mentalités*—the structures of intellectual thought that determined much of how individuals and groups act—and individual deviations from those beliefs.

Trained as a medievalist, Bloch's interests were even more wide ranging. His research moved from the emancipation of the serfs on Capetian land to why and how people came to believe that the kings of France had the ability to heal scrofula (a belief that survived for more than eight centuries in France), to the fundamental factors that had determined the country's agrarian history. Bloch's most important, although not his most famous, work was *Les Caractères originaux de l'histoire rurale française,* published in 1931 (translated into English in 1970 as *French Rural History: An Essay on Its Basic Characteristics*). In it, Bloch explored "the technicalities of farming"—the topography of the land, the size and shape of fields, the rotation of crops and fallow, the size and shape of plows, the amount of manure produced by scrawny cows and pigs, the availability of water—and "the customs by which rural life was to a greater or lesser extent governed": communal arrangements for planting and plowing, the relationship between *seigneur* and peasants, access to the common land, the physical arrangements of villages and hamlets, land tenure systems, the form of rent payments, and reactions to external changes in the economy, politics, or the law from the fourth to the nineteenth century. The primary characteristics of *Les Caractères originaux*—the crossing of disciplinary and chronological boundaries, and the constant search for why things were the way they were, how they got to be that way, and what their significance was in the life of human beings—were to become the hallmarks of the new history in which Marc Bloch and Lucien Febvre were pioneers.

The *Annalistes* believed that historians should use the most refined techniques of the mathematician and statistician, as well as the standard analytic techniques of historians. Whatever could be measured should be measured, whatever could be counted should be counted, including rainfall and temperature, births and deaths, harvest yields and prices, acreage planted and not planted, land sales and taxes. Only then could a complete picture of the past begin to emerge.

Over the years, the name and the focus of the *Annales* changed several times until in 1946 it became the *Annales: Économies, sociétés, civilisations,* a title it has retained to the present. While the name changes signaled shifts in the contents and goals of the *Annalistes,* in the most important sense the journal remained true to Febvre's and Bloch's vision of comprehensive, analytic, interdisciplinary history.

The most monumental and best-known of the works produced within the *Annales* philosophy of history is Fernand Braudel's *La Méditerranée et le monde méditerranéen à l'époque de Philippe II,* published in French in 1949, revised in 1966, and translated into English as *The Mediterranean and the Mediterranean World in the Age of Philip II* in 1973. Braudel was a second-generation *Annaliste.* He was only seventeen when Marc Bloch and Lucien Febvre were meeting at the University of Strasbourg in 1919. In true French style, he taught at a lycée (in Algeria) in the 1920s and 1930s while he worked on his doctoral thesis on Philip II of Spain. As he worked, he grew less interested in Philip II and more interested in the Mediterranean. Inspired by the work of Lucien Febvre and Henri Pirenne, he explored archives in Spain, Italy, Brazil, and France; as he did, a historical conception of enormous scope began to take shape in his mind.

La Méditerranée would have been an epoch-making book no matter how or when it was written, but Braudel's accomplishment was all the more remarkable since he wrote the book without notes in a German prison camp during World War II. As Samuel Kinser noted in 1981, "if the Nobel Prize were given to historians, it would almost certainly have been awarded to Fernand Braudel" ("*Annaliste* Paradigm? The Geohistorical Structuralism of Fernand Braudel"). Cutting across all political boundaries, examining all of the information about the Mediterranean Sea and the people who lived by it and traveled on it, and sweeping across centuries of time to establish the geographical context for the study of the sixteenth century, *La Méditerranée* embodied the philosophy of the *Annalistes* in a way that no other single work has.

Braudel conceived of the history of the Mediterranean as three interrelated and yet independent layers of activity. Like the tectonic plates that make up the earth's surface, each plate could move independently of the others, but the movement of one plate might produce some movement in the others. The first, and perhaps most important layer from Braudel's point of view, was the physical environment. Frequently referred to as geohistory, changes in this layer occurred very slowly. This was history of the *longue durée* (long wave), of the physical structures of the region—the terrain, climate, seasons, diseases—and the constraints they placed on human movement: land and sea routes, the difficulty of winter travel and shipping, the location of towns and cities, population growth and migration. Unlike many histories that set the geographical stage at the beginning of the work and then proceed to other matters, Braudel's environmental or geographical history interacted constantly with the other levels of history. The environment affected human life; it determined the crops that could be grown; the relative isolation or transmission of culture and technology; the size, growth, and decline of population and towns; the seasonal rhythms of life.

Braudel's second layer of history was that of collective destinies and general trends, what most people mean when they refer to social and economic history. This was history of the *moyenne durée* (medium wave). Here Braudel's focus was on groups, not individuals. He analyzed the structure of Mediterranean trade and agriculture, the impact of the arrival of gold and silver in the region, the causes and consequences of rising prices, the size of ships and their owners, the rise of empires, the spread and clash of religions and cultures, forms of warfare, and the structure of society (for example, nobles, peasants, bourgeois merchants, slaves, and bandits).

The third and, from Baudel and the other *Annalistes'* perspective, least interesting and least important layer of history was that of the *courte durée* (short wave), the *evénementielle* (event). Here Braudel turned to the political, diplomatic, and military narrative history that had dominated traditional historiography. He explored the impact of events and individuals on the organization and quality of human life. While he knew that the events that occurred in this layer of history were the ones that had filled the consciousness of people at the time, he also regarded them as ultimately the most ephemeral and the least important.

Weaving these three layers of history together was a considerable task and not one that Braudel accomplished completely. Nor was his vision of the past as complete and all-encompassing as he desired. Long as *La Méditerranée* is, it emphasizes economic history and gives rather short shrift to cultural, intellectual, demographic, and social history. But the book remains a model of what one of the finest thinkers of this century could accomplish when he shook off the constraints of the old political and diplomatic historiography and applied the questions and tools of the other human sciences to the study of the past.

Under the successive leadership of Febvre and Braudel, the Sixth Section of the École des Hautes Études became the home of the *Annales* approach to history. Collectively, the *Annalistes'* work has ranged widely through the past, while individual works have focused on particular issues and time periods. Febvre's major contributions fell in the area of mentalités; Bloch focused on economic and agrarian history; Braudel on economic and total history. Ernest Labrousse used sophisticated quantitative methods to examine price series in the eighteenth century and France's economic crisis on the eve of the Revolution. Emmanuel Le Roy Ladurie, one of the most prolific of the *Annalistes,* focused on the history of climate, mentalité, folk culture, and religion in the sixteenth and seventeenth century. Like Braudel's *La Méditerranée,* his study of the region of Languedoc in the sixteenth and seventeenth centuries aspired to be total history.

Georges Lefebvre directed his attention to the French Revolution. In his 1970 *La Grande Peur* (translated as *The Great Fear,* 1973), he combined the study of geography with collective mentalité to analyze the peasant fear that brigands were coming to burn their crops at the beginning of the French Revolution, and the routes along which their panic moved from village to village. Unlike most of his fellow *Annalistes,* who perceived class struggle as a product rather than as a cause of economic and social developments, Lefebvre saw it as a prime variable to be analyzed and as a significant cause of the French Revolution. Lefebvre's interest in class struggle, as well as the quality of his scholarship, made his work especially interesting to British labor historians, and made him the logical choice for the French adviser to the editorial board of the social history and Marxist-oriented journal *Past and Present* when it was introduced in 1952.

Lefebvre's interest in the social history of the French Revolution was not an isolated phenomenon in France. Most prominent among other studies by French Marxists was Albert Soboul's study of the *sans-culottes,* the artisan and working-class men (and to a lesser extent women) of Paris (*Les Sans-culottes parisiens en l'an II,* 2d ed., 1962).

To summarize the work of the *Annalistes* does not begin to do justice to the significance and scope of their contributions to our understanding of the past or to their impact upon the historical profession. Neither the first nor second generation of

Annalistes may have achieved the goal of writing total history, but their methods, questions, and creative vision altered the way historians around the globe think about the past; these questions lie at the core of what is generally defined as social history.

THE BRITISH MARXISTS

Like the *Annalistes,* the mid-twentieth-century British Marxist historians took long views, crossed the subdisciplinary boundaries within history, and undertook large research projects. They eschewed traditional political history and began with the material and historical environment. They examined the relationships between intellectual, economic, social, political, religious, and cultural developments. They focused on groups rather than on individuals. And they moved toward a more complex understanding of the past than had previously been the case in British historiography. But the British Marxists also differed from the *Annalistes:* they focused more on human agency, on the ways in which men and women made their own history, than on the geological, economic, and cultural structures that constrained human action. And above all, they were centrally concerned with class struggle and the rise of capitalism.

The first histories of the working-class were written in Britain between the 1860s and the 1920s; notable authors are Sidney and Beatrice Webb, John and Barbara Hammond, R. H. Tawney and G. D. H. Cole. The respect their prior work had earned made it possible for the Marxist historians to find acceptance in the academy more easily than the *Annalistes* did in France. This is not to imply that there were no disputes, no disagreements, no arguments among British historians over their understanding of the past. The younger Marxist historians disagreed quite profoundly with their predecessors in the field of labor and economic history about a number of issues, but the men and women who challenged the older paradigm did so more from inside the discipline than was the case in France.

The writings of the older generation of economic/labor historians were moralistic in tone and institutional in focus. Written by scholars who themselves were political activists, these histories analyzed the development of social insitutions like the Labour Party, trade unions, and the Fabian Society, and carried strong moral messages about how workers should act. Cole, in particular, who in the view of many, "practically invented labour history as a subject," wrote biographies of labor leaders, histories of unionism, Chartism, the Labour party and Cooperation, as well as a five-volume study of socialist thought. What received little or no attention in these works was popular beliefs and working-class life. In what we might regard as almost a natural progression toward unexplored territory, it was precisely these aspects of labor history that would consume the attention of the next generation of labor historians.

The most influential of the Marxist historians were Christopher Hill (b. 1912), Rodney Hilton (b. 1916), Eric Hobsbawm (b. 1917), E. P. Thompson (b. 1924), and George Rudé (b. 1910).

The social and political consciousness of the younger Marxist historians was formed during the Great Depression of the 1930s and Britain's World War II struggle against Nazism and fascism. Between 1946 and 1956, all were members of the Communist party's Historians Group. Marice Dobb and Dona Torr played particularly important roles in the intellectual development of the Marxist historians associated with the Communist party. Indeed, their roles were similar to that played by Berr in the formation of the ideas of the *Annalistes.* Torr was interested in the ideological and political aspects of what she saw as a long transition to capitalism which began in the sixteenth century, and in its impact on ordinary people. Dobb was a theorist with a strong interest in empirical research. In their works, a complex new understanding of the transition to capitalism began to emerge, one in which the experiences and culture of workers took center stage. Inspired by Torr and Dobb, the younger generation of scholars pursued a wide variety of questions about the development and influence of capitalism and the creation of a working class, especially, but not exclusively, in Britain.

While membership in the Communist party was intellectually stimulating and formative for a generation of social historians, it was not without its costs. Beginning in 1948, the ostracism that social historians suffered in France in response to their interdisciplinary approach to history, was suffered by these scholars as well due to their politics. Party members who did not already have academic positions were blacklisted and frozen out of the academy for a decade or more. Then in 1956, with the revelation of the Stalinist purges and the Soviet Union's invasion of Hungary, a new crisis was posed for the members of the historians group; most left the Party (Hobsbawm and Dobb did not).

In 1952, the Marxist historians created a journal, *Past and Present.* The editorial board and list of editors reads like a past and future who's who in British history. Included were Geoffrey Barraclough, Maurice Dobb, Christopher Hill, Rodney Hilton, John Morris, and Eric Hobsbawm (and Georges Lefebvre). Like the *Annales, Past and Present* was created to provide a forum for new research and new perspectives on the past, and to counteract what its editors saw as profoundly disturbing tendencies in historical research and writing—the reduction of historical change to a series of mechanical, logical, inevitable developments by those who explained it purely in terms of the natural sciences, and the reduction of history to a series of inexplicable and unpredictable, irrational, or providential happenings. In contrast, the editors of *Past and Present* set out to publish historical writing that examined the past systematically and rationally yet took the complexity of human behavior and motivation into consideration. Following explicitly in the footsteps of Bloch and Febvre, they promised to proceed "'not by means of methodological articles and theoretical dissertations, but by example and fact'" (*Past and Present* 1, p. i). The measure of their success lies in the fact that *Past and Present* still remains one of the most respected historical journals in the world.

The single most influential book written in the British Marxist historical tradition is E. P. Thompson's *The Making of the English Working Class* (1963), which is to British Marxist history what Braudel's *La Méditerranée* is to *Annaliste* history—an idiosyncratic and magnificent model of its genre. In a virtuoso performance, Thompson broke free of static definitions of class and told a powerful story of how the English working class made itself. Thompson had two essential goals in writing it. One was to flesh out his theory that class is not a structure or a category or a thing but "something which in fact happens . . . in human relationships." "Class happens," he wrote, "when some men, as a result of common experiences (inherited or shared), feel and articulate the identity of their interests as between themselves, and as against other men whose interests are different from (and usually opposed to) theirs" (p. 9). The book tells the story of this "happening" in Britain in the eighteenth and nineteenth centuries.

Thompson's second goal was essential to accomplishing the first. He wanted "to rescue the poor stockinger, the Luddite cropper, the 'obsolete' hand-loom weaver, the 'utopian' artisan, and even the deluded follower of Joanna Southcott, from the enormous condescension of posterity" (p. 12). By rescuing these workers, by telling their stories as he saw them, he would establish their humanity and agency.

Thompson's work has been one of the most widely read of histories. It inspired a large number of British and American historians to investigate the effects of the industrial revolution on human life and relationships. It moved labor historians away from studying the leaders of the labor movement to a focus on the men and women who lived during the transition to industrialization. And it challenged historians both to come to grips with its sweeping story and to analyze how Thompson's vision itself created as much as it recounted the history of the working class. (See Scott, "Women in *The Making of the English Working Class,*" in her *Gender and the Politics of History,* 1988).

While E. P. Thompson may be the most widely read of the British Marxists, his works are only part of the path-breaking studies of class struggle written by this generation of British Marxists. Rodney Hilton shifted the focus of medieval history from the study of legal issues and the relationships between lords and vassals to the study of peasants and lords. Examining what he saw as "the exploitative relationship between landowners and subordinated peasants," in the feudal era, he challenged the general opinion that individualism is a bourgeois value by tracing the struggle for freedom and equality back to that of the feudal serfs against the control of the lords (*The Economic Development of Some Leicestershire Estates,* 1947).

Christopher Hill directed his attention to the seventeenth century and in particular to the English civil war. Again refocusing historians' concerns from their traditional concern with legal and political affairs, Hill argued that the English Revolution was a social rather than a political or religious revolution (*Society and Puritanism in Pre-Revolutionary England* [1964]); that it was a bourgeois revolution not unlike the French Revolution (*The World Turned Upside Down* [1975]); and that it furthered the development of capitalism (*Intellectual Origins of the English Revolution* [1965]).

Moving further in his historical interests, Eric Hobsbawm explored subjects ranging from the seventeenth to the nineteenth century, from Britain and the Continent to Latin America, and from workers to peasants, from skilled artisans to machine-breaking Luddites, from social bandits to modern revolutionaries. He entered the debate over the effects of the industrial revolution on the standard of living in Britain, explored the relationship between Methodism and working-class radicalism (*Labour-*

ing Men [1964]), analyzed the role of the labor elite or aristocracy in the creation and development of the working class (*Primitive Rebels* [1959]), and studied the effects of industrialization on peasants (*The Age of Revolution, 1789–1848* [1962]). Like Thompson, he moved away from institutional and political working-class history toward the experiences of working-class people. He placed the development of British industrial capitalism in the context of worldwide developments (*Industry and Empire* [1969]), and the development of the British working class in the context of the social, political, and economic development of Britain.

George Rudé directed his attention to the participants in the great and small revolutions of the nineteenth century. He was interested, like his colleagues, in seeing history from the bottom up rather than from the top down. In *The Crowd in the French Revolution* (1959), *The Crowd in History* (rev. ed. 1981), and (with Eric Hobsbawm) *Captain Swing* (1969), he examined arrest records to see what he could learn about the class backgrounds and motivations of the men and women involved in demonstrations, riots, and revolutions in France and England.

The success of these Marxist historians in focusing attention on working-class and peasant culture and experience is evident throughout the English-speaking world. Not only are their books and articles widely read, but two additional journals dedicated to publishing social history appeared in 1976 and have since become mainstays of the field. In its inaugural issue, *Social History* harkened back to Lucien Febvre when it stated its dedication to "a new kind of history," one that is "iconoclastic, corrosive of received explanations, creative in producing new concepts and devising new methods; and aggressive, encouraging incursions into all fields of historical analysis" (p. 1). Almost simultaneously, a group of historians which had been holding history workshops at Ruskin College, Oxford, decided to produce *History Workshop: A Journal of Socialist Historians.* Like the *Annalistes* and Marxists before them, they objected in their first issue to the "territorial rights and pecking orders" of historians and that "the great bulk of their writing was never intended to be read outside the ranks of the profession" (p. 1). And while *History Workshop*'s editors openly avowed their politics in a way that their predecessors had not in creating *Past and Present,* they followed in the older Marxists' wake in declaring that their socialism determined their threefold concerns: with "the common people in the past, their life and work and thought and individuality, as well as the context and shaping causes of their class experience"; with capitalism (p. 3); and with "bring[ing] the boundaries of history closer to people's lives" (p. 1). The author and topic of the premier article in the first issue—"Feudalism and the Origins of Capitalism" by Rodney Hilton—further established the link with the older historians.

Although British Marxist historians were still critical of the historical establishment and would not identify themselves with it, by the mid 1970s they had made their mark on the field: the prestige of publishing in the *Annales* and *Past and Present,* the success of the two new journals, and even a glance at the list of books reviewed in the first *Social History* attest to this. The experiences of the ordinary people of the past—whether workers or peasants, men or (as was also becoming apparent) women, revolutionaries or law-abiding citizens—had become a major subject of research and writing.

DEMOGRAPHIC HISTORY

In the 1950s and 1960s, while the *Annalistes* were shifting the focus of historical research from political to social, economic, environmental, and cultural questions in France, and while British Marxists were exploring working-class culture and class struggles, demographers in a variety of countries were focusing attention on population patterns and changes in the demographic behavior of western Europeans. In contrast to the *Annalistes*' and British Marxists' theories and methods, which are identified with particular countries, demographic research involved historians on both sides of the English Channel as well as on both sides of the Atlantic. Quantitative in its very essence, historical demography, when it is not linked to social and economic history, can be almost unintelligible to the average historian. But, as many of its practitioners have demonstrated, when demographic research is combined with social, economic, and cultural history, it provides information about human lives and decisions and the consequences of other changes that is of central significance to our understanding of the past.

The work of J. Hajnal and Michael Anderson is illustrative of the range of interests and discoveries of twentieth-century demographers. In 1965, Hajnal published an article which argued that the eighteenth-century female marriage pattern in western Europe was different from that found anywhere else in the world, then or since. In an article that compared marriage ages and adult celibacy for a wide range of countries, Hajnal presented data that demonstrated that western European women had uniquely high adult celibacy rates and marriage ages ("European Marriage Patterns in Perspective," in Glass and Eversley, *Population in History* [1965]). These findings continue to be generally accepted. The questions Hajnal did not fully explore, which are of crucial importance to social historians, are why the marital pattern was different in western Europe and what the significance of that difference is for the lives of women, men, and families.

Michael Anderson, in a study confined to the textile-manufacturing city of Preston in Lancashire, England, during the period of industrialization, used the most difficult of demographic techniques—record linkage—to recreate the neighborhoods and housing patterns of workers and to trace the effects of rural-urban migration on individuals and families (*Family Structure in Nineteenth-Century Lancashire* [1971]). He argued that continuity rather than disruption marked the experience of rural families as they moved to the city, sought jobs, and found places to live. By combining demographic data with information about households, families and work patterns, Anderson moved from the realm of the purely demographic to social history.

In France, Britain, and the United States, demographers, working together on collective projects, have created large databases from which to answer basic questions about demographic behavior. In France, demographic history is associated with the *Annales* historians who aspired to examine all aspects of life, but is centered at the Institut National d'Études Démographiques (INED), which has gathered data on four hundred communes for the years 1740 to 1829. In Britain, the Cambridge Group for the History of Population and Social Structure enlisted the aid of a network of local historians to record and aggregate monthly totals of marriages, baptisms, and burials from Anglican parish registers between 1541 and 1871. In the United States, the Office of Population Research at Princeton University collected data for a variety of European countries.

French and British demographers have tended to focus on the peculiarities of their own countries' demographic patterns, especially in terms of population growth or stagnation. In addition, British demographers have concentrated on questions about household structure and illegitimacy, while French demographers have focused less on industrialization and more on peasant behavior. Demographers working in the United States have engaged those in France and Britain in dialogue, often challenging the findings of their European peers, and have provided information about the general population structures, marriage patterns, and the effects of nutrition on fertility rates.

Research in France, led by Louis Henry, Michel Fleury, and Pierre Goubert, has revolved around (although it has not been confined to) the question of why the French were the first European population to practice family limitation on a widespread basis. The most significant analytic method employed by these demographers has been family reconstitution. In 1958 Louis Henry, in collaboration with Etienne Gautier, first employed this method in a study of the parish registers for a village in Normandy named Crulai. Family reconstitution consists essentially of constructing family trees for the residents of a particular area (or for a subgroup, such as members of an occupation) from the raw demographic data contained in birth (or baptismal), marriage, and death (or burial) records. Parish registers of vital events were kept by parish priests throughout France from the seventeenth century to the French Revolution, at which point the state took over the recording of demographic events in the *État civil.* Both the church and the state kept remarkably complete records, although the amount of information in them varies from era to era and recorder to recorder. In some places, for instance, village priests recorded stillbirths, in others they did not.

The advantages of family reconstitution over other forms of demographic analysis are considerable. By creating family trees, the historian can determine a wide variety of demographic patterns as well as changes in these patterns. She or he can determine the ages at which women married, the number of children women bore, the average interval between marriage and the birth of the first child, the length of subsequent birth intervals, the number of couples that experienced the death of an infant or child, how many children in a family married and in what order, how many men and women remarried after the death of a spouse and how long they waited, the number of adult women and men who did not marry, and the frequency of illegitimate births—to list only a few.

The parish and civil registers of France contain information about occupational and geographical mobility as well as about vital events. Marriage records, for instance, list the places of birth of the bride and groom, the occupations of the couple and their parents, and the residences and occupations of the witnesses to the wedding. Birth and death records similarly contain occupational information for the parents of children and for the deceased. From these records, the reconstitution of families yields information about occupational endogamy, family occupations, the sexual division of labor, the relative importance of various occupations in the town, village, or region, the rise and fall of occupations, occupational change across a lifetime, and the relationship between the occupations of parents and children, as well as about the geographical mobility of young men and women before marriage.

Family reconstitution, like all of the work pioneered by historians associated with the *Annales,* is a time-consuming research technique. It calls for the researcher to record all of the available data for a particular population for a given period of time, and then to organize it by family, before beginning to analyze it. Given the uncertainty French peasants had about how to spell their names, and their tendency to add or subtract articles (le, la, de) from their names, the sheer act of linking records over the course of decades or centuries can be daunting. In addition, of course, the technique results in the analysis of the geographically most stable families since migration, even over short distances, removes people from the registers being studied. Even so, the reconstitution of families has given historians what they never had before: a sense of marital age and frequency, fertility and contraceptive rates, infant and adult mortality rates, and occupational patterns.

Research in Britain has been led by Peter Laslett, Richard Wall, E. A. Wrigley, and Roger Schofield. In a widely read book, *The World We Have Lost* (1965), Laslett combined demographic analysis with social history to re-create life in rural preindustrial England. The book proceeds as a series of challenges to common mid-twentieth-century assumptions about life in the past, including marriage age (Laslett declares that in preindustrial England child marriage and young teenage marriage did not exist), household size (extended families did not exist), life expectancy (very low at birth), remarriage (occurred quickly after the death of a spouse), and premarital sexual activity (more than half of the children born in the first year of marriage were conceived prior to marriage). While not all of Laslett's arguments have been accepted without challenge, and his estimates of ages and rates have been refined in subsequent analyses, *The World We Have Lost* alerted historians to the significance of demographic analysis for understanding the past.

The issues that most interested Laslett in *The World We Have Lost*—the origins of the nuclear family, and the prevalence of pre- or extramarital fertility—have continued to inform his research. Laslett and Richard Wall have encouraged numerous researches, based on census and census-type lists (such as land and tax records), into the size and composition of households in early modern and modern European history. From their perspective, the data point to the overwhelming prevalence, from well before the industrial revolution, of the nuclear family over other types of family organization (such as multigenerational extended or stem families in which grandparents live with their children and grandchildren, or multiple families in which married siblings and their spouses and children live together). Lutz Berkner, in direct conflict with Laslett, argued that such large aggregated studies obscure the family developmental cycle and the effects of various inheritance systems on family living arrangements and hence on household structures ("The Use and Misuse of Census Data for the Historical Analysis of Family Structure"). Berkner's argument with Laslett is part of a general disagreement within the demographic community about the significance of the general patterns and trends revealed by large aggregated studies versus the greater variety that appears to emerge from smaller studies.

One of the largest research projects undertaken by demographers has been E. A. Wrigley and Roger Schofield's study, *The Population History of England, 1541–1871* (1981). This project is based on the parish register data accumulated by local historians throughout England. It documents a markedly increased rate of population growth in England in the eighteenth century, and attempts to account for it. Wrigley and Schofield argue that this increase was the result *not* of a decrease in mortality rates but rather of an increase in fertility rates, itself a result of changes in marital frequency and age stemming from changes in the economy. Although the primary documentation of the study—the increased rate of population growth in eighteenth-century England—is widely accepted by historians, Wrigley and Schofield's explanations, both in terms of other changes in demographic behavior and in terms of economic changes, have been challenged. Richard M. Smith believes that the long swings in nuptiality and fertility rates identified by Wrigley and Schofield were the product of the English rules for household formation ("Three Centuries of Fertility, Economy and Household Formation in England" [1981]). Nancy Birdsall points to changes in the labor market to explain changes in nuptiality and fertility patterns ("Fertility and Economic Change in Eighteenth and Nineteenth Century Europe" [1983]). David Weir introduces a fuller comparison between England and France and argues that the differences in population growth between the two countries was a product of different economic conditions. Like Berkner, he also argues for breaking down the aggregate data in ways that would allow for the variety of economic experiences and demographic responses to emerge, and for greater use of family reconstitution to supplement the aggregated data. ("Life Under Pressure" [1982]).

In 1972 Franklin Mendels (French-born but American-trained) directed his attention to the demographic consequences of the expansion of the "putting-out" system that occurred in western Europe in advance of the industrial revolution ("Proto-industrialization" [1972]). Since then, considerable attention has been paid to the phenomenon, which Mendels identified as "proto-industrialization," as one of the forces leading to the population explosion of the nineteenth century.

Proto-industrialization, as Mendels defined it, was organized by urban merchants who put raw materials out into the rural countryside to be transformed into manufactured goods by peasants and artisans working in their own homes with traditional tools. The manufactured goods were then returned to the city, where they were shipped to ever-more-distant national and international markets. Unlike their small-scale, cottage-industry predecessors, proto-industries dominated local labor markets. The availability of manufacturing work allowed rural workers to marry younger and more frequently than had previously been the case and consequently resulted in higher fertility rates and population increase.

A variety of studies supported Mendels's early findings and argument, most notably David Levine's comparison of two villages in Leicestershire, England (*Family Formation in an Age of Nascent Capitalism* [1977]), Pierre Deyon's "La Diffusion rurale des industries textiles en Flandre française" (1981), and Hans Medick's "The Proto-Industrial Family Economy" (1976).

Inevitably, refinements of Mendels's, Levine's, and Medick's arguments about the demographic consequences of proto-industrialization also began to appear as more case studies were completed by historians. Chief among these have been James Lehnings's *The Peasants of Marlhes* (1980), which emphasized the multiplicity of changes that affected rural areas in the nineteenth century and the continuity of family strategies for coping with those changes; and Gay L. Gullickson's *Spinners and Weavers of Auffay* (1986), which emphasized the mitigating effect that sexual divisions of labor can have on the demographic impact of proto-industrialization. In communities where proto-industries employed women rather than entire families, demographic behavior remained relatively stable.

WOMEN'S HISTORY

In the last quarter of the twentieth century, the parish records, civil registers, manuscript censuses, and factory time sheets used by social historians became the sources of information for historians interested in women's experiences. Social historians' initial focus on men rather than on both sexes resulted from two assumptions: first, that women's lives had been largely unaffected by economic and political developments such as industrialization; and second, to the extent that they were affected by such developments these effects were either unrelated to, or insignificant for, the general course of history. British and European historians, like others of their culture, had relegated women to the domestic sphere, which they defined as unchanging and unimportant. History might act upon women, but women themselves were rarely if ever seen as actors in history. The revival of the feminist movement in the United States, Britain, and western Europe in the late twentieth century, combined with the development of social history as an approach to the past, gradually focused historians' attention on women's lives, ideas, and actions.

Although the advent of women's history is closely tied to, indeed has become an integral part of, social history, the writing of women's history has its own history. As was the case in the 1970s, the feminist movement of the late nineteenth and early twentieth centuries inspired a generation of female historians to explore women's experiences. Chief among these historians are Alice Clark, Ivy Pinchbeck, and Frances Collier, whose studies of the effects of industrialization on women workers are still read today. Clark focused on the seventeenth century; Pinchbeck and Collier, on the mid eighteenth to mid nineteenth. Their research forms an important part of the early literature on the working class and provides information about an otherwise missing group—women workers. Of the three works, Pinchbeck's *Women Workers and the Industrial Revolution, 1750–1850* (1930) is the largest and most important. Examining the effects of the agricultural and industrial revolutions on workers in a wide variety of occupations between 1750 and 1850, Pinchbeck developed a complex argument about the short-term losses and the long-term advantages of the industrial revolution to women. She contrasted the removal of work (and its grime) from the home and the gradual rise in wages—which made it easier for single women to support themselves—with the dangerous and unhealthy conditions in which women worked and the disastrous effects of the sexual division of labor on women's access to jobs and a living wage.

The effects of industrialization on women, especially peasant and working-class women, again became a major research focus when the history of women was revived in the late twentieth century. New research added nuances and complexities to the picture drawn by the earlier generation of women's historians. Trained as social historians, women's historians used demographic analysis to answer questions about the role marriage and childbearing played in women's lives and the ways in which they and their families both adjusted to, and influenced, the development of capitalism and factory production. Local studies revealed the variety of women's experiences on peasant farms, in small villages, and in large cities. Inspired by the British Marxists, many historians asked questions about the female members of the working-class and bourgeoisie. Inspired by the *Annalistes,* they explored the constraints that economic systems, geographical location, culture, and mentalité placed on women's options and opportunities. Inspired by feminists, they asked questions about patriarchal culture, women's status, and conceptions of femininity and masculinity.

In 1975, Olwen Hufton, a British historian of early modern French history, analyzed the importance of women's paid and nonpaid contributions to the survival of their families and implicitly offered an explanation for the high celibacy and high marriage age of French women—the need to earn a dowry of household goods before marriage and the precarious ability of women to do so ("Women and the Family Economy in Eighteenth-Century France" [1975]). Using the concept of the family economy that the Russian historian A. V. Chayanof first introduced in *Theory of Peasant Economy* (1966), Hufton's work made the family economy of central significance in subsequent analyses of peasant and working-class history.

In 1978 Louise Tilly and Joan Scott, American historians of French history, presented an overview of women's history from 1750 to approximately 1950 in Britain and France (*Women, Work and Family* [1978]). Making distinctions in women's experiences by marital status, age, class, and geographical location, Tilly and Scott explored the impact of the industrial revolution on women's employment opportunities, family responsibilities, and values. Weaving together three of the major concerns of social historians—economic change, demographics, and legal and cultural traditions—and using a life-cycle analysis, they argued persuasively that women's decisions about whether to work and what kind of paid work to do can only be understood in the context of their family responsibilities and relationships.

Subsequent research has added further complexity to historians' understanding of the relationship between the industrialization process and women's lives and work, but it has generally upheld Tilly and Scott's thesis. It has also, however, challenged the accuracy and adequacy of histories that address only men's experiences. Brenda Collins's research on the putting-out system in Ireland, for instance, has demonstrated that historians' focus on factory work and factory workers has led to overemphasis on the significance of that (largely male) workplace on family organization, income, and class consciousness, and has obscured the often larger (female) labor force who worked for the same employers and without whose labor the factories could not have succeeded and families could not have survived ("The Organization of Sewing Outwork in Late-Nineteenth-Century Ulster" [1991]).

British Marxist feminist historians have gone beyond general challenges to direct confrontations with their fellow Marxist historians. The problem for Marxist analysis is well demonstrated in a short article by Anne Phillips and Barbara Taylor. Phillips and Taylor argued that the skill categories established by capitalism were not a result of "objective economic fact[s]," but were "ideological" distinctions "imposed on certain types of work by virtue of the sex and power of the workers who perform it" ("Sex and Skill," p. 79).

The response of many younger British Marxist and socialist historians to the questions raised by feminist historians has been positive. In 1982, *History Workshop* acknowledged that "feminist ideals and demands cannot simply be subsumed under the socialist label" (no. 13 [Spring 1982] p. 1) as the editorial group had thought in 1976, and changed the subtitle of the journal from *A Journal of Socialist Historians* to *A Journal of Socialist and Feminist Historians*. Taking its new name seriously, the editors agreed that

> describing the *Journal* as feminist has major implications for *all* its contents. . . . Just as socialist history means not merely the history of socialist movements or labour organisations, but the reinterpretation of all dominant social and cultural institutions in terms of a class perspective, so a historical analysis influenced by feminism demands that we ask new questions of the past, challenge old assumptions, and become sensitive to the central significance of sexual divisions in the shaping of both past and present. (p. 2)

As one might expect, French historians have been less drawn to the questions raised by Marxists and more drawn to those raised by the *Annalistes*. Bonnie Smith, an American historian of France, explored the issue of mentalité in her study of the domestic world created by the bourgeoises of the Nord, and compared their value system with that of their husbands. In contrast to the men's increasingly secular, republican, progressive, and economically prudent beliefs, the bourgeoises were increasingly religious, hierarchical, monarchic, fatalistic, profligate. Smith's work implicitly raises questions about the gendered nature of definitions of class and the adequacy of definitions built solely on male experiences and values (*Ladies of the Leisure Class* [1981]).

In France, historical research on the social history of women has remained within the *Annales* paradigm. Articles focusing on women have appeared in all of the journals associated with the *Annalistes*. Exemplary of the French approach to women's history are works by Madeleine Guilbert, Martine Segalen, and Alain Corbin.

In 1989, the adequacy of the social historians' approach to the European past in general and to women's history in particular was questioned by the American social historian of France, Joan Scott. Scott's early work on the *Glassworkers of Carmaux* (1974) explored, in the tradition of E. P. Thompson, the role of skilled artisans in creating the French working-class; her middle work analyzed the effects of industrialization on women. Her later work, though, critiqued social history from a poststructuralist perspective. She challenged social historians to analyze the way their writings have relied on, hence perpetuated, the gender conceptions of their subjects (which place the masculine in a dominant and the feminine in a subordinate position). She critiqued the work of Thompson and Gareth Stedman Jones as presenting a gendered construction of class which defines women's experiences as marginal and deviant in relationship to those of men (*Gender and the Politics of History* [1989]).

Scott's writings have challenged not only the adequacy of the social historian's understanding of the past, but also that of women's historians—including, at least implicitly, her own co-authored study, *Women, Work and Family*. Scott's approach has troubled many social historians who see it as a rejection of research that focuses on the experience they see as the heart of social history. Such criticism seems to miss the gist of Scott's argument: she neither ignores experience nor suggests that others do so. Instead, she calls for a rewriting of the master narratives by which we have organized and made sense of the past. She is not content with a social history that integrates women's experiences with those of men but leaves the major narrative—the development of capitalism—unchanged; nor is she content with a separate women's history that develops its own narrative and again leaves the basic storyline of male history unchanged. (See William Sewell's review in *History and Theory* 29 [1990] for an elegant critique of Scott's book and of its critics.)

Scott's focus on gender rather than on women constitutes a major shift in the writing of women's history. It is not without its links to earlier developments in social history, however. Of the subjects that interested the *Annalistes*—economies, societies, and mentalité—the one that received the least attention in the beginning was mentalité. The same could be said of women's history. Having begun with questions about women's experiences women's historians have now begun to explore the constraints placed on women's (and men's) activities by the culture's gender constructions—in short, by their mentalité.

THE FUTURE OF SOCIAL HISTORY

In the last decade of the twentieth century, the Rubaiyat of Omar Khayyam's observation that "the moving finger writes; and, having writ, moves on," may be an apt description of the state of European and British social history. For close to a century, each new generation of historians built upon the work of its predecessors, slightly shifting the questions and focus of research in the process. The *Annalistes* became increasingly interested in mentalité. Marxist feminists challenged their fellow Marxists to rethink their male-oriented theories of class and to pay attention to women as well as men workers. Women's historians, *sui generis,* drew attention to the experiences of women in all classes and eras.

In the final decade of what we historiographically might call the "century of social history," a challenge to the social historians' view of the past has arisen which may result in a major shift in the discipline like the one that produced social history in the first place. The new challenge, known generally as poststructuralism, again comes from France, the land of revolution, and has its origins in the work of Michel Foucault, Jacques Derrida, and Jacques Lacan; it involves a focus on language and a radical questioning of what we know about the past. Some social historians have responded positively to the challenge to write poststructural, linguistically informed history, seeing it as a way to understand more fully the meaning that people attached to their experiences (see the work of Jacques Rancière, William Sewell, Gareth Stedman Jones, and Joan Scott). Others have resisted what they see as a reversal of, rather than a complement to, their previous work in social history. It remains to be seen how much this shift of focus from the experiences of the common man and woman to the language in which they described, organized, and made comprehensible their experiences will affect the writing of social history; but in 1992 at least some of the fingers that have written social history are moving on to new methods and questions.

BIBLIOGRAPHY

"The Annalistes"

Annales d'histoire Économique et Sociale (1929–1938).

Annales d'histoire Sociale (1938–1941).

Annales d'histoire Sociale (1945).

Annales: Économies, sociétés, civilisations (1946–).

Bloch, Marc. *Les Rois thaumaturges: Étude sur le caractère surnaturel attribué à la puissance royale, particulièrement en France et en Angleterre* (1924). Translated as *The Royal Touch* (1973).

———. *Les Caractères originaux de l'histoire rurale française* (1931). Translated by Janet Sondheimer as *French Rural History: An Essay on Its Basic Characteristics* (1970).

———. *La Société féodale.* 2 vols. (1939, 1940). Translated by L. A. Manyon as *Feudal Society.* 2 vols. (1961).

———. *Apologie pour l'histoire, ou Métier d'historien* (1949). Translated by Peter Putnam as *The Historian's Craft* (1953).

Braudel Fernand. *La Méditerranée et le monde méditerranéen à l'époque de Philippe II.* (1949; 2 vol, rev. ed. 1966). Translated by Siân Reynolds as *The Mediterranean and the Mediterranean World in the Age of Philip II.* 2 vols. (1973).

———. "Personal Testimony." *Journal of Modern History* 44, no. 4 (1972).

Febvre, Lucien. *Philippe II et la Franche-Compté: Étude d'histoire politique, religieuse et sociale* (1911; repr. 1970).

———. *La Terre et l'évolution humaine: Introduction géographique à l'histoire* (1922, repr. 1949). Translated by E. G. Mountford and J. H. Paxton as *A Geographical Introduction to History* (1925).

———. *Un Destin: Martin Luther* (1928; repr. 1968).

———. *Le Problème de l'incroyance au XVI*[e] *siècle: La Religion de Rabelais* (1942).

Forster, Robert, and Orest A. Ranum, eds. *Biology of Man in History: Selections from the* Annales, *Economies, Societies, Civilizations* (1975). Translated by Elborg Forster and Patricia Ranum.

———. *Family and Society: Selections from the* Annales, *Economies, Societies, Civilizations* (1976). Translated by Elborg Forster and Patricia Ranum.

———. *Rural Society in France: Selections from the* Annales, *Economies, Societies, Civilizations* (1977). Translated by Elborg Forster and Patricia Ranum.

———. *Deviants and the Abandoned in French Society: Selections from the* Annales, *Economies, Societies, Civilizations* (1978). Translated by Elborg Forster and Patricia Ranum.

———. *Food and Drink in History: Selections from the* Annales, *Economies, Societies, Civilizations* (1979). Translated by Elborg Forster and Patricia Ranum.

———. *Medicine and Society in France: Selections from the* Annales, *Economies, Societies, Civilizations* (1980). Translated by Elborg Forster and Patricia Ranum.

———. *Ritual, Religion, and the Sacred: Selections from the* Annales, *Economies, Societies, Civilizations* (1982). Translated by Elborg Forster and Patricia Ranum.

Goubert, Pierre. *Beauvais et le Beauvaisis de 1600 à 1730: Contribution à l'histoire sociale de la France du XVII*[e] *siècle.* 2 vols. (1960).

Labrousse, Camille Ernest. *Esquisse du mouvement des prix et des revenus en France au XVIII*[e] *siècle.* 2 vols. (1933).

———. *La Crise de l'économie française à la fin de l'ancien régime et au début de la révolution* (vol. 1, 1943).

Lefebvre, Georges. *La Grande peur de 1789* (1970). Translated by Joan White as *The Great Fear* (1973).

Le Roy Ladurie, Emmanuel. *Le Territoire de l'historien.* 2 vols. (1973, 1978). Translated by Ben Reynolds and Siân Reynolds as *The Territory of the Historian* (1979) and *The Mind and Method of the Historian* (1981).

———. *Les Paysans de Languedoc* (1966). Translated by John Day as *The Peasants of Languedoc* (1974).

———. *Montaillou, village occitan de 1294 à 1324* (1975). Translated by Barbara Bray as *Montaillou: The Promised Land of Error* (1978).

———. *Le Carnaval de Romans* (1979). Translated by Mary Feeney as *Carnival in Romans* (1979).

Mélanges d'histoire Sociale (1942–1944).

Demographic History

Anderson, Michael. *Family Structure in Nineteenth-Century Lancashire* (1971).

Berkner, Lutz K. "The Uses and Misuses of Census Data for the Historical Analysis of Family Structure." *Journal of Interdisciplinary History* 5, no. 4 (1975).

Birdsall, Nancy. "Fertility and Economic Change in Eighteenth and Nineteenth Century Europe: A Comment." *Population and Development Review* 9, no. 1 (1983).

Coale, Ansley, and Susan Cotts Watkins, eds. *The Decline of Fertility in Europe* (1986).

Flandrin, Jean-Louis. *Families: Parenté, maison, sexualité dans l'ancienne société* (1976). Translated by Richard Southern as *Families in Former Times: Kinship, Household, and Sexuality* (1979).

Gautier, Etienne, and Louis Henry. *La Population de Crulai, paroisse normande: Étude historique* (1958).

Goubert, Pierre. "Historical Demography and the Reinterpretation of Early Modern French History: A Research Review." *Journal of Interdisciplinary History* 1, no. 1 (1970).

Hajnal, J. "European Marriage Patterns in Perspective." In *Population in History,* edited by David V. Glass and D. E. C. Eversley (1965).

Henry, Louis, and Michel Fleury. *Nouveau manuel de dépouillement et d'exploitation de l'état civil ancien* (1965).

Laslett, Peter. *The World We Have Lost: England Before the Industrial Age* (1965).

Laslett, Peter, and Richard Wall, eds. *Household and Family in Past Time* (1972).

Levine, David. *Family Formation in an Age of Nascent Capitalism* (1977).

Medick, Hans. "The Proto-Industrial Family Economy: The Structural Function of Household and Family During the Transition from Peasant Society to Industrial Capitalism." *Social History* (1976).

Mendels, Franklin. "Proto-Industrialization: The First Phase of the Industrialization Process." *Journal of Economic History* (1972).

Schofield, Roger, and E. A. Wrigley. *The Population History of England, 1541–1871* (1981).

Smith, Richard M. "Three Centuries of Fertility, Economy, and Household Formation in England." *Population and Development Review* 7, no. 4 (1981).

Weir, David R. "Life Under Pressure: France and England, 1670–1870." *Journal of Economic History* 44, no. 1 (1984).

Wrigley, E. A. "Family Limitation in Pre-Industrial England." *Economic History Review* 2d ser., 19, no. 1 (1966).

———. *Population and History* (1969).

British Marxists

History Workshop: A Journal of Socialist Historians (1976–1982).

History Workshop: A Journal of Socialist and Feminist Historians (1982–).

Hill, Christopher. *Society and Puritanism in Pre-Revolutionary England* (1964).

———. *Intellectual Origins of the English Revolution* (1965).

———. *The World Turned Upside Down* (1975).

Hilton, Rodney. *The Economic Development of Some Leicestershire Estates in the Fourteenth and Fifteenth Centuries* (1947).

Hobsbawm, Eric. *Primitive Rebels* (1959).

———. *The Age of Revolution, 1798–1948* (1962).

———. *Labouring Men* (1964).

———. *Industry and Empire* (1969).

Hobsbawm, Eric, and George Rudé. *Captain Swing* (1968).

Past and Present (1952–).

Rudé, George. *The Crowd in the French Revolution* (1959).

———. *The Crowd in History: A Study of Popular Disturbances in France and England, 1730 to 1848* (1980, rev ed. 1981).

Social History (1976–).

Thompson, Edward P. *The Making of the English Working Class* (1963).

———. "Time, Work-Discipline, and Industrial Capitalism." *Past and Present,* no. 38 (1967).

———. "The Moral Economy of the English Crowd in the Eighteenth Century." *Past and Present,* no. 50 (1971).

Women's History

Clark, Alice. *The Working Life of Women in the Seventeenth Century* (1919; repr. 1982).

Collier, Frances. *The Family Economy of the Working Classes in the Cotton Industry, 1784–1833* (1964).

Collins, Brenda. "The Organization of Sewing Outwork in Late-Nineteenth-Century Ulster." In *Markets and Manufacture,* edited by Maxine Berg (1991).

Corbin, Alain. *Les Filles de noce: Misère sexuelle et prostitution aux 19e et 20e siècles* (1978).

Davidoff, Leonore, and Catherine Hall. *Family Fortunes: Men and Women of the English Middle Class.* (1987).

Guilbert, Madeleine. *Les Femmes et l'organisation syndicale avant 1914* (1966).

Hufton, Olwen. "Women and the Family Economy in Eighteenth-Century France." *French Historical Studies* 9, no. 1 (1975).

Phillips, Anne, and Barbara Taylor. "Sex and Skill." *Feminist Review,* no. 6 (1980).

Pinchbeck, Ivy. *Women Workers and the Industrial Revolution, 1750–1850* (1930; repr. 1969).

Ross, Ellen. "'Fierce Questions and Taunts': Married Life in Working-Class London, 1870–1914." *Feminist Studies* 8, no. 3 (1982).

Smith, Bonnie. *Ladies of the Leisure Class: The Bourgeoises of the Nord* (1981).

Taylor, Barbara. *Eve in the New Jerusalem: Socialism and Feminism in the Nineteenth Century* (1983).

Tilly, Louise, and Joan Scott. *Women, Work and Family* (1978).

Walkowitz, Judith. *Prostitution and Victorian Society: Women, Class, and the State* (1980).

Linguistically Informed Social History

Darnton, Robert. *The Great Cat Massacre and Other Episodes in French Cultural History* (1984).

Davis, Natalie Zemon. *Fiction in the Archives: Pardon Tales and Their Tellers in Sixteenth-Century France* (1987).

Ranciere, Jacques. *The Nights of Labor: The Worker's Dream in Nineteenth-Century France* (1989).

Scott, Joan Wallach. *Gender and the Politics of History* (1989).

Stedman-Jones, Gareth. *Language of Class: Studies in English Working Class History, 1832–1982* (1983).

Historiographical Studies

Parker, Harold T. "Great Britain." In *International Handbook of Historical Studies: Contemporary Research and Theory,* edited by George G. Iggers and Harold T. Parker (1979).

Fink, Carole. *Marc Bloch: A Life in History* (1989).

Hexter, J. H. "Fernand Braudel and the *Monde Braudellien. . . .*" *Journal of Modern History* 44, no. 4 (1972).

Johnson, Richard. "Culture and the Historians." In *Working-Class Culture: Studies in History and Theory,* edited by J. Clarke, et al. (1979).

Kaye, Harvey J. *The British Marxist Historians: An Introductory Analysis* (1984).

Kinser, Samuel. "*Annaliste* Paradigm? The Geohistorical Structuralism of Fernand Braudel." *American Historical Review* 86, no. 1 (1981).

Scott, Joan W. *Gender and the Politics of History* (1988).

Stoianovich, Traian. *French Historical Method: The Annales Paradigm* (1976).

Trevor-Roper, H. R. "Fernand Braudel, the *Annales,* and the Mediterranean." *Journal of Modern History* 44, no. 4 (1972).

SEE ALSO **Socialist and Communist Movements; Women and Work**; and various essays in the sections **"Family History"** and **"Processes of Social Change."**

AMERICA AS INTERPRETED BY FOREIGN OBSERVERS

Robert Lawson-Peebles

SEEKING AMERICA

IN 1772 A YORKSHIRE farmer named Charles Varlo struck gold in Dublin. He bought Long Island at a knockdown price. He had discovered a document apparently substantiating a grant from King Charles I of land called New Albion, and he purchased a one-third share in it. In 1784, the Revolution safely over, Varlo traveled to the United States to take up his claim. A broadsheet offering "the Finest Part of America, to be Sold, or Lett" indicates his high hopes. Unfortunately, he found not only that King Charles I's geography was vague but also that King Charles II had granted the same land to others. The law courts of what was now (in his view "corruptly") called New Jersey rejected his claims. So Varlo went on the road, traveling from Virginia to New England and taking notes. The resulting essay, published at London in *Nature Display'd* (1794), shows that his financial disappointment had colored his view of America. He disliked much of what he saw. The land south of Philadelphia was a repository of fevers and agues, while the expanse from New York to Boston was thin and rocky, "a very disagreeable uncouth country" (*Nature Display'd,* p. 124). Many of the nation's roads were poor; its inns were extravagantly expensive; and the alcohol they served was bad. Even America's reptiles were inferior. Much had been written about the deadliness of the rattlesnake. Nonsense, said Varlo; many people had been bitten and had lived to tell the tale. In contrast, Varlo concluded that he had no tale to tell about the United States. Dismissing the preceding forty pages of his "Author's tour thro' America," he asserted that "after all my travels . . . I saw nothing worth attention, except raising tobacco and Indian corn" (*Nature Display'd,* p. 154).

In 1919 the American writer Waldo Frank found plenty worth attention in America. Like Varlo he looked closely at the terrain, but he came to a different conclusion. *Our America* sees an intimate relationship between "the soil of the land" and "the soul of man" (p. 231). The book is a quasi-religious work which laments the nation's materialism but looks forward to a new era of artistic spirituality when Americans will respond appropriately to the "physiography" of their country, which is "vivid and vibrant beyond the scales of temperate Europe" (p. 6). This was a message that was popular in America. The book sold well and went into a second edition the following year. It was also popular in Europe; it was translated into French in 1920, and a new edition was published in Britain in 1922. Indeed, the book had been written with Europe in mind, in response to a request from two French journalists with whom Frank had worked on the *Nouvelle Revue française.* Their encouragement and their angle of vision had been vitally important to him. "As Frenchmen," he said, "they helped me to see America" (p. xi). He concluded: "We go forth all to seek America. And in the seeking we create her. In the quality of our search shall be the nature of the America we create" (*Our America,* p. 10).

These last three sentences are the motto of this essay, which has begun with Varlo and Frank for two reasons. First, nobody has ever visited America in a state of innocence. Visitors have brought with them expectations and preconceptions which affected their view of America and its inhabitants. Varlo traveled to America with hopes of great gain. When those hopes turned to dust, they transformed his America into a dustheap. This is a distressingly common experience. Varlo was far from being the first hopeful traveler to change his mind about his destination and, as we shall see, he was not the last.

The second point is more general. Observing America is far from being a simple one-way process. It is part of what Christopher Mulvey has called "a textual system" ("Écriture and Landscape," pp. 100–101), elements of which include the author's sense of a potential audience, the genre in which the text locates itself (travel account, novel, television documentary, and so on), and its relationship to earlier texts about America or about traveling in general. It is also part of a transatlantic (and, in later years of United States history, a Pan-American and transpacific) dynamic, which includes such factors as the cultural, social, national, and ethnic background of the observer, and the relationship of that background to the people and places observed.

Waldo Frank's *Our America,* which would otherwise be disqualified from this survey because the author is a native-born American, makes the point plainly. Written in the wake of the Franco-American alliance of World War I, it warmly acknowledges a debt of gratitude for what might be called the gift of stereoscopic vision. The addition of a foreign perspective gave Frank a depth of field and made some aspects of his home country, otherwise flat and dull, leap into vivid focus. *Our America* shows that through the eyes of others you can be an acute observer of your own land.

Unfortunately, binocular vision can lead to blindness as well as insight. An example is *Whicker's New World* (1985), a series of interviews by the television journalist Alan Whicker with Britons who live and work in the United States. With a few notable exceptions, the interviewees emerge as alienated people, ill at ease in the New World and with an ossified view of the Old. Their attitudes, in consequence, seem like clichés. Their collective view of America is of a lotusland stalked by muggers and predatory women. Britain, in contrast, is remembered as the cloud-covered site of the last medieval joust, with Prime Minister Margaret Thatcher as St. George and union leader Arthur Scargill as the dragon. These discontented drifters make the negative side of Frank's point. They have reversed the old adage that travel broadens the mind, and their search has created a cramped America and a meager Britain.

We go forth all to seek America. Some sense of the scope of the search may be obtained by comparing contemporary views of New York by the English writers Rupert Brooke (1887–1915) and Israel Zangwill (1864–1926). Brooke, the poet immortalized by his good looks and early death, visited the United States in 1913, writing dispatches for the *Westminster Gazette* which were subsequently published in 1916 as *Letters from America.* The arrival in America is not promising. As his ship docks, he looks down into the water and recoils from the detritus of New York City, which in addition to all the usual filth and flotsam includes "occasionally a dead cat or dog, hideously bladder-like, its four paws stiff and indignant towards heaven" (*Letters,* pp. 50–51). This pungent initiation resembles the first stage of Dante's descent into hell. Brooke's impressions of the city are lurid, a chiaroscuro of "merciless lights" and buildings soaring into the stygian black, accompanied by a sound track of shrieking automobiles, clanging elevated trains, and wailing newboys, all presided over by a strange god, the electric outline of a woman's head, its left eyelid winking in an invitation to buy pepsin chewing gum.

Brooke records his stay in New York as a catalog of perversions. Largely to blame for this vision of hell is democracy. The word lies like a threat on his pages. In England he may have been an advocate of the theory of democracy. In America he finds himself, to his dismay, drawn into its "grimy and generous embrace" and chafed by its fustian (*Letters,* p. 56). He escapes to Harvard, which bears some relationship to his beloved alma mater, Cambridge, although its baseball games are not exactly cricket, and then to Canada, where to his relief he discovers "the English way of doing things" (*Letters,* p. 92). The English way, maybe, but once again not exactly English. Lying behind Brooke's view of North America is nostalgia for his comfortable, upper-middle-class England of Rugby (the elite private school), Cambridge, and the leisured life of the Old Vicarage at Grantchester where, in the words of his poem, the church clock forever stands at "ten to three" and there is "honey still for tea" (*Collected Poems,* p. 57). In another poem, the eerily and movingly prophetic "The Soldier," Brooke foresees "some corner of a foreign field" transformed by his dust into England (*Collected Poems,* p. 9). New York, indeed much of the North American continent, was clearly not England, and Brooke could not forgive that failure.

Israel Zangwill's impression of the same New York could not be more different. The son of a Russian Jewish refugee, he was deeply influenced by his childhood in the East End of London, which he characterized in his novel *Children of the Ghetto* (1892) as "a region where, amid uncleanness and squalor, the rose of romance blows yet a little longer" (p. 1). Zangwill was a fervent Zionist, yet for him the rose of romance was not blown, but blooming, in America. His introduction to *From Plotzk to Boston* (p. 8) by Mary Antin (best known for her autobiographical *The Promised Land*) tells of "the magic vision of free America" that inspired Russian Jews to make the difficult, often dangerous journey from one side of the world to the other. His popular and influential play *The Melting-Pot,* first performed in 1908, tries to realize that magic vision. It concerns a love affair between a Jewish musician orphaned by a pogrom in Russia and a radical Russian aristocrat who works in a New York settlement house. The young couple overcome the barrier of religion and the objections of both families, and the much-quoted closing scene achieves an appropriate apotheosis. The stage setting provides a vision of New York that is the polar opposite of Brooke's. The sunset etches the streets with "narrow lines of saffron and pale gold" while "the whole sky is one glory of burning flame" (p. 198). The hero, "prophetically exalted by the spectacle," talks of New York as "the great Melting-Pot" where all the different races, religions, and nations are united "to build the Republic of Man and the Kingdom of God" (p. 199). America generally is compared favorably to Rome and Jerusalem: in the Old World people go to worship and look back, while in the New "all races and nations come to labour and look forward!" (p. 199). These final words are spoken against a backdrop of skyscrapers, and the presiding deity is not a winking lady peddling gum but the Statue of Liberty, with the Emma Lazarus poem on its base.

THE PLAYGROUND OF THE EUROPEAN IMAGINATION, 1492–1776

It is not at all uncommon to regard America either as heaven or as hell. The vision of America as heaven came first. Columbus's first description of the New World talked of a green and fertile country, a land of pine groves and honey, inhabited by gentle natives and a thousand different songbirds. Columbus was another hopeful traveler and, unlike Varlo, he was fortunate. The land responded kindly to his expectations, although at one point he hallucinated when he reported hearing a nightingale, a bird not native to America. His good fortune and that of subsequent explorers was embroidered by such writers and editors as Peter Martyr (d. 1526), Richard Hakluyt (ca. 1552–1615), and Thomas Harriot (1560–1621). They made up in scholarship what they lacked in experience, describing America in terms of two myths: the Christian Garden of Eden and the classical golden age. Such descriptions made a deep impact. They encouraged the further exploration which many of them were written to promote; they initiated the theme of plenty which became so important in American culture; and they gave rise to the first modern example of a literary genre, utopian fiction. The narrative framework of Thomas More's *Utopia* (1516) begins when Raphael Hythloday accompanies Amerigo Vespucci on his fourth voyage, then stays behind in the New World to indulge his taste for travel and to discover laws and customs which would profitably be adopted in England.

It would be wrong to suggest that the first views of America were entirely positive. Raphael Hythloday reported that he "saw much to condemn" there (*Utopia,* § 40), and Hakluyt disparaged one of the New World's first exports, tobacco, which he called "a pestiferous and wicked poison" (quoted in Honour, *New Golden Land,* p. 42). But it was not until 1605 that the paradisal vision received its first direct answer. Bishop Joseph Hall's *The Discovery of a New World* may well be the first dystopian fiction. Its purpose is the same as *Utopia*—to highlight English social and political problems—but the method is the opposite of More's. Hall agrees that America is fertile, but fertility only encourages gluttony. The favorable conditions in America merely accentuate the foolishness and knavery that is part of the human condition. Humankind is damned; no New World can paint over an old sin. Hall had begun the jeremiadic tradition even before the Puritans landed on Plymouth Rock.

More and Hall used America simply as a guinea pig. So did Charles Louis de Secondat, baron de Montesquieu (1689–1755). Like the two earlier writers, Montesquieu never visited America. Nor, he felt, did he need to. For him the New World was a vehicle for generating an environmentally grounded discussion of primitivism and civilization. *The Spirit of the Laws,* first published in

Montesquieu's native French in 1748, was soon translated into English (1750) and subsequently into most of the other major European languages. Along with Edward Gibbon's *Decline and Fall of the Roman Empire* (1776–1788) and Adam Smith's *Wealth of Nations* (1776), it became one of the most popular and influential books of the eighteenth century, and for similar reasons. All three books seemed to provide objective, scientific reasons for the constitution and variety of civilized societies. This is not to say that Montesquieu eschewed moral judgment. He followed Bishop Hall in condemning those who used America's fertility as an excuse for sloth. He also followed John Locke in distinguishing between natural and civil societies. Those who lived in a state of nature merely hunted, while those who were civilized "rendered the earth more proper for their abode" by tilling it (*The Spirit of the Laws,* p. 274). This distinction between hunters and farmers would be emphasized in *The Law of Nations* (1758, translated into English 1759–1760) by the Swiss jurist Emmerich de Vattel, and would find its place in the thought of Thomas Jefferson and, later, Francis Parkman and Frederick Jackson Turner.

Science can be fascinating for intellectuals, but it is bad news for guinea pigs. Montesquieu's fondness for farming would become an excuse for dispossessing and removing Native Americans. The connection he drew between climate and character would be similarly abused. Montesquieu thought that hot, moist climates made people lazy, passionate, and servile. An authoritarian government was therefore appropriate for such places and peoples. This argument was later taken up by apologists for slavery and, after emancipation, by those who adopted racist practices. *The Spirit of the Laws* also had an impact on white Americans, one which was more immediate if not so catastrophic. The colonists became widely regarded as mentally and physically deficient. Inevitably such attitudes caused much resentment and helped to polarize the governed and the governing before and during the Revolution.

This sad state of affairs materialized because Montesquieu's theories were blurred by a number of European writers who discussed America as an entity in itself. In a series of steps they eroded the distinction he had made between hunters and farmers, natives and settlers. The first step was taken, just one year after the publication of *The Spirit of the Laws,* by another French philosopher, Georges Louis Leclerc, comte de Buffon. His *Natural History* (1749–1804) modified Montesquieu's cause and effect, suggesting that America had a damp, cold climate because it was so sparsely occupied. The Native Americans, he said, had been badly affected; they were stupid, lazy, and impotent. Yet he, too, distinguished between aborigines and immigrants, and confirmed his countryman's assertion that when it was properly farmed, America would become one of the most wholesome places on earth. Three years later, in 1753, the Swedish scientist Per (or Pehr) Kalm (1715–1779) took another step beyond Montesquieu. In his *Travels into North America* he said that the climate affected all of America's inhabitants; nobody was exempt. Disease was common among natives and settlers alike. White women ceased bearing children earlier than their counterparts in Europe; the men were weaker; and everyone aged more rapidly. Even imported animals declined in size.

The work of Montesquieu, Buffon, and Kalm led directly to the most complete vision of America as hell, depicted by Cornelius (Corneille) de Pauw (1739–1801) in his *Recherches philosophiques sur les Américains.* First published in 1768–1769, the book created an immediate stir, was extensively reviewed by British periodicals, and was translated into English in 1775. For the next forty years de Pauw became the oracle for those who wished to disparage the New World. The land, he said, was so sterile that the first settlers had been forced into cannibalism. Its atmosphere was so malignant that it infected all who breathed it with syphilis. The only creatures that prospered in America were "lizards, snakes, serpents, reptiles, and insects that were monstrous by their size and the power of their poison" (Stearn, *Broken Image,* p. 6). The continent was so much the home of original sin that Columbus regretted his discovery.

De Pauw's *Recherches* influenced many European intellectuals, including Voltaire, Goethe, and Kant. It did so because it fitted easily into three interlocking textual systems: Bishop Hall's dystopia, Montesquieu's philosophy, and the tales, as old as travel itself, of natural monstrosities. Columbus reported people in Havana born with tails. George Sandys, an administrator in Virginia from 1621 to 1625, believed that there were hermaphrodites in Florida. Such stories were so common that even as reputable a scientist as Kalm was led astray. During his visit to the middle British colonies from 1749 to 1751 he fell victim to a number of tall tales. One told of deadly rattlesnakes that bewitched squirrels into jumping, obligingly, into their jaws. (One can almost hear Charles Varlo snorting in derision.) Another told of bears that killed cows by biting a hole in the hide and blowing into the hole "till the animal swells excessively and dies" (*Travels into North America,* vol. 1, pp. 116–117). Presumably bears took the precaution of tethering their prey first, or the New World would have possessed another monstrosity, the flying cow.

Kalm's tall tales suggest that the New World was the playground of the European imagination. We should not forget, though, that play is a vital intellectual activity, intimately related to the most serious questions. Kalm was trying to apply Linnaean taxonomy to a continent which was still little known. Buffon and de Pauw were speculating on the relation of the New World to the biblical story of the Flood. America, indeed, seemed to many to provide a model of an embryonic civilization. In a conscious echo of the Book of Genesis, John Locke remarked in 1690 that "in the beginning, all the world was America," and he used it to imagine a premercantile society ("The True End of Civil Government," ss. 48–49). Eighty-six years later, Adam Smith developed Locke's mercantilist model. He considered the discovery of America and the passage to India to be "the two greatest and most important events in the history of mankind," and his *Wealth of Nations* (1776) devotes much space to discussing the revolution in Europe's commerce brought about by the colonization of America. Smith was concerned about the discord between Britain and the colonies, and at the close of the book he argued either for union or for complete separation.

In contrast, Tom Paine's mind was made up. In *Common Sense,* published in the same year as *The Wealth of Nations* but having a much more immediate political effect, he argued vehemently for independence. Like Locke, Buffon, and de Pauw, Paine depicted America in terms of the book of Genesis, using the story of Noah to celebrate "our power to begin the world over again" (*Common Sense,* p. 120). Even those who were opposed to independence recognized the magnitude of the event. Thomas Pownall, a British member of Parliament and an acknowledged expert on colonial affairs, published *A Memorial Addressed to the Sovereigns of America* in 1783, reluctantly accepting the new nation but anticipating, in a striking passage which looked back to Adam Smith and forward to Israel Zangwill, that "the Wealth of Nations must flow in upon them" and that "all the oppressed and injured of every nation will seek . . . refuge" with them (p. 138).

THE AMERICAN EXPERIMENT

After independence, French and British commentary still tended to focus on questions of the development of American civilization, but now inevitably cast them in a political light. Of the two, French accounts tended more towards philosophy. Michel-Guillaume Jean (J. Hector St. John) de Crèvecoeur's *Letters from an American Farmer* (1782) fleshes out Montesquieu's environmental determinism by comparing four regions: the agricultural middle provinces, the fisheries of the Northeast, the frontier West, and the slaveholding South. Thomas Jefferson, who knew and admired Crèvecoeur, doubtless approved the verdict in favor of farming. He could not have been pleased with the book's politics, for Crèvecoeur suggests that the American farmer flourishes best under a mild colonial system and regards the Revolution with terror, as a fratricidal civil war. Perhaps because of this, the first American edition, which appeared in 1793, was a failure, and for a century the book went out of print on both sides of the Atlantic. It was reprinted in 1904 at the behest of a Columbia University professor who praised Crèvecoeur as a "poet-naturalist," and it has since become one of the two major French commentaries on America, possibly as a result of two partial readings. The first sees the book as an unshadowed bucolic idyll, a hymn of praise to American agrarianism. The second rips out of context Letter III, "What Is an American?," which, with its melting-pot imagery and invocations of renewal and self-reliance, is turned into an anticipation of later American ideology.

The other major French commentary is, of course, Alexis de Tocqueville's *Democracy in America* (1835–1840). While it never disappeared as completely as *Letters from an American Farmer,* it, too, enjoyed mixed fortunes before reaching its present prominence. Like its predecessor, *Democracy in America* can be read in several ways. Volume 1 produces a cozily organic view of American democracy by locating its origins in the New England town meeting, from which the events of 1776 become an evolution rather than a revolution. Its tone is generally optimistic, and it ends with a vision of the future in which "the destinies of half the globe" (*Democracy in America,* vol. 1, p. 452) will be dominated by the Russians and the "Anglo-Americans," a term Tocqueville uses frequently. Volume 2 differs in focus and tone. Tocqueville now looks at the cultural consequences of democracy, and his view is less sanguine. The darker hints in volume 1, contained in such phrases as "the tyranny of the majority" (p. 269), develop into a vision of an insipid utilitarian society where the pressures to conform create a nervous individualism which has no room for eccentricity or excellence. This time the conclusion is equivocal, uncertain if the "principle of equality," which Tocqueville regards as inevitable, will lead "to servitude or freedom, to knowledge or barbarism, to prosperity or wretchedness" (vol. 2, p. 352). Together, the two volumes make Tocqueville a prophet for many seasons, fodder at one time for those who believe in the destinies forged by the "special relationship" between Britain and America, at another time for those who fear the declension of democracy into totalitarianism, and at others for those who seek the roots of such important analyses of America as Frederick Jackson Turner's frontier thesis, David Riesman's *The Lonely Crowd: A Study of the Changing American Character* (1950), Christopher Lasch's *The Culture of Narcissism* (1979), and Robert N. Bellah's *Habits of the Heart* (1985).

In contrast with those of the French, British accounts of America have tended toward sociology. One of the best known, Charles Dickens's *American Notes* (1842), is a case in point. Dickens first visited America in 1842, ten years after Tocqueville and with one aim in common: to see American prisons. His report of the tour, published promptly on his return to Britain that same year, differs markedly from Tocqueville's. The Frenchman mentions prisons briefly, on just one occasion. Dickens writes about them at length, and about such other institutions as asylums for the blind and the insane. Unfortunately, his pleasure at the cleanliness and good order he found in most institutions does not extend beyond their walls. "This is not the Republic of my imagination," he wrote to a friend, the actor William C. Macready. America was a disappointment. Its society seemed dull and degraded, and so did the terrain, particularly the famous beauty spots. His description of the Ohio River, often known as "la Belle Rivière," makes it indistinguishable from the Mississippi, whose enormous size and destructive power prompted horror and disgust in many tourists. Looking-Glass Prairie, at the far western point of his travels, has none of the grandeur that he expected but is instead "oppressive in its barren monotony" (*American Notes,* p. 226). Dickens's reaction against America infected his next novel, *Martin Chuzzlewit* (1843). Its American chapters are populated by an array of uncouth, noisy, irascible braggarts whose "smart" sharp practices create, among other things, a hellhole ironically named Eden, the slimy, miasmic speculators' paradise based on Dickens's memory of Cairo, Illinois.

There are three related reasons why Dickens's America is bleaker than Tocqueville's. The first is social. Tocqueville's place in the French aristocracy insulated him from the seamy side of American economic mobility, while Dickens, with his origins in the insecure petite bourgeoisie, was highly sensitive to it. Second, Tocqueville employed the French deductive method, while Dickens regarded himself as an English empiricist, resisting deductions until the final brief chapter of his deliberately named *American Notes.* Therefore, while both writers drew attention to American love of money, Tocqueville deduced from it the principle of sovereignty of the people, and Dickens depicted its various facets in a range of brilliantly detailed characters. Third, *Democracy in America* is part of a speculative textual system which stretches back beyond Montesquieu and the philosophes to Montaigne's "Of the Cannibals." *American Notes* engages with a shorter and more strident tradition, which looks back to British metropolitan condescension toward the American provinces, updated by a number of post-Revolution assessments of the new nation, including those by such members of the *Edinburgh Review* as Francis Jeffrey and Sydney Smith ("who reads an American book?"), and such travelers as Harriet Martineau, Thomas Hamilton, Basil Hall, and, most notoriously, Frances Trollope, who in *Domestic Manners of the Americans* (1832), insisted at length that they had none.

I would not want to make an absolute distinction between the French philosophical and the British sociological views of America. The British, in particular, paid close attention to their neighbors across the Channel. William Robertson's *The History of America* (1777) was influenced by Buffon. *Travels in North America* (1786), a positive view of America by François Jean, the marquis de Chastellux, one of the senior French officers at Yorktown, met its prompt reply in *Remarks on the Travels* (1787) by a senior officer on the British side, John Graves Simcoe. Nevertheless, more recent observers have tended to adhere to their national traditions, following the separate paths trod by Dickens and Tocqueville. James Bryce's exhaustive political analysis, *The American Commonwealth* (1889), therefore began by rejecting the model offered by Tocqueville as too "general and somewhat speculative" (vol. 1, p. 4), a point repeated by Harold Laski in his shorter and more wide-ranging *The American Democracy* (1948), while the British empiricist tradition was probably taken to its limit when Stephen Brook, in *New York Days, New York Nights* (1984), penetrated the darkest recesses of a bathhouse in those elevated times before AIDS began to take its toll. For their part, the French continued to employ the speculative method. In some instances, America seemed to lend itself all too readily to the process. After visiting America early in the Great Depression, the novelist Georges Duhamel saw it as a system of laws, institutions, prejudices, and myths rather than as a people. In other instances, the system was created in Europe but did not survive the Atlantic crossing. The philosopher Jean-Paul Sartre constructed an exotic, radical existentialist America from Hollywood films, jazz records, and the novels of William Faulkner and John Dos Passos. The racism that he witnessed during his 1945 visit began the disillusion which was intensified by the Joseph McCarthy hearings and the Korean and Vietnam wars. D. H. Lawrence, the English writer who came closest to creating a French grand design, made the point succinctly when he remarked in 1923 that it is easier to love America "when you look at it through the wrong end of the telescope, across all the Atlantic water" (*Studies in Classic American Literature,* p. 56). When he arrived in America, like Dickens before him, his utopian expectations were shattered.

THE AMERICAN CENTURY

As the twentieth century progressed, it became less easy to love America from abroad. Previously, most foreign interpretations adhered to the patterns exemplified by French philosophy and British sociology. The Hungarians Sándor Farkas Bölöni and Ágoston Mokcsai Haraszthy, for instance, discussed America in Tocquevillean terms as a model republic. The Russians Pavel Svin'in, Aleksandr Borisovitch Lakier, and Maxim Gorky resembled Dickens in their assessments of American institutions and in their awareness of the power of the almighty dollar. In the twentieth century, however, new interpretations emerged, owing much of their force to the awareness of the growing international role of the United States. Its hegemony had already spread over the American landmass, with the result that the terms for the nation and the continent became interchangeable. Now it spread further, with the result that the United States became the scapegoat for the twentieth century.

One interpretation comes from the Soviet bloc. Lenin's "Letter to American Workers" (1918) within two sentences expresses admiration of "the productive forces of collective human endeavor" which are creating "the wonders of modern engineering," and contempt at the gap "between the handful of arrogant multimillionaires who wallow in filth and luxury, and the millions of working people" who live on the edge of poverty (quoted in Stearn, *Broken Image,* p. 210). This view, oscillating between envy of American productivity and contempt at the capitalist system, remained the official Soviet line until the collapse of Communist power. We now know that the official line was no more than that. Beneath it existed widespread popular enthusiasm for American cultural exports like jazz, jeans, rock and roll, and hamburgers. Such exports were sometimes suppressed, sometimes grudgingly granted official tolerance. Their natural medium was the black market, which inevitably endowed them with added glamour. When, for instance, the first American jazz band, led by Benny Goodman, toured the Soviet Union in 1962, the concerts were sold out and the musicians treated as heroes and mobbed for souvenirs. It may well be that the most radical reform of the 1980s was neither *glasnost* nor *perestroika* but rather the arrival of McDonald's in Moscow.

Third-world analyses of the United States tend to ignore the wonders of its productivity and the glamour of its exports. The result is a view more negative than Lenin's. Frantz Fanon (1925–1961), born in the French Antilles and a major figure in the liberation of Algeria, regarded the United States as the most recent colonial power, a nation where "the taints, the sickness and the inhumanity of Europe have grown to appalling dimensions" (*The Wretched of the Earth,* p. 252). Fanon's last days in a hospital in Washington, D.C., did nothing to change his loathing of a nation he regarded as inherently racist. John Pepper Clark (b. 1935) spent a year at Princeton University and returned home to Nigeria with a view as sour as Fanon's. By 1964 racism did not seem too firmly entrenched in the United States. On the other hand, the nation's role as leader of the so-called free world had made it narcissistic and ignorant, demanding that others believe that the American was the best—indeed the only acceptable—way of life (*America, Their America,* pp. 139–142).

This analysis was taken further by Cyril L. R. James (1901–1989), a Trinidadian who was both a Marxist and a long-term cricket correspondent for a major English newspaper. These two interests intertwined to produce an idiosyncratic, troubling critique of the United States. To James, cricket was a way of life, and its inherently democratic ethic of fair play was an antidote to narcissism and the degrading conditions of modern industrial life. On both counts the English had failed to live up to the game; the Americans did not play it. The implications are apparent in James's study of Herman Melville's *Moby-Dick.* He sees the ship's crew as working-class victims destroyed by their failure to articulate an alternative to Captain Ahab's monomania, which begins as ceticide and ends as homicide. Melville's 1851 novel therefore predicts modern political conditions where a "society of free individualism would give birth to totalitarianism and be unable to defend itself against it" (*Mariners, Renegades, and Castaways,* p. 60). In James's view the self-regarding distinction between the "free" and "unfree" worlds begins, frighteningly, to dissolve.

Contemporary Western European views of the United States have often seen it as the source of all the impedimenta of modernity. The English journalist William T. Stead gave such views a name when in 1901 he predicted the "Americanization" of the world. "Americanization" is more often used pejoratively. The English literary critic F. R. Leavis was one of many who blamed America for the development of mass production and a consequent debasement of human relations, while the popular philosopher C. E. M. Joad blamed it for cinema, advertising, and slang. Even Stead, who hoped for the emergence of an Anglo-American superstate, looked bleakly at the United States in *If Christ Came to Chicago!* (1894), seeing that city as a paradigm of all the evils of urbanization. The literature of anti-Americanism is large and sometimes strident, frequently proclaiming its theme in titles like *America, the Menace* (1931), by Georges Duhamel, and *The Moronic Inferno and Other Visits to America* (1986), by Martin Amis.

However, a number of European intellectuals responded positively to Americanization. They welcomed the reversal of the old polarity, explored most fully by the novelist Henry James, of a virtuous but superficial New World and a corrupt but sophisticated Old World. They believe that America is no longer an embryonic civilization; that in the words of the French political scientist André Siegfried it has come of age; and that its maturity is to be found in such cultural phenomena as jazz, the Hollywood cinema, and the musical. The belief is reflected in some films of French "new wave" directors like Jean-Luc Godard, Louis Malle, and François Truffaut, and in the work of British novelists like Malcolm Bradbury, David Lodge, and Julian Mitchell. It is reflected, too, in the attention paid to the French sociologist Jean Baudrillard. Baudrillard regards the synthetic spaces of Disneyland as a microcosm of Western civilization, a point confirmed economically when, in 1991, Disney entered the Dow Jones industrial average as one of the thirty most important American companies.

Despite all its negative aspects, there is still much popular enthusiasm about the United States. The English novelist E. M. Forster speaks for this popular view. He visited America for the first time at the age of sixty-eight. On his return he gave a talk which echoes the remarks made some thirty-eight years earlier by Waldo Frank and which shows that the country can still be a place of wonder:

> America is rather like life. You can usually find in it what you look for. If you look for skyscrapers or cowboys or cocktail parties or gangsters or business connections or political problems or women's clubs, they will certainly be there. You can be very hot there or very cold. You can explore the America of your choice by plane or train, by hitch-hike or on foot. It will probably be interesting, and it is sure to be large. (*Two Cheers for Democracy,* p. 339)

AMERICA AS INTERPRETED BY FOREIGN OBSERVERS

BIBLIOGRAPHY

Works Quoted or Cited

Amis, Martin. *The Moronic Inferno and Other Visits to America* (1986).

Antin, Mary. *From Plotzk to Boston* (1899).

Baudrillard, Jean. *America.* Translated by Chris Turner (1988).

Brook, Stephen. *New York Days, New York Nights* (1984).

Brooke, Rupert. *The Collected Poems of Rupert Brooke: With a Memoir by Sir Edward Marsh* (1918).

———. *Letters from America.* Preface by Henry James (1916).

Bryce, James. *The American Commonwealth.* 2 vols. (2d ed. 1889).

Buffon, Georges Louis Le Clerc, comte de. *Natural History.* Translated by William Smellie. 9 vols. (2d ed. 1785).

Clark, John Pepper. *America, Their America* (1964; 2d ed. 1969).

Columbus, Christopher. *The Four Voyages of Christopher Columbus.* Edited and translated by J. M. Cohen (1969).

Crèvecoeur, J. Hector St. John de (Michel-Guillaume-Jean de). *Letters from an American Farmer.* Edited by Albert E. Stone (1981).

Dickens, Charles. *American Notes.* Edited by John S. Whitley and Arnold Goldman (1972).

Duhamel, Georges. *America, the Menace: Scenes from the Life of the Future.* Translated by Charles M. Thompson (1931).

Fanon, Frantz. *The Wretched of the Earth.* Preface by Jean-Paul Sartre. Translated by Constance Farrington (1967).

Farkas, Sándor Bölöni. *Journey in North America.* Edited and translated by Arpad Kadarkay (1978).

Forster, E. M. *Two Cheers for Democracy.* Edited by Oliver Stallybrass (1976).

Frank, Waldo. *Our America* (1919).

Hall, Joseph. *The Discovery of a New World.* Edited by Huntington Brown, translated by John Healey (1937; repr. 1972).

James, Cyril L. R. *Mariners, Renegades, and Castaways: The Story of Herman Melville and the World We Live In* (1953; 2d ed. 1984).

Joad, C. E. M. *The Babbitt Warren* (1926).

Kalm, Per (Pehr). *Travels into North America.* Translated by John R. Forster. 3 vols. (1770).

Lakier, Aleksandr Borisovich. *A Russian Looks at America: The Journey of Aleksandr Borisovich Lakier in 1857.* Edited and translated by Arnold Schrier and Joyce Story (1979).

Lawrence, D. H. *Studies in Classic American Literature* (1923).

Leavis, F. R. *Mass Civilisation and Minority Culture* (1930).

Locke, John. "An Essay Concerning the True Original, Extent and End of Civil Government." In *Social Contract: Essays by Locke, Hume and Rousseau,* edited by Sir Ernest Barker (1976).

Montesquieu, Charles de Secondat, Baron de. *The Spirit of the Laws.* Translated by Thomas Nugent (1949).

More, Thomas. *Utopia.* Translated by Paul Turner (1965).

Mulvey, Christopher. "Écriture and Landscape: British Writing on Post-Revolutionary America." In *Views of American Landscapes,* edited by Mick Gidley and Robert Lawson-Peebles (1989).

Paine, Thomas. *Common Sense.* Edited by Isaac Kramnick (1776; rev. 2d ed. 1976).

Pownall, Thomas. *A Memorial Addressed to the Sovereigns of America* (1783).

Siegfried, André. *America Comes of Age.* Translated by H. H. Heming and Doris Heming (1927).

Simcoe, John Graves. *Remarks on the Travels of the Marquis de Chastellux in North America* (1787; repr. 1931).

Smith, Adam. *The Wealth of Nations.* Edited by R. H. Campbell and A. S. Skinner (1776; repr. 1976).

Stead, William Thomas. *If Christ Came to Chicago!* (1894).

———. *The Americanization of the World* (1901).

Stearn, Gerald, ed. *Broken Image: Foreign Critiques of America* (1972). A very useful collection of negative images, including, among those cited in this essay, ones by Cornelius de Pauw, Sydney Smith, Thomas Hamilton, W. T. Stead, Maxim Gorky, V. I. Lenin, and Georges Duhamel.

Svin'in, Pavel Petrovich. *Picturesque United States of America, 1811, 1812, 1813.* Introduced by R. T. H. Hasley (1930).

Tocqueville, Alexis de. *Democracy in America.* Edited by Phillips Bradley. 2 vols. (1945).

Varlo, Charles. *Nature Display'd* (1794).

Whicker, Alan. *Whicker's New World: America Through the Eyes and Lives of Resident Brits* (1985).

Zangwill, Israel. *Children of the Ghetto* (1892; repr. 1898).

———. *The Melting-Pot* (1909).

Background Reading

Elliott, John H. *The Old World and the New, 1492–1650* (1970).

Gerbi, Antonello. *The Dispute of the New World: The History of a Polemic, 1750–1900.* Translated by Jeremy Moyle (rev. and enlarged ed. 1973). Comprehensive discussion of the negative attitudes to America.

Gutman, Huck, ed. *As Others Read Us: International Perspectives on American Literature* (1991).

Honour, Hugh. *The New Golden Land: European Images of America from the Discoveries to the Present Time* (1975). Superbly illustrated survey.

Mulvey, Christopher. *Transatlantic Manners: Social Patterns in Nineteenth-Century Anglo-American Travel Literature* (1990).

Pachter, Marc, ed. *Abroad in America: Visitors to the New Nation, 1776–1914* (1976). A collection of essays on many major figures.

Rose, Richard, ed. *Lessons from America: An Exploration* (1974).

Schwartz, Morton. *Soviet Perceptions of the United States* (1978).

Spender, Stephen. *Love-Hate Relations: A Study of Anglo-American Sensibilities* (1974).

Starr, S. Frederick. *Red and Hot: The Fate of Jazz in the Soviet Union, 1917–1980* (1983).

SEE ALSO American Social and Cultural Geography; The Antebellum Era; Anthropological Approaches to History; English-speaking Protestants; The Early National Period; German Speakers; Native Peoples and Early European Contacts; Social History in Great Britain and Continental Europe.

ANTHROPOLOGICAL APPROACHES TO HISTORY

Margaret Washington

ANTHROPOLOGY, RACIOLOGY, AND "PRIMITIVE" FOLK

SOCIAL HISTORIANS HAVE recently discovered the significance of anthropological methodology and theories of culture in interpreting the lives of the "folk," the "oppressed," and the "dispossessed." Such Americans were once referred to as "inarticulate" by mainstream historians, who insisted they left few records essential to resurrecting their past. African Americans, American Indians, women, and blue-collar workers were among the groups whose histories were for generations either ignored, presented in a truncated fashion, or explored via their subordinate status to the dominant socioeconomic group. Professionally, anthropology's focus, as it developed into a science, was no less ethnocentric than that of history. While historians ignored the past of the "folk," anthropologists studied folk cultures almost exclusively, but from a dismissive, dominant, racialist position. Folk culture was viewed by most anthropologists as inferior to white American culture. It is difficult to say whether historians or anthropologists assumed the most elitist position in regard to "folk" culture. Anthropology began with a distinct racialist agenda, particularly in its studies of so-called primitive societies, although by the turn of the century, detractors to this ethnocentric approach emerged. Racialism in the historical profession, though more implicit than explicit, still denied folk culture its place as a viable area of examination and research. It is nevertheless ironic that anthropology, which began the study of folk culture from a racialist perspective, would be the science appropriated by historians wishing to challenge the profession's long silence regarding the cultures of non-elites in America. This irony speaks to the progressive growth and development of both anthropology and history. Ultimately both disciplines realized the limitations of their perspectives, broadened their methodology and theory, and confronted the narrowness of their worldview.

In recent years, anthropology, the study of humankind, has greatly affected how social historians study and interpret folk cultures, especially in but not limited to nonliterate societies. Ethnography, the branch of anthropology that describes and interprets cultures, began as a "science" in the late nineteenth century and was particularly concerned with cultures of American Indians. During these years, the scholarly and scientific community had developed a science of ethnology based on racial difference and what anthropologist Marvin Harris calls the "biologization of history." By the early twentieth century, the study of comparative anatomy and the belief in the polygenetic origins of humanity convinced social scientists that race determined the level of human progress, particularly between so-called civilized and primitive societies. And anthropology, as the science of "man," engaged in comparisons of anatomy, physiognomy, culture, and environment, proving through "scientific" fact long-held basic assumptions about the racial inferiority of so-called primitive people. At the beginning of the twentieth century, however, this interpretive framework was challenged by the rise of cultural anthropology, which discredited racial theories in assessing peoples' ways of life.

ANTHROPOLOGISTS DISCOVER HISTORY

The cultural anthropologist most responsible for the modern scientific examination of folk cultures and the historical study of ethnography is Franz Boas (1858–1942). Born in Germany of Jewish ancestry, trained as a physicist and geographer, Boas changed his discipline to anthropology as a result of fieldwork among the Eskimos and Pacific

Northwest Indians. Arriving in the United States in the 1880s, Boas received a teaching appointment at Columbia University in 1896 (where he remained until 1941). He soon founded Columbia's anthropology department, organized the first comprehensive anthropology graduate program in the country, and created his own anthropological style. His thinking shaped the course of twentieth-century cultural anthropology and gave rise to a generation of prominent professionals who would dominate the field. Not only responsible for professionalizing and modernizing anthropology, Boas founded the American Folk-lore Society (1888) and the American Anthropological Association (1902), and he revitalized the American Ethnological Society.

Boas challenged raciology and evolutionism, insisting that empirical evidence revealed that the so-called primitive and civilized minds operated in the same way. He took issue with the use of the term "culture" as synonymous with the Western concept of "civilization," a configuration that excluded other societies. Boas popularized a switch to the plural inclusive use of culture, dismissing the implicit moral judgment of the Western interpretation in favor of an emphasis on diversity, relativism, and functionalism. Boas's theoretical approach emphasized the significance of history on culture, the necessity of extensive fieldwork, and the organic nature of a single culture over the superficiality of the cross-cultural comparative approach. Boas furthermore dismissed the preference for "conjectural" history and nomothetic laws. For Boas ethnography involved understanding a culture from the inside, a method that required the anthropologist to "feel" the culture under observation through long-term commitment and investigation. This approach demanded in-depth study of language, customs, rituals, social organization, and patterns of behavior. In other words, Boas advocated an interpretation of culture that was free from the anthropologist's value system, or would at least disavow any moral superiority.

Boas maintained that historical causation and "psychological processes" were responsible for the formation of customs that shaped a people's culture, and were integral to understanding worldview and interpreting meaning. A staunch egalitarian at a time of racism and nativism, Boas advocated historical investigation of the cultural life of nonliterate peoples to combat popular theories of ethnic inferiority. He encouraged students to examine folktales, folk songs, and belief systems as well as customs and patterns of behavior in a search for meaning. He called for an interpretation of the interplay of history and culture to dispel his era's prevailing evolutionist theories of white Anglo-Saxon Protestant cultural superiority.

However, while Boas elevated anthropological research to a new level of quality that stressed the empirical study of the folkways of a people, he was limited by his reluctance to draw conclusions or make generalizations from his data. Boas collected historical facts on folk culture but developed no anthropological school of thought based on his findings or those of his students, nor did he formulate a concept of culture in a modern anthropological sense. Boas was a domineering figure who expected loyalty from his students—his more notable students included Ruth Benedict, Melville Herskovits, Zora Neale Hurston, Alfred Kroeber, Robert Lowie, Margaret Mead, Ashley Montagu, and Paul Radin. Theoretical and ideological differences did occur among Boas's students, but they strengthened the paradigms of their mentor even as they formulated their own ideas. Although Boas himself avoided a theoretical synthesis, his students continued and expanded the trend of historical anthropology, often testing and employing the themes introduced by Boas.

CULTURE, ACCULTURATION, AND HISTORY

Anthropology was far in advance of American history in realizing the significance of folk culture. Anthropologists studied aboriginal and folk cultures through field research, by compiling information from live informants, studying the dynamic aspects of cultural change, observing folkways, and examining the historical process. From the turn of the century through the 1960s, American historians had limited their research to documents, manuscripts, and diverse sources in libraries and other places of public record. A conservative reading of what historians considered evidence, along with the racial climate within their profession, hampered serious attempts by most historians to examine folk culture historically or to realize that elite whites were not the only makers of American history.

Although far from being value free, the nature of cultural anthropology as a discipline prevented disdain of folk sources as part of the historical record. Anthropologists expanded and revised the theories and methodologies introduced by Boas, refining the study of folk culture to encompass a number of innovations that included the scientific analysis of cultural processes. Alfred Kroeber and Clyde Kluckhohn identified and defined distinguishing features of culture and assigned them to categories. Kroeber and Kluckhohn theorized methods by which each culture might be understood on its own terms as an integrative whole rather than unfavorably evaluated relative to Western culture (*Culture: A Critical Review of Concepts and Definitions,* 1956). Challenging currents that rejected a historical interest in ethnology, Kroeber in "History and Science in Anthropology" repudiated the value of nonselective scientific method in the study of cultural phenomena, insisting that culture was a "superorganic phenomenon" and the individual was subordinate to patterns of culture. He also criticized Boas for what he considered a superficial use of historical method. According to Kroeber, Boas employed pseudohistorical techniques, produced no historical results, no "descriptive integration," and little "historical reconstruction" (pp. 545–548). Since all historical data was not relevant to interpretations and evaluations of cultural phenomenon, Kroeber maintained that investigators should make selective use of materials and omit those not needed to produce a "reasonable culture-historical reconstruction" (p. 556).

Similarly, Paul Radin in *The Method and Theory of Ethnology* (1933) criticized Boas and his followers for failing to incorporate the historically based theories of Karl Marx and Max Weber into their work. Thus, among other shortcomings, Radin felt anthropology was not meeting current intellectual challenges of Western thought. Radin confronted issues of religion, psychology, and individuality in his work. He stressed the need to study individual responses to religious belief systems and the role of economic determinism in religious orientation. The visions and prayers of a particular Crow Indian, the singular conversion experience of a former African American slave were psychological responses with implicit meaning for social control. Radin's position on "primitive" religion was equivocal. He accepted a Marxist interpretation of the power of religion to exploit and dominate individual thought (via shamans and priests). Yet he also emphasized the role of the "trickster," as reflective of the dual image of God, and sometimes the antithesis of the dominant power. Radin's interpretation of the trickster and his analysis of the sacred in "primitive" societies and in folk culture were major contributions to anthropology. Moreover, social historians, particularly those studying African American culture, borrowed extensively from Radin's analytical constructions and imaginative historical perspectives.

Melville Herskovits's and Robert Redfield's analysis of acculturation, historical reconstruction, folk culture, and community were major additions to cultural anthropology and heavily influenced subsequent historical methodology. Acculturation comprehended "those phenomena which result when groups of individuals having different cultures come into continuous first-hand contact, with subsequent changes in the original cultural patterns of either or both groups" (Herskovits et al., p. 149). At a time when anthropologists studied "uncontaminated" cultures, Herskovits called for understanding the process of cultural development through "actual recorded history." He maintained that the historical continuum and interrelated cultural dynamics dictated the conditions that influenced behavior, personality, and habits of belief. Studying acculturation in this manner brought an understanding of "the consequence of a subsequent cultural contact as found in the life of the people."

Redfield's ethnological studies of Mexican cultures defined anthropological concepts of community. His fieldwork revealed how communication, integration, harmony, and sense of obligation formed the basis of social organization. Community included social structure, individual biography, worldview, and history. Community, according to Redfield in *Peasant Society and Culture* (1956), should come from "inside" the group and be the people's own story as they conceived it. Redfield's thematic construct of community was, as he later admitted, too self-contained, ideal, and distinct. It allowed little room for mobility, change, or complexity. Redfield's paradigm was expanded to include social interaction involving associations and institutions occurring beyond a group's geopolitical area. His theoretical discussions provoked controversy and comment that allowed his themes to be broadened as well as contradicted.

In the field of history, Redfield's work led to exciting advances in community studies scholarship. Community studies created a conceptual universe that emphasized understanding cohesive structures, ethnic minorities, and resistance to mechanisms of social control by the larger society. By the 1950s massive accumulation of ethnological data produced voluminous monographs and texts on folk cultures and community studies. These studies, despite their expanded historical orientation, usually failed to stress cultural changes from a dynamic perspective of time and place. Nevertheless, anthropology and ethnography provided fruitful grounding for the new social historians to challenge the "consensus" interpretation of American history. Consensus historians such as Daniel Boorstin, David Potter, Richard Hofstadter, Bernard Bailyn, Louis Hartz, and Robert and Katherine Brown stressed "conformity," "unity," and "solidarity" in American history and society within a liberal tradition.

The trend toward community studies in the historical profession began with examinations of colonial America. As historian John Higham has pointed out, historians adopted the community model as they began rejecting the consensus means of interpreting American history. Focusing on Redfield's insistence that communication was the sine qua non for community, historians of the 1960s attempted to comprehend colonial society on the local level across patterns of family, class, and institutional development. They examined manuscripts, church records, tax records, marriage records, and wills for insights into diversity, demography, and life-style within a geopolitical structure. But these community studies lacked theoretical concepts that explained ethos, culture, or social organization. Hence they did not imbibe the anthropological methodology previously discussed.

Just as Redfield's anthropological paradigms affected community studies in history, Herskovits's work helped define issues of major importance for African American history. As an African American anthropologist studying acculturation among blacks in America, Herskovits's insistence on examining the black past had profound implications, and his work on blacks in the diaspora significantly influenced African American history. His *Myth of the Negro Past* (1941) became a model for interpreting African cultural retentions and acculturation among blacks in the United States. His was a major effort to dispel sociological bias in favor of white culture espoused by black sociologist E. Franklin Frazier and by the R. E. Park School at the University of Chicago, which denied that blacks had a usable African heritage or memory. But it is important to note that during the lifetimes of both Frazier and Herskovits, the controversy over Africanisms was not taken up by many historians since few even considered the possibility of a significant black history.

Nevertheless, Herskovits's work has probably had greater impact in the historical profession than among anthropologists in terms of the controversy over African retentions and the nature of the African heritage in the diaspora. While most historians agreed that Africanisms could be found where a sizable black population existed, few recognized the presence of Africanisms inside the United States. In *Slavery: A Problem in American Institutional and Intellectual Life* (1959), Stanley Elkins ushered the debate over Africanisms into the historical profession. He supported the Frazier perspective, maintaining that capture in Africa, the long march to the sea, and the traumatic transatlantic voyage called the Middle Passage so devastated the African psyche that all memory was lost. Elkins then extended the argument by suggesting that the plantation experience further debilitated African Americans, so that their personalities were shaped only by their dependent relationship with their slave masters. The plantation society was described as a "closed" system by Elkins, and the dominant African American personality type as "Sambo." The implicit conclusion of this analysis was that since African Americans had no past and were "child-like" dependents, they were merely creations of the slave system that oppressed them.

Elkins's thesis was not immediately challenged. Certainly his interpretation fit the reigning paradigm of the era. College history classes routinely ignored not only the story of American minorities, but African American, Asian American, Mexican American, and American Indian scholars were excluded from employment in most history departments.

Opposition to the consensus interpretation of American history converged with the sociopolitical turmoil and conflicts that swept the nation in the civil rights era. A "new" social history emerged, and as an expression of discontent, affected the academy in a number of ways. Students and professors demanded a more democratic university and an educational experience that more accurately reflected the pluralistic history and heritage of America. They also called for a more diverse faculty and student body. These urgencies changed the complexion of America's campuses and expanded the agendas of various social science and humanities disciplines.

In the historical profession, some scholars devoted to the new social history reached back to anthropology (and other disciplines) in search of methodologies, research techniques, and conceptual analyses to incorporate the histories of so-called dispossessed groups previously unrepresented or misrepresented in historical scholarship. Because of the work of Elkins, the Frazier-Herskovits debate entered the historical arena and profoundly transformed new scholarship on the African American experience. It also raised more expansive issues pertinent to the histories of all oppressed and marginalized people in America. The historical debate touched many areas of study including religion and family, language and folklore, work and play.

HISTORIANS DISCOVER ANTHROPOLOGY: AFRICAN AMERICAN LIFE

Historians of black America were among the first to incorporate anthropological methods, techniques, and theories to obtain knowledge about common folk and their cultures, and to find ways of interpreting those experiences. African American history was gradually recognized as a legitimate field of study as scholars in the late 1960s successfully refuted arguments that the black past was undocumented and therefore unknowable. Challenging the assertion that African Americans had no historical voice, scholars employed folklore, folk customs, and the oral tradition to illustrate blacks' role as actors in their own historical experience. In his 1968 article "Through the Prism of Folklore," Sterling Stuckey insisted that African American folk culture was not only a window into black history, but it also allowed blacks to speak with their own voice. Years later, Stuckey's *Slave Culture: Nationalist Theory and the Foundations of Black America* (1987) merged anthropological evidence with historical reconstruction. Stuckey used the Herskovits model to explain the roots of black American culture and nationalism. Through cultural continuity and collective memory, Stuckey argued, blacks clung tenaciously to African folkways, behaviorisms, and artistic forms. For Stuckey, folk culture had as its goal unity, solidarity, and resistance to oppression.

Lawrence Levine's 1971 article "Slave Songs and Slave Consciousness" investigated African American spirituals as a means of comprehending black resistance and sense of community. By analyzing the meaning of spirituals created by the enslaved people—in the tradition of earlier anthropologists—Levine noted the message of hope and resistance in song that ostensibly spoke merely of worldly transcendence. The article was a prelude to Levine's impressive *Black Culture and Black Consciousness: Afro-American Folk Thought from Slavery to Freedom* (1977). In this volume, Levine employed massive anthropological and historical evidence on the dynamic nature of black culture, the historical worldview of Africans in America, and processes of acculturation in rural and urban contexts. Levine's orientation was historical, but much of his method was anthropological. He rejected static concepts of culture and traced the African influence of black American thought, particularly in terms of an ethos that fused the sacred and secular. He embraced anthropology's acculturative model by demonstrating transformations in black culture, especially as emancipation brought more intense culture contact and mitigated the "cultural containment" of earlier generations. Levine investigated numerous aspects of black culture as practiced, transformed, and internalized by African Americans. His evidence consisted of folklore, songs, jokes, toasts, legends, linguistic patterns, and oral histories. He offered analytical constructs of a sacred and temporal worldview to demonstrate the tenacity of an African ethos and ontology among enslaved African Americans. Moreover, Levine's conceptualization of how black people interpreted Christianity was based on Radin's insight that rather than embracing a Christian God, African Americans' adaptive capacity involved converting the Christian deity into their sacred system. Levine also relied on urban anthropology, particularly the work of Claudia Mitchell-Kernan, in interpreting linguistic patterns in black oral tradition. *Black Culture and Black Consciousness* represented an important merger of anthropological method with history to produce a sweeping historical interpretation of black culture.

Historians interested in folk culture, acculturation, and adaptation have also relied on paradigms suggested by Sidney Mintz and Richard Price. The publication of Mintz and Price's *An Anthropological Approach to the Afro-American Past: A Caribbean Perspective* (1976) represents the most sophisticated theoretical expansion of the Herskovits model. Calling for more subtlety of analysis and greater sociohistorical research than was present in the Herskovits model, Mintz and Price offered ideas that illustrate important considerations for historically oriented cultural anthropologists. While their work dealt specifically with the Caribbean, historians of the United States have adopted Mintz's and Price's methodologies and thematic suggestions. Like Herskovits, Mintz and Price insisted on recognition of the significance of the African background as a starting point for studying culture. But they did not believe in a generalized heritage as postulated by Herskovits. Nevertheless they maintained that Herskovits's formulation was exemplary and mainly needed to be defined in less concrete terms by focusing more on values and common orientations and "the way the world functions phenomenologically" (p. 5). Mintz and Price wrote that "deep-level cultural principles, assumptions and understandings which were shared by the Africans in any New World colony would be a "crucial resource" and "catalyst" in the processes by which individuals from diverse societies forged new institutions (p. 7).

Mintz and Price's contention that culture must be studied in terms of broadly conceived Old and New World continuities was applied by Herbert Gutman in *The Black Family in Slavery and Freedom, 1750–1925* (1976). Gutman recognized his debt to cultural anthropology, and particularly to Sidney Mintz, for prodding him to explain the sources of belief and behavior. Using Mintz and Price (and other anthropologists), Gutman explored family structures among American slaves. His research supported Mintz and Price, who speculated that adaptive kin networks were rooted in antecedent beliefs about kinship and social relations; kinship was an important means of cultural transmission and transformation of West African beliefs. Mintz and Price singled out "the sheer importance of kinship in structuring interpersonal relations and in defining an individual's place in his society" (p. 34). In the slave community, Gutman pointed out, kinship was a vehicle of individual and collective identity autonomous from enslavement. One important example of how kinship engendered solidarity may be found in Gutman's discussion of naming practices. The process of naming reflected kin obligation and expanded into the social obligation of slaves, regardless of whether African or American names were used. Naming children after parents and necronymic naming (naming children after dead siblings) reinforced kinship, even when slaves were separated by death or sale. According to Gutman, naming children for blood relations in the extended family also suggests that "slaves incorporated elements of the traditional lineal orientation of their West African forebears into their new belief systems" (p. 197–198). Using the anthropological African American model of Mintz and Price, Gutman elevated naming patterns to an important historical tool for studying folk culture.

While Stuckey, Levine, and Gutman borrowed from anthropological interpretations, other historians eschewed such conceptualizations but adopted anthropological methods of research. This has legitimized as source material certain types of documentation previously considered invalid. Among this group are narratives of fugitive slaves, slave songs, folktales, sermons, jokes, and various types of oral histories. George P. Rawick made an unprecedented contribution to historical studies of folk cultures by editing and publishing *The American Slave: A Composite Autobiography* (1972). This multivolume work consists of oral interviews of former slaves, collected from 1936 to 1938 as part of the Federal Writers' Project of the Works Projects Administration (WPA). Portions of these interviews had appeared previously in a number of forms, but never as a complete set. Hence, publication of the collection was a pioneering achievement making available the life stories of thousands of former slaves of seventeen states.

Historians have made extensive use of this rich but neglected documentation of antebellum black life. In his Pulitzer Prize–winning book, *Been in the Storm So Long: The Aftermath of Slavery* (1979), Leon F. Litwack used the Rawick narrative collection extensively to recreate the social and economic dimensions of emancipation prior to Reconstruction. Litwack did not use anthropological methodology in *Been in the Storm So Long,* but by relying on the oral interviews for documentation, he adopted a view of what constitutes "evidence" in writing history not previously accepted by mainstream historians. This type of data gathering has recently become part of the historian's craft but has long been part of anthropological data.

Similarly, in *Slave Religion: The "Invisible Institution" in the Antebellum South* (1978), Albert J. Raboteau did not employ anthropological methodology, yet the impact of anthropology was revealed in the structure of his study and his documentation. The significance of the African background was important to Raboteau's presentation of slave religion, as was his preoccupation with the Frazier-Herskovits deculturation issue. Moreover, Raboteau used the WPA narratives compiled by Rawick, the antebellum fugitive slave narratives, African American spirituals, and folklore. Folk culture among African American slave women was the theme of Deborah Gray White's *Ar'n't I a Woman?: Female Slaves in the Plantation South* (1985). White illustrated that despite the dual burdens of racism and sexism, the importance of the slave family, the community, and the female network dominated the lives of black women in bondage. This study of folk life from the perspective of slave women was possible because White employed both nineteenth-century slave narratives and twentieth-century oral histories. Slave sources allowed White to reveal how black women created collective autonomous experiences from life in bondage despite the confining nature of enslavement and the violence of sexual exploitation. Oral histories and narratives demonstrate how slave women bonded together in support of the integrity of the slave community and the black family.

After publishing *The American Slave,* Rawick wrote a study of slavery entitled *From Sundown to Sunup: The Making of the Black Community* (1972). Using material compiled from the slave interviews, Rawick wrote his history of the "creation of the black community under slavery" (p. xix), emphasizing life outside of work relations and employing an interdisciplinary approach. Beginning with the African background, as discussed by former slave informants, and ending with a sociological discussion of racism, Rawick employed anthropological and sociological techniques to interpret black society and culture historically from the perspective of African American people in bondage. In his efforts to raise questions and to develop an appropriate methodology for studying slave society through the voice of the slave, Rawick helped provide a model for future historians of the African American experience interested in folk culture or community studies.

John Blassingame's *The Slave Community: Plantation Life in the Antebellum South* (1972) appeared at the same time as Rawick's works. Blassingame's study represented the first extensive use of the fugitive slave narratives. Beginning with the Herskovits theme of acculturation, elaborating the existence of a viable community among African Americans in the slave quarters (a refutation of Elkins), Blassingame further supported the need to change the traditional, static concepts of "evidence" in historical writing. Blassingame emphasized the need to allow the slaves to speak for themselves rather than through the sources left by their masters.

Another historian who made extensive use of narrative sources and applied an interdisciplinary perspective to historical writing was Eugene D. Genovese, whose major work on African Americans is *Roll, Jordan, Roll: The World the Slaves Made* (1974). In a conservative perspective on black-white relations Genovese perceived African American slaves as accommodating to slavery and succumbing to planter hegemony. The slaveholder's sense of "duty" and obligation toward the slave and the slave's accommodations created a complex web of "paternalism," according to Genovese. He used numerous social science theories and an array of fugitive slave and WPA narratives to support his analyses. Although Genovese argued that acceptance of planter paternalism severely limited the slave's ability to assert autonomy, his work further revealed the complexity of African American slavery that Elkins had denied.

FOLK CULTURE, COMMUNITY, AND SYMBOLIC ANTHROPOLOGY: WOMEN AND WORKERS

Historians employing anthropological methods have borrowed terminology from anthropologists and used that discipline's investigative techniques to create historical paradigms. This new direction has been greatly facilitated by the work of anthropologists such as Victor Turner, Mary Douglas, Clifford Geertz, and Anthony Wallace. Anthropologists like Turner and Douglas used symbols and rituals as mirrors of social process and transformation. Their work begins with the assumption that society is involved in a perennially conflicting struggle for status and power.

Feminist historian Carroll Smith-Rosenberg's *Disorderly Conduct* (1985) demonstrated how symbolic anthropological perspectives help us to interpret gender conventions, particularly sexual images and symbols. Informed by Turner and Douglas, Smith-Rosenberg used rituals and symbols of the physical body as a metaphor for the "body politic" in an essay entitled "Davy Crockett as Trickster." The macabre, brutal, racialist exploits of Davy Crockett are cited as they appeared in popular literature, and they are interpreted according to anthropological constructs about society. The Crockett legends depict an alienated, individualistic wave of westerners scornful of the emerging "American bourgeoisie." This theme is played out in comic relief through the Davy Crockett almanacs that appeared in the 1830s and 1840s. In the fabled Crockett world, men and women humorously violate all eastern taboos, ostensibly disdaining whatever is "proper" and "progressive." The almanacs are replete with symbols of cannibalism, sexuality, and homoerotic behavior. Smith-Rosenberg interpreted the Crockett myth as exemplary of the nineteenth-century patriarchal racism and sexism in Jacksonian America. Here, white folk culture is animalistic, lewd, brutal, and racist. In one account Crockett killed an Indian "by chewing through his jugular and letting him bleed to death" (p. 98). Mrs. Crockett, true to the tradition of the West, kept the Indian's scalp "fastened to a stick to brush the flies off the table when we were at dinner" (p. 98). These stories were published as humorous parodies.

Smith-Rosenberg adopted Mary Douglas's perspective that humor could challenge the social order of the eastern bourgeoisie, but not overthrow it. Thus, the stories are about inversion: the Crockett myth offered young men a fabled frontier of the imagination rather than economic power. More significantly the Crockett myth upheld violence against women and inhabitants of the wilderness—Indians, Mexicans, and escaped slaves. For Smith-Rosenberg the concept of "folk culture" is problematic. Her folk evoke not communal warmth but misogyny and bloodlust. Smith-Rosenberg eschews romanticization and reveals that the "folk" are not necessarily a positive element in society, as most social historians present them. So here is the first sign of rift in historical use of an anthropological concept: "folk" culture may serve to glorify oppression as well as celebrate the capacity of the oppressed to create an autonomous world of their own or to deal with oppressors from a position of power.

The history of women, like that of ethnic minorities, was among the last to be recognized as significant. Scholars of women's experiences were not only recovering women's past and integrating it into the American experience, they were interpreting historical meanings of female past using models outside the discipline of history. In another article from *Disorderly Conduct,* entitled "The Cross and the Pedestal," Smith-Rosenberg illustrated nineteenth-century female religious experiences as "anti-ritualism," a term borrowed from Mary Douglas. The hypothesis here centers on the relationship between cultural forms and social experience; it fuses "anthropology's sensitivity to ritual and anti-ritual as symbolic languages, and history's awareness of heterogeneity, change and conflict" (p. 161).

For Smith-Rosenberg, anti-ritualism represented women's repudiation of formal religious structure and theology, in preference for intuitive, instinctive, enthusiastic behavior. As Victor Turner has argued, anti-ritual events (that is, inversions or violations of powerful social rules) are frequent at times of social upheaval, especially among poor or marginalized groups. Again, like Douglas and Turner, Smith-Rosenberg used ritual and symbols to depict conflicts in society. She focused on "form" rather than belief, analyzing how the metaphoric language of religious enthusiasm suggests women's response to family stress, power, gender relations, and social change. Douglas's view that religious enthusiasm repudiates existing social order, challenges authority, and defies hierarchy is central to Smith-Rosenberg's analysis of women in Jacksonian America. The Shaker communities were exemplary according to Smith-Rosenberg. Led by Ann Lee, Shakers "transfigured the epitome of marginality and powerlessness . . . into God's Second Incarnation" (p. 141). Shakers worshiped the "Father of Power" (God) and the "Mother of Wisdom" (Lee). They communicated with the "Woman Clothed in the Sun," denounced the emerging capitalist order, as well as the nuclear family (p. 141). In religious meetings, "each Shaker sang, danced, spoke in tongues, prophesied, sat silently, or spun in circles for hours, as the Spirit directed" (p. 132).

Douglas's microcosmic perspective takes Smith-Rosenberg only so far; anti-ritual groups she indicates, once outside the new economic and institutional order, gradually re-embraced it, leading to a Victorian consensus. Smith-Rosenberg turned to Victor Turner's conceptualization of rites of passage to analyze why bourgeois mobility among women (as discussed in Mary Ryan's *Cradle of the Middle Class* [1981]) was accompanied by anti-ritualism, but ultimately led to reintegration. According to Turner, the first stage of any rite of passage, "separation," was symbolic detachment. The second, "liminality," represented limbo and disorder, where the neophyte was outside social constraints, but seeking to recover herself. The final phase, "aggregation," was reintegration into the social order. These three components depict a conservative process involving formal recognition, but also symbolizing control and authority. Smith-Rosenberg was particularly concerned with the liminal stage, comparing it to nineteenth-century Christian evangelical revivals. The liminal, disorderly, intense experience of women, "their bitter confrontations with conservative male spiritual and social leaders, bespoke the attraction that spiritual autonomy, powerful new roles, the very right to speak after years of silence, held for her" (p. 155). This liminal experience (anti-ritualism) was such a threat that "society enveloped that reaggregation with the elaborate rituals of the Victorian era—especially since the new male establishment had chosen her silence, so hard to secure, as the symbol of their hegemony" (p. 155).

Because Jacksonian women returned to bourgeois society changed beings, they thereby changed their world. Their experiences, says Smith-Rosenberg, "constitute a perfect example of Turner's thesis that radical actions, though rooted initially in social paradigms, can break those paradigms, restructuring both the actor and the actor's world" (p. 155). Some women did break loose and remained outside the hegemonic paradigm, becoming women's rights advocates and calling for diverse reforms in American society. But most women assumed acceptable positions in society and became "symbols of stability" for the new order (p. 164).

Clifford Geertz's perspectives on symbolic anthropology contain subtle differences from Turner and Douglas. In the early 1990s, Geertz was perhaps the most influential anthropologist among historians. Geertz emphasized symbols, rituals, and meaning, but focused on culture rather than society. A Harvard-trained anthropologist from the prestigious (interdisciplinary) Department of Social Relations, Geertz's main field of research was Indonesia and Morocco. But his analysis of rituals and symbols as these affect interpretations of cultures struck a kindred note outside his area of study. Geertz's influence reached its crest following the 1973 appearance of a collection of essays entitled *The Interpretation of Cultures*. The essay that most influenced historians was "Thick Description: Toward an Interpretive Theory of Culture." Borrowing the term "thick description" from anthropologist Gilbert Ryle, Geertz described it as a discovery and reconstruction of deep layers of meaning involved in human interaction. Much of "thick description" involves diverse perceptions and perspectives of events, even over time. Cultural analysis, wrote Geertz, involved "guessing at meanings, assessing the guesses, drawing explanatory conclusions from the better guesses" (p. 20). An obscure event or a mundane episode can lead to broad insights into the wider perceptions of an individual or a people; one might compile bits of human behavior and extract revelations about a culture. Geertz's model can be employed where symbols, rituals, institutions, or some specific mode of discourse exist and have interpretive meaning. His analytical perspective and stated methodology provided historians with a means of expressing theoretically and coherently their own insights about ideology, belief, ethos, community structure, and order in society.

In some ways Geertz was a reification of the Boas school, as he argued for a thick, rich description of people's cultures from the perspective of the social actors. And he rejected the cultural approaches of Kroeber, Kluckhohn, and others of the "consensus gentium" school ("Culture: A Critical Review," p. 39), who tended to see culture in everything and emphasized universals. But unlike Boas, or even Herskovitz, Geertz called for the study of meaning over behavior. He further stressed interpretations over causality and "microscopic" over large-scale ethnographic interpretations. Geertz called for the interpretation of cultures through their public symbols, which he believed articulated their cosmology and their worldviews, and determined their interrelationships. Symbols could be as simple as a wink, as complex as a poem or slave spiritual. They communicate how social actors feel or think, and they convey specific cultural meanings that are guides to human behavior.

Geertz's contribution has reinforced the idea among historians that common folk, poor people, non-Western people, and nonliterary people are not "inarticulate," and that many symbols, not merely the written word, can be interpreted as a text. Geertz's work not only suggested new insights, but offered useful terminology that helped historians articulate more clearly their lines of interpretation. American historians writing after 1975 have incorporated Geertz's concepts into analytical and interpretive works on religion and social conflict and community studies. Studies on African American religion and culture, American Indian history, American intellectual history, agrarian class structure, and working-class culture include some of the topics that have borrowed Geertz's ethnographic technique and perspective and fused them with historical methodology as a means of studying folk cultures.

Herbert Gutman's work on the white working class represented an effort to expand labor history, which prior to the 1960s had neglected workers outside the fold of trade unions. In his title article "Work, Culture, and Society in Industrializing America" Gutman uses notions of culture and society to explain human behavior—in this case, working-class behavior. Culture was the "resource." Society was the "arena." By studying culture and society, he found that "powerful cultural continuities and adaptations . . . shape the historical behavior of diverse working-class populations" (p. 18). This is especially true in examining "premodern work habits of diverse American men and women" in an alien, machine society (p. 18). Gutman integrated workplace experiences with the idea of cultural ethos, and thereby eschewed a merely economic focus in studying industrial workers. The cultures, work ethos, and life-styles of working people are interpreted through time and place. Gutman employs "thick description" (songs, poems, workers' sketches, and journals) as insights into collective and individual behavior, expectations, and the social process that revealed conflicting tensions between the industrial work routine, its concomitant poverty, and the "rhythms and feelings" of people's reactions to machine society.

In the field of African American history, Geertz's theoretical model and interpretive framework has influenced folk-culture studies, especially that of African American slaves. Margaret Washington Creel's work on the South Carolina Sea Island slaves demonstrated how religion and ritual are used in the historical development of a community. In *"A Peculiar People": Slave Religion and Community-Culture Among the Gullahs* (1988), Creel analyzed the Gullah slave society and maintained that their community culture was a fusion of spiritual and secular ethos. Language development, burial practices, spirituals, ring shouts, and internal systems of justice in the slave quarters were analyzed for their symbolic meaning and their role in resistance to slavery, cultural formation, and community cohesion. The rituals and symbols in Gullah culture represent the worldview of African American bondspeople. The worldview is cast in African spiritual traditions and cosmology and fused with Christianity. Creel employed "thick description" and adopted Geertz's view that religion casts a "lunar light" over a people's secular life. The Gullah community was created out of this fusion that resulted in spiritual as well as secular cohesion.

"A Peculiar People" also merged historical and anthropological approaches by using Herskovits's methodology, but went beyond him in the manner suggested by Mintz and Price. African retentions and behaviorisms were not as important for Creel as the meaning of rituals and symbols, features of kinship, cosmological perceptions, ontology, and ethos as these influenced the Gullah historical experience. She argued that these perceptions had strong African antecedents. African anthropologists who interpret the significance of cultural association provide supportive evidence for Creel's discussion of the relationship of African secret societies and Gullah socioreligious heritage. Using work by anthropologists such as Kenneth Little and Warren d'Azevedo, Creel described the sacred and secular function of mandatory secret associations in Sierra Leone, Liberia, and parts of Gambia, arguing that these areas were major regions of origin for Gullah slaves. She compares these associations—Poro for men and Sande for women—with Gullah folk culture, Gullah religious expressions through symbols and rituals, and the structure of Gullah community within the slave quarters.

As Smith-Rosenberg adopted Victor Turner's concept of the rite of passage to explain anti-ritualism among marginalized white women and its negative impact, Creel employed the rituals in the African American experience as symbolic of community cohesion, but in a positive sense. For African Americans, Christian conversion was an inverted rite of passage that forged accountability and structure in the slave community. It served a counter-hegemonic function in Creel's study, while in Smith-Rosenberg's interpretation, rites of passage supported a hegemonic social order. Nevertheless, both historical studies demonstrate how central anthropological approaches are to social historians, particularly those interpreting the experiences of marginalized groups.

Not all historians who use anthropological approaches write about marginalized Americans. In a 1977 article entitled "The New Social History and the Search for 'Community' in Colonial America," Richard Beeman suggested that rather than apply techniques of sociology or political science, historians of colonial America turn to anthropology for methodological and theoretical guidance. Beeman recognized that cultural anthropology, more than any other social science discipline, studied social organization in well-defined localities, used history-related data gathering, and examined culture as a historical, dynamic process. Beeman also pointed out the "actor-oriented" analytical approach of anthropologists. Yet historians, wrote Beeman, "have no viable 'theories' of social organization for colonial America" (p. 426) and have failed to define "community." He suggested that colonial historians examine the theoretical perspectives of Geertz, Redfield, and Turner to position "the organization, operation, and ethic of early American communities" (p. 428). Redfield's community was a group bound by shared values, obligations, and expectations, whose relationships were based on communication rather than physical space. Geertz emphasized social action, cultural meaning, and ritual analyzed in a semiotic domain. Turner explained contrasting types of social arrangements and interactions, structural and hierarchical relationships as a dialectical process involving alternatives to power (p. 443). Collectively they offer the historian "a three-tiered analysis," whereby anthropological theory merges with "the special skills of those individuals engaged in 'the new social history.'" Historians are able to discern meaning from "barren documents" such as "court and probate records, land and tax lists" and reconstruct the past in an interpretive framework (pp. 442–443).

One example of the use of historical ethnography by colonial historians can be found in Rhys Isaac's *The Transformation of Virginia, 1740–1790* (1982). As a historian convinced that "reconstruction of the distinctive mentalities of past peoples" (p. 323) is an important part of his task, Isaac experimented with strategies and methodologies employed by anthropologists. Rather than focusing on comparison, as some social historians using ethnography do, Isaac employed anthropological methodology to understand and explain "unfamiliar societies and systems of meaning" (p. 323). His work was a fifty-year study of socioreligious and political life in Virginia. Neither Isaac's sources nor his descriptions of life or accounts of events in Virginia were original. But his use of artistic forms, his discussion of social patterns, institutions, labor, and hierarchy were richly and dramatically presented in an interpretive pattern of "thick description." Codes of conduct, routines, posture, apparel, architecture, and beliefs of those who interact culturally conveyed internal semiotic meanings. Isaac's interpretation of empirical evidence elaborated context to reconstruct the world of white colonial Virginians as they themselves perceived it. This ethnographic outlook viewed society as a product of the activities of its members. It also viewed society as shaped by the perceptions of participants and their interpretation of the performance of others.

ETHNOGRAPHY, ANTHROPOLOGY, AND NEW INDIAN HISTORY

The study of American Indians has been more within the academic purview of anthropology departments than history departments. Anthropologists have been criticized for cultural imperialism and for imposing value judgments in their works on American Indians in some cases, and of pure racism in other instances. Thus anthropology's contribution to the study of American Indian history has been both significant and controversial. American Indian scholars have further lamented the fact that in the hands of anthropologists, and to a lesser extent historians, Indian history reaches backwards without using the past to explain the present. Hence modern problems facing American Indians are not integrated into the Indian experience.

Since the 1960s, some scholars have endeavored to move beyond merely using ethnographic fieldwork as data and making judgmental conclusions in evaluating the American Indian experience. Anthropologists have taken historical perspectives in examining acculturation, life-style, change and continuity, status, and hierarchy. They rely on documentary evidence and public records as well as fieldwork and oral history to amplify their historical reconstructions. A merger between historical and anthropological approaches to the study of American Indians was formalized in the 1950s by the establishment of the American Indian Ethnohistoric Conference, now called the American Society for Ethnohistory. The Society's publication, *Ethnohistory,* embraces the study of ethnicity from a humanistic and scientific perspective. It encompasses a number of disciplines, but most specifically history and anthropology.

In a 1969 article entitled "The Political Context of a New Indian History," Robert F. Berkhofer, Jr., called for a movement away from the missionary perspective; he asserted that scholars must reject moralizing, ethnic bias, and simplistic concepts like assimilation. In moving away from old themes, largely the purview of anthropologists, Berkhofer suggested that a new direction "ought to be the remarkable persistence of cultural and personality traits and ethnic identity in Indian societies in the face of white conquest and efforts at elimination or assimilation" (p. 102). This approach focuses on Indian-Indian relations as well as white-Indian contact. It also broadens the picture spatially and temporally—back in time to pre-white contact, or "beyond the reservation" to the "urban ghetto and national Indian organizations" of the modern era (p. 102).

In discussing the achievement of this aim, Berkhofer suggested that movement from the past into the present is both the responsibility of anthropology and history. The dilemma for both disciplines was how to reconcile change with continuity in American Indian societies. Anthropologists and historians need to look beyond the tribe, which

Berkhofer viewed as an abstract conception and "an artificial unit of analysis" (p. 113). What is more important is political behavior which, "as a result of the rise of political anthropology" (p. 108), reveals how aspects and degrees of change are "inextricably entwined with questions of politics and power" (p. 108). But Berkhofer cautioned historians about evaluating the data and the "political processes that produced it" and the importance of scrutinizing evidence and conclusions coming from political anthropological perspectives (p. 113). Yet political anthropology's emphasis on process as opposed to the previous preoccupation with formal structure is useful to historians. Such perspectives can embrace social, political, religious, or economic conflict and resolution, and it is not group restrictive. Within this context, the "tribe," a configuration of post-white contact, represents only one analytical unit, but obscures other relationships both internal and external.

Major themes of political anthropology are the distribution of power and governance structure within Indian society. Factionalism according to Berkhofer is important in understanding the complexities of Indian political systems; the concept also helps us recognize how particular informants are situated in power relationships. "A creative response to external white pressures as well as to internal cultural values," by chronicling factionalism the historian "provides an Indian view of an Indian way of handling change and persistence" (pp. 123–124). Berkhofer suggested ways of writing American Indian history from the vantage point of internal issues related to power and government, using a broad understanding of political anthropology in interpreting historical evidence and ethnography. He suggested that political perspectives offer one means of reconstructing, interpreting, and organizing the study of American Indians, and offered a broader, more complex historical vision. Historians and anthropologists have directly and indirectly merged anthropological theory and historical documentation in writing the new Indian history.

An example of anthropological and historical approaches in American Indian history is Loretta Fowler's *Shared Symbols, Contested Meanings: Gros Ventre Culture and History, 1778–1984* (1987). Fowler, an anthropologist, used Geertz's concept of culture—an established set of meanings embodied in certain symbols that create a social reality from which people explain their society and their position within it. Fowler was concerned with cultural change and continuity as she examined the political, ritual, and sacred symbols of Gros Ventre and Assiniboine Indians on the Fort Belknap reservation in Montana. Within the two groups, and among those of various ages, differences occurred in interpretation of the symbols. Fowler's investigation of their history and culture over two centuries explained how different and opposing meanings evolved among people sharing cultural symbols, and how these differences affected identity.

Fowler's study exemplified the range of available historical sources, including archival and unpublished state and federal documents, missionary records, court records, newspapers, Canadian correspondence, and state papers as anthropological sources. Her evidence also included field study, ethnohistory, and folk history. She was particularly critical of anthropological approaches that commonly isolate one specific group; search for "idealized" cultural commonality; view Indian society in terms of acculturation and assimilation into white society; present disagreements as factionalism, rather than analyzing meanings and cultural differences; and view multitribal communities from a "pan 'Indian'" cultural perspective.

Fowler considered many scholars' analytic categories to be stereotypes and oversimplifications, none of which fit the Gros Ventre and Assiniboine experiences. Their struggle to maintain cultural distinction is revealed in their folk histories, their group identity, and their response to change. The issue of internal group dynamics, her placing the Indian experience at the center of the study, the focus on two groups as opposed to one, her extensive use of historical sources, and her analysis of change over a long period of time are all answers to the call for new directions in the morphology of the study of American Indians. Her work is an excellent example of using anthropological theory to write an historical study and incorporate new vistas.

Historian Ramon A. Gutierrez's work on Pueblo Indians uses anthropological theory and analyses of power relations. *When Jesus Came, the Corn Mothers Went Away: Marriage, Sexuality and Power in New Mexico, 1500–1846* (1991) presents the "conquest" period as a cultural dialogue. Using journals, expedition itineraries, provincial records, and papers produced by conflicts over jurisdictional control of Indians, Gutierrez focuses on three models of marriage to interpret the social, political, and economic composition of New Mexico. This rite of passage reveals the contours of class and status, gender, sexual relations, self-identity, and adulthood. The sociopolitical implications of power relations between the sexes, the races, old and young, rich and poor, slave and free, imply an interdependency that challenge traditional notions of "conquest." The analytical model employed by Gutierrez is shaped by cultural anthropologists Jane Collier and Sylvia Yanagisako, who argue that all societies are unequal within themselves. Collier and Yanagisako maintain that exposing the various forms of inequality in a given society over time is more important than explaining why such inequality exists. Symbols and meanings surrounding marriage and sexuality, for example, are related to other forms of social inequality that involve specific disbursements of authority, hegemony, and prerogative.

Gutierrez's study shows how the symbolic meanings behind gift giving and sociosexual relations perpetuated inequality and control among preconquest Pueblo Indians. The cosmic world, as understood through Pueblo Indian ontology, defined masculinity and femininity as balanced, but the social world did not. Gender roles specified "the power women enjoyed by virtue of their control over household, feeding, and sexuality," but men countered with their "control over the community's relationships with its gods". Men, then, were the true forces of power. But sexual intercourse was "the symbol of cosmic harmony" because "it united in balance all the masculine forces of the sky with all the feminine forces of the earth". Symbols representing this analysis included fecundity initiation ceremonies, various dances, feeding, the spatial and ceremonial significance of the "kiva" (religious place), and the Snake Dance. This guiltless fusion of the sexual and the sacred was repugnant to Spanish missionaries, while the mystical marriage of the friars to Christ seemed incomprehensible to both Indians and Spanish soldiers. The inequality inherent in marriage came into full focus theoretically and historically in eighteenth-century New Mexico with resident nobility, landless peasants, and Indian slaves.

Historian Richard White also pursued a complex analysis of Indian-white interdependency. His book *The Middle Ground: Indians, Empires, and Republics in the Great Lakes Region, 1650–1815* (1991) is a search for accommodation and common meaning in Indian-white relations. He articulated how whites and Indians constructed mutuality that ultimately fragmented. The acculturation of one group to another is not White's theme, but rather the coming together of two groups in a middle place, "in between cultures, peoples, and in between empires and the nonstate world of villages." Accommodation and change occurred in this middle ground because of mutual dependency, not because of a process of dominance. The two cultures formed an alliance that served the interests of both. The "sinews" of the alliance were "rituals and ceremonials based on cultural parallels and congruences" (p. 93). For Indians, the crisis and disintegration began when they lost the power to maintain this middle ground. This started with the creation of the American Republic and culminated in the death of their charismatic leader, Tecumseh, during the War of 1812.

CONCLUSION

In the study of blacks, women, and other marginalized groups, historians and anthropologists with historical vision have placed historical actors once silenced or considered passive in the center of their own experience, and revealed the efforts of these groups to assert autonomy and power. These scholars have broadened the concept of what constitutes documentation, and thereby heard the voices of those whom previous scholars had labeled inarticulate. Material anthropologists have criticized cultural anthropologists like Geertz for ignoring the issue of power. Yet most scholars of ethnic and women's history who employed cultural anthropological methodology and terminology have avoided this pitfall. Instead they used "thick description" to define power relations rather than accept as a given the hegemony of those who politically and economically dominate society. Anthropologists who followed the Durkheim school such as Mary Douglas and Victor Turner asserted conclusions more in keeping with historians seeking articulation of power dynamics among groups defined outside the status quo.

Nevertheless, most historians are ever mindful of the cautionary suggestion of Robert Berkhofer to "Beware of the anthropologists bearing conclusions" (p. 120). Historians and anthropologists may share investigative techniques, conceptual frameworks, methodologies, and even terminologies, but still reach independent conclusions and assessments, particularly in regard to power. Still, history is indebted to anthropology. The fusion of anthropological approaches with historical studies of folk culture has helped democratize American historical writing and compelled historians to recognize diversity.

BIBLIOGRAPHY

Anthropological Works

Boas, Franz. *Social Organization and the Secret Societies of the Kwakiutl Indian* (1895).

———. *Race, Language and Culture* (1940).

Brinton, Daniel. *Races and Peoples: Lectures on the Science of Ethnography* (1890).

Douglas, Mary. *Natural Symbols: Explorations in Cosmology* (1970).

Geertz, Clifford. *The Interpretation of Cultures: Selected Essays* (1973).

Harris, Marvin. *The Rise of Anthropological Theory: A History of Theories of Culture* (1968).

Herskovits, Melville J. "The Significance of the Study of Acculturation for Anthropology." *American Anthropologist* 39, no. 2 (1937): 259–264.

———. *The Myth of the Negro Past* (1941).

Herskovits, Melville J., Ralph Linton, and Robert Redfield. "Memorandum for the Study of Acculturation." *American Anthropologist* 38 (1936): 149–152.

Herskovits, Melville J., ed. "The Interdisciplinary Aspects of Negro Studies." *American Council of Learned Societies Bulletin,* no. 32 (1941).

Kroeber, Alfred. "History and Science in Anthropology." *American Anthropologist* 37 (1937): 539–569.

Kroeber, Alfred, and Clyde Kluckhohn. *Culture: A Critical Review of Concepts and Definitions. Harvard University Papers of the Peabody Museum of American Archeology and Ethnology* 47 (1952).

Mintz, Sidney W. "Toward an Afro-American History." *Journal of World History* 13, no. 2 (1971): 317–332.

Mintz, Sidney W., and Richard Price. *An Anthropological Approach to the Afro-American Past: A Caribbean Perspective* (1976).

Redfield, Robert. *The Folk Culture of Yucatan* (1941).

———. *The Little Community: Viewpoints for the Study of a Human Whole* (1955).

———. *Peasant Society and Culture: An Anthropological Approach to Civilization* (1956).

Turner, Victor. *The Forest of Symbols: Aspects of Ndembu Ritual* (1967).

———. *The Ritual Process: Structure and Anti-structure* (1969).

———. *Dramas, Fields, and Metaphors: Symbolic Action in Human Society* (1974).

Historical Works

Beeman, Richard R. "The New Social History and the Search for 'Community' in Colonial America." *American Quarterly* 24 (1977): 422–433.

Bender, Thomas. *Community and Social Change in America* (1978).

Berkhofer, Robert F., Jr. "The Political Context of a New Indian History." In *The American Indian: Essays from the Pacific Historical Review,* edited by Norris Hundley, Jr. (1974).

———. *The White Man's Indian: Images of the American Indian from Columbus to the Present* (1978).

Breen, T. H. "Horses and Gentlemen: The Cultural Significance of Gambling Among the Gentry in Virginia." *William and Mary Quarterly* 34, no. 2 (1977): 239–257.

Calhoun, C. J. "History, Anthropology and the Study of Communities: Some Problems with Macfarlane's Proposal." *Social History* 3, no. 3 (1978): 363–373.

———. "Community: Toward a Variable Conceptualization for Comparative Research." *Social History* 5, no. 1 (1980): 105–129.

Creel, Margaret Washington. *"A Peculiar People": Slave Religion and Community Culture Among the Gullahs* (1988).

Gutierrez, Ramon A. *When Jesus Came, the Corn Mothers Went Away: Marriage, Sexuality, and Power in New Mexico, 1500–1846* (1991).

Gutman, Herbert G. *The Black Family in Slavery and Freedom: 1750–1925* (1976).

———. *Work, Culture, and Society in Industrializing America: Essays in American Working-class and Social History* (1976).

Higham, John. "Hanging Together: Divergent Unities in American History." Presidential Address, Organization of American Historians, 18 April 1974.

Higham, John, and Paul K. Conkin, eds. *New Directions in American Intellectual History* (1979).

Holloway, Joseph, ed. *Africanisms in American Culture* (1990).

Isaac, Rhys. *The Transformation of Virginia, 1740–1790* (1982).

Levine, Lawrence W. "Slave Songs and Slave Consciousness." In *Anonymous Americans,* edited by Tamara Hareven (1971).

———. *Black Culture and Black Consciousness: Afro-American Folk Thought from Slavery to Freedom* (1977).

Rawick, George P. *From Sundown to Sunup: The Making of the Black Community.* Contributions in Afro-American and African Studies, no. 11 (1972).

Rawick, George P., ed. *The American Slave: A Composite Autobiography.* Supplement 2, no. 19 (1972).

Smith-Rosenberg, Carroll. *Disorderly Conduct: Visions of Gender in Victorian America* (1985).

Stuckey, Sterling. "Through the Prism of Folklore: The Black Ethos in Slavery." *Massachusetts Review* 9, pt. 2 (1968): 417–437.

———. *Slave Culture: Nationalist Theory and the Foundations of Black America* (1987).

White, Richard. *The Middle Ground: Indians, Empires, and Republics in the Great Lakes Region, 1650–1815* (1991).

SEE ALSO **Community Studies; Feminist Approaches to Social History; Material Culture Studies; The Old Social History and the New; Poststructural Theory; Racial Ideology; The Social History of Culture.**

COMMUNITY STUDIES

Dwight W. Hoover

THE TERM "COMMUNITY STUDIES" encompasses several disciplines with a variety of research strategies, all of which can trace their origins back to the nineteenth century. These include, but are not restricted to, anthropology with its emphasis on field ethnography, sociology with its instrument of the social survey, and history with its reliance upon archival research. All these disciplines and methods persist to this day, although with increased sophistication and greater support. One difference has emerged, however: disciplinary lines have blurred so that community studies may be done with several of the above techniques.

The interest in community studies reached its peak in the second quarter of the twentieth century and then declined as researchers moved in two completely different directions: into micro and macro studies. Some, despairing of making sense of an entire community, began to analyze parts rather than wholes—population movement, the neighborhood, the political system, or the role of technology in one setting. Others, believing the study of a single community to be wasted effort because it supposedly failed to reveal much of larger trends, opted to take the entire nation as a subject and to bypass the local community altogether.

Great Britain and the Commonwealth have seen a return in sociology to "locality studies," a name preferred to "community studies" although covering the same ground. To a lesser degree, a renaissance has occurred in the United States because of the realization that the study of social change based on national data homogenizes the very real differences between localities and, hence, cannot measure the significance of changes in people's lives.

SOCIOLOGY AND ANTHROPOLOGY

The roots of community studies in sociology go back to the reform impulse at the turn of the century in England and the United States. The major influence was Charles Booth's *Life and Labour of the People in London* (1889–1903), which prompted American reformers to undertake exhaustive surveys of their own communities for the purpose of reforming them. Among early efforts was that of Jane Addams at Hull-House, where she sought out the realities of housing and services in Chicago neighborhoods. The culmination of the early American social survey was the six-volume Pittsburgh survey of 1907 to 1909, which described industrial life in the steel town. All these surveys emphasized the problems caused by low wages, poor housing, inadequate public health facilities, and unsafe working conditions for the laboring classes.

Perhaps the major nineteenth-century study done by a professional historian was W. E. B. DuBois's *The Philadelphia Negro* (1899). DuBois studied nine thousand black Philadelphians from the city's Seventh Ward in 1896–1897, using techniques that would later become standard in scientific community research. He interviewed knowledgeable residents, examined records and official statistics, attended all kinds of social gatherings, visited homes, and personally observed everyday life in addition to collecting survey data.

The reformist tradition became institutionalized in the journal *Charities and Commons,* later renamed *The Survey,* which continued to publish survey findings. In sociological circles the detachment of the social reform impulse from the survey was first accomplished at the University of Chicago under the leadership of Robert Park.

The Chicago School and Middletown The Chicago school of sociology, as it came to be known, took Chicago as its laboratory for the study of urban phenomena in a scientific fashion. Since the city was so large, the studies inevitably took only certain aspects as appropriate for examination, among them ethnic and racial groups. One of the first such works was *The Polish Peasant in Europe and America* (1918), by William I. Thomas and Florian Znaniecki. In this epochal work, the authors argued that the Polish peasants who migrated to Chicago from rural villages in Poland became the victims of social disorganization when the primary institutions of eastern Europe were weakened in the transit to the New World. Another important book was *The Negro in Chicago* (1922), a report of the Chicago Commission on Race Relations written largely by Charles Spurgeon Johnson, a graduate student in the sociology department, although Johnson was not acknowledged as principal author. This pioneering description of the conditions of African Americans was complemented later by E. Franklin Frazier's *The Negro Family in Chicago* (1932), a dissertation written to apply the ideas of Park and Ernest W. Burgess, another Chicago sociologist, regarding urban ecology and African Americans.

One of the most influential members of the Chicago school was Louis Wirth, a student of Park, who analyzed the Jewish community in Chicago in his book *The Ghetto* (1928). This volume emphasized the yeasty nature of that community as Jews assimilated into the larger society. His most significant work, however, was "Urbanism as a Way of Life" (*American Journal of Sociology* 44, no. 1 [1938]). A theoretical article that defined urbanism in such a way as to make it possible to study standard elements of every community. Urbanism, according to Wirth, was composed of three necessary factors: physical structure (population, technology, ecology), social organization (status groups, institutions), and collective behavior (group attitudes, ideologies). Later scholars concentrated upon one or another of the three and not upon the entire community.

In the 1920s, at the same time that the Chicago school was at its peak, Robert S. and Helen M. Lynd began a study of an entire community, later published as *Middletown: A Study in American Culture* (1929), which was to have a major impact upon community studies. The Lynds were not trained social scientists—Robert Lynd had graduated from Union Theological Seminary and Helen Lynd had obtained a degree in social philosophy from Wellesley—but they decided to adapt an anthropological model developed by the British social anthropologist W. H. R. Rivers to study primitive societies in the Pacific in their study of Muncie, Indiana, a town of thirty-seven thousand people. This model divided human activities into six categories: getting a living, making a home, using leisure, engaging in religious practices, training the young, and engaging in community activities. The Lynds moved to Muncie and obtained data for each of these categories by using surveys, historical research, and ethnological techniques.

The Lynds followed *Middletown* with *Middletown in Transition: A Study in Cultural Conflicts* (1937), a study of Muncie ten years after the first, while the city was in the throes of a severe economic depression. Both books had the same theme: the pernicious impact of urbanization and industrialization on a traditional community. Both were pessimistic concerning the future of the town and its citizens, who were unable to resist the blandishments of advertisers. Class antagonisms were muted by the pursuit of consumer goods.

Studies of Smaller Communities In the mid 1930s, at the same time the Lynds returned to Muncie, William Lloyd Warner, a sociologist informed by anthropological ideas, journeyed to Newburyport, Massachusetts, a town half the size of Muncie, with a team of sociologists to study that industrial community. Warner named the town Yankee City and, with his colleagues, published several volumes of his results. Among these were *The Social Life of a Modern Community* (1941) and *The Status System of a Modern Community* (1942), both written with Paul S. Lunt.

Warner's findings were not too different from those of the Lynds. Newburyport's way of life had changed as industrialization had eliminated craftsmen, turning them into industrial workers and thereby lowering their status and limiting their social mobility. The paternalistic preindustrial system of production had given way to an impersonal one run by managers for absentee owners.

Warner next undertook a study of a community one-third the size of Newburyport, an Illinois town with a population of 6,200 that he called Jonesville. Like Yankee City, Jonesville had a class system difficult to surmount, but it also had a system in which acculturated Norwegians were being assimilated into the Yankee elite. In addition, the older distinction between town and country was fading. These results, published as *Democracy in Jonesville: A Study in Quality and Inequality* (1949), attacked the myth of the egalitarian small town.

Another aspect of life in Jonesville was the topic of another book published in the same year,

Elmtown's Youth: The Impact of Social Classes on Adolescents (1949), by August B. Hollingshead. The Committee on Human Development at the University of Chicago sponsored the study, which was conducted in 1941 and 1942. While technically Hollingshead was under the supervision of Dean Robert Redfield, he worked closely with Warner.

Elmtown's Youth, as the title implies, was a study of adolescents and their behavior in relation to the social stratification of the community. Hollingshead took one high school "generation," all those who been in school between 1938 and 1941, as his base. He then determined their class position and compared it to their behavior in school, on the job, in their cliques, in dating, and in sexual situations. He proved to his satisfaction that the information gained from his surveys and interviews demonstrated a functional relationship between class and behavior.

The data accumulated by the Committee on Human Development yielded a more social-psychological study, *Adolescent Character and Personality* (1949), by Robert J. Havighurst and Hilda Taba. Havighurst also published a book with H. Gerthon Morgan on another small community, Seneca, Illinois. *The Social History of a War-Boom Community* (1951) analyzed the changes in the social structure of a town of 1,200 residents created by a fivefold expansion during World War II and a subsequent shrinkage to its prewar size.

Another study of a Midwest community of about the same size as Seneca was Carl Withers's *Plainville, U.S.A.* (1945). The locale was a Missouri town of about one thousand people. *Plainville, U.S.A.,* which Withers published under the pseudonym of James West, pictured a place where the class system was so fixed that social mobility could be achieved only by leaving, and where the working class was so socialized into its position that the highest aspiration of its members was a factory job.

Studies of the South The Midwest was not the only region to be scrutinized. Studies done on the South were informed more by anthropological techniques such as participant observation than by the survey data used by sociologists. The first to be published was John Dollard's *Caste and Class in a Southern Town* (1937), based upon research in a town of 2,500 that Dollard dubbed Southerntown. His main object was to investigate the forces that kept both African American and white residents conforming to a system which denied the basic American value of equality. He proceeded to do this by using psychological insights into the personalities of members of both races that were based upon everyday social contacts with whites and daily interviews, almost qualifying as therapy sessions, with African Americans.

The second study was *Deep South* (1941), by Allison Davis, Burleigh B. Gardner, and Mary R. Gardner, a look at a town called Old City, a trade center of about ten thousand residents. The researchers relied heavily upon participant observation, although in a less psychologically oriented manner. After studying the social organization that defined the caste separation between African Americans and whites, they determined that all the institutions in Old City focused upon the task of keeping African Americans in their place.

In the late 1940s, the Institute for Research in Social Science at the University of North Carolina, directed by the anthropologist John Gillin, undertook a series of community studies partially financed by the Julius Rosenwald Fund under the rubric of Field Studies in the Modern Culture of the South. The first involved a hamlet of three hundred families, identified as Plantation Town, in a county of twenty-five thousand called Plantation County. Morton Rubin, the investigator, did what was basically an ethnographic study relying upon middle- and upper-class whites in an area that was heavily populated by blacks. As a result *Plantation County* (1951) analyzed plantation culture and the process of enculturation with a bow to identifying the community's stratification system.

The next study in the Modern Culture of the South series was *Blackways of Kent* (1955). Kent was a county seat of four thousand people located in the southern Piedmont that had textile production as its economic base. Unlike Plantation Town, it was predominantly white. *Blackways of Kent,* however, concerned the minority community; and, according to its author, Hylan Lewis, "The study was conceived as a comprehensive treatment of culture in a subgroup" (p. 5). His method of field study owed much to the social anthropologist A. R. Radcliffe-Brown, and his objects of scrutiny were cultural complexes: courtship, marriage and the family, education, government, and social control in order to determine cultural imperatives.

A fellow researcher, John Kenneth Morland, produced a companion volume, *The Millways of Kent* (1958), on the white working class. Like Lewis's work, it was done in the late 1940s; used the same method, participant observation; and had the same goal, the study of a subculture. The subculture in this case was that of the mill villager, a member of the industrial working class.

A Concern with Mental Health By the 1950s, there had been a plethora of community studies done by sociologists and social anthropologists using survey techniques and field studies. It appeared that the two disciplines had melded; certainly this was the hope Robert Redfield expressed in his Gottesman Lectures given at Uppsala University and published as *The Little Community* (1955). In this significant theoretical statement, Redfield drew upon his experiences as an ethnologist in the Yucatecan village of Chan Kom and the Mexican village of Tepoztlán. He proposed that communities be viewed from several different perspectives—ecology, social structure, outlook on life, and history. His words might have persuaded a reader that the future of community studies was assured. Such was not the case.

Social scientists continued to study whole communities in the 1950s. Herman R. Lantz, a sociologist, studied a small southern Illinois coal town with a team of researchers financed by the Graduate School of Southern Illinois University. According to Lantz, the methods used included those "employed in history, sociology, social psychology, and anthropology," although he conceded that the most important source of data was the personal interview. In *People of Coal Town* (1958), Lantz analyzed attitudes, social-class structure, family patterns, and the perceived meaning of mining. He concluded that the declining economic prospects of the town had imposed a way of viewing life that resulted in feelings of inadequacy and a high incidence of mental illness among its residents. His book marked a subtle shift to a concern with mental health in American communities.

This shift is evident in *Small Town in Mass Society* (1958), by Arthur J. Vidich and Joseph Bensman; the study was sponsored by Cornell Studies in Social Growth, which in turn was under the auspices of the Department of Child Development and Family Relationships of the New York State College of Home Economics. The National Institute of Mental Health, the United States Public Health Service, and the Social Science Research Council provided the necessary funds.

Vidich and Bensman selected an upstate New York town of about one thousand residents near Ithaca that they named Springdale. A community in economic decline, its small retail stores lost customers to chain stores in larger towns. The political boss of Springdale, a farm implement dealer and feed mill owner, ran the town parsimoniously and with a rhetoric of self-help while eagerly seeking federal and state aid. The residents deceived themselves into believing that their town was democratic, self-sufficient, and self-reliant, although in reality it was socially stratified and dominated economically and politically by a small elite. Vidich and Bensman derived these conclusions through a variety of methods, including informant interviews, which created problems when the substance of some interviews became public.

By the time that *People of Coal Town* and *Small Town in Mass Society* appeared, the direction of social science research had changed. The attempt to study whole communities had been shelved in favor of studying either segments of larger communities or one phenomenon in a town or city. Typical of these was the account of upper-middle-class life of the residents of a Toronto suburb portrayed in *Crestwood Heights* (1956), by John R. Seeley, R. Alexander Sim, and Elizabeth W. Loosley, all trained sociologists. *Crestwood Heights* explored the psychic costs of living in a fifteen-thousand-person suburb undergoing a transition from a Gentile to a Jewish community.

Segments and Discrete Phenomena Another kind of community study being undertaken by political scientists was the exploration of community power structures. Two such studies were Floyd Hunter's *Community Power Structure* (1953), an examination of the small elite which Hunter claimed controlled Atlanta, and Robert A. Dahl's *Who Governs? Democracy and Power in an American City* (1961), a study of New Haven which contradicted Hunter's thesis by showing how power was shared by several groups.

Why had the study of a suburb or the power structure of a city supplanted the study of entire small towns? There are several reasons. The social sciences had become more rigorously mathematical, and the results of participant observation were difficult to quantify. Moreover, the latter was quite expensive, requiring considerable institutional support. Another reason is that most of the communities analyzed were quite small, and investigators chose smaller ones as time progressed. The concentration upon small-town life had come in part from the fascination with—and the revolt against—it in the 1920s. The revolt highlighted the negative side of that life: its prejudices, its class or caste consciousness. Although there was no explicit recognition of this attitude, it resonated in all the studies.

The citizens of Middletown, Yankee City, Kent, Elmtown, Old City, Plainville, Coal Town, and Springdale all seemed to be living in a premodern world, clinging to out-of-date values and behaving in a manner inconsistent with those values.

These unfavorable portraits provoked almost uniformly angry responses. Irate residents of the communities claimed that the studies were distorted and that the interviews either were of unrepresentative residents or misrepresented the actual situations or both, and they threatened to sue. The anger was not confined to the local citizenry. In the case of Middletown, the sponsoring group objected because it believed the effort sensationalized religion by reporting on a revival meeting at the town's most prestigious church. In the case of Springdale, the project director at Cornell, Urie Bronfenbrenner, objected because Vidich wrote the book after he left Cornell; because he used data he had not personally collected; and because, Bronfenbrenner claimed, he described individuals in a manner that made them easily identifiable, despite the project's assurance of anonymity to participants.

Although the 1960s and 1970s saw fewer studies of the type that had fascinated social scientists earlier, there were exceptions. Everett C. Ladd used three Connecticut communities in his *Ideology in America: Change and Response in a City, a Suburb, and a Small Town* (1969). Supported by grants from the National Science Foundation, the Social Science Research Council, and the University of Connecticut Research Foundation, Ladd analyzed political ideas in three communities of different sizes through demographic data, surveys, interviews, and community histories. Ladd's interest was not in class or caste, but in liberal or conservative political ideas. He also deviated from the tradition of past community studies in that he used no pseudonyms; he named his informants and his communities.

Return to an Older Style In the 1970s, however, there was a return to the older style of community studies, although it was informed by newer intellectual developments. Hervé Varenne, a French-born anthropologist trained at the University of Chicago, obtained a grant from the Wenner-Gren Foundation to study a community he named Appleton. A small town of 3,160 situated between Peoria, Illinois, and Dubuque, Iowa, Appleton resembled Elmtown in size, although Varenne's book, *Americans Together: Structured Diversity in a Midwestern Town* (1977), was a far cry from *Elmtown's Youth*.

Informed by Claude Lévi-Strauss's structuralism, Varenne lived in Appleton for a year and joined the life of the community. He wished to discover the culture of an American small town by concentrating upon the "exoticism of our everyday life and its structure." The result was a book consisting of information gathered about certain general topics, among them individualism, community, and love. Under these general headings, Varenne subdivided his analysis into such categories as the social structure, religious ideology and organization, and government democracy. Although his topics varied somewhat from those used by the Lynds, Warner, and Hollingshead, the major difference lay elsewhere. Believing that anthropology had advanced since earlier studies were made, Varenne conceived of his study as concerned with American culture in general through the structure that generated it rather than with one community.

And, for the first time, in the 1970s a group of researchers proposed to replicate an earlier study. The group called Middletown III returned to study Muncie fifty years after the first study. A team of three sociologists—Theodore Caplow, Howard Bahr, and Bruce Chadwick—funded by the National Science Foundation responded to a question posed by Colin Bell: why replication, so central to the scientific method, was so infrequently employed in sociology.

Middletown III conducted more surveys and used much more sophisticated statistical data than had the Lynds, but it also duplicated many of the techniques utilized by them. It spent more time, money, and effort than had gone into *Middletown* and *Middletown in Transition*. The findings were much more conservative and, from the standpoint of the community's residents, much more positive. In a series of papers, in articles, and in two books—*Middletown Families* (1982) and *All Faithful People* (1983)—the authors argued that modernization was slowing down, the class differences were narrowing, and that both the family and organized religion were stronger in the Muncie of the late 1970s than in the 1920s and 1930s.

The Middletown III project is still unfinished, but the early response to the publications was mixed, reflecting doubt about the appropriateness of community studies. According to David Riesman, "Community studies such as the Middletown project do not have the influence they once had because there is less interest among social sciences in the kind of broad, cross-sectional comparisons such studies yield" (Ellen K. Coughlin, "'Middletown'

Much the Same After 50 Years, Study Finds, but Sociology Greatly Changed," *Chronicle of Higher Education,* 17 March, 1982). Other sociologists also had reservations; Charles Page argued that field observation had fallen into disrepute, and Peter H. Rossi claimed that it was impossible "to replicate what is essentially a qualitative study" ("The Muncie Papers: Some Comments on the 'Middletown' Series," comments made at the Community Section Meeting of the American Sociological Association, 1 September, 1983).

Whether this criticism signals the complete end of empirical sociology's interest in community studies is difficult to ascertain. In other places, interest is increasing. In Great Britain the return goes under the rubric of "locality studies" and is exemplified by two large-scale projects—one of the Isle of Sheppey in Kent and the other of the South Wales town of Port Talbot. Sociologists involved in these efforts have supported field studies and participant observation, arguing that these methods enable the researcher to gain an empathetic understanding that gives such studies a personal quality, to demystify social life, and to strike a balance between data and theoretical abstraction. Whether, like Booth's study of the people of London, locality studies will influence Americans significantly remains to be seen.

HISTORY

The history of communities originated from two different sources that still remain largely separate. The earliest histories were frankly promotional and designed to chronicle the exceptional qualities of the communities and their residents. The promotional aspect, with its amateur air, led most professional historians to regard community history with skepticism and not a little disdain. The advent of the new social history, however, sparked interest in community history and those involved came to regard it as a viable research field. These historians altered the method by limiting their subject and their period. Instead of studying an entire community, they took one group. Instead of tracing developments over several centuries, they studied one decade. Instead of writing descriptive histories, they wrote analytical histories. The two histories did not merge; they remained separate.

Both shared common strengths. Both focused attention on less well-known places, individuals, and groups, bringing their histories closer to the goal of writing the history of more common people. Both suffered the weakness of being local and specific, of not connecting local events into national ones, of not melding micro studies into macro ones.

Can urban history be considered a part of community studies? It can be if "community" is taken to mean, as Darrett Rutman has suggested in "The Social Web" (1973), the network of relationships in a particular locale. This definition is, however, a 1970s one, informed by several generations of social science theory. Earlier historians thought they were doing community studies when they wrote histories of their towns.

Before professional historians became interested in urban history in the twentieth century, amateur historians already were digging into their communities' past. Many of their publications date from the nineteenth century and come from New England, which had a strong antiquarian tradition. An occasional professional historian ventured to write an urban biography under the stimulus of a search for Germanic origins of the American colonial towns. One of the first was Charles Andrews's *The River Towns of Connecticut* (1889).

Urban History In the twentieth century, the first urban historians wrote biographies of individual cities. Among these pioneers were Bessie Pierce, who studied the history of Chicago; Constance McLaughlin Green, who studied Holyoke, Massachusetts; and Blake McKelvey, who studied Rochester, New York. These pre–World War II urban biographies concentrated primarily upon reasons for economic growth, were descriptive rather than analytical, and were narrative in form.

When the Urban History Group was formed in 1953, the emphasis had shifted to the incorporation of social science techniques and models into its work. A good example of such a study was the Kansas City project. Its guiding scholar was R. Richard Wohl, who wished to apply sociological precepts to the historical study of entrepreneurship. Wohl, who taught social science at Chicago, was influenced by Havighurst and his colleagues, who regarded themselves as the successors to the Chicago school of sociology but had decided Chicago was too "complex" to study in their time and had chosen Kansas City instead. Havighurst had begun a study of aging in the latter city in 1953; Wohl received a Rockefeller Foundation grant to write a history of Kansas City to accompany Havighurst's project. Wohl did not complete the project himself, but other historians did write several volumes of the desired history. Perhaps the best-known of these was Charles N. Glaab's *Kansas City and the Railroads* (1962), which focused on the business leadership of the frontier town that made it into an important rail center.

The most revealing example of what was to come, however, was a pioneering effort by Merle Curti, an intellectual historian, who applied statistical methods to the study of a rural Wisconsin county. His *The Making of an American Community: A Case Study of Democracy in a Frontier County* (1959) is rightly regarded as one of the first books in the new social history as well as in the new community studies.

By the 1960s, the floodgates had opened and urban historians rowed off in almost every direction. Some wrote urban biographies; others did comparative studies of several towns; still others studied various developments in sections of larger cities.

The most influential community study of the early 1960s was Stephan Thernstrom's *Poverty and Progress* (1964), a look at historic Newburyport that demonstrated the essential ahistoricism of Warner's Yankee City series. Using manuscript census schedules and a variety of local records, Thernstrom analyzed occupational, geographical, and intergenerational mobility among workers. His conclusion was that Warner's assumption of an open class system in the nineteenth century was just that—an assumption. Workers in that era had no more mobility than they did in the 1930s.

Thernstrom's model became a popular one that was much replicated. In *Nineteenth-Century Cities: Essays in the New Urban History* (1969), a collection of essays edited by Thernstrom and Richard Sennett, there appeared a definition of the new urban history. It was the history of population movement in urban areas with an emphasis upon the inarticulate through the use of quantitative data. Among the books in that tradition are Peter A. Knights's *The Plain People of Boston, 1830–1860* (1971); Howard P. Chudacoff's *Mobile Americans: Residential and Social Mobility in Omaha, 1880–1920* (1972); Stephan Thernstrom's *The Other Bostonians: Poverty and Progress in the American Metropolis* (1973); and Dean Esslinger's *Immigrants and the City: Ethnicity and Mobility in a Nineteenth Century Midwestern Community* (1975), a study of South Bend, Indiana.

The Colonial Town In addition to the study of mobility in nineteenth-century American cities, there was a spate of studies of colonial New England towns, several of which had their origins in graduate seminars at Harvard. Most examined the small towns for a limited time period and chronicled their transformation from English agricultural villages to a more modern town form. Two good examples are Kenneth A. Lockridge's *A New England Town: The First One Hundred Years* (1970), a study of Dedham, Massachusetts, and Philip Greven, Jr.'s *Four Generations: Population, Land, and Family in Colonial Andover, Massachusetts* (1970). A similar work published the same year, John Demos's *A Little Commonwealth: Family Life in Plymouth Colony* (1970), took a somewhat more psychological approach that attempted to relate material culture to the life lived in that colony.

Other historians opted for a comparative approach, including several communities in works that emphasized common denominators among them. Examples of these are Michael Zuckerman's *Peaceable Kingdoms: New England Towns in the Eighteenth Century* (1970) and Bruce C. Daniels's *The Connecticut Town: Growth and Development, 1635–1790* (1979), which described all 101 towns in that colony.

Not all community studies of this genre were of New England towns; a few considered other regions. Stephanie Grauman Wolf's *Urban Village: Population, Community and Family Structure in Germantown, Pennsylvania, 1683–1800* (1976) applied the same methods to a settlement in the middle colonies.

The Small Industrial Town The analysis of family structure in small towns in the seventeenth and eighteenth centuries shaded into another, similar kind of community study in the 1970s, one that emphasized the urban working class. The kinds of issues involved were articulated best in Herbert Gutman's *Work, Culture, and Society in Industrializing America* (1976). By examining family and kinship relations as well as working-class culture in an urban setting, these historians could discover the resilience of the family in the face of changing lifestyles and the stubbornness of workers in clinging to preindustrial work patterns.

Among those exploring such themes were participants in the Harvard Studies in Urban History project. They included Stuart M. Blumin, who studied Kingston, New York, in *The Urban Threshold: Growth and Change in a Nineteenth-Century Amer-*

ican Community (1976); Clyde and Sally Griffen, who studied Poughkeepsie, New York, in their *Natives and Newcomers: The Ordering of Opportunity in Mid-Nineteenth Century Poughkeepsie* (1978); and Michael B. Katz, who studied Hamilton, Ontario, in *The People of Hamilton, Canada West* (1975). These studies represented an extremely quantitative approach to the problem of determining social structure. Perhaps the most successful of this type of community study was Mary P. Ryan's *Cradle of the Middle Class: The Family in Oneida County, New York, 1780–1865* (1981).

Other studies focusing more directly on working-class issues are Tamara K. Hareven and Randolph Langenbach's *Amoskeag: Life and Work in an American Factory-City* (1978), a collection of life histories of textile workers in a New Hampshire town; Alan Dawley's *Class and Community: The Industrial Revolution in Lynn* (1976); Daniel Walkowitz's *Worker City, Company Town: Iron and Cotton-Worker Protest in Troy and Cohoes, New York, 1855–84* (1978); and Susan E. Hirsch's *Roots of the American Working Class: The Industrialization of Crafts in Newark, 1800–1860* (1978). All of these showed the resistance to the transformation from craft workers to industrial workers and the creation of working-class communities in small industrial towns. The interest in such a transformation was not confined to historians. The anthropologist Anthony F. C. Wallace used a larger cultural emphasis in his description of the battle waged by workers against manufacturers' hegemony in a Pennsylvania textile mill town in the nineteenth century in *Rockdale: The Growth of an American Village in the Early Industrial Revolution* (1978).

Community Formation At the same time, there was a return to the examination of community formation in the nineteenth century prior to industrialization. These studies, using more sophisticated methods and informed by sociological insights, looked at small Midwest communities. They also shaded into a new interest in rural history. The two most impressive were Don Harrison Doyle's *The Social Order of a Frontier Community: Jacksonville, Illinois, 1825–70* (1978) and John Mack Faragher's *Sugar Creek: Life on the Illinois Prairie* (1986). Doyle, influenced by Max Weber, argued that the exercise of power by "communities of limited liability" integrated a heterogeneous society and provided social control. Faragher examined "the first generation of a midwestern community, in the six decades before the American Civil War," using family history. He described his work as a local study in the British tradition of William Morgan Williams's *A West Country Village: Ashworthy* (1963) and Ronald Blythe's *Akenfield: Portrait of an English Village* (1969). Because of this, Faragher's work comes closest to melding British locality studies with American historical community studies.

Studies of early colonial communities resemble studies of Illinois. Inspired by Darrett B. Rutman's seminal article, "Community Studies," historians used network analysis (a study of the interaction of individuals in business, religion, marriage, and other social groupings) to study local society. This method, which Rutman believed overcame the fuzzy definition of community used by historians of New England, was more openly quantitative and borrowed much from sociological methods. Books based upon this technique include Darrett B. Rutman and Anita Rutman's *A Place in Time: Middlesex County, Virginia, 1650–1750* (1984) and James R. Perry's *The Formation of a Society on Virginia's Eastern Shore, 1615–1655* (1990). Both analyze communities that could scarcely be called urban in any sense but which fit Rutman's definition.

No consideration of the problem of community studies is complete without mention of the best theoretical volume on the topic. Thomas Bender's *Community and Social Change in America* (1978) provides useful definitions and discriminating views of the issues involved. Bender argues persuasively that the traditional distinction between the village and the city, upon which much of community studies is based and which was inherited from German sociology, is flawed. Both the village and the city possess elements of the other. As a result, Bender calls for new and more powerful theories and methods.

Bender's insights point the way to the future. The return to field studies and participant observation done in English locality studies and by Varenne in Wisconsin signals the seeming exhaustion of rigidly quantitative studies in sociology and anthropology and a return to earlier methods. On the other hand, further refinement of such social science techniques as network analysis suggests a continuing fascination with quantitative data. The disparity noted at the beginning of this article has continued and appears to be widening. Unless a powerful new all-encompassing theory becomes accepted, community studies will remain disparate.

BIBLIOGRAPHY

Anthropology and Sociology

Bell, Colin, and Howard Newby. *Community Studies: An Introduction to the Sociology of the Local Community* (1972).

Chock, Phyllis Pease. "Irony and Ethnography: On Cultural Analysis of One's Own Culture." *Anthropological Quarterly* 59 (April 1986).

Gillin, John. "The Application of Anthropological Knowledge to Modern Mass Society: An Anthropologist's View." *Human Organization* 15, no. 4 (1957).

Spindler, George D., and Louise Spindler. "Anthropologists View American Culture." *Annual Review of Anthropology* 12 (1983).

Stein, Maurice. *The Eclipse of Community: An Interpretation of American Studies* (1960).

Szacki, Jerzy. *History of Sociological Thought* (1979).

Van Maanen, John. *Tales of the Field: On Writing Ethnography* (1988).

History

Beeman, Richard. "The New Social History and the Search for 'Community' in Colonial America." *American Quarterly* 29, no. 4 (1977).

Bender, Thomas. *Community and Social Change in America* (1978).

Conzen, Katheleen Neils. "Community Studies, Urban History, and American Local History." In *The Past Before Us,* edited by Michael Kammen (1980).

Dykstra, Robert R., and William Silag. "Doing Local History: Monographic Approaches to the Smaller Community." In *American Urbanism: A Historiographical Review,* edited by Howard Gillette, Jr., and Zane L. Miller (1987).

Ebner, Michael. "Urban History: Retrospect and Prospect." *Journal of American History* 68, no. 1 (1981).

Frisch, Michael. "American Urban History as an Example of Recent Historiography." *History and Theory* 18, no. 3 (1979).

Mohl, Raymond A. "New Perspectives on American Urban History." In *The Making of Urban America,* edited by Mohl (1988).

Russo, David J. *Families and Communities: A New View of American History* (1974).

Rutman, Darrett B. "The Social Web: A Prospectus for the Study of the Early American Community." In *Insights and Parallels: Problems and Issues of American Social History,* edited by William L. O'Neill (1973).

———. "Community Studies." *Historical Methods* 13, no. 1 (1980).

Thernstrom, Stephan. "Reflections on the New Urban History." *Daedalus* 100 (Spring 1971).

SEE ALSO **The City**; **Communitarians and Counterculturists**; **Immigration**; **Urbanization**; and various essays in the sections "**Regionalism and Regional Subcultures**" and "**Space and Place.**"

AMERICAN SOCIAL AND CULTURAL GEOGRAPHY

Wilbur Zelinsky

THE PRACTICE OF SOCIAL and cultural geography in the United States has never been more energetic, interesting, and productive than it is at the present time. But any such roseate observation must be tempered by more than a single qualification: that much debate and confusion persist as to the nature, aims, and methods of this scholarly enterprise; that its practitioners have an immense, ever-expanding agenda of items still to be addressed adequately, or at all; and that this brand of geography has not yet had the sort of impact upon geographers of other persuasions, the academic community at large (including social historians), or the general public it arguably merits or that one might ideally desire.

If, for the sake of brevity, we simply define geography as the study of all those phenomena on this planet that can be usefully analyzed using a spatial approach or that have some relationship to the concept of place (a definition that leaves out surprisingly little), cultural geography is the subfield that applies the idea of culture to geographic problems. Similarly, social geography exploits the idea of society, or sociological principles, in treating a broad range of spatially specified matters. Taken as a whole, the study of geography is perhaps the most catholic, or imperialistic, of academic disciplines in terms of its topical reach in both principle and practice.

THE STUDY OF GEOGRAPHY BEFORE WORLD WAR II

Geography has been a slow, late-blooming phenomenon on the American scene, especially as compared with the parental European developments. (For an informative survey of the evolution of geographic thought, at least up to 1970, see Preston E. James, *All Possible Worlds,* 1972.) Even though one can now lay claim to such isolated pioneers as George Perkins Marsh (1801–1882), whom many regard as the founding father of modern cultural ecology, as premature but authentic geographers, more or less scientific geography materialized in a few American colleges only in the waning years of the nineteenth century. And it did so largely at the instigation of geologists, whose influence caused physical geography and, indirectly, the doctrine of environmental determinism to dominate the field during the first decades of the twentieth century.

The only other specialty, aside from physiography and climatology, to achieve much prominence in the pre–World War II era was a narrowly conceived economic geography. However, some attention was paid to developing political geography, albeit at a somewhat simplistic level, thanks in large part to the towering figure of Isaiah Bowman (1878–1950), who was so instrumental in redrafting the international boundaries of post-Versailles Europe.

Regrettably, geographers have played only a minor role in perhaps the liveliest, most enduring of debates in American social history, one that began in 1893 with the promulgation of the Turner thesis, that quintessentially historical-geographic argument on the shaping of American life and institutions through the frontier experience. However, one may contend that Frederick Jackson Turner (1861–1932) was, in actuality, a geographer despite his nominal title of historian.

As much as anything else, an emphasis on things that appear on physical, land-use, political, and other conventional maps or in census statistics militated against serious involvement in the rather less tangible aspects of culture and society. The one great productive exception to such lack of interest was the work initiated at the University of California from the 1930s onward, the so-called Berkeley school. It was largely the doing of the charismatic

Carl O. Sauer (1889–1975), who had been trained originally as a geologist. Through his teaching and writings, which incorporated much of the attitude and subject matter of cultural anthropology as well as strong preoccupation with history and prehistory, and the activities of a sizable corps of his students, many new lines of investigation were opened into cultural landscapes past and present and into a broad range of largely premodern human activities (John Leighly, ed., *Land and Life,* 1963). The impact of the Sauer tradition, especially in the field of cultural ecology, is still expanding.

However seminal the stirrings in Berkeley may have been, prewar geography in America, as a whole or viewed in terms of particular specialties, comprised a relatively small segment of the academic totality. And if the sociology of knowledge and organizations is germane, one must also note that the earlier generations of American geographers were emphatically WASP in makeup, Middle Western in origin, and overwhelmingly male in gender. There had been scant contact with other disciplines, except geology and meteorology, and minimal attention to contemporary thought overseas.

Because of the deep involvement of nearly the entire geographic community in the war effort—principally in map preparation and intelligence gathering and evaluation—1941 to 1945 may be regarded as a watershed period. But the maturation of the discipline did not happen overnight, and indeed new values and directions took some years to become manifest. To a marked degree they seem to reflect the ongoing restructuring of our larger society and collective psyche. In any event, from this point onward, it makes more sense to deal with a number of larger themes rather than to view developments in strict chronological sequence.

THE RISE OF HUMAN GEOGRAPHY

The most obvious development has been quantitative growth in membership in the discipline. Noteworthy also are the shifts in population structure, with a steady climb in female participation and stronger representation of various ethnic groups. But more interesting than the quantitative have been the qualitative changes. Perhaps the most striking of these has been what might be called the cosmopolitanization of the discipline. Indeed it is no longer easy to specify what is truly American in current geographic practice in this country when so many established scholars and graduate students from other nations have migrated or circulated here—and when a reverse flow is also much in evidence. Even more meaningful may be the sharing of publications, themes, technologies, and concerns of all sorts across national borders. The connections have been most intimate and fruitful with colleagues and ideas in Canada and the British Isles (where intellectual ferment in geography has been notably lively of late); but other anglophone countries are part of this latter-day collectivity, along with geographers in virtually all of Europe, the Soviet Union, and southern and eastern Asia. But, however global the conduct of geography has become recently, there is little doubt that, in contrast to the prewar epoch, when Germany and France contended for leadership, the United States has become, and remains, the dominant breeding ground and market for new ideas, themes, and techniques.

In similar fashion—and in contrast to the intellectual isolationism of the prewar years—recent decades have witnessed a marked interdisciplinary outreach. Such cross-pollination, which has been initiated from both sides of disciplinary fences and is still growing in scope, has enriched mutual understanding and the quality of production in a number of areas, including, among others, sociology, demography, anthropology, folklore, philosophy, history of all sorts, economics, market research, psychology, landscape architecture, and American studies. If any single event best exemplifies this collegiality, it may be the symposium, prominently involving geographers along with members of several other disciplines, that led to the publication of *Man's Role in Changing the Face of the Earth,* edited by William L. Thomas, Jr., in 1955. It is a volume with much value for students of social history at the world scale as the first extended, amply documented statement, couched in both historical and regional terms, of human agency in transforming this planet's ecosystem. One consequence of all this hybridization is the frequent difficulty of assigning a particular individual or publication unambiguously to a given field, whether geographic or not.

This account would be incomplete without some mention of the ongoing technological advances that have greatly affected the ways in which geographers ply their craft. Like their colleagues in so many other pursuits, they have become addicted to electronic computers and their data-handling wonders, and are busily probing the dazzling frontiers of computer mapping. The remote sensing of terrestrial features using esoteric as well as traditional modes of observation and the related emergent GIS (geographic information systems) technology is especially appealing to many in the geographic guild. Cultural and social geographers have not yet exploited these novel capabilities as avidly as their neighbors involved in economic, biotic, and other physical topics, but they have certainly begun to do so; the potentialities for the elucidation of all manner of relevant questions, historical as well as contemporary, are impressive.

Contemporary geography resembles other disciplines in the way it has been splintering into an ever-growing swarm of specializations. A reflection of the trend is visible in the very structure of the Association of American Geographers, which now houses no fewer than thirty-nine specialty groups, some fourteen of which are in varying degree concerned with social and cultural matters. Remaining uncounted are the many ad hoc groups, special symposia and workshops, and, of course, the numerous "invisible colleges" of like-minded students where fresh ideas are often germinated and hatched. The proliferation of specialized journals, along with many newsletters and monograph series, attests to the vigor of such branching out. Examples of the former (limited here to the human side of the discipline) include *Applied Geography, Journal of Historical Geography, Landscape, Political Geography Quarterly, North American Culture, Environment and Planning, Regional Studies, Urban Geography, Journal of Regional Science, Geographical Analysis, Antipode, Journal of Cultural Geography,* and *Environment and Behavior.*

Perhaps more relevant to the present discussion than any of the other grander developments has been a growing sensitivity to the human factor and to social issues among American geographers and a consequent curiosity directed toward both historical and current situations within the human realm. A regrettable immediate consequence of this redirection of efforts was a deepening gap between human geography and traditional physical geography, and the near-eclipse of the latter or its abandonment to the cognate physical sciences during the first decades of the postwar period. Fortunately, a healthy corrective trend emerged, a physical geography in which human agency receives its proper due. One result has been closer attention to past, as well as ongoing, man-induced changes in drainage systems, plant cover, soils, shorelines, and landforms—items that social historians would do well to place on their agenda. In any event, what one might term the "socialization" of geography is one of those structural alterations in a disciplinary mind-set that cannot be attributed to any given person, publication, or event, but rather seems to resonate to the general zeitgeist within the wider intellectual community.

But if a preoccupation with the human condition, past and present, and in both theoretical and practical terms, may be *the* dominant theme among American geographers today, such supremacy did not come about without a certain amount of ideological turmoil. Beginning in the late 1950s, American geography (and, after a short time lag, its overseas affiliates) experienced what is commonly called the "quantitative revolution," a paroxysm that climaxed in the late 1960s and early 1970s (a time, not too coincidentally, of profound unrest in other phases of public life). Generated by a bright, energetic corps of Young Turks who were acutely and properly disenchanted with the state of the mainstream geography they had inherited, this rebellious generation sought to replace a largely descriptive, atheoretical pattern of scholarship—one all too frequently embodied in the deadly cookbook type of regional monograph—with a rigorously scientific spatial praxis. This discredited ideographic mode of inquiry, which usually gave temporal considerations short shrift, tended to be localistic or descriptive in approach, and all too often consisted of little more than filling out a checklist of topics, beginning with geology and ending with settlement patterns or commerce. Adopting a powerful arsenal of mathematical weapons and relying heavily on a positivistic philosophy, the scholars in question sought diligently to formulate a set of general laws that would describe, explain, and predict all significant patterns of human behavior on the face of the earth. Needless to say, such universal formulas would take little or no cognizance of history or culture.

There were some interesting achievements along the way. The two most prominent were central place theory, as embodied in the work of Brian J. L. Berry and many others, and the diffusion of innovations, as promulgated by the Swedish geographer Torsten Hägerstrand and eagerly emulated by numerous English and American scholars. Berry's work sets forth a scheme whereby the geometric array of agglomerated settlements and retail functions can be predicted on a level, undifferentiated plain while Hägerstrand's describes or predicts the spatial progression over time of the acceptance of a new idea, device, or practice from point of origin to adjacent territories. Under ideal circumstances, both formulations have some validity, but ideal circumstances rarely present themselves. In any case, it became obvious within a few years that the larger goals of the quantifiers were not only practically unattainable but were also untenable in philosophical terms and by the very nature of human reality.

The most valuable legacy of the flawed quantitative revolution has been a receptivity to new ideas and attitudes, a willingness to experiment with all manner of approaches to the bewilderments of a complex human world. In the broadest terms, this has meant that commitment to understanding, and presumably coping with, the real patterns and problems of society noted a few paragraphs earlier. As has happened in all the social sciences in America and overseas (and in some humanistic areas as well), the keener geographic minds during the past decade or two have immersed themselves, or at least dabbled in, some form of Marxist thought—be it orthodox, revisionist, neo-, post-, or whatever—but not to the exclusion of other philosophical schools, such as phenomenology. To date no controlling paradigm has triumphed, nor do we have any single, universally acknowledged leader heading up the parade. However, as emblematic and influential a thinker as any is the British-American geographer David Harvey, whose influence ranges well beyond the boundaries of his nominal discipline and whose intellectual odyssey has carried him from the halcyon days of the quantitative revolution through a Marxist conversion to an ongoing effort at some type of postmodern Marxist synthesis.

In writing of the present-day confusion and rapid turnover of fashions in the bazaar of ideas, Harvey offers an observation that need not be limited to geographers:

> the competitive marketing of ideas, theories, models, topic thrusts, generates color-of-the-month fashions which exacerbate rather than ameliorate conditions of rapid turnover, speed-up and ephemerality. Last year it was positivism and Marxism, this year structurationism, next year realism and the year after that constructivism, postmodernism, or whatever. It is easier to keep pace with the changes in Benetton's colors than to follow the gyrations of ephemeral ideas now being turned over within the academic world. ("Between Space and Time," p. 431)

Thus any attempt at characterizing the present-day theoretical landscape would be foolhardy and would surely be obsolete by the time these words are printed. Suffice it to say that in 1991 the current mantra is "critical social theory," however one might wish to translate that concept. I must also note that much of the jargon used in numerous programmatic statements is virtually impenetrable, and that much more verbiage has been expended in exhortation than in empirical demonstration by the exhorters.

But if the ideological arena in human geography is in a state of chaotic flux and if the theoreticians are marching off in all directions, there is still much substantive work being done by social and cultural geographers that has considerable value directly or indirectly for the social historian. The philosophical debates have only modestly affected choice of topic and type of approach. And the most effective way of dealing with this relevant material is to take it up topic by topic. (This review excludes a number of thriving specialties that are of minimal interest to the historian, for example, regional planning, tourism, energy, and hazards.)

HISTORICAL GEOGRAPHY

The oldest specialized focus and the one offering the richest immediate rewards to the social historian is that inhabited by persons calling themselves historical geographers. (For detailed surveys of recent activity in this and most other geographic specialties, see Gaile and Willmott, *Geography in America,* 1989.) Although many are members of, or are genealogically linked with, the Berkeley school, the historical-geographic approach emerged spontaneously from a number of different sources, another example among many of the independent invention of an idea whose time had come.

Especially influential has been the work of Andrew H. Clark (a Berkeley Ph.D.) at the University of Wisconsin–Madison on Maritime Canada and other areas, but especially the output of his large cohort of productive disciples. The latter have generated an impressive series of studies of the historical development of specific regions, usually with an emphasis on economic factors. This list includes James Lemon (1976) on southeastern Pennsylvania, Carville Earle (1975) on the Chesapeake Bay country, Roy Merrens (1964) on North Carolina, Cole-brook Harris (1966) on seigneurial Quebec, and Robert Mitchell (1977) on the Shenandoah Valley. Any historian, social or otherwise, who deals with any of these localities must reckon with these publications. Despite much wrangling over the precise nature and mission of historical geography, it seems clear enough that its adherents are intent on reconstructing past geographies and/or the processes whereby geographic change has come about in the past and helped shape our contemporary world. Furthermore, their work is involved with the unspoken axiom that all geography is temporal as well as spatial in nature. If there is any central argument in this essay, it is emphatically that space matters, and place as well, indeed that such territorial attributes matter a great deal in human affairs—and are coequal with time in importance. Consequently, if geographers dare not ignore history (although many have not yet learned that elemental lesson), practitioners of history and the other social sciences and humanities must reciprocate by taking the spatial factor into full account in their endeavors. Indeed, the ideal approach is one in which the spatial and temporal are inextricably blended. The fact that this ideal is too infrequently realized reflects the dominance of historicism in modern Western thought, for reasons too complicated to be pursued here. The great numerical disparity between the ranks of professional historians and geographers here and elsewhere presents strong testimony of the prevailing mind-set.

If there are two individuals in competition for the godfatherhood of historical geography, they are undoubtedly John K. Wright (1891–1969) and Ralph H. Brown (1898–1948). Wright, who received his early training as a historian, was associated with the American Geographical Society of New York during a long, fruitful career and was one of the editors (with Paullin) of the *Atlas of the Historical Geography of the United States* in 1932. It is a scholarly tour de force involving joint efforts by historians and geographers that has lost little of its value since its publication in 1932. The volume has also inspired a number of later atlases of a historical character at the national or regional scale. Two efforts that merit special notice are the National Geographic Society's lavish *Historical Atlas of the United States* (edited by Wilbur E. Garrett, 1988) and the exemplary *Historical Atlas of Canada* (edited by R. Colebrook Harris, 1987), the first volume of which illuminates our knowledge of the territory that eventually became the United States as well as setting the stage for modern Canada. Writing at the University of Minnesota, Ralph Brown generated a book-length *Historical Geography of the United States* (1948), a heroic initial attempt to deal with the exploration, settlement, and economic evolution of America in a chronological-cum-spatial format up to about 1870, one that inspired much subsequent scholarship.

By all odds the most outstanding achievement in American historical geography to date is Donald W. Meinig's monumental *Shaping of America* (1986). Even though only the first volume of what promises to be a tetralogy has appeared to date, it is plain that this will be much more than the consummation of Brown's relatively rudimentary project—as close to a definitive statement of the development of American society and culture over time and space at both the continental and regional scales as one could hope for. By viewing the United States as a dynamic geographic formation, as a continually changing, complex set of regions, interacting spatially among themselves and with more distant places, Meinig offers a restaging of the American past that reinterprets familiar themes, one that in part complements but in larger measure challenges more orthodox histories. In this initial volume, we meet such major themes as human migrations, racial encounters, cultural patterns, the salience of particular habitats, and the exercise of power over wide spatial intervals. Meinig focuses in particular on how an immense diversity of ethnic and religious groups—Europeans, Africans, and Native Americans—came to be sorted into a set of distinct regional societies, all against the backdrop of the greater Atlantic world of Europe, Africa, and Latin America. The intellectual heft and thrust of this work invites comparison with Immanuel Wallerstein's world-systems project, and could ultimately have the same impact on modes of historical and geographic inquiry.

But Meinig has not been working in isolation; one must also acknowledge at least two other publications, both collections of original essays, that seek to span the entire spectrum of American historicogeographic experience: those edited by Robert D. Mitchell and Paul A. Groves (1987) and by Michael P. Conzen (1990). The historian can profit richly from both. The former portrays the evolution of the American land and society chronologically at both the continental and regional scales, while the latter deals with the fashioning of the visible landscape over time, using such diverse approaches as the varied European legacies, the impact of technology and urbanization, encounters with unfamiliar environments, the role of the ethnic immigrants, and the imprint of social class and of central authority.

This is an opportune point at which to raise the possibility that both human geographers and social historians may have been energized recently, however subconsciously for the most part, by a pervasive mood clearly evident throughout the general population as well as in corners of the world of learning: a nostalgic yearning for things past and a revulsion against placelessness. Thus we can note the burgeoning of historical preservation in America as elsewhere (a movement in which geographers have played an honorable part), certain retrospective trends in residential and commercial architecture and in patterns of personal names, the boom in genealogy and antiques, the proliferation of historical-cum-regional museums, festivals, periodicals, and study centers, and regional strategies in many advertising campaigns. And within the geographic vanguard, a new, sophisticated regional approach to social and economic analysis has suddenly become trendy after so many years in which any sort of regional study was treated with disdain. Michael Steiner and Clarence Mondale's annotated bibliography (1988) is a splendid guide to the literature on all aspects of American regionalism.

OTHER SPECIALTIES

Other specialties may not be explicitly historical in orientation, but most do contain a significant historical component. The least temporally sensitive of these interest groups, but one too conspicuous to ignore, is that clan of geographers who characterize themselves as "behavioral." Using a psychological, present-oriented approach (originally inspired by J. K. Wright) and occasionally a phenomenological stance, they have vigorously researched the ways in which individuals perceive their habitats and the resulting forms of behavior. But they have not yet bridged the gap between the person or small group and the larger society.

Population geographers have had more to say about both society and history. We can date the founding of the American specialty with precision: Glenn T. Trewartha's presidential address before the AAG in 1953. Since that time, a small but devoted group of scholars, who are quite aware of what their demographic counterparts have been up to, have pursued such themes as population distribution and change and especially migration and mobility, but have tended to bypass questions of fertility, mortality, marital attributes, and household composition. For a reasonably complete summary of developments and directions, see George A. Schnell and Mark S. Monmonier's *The Study of Population* (1983). It and other publications in the genre often examine past population patterns and movements as well as changes over time. An example thereof is Wilbur Zelinsky's "Hypothesis of the Mobility Transition" (1971), an essay that has prompted much subsequent research by both geographers and demographers. Turning to another aspect of demography, historians specializing in the colonial and early republican periods should regard as indispensable Herman Friis's minutely detailed maps depicting the distribution of the American population from 1625 through 1790.

Pursuit of demographic phenomena led some geographers, quite naturally, into the neighboring field of medical geography, a specialty that has been gathering momentum and substance of late. Melinda S. Meade offers one of the better introductions to the status of a field in which there have been two dominant concerns: the spatial attributes of diseases and the geography of the provision of health care. The historical dimension has figured in only a small fraction of the literature. That statement applies even more forcefully to the thriving new specialty that delves into the geography of aging. However, the potential value of such an approach—and one of special relevance to chroniclers of bygone societies—is illustrated by John Florin's analysis of cause of death in New England at the town level over a span of three centuries (1971).

Another predictable result of the turn to the demographic on the part of geographers has been the cultivation of ethnic and racial studies, which not infrequently examine bygone situations along with changes over time and migratory flows. Among many possible examples, one may cite Robert Ostergren's account of the locational patterns of Scandinavian settlement in the upper Middle West (1988) or Zelinsky's charting and explication of the changing spatial array of free Negroes from 1790 to 1860 ("The Population Geography of the Free Negro," 1950). The key document within this literature (and one indispensable to the social historian) is James P. Allen and Eugene J. Turner's *We the People* (1988), which deals as comprehensively as possible with virtually every immigrant group, as well as native-born Americans, at the national, state, and county levels. Although it concentrates largely on 1980 data, there is ample coverage in text and graphics of pre-1980 materials. We also encounter many items that analyze ethnic and racial communities at the micro scale in the vigorous literature on urban social geography that is discussed below. As one might anticipate, the African American population, past and present, has received special scrutiny from geographers. Molefi Asante and Mark

Mattson's *Historical and Cultural Atlas of African Americans* quite effectively summarizes knowledge as of 1991. Our understanding of the great outward twentieth-century surge of southern blacks or such varied phenomena as voting patterns, lynching, participation in sports, or demographic traits remains woefully incomplete until we examine the place-specific data displayed in its plates—maps that may raise more questions than we are now prepared to answer.

Although they were a bit tardier than other social scientists in recognizing the salience of gender studies, human geographers have been scurrying to make up for lost time in their investigations concerning the geography of women—and the status of females within the profession—during the last decade or two. Great Britain may have become the epicenter of the feminist movement among geographers, but the intensity of American activity—as surveyed by Wilbur Zelinsky, Janice Monk, and Susan Hanson—is also impressive. Once again, some of the work in question is historically oriented, as, for example, the coverage of the historical geography of the women's suffrage movement in Barbara Shortridge's comprehensive atlas (1987). The fact that women first won the right to vote in Wyoming and that their enfranchisement followed shortly thereafter in other nearby western states but was never realized in the Southeast before the Nineteenth Amendment was ratified in 1920 compels us to pose significant questions about American social history that would remain invisible, or much less insistent, in the absence of maps.

A great deal of the most intellectually adventurous work by human geographers nowadays has to do with the social geography of cities. It represents a genuine departure from an ample earlier body of geographic literature that treated cities rather narrowly as economic entities, as points of varied size and function within a spatial matrix, or as places segmented into sectors by spatial and land-cost factors following the model postulated by the sociologists Park and Burgess, or variants thereof. But if we can report notable advances in elucidating the historical geography of the urban economy at the continental scale by such scholars as Allan Pred and James E. Vance, Jr., the more fully rounded social-cultural approaches that are being ardently pursued currently are even more exciting. For it is in the urban theater that all the pressing concerns of the more venturesome human geographers converge—the humanistic, political, perceptual, demographic, questions of gender, class, ethnic, and other power relationships, of housing, and landscape, sense of place, historic preservation, and quality of life. David Ley's sensitive textbook *A Social Geography of the City* (1983) is a fine overview of this latter-day school of urban geography.

For specific localized examples, one can do no better than to turn to William Bunge's exploration of a single square mile of Detroit (1971), Peirce Lewis's lively account of an evolving New Orleans (1976), or Sherry Olson's definitive geographic and historical chronicle of Baltimore (1980). Of more recent vintage is Edward Soja's thought-provoking neo-Marxist dissection of the Los Angeles metropolitan area, that bellwether of a postmodern urban world (1986). We learn from such monographs that easy generalizations about urban history must yield to the reality that their subject areas are intricate mosaics, in physical as well as social space, and that societal change has followed a complex territorial scenario one must decipher in order to grasp the actual contours of historical evolution. Going beyond both city and geography, but rooted in both, is David Harvey's *The Condition of Postmodernity* (1989), which deals with a swiftly transformative social geography and a social history that is galloping along before our eyes with breathtaking speed. Antedating all these items is Jean Gottmann's *Megalopolis* (1961), the most influential of geographic statements about modern urbanization and a volume saturated with history. In this account we can trace the emergence and consolidation of the world's largest conurbation, and view the process, in all its many demographic, economic, transport, political, and land-use dimensions, with the aid of scores of maps. The Russian-born author has spent his working life in France, the United States, and England, a peripatetic career characteristic of so many of the leading lights in geography.

POLITICAL GEOGRAPHY

As has happened in other geographic endeavors, there has been a welcome metamorphosis in political geography recently. An exclusive obsession with geopolitics at the grand global scale or the plotting of international boundaries that was so prevalent as of yesteryear has been replaced by a multidimensional political geography into which social factors enter in meaningful fashion. This is apparent in many analyses of electoral patterns (not all necessarily recent) and of power struggles at the local level over all kinds of issues. A useful fraction of this work is historically tinged, but special note must be taken by social historians of a remarkable new data resource, Kenneth Martis's massive historical atlas of congressional districts. It delineates the boundaries of each district for each Congress from 1789 through the 1980s, then indicates which political party represented specific districts and states over the entire period, and finally maps the votes on a number of especially important pieces of legislation. The analytical possibilities latent in this resource are of inestimable value for the social as well as political historian.

Rivaling the urban-social frontier in terms of intellectual appeal are the ongoing developments in cultural ecology, an area in which American geographers have shared the spotlight with historians (such as William Cronon), archaeologists (such as James Deetz), and biologists in explicating the interactions of man and habitat over time and space. Their efforts have been so diverse in terms of specific problems and locale (more often than not outside the United States) that, for lack of space, I can cite only some of the more prominent actors in this project and urge the interested reader to seek out their works: Karl W. Butzer, William M. Denevan, Susanna Hecht, Terry G. Jordan, Bernard W. Nietschmann, Philip W. Porter, Carl O. Sauer (again), Frederick J. Simoons, Joseph E. Spencer, Billie L. Turner II, and Bret Wallach. Given the nature of the subject, most of their output is notable for considerable time depth, sometimes connecting contemporary ecosystems with the distant historic, or even prehistoric, past. Many of the younger cohort publishing within this specialty place so much stress on political and economic externalities that they prefer to label it "political ecology." As a sample of this thriving genre, consider Bret Wallach's 1991 collection of essays dealing with the ecological mischief, and occasional conservationist triumph, perpetrated by Americans in northern Maine, the mountains of East Tennessee, the Elk Hills oil field of Kern County, California, the Columbia Basin Project, the Little Missouri National Grassland, the Texas Panhandle, and the sheep country of Wyoming.

CULTURAL GEOGRAPHY

Rounding out this inventory of historically pertinent topics in the repertory of contemporary American geographers, we come to that group conventionally classified as cultural. Cultural themes have their ardent advocates with a fair quota of interesting accomplishments to their credit, but it is also fair to say that these specialties are less well developed than most of the others already discussed as well as being less fully integrated into mainstream practice.

Three publications offer a useful general introduction to the subject. The earliest, but still valuable, Philip L. Wagner and Marvin W. Mikesell's *Readings in Cultural Geography* appeared in 1962. Culture history is one of the five themes emphasized in this carefully edited collection, along with the concept of culture, culture area, cultural landscape, and cultural ecology; and, as it happens, most of the essays treat their material in considerable time depth. A quite successful textbook by Terry G. Jordan and Lester Rowntree (1990) fills in the decades since Wagner and Mikesell and offers innovative chapters on such relatively neglected areas as folk and popular culture, along with nine other major topics. Each of its chapters also cleverly exploits five themes—region, diffusion, ecology, cultural integration, and cultural landscape. If the element of time is seldom neglected in any of these approaches, it is made especially explicit in discussing the cultural landscape. For a specific focus on the American scene, Wilbur Zelinsky's *Cultural Geography of the United States* (1973) is perhaps the best recourse. Offering a different, stimulating approach that excites many of our more venturesome younger practitioners, is Peter Jackson's 1989 review of, and prospectus for, cultural geography, one that joins the subject in an intimate liaison with social geography. The work discussed or proposed therein is mostly politically contentious in character or localized in scale.

If it has taken geographers a long while to appreciate the prominence of religion in human affairs, a small band of them in the United States and elsewhere have taken up the challenge by charting the spatial attributes of various faiths and, in the process, usually recognizing historical trends and forces. Key figures in this country have been David E. Sopher (1967) and James R. Shortridge (1977). They and their followers have been handicapped by severe limitations in American statistical data for all time periods and the difficulties of carrying on field work over extensive areas, as has been true also for such religious historians with a geographic bent as Edwin S. Gaustad (1976). But various geographers, including Donald W. Meinig (1965) and Richard H. Jackson (1978), have been able to elucidate the historical geography of a major section of the American West by tracing the spatial fortunes of a particularly influential denomination, the Mormons.

Anthropologists may regard language as the most central component of culture, something linguists would also be inclined to profess, of course, but with the exception of one notable subtopic, geographers in the United States and other countries have contributed only modestly to scholarship in this area. Most of what they have done concerning the general geography of language has been the simple mapping of languages and dialects and treatments of the relationships between language and political matters. Their greatest initiative has been in toponymy, the study of place-names. And, given the inertial nature of the great majority of such items, and also the clues they present to earlier flows of people and ideas, the historical dimension has entered strongly into their research agenda. For many years the dominant figure in toponymic scholarship was George R. Stewart, a closet geographer masquerading as English professor and novelist, who also made solid contributions to other branches of cultural geography. Within the broader field of the American language, it is impossible to ignore the monumental *Dictionary of American Regional English* being edited by linguist Frederic Cassidy, a document based upon extensive field interviews and an exhaustive documentary search and overflowing with riches for geographer and historian alike.

The geographic analysis of music is still in its infancy and largely confined to the American scene, where George O. Carney and his students have led the way, with special attention to folk and popular music and the historical development thereof. The same observation applies to the belated genesis of a geography of sport and recreation. Once again, a solitary pioneer, John F. Rooney, Jr., along with his protégés, has blazed the trail. The output of this group is frequently historical in character, and in any case it is difficult to conceive of a well-rounded social history of America that does not reckon with the role of sport among its inhabitants.

It is only quite recently that a few cultural geographers have become curious about the intersections between literature, the fine arts, and geography and have made some tentative sorties into what is still largely terra incognita. We can expect progress, and since the authors and artists to be investigated, as, for example, William Faulkner (for whom we already have some useful studies), have necessarily depicted landscapes of the past, the results should be grist for the historian's mill.

We are left with several lacunae on the cultural-geographic front. The most mystifying is the thinness of scholarship on the historical geography of communications in America. It is hard to imagine a more crucial element in the operation of a cultural system. Geographers have just begun to nibble at the ways American foodways have evolved over space and time, and there seems to be a compete blank when we seek material in the geographic cupboard on costume or sexual behavior in this country. A respectable beginning has been registered in charting the temporal, geographic, and cultural dimensions of American cemeteries, most notably by Terry Jordan (1982), but the volume of unfinished business is staggering.

Despite the gaps just noted and the remaining inadequacies in some of the better-cultivated branches of social and cultural geography, the prospects are reasonably bright for further advances into known and unknown territory. Moreover, the existing body of knowledge relating to the American scene is already substantial, so that it behooves the social historian to become more familiar with this literature and its authors than seems to be the case today. The synergistic benefits for both geographer and historian could be noteworthy.

BIBLIOGRAPHY

Allen, James P., and Eugene J. Turner. *We the People: An Atlas of America's Ethnic Diversity* (1988).

Asante, Molefi, and Mark Mattson. *The Historical and Cultural Atlas of African Americans* (1991).

Berry, Brian J. L. *Geography of Market Centers and Retail Distribution* (1967).

Brown, Ralph H. *Historical Geography of the United States* (1948).

Bunge, William. *Fitzgerald: Geography of a Revolution* (1971).

Carney, George O., ed. *The Sounds of People and Places: Readings in the Geography of Music* (1978).

Cassidy, Frederic G. *Dictionary of American Regional English.* Vol. 1, *Introduction and A–C* (1985).

Conzen, Michael P., ed. *The Making of the American Landscape* (1990).

Earle, Carville V. *The Evolution of a Tidewater Settlement System: All Hallow's Parish, Maryland, 1650–1783* (1975).

Florin, John W. *Death in New England: Regional Variations in Mortality* (1971).

Friis, Herman R. *A Series of Population Maps of the Colonies and the United States, 1625–1790* (1968).

Gaile, Gary L., and Cort J. Willmott. *Geography in America* (1989).

Garrett, Wilbur E., ed. *Historical Atlas of the United States* (1988).

Gaustad, Edwin S. *Historical Atlas of Religion in America* (1976).

Gottmann, Jean. *Megalopolis: The Urbanized Northeastern Seaboard of the United States* (1961).

Harris, R. Colebrook. *The Seigneurial System in Early Canada: A Geographical Study* (1966).

———, ed. *Historical Atlas of Canada.* Vol. 3, *From the Beginning to 1800* (1987).

Hägerstrand, Torsten. *Innovation Diffusion as a Spatial Process* (1967).

Harvey, David. *The Condition of Postmodernity: An Enquiry into the Origins of Cultural Change* (1989).

———. "Between Space and Time: Reflections on the Geographical Imagination." *Annals of the Association of American Geographers* 80, no. 3 (1990).

Jackson, Peter. *Maps of Meaning: An Introduction to Cultural Geography* (1989).

Jackson, Richard H., ed. *The Mormon Role in the Settlement of the West* (1978).

Jakle, John A., Stanley Brunn, and Curtis C. Roseman. *Human Spatial Behavior: A Social Geography* (1976).

James, Preston E. *All Possible Worlds: A History of Geographical Ideas* (1972).

Jordan, Terry G. *Texas Graveyards: A Cultural Legacy* (1982).

Jordan, Terry G., and Lester Rowntree. *The Human Mosaic: A Thematic Introduction to Cultural Geography.* 5th ed. (1990).

Leighly, John, ed. *Land and Life: A Selection from the Writings of Carl Ortwin Sauer* (1963).

Lemon, James T. *The Best Poor Man's Country: A Geographical Study of Early Southeastern Pennsylvania* (1972).

Lewis, Peirce F. *New Orleans: The Making of an Urban Landscape* (1976).

Ley, David. *A Social Geography of the City* (1983).

Martis, Kenneth C., and Ruth A. Rowles, eds. *The Historical Atlas of U.S. Congressional Districts, 1789–1983* (1982).

———. *The Historical Atlas of Political Parties in the United States Congress, 1789–1989* (1988).

Meade, Melinda S., ed. *Conceptual and Methodological Issues in Medical Geography* (1980).

Meinig, Donald W. "The Mormon Culture Region: Strategies and Patterns in the Geography of the American West, 1847–1964." *Annals of the Association of American Geographers* 55, no. 2 (1965).

———. *The Shaping of America: A Geographical Perspective on 500 Years of History.* Vol. 1, *Atlantic America, 1492–1800* (1986).

Merrens, Harry Roy. *Colonial North Carolina in the Eighteenth Century: A Study in Historical Geography* (1964).

Mitchell, Robert D. *Commercialism and Frontier: Perspectives on the Early Shenandoah Valley* (1977).

Mitchell, Robert D., and Paul A. Groves. *North America: The Historical Geography of a Changing Continent* (1987).

Olson, Sherry H. *Baltimore: The Building of an American City* (1980).

Ostergren, Robert C. *A Community Transplanted: The Trans-Atlantic Experience of a Swedish Immigrant Settlement in the Upper Middle West, 1835–1915* (1988).

Pred, Allan R. *Urban Growth and City Systems in the United States, 1840–1860* (1980).

Rooney, John F., Jr. *A Geography of American Sport: From Cabin Creek to Anaheim* (1974).

Schnell, George A., and Mark S. Monmonier. *The Study of Population: Elements, Patterns, Processes* (1983).

Shortridge, Barbara G. *Atlas of American Women* (1987).

Shortridge, James R. "A New Regionalization of American Religion." *Journal for the Scientific Study of Religion* 16, no. 2 (1977).

Soja, Edward W. "Taking Los Angeles Apart: Some Fragments of a Critical Human Geography." *Environment and Planning D: Society and Space* 4, no. 3 (1986).

Sopher, David E. *Geography of Religion* (1967).

Steiner, Michael, and Clarence Mondale. *Region and Regionalism in the United States: A Source Book for the Humanities and Social Sciences* (1988).

Stewart, George R. *Names on the Land: A Historical Account of Place-Naming in the United States.* 4th ed. (1982).

Thomas, William L., Jr., ed. *Man's Role in Changing the Face of the Earth* (1955).

Trewartha, Glenn T. "A Case for Population Geography." *Annals of the Association of American Geographers* 43, no. 2 (1953).

Vance, James E., Jr. *The Merchant's World: The Geography of Wholesaling* (1970).

Wallach, Bret. *At Odds with Progress: Americans and Conservation* (1991).

Wagner, Philip L., and Marvin W. Mikesell, eds. *Readings in Cultural Geography* (1962).

Zelinsky, Wilbur. "The Population Geography of the Free Negro in Ante-Bellum America." *Population Studies* 3 (1950).

———. "The Hypothesis of the Mobility Transition." *Geographical Review* 61, no. 2 (1971).

———. *The Cultural Geography of the United States* (1973).

Zelinsky, Wilbur, Janice Monk, and Susan Hanson. "Women and Geography: A Review and Prospectus." *Progress in Human Geography* 6, no. 3 (1982).

SEE ALSO **Immigration**; **Landscapes**; **National Parks and Preservation**; **Regionalism**; and various essays in the sections "**Regionalism and Regional Subcultures**" and "**Space and Place.**"

FEMINIST APPROACHES TO SOCIAL HISTORY

Mari Jo Buhle

GROUPS OF FEMINIST scholars began in the late 1960s to define themselves by a particular choice of subject—women—and by the goals and methods of social history. In the pathbreaking essay "New Approaches to the Study of Women in American History" first published in 1969, Gerda Lerner explained that feminist historians and social historians share a prevailing interest in groups out of power. They also face, she noted, a common set of problems associated with constructing a conceptual framework distinct from the contours of political, diplomatic, and military history—that is, the conventional narratives of "great events" or presidential administrations. Lerner and the feminist scholars who pioneered the field of women's history thus regarded social history as a kindred venture. They joined many other scholars, some influenced by the New Left, to reconsider history "from the bottom up," to give voice to those rendered "inarticulate" in standard texts and to show how ordinary people distant from the sources of formal power actively affected the course of historical development. By 1973, when feminist scholars gathered at the first Berkshire Conference on the History of Women, held at Douglass College (New Brunswick, N.J.), the papers presented affirmed the field's strong link with social history.

THE SOCIAL HISTORY AGENDA

The goal of feminist scholars, Joan Kelly-Gadol stated, is simple: "to restore women to history and to restore our history to women" ("The Social Relation of the Sexes: Methodological Implications of Women's History," *Signs* 1, no. 4 [1976]:809; reprinted in *Women, History, and Theory*). To carry out this work, feminist scholars emphatically rejected "contribution" or "compensatory" history, which rested on the premise that only when women acted publicly did their story merit recording. The study of "woman worthies"—that is, women who had resembled men in their achievements or valor—would not do. Not even the historic woman's rights movement could command the respect of the proud feminist scholars who self-consciously carried the movement's mantle into the late twentieth century. The history of the struggle for woman suffrage fit too comfortably, they reasoned, alongside the usual subjects of politics and power. Rather than making heroes of those few luminaries or groups of women who had left their mark on public affairs, feminist scholars set out to tap the collective experience of "ordinary" women.

The turn away from the public realm placed feminist scholars on course with the new social history and its emphasis on the ostensibly private arenas of the family, household, and community. By introducing the concepts and concerns of the behavioral and social sciences, such as life cycles, child-rearing practices, sexual practices, and geographical mobility, social historians considerably expanded the terrain of historical investigation and ushered in subjects compelling to feminist scholars. Feminists gained insight into new types of sources for documentation and analysis beyond the usual archival troves collected and organized to shed light on matters of public policy. Quantitative or aggregate data analysis and techniques of family reconstitution, among others, yielded precisely the kind of data that feminist scholars were looking for. Social historians opened windows to popular culture, media and mass communication, the built environment, and iconography, among other areas. Feminist scholars thus gained novel methodologies as well as sanction to explore areas rarely studied by traditional historians.

Some of the earliest publications in the new scholarship of women's history gave a foretaste of this tendency. None was more prescient than the oft-cited "The Cult of True Womanhood: 1820–

1860," published in 1966. In this brief essay, Barbara Welter delineated the cardinal tenets of nineteenth-century femininity—piety, purity, submissiveness, and domesticity—as functional adaptations to changes in men's role with the onset of the industrial revolution. Based mainly on a reading of prescriptive literature, such as sermons and periodicals, Welter's argument centered on marriage and family in relation to the emergence of new sex roles among the middle class. Anne Firor Scott's *The Southern Lady: From Pedestal to Politics* (1970) sprang from the author's interest in women's political activism prior to suffrage but issued in a pathbreaking study of female role conflict in the antebellum South. Scott carefully examined the myth of the Southern lady in juxtaposition to the actual experiences of the plantation mistress and, like Welter, she emphasized the private realm of the household. Even William L. O'Neill's *Everyone Was Brave: The Rise and Fall of Feminism in America* (1969) cast the history of the historic woman's movement in social terms. Unlike earlier studies that unproblematically linked women's accession to the ballot to the expansion of democracy in the United States, O'Neill's revision explained the emergence of the crusade for woman's rights as a response to the contraction of female roles with the onset of industrialism. A political history filled with cameo biographies of "notable" women, *Everyone Was Brave* nevertheless dwelt on affairs of the heart and hearth and vividly illustrated the influence of social history within the field.

Despite their own predilections, feminist scholars were not uncritical of the new social history and sought to stake out their own dominion. The majority of social historians, they charged, proved insufficiently attuned to feminists' concerns. The growing number of works on marriages and families, factories and labor unions, churches and religious revivals, prisons, hospitals, schools, and asylums of various kinds could not help but note the presence of women therein. Yet these otherwise useful studies did not advance a systematic analysis of women's experience or provide a conceptual framework suited to feminists' goals.

Feminists observed that the new social historians continued to make men and men's affairs the main component of their analyses. The new studies in family history proved a case in point. Because historians of the family deal primarily with the private rather than public sphere, with daily life rather than watershed events, feminist scholars anticipated a fruitful collaboration. By the early 1970s, however, they had recorded their disappointments. Many family historians, deriving their categories of analysis from sociological studies of family disorganization, dysfunction, or breakdown, discussed parental roles, adolescent rebellion, and problems of the aged without particular reference to gender distinctions. Moreover, feminist scholars noted, family historians often utilized research strategies that tapped evidence restricted to men's activities, as exemplified by the studies of inheritance patterns and transference of property that focused on fathers and sons or of social mobility based on the tax or census records of male household heads. Acknowledging the "rich cross-fertilization" between the two fields, Lerner, for one, refused to subsume women's history under "the larger and already respectable field of social history" ("Placing Women in History," p. 8; reprinted in *The Majority Finds Its Past,* p. 150).

The main objection to the trajectory of the new social history, according to Carroll Smith-Rosenberg, concerned its relative indifference to "one of the most basic forms of human interaction—that between the sexes" ("The New Woman and the New History," p. 189). Feminist scholars who charted the field of women's history but identified themselves primarily as social historians thus placed at the top of their agenda the study of the social relationships defined by sex, not only relationships between men and women but also among women themselves. In defining their enterprise as a history of social relationships, feminist scholars placed themselves squarely within the realm of social history.

Feminist scholars set out to define a distinctive conceptual framework for this study of social relationships. The main problems were familiar to most other social historians: redefining and reevaluating the major periods of American history, formulating the basic categories of social analysis, and testing theories of causation or social change.

Lerner's "The Lady and the Mill Girl: Changes in the Status of Women in the Age of Jackson" (reprinted in *The Majority Finds Its Past*) illustrated these early attempts to construct a conceptual framework. Publishing in 1969, Lerner challenged the customary interpretation of the Age of Jackson as an era marked by extension of democratic rights and progress in general. If viewed from women's perspective, the period was, she contended, the nadir of American history. Lerner came to this conclusion not simply by noting the absence of women from the ranks of new voters but by focusing on the industrial revolution and its impact on the relationships between the sexes and among women.

Lerner advanced an argument that would become basic to many later historical works. As production moved outside the household, she explained, the workplaces of men and women diverged, with the new capitalist order assigning primary value to the waged or salaried work of men. In this new schema, women became the singular guardians of home and family but in consequence lost their productive role and the status and authority it had previously conferred upon them. This narrative applied, Lerner pointed out, to the rising middle class of Jacksonian society. There was, however, an equally compelling story to tell about the situation of working-class women. The industrial revolution, while creating the "lady," pushed poor women into the new textile mills of Lowell, Massachusetts, and elsewhere. The "mill girl" thus came to embody the antithesis of middle-class domesticity and, consequently, the new norm of "respectable" femininity. Where women did work for wages, in other words, they were locked into extremely low-paying, low-status jobs. The Age of Jackson thus reordered the relationship between the sexes and formed new barriers between groups of women.

In the wake of Lerner's essay, feminist scholars reassessed the meaning of major events and periods of American history in terms of women's status. Several asked whether the American Revolution marked a watershed in the history of women. Some examined the impact of the Civil War and the world wars on women's status, while still others argued over whether the Great Depression or World War II denoted a more significant period of change in the status of twentieth-century women. In mounting numbers of publications, feminist scholars had "unsettled," as Kelly-Gadol put it, the customary appraisal of historical periods. Ultimately, feminist scholars believed, a wholly new vision of history would emerge.

As feminist scholars began to demonstrate the vitality of sex as a category of historical analysis, they surpassed other social historians in grappling with the theoretical subtext of their own enterprise: the grounds for considering women a discrete group. Although most scholars conceded that all women throughout American history shared a status secondary to men's, they nevertheless rejected the concept of "oppression" as a foundation for historical analysis. The patent difference between the situations of the plantation mistress and female slave undermined all notions of common oppression. As Lerner's essay showed, a period of history or a major event also held divergent meanings for women of different classes of the same race. It was clear in these instances that individuals or groups of women may claim greater interest with (or even share power with) men of their class, race, or ethnicity than with other women.

Early feminist scholars thus rejected analogies based on either the sociological concept of "caste" or the Marxist notion of "class." Women constitute a category in themselves, Lerner insisted. Kelly added, "Women have to be defined as women. We are the social opposite, not of a class, a caste, or of a majority, since we are a majority, but of a sex: men" ("The Social Relation of the Sexes: Methodological Implications of Women's History." *Signs* 1, no. 4 [1976]:814; reprinted in *Women, History, and Theory*). Although scholars like Lerner and Kelly insisted that sex carry the same weight in historical analysis as race or class, they nevertheless maintained that it was the intersection of sex and other social categories that stood at the forefront of feminist endeavors. In short, Lerner remarked, "the subject 'Women' is too vast and diffuse to serve as a valid point of departure" ("New Approaches to the Study of Women in American History," *Journal of Social History* 3, no. 1 [1969]:pp. 59–60; reprinted in *The Majority Finds Its Past*). Such a project would require a sturdy bridge between feminist scholarship and other areas of American social history.

During the formative period of feminist scholarship, the new labor history, itself a subfield of social history, provided a complementary model of analysis. The new labor historians, in the wake of E. P. Thompson's *The Making of the English Working Class* (1963), had subordinated the conventional study of labor unions and political parties to workers and work. Most important, they explored Thompson's understanding of class as an experience shaped by productive relations but "handled in cultural terms: embodied in traditions, value-systems, ideas, and institutional forms." This insight allowed American labor historians to chart the particular and often unique processes of class formation within one community, workplace, industry, or group informed by race or ethnic ties.

Although feminist scholars disallowed any simple analogy beteen class and sex, they nevertheless recognized in the new labor history the rudiments of a felicitous mode of analysis. Labor historians had begun to define class not as a determinant group but as a social relationship. They had taken up the study of the processes by which class relations change, how these processes condition an awareness of class relations, and how people in particular situations act upon this understanding. Feminist scholars similarly approached the study of the relationships between the sexes, rejecting biological determinism as labor historians did economic determinism. They likewise addressed theories of social change and causation, similarly focusing to a large degree on modes of production. The decline of the household as a principal site of labor played as central a role in early feminist scholarship as it did in labor history. Many of the early feminist scholars—Linda Gordon, Maurine Greenwald, Alice Kessler-Harris, and Gerda Lerner, among others—had prior interest in the history of class relationships. Most maintained collegial ties with labor historians, while a growing number made the study of women and work their primary field.

By the early 1970s, then, feminist scholars had introduced sex as a fundamental category of historical analysis. They argued that the relation of the sexes, like those of class and race, were socially rather than naturally or divinely constructed and constituted the heart of their scholarly inquiry. The import of this development showed itself in many ways. To give one example, a standard anthology of readings in the new social history, *The American Family in Social-Historical Perspective,* which appeared first in 1973, gathered three essays on women and the family under the subheading "Women: Roles and Relationships." The second edition, published in 1978, retained the rubric but expanded the number of selections to reflect the growth of scholarship in this area. By 1983 the third edition organized these readings under a new heading, one more suited to the feminist project—"Relations Between the Sexes."

OLD SCHOLARSHIP AND SOCIAL HISTORY

Although feminist scholars allied themselves methodologically and conceptually with the new social history, including the new labor history, they also drew on their own historiographical traditions. A century-long study of women had generated a large number of books and articles, the overwhelming majority written by women and men outside the historical profession. The woman suffrage movement in particular had inspired scores of participants to give witness to its historical importance. A sizable portion of the books in this field concerned women's efforts to expand their sphere and to play a larger part in American political life. Biographies of prominent women abounded. Amid these often quaint but nevertheless valuable publications was a scattering of social histories influenced as much by the old social history as the campaign for woman's rights.

With the rise of Progressivism at the turn of the century, historians and kindred scholars expanded their range of research to those subjects now covered under social history, and a handful of skillful writers contributed works centered on women's experience. Alice Morse Earle (1851–1911), author of nearly twenty books and more than thirty articles, wrote extensively on childhood and domestic life. Earle's *Home Life in Colonial Days* (1899) provided rich details on household production, its tools and processes. Lucy Maynard Salmon (1853–1927), who taught at Vassar College, produced a pioneering statistical study, *Domestic Service* (1897). Helen Sumner Woodbury (1876–1933) fashioned the first full-length narrative in women's labor history, "History of Women in Industry in the United States," published by the U.S. Bureau of Labor in 1910. These mainly descriptive and documentary texts proved invaluable to the generation of social historians coming to the fore in the late 1960s.

More instrumental were the works that flowed directly from the first wave of social history. In 1922 Arthur Meier Schlesinger lamented "the pall of silence" over the subject of women and called upon his colleagues to make up for past neglect. From reading standard history textbooks, he wrote, one might conclude "that one-half our population have been negligible factors in our country's history," and went on to predict that this situation would soon change (*New Viewpoints in American History* [1922], p. 126). During the 1920s and 1930s the first books fashioned self-consciously as social history of women appeared. Mary Sumner Benson foreshadowed Welter in her *Women in Eighteenth-Century America* (1935), which utilized religious and periodical literature as well as fiction to discuss ideals of womanhood. Elisabeth Anthony Dexter's *Colonial Women of Affairs* (1924), a broad survey of women in the professions, presaged Lerner in documenting the decline in women's status as the nineteenth century opened. Julia Cherry Spruill produced a richly detailed study of regional society, *Women's Life and Work in the Southern Colonies* (1938), which covered such topics as wardrobe and toilet, schooling, courtship and domestic discord, and criminality among white women. Schlesinger himself predicted that future students of American social history would turn frequently to Spruill's important work.

The group of social historians of women who practiced in the decades between the world wars—when the proportion of women earning higher degrees peaked before it declined precipitously—had a direct influence on their successors. They had not only expanded the terrain of documentation of daily life begun by their predecessors at the turn of the century but had introduced broader conceptual and interpretive concerns. Dexter, for example, had challenged the simplistic notion that women gained in status and rights as American democracy inevitably expanded. She argued, to the contrary, that women as a group lost ground after the American Revolution and offered a preliminary explanation of the processes causing this decline in status.

Of this generation of historians of women, no one proved more compelling to later feminist scholars than Mary Ritter Beard (1876–1958). Beard's own work on women spanned nearly fifty years and took its special form during the first decades of the century. She had taken a strong stand against those historians who had emphasized the limitations placed on women by men's rule of public life and who envisioned women's history primarily as a century-long struggle to gain entry into the political arena. Women's history was not "a history of repeated injuries and usurpations on the part of man toward woman, having in direct object the establishment of an absolute tyranny over her," as the Declaration of Sentiments adopted at Seneca Falls in 1848 claimed (Mari Jo Buhle and Paul Buhle, eds., *The Concise History of Woman Suffrage,* p. 94). Beard's "long view" of history, advanced in *Woman as Force in History* (1946), revealed that women stood at the very center of civilization.

Although Beard affirmed Schlesinger's wisdom, she sought to move beyond his interest in women's contribution to the progress of the American nation. Beard agreed with Schlesinger that women had played important roles in the civic affairs of their communities far in advance of their accession to the vote, an idea that Anne Firor Scott later adapted to her studies of Southern women and voluntary organizations. Beard's own *Woman's Work in Municipalities* (1915) aptly illustrated this contention. Beard, however, pushed beyond the boundaries of the public sphere to contend that within the private arena of home and family, women held the key to human survival. Beard showed that women historically wielded significant power as care-givers and nurturers and argued, moreover, that their affairs equaled and perhaps even outweighed those of men on the scale of historical significance.

Woman as Force in History, reissued in a paperbound edition in 1962, appeared just in time for the rebirth of feminist scholarship at the end of the 1960s. Beard had questioned the standards that historians conventionally employed in designating the important subjects of inquiry. She argued, moreover, that women could rightfully claim principal responsibility for whatever civility humanity had achieved. In highlighting the importance of the affairs of everyday life—that is, the private sphere relegated mainly to women—Beard not only fortified the agenda of social history but brought it back into the realm of politics. "If this phase of woman's force in history is to be capitalized as against barbaric propensities and activities," she wrote in the shadow of World War II, "then an understanding of women's past history . . . must be regarded as indispensable to the maintenance and promotion of civilization in the present age" (*Woman as Force in History,* pp. 331–332).

The feminist scholars who found immediate inspiration in Beard's work took away two major ideas. The affairs of private life do not constitute the details of arcana but instead directly determine all historical developments. Translated into the words of contemporary feminism, Beard's message read simply, "The personal is political." Second, the pursuit of this history was no mere professional exercise or intellectual hobby but vital to human survival. *Woman as Force in History* thus predicted both the premises and spirit that would inform feminist scholarship as it emerged at the close of the 1960s.

CONTEMPORARY FEMINISM AND ITS INFLUENCE

The feminist scholars who shaped the field in the 1970s pursued social history, one might say, for political purposes. Linda Gordon recalled in 1978 that at first she and her peers thought of themselves as "propagandists for the women's liberation movement" ("What Should Women's Historians Do," p. 129). Polemics soon fell out of fashion, however.

Gordon advised historians to take their questions from the feminist movement but not their answers. This strategy helped to produce ground-breaking studies on subjects central to the women's liberation movement, Gordon's own works on the history of birth control and domestic violence being prime examples. Histories of housework, childbirth, sexual preference or identity, professional advancement, and educational attainment—issues of central concern to contemporary women—appeared within the decade.

Despite the commitment to social history, politics remained an underlying theme in feminist scholarship. As Gordon explained, the study of social change demanded a political context. "Since social change only happens through power conflict," she reasoned, "it cannot be apprehended without attention to politics. A social history that excludes politics risks becoming ahistorical" ("What Should Women's Historians Do," p. 133).

The dictum that "the personal is political" encouraged feminist scholars to search for connections between the private and public spheres, the family and civil society. Anthropologists led the way toward initial interpretations. Michelle Zimbalist Rosaldo (in "Women, Culture, and Society") noted a universal sexual asymmetry in human societies but pointed out that relationship between the roles and spheres of men and women varies considerably across cultures. She further reasoned that this structural relationship determined to a large degree the relative status of each sex. When the differential between the domestic and public spheres is sharp, women rank low in status and value. To raise their position, women had two choices, Rosaldo surmised: they could enter men's sphere or they could transform their own sphere into a public arena.

The historical scholarship produced in the 1970s followed Rosaldo's trajectory. One large sector analyzed the movement of women into the public sphere, not primarily to record their "contribution" to the commonweal or celebrate their "progress," as had earlier historians, but to pinpoint the structural determinants of change in women's status. A second contingent focused on shifts in the private sphere. The emerging conceptual framework took shape, then, as the relationship between the "private" and "public" spheres or arenas of social life.

Although historians studied a variety of means by which women "entered" the public sphere—education, profession, civil rights, among others—the largest number focused on labor. Part of the inspiration came from liberal feminism. As represented in Betty Friedan's *The Feminine Mystique* (1963), liberal feminists located the source of contemporary women's discontent in their relegation to domesticity and sought to document historically the means by which women gained access to work and especially professional attainment outside the home. Marxist feminism also helped to set this course. A sizable number of pioneering scholars of the early 1970s traced their political roots to the New Left as well as to the women's liberation movement of the preceding decade, and they were heavily influenced by social theorists who put the importance of labor in human activity in the foreground.

Contemporary scholars drew from a long tradition dating to the mid nineteenth century, when feminists in western Europe and in the United States began to extol woman's right to labor as fundamental to their freedom. Socialists such as August Bebel, in *Die Frau und der Sozialismus* (1883), argued that as women left the domestic sphere for wage labor, they would join the proletariat in its fight against capitalism and achieve through financial independence their emancipation from male tyranny. These ideas continued to resonate for both liberal and Marxist feminists and provoked scholars to test them through new historical research. The European historians Louise Tilly and Joan Wallach Scott directly challenged this thesis in their highly influential *Women, Work, and Family* (1978). They found that wage-earning women in the nineteenth century rarely earned enough to claim independence and instead found themselves increasingly subject to masculine authority. Leslie Woodcock Tentler's *Wage-earning Women: Industrial Work and Family Life in the United States, 1900–1930* (1979) echoed this argument, adapted to American conditions. Tentler found that the low wages women earned in tedious jobs under male supervision reinforced their low status and actually encouraged women to seek in marriage and domesticity an alternative source of authority. Thomas Dublin, in *Women at Work: The Transformation of Work and Community in Lowell, Massachusetts, 1826–1860* (1979), in contrast, argued that daughters gained a modicum of freedom from paternal authority when they filled the ranks of industrial workers in the early textile mills. Despite the polarity of evaluations here, the significance of wage labor to women's status remained firm.

The main conceptual innovation lay, however, in the scholarship linking women's labor-market advances (or setbacks) to their continuing maintenance of the private sphere, the home or household. In 1969 Margaret Benston argued that women's domestic work—housework, consumer functions, supervision of boarders, child care, sexual and emotional services to spouses—shape feminine identity and affect market relations, and, second, that these activities are not insignificant but central to the overall system of capitalist production. Scholars in several disciplines elaborated Benston's thesis into a forceful argument affirming the importance of women's role in "social production," or what Marxists termed "the reproduction of labor power" ("The Political Economy of Women's Liberation").

Feminist scholars thus forced the connections between the ostensibly "private" and "public" dimensions of women's lives. Their researches into the history of women and work included conventional areas of collective actions, strikes, and unions as well as novel domestic concerns of family, reproduction, and sex-role stereotypes. This perspective expanded the story of important events in American labor history. For example, the Lawrence, Massachusetts, textile strike of 1912, a landmark in the history of labor protest, gained a new context in the wake of feminist research. Ardis Cameron, in *The Laboring Women of Lawrence* (1991), skillfully reframed the questions concerning trade unionism to include the affairs of women outside the labor force. By using manuscript census data to reconstitute neighborhoods, and court newspaper records to identify protest leaders, Cameron uncovered a network of women that spanned household and factory to play the instrumental role in organizing and sustaining the strike. An interpretation of collective action and trade unionism thus depended, in Cameron's model, on the historians' observance of the details of life in the private sphere.

The historians who focused on women's position vis-à-vis the public sphere, including those who produced scores of studies on women and labor, helped to formulate the central—soon to emerge at its most problematical—concept of the early scholarship in the field, "woman's culture." Although both Welter and Lerner had noted that a unique ideal of womanhood developed during the early nineteenth century, neither historian had attached positive significance to this development. Before one decade had passed, however, scholars had begun to revise the unique-ideal interpretation. For the most part, they retained the industrial revolution as the watershed event, the force behind the epochal separation of "private" from "public," of men's sphere from women's. But rather than focusing on the ramifications of this change for women's standing in the public sphere, these scholars found in a greatly enhanced definition of domesticity their most compelling subject.

Nancy F. Cott's *The Bonds of Womanhood: "Woman's Sphere" in New England, 1780–1835* (1977) is the signal monograph in this genre. Cott opened with a chapter analyzing the economic activity that set middle-class men in public careers and their wives in domesticity. She quickly moved on to assess its social ramifications. Woman's sphere constituted, she argued, a subculture among women. Cott found in the emerging "cult of domesticity" the source of women's collective identity as a group defined by subordination to men as well as shared experience. She thus inscribed her study with Sarah M. Grimké's salutation "Thine in the bonds of womanhood" to underscore the dual meaning of nineteenth-century womanhood. In Cott's words, the ideology of woman's sphere "bound women together even as it bound them down" (p. 1) and served, therefore, as a precondition for feminism. Cott explained that the "doctrine of woman's sphere opened to women [reserved for them] the avenues of domestic influence, religious morality, and child nurture. It articulated a social power based on their special female qualities" (p. 200). From this position, women moved into reform activity, such as the antislavery movement and ultimately the movement for woman's rights.

In *The Bonds of Womanhood,* Cott followed Lerner and Welter to delineate the restrictions placed on middle-class women with the rise of industrialism but broke step by acknowledging fruitful aspects of this development. Equally important, she assigned to women themselves an important role in fashioning the new ideology of womanhood. Kathryn Kish Sklar's *Catharine Beecher: A Study in American Domesticity* (1973) had provided a vivid illustration of female agency in the biography of one of its principal architects.

The concept of woman's culture appeared in its fullest delineation in Carroll Smith-Rosenberg's "The Female World of Love and Ritual: Relations Between Women in Nineteenth-Century America," which, following its publication in *Signs* in 1975, became the most frequently cited article in the field. Through a sizable collection of letters and diaries of middle-class white women, Smith-Rosenberg discovered that women of the eighteenth and nineteenth centuries habitually enjoyed intimate friendships which in terms of emotional intensity often exceeded their attachments to men. Through these friendships, women built for themselves supportive networks that were in turn institutionalized through the rituals marking the important events in women's lives from birth through death. "Within such a world of emotional richness and complexity," Smith-Rosenberg wrote, "devotion to and love of other women became a plausible and socially accepted form of human interaction."

Although Smith-Rosenberg used the phrase "female world" rather than "woman's culture" to denote the consequence of these relationships, she, too, located their origins in the rigid gender-segregation of American society at the time—that is, in "separate spheres." Like Cott and Sklar, Smith-Rosenberg found positive values in the social structure and worldview that fostered this division. Nineteenth-century women enjoyed "a wide latitude of emotions and sexual feelings," perhaps greater freedom to satisfy their needs than their descendants in the twentieth century ("The Female World of Love and Ritual," pp. 9, 29).

The notion of woman's sphere or woman's culture supplied the basic framework for the bulk of feminist scholarship produced in the 1970s. It established a structural mode of analysis, locating sex roles and gender definitions on the shifting planes of private and public spheres. But rather than evaluate these changes directly in terms of their implications for women's status, as earlier historians had done, scholars in the 1970s discussed their experiential meaning or, as Smith-Rosenberg put it, "the emotional realities of daily routine." As Cott's and Sklar's works also attested, feminist scholars sought to uncover "gender consciousness," or how women themselves interpreted and acted upon the structure of woman's sphere.

Feminist scholars thus reaffirmed the necessary connection between social history and political history in their endeavor. They explicitly distanced themselves from those historians who in the *Annales* tradition of French social history adhered to empiricist modes, collecting massive amounts of "objective" data to the neglect of its "subjective" meaning. As Smith-Rosenberg insisted, statistical data cannot "answer questions about the experiential meaning of autonomy" ("The New Woman and the New History," p. 191). Cott and Elizabeth H. Pleck similarly attested that all questions engaging feminist scholars "involve women's consciousness; that is, they ask not only how gender defines women's treatment, occupations, and so on, but also how women themselves perceive the personal, social, and political meanings of being female" ("Introduction," in Cott and Pleck, eds. *A Heritage of Her Own,* 20). As in the new labor history, where the study of working-class consciousness culminated in collective action, the new scholarship in women's history developed a discernible sense of a goal.

The importance of subjectivity underscored by the research on woman's culture also shaped new studies on sexual behavior and sexual identity. While Smith-Rosenberg's "The Female World" revealed an intimacy and love between nineteenth-century women that rivaled and perhaps surpassed their relationships with men, other contributions documented the persistence of these "homosocial" (Smith-Rosenberg's term) bonds into the twentieth century. Historians documented tender and romantic attachments between, for example, settlement-house residents, trade unionists, college teachers and administrators, suffragists, athletes, as well as government officials. Whether to use "female friendship" or "lesbian relationship" as a descriptive terminology became an item of disagreement. Some historians downplayed the importance of genital contact as the determining factor in lesbianism. Others insisted that it was the sexual behavior as well as the self-identity of women that determined the meaning of lesbianism. For most scholars, it was subjectivity rather than behavior alone that governed their analyses.

The import of this orientation showed itself clearly in the shifting feminist interpretations of the American West. Scholars mined a rich vein in this area, spinning off originally from Frederick Jackson Turner's "frontier thesis." Many of the earliest writers, noting the early granting of woman suffrage in western states, reasoned that the frontier allowed women greater opportunities than found in the developed areas of the East and Midwest. The frontier served, to paraphrase Turner, as a "safety valve" for their grievances against a restricted sphere. Other historians appeared to follow Mary Beard's line of argument, attributing whatever stability western areas achieved to women's "civilizing" influences. Dee Brown's *The Gentle Tamers: Women of the Old Wild West* (1958) best illustrated this interpretation. In 1975 Johnny Faragher and Christine Stansell established the new line of analysis. Faragher and Stansell agreed with the previous historians who documented an expanded realm of opportunity for women as they migrated west. By necessity, the spheres of men and women broke down, they recognized, on the rugged terrain of the trail. But rather than enjoying a greater equality with men, Faragher and Stansell argued, "most women did not see the experience in this way." Rather, women on the Overland Trail "experienced the breakdown of the sexual division of labor as a dissolution of their own autonomous 'sphere.'" ("Women and Their Families on the Overland Trail," p. 151). Like Smith-Rosenberg, Faragher and Stansell used manuscript letters of pioneering women to their female friends back home and found manifold expressions of resentment toward their husbands and longing for the lost female world. Feminist scholars like Faragher, Stansell, and Smith-Rosenberg sought to interpret both objective and subjective realities.

The emphasis on subjectivity or consciousness implied a shift in paradigm. Whereas woman's sphere connoted a man-made ideology, a by-product of industrialism or modernization, woman's culture suggested that women enjoy a certain amount of autonomy in shaping social relationships and in defining the meaning of gender. This interpretive development complemented Beard's teaching, focusing feminist inquiry clearly on women as subjects of history.

By the end of the decade, scholars began to assess the heuristic value of this paradigm. In a symposium on politics and culture in women's history published in *Feminist Studies* in 1980, Ellen Carol DuBois charged that the studies of woman's culture went too far in isolating women from the structures of male domination and in romanticizing their situation. Although woman's culture derived ultimately from women's exclusion from the public sphere, the concept nevertheless dispelled the oppressive qualities of this experience. Contrary to earlier interpretations, DuBois suggested that domesticity now connoted a set of positive qualities or behaviors amounting to a nurturant, loving, mutually supportive network of domestic women. She feared that the growing attention to woman's culture would eventually deracinate feminist inquiry of its political character. "There is a very sneaky kind of antifeminism here," she contended, "[one] that criticizes feminism in the name of the common woman, and political history in the name of social history" ("Politics and Culture in Women's History," p. 33). The other historians participating in the forum disagreed, Lerner contending that "there is no point to counterposing [woman's culture] to 'feminism'" ("Politics and Culture in Women's History," p. 53).

The concept of woman's culture, in affirming both the importance of the private sphere and woman's agency, actually enhanced political history, giving it a clear social or cultural dimension. Estelle Freedman picked up on Michelle Zimbalist Rosaldo's discussion of two strategies for overcoming gender asymmetry—entering the public (masculine) realm or creating a separate public female sphere—and noted that at certain historical periods, the latter might be "the only viable political strategy for women." Freedman thus used the concept of woman's culture, including its delineation of friendships and female networks, rituals, and relationships, as a basis to discuss women's collective efforts to gain leverage in civil society. "A separatist political strategy . . . emerged from the middle-class women's culture of the nineteenth century," suggesting, Freedman wrote, that "women's culture can be integral to feminist politics" ("Separatism as Strategy," p. 513).

Freedman spoke for dozens of feminist scholars pursuing this lead. By analyzing the values informed by nineteenth-century domesticity, historians gained new insights into the means by which women acted to create networks of female power and to gain access to the channels of political influence. The Woman's Christian Temperance Union (WCTU) served as the most vivid example. Feminist scholars discarded the prevailing "social control" motif of temperance historiography to study the emergence of the WCTU as a massive, powerful, and "separatist" women's institution. Its famous "Home Protection" campaign fit comfortably into the interpretive paradigm: women rallied the values associated with the domestic sphere to impose their will on the civil society. The WCTU mobilized more women than any other single campaign in the nineteenth century and brought them into a broad spectrum of activities, ranging from temperance agitation to prison reform, social purity, and woman suffrage. The connection between culture and politics appeared explicit. Its long-term president Frances E. Willard explained, "[Women] must first show power, for power is always respected whether it comes in the form of a cyclone or a dewdrop" (*President's Address to the Annual Meeting of the National Woman's Christian Temperance Union, 1892* [n.d.], p. 6). This perspective informed several new studies of the WCTU, including Ruth Bordin's *Woman and Temperance: The Quest for Power and Liberty, 1873–1900* (1981).

Scores of other studies appeared, charting the trajectory from domesticity to public activism. From antebellum benevolent activities, including moral reform and antislavery, to the plethora of women's organizations in the Gilded Age—women's colleges, women's clubs, female missionary societies, and social settlements and women's hospitals—the paradigm of woman's culture / politics prevailed. Several scholars utilized the concept to discuss women outside the middle class. Studies of women in the Knights of Labor, agrarian radicalism, socialism, and trade unionism followed an analogous line of argument, mooring political activism not in the middle-class cult of domesticity but nevertheless in the particular set of social relationships of the working-class household. The malleable concept of woman's culture appeared in studies of women's dramatic role in bread riots, rent strikes, and other forms of neighborhood activity, including prostitution. The notion also served to explain how women on occasion cooperated across the barriers of class and, to a more limited extent, of race.

The woman's culture–woman's politics trajectory in historical scholarship complemented an important shift of contemporary feminism in the 1970s. As Alice Echols suggested in *Daring to Be Bad: Radical Feminism in America, 1967–1975* (1989), cultural feminism, which by 1975 had become the dominant tendency in the women's liberation movement, emphasized the differences between the sexes and attributed to all women a distinctive set of values and virtues associated with their unique reproductive capacities. On this common ground, cultural feminists reasoned, women might yet realize a universal sisterhood. Although few historians ascribed to the biologically essentialist tenets of cultural feminism and instead built their analytic model on the historical constructions of woman's sphere / woman's culture, most had nevertheless made gender their principal category of analysis and sought ways to organize the history of all women into a single comprehensive conceptual framework. "By gendering the Victorian landscape and evaluating historical patterns and processes in women's own terms," Nancy A. Hewitt noted, "the historians of bourgeois womanhood have established concepts and categories that now shape the analysis of all groups of American women" ("Beyond the Search for Sisterhood," p. 301).

BEYOND SISTERHOOD

By the early 1980s, historians who had deliberately stood outside the mainstream of the contemporary women's liberation movement began to advance a new case for the importance of difference. In 1983 Bonnie Thornton Dill, in reviewing the past decade, noted that the maxim "Sisterhood is powerful!" enlisted only a limited population of American women. "Black, Hispanic, Native American, and Asian American women of all classes, as well as many working-class women, have not readily identified themselves as sisters of the white middle-class women who have been in the forefront of the movement." Dill observed that black women themselves enjoy a long history of a sisterhood that took institutional form in, for example, churches and women's clubs as well as strong female kinship ties in extended families. Nevertheless, she argued, black women have not used sisterhood as "the anvil to forge our political identities." Race, not gender, galvanized African American women. Dill went on to point out that sisterhood that brought white women together in the woman suffrage movement was not so inclusive as to preclude active discrimination against other women on the basis of race. She recommended "a more pluralistic approach that recognizes and accepts the objective differences between women." In Dill's lexicon, "difference" referred not simply to disparities based on gender but to the manifold contradictions that separate women from one another ("Race, Class, and Gender," pp. 131, 134, 146).

Historians of African American women did not altogether abandon the woman's culture paradigm but instead grounded it in the specific social relations of the black experience. Deborah Gray White's *Ar'n't I a Woman?* (1985) detailed a specific form of gender relationships shaped by the legacy of African matrifocal kinship patterns and the sexual division of labor in plantation slavery. In the slave community, women stood at the center of the family, and the mother-child bond transcended that of any other relationship, including the husband-wife relationship. Jacqueline Jones also emphasized the sex-segregated nature of slave labor and observed that black women created their own value system and worldview distinct from that of black men and white women. As Jones underscored, black women "nonetheless maintained a racial self-consciousness and loyalty to their kin (reinforced by white hostility) that precluded any interracial bonds of womanhood" (*Labor of Love, Labor of Sorrow,* p. 6).

By the mid 1980s, gender no longer stood as the principal social category of analysis. Nor did the relationships between the sexes (in Kelly's phrase) serve to guide scholars in their historical explorations. Even the theoretical search for an adequate conceptual framework to place women in history fell into disrepute. DuBois and Vicki L. Ruiz summed up the situation:

> Most of the early work in U.S. women's history paid little attention to race and assumed instead a universal women's experience, defined in contrast to "man's" history. While a stark focus on the difference between the male and female past helped to legitimize women's history, the past it explored usually was only that of middle-class white women. In this uniracial model, the universal man of American history was replaced with the universal woman.

DuBois and Ruiz advocated a biracial or multicultural approach, one that "shatters the notion of a universal sisterhood" and allows historians "to explore the dynamics through which women have oppressed other women" ("Introduction," in DuBois and Ruiz, eds., *Unequal Sisters,* pp. xi, xii).

After two decades of scholarly practice, feminist scholars took stock of their basic premises and concluded that too much emphasis had been placed on gender as a unifying concept. This sensibility showed itself most dramatically in October 1988 at a gathering of sixty-three leading teachers and writers. Sponsored by the National Endowment for the Humanities and the Johnson Foundation, the conference focused primarily on graduate training in women's history in the United States but raised for general discussion the most pressing theoretical matter facing everyone in the field. "Without a doubt," organizers Gerda Lerner and Kathryn Kish Sklar reported, the workshop that "generated the most concern and energy" addressed questions of difference among women. The participants sought to reconceptualize the meaning of difference by focusing on social categories of analysis beyond gender, such as class, region, race, and ethnicity. They rejected "cultural pluralism" as a suitable approach, deeming it merely descriptive or possibly celebrative of diversity and insufficiently attentive to the inequality of power that governs the relationships among groups of women.

Although these feminist scholars reached a consensus on the multiracial or multiethnic goal of their forthcoming endeavors, they could not derive a conceptual model to replace the popular woman's sphere / culture paradigm. Many in fact rejected on principle all "universalizing" frameworks and advocated instead "multiple narratives." Of particular concern were biracial versus multiracial assumptions. Scholars asked whether white-black relations should predominate, given the historic importance of slavery and its repercussions, or should all ethnic and racial groups figure equally in historical narrative. The conference participants could not resolve this matter but implied that race as a conceptual category of difference superseded all others. Many of the scholars echoed Linda Gordon, who had earlier advised feminist historians to frame their research to highlight the significance of race. "It will no longer do," Lerner later resolved, "to design a research project or to teach without taking the differences among women into account" (Gerda Lerner, "Reconceptualizing Differences Among Women," p. 107).

As Lerner and Sklar noted, other constructions of difference among women received far less attention from conference participants than race or ethnicity. Some scholars noted in passing the problems of framing the historical experience of lesbians. Others pointed out that anti-Semitism deserved more attention, while yet others referred to age or ageism as an important designation of difference among women. Perhaps most surprising, given the legacy of research on wage-earning women, questions concerning the importance of class differences roused affirmation but relatively little deliberation.

The conference on graduate training in American women's history produced a set of sixteen recommendations for action by individual faculty and departments, the first two of which read:

> 1. Reshape our syllabi and courses to include difference among women as a core concept.
>
> 2. Create courses on feminist theories and methodologies that make explicit the differences among women as well as the differences, structural and historical, between women and men. (Gerda Lerner and Kathryn Kish Sklar, *Graduate Training in U.S. Women's History,* p. 47)

No specific set of guidelines or program accompanied these resolutions, but the intent was clear.

Although feminist scholars had early on recognized no common thread binding the history of all women, the emphasis on "difference" emerging in their second decade of practice was new. Lerner had, for example, carefully delineated the varying constructions of womanhood formed during the Jacksonian era, her lady-and-the-mill-girl prototype providing a vivid illustration of class disparities. Most historians had nevertheless sought to illuminate incidences of "sisterhood," events or causes that allowed women to cross class barriers and to unite for common purposes. Studies of settlement-house workers or the Women's Trade Union League, for example, that carefully noted class differences, brought into bold relief the points of agreement between working- and middle-class women. Feminist scholars coming to the fore at the end of the 1980s emphasized instead conflict among women. Christine Stansell's *City of Women: Sex and Class in New York, 1789–1860* (1986) foreshadowed this development. Stansell not only contrasted middle-class domesticity with the situation of poor women but stressed the oppositional quality of the experiences of these two groups. Middle-class women acted on their own conception of womanhood, she alleged, to restrict the behavior of their working-class contemporaries. Other historians, such as Mary P. Ryan and Nancy A. Hewitt, identified a similar theme in the relationship between gender, reform activity, and class politics in the antebellum period.

Recent works of feminist scholars tend to interrelate gender and class or racial formations. Lori D. Ginzberg studied a middle-class ideology that merged femininity and morality and thereby supported women's social activism during the antebellum period. She acknowledged the contributions of her graduate adviser, Nancy F. Cott, in delineating the connections between the concept of woman's sphere, the emergence of gender consciousness, and the participation of middle-class white women in an expanding realm of social activity. Ginzberg nevertheless drew out the significance of this history in class terms. She focused on the ideological transformation of benevolence as succeeding generations of reformers adapted their activities "to an increasingly class-stratified and class-conscious society—indeed, how they refashioned the ideology of benevolence itself from an analysis of gender to one of class." Ginzberg intended, in sum, to reevaluate "changes in the ideology and practice of a specifically female benevolent activism in light of the essentially class nature of benevolence" (*Women and the Work of Benevolence,* pp. 5, 7).

Following the lead of historians of African American women, feminist scholars like Stansell and Ginzberg now call into question Joan Kelly's earlier statement that gender is "a category as fundamental to our analysis of the social order as other classifications, such as class and race" ("The Social Relation of the Sexes," p. 816). Ginzberg concluded her important study by identifying a major conceptual problem in current scholarship, the hesitancy of feminist historians "to sacrifice the assumption that gender forms women's primary self-identity" (*Women and the Work of Benevolence,* p. 220). A pioneer in the field, Alice Kessler-Harris asked a complementary question: "Does gender constitute the single most important level at which men and women self-identify in a given historical period or at a particular phase in these lives?" ("Gender Ideology in Historical Reconstruction," p. 33). Although both historians affirmed their faith in gender as an important category of analysis, neither vouched for its predominance and both suggested instead that other social categories may surpass gender.

Outside the realm of social history, women's historians face yet another challenge to basic assumptions. Scholars shaping a new subfield sometimes called "gender history" have developed a practice derived in part from post-structuralists such as Jacques Derrida and Michel Foucault and focus on gender in language or discourse. In their presentations, the actual experience of women stands as unknowable, forever beyond the reconstructive reach of historians. All that remains is the representation of gender in discourse, however broadly defined. This type of analysis discounts the culture-and-politics paradigm of earlier scholarship, not for its inability to encompass cultural diversity, but for its philosophical shortcomings. Joan W. Scott has defined the principles of this new departure: "Experience is not seen as the objective circumstances that condition identity; identity is not an objectively determined sense of self defined by needs and interests. Politics is not the collective coming to consciousness of similarly situated individual subjects" (*Gender and the Politics of History,* p. 5). Historians influenced by post-structuralism, such as Scott and Carroll Smith-Rosenberg, have thus severed the connection between women's history and social history.

Despite these conceptual fragmentations, feminist scholarship had, at its quarter-century mark, reshaped the writing of American social history in many ways, foremost perhaps in college textbooks, to a lesser degree in specialized monographs in fields such as labor, ethnic, and racial history. Simply put, the overview of American life cannot be written in the 1990s as it was before the 1960s. Outstanding women from Harriet Tubman to Gloria Steinem find their way into political studies; the woman suffrage and feminist movements become a part of social protest; and working women figure prominently both in eras of labor discontent and periods of economic growth.

But feminist scholarship cannot be said to have approached its initial goal of transforming the standard narrative. The expectation or hopes of drastically changing the focus upon subject, periods, and underlying premises could not be realized. In the large world of American social history, the fundamental challenges of feminist scholarship seem lost. For example, feminists had argued that the history of modern economic development cannot be fully understood unless the relationship between wage labor and the family economy be at the center of analysis. While many labor historians now use gender to differentiate among various types of workers, few have departed from the conventional framework that puts the factory and the paycheck in the foreground. In the larger sense, gender has been "included" without unsettling the foundations of established practices.

Feminist scholars have contributed mightily, however, to the internal dialogue about the meaning of history. From the onset, they called into question the conventional measures of significance. They have persistently interrogated their own practice, most prominently along the lines of race and class. Perhaps more than any other sector of historians, feminists have contributed to a "decentering" of historical process by which the major narratives have been constructed. First, they joined other social historians in shifting the emphasis from the elites to ordinary people, from the "great events" of political history to the experiences of the anonymous masses. Next, they called into question the very concept of historical "progress" or "development," raising the possibility that for large numbers of people—perhaps a majority of the world's population—these terms had no real meaning. They rejected the notion of a universalizing framework, not least for their own study of women and gender. Feminist scholars, in sum, made the theory of history as important as the practice of history.

BIBLIOGRAPHY

Collections of Related Essays

Aptheker, Bettina. *Woman's Legacy: Essays on Race, Sex, and Class in American History* (1982).

Carroll, Berenice, ed. *Liberating Women's History: Theoretical and Critical Essays* (1976).

Cott, Nancy F., and Elizabeth H. Pleck, eds. *A Heritage of Her Own: Toward a New Social History of American Women* (1979).

DuBois, Ellen Carol, and Vicki Ruiz, eds. *Unequal Sisters: A Multi-Cultural Reader in U.S. Women's History* (1990).

Eisenstein, Zillah R., ed. *Capitalist Patriarchy and the Case for Socialist Feminism* (1978).

Hartman, Mary S., and Lois Banner, eds. *Clio's Consciousness Raised: New Perspectives on the History of Women* (1974).

Kelly, Joan. *Women, History, and Theory: The Essays of Joan Kelly* (1984).

Lerner, Gerda. *The Majority Finds Its Past: Placing Women in History* (1979).

Nicholson, Linda J., ed. *Feminism/Postmodernism* (1989).

Essays on Historiography

Bock, Gisela. "Women's History and Gender History: Aspects of an International Debate." *Gender and History* 1, no. 1 (1989).

Buhle, Mari Jo. "Gender and Labor History." In *Perspectives on American Labor History: The Problems of Synthesis,* edited by J. Carroll Moody and Alice Kessler-Harris (1989).

DuBois, Ellen Carol et al. "Politics and Culture in Women's History." *Feminist Studies* 6, no. 1 (1980).

DuBois, Ellen Carol, Gail Paradise Kelly, Elizabeth Lapovsky Kennedy, Carolyn W. Korsmeyer, and Lillian S. Robinson. *Feminist Scholarship: Kindling in the Groves of Academe* (1985).

Fox-Genovese, Elizabeth. "Placing Women's History in History." *New Left Review* 133 (1982).

Gordon, Linda. "What Should Women's Historians Do: Politics, Social Theory, and Women's History." *Marxist Perspectives* 1, no. 3 (1978).

———. "What's New in Women's History." In *Feminist Studies–Critical Studies,* edited by Teresa de Lauretis (1986).

Jensen, Joan M., and Darlis A. Miller. "The Gentle Tamers Revisited: New Approaches to the History of Women in the American West." *Pacific Historical Review* 49, no. 2 (1980).

Norton, Mary Beth. "American History." *Signs* 5, no. 2 (1979).

Sicherman, Barbara, "American History: Review Essay." *Signs* 1, no. 2 (1975).

Tilly, Louise. "Women's History and Family History: Fruitful Collaboration or Missed Connection?" *Journal of Family History* 12, nos. 1–3 (1987).

Walkowitz, Judith, Myra Jehlen, and Bell Chevigny. "Patrolling the Borders: Feminist Historiography and the New Historicism." *Radical History Review* 43 (1989).

Conceptual Contributions

Benston, Margaret. "The Political Economy of Women's Liberation." *Monthly Review* 21, no. 4 (1969).

Butler, Judith. *Gender Trouble: Feminism and the Subversion of Identity* (1989).

Christian, Barbara. "The Race for Theory." *Feminist Studies* 14, no. 1 (1988).

Davis, Angela. *Women, Race, and Class* (1981).

Dill, Bonnie Thornton. "Race, Class, and Gender: Prospects for an All-inclusive Sisterhood." *Feminist Studies* 9, no. 1 (1983).

Fox-Genovese, Elizabeth. "The Personal Is Not Political Enough." *Marxist Perspectives* 2, no. 4 (1979–1980).

Freedman, Estelle. "Separatism as Strategy: Female Institution Building and American Feminism, 1870–1930." *Feminist Studies* 5, no. 3 (1979).

Gordon, Ann D., Mari Jo Buhle, and Nancy E. Schrom [Dye]. "Women in American Society: An Historical Contribution." *Radical America* 5, no. 4 (1971).

Hewitt, Nancy. "Beyond the Search for Sisterhood: American Women's History in the 1980s." *Social History* 10 (1985).

Higginbotham, Evelyn Brooks. "Beyond the Sound of Silence: Afro-American Women in History." *Gender and History* 1, no. 1 (1989).

Kerber, Linda K. "Separate Spheres, Female Worlds, Woman's Place: The Rhetoric of Women's History." *Journal of American History* 75, no. 1 (June 1988).

Kessler-Harris, Alice. "Gender Ideology in Historical Reconstruction: A Case Study from the 1930s." *Gender and History* 1, no. 1 (1989).

Lerner, Gerda. "Reconceptualizing Differences Among Women." *Journal of Women's History* 1, no. 3 (1990).

Poovey, Mary. "Feminism and Deconstruction." *Feminist Studies* 14, no. 1 (1988).

Rosaldo, Michelle Zimbalist. "Woman, Culture, and Society: A Theoretical Overview." In *Woman, Culture, and Society,* edited by Michelle Zimbalist Rosaldo and Louise Lamphere (1974).

Scott, Joan W. "On Language, Gender, and Working-Class History," and responses by Bryan D. Palmer, Christine Stansell, and Anson Rabinbach. *International Labor and Working-Class History* 32 (1987).

———. *Gender and the Politics of History* (1988).

Smith-Rosenberg, Carroll. "The Female World of Love and Ritual: Relations Between Women in Nineteenth-Century America." *Signs* 1, no. 1 (1975).

———. "The New Woman and the New History." *Feminist Studies* 3, no. 1/2 (1975).

Welter, Barbara. "The Cult of True Womanhood: 1820–1860." *American Quarterly* 18, no. 2 (1966).

Other Works of Women's History Discussed in Text

Beard, Mary Ritter. *Woman as Force in History* (1946).

Bordin, Ruth. *Woman and Temperance: The Quest for Power and Liberty, 1873–1900* (1981).

Buhle, Mari Jo, and Paul Buhle, eds. *The Concise History of Woman Suffrage* (1978).

Cott, Nancy F. *The Bonds of Womanhood: "Woman's Sphere" in New England, 1780–1835* (1977).

Dexter, Elisabeth Anthony. *Colonial Women of Affairs* (1924).

Dublin, Thomas. *Women at Work: The Transformation of Work and Community in Lowell, Massachusetts, 1826–1860* (1979).

Echols, Alice. *Daring to Be Bad: Radical Feminism in America, 1967–1975* (1989).

Faragher, Johnny, and Christine Stansell. "Women and Their Families on the Overland Trail to California and Oregon, 1842–1867." *Feminist Studies* 2, no. 2/3 (1975).

Ginzberg, Lori. *Women and the Work of Benevolence: Morality, Politics, and Class in the Nineteenth-Century United States* (1990).

Jones, Jacqueline. *Labor of Love, Labor of Sorrow: Black Women, Work, and the Family from Slavery to the Present* (1985).

O'Neill, William L. *Everyone Was Brave: The Rise and Fall of Feminism in America* (1969).

Scott, Anne Firor. *The Southern Lady: From Pedestal to Politics* (1970).

Scott, Joan, and Louise Tilly. *Women, Work, and Family* (1978).

Sklar, Kathryn Kish. *Catharine Beecher: A Study in American Domesticity* (1973).

Stansell, Christine. *City of Women: Sex and Class in New York, 1789–1860* (1986).

Tentler, Leslie Woodcock. *Wage-earning Women: Industrial Work and Family Life in the United States, 1900–1930* (1979).

White, Deborah Gray. *Ar'n't I a Woman?* (1985).

SEE ALSO **Gender; Gender Roles and Relations; Social Reform Movements; Reproduction and Parenthood; Women and Work; Women's Organizations.**

RACIAL IDEOLOGY

Eugene Y. Lowe, Jr.

THE SEARCH FOR A COMMON PAST

THE INTERPRETATION OF the past is an expression of the values, tensions, and concerns of the time in which the interpretation is undertaken. For this reason, understanding the history of historical interpretation can be as revealing as getting at the substance of the matter manifestly under consideration. For the most part, the writing of American history has reflected a unitive tendency to overlook difference in favor of promoting a shared vision of the nation's destiny. During the twentieth century, the frontier thesis, first articulated by Frederick Jackson Turner, in his essay "The Significance of the Frontier in American History" (1893), was an important impetus in the search for an overarching view of American history. Turner's influential vision of the past implied a view of American history that supported a quest for a common identity.

More recently, social history has focused on different spheres of experience, including local and community history, the history of women, and the history of minority groups. However, throughout most of American history, the process of historical reconstruction has been dominated by ideologies associated with Manifest Destiny, imperialism, and the cultural superiority of the white, Anglo-Saxon, Protestant heritage. These unexamined beliefs constituted a conventional wisdom that shaped conscience and consciousness for generations of Americans. The recent changes in the practice of social historiography reflect a decisive shift in consciousness about the meaning of the diversities that have from the beginning constituted the American experience.

From the earliest years of the nation's life, there has been a countervailing notion to the dominant ideology—that out of many backgrounds and cultures America makes a new people, freed from the oppressions and divisiveness of the past. The nineteenth-century French statesman Alexis de Tocqueville, whose *Democracy in America* (1835) describes his observations on American society, was not the first to remark on the unreconciled tensions in the American ethos between the assertion of dominance and the embrace of diversity. Though institutionally separated, religion and politics mutually reinforced the conviction that God's providential order manifested itself more fully in the American destiny than at any other point or place in human history. Indeed, America was the new Israel, and Americans the chosen people.

The power and the vitality of these conceptions buttressed American culture well into the twentieth century. The conventional wisdom was that those who were part of the extraordinary immigration that helped double the population between 1880 and 1920 would be assimilated in succeeding generations under the rubric of the "melting pot." Differences of background, culture, and language would be overcome in the creation of a new people. While all Americans were not the same to begin with, there was a common identity to which they could aspire. The result of this assimilation would not be the renunciation of distinctive histories; in fact, memories and traditions would continue to fortify ethnic and national subcommunities. In *Protestant, Catholic, Jew* (1960), a classic review of the religious situation in mid-twentieth-century America, the sociologist Will Herberg observed that religious differences were increasingly less important than a shared experience and commitment to "an American way of life."

The election of a Roman Catholic, John F. Kennedy, to the presidency in 1960 signaled, for many observers, the confirmation of the assimilationist ethos. However, the sixties were also the decade in which other, previously submerged, forces in the culture achieved visibility. These forces countered the melting-pot theory by compelling the nation to recognize how persistently its understanding of progress had excluded people of color, particularly black Americans who, in the century following the Civil War, had been subjected to a caste system based on white superiority. An important consequence of this development was the search for a past that was distinctively focused on the needs, hopes, and aspirations of the black community. This history derived its energy and focus from its recognition of difference and its embrace of pluralism and was intended to be critical of conventional and established historical interpretations. The acknowledgment of the need to recover a distinctive African American past led to both a reexamination of the ways in which the past had been conceived and a search for sources and data to illuminate a sector that had been obscured or neglected in the effort to chronicle a common past.

THE AFRICAN AMERICAN EXPERIENCE BEFORE 1896

American ambivalence about slavery was clearly illustrated in the United States Constitution. The divisiveness of the slavery issue for the delegates to the Constitutional Convention in Philadelphia in 1789 was manifested in what became known as the Three-Fifths Compromise, which provided that, for purposes of representation and taxation, each slave would be counted as three-fifths of a person in calculating the populations of the states. The acknowledgment that slaves were, for these pragmatic purposes, fractionally comparable to whites was a compromise with immense symbolic resonance for the century and a half ahead. From the standpoint of the white majority, the admission that a slave was enough of a person to count, but not enough to consider an equal, was an equivocation impossible to sustain without a significant measure of emotional and moral compromise. For blacks, this *tertium quid* became the source of the "twoness," which W. E. B. Du Bois referred to in *The Souls of Black Folk* (1903) as the ontological condition of the black person in the United States.

The growth of the nation after 1789 and the careful attention to maintaining the balance of free and slave states perpetuated and exacerbated this tension. The principal drafter of the Declaration of Independence, Thomas Jefferson, struggled futilely in both his political and his personal life to reconcile the Declaration's assertion that all men are created equal with the imperatives and mores of southern culture regarding slavery. Political tensions were reinforced by the power of another pervasive social dynamic: the problem for professed Christians of holding in a condition of involuntary servitude human beings who were Christians created in the image of the same God who had created whites. On political and religious grounds, the United States was mired in a dilemma that would not be settled legally until Reconstruction, and which to this day has eluded decisive cultural or political resolution.

This fundamental ambivalence, reflecting the experience of a people who had rallied energies and resources to overthrow the bondage of British rule and who at the same time had to rationalize on political and religious grounds the existence of masters and slaves, affected the development of American history from its beginnings. While not all blacks were slaves, the terms defining the existence of slaves affected all blacks. The invention of the cotton gin, which made slavery a profitable contributor to the southern economy, precipitated a divisive moral crisis in the young republic. Southern apologists for slavery, recognizing the tension between the bondage upon which a way of life was based and the claims of the Bible that all human beings were creatures created in the image of God, began during the Second Great Awakening (1800–1850) to construct an elaborate justification for slavery as a mechanism to convert the heathen black to Christianity. Some went so far as to suggest that God had ordained the institution of slavery as a means to acculturate and convert Africans to Christianity and civilization. The plantation was to be understood not only as a social or an economic organism but also, and even most fundamentally, as a religious system.

On the other hand, some voices in both the South and the North began to understand the constitutional tolerance of slavery as an egregious and sinful compact with Satan, an institution that undermined the moral foundation of the new nation. Christianity and natural rights philosophy were in accord in both their complementary assertions of the equality of all persons before God and their belief in the necessity of confession and conversion for all.

Between 1800 and 1850, decisive battle lines were drawn between two fundamentally antagonistic views about the significance of slavery and the destiny of the nation. One view sought to accommodate the institution of slavery to the emerging cultural imperatives of the southern way of life; the other sought its abolition as a step along the way in the American pilgrimage toward freedom.

Neither of these movements was free of the racism that for centuries had sanctioned the view that blacks were an inferior race within the human species. This view was reflected, for example, in the motivations of the founders of the American Colonization Society, who protested chattel slavery but also believed that blacks would never be successfully assimilated in American society and therefore sought ways to return blacks to Africa. (Their efforts contributed to the founding of Liberia in 1822.)

THE QUEST FOR AN AFRICAN AMERICAN PAST

The patterns of historical interpretation that emerged toward the end of the nineteenth century reflected in different measure these early views about race, freedom, and the American destiny. The conviction, given arithmetic precision in the three-fifths compromise, that black slaves counted less than others shaped the consciousness of the nation and, consequently, the ways in which the history of the nation was charted and understood.

The 1896 decision of the United States Supreme Court in *Plessy* v. *Ferguson* endorsed the principle that the Fourteenth Amendment's guarantee of equal protection under the law was secured if blacks and whites were accorded "separate but equal" provision of resources and opportunity by states and the federal government. This decision, which codified the post-Reconstruction settlement of race relations in the South, symbolized the resistance of the dominant culture to the inclusion of blacks in mainstream American society and that society's determination to provide blacks with the opportunity to form separate communities and institutions. A latter-day version of the ethos of the Colonization Society, this notion sanctioned the development of a subculture that would enable blacks to take some responsibility for determining their destiny in a segregated society.

THE RISE OF AFRICAN AMERICAN HISTORIOGRAPHY

John Hope Franklin has suggested that the two-volume work *A History of the Negro Race in America from 1619 to 1880: Negroes as Slaves, as Soldiers, and as Citizens,* published in 1882 by George Washington Williams, marks the beginning of the study of African American history in the United States. Williams's work sought to place the experience, the sufferings, and the achievements of black slaves in the context of a biblical ethnology and an African past. In the first volume, Williams detailed the history of the American Negro through the revolutionary period; in the second, he focused on slavery, the antebellum period, and the Civil War. Having served as a soldier in the Union army, Williams was particularly interested in identifying the contributions of blacks during the American Revolution and the Civil War to the achievement of goals from which blacks were then constrained from benefiting.

While Williams served as a catalyst, others—including most notably W. E. B. Du Bois (1868–1963) and Booker T. Washington (1856–1915)—served as focal points not only for scholarly endeavors but also for activism directed toward racial uplift. Du Bois, a graduate of Fisk University who grew up in Great Barrington, Massachusetts, became the first black to earn a Ph.D. at Harvard University. Author of several important works about slavery and the current status of the Negro, Du Bois was a founder of the National Association for the Advancement of Colored People serving also for many years as the editor of the *Crisis.* Like Du Bois, the educator Booker T. Washington was an activist. In his autobiography, *Up from Slavery* (1901), Washington used the story of his own emancipation, education, and successful career to inspire southern blacks who had been denied opportunity for education and self-improvement. This theme was carried forward in *The Story of the Negro: The Rise of the Race from Slavery* (1909).

Within the black community, Du Bois and Washington came to represent two opposite modes of comprehending and adjusting to the American experience. Intellectually rebellious and critical, Du Bois insisted that the exercise of political responsibility, the use of the right to vote, and the pursuit of education for the most able members of the race—the "talented tenth" had to be at the forefront of the agenda for racial reform. Washington, on the other hand, deemphasized politics in favor of the importance of cultivating sound habits and character so that blacks, having prepared themselves educationally and culturally for the responsibility, would be seen by whites as meriting civil rights. More accommodationist in orientation, Washington, a personal symbol of the idea of progress, became the most influential black in the United States during the first decade of the twentieth century and a principal source of patronage during the Republican administrations of Theodore Roosevelt and William Howard Taft.

The tension between Du Bois and Washington—arguably more notable for its political than for its intellectual significance—framed a set of questions that would resonate in succeeding generations—questions about the role of the Negro in American life, the nature of "equality," and the relationship between intellectual and racial progress. In the context of a society prepared to sanction both the pursuit of equality and the separation of the races, blacks sought to find and to make a history within boundaries established by the dominant culture of the land. In a period marked by incipient professionalism in the historical guilds and in the colleges and universities that supported the work of historians of white culture, the search for a distinctive African American past was carried on outside the academy to furnish a memory for a people on the brink of losing their past. The goal of these early efforts was both practical and intellectual; the object was not the pursuit of knowledge for its own sake, but the pursuit of the past for the sake of affecting the present and the future of blacks, even if separated from the mainstream American culture. In this generation, the study of the African American past was joined to the responsibility of creating an African American future, and this activist legacy persisted well into the twentieth century.

HISTORIOGRAPHY AS INSPIRATION (1915–1940)

Du Bois, who lived until 1963, was influential during what John Hope Franklin calls the "second generation" of African American scholarship, spanning roughly the twenty-five-year period beginning in 1915, during which Carter G. Woodson (1875–1950) provided intellectual leadership as the head of the Association for the Study of Negro Life and History. Established in 1915, this academic group was dedicated to the idea that the scientific study of history would promote race progress by enhancing the self-esteem of blacks and eliminating the prejudice of white Americans. In the same year Du Bois published *The Negro,* in which he initiated an exploration of the impact of the African past, seeking to analyze the persistence of distinctive African cultural traits in order to better understand the black experience on its own terms and not in relation to dominant cultural patterns.

The intensification and institutionalization of the legalized segregation against which black scholars had to struggle were reflected in a number of ways: neither Du Bois nor Woodson had the opportunity to teach in any of the white colleges or universities in the land, nor would the nascent American Historical Association endorse the study of the Negro as a legitimate field of inquiry. From the standpoint of the academy and the guilds in which both these men were trained, the study of the black race, on whatever terms, was like the race itself, relegated to the margin in a fashion consistent with the pervasive belief that blacks were essentially inferior and not easily assimilated into American culture.

Consistent with the dominant convictions of the culture was the portrayal of blacks in the pioneering motion picture *The Birth of a Nation* (1915), based on a novel of Reconstruction by Thomas Dixon, which pandered to the worst prejudices of white Americans about the moral and intellectual incapacities of blacks. Within the mainline academy and the historical guild, the most important interpretation of slavery and of southern history was developed by the gifted historian Ulrich Bonnell Phillips (1877–1934). A native of Georgia, Phillips studied at the University of Georgia and completed his Ph.D. at Columbia in 1902. His most important works, *American Negro Slavery* (1918) and *Life and Labor in the Old South* (1929), promoted a view of slavery as a social and economic system that civilized the heathen black and supported an agricultural civilization. Unabashedly, Phillips, who taught at Wisconsin, Michigan, Tulane, and Yale, suggested that the Negro was essentially "a child," who "must be guided and governed, and often guarded against himself, by a sympathetic hand." With a perspective reminiscent of the apologists for the plantation mission, Phillips took as a starting point for his scholarship the essential inferiority of the Negro to the Anglo-Saxon. Du Bois published one of the few dissenting reviews of the otherwise highly acclaimed *American Negro Slavery,* which, Du Bois observed, completely ignored sources that set forth the slave perspective and which constructed a benign view of plantation life in which "subhuman" slaves and "superhuman" masters coexisted in a necessary institutional equilibrium. Although Phillips responded later in his career to some of Du Bois's contentions, the Georgia native was fundamentally unaware of most of the work being undertaken by Du Bois, Woodson, and others about the history of slavery and of African Americans. The worlds and the views of established and African American scholarship were—consistent with the ethos of the time—separate and, in the view of the dominant academic culture, unequal.

Black scholars found an outlet for their rebuttals to this racist scholarship in the *Journal of Negro History,* founded by Woodson in 1916. For nearly fifty years, the *Journal* served as the principal forum for students of African American history. Like Woodson's *The Negro in Our History* (1927) and his study of the black church, it highlights the extent to which the ideology of separation informed academic reflection during this period. Woodson, whose efforts were endorsed by the editor of the *American Historical Review* and initially supported by a number of white philanthropies, sought over time to diminish his dependence on white sources of support, first cultivating and then appealing for support to a network based in the black community. The Harlem Renaissance and the rise of the black nationalist Marcus Garvey in the 1920s, with their emphasis on the theme of black cultural renewal, provided what seemed a promising backdrop for such a strategy. At the same time, Woodson's efforts were in line with those of progressive historians such as Charles and Mary Beard and Carl Becker, who viewed history as a discipline to help address contemporary problems and who looked to the social sciences as cognate disciplines for historical interpretation. Like his predecessors, Woodson insisted that the study of Negro history was not only a fundamental necessity for the development of the black community but also an essential corrective to mainline historians' habit of overlooking or caricaturing the role of blacks in American history. For Woodson, history was both disinterested and objective. By personal inclination, he was an independent practitioner; further, the cultural mores of his time made it virtually impossible for him to collaborate with his peers in the historians' guild. He continued to believe with them that the truth—the historical truth—gleaned and analyzed would overcome prejudice and lift the spirits of those whose history he worked to recover and present.

BLACK HISTORY AS PART OF A BROADER WORLD VIEW

The seeds for the work of the next generation of chroniclers of African American history were sown during the Great Depression and World War II. A number of scholars outside Woodson's circle began to reflect and consolidate the gains of his effort and the efforts of others in light of the country's experience of economic hardship and international conflict. Du Bois, who had begun to be influenced by Marxist thought, published *Black Reconstruction* in 1935, arguing that the constructive role played by blacks in the South following the Civil War had not been adequately noted. Du Bois's socialist leanings made for controversial historical interpretation in some specific areas; however, he gave expression to long-held ideas about human equality that would soon be shared by a number of influential historians—black and white—in the postwar period.

During the Depression years, interest in socialism and in Marxist thought had increased in light of the failure of the economy to provide security for the nation. Within the academy and among a significant number of intellectuals, a newly critical temperament made ideas that would not have gotten a hearing in the previous decade seem more plausible. The wartime experience in Europe and the struggle against a power that preached Aryan superiority also had an impact on American thinking. ("Separate but equal" was, however, still the guiding norm; American troops fought in segregated units throughout World War II.)

During this period, the academy, particularly at some elite institutions, became more open to progressive views about race. The work of two white historians, C. Vann Woodward (b. 1908) and Vernon Lane Wharton (1907–1964), both of whom received doctorates from the University of North Carolina during the 1930s, was influential in establishing a different perspective about race and the black experience. Woodward, later Sterling Professor of History at Yale, wrote Du Bois in 1938 in appreciation for his "admirable book, *Black Reconstruction.*"

The increasing interest and commitment of white scholars were characteristic of this third period in the development of an African American historiographical tradition. In 1937 the Carnegie Corporation of New York commissioned the Swedish social scientist Gunnar Myrdal to undertake a systematic study about the condition of Negro life in the United States. Published in 1944, *An American Dilemma* became the standard reference on race relations in the social science canon in the United States. This work, which, like so many earlier studies about race, combined poignant analysis and moral outrage, brought into clearer focus the consequences of racism and segregation for black Americans. *An American Dilemma* had, in the view of the black writer Ralph Ellison, another impact: its dramatic portrayal of blacks as victims rather than creators of history, a problem that would preoccupy many black and white historians a generation later when the civil rights movement achieved its most important victories.

During the 1940s, two distinguished black historians who continue to influence black historiography, began their academic careers. The first, Benjamin Quarles (b. 1904), published a biography of the black abolitionist Frederick Douglass. Influenced deeply by Douglass's views, Quarles based his work on his belief, at odds with the prevailing Beardian emphasis on economic factors, in the moral dynamic of human history. Like Woodson, Quarles understood black history as a tool to strengthen interracial understanding and to restore a sense of the centrality of black experience within the American story. Both the Douglass biography and Quarles's subsequent work were grounded in an expectation that the United States would overcome its racist and segregationist past.

The second major black historian of this period, John Hope Franklin (b. 1915), has exercised profound influence since the 1947 publication of *From Slavery to Freedom: A History of Negro Americans*. Franklin, who has defined himself from the beginning as a historian of the South, has insisted throughout his career—as has Quarles—that the study of black history must be integrated into the broader study of the American past. After completing his undergraduate work at Fisk University in Memphis, Franklin completed his Ph.D. at Harvard, where Arthur M. Schlesinger was an important mentor. In contrast to Quarles, who has tended to seek and identify in his subjects a spark of sensibility that yearns for the elimination of racism, Franklin has focused on the complexity of black and white interaction in American history. Unlike some of his predecessors, Franklin has resisted the practice of using black history as a tool for developing racial pride. Not only, he has argued, must scholars overcome the tendency to understand black history in a vacuum; they must also mitigate the tendency to search only for heroes and heroines. The history of blacks has unfolded and taken shape as part of a more encompassing community of human experience; as in the wider community in which there is failure and imperfection, the black community has its share of human weakness and frustration. Like so much in the human situation, history represents an admixture of the good, the intriguing, and the problematic. This recognition, along with an insistence on integration and interactivity, has been a hallmark of Franklin's historiographical pattern.

Franklin's disavowal of the notion of separated histories indirectly prefigured the arguments that would be considered by the United States Supreme Court, which in the case of *Brown* v. *Board of Education of Topeka* (1954) unanimously overturned *Plessy* v. *Ferguson*. Declaring that "separate but equal" is inherently unequal and that racial segregation in public schools is inconsistent with the Fourteenth Amendment's guarantee of equal protection under the law, the Court embarked on a new course, setting the stage for a generation of judicial activism in constitutional interpretation.

This rebellion against the racial status quo could be said to have had a number of antecedents, including the work of Du Bois, who continued to exercise significant influence during this generation. Although Herbert Aptheker's *American Negro Slave Revolts* had been published in 1943 and a number of scholars were questioning Ulrich Bonnell Phillips's racist interpretation of plantation life, the 1940s did not produce a definitive response to his synthesis. Aptheker (b. 1915), whose forays into communism and social radicalism had been directly stimulated by his recognition of the reality of racial injustice, prepared the way for a reconsideration of Phillips's work by asserting that there had been periodic episodes of protest and rebellion against slavery in which blacks like Nat Turner had organized to claim their freedom at enormous personal risk.

As a junior historian, Kenneth Stampp (b. 1912) had been provoked by Aptheker's interpretation of slave resistance. Impatient with the tradition of southern scholarship on slavery, Stampp began research on *The Peculiar Institution* in 1948, the year the southern Dixiecrats bolted the Democratic presidential nominating convention because of the civil rights plank insisted upon by President Harry S. Truman. Published in 1956, two years after the *Brown* decision and in the midst of the Montgomery bus boycott led by the Reverend Martin Luther King, Jr., Stampp's study was greeted with relief and enthusiasm in a social and intellectual climate prepared to consider the brutality of slavery and to appreciate the humanity of the slaves themselves.

The historiographical discussions of the 1950s focused on the problem of slavery against a backdrop of anxiety about how and why segregation had come to be embraced as the law of the land. C. Vann Woodward's *The Strange Career of Jim Crow*

(1955) represented a self-conscious effort to use history to provide leverage and hope as the nation confronted the necessity of desegregating its schools. Stampp's *Peculiar Institution* was the first effort by a white historian since Phillips to probe the world of slaves. Phillips had sought to address the economic and environmental constraints that influenced the development of a social system; Stampp, on the other hand, focused on how the experience of the Negro after the Civil War was connected to the experience of slavery. Stampp's view of slavery incorporated conflict and complexity in the relations of masters and slaves; his own sense of the immorality of the system pervades the narrative.

Stampp's assumption of continuity of experience across racial groups was manifested in his assertion that for purposes of his analysis, he would assume "that innately Negroes are, after all, only white men with black skins, nothing more, nothing less." This observation, which has been widely discussed, poignantly epitomizes a dilemma that would emerge with some starkness in the decades ahead: the tension between egalitarian convictions and cultural differences. The case for "separate but equal" had been based in part on the assumption that Negroes were different; the case for integration had, therefore, to adopt a strategy that repudiated every trace of racist ideology.

The persistence of the effort to understand the black experience as part of a more encompassing consideration of oppression was also represented in Stanley Elkins's *Slavery: A Problem in American Institutional and Intellectual Life* (1959). Unlike Stampp, who undertook extensive research in primary source materials about slavery, Elkins presented an analysis that compared the slave experience in the United States with the experiences of Latin American slaves and of Jews in Nazi concentration camps. Stampp had been impressed with the immorality of the system and the patterns of resistance that emerged with some regularity; Elkins was stimulated to reflect on the stability of the slave system and the ways in which it secured the acquiescence of its victims. Elkins mused about the compensatory psychological adjustment that allowed the slaves to internalize an acceptance of or an accommodation to their situation—the development of the childlike, carefree, and self-deprecating characteristics Elkins associated with the character Sambo. In a broad sense, Elkins's work was an effort to understand how closed, totalitarian systems rationalize and perpetuate themselves, how paternalism and repression can coexist within the same social system, and how nineteenth-century American culture mediated conflict about moral and political ideals.

Elkins's book appeared just before the sixties erupted. Its arguments implicitly sustained a theme that a number of scholars—beginning with Myrdal in *An American Dilemma*—had stressed: the victimization of the Negro in American life. This emphasis, which emerged in the work of a number of distinguished scholars, was, in part, a function of the concerns that had led to the *Brown* decision, namely that segregation had deprived blacks of equal opportunity. It also reflected a corrective bias among white historians, for whom slavery and the African-American experience had not, prior to the 1950s, been central concerns.

The scholarly discussion during the 1960s reflected the experience of the time, which called into question not only the adequacy of the model of victimization, but also the implication that blacks and whites were, except for skin color, essentially the same. The ideology of integration became subject to question at the same time that a political consensus emerged to support the civil rights movement. One barometer of the situation was a nagging sense that neither the Stampp nor the Elkins model of slavery seemed to elucidate fully what people believed about slavery. Although Stampp had succeeded in developing a view of slavery that incorporated the perspective of slaves, his interpretation did not provide, as Elkins's had, an explanation for the viability of the system. Reviewing Elkins's work, many took exception to his provocative formulation comparing the experience of slavery to the Holocaust, an analogy that, they believed, was not supported by enough of the kinds of evidence that both Stampp and Phillips had assembled. What seemed lacking to many historians was an interpretation of slavery that incorporated both a sophisticated appreciation for the dynamics of oppression and a careful analysis of the range of data available from sources providing testimony from whites and blacks alike. Historians confronted the decade of the 1960s hoping that the cause of social justice and the search for a new consensus about the past could be joined.

The successes of the black-led civil rights movement—in which many academics participated—stimulated an appreciation of the dynamics of power relations and of the leverage that can be mustered from a position of weakness. The strategy of nonviolent confrontation, which Martin Luther

King, Jr., so actively promoted, provided ample contemporary evidence for a more complicated understanding of social and political power than was suggested by an analysis that stressed either rebelliousness or accommodation. Furthermore, the commitment of the black power movement, which emerged with more prominence in the mid 1960s, to an enhanced sense of black cultural sovereignty reinforced the growing tendency to view blacks as having the ability to determine for themselves both their situation and their destinies.

The emergence of the civil rights movement prompted interest in black activism in and around the Civil War period. The work of August Meier (b. 1923) in black intellectual and social history, notably *Negro Thought in America: 1880–1915* (1963), represented an important refocusing of a problem that had generally been cast in terms of black victimization. Meier analyzed meticulously the basis of the argument between Washington and Du Bois during the post-Reconstruction period. The roles of black and white abolitionists were also explored by James McPherson (b. 1936) in *The Struggle for Equality* (1964). In *Rehearsal for Reconstruction* (1964), Willie Lee Rose (b. 1927) described the roles and aspirations of freed blacks and their contribution to the development of the sharecropping system that developed after the Civil War.

As had been the case during the New Deal and the World War II years, the events that took place during the 1960s—a decade marked by an explosion of social consciousness—provided a backdrop for a change in the conventional thinking about history. The pent-up anger of residents of the inner cities of Los Angeles, Newark, and Detroit erupted into riot, a dramatic reminder of the failure of progress during a period of heightened expectations. President Lyndon B. Johnson appointed a commission, led by Governor Otto Kerner of Illinois, to investigate the causes of, and make recommendations to alleviate, the violent conflicts that plagued the urban ghetto. The conclusions of the National Advisory Commission on Civil Disorders in 1968 stressed the implacability of white racism as a social force continuing to constrain the opportunities available to black citizens.

The realities of the present again were reflected in the direction of historical research. August Meier collaborated with sociologist Elliott Rudwick (b. 1927), to publish a survey of black history, *From Plantation to Ghetto* (1966). This title signaled a shift in the focus of black history away from slavery and toward the urban centers of the nation while continuing to emphasize the theme of victimization. A desire to understand the urban ghettos led two other historians to undertake important investigations of the origins and experiences of black communities in northern cities. Gilbert Osofsky (1935–1974) published *Harlem: The Making of a Ghetto, 1890–1930* in 1966. Osofsky had first been interested in exploring minority group oppression as experienced within the immigrant Jewish community in New York. Following the suggestion of one of his mentors, he decided to focus on the black community in New York as a case study of segregation in the north. Allan Spear (b. 1937) undertook a similar study about the impact of racism on the development of an urban community, published in 1967 as *Black Chicago: The Making of a Negro Ghetto, 1890–1920.* In both city-specific studies, the theme of migration to the North—and the attendant dashed hopes and expectations—played a significant role in the interpretation of the black experience. While black life continued to be riddled with unfulfilled aspirations, the movement to the cities meant that blacks were becoming an urban people.

During this period, Winthrop Jordan (b. 1931) completed his extensive, award-winning study of the origins of prejudice against blacks in America, *White over Black: American Attitudes Toward the Negro: 1550–1812* (1968). Jordan carefully dissected a centuries-old pattern of debasement of darker-skinned people and the conflicts created by this practice during the revolutionary and constitutional eras. He suggested that white men's conviction of inherent superiority could not be maintained without a high level of anxiety that left them in a peculiar and paradoxical position of domination and insecurity, caught between a need to be in control and an incipient belief that natural rights philosophy and Christianity made slavery and human inequality difficult to sustain in principle.

By the end of the decade, as reaction to the convulsions of the 1960s began to find political expression, historians—white as well as black—were prepared to embrace African American history as an integral part of the study of American history. Indeed, as the period encompassed in John Hope Franklin's delineation of the third generation of African American history drew to a close, the consensus about the boundaries of the discipline had expanded to include what Franklin himself had argued in *From Slavery to Freedom:* that African

American history is part of American history and that the history of blacks and whites in the United States must be understood as they relate to one another if the American story is to be understood in its fullest complexity, richness, and tragedy. Although slavery would continue to be a dominant focus for historical work, the continuing dilemmas associated with the development of the black experience in the United States suggested powerfully that freedom was not enough to overcome the lack of social and economic constraints imposed by the various forms of institutional racism that continued to affect black Americans.

CONTEMPORARY BLACK HISTORIOGRAPHY

Current research about African American history—like that of the preceding period—has been marked by distinctive contributions by white and black scholars. While generalizations are difficult, salient features of the work of the post-1970 generation include the overcoming of the stress on victimization in black history and the emphasis on the capacity of blacks to shape their own destiny; an interest in family life and religion; a concern to distinguish the experiences of black women and black men; and an exploration of the proposition that differences in culture, ethnicity, and gender constitute important variables in human experience that historical analysis must take into account. The "mainstreaming" of African American history—with the attendant tension between inclusion and difference—raised important questions about the contents of the mainstream itself.

Soon after completing his study of Harlem's transformation, Gilbert Osofsky edited *Puttin' On Ole Massa: The Slave Narratives of Henry Bibb, William Wells Brown, and Solomon Northup* (1969). In this volume, Osofsky presented the autobiographies of three men who had escaped from slavery, two of whom later played important roles in the antislavery movement before the Civil War. The collection presented former slaves, each a distinctive personality, speaking in their own voices, actively taking responsibility for their own lives and for those of fellow blacks. In *The Slave Community: Plantation Life in the Antebellum South* (1972), John Blassingame argued that family life among slaves was more stable than was generally assumed and that, for example, most slaves lived as children with two parents. These findings were further supported by the work of Herbert Gutman, who in *The Black Family in Slavery and Freedom, 1750–1925* (1976) also suggested that, though many slave marriages were never officially sanctioned, men and women made **de facto** enduring commitments to each other and to their offspring.

A controversial study, *Time on the Cross: The Economics of American Negro Slavery* (1974) by Robert Fogel and Stanley Engerman, sought to demonstrate that slavery was profitable in the South on the eve of the Civil War and that, while slavery was a detestable institution in principle, life on the plantation was not so terrible as many assumed. Fogel and Engerman, revisiting themes that Ulrich Bonnell Phillips had explored, argued that the slave system was characterized by economic rationality. Unlike Phillips, they appreciated the ways in which blacks achieved a measure of dignity and communal stability under adverse circumstances.

The creative power of the slave community to sustain itself was nowhere better exemplified than in its religious life. In this sphere of experience, slaves were able both to share in the culture of their masters and to fashion a distinctive tradition drawing on patterns of African culture and evangelical Christianity. In *Roll, Jordan, Roll: The World the Slaves Made* (1974), Eugene Genovese delved deeply into slave culture and life, arguing that slave religion provided the community with a heritage and a resource that facilitated both accommodation and resistance to the slave system. While much of slave religious observance took place under white supervision, other dimensions of religious practice made it possible for blacks to bond in the knowledge that they—like whites—were created in the image of God. In this conviction they found support to withstand the degradations inflicted upon them and the energy to hope for a different future. Genovese, whose earlier work had focused on the political economy of slavery, reflected in *Roll, Jordan, Roll* a wider and deeper appreciation for the texture of human experience. This interpretation represented the most comprehensive and, in many respects, the most compelling portrait of the world of slavery yet developed. Genovese's arguments encompassed the experiences of masters and slaves in their connections and in their differences and provided a nuanced and provocative portrait that allowed for the interplay of irony, paradox, and ambiguity.

A more focused inquiry was undertaken in *Slave Religion: The "Invisible Institution" in the Antebellum South* (1978) by Albert J. Raboteau. Raboteau effectively demonstrated how social-scientific approaches to religious studies could be used to illuminate historical data. Beginning with a nuanced consideration of the influence of the slaves' African background on their religion and culture, Raboteau then explored Roman Catholic and Protestant influences on slave religion. Raboteau's work has persuasively established the significance of religion as a means of forming community, expressing interdependence, and asserting autonomy. Like Genovese, Raboteau argued that the Christianity shared by masters and slaves was put to quite different uses by whites and blacks. The Exodus story is paradigmatic: for whites the journey to the New World meant deliverance from bondage, whereas for blacks, that journey represented deliverance into bondage. Blacks and whites could tell the same story but attach opposite meanings to its significance. Raboteau's recognition of this kind of shared text with divergent interpretations cast a different shadow on the older debates about patterns of accommodation and rebelliousness in slave cultures, suggesting that a different dynamic of cultural self-determination under oppression was taking place.

A similar argument emerged in another important study, Lawrence W. Levine's *Black Culture and Black Consciousness: Afro-American Folk Thought from Slavery to Freedom* (1977). Influenced by his own experience in the culture of Orthodox Judaism after the Holocaust, Levine described an enduring and sustaining folk culture that originated in slavery and that was characteristically African American. Stimulated by an observation by Imamu Amiri Baraka (formerly LeRoi Jones) that the core of black culture was to be found in song, spirituals, and riddles, Levine studied how the black response to exploitation, racism, and segregation had bound and sustained the community in slavery and its aftermath.

The shift from the 1960s' characteristic emphasis on the treatment received by blacks to a more contemporary focus on black responses to oppression can be seen in the work of Leon F. Litwack. In *North of Slavery* (1961), thematically ordered by a concern with describing racism in the North, Litwack identified continuities between southern and northern patterns of discrimination. In *Been in the Storm So Long* (1979), he focused on black contributions to Reconstruction, highlighting the vitality and distinctiveness of cultural cohesion and self-determination among former slaves.

A number of works, including *Ar'n't I a Woman?: Black Women, Work, and the Family from Slavery to the Present* (1985) by Deborah Gray White, *Labor of Love, Labor of Sorrow: Female Slaves in the Plantation South* (1985) by Jacqueline Jones, and *Within the Plantation Household: Black and White Women of the Old South* (1988) by Elizabeth Fox-Genovese, have explored gender relations and the distinctive contributions of black women during the antebellum period. In addition, William L. Andrews edited *Sisters of the Spirit: Three Black Women's Autobiographies of the Nineteenth Century* (1986), that parallels Osofsky's *Puttin' On Ole Massa* but is explicitly concerned with the role of women and religion before the Civil War. This development reflects the permeability of the boundaries between African American and American history, both of which are subject to revisionist pressures catalyzed by feminist political and intellectual sensibilities. The significance of these studies is that they represent a continuing stimulus to value the past in both its complexity and its heterogeneity. As civil unrest and other contemporaneous events influenced the writing of history in earlier periods, so it may be said that gender-sensitive explorations of both the present and the past have marked the 1980s in a distinctive way. In addition, the acceptance of the importance of African American history has invited questions of how other people's experiences of hyphenated "Americanness" should be incorporated within the larger history of the peoples of the United States. A precursor to this kind of consideration is represented in the work of Ronald T. Takaki in *Iron Cages: Race and Culture in Nineteenth-Century America* (1979) and *From Different Shores: Perspectives on Race and Ethnicity in America* (1987). Takaki's concerns have focused generically on the histories of Native Americans, Asians, Hispanics, and African Americans as they have represented contrapuntal tendencies within a historical torrent dominated by white male forces—forces who invaded, conquered, and, they believed, civilized a continent and who defined themselves as the chosen people over and against those who were different. Hispanic Americans—a heterogeneous group that includes Puerto Ricans, Cuban Americans, Mexican Americans, and others from the different countries of Latin America and that is soon to become the most numerous of America's ethnic minorities—have begun to define their own distinctive tradition for historical examination. Among the issues raised by this group was its challenge to the reigning interpretations of the achievements of Christopher Columbus on the five hundredth anniversary of the "discovery" of America.

Increasingly, historians and, indeed, society at large are challenged to construct a vision of the whole that serves to synthesize the experience of diversity in American life. The assimilationist-inspired metaphor of the melting pot seems ever more problematic as the nation discovers anew the extent of its heterogeneity and anticipates the more challenging pluralisms of the twenty-first century. The questions likely to engage the widest discussion will focus on the meaning and the significance of difference—of race, gender, and class—in a nation that has claimed to make out of many, one people.

BIBLIOGRAPHY

General Works

Abzug, Robert H., and Stephen E. Maizlish, eds. *New Perspectives on Race and Slavery in America: Essays in Honor of Kenneth M. Stampp* (1986).

Berlin, Ira, et al., eds. *Freedom: A Documentary History of Emancipation, 1861–1867* (1982).

Blassingame, John W. *The Slave Community: Plantation Life in the Antebellum South* (1979).

Bodnar, John. *Immigration and Industrialization: Ethnicity in an American Mill Town, 1870–1940* (1977).

Dolan, Jay P. *The Immigrant Church: New York's Irish and German Catholics, 1815–1865* (1975).

Foner, Eric, ed. *The New American History* (1990).

Fox-Genovese, Elizabeth. *Within the Plantation Household: Black and White Women in the Old South* (1988).

Franklin, John Hope. *George Washington Williams: A Biography* (1985).

———. *Race and History: Selected Essays 1938–1988* (1989).

Franklin, John Hope, and Alfred A. Moss, Jr. *From Slavery to Freedom: A History of Negro Americans* (6th ed. 1988).

Gann, Lewis H., and Peter J. Duignan. *The Hispanics in the United States* (1986).

Genovese, Eugene. *Roll, Jordan, Roll: The World the Slaves Made* (1974).

Glazer, Nathan, and Daniel Patrick Moynihan, eds. *Ethnicity: Theory and Experience* (1975).

Grossman, James R. *Land of Hope: Chicago, Black Southerners, and the Great Migration* (1989).

Gutman, Herbert G. *The Black Family in Slavery and Freedom, 1750–1925* (1976).

Handlin, Oscar. *Boston's Immigrants, 1790–1880* (1971).

Higham, John. *Strangers in the Land: Patterns of American Nativism, 1860–1925* (1955).

Hines, Darlene Clark, ed. *The State of Afro-American History: Past, Present, and Future* (1986).

Jordan, Winthrop D. *White over Black: American Attitudes Toward the Negro, 1550–1812* (1968).

Levine, Lawrence W. *Black Culture and Black Consciousness: Afro-American Folk Thought from Slavery to Freedom* (1977).

McPherson, James M., et al. *Blacks in America: Bibliographical Essays* (1971).

Meier, August, and Elliott Rudwick. *Along the Color Line: Explorations in the Black Experience* (1976).

———. *Black History and the Historical Profession, 1915–1980* (1986).

Moore, Joan W., and Pachon, Harry. *Hispanics in the United States* (1985).

Osofsky, Gilbert. *Harlem, the Making of a Ghetto: Negro New York, 1890–1930* (1966).

Polenberg, Richard. *One Nation Divisible: Class, Race, and Ethnicity in the U.S. Since 1938* (1980).

Quarles, Benjamin. *Black Mosaic: Essays in Afro-American History and Historiography* (1988).

Raboteau, Albert J. *Slave Religion: The "Invisible Institution" in the Antebellum South* (1978).

Takaki, Ronald T. *Iron Cages: Race and Culture in Nineteenth-Century America* (1979).

Villafañe, Eldin. *The Liberating Spirit: Toward an Hispanic American Pentecostal Social Ethic* (1992).

Zunz, Olivier, ed. *Reliving the Past: The Worlds of Social History* (1985).

SEE ALSO **Intellectuals and the Intelligentsia**; and various essays in the sections "**The Construction of Social Identity**," "**Ethnic and Racial Subcultures**," "**Periods of Social Change**," "**Popular Culture and Recreation**," and "**Work and Labor**."

MODERNIZATION THEORY AND ITS CRITICS

Melvin L. Adelman

IN THE 1960s, many historians in America began increasingly to place their research within a modernization framework. Two changes occurring within the historical profession influenced the adoption of this approach. One was the emergence of the view that interdisciplinary connections with the social sciences would enhance historical scholarship. This vision led a number of historians to incorporate into their works elements of modernization theory, the dominant paradigm in the social sciences in the two decades after World War II. Another stimulant was the rise of new fields of historical inquiry and a dramatic explosion in the number of historical topics being examined. Historians now found the modernization framework more attractive because it promised a holistic conception of society and a multifaceted vision of the process of social change. The expanded approach appeared better suited to frame the questions, contextualize the analysis, and encompass a broad range of subjects, including many of the new research topics.

At the same time that historians started to employ a modernization framework, social scientists mounted a growing criticism of modernization theory. By the early 1970s they had presented a significant critique of some of its underlying assumptions. The criticisms quickly spilled over into the history discipline, and questions surfaced concerning the utility of the modernization framework to the conduct of research in this field. Critics charged that the theory had been applied in a manner that was both reductive and deterministic and that it had been totally discredited by social scientists. Supporters of modernization conceded that problems existed with the theory and some even questioned whether it was a theory at all. However, they insisted that as a conceptual framework modernization aided in organizing and synthesizing historical data, that it facilitated the much needed demonstration of societal linkages, and that the objections raised to this approach were more often stated than substantiated. Nevertheless, after nearly two decades of contributing to historical writings, by the mid 1980s the influence of the modernization perspective diminished as an increasing number of historians turned to another approach to explicate new questions and reexamine older ones. This new orientation aligned history more with anthropology than sociology and was concerned more with questions of culture than structure. While the findings that have emerged from this new framework have enriched historical scholarship and presented exciting challenges to existing literature, the modernization approach remains a valuable method to explicate historical continuity and change.

THE DEVELOPMENT OF MODERNIZATION THEORY

Modernization theory was constructed only after World War II, but its antecedents can be found as early as the seventeenth century, when the term modern was used to denote a historical era distinct from the ancient and medieval periods. By the end of the following century the influence of Enlightenment thought, economic change, and the French Revolution had coalesced to intensify the vision that older ways of life were yielding to new social arrangements. These developments engendered a new conception of society, as traditional and modern came to represent distinct social orders.

During the nineteenth century, questions about the nature of modern life, its development, and its consequences came to the forefront of social thought, especially in the emerging field of sociology. To explicate the character of modern life scholars constructed various typologies based on a dichotomous conception of traditional and modern society. Despite employing different terminologies to conceptualize these varying social orders—Henry Maine's (1822–1888) status and contract, Émile Durkheim's (1858–1917) mechanical and organic solidarity, and Ferdinand Tönnies's (1855–1936) Gemeinschaft and Gesellschaft—they painted fundamentally similar portraits. Traditional society was envisioned as stable, with limited differentiation, an agrarian economy based on a mechanical division of labor and ruled by an ascriptive elite. The traditional community was marked by personal contacts: ritual flowed through its entire experience, and the repetition of past ways rather than innovative action was encouraged. By contrast, modern society was characterized by a high division of labor consistent with industrial change: it was a functional social structure that conformed to shifting political and economic patterns, and it was governed by rulers who were accountable in terms of secular values of justice, freedom, and efficiency. Premodern life was static, hierarchical, homogeneous, ritualistic, and tradition-bound. Modern life was dynamic, cosmopolitan, impersonal, and oriented to change, innovation, and rationality.

Max Weber (1864–1920) insisted that typological constructs, or what he called "ideal types," were not perfect reflections of any existing society, but a heuristic device designed to facilitate analysis. He expressed concern that ideal types and reality would be confused with each other; the fallacy did arise in the works of various scholars. The popularity of evolutionary thought contributed to this trend and it also encouraged scholars to adopt a linear vision of social change, one in which modern characteristics inevitably replaced traditional ones. While works as diverse as Maine's and Karl Marx's (1818–1883) were representative of this genre, several of the classical sociologists rejected sharp dichotomies between "primitive" and "advanced." Weber, among others, pointed out that Gemeinschaft and Gesellschaft were in reality not mutually exclusive types, but that both continued to coexist within modern society.

During the first half of the twentieth century, American sociologists such as Charles Cooley (1864–1929), Louis Wirth (1897–1952), Talcott Parsons (1902–1979), and Robert Redfield (1897–1958) drew upon the works of their European counterparts to construct their own typologies to analyze social change. Each employed their own terminology, but the fundamental picture they presented was remarkably similar. Nor did it differ significantly from what Maine, Durkheim, and Tönnies had offered. In addition, most American sociologists also articulated a vision of change in which communal patterns of life were increasingly being replaced by more functional, associational, modern patterns. Nowhere is the theme of community breakdown and replacement more eloquently treated than in Wirth's classic article, "Urbanism as a Way of Life." However, it was the works of Parsons and other structural-functional writers that profoundly influenced how modernization theorists framed their examinations and explanations of the process of social change.

While modernization theory had a lengthy prehistory, this approach really developed only after World War II. Its emergence among American social scientists was stimulated by the onset of the cold war, the breakdown of European colonial empires, and the increased importance of "third world" countries. To construct a model that assessed economic, political, and cultural developments in these countries, scholars amalgamated the ideas of several eminent thinkers, including Weber's thoughts on rationality, W. W. Rostow's (1916–) on investment, Joseph Schumpeter's (1883–1950) on entrepreneurship, and Parsons's on deviance. However, the creation of the modernization theory was more than just a scholarly undertaking. For some of its proponents it was a concerted effort to respond to Marxist thought and to provide the ideological justifications and the policy implementations for making third-world countries become more like capitalistic America. Nowhere was the procapitalist dimension of this theoretical orientation more strongly articulated than in W. W. Rostow's *The Stages of Economic Growth*.

In their analyses of third-world countries, modernization theorists sought to explicate the characteristics of traditional and modern societies, and they constructed several indexes to measure the degree to which they could be differentiated. This research elaborated on the traits of both societies, but the portrait presented was remarkably similar to what the classic sociologists had created. Nevertheless, significant differences existed in the tone of the two scholarly groups. Whereas the views of nineteenth-century scholars were often shaped by a romantic vision of traditional society, the perceptions of their twentieth-century counterparts were often predicated on the belief that modernity was the ultimate expression of rationality, progress, and liberal democracy. The ambivalence to the emergence of modern industrial society in the writings of Durkheim, Tönnies, Marx, and Weber was absent in the works of the modernists. However, the major distinction between the modernization theorists and the classic sociologists was not the alteration in tone but the shift in the focus of the scholarship. The new scholars moved away from exploring the characteristics of society to examining the conditions required for the emergence of a modern one and how modernization might be induced in third-world countries. This more expansive focus, with its greater emphasis on theory, prediction, and policy making, marked the break between modernization theorists and their predecessors.

Modernization theorists adopted a systemic approach to investigate the process of social change. This orientation closely linked them with structural-functionalism and reinforced the ideal-type construction of traditional and modern societies as mutually exclusive systems. The systemic approach was rooted in the premise that the qualitative characteristics and institutional structures of modern life enabled it more effectively to adapt to the new and wider variety of societal alterations and problems. Modernization theorists further asserted that a strong degree of interconnection existed among the various institutional areas. As a result, the modernization of one component of society influenced the modernization of another and created similar types of structural patterns.

This combination of evolutionary and systemic perspectives led scholars to several conclusions about how social change took place. They felt that once the institutional kernels of the modern system were put in place, their internal and logical "needs" would generate specific structural and organizational developments. They asserted that all societies undergoing modernization would pass through several similar stages. The assumption that a sequential pattern existed led researchers to explicate what propelled the takeoff toward modernity. While the initial emphasis focused on economic developments (Rostow's work was the most important one of this genre), this orientation was quickly abandoned when it was realized that the economy alone did not explain the process. A more influential book along these lines was Daniel Lerner's *The Passing of Traditional Society,* which argued that a sequence of demographic, economic, and social changes stimulated political modernization. Other social scientists theorized that although somewhat divergent paths toward modernity existed, the universal characteristics of modern industrial systems would inevitably produce convergence among modern industrial societies. The result would be that they would all take on similar institutional characteristics and forms.

THE HISTORIAN AND MODERNIZATION

While after 1960 an increasing number of American historians came to rely on a modernization framework, this perspective never coalesced into what may be described as a school of historical thought. Several interacting reasons exist for this absence, not the least of which was that historians were exceedingly eclectic in what they extracted from the modernization literature. Some drew upon works that emphasized structural modernization while others extrapolated from those that analyzed behavioral modernization. This diversity was itself intimately linked to the wide range of historical topics to which the modernization framework was applied. So we are dealing here not with a unified theory, or a clearly defined intellectual tradition, but with a set of related motifs; modernization is more an orientation than a monolithic interpretive framework.

While historians varied in how they used this approach, the biggest differences among them tended to be between those scholars examining developments in Western and non-Western countries. Historians who used a modernist perspective to focus on nonwestern countries generally were more reliant on the writings of modernization theorists and were more explicit in their advocacy of a modernization perspective. Those scholars who focused on western countries were less explicit in their use of this framework, and they were more likely to be informed by the writings of Weber, Wirth, and, to a lesser extent, Parsons.

While historians applied a modernization framework to a variety of different fields, its influence was most strongly felt in such new areas of research as comparative history. Given the global dimension of modernization and the assumption that it possessed universal characteristics, it is not surprising that historians engaged in cross-cultural research found this approach attractive. During the 1960s and 1970s modernization emerged as a major paradigm in this field largely as a result of Cyril E. Black's (1915–) efforts. Black's *Dynamics of Mod-*

ernization was among the first works to advocate the use of this orientation for historical study. At the same time, he sought to demonstrate how a historical analysis of modernization corrected some of the limitations of modernization theory as articulated by social scientists. Examining modernization on a worldwide basis, Black concentrated his attention solely on its political dimension. He explored four universal phases/problems that modernizing societies confronted, and he identified seven distinct historical patterns of political modernization. Despite Black's effort to surmount some of the problems with modernization theory and his repeated calls to be judicious in its application, he was, finally, too uncritical of the paradigm. As a result, his version of the fruits of the modernizing process was far too sweeping. From the perspective of a quarter of a century later, *Dynamics* appears as a quaint work filled with many of the flaws that the antimodernists have raised against this orientation. However, it should be noted that Black's short work was designed more to be suggestive than definitive, and he was quick to concede that he outlined a general rather than a specific vision of political change. In addition, he was concerned as much with the promotion of a comparative approach to historical inquiry as he was with an effort to explicate the process of modernization.

Nearly a decade later, Black collaborated with scholars from a variety of disciplines to produce the thoroughly comparative work, *The Modernization of Japan and Russia.* In 1980, George Fredrickson praised this work for the way that it incorporated a deeply detailed and richly textured historical study within a consistent theoretical framework. He stated that it was the most successful example of comparative history and that it demonstrated that interdisciplinary scholarship was the wave of the future.

During the 1960s, American historians took up the comparative banner and began to apply modernization theory to Japan. The popularity of this approach was tied to the vibrant interdisciplinary heritage that existed within this historical field and because Japan's transformation in the century following the Meiji Restoration (1868) was the central focus of much of the scholarship from the 1950s to the 1970s. Within this context, historians also drew on the modernization perspective as a way to transcend the view that these changes derived merely from Japan's effort to westernize or were solely the product of intense class struggles.

While some historians adopted a modernist framework to examine developments in several underdeveloped countries, others used it to explicate different dimensions of European history. None did so more brilliantly than Eugen Weber in his *Peasants into Frenchmen.* Unlike the comparative and Japanese historians, Weber eschewed any ties to the literature on modernization theory or even to the writings of the classical sociologists when framing his scholarship. Yet in his richly textured, well-documented, and judiciously examined work, Weber indicates how a variety of social, cultural, and economic forces coalesce to modernize rural France in the half-century prior to World War I.

A modernization framework was also applied to a variety of fields in American history, but especially in the new areas of historical inquiry. The major exponents of this orientation came out of Harvard University, specifically Oscar Handlin and Bernard Bailyn and their students. Handlin had been a leading champion of the marriage of history with the social sciences, and at Harvard he was connected with the interdisciplinary Department of Social Relations, which was strongly associated with Talcott Parsons. During the 1960s and 1970s the modernist perspective profoundly influenced the study of urban and community history as historians investigated the meanings and consequences of the transitions of America from traditional to modern during different time periods and in different locales. The most significant work of this genre was Robert Wiebe's *A Search for Order.* Interestingly, Wiebe was one of the few historians writing from this perspective who was not associated with Harvard. In this now classic study, Wiebe detailed the replacement of the "island" (traditional) community by a bureaucratic modern society, and explicated its significance. He asserted that the transformation was part and parcel of the triumph of a "new" middle class and its values and that this group was at the forefront of the Progressive movement.

The modernization framework also influenced business history, but here as well the orientation was almost totally implicit. Louis Galambos placed the research in this field and related areas, such as the histories of technology and the various professions, within the context of an organizational framework. Despite some differences between the modernization and organizational paradigms, they shared much in common as evidenced by Wiebe's work being significant to both. In fact a case can be made that the organizational approach is to a large extent a subcategory of modernization. Galambos's call for historians to integrate Parsonian thought into their scholarship reveals the kinship of these two analytical frameworks.

The presence of the modernization perspective in business history can also be illustrated from a quick glance at the training and scholarship of Alfred D. Chandler, Jr., the preeminent figure behind the surge in this field of historical inquiry. At Harvard, Chandler had been profoundly influenced by his course work with Parsons and deeply admired his structural-functional approach and emphasis on role theory. Throughout Chandler's subsequent research, he continued to be informed by Parsonian as well as Weberian sociology. In both *Strategy and Structure* and *The Visible Hand,* he employed a systems approach to explicate the rise of the modern business enterprise and administration. Chandler also shared with many of the modernists an appreciation for comparative scholarship. In his research on American business, he examined a variety of different types of companies and, along with Herman Daems, he edited a book that provided a cross-cultural comparison of business management. The essays in this work paralleled the writings of the early modernization theorists in that they emphasized the structural similarities that business firms achieved in the different countries rather than the impact of cultural differences on them.

Both the modernization and organizational frameworks essentially sought to shift the centrality of American history away from its political emphasis and to have the scholarship transcend the dispute between the conflict and consensus schools of thought. For the organizationalists, the major questions of American history naturally revolved around the changes and consequences of organization building and the emergence of new formal hierarchical structures of authority. Within this framework, America's rendezvous, as Galambos so aptly phrased it, was not with the liberal society, but with bureaucracy.

Not all historians who employed a modernization framework focused on organization building, but this approach significantly shaped how they examined a variety of institutional developments, from schools to hospitals, libraries to sport. The emergence of the modernist perspective at the center of this scholarship can best be understood against the backdrop of the dramatic rise of social history. While this new field legitimized the study of heretofore unexplored and even previously taboo topics, it also demanded that they be linked to broader sociocultural trends. The modernization orientation fit this requirement well as its "before and after" model of social change enabled historians to explain institutional developments as both a result of and response to the societal transformation. In a host of works they presented the creation of modern institutions in terms compatible with Parsonian pattern-maintenance. This vision emerged among the profession's conservative-moderate wing as well as their liberal-leftist counterparts. They agreed that the new structural forms had been critical in shaping how America's adjustment to economic and social order change, but they differed about who benefited from this process.

By the 1970s, liberal and leftist historians challenged the view that the new organizations promoted humanitarian goals and established a more equitable system. Instead they asserted that bureaucratic institutions were created to foster the prerogatives and power of the privileged class. While this critique remained rooted in the systemic orientation of the modernization framework, what was innovative about it was that it shattered the unquestioned alliance American modernists, both in history and the social sciences, had forged with the assumptions of Progressive thought. To different degrees and for different reasons, liberal and leftist historians had resurrected in their works the ambiguity that the classical sociologists had expressed about the onset and consequences of modernity.

Early social history research on institutions generated some interesting questions and produced innovative works, such as David Rothman's *The Discovery of the Asylum.* Nevertheless, this scholarship was limited by the academic milieu in which it emerged. Since the essence of the new social history was to establish broad patterns of relationships between social phenomena, scholarship centered more on explicating external influences, in most cases community breakdown, rather than focusing internally on institutions themselves.

The history of sport, for example, was an area inhibited by an almost exclusive focus on the impact of societal forces and transformations. The use of this external orientation was not accidental since sport had long been considered unworthy of scholarly inquiry. Given this outlook, it is understandable why early sport historians often legitimized their subject by enunciating that its utility derived from how sport elucidated other societal themes. The application of this outside-in approach enabled them to frame sport in its societal context, something glaringly absent in the numerous popular sport histories. Nevertheless, it also resulted in historians reducing sporting change to a by-product of societal alterations. Their analysis lacked an internal perspective that would examine how the institutional and structural characteristics of athletics were implicated in influencing the tone and direction of sport.

Allen Guttmann's *From Ritual to Record* (1978) established modernization as a major paradigm within the sport studies field not only in the United States but worldwide. His book provided an insightful investigation into the characteristics of premodern and modern sport which he then used to examine his twofold thesis. One is that premodern and modern sport are fundamentally different. The other is that the quest for records, the essential characteristic of modern sport, which has its roots in the triumph of Enlightenment science, has generated a sport system which in Parsonian terminology is more universalistic than particularistic. *Ritual to Record* shares many of the same traits as *Dynamics of Modernization.* Similar to Black's book, its brevity makes it more suggestive than conclusive. Despite this limitation, Guttmann's book was important because it brought a global dimension to an emerging field of historical inquiry. In it he wove together a discussion of sport from primitive times to the present and constructed a cross-cultural analysis of sport in contemporary society.

In *A Sporting Time* (1986), Melvin Adelman explicitly applied a modernization framework to a discrete time and place, mid-nineteenth-century New York City. He combined external and internal approaches to analyze sporting developments. This perspective facilitated an examination of sport on two distinct but interrelated and interacting levels: the relationship between sport and the modernization of society and the evolution of modern sport structures and ideology. Adelman's research on sport revealed that the emergence of modern sport structures was the result of more than just societal change. Rather, the development of each particular sport was also profoundly influenced by a combination of internal events, notably the rate of its growth, the degree to which it became a competitive activity, and the extent to which it emerged as a commercial undertaking.

Sport history, of course, was but one front of modernization. By the 1980s the continued growth of social history emboldened historians to take a more in-depth look at modern institutions. Many agreed with Neil Harris that this research needed to move beyond its context within the Progressive–social control debate and that it should focus on reconstructing the choices confronted by those involved within the institutions. This vision naturally encouraged historians to give greater expression to an internal perspective, but it did not detract from their commitment to illustrate how institutions were connected to the larger society. The amalgamation of internal and external approaches generated important studies about the nature and workings of modern institutions and their societal influences. What was particularly innovative about this scholarship, much of which took place off the beaten path of historical research, was the way in which it attacked some of the limitations of modernization theory. These historians still viewed institutional structures as possessing some degree of "autonomy," but they rejected the systemic approach and its machine-like imagery. Rather they envisioned structures as embedded in cultural constructs.

Paul Starr's *The Social Transformation of American Medicine* is one of the best examples of this new orientation. His study indicates that the dynamics that enabled medicine to emerge as an authoritative profession emanated from the interactions between both its internal developments and broader economic and social changes. Starr's analysis began by rejecting the functionalist account of structures. Instead, he sees their development as the outcome of historical actors pursuing their interests and ideals. As a result, his work alternates dialectically between structure and human agency to indicate how the cultural authority of the medical profession emerged and how it was converted into control of markets, organization, and government policy.

Charles Rosenberg's *The Care of Strangers* is another fine illustration of the new approach to studying modern institutions. He maintains that the influences that shaped the growth and changes in American hospitals were mainly internally driven. Rosenberg does not present the hospital as an institution that was primarily swayed by its functional needs and priorities. Rather, he points out, it was the culture of the doctors—their values, rewards, career patterns, and knowledge base—that most determined the direction of hospitals in this country. Rosenberg's study reflects important trends in recent scholarship on modern institutions. First, historians are once again giving attention to the important role of ideas in shaping organizational developments. Second, scholars no longer see modern institutions as expressing either triumph or tragedy but as possessing their own contradictions and tensions.

Historical scholarship has revealed far more complex and variegated patterns than modernization theorists had initially advanced. Research in family history illustrates this. Several American scholars, along with their English counterparts, rejected the simple view of family transition from an extended kinship pattern to a nuclear family. For example, in a number of studies Tamara Hareven was exceedingly sensitive to how continuity as well as change characterized family life and how such variables as gender and class, among others, contributed to the interaction and maintenance of traditional family patterns and the emergence of modern ones. In addition, her article, "Modernization and Family History" (1976), remains one of the best articulations of the utility of the concept of modernization as a means of organizing and synthesizing the research in a particular historical field.

Historians also investigated changes in sexual practices and attitudes within a modernization context. Maris Vinovskis and Robert Wells examined the influence of modern values on the decline of fertility rates in mid-nineteenth-century America. Jayme Sokolow placed his discussion of sexuality in Victorian America within this framework. He maintained that the repressive views of health reformers expressed their concerns about the consequences of modernization and their solutions of how best to respond to it. W. Andrew Achenbaum along with Peter Stearns examined modernization and the aging process. All of this scholarship indicated the vitality of the paradigm, even as the multitextured pattern challenged the earlier, linear and monocausal modernization perspective.

While many historians used a modernization perspective to interpret research on a variety of topics, this framework achieved its strongest advocacy and broadest articulation in Richard Brown's 1976 publication, *Modernization: The Transformation of American Life, 1600–1865*. Brown stated that the concept of modernization offered a new way to organize and synthesize the burgeoning and diverse historical literature that was emerging in a variety of fields, but especially in social history. He was well aware of the limitations of modernization theory as social scientists voiced it, even though he essentially accepted their "ideal-type" constructions. Brown knew the criticisms of his colleagues, but while he did not deny the validity of their concerns he maintained that modernization merited serious consideration because it was a framework that had the potential to amalgamate a variety of historical phenomena.

Brown demanded much of the modernization framework in his effort to demonstrate that it offered unique possibilities for understanding American history. He insisted that an examination of the uneven and incomplete process of modernization provides new ways to compare northern and southern colonies, construct linkages between different time periods, and to comprehend the meaning of the Civil War. Brown scrutinized how both structural and attitudinal changes over the course of two and one-half centuries influenced developments, but he was more interested in the latter than the former. While he paid proper attention to organizational and material alterations, it is the gradual unfolding and triumph of the modern personality that was at the center of his work. Similar to Seymour Lipset and Michael Zuckerman, Brown felt that the seeds for this outcome existed almost from the outset, and he focused on how political, demographic, economic, and other societal shifts continued, albeit unevenly, to nurture its maturity. By the 1820s the modern personality had emerged as the prevailing one in America, but it was the northern victory in the Civil War that completed the triumph of the modern way of life in this country.

THE CRITIQUE OF MODERNIZATION

Brown had hoped that his suggestive work would lead historians to more frequently and explicitly apply a modernization framework to their research, but this did not prove to be the case. While this perspective still had its champions and some scholars continued to use it, questions of its utility for historical research surfaced simultaneously with the appearance of Brown's book. The antimodernists cogently pointed out some significant problems that resulted from the reliance of historians on this framework, but much of their criticism of modernization did not distinguish between its sociological construct and his historical application. Peter Stearns argued in 1980 that critics of the modernization concept articulated a sense of dissatisfaction with this approach, but that they had not marshaled the evidence to indicate its systemic limitations. Stearns comments remain valid.

Even before historians postulated their problems with modernization, social scientists had posed their own challenges to this theory. By the late 1960s shifts in the political climate contributed to the growing rejection of this approach as critics objected to its connection to cold-war ideology and its promotion of American imperialism. They also opposed modernization theory because it projected a Western ethnocentric vision on the process of social change. In addition, the disenchantment with the theory was an extension of uncertainty about many of the values associated with modernity, most notably rationality and progress.

However, the mounting criticism of modernization was not primarily externally driven. Even by the end of the 1950s, social scientists had raised serious questions, and the attacks intensified in the subsequent decade. They indicated that a variety of problems emanated out of the tradition-modernity dichotomy. Sociologists showed that the initial research had erroneously portrayed a monolithic traditional society and failed to appreciate the diversity of cultures and societies. Similarly the model did not account for the persistence of traditional patterns and symbols in modern society or for the interacting influences traditional and modern ways had on one another. Intimately linked with these charges were complaints that the explanatory powers of modernization were severely limited by its lack of attention to cultural forces and its ahistorical quality. Marxist scholars, in particular, maintained that the lack of attention to the historical dimension had resulted in the failure of modernization theorists to envision this process as an extension of capitalistic expansion, which implicated it in a new international system and the power relations that emerged from it. Several social scientists also pointed out that the increased emphasis on the historical experience of modernization challenged the deterministic vision of a universal systemic character and made the convergence theory of modern society impossible to accept.

By the 1970s, social scientists had attacked the basic tenets of the modernization theory as well as the structural-functional thought on which it rested. Given the difficulties with this theory, several scholars called on their colleagues to abandon it. None did so more thoughtfully than Dean Tipps. He outlined several problems with modernization theory, but the most critical ones recited were at the metatheoretical level. He insisted that exponents of this theory erred by trying to incorporate disparate processes of social change within a single concept; that it encouraged certain tendencies that inhibited scholarly insights, including perpetuating a gap between theory and research; and that the major failing of modernization theorists was their inattention to define what they wanted the theory to explain.

Raymond Grew was one of a number of scholars who acknowledged that problems existed with modernization theory but who were unwilling to dispense with it entirely. He charged that many of the attacks on modernization were spurious, that they unfairly critiqued positions that no serious scholar ever adopted, and that they often ignored subtleties in the arguments of those who cleaved to the paradigm. Grew insisted that modernization was not a theory and that it certainly had no predictive powers. However, he maintained that the concept defines categories that describe the organization of society and its constituent parts, and that it very broadly defines the direction of change that may occur within these categories. The framework also relates how changes in one category are connected to changes in another, indicates how social groups respond to such alterations, and identifies shifting patterns of organization and behavior. Grew articulated other critical reasons for retaining the concept of modernization. He noted that since the eighteenth century many similar changes (albeit at different times, degrees, and rates) have occurred worldwide, and that modernization has generally emerged as the term to describe these changes. He argued that the concept is essentially historical in its concern for change over time and the interrelatedness of change among different components of society, and that it has long been embedded within an interdisciplinary heritage and vocabulary. Finally, the concept facilitates comparisons between social groups, countries, and time periods.

By the mid 1970s, historians began to raise questions about modernization as it pertained to the writings within their own profession. However, their criticism hardly differed from the points their social-science colleagues had already made. Historians essentially leveled three interrelated charges against modernization: that it was an ahistorical construct; that the traditional-modern dichotomy had at best simplified the historical process and at worst distorted it; and, that modernization emphasized structure at the expense of culture and human agency. By the 1980s, these allegations had become common fare within the historical profession. This climate contributed to historians being defensive about, and shying away from, writing within the context of a modernization framework. This trend can be observed in Jack Temple Kirby's outstanding study of the rural modernization in the South. Despite his exceedingly sensitive presentation of how structural and cultural influences interacted to shape this development, Kirby makes no effort to place his work within or relate it to the literature on historical modernization.

There was certainly some merit to the charges raised about the application of a modernization framework to historical research, but it was premature to call it a false synthesis, as James Henretta did in his review of Brown's book. What is particularly striking is that the current view has emerged despite very little analysis of the incorporation of a modernization perspective into historical scholarship. Nevertheless, one- or two-line complaints against modernization can still be found in reviews of works as certain proof that a problem exists. Moreover, support for the antimodernization position is often done by citing articles that are now nearly fifteen years old, without noting that these critiques contain their own drawbacks. Many were ill-focused, failed to account for revisionist tendencies already underway, and had their own contradictions and inconsistencies. Although many critics simply brushed off modernization, they did not demonstrate its systemic limitations.

The most familiar charge against modernization was that it is ahistorical. An example is Sean Wilentz's complaint that this theory was embedded in the substitution of functionalist teleology for historical process, static and reified ideal types for complex social realities, and temporal labels for social categories. While Wilentz, like many of his antimodernist colleagues, had too easily ignored the revisionist writings on modernization, he had a point. As a theoretical construct modernization is ahistorical. Given its sociological origins this is neither surprising nor could it have been otherwise. Nevertheless, Neil Smelser, one of the early exponents of modernization theory, recognized from the outset that important differences existed between the model and actual historical experiences. In fact, the theory was not designed to match reality or explain the unfolding of a series of events as historians conceptualize this process. However, when modernization is understood as a concept designed to help frame coherent patterns, it is, as Raymond Grew pointed out, distinctively historical.

Daniel T. Rodgers was among the first historians to express concern that his colleagues had too easily accepted the linear view of social change expressed in modernization theory. As he pointed out, even leftist and Marxist scholars, including E. P. Thompson (1924–), had accepted the basic contours of the modernization argument. Rodgers correctly indicated the fallacy of modern structures and values inevitably replacing traditional ones; scholars in other fields, including Clifford Geertz, also made this point. However, dropping the either-or view of social change does not require the abandonment of a modernization approach. In *Community and Social Change in America* (1978), Thomas Bender explicated the benefits of examining change in terms of the tensions and interactions between Gemeinschaft and Gesellschaft. Peter Stearns also proclaimed that one of the values of the concept of modernization is that it embraces contradictions, illustrating as it does the complexities of modern life.

Modernization theory, Elliot Gorn remarked, tended to generate a history without people and without human agency since impersonal institutions and social forces were responsible for the major decisions. The modernization perspective has been, and probably always will be, more concerned with the collective than the individual. It was precisely this focus that made it attractive to social historians at a time when they sought to enhance historical scholarship by moving its emphasis beyond the particular to examine connections to larger social systems. As historians entered new terrain and used different kinds of source materials to map out structural developments and explicate their significance, a mechanistic vision crept into their analysis although the best works sought to guard against it.

Some of the early historians who adopted a modernization perspective succumbed to the tendency to merely insert the data within the contours of modernization theory. However, the limitations of execution should not be construed as a limitation with the approach. Despite the erroneous tendency of some critics to see modernization as a deterministic model, Parsons was always well aware of the existence of knowledgable human actors. He did not give priority to society over the individual, and he recognized that human choices influenced the system. In addition, Zygmunt Bauman is correct in reminding us that Parsons did not subscribe to the view that the social system contained its own imperative demand. It is not surprising, as already noted, that the recent historical scholarship has demonstrated that understanding people's actions and beliefs enhances and is compatible with a modernization orientation.

Over a decade ago, Peter Stearns presented an exceedingly thoughtful case for the utility of modernization as a conceptual tool in both teaching and researching social history, at least within the context of the Western experience. Many of Stearns's claims for modernization have been pointed to throughout this article. What bears reemphasizing is his support for the concept because it serves as an integrating device. Stearns recognized that modernization is not the only framework than can perform this worthy objective, but he did insist that it was modernization's synthetic potential that is among its most significant virtues. From the outset, it has been this dimension that has made it attractive to scholars seeking to construct broader sociocultural connections.

Certainly early proponents of modernization claimed too much on behalf of both the theory and the concept, insisting that it would amalgamate political, economic, and social elements into one neat picture. Even the strongest supporters of modernization should be aware that the complexities of modern life make it easier to articulate the scholarly need for making connections between social units than actually demonstrating them. Despite the inevitable discrepancy between the ideal and reality, modernization offers a way of integrating three concomitant sets of processes: the modernization of structures, the modernization of public beliefs, and actual popular mentalities. In a profession whose scholarship is increasingly fragmented, the modernization paradigm, with all of its flaws, still gives us powerful insight into American social history.

BIBLIOGRAPHY

Achenbaum, W. Andrew. "Further Perspectives on Modernization and Aging: A (P)review of the Historical Literature." *Social Science History* 6 (1982): 347–368.

Achenbaum, W. Andrew, and Peter N. Stearns. "Modernization and the History of Old Age." *The Gerontologist* 18 (1978): 307–313.

Adelman, Melvin L. *A Sporting Time: New York City and the Rise of Modern Athletics, 1820–70* (1986).

Bailyn, Bernard. *Education in the Forming of American Society* (1960).

Bauman, Zygmunt. "Hermeneutics and Modern Social Theory." In *Social Theory of Modern Societies: Anthony Giddens and His Critics,* edited by David Held and John B. Thompson (1989).

Bender, Thomas. *Community and Social Change in America* (1978).

Bendix, Reinhard. "Traditional and Modernity Reconsidered." *Comparative Studies in Society and History* 9 (1967): 292–346.

Black, Cyril E. *The Dynamics of Modernization: A Study in Comparative History* (1966).

Black, Cyril E., et al. *The Modernization of Japan and Russia: A Comparative Study* (1975).

Brown, Richard D. *Modernization: The Transformation of American Life, 1600–1865* (1976).

Chandler, Alfred D., Jr. *Strategy and Structure: Chapters in the History of Industrial Enterprise* (1962).

———. *The Visible Hand: The Managerial Revolution in American Business* (1977).

Chandler, Alfred D., Jr., and Herman Daems. *Managerial Hierarchies: Comparative Perspectives on the Rise of the Modern Industrial Enterprise* (1980).

Eisenstadt, S. N. *Tradition, Change, and Modernity* (1973).

———. "Studies of Modernization and Sociological Theory." *History and Theory* 13 (1974): 225–252.

Fredrickson, George M. "Comparative History." In *The Past Before Us: Contemporary Historical Writing in the United States,* edited by Michael Kammen (1980).

Galambos, Louis. "Parsonian Sociology and Post-Progressive History." *Social Science Quarterly* 50 (1969): 25–45.

———. "Technology, Political Economy, and Professionalization: Central Themes of the Organizational Synthesis." *Business History Review* 57 (1983): 471–493.

Geertz, Clifford. *Peddlers and Princes: Social Change and Economic Modernization in Two Indonesian Towns* (1963).

Gorn, Elliott J. "Doing Sports History." *Reviews in American History* 18 (1990): 27–32.

Grew, Raymond. "Modernization and Its Discontents." *American Behavioral Scientist* 21 (1977): 289–312.

———. "More on Modernization." *Journal of Social History* 14 (1980): 179–187.

Gusfield, Joseph. "Tradition and Modernity: Misplaced Polarities in the Study of Social Change." *American Journal of Sociology* 72 (1967): 351–362.

Guttmann, Allen. *From Ritual to Record: The Nature of Modern Sports* (1978).

Hareven, Tamara. "Family Time and Industrial Time: Family and Work in a Planned Corporation Town, 1900–1924." *Journal of Urban History* 1 (1975): 365–389.

———. "Modernization and Family History: Perspectives on Social Change." *Signs* 2 (1976): 190–206.

Harris, Neil. "Cultural Institutions and American Modernization." *Journal of Library History* 16 (1981): 38–48.

Henretta, James A. "'Modernization': Towards a False Synthesis." *Reviews in American History* 5 (1977): 445–452.

Inkeles, Alex, and David H. Smith. *Becoming Modern: Individual Change in Six Developing Countries* (1974).

Kammen, Michael, ed. *The Past Before Us: Contemporary Historical Writing in the United States* (1980).

Kirby, Jack T. *Rural Worlds Lost: The American South, 1920–1960* (1987).

Lerner, Daniel. *The Passing of Traditional Society: Modernizing the Middle East* (1958).

Lipset, Seymour. *The First New Nation: The United States in Historical and Comparative Perspective* (1963).

Lloyd, Christopher. *Explanation in Social History* (1986).

———. "The Methodologies of Social History: A Critical Survey and Defense of Structuralism." *History and Theory* 30 (1991): 180–219.

Nugent, Walter. *Structures of American Social History* (1981).

Rodgers, Daniel T. "Tradition, Modernity, and the American Industrial Worker:

Reflections and Critique." *Journal of Interdisciplinary History* 7 (1977): 655–681.

Rosenberg, Charles. *The Care of Strangers: The Rise of America's Hospital System* (1987).

Rostow, W. W. *The Stages of Economic Growth: A Non-Communist Manifesto* (1960).

Rothman, David J. *The Discovery of the Asylum: Social Order and Disorder in the New Republic* (1971).

Smelser, Neil. *Social Change in the Industrial Revolution* (1959).

Smith, Daniel Scott. "'Modernization' and American Social History." *Social Science History* 2 (1978): 361–367.

Sokolow, Jayme A. *Eros and Modernization: Sylvester Graham, Health Reform, and the Origins of Victorian Sexuality in America* (1983).

Starr, Paul. *The Social Transformation of American Medicine* (1982).

Stearns, Peter. "Modernization and Social History: Some Suggestions, and a Muted Cheer." *Journal of Social History* 14 (1980): 189–209.

Tipps, Dean C. "Modernization Theory and the Comparative Studies of Societies: A Critical Perspective." *Comparative Studies in Society and History* 15 (1973): 199–206.

Vinovskis, Maris A. "Socioeconomic Determinants of Interstate Fertility Differentials in the United States in 1850 and 1860." *Journal of Interdisciplinary History* 6 (1976): 375–396.

———. "Recent Trends in American Historical Demography." *American Review of Sociology* 47 (1978).

Weber, Eugen. *Peasants into Frenchmen: The Modernization of Rural France, 1870–1914* (1978).

Wells, Robert V. "Family History and Demographic Transition." *Journal of Social History* 9 (1975): 1–19.

Wiebe, Robert H. *A Search for Order, 1877–1920* (1967).

Wilentz, Sean. "On Class and Politics in Jacksonian America." *Reviews in American History* 10 (1982): 45–63.

Wirth, Louis. "Urbanism as a Way of Life." *American Journal of Sociology* 44 (1938): 1–24.

Wrigley, E. A. "The Process of Modernization and the Industrial Revolution in England." *Journal of Interdisciplinary History* 3 (1972): 225–260.

Zuckerman, Michael. "The Fabrication of Identity." *William and Mary Quarterly* 34 (1977): 183–214.

SEE ALSO various essays in the section **"Processes of Social Change."**

QUANTIFICATION AND ITS CRITICS

Stanley L. Engerman

QUANTIFICATION, LOOSELY DEFINED as counting, has long been a familiar tool used by many historians. The early Greek historians used numbers to describe the size of armies and other critical factors in order to present relevant orders of magnitude and to provide some basis for comparisons. Even basically nonquantitative historians have presented quantitative measures—such as population size, the numbers of business firms, the numbers of laborers on strike, and breakdowns of votes—and indicated their importance. A standard late-nineteenth-century work on historical method, for example, posits the need for quantitative measures to establish the importance of nonquantitative observations:

> Descriptive formulae relating to characters, being merely qualitative, only give an abstract idea of the facts; in order to realise the place they occupied in reality, quantity is necessary. It is not a matter of indifference whether a given usage was practised by a hundred men or by millions. (Langlois and Seignobos, *Introduction to the Study of History,* p. 274)

The eminent British economic historian Sir John Clapham, in terms generally applicable to any attempt to place an observed pattern in broader historical perspective, stated: "Every economic historian should, however, have acquired what might be called the statistical sense, the habit of asking in relation to any institution, policy, group or movement the questions: how large? how long? how often? how representative? ("Economic History as a Discipline," p. 328). A useful role for the statistical method was also suggested by the economist Joseph Schumpeter: "We need statistics not only for explaining things but also in order to know precisely what there is to explain" (*History of Economic Analysis,* p. 14).

These broad statements about quantification indicate both its long use in historical studies and its important role as a supplement to, and not a substitute for, other types of historical approaches. In brief, quantification is used to help determine the nature of the historical events to be explained, as well as to determine how typical (or representative, or important) these happenings and episodes were. More generally, the statements quoted above indicate that quantitative methods represent a useful component of most historical interpretations while not being the sole or exclusive basis of historical understanding.

These descriptions also point up quantification's diverse approaches and methods. These include "simple" counts of the number of occurrences, such as the number of slaves transported to the New World in the transatlantic slave trade (the preparation of a simple count may, however, include rather complex interpolations or extrapolations); calculations of distributions of various categories, such as income and wealth within a population, to permit determinations of relative positions; and measures of the importance of relations among different causal factors, such as the contribution of changes in education and income to the declines in American fertility (such measures entail the use of regression analysis and other complex statistical procedures). Clearly the benefits of quantification, as well as the criticisms of its use, would be expected to vary with the specific nature of the quantitative procedure employed as well as with the appropriateness of its application to the specific historical issue.

THE EXPANSION OF QUANTIFICATION

Quantification has long been used in social history and other types of history, in the United States and elsewhere. In the United States, for example, much of the work of Frederick Jackson Turner, as well as of his followers and critics in the first part of the twentieth century, utilized some variant of quantification (see, for example, Swierenga, *Quantification in American History,* pp. xii–xv). Nevertheless, the great expansion of quantification both in historical studies and in the study of social history came in the late 1950s and the 1960s.

The expansion of quantification in social history was due to several factors. First, the computer, with its ability to handle large data sets and complicated statistical analysis, played an obviously central role. Curiously, several of the most important of the early quantitative social history studies did not initially use computers but, rather, calculators and adding machines. Second, there were developments in statistical methods and a greater acceptance of sampling to answer questions when the examination of the full population would have been prohibitive in terms of time, money, and intellectual concentration. This meant that, for some questions, it was possible to use quantitative methods to reach acceptable interpretations even with limited data. Third, and perhaps most important, was the framing of new questions by social historians that could best be answered in terms of Clapham's queries: how large? how long? how often? These questions, often requiring the use of data about individuals and families, were generated by Marxists and other critics of the American experience, as well as by scholars who had some background in the empirical methods of the social sciences. Many of the latter were initially more concerned with using quantitative methods to study the historical record to understand the past than with using them to test social scientific theories of human behavior.

The influential early studies, even when dealing with diverse topics, claimed a similar method of approach, and the basic research began within a limited time span in the late 1950s. The central questions of social mobility, demographic and family behavior, and income and wealth distribution were studied using data about individuals and families. These included data from the manuscript schedules of the federal and state censuses, tax lists, city directories, and related sources, which could be examined most effectively with the help of computers. Not all social history is quantitative, as not all social science is quantitative. For many of the questions of concern for social historians in this period, however, some degree of counting and quantification appeared necessary in order both to describe what had happened in the past and to provide a way of explaining it.

The first major studies using quantification in social history ran the full gamut of the social-history questions then asked. Quantification was employed in the study of topics such as social mobility, family patterns, and the social basis of voting behavior, and it played a role in the study of various histories: immigration, ethnic, black, women's, labor, and urban. Moreover, quantitative work in other areas, such as economic history and political history, played a major role in the examination of issues in social history. As with all types of historical study, debates about the usefulness of a particular approach, the precise meaning of particular concepts and questions and their interpretation, and the manner in which results and conclusions fit into the broader historical context, arose. At times, debates about the specifics of studying a particular issue merged with arguments about methods in general. I shall return to these general issues after discussing several of the major earlier works that significantly influenced subsequent works in social history, works dealing with issues that were heatedly debated and of key interest to historians—then and now.

THE USES OF QUANTIFICATION

Studies of Mobility Perhaps the most influential early studies in social history using quantification were writings on social, occupational, and geographic mobility. The most influential, because of its explicit concern with method, was Stephan Thernstrom's *Poverty and Progress* (1964), an examination of intra- and intergenerational change in occupational status and of geographic mobility in Newburyport, Massachusetts. He used a data source earlier employed by Oscar Handlin in *Boston's Immigrants, 1790–1865* (1941) and utilized by James Malin in "The Turnover of Farm Population in Kansas" (1935), by Merle Curti and others in *The Making of an American Community* (1959), and by Allan Bogue in *From Prairie to Cornbelt* (1963) in studies of the nineteenth-century Midwest. Thernstrom drew upon the manuscripts of the federal census schedules to determine how many and which members of the male population departed from Newburyport for other locations within each ten-year period between censuses; what happened to the occupational status of those who remained; and what was the relation of the occupations of the sons who lived in Newburyport to the occupations of their fathers.

There were difficulties in undertaking and interpreting such measures, as Thernstrom indicated, but his work represented a major step forward in answering many of the central questions raised about the impacts of social and economic change on the native-born and immigrant population of late-nineteenth-century America: Were people locked in place for life or did they move frequently, possibly in response to opportunities elsewhere? Was mobility low—a presumed sign of a continued community—or was it so high that it would be difficult to sustain any labor or reform movements, as well as any communal existence? Did lower-class individuals lose status in the process of economic growth, or was there upward mobility in status as determined by occupation (if not in wealth or in wages)? If upward mobility, both within a generation or over generations, was possible, did this dilute American protest movements or, at least, lead to forms of protest different from those in Europe, where (as was then believed) social mobility seemed more limited? (This latter view was modified when European quantitative studies suggested that rates of mobility in Europe and in America were closer than had been believed.)

Thernstrom's study pointed to the high degree of geographic mobility of the population, particularly those of lower economic status, many of whom left in the ten-year interval between censuses, as well as the apparent high degree of occupational mobility of those who remained, both for fathers and for their sons. There was both agreement on these basic findings and debates about broader implications for American social and political life, but these could now be conducted on a more solid historical basis.

The questions asked were, as Thernstrom pointed out, not new. Also, their importance to historians was seen in light of their politically charged nature. Thernstrom's use of census data provided a measure of frequencies of occurrence with which to begin to answer frequently asked questions. His presentation of data did not imply that mobility was a "good" thing, as had earlier been argued by others, nor even that all individuals should want to seek upward mobility. Tastes in regard to economic and social advancement might differ among individuals and groups, meaning that earlier discussions of the problem of mobility had been incomplete. Indeed, one of the significant conclusions of Thernstrom's work here and elsewhere (see, for example, his *The Other Bostonians*) was precisely that not all individuals and ethnic groups valued upward social and economic mobility. Rather, they had made choices when confronted with a trade-off between different desirable ends and values, and they faced the consequences—and benefits—of their choice.

While specific interpretations linking estimated magnitudes of mobility and individual belief and behavior are still questioned, the work on social mobility has provided the essential framework for many subsequent studies in social, urban, educational, women's, ethnic, and labor history. In each, the observations of behavior, as described by quantitative or other methods, are used, supplemented by other sources, to infer the beliefs and motives of individuals. These studies include important examinations of related issues by Elizabeth Pleck in *Black Migration and Poverty* (1979), Theodore Hershberg and others in *Philadelphia* (1981), Michael Katz and others in *The Social Organization of Early Industrial Capitalism* (1982), Alexander Keyssar in *Out of Work* (1986), and Joel Perlmann in *Ethnic Differences* (1988), among others. These studies have, in general, pointed to what seem to be high rates of geographic mobility and generally upward social and economic mobility over the course of the nineteenth century, as well as significant differences among racial and ethnic groups. Further, studies of wealth using tax lists (see, for example, "The Progress of Inequality in Revolutionary Boston" by Allan Kulikoff), probate estate records (by, among others, Alice Hanson Jones in *Wealth of a Nation to Be* (1980) for the pre-Revolutionary era), and manuscript census schedules (by Lee Soltow in *Men and Wealth in the United States* (1975) for the mid nineteenth century) have permitted studies of changing wealth holdings and their distribution over time.

These studies have made important contributions by pointing to the role of age and life-cycle status in changing social and economic positions. On issues of direct concern to labor historians, there have been more studies, using census data, military records, newspapers, and firm records, to detail changing patterns of real wages in different occupations and locales (see, for example, Robert A. Margo and Georgia C. Villaflor's "The Growth of Wages in Antebellum America" and Winifred Rothenberg's "The Emergence of Farm Labor Markets"). More recently, state and federal labor reports, mainly for the late nineteenth century, have been used to provide better estimates of the nature of labor turnover and job persistence, measures critical for discussions of the causes for the weakness (or strength) of the American labor movement.

The History of African Americans African American history became an important area for quantitative social history beginning, in some measure, with the work of Philip Curtin. In 1969, Curtin, as a result of undertaking some needed background calculations for an essay on the slave trade, published *The Atlantic Slave Trade: A Census.* This book has raised questions central to the historical studies of four continents. Curtin's quantification was intended to provide the details found in a census—a total count of the number of slaves who left Africa for the New World, with details on points of departure, points of arrival, and nationalities of carriers. All that was initially intended was a simple counting, although given the incompleteness of the data available, various interpolations and extrapolations were required to present a complete picture.

In his first chapter Curtin demonstrated that historians had long considered the question of the total numbers leaving Africa for the Americas to be important. He also anticipated critics who might ask why it was necessary to prepare new estimates for a series of data long available and used by tracing the then most frequently cited estimate of the magnitude of the slave trade back to an obscure American publicist, Edward E. Dunbar, writing in 1861, who clearly lacked much of the evidence available in the twentieth century. Curtin's estimates of about ten million Africans arriving as slaves in the New World triggered extensive research and analysis. Because of the discoveries of new archival information and the use of different extrapolation methods, there have been some modifications of his initial totals and breakdowns, but all of this has helped to cast new light on American, European, and African history (see, for example, Herbert S. Klein's *The Middle Passage,* Paul E. Lovejoy's *Transformations in Slavery,* and Patrick Manning's *Slavery and African Life*).

The count of the slave trade, in conjunction with counts of white migration, served, as pointed out by David Eltis in "Free and Coerced Transatlantic Migrations" (1984), to generate new pictures of the relative importance of black and white migration to the Americas, with more than four times more blacks than whites arriving until the early years of the nineteenth century. And the analytical use made of the records of indentured servants by David Galenson in *White Servitude in Colonial America* (1981), and by Bernard Bailyn in *Voyagers to the West* (1986) and by others, has provided more information on the English background to this important stream of white migrants. All these findings have been fitted in with reconstructions of the Native American population prior to settlement (and its rapid decline after transatlantic contact) to recast the history of the settlement period.

Yet Curtin's work had an even more significant influence upon the study of the social history of African Americans in the period of slavery. By comparing the total number of slaves brought to the United States with the population of blacks in the United States in 1950, Curtin highlighted a demographic puzzle that had been put aside for over a century. The slave population of the United States had an extremely high rate of natural increase, unique for a major slave population and unusual even compared with free populations elsewhere. The slave populations in the Caribbean and throughout most of South America, however, must have experienced significant rates of natural decrease—mortality exceeding fertility. These comparisons hold significant implications for the study of African American culture. There was a higher proportion of native-born slaves in mainland North America than in the Caribbean and in South America during the era of the slave trade.

There were clearly other streams opening up the social history of black America in the 1960s and 1970s. The presentation of this demographic contrast by Curtin became a central part of ongoing work describing the comparative treatment of slave populations. It was also important for the examination of the different rates of natural increase, and the analysis of the comparative rates of fertility and mortality for slaves in the United States and elsewhere. Factors that were examined included work routines, slave-owner interference with slave reproductive patterns, slave-family stability, the physical treatment of slaves, their nutrition and diet, and the impact of migration by sale and/or geographic relocation. Influenced in part by Curtin's findings, writings on the antebellum slave experience by, among others, Eugene Genovese in *Roll, Jordan, Roll* (1974), Robert Fogel and Stanley Engerman in *Time on the Cross* (1974), Herbert Gutman in *The Black Family in Slavery and Freedom* (1976), and Robert Fogel in *Without Consent or Contract* (1989) dealt with these issues, often on the basis of quantification derived from sources including census manuscripts, plantation records, shipping data relating to slaves, and invoices of slave sales.

Perhaps the most intense debate, relating to both method and substance, arose after the publication of Fogel and Engerman's *Time on the Cross*. This work dealt with the development of the overall southern economy in the antebellum period, the material treatment of the slave population, and the nature of the plantation economy. Criticisms of specifics related to the usability of the different sources employed, the possibilities of sampling biases, and the implications to be drawn from competing assumptions of individual behavior in reaching conclusions (see, for example, Paul A. David et al., *Reckoning with Slavery*). Other historians argued against the possibilities of using historical methods, including quantification, to reach any interpretation of an immoral institution. The controversy did suggest that many of the criticisms raised about quantitative methods were equally applicable to other approaches, and that the quantitative measures were often more amenable to detailed critical evaluation than were others.

There were other strands leading to these broader developments in the social history of slavery. These included the anthropological approach to the behavior of lower classes inspired by E. P. Thompson's *The Making of the English Working Class* (1963), the economic analysis of the profitability of slavery in the United States by Alfred Conrad and John Meyer in "The Economics of Slavery" (1958), and the shifting of attention to the beliefs and behavior of black slaves, earlier advocated by black and white historians. Not all questions could be discussed in quantitative terms. Yet it was possible to use quantitative methods to extract considerable new information from previously underutilized sources.

Demographic and Family History As in the study of black slaves, the use of various types of documents susceptible to the application of quantitative methods helped to give voice to groups that had often previously seemed voiceless—women, lower-class workers, immigrants, and minority groups. The census data generated new information about the outcome of behavior—fertility patterns, family structure, occupations, wealth—and their changes over time, and provided access to these and other aspects of human life. As a complement to the use of other sources, quantitative methods helped to indicate the critical issues necessary to describe those for whom more traditional sources were less frequently available and more difficult to place in an appropriate historical context.

One of the major developments of quantitative social history in Europe since the 1960s is the study of demographic and family history, especially in France and England. It is from England, most notably the so-called Cambridge Group including Peter Laslett, E. A. Wrigley, and Roger Schofield, that the larger impact upon demographic studies in the United States has come. Laslett's initial substantive contribution, *The World We Have Lost* (1965), fit into the confines of both family and demographic history. Having examined English household lists and town and village censuses for several centuries, he argued that there had been no transition from a larger, extended preindustrial family to a smaller, nuclear industrial family. Rather, the smaller nuclear residential pattern had long been predominant. This conclusion led to further questions, some taken up by Laslett. One concerned the relation of life cycle and residential patterns and the frequency with which individuals lived part of their lives in an extended family (whatever pattern was most frequent at any given time). Another question related to the nature and frequency of closeness to kin and other sources of support for nuclear families.

The focus on family structure also served to underpin studies, using other sources, of relations among individuals and of emotional life within the family. Extended comparison of family size and age at marriage in "European Marriage Patterns in Perspective" (1965) led John Hajnal to distinguish a western European marriage pattern from marriage patterns in other parts of the world, a distinction that has been used to explain why western Europe and England experienced modern economic growth earlier than other regions. Laslett used parish registers to determine marriage ages in early modern England, finding that the age for females was in the mid twenties rather than the teens (as exemplified by Shakespeare's Juliet). This relatively late marriage age for English men and women, with apparently limited illegitimate births, raised questions concerning social life and sexual patterns that were explored by Laslett and others using more traditional sources. Questions such as these have been important to American social historians, particularly given the earlier marriage ages and larger family sizes in the United States during the early colonial era.

In *The Population History of England* (1981), E. A. Wrigley and R. S. Schofield utilized British censuses, parish registers of births, deaths, and marriages, and related sources to provide a massive study of British demographic development from 1541 to 1871. This project involved some complex procedures to interpolate missing data, but their book is a model (for all historians) of how to test for the sensitivity of outcomes resulting from various estimating procedures and assumptions, and how to arrange for such tests with available data. In addition to preparing the overall estimates, they examined the relative contributions of fertility and mortality changes to population variability, and the impact on fertility change of changed age at marriage and of variations in the avoidance of marriage. They then related these changes to real wages, to determine how the demographic changes were related to economic variables, and to see if things behaved as Malthus had predicted. Striking in their findings were the frequent variations in fertility and mortality, providing a demonstration that periods of long-term constancy in these variables did not exist, and that no simplistic Malthusian pattern had preceded the modern era.

In a related set of demographic studies, starting in 1963, the fertility transition in Europe was studied by the Princeton European Fertility Project, under the direction of Ansley Coale (see Ansley J. Coale and Susan C. Watkins, *The Decline of Fertility in Europe*). Using measures drawn from various national censuses, several volumes examined the timing of the fertility decline within specific countries and dealt with some of the explanatory factors. Rich in empirical detail, they provided methods and issues for demographers elsewhere, as well as numerous questions for social historians interested in family and demographic issues. This served to provide a firmer empirical basis for describing the impact of the many changes that have characterized the modern era.

Another topic of importance for demography has been height, which has been studied by, among others, scholars associated with the Development of the American Economy program of the National Bureau of Economic Research, under the direction of Robert Fogel. The first major book on this subject, *Height, Health and History* (1990) by Roderick Floud, Kenneth Wachter, and Annabel Gregory, used military and philanthropic data on the heights of British males to describe the variations in one aspect of the changing British standard of living between 1750 and 1980. Other studies for the United States (slave and free), the Caribbean, Europe, and Africa have dealt with changes in height, nutritional status, and mortality.

The key demographic issues in European contexts had obvious importance for the United States. Similar questions have been studied by similar methods, and the use of similar methods has led to comparative studies between the United States and elsewhere.

In the United States, the first major studies by social historians dealing with demographic issues concerned the colonial period. Using various quantitative sources, such as town census lists and registers of births, marriages, and deaths, John Demos in *A Little Commonwealth,* Philip Greven in *Four Generations,* and Kenneth Lockridge in *A New England Town* (all published in 1970) described the demographic and family patterns of seventeenth- and eighteenth-century colonial New England, examining ages at marriage, fertility, and family patterns, and mortality. Maris Vinovskis, in *Fertility in Massachusetts* (1981), extended the study of the fertility decline in Massachusetts up to the Civil War. Subsequent studies of the Chesapeake by Russell Menard, Lois Carr, Lorena Walsh, and others made it possible to highlight certain significant differences in settlement patterns, in life expectancy, and in family formation among regions more precisely than before. They noted the unusual demographic experience of New England and other areas of the American colonies: the colonies had extremely high rates of natural increase, due to the high rates of fertility, particularly among native-born women. New England also had low mortality in comparison with other sections in the Americas and with Europe. Social historians were now more able to draw out implications of the differing settlement and demographic patterns among the colonies for social, political, and cultural life.

Economic and Political History Several important quantitative studies influenced the study of social history and emerged in other subfields of history. Economic history has long been, on the basis of questions studied and data used, about the most quantitative of the subfields of history. Its quantitative nature was confirmed by the publication in the early 1960s of works by Douglass North (*The Economic Growth of the United States*) and Robert Fogel (*Railroads and American Economic Growth*), and the subdiscipline came to be called the "new economic history" and "cliometrics" by its proponents.

Much of the early work in quantitative economic history was undertaken at the National Bureau of Economic Research, and several influential quantitative essays in economic history were first published under its auspices in two conference volumes, *Trends in the American Economy in the Nineteenth Century* (1960) and *Output, Employment, and Productivity in the United States After 1800* (1966). Also instrumental in expanding the range of social and economic history was the initiation by William N. Parker of the collection of data for over five thousand southern farms in 1860 from the manuscript census schedules of the federal census. When the collection was completed, under the direction of Parker and Robert E. Gallman, and made accessible to scholars in the late 1960s, the importance of linking the manuscript census schedules containing economic and demographic data became apparent and numerous scholars have subsequently undertaken similar work to deal with major historical problems.

In major work, building upon census data on production after 1840, Robert Gallman, in "Commodity Output" (1960), prepared detailed estimates of national income, including its total and its sectoral breakdowns, for the years after 1840. He linked these estimates with the pioneering estimates of Simon Kuznets to most of the nineteenth century, and with those of Kuznets and the Department of Commerce to bring estimates of national income up to date. Gallman's initial work posed several key problems for social historians, among them the early onset of American economic growth and the relatively high (by international standards) level of per capita income at its starting point.

Moreover, as Thomas Cochran had suggested in "Did the Civil War Retard Industrialization?" (1961), not only had rapid economic growth preceded the start of the Civil War, but the wartime decade itself was one of slow economic growth. This meant that economic growth had started earlier, ending arguments about the impact of the Civil War as the initiator of American economic growth. Related studies by other economic historians, on the basis of census data for the nineteenth century, were Stanley Lebergott's *Manpower and Economic Growth* (1964) and Thomas Weiss's "Revised Estimates of the United States Workforce" (1986), detailed breakdowns of the labor force by sector pointing to an early, rapid movement of labor out of agriculture. In "The Growth of Real Product in the United States" (1967), Paul David used the Gallman and Lebergott estimates to infer high and varying rates of economic growth between 1800 and 1840. Richard Easterlin in "Regional Income Trends" (1961) estimated regional incomes for census years after 1840, pointing to a pattern that he interpreted as showing a relatively more favorable income position for the South before the Civil War than after. This has helped to frame discussions of the social and economic patterns of change in the South under slavery and in the economic adjustments to the emancipation of the slaves.

The questions studied by social historians were also influenced by quantitative studies of political behavior, particularly Lee Benson's *The Concept of Jacksonian Democracy* (1961), that stressed the role of ethnocultural factors in voting. These studies led to renewed attention to religion and ethnicity as determinants of voting patterns, an analysis of influences on voting that went beyond simple arguments dealing only with economic factors. The attention to religion and ethnicity then spread beyond the study of political behavior to describe the basis of broad social movements and reform arguments, including the emergence and ultimate success of the northern abolition movement. These arguments pointed to a role for religion as a social factor in describing other changes, and not isolating religion as a narrow intellectual issue. While there were other influences in these, as in all the other developments described, the impact of quantitative voting studies helped demonstrate the importance of the ethnocultural factors for the analysis of many social-history questions, such as the abolition of slavery (see Fogel, *Without Consent or Contract*), educational performance (see, for example, Perlmann, *Ethnic Differences*), and the emergence of distinct political cultures (see, for example, Paul Kleppner, *The Third Electoral System*).

THE DEBATE OVER QUANTIFICATION

Disagreements, questionings, and the use of new findings to raise new questions are in the general nature of historical work, and quantification has been no exception to this. Errors of analysis and interpretation arise in quantitative, nonquantitative, and antiquantitative scholarship. There has been some literature (see, for example, Barrington Moore's *The Social Origins of Dictatorship and Democracy,* Lawrence Stone's *The Past and the Present,* and Theodore S. Hamerow's *Reflections on History and Historians*) that argues specifically about quantitative methods on apparently general principles. Such exercises seem, however, to be misleading as a historiographic strategy, since it is on the specifics of analysis that debates should rest. Further, many of the points raised are equally applicable to any method of historical study, not just to quantification, and important questions of method should concern all historians.

The debates on the more general criticism of quantification in history thus have come to resemble the familiar debates between those who advocate employing newer methods (or employing older methods more explicitly and to a greater extent) and those who deny the value of any but the most traditional methods. To defenders of older methods, any new method seems to be misleading historically, causing the asking of wrong questions, omitting the essence of what might be considered historically important, studying issues only because they are dictated by the method, and not providing anything more than what is already known. Advocates of any new method, in arguing for the usefulness of their approach to study long-standing historical problems, would point to its benefits in broadening the horizons of the historian; in being more precise in asking questions and defining concepts (even if initially the issues and the range of factors considered seem narrow); in opening a greater part of the historical record, with the preparation of new data bases and new data collections; and in being able to apply the method to answer older questions.

At the general level, debates about method often pit defenders of older methods who seem to deny any benefits from the new against advocates of newer methods who believe that they can be broadly applied to old (and new) historical questions. The broad debate muted as quantitative history like other historical innovations, became part of the mainstream of historical studies; the debate shifted to what is, in any particular case, good historical scholarship. By the 1990s, it was accepted that there are some issues that cannot be dealt with quantitatively, some that are inherently quantitative, and many to which quantification can make some contribution when used in conjunction with other methods.

Since quantification includes many different procedures and plays a number of quite different roles in historical studies, the earlier blanket condemnation (and praise) of quantitative methods in general has more appropriately narrowed to discussions of their use in specific cases to study specific questions. In this it resembles, for the most part, critiques of other types of historical examination. That this should be so is not surprising. History proceeds by stages, from collection and examination of data to establish what happened, to attempts to understand what the data meant to contemporaries and subsequent scholars, and to dealing with broader implications and generalizations. Each scholar usually performs some of these steps, and is aided by other scholars who perform complementary or related studies that help fill out the broader picture. The great Scottish moral philosopher Adam Smith pointed to the advantages of a division of labor in producing for the economy, and there are similar advantages in various academic disciplines, including history. Quantification can have considerable importance for some studies in social history (imagine, for example, studying the history of labor without quantitative information on numbers in different occupations, wages and incomes, labor force participation, and laborer voting patterns), less importance for others, and little or no importance for still others. Thus, the very existence of general arguments about quantification is itself an interesting question for the social history of history.

BIBLIOGRAPHY

The quotations at the beginning of the article, in sources still worth reading on many issues, are from the following:

Clapham, J. H. "Economic History as a Discipline." In *Encyclopaedia of the Social Sciences.* Vol. 5 (1937).

Langlois, C. V., and C. Seignobos. *Introduction to the Study of History.* Translated by G. G. Berry (1898).

Schumpeter, Joseph A. *History of Economic Analysis* (1954).

QUANTIFICATION AND ITS CRITICS

Books

Bailyn, Bernard. *Voyagers to the West: A Passage in the Peopling of America on the Eve of the Revolution* (1986).

Benson, Lee. *The Concept of Jacksonian Democracy: New York as a Test Case* (1961).

Bogue, Allan G. *From Prairie to Cornbelt: Farming on the Illinois and Iowa Prairies in the Nineteenth Century* (1963).

Coale, Ansley J., and Susan Cotts Watkins, eds. *The Decline of Fertility in Europe* (1985).

Conference on Research in Income and Wealth, *Trends in the American Economy in the Nineteenth Century,* edited by William N. Parker (1960).

———. *Output, Employment, and Productivity in the United States After 1800,* edited by Dorothy S. Brady (1966).

Curti, Merle, with the assistance of Robert Daniel, Shaw Livermore, Jr., Joseph Van Hise, and Margaret W. Curti. *The Making of an American Community: A Case Study of Democracy in a Frontier Community* (1959).

Curtin, Philip D. *The Atlantic Slave Trade: A Census* (1969).

David, Paul A., Herbert G. Gutman, Richard Sutch, Peter Temin, and Gavin Wright. *Reckoning with Slavery: A Critical Study in the Quantitative History of American Negro Slavery* (1976).

Demos, John. *A Little Commonwealth: Family Life in Plymouth Colony* (1970).

Floud, Roderick, Kenneth Wachter, and Annabel Gregory. *Height, Health and History: Nutritional Status in the United Kingdom, 1750–1980* (1990).

Fogel, Robert William. *Railroads and American Economic Growth* (1964).

———. *Without Consent or Contract: The Rise and Fall of American Slavery* (1989).

Fogel, Robert William, and Stanley L. Engerman. *Time on the Cross* (1974).

Galenson, David. *White Servitude in Colonial America: An Economic Analysis* (1981).

Genovese, Eugene. *Roll, Jordan, Roll: The World Slaves Made* (1974).

Greven, Philip J., Jr. *Four Generations: Population, Land, and Family in Colonial Andover, Massachusetts* (1970).

Gutman, Herbert G. *The Black Family in Slavery and Freedom, 1750–1925* (1976).

Handlin, Oscar. *Boston's Immigrants, 1790–1865* (1941).

Hershberg, Theodore, ed. *Philadelphia* (1981).

Jones, Alice Hanson. *Wealth of a Nation to Be: The American Colonies on the Eve of the Revolution* (1980).

Katz, Michael B., Michael J. Doucet, and Mark J. Stern. *The Social Organization of Early Industrial Capitalism* (1982).

Keyssar, Alexander. *Out of Work: The First Century of Unemployment in Massachusetts* (1986).

Klein, Herbert S. *The Middle Passage: Comparative Studies in the African Slave Trade* (1978).

Kleppner, Paul. *The Third Electoral System; 1853–1892: Parties, Voters, and Political Cultures* (1979).

Laslett, Peter. *The World We Have Lost* (1965).

Lebergott, Stanley. *Manpower and Economic Growth: The American Record Since 1800* (1964).

Lockridge, Kenneth A. *A New England Town: The First Hundred Years, Dedham, Massachusetts, 1636–1736* (1970).

Lovejoy, Paul E. *Transformations in Slavery: A History of Slavery in Africa* (1983).

Manning, Patrick. *Slavery and African Life* (1990).

North, Douglass C. *The Economic Growth of the United States, 1790–1860* (1961).

Perlmann, Joel. *Ethnic Differences: Schooling and Social Structure Among the Irish, Italians, Jews, and Blacks in an American City, 1880–1935* (1988).

Pleck, Elizabeth Hafkin. *Black Migration and Poverty: Boston, 1865–1900* (1979).

Soltow, Lee. *Men and Wealth in the United States, 1850–1870* (1975).

Thernstrom, Stephan. *Poverty and Progress: Social Mobility in a Nineteenth-Century City* (1964).

———. *The Other Bostonians: Poverty and Progress in the American Metropolis, 1880–1970* (1973).

Thompson, E. P. *The Making of the English Working Class* (1963).

Vinovskis, Maris A. *Fertility in Massachusetts from the Revolution to the Civil War* (1981).

Wrigley, E. A., and R. S. Schofield. *The Population History of England, 1541–1871* (1981).

Articles

Carr, Lois Green, and Russell R. Menard, "Immigration and Opportunity: The Freedman in Early Colonial Maryland." In *The Chesapeake in the Seventeenth Century: Essays on Anglo-American Society,* edited by Thad W. Tate and David L. Ammerman (1979).

Carr, Lois Green, and Lorena S. Walsh. "The Planter's Wife: The Experience of White Women in Seventeenth-Century Maryland." *William and Mary Quarterly,* 3d ser., 34, no. 4 (October 1977):542–571.

Cochran, Thomas C. "Did the Civil War Retard Industrialization?" *Mississippi Valley Historical Review* 48, no. 2 (September 1961):197–210.

Conrad, Alfred H., and John R. Meyer. "The Economics of Slavery in the Ante Bellum South." *Journal of Political Economy* 66, no. 2 (April 1958):95–130.

David, Paul A. "The Growth of Real Product in the United States Before 1840: New Evidence, Controlled Conjectures." *Journal of Economic History* 27, no. 2 (June 1967):151–197.

Easterlin, Richard A. "Regional Income Trends, 1840–1950." In *American Economic History,* edited by Seymour Harris (1961).

Eltis, David. "Free and Coerced Transatlantic Migrations: Some Comparisons." *American Historical Review* 88, no. 2 (April 1983):251–280.

Gallman, Robert E. "Commodity Output, 1839–1899." In Conference on Research in Income and Wealth, *Trends in the American Economy in the Nineteenth Century* (1960).

———. "The Pace and Pattern of American Economic Growth." In *American Economic Growth,* edited by Lance E. Davis, Richard A. Easterlin, and William N. Parker (1972).

Hajnal, John. "European Marriage Patterns in Perspective." In *Population in History,* edited by David Glass and D. E. C. Eversley (1965).

Kulikoff, Allan. "The Progress of Inequality in Revolutionary Boston." *William and Mary Quarterly,* 3rd ser., 28, no. 3 (July 1971):375–412.

Malin, James. "The Turnover of Farm Population in Kansas." *Kansas Historical Quarterly* 4, no. 4 (November 1935):339–372.

Margo, Robert A., and Georgia C. Villaflor. "The Growth of Wages in Antebellum America: New Evidence." *Journal of Economic History* 47, no. 4 (December 1987):873–895.

Rothenberg, Winifred. "The Emergence of Farm Labor Markets and the Transformation of the Rural Economy: Massachusetts, 1750–1855." *Journal of Economic History* 48, no. 3 (September 1988):537–564.

Walsh, Lorena S., and Russell R. Menard, "Death in the Chesapeake: Two Life Tables for Men in Early Colonial Maryland," *Maryland Historical Magazine* 69, no. 2 (Summer 1974):211–227.

Weiss, Thomas. "Revised Estimates of the United States Workforce, 1800–1860." In *Long-Term Factors in American Economic Growth,* edited by Stanley L. Engerman and Robert E. Gallman (1986).

Discussions of Quantification

Aydelotte, William O. *Quantification in History* (1971).

Fogel, Robert W. "The Limits of Quantitative Methods in History." *American Historical Review* 80, no. 2 (April 1975):327–350.

Hamerow, Theodore S. *Reflections on History and Historians* (1987).

Kousser, J. Morgan. "Quantitative Social-Scientific History." In *The Past Before Us: Contemporary Historical Writing in the United States,* edited by Michael Kammen (1980).

———. "The Revivalism of Narrative: A Response to Recent Criticisms of Quantitative History." *Social Science History* 8, no. 2 (Spring 1984):133–149.

Moore, Barrington, Jr. *Social Origins of Dictatorship and Democracy: Lord and Peasant in the Making of the Modern World* (1966).

Stone, Lawrence. *The Past and the Present* (1981).

Swierenga, Robert P., ed. *Quantification in American History* (1970).

SEE ALSO **Community Studies; Ethnicity; Family Structures; Geographical Mobility; The Old Social History and the New; Race; Slavery; Social Class; Social History in Great Britain and Continental Europe** and various essays in the section on "**Family History.**"

MARXISM AND ITS CRITICS

Paul M. Buhle

MARXIST IDEAS HAVE permeated and substantially influenced the writing of United States social history, especially since 1965, often in ways that neither avowed Marxists nor opponents of Marxism anticipated. Repeatedly in the course of the twentieth century, "Marxism" as a method of analyzing history has been detached from expectations for some future proletarian triumph, and turned instead into a component of the progressive or "radical" sociohistorical perspective. In that light, many of its proponents have emphasized not only the significance of class and race, but also—and contrary to much of the older Marxism—of gender and ethnicity. They have also refocused leftist criticism on the historic role of American elites and have helped make possible a synthesis of varying methodological outlooks.

Through these shifts, the theoretical underpinnings of Marxist models for historical study have been transformed where they have not given way entirely. Orthodox Marxist interpretations rested upon the specification of a rising bourgeoisie displacing its forerunners and even itself. Capitalism's steady expansion created, according to the model, a proletarian army within the factories and fields, while contradictions within the system of production manifested themselves in periodic crises. For these Marxist scholars, history should yield both "lessons" of class struggle from the prebourgeois epoch and explanations of contemporary inequalities. These verities could not survive generations of disappointed promises, but elements of Marxist methodology did remain relevant within the reworked critique of capitalism.

Critics of Marxist-influenced writing, especially liberal intellectuals frantic to separate their political causes and historical outlook from the Left, have repeatedly sought to expunge or discredit the scholarship and the scholars they deplore. Since the 1940s treating radical critics of various kinds as disreputable if not actually disloyal, these critics have in recent years turned their pens against the phenomenon known as "multiculturalism." The egalitarian (if scarcely Marxist) alternative to the traditional narrative of heroic national (white, male) triumph has thereby become, in more than one way, Marxism's lineal successor.

ORIGINS OF MARXIST HISTORY

The influence of Marxist historians on the scholarly mainstream remained very limited until, at least, the middle 1930s. The reason for this lack of influence cannot be simply attributed to an absence of serious studies, as John Higham argues in "Changing Paradigms: The Collapse of Consensus History." Such a judgment misconstrues the nature and value of most Marxist scholarship before the 1930s and even after. Marxist historians, by and large self-taught writers seeking a political rather than a scholarly audience, often managed remarkable studies, sometimes with a wide public acceptance. Indeed, popularized history served better than any other discipline (including economics) to explain the socialist cause. Professional scholars remained oblivious to or contemptuous of such achievements.

The founders of Marxism, and their immediate disciples, established some important if incomplete and often ambiguous models for historical study. Friedrich Engels's *Peasant War in Germany* (1926) drew from secondary sources the historical "lessons" of the previous revolutionary wave in the sixteenth and seventeenth centuries; he later regarded it as oversimplified and he planned (though never managed) to revise the text. Among other nineteenth-century writers, Engels's disciple, Karl Kautsky, the future "revisionist" Eduard Bernstein, the English socialist E. Belfort Bax, and the American C. Osborne Ward all developed texts treating ancient and medieval uprisings. These texts provided details of conflict consistent with the Marxist thesis that all history is a history of class struggle. These writers often situated their protagonists' efforts as heroic acts of will, though, and attributed their failures to premature material conditions according to Marxist historiography. This solution neatly avoided the many difficulties of interpretation and precise implications for contemporary political action.

The earliest tracings of Marxist histories of American life can be found in the nineteenth- and the early-twentieth-century socialist and anarchist ethnic press. Essayists took over the materialist framework of Marx to explain the development of capitalism and the promise of a future revolution. They also sought to account for the strength of American capitalism and the peculiarly difficult situation of the immigrant worker-reader. These ruminations, based on personal observation as much as on scholarship, contained a wealth of insight into the nature of the job market and craft unions, and into the coerced cultural assimilation that often destroyed the folk wisdom of centuries within a single generation.

English language and especially American-born Marxist writers of the early twentieth century developed their ideas in a very different context, that of "progressive" historiography. By the 1910s many younger historians, uncomfortable with the genteel character and generally unreflective conservatism of their profession, set out with a new agenda. Influenced by journalistic muckraking and public disillusionment with corruption, these scientifically minded scholars re-examined available evidence, revealed the economic interests behind American ideals, raised serious questions about the heroic quality of the constitutional framework and the Civil War, and generally sought to counterbalance existing scholarly prejudices.

Charles Austin Beard, by far the most important of the younger scholars, published his controversial *An Economic Interpretation of the Constitution* in 1913 and *The Economic Origins of Jeffersonian Democracy* two years later. Socialist historians had already been working along similar lines, but Beard's popularity boosted socialist confidence, while his determined search for "causation" in history ran parallel with a Marxist, materialist estimation of society's inner purpose.

Only a handful of writers emerged from this milieu to write full-length works. Marxist correspondent Hermann Schlüter, an editor for many years of the daily *New Yorker Volkszeitung*, produced a fine history of the socialistic brewery workers' union, a balanced documentary study of Lincoln and slavery, and a closely written history of the First International in the United States. His counterpart in the Yiddish daily press, former Hebrew teacher Philip Krantz, penned *All America: History of All the Countries in the New World* (1915), two volumes with heavy emphasis on material conditions but also containing many anthropological sidelights on Native American life. These writers lacked the sophistication of later academic Marxists. But for their radical, working-class audience, their essays and random commentaries on American social history in the German, Italian, Slavic, Finnish, and Yiddish press, were extremely instructive.

English-language socialists lifted the historical progressivism of Beard and others to a higher degree of criticism against contemporary capitalism, and tacked onto this history a radical political agenda. A. M. Simons, a Wisconsin undergraduate during the 1890s and a rapt admirer and student of Frederick Jackson Turner, wrote a lengthy pamphlet overview and study guide, which he delivered to Socialist party activists, *Class Struggles in American History* (1903). Serialized in the *Appeal to Reason*, with a circulation of 200,000, the booklet prompted the formation of some 5,000 study classes for its discussion.

A full-length version, *Social Forces in American History* (1911), drew heavily on the progressive historians (including Woodrow Wilson), W. E. B. Du Bois, and a scattering of primary sources, to reveal the patterns of class repression and deceit, and to praise the mass democratic strivings from below. Significantly, Simons, like the progressive historians, saw neither the American Revolution nor the Civil War as democratic triumphs, but rather as manipulations by the elite, with a heavy rhetorical overlay.

This was history of the kind that socialist literary comedian Oscar Ameringer perfected in his humorous *The Life and Deeds of Uncle Sam: A Little History for Big Children* (1912), which sold more than a half-million copies in ten languages. When national leaders "talk about fighting for justice, eternal right, glory, the flag, God, fatherland or avenging an insult to the nation, watch out," Ameringer warned. These events actually take place because of "selfish material interests of classes which strive against other classes in an endeavor to make an easier living" (pp. 1–2). Historical materialism located and explained the real causes. Muckraker Gustavus Myers devoted his three-volume *History of the Great American Fortunes* (1909) to the same large purpose of cutting through the claims of apologists to reveal the sordid origins of the American plutocratic class. Journalist Allan Benson actually wrote his way to the 1916 Socialist party nomination for president with his best-selling exposé, *Our Dishonest Constitution* (1914). Socialist historical novelists, such as best-selling author Upton Sinclair, molded the same iconoclastic clay around issues of the hour.

Simons, commended by Charles Beard for his insight into historical processes, remains the most interesting of all these writers for his academic sophistication. Simons sought to weave, through the use of Marxist methods and socialist political teleology, the tale of an heroic and tragic struggle for community. Even more than his mentor Turner, Simons was convinced of the "communistic character" of frontier life (and of pre-Columbian Native American life), later destroyed by the intrusion of the market and the cities. The artisan farmer and his cousin the skilled worker, the backbone of real democracy in modern America, had been deprived increasingly of their hard-won victories. Only socialism could remedy this decline of democracy. Simons held impressive Marxist bone fides—he was editor and translator of European Marxist writings in the prestigious *International Socialist Review*. But he actually sought to reconcile modern scholarship, both "bourgeois" and Marxist, with the spirit of the nineteenth-century democratic polemicists such as novelist-journalist George Lippard, who had held up American dreams of a radical republic against the bitterness of capitalist reality.

This school of historical scholarship could not endure. World War I, the split and collapse of the Socialist party, and the accompanying government repression devastated the demi-Marxist historians. The avowed Marxist writers on historical topics for the next twenty years were for the most part communists based in ethnic traditions, or they were intellectual isolates.

Lithuanian-born communist editor Anthony Bimba was the most prominent of the first type. His *The History of the American Working Class* (1927), based on secondary sources, was used widely in Communist study circles; he also published a somewhat more original but small study, *The Molly Maguires* (1932), before returning to historical topics in his native Lithuanian language.

Among the second type, the independent self-trained, nonacademic Marxist historians gradually diminished with the decline of nonuniversity scholars and scholarship generally. Fewer American radical publications existed for work done outside of academia for a nonscholastic audience.

Much subsequent extra-academic work represented the completion of lengthy earlier efforts. For instance, the massive two-volume *Government by Judiciary* (1932) by the prominent civil defense lawyer (and former Marxian theorist of note) Louis B. Boudin sought to contextualize Supreme Court decisions in the political economy of the age and the ideology of increasingly arbitrary court authority. Boudin's onetime editorial collaborator before 1920, former communist leader Lewis Corey, was a self-educated economist with a strong historical bent. His *The House of Morgan* (1930) offered a powerful institutional study of Gilded Age banking, and in *The Crisis of the Middle Class* (1935) he analyzed the intermediate classes as carriers of democratic ideas throughout American history—at this point a novel approach for a Marxist. *Modern Quarterly* editor V. F. Calverton's *The Liberation of American Literature* (1932) and his subsequent works sought similarly to portray intellectual history against the background of a changing capitalism.

Although these books fell into obscurity quickly, the extra-academic and independent radical tradition produced two popular classics. Matthew Josephson, erstwhile bohemian who remained as much a journalist as a popular historian, delivered in 1934 the remarkable *Robber Barons: The Great American Capitalists, 1861–1901*, a more comprehensive and vastly more popular treatment of the phenomenon pinpointed by Corey's *House of Morgan*. Josephson's work appeared at a time of extreme popular disillusion with contemporary capitalism. Widely praised in the popular liberal and radical press, *The Robber Barons* encouraged young scholars to adopt radical approaches. It was dedicated to Charles and Mary Beard.

Far more important in the long run, W. E. B. Du Bois's *Black Reconstruction . . . in America, 1860–1880* (1935) simultaneously revolutionized the study of African Americans and showed how very far historians still had to go in grasping the meaning of the black experience for United States life at large. The book's afterword, a scathing and unprecedented polemic against the ruling racial assumptions among scholars of the South and of Reconstruction generally, would prove to be one of the most embarrassing for professional historians. The truth lay almost entirely on Du Bois's side.

Contrary to the predominant scholarly assumptions that blacks had been largely passive during the Civil War, then brutes of the Reconstruction South overthrown by white recuperation of civilized institutions, Du Bois showed that African American actions were vital to the Northern victory and central to hopes for a democratically reconstructed America. To make his points, Du Bois had employed an often clumsy Marxist jargon, rendering the fleeing from wartime plantations a "general strike" and Reconstruction black rule a "dictatorship of the proletariat"; on the other hand, his analysis owed a great deal to the basic methods of Marxist materialism and to the Leninist theme of anticolonialism.

Du Bois had been moving in this direction from his earliest studies of the slave trade and its consequences. World War I and the Russian Revolution, with evidence of European bankruptcy and a turn in the tides for the world's people of color, propelled him to reconsider radical Reconstruction as a central event of Western history. In *Black Reconstruction,* for the first time a prominent author could write, without straining basic Marxist categories, that American civilization—tragically including its white working classes—had failed the test of democracy. The unease with which American communist leaders met these implications is exemplified in James S. Allen's *Reconstruction: The Battle for Democracy* (1937), which emphasized the (substantially exaggerated) importance of a "Popular Front" of whites and blacks inside the South. Most American historians who took notice of *Black Reconstruction,* though, responded with indifference or hostility.

THE POPULAR FRONT AND THE COLD WAR

The mutual isolation of Marxist scholars and academics eased suddenly in the late 1930s, when Communists redirected their energy toward a "Popular Front" of all democratic forces against the growing tide of fascism. Marked with ambiguities and internal contradictions, the Popular Front nevertheless permitted Left-leaning intellectuals to seek alliances with liberals, and for liberals in turn to accord Communists and Communist sympathizers a niche in the respected intellectual community.

Communist and leftist publications, their status further enhanced by leftist participation in the organization of industrial unions and in the support of the Spanish Republic, rapidly came into vogue. At the same time, however, the very alliance of communists with the New Deal tended to dull the radical edge of criticism. Imperialism, racism, and class exploitation still seemed enemies of humankind, but capitalism itself sometimes appeared a mere remnant of privilege upon an historically progressive American democracy.

The new journal *Science and Society,* founded in 1936 by a group of prominent academics close to the Communist party, enrolled a number of important historians within and outside the academy. Its contributing editors included Broadus Mitchell and Fulmer Mood, while regular contributors included Josephson, labor historians Henry David and Samuel Yellen, early national period specialist George Dangerfield, economic historians Paul Birdsall and Curtis Nettls, and colonialism specialist Irving Mark. With the 1939 Nazi-Soviet Pact, *Science and Society*'s character decisively narrowed; the above-named editors and contributors dropped off almost entirely. Only one young intellectual, Herbert Aptheker (destined to remain for most of his life outside the academic world), remained in the milieu of the journal.

Popular Front Marxism had its critics. Louis Hacker, the Beardian economic historian with Marxian pretensions, charged with great acuity that traditionally Marxist judgments of class and its role in the state had already been sacrificed by the Popular Front to political ends. Indeed, Communist party leader Earl Browder, in his *Traitors in American History: Lessons of the Moscow Trials* (1938), had insistently cast the Founding Fathers of the United States as communist-like leaders of democratic change, their opponents conspiratorial conservatives (or precursors of Leon Trotsky!). Hacker's specific complaints, however, missed a more important point.

During the last half of the 1930s, communists, liberals, and many writers and artists, irrespective of their other differences, had embraced American democratic historic and folkloric themes in a darkening world. (Hacker, author of several historic studies that were critical of American economic institutions, changed his own mind in *The Triumph of American Capitalism* [1940], hailing the system's success in providing material goods.) Boosters of democratic inclusionism made the most of the moment. In the popular presentation of history presented by Works Progress Administration (WPA) murals, chorale and folk or concert hall music, community theater, and Left-scripted Hollywood film, many groups were seen to contribute to the great democratic saga of American life. "Public history" arguably achieved its greatest triumph through the efforts of musical masters Paul Robeson, Aaron Copland, and Earl Robinson; muralists Ben Shahn and Rockwell Kent; and Hallie Flanagan's Federal Theater. All bore a remote version of a Marxist perspective, heavily filtered through the Popular Front lens.

The contradictions of this view were obscured by the impending crusade against international fascism and against racist or semifascistic (such as anti-Semitic) views at home. During this historic moment, communist allies and liberals could join together to lobby for Negro History Week in public schools and to organize immigrant groups (such as Jews, Italians, and Slavs) to lobby for their own respective recognition. However, no systemic analysis of racism or other forms of oppression and discrimination was permitted to cloud the optimism. Any severe and pessimistic historical treatment of American society, such as Du Bois's critique of Reconstruction's defeat as a crushing national failure, were again almost completely marginalized.

Wartime sentiments extended the illusion of continued Marxist influence. The war's boost to democratic inclusion had a dire effect on the writing of history in Marxist terms, and two works together signaled a virtual end to the troubled academic beginnings of the later 1930s. *American Renaissance* (1941), by literary scholar F. O. Matthiessen, was a monumental effort to place the Concord literary radicals of the 1830s in their precise cultural context. One of Matthiessen's students, Arthur Schlesinger, Jr., who would later become a hostile and demeaning critic of his former teacher wrote a mainstreamed political history counterpart in *The Age of Jackson* (1945), heralding a victorious nineteenth-century people's coalition. The two works might be taken together as the demi-Marxist tributes of academics to the promise of the 1830s and their hopes for an ongoing New Deal to usher in a more cooperative social order. It was notable, though, that Marxist Matthiessen never strayed far from standard literary analytical methods, and that Schlesinger glossed over Andrew Jackson's mass murder of Native Americans in his lengthy volume. Matthiessen would be dead from a suicide, a victim of the cold war, by 1951. Schlesinger, a veritable champion of the cold war, would pronounce a formal end to his radicalism with a spirited anti-Marxist text, *The Vital Center* (1949).

By the early 1950s, American communism had been discredited in the eyes of most of its former adherents. And yet the lingering, positive reflections of the Popular Front and especially of its emphasis on support for blacks, labor, and progressive ethnic nationalism would remain in individuals and take on new meaning in the years to follow. David Montgomery, Herbert Gutman, Alexander Saxton, and hundreds of lesser-known teacher-scholars had passed through the Communist party or its fraternal, youth, or social peripheries, or through the last great cause of the 1940s Left generation, the Henry Wallace presidential campaign of 1948. Senator, sometime labor historian, and future presidential nominee George McGovern was only the most prominent of the Wallace boosters who also contributed to historical scholarship.

Nonetheless, during the 1950s, the prospects for Marxist historiography dramatically darkened. Its political status defamed on campus—the academics supporting Henry Wallace faced severe personal attacks for years to come—and its Popular Front expectations of democratic advance lost, the Marxist study of history all but disappeared for a decade. Surviving traces could be found by close observers, but only by carefully unpacking the intentions concealed in such works as Ray Ginger's compelling biography of Eugene Debs, *The Bending Cross* (1949); by searching among the very small circle of communist and semicommunist historians (several of the most sensitive among them Jewish literary scholars writing in Yiddish); or by examining the Marxist-influenced antiradicalism of the "counter-progressives."

Communists Herbert Aptheker and Philip S. Foner, both denied academic positions because of their political beliefs, worked frantically to fill the historiographical gap. Aptheker's landmark *American Negro Slave Revolts* (1943) earnestly sought to deduce slave resistance from the material conditions of extreme oppression and the (often slight) evidence of unrest. His subsequent series of works on African American history set out to follow the tradition of Du Bois (eventually he became Du Bois's literary executor, and the editor of many volumes of Du Bois's papers). His more general works on United States history seemed, however, simplistic and overdrawn.

Foner showed less interest in discussions of Marxist methods but a fanatic devotion to the Left version of old-fashioned, institutional studies of labor history. The basic story of class struggle seemed virtually unchangeable across time and circumstance in his works, and communists (or their presumed predecessors, as specified by Foner) appeared perpetually to emerge as the proper leaders of the masses, almost always wrongfully denied their historic opportunity. Foner's multivolume history of American labor and more than a hundred other works on labor, African Americans, and women, among other topics, were only coincidentally social history, by virtue of the detail added to flesh out a standard political- or institutional-style narrative. But Foner presented such a vast amount of detail that readers might glean an approximate social history of labor with a loosely Marxist perspective.

Not only were Marxists themselves marginalized in this era, but an intellectually prestigious countercurrent gathered force. Former radicals fused Marxist ideas they had learned with subtle methodological innovations (principally the study of psychological motivation) to help push the profession toward "consensus" history. In this counter-progressive paradigm, the vast majority of Americans had agreed on common goals, disputing only the means by which these might be accomplished. Richard Hofstadter, chief synthesizer, was for almost a decade between the mid-1950s and mid-1960s a virtual reigning force in American political history. A Communist in his youth and later a close sympathizer with the quasi-Trotskyist, anarcho-Marxist magazine *Politics,* he became a clever and lucid commentator on the national epic.

Written with an almost aristocratic elegance, Hofstadter's *The American Political Tradition* (1948) and *The Age of Reform* (1955) turned progressive historical assumptions on their heads. In Hofstadter's version, Americans had always shared a business mentality ("a democracy in cupidity rather than a democracy of fraternity"); dissenters from this tradition were necessarily outsiders, usually unwelcome ones; and the only truly class-conscious or fully conscious group worthy of note and admiration existed among the wealthy and conservative. A materialist, Hofstadter might have argued (although he did not), could only come to this conclusion in mid-century United States.

By this standard—as Hofstadter drew on the psychological literature of the 1950s—reformers necessarily had motivations very different from the noble ones usually attributed to them. Brahmin elites so prominent in nineteenth- and early-twentieth-century struggles—abolitionist to anti-imperialist to progressive—actually sought to solidify their eroded class status. Populists, viewed by communists as the great egalitarians of the nineteenth century, were victims of hateful rural irrationalities and proponents of impossible visions of community.

Hofstadter had constructed, to his own satisfaction, a radical critique of American limitations, severely marked by an inability to accommodate reasonable structural reform. His work could be seen both as an extension of Marxist hypotheses, and simultaneously as a critical response toward them. Hofstadter himself remained ambiguous about his intentions, shifting ground repeatedly.

In the political climate of the time, Hofstadter's conclusion seemed to echo familiar cold war themes of America the great and homogenous democracy armed against the enemies of freedom. Vulgarized by historians like former communist Daniel Boorstin, consensus views became mere scholarly propaganda. Boorstin testified against his college roommates and advisers, assured a congressional committee that communists should never be allowed to teach college history, went on to write *The Genius of American Politics* (1953) and later to serve as Librarian of Congress. Both Hofstadter and Boorstin affirmed the certainty of consensus, however they judged it. Not surprisingly, the Mississippi Valley Historical Association (forerunner of the Organization of American Historians) awarded the coveted Bancroft Award in 1950 to an otherwise undistinguished and badly researched volume, Arthur Holcombe's *Our More Perfect Union: From Eighteenth-Century Principles to Twentieth-Century Practice,* which "proved" the utter impossibility of Marxist historical interpretations.

By contrast, Hofstadter's Marxism manqué salvaged an element of radical openness for alternatives to consensus history, past and future. Despite his avowed conservatism, Hofstadter retained his admiration for Charles Beard, whom cold war–minded historians had bitterly denounced for opposing President Roosevelt and the cold war. Hinting at his personal shift leftward once more, this time in the context of a vibrant 1960s, Hofstadter's final monograph, *The Progressive Historians*

(1968), even suggested that a new history might come out of a ferment similar to that which had made the progressive historians possible.

The study of race relations and politics by a relatively small group of historians meanwhile demonstrated that within sharp limits, a radical critique had already become acceptable. C. Vann Woodward, most prominent among scholars of the American South, had visited the Soviet Union in the 1930s and been drawn toward Marxist hypotheses (if not necessarily accepting Marxist conclusions, and repelled by Communist political tactics) by the sheer exploitative character of slavery and the starkness of racism in his native American South. His *Tom Watson: Agrarian Rebel* (1938), even more than his later works, revealed Woodward's effort to tease out the radical, but emphatically non-Marxist, character of southern Populism. By the 1950s, the civil rights movement raised historical questions which neither the progressive tradition of Beard nor the consensus interpretations of Boorstin could satisfactorily answer, but to which Woodward's approach seemed increasingly relevant.

NEW LEFT MARXISM TAKES SHAPE

A new and unique Marxist-influenced history grew up within the final strongholds of progressive history, and moved to prominence as social conflict returned to the center of American political life. Unlike its predecessor, it not only lacked any significant links with communism but tended to regard Marxism as scarcely more than one current within available radical thought, and the working class as no more than one constituency in a mosaic of social change.

The young generation of Marxist scholars took shape, more than anywhere else, at the University of Wisconsin, in Madison. There, where historians of earlier generations had been in close touch with two La Follette governors and a deep, popular antiwar sentiment, the cold war was resisted and its crushing effects on intellectual life were mitigated. For a quarter century or more after World War II, graduate students in American history emerged eager to engage with radical (including Marxist) theories and fresh methods to rewrite history.

Their earliest and most long-standing mentor, Merle Curti, was the radical (if non-Marxist) champion of lost causes during the 1930s and 1940s. Pacifist, student of Frederick Jackson Turner at Harvard during the 1910s, author of the Pulitzer Prize–winning *Growth of American Thought* (1943) as well as notable studies of antiwar activism, Curti had devoted his 1953 presidential address at the American Historical Association to the then-unpopular task of vindicating Charles Beard and the progressive tradition. Among those joining him in Madison, also deeply influential for the next generation of historians, were Merrill Jensen, the last of the major progressive historians drawn to the democratic decentralism of the pre-constitutional era; Fred Harvey Harrington, a progressive diplomatic historian; and European historians George Mosse and Harvey Goldberg, whose radical slant on Continental politics and culture provided a way to appreciate Marxism's historical role abroad. These scholars—and one of their students in particular—nurtured a remarkable cadre of graduate students who by the early 1970s would change the writing of United States history.

William Appleman Williams, a former Naval commander, studied history at Madison with Harrington, and sociology with Hans Gerth, a Marxist-inclined German intellectual refugee, before returning in 1960 to teach. From the early to middle 1960s, Williams primed the most influential single bloc of foreign policy scholar-critics for the next era, including Lloyd Gardner, Gar Alperovitz, Walter LaFeber, and Thomas McCormick. Together, their "revisionist" treatment of United States foreign policy provided overwhelming evidence for the economic basis of foreign engagement and the imperial intentions of foreign policy.

Williams's own works—scorned by the likes of Oscar Handlin and Arthur Schlesinger, Jr., and decades later still savaged in the neoliberal *New Republic*—and his influence got him elected president of the Organization of American Historians in 1981. His devotees claimed for this self-avowed Marxist the greatest influence on American history of any figure since Frederick Jackson Turner and Charles Beard.

Williams's extremely influential *Tragedy of American Diplomacy* (1959) had set the tone for later studies, through an internal critique of United States policy objectives. The elites, he asserted, had denied to other nations the autonomy that U.S. policymakers feared might bar the Americans commercial access (the "Open Door"). This compulsion, more than any other world dynamic, had effectively triggered the nuclear arms race and drowned in blood and corruption the third world's hopes for real economic independence. Williams's graduate students proceeded to detail the opening of the cold war in Europe and Asia, and the American determination to seek supremacy; the crushing weight that its economic and military policy placed upon subservient Latin American nations; and the horrific yet unsuccessful war it had waged in Southeast Asia. With scholarly rigor, a close eye for detail, and a skillful popularization of radical ideas, Williams's protégés collectively exceeded the output and the influence of previous American Marxist historians. Above all, they developed the theme of American society's failure according to its own terms—the implementation of democratic aspirations. Their works collectively displaced or altered the traditional portrait of American foreign policy found in standard treatments, substituting for their emphasis on heroism and idealism one of economic motives implemented with sordid cruelty—at best an indifference to the sufferings of nonwhite peoples.

Williams influenced the writing of American history in two other large and Marxian-related ways. Breaking with Turner, Beard, and Simons's treatment of historic western movement as a democratizing process, Williams depicted the "frontier" as the escape from the social responsibilities of nationhood. Beard, in particular, had placed the antidemocratic impulses within American life in the late nineteenth century, with the rise of monopolies and an overseas empire. He had cast the democratic response as a people's movement (populism, progressivism, and finally the New Deal) against the usurpacious "interests." In the view of Williams and his disciples, frontier settlement had meant displacement of indigenous peoples at high human cost, and high cost to democratic aspirations as well. This interpretation dated the rise of empire to a much earlier moment, and posed imperial policy as an inevitable and continuous part of the construction of the United States.

Williams had, in fact, drawn from consensus historians' emphasis on capitalist values as the building blocks of American identity. But while accepting and even admiring American statesmanship within the eighteenth- to mid-nineteenth-century world as creating an island of relative liberty, Williams came to less sunny conclusions about the next century, going so far as to title one of his books *Empire as a Way of Life* (1980). He insisted that Marxism had been an essential informative method in his work, and he devoted a little volume, *The Great Evasion* (1964), to demonstrate its utility. His perceptive critics and friends often concluded, however, that a fundamentally Christian Socialist perspective, with its goal of community in opposition to anomic and rapacious individualism, had permitted Williams to interrogate the dark side of American character.

Williams's other great influence built upon this one. *The Contours of American History* (1961) outlined the background and development of what graduate student Martin J. Sklar would dub "corporate liberalism," the single most influential scholarly phrase for a generation of antiwar activism. By arguing that modern liberalism had been a regulative part of the corporate thrust rather than contrary to its essential logic, Williams again borrowed from the insights of the consensus historians, once more turning these ideas around for radical purposes. The federal government as a taxing, service-dispensing, and war-making instrument established the formidable role of the liberal bureaucrat who sought to preserve the economic system by filling gaps in its social relations. Liberals in the presidency and Congress—that is, centrist Democrats, as Williams's students and readers would argue—had become true agents of corporatism at its highest level, through international intervention. Here again, Williams had made a "Marxist" point as immanent critique, and with a systemic clarity that the Popular Front Communists (wedded as they were, before and after 1948, to liberals in the Democratic party) could not muster.

Finally, Williams helped a political milieu of scholarship to coalesce around similar ideas. In 1959 a group of mostly former communist youth and Williams's students at the University of Wisconsin formed *Studies on the Left,* a scholarly journal with a strong historical bent and a radical political commitment. Shaking off their own past dogma but retaining kernels of Marxist critical thought, these young intellectuals elaborated a wide-ranging critique of corporate-liberal America. Leading member Sklar's *The Corporate Reconstruction of American Capitalism, 1890–1916: The Market, the Law, and Politics* (1988) fairly epitomized, in its publication decades later, one side of their collective accomplishment. James O'Connor's close studies of the state (and his own later journal, *Kapitalistate*) elaborated a similar perspective. James Weinstein's political popularizations of Williams's views, in the former's weekly newspaper, *In These Times,* have shown that paper's importance in continuing to link a particular style of Marxist-influenced radical history and politics from the 1970s and into the 1990s.

Studies on the Left also included among its prominent writers and editors two important social historians also drawn to the corporate-liberal paradigm: Gabriel Kolko and Eugene Genovese. Kolko, a Wisconsin graduate student of the early 1950s, had arrived at a similar perspective on his own and elaborated it eloquently in *The Triumph of Conservatism: A Reinterpretation of American History, 1900–1916* (1963). Placing iconoclastic American radical Thorstein Veblen above Marx as a source of historical insight, Kolko calculatedly showed the role of reform in preserving the troubled transition to modern capitalism. Farsighted elites had overseen this process, effectively eclipsing radical possibilities. In later volumes on United States foreign policy Kolko slipped into a more straightforward Marxist approach of military conflict mediating class conflicts in the international arena, with the United States as the chief capitalist of the world. Joyce and Gabriel Kolko's *The Limits of Power* (1972) considered the early cold war in great detail, while Gabriel Kolko's study *Anatomy of a War: Vietnam, the United States and the Modern Historical Experience* (1985) analyzed the reasons for the unprecedented defeat of an American intervention by a third-world people.

Genovese, a former Communist youth leader in Brooklyn, made his fame in the late 1960s by proclaiming his hope for the victory of the National Liberation Front over the American forces in Vietnam, and by analyzing the antebellum South as an arena of highly mediated class-race distinctions. Also drawing on the consensus historians, but from still another angle, Genovese the avowed Marxist (and devotee of Antonio Gramsci) bitterly disputed Herbert Aptheker's model of slave-master conflict. Rather than barely subdued warfare, he argued, the "master class" had practiced what Gramsci described as "hegemony," rule by informal consent. In *The Political Economy of Slavery* (1965) and later volumes culminating in *Roll, Jordan, Roll* (1974), Genovese elaborated a careful study of slave economic and social conditions, in terms that overlaid a version of historical materialism on a set of assumptions allied with those who espoused the Marxism spawned by the journal *Studies on the Left*.

The increasing attention of Genovese to another side of slave life owed much to a Marxist-oriented school of historical studies otherwise distant from the assumptions of Williams and the *Studies on the Left* school. George Rawick, expelled from the Young Communist League in the late 1940s and drawn into the Trotskyist youth movement as he passed through graduate school in Madison, Wisconsin, in the early 1950s, had subsequently moved into the intellectual orbit of C. L. R. James. Author of *The Black Jacobins* (1938), a Pan-Africanist veteran, Marxist philosopher, and Caribbean literary pioneer of the 1930s, James was also a famed cultural critic. (His study of cricket, *Beyond a Boundary* [1963], remains an outstanding social analysis of sports' role in popular life.) He had been expelled from the United States on a passport violation during the McCarthy era, but kept in close touch through a small group of followers, and returned after 1969 to lecture for nearly ten years as black Marxist éminence grise at American universities.

James had, like Du Bois, argued during the 1930s to the 1940s when such views were rarely heard that blacks had played a unique and central role in American life. More self-consciously Marxist than Du Bois (who had long emphasized the role of the black elite, and came to communism only late in life), James insisted that black history had been formative to modern economic and social life. Slave plantation labor presaged and predicted factory labor, while creating the economic surplus that made the blossoming of Western capitalism possible. Again and again, from abolitionism and radical reconstruction to populism and the involvement of African Americans in twentieth century industry, black activity had threatened to unify the splintered American working class from the bottom upward.

Seeking out what Marx had called "self-activity" (or self-directed activity) among ordinary people, James pointed Rawick in the direction of unpublished slave narratives. Rawick collected these narratives into nineteen volumes, adding in his own book-length essay an interpretation of what Rawick dubbed slave life "from sundown to sunup," away from master controls.

By the late 1960s, James's work shared American devotees with that of another heterodox communist living in England: E. P. Thompson. Author of the massively influential *The Making of the English Working Class* (1963) and a former labor educator, Thompson had sought, with great literary imagination, the conscious role of the lower classes in their own "making." Together with colleagues (especially Eric Hobsbawm) and through their journal,

Past and Present, Thompson and his circle offered to like-minded American intellectuals models for the study of working-class life.

James and Thompson together influenced a second, more diffuse but also vital, Madison efflorescence of specifically New Left social history. The acceleration of the Vietnam War and the rise of the protest movement with its graduate student component—intellectual leaders, sometimes detached from undergraduate militants but often in the avuncular role of advisers—suddenly placed an odd premium on United States history. While "revolution," armed struggles, or at least mass labor strikes took place in other countries, young American radicals felt the need to search out antecedents for an indigenous radicalism. The journal *Radical America,* as signaled by its very name, meant to answer that call.

For a decade or more after its founding in 1967, James and Thompson's *Radical America* offered lodestars of intellectual influence and inspiration for labor history, women's history, and African American history. James himself (through his writings and devotees), Thompson, Rawick, Staughton Lynd, Manning Marable, Linda Gordon, and Mari Jo Buhle figured among major contributors and editorial intimates. As activist waves moved swiftly by, and political turmoil died down into despair and scholarly repose, these writers and the journal itself—supplemented and finally supplanted to a great extent by the *Radical History Review*—helped greatly to offer younger radical graduate students a social history orientation, and a vision of scholars with continuing activist commitment.

Two other intellectual figures, both close to *Radical America* environs by the 1970s, played a related role from the center of the university system. Herbert G. Gutman, with a youthful experience at the fringes of the communist fraternal apparatus, spent his graduate years at Madison in the early 1950s. Inspired in part by Curti's far-ranging methodological searches, Gutman pursued the concept of class through the interdisciplinary methods just becoming popular with the consensus historians. Avoiding the old paths of Marxist historians—valorizing individual leaders or conflicts, or alternatively, muckraking wealth and power—Gutman followed out the anthropologists' "thick description" of community life into discrete, often minute, studies of class and conflict.

David Montgomery took the more traditional Marxist tack of shopfloor studies in a new direction. Former communist machinist, a Ph.D. from the University of Minnesota in the middle 1960s who was also heavily influenced by the British Marxist historians, Montgomery added an impressive political history text to labor studies with *Beyond Equality: Labor and the Radical Republicans, 1862–1872* (1967). His subsequent work, solidly rooted in Marxist theoretical concerns, sought to explain the responses of different types of workers—chiefly skilled ones—to the changing modes of production. His discovery of increasingly tight webs of corporate and government restrictions was not in itself startling. But his detailing of the process shed much light on the logic of production and the understanding by the workers themselves of the ongoing process.

By the early 1970s, radical history, and by extension Marxist influences within radical history, had reached a new stage of consolidation. Williams's influence, despite continued professional resistance, had reached a wide third generation of students, including activists within the doomed McGovern presidential campaign. Eugene Genovese, for his part, received increasingly high marks from conservative colleagues (grateful, in part, that Genovese himself disparaged student antiwar activism on the campus). Radical-minded black scholars such as Vincent Harding (also heavily influenced by C. L. R. James) began to reframe the writing of black American history. Herbert Gutman's widely hailed journal essays describing immigrant working-class life across the nineteenth and early twentieth century effectively validated a new, "cultural" historical study of the lower classes. Meanwhile, a single lengthy pamphlet reprinted from *Radical America*—"Women in American Society" (1971) by Ann D. Gordon, Nancy Schrom Dye and Mari Jo Buhle—served as a study guide for hundreds of women's history classes.

It would not be possible to say precisely what Marxism had to do with this swift if still preliminary rewriting and reorganizing of American history. The practitioners had practically all been effected by Marxian or semi-Marxian influences of one kind or another, but they had chosen, both consciously and unconsciously, not to place this element in the foreground. Rather, as "Women in American Society" stresses, the determination to see the subordinate status of any group as a "situation" (historically rooted, and subject to change) rather than a "condition" (biological and changeless) consistently marks the approach to research and writing. After world revolution failed to rise out of the postwar world of the 1940s, Marxism could only have become conditional and, in a certain way, existential. It now expressed possibilities and attitudes, not "scientific" certainties and not even necessarily an optimistic view of humankind's future. That Marxism had resurfaced in new ways at all, amid a radicalization that scarcely touched the working class (save for racial minorities, and then not often in a clear class form), was the wonder.

The analysis of "periodization," or the placing of key developments within the past illustrates the ambiguous and changing uses of Marxism. In the "classical" Marxist version of American history, modern industrial class struggle arrived in the United States in the late nineteenth century, and the formation of a mass socialist political movement was sure to follow. As "Women in American Society" suggested, women's history turned instead upon an earlier moment, when the household mode of production and its social relations were set aside by the rise of wage-labor and "commodity fetishism," to use a Marxist phrase.

Gutman, leaning on E. P. Thompson's British work and the influence of the Marxist-influenced French *Annales* school of close historical examination, proposed something similar in the accommodation of the preindustrial worker to the pace and problems of waged productive life. The receding or outright disappearance of any approaching climactic moment of class struggle in the present day signaled the scholarly refocus on the change of habits and perceptions more than any decisive class reconsolidation in the past. Picturesque and important developments did not lose their value if they led to no happy outcome. From another and less rosy standpoint, scholars' renewed appreciation of Du Bois's *Black Reconstruction* drove a similar point home. Heroic struggles for democratic changes in American society had been crushed, in no small part because of popular complicity with racial dominance. The historical message continued into the present, promising more moments of truth—but not necessarily any happy endings.

HISTORY REWRITTEN

"We regard methodology as the key to radical history," University of Wisconsin graduate student James P. O'Brien wrote in the introduction to a special issue of *Radical America* entitled "Radical Historiography" (vol. 51, November 1970). But he added that while Marxism promised a useful starting point, "there are no magic methodological formulas that serve to make the job of writing history an easy one." Lack of theoretical sophistication of any kind among historians was a barrier, but theory could never substitute for the hard work of evidence-gathering, evaluation, and writing a coherent narrative.

This overview proved shrewd as a generational statement of purpose, among the very large number of radical apprentice-historians, but even more shrewd as prediction. Marxist-influenced historical study over the next twenty years achieved more and more respectability within the profession and its journals; in the burgeoning field of university press monographs, exhibits, conferences; and even in prestigious prizes and appointments. The process involved, however, mainly a drastic reduction in the distance between an increasingly dilute Marxism and the shifting mainstream of the profession. Perhaps Marxism had become, by and large, a partner—in many circumstances a silent partner—to new versions of progressive history both seemingly very different from and subtly continuous with the older school.

The signs of continuity could be seen clearly enough in the professionalization and institutionalization of former campus radical moods of the 1970s. Not so ironically, the collapse of antiwar protest, the suppression and dissipation of the black power movement, and the emergence of a women's liberation (and to a lesser extent, also a gay liberation) force within a relative political vacuum, refocused the attention of most intellectual radicals onto the campus scene. Working at their craft, engaging with students and colleagues, they felt compelled toward scholarly concentration.

The accomplishments of labor history in this period illustrate the powerful effect of Marxism, interpreted mainly by way of E. P. Thompson and the *Past and Present* British milieu. In *Class and Community* (1976), prize-winning author Alan Dawley Bancroft, for instance, examined the history of the skilled working class of Lynn, Massachusetts, as it was overtaken by fundamental changes in the nature of production, the politicized response of that class, and the demise of its challenge. Many other authors rushed in with detailed statistical studies, merging the demographic "new social history" with the new concerns of Marxist-influenced historians.

The problematic nature of labor history best illustrated the difficulties of Marxism's further adaptations. Paul Breines argued in an essay significantly titled "Uncertain Marxism" that the once-fundamental belief in history being on the side of the working class had fallen away, leaving little of certainty behind. That daunting conclusion did not diminish the intellectual energy of graduate students working with Herbert Gutman, David Montgomery, and many other labor historians. But it shaped and finally limited their work.

Some years down the road, at the close of the 1980s, the journal *International Labor and Working Class History* (edited, for a time, by David Montgomery) conducted important and searching symposia on the consequences of vanishing paradigms. For labor historians, the long-assumed "conceptual building blocks" of the field, occupational histories and associated data sources, had been both the most useable by Marxist historical materialist methods, and the ones which gave way at once to methodological challenges. Joan W. Scott, one of the most prominent historians of European labor, posed the problem most directly by insisting on the sharp separation of gender experiences within labor, effectively eradicating any absolute class interpretations. She also raised the centrality of language to any reexamination, further demanding more than the familiar Marxist models could provide ("On Language, Gender and Working-Class History," *ILWCH,* no. 21 [Spring 1987]). French historian Jean Quataert concludes the discussion wisely with the observation that the old theoretical certainties had indeed faded into the necessity for closer, discrete examinations ("The End of Certainty—A Reply to Critics," *ILWCH* no. 35 [Spring 1989]).

Many observers, including Casey Blake in his "Where Are All the Young Left Historians?," noted that beneath the level of lively discussion, a "stagnation of interpretive work" had been under way since at least the early 1980s. Fragmentation if not stagnation sooner or later struck at every quarter of radical history as the decade wore on, raising the same methodological or conceptual difficulties that labor historians faced. Indeed, one could see the progressive shift outward from the more Marxist categories in labor history to different but no less radical approaches in newer fields.

Women's history offered a most persuasive case in point. During the early years in the field, crusading interpreters carried a vital message of recovering lost experience and lost movements for the current generation and those to follow—as Joan Kelly put it in "The Social Relation of the Sexes," "to restore women to history and to restore our history to women." The connection of women's history with labor history, most vital at an early point, underlined the real similarities of class themes, while at the same time differentiating women's experience of class from men's. Under this rubric, many original and valuable monographs and essays appeared. Frequently, outstanding scholars such as Kelly found themselves stressing the break with Marxist categories required for understanding women's life and labor.

Practitioners of black, Chicano, Asian, and other racial and ethnic fields likewise felt compelled, in many cases, to stress their differences from Marxism in order to concentrate attention on the unique qualities of their particular subject. Younger scholars in these fields, themselves often distanced from the era of political rebellion, experienced Marxism only at second remove, as another "white" ideology. And yet the continuing socioeconomic difficulties of these communities, as well as an intellectual maturation of the scholars, encouraged partial rapprochements with "radical" or "progressive" history if not "Marxism."

The development of the field of cultural history might be described as an attempted response of veteran Marxist radicals to the burgeoning of racial and ethnic studies along with the growing influence of anthropological and ethnographic theory. In some unexpected ways, newer developments marked a final narrative break with the old "myth and symbol" school of 1950s American studies (by which the meaning of an "age" might be captured through examination of symbols) as the newer radical history had broken earlier from the consensus school. Cultural history brought Marxist insights into the interpretation of dissenting or minority currents that had posed challenges to sensibilities of the dominant order. Here, the demi-Marxism of the Frankfurt school (represented by Herbert Marcuse, Theodor Adorno, and others) and the British New Left Marxism of the Centre for Contemporary Cultural Studies (especially of its sometime director, Stuart Hall) came strongly into play, joined to a critique of symbolic language associated with the Russian Marxist literary critic, Mikhail Bakhtin.

Cultural historians, by insisting with Bakhtin on the "dialogic" or dialoguelike nature of all speech (and implicitly, all action), most effectively renewed the Marxist notion of the human experience as essentially social. If human consciousness could be seen as an ensemble of social relations (as Marx and Engels related in *The German Ideology*), an important element of the Marxist legacy might yet be vindicated. The most political-minded of the cultural historians responded to the vanishing destiny of the proletariat by seeking the catch springs of that consciousness in subordinate groups.

In an exemplary effort of this type George Lipsitz's *Time Passages: Collective Memory and American Popular Culture* (1990) examines various discrete phenomena from early 1950s "ethnic" television (*I Remember Mama*) to 1980s Chicano popular music. His work proposes a potential recovery of collective memory—not of a now-distant "folk" culture but of the subordinate groups' "marginal" cultures that endlessly intersect with each other and with conflicting contemporary society. Robin D. G. Kelley's notable history of a very particular 1930s Left, *Hammer and Hoe: Alabama Communists During the Great Depression* (1990), employs some of the same methods to pinpoint the merging of religious and political traditions of rural blacks into a revolutionary quasi Marxism largely of their own imagination.

These studies do not escape the familiar problems of Marxist scholarship. Even the most effective "countermemory," or successful historical reconstruction of the repressed and marginal, cannot reestablish the vanished certainty of the older Marxist class-historical perspective. Indeed, the verve of countermemory evidence may disguise some familiar problems of the older Marxism, such as failure to grapple with what Du Bois had called the "American Assumption," the permeation of materialist cupidity and race bias among wide populations certain in their own minds that unhindered economic expansion would solve all problems that (white) Americans might face.

Prestigious critics of these newest shifts in Marxist or post-Marxist thought complained that Italian Marxist Antonio Gramsci's concept of "hegemony" (popularized among American historians by Eugene D. Genovese) had been substituted for the simplistic Marxist concept of "false consciousness," by which the masses failed to perceive their own proper interest. The "consensus" mentality that Alexis de Tocqueville had observed as early as the 1830s had not been shaken even by a recurrently bad reality.

Cultural Marxists and their co-thinkers responded that the critics had assumed what needed to be demonstrated: the "real" 1830s or 1930s America that the traditional historians and Tocquevillian observers had portrayed in fact corresponded with the lives and observations of the population as a whole. Not only racial minorities and women but large sections of poor and middling white men were relatively powerless and often unpolled. Their sentiments had not been recorded in the official documents and elite memories that formed the contemporary and scholarly "construction" of official reality. Against the background of Ronald Reagan's America with its manipulated public opinion and mass political apathy, such arguments gained scholarly credibility.

The older Marxism had, in this response and in many newer studies at large, given way to radical examinations of how meaning is created in the historical process. If Marxism's descendants could claim no more certainty than this, they nevertheless had the capacity to document the various "stories" of which "history" remained only the official version of the history's victors. That latter version also obviously represented the vindication of the historic uses of power by contemporary admirers of the powerful; radical scholars, however persuasive, could not destroy the charisma of power and its lure for conservative and liberal historians alike. At present, they could give counterevidence.

This approach had a special potential value for those whose historical experiences had hardly appeared hitherto in the history books. Not by accident, studies of Native American life had flourished to such a degree that the tiny corpus of sympathetic (mostly condescending) monographs available in 1960 had grown to a considerable cross-referenced library of anthropological, ethnographic, and other interdisciplinary contributions. The same might be said, in lesser degrees, about many other fields.

On a less theoretical or commonsensical level, the spirit of diversity found its way through administrators, teachers, and eager students into schools, museums, and "public history" programs of many kinds. Here, more than in works primarily by and for intellectuals, quasi-Marxist concepts and many of their former proponents merged with broader democratic sentiments and projects in unbroken hopes for a different America. In one remarkable example, "gay history" grew out of networks of activists close to sympathetic historians, through slide shows, exhibits, and finally, scholarly works that owed much to the rebel spirit of the 1960s but little, in any direct sense, to Marxism proper.

Conservative scholars, several noted liberals, and even an occasional erstwhile Marxist saw much of the continuing New Left scholarship and the subsequent "multiculturalism" of historical theory and college or elementary curriculum as the hated spawn of the "politically correct" scholars. They denounced this tendency—especially evident in women's studies, black studies, Chicano studies, and cultural studies of various kinds—with a fury once reserved for purported "Communist subversion." Indeed, many of the arguments of Schlesinger's *The Vital Center* were rehearsed here once again. Economic and military expansionism, including land expropriations affecting Native Americans and Mexican Americans, were defended as building blocks of democracy; the cold war, with all its human and environmental costs, demanded unflinching vindication even in the face of the collapse of the Soviet threat. Refusal to accept sturdy traditional views was blistered once more as an attack on democracy, even a form of moral treason. It was not hard to perceive that for these aging but still powerful figures, Marxist thought had continued to do its nefarious work, however disguised among the latest revisionist tamperings with the canon.

This frontal attack on radicalism placed the descendants of Marxism in a dilemma. To their avant-garde left, the purveyors of "postmodern" theories tended to deny the meaning of all collective experience; on their right, highly prestigious and senior academic figures with institutional clout charged them with being party to the destruction of meaningful historical interpretations of American life.

A stubborn refusal to accept the familiar, mainstream version of American triumphalism, then, redoubled the need somehow to formulate a new synthesis that gave meaning, even in a preliminary sense, to the welter of interpretations. That need coincided with another facing all historians: to absorb and go beyond the vast detailed work that proliferating monographs of the previous quarter century had made available. Writing at the dawn of the 1980s, Herbert Gutman had noted, "We know much more about the American past as we enter the 1980s than we did when we entered the 1960s. And yet the past is more inaccessible to nonhistorians than it was thirty or fifty years ago" ("Whatever Happened to History," *The Nation,* 26 November 1981). Ultimately, the social utility and powers of persuasion in Marxist (and post-Marxist) ideas would be tested in the resynthesis of large areas of American history.

By the early 1990s, that task had hardly begun. Eric Foner's *Reconstruction: America's Unfinished Revolution, 1863–1877* (1988), winner of awards and the object of rare public attention for a historical work, could be seen, not improperly, as a descendent of Du Bois's *Black Reconstruction.* The black intellectual giant's struggle to fit Marxism into the historical understanding of African American life had acquired a devotee's patient updating of concept and object. From another angle, Foner (junior member of a prominent family of Marxist historians) had drawn the lessons of a generation of radical scholars working frantically at the details of a crucial era in the nation's troubled race relations. The 1993–1994 president of the Organization of American Historians, Eric Foner, had no need to wear Marxism on his sleeve. Some of Marxism's key elements had become truly a part of the methods and motives of historical examination.

Eric Foner, along with his political colleagues and counterparts, had returned in another sense not to Marx so much as to Charles and Mary Beard and Du Bois, all cartographers of American experience and democratic aspiration. The Beards—to rehearse a perception rooted in the early twentieth century—demolished illusions about the historical sanctity of the Constitution, pinpointed the misdeeds of the powerful, and argued vigorously for the inclusion of at least one crucial group in American society, women. Du Bois had worked against the illusions in his own way. The work of these writers had fallen short in modern eyes, for many reasons. Yet the public engager, the antiwarrior, the determined synthesizer, remained a model of activist and public historian that later scholars influenced by Marxism had followed even when they had not clearly seen their lineage.

What the newer radical scholars would add to these equations only became clear as the political cohort of the 1960s passed through early middle age amid an era of revanchist conservatism. But the new contribution was as much rooted in the conflicts and cataclysms of its era as earlier formulations were the product of the radical social ferment of the Progressive era and the New Deal. Marxism, but not the Marxism of the 1910s or 1930s, would surely be something more than a personal background or a mislaid tool in Rosa Luxemburg's famed "lumber room" of theory. How much more, remains to be seen.

MARXISM AND ITS CRITICS

BIBLIOGRAPHY

Early Marxist Histories, 1900–1940

Allen, James S. *Reconstruction: The Battle for Democracy, 1865–1876* (1937).

Benson, Allan Louis. *Our Dishonest Constitution* (1914).

Bimba, Anthony. *The History of the American Working Class* (1927; 2d ed. 1934).

———. *The Molly Maguires* (1932).

Boudin, Louis B. *Government by Judiciary.* 2 vols. (1932).

Browder, Earl. *Traitors in American History: Lessons of the Moscow Trials* (1938).

Calverton, V. F. [George Goetz]. *The Liberation of American Literature* (1932).

Corey, Lewis [Louis C. Fraina]. *The House of Morgan: A Social Biography of the Masters of Money* (1930).

Du Bois, W. E. B. *Black Reconstruction in America, 1860–1880* (1935).

Josephson, Matthew. *The Robber Barons: The Great American Capitalists, 1861–1901* (1934).

Mark, Irving. *Agrarian Conflicts in Colonial New York, 1711–1775* (1940).

Myers, Gustavus. *History of the Great American Fortunes* (1909).

Simons, A. M. *Class Struggles in America* (1903).

———. *Social Forces in American History* (1911).

Ward, C. Osborne. *The Ancient Lowly: A History of the Ancient Working People* . . . 2 vols. (1879).

Recent Radical Texts, 1940 to the Present

Aptheker, Herbert. *American Negro Slave Revolts* (1943).

Genovese, Eugene D. *The Political Economy of Slavery: Studies in the Economy and Society of the Slave South* (1965).

———. *Roll, Jordan, Roll: The World the Slaves Made* (1974).

Ginger, Ray. *The Bending Cross: A Biography of Eugene Victor Debs* (1949).

Gutman, Herbert G. *Work, Culture and Society in Industrializing America: Essays in American Working-class and Social History* (1976).

Harding, Vincent. *There Is a River: The Black Struggle for Freedom in America* (1981).

Hofstadter, Richard. *The American Political Tradition and the Men Who Made It* (1948).

———. *The Age of Reform: From Bryan to F. D. R.* (1955).

———. *The Progressive Historians: Turner, Beard, Parrington* (1968).

Kelley, Robin D. G. *Hammer and Hoe: Alabama Communists During the Great Depression* (1990).

Kelly, Joan. "The Social Relation of the Sexes." *Signs* 1 (1976).

———. *Women, History, and Theory: The Essays of Joan Kelly* (1984).

Kolko, Gabriel. *The Triumph of Conservatism: A Reinterpretation of American History, 1900–1916* (1963).

Lipsitz, George. *Time Passages: Collective Memory and American Popular Culture* (1990).

Matthiessen, F. O. *American Renaissance: Art and Expression in the Age of Emerson and Whitman* (1941).

Montgomery, David. *Beyond Equality: Labor and the Radical Republicans, 1862–1872* (1967).

Radical America: Fifteen Years of Radical America: An Anthology. 16, no. 2 (1982).

Rawick, George. *The American Slave: A Composite Autobiography.* Vol. I: *From Sundown to Sunup, the Making of the Black Community* (1972).

Saxton, Alexander. *The Rise and Fall of the White Republic: Class Politics and Mass Culture in Nineteenth-Century America* (1991).

Schlesinger, Arthur M., Jr. *The Age of Jackson* (1945).

———. *The Vital Center: The Politics of Freedom* (1949).

Sklar, Martin J. *The Corporate Reconstruction of American Capitalism, 1890–1916: The Market, the Law, and Politics* (1988).

Weinstein, James, and David Eakins, eds. *For a New America: Essays in History and Politics from* Studies on the Left, *1959–1967* (1970).

Williams, William A. *The Tragedy of American Diplomacy* (1959).

———. *The Contours of American History* (1961).

Historiographical Studies

Abelove, Henry, et al., eds. *Visions of History* (1984).

Blake, Casey. "Where Are All the Young Left Historians?" *Radical History Review,* nos. 28–30 (1984): 114–123.

Breines, Paul. "Uncertain Marxism." *Radical History Review* 22 (1979–1980).

Buhle, Paul. "American Marxist Historiography, 1900–1940." *Radical America* 4, nos. 9–10 (1970).

Buhle, Paul, ed. *History and the New Left: Madison, Wisconsin, 1950–1970* (1990).

D'Emilio, John. "Not a Simple Matter: Gay History and Gay Historians." *Journal of American History* 76, no. 2 (1989): 435–442.

Diggins, John Patrick. "Comrades and Citizens: New Mythologies in American Historiography." *American Historical Review* 90, no. 3 (1985): 614–638.

Gordon, Ann D., Nancy Schrom [Dye], and Mari Jo Buhle, "Women in American Society: An Historical Contribution." *Radical America* 5, no. 4 (1971).

Higham, John. *Writing American History: Essays on Modern Scholarship* (1970).

———. "Changing Paradigms: The Collapse of Consensus History." *Journal of American History* 76, no. 2 (1989).

Lears, T. Jackson. "The Concept of Cultural Hegemony: Problems and Possibilities." *American Historical Review* 90, no. 3 (1985): 567–593.

Lemisch, Jesse. *On Active Service in War and Peace: Politics and Ideology in the American Historical Profession* (1975).

Novick, Peter. *That Noble Dream: The "Objectivity Question" and the American Historical Profession* (1988).

O'Brien, James P. "Editorial Introduction." *Radical America* 5, nos. 9–10 (1970).

Roper, John Herbert. *C. Vann Woodward, Southerner* (1987).

Wiener, Jonathan M. "Radical Historians and the Crisis in American History, 1959–1980." *Journal of American History* 76, no. 2 (1989): 399–434.

SEE ALSO **Intellectuals and the Intelligentsia; Socialist and Communist Movements**; and various essays in the sections **"Methods and Contexts," "Periods of Social Change,"** and **"Processes of Social Change."**

MENTALITÉ AND THE NATURE OF CONSCIOUSNESS

Christopher Clark

WHEN THEY FOUNDED the journal *Annales d'histoire économique et sociale* (since 1947, *Annales: économies, sociétés, civilisations*) in 1929, the French scholars Lucien Febvre and Marc Bloch envisaged a "total history" embracing all aspects of human society and experience. Rejecting historians' then-exclusive focus on events and on holders of power, they helped encourage the extraordinary broadening of scope that has since taken place in historical studies. Developments in the so-called *Annales* school took two major directions, each of which has, since the late 1960s, had a significant effect on American social history.

First, quantitative studies of geography, economics, demography, and social structure, which French historians such as Fernand Braudel sought to unite in a single analytical model, helped inspire the regional community studies, such as those of Kenneth Lockridge, Philip Greven, and John Demos on colonial Massachusetts, which became an important genre in the field. Second, "total history" would include a broad examination of human mental structures and emotions. In 1941, Febvre urged the need for studies of love, death, pity, cruelty, joy and fear, "the fundamental sentiments of man and the forms they take," without which, he wrote, "there will be no real history possible" ("Sensibility and History," p. 24). A later generation's acceptance of this challenge to explore the *mentalités* and consciousness of people in the past has exercised an increasing influence on American social historians. Indeed the effects of this second strand of inspiration from *Annales* have probably, by the early 1990s, become more widespread than the first.

Few social historians, it seems, would not acknowledge some debt to the French enthusiasm for *l'histoire des mentalités.* Interest in reconstructing the attitudes, values, and perspectives of historical groups and individuals has never been greater, and historians have welcomed the opportunity it offers to interpret the social structures and processes they had long been able to measure. Following the French historian Robert Mandrou, some moved intellectual history into the social realm, to uncover the less conscious, less rational influences upon the men (and sometimes women) whose ideas had long been a subject for study. But two facets of *l'histoire des mentalités* would particularly define its importance to social historians and create problems that they had to address. Because it helped open up the mental worlds of people traditionally left out by historians—the obscure, the poor, and socially marginal—it has been advanced by the rapid growth since the 1960s of a social history dedicated to uncovering the lives of ordinary people in the past. Secondly, however, the purpose of *Annales* historians was to redefine the often crude assumptions of economic determinists and "vulgar Marxists" that culture and consciousness were primarily shaped by, and dependent upon, material conditions. These two themes, history "from below" and the relationships between consciousness and circumstances, have powerfully shaped American acceptance of the French interest in *mentalités,* both curbing its adoption and inspiring a process of creative adaptation.

MENTALITÉS: POTENTIAL AND CRITIQUES

The history of *mentalités* concerns peoples' "visions of the world." Not readily translatable into English, the term connotes a range of mental attributes and structures that the word "mentalities" only inadequately conveys. It includes the study of what James A. Henretta has called "the *conscious-*

ness of the inhabitants, the mental, or emotional or ideological aspects of their lives," their "motivations, values and goals" ("Families and Farms," p. 3). The possibility of uncovering evidence about such things, even about obscure people in the past, was demonstrated in the United States by Europeanists, such as Natalie Zemon Davis, whose collected essays in *Society and Culture in Early Modern France* (1975) imaginatively reconstructed the elements of everyday cultural experience. Subsequently, Americanists were influenced by Emmanuel Le Roy Ladurie, an *Annales* historian who shifted his focus from quantification to *mentalités* in the 1970s, and by Carlo Ginzburg's *The Cheese and the Worms: The Cosmos of a Sixteenth-Century Miller* (English translation, 1980), which traced the beliefs and dreams of Menocchio, a miller in the Friuli region of northern Italy, from inquisitorial records of his examination for heresy. More recently Robert Darnton and Roger Chartier have obtained similar followings outside their immediate fields and have contributed to a broadening interest in *l'histoire des mentalités* among social historians in general.

Americanists began to read French studies of *mentalité* as they founded the new social history in the 1960s and early 1970s and began to study the types of topic Febvre had once referred to (although Febvre's essays were translated only in 1973, after interest in such topics had started to grow). Theses, books, and articles on love, courtship, sexuality, childhood, old age, violence, witchcraft, and a host of other themes multiplied. Philippe Ariès's *Centuries of Childhood* (1962) helped inspire John Demos, Tamara Hareven, and other American pioneers in the field of family history, while his later work on attitudes toward death strongly influenced David E. Stannard's exploration of colonial New England in *The Puritan Way of Death* (1977). Historians' views of what constituted suitable objects for study broadened considerably. Works such as Ariès's were also among the earliest interdisciplinary influences on social historians that did not derive purely from the other social sciences and that thus conveyed a specific historical viewpoint.

Other facets of *l'histoire des mentalités* in Europe also helped shape its adoption in America. An approach best suited to exploring cultures quite different from those of modern industrial societies, its usual application was to early modern Europe. Similarly, it has more commonly been embraced by historians of early America than by modernists; most studies of *mentalités* concern the seventeenth, eighteenth, and early nineteenth centuries. It alerted historians to new uses that could be made of studies of specific documents or events. Both Ginzburg's use of legal records of one man's beliefs in *The Cheese and the Worms* and Le Roy Ladurie's study of a single episode of festival and riot, in *Carnival in Romans* (1979), were designed to throw light on whole cultures, treating these not as individual, or even representative, events, but as keys to understanding the strange mental worlds of the past. Drawing on methods of anthropologists and literary critics, scholars of *mentalités* unearth implicit and symbolic meanings in events and texts, and "read" events themselves as "texts" revealing assumptions about social structures and relationships.

American historians did not, however, simply borrow French ideas and apply them uncritically. Interest in *mentalités* entered American history through doors already opened for it, because it suited scholars' existing purposes. In the early 1960s the sociologist Daniel Bell had proclaimed "the end of ideology," but many historians, dissatisfied with purely quantitative or materialist approaches, continued to hold that the study of peoples' outlooks on the world could lead to significant historical explanations. Psychohistory, at first the most promising means of understanding the minds of dead people, came under attack for its methodology and for its inability to say much about men and women whose lives were not well documented. The study of *mentalités* filled the gap, in part because it pointed scholars toward new topics of study and source materials more firmly than it prescribed how to use them.

Americanists were aware of the criticisms that could be leveled at *l'histoire des mentalités:* that it can merely multiply subjects for study; that it is often ill-contrived to explain historical change; that this derives from its French structuralist assumptions, which are themselves ahistorical (early practitioners regarded their task as laying bare the deeply encoded mental structures of a given culture); and that its focus on commonly held past assumptions and beliefs favors the study of consensus rather than of conflict. Some American studies influenced by the genre are subject to similar objections. But it has been more of an inspiration than a model to American social historians, because awareness of the need to meet these criticisms and the wish to adapt its insights to their own purposes has caused them to adopt French historical method with caution.

Indeed, since the early 1970s, historians of popular thought and consciousness have used a variety of methods of analysis. Historians opening up the so-called "history of the inarticulate" from the late 1960s onward—exploring the lives and actions of the middling and poor—derived more inspiration from English Marxists such as E. P. Thompson than from French historians; Thompson's studies of workers' agency and experience were also helping to transform American labor history from a study of institutions into the social history of working people. Similarly, the scope and force of Natalie Zemon Davis's insights into the world of early modern France derived much from her use of symbolic anthropology, and she helped greatly to introduce historians to the ideas and writings of anthropologists such as Clifford Geertz and Mary Douglas. Concern with *mentalités,* therefore, did not imply subscription to any firm set of approaches to the past. More a choice of topic than of a particular method, the influence of the study of *mentalités* on American social history has been broader than it has been deep.

Opinions have differed widely about its implications for the issue of the relationship between social being and social consciousness, which the original *Annales* historians sought to reevaluate. Some historians, including Philippe Ariès, appear to have regarded the mental and material worlds as essentially separate from one another. Recently others, including Roger Chartier, have argued that while connections exist between the two, the realm of *mentalités* plays a determining role, because "the representations of the social world," in language, belief, and expression, "themselves are the constituents of social reality" ("Intellectual History or Sociocultural History?" p. 41). Still others, including many American social historians influenced by Thompson, regard *l'histoire des mentalités* as an approach that can illuminate the complex interconnections between being and consciousness, and continue to regard material influences as of equal or greater significance. And while many Americanists would accept Michel Vovelle's definition of *l'histoire des mentalités* as the study of "the mediations and dialectical relationships between objective conditions . . . and the ways in which people narrate [life] and even live it" (*Ideologies and Mentalities,* p. 12), they would probably resist his firm distinction between that and "ideology," defined as the result of systematic thought. It is in the subtle shifts between thought and belief, rational and irrational, material and emotional, that they seek to explore the significance of the mental worlds of people in the past.

MENTALITÉS AND AMERICAN SOCIAL HISTORY

A straightforward example of interest in *mentalités* may be found in the traditional field for concern with beliefs, religious studies. In *Worlds of Wonder, Days of Judgment: Popular Religious Belief in Early New England* (1989), David D. Hall was concerned precisely with the interaction between formal thought and popular belief and ideology, showing how the intellectual Puritanism of the clergy was shaped in practice by the fears and visions of believers and by the rituals and means of communication of early colonial society. These same influences, however, also shaped popular belief; Hall argues that there was a broad acceptance of the word, derived from the Bible, even among the illiterate, and implies that the mental worlds of clergy and laity, wealthy and poor shared much in common from both intellectual and visionary sources of belief.

Other American social historians had already incorporated into their work the technique of "reading" both documents and events as "texts" of broader cultural significance. Mary Ryan, Edward Countryman, and Sean Wilentz, for example, demonstrated how maps and pictures, as well as written sources, contained encoded information that could be incorporated into a broader social history, although this approach remained supplementary to other methods of analysis in their work. Ryan's recent writing, however, exploring nineteenth-century rituals such as parades, focuses more explicitly on these techniques and follows the example of similar work in France by Robert Darnton and others, while clearly noting differences in the American context. The makeup, ordering, and conduct of parades, she argues, embodied public conceptions of the social order and its boundaries. She traces shifts over time, from early emphases on corporate and craft membership, to the point, by the 1870s, at which the urban parade was virtually "an ethnic festival" ("The American Parade," p. 145).

The character and significance of parades, Ryan suggests—what they celebrated, who they included and who they left out—constitute a set of texts for the scholar to interpret or "decode," a "social vocabulary" (p. 139) that nineteenth-century people inscribed on their city streets and with which they provided public representations of their own view of social reality.

The broadest recent exploration of early American culture, David Hackett Fischer's *Albion's Seed* (1989), is a massive study of the influence of four British regional cultures in the early white settlement of North America. Though less explicitly influenced than Ryan by studies of France, its focus on "folkways"—"the normative structure of values, customs and meanings that exist in any culture" (p. 7)—has close parallels with many French scholars' structuralist view of *mentalités*. Distinctive, well-rooted patterns of belief, speech, behavior, and social organization, these regional "folkways," Fischer argues, have continued to influence American society since; even though they have been overlain by other influences and other cultural groups, fundamental regional differences in the contemporary United States can still be traced back to these deeply embedded habits and values. Yet to most Americanists what the French historian Michel Vovelle has called the "inertia of mental structures" (*Ideologies and Mentalities,* p. 8) seems inadequate to explain such a rapidly growing, dynamic culture as early America. Many recent studies of early white-Indian cultural interaction, of rural societies, and of political change point toward significant adaptations from existing European, pre-Columbian, or African cultures. James H. Merrell in *The Indians' New World* (1989), a study of the Catawba and their connections with white settlers in the eighteenth-century Southeast, chose to emphasize not the residual patterns that Fischer begins with, but the constant processes of cultural interaction and change that took place in both Indian and white societies from the start of settlement. Structuralism seems a poor tool for analyzing dynamic societies where few residual values remained undisturbed or unchallenged.

A second criticism of Fischer, that his work pays insufficient attention to economic issues, reflects an attachment to materialist explanations that has, paradoxically, underpinned much of the American interest in *l'histoire des mentalités.* A central concern of many historians, the uncovering of essential social, economic, and cultural values and their effects on significant events or movements, was first addressed by James A. Henretta, whose 1978 article "Families and Farms: *Mentalité* in Pre-Industrial America," helped open up new approaches to early American rural history and the study of American capitalism.

Henretta's contribution had two important parts. First, he showed that existing studies of early American economic life, though not examining values and attitudes specifically, in fact ascribed powerful cultural attitudes to their subjects, which became central to their analyses. Historians assumed, for instance, that all Americans were motivated by individualism, by the wish to maximize economic returns, and by the entrepreneurial instincts that John D. Rockefeller would understand. Indeed, he implied, there already existed a well-established *histoire des mentalités* of early Americans, but one made up of assumptions, rather than evidence, and corresponding very closely to popular myths that Americans held about their own past.

Second, Henretta presented evidence about the economic behavior, settlement patterns, family life, inheritance practices, and naming patterns of farm families to support his argument that their values and attitudes differed markedly from those usually ascribed to them. Rural people, he suggested, were motivated more by attachment to their family line and to their membership within it than to individual advancement, and these motivations formed an important part of their *mentalité.* While economic historians have disputed Henretta's view, and subsequent studies have modified his precise findings, this has not altered the conceptual importance of his argument. Past values and views of the world could be, and should be, explored, not ascribed. These values influenced the outcome not only of specific events but whole economic systems. Evidence about them was to be uncovered in letters, diaries, legal documents, account books, tax records, genealogies, and material artifacts.

Another historian, T. H. Breen, took the study of cultural values and their material context in a different direction. In *Tobacco Culture,* an analysis of the mental world of eighteenth-century Chesapeake planters, Breen's ultimate purpose was to explain why the Virginia elite helped foment the American Revolution, but he commenced his study by tracing the material roots of planters' mentality in the rituals and processes of tobacco cultivation itself. Broadening into a wider look at standards of behavior, manners, and customs, Breen demonstrated how attitudes and ideologies were connected to the web of social and productive relationships planters were engaged in. Debt, in particular, was not purely a legal or economic burden, but a cultural phenomenon, testing relationships and provoking new desires for economic and political independence from English and Scottish influence. The value of this type of approach lies, not least, in its ability to demonstrate the force of conjunctions of social, economic, and ideological influences—too often handled separately by historians—which in this particular case had political effects of great significance.

Yet both Henretta's and Breen's studies remain open to the common criticisms of histories of *mentalités:* that they emphasize consensus and inadequately explain change. If Henretta's early American farmers were agreed on the importance of the linear family, what were the sources of conflict and change in rural societies? To Breen, the principal sources of change in Virginia came from outside the culture itself, from planters' encounters with British economic and political adversaries, though these influences were refracted by the rules and attitudes of the elite. Moreover Breen's focus on the discontent planters felt toward Britain says little about conflicts within Virginia itself. Rhys Isaac, by contrast, in *The Transformation of Virginia,* located crucial differences in mental and ideological outlook between groups in colonial society, as poor settlers and immigrant groups influenced by the revivalism of the Great Awakening challenged the elite's Anglican religious, social, and political orthodoxy and precipitated a significant cultural conflict.

Precisely because American social historians are generally concerned with change and with conflict, and because it is among such historians that interest in *l'histoire des mentalités* has been greatest, the genre has undergone significant changes in its translation from France to the United States. Most of its American exponents have come from the direction of the "new social history's" attacks on the older "consensus" history of the 1950s. Consequently, they have been more interested in the worldviews of particular social groups and in the genesis of ideological conflict and opposing forms of consciousness.

Yet the modified history of *mentalités* in America, while rebutting some of the criticisms leveled at French practice, still faced a dilemma. On the extent to which cultural issues and ideology may be understood separately from other social, economic, or material issues, American historians—as we saw—tended to move toward the materialist end of the spectrum; few would detach cultural from broader social or economic concerns. However, in taking this position, they also begged the question of the relative autonomy or interdependence of worldviews among different social groups. Studies of class, in particular, and race and gender too, have been divided as to whether subordinate cultures were essentially autonomous or primarily shaped by the values of those with power over them.

SOCIAL RELATIONS: CLASS, RACE, AND GENDER

A preoccupation of the "new social history" has been the study of class in America, a country whose popular mythology and mid-twentieth-century scholarship so often declared was free from the class barriers and tensions that dogged older European societies such as Britain. Debates in three fields particularly stimulated discussion of values and consciousness: social conflict in the American Revolution; class and community in the nineteenth-century North; and slavery in the South.

The combined influence of the work of George Rudé on eighteenth-century English and French crowds and of critics of "consensus" interpretations of the American Revolution greatly altered discussions of that event even as its bicentennial was being celebrated. "Mob" actions in prerevolutionary society, formerly dismissed as marginal or irrelevant to the process of political change, came in the hands of scholars such as Alfred F. Young, Gary B. Nash, and Dirk Hoerder to be seen in a new light. Not only were they purposive activities, whose social composition and political intent could be measured from the evidence, but their varied social coherence and fragmentation revealed adherence to different levels of ideology, frequently distinct from that of elite writers on politics and often displaying antagonism to wealth and privilege. Following Thompson in England, scholars uncovered a "moral economy" of the American crowd, which, in its rituals and symbolism, revealed popular conceptions of the bounds of legitimate social action. Only during the Revolution, according to most historians, and not even then, according to others, did these notions of popular rights to riot against violations of legitimate economic or political behavior become subsumed in the political activities of republican governments. Central sources of these values of legitimate popular protest were artisans of the major port towns, soon to become the nucleus of a new American working class.

The concepts of class and consciousness share common conceptual roots in Marxist analysis of class struggle. American scholars in the past twenty years have made a particularly creative adaptation of older, and European, historical ideas to the American context, at once placing class back on the agenda for social history and investing it with a new cultural content. Again, the influence of Thompson was crucial, but not exclusive. The early social history of the American working class owed most to the pioneering work of Herbert Gutman, who in successive essays traced material and cultural influences on workers' lives and experience, from religious beliefs to the cultural dimensions of work and the adaptation to American industrial capitalism of successive generations of immigrants. But the new social history has also focused on the early experience of industrialization: the demands placed on artisans by new forms of production and the increase in urban, manufacturing work forces. Studies of this process by Alan Dawley, Paul Faler, Sean Wilentz, and others, placed strong emphasis on change in the means of production as an influence on workers' lives, but nevertheless also examined the broader cultural and political dimensions of change. Both in large cities like New York and growing manufacturing towns like Lynn, Massachusetts, workmen's ideology, consciousness, and politics were forged in the context of community and collective identities.

Studies dealing with both middle and working-class experience, however, were rarer, and often relied on crude "social control" models to suggest that working-class behavior was made the tool of middle-class interests and ambitions. Paul Johnson, in his 1978 book on religious revivalism in Rochester, New York, in the 1820s and 1830s, sought to recast the issue, and to explain the connections between cultural and material changes without either abandoning class analysis or relying exclusively on the mode of production as a fundamental explanation. In an expanding commercial and industrial capitalism in which middle-class families were breaking existing paternalist ties to their employees and creating separate bourgeois and working-class worlds of work, residence, and leisure, evangelical revivals both reflected middle-class "beliefs and modes of comportment" (p. 138) and legitimated its social power. Yet this was not a simple imposition of values on workers for the purposes of social control; the doctrine of free will propounded by the revivals left it to individuals themselves to decide whether to participate, while at the same time permitting converts to exclude men and women who had not accepted the path to salvation. Johnson's argument that the dominant group, the evangelical middle class, did not exercise direct control over workers but rearranged the rules for class interaction, to a significant extent preserved the concept of class domination without resorting to mechanistic explanations for its power. Indeed, it was in the realm of *mentalités*—belief, behavior, and consciousness—that power was exercised.

All these studies drew in part from Thompson's explorations of the mentalities and ideologies of working people in eighteenth- and nineteenth-century England, and his attention to the actions, moral universe, and attitudes to authority of subordinate groups in a class society. By the 1970s the same issues had become central to studies of American slavery. Slaves had traditionally been portrayed merely as the victims of oppression, effectively without culture. The work of John W. Blassingame, Eugene D. Genovese, Herbert Gutman, and other historians radically revised this assumption, and explored the rich and complex world of slaves' beliefs, family and kinship patterns, music, oral culture, and humor that sustained an independent consciousness and a degree of everyday resistance to oppression. Like historians of the working class, they stressed a subordinate group's self-activity, and the role of slave culture not only in sustaining its members under oppression but in shaping, to some extent, the very character of the system that bound them. *Mentalités* and consciousness were crucial to an understanding of slavery.

Precisely what emphasis should be placed on them nevertheless became a matter for debate. Herbert Gutman's study of African American values and behavior, including the marriage patterns of former slaves after the Civil War and the evolution of the family in slavery and after, tended to stress the autonomous character of a culture drawn in upon itself by the twin oppressions of class and race. Genovese, on the other hand, had written a sophisticated analysis of law, religion, and values into his studies of slave-planter relations; instead of emphasizing the autonomy of black culture, he traced the hegemonic character of planter power in a relationship that slaves, nonetheless, did much to influence. The debate over slave culture, perhaps more than any other in American social history, emphasized the difficulties facing any historian of *mentalités:* the tensions between cultural autonomy and cultural domination. However, the dynamic context of class and race relations within which these studies operated made them more revealing of the interconnections of culture and society than static, often consensual, formal *histoires des mentalités* could achieve.

Particularly successful in striking a balance between autonomy and subordination was Lawrence Levine's study *Black Culture and Black Consciousness* (1977), which extended the discussion from the mid nineteenth into the twentieth century by focusing on the ramifications of "verbal art"—preaching and spirituals, stories and songs, jokes and aphorisms. Levine stressed the syncretism of Christian with African and other folkloric traditions, the links between the African American sacred world and the incidents of daily experience, and the structural relationships between different forms of cultural expression. This culture was formed, he wrote, "upon the hard rock of racial, social and economic exploitation and injustice" (p. xi); domination was ever-present, but the realms of religion, music and storytelling provided areas of control or autonomy for black Americans within the framework of oppression.

Studies of class and class consciousness might incorporate elements of *l'histoire des mentalités* and at the same time move beyond it, but the issues posed by race and gender relations seem, for the time being at least, to have been less affected by it. Each has concerns considerably removed from the European social and intellectual contexts in which the *Annales* school was established and flourished. One factor is the *Annales'* origins as an effort to develop Marxism: the problems of materialism and consciousness posed by Marxism's central emphasis on class struggle were not precisely replicated in other areas of relations and conflict.

Not only do America's unusual triracial origins make for complex cross currents of cultural influence poorly suited to an analysis with structuralist-type, static, or ahistorical roots, but debates in particular fields associated with race have addressed concerns far removed from those of most studies of *mentalités.* Central issues in African American studies, for instance, have included the strength or weakness of African influences on black Americans' experience, and the importance, in turn, of this experience in the formation of American culture in general. Fischer's *Albion's Seed* has been criticized for focusing entirely on British ethnic cultures in early America, and ignoring the effects of racial and ethnic interaction with native Americans and Africans, even upon the cultural continuities that it emphasized. Again, Levine showed that African American culture was not static, but always revitalizing itself in the changing circumstances of the shift from slavery to new forms of domination, from farm to factory, from country to city. This revitalization, Levine argued, drew on both old and new cultural forms, on African and American sources. The key to the distinctiveness of cultural forms was not their origins as such, but the "communal milieu" in which African American culture and consciousness were forged: *mentalités,* in other words, are best understood in their complex social contexts. Many other studies of race and ethnicity, however, have had to come to terms with the problems and tensions associated with assimilation and cultural autonomy, which can call cultural identity itself into question. In such cases, the issues of values, beliefs, and "worldviews" confidently assigned by Europeanists to the category "*mentalités,*" are precisely those most fragmented by disagreements and uncertainty.

In studies of gender relations, again, complexity and dynamism outran the capacity of an approach that was, in any event, formulated well before gender emerged as a significant analytical category. Here French influences come from Michel Foucault, Jacques Lacan, and post-structuralist linguistic and literary theorists, whose work developed from, and in parallel to, that of historians of *mentalités.* A major survey of literature in the field, published by Joan W. Scott in 1986, cited not one example of a study inspired by the *Annales* school, and although the essays of Natalie Zemon Davis may be an exception, we have already noted the important influence of social anthropology on her work. As in the case of race, the history of *mentalités* is limited by its lack of a compatible method: gender studies are, above all, dominated by the search for analytical approaches that can shed light on the social and cultural constructions of gender over time. Among the first American historians to enter this field, Carroll Smith-Rosenberg has explored the cultural boundaries between women's and men's worlds in the nineteenth century, the construction of concepts of gender in language and myth, and "the way gender channeled the impact of social change and the experience and exercise of power" (*Disorderly Conduct,* p. 45). At the time of writing there is increasing interest in Lacanian approaches to the symbolic order embedded in language and in Foucault's analyses of the power relationships embedded in discourse and systems of thought, both of which are congruent with the view that gender (and similar categories) are malleable and culturally constituted, not structurally embedded in human experience.

Indeed, various historians have emphasized the need to study race, class, and gender, not separately, but as they constitute one another. Christine Stansell's *City of Women* (1986), on the women of early-nineteenth-century New York City, and Mary Blewett's *Men, Women, and Work* (1988), on New England shoemakers, both demonstrate the complex interconnections between productive relations, class consciousness, and gender. Blewett, for instance, traces the different attitudes toward strike action taken by factory-employed and outworker women shoemakers, relating them to different perceptions of roles, both in the labor force and in the family economy. Jacqueline Jones's *Labor of Love, Labor of Sorrow* (1985), on black women from slavery to the present, focuses on the complex contradictions and interconnections between her subjects' work, gender, class, and race and suggests the need to understand consciousness not as a fixed set of mental categories, but as dynamic and multilayered.

CONCLUSION

Dominick LaCapra, one of the sharpest critics of *l'histoire des mentalités* from the direction of literary theory, has argued that "everyone is indeed a *mentalité* case," but never in precisely the same way (*History and Criticism,* p. 93). One implication of this is the need for a multiplicity of studies, which explore the experiences of individual men and women for what they reveal about worldviews of their particular time and place. Interest in this approach is indicated in the success of Laurel Thatcher Ulrich's book *The Midwife's Tale* (1990), about the late-eighteenth-century Maine midwife Martha Ballard. Such studies, and the continued output of works on the sorts of topics Febvre identified when he helped direct attention to the field of *mentalités* fifty years ago, will keep us conscious of the *Annales* school's greatest achievement, that of waking historians up to the extraordinary range, variety, and richness of their own discipline.

If we ask, however, how *l'histoire des mentalités* might contribute to the achievement of broader synthesis in American social history, it is likely that the methods used will take one of two forms. It could follow a Foucaultian approach, tracing the creation of systems of thought and cultural categories and their impact on social relations through discursive structures. Some historians are already using such an approach, in studies of sexuality, medicine, and changing understanding of the workings of the human mind and body in the past; this is often done in conjunction with other methods, because among many criticisms directed at Foucault was the disembodied character of his systems of thought, which were rarely attributable to individuals or groups. An alternative will follow the method adopted by Henretta, who made the assumption that "behavior . . . constitutes a crucial (although not a foolproof) indicator of . . . values and aspirations" ("Families and Farms," p. 20). Tracing everyday economic life and behavior through a multitude of documentary sources might be most amenable to the common habits and preferences of the social historian, especially one not particularly worried by the essentially positivist assumptions of this approach. One might venture to predict that for some time to come this will remain the most common application of *l'histoire des mentalités* in American social history.

BIBLIOGRAPHY

Methodology

Chartier, Roger. "Intellectual History or Sociocultural History? The French Trajectories." In *Modern European Intellectual History: Reappraisals and New Perspectives,* edited by Dominick LaCapra and Steven L. Kaplan (1982).

Febvre, Lucien. "Sensibility and History: How to Reconstitute the Emotional Life of the Past" (1941). In *A New Kind of History and Other Essays.* Edited by Peter Burke. Translated by K. Folca (1973).

LaCapra, Dominick. *History and Criticism* (1985).

Scott, Joan W. "Gender: A Useful Category of Historical Analysis." *American Historical Review* 91, no. 5 (1986).

Stoianovich, Traian. *French Historical Method: The Annales Paradigm* (1976).

Vovelle, Michel. *Ideologies and Mentalities.* Translated by Eamon O'Flaherty (1990).

Social History

Breen, T. H. *Tobacco Culture: The Mentality of the Great Tidewater Planters on the Eve of the Revolution* (1985).

Fischer, David Hackett. *Albion's Seed: Four British Folkways in America* (1989).

Genovese, Eugene D. *Roll, Jordan, Roll: The World the Slaves Made* (1974).

Henretta, James A. "Families and Farms: *Mentalité* in Pre-Industrial America." *William and Mary Quarterly,* 3d. ser., 35, no. 1 (1978).

Gutman, Herbert G. *The Black Family in Slavery and Freedom, 1750–1825* (1976).

———. *Work, Culture, and Society in Industrializing America* (1976).

Isaac, Rhys. *The Transformation of Virginia, 1740–1790* (1982).

Johnson, Paul E. *A Shopkeeper's Millennium: Society and Revivals in Rochester, New York, 1815–1837* (1978).

Jones, Jacqueline. *Labor of Love, Labor of Sorrow: Black Women, Work, and Family from Slavery to the Present* (1985).

Merrell, James H. *The Indians' New World: Catawbas and their Neighbors from European Contact Through the Era of Removal* (1989).

Ryan, Mary. "The American Parade: Representations of the Nineteenth-Century Social Order." In *The New Cultural History,* edited by Lynn Hunt (1989).

Smith-Rosenberg, Carroll. *Disorderly Conduct: Visions of Gender in Victorian America* (1985).

Young, Alfred F., ed. *The American Revolution: Explorations in the History of American Radicalism* (1976).

SEE ALSO **Anthropological Approaches to History; The Old Social History and the New; Social History in Great Britain and Continental Europe.**

ORAL HISTORY

Douglas DeNatale

THE TERM "ORAL HISTORY" is applied both to a method of eliciting spoken testimony concerning historical events from living individuals and to the development of a subdiscipline within the historical profession that promotes this method as a viable tool for historical research. Oral historical method was first developed among American historians in the late 1940s. It was not until the 1970s that oral history gained widespread public appeal, and the concurrent impact of the new social history gave the method greater credibility among historians. Oral history has strongly influenced the writing of social history in a number of fields, and may further influence theoretical thought on the construction of historical discourse.

ANTECEDENTS

Oral history relies on an interview method that did not originate within the historical profession. Early-twentieth-century American anthropologists pioneered the use of the personal interview to gather information concerning customs, beliefs, and social organization among nonliterate peoples. Anthropologists also elicited historical narratives to supplement their information gathering. Personal narratives of Native American war parties were published by A. L. Kroeber as early as 1908. Paul Radin published the first autobiography based on oral testimony in a 1913 article. Radin later developed his interviews with a Winnebago Indian, Crashing Thunder, into a book-length autobiography published in 1926. Anthropologists also pioneered the use of sound recording for oral interviews, beginning with the wax cylinder recordings made by the Bureau of American Ethnology in the 1890s.

Widespread use of oral autobiography within anthropology began with the development of the culture and personality school in the 1920s. Led by Edward Sapir, the school explored the relationship between individual psychology and cultural dynamics, and constructed individual biographies based on interviews for this purpose. Among the best examples of the genre of anthropological life history that flourished in the 1930s and 1940s are Walter Dyk's *Son of Old Man Hat* (1938) and Leo W. Simmons's *Sun Chief* (1942). Oscar Lewis was a later proponent of the life history, exerting great influence on oral historians in works such as *The Children of Sánchez* (1961) and *Living the Revolution* (1977).

A related subdiscipline within anthropology is ethnohistory, which employs oral testimony, artifactual evidence, and outsider accounts to reconstruct the history of nonliterate peoples. Ethnohistory shares with oral history a concern for determining the truth value of oral testimony. A leading proponent of ethnohistory is Jan Vansina, whose work in African ethnohistory has had a major influence on oral history. Vansina developed a methodology for evaluating oral testimonies, summarized in his *Oral History* (1965), that involves establishing an unbroken chain of testimonies back to the event reported, textual comparison, and comparison of the circumstances of transmission.

European ethnologists made other early attempts to record historical information from living individuals. The Irish Folklore Commission (established in the 1930s), the School of Scottish Studies at Edinburgh University (1951), and the Welsh Folk Museum (1957) each conducted extensive interviewing projects to document traditional customs, beliefs, and expressive narratives. Documentation of folklife in the United States focused on oral expression, particularly song. The Archive of American Folk Song, established at the Library of Congress in 1928, amassed a large collection of recorded oral material.

In sociology, the long-term study of Polish immigration to America by William I. Thomas and

Florian Znaniecki, published as *The Polish Peasant in Europe and America* (1918–1920), was another path-breaking work. In addition to diaries, letters, and other written evidence, the authors relied upon oral testimony to compile a comparative view of peasant and immigrant communities.

The narrative compositions compiled during the 1930s for the Federal Writers' Project, a program of the Works Progress Administration (WPA), have received much attention as the first widespread attempt to record the details of everyday life among representative Americans. Participants in the regional programs of the Writers' Project were given a set of instructions and an outline of topics to be covered, then sent out to interview a range of individuals, including farmers, industrial workers, miners, and, in a separate project, former slaves. From notes taken during these interviews, the writer composed a first-person life history in the interviewee's voice, with descriptive details of the interviewee's surroundings added. Historians have variously rejected the WPA life histories as synthetic fabrications with little historical value or embraced them as valuable documents of life in Depression-era America, with a ring of authenticity despite the manner in which they were collected.

Within the American historical profession, there were forerunners of oral history. The Mormon church historian Andrew Jenson (1850–1941) began interviewing church elders in 1888. Jonas Bergren, a member of a Swedish utopian community in Illinois, made cylinder recordings of interviews with early settlers at the turn of the century. The Wisconsin historian Lyman C. Draper (1815–1891) compiled hundreds of volumes of interview notes. In California, Hubert Howe Bancroft (1832–1918) employed stenographers to record accounts by early settlers. Charles T. Morrissey traces the earliest known appearance of the term "oral history" to an address by Winslow Cossoul Watson to the Vermont Historical Society in 1863. Joe Gould, a Greenwich Village bohemian, published a number of pieces in 1929 under the heading "From Joe Gould's Oral History."

Although a number of the historical projects pursued by these individuals had aims similar to those of the later organized oral history movement, they did not constitute a consistent methodology or movement. The development of oral history as a programmatic research method originated with the establishment of the Columbia Oral History Research Office by Allan Nevins in the late 1940s.

THE COLUMBIA ORAL HISTORY MODEL

Allan Nevins (1890–1971) was a prolific biographer and historian. Educated at the University of Illinois, he was initially a journalist. Between 1913 and 1931, he held editorial positions on the *New York Evening Post,* the *Nation,* the *New York Sun,* and the *New York World.* While on the staff of the *World,* Nevins taught history at Cornell University before assuming a position in 1928 as associate professor at Columbia University, where he remained until his retirement in 1958. Nevins's biographies included studies of John Frémont, Grover Cleveland, John D. Rockefeller, Abraham Lincoln, Eli Whitney, and Henry Ford. Among his best-known works are *The Gateway to History* (1938), a historiographical treatise, and his Civil War studies, *Ordeal of the Union* (1947–1971) and *The War for the Union* (1959).

Nevins's first proposal for something approaching oral history appeared in his preface to *The Gateway to History,* in which he expressed a desire for "some organization which made a systematic attempt to obtain, from the lips and papers of living Americans who have led significant lives, a fuller record of their participation in the political, economic, and cultural life of the last sixty years" (p. iv). Nevins and a research assistant conducted their first oral history interview with a New York banker, George McAneny, on 18 May 1948. According to some accounts, on their way to the interview, Nevins's assistant asked him what they should call their enterprise. "Professor Nevins, striding across the Morningside campus at that moment, said he thought, 'Oral History' about as good a name as any" (Louis M. Starr, *Oral History at Columbia,* p. 11). In his diary for the day, Nevins noted, "In the afternoon I took my student Albertson down to an interview with old George McAneny at his apartment in the middle East Side; an interview that inaugurates my scheme for setting down oral history" (quoted in Charles T. Morrissey, "Why Call It 'Oral History'?" p. 35).

Nevins's brainchild combined his journalistic background and biographical leanings. His interest in oral history was frankly experimental and oriented toward recording isolated pieces of data. He did not use a tape recorder but instead employed two investigators, the historian and a note taker, because "many men of distinction expect some person of whom they have heard, and not a mere secretary, to talk with them; because expertness is needed in framing questions; and because two pairs of ears are better than one" (quoted in Morrissey, p. 36).

The Columbia orientation was further developed by Nevins's successor, Louis M. Starr (1917–1980), who shared Nevins's background in journalism and his emphasis on oral history materials as raw data for historical research. After working as a reporter for the *Chicago Sun,* Starr received a Ph.D. in history from Columbia in 1954. While a graduate student, he was an interviewer for the Oral History Research Office, and he became director upon Nevins's retirement in 1958.

Starr was a leading advocate for methodological rigor in oral history. Under Starr, the Columbia program began to tape-record interviews and established a process of producing interview transcripts that were returned to the interviewee for fact checking. Because of the program's emphasis on data collection and the history profession's traditional reliance on the written record, the program's early recordings were viewed as mere aids in this process, and were erased once the transcript had been corrected. Starr was a strong proponent of the validity of historical data taken from oral history interviews, as long as this information was measured against documentary evidence.

The Columbia program was established in accordance with the contemporary model of political and economic history, in which the actions of business and political leaders were taken to be the most significant driving force in historical change. Michael Frisch has noted that Nevins's intention was "the 'de-briefing' of the Great Men before they passed on. Its nature was explicitly archival, informational, and elitist" ("Oral History and *Hard Times,*" p. 73). The work of the oral historian was viewed as the ordered collection of interviews that were likely to have value to future historians. The Columbia model did not emphasize the investigation of particular social issues or groups; rather, it viewed the purpose of oral historical methodology to be the compilation of an archival collection of textual documents that might be investigated objectively with the tools of standard historiography.

Between 1948 and the 1960s, the Columbia model predominated among American oral historians. The twenty-nine oral history archives established between 1948 and 1960 focused on the biographies of political and economic leaders, institutional history, and military history. Early programs were established at the Henry Ford Archives (1950), the Forest History Society (1952), the University of Texas at Austin (1952), the Bancroft Library of the University of California, Berkeley (1954), and the Colonial Williamsburg Foundation (1955).

By the early 1960s, Columbia's oral history approach was gaining acceptance among professional organizations for the purpose of documenting institutional history, as well as recording the biographies of leaders in medicine, business, government, and science. Among the professional and business organizations that established oral history programs during this period were NASA (1959), General Motors (1960), International Business Machines (1962), the Mayo Clinic (1963), the American Society of Civil Engineers (1963), the American Institute of Physics (1964), the American Society for Microbiology (1964), the American Psychiatric Association (1965), and the American Medical Association (1966).

The oral history model developed at Columbia with its biographical emphases proved particularly attractive to the presidential libraries, where oral history was increasingly used to supplement the documentary record. The Harry S. Truman Library established the first presidential oral history program in 1961. This was followed by programs at the Dwight D. Eisenhower Library and the John F. Kennedy Library in 1964, and by oral history projects devoted to the presidencies of Herbert Hoover in 1966 and Lyndon B. Johnson in 1968.

Individuals who emerged as leaders in the oral history movement within the history profession found institutional bases at both university and organizational archives. Among these are Willa K. Baum (b. 1929), who assumed the directorship of Berkeley's Regional Oral History Office in 1954; Charles T. Morrissey (b. 1933), who served as oral historian for the Truman and Kennedy libraries; and William W. Moss (b. 1935), director of the oral history program at the Kennedy Library.

A steady increase in the number of oral history programs during the 1960s, in both university and organizational settings, led to the establishment of the Oral History Association in 1967, following two national conferences. The association instituted a series of annual colloquia with published proceedings. In 1973, the published annual proceedings were superseded by *Oral History Review,* which continues to serve as the association's official organ.

DEVELOPMENT OF POPULAR INTEREST

Beginning in the late 1960s, while the oral history movement was constituting itself as a subdiscipline within the historical profession, a number of outside ventures employing oral interviews for historical inquiry seized the American public's interest and presented a dramatic contrast to the Columbia model. The series of "memory books" by Studs Terkel, Alex Haley's *Roots,* and Eliot Wigginton's *Foxfire* project each had a dramatic impact on the professional oral history movement. Together with the growing acceptance of the new social history within the American history profession, these popular oral histories gave the oral history movement cause to reexamine its purpose and methods.

Louis "Studs" Terkel (b. 1912) trained as a lawyer and worked as a civil service employee but turned to broadcasting in 1945. His radio interview program, *Wax Museum,* on WFMT in Chicago, led to an early Chicago television show, *Studs' Place* (1950–1953), which took its title from the nickname Terkel adopted from the fictional character Studs Lonigan. Terkel's membership in a left-wing theater group was used to cut short his television career during the McCarthy era, and he returned to radio interviewing.

After publishing an anthology of interviews with jazz musicians in 1957, Terkel was approached in the 1960s by Andre Schiffrin, an editor for Pantheon Books, with the proposal that he produce a portrait of Chicago modeled on Jan Myrdal's *Report from a Chinese Village* (1965). The resulting work, *Division Street: America* (1967), compiled excerpts from a broad range of interviews to produce a composite portrait of the city. Terkel developed this approach in a series of books that reached a large popular audience. Terkel's subjects included the Great Depression in *Hard Times* (1970); American occupational life in *Working* (1974); and World War II in *"The Good War"* (1984).

Terkel has called his method of producing smooth prose through heavy editing of oral interview transcripts "digging for gold," an endeavor in which editorial judgment leads to a core of truth. Though some oral historians trained in the Columbia model were willing to accept Terkel's anthologies as a valuable new literary genre, many were annoyed by their popular association with oral history, which was still struggling to establish itself as an acceptable historical method.

The publication of Alex Haley's *Roots* in 1976 had a further impact. Haley (b. 1921) was born in Ithaca, New York, where his father was a professor at Cornell University. After serving as a journalist with the Coast Guard for twenty years, Haley turned to free-lance writing in 1959. An interview with Malcolm X for *Playboy* magazine led to Haley's collaboration on *The Autobiography of Malcolm X* (1965).

In stories he had heard from his family in Henning, Tennessee, Haley had received fragmented details concerning his slave ancestors, including a figure identified by the family as "The African," who had taught his children a number of apparently African words that were subsequently passed down, including the African's self-identification as "Kin-tay." Haley's attempts to trace the words led him to ethnohistorian Jan Vansina, who identified the terms as Mandinkan. Haley traveled to Gambia, where government officials identified Kinte as a clan name. Haley later met with Kebba Kanga Fofana, a griot of the Kinte clan, who corroborated Haley's details and identified "the African" as Kunta Kinte.

Haley presented his research to the Oral History Association in 1972, and subsequently published his family's saga in novelized form as *Roots.* The book's enormous popularity and the conjunction of its publication with the American bicentennial helped fuel a surge of interest in family history, which in turn drew popular attention to oral history as a method.

A third development during this period was the widespread growth of cultural journalism projects at the secondary-school level, inspired by the *Foxfire* model developed by Eliot Wigginton (b. 1942) and his students at Rabun Gap, Georgia. Wigginton, the son of a University of Georgia professor, had spent time in the Rabun Gap community as a child, and returned there to teach after his graduation from Cornell University. Wigginton's frustrations with standard teaching methods led to a collaborative approach in which he and his students designed a literary magazine that included pieces on local history and cultural traditions.

The *Foxfire* model developed by Wigginton with his students involved training in interview techniques, transcription, and editing, towards the goal of developing literacy and analytical skills among the students. Wigginton's students produced descriptive articles outlining cultural processes common among an earlier generation. The process has been characterized by Thad Sitton as a type of "salvage ethnography" carried out by insiders to the local culture.

Wigginton and his collaborators attempted to disseminate the *Foxfire* educational model with the assistance of a Ford Foundation grant. The 1972 publication of *The Foxfire Book,* an anthology of articles from the Rabun Gap student magazine, brought the project national renown and inspired a host of *Foxfire*-type school projects. By 1977, eighty schools were involved in the official *Foxfire* training project, and many more independent efforts were under way. Ironically, the popular conception of *Foxfire* as a project concentrating on cultural heritage, supported by the series of *Foxfire* books that followed the first, worked against its underlying educational philosophy as a collaborative student/teacher venture in which cultural journalism was one possible outcome but not the underlying motivation. During the 1980s, the number of *Foxfire*-inspired projects declined in the face of national emphasis on standardized competency tests. More recently, the efforts of Wigginton and his *Foxfire* collaborators have concentrated on refining the underlying educational philosophy and developing a more established network of educators.

The popular appeal of the books by Terkel, Haley, and Wigginton and his students helped fuel national awareness of oral history as a tool for uncovering local and family history. During the early 1970s, the number of oral history archives in local libraries and historical societies significantly increased as popular interest peaked with the United States bicentennial. By 1975, membership in the Oral History Association had risen to twelve hundred, and the association was engaged in a membership campaign to reach the great number of unaffiliated individuals engaged in oral history interviewing.

DEBATES WITHIN THE PROFESSION

From a single approach developed in the 1950s, oral history had by the mid 1970s become a heterogeneous movement that included university professors, high school students, librarians, local historians, and journalists. This transition was accompanied by a shift in the debates within the historical profession concerning the nature and validity of oral history as a method.

Nevins and his successors viewed oral history as a technique for supplementing the documentary record by creating personal memoirs in collaboration with the individual interviewed. They argued that evidence taken from oral history is as valid as written documents produced by the interviewee, providing that proper historiographical principles are employed. This view was countered by such eminent historians as Oscar Handlin and Barbara Tuchman, who suggested that oral history leads to "an artificial survival of trivia of appalling proportions" (quoted in Charles W. Crawford, "Oral History," p. 8). For these historians, the elicitation of narratives long after the events described rendered such evidence inaccurate and irrelevant.

In response, oral historians devoted much attention and internal debate during the 1970s to the development of a theoretical and methodological base for their claim of the factual validity of oral historical testimony. Proponents of oral history accepted the criticism that oral history could produce questionable source material but countered that this was a possibility with any historical source. A common position was stated by Oral History Association President Charles Crawford, who argued that "it may well be that initial errors in the practice of oral history by serving as examples to be avoided will improve both procedures and the product" (Crawford, "Oral History," p. 8). William Moss offered the consensus prescription: "We need more articles that develop theory and we need an exploration of and testing of quality criteria that may be applied to oral history and we need more publication of oral history product by oral historians" ("The Future of Oral History," p. 10).

Within the professional oral history movement, emphasis on methodological rigor increased in direct response to the increasing popular enthusiasm for oral history during the 1970s. Practices developed at the established oral history archives were codified and commercially published in handbook form for the first time during this period. The handbooks include Willa Baum, *Oral History for the Local Historical Society* (1969); Gary Shumway and William Hartley, *An Oral History Primer* (1973); Edward Ives, *The Tape-recorded Interview* (1974); William Moss, *Oral History Program Manual* (1974); John Neuenschwander, *Oral History as a Teaching Approach* (1976); and Willa Baum, *Transcribing and Editing Oral History* (1977). Although the Oral History Association welcomed popular interest, it also struggled for disciplinary order, first through educational outreach and later through attempts to establish professional standards. Beginning in 1975, the association appointed an exploratory standards committee and formed a group of volunteers to evaluate projects upon request. In 1979, the association prepared and adopted a set of professional guidelines, at the same time resisting any suggestion of establishing formal certification procedures.

The attempt to advance methodological rigor brought with it increasing reflection on the nature of oral history communication. The defense against the criticism that oral history is factually unreliable brought the first assertions that oral history involves a new process of constructing historical understandings. Oral history is unique, its advocates argued, because the historiographical process of evaluating source material occurs at the very point when the oral history document is composed. The oral history interviewer brings a body of background knowledge to the interview, and through a process of colloquy and cross-examination during the interview historical truth emerges. William W. Moss and Gary Y. Okihiro suggested that oral history constitutes an extension of existing historiographical theory in which the processes involved in oral historical documentation provide an additional filter.

This strain of inquiry led to serious consideration of the role of long-term memory in the oral history process, with the aim of compensating for its effects. Once oral historians have gained a sufficient understanding of the psychological bases of memory, John A. Neuenschwander and T. L. Brink argued, a reliable extension of historiography can be achieved. By the early 1980s, however, several other strains in the development of oral historical thought had become apparent under the growing influence of social history.

IMPACT OF SOCIAL HISTORY

Although the early development of social history by the French *Annaliste* school, with its reliance on quantitative methods, did not have an immediate influence on American oral historians, the emphasis of social history on those portions of society not well represented in the documentary record found resonance among a growing cadre of historians interested in using oral history to augment the documentary record with accounts by non-elites. When European social historians such as Emmanuel Le Roy Ladurie began to employ qualitative analysis of narrative documents for sociological patterns, the stage was set for social history and oral history to find a common purpose.

American historians had begun to move in this direction in the 1960s with the use of oral history to investigate ethnic and labor history. Early programs in these areas had tended to focus on institutional history and leadership studies, but by the late 1960s attention was beginning to be given to ethnic community life and the experiences of rank-and-file workers. Beginning in 1966, the Doris Duke Foundation funded a number of university oral history programs to recover Native American tribal histories, and a number of significant oral history projects were initiated in Jewish and Asian communities. Labor history programs at Wayne State University, Pennsylvania State University, the University of Michigan, and elsewhere made comparable shifts.

The work of the English historian Paul Thompson and his colleagues at Essex University were particularly influential among American oral historians in this regard. In 1968 Thompson initiated an oral history project examining family life and work experience in pre-1918 England, subsequently published as *The Edwardians* (1975). Drawing upon quantitative methods, Thompson's study was based on a quota sample taken from 1911 census categories. Thompson's active participation in the Oral History Association brought his approach to the early notice of American historians, and his later summary, *The Voice of the Past* (1978), brought it to a wider audience. In 1974, a panel discussion entitled "Taped Interviews and Social History" explored the relationship between oral history and social history at the annual Oral History Association meeting.

During this period a number of young American scholars were pioneering oral history as a means for broadening the scope of historical inquiry. In 1974, Theodore Rosengarten (b. 1944) published *All God's Dangers,* a life history based on an extensive series of oral history interviews with an Alabama sharecropper, Ned Cobb, identified as "Nate Shaw" in Rosengarten's book. Rosengarten's work was criticized by a few oral historians as a portent of scholarly "Terkelism," but it was more generally applauded as a path-breaking model of the power of oral history to illuminate the lives of those poorly represented in the documentary record. Peter Friedlander's *The Emergence of a UAW Local* (1975) represented another important development. Friedlander's thoughtful introductory discussion of the structure of historical memory and his application of a self-conscious collaborative process in the construction of his study drew much attention among oral historians.

The general shift in the historical paradigm brought forth a new generation of scholars eager to apply oral historical methodology to social historical inquiry. Duke University's Oral History Program, established in 1972 by William Chafe and Lawrence Goodwyn under a grant from the Rockefeller Foundation, had as its conscious goal the reformulation of historical scholarship through an application of oral historical methodology. Individual scholars with a social historical orientation began to employ oral history methods in studies of labor, ethnicity, regions, material culture, and women's history.

In labor history, scholars such as John Bodnar, Tamara Hareven, Edward D. Ives, Kenneth Kann, Nell Irvin Painter, Jeremy Brecher, and Jacquelyn Dowd Hall have made important contributions. Ethnic studies by Virginia Yans-McLaughlin, Theda Perdue, Elizabeth Bethel, Emily Wilson, and Helen Epstein have drawn heavily upon oral history. A series of oral histories on the camps in which Japanese Americans were interned during World War II succeeded in bringing this neglected topic to national attention. Regional histories by William Lynwood Montell, Kathy Kahn, and Laura Shackelford have used oral history to gain information not available in the documentary record. Material culture studies by George McDaniel and Charles Martin have synthesized artifactual analysis and oral interviews. Women's histories by Sherna Gluck, Rosemary Joyce, Ruth Sidel, and Kathryn Anderson have employed oral history as a means of exploring the relationships among ideologies, social structures, and gender.

By the late 1970s the social historical paradigm had begun to awaken a new interdisciplinary openness among oral historians. To a degree this was a reawakening. Oral historians earlier had welcomed methodological input from anthropology, folklore, and sociology while largely disregarding the theoretical perspectives that scholars in those disciplines had brought to their attention (see, for example, Richard Dorson, "The Oral Historian and the Folklorist" and Henry Glassie, "A Folkloristic Thought"). A few scholars trained in other disciplines had likewise gained respect for their oral historical scholarship, including folklorists William Lynwood Montell and Edward D. Ives. But it was under the influence of social history that a number of younger historians began to investigate the implications of oral history as a mode of historical understanding.

Two seminal articles, by Michael Frisch, "Oral History and *Hard Times*" (1979) and "The Memory of History" (1981), provided a compelling basis for the new interdisciplinary inquiry. Contrasting the existing tendencies among oral historians that he labeled the "More History" and "Anti-History" approaches, Frisch called for consideration of oral history as a means of exploring issues of the social construction of historical understanding. During the 1980s, serious colloquy between oral historians and scholars in related disciplines helped to transform oral historians' understanding of their endeavor. Much of the discussion took place within the *International Journal of Oral History,* which was founded in 1980.

During the early portion of this discussion, voices from related disciplines asserted the implications that their own theoretical understandings held for oral history. In an influential 1979 article, Sidney Mintz articulated the argument that an anthropological background is necessary for understanding relationships between individual voices and sociocultural patterns, and suggested that the oral history interview was not fully comprehensible outside of ethnographic analysis. Folklorists Charles Joyner, Roger D. Abrahams, and Samuel Schrager defined oral history as a communicative event in which discrepant sociolinguistic patterns and contrasting expressive genres may hinder the oral historian's ability to ascertain the social meaning of narrative.

As oral historians pondered these points, some suggested that the significance of oral history does not lie in its disputed ability to augment the historical record or to recover the undocumented past, but in the fact of its emergence as a new mode of historical discourse. Proceeding from this viewpoint, Ronald Grele distinguished the historian's project from that of the anthropologist, sociologist, or folklorist, and suggested that oral history leads to an examination of the relationship between multiple social constructions of the past, in which the historian as cultural outsider plays a crucial evaluative role:

> While . . . culture may have no gap, to the historian individual historical constructions do and history as an artifact of culture does. . . . It is not that we plug the gap with ideas not part of that culture; rather, we examine why certain individuals and classes of people leave gaps, or don't. (*Envelopes of Sound* [rev. ed., 1985], p. xx)

The work of European oral historians has played a significant role in the development of this train of thought. Among these, Daniel Bertaux and Philippe Joutard in France and Alessandro Portelli and Luisa Passerini in Italy, following the theoretical orientation of the Frankfurt school, rejected the notion of unilateral interpretation. Passerini argued for a radical subjectivism "as the only possible way of establishing some kind of objectivity, or, in the terms used by Theodor Adorno, of re-giving to the object its objective quality" (Passerini, "Oral History in Italy," p. 117). In Portelli's view, the goal of analysis is not "any ultimate history, but a lot of different and partial and temporary histories, each redefining and undermining the others, each 'falling short' of the others and therefore needing them" (in Paul Thompson et al., "Between Social Scientists," p. 39).

This emerging qualitative perspective found resistance among practitioners of social history grounded in quantitative social scientific method. Louise A. Tilly challenged the approach as an analytical move based on a misguided elevation of individual psychological states over social relationships. In his editorial afterword to Tilly's remarks, Ronald Grele acknowledged the emergence of two approaches to oral historical interpretation: hermeneutic and ethnographic. The goal of the hermeneutic approach is "to discover the interpretive power of the text, its levels of discourse, its hidden meanings, and its ability to transmit a message."

> Through this analysis, we find how people manipulate truth, make history, tell stories, and carry on the collective memory. The assumption is that it tells us something about mind in action, something that is shaped by many in the culture either on a formal or an experiential level.
>
> The ethnographic approach seeks to locate the testimony in the society, to study it for what it tells about people and their relations to other people, the world of production. There is, however, also an attempt to relate the levels of discourse, and the use of language, to social domains. (Tilly, pp. 45, 46)

In recent years, analysis of oral historical discourse as a hermeneutic process has centered on the social construction of meaning within the interview context. Viewing the oral history interview as a joint accomplishment, hermeneutic analysis has centered on the process of dialectical questioning that occurs as cultural peers move toward the construction of shared meaning. While acknowledging that the construction of meaning occurs in any cultural interaction, an extensive hermeneutic analysis of oral history discourse by Eva McMahan has focused on interviews with elites. McMahan suggests that the creation of intersubjective reality in the oral history interview is least ambiguous in such a setting. McMahan's analysis solves the issue of the truth-value of oral history, placing it at the heart of the hermeneutic process. It also suggests that the construction of historical discourse through oral interviewing inherently leads to multiple histories in which cultural disjuncture between interviewer and informant exists.

The notion of intersubjectivity has also informed ethnographic analysis employing oral interviews. Radical culture theories developed by anthropologists such as Clifford Geertz, Marshall Sahlins, and David Schneider have given priority to the social construction of meaning. Analysis of ethnographic representation by anthropologists such as James Clifford and George Marcus has centered on the emergence of ethnography as a literary genre in which conventions of representation proceed from cultural assumptions concerning the relationship between ethnographer and informant. In an essay directed to oral historians, anthropologist Micaela Di Leonardo contrasts the generic structure of oral histories and ethnographies, acknowledging that the intersubjectivity of knowledge is the basic epistemological problem for each. Di Leonardo suggests that the ethnographic approach has its own analytical power for analyzing the relationships that impinge on the construction of meaning in any interview setting.

As oral historians continue to grapple with the nature of their enterprise, questions of representation and the construction of discourse have emerged as critical. Such questions have greater implications for the nature of historical discourse, and for this reason the ultimate contribution of oral history may yet be achieved in this regard.

BIBLIOGRAPHY

General Works

Allen, Barbara, and William Lynwood Montell. *From Memory to History: Using Oral Sources in Local Historical Research* (1981).

ORAL HISTORY

Baum, Willa K. *Oral History for the Local Historical Society* (1969; rev eds. 1974, 1987).

———. *Transcribing and Editing Oral History* (1977).

Baum, Willa K., and David K. Dunaway. *Oral History: An Interdisciplinary Anthology* (1984).

Crawford, Charles W. "Oral History—The State of the Profession." *Oral History Review* 2 (1974).

Dorson, Richard. "The Oral Historian and the Folklorist." In *Selections from the Fifth and Sixth National Colloquia on Oral History,* edited by Peter D. Olch and Forrest C. Pogue (1972).

Evans, George Ewart. *Spoken History* (1987).

Haley, Alex. "Black History, Oral History, and Genealogy." *Oral History Review* 1, no. 1 (1973).

———. *Roots* (1976).

Hall, Jacquelyn Dowd. "Documenting Diversity: The Southern Experience." *Oral History Review* 4 (1976).

Havlice, Patricia Pate. *Oral History: A Reference Guide and Annotated Bibliography* (1985).

Ives, Edward D. *The Tape-recorded Interview: A Manual for Field Workers in Folklore and Oral History* (1974; rev. and enl. ed. 1980).

Jefferson, Alphine W. "Echoes from the South: The History and Methodology of the Duke University Oral History Program, 1972–1982." *Oral History Review* 12 (1984).

Meckler, Alan M., comp. and ed. *Oral History Collections* (1975).

Mehaffy, George L. "Foxfire Comes of Age." *Oral History Review* 13 (1985).

Microfilming Corporation of America. *Oral History Guide: A Bibliographic Listing of the Memoirs in the Micropublished Collections* (1976).

Morrissey, Charles T. "Why Call It 'Oral History'? Searching for Early Usage of a Generic Term." *Oral History Review* 8 (1980).

———. "Riding a Mule Through the 'Terminological Jungle': Oral History and the Problems of Nomenclature." *Oral History Review* 12 (1984).

Moss, William W. *Oral History Program Manual* (1974).

———. "The Future of Oral History." *Oral History Review* 3 (1975).

———. "Oral History: An Appreciation." *The American Archivist* 40, no. 4. (1977).

Neuenschwander, John A. *Oral History as a Teaching Approach* (1976).

Nevins, Allan. *The Gateway to History* (1938; rev. ed. 1963).

Passerini, Luisa. "Oral History in Italy After the Second World War: From Populism to Subjectivity." *International Journal of Oral History* 9, no. 2 (1988).

Pogue, Forrest. "Louis Starr: A Remembrance." *Oral History Review* 8 (1980).

Proctor, Samuel. "Oral History Comes of Age." *Oral History Review* 3 (1975).

Shumway, Gary L. *Oral History in the United States: A Directory* (1971).

Shumway, Gary L., and William G. Hartley. *An Oral History Primer* (1973).

Sitton, Thad. "The Descendants of *Foxfire*." *Oral History Review* 6 (1978).

Smith, Richard Cándida. "¿Quién quiere Usted que sea bueno?" *Oral History Review* 14 (1986).

Starr, Louis M. *Oral History at Columbia* (1964).

———. "Studs Terkel and Oral History." *Chicago History* 3, no. 2 (1974).

METHODS AND CONTEXTS

Theory

Abrahams, Roger D. "Story and History: A Folklorist's View." *Oral History Review* 9 (1981).

Anderson, Kathryn, Susan Armitage, Dana Jack, and Judith Wittner. "Beginning Where We Are: Feminist Methodology in Oral History." *Oral History Review* 15, no. 1 (1987).

Brink, T. L. "Oral History and Geriatric Mental Health: Distortions of Testimony Produced by Psychopathology." *Oral History Review* 13 (1985).

Clark, E. Culpepper, Michael J. Hyde, and Eva M. McMahan. "Communication in the Oral History Interview." *International Journal of Oral History* 1, no. 1 (1980).

Di Leonardo, Micaela. "Oral History as Ethnographic Encounter." *Oral History Review* 15, no. 1 (1987).

Faris, David E. "Narrative Form and Oral History: Some Problems and Possibilities." *International Journal of Oral History* 1, no. 3 (1980).

Frisch, Michael. "Oral History and *Hard Times:* A Review Essay." *Oral History Review* 7 (1979).

———. "The Memory of History." *Radical History Review* no. 25 (1981).

———. *A Shared Authority: Essays on the Craft and Meaning of Oral and Public History* (1990).

Fry, Amelia R. "Reflections on Ethics." *Oral History Review* 3 (1975).

Glassie, Henry. "A Folkloristic Thought on the Promise of Oral History." In *Selections from the Fifth and Sixth National Colloquia on Oral History,* edited by Peter D. Olch and Forrest C. Pogue (1972).

Grele, Ronald, ed. *Envelopes of Sound: Six Practitioners Discuss the Method, Theory, and Practice of Oral History and Oral Testimony* (1975; 2d ed., rev. and enl. 1985).

———. "Can Anyone over Thirty Be Trusted: A Friendly Critique of Oral History." *Oral History Review* 6 (1978).

Henige, David. *Oral Historiography* (1982).

Joyner, Charles W. "Oral History as Communicative Event: A Folkloristic Perspective." *Oral History Review* 7 (1979).

McMahan, Eva M. "Speech and Counterspeech: Language-in-use in Oral History Fieldwork." *Oral History Review* 15, no. 1 (1987).

———. *Elite Oral History Discourse: A Study of Cooperation and Coherence* (1989).

Mintz, Sidney W. "The Anthropological Interview and the Life History." *Oral History Review* 7 (1979).

Moore, Waddy W. "Critical Perspectives." *Oral History Review* 6 (1978).

Neuenschwander, John A. "Remembrance of Things Past: Oral Historians and Long-term Memory." *Oral History Review* 6 (1978).

Okihiro, Gary Y. "Oral History and the Writing of Ethnic History: A Reconnaissance into Method and Theory." *Oral History Review* 9 (1981).

Rapport, Leonard. "How Valid Are the Federal Writers' Project Life Stories: An Iconoclast Among the True Believers." *Oral History Review* 7 (1979).

Schrager, Samuel. "What Is Social in Oral History?" *International Journal of Oral History* 4, no. 2 (1983).

Terrill, Tom E., and Jerrold Hirsch. "Replies to Leonard Rapport's 'How Valid Are the Federal Writers' Project Life Stories: An Iconoclast Among the True Believers.'" *Oral History Review* 8 (1980).

Thompson, Paul R. *The Voice of the Past: Oral History* (1978; rev. ed. 1988).

Thompson, Paul R., Luisa Passerini, Isabelle Bertaux-Wiame, and Alessandro Portelli. "Between Social Scientists: Response to Louise A. Tilly." *International Journal of Oral History* 6, no. 1 (1985).

Tilly, Louise A. "People's History and Social Science History" and "Louise A. Tilly's Response." *International Journal of Oral History* 6, no. 1 (1985).

Vansina, Jan. *Oral Tradition: A Study in Historical Methodology.* Translated by H. M. Wright (1965).

Examples of Oral History

Bethel, Elizabeth Rauh. *Promiseland: A Century of Life in a Negro Community* (1981).

Bodnar, John. *Immigration and Industrialization: Ethnicity in an American Mill Town, 1870–1940* (1977).

———. *Workers' World: Kinship, Community, and Protest in an Industrial Society, 1900–1940* (1982).

Brecher, Jeremy, Jerry Lombardi, and Jan Stackhouse, eds. and comps. *Brass Valley: The Story of Working People's Lives and Struggles in an American Industrial Region* (1982).

Epstein, Helen. *Children of the Holocaust: Conversations with Sons and Daughters of Survivors* (1979).

Escott, Paul D. *Slavery Remembered: A Record of Twentieth-Century Slave Narratives* (1979).

Friedlander, Peter. *The Emergence of a UAW Local, 1936–1939* (1975).

Girdner, Audrie, and Anne Loftis. *The Great Betrayal: The Evacuation of the Japanese-Americans During World War II* (1969).

Gluck, Sherna B. *From Parlor to Prison: Five American Suffragists Talk About Their Lives* (1976).

———. "Interlude or Change: Woman and the World War II Work Experience." *International Journal of Oral History* 3 (1982).

Hall, Jacqueline Dowd, James Leloudis, Robert Korstad, Mary Murphy, Lu Ann Jones, and Christopher B. Daly. *Like a Family: The Making of a Southern Cotton Mill World* (1987).

Hareven, Tamara K. *Family Time and Industrial Time: The Relationship Between the Family and Work in a New England Industrial Community* (1982).

Hareven, Tamara K., and Randolph Langebach. *Amoskeag: Life and Work in an American Factory-City* (1978).

Ives, Edward D. *Joe Scott, the Woodsman-Songmaker* (1978).

Joyce, Rosemary O. *A Woman's Place: The Life History of a Rural Ohio Grandmother* (1983).

Kahn, Kathy. *Hillbilly Women* (1973).

Kann, Kenneth. *Joe Rapoport, The Life of a Jewish Radical* (1981).

Lewis, Oscar. *The Children of Sánchez* (1961).

Lewis, Oscar, Ruth M. Lewis, and Susan M. Rigdon. *Living the Revolution* (1977).

McDaniel, George W. *Hearth and Home: Preserving a People's Culture* (1982).

Martin, Charles E. *Hollybush: Folk Building and Social Change in an Appalachian Community* (1984).

Miller, Merle. *Plain Speaking: An Oral Biography of Harry S. Truman* (1974).

Montell, William Lynwood. *The Saga of Coe Ridge* (1970).

Painter, Nell Irvin. *The Narrative of Hosea Hudson: His Life as a Negro Communist in the South* (1979).

Perdue, Theda. *Nations Remembered: An Oral History of the Five Civilized Tribes, 1865–1907* (1980).

Rosengarten, Theodore. *All God's Dangers: The Life of Nate Shaw* (1974).

Shackelford, Laura, and Bill Weinberg, eds. *Our Appalachia: An Oral History* (1977).

Sidel, Ruth. *Urban Survival: The World of Working-class Women* (1978).

Tateishi, John. *And Justice for All: An Oral History of the Japanese American Detention Camps* (1984).

Terkel, Studs. *Division Street: America* (1967).

———. *Hard Times: An Oral History of the Great Depression* (1970).

———. *Working: People Talk About What They Do All Day, and How They Feel About What They Do* (1974).

———. *"The Good War": An Oral History of World War Two* (1984).

Terrill, Tom E., and Jerrold Hirsch. *Such as Us: Southern Voices of the Thirties* (1978).

Thompson, Paul R. *The Edwardians: The Remaking of British Society* (1975).

Thompson, Paul R., and Natasha Burchardt, eds. *Our Common History: The Transformation of Europe* (1982).

Thompson, Paul R., with Tony Wailey and Trevor Lummis. *Living the Fishing* (1983).

Weglyn, Michi. *Years of Infamy: The Untold Story of America's Concentration Camps* (1976).

Wigginton, Eliot. *Sometimes a Shining Moment: The Foxfire Experience* (1985).

———, ed. *The Foxfire Book* (1972).

Wilson, Emily Herring. *Hope and Dignity: Older Black Women of the South* (1983).

Yans-McLaughlin, Virginia. *Family and Community: Italian Immigrants in Buffalo, 1880–1930* (1977).

SEE ALSO **Anthropological Approaches to History; Community Studies; The Old Social History and the New**; and various articles in the section "**Work and Labor.**"

MATERIAL CULTURE STUDIES

Thomas J. Schlereth

A GENERATION AGO only a few American historians would have recognized or have been interested in either social history or material culture as an important research strategy in historical studies. Social history has had a historiography stretching far beyond the emergence of its so-called new practitioners of the 1960s; the history of scholars working with artifactual evidence likewise extends well into the late nineteenth century.

Three North American scholarly journals now carry the term "material culture" on their mastheads: the *Winterthur Portfolio: A Journal of American Material Culture* (Winterthur Museum and the University of Chicago Press), *Material Culture* (Pioneer America Society and the University of Akron), and *Material History Bulletin* (National Museums of Civilization, Ottawa, Canada). The term "material culture," "material life," or "material history" now frequently appears as the disciplinary specialty of scholars, in the titles of monographs, scholarly papers, fellowships, and conferences, and as the subject of undergraduate and graduate courses.

MATERIAL CULTURE STUDIES AND SOCIAL HISTORY: PARALLELS AND PROBLEMS

What is meant by the term material culture? While scholars who use it are continually expanding and contracting the definition, one basic and succinct one would be: material culture is that segment of humankind's physical environment that has been purposely made or modified, consciously or unconsciously, by people according to culturally dictated plans. Material culture entails those artifacts that humankind creates to cope with the physical world, to regulate its social relations, to perform its work, to delight its fancy, and to create symbols of meaning.

Material culture studies is a multidisciplinary form of cultural inquiry that describes the research, writing, teaching, exhibiting, and publishing of individuals who endeavor to analyze and interpret past and present human activity (behaviors, values, attitudes, beliefs) largely, but not exclusively, through extant physical evidence.

Material culture studies is deliberately plural because it comprises several disciplines, among them the triad of art, architectural, and decorative arts history; cultural geography; the history of technology; folklore; historical archaeology; cultural anthropology; and cultural and social history.

The majority of the disciplines that use material culture evidence and material culture methodologies shares with social history a concern for historical explanations of human behavior over time and place. Other affinities exist. For example, both social history and material culture studies challenge the older monocausal view of history as past politics, both have sought to demonstrate the great diversity of the American people and their ways of life, and both have been eager to expand (some would say, explode) the traditional boundaries of American historical scholarship and thereby actually to redefine what constitutes American history.

Students of material culture and social historians tend to agree that most ordinary individuals in the past left few literate records. For the majority of people, the primary historical record of their everyday lives survives as data gathered about them or, as happens even more frequently, as objects made and used and finally discarded by them. Material culture, claim its advocates, is more democratic than literary or statistical documents as well as less sensitive to the subjectivity that every person brought, however unconsciously, to one's written or oral accounting of peoples and events. Such an assertion concurs with social history's concern for a higher degree of representativeness in the evidential basis of all historical explanation.

Historians who work with objects and some social historians use formats of communicating historical information and insight other than the history establishment's venerable rhetorical modes of presentation, the scholarly monograph and the journal article. Just as social historians experimented with different presentation techniques such as quantification and oral history, material culture scholars have likewise sought innovative formats (for example, experimental archaeology and outdoor living-history museums) through which new historical data and information might be most accurately and meaningfully conveyed to a wide sector of the American public.

Despite these several convergent interests, a number of issues separate social historians and historians who have sought to use artifacts as a primary data base. One difference has been their respective publics. Academic social historians have tended to write only for other fellow specialists, showing minimal interest in disseminating their data, methods, and conclusions outside the academic compounds of the universities. Material culture scholars, on the other hand, have usually worked in a more diverse institutional structure, researching and publishing (in exhibits as well as articles) in museums, government agencies, and state historical societies, as well as colleges and universities.

With a few exceptions, most students of material culture have not shared the enthusiasm of those in social history who see quantification as the principal salvation of historical studies. Quantification has been a research tool for a few individuals working with probate inventories, wills, and other statistical collections of objects, but there is still considerable hesitancy on the part of scholars initially trained to study single objects (especially as art objects) to embrace techniques for monitoring and manipulating large aggregates of physical data.

Finally, material culture studies, despite all the methodological creativity demonstrated by some of its most pioneering proponents, is still only beginning to explore the conceptual and analytical potential of its approach to historical study. Traditionally content to collect and to describe objects, many material culture students still resist the methodological necessity of extracting and synthesizing social behavior from such three-dimensional data. Or, to put it another way, many resist the imperative to deduce, wherever possible, the culture behind the material.

In several topical areas, however, scholars in material culture research have made both methodological advances and substantive contributions to contemporary knowledge about American social history. To the neglect of many other topics that might be surveyed—for example, kinship, schooling, ethnicity, aging—and simply because of space limitations, this essay will confine its overview to six topics (residential spaces; domestic artifacts; women's studies; work, working, and workers; life experiences; community landscapes) where the interests of material-culture research and social history coincide.

RESIDENTIAL SPACES

When John Demos devoted part one ("The Physical Setting") of his *Little Commonwealth: Family Life in Plymouth Colony* (1970) to the domestic shelter and artifacts of the seventeenth-century Pilgrim community, he was recognizing a fact crucial to much material culture research: as the elementary unit of humankind is the individual, the elementary artifact on the human landscape is the dwelling. Housing represents social and economic identity, and is a microcosm of domestic culture. Demos, of course, went on to explore the societal implications of architectural evidence (for example, status, privacy, social segregation, repression of familial anger and aggression, and child-rearing practices) in his pioneering application of social and behavioral science concepts to the houses of seventeenth-century Massachusetts.

Although Demos's analysis of the material culture of a single seventeenth-century New England colony was brief, inferential, and only a case study, it does represent one type of social history that has employed housing as significant evidence. Others include Gwendolyn Wright's *Moralism and the Model Home* (1980), David P. Handlin's *The American Home: Architecture and Society, 1815–1915* (1979) and Clifford E. Clark, Jr.'s *The American Family Home, 1860–1960* (1986). Such research eschews the usual approach of the traditional architectural historian in that it avoids mere "facadism" (interpreting a house primarily through its front elevation and aesthetic style) as well as elitism (researching only structures designed by professional architects).

Housing, as well as the house, has become an important material culture subfield. Ever since

Herbert Gans's work *The Levittowners* appeared in 1967, an interest in the material culture of Anglo-American suburbia has steadily increased due to the work of individuals such as the architect Robert Venturi, the landscape historian John Stilgoe, and the architectural historian Alan Gowans. Such work investigates the history of urban middle- and working-class neighborhoods through their extant housing stock. Tenement districts, slums, and even alleys are receiving attention as are such issues as the social meaning of home ownership, housing and property controls, residential class segregation, and subsidized public housing.

Folklorists studying the construction techniques involved in erecting and furnishing housing often explore changes in a community's economic and social organization of work through building practices. In two pioneering books—*Pattern in the Material Folk Culture of the Eastern United States* (1968) and *Folk Housing in Middle Virginia: A Structural Analysis of Historic Artifacts* (1975)—Henry Glassie has researched such historical *processes* in order to understand the *persons* who used them and the *products* that resulted from them. In *Folk Housing,* Glassie approached material culture by means of the paradigm of twentieth-century structuralism, particularly as articulated by Noam Chomsky and Claude Lévi-Strauss.

Glassie, following Chomsky, argued that "culture is pattern in mind, the ability to make things like sentences or houses." Rejecting the concept that objects are the simple products of passive minds, Glassie attempted to develop a systematic model that would account for and help analyze the design abilities of an idealized maker of artifacts. As a case study, he investigated the builders of 156 houses constructed between the middle of the eighteenth century and World War I in a seventy-square-mile (182-square-kilometer) area of central Virginia. His research objective, using almost exclusively material culture data left behind by anonymous builders, was to discover the unwritten boundaries or "artifactual grammar" of the creative process as it was exercised in a particular region's vernacular architecture.

Glassie began his "structural analysis of historic artifacts" with a geometric base structure—the square. Instead of arguing that houses evolve, however, he proposed that it was the ability to design houses that did. He had found such a competency illustrated in some seventeen structural design types and subtypes involving the geometry of the square and reflecting numerous conscious and unconscious individual decisions among the builders of such houses. Combining the basic structuralistic techniques with thorough fieldwork examining housing plans, decorative motifs, and building hardware, he sought to articulate "rule sets" for the collective reasoning behind the construction of the anonymous housing he was investigating.

American material culture structuralism has drawn fire from various camps. Some historians claim that despite its gestures toward tracing a change in minds, the approach, by definition, tends only to work in areas of relative cultural stasis. Fellow folklorists have complained that Glassie's subjective system of binary mental opposites (intellect-emotion, internal-external, complex-simple, and twelve others) merely substitutes one kind of interpretive arbitrariness for another in plotting human behavior patterns. Still others remark that the results from such structural analysis are not adequately comparative.

DOMESTIC ARTIFACTS

In keeping with the folk proverb that claims that a house is not a home, historians have researched the material life of Americans as revealed in patterns of home furnishings, foodways, clothing, and organizations of domestic space as ways of gaining insight into the social past of middle-class and working-class culture. For instance, Carole Shammas's survey, "The Domestic Environment in Early Modern England and America," Katherine O. Grier's *Culture and Comfort: People, Parlors, and Upholstery, 1850–1930* (1989), and Lizabeth Cohen's interpretation of the material culture of American working-class homes between 1885 and 1915 are examples of how the study of the domestic material culture environment can contribute to the historical understanding of the average familial, feminine, and vocational experience of Americans, an understanding that expands on interpretation based primarily on a study of quantified occupations and vital statistics.

Some material culture researchers in the decorative arts have sought such an integration of data. In addition to the standard cultural history surveys of American domestic life, work has been done on a whole range of common household items—parlor furniture, mourning pictures, eating utensils, cleaning devices, family photograph albums, kitchen appliances—that are seen as indices of a society's values as important as its elite artifacts or its literary remains. The material culture of nineteenth-century hallways (hat and clothing stands, mirrors, hallchairs, and card receivers), parlors (especially the ubiquitous home parlor organ), and dining rooms (table settings and eating accoutrements) have been imaginatively analyzed by Kenneth Ames ("Meaning in Artifacts"), while Edward O. Laumann and James S. House ("Living Room Styles") have studied the patterning of material artifacts in the living rooms of twentieth-century working-class families. Still others have attempted to write American social history using wallpaper, silver, ceramics, chairs, and other commonplace domestic artifacts as important evidence in their research.

Several of these studies have also employed quantification techniques in their comparative analyses of past material culture. Such data are found in the form of probate inventories, craftsmen's ledgers, auction lists, wills, deeds, and sales records. Colonial historians were the first to turn to inventories to study social and economic behavior and they have subsequently contributed a substantial corpus of research based upon inventories. Abbott Lowell Cumming's *Rural Household Inventories* (1964), although dealing primarily with the property of wealthy families, contains an excellent discussion of how to interpret the probate inventory as a historical resource for the study of lower- and middle-class households as well.

Photography, an artifact created in the nineteenth century, has also been of immense use to historians interested in American domestic life. George Talbot's *At Home: Domestic Life in the Post-Centennial Era, 1876–1920* (1976) and William Seale's *The Tasteful Interlude: American Interiors Through the Camera's Eye, 1850–1917* (1975) are important examples of such work. Historical photography, when examined closely and in sufficient quantity to ensure a representative evidential sample, provides valuable inferences as to how occupants organized and used space as well as how they interacted with one another. Using photography, much can be learned about family life as lived in residential spaces such as kitchens, bedrooms, hall passages, pantries, inglenooks, nurseries, servants' quarters, as well as in parlors, living rooms, front porches, and dining rooms.

Social historians, whether interested in material culture as evidence or not, have paid scant attention to eating, assuredly one of humankind's most common necessities. Despite the enormous material culture that surrounds this essential experience, it has also been largely ignored by most serious students of material culture. What research has been done focuses primarily on rural and preindustrial communities. In the 1980s, studies by Susan Williams, Harvey Levenstein, and Laura Shapiro have focused on artifacts of twentieth-century food preparation, service, and disposal.

In calling for the integration of foodways (and all other relevant material, statistical, and documentary data) into a cultural, historical, and anthropological approach to material culture, James Deetz has argued for a research paradigm that seeks "the detection and explication of apparently unrelated changes in *all* [my emphasis] aspects of a people's culture, material and otherwise" ("Scientific Humanism," p. 8). Although not directly influenced by the devotees of a *mentalité* approach to the past, he shares this school's interest in the study of popular beliefs, attitudes, customs, sentiments, and modes of behavior as well as its commitment to "thick description"—the technique of bringing to bear upon events of the past a mass of facts of every kind and subjecting them to intensive scrutiny so as to elicit every possible cultural meaning from them.

Yet the Deetz cultural history paradigm does not disregard social-science–research methods such as quantification or model building. In its attempt at as total a reconstruction of past lifeways as possible, its practitioners seek (using all available documentary, statistical, and material data) information about how cultural change is influenced by gender divisions of labor, demographic changes, the impact of technology, or altered kinship patterns. Deetz, a historical archaeologist long associated with the historical reconstruction of Plimoth Plantation (Massachusetts) developed his theory and method in *In Small Things Forgotten: The Archaeology of Early American Life* (1977).

Of particular interest is the challenge Deetz's paradigm presents in *In Small Things Forgotten* to the traditional interpretive claim of political and diplomatic history that the American independence movement was the major cultural watershed of American colonial history. The documentary and material data that Deetz assembled and integrated suggest that the Revolution actually had little impact on American cultural history; in fact, the general American cultural pattern of involvement with English material culture, both before and after the war, remained remarkably constant.

In some ways, Deetz's *In Small Things Forgotten* can be viewed as an American counterpart to Fernand Braudel's *Capitalism and Material Life* (1973). For example, although much briefer and lacking Braudel's extensive documentation, the Deetz interpretation, like Braudel's, stays close to home for its data. The changing domestic technologies of house building, heating, lighting, plumbing, food preparation, and garbage removal are resources in both histories. Extant artifacts are often the only data by which such past behavior can be reconstructed.

In a similar spirit, Albert E. Parr has used lighting and heating fixtures to speculate on how innovations in such domestic technology drastically interrupted the traditional evening orientation of the pre-nineteenth-century family toward a single hearth (a shared communal space), thereby prompting major changes in parent-child and sibling relationships. Others have documented behavior changes in domestic history with the advent of indoor plumbing (especially the appearance of the bathroom) and the installation of central heating.

WOMEN'S STUDIES

Understandably the material culture of the American home has figured in the work of historians of women who, while not always adherents of a social-history approach to their topic, are frequently included in that field's ranks. A special interest among some such scholars in the decorative arts and in the history of technology has focused on kitchen tools and appliances and their roles in defining, confining, or undermining a "woman's place." While various researchers have contributed to this scholarly enterprise, the work of Ruth Schwartz Cowan, Dolores Hayden, and Susan Strasser aptly represent their general concerns.

Cowan's research has moved from the study of a single artifact genre ("A Case of Technology and Social Change: The Washing Machine and the Working Wife," 1974) to kitchen appliances in general ("The 'Industrial Revolution' in the Home," 1976) to women's interaction with technological material culture throughout American history (*More Work for Mother,* 1983). Hayden's interests have been more spatial and environmental than technological. Her *Seven American Utopias: The Architecture of Communitarian Socialism, 1790–1975* (1976) details the social and cultural history of several countercultural societies through their extant structures and sites, as well as through their furniture, household technology, and geography. Hayden's *The Grand Domestic Revolution: A History of Feminist Designs for American Homes, Neighborhoods, and Cities* (1981), provides the social historian with a useful review of the interaction of domestic feminism, cooperative housekeeping, the community kitchen movement, and projects for social reform. Susan Strasser's *Never Done: A History of American Housework* (1982) has set the agenda for future research into basic topics such as food provisioning, housekeeping and housecleaning, and domestic consumerism. On the last topic, Strasser has followed up on her own work and contributed a book, *Satisfaction Guaranteed: The Making of the American Mass Market* (1989), to the material culture of advertising, particularly its orientation toward women consumers.

Mary Johnson's bibliographical essay, "Women and Their Material Universe" (1981), and Martha Moore Trescott's anthology, *Dynamos and Virgins Revisited* (1979) are additional valuable introductions to scholarship using artifacts to explain the social history of American women. Johnson points out, for instance, how public documents and private correspondence rarely mention the tasks of housewifery, daily work that consumed so much of the time, energy, and creativity of women in the past. Her bibliography surveys the literature that—through the interpretation of common household utensils, furnishings, and spaces—has sought answers to a series of questions regarding women's role in household production, activities, servant management, child nurture, and the design, manufacture, and role of clothing.

In the triptych of human necessities—food, clothing, and shelter—clothing has received almost as little attention as has food from professional historians. Despite the insights drawn by Philippe Ariès and John Demos from early modern costume styles and materials, clothing—an artifact frequently made by women—has figured as an important historical resource in only a few innovative studies. The valuable research that has been done has tended to use clothing as historical evidence to plot configurations of social status (for example, Jeanette C. Lauer and Robert H. Lauer, "The Language of Dress," 1979); gender identification (Deborah Jean Warner, "Fashion, Emancipation, Reform, and the Rational Undergarment," 1978), or democratization (Margaret Walsh, "The Democratization of the Women's Dress Pattern Industry," 1979).

The theme of how democratic culture impinged upon material culture permeates Claudia B. Kidwell and Margaret C. Christman's *Suiting Everyone: The Democratization of Clothing in America* (1974), the catalog to a Smithsonian museum exhibition. Kidwell, who has done pioneering social history studies of vernacular clothing such as eighteenth-century short gowns and nineteenth-century bathing attire, uses artifacts to explore two principal themes in *Suiting Everyone.* She examines the economic transformation resulting from the shift from dressing in homemade clothing to ready-to-wear clothing, and the social shift in customs from dressing according to one's class to a new "democratic dress" whereby everyone strives to dress alike. As Thorstein Veblen noted in *The Theory of the Leisure Class* (1899), this style of democratic uniformity in dress created a tension in American society between the ideals of equality and individuality. Kidwell explores the social dimensions of this tension as well as other paradoxes such as the oppressive nature of the sweated industries that produced cheaper and better clothing for an ever-widening segment of the populace. Such themes, plus the issues of gender in costume design and consumer preference, are explored in another volume Kidwell has coedited with Valerie Steele, *Men and Women: Dressing the Part* (1989).

In addition to their traditional occupations of manufacturing all manner of domestic and sartorial artifacts, women have been bearers and rearers of children. Women menstruate, parturate, and lactate; men do not. Yet written history takes little note of these obvious facts and their possible impact upon life as lived in the past. These uniquely female experiences have prompted a wide range of material culture: pessaries, sanitary napkins, tampons, various intrauterine devices, artificial nipples, bottle sterilizers, and pasteurized and condensed milks are only a few.

The social history based upon this unique female material culture evidence has only begun to be explored. With the possible exception of historians researching the technology of contraception, scholars are only now becoming aware of how neglected this topic has been. Virginia Drachman's analysis of the relation between gynecological instruments and surgical decisions in hospitals in late-nineteenth-century America is a helpful work-in-progress report but much more needs to be done. As Ruth Cowan points out, none of the standard histories or bibliographies of American technology contain adequate reference to such a culturally significant artifact as the baby bottle. Here is a simple implement that, along with its attendant delivery system, revolutionized a basic biological process, transformed a fundamental human experience for vast numbers of infants and mothers, and served as one of the more controversial exports of Western technology to underdeveloped countries.

According to Cowan, there is a host of questions that scholars might reasonably ask about the baby bottle. For how long has it been part of Western culture? When a mother's milk could not be provided, which classes of people used the bottle and which the wet nurse, and for what reasons? Which was a more crucial determinant for widespread use of the bottle, changes in milk technology or changes in bottle technology? Who marketed the bottles, at what prices, to whom? How did mothers of different social classes and ethnic groups react to them? Can the phenomenon of "not enough milk," which was widely reported by pediatricians and obstetricians in the 1920s and 1930s, be connected with the advent of the safe baby bottle? Which was cause and which effect?

Similar questions are now being asked about the technologies of childrearing, a function that is not anatomically confined to women but that, in much of the past, has been more or less effectively limited to them by the terms of many unspoken social contracts. To date, however, most students of material culture have focused their energy more specifically on child play than on child nurture. Playthings, for instance, are studied as factors significant in shaping individual personalities and cultural traits. Acknowledging the fact that most toys are made by adults to appeal and to sell to other adults, researchers still see great potential in studying such artifacts for writing a more comprehensive history of childhood. Taking a clue from Johan Huizinga's classic cultural history, *Homo Ludens* (1949), American studies scholar Bernard Mergen has provided would-be researchers with a survey of the topic's potential, a bibliographical guide to past work and resource data, as well as a review of research theories and conclusions resulting from using "toys as hypotheses" in material culture study. Students of the toys available for children in the twentieth century, for example, are struck by two particular facts: first, in selecting toys, children have been encouraged to follow the scientific and technological fads of their elders and, second, these toys were often advertised as being more appropriate for one gender than the other.

WORK, WORKING, WORKERS

Products for one individual's play are, of course, the products of another individual's work. Historians have also begun to study the material culture of American working places. Some of this research takes the form of town or community studies, some has focused primarily on working conditions within mills, mines, shops, and factories. Some has primarily investigated worker's housing. Two fields of material culture studies—the history of technology and industrial archaeology—have contributed to this new brand of labor history.

In an attempt to move beyond the traditional subjects of labor history (among them unionization, strikes, and the personalities of labor leaders), scholars such as Herbert Gutman, David Montgomery, and Jonathan Prude have probed both the specialized work *processes* of American laborers and the total historical experience of such workers as *persons* in the wider society. Many students of work processes and attendant technologies have been labeled functionalists in their approach to material culture evidence. The functionalist paradigm in material culture studies holds that culture is primarily a means of adapting to environment with technology as the most important adaptive mechanism. The utility of artifacts within the context of a technological system, whether it be a kitchen appliance, a Corliss steam engine, or an interstate highway system, provides the key to understanding cultural transmission and adaptation in this approach to material culture research. With only a secondary concern for the origins of artifacts, the functionalists are primarily interested in the ramifications of material culture; they are intrigued with process, change, adaptation, and the cultural impact of objects. Bronislaw Malinowski's and A. R. Radcliffe Brown's approaches to anthropological research provide part of the theoretical base for the functionalist approach to material culture; Lewis H. Morgan, Franz Boas, Ruth Benedict, and especially William Bascom are also cited as methodological progenitors. Within the history of technology the work of Sigfried Giedion, Lynn White, and Carl Condit follows a functional interpretation.

Methodological arguments in support of the functionalist approach in American material culture studies have been put forth in several publications by Warren Roberts, a contemporary folklife researcher. Citing the criteria of "practicality" in a "local context" as the vital determinants in the manufacture and use of artifacts, Roberts and other functionalists tend to sound much like environmentalists (to be discussed below) when they enumerate specific factors such as available materials, weather conditions, technical competencies, support services, family structures, and economic systems, that affect the selection, use, and transmission of material culture. While recognizing the many facets that make up an object's *milieu,* the functionalist is equally concerned with the *maker* of an object. Material culture functionalists try to explain both how an object was "worked" (how its maker functioned in order to make it), as well as how the object itself "works" (how it actually functions in a sociocultural context).

Those who espouse the functionalist approach are anxious to demonstrate that material culture is, at its core, a reflection of the rationality and practicality of the participants in a culture. They argue, therefore, that description of the worker's (maker's) motives best supports the analyst's functional explanation. Oral history fieldwork, not surprisingly, is a frequently employed research tool when dealing with the material culture of still-living memory. But often informant data is not available for cultural activity of the past, leaving the researcher to surmise the functional sequence originally used in the manufacture and use of an artifact. Such a fascination with the "mind of the maker" often allies the functionalist with the structuralists previously mentioned, and the behavioralists to be discussed shortly.

Interest in the cognitive processes involved in the production of past material culture likewise intrigues a group of scholars who now call themselves "experimental archaeologists." The history of their approach has been summarized by Jay Anderson and by Robert Asher, and elaborated by John Coles in his primer *Archaeology by Experiment* (1973). In Anderson's words,

> experimental archaeology was developed as a means of 1) practically testing theories of past cultural behavior, especially technological processes involving the use of tools, and, 2) obtaining data not readily available from more traditional artifact analysis and historical sources. Since experimental archaeology seeks to "imitate or replicate" the original functions or processes involved in using certain artifacts, the technique has also been called "imitative archaeology." (pp. 2–3)

Perhaps the most spectacular and most publicized application of the experimental approach has been the Kon Tiki expedition on which Thor Heyerdahl sought to test his hypothesis that people, with certain available technologies, could have sailed the 4,000 miles (6,400 kilometers) between South America and the Polynesian Islands, transplanting themselves and their culture before A.D. 1100. Other instances of experimental archaeology research include work on tool manufacture, beer brewing, house building, pottery making, and especially on foodways. In each case, a key research objective was to discover how artifacts originally functioned in the society that made and used them.

Ethnicity, often considered an important factor in the study of various artifacts, is now seen by material culturists as a significant element in understanding certain working-class cultures. For example, there has been research on the interrelations between living-room furnishings, ethnic identity, and acculturation among Greek Philadelphians; studies of ethnic differentiation among the West Coast Chinese through their specialized foodways and cultural practices; and work on social stratification patterns of eastern and southern Europeans through family photograph albums. The bulk of this research—done by folklife scholars, architectural historians, and decorative arts specialists—focuses on mainstream immigrant groups such as the Germans, the Scandinavians, and the Dutch. More recent ethnic communities such as those of Pacific Islanders, Laotians, and Puerto Ricans are only beginning to be examined.

LIFE EXPERIENCES

Several useful ethnographic investigations of ethnicity through artifacts can be found in Simon Bronner's *American Material Culture and Folklife: A Prologue and a Dialogue* (1985). The contributors to this volume are also much taken with the possibility of inferring individual human behavior from material culture evidence. Although several of these interpreters begin their historical analyses with artifacts such as country furniture, musical instruments, vernacular houses, and common tools, these things are but a means to an end: the objective is to understand human behavior as influencing and being influenced by such objects. This paradigm, called behavioralistic (not to be confused with behaviorism in psychology), tends, therefore, to focus on the individual creator of objects; it proceeds on the assumption that each individual is unique in his or her beliefs, values, skills, and motivations. In the study of an individual's material culture, the researcher aspires to understand and explain personal creativity, cognitive processes, and aesthetic individuality. The behavioralistic approach to material culture thus emphasizes the diversity of human creative expression and motivation. Although much in debt to the social and behavioral sciences, this perspective also shares a degree of kinship with the traditional art history perspective in its concentration on an object's creator and how his or her individual beliefs, values, and aspirations shape his or her creations.

Folk art has been the material culture genre most thoroughly studied by behavioralists as they have turned most of their attention toward understanding the modern context of material evidence rather than attempting to reconstruct past societies from artifactual remains.

Jones has been a major proponent and practitioner of this orientation in material culture studies. Limiting himself largely to contemporary material culture (for example, furniture made in the Cumberland mountains of southeastern Kentucky or the vernacular housing of "L.A. add-on and re-dos" in southern California), Jones has defined his task as an effort to understand human behavior more fully. Furthermore, Jones maintains that "research into human behavior must begin as well as end with human beings and should focus on the individual." In fact, in his major book, *The Hand-made Object and Its Maker,* Jones concentrated his research primarily on one man, an upland southern chairmaker who went simply by the name of Charley. Jones did this for two reasons. First, he insisted that "an object cannot be fully understood or appreciated without knowledge of the man who made it, and the traits of one object cannot be explained by reference only to antecedent works of an earlier period from which later qualities allegedly evolved" (pp. vii–viii). Second, argued Jones, a researcher cannot divorce what he or she calls "artistic or creative processes from technological ones"; the study of artifacts requires "considerations of both appearance and fitness for use" (pp. vii–viii).

In Jones's behavioralistic analysis, each individual maker of objects personifies a novel complex of skills that defy precise categorization into environmental, regional, or historical divisions. His approach tends to stress the diversity of human creativity rather than its uniformity as sought, say, by the structuralists in their quest for the universal patterns that structure human consciousness. While both perspectives hope to enter the mind of an object's maker, in order to get at the "mental template" of *homo faber,* the structuralists have tended to investigate large aggregates of data (for example, Glassie's 156 middle Virginia houses) whereas behavioralists such as William Ferris, John Vlach, and Simon Bronner have concentrated their attention on a few craftsmen and the products they have made.

By no means do all behavioralistic studies follow the Jones model. Most do share, however, his belief that certain forms of behavior are pervasive, constituting much of the oral, kinesic, and symbolic communication among people in face-to-face interaction. Frequently such behavior is encapsulated in objects but the study of it has often been neglected in traditional American history interpretations.

In an unpublished manifesto, "Toward a Behavioral History" (pp. 7–9), Jones singled out Allan Ludwig's gravestone research as a model application of the behavioralistic perspective to material culture evidence. Ludwig's analysis of the symbolism, rituals, and forms of funerary art in colonial Massachusetts and Connecticut reveals a story different from conventional histories of New England Puritanism based solely on written sources. The strictly verbal evidence depicted the Puritans as an iconophobic, nonmystical people whose piety, while once pronounced, declined dramatically near the end of the seventeenth century. Not so, suggests the cross section of New England gravestones that Ludwig documented, analyzed, and interpreted. The material culture evidence examined appears to lead to at least two other conclusions: (1) that a very strong religious sentiment flourished among inhabitants of New England until well into the nineteenth century, as evidenced by the symbols on their gravestones, and (2) that the Puritans in America created much figural as well as religious art, despite the inference that has usually been drawn from official written sources that they were a highly iconophobic culture.

Using material culture data from the distant American past remains the exception rather than the rule among advocates of the behavioralistic model. Most research (such as Mihaly Csikszentmihalyi and Eugene Rochberg-Halton, *The Meaning of Things,* 1981), deals with contemporary persons, processes, and products, and in order to conduct such research, fieldwork is a sine qua non. The fieldwork component espoused by Jones and other behavioralists in order, for example, to identify the impact of a craftsman's beliefs, values, and aspirations upon the manufacture, use, and sale of his products has a certain affinity with scholarly trends now labeled "the new ethnography." The behavioralistic approach to artifact study also parallels current social-history research on many of life's common occurrences—birthing, growing, marrying, aging, and, as mentioned, dying.

The behavioralistic research orientation also finds like-minded investigators pursuing a corollary approach to material culture study frequently called "performance theory." Advocates of this approach, who are found in the structuralist and functionalist camps as well, are intrigued by the many unexplored interconnections between material and mind. They apply a "performance" or "phenomenological" mode of analysis to artifactual matter. For example, researchers such as Dell Upton and Thomas Adler argue that the human processes involved in conceiving, making, perceiving, using, adapting, decorating, exalting, loathing, and discarding objects are intrinsic elements of human experience. Such experiences, not just the objects involved in them, are what the material culture student should strive to comprehend. To performance theorists, the human processes of creation, communication, and conduct are the important features of material culture research.

In his attempt to get into the minds of the makers of artifacts, Upton has tested the validity of performance theory in his investigation of vernacular architecture of early tidewater Virginia. By studying the "performance" extant in traditional houses, he has attempted to recreate the shapes of patterned behavior within such buildings. In the enterprise, he sought answers to questions such as: From whom does a builder of a house get his ideas? What does he do with such ideas between the time he learns them and the time that he produces a structure? The intention behind creation also determines ex post facto reconstruction of performances. Material culture scholars, using this technique, share affinity with the experimental archaeologists, described earlier as practitioners of the functionalist perspective, and with the process reconstructionists discussed in the cultural history approach.

Adler has proposed that performance theory should apply to the contemporary material culture researcher as well as to the topics he researches. Making specific reference to bluegrass banjos and traditional woodworking tools, Adler suggests the necessity of personal experience with the artifacts that the researcher studies in order to understand more fully how earlier people actually experienced such objects. Thus, in addition to the usual *referential* knowledge (seeing a banjo in a mail-order catalog or reading a description of it in a nineteenth-century diary) and *mediated* knowledge (hearing banjo music played over a radio or at a folk-music concert), a material culture student must also, whenever possible, acquire *experiential* knowledge (playing the banjo). One can best understand performers of the past only by becoming performers in the present.

COMMUNITY LANDSCAPES

Social and environmental psychologists have often claimed a correlation between environments and behavior. The material culture of public buildings, spaces, institutions, landscapes, and transportation networks has been seen as revelatory of certain cultural patterns. Urban historians, folklife researchers, architectural historians, and cultural geographers have sought to explain change through the shifts (for example, in location and in form) of such artifactual data through time and across space. These interpreters have worked at both macro and micro levels of inquiry, seeking to explain past American life by means of interpretations that range in scope from the built environment of entire cities to detailed investigations of urban street-lighting systems. They have been likewise interested in rural, suburban, and urban spaces. In general, they have believed as Philip Wagner and Marvin Mikesell argue, "any sign of human action in the landscape implies a culture, recalls a history, and demands an ecological interpretation; the history of any people evokes its setting in a landscape, its ecological problems and its cultural commitments, and the recognition of a culture calls for the discovery of traces it has left on the earth" (*Readings in Cultural Geography,* p. 23).

Urbanists such as Sam Bass Warner, Blaine Brownell, and Richard Wade have used material culture (public transportation patterns, housing, public works, cartography, urban photography, landscape architecture) in their historical interpretations of American cities; geographers and landscape historians such as David Ward, John Stilgoe, J. B. Jackson, and Grady Clay have done likewise.

These material culture researchers have concentrated their efforts largely on artifacts of urban complexes. Others have narrowed their focus to study the spatial and architectural significance of public institutions such as settlement houses, prisons, asylums, and hospitals. For many, transportation networks have been a key to explaining residential clustering, racial segregation, and occupation patterns; for instance, the hypothesis of Warner's now famous *Streetcar Suburbs* (1962) has spawned many sequels, among them, Oliver Zunz's "Technology and Society in the Urban Environment" (1972). Investigations of early transportation arteries and artifacts—horsecar barns, railroad stations, ferry slips, interurban lines—have all yielded new information about the passengers who used them.

Public structures are the most obvious element for probing the city as a historical site. Yet the topographical and geographical features of the city (particularly its parks, public squares, recreational facilities, waterfronts, alleys, and open spaces) also provided historians with indices for measuring social change. In a review essay, "Social History and the History of Landscape Architecture" (1975), Roy Lubove notes several reasons for examining such data. He argues that the use of landscape artifacts can expand the knowledge of the urbanization process, suggest the interconnections between politics and design as well as between social theory and social reform, and, in general, dramatize the role of proxemic analysis in historical study. In a similar spirit, the editors of the *Radical History Review* devoted their entire fall 1979 issue to "The Spatial Dimension of History," featuring research on nineteenth-century middle-class parks and working-class recreation, industrial archaeology, housing and property relations, the evolution of charity hospitals, and the development of the American department store. Several of the *RHR* essays focus on public works and urban plans as the data by which the politics of spatial design, especially as a vehicle for social control, can be studied.

Historians of town and city planning, with a similar sensitivity to space as an artifact wherein a changing set of social relations takes place, offer perspective on this approach in basic texts by John Reps, Norman T. Newton, and Mellier Scott. Individual case studies of American city planners such as Daniel Burnham of Chicago and Robert Moses of New York have revealed much about the impact of spatial design on the economic, racial, and social past of a city. For example, the two hundred or so low-hanging overpasses on Long Island parkways were deliberately designed by Moses to discourage buses on his parkways. Automobile-owning whites of "upper" and "comfortable middle" classes (as Moses called them) would be free to use the parkways for recreation and commuting. Poor people and blacks, who most often used public transit, were kept off such roads because the twelve-foot-tall buses they normally rode could not get through Moses's overpasses.

In *Cities of the American West: A History of Frontier Urban Planning* (1979), John Reps has extended his research on civic design from traditional urban complexes to more rural communities. Before departing this survey of environmental artifacts as historical evidence, it is important to note that—unlike most mainline social history research to date—a great deal of work by geographers and folklorists has appeared on the artifacts of rural America. For example, many current practitioners concerned with the migration and diffusion of objects such as fence types, barns, field patterns, and farm houses identify with the early work of Carl O. Sauer, who, in turn, had been highly influenced by the cultural anthropologist A. L. Kroeber, a fellow faculty member at the University of California in the 1930s. In addition to the work of Sauer and Kroeber, the interpretations of *The Great Plains* (1936) by a historian like Walter Prescott Webb or *The Grasslands of North America* (1947) by a geographer like James Malin are other examples of what might be called an environmentalist approach to material culture. Perhaps the greatest influence on the current generation of material culturists with this perspective has been Fred B. Kniffen. Numerous contemporary advocates of the environmentalist paradigm—geographers, folklorists, anthropologists—were trained by Kniffen and espouse his interests and his methods.

To study material culture, Kniffen proposed five methodological procedures: identification, classification, arrangement, interpretation, and presentation. The identification of cultural features in the form of artifacts on a particular landscape and, where possible, limited to a specific framework of historical time constitutes the first step toward deriving what he terms a "cultural taxonomy." Classification follows and entails division of the objects into types. Arrangement of the types into complexes enables the analyst to plot the diffusion of a culture through time and space. Interpretation requires examination of the diffusion process to determine origin, dissemination route(s), and the distribution of culture.

The environmentalist approach to material culture research rests on several assumptions. It accepts as axiomatic that culture diffuses across space and acquires and loses elements through the effects of the environment. Advocates of this approach have a particular penchant for vernacular or folk material culture (especially housing) because, as Henry Glassie has claimed, folk artifacts supposedly remain stable over time but variable over space. Belief in such stability, however, tends to attribute to artifacts a superorganic existence, often minimizing the individual's role in their creation. Such a belief also frequently ascribes an innate cultural conservatism to groups that produce such objects. A more doctrinaire diffusionist in his first major publication (*Pattern in the Material Folk Culture of the Eastern United States,* 1968), Glassie has recognized the implicit determinism in this perspective in a subsequent work (*Folk Housing in Middle Virginia,* 1975). He, like several other contemporary environmentalists, now seeks to avoid interpretations of material culture evidence strictly in terms of ecological forces to which individuals must conform or explanations in which the individual's singular creativity and personal cognition play no significant role. As Peter J. Hugill and D. Bruce Dickson point out in *The Transfer and Transformation of Ideas and Material Culture* (1988), diffusion is not a process analogous to a contagious disease but a phenomenon that happens within social contexts. When an idea, an artifact, or a behavior spreads, it does so because people decide it is to their advantage to adopt (or not to adopt) the innovation.

Environmental material culture research sometimes operates under three other presuppositions related to the concept of diffusion: (1) that rural, preindustrial landscapes presumably best preserve artifactual survivals of culture; (2) that such a landscape provides the student of material culture with superior data for ascertaining a succession of regional cultures across time; and (3) that a region's diverse material culture is, at its core, integrative. That is to say, all the culture manifested in a region's material culture can be considered to be an integrated whole. Thus, if one artifact such as a dogtrot house type spreads (diffuses) across a region, it is assumed other artifacts (such as smokehouses, fences, barns) related to the house type will also move or diffuse. In order to monitor and to interpret such movement, contemporary scholars working with material folk culture have resorted to various techniques. Some have employed the work of the cognitive anthropologists in an oral-history approach to informant fieldwork. Others have turned to quantification, particularly when attempting to deal with the classification and arrangement procedures in the Kniffen model. Still others have applied the methodology to high-style artifacts such as Frank Lloyd Wright's prairie houses and their diffusion among the midwestern middle class.

No matter what their individual techniques, these students of material culture are widely interested in the interpretation of ordinary landscapes. As Peirce Lewis recognizes, they are researching the history of "mobile homes, motels, gas stations, shopping centers, billboards, suburban tract housing, the look of fundamentalist churches, watertowers, city dumps, garages and carports" because "such things are found nearly everywhere that Americans have set foot, and they obviously reflect the way ordinary Americans behave most of the time" (*The Interpretation of Ordinary Landscapes,* p. 19).

Such a position, common to the other artifact orientations and material culture paradigms surveyed in this essay, shares many affinities with contemporary social history practice. Perhaps the strongest bonds of common cause between current material culture studies and social history research are a mutual interest in the vernacular, the typical, the commonplace of the past; a desire to make history, as William Makepeace Thackeray once hoped, "more familiar than heroic"; a sense of the potential to expand the traditional domain and discourse of American history; and perhaps, most important, a common concern to bring a wider sociohistorical understanding, as Lewis put it, of "the way ordinary Americans behave most of the time."

BIBLIOGRAPHY

Adler, Thomas A. "Personal Experience and the Artifact: Musical Instruments, Tools, and the Experience of Control." In *American Material Culture and Folklife: A Prologue and a Dialogue,* edited by Simon J. Bronner (1985).

Ames, Kenneth L. "Meaning in Artifacts: Hall Furnishings in Victorian America." *Journal of Interdisciplinary History* 9, no. 1 (Summer 1978).

———. "Material Culture as Non-verbal Communication: A Historical Case Study." *Journal of American Culture* 3, no. 4 (Winter 1980).

Anderson, Jay. "Immaterial Folk Culture: The Implications of Experimental Research for Folklife Museums." *Keystone Folklore* 21, no. 2 (1976–1977).

Asher, Robert. "Experimental Archaeology." *American Anthropology* 63 (1961).

Braudel, Fernand. *Capitalism and Material Life, 1400–1800,* translated by Miriam Kochan (1973).

Bronner, Simon J. "Concepts in the Study of Material Aspects of American Folk Culture." *Folklore Forum* 12, nos. 2 and 3 (1979).

———, ed. *American Material Culture and Folklife: A Prologue and a Dialogue* (1985).

Bronner, Simon J., and Stephen P. Poyser. "From Neglect to Concept: An Introduction to the Study of Material Aspects of American Folk Culture." *Folklore Forum* 12, nos. 2 and 3 (1979).

Carson, Cary, et al. "Impermanent Architecture in the Southern American Colonies." *Winterthur Portfolio* 16, nos. 2/3 (Summer/Autumn 1981). Reprinted in Robert Blair St. George, ed., *Material Life in America* (1988).

Clark, Clifford E., Jr. "Domestic Architecture as an Index to Social History: The Romantic Revival and the Cult of Domesticity in America, 1840–1870." *Journal of Interdisciplinary History* 7, no. 1 (1976).

Cohen, Lizabeth A. "Embellishing a Life of Labor: An Interpretation of the Material Culture of American Working-Class Homes, 1885–1915." *Journal of American Culture* 3, no. 4 (Winter 1980).

Coles, John. *Archaeology by Experiment* (1973).

Cowan, Ruth Schwartz. *More Work for Mother: The Ironies of Household Technology from the Open Hearth to the Microwave* (1983).

Deetz, James. "A Cognitive Historical Model for American Material Culture, 1620–1835." In *Reconstructing Complex Societies,* edited by Charlotte B. Moore (1974).

———. *In Small Things Forgotten: The Archaeology of Early American Life* (1977).

———. "Material Culture and Archaeology—What's the Difference?" In *Historical Archaeology and the Importance of Material Things,* edited by Leland Ferguson (1977).

———. "Scientific Humanism and Humanistic Science." Unpublished paper (March 1981).

Demos, John. *A Little Commonwealth: Family Life in Plymouth Colony* (1970).

Ferguson, Eugene S. "The Mind's Eye: Nonverbal Thought in Technology." *Science* 197, no. 4306 (1977).

Fleming, E. McClung. "Artifact Study: A Proposed Model." *Winterthur Portfolio* 9 (1974).

Giedion, Sigfried. *Mechanization Takes Command: A Contribution to Anonymous History* (1948).

Glassie, Henry. *Pattern in the Material Folk Culture of the Eastern United States* (1968).

———. *Folk Housing in Middle Virginia: A Structural Analysis of Historic Artifacts* (1975).

———. "Meaningful Things and Appropriate Myths: The Artifact's Place in American Studies." *Prospects: An Annual of American Cultural Studies* (1977).

Gould, Richard A., and Michael B. Schiffer. *Modern Material Culture: The Archaeology of Us* (1981).

Gowans, Alan. *Images of American Living: Four Centuries of Architecture and Furniture as Cultural Expression* (1964).

Hayden, Dolores. *Seven American Utopias: The Architecture of Communitarian Socialism, 1790–1975* (1976).

———. "Two Utopian Feminists and Their Campaigns for Kitchenless Houses." *Signs: A Journal of Women and Culture* 4, no. 2 (Winter 1978).

———. *The Grand Domestic Revolution: A History of Feminist Designs for American Homes, Neighborhoods, and Cities* (1981).

Hindle, Brooke. "How Much Is a Piece of the True Cross Worth?" In *Material Culture and the Study of American Life,* edited by Ian M. G. Quimby (1978).

Hugill, Peter J., and D. Bruce Dickson. *The Transfer and Transformation of Ideas and Material Culture* (1988).

Jackson, J. B. *American Space: The Centennial Years, 1865–1876* (1972).

Johnson, Mary. "Women and Their Material Universe: A Bibliographical Essay." Paper, Regional Economic History Research Center, Hagley Museum, Wilmington, Delaware (1981).

Jones, Michael O. "Two Directions for Folkloristics in Study of American Art." *Southern Folklore Quarterly* 32 (1968).

———. *The Hand-made Object and Its Maker* (1975).

———. "Bibliographic and Reference Tools: Toward a Behavioral History." Paper, AASLH Folklore and Local History Conference, New Orleans (1980).

———. "Another America: Toward a Behavioral History Based on Folkloristics." *Western Folklore* 41 (1982).

———. "Folkloristics and Fieldwork." In *American Material Culture and Folklife: A Prologue and a Dialogue,* edited by Simon J. Bronner (1985).

———. "A Strange Rocking Chair . . . The Need to Express, the Urge to Create." In *Exploring Folk Art,* edited by Michael O. Jones (1987).

———. "L.A. Re-dos and Add-ons: Private Space vs. Public Policy." In *Exploring Folk Art,* edited by Michael O. Jones (1987).

Kniffen, Fred. "Louisiana House Types." *Annals, Association of American Geographers* 26 (1936).

———. "American Culture Geography and Folklife." In *American Folklife,* edited by Don Yoder (1976).

Kniffen, Fred, and Margaret C. Christman. *Suiting Everyone: The Democratization of Clothing in America* (1974).

Kniffen, Fred, and Valerie Steele. *Men and Women: Dressing the Part* (1989).

Kouwenhoven, John. *The Arts in Modern Civilization* (1967).

Lauer, Jeanette C., and Robert H. Lauer. "The Language of Dress: A Sociohistorical Study of the Meaning of Clothing in America." *Canadian Review of American Studies* 10, no. 3 (Winter 1979).

Laumann, Edward O., and James S. House. "Living Room Styles and Social Attributes: The Patterning of Material Artifacts in a Modern Urban Community." *Sociology and Social Research* 54 (1970).

Lewis, Peirce. "Axioms for Reading the Landscape." In *The Interpretation of Ordinary Landscapes: Geographical Essays,* edited by D. W. Meinig (1979).

Lubove, Roy. *The Progressives and the Slums: Tenement House Reform in New York City, 1890–1917* (1962).

———. "Social History and the History of Landscape Architecture." *Journal of Social History* 9, no. 2 (Winter 1975).

Mergen, Bernard. "Toys and American Culture: Objects as Hypotheses." *Journal of American Culture* 3, no. 4 (Winter 1980).

Newton, Norman T. *Design on the Land: The Development of Landscape Architecture* (1971).

Prown, Jules David. "Style as Evidence." *Winterthur Portfolio* 15, no. 3 (Autumn 1980).

———. "Mind in Matter: An Introduction to Material Culture Theory and Method." *Winterthur Portfolio* 17, no. 1 (Spring 1982).

Quimby, Ian M. G., ed. *Material Culture and the Study of American Life* (1977).

Rapoport, Amos. *House Form and Culture* (1969).

Reps, John. *The Making of Urban America: A History of City Planning in the United States* (1965).

———. *Cities of the American West: A History of Frontier Urban Planning* (1979).

Roberts, Warren. "Folk Architecture in Context: The Folk Museum." *Pioneer America Society Proceedings* 1 (1973).

Schlereth, Thomas J. *Artifacts and the American Past* (1980).

———. *Material Culture: A Research Guide* (1985).

———. *Cultural History and Material Culture: Everyday Life, Landscapes, Museums* (1990).

———. *Victorian America: Transformations in Everyday Life, 1876–1915* (1991).

———, ed. *Material Culture Studies in America* (1982).

Strasser, Susan. *Never Done: A History of American Housework* (1982).

Upton, Dell. "Toward a Performance Theory of Vernacular Architecture: Early Tidewater Virginia as a Case Study." *Folklore Forum* 12 (1979).

Venturi, Robert, Denise Scott Brown, and Steven Izenour. *Learning from Las Vegas: The Forgotten Symbolism of Architectural Form* (1972).

Wagner, Philip L., and Marvin W. Mikesell, eds. *Readings in Cultural Geography* (1962).

White, Lynn. *Medieval Technology and Social Change* (1962).

Winner, Langdon. "Do Artifacts Have Politics?" *Daedalus* 109 (1980).

Wright, Gwendolyn. *Building the Dream: A Social History of Housing in America* (1981).

Zelinsky, Wilbur. *The Cultural Geography of the United States* (1973).

SEE ALSO **American Social and Cultural Geography; Anthropological Approaches to History; Clothing and Personal Adornment; Foodways; Household Labor; Housing; The Social History of Culture.**

POSTSTRUCTURAL THEORY

Kenneth Cmiel

THERE IS A CERTAIN irony in writing an encyclopedia essay on poststructural theory, for such a summation of methodological precepts is exactly what many poststructuralists are skeptical of. Such an effort to grasp the core of poststructuralism contradicts one of its basic premises—that all thinking is fragmentary and incomplete. To get a clue about the workings of poststructural thought, one should keep in mind how practitioners would be deeply resistant to this very article.

In the late 1970s and 1980s, a number of critical social theories, generally referred to as "poststructuralist" or "postmodern," entered American social thought. A few theorists found American ancestors of the movement—Ralph Waldo Emerson, John Dewey, and William James. Most, however, found the immediate origin in France, but with deeper roots that ran back to the philosophies of Martin Heidegger and Friedrich Nietzsche.

Poststructuralism was a form of "antirealism." It stressed the determinative power of discourse. Critical attention was directed to the ways that rhetoric constructed the categories of our world. Language did not so much describe reality as constitute it. Poststructuralism was also a form of "antiessentialism," emphasizing the inability of any linguistic formulation to grasp the totality or whole of any object of study. In poststructural terminology, the world is "irreducibly multiple." Instead of trying to capture an "essence," poststructural scholarship encouraged the continual elaboration of "difference."

Among Americanists, poststructuralism clearly had its largest impact on literary studies, where, in the course of the 1980s, poststructural discourse theory became mainstream. Other disciplines, however, showed more resistance. Nevertheless, by the end of the decade poststructuralism was attracting increasing attention among those associated with American Studies and had begun to influence a small but growing number of historians and social scientists, although skepticism (and downright hostility) remained high in these disciplines.

THE ROOTS OF POSTSTRUCTURAL THEORY

Friedrich Nietzsche The critical intellectual forebear of poststructural theory was Friedrich Nietzsche (1844–1900). It is important to see how Nietzsche was interpreted by poststructuralists, not as a proto-Fascist committed to the Superman, or as a skeptical naturalist, but as a thinker who unflinchingly worked out the implications of living in a post-Christian, post-rationalist West.

For Nietzsche, the death of God meant that the universe was random. There was no real or true meaning to our existence. Nietzsche, like Kant, spoke of the "chaos of sensations" in the world around us. But unlike Kant, Nietzsche claimed that all concepts and categories used to interpret the world were irredeemably "fictional," made up to give some order to the chaos. Terms like "class" or "nation" did not simply describe external reality. They imposed meaning on the flux of experience.

The absence of inherent meaning also meant that there was no rational moral order to the human world. Nietzsche distrusted Western rationalism as much as Christianity. For Nietzsche, the decision to behave in one way or another was at its core aesthetic.

Nietzsche, then, can be considered a nihilist. But "nihilism" here should not be taken in its everyday sense. Nihilism for Nietzsche is not despairing; it is liberating. Only by pushing the implications of nihilism to its furthest reaches, Nietzsche contended, could we see that we ultimately stood alone; that value and order came from neither God, history, or reason, but from ourselves. A complete nihilism revealed how creative human beings ultimately could be, how fully "aesthetic" their whole existence might actually become.

In *Thus Spake Zarathustra* (1883–1892), Nietzsche pushed these insights in two contradictory directions. On the one hand, there was the will to power embodied in the Superman, who rejected religion, reason, and convention and then completely invented his own self. But elsewhere in the book Nietzsche talked of "the eternal return," claiming that we perpetually repeat our experience and that willing our way out of it was a chimera. These two strains were not reconciled. The first emphasized the creative power of individuals; the second the inability of escaping our own fictions. One celebrated the creative potential of the will; the other suggested that the highest form of will is in submitting to our fate.

Poststructural critics elaborated on these strands of Nietzschean thinking in the 1970s and 1980s, albeit to very different ends. For some, like Hayden White, these ideas implied the radical autonomy of the will. For others, like Walter Benn Michaels, they suggested that we were hopelessly trapped inside our myths. For some the implications were politically radical; for others they suggested a pluralistic acceptance of the world as is.

Michel Foucault No doubt one of the most important poststructural theorists has been Michel Foucault (1926–1984). Foucault's oeuvre was vast; here I will touch on only those strands of thought that most directly contributed to American cultural studies. This was, for the most part, the work that appeared in English in the 1970s, especially *The Birth of the Clinic* (1973), *Discipline and Punish* (1977), *The Archaeology of Knowledge* (1972), and *Power/Knowledge* (1980).

Foucault stressed the determinative power of discourse. In an earlier book, *The Order of Things* (1970) Foucault suggested that it is possible to conceive a posthumanistic social science, one in which "man" did not exist. Since discourse structures our existence, any discussion that takes a category like "humanity" at face value gets it backward. "Humanity" is not something to be discovered but a result of those discourses that coordinate power and practice. The activities of the self are produced by our categories of thought, or, as poststructuralists like to say, the subject is an effect of discourse.

Much of what Foucault said directly echoed Nietzsche. The notion that "man" does not exist was close to Nietzsche's claim that there is no essential humanity. The idea that discourse structures our lives meant that no hard "reality" structures discourse. Yet if there were many parallels with Nietzsche, there were also differences. Foucault's whole intellectual life was dedicated to sympathy for the outcast, a theme completely absent from Nietzsche.

Foucault was developing an anti-Marxist form of critical social theory. Discourse, not socioeconomic relations, was the way that power is coordinated. Moreover, for Foucault ideologies are not "false," not masks for "real" social relations, as certain Marxists claimed. Foucault was interested in how discourse actually generates knowledge that serves specific forms of domination. Knowledge is always connected to some form of power but that did not mean that it is not "true." Nor did it mean that power should not be opposed.

Foucault also argued that power is multiple, harking back to the Nietzschean theme of the essential pluralism of the world. There are various loci of power—workplace, asylum, hospital, school, and prison. And there are innumerable discourses that coordinate power—those of family, gender, normality, sickness, sexual preference, economics, and more. We are enmeshed in a web of countless different power games. Any mainstream effort to write the "total" history of, say, the "Victorian Age" inevitably misses the multiplicity of stories and ways that power operates. Marxist efforts to reduce all struggle to class conflict similarly ignore the sheer diversity of power relations. Focusing on large macro-level concepts like "capitalism," moreover, tend to obscure the precise ways that power is exercised in specific settings.

Foucault, still echoing Nietzsche, also challenged the humanistic Western assumption (both liberal and Marxist) that humanity is progressing. Instead, we are involved in a perpetual war against innumerable forms of power. Liberation from one form of domination does not lead to more freedom so much as to a new sort of despotism. Freedom from torture only led to the prison and the disciplining gaze of the prison keeper. Ending Victorian attitudes toward sex were followed by the pressure to have a slender, tan body.

The reception of Foucault among Americanists was at first largely hostile and his initial impact on American cultural and social history was small. Indeed, as with all poststructural theories, he has had a bigger impact on Europeanists than on Americanists. By the time that Americanists came around to discussing poststructural critical theory, Foucault had already been severely criticized. Consequently, there were not many "Foucaultians" working on American social and cultural history.

Still, Foucault was read widely. And he turned up again and again in footnotes. Foucault was important for suggesting that "class" should not be the only category of critical social analysis, for pointing out the multiplicity of power relations. The genealogy of the recent attention that critical Americanists have paid to "race, class, and gender" as concepts of equal weight indirectly owes much to Foucault. Foucault was also used to help explain how domination constructed itself by means of knowledge and discourse instead of through the barrel of a gun. Finally, Foucault was most important for pushing power itself to the center of critical inquiry. Knowledge, discourse, institutions—they all were bound up in a complex of power relationships. This "ontologization of power," as it has been called, the exploration of the ways that power is crucial to *all* our discourse and practices, has been a very important part of critical poststructuralism.

Criticisms of Foucault Foucault was criticized by both liberal and Marxist scholars for being insufficiently empirical. Foucault analyzed discourse and simply assumed that discourse shaped practice. But, his critics argued, there was no reason to assume that what actually went on inside prisons, hospitals, schools, and other institutions reflected the "official" discourse. Critics also distrusted the agentless history that Foucault wrote. Since the self had disappeared in Foucault's thought, it often seemed as if some disembodied "discourse" itself had become the motor of history instead of real, live people. And by a priori denying that the cause of change could be uncovered, some argued, Foucault was actually refusing to investigate the truth wherever it might be found.

Other critics condemned the bleakness of his thought. With each form of domination simply replaced by another, there was no hope for liberation. Jürgen Habermas, for example, argued that Foucault simply investigated that was wrong with modernity instead of trying to assess both its gains and losses.

Both the empirical and moral criticism, it should be noted, were actually rejections of Nietzsche as much as Foucault. The empirical critique—there *was* some intrinsic order in a given historical situation—was a rejection of Nietzsche's position that the world is a "chaos of sensations" that we order through aesthetic invention. And the moral critique—Foucault had no positive program—was based on the belief that there was some way for "rational" or "progressive" values to be articulated.

Foucault was caught on the hinge of nihilism confronted by Nietzsche a century earlier. In the last phase of his career, Foucault began to suggest ways out of the impasse. He started to articulate an ethic of permanent revolt, which he once called "hyperactive pessimism," whereby we look for aesthetically pleasing moments to break the chains of everyday domination. This and other new strains in his thought were only partially worked out before he died in 1984.

If Foucault was criticized by more traditional scholars, he was also criticized from within the poststructural ranks. While theorists like Hayden White, Jacques Derrida, and Julia Kristeva agreed that the unified self was a mirage, that power was multiple, and that any thinking about totality was essentially repressive, they also differed from Foucault in a number of ways. A cluster of ideas have become important for scholars not content to rest with Foucault. By the mid 1980s, many scholars, including Americanists, were tending to use these notions eclectically, as a set of concepts drawn on as needed. The theoretical writings of Dominick La Capra might be seen as a methodological expression of this eclecticism.

One important notion was that of a radical textualism, first given expression by the French philosopher Jacques Derrida. While Foucault wrote as if discourse directs practice, Derrida claimed that discourse is all we could get at, as he put it in his celebrated phrase, there is nothing outside the text ("il n'y a pas de hors-texte"). This should not be taken to mean that there is nothing but books, but rather that there is no way to get beyond discourse. Since all thought is an aesthetic ordering, it is wrong to suggest (following Foucault) that discourse structures practice. Even saying "discourse structures practice" is itself an aesthetic act, a discursive strategy. While Foucault has been called a worldly poststructuralist, Derrida is far more hermetically textual.

It is misleading to say that for Derrida discourse shapes our sense of reality. For Derrida, there is no such thing as "reality." There is *no* context outside the text. More thoroughgoing textualists directed attention to the ways that linguistic categories ("fat," "thin," "beautiful," "ugly," "man," "woman," "Western," "primitive") create the terms with which we think our lives, indeed, to the ways that such categories *are* our very lives. And while Derrida himself devoted his attention to philosophical texts, other Derridians made broader use of these ideas. The language of popular social movements and institutional authority could be analyzed in this way just as much as any piece of formal literature.

DECONSTRUCTION

This radical textualism was connected to another major pillar of poststructural thought, the notion of "deconstruction." As theory, this idea was most closely associated with Derrida and the Yale literary critic Paul de Man (1919–1983). The latter's reputation fell dramatically at the end of the 1980s when scholars uncovered anti-Semitic essays he wrote during World War II. Still, in the previous decade de Man was vitally important to the transmission of deconstruction to the United States. Deconstruction was deeply skeptical about the fixity of meaning and turned critical analysis to probing the limitations of all texts. Here again the Nietzschean theme of the pluralism of the world came through. Any claim of grasping the totality of meaning was wrongheaded, serving to repress all that was either left out or pushed to the periphery.

While traditional critical studies tried to uncover the meaning of the text, deconstruction took texts apart to analyze their limits, to probe what each text, through its linguistic strategies, wound up marginalizing, subordinating, or ignoring. Interpretation, then, was no longer a matter of "figuring out" the author's intent but of "deconstructing" the supposed coherent meaning of any given work.

But it is wrong to suggest (as some have) that Derrida or de Man claimed that the critic is actually superior to the creative writer. Instead, they realized that interpreters misread as much as any author. Here the fatalistic side of poststructuralism asserted itself. A central tenet of poststructural thinking was that language is hopelessly inadequate to express unequivocal meaning. The rhetorical habits (tropes) of any given moment are more powerful than a writer's intent. We are inevitably trapped by implications of our language that we will never fully understand. There is no way out of this box. But this is not necessarily cause for despair. For as de Man put it, even while our gaps in self-reflexivity limit what we might see, and make us prisoners of language, they also make other, partial insights possible. Blindness and insight are not opposites but intimate relations.

With authorial intent set aside along with the sense that the critic could uncover the "true" meaning of a text, no longer will we worry about a single correct reading. All cultural objects are a product not of the creator but of the succession of interpreters. The connection of this notion of the "death of the author" to the essentially Nietzschian idea of the "death of man" should not be missed. Nor should the inevitability of misreading with the notion of the aesthetic rendering of experience. We are fated to be interpreted the way future discursive practices want.

In their first flush, deconstructive ideas were thought to be antihistorical. Some (notably de Man) asserted that there was no bridge between deconstruction and history. But by the middle of the 1980s, with the increasingly eclectic use of poststructural concepts, deconstructive readings were being introduced to historical works. In the study of American literature and social thought, Walter Benn Michaels provides one good example. Cornel West explored American intellectual history through the lens of poststructuralism. Among historians, the Europeanist Joan Wallach Scott and the Americanist George Lipsitz blended poststructural notions into their explorations of the past. By the end of the 1980s, one even found relatively traditional scholars occasionally making selective use of various critical-discourse theories.

Applications of Deconstruction One way poststructuralism was applied to social analysis was by deconstructing basic binary categories of traditional thought to reveal how such categories conferred privilege on certain groups and subordinated others. Scholars like Henry Louis Gates, Jr., Julia Kristeva, Gayatri Spivak, and Edward Said have explored how terms like "civilized" were used to denigrate third-world peoples as "backward"; how "reason" has been tied to masculinity and "hysteria" to the feminine; how the Western sense of "universal progress" ran roughshod over local cultures. In all these cases the efforts has been to deconstruct elite Western, male categories of thought, particularly that of rationality, and to champion those groups who have been marginalized by that discourse.

For poststructuralism, cultural presence was a product of power. Consequently, the articulation of cultural difference had both a critical and celebratory purpose. When scholars explored how the abstract and universal categories of Western rationalism actually subordinated women, people of color, and the West's own lower classes, the intent was critical. The irreducible pluralism of the world exposed the stupidity and cruelty of Western pretensions. But the elaboration of difference might also be a means of articulating an Other's identity, of empowering a people previously marginalized. So, to take one example, scholars like Houston Baker and Henry Louis Gates, Jr., called for a distinctly African American aesthetic based on an examination of texts indigenous to the African American community.

In keeping with the poststructural notion that all discourse is limited, a notion itself central to the interest in "difference," no category is final. Even oppositional groups are not immune from further differentiation. An African American feminist like bell hooks might point out the racial limitations of white feminist discussions of gender. While feminists might point out the presumed patriarchy of certain African American males. The issue of sexual preference complicated the picture further. There was always the potential for the further elaboration of difference.

The belief that all categories are aesthetic productions of discourse made distinctions based on "nature" especially suspect. Henry Louis Gates, Jr., observed how "race" had become "a trope of ultimate, irreducible difference between cultures" even though it was certainly not rooted in nature. Many feminists discussed "gender" as a cultural, not a biological category. Carroll Smith-Rosenberg, for example, analyzed how nineteenth-century "gender" distinctions were discursive inventions justified through the gloss of biology. And Werner Sollors' *Beyond Ethnicity,* from a very different political perspective, analyzed the ways that Americans textually constructed the category of ethnicity. These supposedly biological categories were reinterpreted as discursive efforts to generate or enforce cultural difference, usually with domination in mind.

THE INFLUENCE OF BAKHTIN

Other ideas integrated into the poststructural canon came from the work of the Russian literary critic Mikhail Bakhtin (1895–1975). There were a number of large differences between Bakhtin and the deconstructionists that cannot be discussed here. For one, though, Bakhtin was far less purely textual than Derrida. In this, at least, he resembled Foucault. Still, if Bakhtin was no forerunner of the deconstructionists, he shared with them certain similarities in outlook. As early as the 1920s, Bakhtin was expressing skepticism about all totalistic forms of thinking. Along with his colleagues, Valentin Voloshinov (1894–1936) (whose *Marxism and the Philosophy of Language* was another important poststructural text), Bakhtin also argued that no speech or text is univocal, but rather part of a dialogue of voices. Deconstructionists focused on how the text is not something with a fixed meaning. Bakhtin and Voloshinov agreed, adding the idea that each text is the result of an implicit dialogue between the author and the intended audience.

One criticism of Foucault was that he never analyzed popular opposition to a given system. His discourses of authority seemed all-powerful. The notion that the meaning of a text is the product of the interpreter, combined with Bakhtin's idea about dialogue, were used by cultural theorists to suggest ways that outsider discourse (that of "the Other") might confront the established order. In American cultural studies, these ideas can be found in George Lipsitz's *Time Passages* (1990). Lipsitz argued that whatever the intent of inventors of mass culture, there is the possibility of antiauthoritarian or "oppositional" readings. For example, those watching television could impose their own meaning on the show (the "text"). Such viewers "read" the program more subversively than the producers had intended. The communication scholar John Fiske interpreted various social phenomena—the torn jeans fad of the 1980s, the fascination with Madonna—in similarly oppositional terms.

Another notion that Bakhtin willed to contemporary cultural studies was that of "carnival," a concept of growing importance in the late 1980s. These popular celebrations, Bakhtin asserted, are subversive responses to the official desire for order. Carnival is disorder, mayhem. It is laughing at serious people, mocking official pretensions. At carnival, the grotesque are treated as the beautiful, the fool as the king.

Cultural analysts used Bakhtin's notions of carnival to develop oppositional readings. While those in power wanted order, carnivalesque disorder was interpreted as a form of rebellion. While Bakhtin himself thought that the decline of real carnivals in the early modern era had disastrous consequences for the literature of carnivalization, other analysts found the spirit of carnival in a variety of places—Susan Davis in popular parades of early nineteenth-century Philadelphia; others in the movies of the

Marx Brothers. By the end of the 1980s, all sorts of "antidecorum" was being analyzed by means of the notions of Bakhtin. Carnival had the advantage of combining the worldliness of Foucault with far more attention to the ways that those on the bottom resisted.

Poststructuralism in general developed a more tolerant attitude toward popular culture than other critical theories. For Americanists, this was not such a radical break, for American Studies had been receptive to popular culture since the 1950s. But for students of literature it was new. The aristocratic disdain of high modernism—whether in its bourgeois or Frankfurt school Marxist form—disappeared from view. One important aspect of this disappearance was a more tender reading of mass culture. Early-nineteenth-century sentimental novels were discussed as a means for middling women to challenge gentry authority. The dime novel was viewed as an expression of plebian utopian longings. Janice Radway gave a favorable reading to the Book-of-the-Month Club, and Andrew Ross criticized post–World War II American intellectuals for haughtily dismissing popular culture. Although the arguments were by no means simply celebratory, the drift of this work was to claim that middlebrow and lowbrow culture are not so bad after all.

The popularity of the "worldly" Bakhtin suggests that not all scholars making use of poststructural theory were radical textualists. Indeed, the increasingly eclectic use of poststructuralism seemed to guarantee it. Recent works like Michael Denning's *Mechanic Accents: Dime Novels and Working-Class Culture in America* (1987) and Cathy N. Davidson's *Revolution and the Word: The Rise of the Novel in America* (1986) have made extensive use of sophisticated discourse theories but at the same time assumed a "realist" frame that situated their texts in "actual" history. It was not only that some notion of context remained in these books. Historical context remained absolutely central to the understanding of the texts studied.

POLITICAL RESONANCES

While much poststructuralism was developed as an anti-Marxist critical theory, a number of writers have linked it to more mainstream politics. For these writers, poststructuralism is epistemologically liberating, freeing us from the chains of scientistic models, but without any inherent political content. The philosopher Richard Rorty has tried to show how poststructuralism is compatible with democracy and bourgeois individualism. He argues that postmodernism means the priority of democracy over epistemology. The literary critic Stanley Fish suggests that poststructuralism will leave modern academic professionalism intact and argues that the movement has no "essential" political component. Hayden White has claimed that the collapse of any sense of "reality" implies a free slate for historians, on which they can write histories without being tyrannized by epistemology. And Allan Megill has asserted that the real end point of poststructural theory is the elimination of any sense of cultural crisis. For these writers, with the exception of Fish, poststructural aestheticism is connected most to the will of the writer to invent his or her own texts. They stress, in one form or another, the personal freedom poststructuralism offers.

This theme has been given an especially American edge in the writings of Richard Poirier, who in his *The Renewal of Literature* (1987) has developed them through the thought of Emerson. For Poirier, Emerson was a philosopher of literature and language, one who understood the limits of language but at the same time the ability of language both to transgress the given social system and to invent a new self. (Despite their many differences, Nietzsche respected Emerson's thought.) The barrenness of American high culture, as Poirier sees it, was actually the ideal setting for Emerson. It allowed him to realize how the inventiveness of language could produce new, unencumbered selves.

A few others besides Poirier searched for roots in American intellectual history. Poirier himself added Walt Whitman, William James, Robert Frost, and Wallace Stevens to his list. Richard Rorty looked to the pragmatists, particularly William James and John Dewey, although he has turned his thought in a more pragmatic liberal direction than that of Poirier's celebration of literary self-invention. Rorty is especially interested in salvaging some notion of community, not only against "individualists" like Poirier but also against more critical poststructuralists. The reason to choose Dewey over Foucault, Rorty claims, is that Dewey, the pragmatist, showed that there is nothing contradictory in affirming solidarity while attacking philosophic essentialism. Foucault's grim critiques, according to Rorty, only leave space for permanent revolt.

Cornel West's *The American Evasion of Philosophy* (1989) is another effort to build an American lineage for poststructuralism. This book is the first to construct a whole history around the confrontation of American intellectuals with the poststructural denigration of realism and essentialism. West looked to Emerson and the pragmatists as the key antirealists. West was further to the left of Rorty, arguing that oppositional thinkers should engage in a critical dialogue with liberalism. He asked for a "prophetic pragmatism," one with a sense of vision and transcendence attached. It was just this utopian strain that West found lacking both in Foucault and in the mainstream liberalism of Rorty.

CRITIQUES OF POSTSTRUCTURALISM

Those critical of poststructuralism continue to make the same "reality" critiques that were addressed to Foucault. There *is* some order to our historical reality. Not everything is an aesthetic rendering. This can take a realist direction, with Marxists like Bryan D. Palmer and Alex Callinicos continuing to assert that the directive force of modern society derives from capitalist social relations. It can also take a softer, more pragmatic direction, with a historian like James Kloppenberg suggesting that while aesthetic rendering is a large part of our experience, it is inevitably checked by harder empirical reality. There is more of an interplay between fact and concept than poststructuralists claim.

There is also criticism of the various political implications of postmodernism. To those who assert the possibility of oppositional readings of mass culture, it has been replied that such readings are not so easy to construct. To those who deconstruct the binary oppositions of Western thought, Barbara Herrnstein Smith has forcefully argued that these oppositions are the categories of *all* thought, not just Western thought. To try to escape them is to try to escape a deeper boundary. And the centrists have been criticized for missing the power of dominant discourses to marginalize outsiders.

As theory, poststructuralism perpetually swings between the poles of invention and fatalism, between liberating aestheticism and the power of discourse to control our lives. So writers like Hayden White and Richard Poirier, who associate poststructuralism with the liberation of the will should be set against Foucault and his "hyperactive pessimism," de Man and his inevitable "blindness," and Walter Benn Michaels and his claim that we literally cannot critique our own social order. These divisions run through all poststructural thought, cutting across the various political and methodological divisions. They are, at bottom, the same tension found in Nietzsche's *Thus Spake Zarathustra.*

The coherent theory of poststructuralism stands or falls with Nietzsche's philosophy. Yet given the nature of contemporary academic life, where practitioners appropriate theory in bits and pieces without rigorously working through deeper implications, there is no reason to think that Nietzsche and poststructuralism will in fact stand and fall together. The increasingly eclectic uses of poststructural concepts, which tend to sever some parts of the theory from the rest, probably makes their separation even more likely.

This eclecticism is itself open to different interpretations. One could point out the contradictions. The radical aestheticism of poststructural thought is just not consistent with any belief that capitalism is the "real" driving force of American history. The increasing eclecticism, however, can be seen in a more tender light—with the excessive claims of poststructuralism now purged, its legitimate insights can be integrated into mainstream scholarship. But there is still a third possible interpretation, a more poststructural one. The use of culture in bits and pieces, the wrenching of fragments out of their original context for deployment elsewhere, is itself considered by poststructuralists to be part of our late twentieth-century condition. This "pastiche" or "bricolage" is eminently connected to what it means to be postmodern. The scholarly bricolage is poststructuralism in action.

But with the integration of poststructuralism into mainstream scholarship, there is the danger that something might be lost. Nietzsche, Foucault, and Derrida, whatever one finally makes of them, were serious and subtle philosophers, worth coming to terms to their thought. The same cannot be said for all the Nietzscheans, Foucaultians, and Derridians at work today in the academic vineyards. Many sophisticated poststructural interpreters are writing today, but there are also many who appropriate poststructural categories ritually and thoughtlessly. Martin Heidegger once observed that when any thought becomes an intellectual movement with a name and agenda it then stands opposed to genuine thoughtfulness. This is a danger that poststructuralism must guard against.

Poststructuralism puts the fragmentary character of all thought in the foreground. Here is the source of its hostility to any holism, of its commitment to irreducible pluralism. However, as the movement passes from its masters to its epigoni, and shifts from being a criticism of culture to an arm of the culture industry, it threatens to become a cliché. As such, it presents itself as "the" truth, becoming, ironically, blind to the partial nature of its own insights and consequently demanding its own deconstruction. Preventing the routinization of poststructural thinking might itself be one of the greatest honors we can pay to it.

BIBLIOGRAPHY

Theory

Berkhofer, Robert F., Jr. "A New Context for a New American Studies?" *American Quarterly* 41, no. 4 (1989). Best single essay on implications for American studies.

Fish, Stanley. *Doing What Comes Naturally: Change, Rhetoric, and the Practice of Theory in Literary and Legal Studies* (1989).

Habermas, Jürgen. *The Philosophical Discourse of Modernity.* Translated by Frederick G. Lawrence (1987).

hooks, bell. *Yearning: Race and Gender in the Cultural Marketplace* (1990).

Kloppenberg, James T. "Objectivity and Historicism: A Century of American Historical Writing." *American Historical Review* 94, no. 4 (1989).

La Capra, Dominick. *Soundings in Critical Theory* (1989).

Megill, Allan. *Prophets of Extremity: Nietzsche, Heidegger, Foucault, Derrida* (1985).

Morson, Gary Saul, and Caryl Emerson. *Mikhail Bakhtin: Creation of a Prosaics.* (1991). The most complete book on Bakhtin.

Norris, Christopher. *Deconstruction: Theory and Practice* (1982). A lucid introduction.

———. *What's Wrong with Postmodernism* (1990). A philosophically sophisticated critique.

Rorty, Richard. *Consequences of Pragmatism* (1982).

———. *Contingency, Irony, and Solidarity* (1989).

Smith, Barbara Herrnstein. *Contingencies of Value: Alternative Perspectives for Critical Theory* (1988).

Veeser, H. Aram, ed. *The New Historicism* (1989).

White, Hayden. *Metahistory: The Historical Imagination in Nineteenth-Century Europe* (1973).

———. *The Content of the Form: Narrative Discourse and Historical Representation* (1987).

Cultural and Social Studies

Conner, Steven. *Postmodernist Culture: An Introduction to Theories of the Contemporary* (1989). Good critical survey of studies of postmodern culture.

Fiske, John. *Understanding Popular Culture* (1989).

Gates, Henry Louis, Jr. *The Signifying Monkey: A Theory of Afro-American Literary Criticism* (1988).

Gates, Henry Louis, Jr., ed. *"Race," Writing, and Difference* (1986).

Lipsitz, George. *Time Passages: Collective Memory and American Popular Culture* (1990).

Michaels, Walter Benn. *The Gold Standard and the Logic of Naturalism: American Literature at the Turn of the Century* (1987).

Palmer, Bryan D. *Descent into Discourse: The Reification of Language and the Writing of Social History* (1990). Marxist critique of poststructural social history.

Ross, Andrew. *No Respect: Intellectuals and Popular Culture* (1989).

Scott, Joan Wallach. *Gender and the Politics of History* (1988).

Sollors, Werner. *Beyond Ethnicity: Consent and Descent in American Culture* (1986).

West, Cornel. *The American Evasion of Philosophy: A Genealogy of Pragmatism* (1989).

SEE ALSO **Intellectuals and the Intelligentsia**; and various articles in the section "**Methods and Contexts.**"

Part III

THE CONSTRUCTION OF SOCIAL IDENTITY

RACE

Peter H. Wood

RACE IS AN idea whose time has almost passed. The last half millennium or so has witnessed the rise, and the beginnings of the fall, of the race concept in Western thought. The long history of this intellectual construct can be tied to the broader story of overseas reconnaissance and conquest that led to the European colonization of much of the world and to the gradual, often begrudging, education of Europeans with regard to their limited place in the broader human family. Significantly, the European conquest of North America and the emergence of the United States as a complex political and social entity paralleled the evolution of race as an important, and sometimes determining, social construction in the modern world.

Race is by no means the immutable truth that many take it for. The modern dogma surrounding the idea has evolved in contradictory and surprising ways over hundreds of years, and only in the twentieth century, with the rise of human genetics and cultural anthropology, has its grip on Western society begun to loosen. Although far from a scientific concept, its emergence has coincided chronologically with the development of post-Renaissance science, and racialist thinking has sought and claimed scientific sanction at numerous points in recent centuries. For that very reason, during the time of resistance to Hitler's Third Reich, the anthropologist Ashley Montagu described "the fallacy of race" as "man's most dangerous myth." The tortuous history, devastating consequences, and intractable nature of this pseudoscientific concept would seem to justify that label.

In the early 1990s, it seems clear to experts that mankind is essentially one, with all human beings evolving from a unified ancestral stock that developed between 600,000 and one million years ago. Rather than being descended from apes, humans represent part of a long evolutionary line, from which monkeys and apes apparently branched off several million years ago. In evolutionary terms, therefore, no human group is significantly closer than any other to mankind's simian relatives, and all human genetic groupings are immeasurably further removed from their nearest nonhuman relations than from one another. What accounts, then, for the discernible groupings, or populations, that exist within the human species? We now know that they differ from each other in the frequency of one or more genes which determine such hereditary traits as height, hair texture, facial formation, and the color of eyes, hair, and skin.

The physical differences we ascribe to the three major human groupings—the Mongoloid, the Negroid, and the Caucasoid—are not fixed; they continue to fluctuate and change over time. But the rate of change is extremely slow, occurring over thousands of years, for evolution depends upon a twofold process. First, genetic variation must occur through the random procedure known as mutation. This takes place during the formation of male sperm and female egg cells, when the molecular structure of a gene is spontaneously altered, rather than being replicated exactly, and the alteration is passed on to offspring. For such a mutation to endure, however, natural selection must also occur, whereby the altered trait proves suitable enough to the organism's changing environment over time that it predominates in future generations and the older, less adaptive trait disappears.

Besides the fact that these relatively separate gene pools fluctuate continuously and exceedingly slowly, it is also important to underscore at the outset three other basic points about them. First of all, these genetic groupings do not coincide in any way with linguistic and religious boundaries, or with national lines of demarcation. Second, they are not connected in any way to the distinctive cultural traits that characterize separate societies or to the varieties of inner temperament and personality that appear in all societies. Third, despite distinctions in outward appearance and physical makeup, there is no perceived difference in intelligence between the world's steadily changing populations.

In the sphere of cultural evolution—in contrast to that of biological evolution—noticeable human differences are deeper and more dramatic, and change can occur infinitely more rapidly. For in the cultural domain traits acquired during a lifetime can be passed directly to the next generation through oral traditions, written instructions, or memorable rituals; and new traits—beliefs, practices, mannerisms—can be learned from a wide variety of sources. In short, the old and tempting theories best associated with the French naturalist, Jean Baptiste, chevalier de Lamarck (1744–1829), regarding the inheritability of acquired characteristics, are simply incorrect. A parent who has received a scar or lost a limb cannot pass this trait on to a child, nor can that parent pass on *biologically* any learned knowledge, skills, or attitudes. But all children are capable, potentially, of acquiring a wide range of traits—whether old ones from parents or new ones from strangers—as their cultural inheritance.

THE RISE OF RACE IN THE EUROPEAN WORLD

Centuries of Western economic change, scientific debate, and political turmoil have spawned modern notions of race. But the general perception of human diversity—often with value judgment attached regarding mental, physical, and moral attributes—is as old as settled human existence. Local practices of interregional trade and warfare dating from prehistoric times shaped attitudes about physical and cultural differences throughout the world, and the records of every ancient society are replete with explicit opinions about neighbors and strangers. The fascinating topic of non-Western understanding of human diversity lies beyond the scope of this essay. Nevertheless, it is helpful to begin with attention to the earliest inhabitants of North America, since they illustrate well the difference between genetic and cultural adaptation, and they figure prominently in the evolution of modern Western beliefs about race.

Scholars now believe that some forty thousand years ago—very recently in terms of human evolution—an extended ice age removed enough water from the oceans to expose a land bridge between Siberia and Alaska, allowing different species to migrate from one continent to another. Ancestors of the camel may have moved westward from America to Asia, while mammoths apparently traveled eastward. Humans who were part of the proto-Mongolian gene pool, which was already well developed by that time, came from Asia in pursuit of these large animals. They probably crossed into America for the first time roughly fifteen thousand years ago—though whether they came earlier or later, by land or sea, in small or large groups, all remain topics of debate.

Less debatable, however, is the relative isolation of these people after reaching the Western Hemisphere. Hence, even as they spread out across the Americas over thousands of years, they still retained genetic characteristics of their proto-Mongolian forebears: straight black hair, dark eyes, light brown or coppery skin tones, limited facial and body hair. In genetic terms, they changed very slowly, retaining numerous common traits despite their rapid dispersal over two amazingly diverse continents. Identifiable blood types persisted, as did the dental characteristic of "shoveled incisors." Predictably, some of the latest migrants from Siberia, the Eskimos, retained physical traits closest to those of modern Asian peoples, including the distinctive eyelid without a fold.

But these continuities were biological rather than social, and the earliest Americans developed markedly different cultures in adaptation to the richly varied climate and geography of two continents. As groups migrated and divided over thousands of years, they evolved hundreds of different languages and diverse customs, taking pride in their separate identities. Occasionally a boatload of strangers may have touched an American coast from Asia, Africa, or Europe. But such arrivals, if and when they appeared, were far too late, too few, and too infrequent to have a widespread genetic or cultural impact. These conditions in America—great cultural diversity combined with virtual genetic isolation from the rest of the world—were altered drastically and irrevocably by the sudden arrival of an expanding stream of newcomers after the late fifteenth century.

The complex facts, summarized so briefly here, about the biology of human differences and the evolution of the first American cultures are now widely understood, and the refinement and dissemination of these insights continues. But none of this modern information was known to the Europeans of Christopher Columbus's generation, nor could it have been. They did not even suspect the existence of the Americas, much less have an adequate framework for understanding the inhabitants. The framework they did have, based almost entirely upon Christian mythology and the interpretation of Biblical texts, was a confining, if reassuring, one. It postulated the descent of all humans from one couple, Adam and Eve, created by God at the same time he had created the world, no more than several thousand years in the past. But this medieval framework was already beginning to undergo serious changes associated with the European Renaissance.

In Christian Europe of the fifteenth century new sailing technologies were allowing increased travel, and Christian rulers were intensifying their competition for the secular wealth, religious glory, and strategic knowledge that could accompany exploration. Marco Polo's journey to Cathay in the late thirteenth century, a succession of crusades to the Near East, and the ongoing caravan trade with sub-Saharan Africa had slowly sensitized European courtiers to the problems and possibilities posed by various peoples beyond the shores of the Mediterranean Sea. It is interesting to note that as a result of these contacts, Italians had started to employ the word *razza* before 1400, and during the fifteenth century the terms *raça* (Portuguese), *raza* (Spanish), and *race* (French) came into use. Englishmen, removed from the Mediterranean and late to enter the theater of overseas exploration, would not utilize the word *race* until shortly after 1500.

Cut off from Asia by Muslim power, Europe's initial outward thrust in the century before Columbus was southward toward the "New World" of the Southern Hemisphere, rather than westward, and European maps and paintings of the period reflect an increasing familiarity with the different-looking people of equatorial Africa. The famed Catalan Atlas (drawn by the Jewish cartographer Abraham Cresques on the island of Majorca and presented to Charles VI of France in 1381 by Pedro IV of Aragon) depicts a handsome black king in West Africa. The image derives from Mansa Mūsā, the king of Mali, who had traveled from Timbuktu to Mecca half a century earlier (1324) with such a fabulous retinue that his fame had spread across both the Islamic and the Christian world. The figure wears a royal crown, carries a scepter, and holds up an enormous nugget of gold in his right hand. "This Negro lord," states the inscription, "is called Musa Mali, lord of the Negroes of Guinea. This king is the richest, most noble lord in all this region on account of the abundance of gold that is gathered in his land."

Militant Christians began to speculate about conquering or converting such distant rulers and locating others who had already acquired the Christian faith in earlier times. Foremost among these was the mythical Prester John, a wise and wealthy Christian ruler living somewhere to the east or south in the vague "Indies" where the Apostle Thomas had preached the Gospel. By the fourteenth century he was considered black and associated with the broad region of Ethiopia. An inscription on the Catalan map described a place south of Egypt where a Saracen king was "always at war with the Christians of Nubia who are under the rule of the Emperor of Ethiopia, of the land of Prester John." In the second quarter of the fifteenth century, therefore, when Portugal's Prince Henry the Navigator (1394–1460) sent ships southward along the African coast in the hope of outflanking Muslim power in the Middle East and reaching Asia by sea, he desired to open up oceanic trade with black Africa, convert Muslim rulers, and establish ties with black Christians in the land of Prester John.

Meanwhile, Pope Eugenius IV, anxious to link the Church of Rome to the Eastern churches in the face of an increasing Ottoman threat, sent out invitations in 1439 to diverse patriarchs and Christian leaders—including "Prester John, illustrious emperor of the Ethiopians"—to convene in Italy. Delegates from an Ethiopian monastery in Jerusalem attended the Council of Florence (1439–1443) in 1441, and the presence of these African dignitaries had an impact on the art of the early Renaissance. It soon became common throughout much of Europe to portray one of the three Wise Men from the New Testament as a pious and wealthy African. Indeed, the Adoration of the Magi became a favorite artistic theme of the late fifteenth century, and the black king, resplendent and devout, was often depicted with an emblem of Africa near him, such as a camel or a chimpanzee. By the start of the sixteenth century, when reports of the explorations of Vasco da Gama and Christopher Columbus were exciting the Renaissance imagination, such masters as Hieronymous Bosch and Albrecht Dürer elevated this black Wise Man, bearing an orb in his hand, into an emblem of the world of discovery that beckoned Europeans.

Not all fifteenth-century depictions of Africans were so regal and positive, though. To be sure, Saint Maurice, the early Christian martyr from North Africa who had become a favored emblem of the Holy Roman Empire, continued to appear as a noble and militant black defender of the faith in the churches of central Europe. But it was also commonplace to depict devils, executioners, and the biblical scourgers of Christ as strong and dangerous African infidels. In the Portuguese conquest of Ceuta in North Africa in 1415, often taken to mark the beginning of successful European overseas expansion, the chronicler Gomes Eanes de Zurara described a Moor, "very tall and of a most threatening complexion," who led the defense until pierced by a Portuguese lance. "The aspect of this Moor was such as to inspire terror, since all his body was black as a crow, and he had very long and white teeth, and his lips, which were fleshy, were turned back."

In Iberia, the fifteenth century was dominated by the Christian Reconquest, during which descendants of the Muslims who had invaded Spain from North Africa in 711 were gradually driven out of the region, after seven centuries of complex and often friendly interaction between Muslim and Christian, African and European. This protracted counterthrust by militant Christians engendered, and then fed upon, a new racialism. Hence a fresh preoccupation with inherited characteristics appeared at just the moment when, and in just the place from which, Europeans were reaching out most aggressively into the non-European quarters of the globe.

Religion, culture, and skin color mixed in the propaganda of the Reconquest. Spanish Christians had long referred to their invaders as *moros,* or "People of Mauritania"—the Roman term for present-day Morocco, deriving from an ancient Greek word meaning "black." Increased contact down the West African coast led to the term *moros negros,* black moors, or simply *negros* for sub-Saharan Africans, so that well before 1500 the Spanish term for black had become synonymous with African. At the same time, the numerous Jews who were a central element of Moorish Spain came under increasing attack as infidels. Even those *conversos* who had outwardly accepted Catholicism under duress, and who became known as New Christians, were not free from persecution. Fear that these converts secretly retained their Judaism and defiled the church with heresies led to racial laws regarding *limpieza de sangre,* or "purity of blood." Launched with an outbreak of violent pogroms in Seville and elsewhere in 1391, this anti-*converso* racism was finally institutionalized with the establishment of the Spanish Inquisition in 1478.

In 1492 the Reconquest culminated in the official expulsion of the Moors from Granada, and King Ferdinand and Queen Isabella followed their victory by issuing a decree on 31 March which gave professing Jews only four months to leave Spain. The last boatloads of Jewish refugees left Palos for Italy on 31 July, just as Columbus was making final preparations to set sail from the same port. Whether Columbus himself was a New Christian, as some have speculated, is not clear; but his expedition of discovery was more than coincidentally linked to the events of the Reconquest and the Expulsion decree. He was setting out from a place where themes of racial and religious conflict had taken on heightened, and often interconnected, meaning. Inadvertently, his ambitious search for a westward route from Europe to Asia would initiate continuous contact between two previously isolated hemispheres. Not surprisingly, the contemporary Iberian beliefs in militant Christianity and European racial purity would become dominant themes in the European invasion of America that followed the initial voyages of Columbus.

Columbus himself, having previously visited West Africa and perhaps Iceland, shared with most Europeans a sense that skin color correlated readily, if not exactly, with latitude. On 13 October 1492, after sailing west from the Canary Islands until he encountered the Bahamas, the admiral noted of the local inhabitants that "they are not at all black, but the color of the Canarians, and nothing else could be expected, since this is in one line from east to west with the island of Hierro in the Canaries." Believing that he had reached the Indies of Southeast Asia, Columbus designated as "Indians" all those living in the uncharted domain to which he laid claim. Before the enormity of his error became clear in Europe, this colossal misnomer had taken on an irrevocable life of its own.

Confident to the end of his life that he had reached the outskirts of Asia on his four voyages, Columbus felt little surprise regarding the people he had encountered. But the contacts initiated in 1492 presented profound conceptual challenges for both Americans and Europeans. As Columbus's successors admitted the existence of a landmass they had not known (calling it America after the early explorer Amerigo Vespucci), the nature of its residents became more problematic for the newcomers. They had to wonder, as others were wondering of them, whether these unknown beings were mortal or immortal, human or nonhuman. The Christian invaders asked themselves whether these strangers should be exterminated if possible, as dangerous animals with no souls? Or should they be enslaved, following Aristotle's ancient dictum "that some men are by nature free, and others slaves, and that for these latter slavery is both expedient and right"? After all, not only did slavery have sanction from respected ancient philosophers, but also the enslavement of non-Christians had royal and papal approval.

Resolution of these momentous questions did not come quickly. A tome published in Paris in 1510 by a Scotsman named John Major argued that Aristotle's doctrine of natural slavery applied to the Indians. But the following year a Dominican friar in Hispaniola denounced cruel Spanish practices of enslavement in a sermon: "Are these Indians not men?" asked Antonio de Montesinos. "Do they not have rational souls? Are you not obliged to love them as you love yourselves?" In 1537 Pope Paul III decreed that Indians should not "be treated as dumb brutes created for our service . . . incapable of receiving the Catholic faith, . . . nor should they be in any way enslaved." His papal bull entitled *Sublimis Deus* went on to affirm that "the Indians are truly men and that they are not only capable of understanding the Catholic faith but, according to our information, they desire exceedingly to receive it." Five years later the Spanish king prohibited Indian slavery in his colonies, due largely to the effective protests of priests, led by Bartolomé de Las Casas. Nevertheless, forced labor and the expanding practice of importing African slaves continued in New Spain.

The proper place of the Indian was contested most sharply at Valladolid in Spain in 1550–1551, during the extended debate that took place between Las Casas and Juan Genés de Sepulveda. But throughout the century Renaissance humanists, preoccupied with Aristotle's dictum that man is the measure of all things, disputed the origin and place of non-Europeans. For example, Paracelsus, the Swiss-born physician, surmised in 1520 that Negroes and other non-Europeans had not descended from Adam. The French essayist Michel de Montaigne, on the other hand, argued forcefully that human beings were similar and equal, set apart only by minor differences of appearance, widely divergent customs, and deep-seated prejudices. Civilization is largely in the eye of the beholder, Montaigne contended: "each of us labels whatever is not among the customs of his own people as barbarism."

For Montaigne's contemporaries, intent upon understanding the true identity and nature of America's inhabitants, the question of Indian origins emerged as an intriguing and significant issue that would continue to vex future generations of Europeans. A century after Columbus, a Jesuit missionary named José de Acosta, who had spent seventeen years in Peru and Mexico, cautiously surmised that Indians had come to the New World several thousand years ago, pushed by hunger or overpopulation. Building on the ideas of others, he speculated that the Americans had originally arrived from Asia by crossing a narrow strait or using a land connection still unknown to sixteenth-century Europeans. The hypothesis expressed in Acosta's *Historia natural y moral de las Indias* (1590) was successfully countered within Spain by the more vague and contradictory speculations of Gregorio García, who published his *Origen de los indios de el nuevo mundo* in 1607. But Acosta's views received considerable attention elsewhere in Europe.

After all, most Europeans now understood Americans to be human, and all humans were still thought to have descended from Adam and Eve no more than several thousand years ago. If, as Christians believed, the Garden of Eden lay far to the east of the European landmass, then America might be closer to that ancestral garden than Europe itself (indeed, Columbus even speculated that he had found Eden). Acosta's proposition of an Asiatic derivation for the Indians, therefore, kept open the possibility for affirming Holy Scripture, though Acosta himself dismissed the common speculation that Americans represented one of the biblical Lost Tribes of Israel. Acosta's *Historia* appeared in an English translation in 1604, at a time when English interest in colonization and its attendant intellectual and cultural issues was reaching new heights. Within the following decade England established its first permanent foothold in the New World at Jamestown in Virginia, and Shakespeare completed *The Tempest,* his brilliant play that deals fancifully, but profoundly, with the issues of physical and cultural differences.

Having renounced papal authority when the Protestant Reformation reached England in the mid sixteenth century, and having staved off the Spanish Armada in 1588, the English set out to colonize North America in ways that would distinguish them from the conquistadors of Catholic Spain. They translated the lurid descriptions of Spanish atrocities in America penned by Las Casas and used them to motivate early efforts toward Christianization of Indians in New England and elsewhere. The seal of the Massachusetts Bay colony depicted a Native American calling out, "Come over and help us," and early Puritans speculated that the local inhabitants were descendants of the Lost Tribe of Israel. Others, however, hardened by hostile encounters with the Irish in earlier colonization efforts closer to home, suspected that the Indians might instead be imps of Satan, placed in their path to test and torment them.

From the start the English were bent upon founding settler colonies, to which they sent not only young male soldiers but whole families. Relations with Indian women, therefore, were often viewed more as a sinful temptation than as a logical accommodation to circumstance, as in the early Spanish and French colonies. In Virginia, John Rolfe, according to his letters, agonized at length before wedding the youthful Powhatan woman, Pocahontas. For Rolfe and others, the issue turned much more on the heathen religious status of his potential bride than on her non-European features. Sanctioned and unsanctioned liaisons with Indians would remain a part of life in Anglo-America, but the doctrine of intermarriage would never gain such wide acceptance among the settler colonies of the Protestant English of northern Europe as it did among the Catholic French and Spanish, who by the seventeenth century had already developed more extensive contacts with non-European peoples.

At first the English were hesitant to abuse or alienate the various eastern woodland Indian groups upon which they found themselves dependent in the new and unfamiliar American environment. And they maintained pious fantasies of avoiding the hegemonic excesses of the Spanish and perhaps even converting local tribes into loyal Protestant allies against their papist rivals in Florida and the West Indies. When such European diseases as smallpox and measles devastated their Indian neighbors, while sparing most colonists, the English had no knowledge of comparative immunities that could help them understand the phenomenon. Their ministers righteously interpreted the devastation as a further sign of their Protestant God's favor to his chosen people.

Faced with a rapid decline in Indian population and with a decreasing availability of excess labor from England, the settlers gradually turned, during the seventeenth century, to the importation of African laborers. English colonists had partial access to the elaborate Atlantic slaving networks of other European colonial powers, such as the Spanish and Dutch, and by the 1660s they had established their own Royal African Company. At first the rationale for exploiting Africans had little to do with appearance—non-Christians and captives taken in war could be enslaved according to accepted European principles; color had little to do with it. But by these same principles, any laborers who converted to Christianity could demand release from bondage. It soon became clear to planters in Virginia and the Carolinas, aided by Spanish precedent, that if legal status could be tied to skin color, a genetic trait far less changeable than the cultural attribute of faith, then African Americans and their offspring could be confined to perpetual bondage.

RACE AND RACISM IN THE AGE OF ENLIGHTENMENT

By the late seventeenth century, with the wholesale enslavement of Africans and coercion of Native Americans under way in the New World colonies, Europeans at home continued to grope for an understanding of the wider world they were moving so decisively and competitively to exploit. In 1684 the French physician François Bernier suggested that it was possible to classify people not merely by country and region, but also according to differing conformations of the face and body. He divided mankind under four general classifications: Europeans, Far Easterners, Black Africans, and Lapps. For Bernier's generation, the diversity among Europeans paled before their similarities when contrasted with people from other continents. Predictably, Bernier was most judgmental toward the group he knew least well. Having seen only two Lapps in his life, he still felt able to describe them as "quite frightful," with bearish faces, big feet, and large shoulders; but being still less familiar with American Indians, he did not even try to place them in his classification.

Over the next half century, descriptive natural history emerged as an increasingly serious pursuit and found its greatest champion in the botanist Carl Linnaeus. In his *Systema naturae,* first published in 1735, the young scholar put forward his own four-part list regarding humankind. At age twenty-eight, the Swedish naturalist was already embarked upon his lifelong career of describing all living organisms and classifying them into fixed categories. In each separate and immutable species, there existed numerous varieties that had adapted to diverse geographic or climatic conditions. Within the human species, Linnaeus identified four general varieties: *Homo europaeus, Homo asiaticus, Homo afer,* and *Homo americanus.* But these were all variations on a single theme. As the German philosopher Gottfried Wilhelm von Leibnitz (1646–1716) had put it, there "is no reason why all men who inhabit the earth should not be of the same race, which has been altered by different climates, as we see that beasts and plants change their nature, and improve or degenerate."

Georges Louis Leclerc de Buffon (1707–1788), the leading French authority on natural history during the second half of the eighteenth century, proved to be of this opinion. Buffon argued that Africans had been gradually darkened by generations of living in the tropics. If they resided long enough in Europe, he surmised, their color would perhaps lighten eventually to become as white as that of native Europeans. For Buffon and others, such changes were not based upon temperature alone; altitude, diet, and proximity to the ocean seemed to be significant forces shaping appearance, but so did social customs in general and "cross-breeding" in particular.

The problem for these eighteenth-century observers lay in differentiating between human changes caused by environmental, social, medical, and genetic factors. A boy's skin color, for example, might differ from that of his mother because he had been reared in a different climate, or because he had been obliged to work in the fields and was exposed to more sun and wind, or because he had suffered some malady, or because his biological father was of a different color. When similar results could derive from such different causes, it was by no means easy to unravel the underlying rules. Keen to address such problems and to encourage the progress of anthropology at a time of ongoing overseas exploration, a group of prominent French scientists founded the "Society of the Observers of Man" in 1800. Could acquired characteristics be inherited, they wondered; could inherited characteristics be changed? It is not surprising that one of the society's charter members, the naturalist Lamarck, came to the mistaken conclusion that traits obtained in life could be transmitted by heredity.

Another European puzzling over "whether a leopard could change its spots" was Johann Friedrich Blumenbach (1752–1840), a medical professor at the University of Göttingen (who, with Buffon, is often considered to be the father of anthropology). "Innumerable varieties of mankind run into one another by insensible degrees," Blumenbach observed. Yet he was willing to divide humans into five basic varieties: Linnaeus's four, plus the Malays. The division, he believed, went far beyond color, for he collected and studied skeletons from around the world. He was especially interested in crania and originated the comparative study of human skulls. Observing that one skull from the Caucasus Mountains of Russia in his collection resembled the crania of his fellow Germans, he coined the term "Caucasian" to describe light-skinned Europeans. But Blumenbach ridiculed those who tried to rank human differences in any hierarchy, usually one with themselves at the top. "If toads could speak," he wrote, they would no doubt modestly rank themselves as "the loveliest creature upon God's earth."

In English North America, patterns of racial prejudice and discrimination against nonwhites had been well established since the seventeenth century, gaining the weight of legal and intellectual precedent with each succeeding generation. Nevertheless, speculation persisted regarding the adaptability—and even the eventual amalgamation—of Europeans, Africans, and Native Americans in the so-called New World. Plantations and cities near the coast, frontier villages, and Indian towns in the interior provided ample evidence that humans of different "varieties" could procreate at will. Moreover, enlightenment belief in human perfectibility and brotherhood reinforced this egalitarian tendency as the century progressed. In this context, it was hardly surprising for the Declaration of Independence to underscore the ideal that "all men are created equal," even if present circumstances revealed stark inequalities.

After all, most American leaders in the Revolutionary generation shared the environmentalist optimism of Buffon and Blumenbach. In 1787 the Reverend Samuel Stanhope Smith, a Presbyterian minister who later became president of the College of New Jersey, published *An Essay on the Causes of the Variety of Complexion and Figure in the Human Species,* in which he speculated that human physiology was determined by latitude, along with elevation, soil, wind, and other factors. He explained apparent differences between African American field hands and house servants not in terms of any miscegenation in the big house, but rather in terms of the harsh conditions in the fields. Not surprisingly, Smith and others became fascinated with the case of Henry Moss, a former slave from Virginia who, while living in the North after the Revolution, developed white spots on his body. Within the course of several years Moss had nearly turned white, and he was exhibited in Philadelphia in 1795 as a living example of the fact that freedom and a cooler climate could draw out underlying similarities between Africans and Europeans.

Like Blumenbach's toads, these white observers had no hesitancy in seeing their own physical characteristics as the ideal norm. They accepted Buffon's ethnocentric notion that the pale skin of Europeans represented the "real and natural color" of the human race—giving an additional meaning to the term "enlightenment." Dr. Benjamin Rush (1745–1813) of Philadelphia, familiar with the dramatic case of Henry Moss, speculated that blackness might be viewed as a mild disease, an affliction, perhaps derived from leprosy, that could be cured by improved conditions. All mankind, such observers reasoned, had descended from the single creation of Adam and Eve (monogenism). Some human groups, long subjected to harsher environments, had diverged and degenerated more than others. Still, "the history of the creation of man and of the relation of our species to each other by birth, which is recorded in the Old Testament," Rush observed, "is the . . . strongest argument that can be used in favor of the original and natural equality of all mankind."

If the Bible gave credence to the ideas of a single creation and the unity of the human species, then critics of Scripture inevitably posed a challenge to monogenism. Hence François-Marie Arouet, known as Voltaire (1694–1778), the popular French humanist whose attacks on dogmatism often included the Christian church, raised pointed questions about Old Testament ideas of a unified creation. In an essay on "The People of America," he mocked Christian scholars in Europe who had first denied the possibility of accessible land and peoples beyond the Atlantic and then, in the wake of Columbus, had rushed to tie inhabitants of the Americas to Old Testament tribes on the thinnest of evidence. No doubt the famous philosophe had in mind such persons as James Adair, an English Indian agent who spent much of his life in the American Southeast. Building upon earlier theories and his own observations, Adair published an extensive *History of the American Indians* in 1775, arguing that Native Americans resembled the biblical Hebrews in numerous elements of language and culture.

But when Voltaire asked, somewhat rhetorically, whether any hard evidence existed linking Europeans to Indians or to Africans, he concluded that none did. "The negro race is a species of men as different from ours as the breed of spaniels is from that of greyhounds," announced the influential skeptic, adding that, "if their understanding is not of a different nature from ours, it is at least greatly inferior. They are not capable of any great application or association of ideas, and seem formed neither for the advantages nor the abuses of philosophy." The prominent deist reasoned that if Scripture contained allegory rather than literal truth, then there might be separate human species, or races, descended from different Adams. "As the negro of Africa has not his original from us whites," Voltaire asked, "why should the red, olive, or ash-colored peoples of America come from our countries?"

Similar questions troubled Henry Home, Lord Kames, the Scottish jurist and essayist who published *Sketches of the History of Man* in 1774. Just as Julian the Apostate, fourth-century ruler of the Roman Empire, had once doubted "if we were descended from one man and one woman," given the diversity of human appearances and cultures, so Kames found it highly dubious that climate alone could account for the wide differences in mankind. He dismissed the common idea that if two organisms could produce fertile offspring they must belong to the same species, arguing that sheep and goats, hares and rabbits could reproduce effectively. Kames contended that different breeds of dogs amounted to different species, and added, "there are different species of men as well as of dogs: a mastiff differs not more from a spaniel, than a white man from a negro, or a Laplander from a Dane."

Across the Atlantic, an occasional American writer was pondering similar possibilities. Revolutionary egalitarianism could not wipe out generations of racial hostility. For the new empire-builders, patterns of degradation imposed by conquest and enslavement could be viewed smugly as inherent traits in nonwhite peoples. For some, perhaps, the Negro poet Phyllis Wheatley (1753?–1784) in Massachusetts and the black scientist Benjamin Banneker (1731–1806) in Maryland appeared as harbingers of broader assimilation. But others saw them as bizarre exceptions who only proved a general rule of nonwhite separateness and inferiority, much as the transformation of Henry Moss's skin underscored for many the general immutability of color.

It is not surprising that a slaveholder and deist, Thomas Jefferson, came closest to the "polygenist" blasphemies of Voltaire. In his influential *Notes on the State of Virginia* (1785), the master of Monticello imposed a crude hierarchy on perceived differences, finding Africans (whom he had only known in bondage) to be less beautiful, sensitive, artistic, and gifted than Europeans. While placing his own ancestors well above the forebears of his slaves on almost every count, Jefferson still hedged on the crucial issue of separate origins, and admitted his lingering uncertainty. "I advance it, therefore, as a suspicion only, that the blacks, whether originally a distinct race, or made distinct by time and circumstance, are inferior to the whites in the endowment both of body and of mind."

TOWARD "SCIENTIFIC" RACISM

This growing propensity to rank, rather than merely to differentiate, would characterize the nineteenth century. The biological thinking of the late eighteenth century gave rise, in subsequent decades, to an increasingly concrete and damaging racist ideology, as scientists and scholars lent added credence to popular beliefs in the inherent inferiority of nonwhites. The nineteenth century saw the gradual emergence of a pseudoscientific theory that viewed Caucasians as innately and permanently superior. Enlightenment challenges to the literal meaning of the Bible had helped to cast doubts upon the unity of mankind, as traditionally emphasized in the Christian doctrine. It no longer seemed certain, as written in Acts 17:26, that God "hath made of one blood all nations of men for to dwell on all the face of the earth."

Ironically, the leading proponent of polygenism in North America did not emerge from among southern slaveholders, but from the scientific community of Philadelphia. Dr. Samuel George Morton (1799–1851) was a respected physician and geologist whose early study of fossils made him the founder of invertebrate paleontology in the United States. Morton conceded that humans of different skin colors could procreate, but he subscribed to the common misconception of the day that it was difficult for mulatto couples to conceive and to create fertile offspring.

Morton was convinced of the separate origins of the so-called races. Like Blumenbach in Europe, he believed that intensive comparative measurement of skulls (craniometry) could illustrate innate differences, so he amassed a huge collection of skulls from around the world. But unlike Blumenbach, Morton perceived an elaborate hierarchy, headed by Caucasians. In his *Crania Americana* (1839), Morton analyzed 144 Native American skulls and proclaimed them to be quantifiably inferior to a Caucasian ideal. Indians, he asserted, were "slow in acquiring knowledge," as well as being "restless and revengeful." Beneath them he placed the "indolent" Negroes as his "lowest grade" of humanity. Such crass observations were common among white Americans, but Morton gave them added standing, having served as president of the Academy of Natural Sciences in Philadelphia. When Morton died in 1851, the Charleston Medical Journal eulogized: "We of the South should consider him as our benefactor, for aiding most materially in giving to the negro his true position as an inferior race."

Not everyone in the Western scientific community agreed. As physical anthropology continued to take shape, many of the Europeans most interested in human differences and their origins continued to speak out forcefully against efforts to rank the varieties of humans. "Whilst we maintain the unity of the human species, we at the same time repel the depressing assumption of superior and inferior races of men," wrote Alexander von Humboldt (1769–1859). "All are in like degree designed for freedom." It was this moral and political issue of who seemed to be made for freedom that came to preoccupy the debates over race in the nineteenth century. For it is only then that an explicit, pseudoscientific body of racial beliefs emerged as a main current in Western thought, arguing for the innate and unchanging superiority of the white race.

After Morton's death, there were others waiting to pick up his mantle. One of those who had helped him acquire skulls from the Middle East was an Englishman residing in Cairo named George Robins Gliddon. While lecturing in America, Gliddon teamed up with a flamboyant doctor in Mobile named Josiah Clark Nott, and in 1854 the two men published a 738-page book called *Types of Mankind; or, Ethnological Researches,* which they dedicated to Morton's memory. The two authors popularized Morton's polygenism and continued to attack those who took the Bible literally. They argued for multiple creations leading to separate species, or races, and they embraced recent geological findings suggesting that the world was much older than previously suspected. They even included a section by the Swiss-born naturalist, Louis Agassiz, a prominent apostle of polygeny who also contributed briefly to their 1857 volume, *Indigenous Races of the Earth.*

That same year, as the constitutional debate over race and slavery grew more inflamed, the Supreme Court, in *Dred Scott* v. *Sandford,* addressed the question of whether a Negro could ever aspire to the full rights of citizenship in the United States and decided in the negative. The intent of the framers was "too clear for dispute," the Court ruled: "the enslaved African race were not intended to be included." Eager to win the votes of white farmers in the West, Abraham Lincoln sounded a similar note in famous debates with Stephen Douglas in 1858. "There is a physical difference between the white and black races which I believe will forever forbid the two races living together on terms of social and political equality," Lincoln stated. "I as much as any other man am in favor of having the superior position assigned to the white race."

Dramatically changed circumstances, rather than any massive shift in convictions, would prompt Lincoln to issue the Emancipation Proclamation four years later, in the middle of the Civil War. But the altered legal situation of African Americans after the defeat of the Confederacy, and the passage of the Thirteenth, Fourteenth, and Fifteenth amendments to the Constitution during Reconstruction, granting blacks freedom, citizenship, and the right to vote, did nothing to temper or resolve debates about race. Indeed, the specter of black equality unleashed an unprecedented barrage of racist rhetoric among white Americans, both northern and southern. Anxious to find scientific authority to reinforce entrenched public beliefs, pamphleteers hostile to Republicans and Negroes drew heavily upon the writings of Gliddon, Nott, Agassiz, and the French writer, Joseph Arthur de Gobineau, whose four-volume *Essai sur l'inégalité des races humaines* (1853–1855) stressed race as the single greatest determinant of history.

Meanwhile, in 1859 the English naturalist Charles Darwin (1809–1882) had published his controversial new theory of evolution in *On the Origin of Species.* At one level, the long-standing debate over unitary versus multiple "creations" suddenly became irrelevant. But at another level, Darwin's idea of human evolution from a distant common ancestor pushed back the time frame so tremendously that there was more room than ever to speculate about human divergences and separations. To Darwin's dismay, fellow Englishman Herbert Spencer (1820–1903) wasted no time in transposing evolutionary laws of the physical world to society as well. During the first half of the nineteenth century, groups that had been regarded by Europeans as "lower" biologically were now said to be "further back" in their evolutionary development. On both sides of the Atlantic, whites' earlier presumption that their stature, hair, and skin color represented the ideal of human beauty was reformulated: now Caucasians believed themselves to represent the most mature expression of human evolution.

To America's racial theorists, the Negroes remained the least-developed race, and Reconstruction policies represented a dubious and even dangerous experiment that might tax blacks beyond their current capabilities. Josiah Nott speculated in 1866 that "the Freedmen's Bureau will not have vitality enough to see the negro experiment through many hundred generations." In an open letter to the bureau's superintendent, Nott remarked to Major General Oliver Otis Howard regarding "the physical and civil history of the negro race, that it is now, wherever found, just what it was 5000 years ago." "Let us beware," Louis Agassiz warned, "of granting too much to the negro race in the beginning." The outlines of the paternalistic white man's burden toward "less advanced" races had clearly begun to emerge. "I am responsible," wrote Alexander Winchell, a prominent American academic in 1880, "if I grant him privileges which he can only pervert to his detriment and mine; or impose upon him duties which he is incompetent to perform or even to understand."

The same social Darwinists who believed that African Americans might need to be segregated and treated as children, had only slightly higher expectations for Native Americans. Many had concluded that the ancient mounds discovered throughout the Ohio and Mississippi river valleys over the past generation could not possibly have been built by the ancestors of the current Indians, who seemed to be destined to disappear in the ongoing struggle with superior Europeans. Even the forced removal of the five "civilized" tribes from the Southeast to what is now Oklahoma during the Jacksonian era had not been sufficient protection, they argued. The Indians would vanish entirely, it was believed, unless they were confined to reservations or obliged to take up white ways. Just as Negro training schools were established after the Civil War, Indian schools sprang up as well; several institutions, such as Hampton Institute, served both constituencies.

The California gold rush and the expansion of railroads across the continent had also brought an influx of Asian workers to the United States, sparking racist fears of a "yellow peril." Between 1866 and 1869, some ten thousand Chinese dug tunnels and laid track for the Central Pacific Railway in

Nevada and Utah. By 1870 Chinese made up nearly 9 percent of all Californians, and they were being imported into the South to replace departed slaves and into the East to take the place of striking workers. Fear of competition from Asian labor strengthened existing prejudices, especially in the West, and anti-Chinese riots erupted in San Francisco in 1877. "Our experience in dealing with the weaker races—the Negroes and Indians, for example,—is not encouraging," President Rutherford B. Hayes wrote in his diary in 1879. "I would consider with favor any suitable measures to discourage the Chinese from coming to our shores." In 1882 Congress passed an Exclusion Act halting Chinese immigration, followed by further restrictions in 1888 and 1892.

"EMBATTLED ANGLO-SAXONS"

Antagonism toward free Negroes in the South, beleaguered Indians in the Plains, and Asian immigrants in the West was echoed by mounting hostility in the East toward new immigration from Europe. Fear of labor competition fed ethnic and national resentments as the pattern of arrivals from Europe began to shift dramatically. The "old immigration" from northern and western Europe gave way to new movements from southern and eastern Europe. The new stream was larger than the old; it contained fewer persons who spoke English and more who spoke Polish or Italian; it brought fewer who were Protestants, more who were Catholics and Jews. The American elite establishment reacted by stressing, and exaggerating, its Anglo-Saxon heritage. Dropping any pretext of Europeans as a unified genetic or cultural community, the establishment began to discriminate in racial terms between Teutonic and Slavic peoples. Whether the society could absorb and assimilate these newcomers became a real question in the minds of people steeped in a burgeoning ideology of discrimination.

Indeed, for many the questions went further. Would the United States be "overwhelmed" by this new immigration, "dragged down," or irredeemably transformed? Nativist editors, professors, and politicians made much of the fact that immigrant workers were the descendants of serfs and came from undemocratic societies—observations that meant much if one believed the popular neo-Lamarckian view that environmental and cultural influences had a hereditary effect. Moreover, these foreigners seemed to reproduce more rapidly and "indiscriminately" than their elite employers. Besides forming a rash of exclusivist genealogical societies, eastern elites responded with strong calls for limiting immigration. In 1892 Thomas Bailey Aldrich, taking issue with Emma Lazarus, published a popular restrictionist poem in the *Atlantic Monthly* entitled "Unguarded Gates," and Harvard historian John Fiske, an outspoken social Darwinist, became the first president of the Immigration Restriction League in 1894.

Despite voices to the contrary, racial fears became an increasing theme in America's scientific and literary community. The anti-Semitism of popular authors such as Owen Wister (1860–1938) was exceeded by the negrophobia of Thomas Dixon, author of *The Leopard's Spots* (1902). His novel *The Clansman* (1905) was transformed by fellow southerner D. W. Griffith into the popular racist film, *The Birth of a Nation* (1915). The following year a self-styled anthropologist, the blue blood Madison Grant summarized a generation of racialist rhetoric when he published a grandiose and ill-documented tract entitled *The Passing of the Great Race,* arguing that the "Nordic race" in America was on the brink of an abyss, facing virtual extinction unless immigration limits could be enacted. When the end of World War I renewed the press of immigrants from Europe (many of them said to harbor dangerous political views), calls for restriction increased, and in the 1920s Congress enacted a series of stringent anti-immigration laws that severely restricted the immigration to America of all but western Europeans.

In an era of rampant racial antipathy, the sciences continued to play a significant role. One key figure, ironically enough, was Darwin's own cousin, Francis Galton, who published *Hereditary Genius* in 1869 and coined the term "eugenics." Drawing on biographies, conversations, and travel literature, Galton concluded that much as higher and lower grades of person existed in each race, races themselves could be ranked. Participants in the growing eugenics movement suggested that if geniuses sprang from identifiable stock and if feeblemindedness, criminality, and even poverty was deeply influenced by heredity, social engineering was possible and desirable. Philanthropic and reform efforts, they believed, were at best misguided, at worst counterproductive. Eugenicists tended to favor harsher measures: immigration barriers, social segregation, incarceration, stricter marriage laws, even sterilization.

In the United States, organized eugenics took hold in 1904, when delegates to an American Breeders Association meeting urged the application to humans of the same selective breeding techniques known to work for animals and plants. A Eugenics Record Office was founded in 1910, at Cold Spring Harbor, New York, followed by the creation of a Eugenics Research Association. Eugenicists gained fuel for their arguments from the rediscovery, and initial crude uses, of the pioneering work of Gregor Mendel (1822–1884), the Austrian monk whose botanical experiments with peas laid the groundwork for modern genetics. Published in 1866 but ignored for a full generation, Mendel's observations regained notice at the turn of the century, and scientists preoccupied with heredity jumped to the mistaken assumption that hereditary laws governing the shape and size of a pea could apply equally to complicated human characteristics. They speculated that variations in anatomy or behavior must illustrate the dominant or recessive form of a single gene.

Later generations of geneticists would show that elements of the human body depend upon the complex interaction of numerous genes with one another and with the external environment. But simplification typified early-twentieth-century research regarding race, and nowhere was this more true than in the search—not unlike the efforts of craniometry in the previous century—to find a unitary and quantifiable scale of human intelligence. Indeed, it was a practicing craniometrist, the French psychologist Alfred Binet (1857–1911), who first created an intelligence scale using a composite of simple (and we would now say culturally biased) tests to determine the subject's "mental age." When mental age was divided by chronological age (as suggested by the German psychologist William Stern in 1912), the result was an intelligence quotient, or IQ. Such numbers did not, Binet cautioned, represent inborn intelligence, and he rightly feared that his testing device would be misused to categorize children.

The popularizer of Binet's scale in America was Henry H. Goddard (1866–1957), research director of a training school for feebleminded children in New Jersey. Studying these children, as well as samples of immigrants at Ellis Island, Goddard concluded that normal intelligence was governed by a single gene and inherited in a strictly Mendelian fashion, so that mental deficiency could be explained as the inheritance of a recessive intelligence gene. Other social behaviors—violence, criminality, prostitution—were governed by other hereditary genes. In 1916 Stanford professor Lewis M. Terman expanded and popularized the Frenchman's scale with his Stanford-Binet test, which was to become the standard for subsequent IQ testing. As America prepared to enter World War I, Harvard professor Robert M. Yerkes struck upon the idea of mass mental testing for soldiers as a way to assist the mobilization and bolster his fledgling discipline of psychology. Yerkes eventually tested 1.75 million army recruits, and his race-based data became highly influential, despite inherent flaws.

CULTURAL ANTHROPOLOGY, DESEGREGATION, AND BEYOND

Such varied disciplines as psychology, history, sociology, and genetics all contributed to the consolidation of racist ideology in America, which reached its height during the 1920s with the national resurgence of the Ku Klux Klan, the passage of new immigration laws, and the rise of postwar xenophobia. But at least one human science, anthropology, was beginning to move in a different direction. Physical anthropology had been at the forefront of the nineteenth-century obsession with ever more refined comparative measurement of the human anatomy. William Z. Ripley, a lecturer on anthropology at Columbia University, still made use of the cephalic index in his *Races of Europe,* published in 1899, but he cautioned against using such physical measurements to draw moral conclusions. Craniology, he warned, is not an exact science, and he objected to the fact that "vulgar" theories of race had been "made sponsor for nearly every conceivable form of social, political, and economic virtues or ills, as the case may be."

Gradually anthropologists—both amateur and professional, European and American—were beginning to move away from an emphasis on biology as a dominant form of explanation for human activity. Increasingly, they looked instead to questions of social process, and from this the field of modern cultural anthropology slowly took shape. Edward Burnett Tylor (1832–1917) had published *Primitive Culture* in England in 1871, but it was in America that some of the greatest advances in this new field would occur, thanks largely to the forceful example of a single man. Franz Boas (1858–1942) was born in Germany and trained in physics, turning to anthropology after a sojourn at a German meteorological station in Baffinland in 1883. At home with quantification, he became an expert in anthropometry, but he realized at an early stage that measurement was not equally applicable to all realms of human experience. When he moved to the United States in his late twenties, he threw himself into the study of indigenous American cultures and languages.

Living first with the Eskimos, and then with other North American groups, Boas found that complex cultures could not be readily explained by simply invoking logical reactions to specific environments. He sensed the importance of learning the spoken language and living within the culture in order to understand it. It became increasingly clear to Boas that race was not the determinant of culture, and as someone who had proven himself in the field of anthropometry, he was in a unique position to press racialist thinkers for data that could prove their broad and poorly documented assertions. An outspoken opponent of race theorists such as Madison Grant, Boas was joined during the 1920s by a new generation of scientists and social scientists who were finding racist doctrines to be too contradictory, subjective, and unprovable. Unsubstantiated race dogma had reached its zenith in America and was beginning to fall of its own weight. When Madison Grant published his next book in 1933, it met with ridicule.

Beginning in the 1930s, several trends converged during the middle third of the twentieth century to alter racial thinking and race policy in America slowly but dramatically. At home, Great Depression hardships and New Deal programs, followed by the mobilization for World War II, obliged Americans to interact in different ways. Minority groups took advantage of their constitutional rights to begin to press systematically for greater protection through the courts. During the war itself, heightened migration and the necessity of undertaking prodigious common tasks brought America's complex society closer together. Disillusionment with the racist excesses of Mussolini and Hitler soon became virtually complete. On the other hand, discrimination against Japanese Americans and their eventual internment by the United States government showed that many Americans still retained strong beliefs in hereditary racial tendencies. Prejudice against African Americans gave way slowly, and only when sanctioned by the weight of government intervention.

But federal pressure in favor of equal rights—whether from the judicial, legislative, or executive branch—was not always swift in coming. Intellectual argument could help it along occasionally, as when Swedish sociologist Gunnar Myrdal was recruited by the Carnegie Corporation to study the American race problem with an integrated team of social scientists. Their massive report, published as *An American Dilemma: The Negro Problem and Modern Democracy* (1944), influenced Supreme Court decisions on desegregation in the following decade. World opinion was also a factor at times. As the cold war intensified in the 1950s, the American government, eager to find support against Soviet communism in the United Nations and throughout the newly independent countries of the "third world," became increasingly sensitive to charges of racial discrimination at home. But more often, it was grass-roots organizing that forced government intervention to protect nonwhite Americans from legalized and extralegal discrimination. It is a measure of national ambivalence on these matters that different levels and branches of government often worked at cross-purposes.

During the 1950s and the early 1960s grass-roots activities grew into a full-fledged protest campaign, culminating in the 1963 March on Washington (where the Reverend Martin Luther King, Jr., described his "dream" for American integration) and in the 1964 Civil Rights Act. But even as the walls of segregation came down in the nation's schools and other public facilities, Americans wondered whether the changes were merely temporary concessions to pressure or irreversible commitments to creating a nonracial society.

The protracted war in Vietnam, for example, revived deep anti-Asian feeling that had been encouraged during World War II and the Korean War, and that would surface again during the lingering cold war arguments with China and trade war confrontations with Japan in the 1980s and 1990s. Protracted conflict in the oil-rich Middle East gave new life to long-standing "orientalist" stereotypes about the residents of that region. Race also became a factor in hostility towards the increasing number of legal and illegal immigrants from Latin America. Since most were Spanish-speaking, language often became the surface issue marking deeper prejudice, and nativist groups pushed to make English the "official" language of the United States. Moreover, recessions in the Reagan-Bush years intensified competition for jobs and drew out smoldering hostilities among whites to so-called affirmative action policies intended to offset centuries of discrimination. It was no mere coincidence that the 500th anniversary of Columbus's encounter found the

United States embroiled in a noisy debate about how to square the long-standing realities of a multiracial nation with an intellectual inheritance built upon centuries of misguided European race mythology outlined briefly here.

BIBLIOGRAPHY

General Surveys

Anderson, David D., and Robert L. Wright, eds. *The Dark and Tangled Path: Race in America* (1971).

Daniels, Roger, and Spencer C. Olin, Jr., eds. *Racism in California: A Reader in the History of Oppression* (1972).

Fields, Barbara J. "Ideology and Race in American History." In *Region, Race, and Reconstruction: Essays in Honor of C. Vann Woodward,* edited by J. Morgan Kousser and James M. McPherson (1982).

Gossett, Thomas F. *Race: The History of an Idea in America* (1963).

Handlin, Oscar. *Race and Nationality in American Life* (1957).

Harris, Marvin. *Patterns of Race in the Americas* (1964).

Montagu, M. F. Ashley. *Man's Most Dangerous Myth: The Fallacy of Race* (1942; 5th ed. 1974).

Nash, Gary, and Richard Weiss, eds. *The Great Fear: Race in the Mind of America* (1979). Historical essays on issues of race relations.

Rose, Peter I. *The Subject Is Race: Traditional Ideologies and the Teaching of Race Relations* (1968).

Ruchames, Louis, ed. *Racial Thought in America: From the Puritans to Abraham Lincoln* (1969). A useful collection of documents.

Stocking, George W., Jr. *Race, Culture, and Evolution: Essays in the History of Anthropology* (1968).

Terkel, Studs. *Race* (1992). A collection of oral histories.

Historical Studies

Altschuler, Glenn C. *Race, Ethnicity, and Class in American Social Thought, 1865–1919* (1982).

Fredrickson, George M. *The Black Image in the White Mind: The Debate on Afro-American Character and Destiny, 1817–1914* (1971).

Gould, Stephen J. *The Mismeasure of Man* (1981).

Haller, John S. *Outcasts from Evolution: Scientific Attitudes of Racial Inferiority, 1859–1900* (1971).

Higham, John. *Strangers in the Land: Patterns of American Nativism, 1860–1925* (1963).

Huddleston, Lee Eldridge. *Origins of the American Indians: European Concepts, 1492–1729* (1967).

Jordan, Winthrop D. *White over Black: American Attitudes Toward the Negro, 1550–1812* (1968).

Miller, Stuart Creighton. *The Unwelcome Immigrant: The American Image of the Chinese, 1785–1882* (1969).

Myrdal, Gunnar. *An American Dilemma: The Negro Problem and Modern Democracy* (1944).

Sanders, Ronald. *Lost Tribes and Promised Lands: The Origins of American Racism* (1978).

Silverberg, Robert. *Mound Builders of Ancient America: The Archaeology of a Myth* (1968).

Stanton, William. *The Leopard's Spots: Scientific Attitudes Toward Race in America, 1815–59* (1960).

Takaki, Ronald T. *Iron Cages: Race and Culture in Nineteenth-Century America* (1979).

Toll, William. *The Resurgence of Race: Black Social Theory from Reconstruction to the Pan-African Conference* (1979).

Wood, Forrest G. *Black Scare: The Racist Response to Emancipation and Reconstruction* (1968).

The Arts and Popular Culture

Boime, Albert. *The Art of Exclusion: Representing Blacks in the Nineteenth Century* (1990).

Bugner, Ladislas, ed. *The Image of the Black in Western Art* (1976–). This extraordinary four-volume survey is now nearly complete, with the crucial segment on the sixteenth and seventeenth century yet to appear.

Drinnon, Richard. *Facing West: The Metaphysics of Indian-Hating and Empire-Building* (1980).

Honour, Hugh. *The New Golden Land: European Images of America from the Discoveries to the Present Time* (1975).

Parry, Ellwood. *The Image of the Indian and the Black Man in American Art, 1590–1900* (1974).

Van Deburg, William L. *Slavery and Race in American Popular Culture* (1984).

SEE ALSO **Anthropological Approaches; Racial Ideology; Racism.**

ETHNICITY

Edward R. Kantowicz

In 1782, J. Hector St. John de Crèvecoeur, an astute observer of the American colonies then in revolution, penned a classic question: "What then is the American, this new man?" He provided an equally classic answer: "He is either an European, or the descendant of an European, hence that strange mixture of blood, which you will find in no other country... a mixture of English, Scotch, Irish, French, Dutch, Germans, and Swedes" (*Letters from an American Farmer* [1968 ed.], pp. 49, 47).

Crèvecoeur's *Letters* marked the first attempt to analyze the uniquely American problem of the one and the many. Since the time of the American Revolution, the United States has developed a powerful national consciousness that has united a continent-sized country. Yet its people have come from many other countries and have retained at least some habits, customs, and values from their places of origin.

The first federal census, conducted in 1790, seemed to confirm Crèvecoeur's emphasis on the ethnic diversity of the new United States. Only a little less than half the 3,929,000 inhabitants enumerated were of English origin. The second-largest group, African Americans, comprised about 20 percent of the population. The remaining one-third or so were people from the other European nations. American Indians were not enumerated in the census because the United States Constitution excluded "Indians not taxed" from the population base for purposes of representation.

Yet from another point of view, the early United States was not so diverse as these figures might suggest. African Americans would have a profound effect on American history, yet in 1790 nearly all of them were slaves. Apart from a few Quakers, no one in the fledgling nation considered them a component of the "new man" that was forming in North America. (American Indians were considered "domestic dependent nations" and were dealt with as separate entities beyond the pale of American nationality.) If we consider only the white population of the United States, transplanted Englishmen formed a full 70 percent of the populace in 1790. Another 18 percent came from either Scotland or Ireland. That left 12 percent of white Americans whose origins were not in the British Isles. In the late eighteenth century those Germans, Dutchmen, and French Huguenots would have been familiar sights on the streets of London. In short, the white populace of the United States was not much more diverse than that of England.

This situation remained little changed for nearly a century as English Protestants dominated American culture and politics. There were, however, two notable exceptions. In the middle of the nineteenth century, several million Irish Catholics immigrated to the United States, as did an even larger number of Germans. The Irish differed from native-born Americans of English origin in their religion, their poverty, and their dense concentrations in seaboard cities. The Germans dispersed more widely, especially in the Midwest, and generally prospered more quickly than the Irish. Yet in cities of the German triangle—the area bounded by Milwaukee, Cincinnati, and Saint Louis—and in far-flung farming districts they built an impressive subculture that they called *Deutschtum* (Germandom).

On a number of occasions in the nineteenth century, Americans attacked the growing Irish and German subcultures with intolerant nativist movements. Violent nativism was far more common in the older cities of the eastern seaboard, where immigrants confronted a long-entrenched cultural majority such as the Boston Brahmins. In the newer cities of the Midwest, social structures were more fluid and immigrants were "present at the Creation," so to speak. Overall, an unreflective optimism marked American attitudes toward European ethnicity. Scotch Irish and French Huguenots of colonial days had blended effortlessly into the English-speaking Protestant populace that dominated American society; given enough time, perhaps the latest immigrants would, too. Ralph Waldo Emerson spoke confidently of the "smelting pot" that would forge a new American race. In any case, the wide-open spaces and soaring nationalist confidence of the expanding United States in the nineteenth century suggested there was room for all.

As the century came to a close, this easy optimism evaporated. The Civil War and the emancipation of the African American slaves increased the racial and ethnic consciousness of most Americans. Then, shortly after the war, Asian Americans came to the West Coast in large numbers to work on the transcontinental railroads. This influx of nonwhites so alarmed Americans that Congress passed the Chinese Exclusion Act in 1882, the first law barring members of a specific ethnic or racial group from entering the country.

At the turn of the century, the United States experienced its greatest wave of immigration. From about 1896 until the outbreak of World War I in 1914, an average of roughly a million newcomers arrived each year. Even more disturbing to native-born Americans than the sheer numbers was the ethnic composition of the "new immigrants," as they were called. Rather than the Englishmen, Germans, and Swedes from northern Europe so familiar to Crèvecoeur and succeeding generations of Americans, the immigrants who arrived at the turn of the century came largely from southern and eastern Europe. These Poles, Russian Jews, Greeks, Italians, Serbs, Czechs, Portuguese, and many others were darker skinned than their northern European predecessors and spoke languages rarely heard before in London or New York. In addition, few of the "new immigrants" were Protestants.

Because of the prevailing preoccupation with race, both in the United States and in European intellectual circles, turn-of-the-century Americans tended to view the newcomers in racial terms. Supposedly scientific treatises such as Madison Grant's *The Passing of the Great Race* (1916) divided white Europeans into three "races": the Nordic, the Mediterranean, and the Alpine. Grant characterized blond, blue-eyed Nordics from northern Europe as preeminently fighters and legislators, and as naturally superior. Mediterraneans were artistic and creative, but rather unstable and undependable. Alpines, such as the Poles and other eastern Europeans, were to him a stolid peasant people, strong of back but weak of mind. Imbued with such pseudoscientific information, Americans reacted with alarm to the influx of Alpines and Mediterraneans by imposing harshly restrictive immigration quotas in the early 1920s that not only reduced the overall numbers of immigrants but also favored the entry of the old-stock, northern Europeans.

Both before and after the enactment of immigration restriction, the twentieth century has witnessed an outpouring of theories about ethnicity and assimilation. Scholars, politicians, and ordinary citizens have agonized over the proper interpretation of *E pluribus unum* (one from many), the motto on the nation's coins. The question of ethnic identity is an important one, for it cuts to the heart of how Americans view themselves as individuals and as a people.

WHAT IS ETHNICITY?

Horace Kallen, an American Zionist, wrote in 1924 what is still probably the single most famous sentence about ethnicity: "Men may change their clothes, their politics, their wives, their religions, their philosophies, to greater or lesser extent: they cannot change their grandfathers" (*Culture and Democracy in the United States,* p. 116). Unfortunately, the only way Kallen's statement makes any sense is in racial terms. He unconsciously echoed the vociferous racism of his contemporaries. People cannot, of course, change their grandfathers in the genetic, racial sense. Yet they can forget their grandfathers' languages, reject their beliefs and customs, and shun their other descendants. In order to understand ethnicity, we must divest it of all conscious or unconscious racial connotations. Ethnicity may be defined as a collective, inherited, cultural identity, buttressed by social structures and social networks, and often formulated in opposition to competing social groups. Let us consider each element of this definition in turn.

First of all, ethnicity is a collective phenomenon, a "we feeling" that unites a number of people. Ethnic groups may be large or small, and words can seriously mislead us when we talk about them. For instance, when an ethnic group in Africa does not possess a nation-state of its own, it is often called a tribe. Yet a group of similar size in Europe, which happens to form the majority of a political state, will be called a nation. Both ethnic groups (the Greek root, *ethnos,* means "people") are basically the same thing: a collectivity united by a sense of common origin.

Ethnicity is also an inherited trait. An ethnic group is not just a voluntary association that one joins. One is born into and brought up in it. Sociologists may occasionally consider certain groups like intellectuals or young urban professionals (the so-called Yuppies) to be akin to ethnic groups: but this is probably not a helpful analogy. A person earns his or her way into the intellectual or the consuming class, but is nurtured in an ethnic group.

One's ethnic inheritance, however, is cultural, not genetic. A child learns his or her language, values, beliefs, and ways of acting from his or her parents. An Irish child raised by wolves will not grow up to be an Irish Catholic, nor will a child of Polish parents adopted and raised by a Puerto Rican family retain a Polish ethnic consciousness.

The culture inherited by children is powerfully reinforced by social structures and social networks. People with a strong sense of ethnicity will share nearly all their primary, face-to-face, social relations with members of their own ethnic group. They will interact with members of other groups only in secondary, formal relationships at school or work. They are also most likely to choose a spouse from among their own ethnic group.

Ethnic culture is by no means unchanging. The children of immigrants often fuse their parents' language with the English they hear on the streets into freewheeling blends of the old and the new. They retain some culinary and ceremonial traditions, and abandon others. They venerate some patron saints from the old country and adopt additional religious practices in the new. The fact that a culture is inherited does not mean it is static. It is not an unchanging set of traits; it is more like a dowry, which can be preserved, increased, diminished, or wasted.

There is an inherently negative side to ethnicity as well. A group inevitably works out its ethnic identification in conflict with others. A small band of similar people isolated on a desert island would feel no ethnic consciousness, for they would have no one to compare themselves against. They would simply call themselves "the people," as small tribes in isolated regions of the world still do. It is only when different groups encounter one another that they develop an ethnic consciousness.

THE DEVELOPMENT OF ETHNIC IDENTITY: THE POLES

These abstract definitional matters may become clearer if we apply them to a specific ethnic group. The Poles, who have had a long and tangled history both in Europe and America, will serve to highlight the contours of group identity.

In the late Middle Ages, Poland was a large, multinational state sprawling far eastward into what is now Russia. Germans, Lithuanians, Ukrainians, Russians, Jews, and Poles lived within the bounds of the Polish Commonwealth. Nicolaus Copernicus, the early-sixteenth-century cleric who first theorized that Earth and the other planets actually move around the sun rather than vice versa, has been claimed by both Polish and German historians as one of their own. But such nationalistic pride misses the point that ethnic consciousness remained quite undeveloped at the time. Copernicus, who was born in the city of Toruń in what was then part of Poland but later became East Prussia, no doubt spoke both German and Polish; but as a Renaissance scholar he probably thought in Latin and dreamed in Italian.

The Polish *szlachta* (gentry), a large landowning warrior class that dominated both the weak central government and the powerful military, reduced the peasants to serfdom. Over the centuries, the *szlachta* developed a fierce national consciousness as Poland's neighbors gradually whittled away at its borders and then, in the late eighteenth century, partitioned the country, erasing it from the map.

Both in the days of independence and under the partitioning powers, the *szlachta* were in fact the nation, the Polish people. The peasants who toiled on the manors spoke the same language as their lords but did not share their historical memories or consider themselves part of the Polish nation. The *szlachta,* for their part, cultivated the "Sarmatian myth," alleging that they were descendants of the ancient Sarmatians and thus formed a race wholly separate from the peasants. Polish peasants had as little in common with their *szlachta* masters as African Americans did with George Washington or Thomas Jefferson.

Peasant identity was built partly on class grievances. In 1846, for instance, when the gentry led a quixotic rebellion against Austrian occupiers in the province of Galicia, the peasants did not join the revolt but used the occasion to slaughter their masters and burn their manor houses. For the most part, however, the peasants in Polish lands felt little class or national consciousness. They identified mainly with their region or village, the *okolica* (little world) that surrounded their daily activities. The Catholic religion with its annual cycle of rituals helped peasants to define their place in the universe, and this identity as Catholic peasants was reinforced whenever they encountered Jewish shopkeepers in the towns or Gypsies in the countryside. The greater masses who immigrated to the United States from partitioned Poland in the nineteenth century were not Poles in any meaningful nationalist sense. In their own minds they were Catholic village people.

When these peasants immigrated to the United States between 1890 and 1914, they discovered that they were Poles after all. Their language set them apart from the English-speaking Americans and from the Germans and Czechs who settled in the same neighborhoods they did. Although immigrants from the same village often settled close together in American cities, they could not help but meet many Polish speakers from other villages. Clerical and nationalist leaders trumpeted the glories of the Polish nation as they recruited peasant immigrants into such fraternal societies as the Polish National Alliance and the Polish Roman Catholic Union. By encountering strangers, finding other peasant immigrants who spoke their language, and listening to the elite leaders of the emigration, immigrants swiftly began to think of themselves as Poles in America.

The two world wars marked further watersheds in the developing identities of Polish immigrants and their descendants. Before World War I, the Polish National Alliance had worked for the liberation of the homeland from the three partitioning powers—Russia, Austria, and Germany—and had contended that Poles in America formed a "fourth province of Poland." Many American Poles told themselves that if Poland were only free and independent, they would return in an instant.

When war finally came and Poland was reconstituted as a state at the end of the conflict, however, few of the immigrants chose to return. Many of those who did so were disappointed, finding not the Poland of their dreams but a poor country ravaged by disease, starvation, and internal dissension. Some consciously sought to Americanize the new Poland by introducing modern machinery and technical know-how. One group of returning emigrants summed up this mood in homely fashion: "We will put in every house an American bathtub." But the great majority stayed in America, and even some who had returned to the postwar flush of excitement eventually came back to the United States. The Poles in America had become Polish Americans.

The children of the immigrants, the second generation, truly lived in a hyphenated world. They spoke Polish at home with their parents but felt more fully at ease using English outside the home. They imbibed the popular culture of baseball and the movies, and looked down on old-country customs as outmoded. When they grew to adulthood, they usually married a member of their own ethnic group, but they did not teach Polish to their children. Polish-American organizations also felt the tensions of a bipolar world in the interwar years. The ethnic press continued to flourish, but it published more pages in English than previously. Some organizations of Polish professionals held Election Day dinners at which they served corned beef and cabbage while exhorting their members to vote only for Polish American candidates.

After World War II, economic changes accelerated the deterioration of Polish ethnic consciousness. Postwar prosperity and the widespread availability of the automobile allowed Polish Americans to move to the suburbs. The grandchildren of the original Polish immigrants, the third generation, were raised in an English-speaking, television-watching suburban milieu. They became simply Americans of Polish descent.

ETHNIC GHETTOS

It has long been a truism that immigrants like the Poles formed ethnic ghettos in the American cities where they settled. Social workers, journalists, and other observers often compared the immigrant neighborhoods, dominated by the twin spires of church steeple and factory smokestack, to self-contained medieval villages. This perception increased hostility toward immigrants, who appeared to be forming indigestible, unassimilable lumps of humanity in American cities. Later scholars, for example Oscar Handlin and Louis Wirth, have embedded the idea of the ghetto (the word originally applied to the Jewish quarter of a European city) as the primary residence of first-generation immigrants firmly in the historical and sociological literature.

Recently, however, historians such as Sam Bass Warner, Jr., Howard Chudacoff, Thomas Philpott, and Kathleen Conzen have reassessed the ghetto experience, questioning whether immigrants in fact clustered together as closely as they were presumed to have done. Four points emerge from these historical reassessments: (1) the turn-of-the-century immigrants from southern and eastern Europe were the most likely to cluster together in ghettos; (2) even they, however, rarely dominated a whole neighborhood's population; (3) a majority of each immigrant group's members did not reside in a single ghetto neighborhood; and (4) those individuals who did live in residential clusters for a time did not remain there very long but experienced a high degree of geographic mobility.

Economic forces tended to cluster the turn-of-the-century immigrants more than their predecessors. By 1900 American industry had concentrated production in massive factory complexes such as Chicago's Union Stockyards, the McCormick reaper works, and the Pittsburgh steel mills. Peasant immigrants with few skills but a tradition of hard manual labor easily found jobs as unskilled laborers in these places, but low wages and long hours made it imperative for them to live within walking distance of the plant's gates. The housing stock in these older factory neighborhoods was cheap and run-down, often owned by absentee landlords who did not mind renting to foreigners because they did not themselves live in the neighborhood. Economic constraints thus sharply limited immigrants' choices in the housing market.

Yet the clustering of European immigrants was not legally prescribed, as was the ghettoization of Jews in Europe, or forced by threats of violence, as was the segregation of African Americans. Even if economic constraints had been absent, many immigrants would have clustered together for social and cultural reasons. For instance, immigrants often migrated in human chains. Early arrivals sent money and advice to relatives or friends in the old country, who eventually showed up on their doorsteps in America. Naturally, the established immigrants helped the greenhorns find jobs and housing close by. Immigrants wanted to live near people who spoke their language, practiced the same religion, ate the same foods. As their numbers swelled in particular neighborhoods, they founded self-help societies, small businesses, ethnic churches, and other components of an ethnic ghetto.

Despite the reservations of certain recent historians, it is important to emphasize that some ethnic groups did indeed totally dominate whole neighborhoods of American cities. "Polish downtown," concentrated around Saint Stanislaus Kostka church on the northwest side of Chicago, for example, comprised a contiguous area of eleven precincts roughly three-quarters of a mile long and a half mile wide. In 1900 this area was 86.3 percent Polish. One precinct was 99.6 percent Polish, with only one non-Pole among 2,500 inhabitants: a Chinese cook at the Saint Stanislaus rectory.

Other ethnic groups dispersed more widely than the Poles, but most groups formed at least one clearly defined ethnic ghetto in a large city. The Italians in Chicago, for instance, concentrated in a district near Jane Addams's Hull-House on the West Side. Five precincts in this area each had a population about 63 percent Italian at the turn of the century. One-third of all the Italians in the city resided in this ghetto.

Such neighborhoods overwhelmingly dominated by one ethnic group tended, however, to be exceptional. More typical was the Bridgeport neighborhood on Chicago's Near South Side, home to both Richard J. Daley, Richard M. Daley, and several other Chicago mayors. From the late nineteenth century onward, Bridgeport was roughly one-third Irish, one-third Polish, and one-third Lithuanian, with smaller numbers of Germans and Czechs. The neighborhood, which was clearly defined by such natural boundaries as the south branch of the Chicago River and a wide swath of railroad tracks, measured about a mile and a half long by a mile wide. In 1910 roughly 70 percent of Bridgeport's inhabitants were Catholic, with ten Catholic churches founded by five different ethnic groups. Though all the immigrants shared the same religion and the services were conducted in Latin—a language equally incomprehensible to all—each group demanded a parish of its own, for the church was more than a religious organization; it was a vital social center for its community as well.

Bridgeport was a multiethnic area, but it was not integrated. The major ethnic groups tended to live in definable sections of the district. A common measure of residential segregation, called the index of dissimilarity, can usefully summarize this situation. In 1898, 72 percent of the Poles and 96 percent of the Lithuanians in Bridgeport would have had to change residences in order to achieve an even distribution with the Irish.

Even when members of two different groups lived on the same block, they kept largely to themselves, attending different churches, patronizing different grocery stores, and socializing at different bars and clubs. A Polish immigrant in Bridgeport would walk past the Lithuanian church on Sunday to attend Mass in the Polish church. Though residential clustering reinforced ethnic identity, it was not essential to it. Fundamentally, an ethnic ghetto was a social and cultural phenomenon more than a geographic or demographic identity. Most immigrant groups built toward what sociologists call "institutional completeness," that is, they supported a wide range of institutions which could perform nearly all the services that members required—religious, educational, political, recreational, economic—without recourse to the host society.

The process of ethnic community building often began with thoughts of death. Far from the village churchyard where their ancestors lay, immigrants worried about their final resting places; therefore, they organized death-benefit societies. A tiny yearly payment ensured that members of the societies would be given a decent burial. Other kinds of mutual-aid societies quickly proliferated. Sometimes with the aid of church authorities, federations of such societies bought their own cemeteries on the outskirts of cities. They also provided social activities for the living and made building loans to aid immigrants in buying a house.

The most important institution of an ethnic ghetto was undoubtedly the church. Whether Protestant, Catholic, Jewish, or Orthodox, new immigrants desired to worship together, following familiar rituals from the old country. Most Catholic and many Lutheran parishes built a school next to the church where the group's Old World language and culture, as well as its religion, could be inculcated in the younger generation. Jews, Orthodox, and most Protestants organized weekend or Sunday school classes. Pastors of churches from the same ethnic group also cooperated to build high schools, orphanages, and other social welfare institutions for their compatriots. These facilities were often located in the exceptional ethnic neighborhoods dominated by one group, which then served as alternative downtowns for members of that ethnic group, who might come from all over the city to shop and socialize.

The ethnic community also served as a focus for political action. American politics had long been affected by ethnic and cultural concerns. Throughout the nineteenth century the two major political parties, the Whigs/Republicans and the Democrats, were distinguished from each other mainly by their stance on cultural issues. First the Whig party (which disappeared in the 1850s), then the Republicans, adopted a morally activist position, intervening to impose moral standards on society. For instance, they tried to limit or ban slavery, prohibit alcoholic beverages, and close shops and offices on Sunday, a sabbath day. The Democrats, on the other hand, favored a laissez-faire attitude on cultural issues. The more an ethnic group's culture resembled that of the English Protestant majority, the more often it voted Republican. If, on the contrary, an ethnic group felt alien and outside the mainstream, it tended to support the Democrats, whose permissive views seemed less threatening.

Whenever and wherever ethnic groups clustered in geographic ghettos, their political power tended to increase. Political bosses recognized only one law, the law of numbers. If the majority of voters in a district belonged to a particular ethnic group, the politicians catered to that group with jobs, favors, and symbolic gestures such as parades on ethnic holidays. Political machines in many cities were based on ethnic constituencies of the various wards.

About the only realm of life that escaped the immigrants' drive for institutional completeness was the world of work. Some immigrants opened small businesses that provided jobs and services to their countrymen. In this respect eastern European Jews, Italians, and Greeks proved to be more entrepreneurial than the Irish, the Polish, and some others. For example, vast numbers of Jewish "greenhorns" in New York City labored in the sweatshops of the garment industry, largely owned by earlier Jewish immigrants. This pattern was exceptional, however. The vast majority of immigrants worked in factories or shops owned by native-born American individuals or large corporations.

To sum up, an ethnic ghetto did not need a territorial base to survive, though it was certainly useful to have one. It did, however, require institutional completeness, social networks, and cultural bonds.

Historians have recently debated whether the immigrants who lived in ethnic neighborhoods were "uprooted" individuals or members of intact "transplanted" cultural communities. Oscar Handlin's vastly influential book *The Uprooted* (1951) delineated in novelistic detail the bewildering, disruptive experience of immigration on the lives of individuals. No one who has moved from one country to another can deny the truth of these powerful insights or argue that immigration is not a disorienting, alienating experience. Nevertheless, Handlin probably exaggerated and overgeneralized. In particular, he did not realize how successful many immigrants were in "transplanting" their cultural institutions and social networks. Ultimately, like most historiographical debates, the conflict between Handlin and his numerous critics is rather artificial. The literal meanings of the two metaphors, uprooting and transplanting, suggest that both processes took place. A plant cannot be transplanted unless it is first uprooted. So, too, with human beings: immigrants are uprooted from their own soil and transplanted into new ground. Some wither and die, others survive and flourish, and still others mutate and grow into hybrids. Ethnic ghettos were the seedbeds within which these varied processes took place.

THEORIES OF ETHNICITY AND ASSIMILATION

Contemporaries of the immigrant influx at the turn of the century did not debate whether the newcomers were uprooted or transplanted. Rather, they worried about the future of the immigrants and of the country. The first two decades of the twentieth century were the formative period for theories of ethnicity and assimilation in America.

Four theories of ethnic adjustment and adaptation were proposed early in the century. Two of them, the melting pot and Anglo conformity, stressed the eventual unification of peoples. The other two, the federation of nationalities and cultural pluralism, stressed a continuing diversity. In the broadest terms, these theories set the terms of debate on ethnicity for the rest of the century.

The melting pot is surely the most famous figure of speech applied to the immigrant experience. The concept, though not the exact phrase, was implicit in Crèvecoeur's writings at the time of the Revolution. The idea of an easy melting of the immigrant populace into "new men" underlay the unquestioned optimism of the nineteenth century's approach to immigration.

The term "melting pot" was first used by Israel Zangwill, a British Jew, who wrote a play with that title in 1908. The chief characters were immigrants to New York City: a Russian nobleman who had personally conducted pogroms against Jews in the old country, his beautiful daughter, and a young, penniless Jew whose family had been killed in one of the nobleman's pogroms. Naturally, for this was a romantic play, the young Jew and the nobleman's daughter fall in love. Slowly they discover the tragic truth about their parents, but love and the American dream conquer all as they agree to forget the past and be melded into a new American future.

At the end of *The Melting Pot,* David Quixano, the young Jewish protagonist, announces the theme of the drama as he and his beloved gaze into the sunset.

> There she lies, the great Melting Pot—listen! Can't you hear the roaring and the bubbling? There gapes her mouth—the harbour where a thousand mammoth feeders come from the ends of the world to pour in their human freight. . . . Celt and Latin, Slav and Teuton, Greek and Syrian—black and yellow—. . . . Ah, Vera, what is the glory of Rome and Jerusalem where all nations and races come to worship and look back, compared with the glory of America, where all races and nations come to labour and look forward!

"To look forward!" This was the heart of the melting-pot idea. The world was not yet finished, the ideal American was not yet created, a new and better race was being forged.

The melting-pot idea has been so distorted and misunderstood in recent years that it is worth emphasizing its main features. First, it is a two-way process. Both immigrants and natives are thrown into the melting pot; both give up some of their traits and acquire new ones. It is a process of give and take. Second, it is a forward-looking process. The ideal American type lies in the future, and no one knows exactly what he or she will look like. Finally, the melting-pot theory is a hopeful, generous ideology. It is neither coercive nor repressive.

Around the time of World War I, another, not so generous, ideology—that of 100 percent Americanism and Americanization—sprang up. It has been confused with the melting-pot idea ever since. Americanization began as a movement to enforce the loyalty of German Americans and other foreigners during World War I. It continued for a time afterward, and reached its grotesque climax in the agitation of the Ku Klux Klan during the early 1920s. This rise of the Klan was aimed as much at Catholic and Jewish immigrants as at African Americans.

The ideology of 100 percent Americanism, or Anglo conformity, as sociologists call it today, required immigrants to conform to a preexisting Anglo-American ideal type. Like the melting-pot theory, Anglo conformity envisioned the eventual unification of the American people. Unlike the melting pot, however, there was to be no give and take—it must be all give on the part of the immigrant. Whereas the melting pot was forward-looking, to a new race with new ideals and a new culture, Anglo conformity looked to the past. The Americanizers wanted to preserve intact the Anglo-Saxon Protestant culture that had existed around 1776, allowing no new additions or changes.

Two other prominent theories of ethnicity proposed early in the century envisioned a continuing diversity of peoples in America. These two theories, the federation of nationalities and cultural pluralism, have often been confused.

As immigrants clustered in ghetto neighborhoods in American cities, some ethnic leaders dreamed of transforming these ghettos into small states for their own people. Because America already had a federal system of government, these leaders theorized that some of the states might gradually be dominated by individual ethnic groups and become Polish, German, Italian, or Greek states within the federal union. Each immigrant group would live apart in its own community, with its own language, culture, and institutions; but these separate ethnic states would be economically integrated and united loosely in the federal government. Ironically, some of the more extreme racists among the native-born Americans saw some merit in these ideas. If immigrants stayed together in their own separate states, they would keep away from the Anglo-Saxons and not intermarry with them. A kind of *apartheid* would result.

The federation of nationalities had been tried extensively in Europe. Switzerland successfully practiced it for centuries, with French-, German-, and Italian-speaking cantons. The idea proved spectacularly unsuccessful, however, in the Austro-Hungarian Empire of the nineteenth century and the Soviet Union and Yugoslavia of the twentieth. In all three cases the individual ethnic groups demanded that the multinational state be broken up into its constituent parts.

Federations of nationalities never had much chance as a long-term strategy in the United States. The ethnic enclaves were too small, and too few of them were ethnically homogeneous. In contrast with Europe, members of the various ethnic groups in America were all newcomers without historic ties to any particular territory or piece of ground. Serbs and Croats in Yugoslavia, and Russians and Ukrainians in the Soviet Union had resided in the same territories for centuries, and generations of ancestors were buried in their village graveyards. Thus, the members of those groups harbored fierce attachments to their territory. This was not the case with Jewish immigrants on the Lower East Side of New York and Polish immigrants in the Chicago stockyards district. There, rather than fighting to protect their ethnic neighborhoods, many were striving to escape.

The fourth theory of ethnicity formulated early in the twentieth century envisioned a more subtle and complex form of diversity than the federation of nationalities. Cultural pluralists were typically second- or third-generation descendants of immigrants who realized that ethnic groups would not stay together indefinitely in compact, separate neighborhoods. They felt thoroughly at home in the English language and comfortable with America's economic prosperity and democratic political institutions. Yet they wanted to retain their ancestral language, religion, and customs, along with emotional and symbolic attachments to the old country. In short, they advocated a kind of dual loyalty, believing that immigrants should become American citizens and English should remain the language of government and public life, but that each individual ethnic group should preserve its own language and customs in the privacy of home and family.

German American leaders coined a phrase that summed up the cultural pluralism ideal in homely fashion: "Germania meine Mutter, Columbia meine Braut" (Germany my mother, America my bride). The experience of one such German American, a Lutheran pastor named Francis Hoffmann, points up the tensions involved in living such dual loyalties. Hoffmann married a woman of English background, and when he insisted that she learn German and speak in that tongue at the family dinner table, she nearly divorced him. Immigrants and their descendants have long found cultural pluralism as difficult a balancing act as balancing loyalty to one's mother with devotion to one's bride, and usually their children abandon one loyalty or the other.

After the formative period of ethnic theorizing in the first two decades of the twentieth century, interethnic relations experienced a period of quiet consensus on what was called the melting pot but was really Anglo conformity. The immigration restriction acts of the 1920s effectively ended mass immigration from Europe, and Americans hoped that gradually the immigrants would melt into the Anglo-Saxon mainstream. It is important to emphasize that the pressure for conformity was presented in the generous guise of the melting pot, once the Americanization hysteria surrounding World War I died down. Had it continued as overt, coercive pressure, as in the Ku Klux Klan, it probably would have backfired, for it would have galvanized immigrants' resistance. Many of the ethnic groups that came to America had long histories of resisting cultural repression in Europe. Indeed, it seems almost impossible to destroy a people's ethnic consciousness by coercion.

To say this does not, however, mean that ethnic consciousness remained unchanged. Tyrants cannot repress ethnicity with force, but democracies can sap its vitality with blandishments. In the 1920s, 1930s, and 1940s Americans offered assimilation as an opportunity, not a punishment. Their use of the term "melting pot" for what was essentially Anglo conformity helped break down immigrants' resistance. In short, America seduced European immigrants into abandoning much of their own ethnic consciousness and adopting an American national identity.

After World War II, theorists of assimilation noted that ethnic melting had proceeded fairly rapidly and that a different kind of pluralism had also appeared. A Yale sociologist, Ruby Jo Reeves Kennedy, published a series of articles demonstrating that ethnic intermarriage was increasing rapidly but always seemed to stay within religious boundaries. That is, the various Catholic ethnic groups, such as Irish, Poles, and Italians, intermarried freely with each other but did not marry Protestants or Jews. Similarly, eastern European and German Jews intermarried but did not marry Gentiles. Based on this evidence, Kennedy postulated a triple melting pot. Ethnic groups were melting, but the result was not complete unity; rather, it was a kind of religious triculturalism. Will Herberg, a Jewish religious scholar, popularized these sociological findings in his book *Protestant, Catholic, Jew* (1955).

At mid century the "triple melting pot" theory enjoyed brief status as a kind of orthodoxy, for it suited the temper of the times. It assured Americans that the melting process was advancing while accommodating the obvious evidence that not all cultural differences between groups had disappeared. By emphasizing religious rather than ethnic differences, this theory harmonized with the much-noted revival of religious practice of the 1950s.

Nathan Glazer and Daniel Patrick Moynihan made a final refinement to the neo-melting-pot theory in their study of ethnic groups in New York, *Beyond the Melting Pot* (1963). A single line from this book has been much quoted, out of context: "The point about the melting pot is that it did not happen." What the authors meant is that the *single* melting pot did not happen. Glazer and Moynihan accepted the reigning "triple melting pot" theory but made it multiple by adding the variable of race. They agreed, for the most part, with Will Herberg that European ethnic groups had melted in culturally along religious lines, but they noted the obvious fact that black Protestants did not meld with white Protestants. Thus, New York City in the 1960s was a mosaic of groups based on religion and race. Glazer and Moynihan also made the important observation that these religious and racial groupings constituted political interest groups as much as cultural entities.

THE ETHNIC REVIVAL

Shortly after *Beyond the Melting Pot* appeared, its misapprehended statement that the melting pot had never happened became the rallying cry of an ethnic revival. The black civil rights movement of the 1960s was the catalyst for this revival in two ways. First, the black revolt and the sympathy it elicited from wealthy white liberals stirred up great resentment among the lower middle class, who happened to be mainly descendants of European immigrants. They felt ground between the millstones of increasingly politicized inner-city blacks and their white suburban sympathizers, the "limousine liberals." The reaction of lower-middle-class communities was first called white backlash, but later a white ethnic revival.

The second way the black revolution stimulated white ethnics was by example. Black-power leaders gained media attention by being militant, noisy, and offensive, so some white ethnic leaders imitated them. Michael Novak, a Catholic intellectual of Slovak background, summed up this white ethnic assertiveness in his book *The Rise of the Unmeltable Ethnics* (1972), an impassioned polemic that invoked a supposedly more natural, earthy eastern European ethnic past as an antidote to the powerlessness of the white American masses. The political outcome of all this resentment was Alabama Governor George Wallace's independent campaign for the presidency in 1972, which attracted the votes of many northern white ethnics as well as those of his natural constituency of southern whites.

The rage of the lower middle class in the late 1960s and early 1970s was actually based more on class grievances and racial animosity than on ethnicity. Few of the third-generation descendants of immigrants had retained their grandparents' language or customs, and not many followed Novak's urgings to revive them. Nonetheless, ethnicity became all the rage with politicians, academic scholars, and philanthropic foundations.

In 1972 Congress passed the Ethnic Heritage Studies Centers Bill, introduced by Chicago Congressman Roman Pucinski. The law authorized grants to school systems to develop curricula that would teach children from various ethnic groups about their own heritage. Though the congressional funding provided only enough money for pilot programs, the act marked the first time that the federal government had granted official recognition to ethnic groups in the United States.

The Ford Foundation provided more substantial funding for three separate ethnic studies projects, beginning with an extensive series of consultations on ethnicity, arranged by the American Jewish Committee, that brought together academic scholars and ethnic leaders. The second project funded by the Ford Foundation was the Center for the Study of American Pluralism, virtually a one-man think tank organized by the priest-sociologist Andrew M. Greeley at Chicago's National Opinion Research Center. The third institution founded during the ethnic revival was also the work of one man, the Roman Catholic Monsignor Geno Baroni, who started the National Center for Urban Ethnic Affairs. All three of these intellectual manifestations of ethnicity worked to deflect the rage of white ethnics away from protest politics and toward cultural concerns. Their impact on the masses was slight, but they helped spur an outpouring of academic books and articles about ethnic groups in America that has not abated.

In short, the ethnic revival made it respectable and profitable for scholars to write about ethnicity, but it did not signal a widespread renaissance of European ethnic cultures in America.

EVOLVING LATINO CONSCIOUSNESS

Theorists of the 1960s focused primarily on ethnic survival and revival among descendants of European immigrants. Yet at the very time they were writing, a new influx of immigrants was arriving in the United States, mainly from Asia and Latin America. In 1965 Congress passed a fundamental revision of the immigration law that abolished the discriminatory national origins quotas of the 1920s and put all countries of the world on an equal footing. Large numbers from China, Japan, the Philippines, and elsewhere in Asia, as well as from Mexico and Central and South America, took advantage of the new openness. In the 1970s and 1980s, immigration flows again approached the million-a-year level that had been so common in the first years of the century. In addition, many migrants from the American commonwealth of Puerto Rico, as well as numerous illegal immigrants from Mexico—neither group appears in official immigration figures—have swelled the numbers of newcomers to the United States mainland.

The Spanish-speaking nationalities provide an interesting case study in the evolution of ethnic consciousness. Like the European immigrants before them, Spanish-speaking newcomers have tended to cluster in just a few areas. Nearly 75 percent of them reside in five states: California, Texas, Florida, New York, and Illinois. Furthermore, one nationality usually dominates in most of these areas—for example, Puerto Ricans in New York, Cubans in Miami, and Mexicans in California and Texas. Chicago is unusual in that it has received significant numbers of Puerto Ricans and Mexicans, as well as smaller populations of Cubans, Central Americans, and South Americans.

The census and most English-language media employ the word "Hispanic" as an umbrella term to designate all the Spanish-speaking people in America. Yet many community leaders prefer to call themselves "Latinos," because "Hispanic" refers to the Spanish conquerors of Central and South America. Labeling Latin Americans "Hispanics" is akin to calling Irishmen "Britons" simply because they come from one of the British Isles and were long ruled by Great Britain. "Latino" is a more neutral label for all migrants who come from south of the border, a shortened term for "Latin American."

Theoretically, migrants from Cuba, Puerto Rico, and Mexico enjoy several options for forging an ethnic identity. They could remain separate nationalities or melt individually into the American mass. Alternatively, they could join the multiple melting pot in one of two ways, by coalescing into a bloc with other Catholic ethnic groups or by forming a consortium of the oppressed with African Americans and other peoples of color. Many Latin American leaders, however, have pursued the altogether different strategy of "Latinismo," or Latino consciousness. They have tried to unify the various nationalities emigrating from Mexico, Puerto Rico, and Central and South America into one ethnic group based on their common use of the Spanish language and common experience of economic and political discrimination in the United States.

That is, they are trying to forge a Latino melting pot alongside those based on religion and race.

It is impossible to tell how successful this attempt to form an interethnic consciousness has been among Latino groups. As a community organizer remarked to sociologist Felix Padilla: "I try to use Latino as much as I can. When I talk to people in my community, I use Mexican, but I use Latino when the situation calls for issues that have city-wide implications" (*Latino Ethnic Consciousness*, p. 62). "Latino" is an essentially political word, used to unite various nationalities into one political interest group, as Glazer and Moynihan noted. So far only a very tenuous pan-Asian consciousness movement has appeared among recent immigrants from China, the Philippines, and elsewhere in the Far East.

Ethnicity has clearly been an important factor in American history, but there is scant agreement among scholars as to how significant it has been and how much of it remains today.

One way of looking at the role of ethnicity is to consider each major theory of ethnic assimilation as a stage through which most ethnic groups passed in succession. As a rule, newly arrived immigrants, whether Germans in Cincinnati in 1850 or Poles in Chicago in 1900 or Mexicans in Los Angeles in 1970, initially followed the federation of nationalities model, clustering together in ethnic ghettos and building a dense complex of social and cultural institutions. The second generation, the children of those immigrants, abandoned the ghettos and lived in the world of cultural pluralism, speaking English most of the time but using their ancestors' language to communicate with their parents. The third and subsequent generations followed one of the unifying models, either seeking to become carbon-copy WASPS, according to the Anglo conformity theory, or diving into the multiple melting pots of religion, race, or wider ethnic consciousness. The ideal of the single melting pot, a unified American nationality incorporating the best traits of all the immigrants, still functions for many as a beacon for the future.

Some recent immigrants, such as Latinos and Asian Americans, are still in the earlier stages of federation of nationalities and cultural pluralism. However, they may not move on to the unifying stages as swiftly as European immigrants did, since the government now grants more legitimacy to ethnic groups as collective entities than in the past. Since about 1970, African Americans, Latinos, Native Americans, and Asian Americans have been recognized as "official" minority groups, eligible for affirmative action preferences in employment to redress past discrimination. Now bilingual education is legally required for non-English-speaking groups. Though government policy prescribes bilingualism as a transitional strategy designed to ease the adjustment of new immigrants, it may actually lead newcomers to greater maintenance of their language and culture. Furthermore, the homelands of most Latin American immigrants are much closer to the American border than Europe is, and many Latino migrants go back and forth frequently. Some sociologists have noted that Puerto Ricans and Mexicans in particular sometimes maintain what are virtually dual home bases.

Descendants of European immigrants, however, do not seem to retain much ethnic consciousness today. Certainly the old-country languages have not persisted beyond the second generation, and the ethnic heritage studies centers funded by the federal government have been neither very widespread nor very successful in teaching ethnic history.

At the height of the ethnic revival, Rudolph Vecoli, founder of the Immigration History Research Center archives in Minnesota, assessed the status of his own ethnic group, the Italian Americans:

> What in Italian Americans is still distinctively Italian? On the face of it, very little. . . .
>
> To speak, then, of an Italian American cultural heritage is not to refer to "high culture" but rather to an urban culture which is a compound of southern Italian and American working class folkways. . . .
>
> At the risk of caricaturing . . . one can catalogue what appear to be its salient qualities: the obligation of loyalty to family and friends; the emphasis on domesticity . . . ; the dominant role of the male; the importance of cutting a fine figure . . . ; the overflowing hospitality; the passion for good food and drink; the respect for authority figures. ("The Italian Americans," p. 38)

As Vecoli noted, such vestigial cultural traits tend toward caricature and stereotype, and are hardly unique to any one group. Viewed this way, ethnicity is hard to define, but you know it when you see it.

The sociologist Milton Gordon, in the single best book to emerge from the ethnic revival of the 1960s, *Assimilation in American Life* (1964), suggested another approach to explain what is left of ethnicity today. He drew a sharp distinction between cultural assimilation, which he felt was far advanced in American society, and structural assimilation, which had not proceeded so far.

Cultural assimilation, or simply acculturation, means adopting the language, customs, patterns of consumption, values, norms, and belief systems of the host society. Clearly, this has occurred almost universally among descendants of European immigrants. Members of all these groups speak English, pursue conspicuous consumption, receive most of their popular culture—and the majority of their opinions—from television, wave the flag on cue, and act like Americans while traveling overseas.

Structural assimilation means mingling with others in the host society at school and work, as well as in voluntary associations, friendship groups, and social activities. The ultimate stage of structural assimilation is intermarriage. Though Americans of different ethnic backgrounds often mix at work or school, their family, church, fraternal societies, and friendship groups are still structured along ethnic lines.

Taking intermarriage as the ultimate index of structural assimilation, we can conclude that this kind of assimilation is occurring slowly, mostly along the lines of the multiple melting pot. Most studies of marriage patterns in the United States find that intermarriage rates of all kinds are increasing but that racial intermarriage still occurs infrequently, whereas marriage across religious lines is quite common, and nationality intermarriage is the most common of all.

Ethnicity is just one factor that Americans use to construct their social identities. Probably the strongest identities are those which result from the intersection of several different factors, such as class, religion, race, or ethnicity. Milton Gordon coined the word "ethclass" to describe this phenomenon of intersecting identities. Some examples of ethclasses are lower-middle-class Polish Catholics, upper-middle-class Jewish professionals, wealthy Scots Presbyterians, poor African American evangelical Protestants, and working-class Mexican Americans. Perhaps the majority of Americans live out their lives largely within the confines of such ethclasses. There has been much fusing of ethnic groups over the years, but ethnic pluralism and diversity still dominate the American scene.

Amid such diversity, greater knowledge about other groups and a spirit of acceptance of them are essential; and so is a sense of humor. Ethnic jokes are often condemned as pejorative and insensitive, but when they are targeted at a person's own group as well as at others, and delivered with a light touch, they can be powerful solvents of hostility. In a homely version of the melting pot, ethnic humor from many nationalities has long enriched American popular culture.

Louis Adamic, a Slovenian immigrant intellectual and a prolific writer on American culture early in the twentieth century, provided an apt prescription for survival in America in the title of his autobiography, *Laughing in the Jungle* (1932). His conclusion sounds very contemporary and contains good advice:

> Immigration is in no small way to blame for the fact that the United States today is more a jungle than a civilization—a land of deep economic, social, spiritual, and intellectual chaos and distress—in which, it seems to me, by far the most precious possession a sensitive and intelligent person can have is an active sense of humor. (p. ix)

BIBLIOGRAPHY

Theoretical and Interpretive Works

Adamic, Louis. *Laughing in the Jungle* (1932; repr. 1969).

Berkson, Isaac. *Theories of Americanization: A Critical Study, with Special Reference to the Jewish Group* (1920).

Bodnar, John E. *The Transplanted: A History of Immigrants in Urban America* (1985). A reinterpretation of the immigrant experience.

Chudacoff, Howard P. "A New Look at Ethnic Neighborhoods: Residential Dispersion and the Concept of Visibility in a Medium-sized City." *Journal of American History* 60, no. 1 (1973): 76–93.

Conzen, Kathleen Neils. "Immigrants, Immigrant Neighborhoods, and Ethnic Identity: Historical Issues." *Journal of American History* 66, no. 3 (1979): 603–615.

Gordon, Milton M. *Assimilation in American Life* (1964).

Grant, Madison. *The Passing of the Great Race; or, The Racial Basis of European History* (1916).

Handlin, Oscar. *The Uprooted; The Epic Story of the Great Migrations That Made the American People* (1951, repr. 1973). A classic. The single best study of the immigrant experience.

———. *Race and Nationality in American Life* (1957).

Higham, John. *Send These to Me: Jews and Other Immigrants in Urban America* (1975).

Kallen, Horace M. *Culture and Democracy in the United States: Studies in the Group Psychology of the American Peoples* (1924; repr. 1970).

Mann, Arthur. *The One and the Many: Reflections on the American Identity* (1979).

Novak, Michael. *The Rise of the Unmeltable Ethnics: Politics and Culture in the Seventies* (1972). A polemical tract from the ethnic revival.

St. John de Crèvecoeur, J. Hector. *Letters from an American Farmer* (1782; facs. repr. 1968).

Warner, Sam Bass, Jr., and Colin Burke. "Cultural Change and the Ghetto." *Journal of Contemporary History* 4, no. 4 (1969): 173–187.

Case Studies

Greene, Victor R. *For God and Country: The Rise of Polish and Lithuanian Ethnic Consciousness in America, 1860–1910* (1975). Analyzes the development of Polish ethnic consciousness.

Handlin, Oscar. *Boston's Immigrants, 1790–1865: A Study in Acculturation* (1941).

Howe, Irving. *World of Our Fathers* (1976). Jews in New York.

Kantowicz, Edward R. *Polish-American Politics in Chicago, 1888–1940* (1975).

Pacyga, Dominic A. *Polish Immigrants and Industrial Chicago: Workers on the South Side, 1880–1922* (1991).

Padilla, Felix M. *Latino Ethnic Consciousness: The Case of Mexican Americans and Puerto Ricans in Chicago* (1985). Examines the growth of a common ethnic feeling among Puerto Ricans and Mexicans.

Wirth, Louis. *The Ghetto* (1928). Classic sociological study of Chicago's Jewish ghetto.

Comparative Studies

Barton, Josef J. *Peasants and Strangers: Italians, Rumanians, and Slovaks in an American City, 1890–1950,* (1975). Three ethnic groups in Cleveland.

Bodnar, John F., Roger Simon, and Michael P. Weber. *Lives of Their Own: Blacks, Italians, and Poles in Pittsburgh, 1900–1960* (1981). Blacks and ethnic whites in Pittsburgh.

Davis, Allen F., and Mark H. Haller. *The Peoples of Philadelphia* (1976).

Glazer, Nathan, and Daniel Patrick Moynihan. *Beyond the Melting Pot: The Negroes, Puerto Ricans, Jews, Italians, and Irish of New York City* (1963; repr. 1970). New York's ethnic groups.

Greene, Victor R. *American Immigrant Leaders, 1800–1910: Marginality and Identity* (1987).

Holli, Melvin G., and Peter d'A. Jones. *Ethnic Chicago* (1984).

Philpott, Thomas Lee. *The Slum and the Ghetto: Neighborhood Deterioration and Middle-Class Reform, Chicago, 1880–1930* (1978). Blacks and ethnic whites in Chicago.

Thernstrom, Stephan, et al. *The Harvard Encyclopedia of American Ethnic Groups* (1980). Landmark reference book containing both topical essays and articles on individual ethnic groups.

Vecoli, Rudolph. "The Italian Americans." *Center* 7 (July–August 1974): 31–43.

Ward, David. *Cities and Immigrants* (1971). A geographical study of settlement patterns.

SEE ALSO **Immigration**; **Minorities and Work**; **Nativism, Anti-Catholicism, and Anti-Semitism**; and various articles in the section "**Ethnic and Racial Subcultures.**"

SOCIAL CLASS

Ronald Story

SEVENTEENTH-CENTURY EUROPEANS and Native Americans would probably have collided violently under the best of circumstances because the "Indians" inhabited territory the Europeans wanted for themselves. But the fact that European and Native American cultures of the period differed drastically made the collision particularly deadly. The village-oriented subsistence societies of most North American Indians, including those in the eastern forest regions, rested on powerful kinship and tribal ties, common land possession and equitable distribution of wealth, consensus leadership with significant female participation, and a totemistic spiritual reverence for the Earth. Contemporary European society, by contrast, rested increasingly on the male-dominant nuclear family, on private property and the unequal distribution of wealth, on coercive government by the few or by one, and on a utilitarian view of the earth as exploitable for present gain. In England, moreover, while economic and political innovations from sheep-raising and mining to piracy and absolutism rocked the feudal orders and set off an acquisitive scramble among the better-off, artisans steadily lost purchasing power and peasants their place on the land. The gap between rich and poor thus grew more obvious, English society more unstable, the struggle for wealth and power on the one hand and survival and safety on the other more ruthless and desperate, the class divisions and acquisitive individualism of European culture more intense—and the difference between Indians and Europeans more profound. The result, in areas of concentrated early settlement, was the systematic, sometimes brutal displacement of Indian communities.

CLASS DIVISIONS IN THE EARLY COLONIES

The Southern Colonies The early Virginia Company distributed private land to shareholders and settlers, thus duplicating English ownership patterns and establishing the norms for future settlement. The availability of productive land, the rise of a strong European tobacco market, and the uniform grimness of Chesapeake life initially produced significant equality of circumstance and opportunity. Most early landholders, for example, were not well-born; a third of new political officeholders were either illiterate or former indentured servants; and the median wealth of the top fifth of the white population was just forty times that of the bottom fifth, a far lower multiple than in contemporary England. The starkest early class division in this predominantly male society was between those who owned land of whatever amount, and those, chiefly indentured servants, who worked it (more often than not to their death).

As landholdings grew larger and the demand for labor greater, Chesapeake planters came to rely less on indentured servants, who were starting to outlive their indentures and become a public nuisance and political threat, and more on African slaves, who would never become free, could be more directly controlled, and were in any case better workers. In 1670 there were two thousand slaves in Virginia, most from Caribbean island colonies; in 1700 there were twenty thousand, most from Africa itself. The consequences for the class structure were profound. Slaves were more permanent and productive farm laborers than servants, giving a decisive competitive advantage to their owners. And slaves cost more, meaning that ownership would be concentrated among the prosperous. By the early eighteenth century wealthy planters owned two-thirds of all Chesapeake slaves, thus putting real distance between themselves and those below, who now possessed property worth less than one hundredth of that of the top fifth. The planter elite, possessed now of easily transmissible land and laborers, gradually consolidated itself through intermarriage and political alliances and favorable access to English credit, culture, and imperial preferment. Farther down the social hierarchy, large numbers of white farmers (including many former servants) worked usually marginal land with mostly family labor. Restless to the point of rebellion in the 1660s and 1670s, these smallholders grew quieter by the early 1700s, their hope for advancement pinned chiefly on a turn in tobacco prices (which seldom came) or cheap land on the frontier (which took a backbreaking generation to develop), their consciousness and resentment of the wealthy dulled by illiteracy, rural isolation, and the overwhelming fact that, unlike the servile Africans, they were, after all, white and free.

The New England Colonies Puritan New England sought to combat the materialism and economic conflict of the seventeenth century by constructing "Christian Commonwealths" centering on church life and such humble occupations as subsistence farming and traditional crafts. The impact of this attempt at egalitarianism was minimal on the New England Indian communities, which, with few exceptions, were as quickly and decisively displaced as in Virginia. The impact on settler society was more significant. Initial land distributions were remarkably even, and colonial officials frequently imposed either wage or price controls to prevent windfall accumulations of personal wealth. For this reason, and because New England provided fewer ways to attain wealth than did England or the Chesapeake and so attracted fewer ruthless profit-seekers, the distance between rich and poor during the first two generations of settlement was five or six to one, among the narrowest in modern history. Both church and town polity were broadly participatory, moreover, and most landowners could expect to hold local office at some time.

Yet New England society was not wholly egalitarian. A "Standing Order" of ministers and prominent landholders existed from the start; these were gradually joined by merchants in the seaboard towns. The ministry remained important throughout the century, particularly in traditional areas. But as opportunities for trade increased, the merchant group, which could consolidate and bequeath its wealth more easily than ministers could their pulpits, gained in prominence at the expense of the ministers. The Standing Order thus acquired a more commercial, less spiritual hue; in the towns the top tenth of the population owned by 1700 nearly 40 percent of the wealth. Villages meanwhile continued, partly for lack of alternatives, to practice subsistence family farming. For this reason and also because of the persistence of intense piety in backcountry communities, women, though clearly subordinate to men, were integral to New England society—as defenders of the faith, gardeners and household organizers, involved neighbors, deputy husbands, and mothers and grandmothers to extended families—in a way that was not true in the southern colonies.

The Middle Colonies The largest middle colonies followed divergent paths. In New York the Dutch and later the first English governors bestowed vast Hudson River estates on favored families. Tenants gradually occupied this land on long leases. Some used the profits from fur trapping and wheat production to purchase their farms outright. Most, however, remained tenants, leaving to their landlords not only the profit from processing the grain but the capital gains from owning the land. Early New York thus ended up with the closest approximation of feudal relations—great tracts tenanted by a nonowning European peasantry—in British North America. But the Hudson River also funneled all agricultural produce through New York City, leading to rapid urban growth, a thriving merchant elite, and an unusually large artisan community drawn from France and Holland as well as from England. Perhaps reflecting the manorial tradition, wealthy New Yorkers owned more African slaves than other northern elites; by the early eighteenth century Africans comprised one tenth of the population of New York City.

Pennsylvania land tenure differed from New York's in that most land grants went outright to actual settlers, so that this fertile colony consisted from the beginning chiefly of freehold family farms producing grain and other commodities for Atlantic markets. In the early eighteenth century the upper tenth of Pennsylvania's rural population owned only one fifth of the land, a distribution resembling New England's rather than New York's. The colony's chief elite was therefore in Philadelphia, where an aggressive Quaker merchant community was busily making Philadelphia a major center for carrying and merchandising British colonial products. Philadelphia's artisans—including Germans as well as English and encompassing printing, cabinetmaking, and metalworking along with the maritime and building trades—was comparatively large and prosperous in this period, with a well-developed but demanding apprenticeship program that inculcated civic responsibility and old-world craft traditions. Founded on principles of religious tolerance, Pennsylvania's free population as a whole quickly exhibited a singular ethnic and religious diversity. The slave population, far smaller than New York's, was confined chiefly to Philadelphia.

SLAVERY, LAND OWNERSHIP, AND THE FORMATION OF CLASS DIVISIONS

The flourishing of trade within the British imperial system of the eighteenth century had several consequences with regard to the American class structure. One was that as southern staple agriculture (particularly tobacco but also rice, indigo, and cotton) steadily expanded, so did the system of African slavery. By the 1760s slaves numbered two hundred thousand. They constituted a third of the southern colonial population as a whole and 40 percent of the Chesapeake region, where nearly two-thirds of all southerners still lived. The growth of imperial trade, which rewarded the well-connected, and the spread of slave labor, which rewarded the well-capitalized, both worked to concentrate wealth in elite hands. By mid century the richest tenth owned nearly half of southern wealth and, along with representatives of the crown, dominated the colonial governments, courts, and Anglican churches. The great planters of the Chesapeake developed an upper-class gentry standard of living centering on the country estate, the county seat, and the colonial assembly; those of the Carolinas gravitated more towards the urban center of Charleston in an effort to escape the fevers of the rice fields. Both groups, though self-confident and self-conscious in their own right, were also strongly Anglophile, tapping England not only for credit, connections, and contracts but also for ideas, books, fashions, and models of behavior.

A chief source of imperial trading profit was the slaves themselves, whom English and northern colonial shippers imported from West and South-Central Africa for sale to the tobacco and rice planters. Divided by language, custom, and circumstance, united by enslavement and racism, by the mid eighteenth century slaves, a majority of whom were now American-born, had developed a distinctive African American culture whose main features included the creation of extended kinship networks based on "adoption" rituals and the devising of collective methods, ranging from subterfuge to revolt, of resisting the white master. Of the nonslaveholding whites, meanwhile, although nearly one quarter were tenants or wage-earners who owned very little, well over half enjoyed title to their land, still a high figure compared to Europe. These so-called nondescript farmers consumed roughly 60 percent of what they produced and bartered the rest (mostly grain and livestock) for tools and other goods they could not make. Increasingly, such smallholders were to be found in the Appalachian foothills where land remained relatively cheap. Increasingly, the foothills contained not only English but thousands of poor and combative Scotch-Irish, whose emotional Calvinism, hostility to England, and distance from the coast divided them from the seaboard elites even as their economic anxiety and false sense of superiority divided them from the African Americans.

Northern farmers experienced something of a Malthusian crisis in the eighteenth century in which children inherited too little land for viable farming. Three factors prevented widespread rural immiserization. One was increased land productivity, particularly from gardens and orchards. A second was the safety valve of the frontier. Partially protected by British forts, partially peopled by a broad stream of German and Scotch-Irish newcomers, the frontier districts of Vermont, New York, and Pennsylvania were not only sources of profit to land speculators but, as in the South, places for starting new farms. They were also places that bred discontent, not only with absentee landlords and uncaring colonial assemblies but, eventually, with the proclamation of 1763 that seemed to bar further expansion.

But British mercantilism not only made the eighteenth-century American frontier more accessible. It also made American towns and cities more prosperous. Factor three in reducing rural misery thus became the colonial towns and especially the seaports. By the 1760s nearly 15 percent of all northerners lived in places with twenty-five hundred or more people. Boston, New York, and Philadelphia each had more than fifteen thousand people, Providence and New Haven nearly ten thousand, many of them migrants from the hinterlands traveling eastward rather than westward to find competency and fortune.

In one sense urban class divisions were relatively insignificant. Except in its rarified imperial reaches, commerce remained easier to enter than plantation agriculture, particularly for prosperous craftsmen familiar with trade. As commerce flourished, moreover, so did the crafts themselves, with artisans producing not only maritime goods such as boats, sails, ropes, anchors, and barrels but rum and hats for Europe and Africa, silverwork and fine furniture for the elite, and buildings, wagons, horseshoes, candles, and ale for the citizenry. Thriving commerce and crafts, in turn, meant work for the laborers who hauled the materials and cargo and the sailors who manned the ships; apprenticeship programs also enabled some wage earners to enter the crafts. Meanwhile, the proliferation of churches, taverns, and printshops as well as the constant arrival of ships from interesting climes bearing interesting commodities and people made seaport cultural life for all ranks the liveliest and most diverting in the colonies.

In another sense, however, urban class divisions did matter. For one thing, the benefits of prosperity were imperfectly shared. The top 5 percent of the population (the imperial mercantile establishment) owned 25 percent of everything in the 1690s, but 40 percent by the 1770s. At the other end, not only did the share of the lowest two-fifths of the population fall from over 10 percent to less than 5 percent, indicating slippage among the artisans, but the proportion of laborers rose and so did the number of transients and destitute, indicating that towns were neither fully absorbing those who needed work nor adequately paying those who found it. Urban class divisions also mattered because they affected urban politics, in which artisans as well as small shippers and traders and even sailors and laborers had long played a role alongside the elite. Two political changes were especially notable. The number of riots—mass actions against property or representatives of property—increased steadily through the century until they were commonplace by the 1760s. And the rioters increasingly targeted not other gangs or religious denominations or opponents in boundary disputes, as previously, but members of the mercantile establishment and representatives of imperial authority.

THE AMERICAN REVOLUTION AND THE EMERGING ELITE

Social class was also important in another sense. The Americans' revolution occurred in part because Americans succeeded in forging intercolonial unity. And this unity developed in part along class and occupational lines. Thus ambitious lesser merchants in Boston and Providence, particularly those engaged in the coastal trade or new to commerce and the seaports, got to know their counterparts in New York and Philadelphia and joined with them to resist British monopoly power. Master artisans as well as apprentices and journeymen sometimes moved from one colony to another, carrying political information and ideas from one artisan community to another. Artisans also found voice in the almanacs, pamphlets, and broadsides of the era, most of them produced (if not written) by artisan printers and finding special favor with artisan readers. Farmers, the most isolated of the great occupational sectors, united across colonial boundaries chiefly by way of the religious revivalism that swept all of British North America in the 1730s and 1740s, simmered in the 1750s, then erupted anew in middle and southern areas in the 1760s. Though not explicitly class-conscious, the revivals weakened traditional patterns of backcountry deference and revealed (and probably fanned) resentment at the corruption of established churches, including Anglicanism, and the pride of urban elites, including the mercantile establishment.

That Americans managed to unite across class lines as well as along them owed in large measure to the unifying abstractness of the legal and constitutional language in which they thought and talked in these years. They used this language in part precisely because of this convenient abstractness, in part because the constitutional nature of the quarrel with England impelled them to. They also used it because so many colonial leaders, including many plantation owners, had for the first time been trained in the law not in London's Inns of Court but in colonial law offices by American-born lawyers. In this sense the revolution marked the emergence of a dominant new profession, largely at this point a preserve of the elite, that would profoundly shape political rhetoric in future decades. Yet the abstract rhetoric of the lawyers did not encompass everyone, even in revolutionary America. Women played a notable revolutionary role by orchestrating nonimportation agreements, raising money and material for the armies, and running farms and shops while the men fought and died. Women's self-esteem, consciousness, and sense of independence grew, and out of this experience came the first women's academies and therefore the first cohort of well-educated women. The revolution did not bring political or legal rights to women, however. Nor did it liberate the mass of African Americans. The few thousand free blacks, mostly northern, participated, and sometime died, for the patriot cause; northern states moved to end slavery there, and African American urban communities created enduring churches, schools, and associations in these years. But most African Americans were southern slaves. Although the fighting of the late 1770s allowed some slaves to escape and libertarian sentiments led some planters to manumit their slaves, for the vast majority of southern slaves the lawyers' writ of freedom did not run.

While farm and artisan families actively contributed to the revolution's success, the Constitution was largely composed by an elite. Southern planters gained the three-fifths clause, a fugutive slave clause, and the right to import slaves for at least twenty years. Northern merchants gained a vast free-trade market for which Congress would set tariffs, regulate money, standardize weights and measures, require common jurisprudence, and enforce a powerful contract clause. Both groups got a president strong enough to make war and suppress rebellion and a senate, federal judiciary, and electoral college once removed from popular control. But the framers took commoners' interests into account, leaving the states with considerable authority, for example, and promising and delivering a Bill of Rights, and artisans vigorously supported the Constitution and helped ratify it. Most farmers came to support it as well. It provided, after all, authority whereby the transappalachian west might be opened for settlement. Farmers—and planters, too—liked that. The Native Americans of the interior, needless to say, did not. Many of them had supported the British during the war as a way of keeping the Americans at bay. They feared that Britain's defeat put their control of the Ohio and Mississippi valleys and therefore their free-ranging, communal way of life in mortal danger. And they were right.

THE NEW REPUBLIC AND THE DISTRIBUTION OF WEALTH

The withdrawal of British authority affected the formation of a class of elite over the coming decades in several ways. It shook the pro-British Tory establishment that most relied on imperial connections and protection, and cleared the way, particularly in the North, for new men eager to open nonimperial markets and develop alternative commodities. Opportunities also arose to develop new sources of credit, not only in the creation of a national bank and a national debt, but in the state-chartered banks and insurance companies that sprang up to convert accumulated funds into venture capital. And independence focused attention on the continent as well as on the ocean, leading eventually to a far-flung national market protected by tariff barriers and integrated by wagon, water, and rail. Yet all this merely diluted without shattering the seaboard elites. The spread of plantation agriculture through the lower South following the invention of the cotton gin in 1793 left some southeastern planters stranded on worn-out estates. Most, however, benefited from westward expansion by either settling the richest Gulf lands themselves or selling slaves to those who did. Northern capitalists similarly adapted. The opening of the Erie Canal in 1826 poured such wealth into New York that by mid century the city was a major financial center. Merchant capital in Boston and Philadelphia meanwhile flowed into textiles, coal, iron, and machinery as well as banking, insurance, and railroads.

The Antebellum South In 1860 the top 10 percent of white families owned half the South's property and two-thirds of its slaves. In the northeastern cities one tenth of the population owned three-fourths of all property by 1860; the top 1 percent owned half. But despite this similarity of property ownership, the regional elites did not become a united national upper class before the Civil War. The chief reason for this was that the issue of slave versus free labor created a vast chasm between the southerners, whose prosperity rested on huge investments in forced agricultural labor, and their northern counterparts, who prospered by investing in labor-saving industrial machinery. Contrasting ideologies—deferred gratification, superior education, and pecuniary achievement in the North, racist paternalism, rustic chivalry, and personal violence in the South—compounded the problem. Powerful national financial and cultural institutions might have bridged this gap at least temporarily. Instead, the Civil War destroyed the basis of the division by destroying the slave wealth and political power of the great planters and thus their relevance to elite formation.

There were some 4 million slaves by the mid nineteenth century. Slaves comprised about one-third of the population in the fifteen states that permitted slavery and half the population of the "black belt" running from South Carolina through the Gulf states to Texas. Their circumstances varied. One tenth, for example, lived in towns or cities and had greater freedom of movement and a wider range of contacts than in the country. One fourth did domestic, industrial, construction, or other nonagricultural work, often developing significant skills and sophisticated knowledge of white ways, and another 15 percent worked on tobacco, rice, and sugar plantations, where unsupervised task labor was not uncommon, rather than on cotton plantations, where gang labor under an overseer or driver was the norm. Two-fifths worked for planters with ten or fewer slaves, whose standard of living, though precarious, often resembled the master's more than on the big estates. With all this said, however, the lingering stereotype is essentially correct: typical antebellum slaves—over two million of them—did hot, hard, unremitting toil, at another's bidding for no reward, on a large cotton plantation of the Deep South.

In an era where twelve hours of hard labor per day was the rule, slave work was only marginally more arduous than that of free white farmers and workers. Slave prices rose throughout the period, moreover, so that masters had some incentive to provide minimal food, clothing, and shelter and to permit fishing, gardening, and other life-preserving activities on nonwork time. Black life expectancy was shorter than for poor southern whites, but not by much in this unhealthy region. A much greater difference between free and slave labor was that, because masters owned slave workers outright, they maintained labor discipline by physical force rather than by manipulating pay levels and employment opportunity as a businessman would. A good overseer—slavery's "middle manager"—was, first and foremost, one who could flog so as to cause pain (thereby encouraging higher productivity) without damage (thereby resulting in lower value). The whip was thus ubiquitous in the South in a way that shocked northerners. Egregious behavior such as sabotage or flight (or the outright rebellion that sometimes occurred in spite of the white monopoly on weapons) elicited more severe tools of punishment, including the chain, branding iron, and ax. Also stemming from total ownership was the masters' power to sell their workers, thereby forceably separating families and communities, as businessmen, again, could not. Forced separation tended to follow two cycles. One was slumping commodity prices, which triggered slave sales chiefly from hard-pressed small planters in the Upper South. The other was the aging of the large planters of the Gulf states, which triggered slave distributions to sons and daughters or slave sales to settle the division of the estate among heirs and creditors. The result was the violent shattering of as many as one-third of all slave marriages in the late antebellum period.

Because owners were reluctant to damage or kill valuable slaves, could not continually police the fields and especially the quarters, and were sometimes Christian paternalists, slaves had leeway to develop a powerful subculture despite their servitude. Family life—formed by ritual vows drawn from African and Christian sources, extended (to compensate for forced division) by the "adoption" of aunts, uncles, nieces and nephews, cemented by African and ancestral naming patterns—was the single most powerful cultural force among African Americans. Also important was music. African music was rhythmic with distinctive tonality. Slaves incorporated these patterns into work chants that established a beat for steady labor and provided the opportunity to devise short verses with real-life, often sorrowful, references. These songs formed the basis of the "blues" of the post–Civil War period, just as the adapted Christian hymns called "spirituals," often imbued with the same sorrowful air as the work songs, metamorphosed into the jubilee and gospel singing of the late nineteenth century. Christianity itself, introduced into the plantations by white evangelists in the late eighteenth and early nineteenth centuries, was a third great force in slave culture. Tolerated, even encouraged by the planters for several decades, slave preachers and congregations welcomed the emotionalism and interventionist God of evangelicalism, which echoed traits of West African religion. Slaves also identified with the suffering prophets, the compassion of Jesus, and especially the Hebrew trek out of Egyptian bondage, elaborating these themes in call-and-response sermons and demonstrative group prayer. Black preachers came to rival house servants, folk healers, and drivers in status; their congregations became the core of the black churches that shaped African American community life through the late twentieth century.

Northern Society The circumstances of northern white workers, whose numbers increased even more rapidly than the slaves during the economic boom of the early nineteenth century, varied greatly as of mid century. Change was most striking in the world of the artisan. In some sectors, especially in skilled construction and food processing, the nature of the work remained about the same as before 1800, and real wages, pushed by urban residential and commercial construction, went up gradually, if modestly, over the decades to several hundred dollars per year. Elsewhere, however, as output rose to supply expanding markets, some master workmen, particularly those supplying boots, harness, and tools to western planters and farmers, divided the work into specialized steps, added journeymen workers and sometimes machinery to perform this specialized labor, and became bosses of small but growing factories—capitalist manufacturers with debts, production schedules, and payrolls all attuned to maximum profit. The hopes of wage-earning journeymen for becoming masters themselves receded as the capital needed to establish a shop rose, while their ranks swelled with the masters' rush to increase production. Many artisans now plied their trade in hovels at the behest of those who supplied them with materials. Even those who still worked in shops found themselves deskilled by the specialization of tasks and their labor paced faster and faster by boss or machine or both. It was mainly from artisan, and especially journeyman, ranks that the impetus came for the craft unions and city labor confederations that proliferated during the 1820s and 1830s, then slumped in the 1840s before resurging, with the support of craft-conscious German immigrants, to help elect a Republican president in 1860.

One source of trouble for union organizers in this period was the great increase in workers outside the artisan tradition. Roads, canals, and railroads employed tens of thousands of unskilled laborers, for example, many of them desperately poor Irish immigrants; thousands more were hod carriers on urban building projects or dockworkers, porters, and teamsters in city commercial districts. Laborers, whose toil was both seasonal and exhausting, seldom made two hundred dollars a year. And since it required more than two hundred dollars, and thus more than one income, for family survival in most cities, women generally worked, too, often as cooks, cleaners, or live-in maids; children, once they left school at age twelve, did whatever casual work they could find, usually for a dime a day. Women and immigrants—and children—also did "outwork," making hats and clothes, for instance, for piece-rate pay from materials brought to their home or garret by contractors. The introduction of sewing machines dropped piece rates for some outworkers so low that they found themselves working eighteen-hour days. A third nonartisan wage-earner was the factory worker, whose ranks, though still modest, were swelling fastest of all. Initially restricted chiefly to the New England textile industry, where the big mills housed water-driven power equipment, by mid century steam power had made factories with power machinery familiar throughout the Northeast. The early mills employed mostly women and children. The newer ones looked increasingly to immigrants, who had to bear not only the long hours and low pay that characterized all of laboring America but such special burdens of the factory world as the constant close supervision of the foreman and the grinding noise and relentless pace of the machine.

THE RISE OF THE MIDDLE CLASS

The northern middle class of the mid nineteenth century differed from the eighteenth century's "middling interest" in its smaller relative size, its greater absolute prosperity, and its more pronounced self-consciousness. Comprised of urban retailers and small manufacturers in the Northeast, commercial farmers and food processors in the Midwest, and clerks, lawyers, contractors, land speculators, and railroad managers everywhere, this "new" middle class felt different from and fearful of immigrants because it was overwhelmingly Protestant and native-born; superior to and fearful of workers because it consisted of individualistic property-owners; different from, superior to, and fearful of elites because it was self-reliant and cherished economic and political liberty. Middle-class men joined political clubs and fraternal orders and read newspapers; middle-class women attended revivals, joined temperance and tract societies, and read magazines. Both enjoyed the popular theater, musical performances, and nickel museums of the antebellum towns. Together they tried to bequeath their status by limiting the number of children they had and making sure the ones they did have went to school. It was the traits of this articulate, highly-visible class—mobility, competitiveness, ambition, anxiety—that foreign visitors took as representative of American character. Its essence appeared in the phrases of the period: "businessman," "technology," "know-how," "suburb," "self-made man;" and also "every man for himself," "mind your own business," "make a killing."

The victorious Republican coalition of 1860 may have included evangelical reformers, opportunistic politicians, and industrialists seeking the high tariffs and railroad subsidies. But its votes came mainly from artisans and middle-class farmers and businessmen who, despite their racial prejudice, were not only dedicated to a free-market, free-labor, democratic political economy but convinced that they could not compete with an expansionist forced-labor system. The actual fighting of the Civil War showed, in a sense, the opposite—that a free system, despite major divisions, could vastly outproduce as well as decisively outgovern a slave system. In the event, the war ended slavery's threat to individual political and economic rights in the North, thereby fulfilling a Republican party pledge that had helped unify its middle- and working-class supporters. It also intensified the pace of industrialization, most immediately through military contracts and high-interest debt, more fundamentally through pro-business banking, tariff, and transportation laws, thereby favoring the Republicans' urban middle-class wing over their agricultural and working-class wing. This helped produce the stupendous industrial growth of the next half century. It also sped the relative decline of American farming and led to an increase in labor militancy that culminated in a wave of railroad strikes in 1877 so bitter they helped precipitate the end of Reconstruction.

Reconstruction had in any case been problematic. Following a postwar period of extreme uncertainty and hardship, African Americans, who had welcomed and joined forces with the advancing Union troops, started to vote and run for local office under Republican party auspices, to attend Freedmen's Bureau schools, and to form churches, fraternal orders, and benevolence societies in the towns. Black men practiced the trades for their own rather than their owners' ends and did lumbering and other industrial work for wages rather than sustenance. The domestic work of black women, though abysmally paid, now became a significant source of family income. On the land, where the vast majority of African Americans still lived, 20 percent owned their own farms by the end of the 1870s. About 40 percent worked farms that they rented or sharecropped; another 40 percent worked in the fields for wages. This proved to be a high-water mark for black farming. Over the next quarter-century, falling world cotton prices and a terrible boll weavil infestation flattened agricultural income at the same time that federal troop withdrawals reduced the ability of African Americans to preserve their political and civil rights against white terrorists. Falling income meant that independent black farmers gradually became renters, and renters sharecroppers. White domination meant that judges and sheriffs increasingly forced black families into debt bondage, or peonage. The black rural South thus sank into a deep and unremitting poverty that underlay and reinforced the emerging pattern of racial segregation. Equally terrorized, subjected to its own kind of infestation—of Freedmen's Bureau Savings Bank branches whose embezzlement and failure swept hard-earned savings away—the black urban South was not far behind.

INDUSTRIALIZATION

The age of industrialization had begun in America. The emergence of the modern American elite coincided, in fact, with the emergence between the 1870s and 1920s of a mature industrial economy built around transcontinental railroads and urban transit systems, large-scale mining and electric-power generation, and mass-produced, mass-distributed goods and services from copper to freight cars to tires to telephones and magazines. The key to this new industrial order proved to be immense physical and organizational scale. The readiest tool for creating and controlling huge industrial ventures proved to be the corporation, a business form that increased the consolidation of firms and therefore the concentration of industrial ownership and family wealth. By 1920 the two hundred largest corporations held nearly one half of all manufacturing assets; 1 percent of the population meanwhile owned 70 percent of corporate stock. That same 1 percent owned two-fifths of total wealth, including all federal bonds and a fifth of the private real estate. The top tenth of the population, which had owned half of everything in 1860, owned 65 percent by the early twentieth century, and drew a third of the national income besides.

The Upper Class This new upper class was somewhat less homogeneous than the old seaboard elites. Many industries were run by aggressive, contentious men from outside the East. Moreover, some capitalists were Catholic rather than Protestant or Jewish rather than Christian. No major fissures developed, however. One reason for this was that millionaire families in New York and other eastern cities succeeded in setting fashion trends (debutantes, charity balls, brownstone mansions, polo ponies) that other elites, particularly in the Midwest, soon came to imitate. Another reason was that investment bankers in the Northeast began to influence national corporate behavior by means of financial leverage and interlocking directorates, thereby reducing the likelihood of potentially destabilizing industrial conflicts. Most importantly, a kind of "cultural curriculum" emerged consisting of the experience to be gained by passing through a constellation of exclusive institutions. Crucial among these were certain New England boarding schools, with a half-dozen Episcopal schools at their core; the Ivy League colleges, especially Harvard, Yale, and Princeton; and selective yacht, country, and downtown men's clubs in the key cities. This "curriculum" was a vehicle for absorbing wealthy parvenus and their children into elite ranks, and for providing elite youth generally with common knowledge, career training, role models, marriage partners, and business contacts, particularly in banking, corporate or trust law and regulated or monopoly industries. Tribalism nevertheless persisted. Jews developed elite Jewish schools and clubs partly because they were excluded from those of the Christian upper class; women developed elite women's schools and social organizations partly because the upper class was male-dominant, if not misogynist. In politics the class operated largely as a Republican party patriciate, occasionally holding office but more commonly influencing politicians through co-optation, party organizations through campaign contributions, and governments by filling top judicial and administrative posts.

The Working Class Besides generating vast fortunes, industrialization created a vast new industrial labor force. In 1870 there were six million nonagricultural workers, of whom one million were factory workers or miners. By 1910 there were thirty-seven million nonagricultural workers, of whom ten million were factory workers or miners. This tremendous growth meant that virtually all industrial workers in this period came of necessity from the countryside or from Europe in one of the remarkable population movements in history. The most important American element of this great flood consisted of African Americans moving north to escape rural poverty and racial terror. From 1890 to 1920 the black population rose by 10 percent in the South, 40 percent in the Northeast, and 50 percent in the Midwest; and by 60 percent in Philadelphia, 200 percent in Chicago, and 700 percent in Detroit. There were approximately 1.5 million African Americans in the North by 1920, mostly excluded from the better-paying crafts and factory-line work, yet nonetheless wholly enmeshed, many for the first time, in the wage-labor system of industrial society.

Finding themselves still beset by low pay and housing discrimination and victimized by repeated mass violence, African Americans organized in their own defense as best they could. First came two southern-oriented black elite initiatives: the National Urban League, founded in New York in 1911, a business group whose watchword was economic self-help and political accommodation; and the National Association for the Advancement of Colored People (NAACP), also founded in New York in 1909–1910, an organization of reformers and writers insistent on full civil rights. More reflective of the realities of mass wage labor were two organizations of the 1920s: the National Brotherhood of Sleeping Car Porters, the country's largest union of black workers, whose leaders argued that, despite white working-class prejudice, labor solidarity and socialism were African Americans' best long-term hope; and the Universal Negro Improvement Association, a popular New York–based black nationalist movement that collapsed when its costly back-to-Africa schemes failed in the late 1920s. In politics most black Americans voted, when they could vote, for the party of emancipation, the Republicans. They also developed a vibrant, quasi-autonomous mass culture independent of, and in some respects more influential than, politics and reform, including a vigorous press with deep Boston and Washington, D.C., roots, an exciting Chicago blues and jazz scene, and the Harlem Renaissance, a flowering of black writing and art.

Immigrant Labor African Americans failed to get the best industrial jobs mainly because European immigrants—forty million of them from 1870 to 1920—got there first. A first wave of some seventeen million arrived from Germany, Ireland, Great Britain, and Scandinavia before 1890; the rest came mostly after 1890 from southern and eastern Europe and the Balkans. As of 1910 immigrants occupied one-quarter of all American jobs. But they were underrepresented in white-collar occupations, overrepresented in blue-collar ones. They comprised some 10 percent of all teachers and stenographers and 20 percent of salesmen; but 30 percent of railroad and streetcar workers, 40 percent of textile and packinghouse workers, 50 percent of coalminers and steelworkers, and 70 percent of copper and iron miners and garment workers. The vast majority of turn-of-the-century industrial workers were therefore foreign-born or the children of foreign-born. They were, accordingly, a majority of the population within the Boston-Baltimore-Saint Louis-Milwaukee rectangle that was the heart of industrial America, and the urban centers, from Lawrence to Pittsburgh to Gary, Indiana, that were the rectangle's fastest-growing nodes.

Where immigrant groups wound up in the industrial system depended partly on time and place of arrival, partly on connections, skills, and cultural baggage. The Irish initially did unskilled urban labor because construction was booming at a time when they lacked either craft skills or money for land. Sheer proximity later opened the door to the textile mills and coal mines, but they also used their rudimentary construction experience to become carpenters and contractors, their ties to the Catholic hierarchy to build parish churches and schools, and their numbers and facility with English to influence urban politics and gain access to municipal jobs. Irish women meanwhile became mill operatives, telegraphers, and retail clerks as well as domestics, commonly contributing heavily to the Catholic church—which could then afford the building contracts that benefited Irish men. Poles were prominent in the steel mills because they arrived with prior experience in Polish industry at a time when steel output was increasing rapidly. The earliest arrivals, in a kind of "chain migration" that became the norm for immigrant groups, then made sure their fellow Poles got first crack at job openings, local housing, and the like. Jews, prohibited from owning land in most of eastern Europe, exploited their urban background and their experience in garment-making to establish a preponderant position in the needle trades of New York City, which was becoming a fashion and ready-made clothing capital at precisely the time that it served as the main port of debarkation for Jewish immigrants. That same urban background proved a boon in the petty retailing that attended mass industrial production, while an unusually high commitment to literacy facilitated the Jewish climb up the lower rungs of the ladder to the learned professions.

Subcultures emerged in immigrant communities as they did in African American communities. Mutual-aid societies (the early Unione Siciliana, for instance) offered burial and accident insurance; fraternal orders (the Sons of Italy, the Hibernian Brotherhood) held rallies, dances, picnics, and banquets. Saloons became important rest-and-recreation places, insuring conflict with middle-class reformers; union halls became important meeting places, insuring conflict with middle-class employers. The largest non-English-speaking groups sustained as many as a half-dozen foreign-language newspapers with circulations as high as two hundred thousand and appeals varying from intellectual socialist to popular sensationalist to middle-class respectable. Theatrical fare included the English music hall, the Italian popular opera, and the Yiddish drama of the Jews. Because most of the new immigration, and much of the old, was from Catholic Europe, the Catholic church—promoted from Rome, dominated by a conservative, predominantly Irish hierarchy, supported by the modest contributions of millions of poor parishioners—was perhaps the single most significant cultural force in the industrial cities. Because of its strong separatist bent, as reflected in the parochial school system, Catholicism may have divided its members from mainstream America. Within immigrant America itself, it was probably a force for unity despite the establishment of Italian-language parishes and a Polish National Catholic church to protest Irish dominance, and a force for ultimate assimilation because of its great stabilizing effect. Reformed Judaism represented an effort by American Jews to accommodate to American ways without ceasing to be Jewish. Immigrant subcultures generally faded faster than the African American subculture because immigrants lived in slums, not racial ghettoes. Once the income of immigrants rose, as it eventually did through wage gains or occupational mobility, they started to move into better, more diverse neighborhoods where the schools were public and immigrant traditions diluted. African Americans were seldom able to do so.

CLASS CONSCIOUSNESS

Organized Labor The key to the development of class consciousness among workers in this period, as opposed to ethnic or racial consciousness, was trade unionism and labor radicalism. There were plenty of issues around which to organize workers. The most familiar were long hours, which gradually but steadily fell, and low wages, which rose in real terms but nonetheless remained low as compared to increases in productivity and value added and thus profit. Newer issues included hazardous working conditions, especially in industries such as coal mining, meat-packing, steelmaking, and clothing; job control, especially where management introduced technology or supervision that reduced the importance of skilled labor, as in brewing or newspaper production; and unemployment, especially as the cyclical troughs of modern capitalism seemed to deepen. Two very different types of union initially responded to the challenge. The Knights of Labor, begun by shoemakers and garment cutters in 1869, was a national union based on geographical locals open to all workers, whether skilled or unskilled, male or female, white or black. Stressing a shorter workday, the arbitration of wage disputes, and the establishment of producer cooperatives that would eliminate the system of wage labor, Knights membership rose from ten thousand in 1870 to a peak of seven hundred thousand in 1886, when it associated itself with a successful railroad strike and saw members gain local political office across the North. The next rail strike failed, however, and the traditional craft unions now declared their enmity to the heterogeneous, "impractical" Knights. By 1892 membership had dwindled to about fifty thousand; the organization dissolved soon after. Replacing it as the voice of workers was the American Federation of Labor (AFL), an organization based strictly on the principles of craft unionism and skilled labor and dedicated to the use of strikes by skilled workers for their own short-term gain. In 1887, a year after its founding, the AFL's affiliates had one hundred forty thousand members. Bolstered by thousands of small, usually brief job actions, membership totals grew steadily thereafter, as, on balance, did the wages and other benefits of its constituent unions.

A measure of the AFL's success is that during the early twentieth century it grew rapidly enough so that a fairly consistent 10 percent of American wage earners were affiliated. A measure of its failure is that 90 percent, including those in most dire need, were not affiliated. AFL leaders refused to organize unskilled workers because they believed the unskilled could not keep bosses from hiring other unskilled to cross picket lines and break strikes. They refused to organize black and female workers for this reason as well as from racism and sexism. And they opposed socialists and other radicals because they seemed impractical, like the Knights, and could provoke armed retaliation by management. City police, corporate armies, state militia, and the U.S. Army had killed fifty workers between 1890 and 1910; others died after World War I and in the 1930s. But precisely because the great mass of wage earners did remain outside the AFL, labor and political radicals repeatedly arose to organize them, most notably the International Workers of the World (IWW), an anarcho-syndicalist body that accepted all wage earners, conducted several major strikes in the 1910s, formed a branch of the American Socialist party (which drew a million votes in the presidential campaigns of 1912 and 1920), and then collapsed in the aftermath of the red scare in the early 1920s.

The dam started to break, finally, in the 1930s. Several large unions, led by the mineworkers, broke with the AFL to organize workers by industry rather than skill. Beneficiaries of New Deal labor legislation and the benevolent neutrality of a Democratic administration earnestly seeking and getting labor votes, the resulting Congress of Industrial Organizations (in which Communist party organizers as well as socialists and other labor militants played a significant role) had four million members by 1940, 75 percent of them from six basic industries—mining, automobile, steel, apparel, packing and canning, and rubber. The AFL, pressured on its left, now revived as well; it had five million members by 1940, the railroad brotherhoods and other independent unions another two million. The coming of World War II, with its desperate imperative of full production, gave labor leaders still further leverage and increased union membership by another 50 percent. Standing on the shoulders of past generations of union organizers and labor radicals, benefiting from circumstances and opportunities, organized labor was for the first time a full, if junior, partner in the American political economy.

The Middle Class The middle classes also changed. Middle-class families of the 1870s were mostly native-born Protestants living in New England, the Middle Atlantic states, or the Midwest, with income from commercial farming, small-scale retailing or manufacturing, or clerical or small-town professional work. Over the next several decades middle-income Americans worked increasingly in cities and lived increasingly in suburbs, in the process becoming at once more mobile and more cosmopolitan. Small producers and retailers remained important. At the turn of the century, however, they were joined by managers, accountants, and other corporate bureaucrats; engineers, industrial designers, advertisers, and public relations experts serving corporate needs; and salesmen distributing the tide of commodities, from band instruments and sheet music to plate glass and cement, which rolled from corporate production lines. Joining them were government workers, especially at the local and state levels where demands for transportation, schools, and other services were greatest; and, by the 1920s, enough artists, writers, teachers, editors, actors, and other cultural workers to constitute an "intelligentsia" of educated, articulate trendsetters for the rest of middle-income America.

Living in the suburbs meant owning a plot of land with a freestanding single-family house located near a streetcar line or, by the 1920s, with a car in the garage, with both car and garage giving a sense of family independence and autonomy. Not only did middle-class work itself become less autonomous and more bureaucratic, deferential, and routinized, contradicting the suburban illusion of independence, but since the man earned most of the family income alone away from home, it also created functional divisions within the family structure. Middle-class families increasingly defined themselves not as producing, profiting economic units, as in the mid nineteenth century, but as buyers of goods and services, from carpets and plumbing fixtures to radios, hairstyles, and Sunday newspapers, for consumption in and around the suburban home. The ownership of productive property no longer became the hallmark of the middle class, but instead income and the consumer goods that income could buy. "Proper" styles of consumption thus became the chief badge of class status in the same way that, on a different scale, they had become badges of attainment in elite society. Given the bureaucratic nature of the new corporate economy, only white-collar career success could guarantee the income necessary to achieve this sort of status. Since a career was still mostly for males, pressure built throughout the middle class for sons to earn the high-school and college credentials needed to climb the career ladder. Good schools thus became quintessential adjuncts of good neighborhoods, and educational credentials nearly as much a symbol of middle-class belonging as houses, cars, or appliances. Middle-class Americans supported different versions of progressive reform not only to control immigrant drinking habits and regulate the financial markets, but to develop the school systems needed for careers, income, and consumption.

Men and women experienced this new world differently. Socialized to be aggressive and domineering yet forced continually to ingratiate themselves with creditors, supervisors, and customers, men sought to exercise mastery in their own households, find community in service organizations, and release aggression in competitive sports. The freedom and opportunities of middle-class women remained circumscribed for several reasons. For one, a working wife implied that the income of a man alone was insufficient to sustain a middle-class standard of living. Prior to the mid twentieth century, most men, and some women, were unwilling to risk this loss of status even in order to gain more income. Also, suburban living not only made community interaction more difficult for "housewives," it made a child-oriented form of "homemaking" one of their major functions, leaving little energy and less time for work or civic activism. A force for public education and women's suffrage in the early twentieth century, women's chief nondomestic function after 1920 was simply to live in a middle-class life. They did so, on the whole, by buying things for their homes, their families and, especially by way of jewelry and clothing, themselves.

POSTWAR DEVELOPMENTS

Since the 1950s several class developments are notable. With regard to the elite, the new prominence of petrochemicals, aerospace, electronics, and consumer services, much of it driven by a greatly enlarged federal government, shifted economic initiative from older industrial areas to the "sunbelt" stretching from Florida through Texas to California. This produced numerous new elite representatives, including Asian Americans as well as parvenu corporate managers. A long wave of mergers, conglomerations, takeovers, and buy-outs concentrated corporate ownership and control and increased the influence of the New York investment bankers and Washington regulators who financed and favored the deals. But many investment bankers and regulators were themselves new men, some from Irish, Italian, and Jewish families. By the 1980s, moreover, a third of the five hundred richest families did not inherit substantial wealth; two-thirds of top corporate managers were from the middle class; and eastern, upper-class, white-collar professional and managerial families appear to have "skidded" into lower socioeconomic categories more frequently than in the 1880s.

Wealth and Income Distribution Yet if many rich families did not inherit great wealth, most of the one hundred richest did, including 70 percent of those individuals on four or more boards of directors and 60 percent of the directors of major banks. And if some elite white-collar families skidded only slightly, the vast majority did not skid at all. Overall, the contemporary upper class appeared modestly more diverse in terms of ethnicity and religion than a generation before and, as befitted a government-driven, bicoastal Sunbelt economy, less local and more national in orientation. "Society", at first based on exclusivity and formality, was now strongly attracted to personalities from sports, the arts, and especially television, from which the handful of upper-class African American families as well as some of the autonomous corporate women, mainly came. Television itself, a costly but effective medium, made money even more dominant politically than at the turn of the century. Partly for this reason, federal policy on taxes, business regulation, military spending, and interest rates tended to favor the corporate rich after the 1960s. As a result, by 1990 the top 10 percent of the population owned 70 percent of all wealth; the top 1 percent owned 45 percent. Income from rents, dividends, and interest surpassed income from wages and salaries for the first time ever. The top 20 percent of the population—the broader managerial and professional elite—therefore made 50 percent of all after-tax American income, while the top 1 percent—the corporate upper class—made 15 percent. Both figures were the highest in modern American history.

The Working Class For about a quarter of a century after World War Two, workers also fared comparatively well. This was, indeed, one of labor's golden ages. Brisk economic growth meant that per capita income rose rapidly compared to other countries. Modest federal deficits and a strong dollar kept inflation low; unemployment was low and stable. Profits were especially high in oligopolistic or internationally dominant industries that could afford to pay the high wages extracted by unionized workers. By 1970, in fact, union membership was about 30 percent of the nonagricultural labor force, or some twenty-one million, most of them affiliated with a united AFL-CIO. Real earnings therefore rose by half from 1945 to 1970 while the length of the work week fell by a tenth; health and retirement benefits rose as well. The development of suburban tract housing enabled union members to buy single-family homes; the development of an elaborate interstate highway system dotted with campgrounds and motels enabled them to take summer vacations as well. In politics, organized labor, working chiefly through the Democratic party, was the single most important force behind the expansion of the social security system, public higher education, and subsidized medical care, all of which benefited industrial workers.

As it happened, this glowing record of solidarity and accomplishment masked serious problems. One was an attitudinal consequence of previous successes. Workers, now living in the suburbs, traveling on vacation, and sending children to high school and college, began, in a reversion to pre-CIO days and as countless polls showed, to consider themselves middle class. They came therefore to share the middle-class propensity to differentiate themselves from the "poor," to oppose redistributive tax policies, to resist broad-based labor unions, and to vote for pro-business political candidates, including Republicans. A second problem was organized labor's debilitating lack of unity. One price of AFL-CIO unification was the expulsion of Communists and other radicals crucial to the organizing successes of the 1930s and 1940s; the largest single union in the country, moreover, was the Teamsters, whose corruption and gangsterism led to its expulsion as well. There were divisions, too, between the rank and file and the leadership, which sometimes used violence to suppress internal opponents; between white workers and black and other minority workers who, partly because of the seniority system that underpinned union contracts, tended to be "last hired and first fired"; and between male workers and women demanding equal access to the skilled trades and to union leadership posts. The third and perhaps most important problem was the structural transformation of the economy. After 1970 economic and population growth was fastest in Sunbelt regions outside organized labor's stronghold, resulting in a relative decline of union influence. Plant relocation abroad and fierce foreign competition meanwhile devastated American manufacturing and led to the loss of once high-paying jobs within the stronghold itself, leading to absolute decline.

After 1970 union membership fell steadily as a percentage of total workers. So did real wages, wage earners' share of total national income, and wages relative to rents, interest, dividends, and capital gains. Unemployment, however, rose. There were fewer strikes and therefore less income lost to strikes, but this was partly because unions could no longer sustain strikes. Family income held up better than individual income, but only because by the 1980s a majority of working-class women were wage earners, too, adding an income to the family total. New homes and a college education, two of the phenomena that had muted postwar class consciousness, were largely out of reach. By now, however, unions seemed too small, narrowly focused, and circumscribed to rebuild that consciousness. And as organized labor's strength receded, so, finally, did its national political clout and therefore the commitment of the government to labor's traditional twentieth-century agenda: public works, progressive taxation, medical assistance, occupational safety, higher minimum wage and unemployment benefits, and subsidized schools and colleges.

The Middle Class The postwar middle class was almost exclusively well-educated, upwardly mobile, suburban-oriented, and white-collar bureaucratic. This was mostly due to the persistence of the giant corporation, with its heavy reliance on line managers, staff consultants, and field representatives supported by company expense accounts; and to the rapid expansion of government bureaucracies at the state and especially the federal level. A new factor was the emergence of an enormous leisure and entertainment industry, from theme parks to rock concerts to golf courses, with a disproportionately well-educated, white-collar labor force. Also a factor was a greatly expanded system of higher education, another disproportionately well-educated, white-collar industry. The social function of these middle-income groups was, generally speaking, managerial as opposed to commercial, technological in the broad areas of scientific and market research, and cultural in the sense of providing a worldview, producing consumable artifacts, and setting taste trends. There were significant contradictions among postwar middle-income Americans. They tended, more than ever before, to be creative and idiosyncratic by education and intellectual bent, but conformist by condition of employment; affectional by family nurture, but isolated by work and living conditions; nonmaterialistic by education and self-image, but status-conscious consumers by income position. After the early 1970s middle-class families saw their disposable income increase because high interest rates, a booming stock market, and inflated real estate values all rewarded cash flow and property ownership; and also because middle-class women increasingly pursued careers, too, producing not only more autonomous women but "yuppies" (young urban professionals) and "dinks" (double income, no kids). After 1980 family disposable income generally stagnated or declined because of heavy interest payments on consumer debt, high corporate, white-collar unemployment, and sharply rising costs for housing, medical care, and higher education.

Youth, Women's, and Environmental Movements The relative affluence of this class, together with its high educational attainment and commitment to self-fulfillment and community, produced three significant social and political movements. One, the youth movement, rested on the "baby boom," an enormous demographic bulge of fifteen to thirty year-olds frustrated by suburban life, sequestered at routinized residential colleges, subjected to intense media and advertising bombardment, and threatened by induction into the army. The chief cultural manifestation of the youth movement was the "counterculture", an agglomeration of nonconformist dress, speech, music, and sexual styles inspired by minorities and the poor and designed to aggravate and challenge authority, including parents, university administrators, and military officers. The chief political manifestation was the "new left," a movement that arose in the main university centers to oppose racial and sexual inequality, institutional authoritarianism, environmental degradation, and especially the Vietnam War. Based on a large, relatively educated and affluent base, both new left and counterculture influenced mainstream politics and culture. As it turned out, education and affluence also made it possible for middle-class youth to rejoin their class by assuming middle-income jobs, accumulating consumer goods, and having families. When they did so, the youth movement, as such, was over.

More durable, because more related to the fundamental circumstances of the class, were the women's rights and environmental movements. Intertwined with the youth and also the civil rights movements, the leadership and core of the women's movement of the late 1960s and 1970s was young, suburban, college-educated, and relatively affluent. Critical of marriage and the patriarchal family, resentful of wage discrimination, occupational exclusion, legal and political barriers, and gender-biased cultural coding, feminists sought community as opposed to suburbanism, autonomy as opposed to subordination, and self-fulfillment as opposed to sacrifice and service. Unlike the youth movement, the women's movement proved both powerful and durable. It was durable because two of its main goals, economic access and parity and the unrestricted right to inhibit and terminate gestation, were extensions of a key, long-standing practice of the modern middle class—limiting family size in order to enhance career prospects and earning power. It was powerful because its central demands coincided with the needs and desires of wage-earning as well as middle-class women. At its inception and its core the environmental movement, with its concern to protect wilderness, save species, prohibit pollution, and recycle waste, reflected the anxieties of middle-class families who traveled to scenic places, lived in nonindustrial suburbs, owned second homes in forest or waterfront areas, could read and follow ecological news, and felt able to buy recycled products and pay recycling taxes.

Minorities By the 1980s minority status no longer automatically implied lower-class status, as it generally did before 1950. There were two reasons for this. First, the NAACP and the church-based Southern Christian Leadership Conference successfully fomented a mid-century civil rights movement powerful enough to desegregate the South, enfranchise black voters, and open previously restricted occupations to minority participation. By the 1980s African Americans were prominent in politics, sports, and the media, and had made significant inroads in corporate business, the professions, the military, and the construction trades; real per capita income for black families was consequently much higher than it had been twenty-five years before and the spectrum of opportunities far wider. Second, in 1950 the minority population—10 percent of the total population—was almost entirely African American. By 1990 the minority population—20 percent of the total population—was almost evenly divided between African Americans and people of Latin American and Asian descent. A majority of the Latinos and Asians were recent immigrants. Asians in particular, but also Cubans and some other Latino groups, brought with them urban middle-class professional and business skills, access to capital, and a disciplined commitment to family success that, for some, translated into the attainment of middle-class, and in some cases elite, status at a rate almost unprecedented for dark-skinned Americans.

Yet minority representation in corporate business and the professions remained disproportionately low, minority family income remained stalled at about 80 percent of nonminority income, and minority unemployment rates were consistently twice as high as for nonminorities. Among immigrants from non-English-speaking countries, language was a formidable barrier to occupational access. Racism and informal or extralegal occupational restrictions were also barriers, as was the society's tendency since the 1970s to redistribute wealth and income away from poorer households toward richer ones. Equally important, plant relocation and automation eliminated millions of the kind of semi-skilled and unskilled jobs that had sustained earlier waves of poorly-educated urban newcomers. White flight to the suburbs and a shrinking tax base meanwhile weakened the public schools that might have provided white-collar skills. Minority males had difficulty becoming primary providers or even finding employment, drifting instead toward desertion and street crime. Minority households, headed disproportionately by females who themselves suffered wage and occupational discrimination, thus became poorer, and minority neighborhoods, shattered by drug traffickers wielding deadly firearms, more violent and unstable. It remained to be seen whether this was leading, as some argued, to the creation of a permanent "underclass" of the criminal, the dependent, and the destitute, or was merely a down phase or negative aspect within the broad historic sweep of minority advancement.

BIBLIOGRAPHY

Aldrich, Nelson W., Jr. *Old Money: The Mythology of America's Upper Class* (1988).

Axtell, James. *The European and the Indian: Essays in the Ethnohistory of Colonial North America* (1981).

Braverman, Harry. *Labor and Monopoly Capital: The Degradation of Work in the Twentieth Century* (1974).

Countryman, Edward. *The American Revolution* (1985).

Couvares, Francis G. *The Remaking of Pittsburgh: Class and Culture in an Industrializing City, 1877–1919* (1984).

Diner, Hasia. *Erin's Daughters in America: Irish Immigrant Women in the Nineteenth Century* (1983).

Erie, Steven. *Rainbow's End: Irish-Americans and the Dilemmas of Urban Machine Politics, 1840–1985* (1988).

Foner, Eric. *Free Soil, Free Labor, Free Men: The Ideology of the Republican Party Before the Civil War* (1970).

———. *Reconstruction: America's Unfinished Revolution, 1863–1877* (1988).

Fox, Richard W., and T. J. Jackson Lears, eds. *The Culture of Consumption: Critical Essays in American History, 1880–1980* (1983).

Hall, Peter Dobkin. *The Organization of American Culture, 1700–1900: Private Institutions, Elites, and the Origins of American Nationality* (1982).

Harris, William. *The Harder We Run: Black Workers Since the Civil War* (1982).

Heyrman, Christine. *Commerce and Culture: The Maritime Communities of Colonial Massachusetts, 1690–1750* (1984).

Jackson, Kenneth T. *Crabgrass Frontier: The Suburbanization of the United States* (1985).

Kessler-Harris, Alice. *Out to Work: A History of Wage-earning Women in the United States* (1982).

Kulikoff, Allan. *Tobacco and Slaves: The Development of Southern Cultures in the Chesapeake, 1680–1800* (1986).

Laurie, Bruce. *Artisans into Workers: Labor in Nineteenth-Century America* (1989).

McClellan, B. Edward, and William J. Reese, eds. *The Social History of American Education* (1988).

Pessen, Edward, ed. *Three Centuries of Social Mobility in America* (1974).

Philpott, Thomas Lee. *The Slum and the Ghetto: Neighborhood Deterioration and Middle-Class Reform, Chicago, 1880–1930* (1978).

Ryan, Mary P. *Cradle of the Middle Class: The Family in Oneida County, New York, 1790–1865* (1981).

Takaki, Ronald. *Strangers from a Different Shore: A History of Asian Americans* (1989).

Thornton, Tamara Plakins. *Cultivating Gentlemen: The Meaning of Country Life Among the Boston Elite, 1785–1860* (1989).

Ulrich, Laurel. *Good Wives: Image and Reality in the Lives of Women in Northern New England, 1650–1750* (1982).

Warner, Sam Bass, Jr. *The Private City: Philadelphia in Three Periods of Its Growth* (1968).

Withey, Lynne. *Urban Growth in Colonial Rhode Island: Newport and Providence in the Eighteenth Century* (1984).

Wyatt-Brown, Bertram. *Southern Honor: Ethics and Behavior in the Old South* (1982).

SEE ALSO **The Aristocracy of Inherited Wealth; Ethnicity; Gender; Immigration; Marxism and Its Critics; Minorities and Work; Race; The Rise and Consolidation of Bourgeois Culture; The Social History of Culture; Wealth and Income Distribution; Women and Work.**

GENDER

Jane Sherron De Hart
Linda K. Kerber

FASCINATED BY THE DIFFERENCES that divide the American people and the commonalities that make them one, scholars and commentators have long focused on such centrifugal forces as regional loyalties, geographic mobility, and political dissent. They have also examined the ways in which race, class, and culture both bond and divide. Until very recently, however, sexual difference has been largely discounted as a significant factor in the American experience. Whether male or female, members of the same racial, ethnic, and economic groups, experiencing the same great social phenomena, were presumed to share the same historical experience. In many respects, they did. For example, enslavement—primarily of Africans but also, in the early years of European settlement, of Indians—was not restricted to one sex; women and men toiled in the fields together. Similarly, industrial workers, both male and female, relied on their wages for their own support and that of their families; when industrial conditions deteriorated, women were at the forefront of working-class protest.

Yet the historical experience of the two sexes, for all its similarities, has proved upon closer examination to be profoundly different in many important ways. Slaves, for example, were for many years assumed to have been provided with at least adequate diets, but new research suggests that for pregnant women and nursing mothers the slaves' standard diet meant semistarvation. Further, differences in family responsibilities account for divergence in the experience of male and female factory workers. The employment patterns of white women in the New England textile industry illustrate the point. Young single women at the turn of and in the nineteenth century went into the mills to supplement family income, often allowing their brothers to improve their job prospects by staying in school; they withdrew after marriage and childbirth but returned to the mills as mothers of small children when the perilous state of family finances required them to do so. As mothers of grown children, they returned to the mills to stay. In the work force, the jobs to which women were assigned, the wages they were paid, the opportunities for unionization they encountered, and the relationships they forged with government regulators all reinforced fundamental differences between the sexes.

As scholars begin to incorporate the wealth of new information generated by historians of women into their standard accounts of the American experience, women's distinctive experience has required the modification of old generalizations. It also has become apparent that there is a history of social relations between the sexes, just as there is a history of relations between the races. Social differences based on, in a word, gender have thus become as critical as those deriving from race or class to understanding the complex ways in which American society has remained stratified and the challenges that lie ahead if the ideal of equality is to be realized.

Most people, male and female, particularly if they are white and middle class, conventionally have understood difference in terms of sex to mean a female advantage. They have assumed that women were spared heavy physical labor and fierce competitive pressures. Excused from primary responsibility for family support, wives and daughters could spend most of their adult lives at home rather than in the work force, devoting their time to such congenial tasks as caring for children, doing charitable deeds, and socializing with friends. Those who were employed outside the home were thought to work for "pin money" which they could use to indulge their whims as consumers.

Recent research makes it clear that most of these "advantages" were class specific and chimerical. The notion that the home protected working-class housewives from the competitive pressures of the marketplace, and all housewives from real work, was an illusion. The home always has been less a haven than a workplace. It was the site of housework—heavy physical labor and unremitting toil—work that was no less strenuous for all the efforts to deny that it was work at all because it was performed for love of family rather than for wages. Even the middle-class housewife who enjoyed the conveniences of nineteenth-century town life and who may have had a servant to help with the laundry and cooking struggled with an exhausting array of tasks. For rural women the work load was even heavier. Although twentieth-century technology has lightened the onerous physical burden, the equation of homemaking with leisure remains a fantasy carefully nurtured by the advertising industry. If the nature of housework has changed, the time spent doing it has not. In 1960 urban women not employed outside the home were spending fifty-five hours per week in housework—three hours more than rural homemakers in the 1920s. In the 1980s women employed full-time outside the home packed an additional twenty-five hours of work—housework—each week into evenings and weekends, leading one expert to conclude that their workdays were probably longer than were those of their grandmothers.

GENDER AS A SOCIAL CONSTRUCTION

The adverse economic implications for women associated with the old perception that housework was not real work suggest that in this instance, as in many others, difference has in fact meant disadvantage. Women's historians not only have documented this disadvantage but also have sought to explain it. The factors involved are very complex and still imperfectly understood. The explanation traditionally offered has been a variant of biological essentialism. As Supreme Court Justice David Brewer put it in his opinion in *Mueller* v. *Oregon* (1908):

> The two sexes differ in structure of body, in the functions to be performed by each, in the amount of physical strength, in the capacity for long continued labor . . . [in] the self-reliance which enables one to assert full rights, and in the capacity to maintain the struggle for subsistence. (Kerber and Mathews, p. 442)

Woman's "physical structure and a proper discharge of maternal functions" place her at a disadvantage in that struggle, he continued, and justify legislation to protect her.

Justice Brewer's statement reveals a common confusion of sex and gender. To the extent that his view of difference is based on anatomical and hormonal features that differentiate males and females biologically, he is talking about sexual difference. When, however, he speaks of "the self-reliance which enables . . . [men] to assert full rights," "the capacity [of men] to maintain the struggle for subsistence," and the "proper discharge of [women's] maternal functions," he is referring to gender differences. The assumptions that men are self-reliant and women are not, that men struggle for subsistence and women do not, and that women nurture their children and men cannot reflect the ways in which Justice Brewer and most of his generation understood the implications of being male or female.

"Sex" refers to biological differences that are unchanging; "gender" involves the meaning that a particular society or culture attaches to sexual difference. Because that meaning varies over time and among cultures, gender differences are both socially constructed and subject to change. Definitions of what is masculine or feminine are learned as each society instructs its members from infancy through adulthood as to what behavior and personality attributes are appropriate for males or females of a particular generation, class, and social group.

In antebellum America, for example, white southern males, whether members of the low-country planter class or the backcountry working class, identified masculinity with a concept of personal honor, in defense of which duels were fought and fists flew. In the cities of the North, many young working-class males shared their southern counterparts' obsession with physical prowess and bellicosity. So synonymous were masculinity and toughness for those New Yorkers known as "Bowery boys" that when the Bowery boy was represented on stage, he was immediately recognizable by his swaggering gait and aggressive persona. Although the black abolitionist Frederick Douglass would not have been comfortable with the flamboyant aggressiveness and virility flaunted by the Bowery boys as a badge of working-class masculinity, the identification of force and power with manhood was a concept he well understood. In *Narrative of the Life of Frederick Douglass* (1845), Douglass's autobiographical account of his life as a slave and his escape to freedom, the author prefaced a description of his brutal fight with the vicious slave breaker Covey with a single sentence: "You have seen how a man was made a slave; you shall see how a slave was made a man."

Not all social groups defined masculinity in this fashion, even in antebellum America. Although aggressiveness, self-reliance, and competitiveness were cultivated in most boys because these traits were needed in the work world of adult males, families whose values were shaped by evangelical Protestantism emphasized that manliness also involved self-restraint, moral self-discipline, and sobriety. These qualities became even more important in the new urban bourgeois culture of the late nineteenth century. A bureaucratized corporate capitalism would require of the middle class a model of masculinity different from the rougher, more "macho" ideal characteristic of the frontier. A "real" man, while projecting a virile and, if necessary, tough demeanor, also needed to be a "team player"—an attribute cultivated in boyhood games and team sports. Indeed, competitive sports, virility, and masculinity have become so intertwined in the twentieth century, concludes historian Clyde Griffin in *Meanings for Manhood,* that "the boy or man who dislikes competitive sports or virile postures has little choice but to affect 'manly' interests and behavior and to hope these affectations will not be exposed" (p. 203). To behave otherwise was to risk being called a "sissy" or a "queer." Such labels reflected popular assumptions that "real" men were sportsmen and that nonathletes, whether heterosexual or not, were males who wished to have sexual relations only with males, were effeminate, and/or wished to be women.

Because homosexuality has been viewed for most of the twentieth century as a biological deviation from "normal" masculinity or femininity, many Americans fail to appreciate the extent to which sexuality is socially constructed. Anatomical and hormonal characteristics set certain boundaries within which we operate. Within those boundaries, socially constructed scripts provide cues as to how we should respond sexually—what or who should arouse our desire. How sexual preference is first determined or chosen, and when, is a matter experts do not fully understand. But here, too, culture plays a part. It is helpful, historian Carroll Smith-Rosenberg wrote in "The Female World of Love and Ritual," to "view sexual and emotional impulses as part of a continuum or spectrum. . . . At one end of the continuum lies committed heterosexuality, at the other uncompromising homosexuality; between, a wide latitude of emotions and sexual feelings" (Kerber and De Hart, p. 171). Where we place ourselves on that continuum and whether we move along it are affected by cultural norms as well as by biology.

Sexuality has its own history. Conceptions of sexuality and attitudes as to how, with whom, and where sexual feelings should be expressed have been continually reshaped by the changing nature of the economy and politics. In the seventeenth century, for example, women were believed to be more lustful and carnal than men. Female sexuality was seen as a source of power and corruption to be feared and controlled. By the nineteenth century, when the role of both church and state in sexual regulation had diminished and sexual restraints had to be internalized, primarily by women, sexuality was redefined. Women—at least white, native-born, middle- and upper-class women—were viewed as having weaker sexual desires than men. Sensuality was attached to poor or "darker" women—who, by definition, "invited" male advances.

As we begin to uncover the history of sexuality, we can better understand what part sexuality played in women's subordination. We can also see how women tried to devise ways to enhance sexual control and expression. In the nineteenth century, for example, some married women took advantage of the belief that women were passionless to reduce the frequency of sexual intercourse in order to reduce the likelihood of pregnancy and to enhance sexual pleasure. Women who wished to express themselves sexually as well as emotionally in single-sex relationships constructed life-styles that opened up new realms of freedom. Indeed, we are just beginning to understand the ways in which these private relationships sustained the public activities of women such as Jane Addams and Lillian Wald.

GENDER AND ITS IMPLICATIONS

Understanding the difference between sex and gender provides a key to understanding the differences in men's and women's historical experiences. In the workplace, for example, women and men were assigned jobs that reflected the employers' beliefs about the kind of work each sex should do. In a society whose understanding of gender included the conviction that women's primary obligations were familial and their basic talents domestic, female wage earners were persistently channeled into jobs that corresponded to the kind of work done in the domestic sphere or with characteristics long associated with women.

In the preindustrial domestic economy, women did both heavy physical labor (hauling water, slaughtering chickens) and skilled tasks (spinning, weaving, nursing). When women sought new avenues through which to gain economic independence, they followed these chores into the marketplace. As slaves and as "hired help," they toiled on other people's farms; as "mill girls" they tended dangerous spinning machinery for twelve hours a day; as packinghouse workers they labored amid stench and slime.

Upwardly mobile women laid claim to the teaching and nursing professions by emphasizing that the personality characteristics and skills required for such work were precisely those believed to be unique to the female sex. Thus nursing, in pre–Civil War years considered an occupation no respectable woman would enter, was eventually touted as a profession eminently suited to women. Providence, after all, had endowed the fairer sex with what the Raleigh, North Carolina, *News and Observer* called in 1904 that "compassion which penetrate[s] the heart, that instinct which divines and anticipates the wants of the sick, and the patience which pliantly bends to all their caprices." As the economy grew more complex, middle-class women infiltrated the ranks of librarians and secretaries. These occupations had been primarily male but, like teaching and nursing, were later redefined to emphasize the nurturing, service-oriented qualities ascribed to women—with a corresponding decrease in pay. Newer industries provided new job titles but old work categories, as well. Receptionists and social workers were hired by employers still convinced that the tasks required in these jobs were consistent with the personality characteristics and skills traditionally associated with women. New white-collar jobs were also segregated by race, even in the North, where segregation was not officially practiced; for example, stewardesses on national airlines were overwhelmingly white until after the civil rights legislation of the 1960s.

Because gender rather than individual talent or capability has been employers' primary consideration, women have been segregated into certain kinds of work, whether in the professions or in industry. Of the 299 occupations listed by the Bureau of Labor Statistics in 1990, only 56 were thoroughly integrated by sex. Males overwhelmingly dominated 104 occupations, while 79 occupations were predominantly female. It is into these that 80 percent of women workers clustered working as waitress, salesperson, secretary, nurse, and teacher.

Once a form of work has been identified with women, it invariably has become associated with low pay and minimal prestige. "Theoretically, the market treats men and women neutrally, judging only the characteristics of their labor," writes historian Alice Kessler-Harris in *A Woman's Wage*. "In the world of economists, the wage is rooted in the play of supply and demand" (p. 2). In practice, Kessler-Harris continues, "the wage is neither neutral or natural, but . . . reveal[s] a set of social constructs . . . that convey messages about the nature of the world, and about . . . men and women and . . . the relations between them" (p. 2). Nowhere are messages about gender relations more clearly revealed than in the demands of nineteenth-century male trade unionists. Higher pay, they argued, was the due of those for whom work—and the skill and strength to do it—was a measure of masculinity; payment of a "family wage" would allow a man to be sole support of his family, thereby confirming his own and society's idea of manliness. Lower pay was appropriate for people assumed to be marginal workers whose place was in the home, where purity and virtue could be protected and family duties fulfilled.

These gendered assumptions about wages worked to the disadvantage of both men and women, especially in working-class families. By making man the sole provider for the family, men whose wives worked outside the home often felt themselves failures, not just as providers but also as men. Women in the work force—whatever their class, whether they worked as a matter of choice or of necessity—received wages that were often based as much on their sex as on the value of their work or their productivity. In this way, the home subsidized the factory not only in the nineteenth century but even in the late twentieth, when two-paycheck families are the norm and a working wife is no longer viewed as a threat to her husband's masculinity.

Gender was embedded not only in economic relations but in legal relations as well. In the legal tradition that English colonists brought to America, the husband was understood to be the head of the family and to represent it in its dealings with the world. Upon marriage the woman lost her separate civil identity; it was assumed that she had voluntarily forsworn the right to make choices at odds with those of her husband. In a powerful legal fiction, man and wife were understood to be one person; the married woman was the *femme covert,* "covered" with her husband's legal identity in virtually all situations except criminal matters. All personal property that she brought to the marriage became her husband's; he could sell her jewelry or gamble away her money. He could not sell her real estate unless she consented, but he could decide how it was to be used: whether land was to be farmed, rented out, or planted in corn or in vegetables and whether trees on it were to be cultivated or cut down.

Since married women did not own their property, they could not make legal contracts affecting it; they could not buy and sell without their husband's consent. A married woman could not decide whether her children were to be kept at home or apprenticed or, if apprenticed, who their masters would be. She could not sign a contract independently; not until she was a widow could she make a will. So powerful was the fiction that husband and wife are one person that marital rape was inconceivable. Indeed, marital rape was not outlawed anywhere in the world until 1978, when New York State passed a statute prohibiting forced sexual intercourse by a stranger, an acquaintance, or a spouse. As of 1990, only nine states had followed New York's lead. In most states, for husbands to force sex upon unwilling, even resisting, wives is a crime only under certain circumstances. In four states it is not a crime at all.

Gender also defined political relationships. In Anglo-American tradition the right to participate in political activities—voting, holding office, serving on juries—was conditioned on the holding of property. Since married women could not direct the use of their property, it seemed to follow that they could be neither jurors nor voters nor officeholders. That politics is a male domain, that women are not political beings, is an understanding as old as Western civilization. Aristotle, whose writings provide the basic terms by which westerners have understood politics, said that men alone realize themselves as citizens. It is no accident that the civic virtue he extolled derives from the same root as the word "virile." Women, Aristotle maintained, realize themselves only within the confines of the household; their relationship to the world of politics, like their legal status, is derivative—through fathers, husbands, and sons.

The notion of this derivative relationship forced women to carve out a political role that rested upon their ability to influence those who held political power. An ancient practice, this wielding influence was used by women to support a wide range of important social issues and philanthropic causes in the years before 1920, when the Nineteenth Amendment granted female suffrage. The uses of influence continued to be exploited by American women even after they got the vote. As primary adviser and campaign manager to Al Smith, governor of New York for most of the 1920s and presidential candidate in 1928, Belle Moskowitz had enormous impact both on the policies of his administration and on the politics of the Democratic party. But she was uncomfortable claiming power for herself and never ran for political office or accepted an appointive post.

Mary McLeod Bethune, a prominent African American educator, was equally adept in the uses of influence. As president of the National Association of Colored Women (1924–1928) and president of the National Council of Negro Women (1935), Bethune met Eleanor Roosevelt. The First Lady, admiring the effectiveness with which this forceful, articulate black woman championed the needs of her people, used her own influence to secure Bethune's appointment to a number of positions, notably in the National Youth Administration (1935). From her position within that organization, Bethune organized the Federal Council on Negro Affairs, a group of black leaders who worked effectively to focus the attention of the media as well as that of the Roosevelt administration on the desperate problems facing blacks in the Great Depression.

The gendering of politics forced women to clothe their political claims in domestic language. To deflect male hostility to their entry into the political arena, they argued that women should have the vote in order to elect city officials who would see to it that rotting garbage was carted away, decaying meat taken out of markets, and polluted water purified; otherwise, the best efforts of mothers to ensure clean homes and wholesome food for their children would be to no avail. Later, women in the nuclear disarmament movement also used gendered language, naming their organization Mothers Strike for Peace.

UNDERSTANDING GENDER AS A SYSTEM

Economics, law, politics—each, as we have seen, was permeated by assumptions, practices, and expectations that were deeply gendered. So widely shared were these assumptions, practices, and expectations, and so much were they a part of the ordinary, everyday experience, that they acquired an aura of naturalness, rightness, and even inevitability. Common sense dictated that "this is simply the way things are." But "common sense," as anthropologist Clifford Geertz shrewdly observed in *Local Knowledge* (1983), "is not what the mind cleared of cant spontaneously apprehends; it is what the mind filled with presuppositions . . . concludes." The consequence of comprehending the world in this way—whether in the nineteenth century or in our own times—is that it obscures the workings of a system in which economic, political, and cultural forces interact and reinforce each other in ways that benefit one group and disadvantage others. Unable to recognize the system, failing to understand that what shapes and defines our lives has been constructed piece by interlocking piece over time by other human beings, we constantly reproduce the world we know, believing we have no other choice. As a result the inequities persist, becoming more difficult to challenge because they, too, seem as natural and inevitable as the system that has produced them.

To develop a way of looking that enables one to "see" economic and social relationships that are presumed to be neutral and natural as socially constructed arrangements that in fact benefit one group at the expense of others is always a difficult task. That task is made even more difficult by the fact that language has embedded in it the values, norms, and assumptions of the dominant group. Consequently it reflects and re-creates reality as it is perceived by that group. Using language that is not one's own to expose unequal relationships or to create an alternative to those relationships challenges the ingenuity and analytical abilities of even the most clearheaded and imaginative thinkers.

Analytical skills, moreover, are not inborn. They are developed slowly and painfully within an educational process that values and encourages those skills instead of, for example, simple memorization or rote learning. Throughout history women have been explicitly excluded from the intellectual community. Prior to the seventeenth century, when most people were illiterate, elite families in which sons learned to read and write rarely provided such opportunities to their daughters. A major literacy gap existed throughout the world until well into the nineteenth century and, in many underdeveloped countries, persists today. At the time of the American Revolution, when it has been estimated that 70 percent of the men in the northern cities could read, only 35 percent of their female counterparts could do so. Slaves by law were denied access to instruction in reading and writing, lest they learn about alternatives to slavery.

Not until the second half of the nineteenth century were white women admitted to major state universities. Between 1860 and 1890 a few elite colleges were founded to provide upper-middle-class young women an education equivalent to what their brothers were receiving at Harvard, Yale, and Princeton. These new women's colleges reluctantly admitted a few black students; it was left to black women with meager resources—notably Mary McLeod Bethune and Charlotte Hawkins Brown—to develop their own institutions in a rigidly segregated society. Because public schools served black children so badly, these private institutions often began not as colleges but as elementary or secondary schools that later grew into colleges. Only in recent generations have substantial numbers of women, white or black, been able to acquire not only a basic education but also the rigorous training necessary to analyze and question the social and cultural arrangements within which they live.

Another consequence of women's educational deprivation was their ignorance of history and, therefore, of other historical actors, male or female, who had faced challenges that in some way resembled their own. Lacking a history of their own, women had few models, few heroes to emulate or strategies to adopt. The lack of a history in which women were actors made it particularly difficult for even educated women to envision a world other than one in which men—their experiences and needs—were the norm. Marginality in the past thus confirmed and reinforced marginality in the present.

Understanding economic and social relationships that benefit one sex at the expense of another, developing language with which to critique those hierarchical relationships and articulate an alternative vision, and forging the group solidarity necessary to realize that vision have been the tasks of feminism. The term "feminism" came into use in the United States around 1910, at a time when women were engaged in the fight for suffrage as well as for a host of other reforms. As historian Nancy Cott has pointed out in *The Grounding of Modern Feminism,* feminism included suffrage and other measures to promote women's welfare that had emerged out of the nineteenth-century women's movement. However, feminism encompassed a wider range of fundamental changes, amounting to a revolution in the relation of the sexes. "As an *ism* (an ideology)," Cott notes, "feminism presupposed a set of principles not necessarily belonging to every woman—nor limited to women" (p. 3). In other words, not all women would oppose a sex hierarchy that privileged men as a group, nor would all women feel compelled to struggle for sexual equality. On the other hand, some men would join feminist women in their efforts to dismantle a system that conferred on one sex the power to define the other. While this system has been partially dismantled—the goal of suffrage was realized in law in 1920—the wider revolution remains to be accomplished.

RETHINKING THE SOCIAL CONSTRUCTION OF GENDER

Embracing the goals of their feminist predecessors and enriched by current scholarship on gender, contemporary feminists seek to reconstruct social relations between the sexes. To do so, they believe, requires change in both public life and private behavior. This double agenda has a long history.

In 1848, when American feminists drafted their first manifesto, the Declaration of Sentiments, Elizabeth Cady Stanton demanded change in both law and custom. She called for legal change in the form of property rights for married women and voting rights for all women. Recognizing the ways in which women's self-esteem and autonomy were undermined, she also urged women to work for wide-ranging cultural change, such as equal standards of sexual behavior and equal roles in churches.

When twentieth-century feminists began to understand gender as a social construction, they realized that the feminist revolution had to be waged in personal life as well as public life; in home as well as in workplace; in the most intimate relationships as well as the most formal. "It must be womanly as well as manly to earn your own living, to stand on your own feet," observed the feminist Crystal Eastman in *The Liberator* (December 1920) shortly after the national suffrage amendment was passed.

> And it must be manly as well as womanly to know how to cook and sew and clean and take care of yourself in the ordinary exigencies of life.... [T]he second part of this revolution will be more passionately resisted than the first. Men will not give up their privilege of helplessness without a struggle. The average man has a carefully cultivated ignorance about household matters . . . a sort of cheerful inefficiency. (*Crystal Eastman On Women and the Revolution,* edited by Blanche Cook [1978])

But it was fifty years before Eastman's insights became an agenda for action.

Feminists of the 1970s captured national attention with bitter criticisms of parents who gave nurses' kits to their daughters and doctors' bags to their sons and of guidance counselors who urged mathematically talented girls to become bookkeepers and mathematically talented boys to become engineers. Feminists condemned stereotypes that fit children to conventional roles in their adult life and they encouraged the publication of books and the marketing of toys designed to demonstrate to both boys and girls that they need not shape their aspirations to gendered stereotypes. (The popular television show, record, and book *Free to Be You and Me* encapsulated these themes.) Feminists also urged a reorganization of the family to allow both sexes to share more equitably the burdens and pleasures associated with earning a living, maintaining a household, and rearing a family. But gender stereotypes turned out to be more resilient than many had anticipated; socialization is a lifetime process and is not easily reversed.

Feminists themselves had to wrestle with a culture that maintained a hierarchy of values, reserving strength, competence, independence, and rationality for men and nurture, supportiveness, and empathy for women. Questioning both the hierarchy and the dualisms embedded in this gendering of values, feminists argued that these should be viewed as shared human qualities that are not sex specific.

Sexual hierarchy was not the only cultural hierarchy that posed problems. There were also hierarchies of race and class. White feminists in the 1970s were criticized for promoting a vision of feminism that ignored black women and assumed that all women who were impatient with contemporary culture were white and middle class. The upwardly mobile vision was a contested vision. The priorities of women of different classes and races did not necessarily converge. Many black women supported elements of the agenda of middle-class white feminists of the 1970s—equal pay for equal work, access to jobs—but they disagreed on priorities. They were skeptical of those who placed the needs of middle-class women ahead of the needs of working women. Middle-class white women, the employers of domestic workers, were markedly more enthusiastic about the elimination of quotas for female students in law and medical schools than they were about the establishment of minimum wage and social security protection for domestic workers. The first generation of white radical feminists fought vigorously for the repeal of all abortion laws and for safe access to birth control; black feminists saw access to abortion as only one of a wide range of medical services for which many black women struggled.

Differences in sexual preference also posed problems for this generation of feminists. Challenges to traditional gender arrangements have always inspired charges of sexual deviance from those seeking to discredit the movement and trivialize grievances. The 1960s and 1970s were no exception. Concerned about the movement's image, many feminists, rejecting the charge, attempted to push lesbians out of sight. Equality, not sexual preference, was the issue, they insisted. Lesbian feminists disagreed, arguing that autonomy in sexual matters involves more than access to reproductive control. In time, tensions eased as many heterosexual feminists accepted the legitimacy of lesbian involvement in the movement and the validity of the contention that straight/gay divisions constitute a form of cultural hierarchy that reinforces male supremacy.

THE COMPLEXITY OF CREATING EQUALITY

Recognizing the magnitude of cultural and personal change required if each woman were to be free to realize her full potential, feminists of the 1970s simultaneously challenged the institutions and the laws that denied women equal treatment. They launched a barrage of test cases in state and federal courts that challenged unequal responsibility for jury service, unequal benefits for dependents, and unequal age requirements for drinking and marriage. In 1972, in the Idaho case of *Reed* v. *Reed,* which tested who was to be the administrator of a will, feminists persuaded the Supreme Court for the first time in American history to treat discrimination on the basis of sex as a denial of equal protection under the law. But the Supreme Court was reluctant to build on this precedent in subsequent cases. Its refusal to apply as strict a standard for sex discrimination as for racial discrimination prompted feminists to try to add an amendment to the Constitution banning sex discrimination; however, the Equal Rights Amendment, passed overwhelmingly by Congress in 1972, fell three states short of the three-fourths majority required for ratification. A contributing factor to this failure was basic disagreement about whether equality under law requires equality of military obligation.

Vigorously lobbying both Congress and the executive branch, feminists won legal guarantees of equal pay for equal work, equal employment opportunities, and equal access to credit and to education. Building on the tactics and achievements of the civil rights movement, they secured major gains in the 1960s and 1970s. In the process, however, they discovered that guarantees of equality in a system structured with men's needs as the norm do not always produce a gender-neutral result. In many professions, for example, there is enormous pressure to demonstrate mastery of one's field in the early stages of a career, precisely when the physical risks of childbearing are lowest. Although the standard appears to be gender neutral, in practice it presents young women with excruciating choices that do not confront their male peers.

Nowhere was the challenge of achieving gender neutrality in the workplace greater than in the matter of pregnancy. Aware of the long history of discrimination against pregnant employees, feminists successfully attacked regulations that prevented pregnant women from making their own decisions about whether and how long to work. But initial legislative "solutions" raised new complexities that challenged the assumption that equality always requires identical treatment. If employers could no longer fire pregnant women, they still could exclude from the company's disability program those temporarily unable to work during some portion of their pregnancy or at childbirth. Pregnancy, said the Supreme Court in its ruling in *Geduldig* v. *Aiello* (1974) and *General Electric* v. *Martha Gilbert* (1976), was not a temporary disability but a "voluntary physical condition." Outraged at the ruling, feminists and their allies demanded congressional action that would require pregnancy and childbirth to be treated like any other physical event that befalls workers. Responding with the 1978 Pregnancy Discrimination Act that mandates equal treatment in the workplace, Congress required employers to give physically disabled pregnant workers the same benefits given to other disabled workers. The problem, however, was not yet resolved.

If employers denied disability leave to all employees as a matter of company policy, federal legislation mandating equal treatment for both sexes with respect to pregnancy disability would, in effect, penalize female employees unable to work because of pregnancy-related illness. Equality, in this instance, seemed to require special treatment. Lawmakers in California and a few other states agreed and passed legislation requiring employers to provide pregnant workers with disability coverage even if no other illnesses were covered. Employers complained that this constituted "preferential treatment" for women. Some feminists, aware of the ways in which legislation designating women as a special class of employees because of their reproductive capacity had penalized female workers in the past, questioned whether such legislation was in the best interests of women. Would it reinforce sexist stereotypes of men as "natural" breadwinners and women as "natural" childbearers and child rearers, making employers reluctant to hire married women of childbearing age and further marginalizing women as workers? Would it be better strategy to concentrate on extending disability benefits to workers of both sexes? Other feminists were untroubled. Pregnancy is unique to women, they argued, and calls for special treatment in recognition of that uniqueness. Such legislation, they insisted, acknowledges reality at a time when growing numbers of women become pregnant within one year of their employment.

In a 1987 decision, *California Federal Savings and Loan Association* v. *Guerra,* in which the Supreme Court upheld a controversial California law on pregnancy disability benefits, Justice Thurgood Marshall went to the heart of the equality/difference dilemma. Writing for the majority, he noted that "while federal law mandates the same treatment of pregnant and non-pregnant employees, it would be violating the spirit of the law to read it as barring preferential treatment of pregnancy." The California law, he reasoned, "promotes equal employment opportunities because it allows women as well as men to have families without losing their jobs" (479 U.S. 272 [1987]).

The difficulty of determining what is fair treatment for pregnant women dramatically illustrates the complexities involved in reconciling equality and sexual difference. Part of the difficulty has to do with the meaning of equality. Is equality to be thought of, as it has been throughout American history, as equality of opportunity? Or is equality to be defined as equality of results? In either case, do the methods used to achieve equality demand the same treatment or different treatment? The stakes in this debate are high, as the debate over pregnancy in the workplace illustrates, because childbearing impacts so directly on women's struggle for economic independence.

Childbearing is only one aspect of sexual difference that complicates efforts to achieve equality between the sexes. Closely related are other issues surrounding reproduction. In the first half of the twentieth century, access to birth control was the contested issue. Feminists argued that the right to choose if and when to bear children was the foundation on which authentic equality between men and women must rest. The debate was intense and emotionally charged because reproductive issues involve sexuality, ethical and religious values, medical technology, and constitutional rights to privacy as well as economic dependence, physical vulnerability, and state power. In the second half of the twentieth century, particularly in the wake of the Supreme Court's decision in *Roe* v. *Wade* (1973), the battle for reproductive control has been fought over policies governing access to abortion.

Issues of race, class, and gender complicate this effort. For many white middle-class feminists, preserving abortion rights is a top priority. Advocates of birth control, they see abortion as a measure of last resort. Without that option, women's efforts to plan their lives, to set priorities, and to make choices are severely constrained, and constrained in ways that men's are not. For poor women and women of color who have been the subject of involuntary sterilization and who lack access to a wide range of medical services, abortion is only one among many essential needs, and not necessarily the most pressing one. For many other women, abortion is not an essential need at all. Believing that the fetus is a human being from the moment of conception and that motherhood is woman's key reason for being, they deny any connection between equality and access to abortion. They reject the feminist contention that denying women access to abortion is one way men use the power of the state to reinforce their power over women. Whether the state should permit or fund abortions for teenage victims of incest is the most dramatic of the issues in conflict.

Incest is only one aspect of the larger problem of sexual violence, considered by feminists the ultimate expression of male dominance. Sexual violence, they insist, is violence, not sex, and a public, not a private, matter. Rape crisis centers, battered women's shelters, "Take Back the Night" marches—all are expressions of the feminists' insistence that government respond to male violence against women. Feminists also directly attack the notion that female victims of violence are in some measure to blame by virtue of provocative dress and behavior or prior sexual experience. In the late 1970s they convinced policymakers that sexual harassment was a form of economic discrimination and that those who maintained workplaces were legally obliged to take action to prevent it.

Feminists also have exposed the link between sexual violence and pornography. Many of them argue that material that objectifies women and equates violence against them with sexual pleasure is an invasion of their civil liberties. This interpretation represents a radical reformulation of traditional civil liberties arguments and indicates a willingness on the part of some feminists to reconsider the boundaries of protected speech. The controversial nature of pornography and the complex issues of civil rights and civil liberties raised by efforts to deal with it once again exemplify the challenges involved in creating a society where men and women are equal.

THE ANGUISH OF FUNDAMENTAL CHANGE

Reconciling equality and difference, equity and justice involves feminists in a task as consequential as any in human history. Relationships assumed to be the result of choice, even of love, have been exposed as hierarchical constructs involving power and control. Such exposures are always traumatic. "All the decent drapery of life is . . . rudely torn off," complained the British legislator Edmund Burke in his *Reflections on the Revolution in France* more than two hundred years ago. "When ancient opinions and rules of life are taken away, the loss cannot possibly be estimated. From that moment we have no compass to govern us; nor can we know distinctly to what port we steer."

Even those in the vanguard of change can appreciate its difficulty; old habits are hard to break even for those determined to break them. For those who are not the initiators, challenges to long-standing beliefs and behaviors, whether issued now or in the past, can be at best unwelcome, and at worst profoundly threatening. Feminism is no exception. Demands for equal power, resources, and prestige are usually seen as redistributive; giving one party its share of the pie may result in a smaller share for the other. Even individuals who believe in equality in the abstract may find themselves loath to share power and privileges in practice, especially when their own lives are affected intimately.

New governmental policies designed to provide women equal protection in the law, equity in the workplace, and parity in politics have been only part of what feminists are about. Cultural values as well as social institutions are under scrutiny. Even the definition of family has been reevaluated, as the 1980 White House–sponsored Conference on Families made all too clear. "Family" has always been construed to refer to persons who are related by blood, marriage, or adoption. The term is now being broadened to include, for example, two mothers with children, all of whom live together, or an unmarried heterosexual couple who are childless. "Anyone living under the same roof that provides support for each other, regardless of blood, marriage, or adoption" seems to qualify, complained a member of the Reagan administration. To recognize these arrangements as multiple family forms, which many feminists do, is to legitimate people who, from the viewpoint of traditionalists, are living illegitimate life-styles.

From this perspective it is hardly surprising that gender changes that feminists regard as expanding options for women and men alike are seen by traditionalists as rejecting cherished beliefs and practices—as "neuterizing society." Women who believe they have lived useful and admirable lives by the old rules often regard feminists' attacks on traditional gender roles as an attack on a way of life they have mastered, and hence an attack on them personally. In *The Power of the Positive Woman* (1977), Phyllis Schlafly expressed the fear of some women that "a woman who has been a good wife and homemaker for decades" will be "turned out to pasture with impunity" by "a new, militant breed of women's liberationists" (p. 81) prepared to sacrifice justice for equality.

At issue are not just individual economic security and personal identity but also the larger social order. Convinced that biological differences between the sexes dictate "natural" roles, traditionalists see the maintenance of these roles as socially and morally necessary—a source of stability in a world of flux. Thus feminist insistence that women should be able to seek fulfillment in the public world of work and power as well as in the private world of home and family is viewed by traditionalists as an egocentric demand elevating personal gratification above familial duty. "Feminists praise self-centeredness and call it liberation," observed New Right activist Connie Marshner in *The New Traditional Woman* (1982). By the same token, the demand that women themselves be the ultimate judge of whether and when to bear children is seen by some not as a legitimate desire to ensure a good life for those children who are born but as an escape from maternal obligations that threatens the future of the family and ultimately, therefore, of society itself.

To suggest that some Americans find feminism an essential part of their identity and that others define themselves and their lives in terms of traditionalism is not to suggest that the ideological history of woman is bipolar. It embraces many variants. Nor do we suggest that there is nothing on which the two groups agree. Traditionalist women may be as suspicious of male-controlled institutions as feminists are, and as vocal and publicly active on behalf of their goals. Feminists may be just as dedicated to family as traditionalists are. Both groups identify with "sisterhood" and see "women's issues" as special, although they do not consistently agree on what they are or how they should be addressed. Partisans of these issues may unite or divide along class, occupational, or political lines. But no matter where they fall on the ideological spectrum, all American women, not merely feminists, are forging a definition of self—and of gender—that extends beyond the definitions of the past, illustrating in the process that change in relations between the sexes is an intrinsic part of the complex and diverse history of the United States.

BIBLIOGRAPHY

General Works

Degler, Carl N. *At Odds: Women and the Family in America from the Revolution to the Present* (1980).

D'Emilio, John, and Estelle B. Freedman. *Intimate Matters: A History of Sexuality in America* (1988).

Evans, Sara M. *Born for Liberty: A History of Women in America* (1989).

Filene, Peter G. *Him/Her/Self: Sex Roles in Modern America* (2d ed. 1986).

Gilmore, David D. *Masculinity in the Making: Cultural Concepts of Masculinity* (1990).

Jones, Jacqueline. *Labor of Love, Labor of Sorrow: Black Women, Work, and the Family from Slavery to the Present* (1985).

Kessler-Harris, Alice. *Out to Work: A History of Wage-Earning Women in the United States* (1982).

Lerner, Gerda. *The Creation of Patriarchy* (1986).

Scott, Joan W. *Gender and the Politics of History* (1988).

Anthologies

Brod, Harry, ed. *The Making of Masculinities: The New Men's Studies* (1987).

Carnes, Mark C., and Clyde Griffin, eds. *Meanings for Manhood: Constructions of Masculinity in Victorian America* (1990).

DuBois, Ellen Carol, and Vicki L. Ruiz, eds. *Unequal Sisters: A Multicultural Reader in U.S. Women's History* (1990).

Kerber, Linda K., and Jane Sherron De Hart, eds. *Women's America: Refocusing the Past* (1991).

Pleck, Elizabeth H., and Joseph H. Pleck, eds. *The American Man* (1980).

Works Using Gender as a Category of Analysis

Aron, Cindy Sondik. *Ladies and Gentlemen of the Civil Service* (1987).

Benson, Susan Porter. *Counter Cultures: Saleswomen, Managers, and Customers in American Department Stores: 1890–1940* (1986).

Blewett, Mary H. *Men, Women and Work: Class, Gender, and Protest in the Nineteenth-Century New England Shoe Industry, 1780–1910* (1988).

Boydston, Jean. *Home and Work: Housework, Wages, and the Ideology of Labor in the Early Republic* (1990).

Chambers-Schiller, Lee. *Liberty, a Better Husband: Single Women in America, The Generations of 1780–1840* (1984).

Cott, Nancy F. *The Grounding of Modern Feminism* (1987).

Deutsch, Sarah. *No Separate Refuge: Culture, Class, and Gender on an Anglo-Hispanic Frontier in the American Southwest, 1880–1940* (1987).

Faragher, John Mack. *Women and Men on the Overland Trail* (1979).

Fox-Genovese, Elizabeth. *Within the Plantation Household: Black and White Women of the Old South* (1988).

Gordon, Linda. *Heroes of Their Own Lives: The Politics and History of Family Violence, Boston, 1880–1960* (1988).

Gorn, Elliott. *The Manly Art: Bare-Knuckle Prize Fighting in America* (1986).

Hall, Jacquelyn Dowd, Jame Leloudis, Robert Korstad, Mary Murphy, Lu Ann Jones, and Christopher B. Daly. *Like a Family: The Making of a Southern Cotton Mill World* (1987).

Jensen, Joan. *Loosening the Bonds: Mid-Atlantic Farm Women, 1750–1850* (1986).

Karlsen, Carol F. *The Devil in the Shape of a Woman: Witchcraft in Colonial New England* (1987).

Kerber, Linda K. *Women of the Republic: Intellect and Ideology in Revolutionary America* (1980).

Kessler-Harris, Alice. *A Woman's Wage: Historical Meanings and Social Consequences* (1990).

Lebsock, Suzanne. *The Free Women of Petersburg: Status and Culture in a Southern Town, 1784–1860* (1984).

Mathews, Donald G., and Jane Sherron De Hart. *Sex, Gender, and the Politics of ERA: A State and the Nation* (1990).

May, Elaine Tyler. *Homeward Bound: American Families in the Cold War Era* (1988).

Milkman, Ruth. *Gender at Work: The Dynamics of Job Segregation by Sex During World War II* (1987).

Morantz-Sanchez, Regina. *Sympathy and Science: Women Physicians in America* (1985).

Ryan, Mary P. *Cradle of the Middle Class: The Family in Oneida County, New York, 1790–1865* (1981).

Smith-Rosenberg, Carroll. *Disorderly Conduct: Visions of Gender in Victorian America* (1985).

Stansell, Christine. *City of Women: Sex and Class in New York, 1789–1860* (1986).

White, Deborah Gray. *Ar'n't I a Woman?: Female Slaves in the Plantation South* (1985).

Wyatt-Brown, Bertram. *Honor and Violence in the Old South* (1986).

SEE ALSO **Feminist Approaches to Social History**; **Fraternal Organizations**; **Women and Work**; **Women's Organizations**; and various essays in the sections "**Family History**" and "**Social Problems, Social Control, and Social Protest**."

SEXUAL ORIENTATION

Leila J. Rupp

"THIS DAY WE examined 5 beastly Sodomiticall boyes, which confessed their wickedness not to bee named," wrote the Reverend Francis Higgeson on his voyage to New England in 1629 (quoted in Katz, *Gay American History,* p. 20). What did it mean to be a "Sodomiticall" boy? Did these boys have something in common with Native American men who dressed as women and engaged in sexual relations with other men? With nineteenth-century women who expressed their passionate love for their female friends? With contemporary self-identified gay men and lesbians? These are the questions that confront the historian interested in same-sex sexuality or what is often called sexual orientation.

Not all cultures have defined sexual relationships primarily on the basis of the sex of the partners. Throughout history and in different parts of the world, generational and gender differences between sexual partners have been more significant than sex differences. In classical Athens, seventeenth-century Japan, and parts of contemporary New Guinea and Melanesia, age differences were or are the most crucial element of sexual relations between boys and men. In some Native American tribes of North America and in Tahiti, gender differences are most important in sexual relations between individuals who take on cross-gender dress and roles and their same-sex sexual partners, who remain within their gender. In the words of Jesuit explorer Pierre François Xavier de Charlevoix, written in 1721, "men were seen to wear the dress of women without a blush, and to debase themselves so as to perform those occupations which are most peculiar to the sex, from whence followed a corruption of morals past all expression" (quoted in Katz [1976], p. 290). Sexual role—the part one plays in sexual activity—is predetermined in transgenerational and transgenderal relations and also has played a critical part in the Western tradition in defining men's sexual relations with a same-generation, same-gender male: activity as an "inserter" has been acceptable, as an "insertee" unacceptable. In all of these phenomena, something other than sexual-object choice is primary.

So the very concept of sexual orientation is grounded in modern assumptions. How problematic this is lies at the center of an ongoing debate over the nature of sexuality: Is there something essential or inherent about the character of human sexuality, or is sexuality largely or entirely socially constructed? The very notion of a history of sexuality presupposes that changing societal conditions affect sexuality, so it is not surprising that social constructionism is dominant among historians. But the essentialist position raises important questions for the consideration of the history of sexual orientation.

For historians interested in same-sex sexual behavior, the key question is whether or not there have always been "gay people." We know that there has always been same-sex sexual activity (although the purest social constructionist argument would maintain that this is not necessarily so). We also know that societies throughout history have viewed such activity in very different ways. The debate centers on the significance of same-sex sexual activity to those engaged in it. John Boswell, who has written a history of what he calls "gay people" in Europe from the beginning of the Christian era to the fourteenth century, argued that there have always been people "conscious of erotic inclination toward their own gender as a distinguishing characteristic," although he later modified this to people "whose erotic interest is predominantly directed toward their own gender" (quoted in Duberman et al., eds., p. 35). Although Boswell eschews the label "essentialist," he has been so identified by others for this position. In contrast, social constructionists argue that we cannot accurately speak of "gay people" until the formation of a homosexual identity sometime between the seventeenth and the late nineteenth centuries. Previously, same-sex sexual activity had little significance, either in the minds of participants or in the view of society at large, for defining a type of person.

The central issue that emerges from this debate is the relationship between sexual desire, behavior, and identity. Is desire inherent or a social construct? Under what conditions does desire lead to behavior? In what circumstances does identity develop out of sexual behavior? Regardless of one's position on an essentialist-social constructionist continuum, the analytical separation of the concepts of desire, behavior, and identity is essential to a consideration of the history of same-sex sexuality.

"Sexual orientation," then, is a term designed to describe sexual-object choice in a society that distinguishes the categories of heterosexuality, homosexuality, and bisexuality and insists upon the significance of sexual desire and behavior for identity. Recognizing this, we can nevertheless identify a history of same-sex desire and same-sex sexual activity dating back to the origins of what became American society.

SAME-SEX SEXUALITY IN PREINDUSTRIAL SOCIETY

Same-Sex Sexuality in Native American, European, and African Sexual Systems The Native American cultures of North America, despite great tribal diversity, tended to foster sexual expressiveness. Most cultures viewed nudity, sexual activity, and reproduction as natural and positive and condoned sexual experimentation among children. Premarital intercourse, polygyny, and easy divorce characterized the sexual systems of many tribes. Such sex-positive cultures accepted same-sex sexuality as well. Among some peoples, same-sex sexual activity might be a part of a childhood experimentation or even an acceptable form of adult relationship. Among the Iroquois, for example, what Jesuit missionary Joseph François Lafitan called "particular friendships" among young men served as a cohesive social bond. In other Native American cultures as well, intense friendships, same-sex play among children and young adults, and adult homosexuality might be viewed as acceptable emotional and erotic possibilities.

The most prominent form of same-sex sexuality among Native Americans was transgenderal. Tribes scattered throughout what would become the United States, although apparently not in eastern North America, created an institutionalized cross-gender role. Men might take on the dress and social roles of women and engage in sexual relationships with male-gendered men. Less frequently, women might cross gender boundaries as well. The European settlers called a cross-gender man a *berdache,* a French version of Persian and Arabic words meaning a young male slave kept for sexual purposes. In fact, the cross-gender institution had spiritual, social, and economic, as well as sexual, manifestations. What is most significant for the history of sexual orientation is the fact that the cross-gender role institutionalized same-sex (although transgenderal) sexual relations. Despite the fact that cross-gender individuals took on the dress, behavior, occupations, and manners of the other gender, their sexual relationships with non-cross-gender partners were not conceptualized as heterosexual ones. The Mohave language includes a term that refers specifically to the lesbian lovemaking of a cross-gender female and her partner, and the Lakotas have a word for male-male anal intercourse that is derived from the word for a *berdache.* Until contact with Europeans, Native American tribes with institutionalized cross-gender roles accepted same-sex sexual relations between cross-gender and non-cross-gender individuals.

Native American cultures with a cross-gender tradition viewed both gender and sexuality very differently than did European colonists. European culture included no institutionalized cross-gender role and vigorously repressed same-sex sexual experimentation and relationships. Nevertheless, same-sex sexuality was not unknown in the societies from which the European settlers came. Despite long-standing civil and religious condemnation, and the threat of execution, individuals did engage in same-sex sexual behavior in a number of contexts. First, elite men of the nobility or clergy might engage in sexual acts with younger or lower-status men in an atmosphere of privileged sexual license. As the Earl of Rochester put it, "missing my whore, I bugger my page" (quoted in Duberman et al., eds., p. 92). For such casual sexual encounters, subordination by age or socioeconomic status was more important than sexual-object choice. Same-sex relations not differentiated by age or status seemed to occur mostly among the less privileged.

Second, sex-segregated subcultures harbored individuals engaged in same-sex sexual activity, sometimes but not always differentiated by age. Priests (much more rarely nuns) represented one group traditionally associated with such relations, but more important in the period of European overseas expansion were pirates and sailors. Aboard ship, sexual activity could only be solitary or same-sex. From sodomy trials we have evidence that same-sex acts did take place among both sailors and pirates. How consensual they were, whether they were primarily situational or whether men inclined to such relations might have sought out seafaring occupations, and what consequences such relations had for the individuals and the crew we do not know.

Third, cases came to light in which women secretly crossed the gender divide, successfully passing as men and marrying women. Whether they did so primarily for the economic and social freedom that male dress and occupations provided, or whether sexual motivation figured into their decisions, we may never know. In any case, such women fought as soldiers and learned male occupations, met and married women, and only came to light when someone exposed the masquerade. Punishment was swift and severe for the usurpation of male privilege, particularly if it involved the use of what were called "material instruments" to "counterfeit the office of a husband." The law and the public both recognized and denied the existence of women's same-sex sexuality, torn between horror and disbelief centered in a "phallocentric" concept of sexuality.

Fourth, urban subcultures of men interested in same-sex sexual activity, made possible by concentrations of people, relative anonymity, and independence from the family, began to emerge as early as the fifteenth century in Venice. By the early eighteenth century, cities such as London, Paris, and Amsterdam sheltered subcultures of effeminate men who frequented taverns, parks, and public latrines, shared a style of dress and behavior, and could identify each other and be recognized by others outside the subculture. Such "sodomites" or, as they were called in England, "mollies," although subject to arrest and punishment, found sexual partners and company within the subculture. These four phenomena suggest that European culture recognized forms of transgenerational, transgenderal, and occasionally "egalitarian" same-sex relations, although these were not institutionalized in the same sense as cross-gender relations in Native American culture.

Africans, like Europeans, brought developed sexual systems to the New World, although the deliberate attempt by white men to break cultural bonds among enslaved Africans and the conditions of slavery had an impact on African American sexuality. In traditional African societies for which we have information about same-sex sexuality, a variety of forms of relations exist today. In some societies, egalitarian same-sex sexual relations among men during adolescence and among women in polygynous households are viewed as preparation for or a complement to heterosexual relations in marriage. Transgenerational relations are rarer. Among the Nzema of Ghana, "friendship marriage" between a man and a male teenager, and sometimes between two women of different generations, serves as a means of transmitting social and spiritual guidance. Most common are transgenderal relations similar to those found among Native American societies, although these exist primarily in central, southern, and northeastern Africa. As with *berdaches,* spiritual aspects of the cross-gender role are particularly important.

In the colonies, an unequal meeting of these sexual systems took place. Although the European system, with its rigorous condemnation of same-sex relations, would win out, it was not the only way to organize sexuality and it was not the only system to have an impact on individuals living in what became the United States.

Same-Sex Sexual Behavior in the Colonies The European explorers, traders, missionaries, and settlers in the colonies recognized the existence of different sexual systems and denounced those that deviated from the European model as immoral. Sexual expressiveness among Native American societies provoked disgust. Although the *berdache* phenomenon either never existed among the tribes of the northeast or died out by the time of European contact, the Spanish and French, to their horror, encountered cross-gender individuals in the Southeast, on the Great Plains, and in the Southwest and West. Europeans did whatever they could to try to eliminate the cross-gender role in Native American societies.

The legal codes of the early colonies reflected the European condemnation of same-sex sexual relations. As a threat to marriage, family, and reproduction, sodomy represented a serious crime that could, and sometimes did, merit execution in the New England, Middle Atlantic, and southern colonies. Laws in the New England and middle colonies and the English "buggery" statute, adopted by the southern colonies, called for death for "the horrible, detestable sins of Sodomie" or what was sometimes called, with typical disregard of women, "man lying with man" (quoted in Katz [1983], pp. 68, 85). Records document nineteen legal cases involving the charge of sodomy and five executions in the period from 1607 to 1740.

Despite the passage of sodomy laws throughout the colonies, regional differences created varying environments for same-sex sexual relations. In the New England colonies, attempts to build utopian religious communities led to the close supervision of morality in a family-centered world. In the Chesapeake region, in contrast, Europeans came originally to exploit rather than settle, and the area contained, until the end of the seventeenth century, more men than women, scattered settlements rather than concentrations of population, and more differentiated inhabitants, including large numbers of indentured servants and slaves. The sex ratio and preponderance of young single migrants may have led to more premarital and extramarital sexuality, perhaps including same-sex sexuality.

Existing evidence of same-sex sexual behavior in the preindustrial societies of the colonies and early United States is sparse. There were no urban concentrations large enough to allow for the development of male same-sex sexual subcultures, so all of the documented cases concern pairs or small groups, primarily of white men. Many of the cases involve indentured servants, suggesting that relations of subordination may have structured these sexual acts in the European tradition. One wealthy, respected, married citizen of Connecticut, for example, was tried in 1677 for sodomy and attempted sodomy with a series of young men, many of them servants, over a thirty-year period. In the 1650s, the Reverend Michael Wigglesworth, a Puritan divine, found himself tormented by affection, love, and lust for his Harvard students.

That same-sex sexual desire and behavior was not entirely confined to elite white men, however, is clear from the limited evidence concerning African American men and white women. (Not surprisingly, given the bias of the sources, there seems to be no documentation of same-sex behavior among African American women.) What impact the role of same-sex sexuality in the sexual systems of various African societies had in the American colonies remains a mystery. Research suggests that the sexual norms of some of the first African peoples enslaved and brought to the colonies included premarital intercourse and polygyny. Perhaps some accepted same-sex relations as well. Court records reveal two cases of sodomy involving black men; both called for execution. In the early eighteenth century, Pennsylvania legislators revised the colony's sodomy legislation to eliminate the death penalty for white offenders but specifically to prescribe it for blacks.

The courts also made distinctions between women and men: sodomy, in general, was a specifically male crime. Nevertheless, courts in the Massachusetts Bay Colony found a female servant guilty of "unseemly practices betwixt her and another maid" in 1642 and considered the case of two married women engaged in "lewd behavior each with [the] other upon a bed" in 1649 (quoted in Katz [1983], pp. 85–86, 92). In addition to such acts, we have evidence of at least one woman who crossed the line of gender. During the Revolution, Deborah Sampson disguised herself as a man, joined the Continental army, and engaged in romantic relationships with women.

Whether involving women or men, African Americans or whites, same-sex sexual acts did not identify a participant as a certain kind of person. Rather, religious and civil authorities focused on the acts, which they condemned as sinful and unnatural, perhaps more dangerous than but not qualitatively different from other nonmarital and non-procreative sexual behavior. There was no permanent cultural category or identity for those who engaged in same-sex sexual relations. Nevertheless, the existing evidence does suggest the recognition that some individuals regularly engaged in—and preferred—same-sex sexual behavior.

Economic, social, and political developments in the colonies in the eighteenth century, which occurred locally and slowly rolled across regions, laid the basis for changes in the dominant sexual system. The rise of commercialized agriculture, the expansion of trade, and the growth of cities undermined family and community control of sexuality. Religious, political, and intellectual currents reconceptualized sexuality as individualistic, natural, and separable from reproduction. All of these developments had implications for same-sex sexuality: urbanization, geographical mobility, individualism, and the valuing of sexuality apart from reproduction provided the context in which same-sex desires and acts might increase. Complicating the sexual system was an increasing differentiation of sexuality on the basis of race, class, and gender. As commercial capitalism gave way to industrial capitalism, the place of same-sex sexuality within American society changed.

SAME-SEX SEXUALITY IN INDUSTRIALIZING SOCIETY

Transformation of the Sexual System The family dominated both the economic and sexual systems of the preindustrial society established by Europeans in North America. The rise of the factory system in the Northeast accelerated the process, already under way, of shifting the production of goods and services outside the four walls of the home. If the family was no longer a central economic unit, however, it retained its sexual and reproductive functions and even increased its emotional ones.

The economic and social transformation associated with the decline of the family economy had important consequences for the sexual system. First, the dominant nineteenth-century sexual system accepted the separability of sexuality and reproduction. With the decline of the family economy, children became less of an economic asset and required more of a financial investment, at least for the urban middle class. In part as a result, the birthrate for white, native-born, urban middle-class families dropped as the use of contraception and abortion increased. Guardians of sexual morality could less easily proclaim reproduction the sole purpose of sexuality, eliminating one argument against nonreproductive sexual acts, including those engaged in by same-sex partners. Although the decline in fertility was not universal—black slave women, southern white women, white women on the frontier, and immigrant women continued to bear large numbers of children—the trend begun in the urban Northeast spread throughout society.

Second, the transformed sexual system posited a fundamental difference between male and female sexuality. The double standard was nothing new, but traditionally women in Western society had been viewed as just as sexual as—even more sexual than—men. The nineteenth-century sexual system represented an aberration on this point, for it reversed the traditional assumption of female lasciviousness and proclaimed the ideal woman inherently passionless. As a response to the increasing separation of male and female spheres among the urban middle class and the concomitant association of middle-class women with the home and domesticity, the tenet of women's sexual differences from men served to aid middle-class men's sexual self-control within marriage and separate good women from bad. Ironically, the ideology of sexual difference, in conjunction with economic and social sex-segregation, also facilitated same-sex love and sexuality.

Finally, the newly developing sexual system reified differences not only of gender but of race and class as well. Sexuality became associated, in the eyes of the white middle class, with racial and ethnic minorities and the working class. In fact, not all groups conformed to the dominant system. African American slave communities, for example, maintained their own values with regard to courtship, sexuality, marriage, childbearing, and divorce. Mexican women and men on the southwestern frontier, in accordance with a Mexican working-class custom, accepted cohabitation in informal unions as well as marriage. And young, single working-class women in urban areas challenged both older concepts of their depravity and new ones of their asexuality to carve out a culture that had some chance of meeting their own sexual and emotional needs. The association of sexuality, race, and class both facilitated intimate (but presumably nonsexual) same-sex relations among the middle class and eroticized cross-class and interracial relations.

The separation of sexuality and reproduction, the assertion of female and male difference, and the increased differentiation of sexuality along gender, race, and class lines, along with the process of industrial and urban development, had consequences for the expression of same-sex desire. Older forms of interaction—individuals engaged in sexual acts, sexual behavior within sex-segregated subcultures, women passing as men and marrying other women—continued to exist, particularly on the frontier of white settlement. In addition, two new developments were particularly important for the history of sexual orientation: the blossoming of romantic friendship and the rise of urban subcultures.

Same-Sex Sexuality on the American Frontier The processes of industrialization and urbanization had differential regional effects, and in some ways white settlement on the western frontier meant the reestablishment of a preindustrial mode of economic organization. At the same time, the dominant gender ideology of industrializing society, including the sexual system, had an impact on white settlers who moved west. Other factors, too, differentiated the frontier experience: the growth of boom towns around the mining industry, the unbalanced sex ratios created by the predominantly male migration to mining and ranching areas (most extreme among the Chinese population), and the diversity of cultures, including Native American, Mexican, Chinese, and native-born white. All had consequences for the expression of same-sex sexuality.

The numerical predominance of men over women among the non–Native American population had consequences for both women and men. For women, it meant the establishment of a variety of sexual alternatives, both voluntary and forced, to traditional monogamous marriage: polygyny in the case of the Mormons, cohabitation for Mexican women, sexual slavery for Chinese women, and sexual exploitation or prostitution for all groups of women. We know very little about the impact of such arrangements on same-sex sexual relations between women, although the fact that prostitutes sometimes lived together and formed close and loving bonds suggests that at least some frontier prostitutes must have had sex with each other. A story circulated in the Comstock lode in northwestern Nevada, for example, that the infamous Calamity Jane had been ejected from a brothel for corrupting the inmates. In another incident in the area, a male audience at a show discovered that a flirtatious gentleman was really a woman. If frontier conditions created the potential for sexual exploitation of women, particularly those deemed "bad" or available, they also may have led to sexual relations among prostitutes and an increase in the number of women who passed as men.

For men, the frontier sex ratio led to the formation of sex-segregated subcultures in which same-sex relations might flourish. As with pirates and sailors, same-sex sexuality was a response to isolation from women and perhaps in some cases what drew men to—or at least did not deter them from—frontier living. Cowboys, for example, spent most of their time on the range or in camps in all-male company. Some formed deep attachments; in the words of one cowboy whose partner had died, they loved each other "the way men do" but never spoke about it (quoted in Williams, p. 158). Others, as suggested by cowboy limericks and the testimony of early twentieth-century cowboys, engaged in overtly sexual relationships.

The same kinds of attachments may have formed among other groups of men on the frontier. Miners, for example, also lived in isolation from women. The sex ratio among the Chinese population was particularly distorted because of immigration policies designed to prevent family settlement. In California in 1860, for example, there were almost twenty Chinese men for every Chinese woman, most of whom were brought into the country to work as prostitutes. Perhaps Chinese men, coming from a society with a long tradition of homosexuality, engaged in same-sex relations. Certainly the same-sex sexuality of *berdaches* was not unknown on the frontier, since popular writings and reports referred to their existence. Some white frontiersmen who lived in Native American cultures even reported sexual advances from *berdaches.*

Same-sex sexuality in sex-segregated subcultures was not a new phenomenon, but the move west by white settlers in the nineteenth century created more sex segregation. A different kind of separation of the sexes—more ideological than literal—affected women and men of the urban middle class as the processes of industrialization and urbanization proceeded in the settled Northeast. A new phenomenon, known as romantic friendship, emerged in this context.

Romantic Friendship The ideology of sexual difference between women and men laid the basis for societal acceptance of intense, passionate relationships between two women and, less frequently, between two men. If women's and men's polarized natures were, in theory, intended to combine in marriage, the notion of sexual difference might also lead to the glorification of same-sex relations. The sex-segregated social worlds of the upper and middle classes created the context in which such relations flourished.

Romantic friendships among women grew out of a female world of kin and friends bound together by female rituals and institutions. Women might meet their lifelong friends through their families or at school, and they often maintained an intimate friendship into marriage. In general, such attachments seemed compatible with marriage. Until the opening of employment, especially in the professions, provided the possibility of economic independence for middle-class women, marriage seemed the only possibility. Unmarried daughters had little choice except to remain within the family, after their parents' deaths moving to the household of a brother or sister. By the second half of the nineteenth century, however, the expansion of employment opportunities meant that romantic friends might decide to forgo marriage and make a life together. These partnerships between romantic friends, which came to be known as "Boston marriages" because of their prevalence in the urban

Northeast, substituted for heterosexual relationships in a way that ultimately proved threatening to the social order.

But until the late nineteenth century, romantic friendships among women met with not just toleration but approbation. Prescriptive literature advocated such bonds as particularly appropriate for women as emotional, spiritual creatures with little to do in the world. Despite the fact that romantic friendship involved vows of love and expressions of physical affection, the friends' gender and class position removed any suspicion of a sexual component. Thus, even when women expressed their love and need for each other, wrote of kissing and holding each other, and compared their relationships to those of husband and wife, they did not challenge the limits of respectability. Whether or not romantic friendships involved genital contact, they clearly had an erotic component. The complexity of these bonds in a society that did not yet divide "homosexuals" from "heterosexuals" is suggested by an exchange between a woman and her friend's fiancé in 1873. Molly, who loved Helena with "a passion such as I had never known until I saw you," congratulated Richard on their upcoming marriage by writing: "Do you know sir, that until you came along I believe that she loved me almost as girls love their lovers. *I know I loved her so.* Don't you wonder that I can stand the sight of you" (quoted in Smith-Rosenberg, "Female World of Love and Ritual," pp. 8–9).

Romantic friendship among women grew from the association of women with the heart and filled a void in lives shorn of most productive activity, but the homosociality of middle-class society also produced a male variety of romantic friendship. Although male romantic friends shared with female ones the sense that only same-sex friends could truly understand one another, they differed in shedding these bonds after the period of youth. Like women, young men formed ardent and romantic attachments and engaged in touching, kissing, and caressing. But they expected to move beyond such friendships when they became men and married. Kissing, hugging, even sharing a bed could be done openly, with no self-consciousness, because these were expressions of emotional intimacy, not sexuality. As male youth became men, they gave up their romantic friendships in the interests of independence, competitiveness, and emotional austerity, the hallmarks of true men. The socially acceptable same-sex bonds of youth had to be abandoned not because they smacked of eroticism, but because they sat uneasily with manly character.

For both women and men of the middle class, then, romantic friendship represented an emotional and sensual option. Societal acceptance of such bonds, and their compatibility with heterosexual relationships, reveals a very different societal conception of the nature of sexuality itself. Acts that would later be construed as sexual could be engaged in unself-consciously, not only by women assumed to be passionless but also by young men. This was a largely class-bound form of relationship, for the extended youth of middle-class men and the leisure of middle-class women played a central role in shaping romantic friendship, and the association of sexuality with the working class preserved the presumed asexuality of these relations. Outside the middle class, more sexualized urban subcultures were beginning to emerge.

The Rise of Urban Subcultures By the nineteenth century, American cities, like European cities in earlier centuries, began to provide the numbers, mobility, and anonymity that made same-sex sexual subcultures possible. With the development of an urban working class came the formation of a culture in which sexuality was more public and, for women, less confined to marriage than was characteristic of the middle class. Until late in the century this working-class subculture was defined by heterosexuality for women, but men began earlier to make contact with other men for both intra- and interclass sexual encounters. Horatio Alger, Jr., dismissed from his Unitarian ministry for sexual relations with boys in 1866, moved to New York where he took up not only the writing of stories but also participation in the work of "rescuing" working-class boys from the streets. In common with other writers and reformers not known for overt sexual interest in boys, Alger glorified the affection and support of older, powerful men for "gentle" boys from the "dangerous classes."

Within the "dangerous classes," all-male worlds fostered a concept of masculinity that substituted for the middle-class ideal of domesticity, with its emphasis on male responsibility and self-control. If working-class men had lost their economic independence and could not achieve manliness in the workplace, they could still be tough and strong. The "manly art" of prizefighting expressed these working-class values and fostered a homoerotic aesthetic. In an environment of male camaraderie, boxers slugged it out, admired as much for their beauty as their pugilistic skill. As one sporting journal described a boxer, "His swelling breast curved out like a cuirass: his shoulders were deep, with a bold curved blade, and the muscular development of the arm large and finely brought out" (quoted in Gorn, *The Manly Art,* p. 74).

The homoeroticism of male working-class culture attracted upper- and middle-class men interested in same-sex encounters. The poet Walt Whitman, for example, sought out working-class men in the streets of Manhattan, Brooklyn, and Washington. Whitman's writings suggest that he frequented taverns, parks, public baths, and other places where he met men with similar erotic interests, and his diaries record taking men home and sleeping with them. As a nurse during the Civil War, Whitman formed romantic friendships with the soldiers for whom he cared, referring to one attachment as "quite an affair, quite romantic" (quoted in D'Emilio and Freedman, *Intimate Matters,* p. 124). He established ongoing relationships with a series of men, all younger and working-class, and his poems celebrated male sexuality. Yet Whitman denied the homosexual character of his poetry in a letter to John Addington Symonds, an English pioneer of homosexual emancipation, perhaps in response to the developing notion of a deviant homosexual identity. Supporting this interpretation is the fact that Whitman used a code name and feminine pronouns when recording his agonies over a relationship with one of his male partners, Peter Doyle. In any case, what is clear from Whitman's life is that men interested in other men knew where to meet and how to recognize each other in the streets of American cities in the mid nineteenth century.

Commentators on the sexual scene confirm the existence of urban male subcultures by the late nineteenth century. A sex manual for males, written by Dr. George Napheys in 1871, referred to an urban sexual underworld in which men could meet each other for sexual encounters, including "restaurants frequented by men in women's attire, yielding themselves in indescribable lewdness" (quoted in Katz [1983], p. 157). Another doctor, Charles Nesbitt, wrote of beer gardens, dance halls, and city streets in New York and Philadelphia where effeminate men congregated. Some visitors to the underworld reported on gatherings of African American male "perverts." Writing in the early twentieth century, German sexologist and homosexual emancipation leader Magnus Hirschfeld and British sexologist Havelock Ellis both noted the prevalence of homosexual subcultures in the United States.

Such subcultures were a part of the underworld of commercialized sex and vice that grew up in the poor sections of cities. For the most part, they catered to men and not to women, who had less freedom of movement given their domestic responsibilities and the violence of the city streets. Still, Dr. Nesbitt reported meeting women dressed in men's clothes and uninterested in men at a dance hall in the late nineteenth century. Perhaps the most interesting evidence of a female subculture centers on the case of Jeanne Bonnet, a San Francisco woman regularly arrested for cross-dressing. In 1875, Bonnet organized a gang of prostitutes who left the brothels, cut off relations with men, and made a living by stealing. But not until the early decades of the twentieth century did a female public world of same-sex sexuality emerge on anything close to the scale of the male subculture. The scattered reports from the nineteenth-century focus on cross-dressing women, suggesting that previously isolated women involved in what was largely a working-class form of same-sex sexuality for women were beginning to make contact with one another.

The emergence of urban subcultures of men, and eventually women, who acted on their desires for same-sex sexual encounters undermined the societal acceptability of romantic friendships and paved the way for the development of the concept of a homosexual identity. By the last decades of the nineteenth century, American society was moving into the phase of consumer capitalism, and this was accompanied by another transformation of the sexual system with important consequences for the history of sexual orientation.

SAME-SEX SEXUALITY IN THE CONSUMER SOCIETY

The Sexual Revolution The sexual revolution of the turn of the century—or the rise of sexual liberalism—brought greater acceptance of sexual expressiveness. As the existence of prostitution and sexual subcultures in the nineteenth century makes clear, the sexualization of society was a matter of degree. Most significant was the growing acceptance of "respectable" white women's sexuality, the spread of sexual expressiveness from the urban working class to the middle class, and increasing public discussion and expression of sexuality. The shift to a consumer economy, accompanied by the growth of the advertising industry, and the continuing process of urbanization underlay the changes in sexual attitudes and behavior. The ideas of doctors and other theorists of sexuality, who came to advocate expression rather than control of sexuality, both reflected and influenced the new patterns of behavior.

The sexualization of society meant the breakdown of barriers between women and men; young women and men had more freedom to participate in heterosocial leisure activities and form heterosexual relationships outside of courtship and marriage. The sexual revolution had mixed consequences for same-sex sexuality: on the one hand, the increasing awareness of sexuality and especially the recognition of women's sexuality made formerly acceptable romantic friendships suspicious; on the other hand, new ideas about same-sex sexuality helped to publicize a deviant identity, inadvertently contributing to the growth of gay and lesbian subcultures.

For the first time, same-sex sexual desire became a publicly recognized and identifying characteristic of individuals. From the mid nineteenth century on, the medical profession had begun to distinguish among different kinds of nonprocreative sexuality, and this process led to the defining of same-sex sexuality as a particular kind of perversion. During the nineteenth century, the medical literature conceptualized the desire for sexual relations with a member of one's own sex as a symptom—not the defining characteristic—of what was called "inversion." Essentially, inversion referred to transgenderal behavior. According to sexologist George Beard, "men become women and women men, in their tastes, conduct, character, feelings and behavior" (quoted in Chauncey, p. 119). By 1900, sexologists began to move away from the idea of gender transformation and to focus more specifically on same-sex sexual-object choice as the defining characteristic of a new category of "homosexuals." British sexologist Havelock Ellis, for example, in 1913 defined sexual inversion as referring to sexual impulses "turned towards individuals of the same sex, while all the other impulses and tastes may remain those of the sex to which the person by anatomical configuration belongs" (quoted in Chauncey, p. 122). The doctors and psychologists argued about whether such impulses were congenital or acquired, but all agreed, by the early twentieth century, that they served as defining characteristics of individuals.

The sexual revolution, then, had different consequences for what would come to be called heterosexuals and homosexuals. Discussion and expression of different-sex sexuality became more public and accepted; same-sex sexuality also became more public, but it became the defining characteristic of a particular kind of deviant person. Some of the early sexologists were themselves attracted to others of their sex and pushed the congenital model of inversion as the rationale for the decriminalization of same-sex relations. Whatever the interests of individual sexologists, however, the new definitions represented a response to, more than a cause of, an emerging homosexual identity.

The Emergence of Identity The sexologists did not cause individuals who engaged in same-sex sexual behavior to see themselves as "inverts" or "homosexuals." Rather, the existence of urban subcultures, when they came to the attention of the doctors, contributed to the new medical definitions. The complex manner in which a "homosexual identity" came to be created can be seen in the history of an investigation of same-sex sexuality at the Newport Naval Training Station in 1919–1920.

The trial documents generated by the Navy's investigation reveal the competing discourses about same-sex sexuality that coexisted in the first decades of the twentieth century. The Navy, concerned about "immorality" in Newport, recruited "decoys" to seek out, have sex with, and testify against men who self-identified as "queers." Neither the decoys nor the other "straight" men with whom the "queers" had sexual relations were, in the Navy's eyes, "homosexual." Sexual role—taking the "female" or "passive" insertee role in sexual acts—determined one's identity. Among the "queers," who took on other aspects of the female gender role, sexual tastes, in addition to sexual role, distinguished individuals. Queers might be "fairies," who preferred oral sex, "pogues," who sought out anal sex, or "two-way artists," with more flexible preferences. For the Navy, effeminacy in appearance and sexual behavior—a limited kind of transgenderal behavior—marked men as deviant.

The defense in this case introduced a different line of interpretation by implying that sexual-object choice, rather than gender-role inversion, played the critical role in defining an individual as deviant. By calling into question the interests of the decoys, who volunteered to have sex with the "queers," the defense suggested that all men involved in same-sex sexual relations, no matter what sexual role they played and for what purpose, shared a similar status. Effeminacy—either in the form of imitating female behavior or, in the case of a prominent minister and a YMCA worker caught up in the accusations, in the form of nurturing behavior—was less important than participation in a sexual act.

The Newport investigation reveals the process of labeling in flux. Especially noteworthy is the lack of impact of the emerging medical discourse on the sexual identity of working-class men caught up in the Naval investigation and even on the military authorities behind the roundup. It would seem that the preexisting subcultures of the sexual underground may have sparked the medical reconceptualization of same-sex behavior. Only in a world that acknowledged same-sex sexuality as a defining characteristic could individuals embrace an identity based on sexual-object choice. Nevertheless, if the new medical model of homosexuality did not create an identity for individuals, it did help to spark public recognition of the growth of gay and lesbian subcultures.

The Growth of Lesbian and Gay Subcultures
The use of the terms "lesbian" and "gay" to refer to individuals involved in same-sex sexual relations moved from the subcultures to the wider public in the mid twentieth century. "Gay" originally referred to heterosexual prostitution and thus makes the link to the sexual underworld. Like the mainstream culture, the gay and lesbian subcultures of the early twentieth century were more open and more sex-integrated than the urban subcultures of earlier centuries. Despite some female participation in the nineteenth-century male subcultures, it was not until the 1920s that lesbian communities became visible. Women had fewer opportunities for economic independence, fewer chances to leave the family circle. But as what were called "women adrift"—women living apart from kin or employers—flocked to cities, the furnished-room districts that housed them allowed for sexual as well as economic autonomy, within limits. In Paris, where American expatriates gathered after the First World War, in Greenwich Village, in Chicago, and in Harlem, women as well as men congregated, were visible, and had an impact on the larger culture. The case of Harlem reveals the shape of these early-twentieth-century subcultures.

The sexual experimentation accepted within artistic communities gave homosexuality a place in Harlem, as in Greenwich Village and Paris. Prominent homosexual or bisexual writers, artists, and musicians formed same-sex relationships, and their experiences often colored their work. From the unpublished lesbian love poems of Angelina Weld Grimké, who formed romantic friendships with other women, to the circumspect references to homosexuality in the literature of Claude McKay and Langston Hughes, to the homoerotic writing and drawing of Bruce Nugent and the raunchy lyrics of the blues sung by Bessie Smith and others, the dazzling talent of the Harlem Renaissance called attention to the gay option. Those who actually went to Harlem, both African American and white, found a gay and lesbian subculture that offered a language, places to meet, and groups of women and men interested in making contact with others like them.

The blues publicized not only the existence of homosexuals, but a language to describe them. Lucille Bogan's "B.D. Women Blues" referred to "bulldagger" women, and "Sissy Man Blues" was a much-recorded male blues number. Although such songs poked fun at "mannish-acting" women and "lisping, swishing, womanish-acting" men, they served to identify and name individuals who built an identity around same-sex desire, and some of them even celebrated the gay lifestyle (quoted in Garber, "A Spectacle in Color," in *Hidden from History,* p. 320). The terms "bulldagger" (which derived from "bulldyker," referring to women "diked out" in male attire) and "sissy" called attention to the transgenderal aspects of homosexuality, thus making a link to the tradition of crossing women and effeminate men. But the core of identity in the gay and lesbian subculture of Harlem had to do with sexuality.

Private and semi-private parties provided a safe place for lesbians and gays to meet. The "rent party," which provided music, dancing, and the chance to buy bootleg alcohol in return for an admission fee, allowed the host to pay the rent and brought together people, not all of whom knew the host, with similar sexual interests. Gays and lesbians also attended the lavish parties thrown by A'Lelia Walker, the millionaire daughter of Madame C. J. Walker, who made her fortune marketing her hair-straightening process. "Buffet flats," private apartments where rooms could be rented by the night and where after-hours entertainment sometimes featured sex circuses, also might cater to a gay clientele. More public were speakeasies and costume balls, which attracted a racially integrated crowd of both heterosexuals and homosexuals.

Although the onset of the Depression brought an end to the Harlem Renaissance, a gay and lesbian subculture remained, albeit one less open and less racially mixed. What is clear is that the processes of urbanization, the commercialization of leisure, the sexualization of society, and changes in women's roles that had come together to shape the gay and lesbian subculture of Harlem were not unique. People with same-sex sexual desires increasingly had an identity, a name for themselves, and the possibility of finding others like them, at least in large cities.

The Rise of Movements The growth of subcultures in the early twentieth century paved the way for the emergence of a social movement focused on the place of lesbian and gay people in American society. The earliest American homosexual rights organization, the Chicago Society for Human Rights, was founded in 1924 by Henry Gerber, who, as part of the military occupation force in Germany after the First World War, had come in contact with the German homosexual rights movement. Gerber, able to recruit a few members, managed to publish two issues of a paper before the police arrested him and the other officers of the group. Reflecting the current medical views of homosexuality, as well as the American tradition of individual rights, the Society's declaration of purpose proclaimed that the organization would promote and protect "the interests of people who by reasons of mental and physical abnormalities are abused and hindered in the legal pursuit of happiness which is guaranteed them by the Declaration of Independence" (quoted in Katz [1976], p. 387).

In 1930, a German émigré, Ernst Klopfleisch, conceived a plan to form a similar organization in New York. Klopfleisch, like Gerber, knew about the German Scientific-Humanitarian Committee and had made plans while still in Germany to turn a summer resort where he worked into a gathering place for "inverts." He planned to recruit membership through the costume balls and raise money by sponsoring dances. Although the organization never got off the ground, the concept of building an organization through the subculture is significant.

It was not until after the Second World War that an enduring gay and lesbian movement began. The war itself played a critical role in furthering the process of the growth of the gay and lesbian subcultures that proved so crucial to political organizing. Not only did the war bring about increased geographical mobility, removing mobilized soldiers and sailors and war workers recruited to boom towns alike from the confines of small-town life, but the sex-segregated nature of both the military and war industry heightened the possibility that individuals with unexpressed or unacknowledged desires for same-sex sexual contacts would make them. As part of the intensified psychological testing designed to improve the mental health of the armed forces, men inducted into the military encountered frank and potentially consciousness-raising questions about their sexual conduct and desires. Women in the new female branches of the military found a high proportion of lesbians among their colleagues. Women with access to formerly male jobs in industry experienced a loosening of social and sexual control; even respectable white middle-class women socialized in public without men and wore pants publicly without reproach. In the interests of the American war effort, lesbians and gays even found their sexuality tolerated by the military. The result of all of this was a boom in lesbian and gay subcultures. San Francisco, the port of departure for and arrival from the Pacific theater, owes its reputation as a lesbian and gay center to the war years.

Demobilization meant, of course, the reversal of many of these trends. Not only did women find themselves pushed out of high-paying industrial jobs, but lesbians and gay men in the military faced an official drive to eliminate them once the war had been won. Fueling the fire, the anticommunist purges whipped up by Senator Joseph McCarthy linked Communist subversion and "homosexual perversion." Gay men and lesbians lost jobs in government as well as the military, with devastating personal consequences. But the witch-hunts did not destroy the existing subcultures; in fact, public discussion of the "homosexual menace" may even have spread word of their existence.

Lesbian life in the 1950s developed in particularly significant directions. Women—especially middle- and upper-class women—continued to form relationships with other women that neither they nor the larger society labeled "lesbian." But continuing the process begun in the 1920s, a public working-class lesbian culture developed in the world of the bars, providing separate space for avowedly lesbian women in a smattering of cities throughout the country. Although far fewer in numbers than gay bars—in 1963 a gay author estimated that there were only thirty exclusively lesbian bars in the entire country, when there were almost that many for men in San Francisco alone—they played an extremely important role. The bar culture had well-defined norms and modes of dress and behavior. Women identified as either "butch" or "femme," not as a mimicking of heterosexuality but as an erotic statement. Butch and femme couples, on the city streets, proclaimed their sexual orientation publicly. In the world of the lesbian bar, butch and femme roles determined an individual's potential sexual partners and structured relationships between women. Like female drag in the gay male world, butch and femme roles challenged mainstream gender roles and even created a core identity.

In the context of external oppression and cultural resistance, the first phase of the gay and lesbian movement, known as the homophile movement, emerged. In 1950, a small group of gay men with leftist connections formed the Mattachine Society, which in its original secret, cell-like, and hierarchical incarnation was modeled on the Communist party. The organization sponsored discussion groups, developed a theory of homosexuals as a cultural minority, fought police harassment, and even began to publish a magazine, *ONE,* in 1953. But the organization's structure, which facilitated a progressive analysis and militant action, also limited recruitment and made Mattachine extremely vulnerable in the anticommunist climate of the 1950s. In 1953, an internal revolt led to a retreat to respectability. No longer asserting the rights of homosexuals as a cultural minority, the new Mattachine asserted that "the sex variant is no different from anyone else except in the object of his sexual expression" (quoted in D'Emilio [1983], p. 81).

The position of the new Mattachine, which included women but was dominated by men, was similar to that of the first lesbian organization. Daughters of Bilitis, launched in 1955 in San Francisco, had as its original purpose an alternative to the bar scene, which had limited appeal to the coupled women who met originally to form a social club. DOB, and its publication, the *Ladder,* worked to prove the respectability of lesbians and to win acceptance within mainstream society. The issues of police harassment, although relevant to members of the predominantly working-class lesbian bar culture, had little appeal to other lesbians. Thus class differences played a powerful role in dividing the lesbian world.

In contrast, the gay male world, which had a long history of eroticizing class differences, had more success in bridging the chasm between the culture and the movement. Mattachine fought police harassment of bar patrons and entrapment of men involved in public cruising, and bars in San Francisco in the early 1960s served as the source of political mobilization. José Sarria, who performed in drag at the Black Cat bar in San Francisco, ran for city supervisor in 1961, and in 1962, the proprietors and employees of several of the city's gay bars formed the Tavern Guild to fight police harassment. The event that sparked the emergence of the contemporary gay-liberation movement was resistance on the part of drag queens, lesbians, and other bar patrons, many of them people of color, to a routine police raid at the Stonewall Inn in Greenwich Village in 1969. What immediately became known as the first gay riot in history began when a lesbian patron resisted arrest. Onlookers, already jeering the police, began to hurl coins, beer cans, and bottles. The call for "Gay Power" that emerged from the ensuing street fight echoed the demands of militant black activists. In fact, the birth of the Gay Liberation Front in the aftermath of the Stonewall riot can only be understood in the context of the other radical movements of the 1960s.

The events in Greenwich Village came to symbolize self-acceptance, pride, and resistance, in contrast to the assimilationist stance of the homophile movement. The homophile organizations advocated conformity to all but the sexual-object choice standards of mainstream society and focused their efforts on professionals, such as doctors and psychologists, in an attempt to prove the physical and mental fitness of homosexual men and women. Never able to mobilize large numbers in the hostile social climate of the 1950s, the homophile movement nevertheless paved the way for the gay liberationists of the early 1970s through persistent, if cautious, work.

The contemporary gay and lesbian movement, which celebrates its birth in the Stonewall riot, owes its existence not just to its homophile predecessors, but especially to the other social movements of the 1960s: the civil rights movement, the New Left, and the women's movement. Even before Stonewall, a militant wing of the homophile movement had emerged on the East Coast, influenced by the victories of the civil rights movement. The ideology of equal rights for minorities, direct-action protest tactics, and grassroots organizing came from the early civil rights struggle; the call for a total transformation of society, the linking of personal and political change, and pride in a gay or lesbian identity represented responses to the Black Power phase of the civil rights movement, the New Left and the counterculture, and the women's liberation movement.

Shortly after Stonewall, the Gay Liberation Front in New York and similar organizations in other cities emerged to carry the banner of the new radicalism and militance. Demanding immediate and profound change in the system, gay liberationists adopted militant strategies and proudly asserted their right to define their own sexuality.

The years since 1969 have witnessed both phenomenal progress in organizing, community-building, and consciousness-raising, and vigorous and often successful efforts to resist the changes favored by the gay and lesbian movement. The number of gay and lesbian groups multiplied from the fifty or so in 1969 to many thousand by the early 1990s. Gay liberation and gay rights organizations, at first dominated by white middle-class men, increasingly attracted a more diverse membership or spawned groups devoted to a particular constituency (lesbians, people of color, students, people of different religious affiliations) or to a special purpose (politics, health, religion, sports). The AIDS (acquired immune deficiency syndrome) crisis, in particular, mobilized gay men and lesbians and their supporters in an unprecedented fashion and has given rise to a new militance in groups such as ACT-UP (Aids Coalition to Unleash Power) and Queer Nation. Local groups are loosely tied together through contact with national-level organizations, national publications, and cooperation on such events as marches on Washington and National Coming Out Day. At the same time, the gay and lesbian community spawned a wide variety of institutions in addition to the traditional bars: restaurants, bookstores, shops, a wide variety of businesses, business guilds, support groups for those confronting substance abuse, and so on.

The result of such growth, in organizations and community institutions, has been a transformation in gay and lesbian consciousness. The early homophile movement was formed in an atmosphere of public silence on homosexuality, broken only by the occasional attack on the sinfulness, sickness, or criminal nature of same-sex passion. Only the Kinsey report on male sexual behavior, published in 1948, had normalized male homosexual activity by showing how common it was even among men who identified as heterosexual. Kinsey's findings, buttressed by his study of female sexuality published in 1953, led him to propose a continuum of human sexuality ranging from exclusive heterosexuality to exclusive homosexuality, with movement across the continuum, rather than fixed orientation, as characteristic. Public outrage greeted both studies, but, ironically, served to publicize and ultimately institutionalize the continuum notion of sexuality. The homophile movement, timid as it could be, began the process of substituting positive images of gay and lesbian people through its publications. The Supreme Court obscenity decisions of the 1960s made publishing about homosexuality a bit easier. But it was not until after Stonewall that the gay and lesbian movement produced so many resources—newspapers, magazines, novels, self-help books, music, plays, films—that access to positive images of gay and lesbian life had the potential to reach people in every corner of the country.

This is not to say that all people engaged in same-sex sexual activity, or even all people who identify as lesbian or gay, support the movement in the 1990s. But even for those who remain closeted, or who disdain activism, the environment has changed profoundly as a result of the gay and lesbian movement.

In response to such progress in organization, community-building, and consciousness-raising, the forces of opposition changed in the post-Stonewall years. As the movement made strides toward repealing sodomy statutes in some (but not all) of the states, curtailing police harassment, removing homosexuality from the American Psychiatric Association's list of mental illnesses, challenging federal employment discrimination (successfully in all areas except the military and the intelligence agencies), and proposing civil rights legislation at the municipal and state levels, an organized and vocal countermovement arose to challenge these gains. The New Right took on homosexuality as a major issue in the late 1970s, reviving all of the traditional arguments about sin, sickness, and criminality. Organized groups fought against civil rights legislation, greeted the AIDS epidemic as just punishment from God, and called for the (sometimes literal) extermination of homosexuality from American society.

Despite such challenges, and the continued struggle against the state, the police, and professionals, made more intense in the face of AIDS, the gay and lesbian movement has made enormous progress in the years since Stonewall. The impulse to organize gay and lesbian individuals and groups into a social movement, first evident in the early twentieth century, is unlikely to disappear.

CONCLUSION

The contemporary gay and lesbian movement, like the community it represents, is not monolithic. The differences in gender, class, race, and ethnicity that have shaped the history of same-sex sexuality divide the movement and give rise to multiple gay and lesbian communities. Diversity even shapes contemporary understanding of the concept of sexual orientation. Some lesbian feminists, building on the assumption that female sexuality is inherently different from male sexuality, define lesbianism in political rather than sexual terms: that is, they downplay sexuality in favor of bonding between women and resistance to patriarchy as the central core of lesbianism. Other lesbians, including some working-class lesbians and lesbians of color, reject a lesbian-feminist "politically correct" sexuality that smacks of white, middle-class sexual standards and emphasize, instead, a style of dress, demeanor, and relationships that is more expressive of sexuality. Within some ethnic and racial communities—African American and Latino, for example—men can engage in sex with other men, as long as they take the inserter role, and not consider themselves, or be considered, gay. In other words, the concept of sexual orientation has, in the mainstream of American society, come to refer to sexual-object choice, but there is no unanimity as to what defines a man as gay or a woman as lesbian.

The history of same-sex sexuality shows that the process of definition is a historical one. Although there have always been people who express desire for sexual contact with others of the same sex, there has not always been an identity attached to such desires. The society constructed by European colonists disapproved of such sexual conduct but did not single it out from other nonmarital and non-procreative sexual acts. Some Native American cultures, and some African cultures, developed social roles that included the possibility of same-sex sexuality, although gender transformation and spirituality, rather than sexuality, were generally at the heart of those roles. The *berdache* role continues to exist within some Native American cultures, while the mainstream culture has become more sexualized and more conducive to sexual expressiveness, despite continuing legal and social barriers to same-sex sexuality.

Identity based on same-sex sexuality emerged in the United States in the course of the nineteenth century, although such identity was sometimes, at least for men, focused on sexual role rather than sexual-object choice. "Sodomites," "queers," "fairies," and "bulldykes" became "homosexuals," "gay men," and "lesbians" as individuals not only claimed labels for themselves but began to gather with others like them and to assert their right to live and love openly. Cultures ranged from those emerging out of sex-segregation (on the frontier, in boarding schools and colleges) to intentional ones growing up in urban areas around institutions such as taverns, brothels, bars, and lodging places. Gay and lesbian cultures, in turn, formed the foundation of the social movement that sprang up in the 1950s. That movement has helped to define further a gay and lesbian identity—and increasingly, as well, a bisexual identity—that emphasizes the significance of a preference for or orientation toward same-sex sexual relations not just for sexuality but for all aspects of human life. As a consideration of history shows, sexual orientation is a concept shaped not by biology but by large-scale social and economic transformation, ideological developments, collective behavior, and organized protest.

BIBLIOGRAPHY

General Works

Boswell, John. *Christianity, Social Tolerance, and Homosexuality: Gay People in Western Europe from the Beginning of the Christian Era to the Fourteenth Century* (1980). An erudite and controversial study that takes an essentialist perspective.

Bullough, Vern L. *Sexual Variance in Society and History* (1976). A broad survey of Western civilization.

D'Emilio, John, and Estelle B. Freedman. *Intimate Matters: A History of Sexuality in America* (1988). The best and most recent interpretive survey.

Duberman, Martin Bauml, Martha Vicinus, and George Chauncey, Jr., eds. *Hidden from History: Reclaiming the Gay and Lesbian Past* (1989). An anthology that includes articles on gay and lesbian history and culture.

Faderman, Lillian. *Surpassing the Love of Men: Romantic Friendship Between Women from the Renaissance to the Present* (1981). A broad-ranging consideration of lesbianism in Europe and the United States; includes material on crossing women and focuses on romantic friendship.

Greenberg, David F. *The Construction of Homosexuality* (1988). A cross-cultural and transhistorical survey.

Katz, Jonathan. *Gay American History: Lesbians and Gay Men in the U.S.A.* (1976). A classic and extremely useful documentary history.

———. *Gay/Lesbian Almanac: A New Documentary . . .* (1983). A successor to the author's *Gay American History.*

Vance, Carole S. "Social Construction Theory: Problems in the History of Sexuality." In *Homosexuality, Which Homosexuality?,* edited by Dennis Altman et al. (1989). An excellent discussion of the theoretical issues.

Preindustrial Society and Existing Sexual Systems

Baum, Robert M. "Homosexuality and the Traditional Religions of the Americas, Australasia, and Africa." In *Homosexuality in World Religions,* edited by Arlene Swidler (forthcoming).

Blackwood, Evelyn. "Sexuality and Gender in Certain Native-American Tribes: The Case of Cross-Gender Females." *Signs* 10 (1984): 27–42.

Brown, Judith C. *Immodest Acts: The Life of a Lesbian Nun in Renaissance Italy* (1986).

Callender, Charles, and Lee M. Kochems. "The North American Berdache." *Current Anthropology* 24 (1983): 443–470.

Crompton, Louis. "Homosexuals and the Death Penalty in Colonial America." *Journal of Homosexuality* 1 (1974): 227–293.

Gilbert, Arthur N. "Buggery and the British Navy, 1700–1861." *Journal of Social History* 10 (1976): 72–98.

Oaks, Robert F. "'Things Fearful to Name': Sodomy and Buggery in Seventeenth-Century New England." *Journal of Social History* 12 (1978): 268–281.

Rey, Michel. "Parisian Homosexuals Create a Lifestyle, 1700–1750: The Police Archives." *Eighteenth-Century Life* 9, n.s. 3 (1985): 179–191.

Williams, Walter L. *The Spirit and the Flesh: Sexual Diversity in American Indian Culture* (1986).

Industrializing Society

Burnham, John. "Early References to Homosexual Communities in American Medical Writings." *Medical Aspects of Human Sexuality* 7 (1973): 34–49.

Goldman, Marion S. *Gold Diggers and Silver Miners: Prostitution and Social Life on the Comstock Lode* (1981).

Gorn, Elliott J. *The Manly Art: Bare-Knuckle Prize-Fighting in America* (1986). Includes material on the homoeroticism of the working-class sporting underworld.

Moon, Michael. "'The Gentle Boy from the Dangerous Classes': Pederasty, Domesticity, and Capitalism in Horatio Alger." *Representations* 19 (1987): 87–110.

Rotundo, E. Anthony. "Romantic Friendship: Male Intimacy and Middle-Class

Youth in the Northern United States, 1800–1900." *Journal of Social History* 23 (1989): 1–25.

Sahli, Nancy. "Smashing: Women's Relationships Before the Fall." *Chrysalis* 8 (1979): 17–27.

Shively, Charley. *Calamus Lovers: Walt Whitman's Working-Class Camerados* (1987).

Smith-Rosenberg, Carroll. "The Female World of Love and Ritual: Relations Between Women in Nineteenth-Century America." *Signs* 1 (1975): 1–29.

Consumer Society

Adam, Barry D. *The Rise of a Gay and Lesbian Movement* (1987).

Almaguer, Tomás. "Chicano Men: A Cartography of Homosexual Identity and Behavior" *differences: A Journal of Feminist Cultural Studies* 3 (1991): 75–100.

Bérubé, Allan. *Coming Out Under Fire: The History of Gay Men and Women in World War II* (1990).

Carby, Hazel V. "'It Jus Be's Dat Way Sometime': The Sexual Politics of Women's Blues." *Radical America* 20 (1986).

Chauncey, George, Jr. "From Sexual Inversion to Homosexuality: Medicine and the Changing Conceptualization of Female Deviance." *Salmagundi* 58–59 (1982–1983): 114–146.

D'Emilio, John. *Sexual Politics, Sexual Communities: The Making of a Homosexual Minority in the United States, 1940–1970* (1983).

———. *Acts of Creation: Gay History, Politics, and the University* (forthcoming). A collection of essays that includes material on the contemporary gay and lesbian movement.

Duberman, Martin. *Cures: A Gay Man's Odyssey* (1991). An autobiographical account that provides important perspective on the 1950s and 1960s.

Faderman, Lillian. *Odd Girls and Twilight Lovers: A History of Lesbian Life in Twentieth-Century America* (1991).

Haeberle, Erwin J. "A Movement of Inverts: An Early Plan for a Homosexual Organization in the United States." *Journal of Homosexuality* 10 (1984).

Hull, Gloria T. *Color, Sex, and Poetry: Three Women Writers of the Harlem Renaissance* (1987). Discusses the lesbian relationships of Alice Dunbar-Nelson and Angelina Weld Grimké.

Lauritsen, John, and David Thorstad. *The Early Homosexual Rights Movement (1864–1935)* (1974).

Meyerowitz, Joanne J. *Women Adrift: Independent Wage Earners in Chicago, 1880–1930* (1988). Includes material on both heterosexual and lesbian women in the working-class urban subculture.

Nestle, Joan. "Butch-Fem Relationships: Sexual Courage in the 1950's." *Heresies* 3, no. 12 (1981).

The author wishes to thank Irene Ledesma for research assistance and John D'Emilio and Verta Taylor for their careful readings of an early draft.

SEE ALSO **Communitarians and Counterculturalists; Family Structures; Feminist Approaches to Social History; Gender; Prostitution; Sexual Behavior and Morality; Women and Work.**

RELIGION

Charles H. Lippy

SCHOLARS ROUTINELY POINT OUT that many tribal languages have no word for "religion." Because religious belief and activity are so interwoven with other dimensions of corporate life, it is impossible to isolate particular ideas or practices and label them "religious." Religion, politics, economics, and other components of social order are part of a single entity, a cultural whole. In such societies, one's personal identity is inextricably tied to the identity of the entire people. Only as societies become more complex and diffuse, and religion emerges as a discrete phenomenon, is it possible to explore how religion enables individuals to construct a sense of personal identity and how it relates to social identity.

But within the context of such societies, precisely what is religion? Most scholars agree that describing religion is easier than defining it. Sociologists label such descriptions as either "functional" or "substantive." Functional descriptions highlight what religion does for persons or societies; substantive descriptions emphasize particular kinds of beliefs and practices. Both assume that religion deals with the multifaceted ways in which people make sense out of individual and corporate experience, how they endow life with meaning. Functionalists thus label "religious" whatever phenomena people employ to understand and interpret their experience. Those taking a substantive approach insist that only beliefs and practices associated with the supernatural or something "other" than human constitute religion. Generally such beliefs and practices are identified with systems of doctrine, religious institutions such as churches or denominations, sacred texts, and the like. The advantage of functionalism lies in its casting a wide net when scrutinizing how people and societies actually operate. Not every vehicle one uses to imbue life with meaning comes from a fixed doctrine or a church; many are more amorphous. The disadvantage is too-casually labeling "religious" anything associated with meaning in life. Correspondingly, the advantage of the substantive approach comes from its more explicit parameters: there are specific beliefs, institutions, and practices to examine. Its drawback is its failure to look beyond the obvious.

While sociologists have tended to see functional and substantive approaches as mutually exclusive, this essay will draw on both. It presumes that religion most readily relates to beliefs, practices, and institutions that have at their base convictions about God and humanity and about how life should be oriented. But it also presumes that ordinary people draw on other phenomena in their quest to infuse life with meaning and purpose. This essay will look at religious groups and beliefs, as well as at forces such as ethnicity, politics, and economics that have influenced how people called Americans have created for themselves identities as individuals and as participants in a common social order. The governing thesis is that even in the colonial era the connections between religion and social identity began to emphasize the function of religion in fashioning citizens of good character while consigning matters of belief to the private sphere—the realm of individual experience—that this process accelerated as American society became more complex, and that it continues in the present.

THE COLONIAL EPOCH

Among seventeenth-century Europeans who settled in British North America, the Puritans of New England come closest in theory to having a tribal culture that united religion and social identity in a single whole—although most leaders in other colonies were convinced that religious uniformity was necessary for political stability. In New England, that conviction had roots in the Puritans' adaptation of Calvinist thought. In colonies where the Church of England became legally established, the basis was more pragmatic than theoretical.

Puritan leaders such as John Winthrop believed that their corporate purpose was to plant a holy commonwealth in the Massachusetts Bay colony. The heart of their scheme was the idea of covenant or mutual agreement. Everybody was part of the social covenant, the implicit compact that bound people to uphold laws to advance the common welfare. Without the social covenant, individual interest would run rampant, resulting in chaos because sin would propel all to act solely for their own advantage and not for the good of the whole. Those who had inwardly experienced regeneration, who knew that God predestined them among the elect, could own (enter into) the church covenant that bound them not only to human law but also to divine law. Owning the church covenant brought full participation in the public order to men, for until British colonial policy mandated otherwise, only male church members received the franchise.

But there were some internal inconsistencies. From the outset of settlement in the New World, more women than men owned the church covenant even though they were denied full participation in religious and political affairs. Indeed, up to the present women have outnumbered men in formally affiliating with religious groups in the United States. At least two consequences follow. First, formal religious affiliation has played a more significant role in the construction of women's social identity than of men's. Second, the primary role of women in nurturing children—a primacy not seriously challenged until the later twentieth century—gave women major responsibility for inculcating religious values in the young. Studies of the Puritan family suggest that such was the case in the seventeenth century.

Another inconsistency emerged when Puritans dealt with the practical matter of assigning pews in the meetinghouses of colonial New England. Although the covenant theoretically presumed the equality of those who accepted its obligations, social standing within the community was the major determinant in the assignment of pews (as it would be for many years in determining class rank at Harvard College).

Nevertheless, the primacy of the church covenant illuminates how Puritans perceived social identity By placing political control in the hands of church members, Puritans grounded their social vision in an understanding of Scripture and its moral implications. Those not committed to the holy commonwealth had no place in the Puritan enterprise. Within a decade of the initial settlements in Massachusetts Bay, dissenters such as Anne Hutchinson and Roger Williams had been banished, and within forty years some Quakers had been hanged. Even so, not all who were part of the Puritan venture subscribed completely to covenant ideology. Puritan diaries and the poetry of Anne Bradstreet breathe a subtle individualism at odds with the holistic foundation of covenant thinking. At the same time, the insistence that persons must directly experience regeneration in order to own the church covenant brought disagreement about how regeneration transpired and how people could be certain that they were among the elect. Yet laws such as those restricting Sabbath activity (the "blue laws" of later generations) attempted to impose on all a social identity conforming to the ideal. More important, the Puritan consciousness of being a people ordained to create the ideal society embedded in American sensibilities a sense of destiny that had enduring consequences.

In colonies such as Virginia, where the Church of England was the established church, links between religion and social identity worked differently because of the attempt there to create a microcosm of English society. In the mother country, nominal allegiance to the established church brought entrance into political, educational, and certain economic circles. Matters of belief and personal religious experience counted less than tacit adherence to the Church of England. The same attitude prevailed as tobacco plantations began to line Virginia's rivers. Planters who became dominant politically and economically generally gave at least formal acknowledgment to the religious establishment, but records suggest that until well into the eighteenth century, Anglicanism was hardly a vital spiritual presence.

The implications of this arrangement for social identity differ from those grounded in covenant ideology. Here religious identification became a sign of social standing, not a means by which one discerned meaning in individual and corporate experience; it became a symbol that one was a good citizen worthy of public trust, not an indicator of one's spirituality. Demographics fostered this pragmatic connection between religion and social identity in the southern colonies. As the plantation economy took hold, the population became widely dispersed. Parishes frequently encompassed such large geographic areas that clergy could not minister effectively, if clergy were available at all. Population distribution and a weak parish system helped relegate religion to the periphery.

In the eighteenth century, challenges arose to both New England covenant ideology and the more pragmatic arrangements in the southern colonies. But before their impact was felt, another colonial endeavor was under way, one that unwittingly became the paradigm for later American developments. In 1681 William Penn, a Quaker, received a charter for the colony that bore his name. Although Penn hoped that his "holy experiment" would provide a refuge for religious compatriots regarded as dangerous radicals in Britain, he knew that Pennsylvania's success depended on non-Quaker settlers. He advertised widely for prospective colonists, particularly among German groups whose religious beliefs and practices consigned them to the margins of public life.

Penn thus paved the way for ethnicity to become a major ingredient in the American religious mix. His willingness to open Pennsylvania to all who believed in God set the stage for the religious toleration popularly regarded as a hallmark of American life. The implications of that toleration are significant. It minimized the substantive dimension of religion and emphasized the functional; that is, what one believed mattered less than how religion buttressed a sense of civic responsibility and ethics. Although Quakers dominated Pennsylvania public life for many years, Quaker identification gradually became more a matter of status than of piety, in part because of the policy of toleration.

In the eighteenth century, that interplay between substantive and functional dimensions of religion became normative. Three examples are the evangelical surge called the Great Awakening, the influence of the Enlightenment, and the movement of Separate Baptists and others into the valleys just east of the Appalachians.

Historians debate whether the evangelical movement that erupted in the 1740s and 1750s constituted a "great" religious awakening. In New England and the middle colonies, at least, response to the calls for conversion from Jonathan Edwards, the "grand itinerant" George Whitefield (who made several tours of the colonies), William and Gilbert Tennent, and others seemed to signal increased religious interest. Edwards, for example, hoping to revitalize Puritanism's covenant ideology, believed that the religious stirrings confirmed America's divine destiny. In retrospect, the Great Awakening turned the substance of religion increasingly inward. Since the individual alone knew what transpired in the heart, who could question the authenticity of religious experience? The most viable test, as Edwards noted in his *Treatise Concerning the Religious Affections* (1746), was behavior, or how religious experience functioned to foster values that promoted the common good. Conversion became a badge of identity testifying to one's morality and worth to society. The only recourse, then, was to tolerate differences of belief (the substance of religion) if the results of belief were the same.

In a different vein, those influenced by the Enlightenment also advanced the interiorization of religion's substance. New England's Jonathan Mayhew, for example, argued for the "right of private judgment" in matters of belief, while Virginia's Thomas Jefferson edited the New Testament, deleting all he found irrational and retaining what promoted reasonable public morality. The right of private judgment meant that people should decide for themselves what the substance of religious belief was; Jefferson's emphasis on morality also buttressed religion's social function. Both the right of private judgment and the emphasis on morality led to broadly based religious toleration built on the assumption that all rational religion supported the common good.

In the second quarter of the eighteenth century, settlers began pushing southward along the eastern slopes of the Appalachians into Virginia and then the Carolinas. Many of them were Scotch-Irish, the largest ethnic group entering the colonies at that time. Few were drawn to legally established Anglicanism; the Church of England was too closely identified with the status quo that frequently excluded the newer colonists from full representation and participation in the political-economic order. Many were Separate Baptists whose evangelical orientation was consonant with Great Awakening impulses. Their increasing numbers left the Church of England more identified with people of status rather than with the masses. The Separate Baptists' struggle for power in the public sphere had two consequences. First, they emphasized inner experience as the locus of religion's substance, castigating Anglicanism's ordered liturgical tradition as mere "lip service" religion. Second, their quest for a proper place in public affairs helped shatter the foundations of religious establishment itself. They were indeed dissenters, but they were also morally upright citizens whose presence aided acceptance of a religious toleration more interested in what religion did than in what it was.

Events during the era of American independence furthered this view. Separation from Britain necessarily challenged all religious establishments, for was not legal recognition of a single religious body a form of tyranny? Should not all be on an equal footing? Although it took a little more than half a century for the individual states to rid themselves of all vestiges of religious establishment, independence propelled the process. Pragmatism decreed that no single body could be legally established nationally; no one group could claim a majority as adherents. The establishment clause of the First Amendment to the United States Constitution reflected that pragmatism more than the strict "separation of church and state" that later generations have claimed.

But the founding generation did appreciate religion's role in providing a moral base for citizens and in promoting a sense of identification with the nation. George Washington, for example, believed that without the morality rooted in religion there would be no support for laws. Although the Constitution lacked overt reference to the Deity, symbols fraught with religious import readily became part of national life. For example, the reference to the United States as *novus ordo seclorum* (new order of the ages) echoed the Puritan sense of mission and destiny, and the Fourth of July quickly took the form of a religious holiday. In other words, alongside the individual religions, a civil or public religion was developing, vacuous in substance but vital in giving the American people a sense of common identity and purpose.

THE EVANGELICAL ETHOS OF EARLY-NINETEENTH-CENTURY PROTESTANTISM

With independence came expansion of the population westward into Kentucky and Tennessee; the Louisiana Purchase in 1803 added a vast tract for Americans to settle; the opening of the Erie Canal in New York in 1825 facilitated westward movement and industrial growth in northern areas. Immigration in the first half of the nineteenth century added millions to the American population. A burning issue for religious leaders was how to provide for the spiritual needs of those in new areas, those creating civilization out of another American wilderness. The matter was complicated because, unlike the situation in the colonial period, no government support was forthcoming.

Robert T. Handy has referred to this epoch as the time of the "Protestant quest for a Christian America." His label highlights the attempt of evangelical Protestants to impose a particular religious cast on the American enterprise, to promote one constellation of values that would give the American people a common identity and purpose. While the quest failed, the means by which it was pursued illuminate the connections between religion and social identity in the early nineteenth century.

One technique—revivalism—had roots in the Great Awakening. In the nineteenth century, revivalism assumed different forms, the descendants of which endure in American culture. On the frontier in Kentucky, Tennessee, and the Old Southwest, the camp meeting emerged as a vital tool to bring religion to a population so scattered that it was virtually impossible to support religious institutions like churches. Informal and sometimes highly emotional camp meetings drew thousands together for a week or more of preaching and socializing. Calls for conversion rang out, often mixed with debates over fine points of doctrine among preachers of different denominational persuasions.

More important than how camp meetings inculcated the substance of Christian doctrine among pioneers was the social role of both the camp meeting and the conversion experience. Camp meetings brought a sense of cohesion and community—a social identity—to a widely dispersed people. In turn, the conversion experience became a mode of entry into responsible society; the convert left behind an identity marked by the presumed savage brutality of the frontier and assumed a new identity. To be converted was to become civilized. It mattered less whether one associated with Methodists, Baptists, or Presbyterians than whether one could testify to an inner experience of conversion.

In the embryonic urban and industrial areas of the North, revivalists like Charles Grandison Finney adapted the camp-meeting style to a different environment. Holding "protracted meetings," breaking gender barriers by allowing women to pray publicly, preaching in an idiomatic and feverishly emotional manner, Finney and other revivalists offered salvation to all who would accept it. As with camp meetings, the revivals' theological substance was less significant than their social function. The revivals were themselves a civilizing process, creating a community of feeling that gave a disparate people a common identity. If everyone was converted, whether in a frontier camp meeting or in an urban revival, Americans would be one people dedicated to common values and the general welfare.

Concern for the general welfare figured prominently in another mechanism promoting the quest for a Christian America: "voluntary societies." The end of established religion meant that religious groups could not rely on the coercive power of government to advance moral and ethical principles thought to be basic to responsible society. Nor did any single religious body have the resources to do so alone. Cooperation across denominational lines, through the combined efforts of individuals who voluntarily organized to deal with specific problems, harmonized with democratic ideals and seemed likely to succeed in molding a Christian nation.

Beginning with the Connecticut Society for the Reformation of Morals (founded in 1813), a host of societies were formed in the first decades of the nineteenth century, creating what some have called a "benevolent empire." The goal of many was spreading the evangelical Protestant style; both the American Bible Society (1816) and the American Tract Society (1825) initially had this aim. For others, eliminating particular social evils predominated; among the most prominent were the American Temperance Society (1826) and the American Antislavery Society (1833). Women accounted for the majority of members of these societies, although prevailing social patterns restricted leadership to men. The societies were thus both one conduit for the public expression of women's spirituality and a reflection of a social order that denied women full participation in common life.

Even within evangelical Protestant ranks, however, some differences prevailed. Southern Evangelicals had visions of a Christian society that generally supported maintenance of the slave-labor system; they consequently produced a vast literature, much of it by members of the clergy, defending slavery. One result of this defense was to push religion further into the private sphere so that ethics became a personal matter of individual behavior almost devoid of social ramifications. Southern Presbyterians, for example, followed the lead of James Henley Thornwell in championing the "spirituality" of the church, a notion that emphasized the personal, and minimized the social, dimensions of religious belief and experience. That notion became more prominent in the decades following Thornwell's death in 1862 than it had been in his lifetime. Some voluntary societies labored in the South, and hence may be construed as having provided an avenue for action in the public sphere, but the more prominent ones were those which sought transformation of individual behavior, not changes in prevailing social structures.

Camp meetings, revivals, voluntary societies, and regional differences all reveal that the fabric of American society was not cut from a single cloth. Not all Americans found meaning in an evangelical Protestant world centered on camp meetings and revivals; not all shared the values promoted by voluntary societies. Immigration patterns in the first half of the nineteenth century brought to the United States increasing numbers of Roman Catholics and Jews, who stood outside the evangelical circle. There were also thousands who found meaning and social identity in various utopian, communitarian, and tribal groups that had very different visions of the ideal society. African Americans, an integral part of American life since the first slave ship arrived in 1619, were forcibly excluded from sharing the ideals on which evangelical Protestants hoped to pattern their America. The story of all these groups is part of the whole, demonstrating how complex the links between religion and social identity were becoming.

THE ETHNIC FACTOR TO THE FORE: AMERICA'S CATHOLICS AND JEWS

Catholics Roman Catholic immigrants to those areas of the New World which became the United States settled first in Spanish and French territories. But the dominant influence in American Catholicism in the nineteenth century (and later) came from migrants to British possessions. By the Civil War, Roman Catholics constituted the nation's largest religious group. Even then, however, Catholic identity was that of a suspect minority.

Catholic immigrants to British colonial America came primarily to Maryland and Pennsylvania. At its inception, Maryland was intended as a place where English Catholics could practice their religion without the disabilities encountered in a mother country more anti-Catholic than pro-Protestant. But non-Catholic colonists, essential to Maryland's survival, quickly became a majority of the population; the colony's proprietors urged Catholics to make their religion strictly a private concern. Pennsylvania's broader toleration made the Quaker colony a more welcome home. Even so, at the time of American independence, Catholics accounted for only about 1 percent of the nation's population.

What brought Catholicism to the fore and also made ethnicity a key factor in its history in America was immigration from Ireland, which brought more than 1.5 million immigrants to American shores in the 1840s and 1850s alone. Larger numbers came from southern and eastern Europe in the century's closing decades, diversifying the church's ethnic composition. Ethnicity, however, is only one component of the story. Equally important are the hostile environment fostered by Protestantism and how Catholicism adapted to that environment, and its ethnically diverse constituency. In addition, most Catholic immigrants came from nations where Catholicism was dominant, if not legally established, to a Protestant culture where separation of church and state prevailed. In the United States, Catholic identity could not be assumed; it had to be cultivated.

Virulent anti-Catholicism emerged in part because first Irish immigrants, and then others, competed for jobs in a growing but rapidly changing economy. It also stemmed from xenophobia directed toward people whose cultural ways were different. Compounding the hostility were longstanding Protestant misgivings about Catholicism itself, most of them rooted in the conviction that Catholic acceptance of papal authority meant loyalty to a foreign prince that precluded Catholics from being good citizens. Historical records recount numerous violent anti-Catholic outbursts. This anti-Catholicism affected social identity for Catholics and non-Catholics alike. It forced Catholics into a defensive posture, having to prove their worth as citizens. Because anti-Catholic nativism festered whenever large waves of immigration occurred, not until well into the twentieth century did Catholic identity cease to be a social liability. Many historians trace the process of acceptance to strong Catholic support for American endeavors in World War I and see its culmination in the election of the first Catholic president in 1960.

Equally important, anti-Catholicism strengthened the coherence of Protestant social identity. If particulars of belief were being relegated to the private sphere, since religious experience was a personal matter, anti-Catholicism became a negative means of identification; if Protestant Americans disagreed on the substance of religion, they could at least proclaim that they were not the same as foreign, Catholic immigrants.

Ethnic tensions within American Catholicism antedate the wave of Irish immigration, and they continue to the present. Early episodes concerned control of church property and the appointment and dismissal of parish priests. Lay trustees believed that they held this power, regarding it as the only approach to church order compatible with American democracy. But Roman Catholicism's hierarchical structure did not acknowledge such power. The ongoing controversy raised thorny questions about whether Catholicism's substance was compatible with American ideals. In a nutshell, the issue was how *American* Catholicism could be without abandoning its heritage.

Ethnicity, Americanism, and anti-Catholicism intertwined in many ways. The parochial school system is one example. Parish schools emerged in part to provide a Catholic education for Catholic children because common (public) schools were a thinly disguised mechanism for promoting Protestant ideals. In time, parochial schools became a vital means of providing basic education to immigrant children who neither spoke nor understood English, the language of instruction. Parochial schools aided the transition of immigrant children into American life, but many Protestants regarded them as another symbol of Catholicism's incompatibility with American ways. Yet for millions of Catholics until well into the twentieth century, part of their Catholic identity was to have a parochial-school education. By then, with the emergent middle-to-upper-middle-class status of many Catholics that more directly tied Catholic interests to prevailing social patterns, the parochial school system had begun a steady decline that was aggravated by the even more precipitous decline in the number of Catholic women who were becoming nuns. (For sisters from numerous orders had staffed the parochial schools for decades.)

And from Rome's perspective, signs appeared that Catholicism in the United States was becoming too Americanized. Between 1880 and World War I, millions of Catholics from southern and eastern Europe immigrated to a United States that was rapidly urbanizing and industrializing. The same period witnessed the birth of the labor movement, with unions struggling to secure safer and better conditions for workers. Catholic and non-Catholic immigrants willingly joined the factory labor force;

employment offered a mode of entry into American society. Popular Catholic support for unions brought conflict with Roman authorities who saw them as irreconcilable with Catholicism. Rome regarded the American context as identical with what the church confronted in Europe, where labor unions were frequently antireligious because of Catholicism's ties to a nonindustrial economy, and saw Catholic association with non-Catholics in labor unions as eroding a distinctive Catholic identity. Not until near the end of the nineteenth century did church authorities in Rome support Catholic participation in American labor unions. In the twentieth century, Catholic thinker John Ryan offered powerful endorsements of workers' concerns in a number of books solidly based on Catholic theological principles, and many labor union leaders came from the ranks of the nation's Catholics.

Intramural ethnic tensions became more pronounced as the Catholic population grew. While Catholics placed much emphasis on being part of one church with one system of doctrine, immigrants brought different religious styles commingled with folk practices of their home cultures. In the nineteenth century, the less liturgical style of Irish Catholics encountered the more liturgical approach of German Catholics. Increasing ethnic diversity and styles led some to propose organizing parishes along ethnic or national lines. Simply put, German parishes did not respond well to Irish priests, and vice versa. Structuring parishes geographically might acknowledge the unity of the church but destroy its ethnic diversity. Others saw eliminating ethnic divisions as necessary for Catholic acceptance into the larger culture. The movement for separate ethnic parishes failed in theory, though it was often maintained in practice because of the concentration of population.

Catholic demographics have changed in the twentieth century, but ethnic issues remain prominent. In areas where maintaining multiple parishes has become economically infeasible, ethnic rivalries have reappeared if, for example, plans are to merge historically Irish and Italian parishes. More significant has been the growing influence of Hispanic Catholicism, particularly Mexican, Cuban, and Puerto Rican, and the distinctive religious styles each nurtures. For Cuban American Catholics the issue of identity remains much what it was for Irish American Catholics in the 1840s—is one's identity Cuban, American, or Catholic, or some fusion thereof? The response says much about one's social identity.

Jews Similar dilemmas are central to the story of American Jews, but the details differ. At the time of the first census, there were only around fifteen hundred Jews in the population, mostly of Spanish Sephardic origin. During the 1840s and 1850s, when Irish and German Catholic immigration peaked, migrants from Germany and the Austro-Hungarian empire helped swell the total number of Jews to around 150,000 by the 1860 census, and millions of Jews were among the masses coming from southern and eastern Europe between 1880 and World War I. Hence the sources of the American Jewish population brought ethnic diversity, but the process of carving an American identity differed with each cluster of immigrants, as did the response of a culture dominated by Protestants.

Enlightenment influences in Germany had worked to grant Jews fuller participation in public life that bolstered their identification with German culture. The more open legal situation in the United States speeded assimilation into American public life and would do so more profoundly with those who came later from the shtetls and ghettos of central and eastern Europe. Ethnicity meant that German Jews were not comfortable with the ways of English-speaking descendants of the earlier Sephardic immigrants, and so they created an array of social institutions—hospitals, fraternal and social clubs, newspapers, religious schools, and the like—patterned after parallel Protestant institutions. Such organizations eased immigrant adjustment to American life, but they also shifted emphasis within German American Judaism away from the substance of religion. German Jewish communities began to resemble Protestant congregations where particulars of belief were private matters. The emergence of Reform Judaism by the 1870s reflects this shift, for the heart of Reform was the modernization of Judaism, eliminating religious practices, such as keeping kosher, that were once central to Jewish identity but now seemed anachronistic in the United States, thus abandoning whatever would cause German American Jews to "stand out." Religion became ethics; religion's function became more vital than its substance.

While cultural gaps caused these more assimilated American Jews at first to be ambivalent toward those coming later from southern and eastern Europe, xenophobia in the larger culture spurred the development of agencies to meet immigrant needs, especially in the New York City area, where by 1890 over half the nation's Jews lived. Frequently skilled workers, the newer immigrants flocked to light industry, especially the garment industry; upward social mobility quickly followed, aided by the greater educational and political opportunities available. Many were reluctant to abandon Orthodox belief and practice. Few went the route of Reform; more identified with the Conservative movement, which attempted to retain Judaism's essential substance while modifying what was thought superfluous. But although many forsook any religious identification with Judaism, virtually all regarded themselves as Jews. A critical issue for American Judaism became, and remains, whether Jewish identity is a matter of religion or of ethnic culture, or some combination thereof.

In the middle third of the twentieth century, the Holocaust perpetrated by the Nazis, with its near destruction of the European Jewish population, strengthened the desire of many American Jews to affirm their identification with their heritage. Yet at the same time, as the American Jewish population became more geographically diffuse, both because of the increased mobility of the population as a whole and because of the movement from urban ghetto to the suburbs, it became more difficult to maintain the social props needed to buttress a distinctive Jewish identity.

American Jews have long encountered anti-Semitism. Earlier nativism contained anti-Semitic elements, but was far more anti-Catholic. But by the 1920s, Jewish "quotas" for admission to prestigious universities, exclusion of Jews from country club memberships, and the like revealed the extent of anti-Semitism in the United States. Rooted more in resentment over Jewish economic, educational, and political gains than in religious hostility, anti-Semitism remains a blot on American culture. Zionism has fueled it, through Jewish support for the establishment of an independent Jewish state and then for Israel, as has American Judaism's long association with liberal political causes, especially the early labor movement and the civil rights movement.

The stories of Catholicism and Judaism in the United States expose the myth of the melting pot. For both, ethnic identity remains a central factor in social identity. External hostility has forged a more cohesive group identity for both than might otherwise have occurred. Both struggle to determine how a religious identity linked to ethnicity relates to American identity in a culture that has historically defined the latter through categories set by Protestants.

AN IDENTITY APART: UTOPIAN, COMMUNITARIAN, AND TRIBAL RELIGIOUS MOVEMENTS

Westward movement, immigration, population growth, increasing ethnic diversity, and nascent industrialization produced for many Americans a sense of social dislocation. That is, they could not readily identify with the emerging social order because it was in such flux. Some found identity in alternative visions of society rooted in religious ideologies diverging from denominational belief systems. Many withdrew into isolated enclaves to mold their own ideal societies. Others revamped features of the old dream of America as an elect nation to fit a new day. Yet others regarded social change as presaging the end of time. For indigenous tribal cultures, national expansion demolished the integrity of what remained of their own societies; their identity, too, was at stake. Understanding the relationship of religion and social identity requires brief examination of each.

The decades immediately preceding the Civil War were replete with communitarian experiments designed to provide members with a secure social identity within an alternative structure. Two examples are the Shakers and the Oneida Perfectionists.

In 1785, the first Shaker community was organized at Watervliet, New York, inaugurating a process of growth peaking in the 1830s and 1840s, when Shakers had some six thousand members in nineteen communities. Shakers believed that their founder, Ann Lee, was Christ returned to earth in female form. Her teaching demanded celibacy and separation of persons by gender, but gender equality in communal work made the Shakers virtually self-sufficient for many years. Contact with the larger society was kept to a minimum. These practices, Shakers thought, purified them from sin and allowed them to live the life of the millennial age in the present.

In 1848 John Humphrey Noyes and his followers moved from Vermont to Oneida, New York, where their community endured until 1881. Oneidans likewise believed that withdrawal from society permitted members to live the perfect life of the millennial age in the present, but their rationale differed from that of the Shakers. Believing that traditional marriage did not exist in heaven, the Perfectionists practiced "complex marriage," regarding each woman as the wife of each man and each man as the husband of each woman. Outsiders mocked this as "free love," but Oneidans carefully regulated sexual relations. They also practiced "Bible communism," holding all possessions in common.

Both groups shared a vision of the ideal society quite at odds with evangelical Protestantism and American capitalism. Both rejected social norms as corrupt and unworkable; instead they found social identity in radical alternatives to which complete commitment was expected. For them, the larger society produced only alienation, whereas within their communities they had economic security and a clear identity. Both, in their rejection of the institution of marriage, offered women a status denied them in the larger society, one through the theoretical equality of men and women (which never worked as well in practice as in theory) and the other in denying the exclusivity of the marriage relation that regarded the wife as virtually the property of the husband. Both represent a continuing strand in American religion in which identity emerges only in the total renunciation of prevailing social patterns and withdrawal into an isolated community of the faithful.

Others developed different alternatives to the larger culture. One such alternative came with the publication of the Book of Mormon in 1830 and Joseph Smith's subsequent organization of followers into the Church of Jesus Christ of Latter-day Saints. Mormons first clustered in an area of central New York not far from Oneida. More important for this story than the spectacular Mormon growth in the twentieth century or Mormon achievement in establishing an ideal commonwealth in the Utah desert is how certain ideas in the Book of Mormon provided a secure identity for people estranged from the larger society and its religious institutions. For example, the Book of Mormon asserted that Christ appeared after the Resurrection to tribes living in North America. It gave a primordial past and sacred roots to people living amid tremendous social transition who felt that they had no roots and their changing nation no real past. It provided a social identity that transcended the vagaries of empirical reality as well as special sanction to the American enterprise, since Christ's appearance meant divine blessing.

Some at sea in the world around them saw the social flux of the 1830s and 1840s as signaling that the end of time was approaching. William Miller, for example, set several dates for Christ's literal return to earth that would bring history to a close. He and his followers found their identity in a radical millennial hope that devalued present society. After 1844, when Christ did not return on the final date Miller fixed, many millennialists again found their place in the larger society; others formed groups to keep the hope alive, finding their identity in proclaiming the nearness of the end. The Seventh-Day Adventists are one group with a lineage going back to this alternative social identity.

Some tribal societies that the first European invaders encountered in the New World also developed alternative social identities. For them, conquest brought encroachment on sacred tribal lands as Europeans refused to acknowledge the integrity of the indigenous cultures. The "Indian policy" of the federal government that included forced removal of many southeastern tribes to Indian Territory in Oklahoma in the 1820s and 1830s further undermined the ability of tribal ways to provide a viable social identity. Clearly Native Americans were excluded from the vision of Americans as a people with a unique destiny, yet they were still part of the nation.

Two well-known movements that sought to revitalize tribal cultures and increase their utility in providing members with a functional social identity are those associated with Handsome Lake and Wovoka. Handsome Lake, a Seneca, early in the nineteenth century epitomized the loss of identity that had come with the destruction of traditional tribal life. Like others, he had become an alcoholic in desperate response to the devastation of tribal culture. While ill, he had a visionary experience that transformed him into a prophet proclaiming a new religious way that fused features of tribal life with the Christianity of the European American conquerors. For a time, his approach allowed those who followed him to carve a social identity that would provide meaning in a rapidly changing world.

A different approach came with Wovoka, a Paiute, who had visionary experiences in the winter of 1888–1889. Wovoka also showed the influence of both tribal and Christian ways, but he adapted the millennialist strain in Christianity to proclaim the coming destruction of the European Americans and the reestablishment of tribal cultures that heeded his message. The central component of Wovoka's scheme was the Ghost Dance; in this ritual, participants danced themselves into ecstatic frenzies during which they were reunited with ancestors and joined with them in ushering in a new age. Until it was snuffed out in the Wounded Knee massacre of 1890 (though some western and Great Plains groups still practice a muted form), the Ghost

Dance provided a social identity that celebrated the integrity of tribal culture while denigrating the culture of the conquerors.

AFRICAN AMERICAN RELIGION AND SOCIAL IDENTITY

No group was more forcibly excluded from the emerging American culture than Africans brought to America as slaves. Accounts abound of separating Africans who could communicate with one another in a massive effort to destroy remnants of African tribal identity and to render them more pliable to their white owners. The slaves themselves came from a variety of African tribal backgrounds, but amid the degradation of slave life, they were able to sustain some religious practices that proclaimed their humanity and gave them a distinct identity. Owners were ambivalent about seeking the conversion of slaves to Christianity, largely because of doubts as to whether Christians could hold other Christians as property. The issue was resolved legislatively by including in slave codes provisions that Christian baptism did not alter a slave's status.

The evangelical surge of the 1740s and 1750s brought the first serious efforts to Christianize African slaves. Baptists, Methodists, and some Presbyterians launched efforts to convert slaves, who responded to the affective evangelical style. One result was the emergence of the "invisible institution," with converted slaves preaching a message of freedom from the bonds of both personal sin and slavery that was also the focus of the African American spiritual. Early in the nineteenth century, free African Americans in the North formed new denominations, such as the African Methodist Episcopal Church and the African Methodist Episcopal Zion Church, to escape discrimination encountered in white churches, though a handful of separate African American congregations already existed in the North and the South. The "invisible institution" and the African American denominations provided an identity that both affirmed the worth of, and gave meaning to, the experiences of a people excluded from the larger society.

Prior to the Civil War, though, most African American Christians in the South worshiped in white churches, usually relegated to "slave galleries" or balconies. With the legal end of slavery after the war, African American denominations and some northern white denominations sought to add these Christians to their numbers, and a greater number of independent African American denominations emerged. The continuing racism in American society, formally manifested in the "separate but equal" ethos of Jim Crow laws, consigned most African Americans to the margins of society. Within the African American community, the churches and religion assumed a place of primary importance. Clergy, often the only well-educated African Americans, became the natural leaders of the community. Churches became community centers with an array of social-service activities as well as places of worship, outlets where a repressed people could exercise their talents and find confirmation of their dignity and worth. Sectarian groups, often of a pentecostal style, and storefront churches that sprang up in northern cities to minister to African Americans migrating from the South seeking a better life, served similar purposes.

For all of these, the function of religion was as important as, if not more important than, the substance of religion. Through religion, African Americans found a social identity denied them by a racist culture. In the mid twentieth century, when the civil rights movement erupted, religious leaders such as Martin Luther King, Jr., logically moved to the forefront, and many African Americans who became politically prominent, such as Adam Clayton Powell, Jr., Jesse Jackson, and Andrew Young, came from the ranks of the clergy. While forces of secularism have left their imprint as legal racism has receded in recent decades, the churches retain symbolic prominence as centers of African American life, offering a social identity to millions of citizens as they move from the margins to full participation in American society.

But at the same time, many African Americans have come to reject Christianity because of its links to an oppressive culture and its providing racists, from the days of slavery to the present, with a theological rationale for injustice. Among the most prominent religious movements to emerge as an alternative to Christianity is the Nation of Islam, whose adherents are popularly known as Black Muslims. Adapting the traditions of Islam to fit the African American context, Black Muslims have been at the forefront of efforts to bolster the status of African Americans in American life, even if at times such efforts have led to calls for cultural and social separatism.

URBANIZATION, INDUSTRIALIZATION, AND IMMIGRATION

Between 1880 and the outbreak of World War I, immigration to the United States reached its zenith. While the majority of earlier immigrants came from northern and western Europe, immigrants from southern and eastern Europe now came by the millions. Their cultural and religious heritages differed greatly from those of earlier immigrants, for Roman Catholics, Jews, and Eastern Orthodox Christians comprised the bulk of this wave of immigrants. Most entered through the major port cities of the Northeast, especially New York, swelling the populations of cities that were already growing rapidly as industrialization lured people from farms to factories. The impact of this immigration on Judaism and Catholicism in the United States has already been sketched; equally significant was the impact on a Protestant America still holding a vision of a Christian nation with common beliefs and values. Among the various ways white Protestants responded were the Social Gospel, the development of the "institutional church," the emergence of fundamentalism, and the continuing reliance on revivalism.

The Social Gospel If many Protestants had made religion's substance a private affair, those identified with the Social Gospel emphasized the ramifications of belief for common life. Walter Rauschenbusch, for example, witnessed the dehumanizing effects of slum life that were exacerbated by the failure of industries to pay workers sufficient wages to provide adequately for their families, and claimed that biblical doctrines provided an ideology for "Christianizing the social order." Washington Gladden, responding to poor working conditions in factories and repeated use of force against workers who protested, saw the social implications of Christian love as demanding support for labor's cause. For both men, religious identity was tied not only to personal religious experience but also to life in the larger society. Yet even here, the function of religion was vital, for Social Gospel advocates insisted that religion could, and should, effect social transformation, that religious identity meant struggling to erect the ideal society. In the early twentieth century, the political movement of Progressivism took up some of the Social Gospel agenda and may have helped erode its influence. It is also clear in retrospect that the Social Gospel agenda was wedded to the interests of the emerging urban middle class, from which most of its leading advocates were drawn. In the mid twentieth century, heirs of the Social Gospel directed considerable energy to the civil rights movement and other social reform endeavors as a way to recast the character of American society.

Others sensitive to the social implications of religious identity regarded the changes wrought by immigration, urbanization, and industrialization as a distinct threat. Josiah Strong, while accepting the premises of the Social Gospel, argued that the influx of non-Protestant immigrants from cultures whose ethos differed markedly from that of earlier generations threatened to undermine the integrity of American life. Consequently, he called for efforts to convert immigrants to Protestant Christianity so they could secure a religious identity consonant with presumed American ideals. Others, such as Dwight L. Moody, who despaired at the apparent erosion of vital Protestantism, looked to mass revivalism as a panacea. Unlike Social Gospel advocates, who wanted to make social structures compatible with Christianity, revivalists assumed that in a corrupt society, the only recourse was to rescue individuals through religious conversion. For them, religious identity set individuals apart from an evil world. But they could not remain aloof from the social conditions of urban life, and many "city missions" or "rescue missions" owed their origins to revivalism's efforts to relate conversion to social problems.

The "Institutional Church" In many cities, larger congregations sought to adapt ministries to meet the needs of young male and female factory workers by building gymnasiums and community centers offering an array of social-service activities. The belief was that if the church could be a total institution (hence the label "institutional church"), these young adults would retain their religious identities and not fall prey to the corruptions of urban life. A similar rationale undergirded the early work of such organizations as the Young Men's Christian Association and the Young Women's Christian Association. Much of this program has cognates in the efforts of Catholics and Jews to work with their immigrant constituencies.

Fundamentalism New intellectual currents also appeared as a threat, particularly those associated with evolutionary theory and with higher criticism or analysis of Scripture that challenged traditional interpretations. The challenges to orthodox theology implicit in these intellectual shifts may well have contributed to a loss of effective influence among the major denominations that continued well into the twentieth century. In addition, many felt that the theological foundations of the Social Gospel were far too liberal. If urbanization, industrialization, and immigration were changing the world in which Protestant Christianity operated, these new intellectual forces seemed to undermine the very substance of religion. One response was the emergence of fundamentalism, the insistence on adherence to certain doctrines, such as the literal interpretation of Scripture and the physical second coming of Christ. Fundamentalism's roots are too complex for careful analysis here. However, it can be said that many of its early proponents came from the northern urban middle class and were responding to some of the same concerns that propelled many of those calling for a Social Gospel. Those drawn to fundamentalism tended to be more pessimistic about the new directions American culture was taking, regarding the social change under way as destroying a familiar world, while those attracted to the Social Gospel tended to be more optimistic, albeit somewhat simplistically so, seeing social change as an opportunity to fashion a better world. Recent scholarship has suggested that fundamentalism was partly propelled by an effort to reaffirm the traditional roles of women in an age when women were making gains in securing their rightful place in American society—for instance, gaining the franchise. But what is important is fundamentalism's attempt to recapture emphasis on the substance of religion. Ironically, however, fundamentalism strengthened the cultural emphasis on religion's function, for acknowledging belief in religion's so-called fundamentals became a badge of acceptance among those who thought that they were preserving authentic Christianity against so many external threats. It provided a common vocabulary for those who could testify to the dramatic, yet very personal, experience of being "born again."

Religion's links to social identity had other ramifications during the Victorian age. Colleen McDannell has called attention to the influence of religious identity on domestic architecture and gender roles within the family. While styles and approaches differed for Protestants and Catholics, and included distinctive domestic iconography, both groups saw religious identity as nurtured in the home and, for Protestants especially, increasingly as a feminine activity. Indeed, Ann Douglas has referred to this era as bringing about the "feminization of American culture." For this analysis, however, the significance lies primarily in the relegation of explicit religious identity to the home. There, in the private sphere, it was culturally acceptable to show one's personal religious identity and sensibilities; the obverse is implicit: such differences did not belong in the public sphere and thus were not part of one's social identity.

At the same time, for Catholic women especially, an alternative religious identity was possible. One could take vows of obedience, chastity, and poverty and enter a religious order. There, married to the church, one could devote one's life to things spiritual and to the service of humanity. The contribution to American culture of the thousands of Catholic women who became nuns is massive, for they staffed the network of parochial schools, labored among the immigrants who were too often on the brink of poverty, operated numerous hospitals, and engaged in a host of other social-welfare endeavors.

During this same period it is also clear, in retrospect, that among Protestants denominational affiliation was increasingly related to economic status. This should not be surprising. If differences of belief that had once separated denominations had eroded as religion's function became more important than its substance, denominational distinctions had likewise become muted. As H. Richard Niebuhr pointed out in his masterful 1929 study, *The Social Sources of Denominationalism,* what drew Americans to particular denominations was less matters of doctrine and more perceptions of which denominational label was appropriate to one's perceived social status. Hence Episcopalians and Presbyterians tended to draw more from among those who found themselves at the upper end of the socioeconomic scale, and those Niebuhr classified as sectarian groups from among those at the lower end of the scale. Niebuhr's analysis was among the first to draw attention to the role of race, region, and ethnicity in religious identity. But the implication of his appraisal, finally, is that what is important is having a label as a sign of social worth and identity.

World War I had an enduring impact on American religious life. Moves to restrict immigration that went into effect early in the 1920s considerably reduced the numbers of those coming from southern and eastern Europe, and gave decided preference to persons whose national backgrounds accorded more with those of a presumed Protestant America of a generation earlier. At the same time, the devastation of war shattered the optimism implicit in the Social Gospel's hope that a more liberal understanding of Christianity's substance could readily lead to large-scale social reform. The close of the war convinced fundamentalists that they had correctly perceived the threats to American Christianity and led to much contentiousness between fundamentalists and so-called modernists in the 1920s. And, as noted earlier, the 1920s also witnessed renewed nativism in the form of anti-Semitism, and anti-Catholicism briefly appeared in religious attacks on Roman Catholic presidential candidate Alfred E. Smith in 1928. It was as if some of white Protestant America realized that the dream of a nation united around a single set of religious values had already collapsed and desperately needed resuscitation. But in reality, for most people the particulars of religious belief remained consigned to the private sphere; increasingly what became important in the public sphere was whether one had a religious identity at all.

RELIGIOUS IDENTITY IN THE MEDIA AGE

In 1955, in the wake of what many called America's post-World War II "revival of religion," the sociologist Will Herberg published *Protestant, Catholic, Jew,* a scathing critique of the American religious scene. Herberg concluded that, at mid century, it no longer mattered for social acceptance whether one was a Protestant, a Catholic, or a Jew, but simply whether one had any religious label at all to mark one as a worthy, responsible citizen. He decried the erosion of vital piety; in its place, Americans of all religious labels, he claimed, had substituted commitment to the materialism of the "American way of life." While critics rightly find many flaws in Herberg's analysis, his thesis nevertheless reveals the consequences of the increasing privatization of religious substance in American culture and the social emphasis on religion's function in creating responsible citizens. Belief and piety remain private matters; all that concerns social identity is that one have a religious label, regardless of what it is.

Herberg's study appeared at the same time that two other aspects of American religious life were accelerating the privatization of religion: the positive-thinking movement associated with Norman Vincent Peale and the renewal of mass revivalism most obviously identified with Billy Graham. Peale's emphasis on the power of the individual to live confidently and optimistically amid the vagaries of modern life helped spawn a vast genre of religious "self-help" books. In all of them, the substance of differentiated doctrine is virtually irrelevant; one can think positively whether one is a Baptist or a Buddhist. Positive thinking and self-help see individual religiosity as transcending society, and thus push the substance of religion further out of the social sphere and into the private realm. All that matters is how one functions in society.

The calls for a "decision for Christ" echoing in the mass evangelist Billy Graham's appeals for conversion in part represent the continuing reliance on revivalism as a technique to bring religion to individuals. Much has been made of how Graham's ministry and that of other evangelists cross traditional denominational boundaries and how mass revivals often secure support from not only the spectrum of Protestant bodies but from Roman Catholics as well. Two consequences follow. One harks back to the heritage of revivalism that locates dynamic religion in personal experience; religion is a private concern involving only the individual and the individual's relation to the Divine. The second is the ongoing blurring of differences between denominations, once perceived to be guardians of religion's substance; if no group has a monopoly on religious truth, then all groups must be equally legitimate and valid. Both consequences lead to the conclusion that what counts, from a societal perspective, is whether one has a religious identity, not its content.

Perhaps nowhere has this trend become more obvious than in the religious style perpetuated by media preachers, the so-called televangelists. In the privacy of the home, the casual viewer absorbs whatever doctrine a televangelist proclaims, combines it with long-held opinions and prejudices, and fashions them into a private religious perspective. The religious affiliation of the televangelist is of little, if any, consequence. The substance of religion is exclusively private. Persons are free to believe whatever they want to believe. One's social identity is contingent only on having something to believe.

Even phenomena as seemingly disparate as the fascination with new religious movements—many of Asian origin—and the rise of the contemporary charismatic and pentecostal movements have intensified the relegation of religion's substance to the private sphere. Many of the new religious movements, such as the International Society for Krishna Consciousness (better known as the Hare Krishnas), have gradually retreated into isolated enclaves as the communitarians of the nineteenth century did, there to pursue personal religious quests through techniques such as disciplined meditation. The heart of the charismatic experience, such as being ecstatically empowered by the Divine to speak in tongues, is an individual, personal one par excellence that likewise highlights the retreat of religion's substance from the larger society almost to the point that one's religious identity and one's social identity have no necessary connection.

In addition, new immigration patterns in the late twentieth century brought a new pluralism to the religious scene. Perhaps the most significant shift was the steady increase in the number of adherents of Islam entering the country, particularly from Asia and, to a lesser extent, from Africa. Although other groups outside the Judeo-Christian circle had already carved niches for themselves in the United States, none approached the numerical strength that seems to be Islam's destiny, for immigration patterns of the 1970s and 1980s mean that before 2000 there will be more Muslims than Jews in the United States. One result will be a continuing relegation of the particulars of religious belief to the private sector, in part to minimize the potential for overt religious conflict in the public sector.

Demographers of religion at mid century reported that denominational switching among Protestants continued apace, with individuals often paying little heed to historic doctrinal differences when choosing a group, but basing their decision more on status, proximity of church to residence, and the extent to which programs met individual and family social needs. But by the late 1960s, groups that appeared to stress doctrine (generally the more conservative groups) began to experience great growth, while such "mainstream" or "mainline" denominations as Episcopalians and Methodists began to lose members. At first glance, it might appear that the substance of religion was becoming more meaningful than its function, but it is just as likely that the shift reflected the trend to privatize religion long under way. Mainline groups in the 1950s and 1960s had frequently associated themselves with social causes, seeking to discern the ramifications of religious belief for life in society. Hence many became caught up in the civil rights movement, the women's movement, and concerns about American involvement in Southeast Asia. Groups that saw religious identity as having social implications saw membership eroding; those which underscored personal religious experience were growing.

Even within religious bodies it became clear that individuals were intent on determining for themselves precisely what identification with a particular group entailed and how much authority they were willing to concede to a group. One example is the papal encyclical *Humanae Vitae,* which in 1968 reaffirmed the Roman Catholic Church's historic opposition to use of artificial means of birth control. From the church's perspective, Catholic identity precluded their use. Yet public opinion polls consistently report that American Catholics practice artificial birth control methods in the same proportion as the general population. But individual Catholics who do so still identify themselves as Catholic; they are unwilling to grant power to the church to control their private lives, because religion is a private matter.

Dissenting voices have arisen, particularly among those who, for a variety of reasons, see consignment of the substance to the private sphere as undermining any shared values through which the American people could maintain a common identity. In 1967 Robert Bellah's acclaimed essay "Civil Religion in America" appeared. Bellah called attention to a set of beliefs and values, especially belief in a Divine Providence controlling American destiny and setting the United States apart from other nations, that he thought had provided a common substratum to American life from the time of independence. Existing alongside religious institutions, this civil religion had shaped the social identity of all Americans. But Bellah also saw the civil religion as endangered by the social change and conflict marking American life in the late 1960s. Hence his analysis became a lament, an attempt to revitalize what he thought had once worked to give cohesion to American culture.

In a different vein, the emergence of the "new religious-political right," epitomized by Jerry Falwell and the Moral Majority (defunct by the late 1980s), also called for a return to common values once thought to characterize Americans' social identity. But this agenda was more akin to that of nineteenth-century evangelical Protestants, whose dream of a Christian America had been undone by ethnicity, immigration, urbanization, pluralism, industrialization, and regionalism. Examples of the religious right's concerns are Supreme Court decisions in 1962 and 1963 banning prayer and Bible reading in public schools. These decisions tacitly acknowledged that because prayer and Bible reading were religion-specific, in the American cultural context they had no bearing on social identity and therefore belonged in the private sphere. For Falwell and his associates, such prohibition sabotaged what they believed to be the religious foundations of American society; only by making prayer and Bible reading legal could the nation proceed again on its divinely ordained course.

But it is hard to undo history. The process of regarding the substance of religion as a personal, private matter had roots in the Puritan enterprise, although it has been commingled with visions for the character of the whole culture. The development of American society over nearly four centuries has continued to view intricacies of religious belief as a private, personal matter while recognizing that religious identity—having a religious label—has a valuable social function in marking persons as responsible citizens. The particular label one wears is unimportant; it is having a label that counts.

For some, that label has been found in the recovery of ancient religious practices often, ironically, labeled "New Age." Many come from pagan rites associated with a sense of oneness with the earth. Particularly among women, so long excluded from full participation and leadership in organized religious groups, there has been a renewed interest in wicca, goddess worship, and other forms of what is popularly called paganism. For these women, the search for an alternative spirituality represents not only an individual, and hence highly personal, quest but also an abiding awareness that much of the way religion has defined social identity in the United States over the centuries has come from a masculine perspective. Yet many combine a distinctively feminine spirituality with identification with more traditional religious approaches. To that extent, they epitomize the American penchant for constructing an individual, private religious world.

THE INVISIBLE RELIGION

In the late 1960s, the sociologist Thomas Luckmann offered a penetrating analysis of the role of traditional religion in complex urban, industrial societies. His contention was captured in the title of his analysis, *The Invisible Religion.* In such societies, religion in its organized, institutional form—religion seen as churches or denominations—had ceased to be the locus of popular religiosity. Rather, individuals drew from a wide range of human associations and groups that might include ethnic heritage, regional identity, political affiliation, and, more obviously, religion (such as membership in a religious group) to formulate personal, intensely private sets of beliefs and values. Tacit allegiance to a particular religious body may be part of this "invisible religion," but only a part; such allegiance may or may not include formal membership in a religious group. Luckmann was essentially writing about the substance of religion, for he regarded the private worldviews as still carrying out religion's age-old function of providing a framework of meaning for individual experience. From another vantage point, Robert Bellah arrived at a similar conclusion, particularly in the jointly authored *Habits of the Heart,* where he called attention to the tension between individuality and community that has been a hallmark of the American religious experience. Drawn to religious institutions, Americans nevertheless continue to create individual worlds of meaning.

Americans indeed identify with religious institutions; in 1990 some 350,000 local congregations dotted the American landscape, and around 60 percent of adult Americans claimed affiliation with a particular religious group. While religious affiliation remains a vital dimension of individuals' identity, it may account for only a portion of the many worldviews on which Americans rely to explain and interpret their experience. If the thesis advanced in this essay is a plausible interpretation of the role of religion in American social history and of the ways religion and social identity have interacted over the centuries, then the substance of religion has become ever more invisible, but having some sort of private, invisible religion remains fundamental to one's social identity as a responsible member of American society.

BIBLIOGRAPHY

Bellah, Robert N. "Civil Religion in America." *Daedalus* 96 (1967).

———. et al. *Habits of the Heart* (1985).

Butler, Jon. *Awash in a Sea of Faith: Christianizing the American People* (1990).

Carter, Paul A. *The Spiritual Crisis of the Gilded Age* (1971).

Cross, Robert D. *The Emergence of Liberal Catholicism in America* (1958).

Dolan, Jay P. *The Immigrant Church: New York's Irish and German Catholics, 1815–1865* (1975).

Douglas, Ann. *The Feminization of American Culture* (1977).

Feingold, Henry. *Zion in America: The Jewish Experience from Colonial Times to the Present* (1974).

Fishburn, Janet Forsythe. *The Fatherhood of God and the Victorian Family: The Social Gospel in America* (1981).

Hadden, Jeffrey K., and Charles Swann. *Prime Time Preachers: The Rising Power of Televangelism* (1981).

Hall, David D. *Worlds of Wonder, Days of Judgment: Popular Religious Belief in Early New England* (1989).

Handy, Robert T. *A Christian America: Protestant Hopes and Historical Realities* (1971).

Hatch, Nathan O. *The Democratization of American Christianity* (1989).

Hennesey, James. *American Catholics: A History of the Roman Catholic Community in the United States* (1981).

Herberg, Will. *Protestant, Catholic, Jew: An Essay in American Religious Sociology* (1955).

Higham, John. *Strangers in the Land: Patterns of American Nativism, 1860–1925* (1955; 2d ed., 1963).

Holloway, Mark. *Heavens on Earth: Utopian Communities in America, 1680–1880* (1951; rev. ed., 1966).

Lippy, Charles H., and Peter W. Williams., eds. *Encyclopedia of the American Religious Experience.* 3 vols. (1988).

Luckmann, Thomas. *The Invisible Religion: The Problem of Religion in Modern Society* (1967).

McDannell, Colleen. *The Christian Home in Victorian America, 1840–1900* (1986).

Niebuhr, H. Richard. *The Social Sources of Denominationalism* (1929).

Roof, Wade Clark, and William McKinney. *American Mainline Religion: Its Changing Shape and Future* (1987).

Shipps, Jan. *Mormonism: The Story of a New Religious Tradition* (1985).

Smith, Timothy L. *Revivalism and Social Reform in Mid-Nineteenth Century America* (1957).

White, Ronald C., Jr., and C. Howard Hopkins. *The Social Gospel: Religion and Reform in Changing America* (1976).

Williams, Peter W. *Popular Religion in America: Symbolic Change and the Modernization Process in Historical Perspective* (1980).

Wilmore, Gayraud S. *Black Religion and Black Radicalism* (1972; rev. ed., 1983).

Wilson, Bryan R. *Magic and the Millennium: A Sociological Study of Religious Movements of Protest Among Tribal and Third-World Peoples* (1973).

Wilson, John. "The Sociological Study of American Religion." In *Encyclopedia of the American Religious Experience,* edited by Charles H. Lippy and Peter W. Williams. Vol. 1 (1988).

Woolverton, John F. *Colonial Anglicanism in North America, 1607–1776* (1984).

SEE ALSO **The Clergy**; **Communitarians and Counterculturists**; **Ethnicity**; **Nativism, Anti-Catholicism, and Anti-Semitism**; and various essays in the section "**Ethnic and Racial Subcultures.**"

REGIONALISM

George B. Tindall

"THE CONCEPT OF REGIONALISM," Michael O'Brien wrote in *The Encyclopedia of Southern Culture* (1989), "is a recent adaptation of the cultural theory of romantic nationalism and the lineal descendant of the idea of sectionalism" (p. 1121). It is an adaptation of a theory first systematized, in the late eighteenth century, by the Romantic German philosopher and writer Johann Gottfried von Herder (1744–1803), in reaction to the universalism championed by the Enlightenment.

Regionalism is, of course, not merely an adaptation of romantic ideas. From certain perspectives, as in the administration of governmental or other large-scale organizations, it has been a practical convenience if not a necessity. The United States Census, for instance, breaks down its figures by regions; the Federal Reserve System has twelve regional Federal Reserve Banks; the Federal Bureau of Investigation maintains regional offices. But in no case are the regional definitions the same.

For geographers and geologists, regionalism is an inescapable fact. Efforts to explain regional differences in human societies are based on the effects of environment (climate and geography) and on acquired characteristics of peoples (historical development). Differing geographic and climatic conditions affect the human condition and define certain possibilities, but historical development may lead peoples to make quite different uses of similar climates—witness metropolitan Japan and the American South.

Regionalism and sectionalism have influenced a variety of subject areas: literature, anthropology, economics, political science, sociology, and so on. As a theoretical construct, it had its heyday in the United States from about 1920 to 1950. The regional approach first issued from academic circles in the West and the South, led by historian Frederick Jackson Turner at the University of Wisconsin, by the literary group at Vanderbilt University known first as the *Fugitives* and then as the Agrarians, and by the Chapel Hill Regionalists, sparked by sociologist Howard W. Odum at the University of North Carolina.

THE COLONIAL PERIOD AND THE EARLY REPUBLIC

Although the word "regionalism" came into common usage only in the twentieth century, the phenomenon was a fact of American society almost from the beginning. The varied cultures of pre-Columbian peoples reflected it in, for instance, the Adena-Hopewell culture of the Northeast (800 B.C.–A.D. 600), the Mississippian culture of the Southeast (A.D. 600–1500), and the Pueblo-Hohokam culture of the Southwest (400 B.C.–present). None of these ever reached the levels of development attained by the classic cultures such as the Mayas of Middle America (300–900 A.D.), although they showed strong influences from the Mayas, Aztecs, and Incas.

And fairly early in the years of English colonization, regionalism developed in the recognition of the southern, New England, and middle colonies as distinctive areas on the basis of their differing geographies and developments in peopling, economies, and societies that grew up in them. Different regions of America were peopled at first by emigrants from different regions of England. Geographically the southern colonies had a unique advantage in climate. They could grow exotic crops that withered in northern latitudes and were prized by the mother country: tobacco around the Chesapeake, rice and indigo farther south.

A plantation society that supported a planter gentry, especially near the coast in the Tidewater, developed on the basis of indentured servants and slavery. New England early had the stamp of Puritanism, but on land suited mainly to hardscrabble agriculture, it exploited forests and fisheries and turned to shipping and commerce. Both geographically and culturally the middle colonies stood in between, and more completely reflected the diversity of colonial life and more fully foreshadowed the pluralism of the later nation. The crops were those of New England but more bountiful, and these colonies became the breadbasket of America.

By the end of the colonial period there had come to be recognized a North and a South, variously divided at the Mason-Dixon Line (after the surveyors of the Maryland-Pennsylvania boundary) or at the Potomac River. In 1785 Thomas Jefferson pointed out to the Marquis de Chastellux some differences between the inhabitants of the two regions:

In the North they are	In the South they are
cool	fiery
sober	voluptuary
laborious	indolent
independent	unsteady
jealous of their own liberties, and just to those of others	zealous for their own liberties but trampling on those of others
interested	generous
chicaning	candid
superstitious and hypocritical in their religion	without attachment or pretensions to any religion but that of the heart

These characteristics, Jefferson asserted, shaded off as one moved toward the middle, so that one could judge the latitude by the attitude of the people. In Pennsylvania the two characters blended "to form a people free from the extremes both of vice and virtue" ("Letter to the Marquis de Chastellux [c. 1789]).

As sectional conflict developed between North and South, particularly over slavery, each section sought to make an ally of the West (by then the third of the three American regions) in order to dominate the country. The spread of upland cotton culture after the invention of the cotton gin in 1793 carried the institution into the Southwest, while, beginning with the Northwest Ordinance of 1787, the Northwest became free territory. The great interior of the continent was largely dependent for transportation on the Mississippi River and its tributaries, which tied the Northwest to the South. By the 1850s, however, the outcome was becoming clearer after the completion of the Erie Canal (1825), which finally linked New York City with the Great Lakes, and the development of east-west railroad lines, which brought transportation links and other ties to the Northeast.

Meanwhile, a movement for southern nationalism paralleled and contradicted the movement for American nationalism. The South as a region or section came to differ from other sections in that it had a nationalist as well as a sectional or regional tradition. To the average American, and apparently to the writers of most school textbooks, the word "section" applies only to the struggle of the North and South over the questions of slavery, state sovereignty, and eventually disunion. But the Civil War was only the most dramatic and most tragic manifestation of sectionalism.

TURNER, ODUM, AND THEIR FOLLOWERS

Frederick Jackson Turner is remembered best for the frontier thesis he first set forth in perhaps the best-known essay by an American historian, "The Significance of the Frontier in American History," presented at the meeting of the American Historical Association held during Chicago's Columbian Exposition of 1893, which celebrated (a bit late) the four-hundredth anniversary of Christopher Columbus's first voyage of discovery. After the 1890 population count the superintendent of the census had noted that he could no longer locate a continuous frontier line beyond which population thinned out to less than two per square mile. Turner wrote:

> The existence of an area of free land, its continuous recession, and the advance of American settlement westward, explain American development.... The result is that to the frontier the American intellect owes its striking characteristics. That coarseness and strength combined with acuteness and inquisitiveness; that practical, inventive turn of mind, quick to find expedients; that masterful grasp of material things, lacking in the artistic but powerful to effect great ends; that restless, nervous energy; that dominant individualism, working for good and for evil, and withal that buoyancy and exuberance which comes with freedom—these are the traits of the frontier, or traits called out elsewhere because of the existence of the frontier. (*The Frontier in American History* [1920], pp. 1, 37)

In 1893, Turner concluded, "four centuries from the discovery of America, at the end of a hundred years under the Constitution, the frontier has gone, and with its going has closed the first period of American history" (p. 38).

With the frontier gone as an active force in American history, Turner cast about for some other unifying concept that would help explain the nation which had come into being. He found it in the development of sectionalism, which seemed to him a permanent characteristic of the American scene firmly based on historical experience and on differing interests that could be projected into the future.

"That sectionalism is not dying away in the United States," he wrote, "will be clear enough to anyone who examines the newspapers and reads the debates in Congress, not to speak of analyzing the votes in that body." At the University of Wisconsin, shortly after the turn of the century, Turner instituted courses in the regional history of the American West, the South, and New England. In "The Significance of the Section in American History," first published in the *Wisconsin Magazine of History* (March 1925) and reprinted in 1932 in a volume titled *The Significance of Sections in American History,* Turner adopted as a definition of "section" the one that philosopher Josiah Royce of Harvard had applied to a province: "any one part of a national domain which is geographically and socially sufficiently unified to have a true consciousness of its own ideals and customs and to possess a sense of its distinction from other parts of the country." It was Royce's opinion that "the world needs . . . vigorous development of . . . provincial life to serve as a check upon mob psychology on a national scale, and to furnish that variety which is essential to vital growth and originality" (*The Significance of Sections,* p. 45). There was, of course, always the danger that the province might come to think of itself as the nation—not a desirable option, in Royce's or Turner's opinion.

But the United States had become a congeries of sections that in their extent, and to some degree in their relations, bore a distinct resemblance to the European nations. Much of the legislation of Congress, from the multiplicity of sectional interests that played upon its drafting, resembled treaties negotiated between sovereign nations. Turner wrote:

> The significance of the section in American history is that it is the faint image of a European nation and that we need to reëxamine our history in the light of this fact. Our politics and our society have been shaped by sectional complexity and interplay not unlike what goes on between European nations. The greater sections are the result of the joint influence of the geologists' physiographic provinces and the colonizing stocks which have entered them. . . . Of course the boundary lines are not definite and fixed. Neither are those of European nations. These larger sections have taken their characteristic and peculiar attitudes from American civilization in general. (*The Significance of Sections,* pp. 50, 51)

Meanwhile, two new and disparate views of southern life arose, each with the novel feature of academic affiliations: Agrarianism, centered at Vanderbilt, and Regionalism, centered at the University of North Carolina. The Vanderbilt Agrarians were the first to perfect their arguments. Their manifesto, *I'll Take My Stand,* appeared in 1930. In reaction against both the progressive New South and H. L. Mencken's image of the benighted South, the Agrarians championed, in Donald Davidson's words, "a traditional society . . . that is stable, religious, more rural than urban, and politically conservative," a society in which human needs were met by "family, bloodkinship, clanship, folkways, custom, community."

In the end, Agrarianism proved less important as a social-economic force than as a context for creative literature. The central figures in the movement were the *Fugitive* poets John Crowe Ransom, Donald Davidson, Allen Tate, and Robert Penn Warren. As Louis Rubin has written, their image of the agrarian South provided "a rich, complex metaphor through which they presented a critique of the modern world." In contrast with the hurried, nervous life of cities, the image of the agrarian South was of a life in which human beings existed serenely and harmoniously. Their critique of the modern frenzy "has since been echoed by commentator after commentator."

Turner's essay "The Significance of the Section in American History" offered a manifest basis in history for the regionalism that Howard Odum was then developing at the University of North Carolina, derived from a focus on the South, in contrast with Turner's emphasis on the West. In 1929 Odum's protégé and colleague Rupert B. Vance produced the first major work of the Regional school: a social history of the cotton complex titled *Human Factors in Cotton Culture,* which yielded a view of an economic and social system on the verge of collapse. Three years later Vance's *Human Geography of the South* (1932) presented an overview of the South at the time, based largely on the 1930 census. In it Vance set forth in some detail the "eclectic tasks" of a new regionalism that would look to "both orderly industrial development and agricultural reform." Research and planning would be the key to a material and cultural renaissance of the South.

Odum had meanwhile published *An American Epoch: Southern Portraiture in the National Picture* (1930), which foretokened his more mature regionalism. The book grew from a creative insight that pictured the evolution of folk life with a skill few historians could muster. Through two semifictional characters, "Uncle John" and "the old Major," and their numerous progeny Odum presented an impressionistic view of southern folk through four generations. In 1931 the General Education Board made a grant to the Social Science Research Council for a southern regional study (*Southern Regions of the United States*) that was to run for three years. The following year, the same year that Turner's *Significance of Sections* appeared, the study was entrusted to Odum. Its title derived from Odum's division of the United States into six regions on the basis of several hundred "objective" indices.

While sectionalism, as conceived by Turner, was a manifestly valid approach to American history, and while it laid a foundation for Odum's regionalism, it did not, for Odum, provide the method of achieving the potentialities of American life. He considered sectionalism to be the source of infinite evil. It abounded in conflict, drawing into controversy the talent and energy that should be expended in rational study and development. "Regionalism" was the word that would exorcise the evil spirits of sectionalism. Regionalism would seek to ameliorate conflict, to integrate the region into the nation, recognizing the differences and encouraging diversity in the context of the general national welfare.

This difference, which represented part of his disagreement with the Vanderbilt Agrarians, was to become for Odum one of the fundamental tenets, if not the central theme, of Regionalism. One of its most trenchant criticisms came from Donald Davidson of the Agrarians in a letter that bespoke a realism not always attributed to the Agrarians: "Odum, I am sure, must realize that pure politics, pure science, pure art never remain pure very long. . . . Odum will not escape the political aspects of Southern economic and cultural problems simply by insisting that he has a regional, not a sectional, program." Odum's distinction might be useful for purposes of study, he wrote, but "sectionalism offers the political approach, which is the natural approach that our history and governmental habits invite" (Davidson to [John Donald] Wade, 3 March 1934 copy in Howard W. Odum, Papers, Southern Historical Collection, University of North Carolina at Chapel Hill).

Regionalism was, of course, more than an attack on sectionalism. It was a concept with implications in literature, geography, history, ecology, anthropology, psychology, economics, political science, and sociology. In Odum's *Southern Regions of the United States* (1936) and more explicitly in his *American Regionalism,* written with Harry E. Moore (1938), these multiple implications are brought forward. Regionalism was a means toward synthesis of all the social sciences and, to some extent, of the humanities. It was a method whereby one could see society as a whole, not in bits and snatches from the viewpoint of some specialty.

Regionalism was, however, too divorced from the mainstream of sociological thought to survive, except marginally, even in the department that Odum founded. And unlike Henry Grady, whose classic speech "The New South" (1886) held before his fellow Southerners a vision that became a motivating force in history, Odum hardly proved to be the prophet of a post–New South. His vision, in fact, built solidly on the New South creed of economic development. After all, were not most of the region's problems rooted ultimately in poverty?

The region was a more manageable frame of reference for interdisciplinary study than the nation as a whole, but it was more than an academic exercise. It was a practical basis on which to pursue social planning. Fundamentally, southern Regionalism was a concept of the "problem South," which President Franklin D. Roosevelt labeled "the nation's economic problem no. 1," a region with shortcomings but with potentialities that called for constructive attention and the application of rational planning.

Odum held to the idea, widely unfashionable then as now, that academic research might be, to quote the title of Guy Johnson and Guion Johnson's history of Odum's Institute for Research in Social Science, *Research in Service to Society* (1980).

REGIONALISM AND THE NEW DEAL

Through the disciples of Odum, as well as agencies of the New Deal, the vision of Regionalism inspired a flood of social-science monographs and programs for reform and development. It is "almost impossible to generalize about the other regionalists," says John Shelton Reed in the *Enduring South* (1972). "Odum was the school's founder, guru, and undisputed leader, but, to his credit, he was not out simply to clone himself. He gathered around him, and nurtured . . . a variety of men and women who did many different kinds of regional sociology, and many different things in addition."

In the end, Odum's chief contribution was that he, like the Agrarians, supplied the impetus of an idea. Agrarianism quickened a generation of southern writers with its vision of southern tradition beset by change, which became the central theme of the Southern Renaissance in literature just a hundred years after the flowering of New England. Regionalism quickened a generation of social scientists with its vision of the "problem South."

Whether regionalism had real potentialities beyond academic study, Odum never contented himself with it as a purely academic discipline. He therefore sought, but never achieved, the establishment of some sort of organized research and planning, through the Council on Southern Regional Development, to push the "national-regional" approach to take the place of the "sectional-local." But the program ran afoul of dangerous and confusing crosscurrents in the late 1930s. Sectionalism reasserted itself in conflict between the New Deal and southern conservatives but also, as Odum put it, "the Southern Conference for Human Welfare, and twenty other groups that are literally taking the lead to do what the Council ought to do."

Among the diversified groups in the field, the New Deal state-planning boards offered a fleeting promise of regional planning, and most of them went the way of all flesh when they evolved into "industry-hunting" boards, in effect official chambers of commerce. In 1932, however, President Roosevelt had suggested programs to combine state planning with overall national planning. In 1933 Interior Secretary Harold Ickes established the National Planning Board to help prepare a public-works program. It grew successively into the National Resources Board and the National Resources Committee and the National Resources Planning Board. In 1935 the Board issued a report, *Regional Factors in National Planning and Development,* that for a time suggested development along the lines endorsed by Odum. However, the board expired in 1943, a casualty of World War II and of a conservative reaction against the New Deal that gained strength during the war.

The outstanding initiative of the New Deal in the field of regional planning was the Tennessee Valley Authority (TVA). It grew less out of a doctrinaire concept, however, than out of events that followed government effort to use Muscle Shoals in Alabama to provide electricity for extracting nitrates during World War I; it evolved through the 1920s into nitrate fertilizers, industrial development, and cheap public power. Waterpower development pointed inevitably toward the problem of navigation, of regulating stream flow for flood control, and of the conservation of soil and forests. The chain of connections led to overall planning for an entire watershed, a total drainage area of 40,569 square miles (105,074 square kilometers) in seven states, four-fifths the size of England.

The first chairman of the TVA, Arthur E. Morgan, president of Antioch College, was a self-made engineer who had a utopian bent. Years before, he had developed a gigantic drainage project in Arkansas, which for want of proper social concern had become the center of some of the most miserable sharecropping anywhere. He therefore hoped to make the TVA a vehicle for both physical and social engineering.

Morgan shared the hope of many at the time that TVA might promote the back-to-the-land movement so popular during the Great Depression. He sought to stimulate handicraft industries and cooperatives—in short, the simple life. The town of Norris, Tennessee, built near the first TVA dam, was modeled on an English garden city. Morgan hoped that Norris would serve as an example to neighboring mountaineers of what they could achieve. Instead, he confronted resentment at a town planned by outsiders.

Other New Dealers saw the TVA in less utopian terms: as a way to restore the economy of the region, not as a social revolution. Morgan in the end lost out to David E. Lilienthal, whose purpose was mainly to provide cheap electricity and fertilizer for the Tennessee Valley. Throughout the 1930s, ardent New Dealers continued to promote the establishment of similar authorities in major river valleys all over the country, but the TVA remained unique—and eventually became more a public utility company than an experiment in social planning.

New Deal programs had literary effects as well. They nourished what critic Alfred Kazin called the "now innocent, now calculating, now purely rhetorical, but always significant experience in national self-discovery" that occurred in the 1930s: The New Deal, through the Works Progress Administration's Federal Writers' Project, among other things contributed to the collection of a "vast granary of facts" in fifty-one state and territorial guidebooks, catalogs of archives, collections of folklore and folksongs, and even records of tombstone inscriptions. The Writers' Project pioneered in the oral history of the "inarticulate" (*On Native Grounds* [1942]). In *These Are Our Lives* (1939), the Federal Writers' Project in North Carolina, Tennessee, and Georgia gathered case histories of white and black workers and sharecroppers. *Lay My Burden Down* (1945) presented the life stories of former slaves as recorded by Writers' Project interviewers. Under the direction of Roy Stryker, the Farm Security Administration built up an enormous photographic documentation of everyday life in America. Pare Lorentz pioneered the motion-picture documentary in *The Plow That Broke the Plains* (1936) and *The River* (1937).

In the 1930s Americans learned that, like it or not, they had a culture and had had one all along—it had simply been overlooked. Now they tried to make up for lost time by tracking down the culture, recording, restoring, and celebrating it.

But the regional focus faded rapidly as the inward-looking Americans found their attention drawn to Munich, Poland, China, and Pearl Harbor. After the death of Odum in 1954, regionalism virtually vanished for several decades. Odum's colleague Rupert Vance observed: "Many of the pertinent demands of the regional movement of the thirties have evaporated. The New Deal has been dealt; what is the fighting all about? As the affluent society crosses the Mason-Dixon line, the regionalist of the 1930s turns up as just another 'liberal without a cause.'"

REGIONALISM AND PLANNING

The one kind of social planning that did flourish and provide employment for large numbers of people was city and regional planning, "regional" in this case referring to larger metropolitan areas, and such agencies as city-planning boards and administrative agencies like the Port of New York Authority, created by interstate compact in 1921. City planning in a sense had existed since the beginning of cities, but it became a specialized vocation in the twentieth century. Although the modern movement was often captured or manipulated by commercial interests, it had a rationale related to that of the conservation movement, ranging from planned land management to wilderness preservation, which dated back at least to the creation of Yellowstone National Park in 1872.

The pattern of urban growth in the nineteenth century often became a sprawl, since it usually took place without plan, in the interest of a fast buck, and without thought to the need for parks and public services. But some cities and developers had the wit to look ahead. In the early 1850s New York had set up a park commission that hired Frederick Law Olmsted as chief architect of Central Park. He later planned parks and subdivisions in San Francisco, Brooklyn, Chicago, and other cities.

Chicago's World's Fair, the World's Columbian Exposition of 1893, gave impetus to the "City Beautiful" movement. The fair was of such size that a whole new city was built on Chicago's South Side lakefront. Olmsted helped with the choice of a site, and the planning brought together leading architects and engineers of the time.

The success of what visitors took to calling the "White City" stirred a new interest in city planning, which eventually came to be known as city and regional planning. In 1901 Washington set out to celebrate the city's centennial (1900) by completing Pierre L'Enfant's plan for a mall from the Capitol to the Potomac. The effort also led to the creation of new monuments and of Rock Creek Park. New civic centers sprang up in the larger cities. Hartford, Connecticut, created the first city-planning commission in 1907, and the idea spread rapidly to smaller towns. Shortly before that, Chicago's Commercial Club in 1906 had engaged a group to work out a comprehensive plan for the city. Adopted by the city council in 1910, the plan influenced the city's development for many decades. In 1916 the American City Planning Institute, a professional organization, met for the first time. A related movement to increase the efficiency of city government sprang up early in the century, based on the idea of having city managers run local government under the direction of a mayor and city council. First undertaken in Staunton, Virginia, in 1908, and copied by Dayton, Ohio, in 1913, the idea spread widely. City managers increasingly were professionals trained in schools of planning.

A more advanced kind of city planning was promoted after 1923 by the Regional Planning Association of America, founded by such social theorists and planners as Benton MacKaye and Lewis Mumford, and inspired by the garden-city movement of British reformers Patrick Geddes and Ebenezer Howard around the turn of the century. MacKaye, designer of the Appalachian Trail, looked to New England small towns as a likely model for bringing urban living into equilibrium with the environment. Mumford, less radical, sought to derive from the movement lessons for the existing metropolis but cooperated in the movement for garden cities, which reached fruition in New Deal plans for several such communities, including Greenbelt, Maryland, and Greendale, Wisconsin, and, later, Reston, Virginia. Such communities, however, most often turned into commuter suburbs rather than the self-contained towns envisioned by the idealists.

The idea, in fact, was not as new as it seemed. Planned towns dated from the ancient world and from the earliest days of European settlement in America, the earliest within the present United States being the Spanish towns of Saint Augustine and Santa Fe. New England towns followed the pattern of peasant villages. James Oglethorpe had planned Savannah before it was built.

Regional planning on Odum's scale reached its peak during the New Deal period, when regionalism seemed the massive fact of society, literature, politics, and art. Leading literary periodicals were filled with references to regional writers. Little magazines with a regional flavor flourished. In the 1930s, however, the rise of literary regionalism was accompanied by a revolt against the local-color school in favor of a "new provincialism" with a universal outlook seeing, as critic and poet Allen Tate put it, "a region with some special characteristics, but offering as an imaginative subject the plight of human beings as it has been and will doubtless continue to be, here and in other parts of the world." Regional authors like Thomas Wolfe and Willa Cather had experienced separation from their origins, had outgrown their communities, and looked back from new perspectives acquired through travel and education.

REGIONALISM AND ETHNICITY

But regionalism, like fundamentalism (otherwise a very different phenomenon), proved to be not dead but dormant—and continued to stir below the surface of popular awareness. It was with folk culture that Odum began his study of regional sociology, the collection of black folk songs and folk culture; he ended it in the unfinished effort to develop a sociological theory of regional folk culture. And when interest began to stir once again, its focus was on regional cultures, in both the anthropological sense and the aesthetic.

The rebirth paralleled a rising interest in ethnicity. In his *Outlines of a Philosophy of the History of Man* (1784–1791), Johann Gottfried von Herder, an eighteenth-century German Romantic, asserted that each national or ethnic group had a distinctive *Volksgeist,* literally a spirit of the people, a cultural life that derived from a shared geography and historical experience. The diversity of such cultures enriched the world. The enrichment was one of Odum's most important defenses of regionalism, which had more in common with nationalism and ethnicity than was immediately apparent. In world history since his time such national and ethnic cultures have shown a surprising resistance to influences that might be expected to work toward more unified cultures. And had not Frederick Jackson Turner said that the section was "the faint image of the European nation"?

So it was with the American "melting pot." During the time of the civil rights movement (itself largely regional in character) and the Vietnam War in the 1960s, a severe case of war weariness—involving wars foreign and domestic—seized the nation. Amid the tumult, the mass media, often thought to be agents of conformity, fostered counterforces instead: black revolt, student rebellion, women's liberation, food fads, hard rock. These were harbingers of a broadening interest in ethnic identity. In the early 1970s "the new ethnicity" became the latest bandwagon, detailed in Peter Schrag's *The Decline of the WASP* (1971), Andrew M. Greeley's *Why Can't They Be Like Us?* (1971), and Michael Novak's *The Rise of the Unmeltable Ethnics* (1972). The theme cropped up in newspapers, in magazines, and in films like *The Godfather.*

In 1954, the *Washington Post* eulogized Howard Odum as "the Eli Whitney of the Modern South. He inspired a revolution. Certainly there was no one—unless it was Franklin D. Roosevelt—whose influence was greater than Odum's on the development of the region below the Potomac" (14 November 1954, p. 4B). Yet by the 1970s nearly half of a sample of new Ph.D.s in sociology confessed that they had never heard of this former president of the American Sociological Association. Another third found his name vaguely familiar but knew nothing of his work.

The exception, in academic circles, to this ignorance was historians specializing in the South. In the 1980s a spate of histories focused on the sudden cultural awakening of the South during the interwar years, and each gave extended attention to Odum, most notably Daniel J. Singal's *The War Within: From Victorian to Modernist Thought in the American South* (1982), which features a chapter on Odum and two more that focus mainly on the sociology department he founded and the University of North Carolina Press, which in those years was one of the most innovative in the country. Singal's work, added to Morton Sosna's *In Search of the Silent South* (1977), Richard H. King's *A Southern Renaissance* (1980), and Michael O'Brien's *The*

Idea of the American South (1979), is part of an impressive list that should also include several pieces by Odum's successor at Chapel Hill, John Shelton Reed, one of the last regional sociologists.

Reed has noted a revival of interest in regionalism among sociologists, geographers, and other social scientists. Reed's *The Enduring South* (1972) applied quantification to opinion polls to show that southerners do not think like other Americans. Lewis Killian, in his study *White Southerners* (1970), which treated them as an ethnic group, found that they did not vanish into the mainstream when they moved north or west. It was more likely to be the mainstream that vanished. Nor was the growing interest confined to students of the South. In his book *Cultural Regions of the United States* (1975), Raymond Gastil supplied a sociological essay on American culture as gallimaufry of regional cultures. Courses on regional topics began to reappear, mostly on the southern region—and in such unlikely places as Boston, Lawrence, Kansas, and Walla Walla, Washington.

More recently there have been further signs of reviving interest. A Canadian, Ralph Matthews, has treated the regionalists at some length in *The Creation of Regional Dependency* (1983). A special issue of *The Review of Radical Political Economics* looked at the South in the light of such regions as Wales, Galicia, Brittany, Catalonia, and Quebec, and discussed socialism as being "the spectre of regionalism." Another assessment appears in a book by Ann Markusen, a radical economist, *Regions: The Economics and Politics of Territory* (1987). The terms "region" and "regionalism" have come to be widely used by students of international affairs.

One of the most interesting linkages surfaced at a session of the Southern Historical Association, which in 1986 observed the fiftieth anniversary of *Southern Regions*. David Goldfield remarked in a lengthy paper delivered at that session: "Regionalism languished as a research methodology except in France, where the Annaliste school [a name derived from the French historical journal *Annales d'histoire sociale*], produced monumental works like Fernand Braudel's epic *La Méditeranée* (1949), carried a geohistorical survey of the Mediterranean region focusing on the development of a regional urban system" and intensive local studies like Emmanuel LeRoy Ladurie's *Montaillou: The Promised Land of Error* (1978).

Like the Annalistes, Odum spelled out the multiple implications of a discipline that would become a means of synthesizing all the social sciences and, to some extent, the humanities, a method whereby one could study society and see it whole. In *An American Epoch* Odum undertook a treatment of what is today called mentality, from the long-term view. He presented the realities of folk life in the New South with a vividness that no formal historian could hope to achieve. In the 1920s Odum wrote an almost poetic trilogy about a wandering "black Ulysses," a figure inspired by Left-Wing Gordon, a one-armed highway crewman. Three small volumes caught, as no academic study or compendium could, the spirit of the black folklore that had occupied Odum's attention over the years: *Rainbow Round My Shoulder* (1928), *Wings on My Feet* (1929), and *Cold Blue Moon* (1931).

The 1970s was also the decade of the ethnics through the growth of immigration. While old ethnic groups renewed their self-awareness, new ethnic groups were rising as floods of newcomers, predominantly Asian and Hispanic in origin, arrived in numbers that, by some estimates which include the undocumented, surpassed the 8.7 million who came in the first decade of the century (previously the largest number). The flood continued into the 1980s. In several recent years, according to the Immigration and Naturalization Service, the influx has approached the number who came in 1901–1910. Between 1980 and 1986 the number of residents of a race other than black or white increased by 45 percent and the share of immigrants from Europe declined to less than 12 percent. If present rates continue, sometime early in the twenty-first century Americans of European descent will be a minority.

The newest immigrants have different origins, and they are going to different destinations, more than ever to the West and the South. In the South this has reversed a pattern that prevailed for nearly two centuries after the 1770s, when little immigration entered a region that in the colonial period had perhaps the most ethnic diversity—black, white, and Native American—of any region.

This has created fears and responses similar to those of earlier periods of immigration. The demands for English as an official language parallel a campaign, that occurred in the late nineteenth century, to forbid foreign-language schools. That campaign affected mainly the Middle West and German schools. By early 1989 seventeen states had adopted English as their "official language," without spelling out clearly what that meant. Applied dogmatically, such laws could sacrifice a precious heritage of cultural diversity and a precious resource of bilingualism. One irony is the frequency with which bilingualism is promoted by immigrants. Greek Americans have set an example of combining assimilation with preservation of the old culture by sending their children to both public schools and parochial schools where they learn Greek. But they have never sought to make bilingualism an official requirement, although some Hispanics and Asians have.

The more likely outcome is a pattern of second-generation Americans rejecting the old language and the old culture in order to be accepted as Americans. For instance, Haitians in Miami seem particularly intent on learning English. Some 40 percent of those who read newspapers say they read the *Miami Herald* rather than French or Creole papers. One should not generalize too much from California, perhaps, but a study by the Rand Corporation showed second-generation Hispanics finishing high school at nearly the same rate as the state average, and the third generation more at home in English than in Spanish, more inclined to attend college and enter the professions. Cuban Hispanics in Miami have tended on the whole to occupy a higher social and educational standing than the broader population.

Anthropologist James L. Peacock III has remarked on how quickly diverse ethnic groups have assimilated not only English but also regional accents. Students from Korea and India, for instance, who spent their teenage years in small North Carolina towns talk like natives of those towns. The phenomenon of assimilation to regional patterns has long been noted on the part of ethnic groups with deeper roots in the South. Moreover, to change is not necessarily to lose a distinctive identity; it is often to enrich it through syncretic combinations, as with Jewish Southerners whose roots go back to the colonial era, or African American Catholics, or Japanese war brides, whose worldview has been found to combine southern evangelical and Japanese Buddhist themes.

In the absence of a common national culture, the adaptation of immigrants to the available regional culture has been a common experience. In 1973 cultural geographer Wilbur Zelinsky referred to the "Doctrine of First Effective Settlement." This was the hypothesis that the first European or native white American population had a decisive and persistent effect on later patterns of culture. This theory, however, does not rule out enormous changes, such as the evolution of New England from predominantly English Puritan to predominantly Irish and Italian Catholic without the loss of its distinctive regional self-awareness.

Speech differences are one fundamental of regional distinction. An ambitious project, sponsored by the American Dialect Society, is the publication, under the editorship of Frederic G. Cassidy, of *Dictionary of American Regional English,* which has so far appeared in two volumes (A–H; 1985–1991). A project that began to reach fruition earlier was *Linguistic Atlas of the United States and Canada,* a series of regional volumes concerned more with pronunciations and phonetics than with dialect expression, which began under the sponsorship of the American Council of Learned Societies (1930) and the general direction of Hans Kurath.

An ambitious project seeks to reconcile the "new" social history and traditional narrative, as well as the ethnic and the regional approaches. David Hackett Fischer has produced the first volume of his projected multivolume cultural history of the United States. *Albion's Seed: Four British Folkways in America* (1989) adopts, without using the term, Zelinsky's "Doctrine of the First Effective Settlement" as applied to the colonial era. In summary, Fischer asserts that Puritans "from East Anglia established a religious community in Massachusetts (1629–40); royalist cavaliers . . . from the south and west of England built a highly stratified agrarian way of life in Virginia (1640–70); egalitarian Quakers of modest social standing from the North Midlands resettled in the Delaware Valley and promoted social pluralism (1675–1715); and . . . the fourth great migration came from the borderlands of North Britain—an area which included the Scottish lowlands, the north of Ireland, and England's six northern counties."

Fischer, however, does not ignore further complexities, such as the distinctive coastal culture of South Carolina, with founding families of English from Barbados, Huguenots from France, emigrants from tidewater Virginia, and a black majority mainly from Angola (hence the Gullah dialect) and the Congo.

Complexities abound in the westward migration of the colonial cultures and the new influences brought to bear, including ethnic pluralism, which did not diminish regional identities but enhanced them. The new immigrants, Fischer notes, "did not assimilate American culture in general. They tended to adopt the folkways of the regions in which they settled." Instead of one American melting pot, there were many.

Multiculturalism, about which much has been heard, is a phenomenon that embraces much more than ethnicity. Regionalism, long viewed as an aberration, a remnant of the 1930s, seems to be returning, perhaps as the central fact of American cultural history.

BIBLIOGRAPHY

General

Bailyn, Bernard. *The Peopling of British North America: An Introduction* (1986).

———. *Voyagers to the West: A Passage in the Peopling of America on the Eve of the Revolution* (1986).

Bogue, Donald J., and Calvin L. Beale. *Economic Areas of the United States* (1961).

Bradshaw, Michael. *Regions and Regionalism in the United States* (1988).

Burleson, Clyde W. *Interstate Commerce: Regional Styles of Doing Business* (1987).

Cassidy, Frederic G., ed. *Dictionary of American Regional English,* 2 vols. (to date) (1985–1991).

Clark, Dennis. *Hibernia America: The Irish and Regional Cultures* (1986).

Fischer, David Hackett. *Albion's Seed: Four British Folkways in America* (1989).

Gastil, Raymond D. *Cultural Regions of the United States* (1975).

Goldfield, David R., and Blaine E. Brownell. *Urban America: A History,* 2d ed. (1990).

Jensen, Merrill, ed. *Regionalism in America* (1951).

Lubove, Roy. *Community Planning in the 1920s: The Contribution of the Regional Planning Association of America* (1963).

Markusen, Anne. *Regions: The Economics and Politics of Territory* (1987).

Matthews, Ralph. *The Creation of Regional Dependency* (1983).

Odum, Howard W., and Harry E. Moore. *American Regionalism: A Cultural-Historical Approach to National Integration* (1938).

Turner, Frederick Jackson. *The Frontier in American History* (1920).

———. *The Significance of Sections in American History* (1932).

Watkins, Floyd. *In Time and Place: Some Origins of American Fiction* (1977).

Webb, Walter Prescott. *The Great Frontier* (1964).

White, C. Langdon. *Regional Geography of Anglo-America,* 6th ed. (1985).

Zelinsky, Wilbur. *The Cultural Geography of the United States* (1973).

Middle West

Allen, Harold Byron. *The Linguistic Atlas of the Upper Midwest,* 3 vols. (1973–1976).

Shortridge, James R. *The Middle West: Its Meaning in American Culture* (1989).

Webb, Walter Prescott. *The Great Plains* (1931).

New England

Black, John Donald. *The Rural Economy of New England* (1950).

Brooks, Van Wyck. *The Flowering of New England* (1937).

South

Brooks, Cleanth. *The Language of the American South* (1985).

McDonald, Raven I., Jr., ed. *Linguistic Atlas of the Middle and South Atlantic States* (1980).

Odum, Howard W. *Southern Regions of the United States* (1936).

Pederson, Lee A., et al., eds. *Linguistic Atlas of the Gulf States*, 5 vols. (1986–1991).

Reed, John Shelton. *The Enduring South: Subcultural Persistence in Mass Society* (1972).

———. *One South: An Ethnic Approach to Regional Culture* (1982).

———. *Southern Folk, Plain and Fancy: Southern White Social Types* (1986).

Taylor, William Robert. *Cavalier and Yankee: The Old South and the American National Character* (1957).

Thompson, Edgar T. *Perspectives on the South: Agenda for Research* (1967).

Tindall, George Brown. *The Ethnic Southerners* (1976).

Vance, Rupert B. *Human Factors in Cotton Culture* (1929).

———. *Human Geography of the South: A Study in Regional Resources and Human Adequacy* (1932).

West

Smith, Henry Nash. *Virgin Land: The American West as Symbol and Myth* (1957).

SEE ALSO various essays in the sections "**Ethnic and Racial Subcultures**," "**Methods and Contexts**," "**Periods of Social Change**," "**Regionalism and Regional Subcultures**," and "**Space and Place**."

Part IV

PROCESSES OF SOCIAL CHANGE

THE MARKET REVOLUTION

Paul E. Johnson

THE DEBATE on the market revolution (the transition to capitalism) in American history is of remarkably recent vintage. The first professional social historians argued that the slow progress of the market in early America was due only to geographical and physical brakes on the individualistic, acquisitive nature of Americans. Self-sufficient households and neighborhoods gladly changed their ways when nineteenth-century improvements in transportation made a market society possible. The assumption that liberal-capitalist values were dominant among early Americans was unchallenged through the 1950s and 1960s, when it was a cornerstone of the consensus history championed by historians of the cold war generation. As a result, the market revolution was not a subject of scholarly inquiry, or was presented in narrowly economic terms as a question of building better roads. The most important work in the field was George R. Taylor's aptly titled 1951 work, *The Transportation Revolution.* The term "market revolution" (much less the more provocative "transition to capitalism"), with its implications of fundamental social and ideological transformation, did not enter the conversation among American historians until the 1970s.

The present debate began with the appearance of seminal articles by Michael Merrill and James Henretta in 1976 and 1978, respectively. Arguing with different vocabularies and from different kinds of evidence, both claimed to have excavated a precapitalist mentality in the colonial and early national countryside, a mentality based on the demands of long-term family security and neighborly cooperation that—along with bad roads—inhibited the transition to market society until well into the nineteenth century. Subsequent studies have added republican notions of patriarchy, citizenship, and independence to the motives that undercut possessive individualism in early America.

The argument for a preindustrial, precapitalist moral economy in eighteenth- and early-nineteenth-century America has been countered most directly by James Lemon, Joyce Appleby, and Winifred Rothenberg. These and others have demonstrated the pervasiveness of local, regional, and international market activity since at least the mid eighteenth century. Insofar as historians of the "moral economy" school have argued for the absence of markets and the self-sufficiency of early American households and neighborhoods, historians of the market have severely damaged their case. The latter sometimes go on, however, to assume the existence of profit-oriented individualism from the existence of markets; market activity, in some studies, is a certain indicator of popular market values that preclude the existence of a familistic, communitarian moral economy. Historians of moral economy counter with an argument for social history: rather than assume that the market's invisible hand creates the human beings that it needs, they conceive the market itself as a social/historical process in which farmers, merchants, artisans, and their families were conscious agents; they try, in short, to reconstruct the social and cultural history of the market.

Allan Kulikoff labels these scholarly combatants "market historians" and "social historians." Market historians, often working with quantitative evidence, reconstruct the history of the market as an objective fact. Social historians apprehend the market as a complex process involving not only economic but also social and ideological change at its most comprehensive and fundamental. In particular, they deny that the presence of market exchange presupposes any particular mentality. They try instead to reconstruct the motives that led Americans to use or avoid market relations as they became available. Working with those methods and assumptions, they have identified a full-scale market revolution that was the central, transforming process in American social history between the Revolution and the Civil War.

Readers should be warned that this essay, while it begins with the work of the market historians, favors the methods and conclusions of the social historians—precisely because they insist that market history be comprehended in social historical terms.

PATTERNS OF ECONOMIC GROWTH, 1760–1860

We turn first to the economic history of market growth between 1760 and 1860, where we find that market activity developed in two stages. In the first stage, which ended in 1815, American agriculturists produced foodstuffs for export to Europe and the slave islands of the Caribbean. The export trade grew dramatically between 1793 and 1815, when the Wars of the French Revolution (1792–1802) and the Napoleonic Wars (1803–1815) disrupted European agriculture. The export trade, however, was an extension of North America's colonial relationship with the Old World: northeastern merchants made personal fortunes and created a financial infrastructure that would later be put to other uses; but increased exports did not—except in the South's nascent Cotton Belt—alter rural social relationships in ways that could be called a market revolution.

Social historians reserve the term "market revolution" for a cluster of events that occurred, largely in the North and the West, after 1815: town-country symbiosis, the development of internal markets for both food and manufactured goods, increased dependence of most households on a money economy, and a cultural ethos that rewarded individual ambition. The South, on the other hand, experienced the market revolution very differently. There the cotton economy committed the region to a highly commercialized agriculture that excluded or marginalized many whites and did not produce a capitalist ethos or a market society.

The Postcolonial Economy, 1760–1815 Market historians are correct in arguing for the early and widespread existence of markets in British North America. Indeed, the beginnings of British settlement in the seventeenth century were tied closely to the beginnings of British market society; the founders of every colony included men who considered colonization a business venture. Southern colonies committed to staple-crop plantation agriculture—which made no sense without external markets. Europe's inability to feed its growing population provided expanding markets for American grain from the 1750s through the 1830s. The Middle Atlantic colonies provided surplus wheat and corn to this market, and the Chesapeake's transition from tobacco to grain was in large part due to the availability of lucrative foreign markets for food. The farmers of New England were relatively slow to enter this trade. Nevertheless, Winifred Rothenberg and Bettye Hobbs Pruitt demonstrate the existence of a brisk regional grain market by the time of the Revolution. Thus, while export markets were most important in the South and Middle Atlantic colonies, markets were a presence in the agriculture of every region.

Foreign markets for American foodstuffs expanded dramatically from 1793 through 1815. The Wars of the French Revolution severely disrupted Europe's already weakened ability to grow its own food. At the same time, hostilities made it dangerous and difficult for British, French, and Spanish ships to supply the plantation islands of the Caribbean or to transport the products of those islands to the home countries. Thus the war in Europe led to significant increases in both the direct export of American foodstuffs to Europe and the islands, and in the reexport trade between the islands and their European colonizers. Both of these trades were subject to regulations and periodic prohibitions by the warring governments of Britain and France, and agricultural exports and the reexport trade suffered dizzying ups and downs. But despite its insecurities, wartime expansion was a source of big profits for Americans.

The most lasting effects of wartime trade between 1793 and 1815 were in the seaport cities, whose merchants organized foreign commerce and reaped its greatest rewards. During the Napoleonic Wars, American cities, for the first time, grew faster than the countryside. Nearly all of that growth was in the seaport towns. Boston grew from 18,320 in 1790 to 38,746 in 1810; Philadelphia, from 44,096 to 87,303; Baltimore, from 13,503 to 46,555. New York City, which became the principal entrepôt for the European trade, grew from 33,131 persons in 1790 to an astronomical 100,775 in 1810. Maritime growth in these years created the private fortunes and the financial infrastructure that would soon take up the task of commercializing and industrializing the northeastern United States. Old merchants like the Brown brothers of Providence, Rhode Island, and Elias Hasket Derby of Salem, Massachusetts, grew richer, and newcomers, led by the immigrant John Jacob Astor, built stupendous personal fortunes.

Alongside these fortunes were new institutions that made and administered money. Seaport docking and warehousing facilities expanded dramatically in these years. Untrained bookkeepers were replaced by accountants familiar with new double-entry methods of keeping accounts, and the risks and rewards of wartime commerce, along with the huge amounts of money involved, spurred the development of the American banking and insurance industries. All of these would come into play during the thoroughgoing market revolution that occurred after 1815.

The export economy did not, however, add up to an internal market revolution. Despite the growth of the seaports, domestic markets for food remained small. The urban population of New England (defined by the census as the proportion of the population living in towns of 2,500 or more) rose from 7.5 percent of the total in 1790 to 10.5 percent in 1820. In the Middle Atlantic colonies urban population rose from 8.7 percent to 11.3 percent in these years; in the South, from 2.3 percent to 5.5 percent. These were significant gains, but the overwhelming majority of the population remained in the countryside, growing foodstuffs for which domestic markets were decidedly limited. The cities and the accumulations of merchant capital did little to encourage American manufactures. The seaports existed to administer foreign commerce. The nation's financial institutions were geared to that commerce, and a federal government that derived 90 percent of its income from the tax on imports did little to encourage the American production of finished goods.

Thus the significant economic growth that occurred between 1793 and 1815 was different in kind from the market revolution that succeeded it. In Emmanuel Wallerstein's helpful terminology, the United States remained on the periphery of the world economic order. American farmers either provided foodstuffs and raw materials to the European (very largely British) core or remained outside the market altogether. Rapid economic development between the Revolution and 1815 produced growth without altering that relationship. Indeed, these years are best understood as a culminating high-water mark in America's colonial relationship to the Old World.

The Transportation Revolution, 1815–1860 The defining economic development of the years 1815 to 1860 was the emergence of regional and increasingly national market economies. In the North, a symbiotic growth of commercial agriculture and urban places created significant internal markets for food, manufactured goods, labor, and capital; at the same time, activist state governments built a transport network that made the market revolution possible and channeled its development. The southern states experienced an equally profound economic transformation that had very different results: the cotton boom that began in the 1790s accelerated rapidly after 1810 until it dominated the commercial sector of southern agriculture. Cotton was an export staple with its own developmental logic, and the southern commitment to that crop resulted in mushroom economic growth without changing the region's peripheral/colonial status, and without generating an internal market revolution. The result, apparent by the 1830s, was a thoroughgoing transformation of the North and the West, while the South experienced more growth than change.

Spectacular improvements in transportation after 1815 were essential both to the market revolution and to alterations in the economic geography of the United States. Transportation's clearest contribution was a reduction in the time, effort, and money spent moving goods and people. In 1816 a Senate committee estimated that it cost $9 to move a ton of goods across the three thousand-mile-wide expanse of the Atlantic Ocean; the same nine dollars would transport the same ton of goods only thirty miles inland. A year later, the cost of transporting wheat overland from the infant settlement of Buffalo to New York City was three times the selling price of wheat in New York. Simply put, the costs of transportation made large-scale market agriculture an impossibility for most American farmers; only on farms near the seaports or with easy river access to the coast could food crops be grown for profit.

Transportation, particularly in the interior, was as difficult as it was expensive. Transportation between western Pennsylvania and Ohio and the northeastern cities, for example, was an epic adventure. Backcountry farmers put their produce onto flatboats that traveled the full length of the Ohio and Mississippi rivers to New Orleans, from which it was trans-shipped to northeastern seaports. Upstream travel was nearly impossible, so the boatmen knocked down their flatboats and sold the lumber in New Orleans, then walked home via the difficult and dangerous Natchez Trace. Finished goods were brought into the West overland through Pennsylvania, and they sold at very high prices. Thus the trans-Appalachian settlements—home to between one in four and one in five Americans—remained outside the market economy. By 1815 New Orleans transshipped about $5 million in western produce annually—a mere $15 per farm family in the interior.

Between 1815 and 1860 improved roads, the introduction of steamboats on the Ohio-Mississippi river system and the Great Lakes, the construction of canals, and the building of railroads cut transport costs by an average of 90 percent, with concomitant increases in the ease and speed of transportation and communications. The old overland route between Cincinnati and New York City, for instance, (by keelboat up the Ohio River to Pittsburgh, then by wagon to Philadelphia and wagon or wagon and river to New York) required fifty-two days. In the 1850s steamboats and fast-sailing packets reduced the trip from Cincinnati to New Orleans and transshipment to New York to twenty-eight days. By 1852, when a trans-Ohio canal linked Cincinnati to Lake Erie, and thus to New York's Erie Canal and Hudson River, travel time dropped to eighteen days. In the same year, the Erie Railroad and its connectors linked Cincinnati directly with New York, carrying freight between those cities in six to eight days. These improvements, with concomitant reductions in freight rates, removed the principal structural brake on the market revolution. As early as the 1830s, grain grown in Ohio could be sold at a profit in New York City.

Markets and Regions, 1815–1860 Such interregional possibilities, however, can be misleading. Until at least 1840 the increase in market activity was more pronounced within regions than between them. Douglass North in particular posits a regional interdependence in which the West grew food for the North and the South, the South grew cotton for northern manufacturers and export merchants, and the North provided manufactured goods and financial services for the South and the West. Diane Lindstrom and others, however, have demonstrated the primacy of regional over interregional trade through at least 1840. The South in particular was self-sufficient in food: plantations either grew their own foodstuffs or bought from local farmers. Eastern farmers also supplied most of their region's needs, and they were by far the largest market for nonagricultural goods produced in their region. For all its potential to tap the wealth of the West and divert it to New York, until 1847 the Erie Canal carried significantly more produce from New York State than from the western states. Western farmers traded primarily within their own region until at least the railroad boom of the 1850s.

This increased trade in foodstuffs was handled by new interior cities that grew in symbiosis with a commercializing agriculture. While urban growth up to 1815 was concentrated in the seaports, urbanization between 1820 and 1870—years that witnessed the most rapid urbanization in American history—was concentrated in the marketing and manufacturing towns of the interior. By 1860, 36.6 percent of New England's population lived in urban places. The Middle Atlantic States were 35.4 percent urban, and the states of the old Northwest were from 13 to 14 percent urban in 1860. Only the South remained overwhelmingly rural: 88.5 percent of its people were in the countryside in 1860; fully 94.1 percent of the Old Southwest's population lived in communities of less than twenty-five hundred in that year.

Thus the transportation revolution created not a national economy but a series of distinctive regional market revolutions—a situation that persisted at least until the 1850s, when railroads linked the Northwest and the Northeast in ways that profited both and portended serious trouble for the South. The market revolution was thus experienced in distinctive ways by the peoples of the North, the West, and the South, and it is to the social histories of those regions that we now turn.

THE RURAL NORTH AND WEST, 1780–1860

Households and Markets, 1780–1815 We begin with a crucial fact about early America: most whites lived and worked on family-owned farms; decisions about the allocation of agricultural resources were made not by governments, large landholders, or peasant communities but by individual heads of households. Among the motives that shaped those decisions, the first was the yearly subsistence of the household. Second was protection of the family's ability to pass farmland to succeeding generations. Third, recent studies suggest that the imperatives of subsistence and succession gained ideological force from a revolutionary republicanism that privileged male equality and independence, and that disparaged dependence, luxury, greed, and exploitation. Together, these three components formed a powerful commitment to household independence, freehold ownership of land,

and the family's (the father's) power to make its own economic choices.

From New England through the Middle Atlantic colonies/states and on into the southern piedmont and backcountry, few farmers in post-Revolutionary America thought of their farms as businesses. Their goal was what rural people called a "competence": the ability to live up to neighborhood standards of material decency while protecting the long-term independence of the household. For most, this imposed a "subsistence-plus" agriculture in which farmers grew foodstuffs, ate most of what they grew, traded much of the rest within neighborhoods, then sent small surpluses to regional and international markets.

The yeomanry of the Revolutionary and early national United States romanticized its sturdy independence, and some historians have done the same. We must note, however, that the independence of households rested upon the uncontested dominance of their white male heads over their dependents. The commitment to equality and independence empowered fathers and not sons, husbands and not wives, slaveholders and not slaves, masters and not servants. Between the Revolution and 1815 in particular, household heads maintained their independence and their ability to pass their status on to their sons by exploiting family labor in unprecedented ways. Thus the most powerful effects of the expansion of external markets between 1790 and 1815 were within rural households.

The Crisis of Inheritance, 1780–1815 The patriarchal republic of the late eighteenth century rested on widespread farm ownership and on a rough equality among white male householders. Even as that vision was formulated in the Revolutionary era, its bases in society were falling apart. Fathers were judged by their ability to support and govern their households, to function as neighbors, and to pass land and independence on to their sons. In the years 1790–1815, fewer and fewer rural fathers were able to do that. Put simply, farmers in the older settlements possessed small farms and large families, and were increasingly unable to provide a competence for all their offspring.

It was a tragedy on more than one level: fathers could not consider themselves successful patriarchs, sons could not count on workable inheritances, and thus fathers could no longer control the labor of their sons. The erosion of rural patriarchy was not due to any lack of trying. Fathers strove mightily to provide for all their heirs (generally by leaving land to sons and personal property to daughters). Very few gave all their land to one son, and an increasing number of wills stated that sons must share barns, cider mills—even houses—on farms that could no longer be subdivided. The increase in shared use rights and labor obligations stipulated by paternal wills fit well with a rural culture that guaranteed the independence of household heads through reciprocal, cooperative relations with kin and neighbors. But divided houses and barns also signified that the system of partible inheritance in the older settlements had reached its limit.

Fathers with money bought farms for their sons—sometimes in the neighborhood, more often in new communities. In old settlements south and west of New England, farm tenancy increased. In parts of Pennsylvania (and very likely in other areas as well) farmers often bought extra farms in their neighborhoods, let them to tenants to increase their household income, then gave them to their grown sons. The sons of poorer farmers became tenants in hopes of saving enough money to buy farms. Some succeeded, some did not. Other fathers bought tracts of unimproved land in the backcountry—sometimes on speculation, more often to provide sons with the raw materials from which to make farms. Still others paid for educating their sons, or arranged apprenticeships and other jobs that got them out of agriculture. As a result of all these efforts, young men left the old farming settlements; the populations of settled rural communities became older and more female, while the rapidly growing frontier settlements and seaport towns became young and male. Young men who stayed in the old settlements often faced lifetimes as tenants or farm laborers.

Farmers countered this crisis of long-term independence by tapping into world markets. West Indian and European demand for American foodstuffs had grown steadily since the mid eighteenth century; it expanded dramatically when war disrupted European agriculture between 1793 and 1815. The new markets played into the hands of American farmers, for they could increase their cash incomes (and thus subsidize their children's futures) without changing their status as fathers and neighbors. Farmers in these years simply produced more food. They continued to eat much of what they grew and to trade locally; but they sent increased surpluses into high-priced markets. Through this strategy farmers in the northern and Middle Atlantic states and in many areas of the upper South and the new trans-Appalachian West profited from world markets for food without becoming dependent on them.

Change Within Households, 1780–1815 Market agriculture in these years did, however, introduce change into rural family life. The combination of overpopulation and markets for surplus food encouraged farmers to clear new land—both forest land in the West and marginal land in the older settlements—and to cultivate their lands more intensively. Among the results were changed relations between women and men on American farms. Men worked in the fields and with pastured livestock, and market involvement both intensified that labor and made it more exclusively male. In the grain-growing regions—particularly in the Middle Atlantic states—the long-handled scythe was replacing the sickle as the principal harvest tool. The sickle had been used as efficiently by women as by men. The long, heavy scythe was designed to be operated by men, and farmers' preference for it stemmed not only from its efficiency but also from a growing cultural prejudice against women working in the fields, coupled with increased demands for female labor on other parts of the farm. The transition from hoe agriculture to plows had the same causes and effects, and visitors to the long-settled farming regions (with the exception of some Middle Atlantic German communities) seldom saw women working in the fields. In his travels through France, Thomas Jefferson judged peasant communities harshly when he saw women laboring in grain fields.

While market agriculture drew men into field labor, responsibilities for household subsistence fell increasingly to women. During these years dairying and intensive gardening—overwhelmingly female activities—added not only to farm incomes but also, and more immediately, to the variety of rural food supplies. Bread and salted meat remained staples throughout rural America. The bread was the old mix of Indian corn and coarse wheat ("rye and Injun," the farmers called it), with crust so thick that it was used as a scoop for soups and stews. Improved brines and pickling techniques extended the supply of salt meat throughout the year, but farmers' palates doubtlessly told them it was the same old salt meat.

A more dramatic change was in the variety of foods on rural tables. By the 1790s improved winter feeding for cattle and better techniques for making and storing butter and cheese kept dairy products on the more prosperous tables throughout the year. Chickens became more common, and farm women began taking household gardens more seriously: they fenced and manured the plots and planted them with an astonishing variety of foods. In the 1790s Martha Ballard of Hallowell, Maine, filled her kitchen garden with a variety of beans, lettuce, beets, cabbages, and onions, along with new culinary niceties such as saffron, coriander, parsley, anise, sage, carrots, "French turnips," and many others. Confined increasingly to housework, dairying, and gardening, farm women enlarged not only the supply of marketable goods but also the variety and nutritional value of foods on their own tables.

Outwork Farm families between 1780 and 1815 protected their independence and improved their standards of living by exploiting their resources—freehold land and household labor—more intensively than in the past. Industrial outwork provided another way to exploit family labor. From the 1790s on, merchants with access to widening markets provided farm families with raw materials and paid them for finished shoes, cloth, brooms, and other handmade goods. It was a huge enterprise. Samuel Slater, who began manufacturing cotton yarn near Providence in 1793, maintained an outwork system stretching more than two hundred miles from his home base; in Marple, Pennsylvania, a farming town near Philadelphia, fully one-third of households were engaged in weaving, furniture making, and other household industry.

Outwork was concentrated in families that were large and relatively poor. With few exceptions, it was organized in ways that shored up the authority of fathers. When young Caleb Jackson and his brother began making shoes for a Massachusetts merchant in 1803, the account was kept in their father's name. Merchants who distributed raw materials that New Hampshire women fashioned into hats followed the same practice: women and girls did the work, but the accounts were kept in the names of their husbands or fathers. In general, outwork was a part-time activity performed by dependent members of the household. Even when it became the family's principal means of support, the outwork was viewed as a means of sustaining household independence, and it was arranged in ways that kept lines of dependence within households intact. In eastern Massachusetts, for example, thousands of farmers on small plots of worn-out land became household shoemakers in the 1790s. They were careful, however, to maintain a rigid gender division of labor: men performed the skilled work of cutting leather and shaping the uppers; women employed traditional skills as sewers and binders. In the town of North Reading, the family of Mayo Greenleaf Patch made shoes throughout the 1790s. Patch was a poor man who drank too much and lived on land owned by his father-in-law; the family income came largely from shoemaking. When asked to state his occupation, however, Patch called himself a "yeoman." As it was for many others, the title—with its connotations of patriarchy and proprietorship—was a fiction subsidized by the labor of Patch's wife and children.

Neighbors Among the market historians' greatest contributions has been their systematic destruction of the myth of the "self-sufficient yeoman." They have demonstrated conclusively that only the wealthiest farmers controlled the equipment and labor to produce what they needed. The alternative was exchange beyond the household, and from this some market historians have assumed that economic choices were market-driven from at least the late eighteenth century.

Social historians, however, seldom claim that rural households were self-sufficient. Indeed, their principal contribution has been the excavation of a system of neighborhood exchange that subsidized household independence with neighbors and kin—a level of local, cooperative exchange that mediated between the historians' artificially neat categories of "subsistence" and "commercial" agriculture. Farmers routinely "changed work," borrowed oxen and plows and other tools, and exchanged surpluses of one kind of food for surpluses of another. Women traded ashes, herbs, butter and eggs, garden produce, seedlings, baby chicks, goose feathers, and the products of their spinning wheels and looms, a lively exchange of women's goods and services that was crucial to the workings of rural households and neighborhoods. Some exchanges of work—house and barn raisings, husking bees, harvest frolics, spring road repairs—brought whole neighborhoods together, transforming economic necessities into pleasurable social events. The gossip, drinking, and dancing that accompanied communal labor strengthened a local social system that rewarded cooperation and not competition.

Remarkably little of the neighborhood economy involved money. Indeed, there was no state or federal paper money in 1790, and the widespread use of Spanish, English, and French coins testified to a constant shortage of specie. In New England, farmers kept more or less careful accounts of neighborhood debts. In the South and West, farmers used the "changing system" in which they simply remembered what they owed; when confronted with the New England system, they condemned it as another manifestation of Yankee greed and lack of character. But in all sections farmers relied more on barter than on cash, even to the point of bartering debts to and from each other. Brissot de Warville, a French traveler, observed:

> Instead of money incessantly going backwards and forwards into the same hands, they supply their needs reciprocally in the countryside by direct exchanges. The tailor and the bootmaker go and do the work of their calling at the house of the farmer, who requires it and who, most often, provides the raw material for it and pays for the work in goods. These sorts of exchanges cover many objects; they write down what they give and receive on both sides and at the end of the year they settle, with a very small amount of coin, a large variety of exchanges which would not be done in Europe other than with a considerable quantity of money. (Quoted in Clark, *Roots of Rural Capitalism,* p. 33)

The mother of the Mormon prophet Joseph Smith revealed the same system when she gave her debt-ridden husband this advice: "he might get both his creditors and debtors together, and arrange matters between them in such a way as to give satisfaction to all parties concerned" (quoted in Bushman, *Joseph Smith,* p. 41).

The neighborhood economy sustained itself through elaborate networks of debt in which nearly every household participated. In Kent, Connecticut, for instance, farmers averaged twenty creditors at the time of death. Such debts were not, however, indications of exploitation, class division, or—in most cases—economic desperation. Instead, they signified a highly structured and absolutely necessary system of neighborly cooperation. Christopher Clark demonstrates that local exchange involved neighbors and relatives, and that localities encouraged creditors to consider debtors' ability to pay. In Kent there were few foreclosures; the one debtor who was bound out was an Indian—a situation that says less about debt than about the town's racial system. Creditors, in short, were expected to behave like neighbors. Even storekeepers participated in the neighborhood system, routinely crediting the accounts of creditors when debtors brought in farm produce and other goods. The crossroads store was thus an agent both of regional markets and of a reciprocal and cooperative system of neighborhood exchange.

The Market Revolution, 1815–1850s The market revolution was a process and not an event; it is difficult to pinpoint when a household, neighborhood, or region stepped out of household production and neighborhood exchange to become "market-oriented." Social historians have found it helpful, however, to isolate the point at which economic decisions were coerced by the market, often at the expense of traditional household and neighborhood considerations. We have seen that most farmers did not cross that line when they produced for foreign markets before 1815; increased market activity in those years simply increased the comfort and security of the old household economy. The most careful analyses of northern and western rural history, as well as the models developed by economic historians, associate the market revolution with the development of domestic markets and complex intraregional divisions of labor that became clearly visible in the 1820s and 1830s. It was in those years that northern farmers were forced to think like nineteenth-century businessmen and not like eighteenth-century husbands, fathers, and neighbors.

The transition to market agriculture had its origins in the final collapse of traditional family obligations. In the trans-Appalachian West and in other new farming areas, settlement began with family-sized farms, many of them encumbered with mortgages. First-generation fathers could settle only one heir on the family farm; others received down payments on farms further west, educations, or apprenticeships that got them out of agriculture—or, increasingly, nothing at all. Toby Ditz demonstrates similar patterns existed in Connecticut. In upland, nonmarket towns, fathers continued to divide their holdings among all their sons (though disparities between favored sons and others grew), and they enforced obligations and elaborate forms of family cooperation in their wills. By the 1820s, however, this system did little more than multiply and sustain rural poverty.

In more prosperous commercial areas, fathers divided estates equally among heirs (including daughters), often by selling their farms and allotting the cash. Grown children received inheritances that were unencumbered with shared use rights or other forms of reciprocal obligation with their siblings; receiving them not as members of families but as individuals. Thus farms in the North and the West were increasingly operated by discrete families that were outside the traditional constraints of family and kinship. They were, however, constrained to produce cash incomes: inheritances came in the form of down payments and not of farms, and vastly increased numbers of farmers required cash incomes to service mortgages and other debts payable in money, to pay increased state and local taxes, and to provide cash inheritances for their children. Thus land, always the center of complicated household and kin obligations, was detached from those obligations and became a means of making money.

Farm families who relied on cash-producing activities relinquished control over economic choices. Outwork, for instance, was taken up by families needing supplementary income. Before the 1820s, however, families generally produced goods in spare time with spare household labor, and sold the finished products to merchants—who often complained that families kept their best work for themselves and for neighborhood exchange. In New England, most outwork consisted of textiles and shoes produced from local flax and leather. Beginning in the 1820s, textiles and shoemaking concentrated in factories that hired surplus labor from the countryside. Merchants now provided outworkers with raw materials from which to make such items as buttons and palm leaf hats (imported raw materials that only merchants could supply), then governed the pace of labor and the quality of finished goods. In the 1830s fully thirty-three thousand New England women fashioned palm leaf hats in their homes, far more than the twenty thousand who worked in the region's much-publicized cotton mills. The new forms of outwork continued to subsidize the independence of the poorer rural household, but they did so in ways that gave control of family labor to merchants and other agents of the regional market economy.

In the years after 1820, patterns of farm production and consumption suggest vastly increased dependence on distant markets, and decreased concern with household subsistence and neighborhood exchange. Farmers in western Massachusetts, for instance, increased production substantially, but their efforts went more and more into fattening cattle for market and growing Indian corn. They seldom attempted to grow other grains, and women in their households ceased the manufacture of cloth. Storekeepers in the area now stocked foodstuffs and drygoods that farm families no longer produced for themselves. The storekeepers of Northampton, for instance, had increased their stock in trade about 7 percent per decade since the late eighteenth century. Their stock increased fully 45 percent in the 1820s, and it now included not only bolts of finished cloth but also flour from the mills in Rochester, New York. And the wheat producers of western New York worked their fields wearing Massachusetts palm leaf hats, shirts made of Lowell cotton and fastened with New Hampshire buttons, and cheap work shoes produced in Lynn. They also counted on the East for some food items: the first westbound boats on the Erie Canal carried barrels of oysters and iced radishes.

Increased reliance on cash crops and distant markets was associated with a sharp drop in rural birthrates. In the Hudson Valley, birthrates dropped 30 percent in the first half of the nineteenth century. In western Massachusetts, fertility dropped after 1820, particularly in the more prosperous households. Families seem to have remained large only on the frontier, where farmland seemed more available than in the congested East, and among the poorer families of the East. Nancy Folbre contends that poor fathers continued to sire large families because they needed family labor—suggesting that poor families sacrificed the long-term well-being of their children to the short-term subsistence of households.

Old patterns of neighborhood exchange also became attenuated. Neighbors continued to exchange goods and labor, and to contract debts that went unpaid for years. But increasing proportions of debts involved profit-minded storekeepers and distant creditors, and even local debts were often payable in cash. At the same time, the new agricultural press preached efficiency to commercializing farmers. Harvest parties, husking bees, dances, communal labor—all with their attendant drinking and socializing—were branded not as neighborly rituals that cemented social networks but as inefficient and morally suspect wastes of time. *The Farmer's Almanack* of 1833 warned New England farmers, "If you love fun, frolic, and waste and slovenliness more than economy and profit, then make a husking" (Jack Larkin, *The Reshaping of Everyday Life,* p. 298).

The efficient farmer of the 1820s and 1830s increased production of goods that were marketable outside the neighborhood, and used his cash income to increase his family's material comforts and to provide cash inheritances for his children. Though the household and neighborhood economic spheres survived, families sustained themselves and maintained their independence not through those spheres but through new forms of dependence on the outside.

THE MARKET REVOLUTION IN THE SOUTH, 1790–1860

The South had produced staple crops for international markets since the seventeenth century. But the transition to short-staple cotton as the region's primary cash crop introduced broad transformations into slavery and southern society—transformations that must be comprehended as a distinctively southern market revolution between the Revolution and the Civil War. The rise of the cotton economy had enormous implications for southern social development. First, it solidified the region's commitment to chattel slavery and plantation agriculture. While that commitment resulted in a profitable commercial agriculture, many whites were excluded from its benefits as profits were monopolized by a smaller and smaller proportion of the white population. The result was a partial and somewhat misshapen market revolution in the South. By the 1820s and 1830s, cotton and slavery had produced a dual economy: a Black Belt committed to plantation agriculture and governed by a small planter elite, and an upland society of freehold farms that remained peripheral to world and regional markets.

Cotton and the Commitment to Slave Labor In 1790 the future of agriculture in the Chesapeake was uncertain. Markets for tobacco had been precarious since before the Revolution, and they continued to decline after 1790. Tobacco depleted the soil, and by the late eighteenth century, tidewater farms and plantations were giving out. At the same time, lands west of the Appalachians opened to settlement; white tenants, laborers, and small farmers left the Chesapeake in droves. Planters were left with a large slave population and an uncertain future.

With the tobacco economy in decline, Chesapeake planters switched to grain and livestock, and tapped new European and West Indian markets for food. Some divided their holdings into small plots and rented both farms and slaves to white tenants; others, particularly in Maryland, created a class of black tenants from the growing ranks of freed slaves. But grain crops required little tending between spring planting and autumn harvest, and thus were better suited to free than to slave labor. Agricultural diversification and the migration of the poorer whites solved many problems in the Chesapeake, but they did not address the question of slavery.

The problem was solved by cotton. British industrialization created a steady demand for cotton from the 1790s on; southern agriculturists knew that they could sell all the cotton they could grow. In 1793 Eli Whitney constructed a cotton gin (a hand-operated machine that separated cotton fibers from cotton seeds) that, for the first time, made short-staple cotton a profitable crop. Working by hand, an adult slave had cleaned a single pound (0.45 kilograms) of cotton daily; with Whitney's gin the figure leaped to 50 pounds (22.5 kilograms) a day. And with that, short-staple cotton became the great southern cash crop and the savior of plantation agriculture. The 3,000 bales of cotton produced in the United States in 1790 leaped to 73,000 in 1800; by 1810 the figure stood at 178,000, and by 1820, 334,000. As early as 1820 cotton accounted for more than half the value of American agricultural exports, and its proportion continued to grow. Between 1815 and 1860 the value of cotton exports increased from $17.5 million to a stupendous $191.8 million—even though northeastern textile mills provided significant and increasing markets for southern cotton.

Short-staple cotton was a remarkably democratic crop. It was suited to the hot, humid climate and the long growing season of the region, and it grew almost anywhere: in the rolling piedmont country east of the Appalachians, in the old coastal lowlands, and—especially—in the new lands of the Old Southwest. It was also a labor-intensive crop that could be grown in large or small quantities. Farmers who owned few or no slaves could profitably grow an acre or two of cotton, while those with large amounts of land and slaves could commit their resources to cotton and profit immensely. Best of all, the factories of England and, increasingly, the northeastern United States exerted a seemingly endless demand for southern cotton.

The result was a rejuvenation of plantation slavery and its spread into new regions. The Chesapeake continued to diversify, and grew little cotton. In Maryland and Delaware, farmers continued to divest themselves of slaves; by the time both states sided with the Union in 1861, over half the blacks in Maryland and three-quarters of those in Delaware were free. The situation in Virginia was different. Virginia planters, with a huge and endangered investment in slave labor, sold slaves to planters to the south and west in order to finance their own transition to more diverse forms of agriculture. Until about 1810 most migrant Virginia slaves left the Old Dominion with masters who were moving to Kentucky or Tennessee. After that date, most left their home plantations as commodities in a new and burgeoning interstate slave trade, and their destinations were the new cotton lands of inland Georgia, Alabama, and Mississippi. The movement of Chesapeake slaves into new territory was immense. In the 1790s one Chesapeake slave in twelve moved south and west. The figure rose to one in ten between 1800 and 1810, and fully one in five between 1810 and 1820. In all, approximately a quarter of a million slaves moved south and west out of the Chesapeake between 1790 and 1820. The result was a fundamental change in the geography of American slavery. In 1790 planters in Virginia and Maryland held 56 percent of American slaves; by 1860 that figure had plummeted to 15 percent.

The post-Revolutionary years witnessed a recommitment to slave labor in the other center of eighteenth-century slavery: coastal South Carolina and Georgia. There the principal crop was rice, which experienced increased international demand along with other North American foodstuffs. As a secondary crop, most planters switched to cotton. The result was renewed confidence in the future of slavery and an increase in the demand for slaves. Lowland planters had lost thousands of slaves during the Revolution, and they faced the prospective end of the African slave trade in 1808. With slave prices rising and slave-produced crops becoming steadily more profitable, lowland planters imported new slaves from Africa. Between 1788 and 1808, 250,000 African slaves entered the country through the ports of Charleston and Savannah. That figure equaled the total number imported during the whole prior history of the African slave trade.

Many of these new slaves remained on lowland rice and cotton plantations. But many others joined Chesapeake slaves in the vast and growing region that grew short-staple cotton. Beginning in the piedmont of Virginia and North Carolina and thickening in upland South Carolina and Georgia, the emerging Black Belt widened to cover vast portions of the Old Southwest. The mushroom growth of this region and its firm commitment to cotton and slavery startled contemporaries. The land that became Madison County, Alabama, for instance, was not ceded by the Cherokees until 1806. The federal government established a land office at Huntsville in 1809, and a land boom went into full swing. By 1820 the new county's population was 19,501, almost half of whom were slaves. Travelers who went outside town and into the rich cotton lands that surrounded it saw tended fields stretching to the horizon on land that had been wilderness a few years earlier. The conversion of untamed nature into cotton land was repeated wherever there was tillable land with access to a navigable river. As early as 1820, plantations west of the Appalachians held almost a third of a million slaves and grew more than half the American cotton crop. By that date it was clear that cotton had saved the South's investment in slavery, and that it was making a new slave-labor civilization in the piedmont and the new lands of the Old Southwest.

The Varieties of Slave Labor In the old areas of the Chesapeake, the transition from tobacco to grain and livestock imposed a new and elaborate gender division of labor upon the slaves. The switch to wheat, for instance, replaced hoe agriculture with the plow and grain cradle—both of which required the upper-body strength of adult men. The grain economy also demanded carts, wagons, mills, and better roads, and thus created a diverse economy that increased the numbers of skilled slaves—nearly all of whom were men. In the new Chesapeake economy male slaves plowed, sowed, ditched, carted, and performed most of the artisanal tasks; this was work that required relatively high skill levels and was performed alone or in small groups with minimal white supervision. Slave women, on the other hand, experienced a relative deterioration in their conditions of labor. Contrary to legend, few slave women in the Chesapeake worked as servants in the big houses of the planters. Instead, they took up the menial and repetitive tasks created by economic diversification. Some new artisanal tasks—cloth manufacture, sewing, candle molding, and the preparation of salt meat—fell to women. But most Chesapeake slave women continued to work on farms. They hoed, weeded, spread manure, and cleaned stables and barnyards—work that was unskilled, monotonous, and generally performed as in gangs under close supervision. This new gender division of labor was starkly dramatized during the wheat harvest. On George Washington's farm prime male harvesters, often working beside white hired laborers, moved in a broad line, mowing down the grain; they were followed by gangs of slave children and women who worked bent over and on hands and knees, binding the wheat into shocks.

On the rice and sea island (long-staple) cotton plantations of lowland South Carolina and Georgia, planters faced labor problems of a different order. Plantations and slave populations in the low country were huge, and the crops demanded intensive labor on low, wet land that bred disease in whites and blacks alike. Planters avoided the dangers and difficulties of supervision by adopting the "task system": each morning the owner or overseer assigned a specific task to each slave; when the work was done, the remainder of the day belonged to the slave. Slaves who did not finish their tasks were punished, and when too many slaves finished early, the owners increased the tasks. With the growth of markets the tasks were increased. In the eighteenth-century rice country, for instance, each slave was expected to tend three to four acres. In the early nineteenth century the expected acreage increased to five.

Low-country planters liked the task system because it encouraged slaves to work hard without supervision. Slaves, however, turned the system to their own uses. Often they did their tasks cooperatively—five slaves, for instance, worked together until all their tasks were completed. It was also common for young, strong, and skilled slaves who had finished their tasks to help older and weaker members of the community with theirs. But while low-country slaves shared their hard-earned free time with each other, they jealously guarded it from their masters. A Jamaican visitor to the low country remarked that planters were "very particular in never employing a negro, without his consent, after his task is finished, and agreeing with him for the payment which he is to receive" (quoted in Innes, *Work and Labor,* p. 212). Slaves won the right to cultivate plantation land as "private fields"—not the little garden plots worked by Chesapeake slaves but farms of up to five acres on which they grew produce and raised livestock for market. There was a lively trade in slave-produced goods, and by the end of slavery the bondsmen of the low country not only produced and exchanged property but also inherited it.

Students of slave culture have long noted that the blacks of low country South Carolina and Georgia preserved West African cultural forms more fully than did blacks in other parts of the South. This was due largely to the arrival of new Africans before 1808 and to the fact that there were few whites in the low country. But it was also due to an organization of labor that allowed slaves cultural autonomy not only at night but also during the workday. The owners of low-country slaves tolerated this autonomy for a simple reason: slaves on the task system worked hard, required minimal supervision, and made money for their owners. The owners of the coastal rice and cotton plantations were among the richest men in North America.

Work was organized very differently on the cotton frontier. The enormous labor of turning wilderness into plantations demanded gang labor, as did short-staple cotton cultivation. Cotton required constant attention: the plants were sowed individually, the fields had to be "chopped" (weeded with hoes), and at harvest time the cotton ripened unevenly and thus was handpicked by gangs of slaves who combed the fields repeatedly. Thus in the Cotton Belt—the largest and fastest-growing region of the South—slave labor was organized in gangs that worked under the close supervision of slave foremen, white overseers, and owners.

Both whites and blacks agreed that slavery on the cotton frontier was more brutal than in the older plantation areas. There was, of course, variation from farm to farm. But it is noteworthy that unexplained infant crib deaths (often called "smothering"), almost certainly a product of maternal exhaustion and malnourishment, were four times as prevalent among slaves in Georgia's cotton growing counties as in the same state's coastal rice counties. During the transition years from the 1790s through the 1820s, slaves in the Old Southwest confronted their new situations with few resources. Most had been torn from families and social networks in the Chesapeake, the low country, and West Africa, and they worked and lived in small groups of strangers. In the cotton counties of upland Georgia, for instance, between the 1790s and 1810 more than half the slaves lived on farms with fewer than ten slaves; only one in six lived in a group of twenty or more. While the slaves of the Cotton Belt would eventually reconstruct families and cultural resources, the cotton frontier of the early nineteenth century was typified by small plantations peopled by ambitious whites and uprooted blacks, and governed by a labor system that denied slaves time or space that they could call their own. Little wonder that masters in the older areas were learning to threaten unruly slaves with the worst of punishments: sale into the hellish conditions of the cotton frontier.

The Southern Yeomanry, 1790–1860 Cotton rewarded economies of scale: planters with large slave labor forces and big farms competed more efficiently and profitably than men who owned small farms and few or no slaves. And with the price of slaves and good land constantly rising, wealth became progressively more concentrated, and fewer and fewer whites reaped the profits of the cotton economy. In 1860 median farm size in the South was about the same as in the North; the average southern farm, however, was double the size of its northern counterpart. Put simply, these figures suggest that by 1860 the South was dominated by large landholdings. The big plantations occupied the best soils (farm value was much more disparate than farm size) and had most of the region's slaves. In 1861 only one in four white households owned slaves. Even in the cotton-growing counties, only half the white families were slaveholders. The antebellum market revolution had created a massive commercialization of southern agriculture. The market revolution, however, involved a shrinking proportion of the white population. The result was not simply an undemocratic distribution of wealth among rural whites but the creation of a dual economy: a commercialized planter elite in the Black Belt and a white yeomanry that remained peripheral to the market throughout the antebellum years.

There were, of course, many small farmers in Black Belt counties—generally on the poorer lands away from navigable rivers. They tended to be commercial farmers growing cotton with the labor of their families and/or a few slaves, and functioning as part of plantation belt society. Often the poor relatives of planters, they voted the great planters into office, used the planters' cotton gins and tapped into their marketing mechanisms, worked for them in a variety of capacities, sold food to the plantations, and helped the planters control slave populations that were usually local majorities. Although economic disparities between planters and farmers in the Black Belt continually widened, farmers continued as participants in the cotton economy.

A large proportion of southern whites, however, lived outside the plantation belt and maintained a yeoman society that was separate from the world of the planters. The southern yeomen shared many of the characteristics of their northern counterparts in the eighteenth century, but they continued in a safety-first, household-and-neighborhood-centered agriculture until the Civil War and beyond. Indeed, many southern households stayed outside the market almost entirely. The mountaineers of the southern Appalachians allowed a trickle of livestock, produce, and timber to flow out of their neighborhoods, but the market bypassed their region until the coming of big-business coal mines in the late nineteenth century. Farmers in large parts of the upland South preferred raising livestock to growing plants. Farmers planted unkept cornfields and let their pigs and cattle run loose in the forest and on unenclosed private land. In the late summer and fall farmers collected their animals and sold them to drovers, who transported them out of the region to be sold to flatland merchants and planters. Thus southern herdsmen were indirect participants in market operations. Animal husbandry was a form of agriculture that made possible large amounts of leisure time and nearly complete household independence, and in large regions of the upland South it was the preferred way of making a living.

Most southern yeomen, however, practiced mixed farming geared toward household subsistence and neighborhood exchange, with the leftovers from those two functions entering outside markets. As in the North, most farmers owned the land on which they worked; indeed, the appropriation of new farmland in the backcountry and the Old Southwest reversed the trend toward white tenancy that had been growing in the eighteenth-century Chesapeake. The upland yeomen were farm owners who made their own economic choices, and the majority of them were without slaves. In the upland Georgia counties studied by Steven Hahn, between seven in ten and nine in ten households were headed by non-slaveholding whites. Farmers in these areas practiced a "subsistence-plus" agriculture that was complicated by the nature of southern cash crops. Northern farmers before 1815 grew grain and livestock with which they fed their families and traded within their neighborhoods, then sent their surplus food into outside markets. Cotton, like tobacco and other southern market crops, was not a food; land committed to cotton was committed to outside markets. The middling and poor farmers put most of their land into food crops and livestock, cultivating only a few acres of cotton. The acreage devoted to cotton seems to have increased when transportation made markets more accessible—particularly when railroads penetrated the piedmont in the 1850s—but few antebellum yeomen became wholly dependent on markets. Limited cash crops paid debts and taxes and provided income for such supplemental items as coffee, tea, tobacco, ready-made cloth, and shoes. But, unlike the rural North, southern neighborhoods produced their own necessities. Widespread farm ownership and a safety-first mentality—along with the steady world market for cotton—allowed southern yeomen to enter and leave the market for their own purposes. Under these conditions the market served the interests of southern yeomen; it seldom dominated them.

Even more than in the North, the culture of southern whites and the social organization of rural neighborhoods inhibited individual ambition and acquisitiveness. Few farms were self-sufficient, and farmers routinely traded labor and goods. In the plantation belt, such neighborly help tended to reinforce the authority and power of planters who put some of their resources at the disposal of their poorer neighbors. In the uplands, cooperation reinforced neighborliness and the commitment to local autonomy. As one upland yeoman put it, "Borrowing . . . was neighboring" (Steven Hahn, *Roots of Southern Populism,* p. 55). Debts contracted within the network of kin and neighbors were generally paid in kind or in labor, and often creditors allowed their neighbors' debts to go unpaid for many years.

The most distinctively southern restraint on acquisitiveness and private property was the region's attitude toward fences. Northern critics never tired of contrasting the neatly fenced farms of the commercialized North with the dilapidated or nonexistent fences of the South. In the bourgeois North, well-maintained fences were a sure sign of ambitious, hardworking farmers; southern fences, on the other hand, signified laziness and lack of planning. The lack of fencing in most southern neighborhoods was, however, the result of local custom, neighborliness, and state law. Georgia, for instance, required farmers to enclose their planted fields; the remainder of their land remained unenclosed by law. In rural neighborhoods where many households depended on hunting and fishing as sources of food, and where most families allowed livestock to roam freely, enclosed private property conflicted with the neighborhood economy that required common use rights in privately owned land. In this sense the northern critics were right: the lack of fencing in the antebellum rural South spoke strongly of neighborhood constraints on the private use of private property. Such constraints, however, were necessary to the subsistence of households and neighborhoods as they were organized in the upland South.

Thus a large proportion of southern agriculturists remained marginal to market society. They entered it only after 1865, and then under adverse conditions created by the South's defeat in the Civil War. Formally freed blacks entered the market as tenants and sharecroppers; most upland whites were forced to mortgage their crops under the crop lien system. In both cases, landowners and merchants dictated that farmers grow cotton for market rather than foodstuffs for household consumption, and that they enter marketing and rental arrangements that kept them poor. While many northerners imagined the market as a liberating force, southern agriculturists, both black and white, experienced market society as a new form of bound labor.

CONCLUSION: WINNERS AND LOSERS

The costs and benefits of the market revolution must be assessed at many levels. It is certain that economic productivity increased dramatically in the first half of the nineteenth century. By 1860 the United States was the second largest industrial nation on earth. Exact figures are unavailable, but it is almost certain that American agriculture in that year was the most productive in the world. The distribution of that productivity and its rewards, however, was decidedly uneven. Per capita income from commodity production averaged $65 nationally in 1840. In the New England states, it averaged $83, and rose to $107 and $118, respectively, in Massachusetts and Rhode Island—the only two states in which industry outproduced agriculture by wide margins. Per capita income averaged $77 in the Middle Atlantic states and between $46 and $51 in the Northwest. In the South, there were huge divisions between the older seaboard areas, which averaged $55 per capita and the Cotton Belt of the Old Southwest, where per capita income rose to an impressive $104. Thus participation in the market revolution and enjoyment of its rewards were concentrated in the commercialized (and increasingly industrialized) Northeast and among the planters of the Cotton Belt.

Within regions, the market revolution had uneven social consequences. In the South, the benefits of the cotton boom were closed to large numbers of whites. The impressive productivity of the Southwest enriched a very few planters. Indeed, the commitment to cotton not only worked against economic democracy within the region but also stunted internal economic development and, by recommitting the region to slave labor, isolated the region politically in ways that led to disaster.

The market revolution among northern whites created both a rise in standards of living and greater disparities between rich and poor. The differences were sharpest in the cities, where slum neighborhoods took shape early in the century, and where class-segregated neighborhoods were standard even in the new cities of the interior by the 1820s and 1830s. In the countryside, estate inventories reveal both rising standards of living and increased inequality. For instance, the market revolution put tables, chairs, and individual table place settings into most northern homes. But some of those homes were bigger than others, and they tended to have glazed windows for light during the day and candles for light at night, painted exteriors, wallpaper, and upholstered furniture. Thus the result was a reduction in the proportion of rural northerners who lived at or below subsistence levels and a multiplication of the number of those who felt poor. Within households, commercialization resulted in subtle change. Men defined themselves less as patriarchs and more as breadwinners, and cash farming often led them to distinguish between paid (male) and unpaid (female) labor. Thus the creation of a domestic sphere within northern farm families (the house, garden, and dairy) was accompanied by a devaluation of women's work. At the same time, increased domestic cleanliness and comfort were often imposed by women and paid for with the "butter and egg money" that they earned and controlled. Perhaps the ambiguities of gender were resolved most forcefully by young women who left their fathers' farms to work in factories or schools: few of them returned to the countryside.

The worst results of the market revolution were suffered by nonwhites, for whites subsidized economic growth with unprecedented levels of expropriation of native lands and exploitation of slave labor. Between the 1790s and the 1850s whites "civilized" the land between the Appalachians and the Mississippi. By the 1830s Native American titles to almost all the land east of the Mississippi were extinguished, and survivors of one-sided wars and devastating epidemics had been removed to poorer lands in Oklahoma and Arkansas. In the new South, they were replaced by legions of slaves whose unpaid labor underwrote the impressive productivity of the region. It is no overstatement to insist that the market revolution was based directly on the theft of Indian land and African American labor.

THE MARKET REVOLUTION

BIBLIOGRAPHY

Collections and Surveys

Appleby, Joyce. "Commercial Farming and the 'Agrarian Myth' in the Early Republic." *Journal of American History* 68, no. 4 (1982):833–849.

Bushman, Richard L. *Joseph Smith and the Beginnings of Mormonism* (1984).

Ditz, Toby L. *Property and Kinship: Inheritance in Early Connecticut, 1750–1820* (1986).

Hahn, Steven, and Jonathan Prude, eds., *The Countryside in the Age of Capitalist Transformation: Essays in the Social History of Rural America* (1985).

Henretta, James A. "Families and Farms: *Mentalité* in Pre-Industrial America." *William and Mary Quarterly* 3rd ser., 35, no. 1 (1978):3–32.

Hoffman, Ronald, John J. McCusker, Russell R. Menard, and Peter J. Albert, eds. *The Economy of Early America: The Revolutionary Period, 1763–1790* (1988).

Innes, Stephen, ed. *Work and Labor in Early America* (1988).

Kulikoff, Allan. "The Transition to Capitalism in Rural America." *William and Mary Quarterly* 3rd ser., 46 (January 1989):120–144. The fairest and most thoughtful introduction to the subject.

Merrill, Michael. "Cash Is Good to Eat: Self-Sufficiency and Exchange in the Rural Economy of the United States." *Radical History Review* 4, no. 1 (1976):42–71.

North, Douglass C. *The Economic Growth of the United States, 1790–1860* (1961). No section of North's book has gone unchallenged, but it remains the best one-volume introduction to the economic history of these years.

Pred, Allan R. *Urban Growth and the Circulation of Information: The United States System of Cities, 1790–1840* (1973).

Sellers, Charles G. *The Market Revolution: Jacksonian America, 1815–1846* (1991). Published too late for consideration in this essay, this book is the first full length social, economic, and political history of the market revolution.

Taylor, George Rogers. *The Transportation Revolution, 1815–1860* (1951).

Wallerstein, Immanuel. *The Modern World System.* 3 vols. (1974–1989).

Northern Studies

Bidwell, Percy Wells. "Rural Economy in New England at the Beginning of the Nineteenth Century." *Transactions of the Connecticut Academy of Arts and Sciences* 20 (April 1916):245–399.

Clark, Christopher. *The Roots of Rural Capitalism: Western Massachusetts, 1780–1860* (1990). The best northern community study.

Cronon, William. *Nature's Metropolis: Chicago and the Great West* (1991). A pathbreaking ecological history.

Faragher, John Mack. *Sugar Creek: Life on the Illinois Prairie* (1986).

Folbre, Nancy R. "The Wealth of Patriarchs: Deerfield, Massachusetts, 1760–1840." *Journal of Interdisciplinary History* 16, no. 2 (1985):199–220.

Gross, Robert A. "Culture and Cultivation: Agriculture and Society in Thoreau's Concord." *Journal of American History* 69, no. 1 (1982):42–61.

Jensen, Joan M. *Loosening the Bonds: Mid-Atlantic Farm Women, 1750–1850* (1986).

Larkin, Jack. *The Reshaping of Everyday Life, 1790–1840* (1988). Valuable synthesis of work on the material culture of New England.

Lemon, James T. *The Best Poor Man's Country: A Geographical Study of Early Southeastern Pennsylvania* (1972).

Lindstrom, Diane. *Economic Development in the Philadelphia Region, 1810–1850* (1978).

Osterud, Nancy Grey. *Bonds of Community: The Lives of Farm Women in Nineteenth-Century New York* (1991).

Pruitt, Bettye Hobbs. "Self-Sufficiency and the Agricultural Economy of Eighteenth-Century Massachusetts." *William and Mary Quarterly* 3rd ser., 41, no. 3 (1984):333–364.

Rothenberg, Winifred B. "The Market and Massachusetts Farmers, 1750–1855." *Journal of Economic History* 41, no. 2 (June 1981):283–314.

Ulrich, Laurel Thatcher. *A Midwife's Tale: The Life of Martha Ballard, Based on Her Diary, 1785–1812* (1990). A densely researched, loving portrait of rural life.

Southern Studies

Beeman, Richard R. *The Evolution of the Southern Backcountry: A Case Study of Lunenberg County, Virginia, 1746–1832* (1984).

Berlin, Ira, and Ronald Hoffman, eds. *Slavery and Freedom in the Age of the American Revolution* (1983).

Burton, Orville Vernon. *In My Father's House Are Many Mansions: Family and Community in Edgefield, South Carolina* (1985).

Fogel, Robert William, and Stanley L. Engerman. *Time on the Cross: The Economics of American Negro Slavery.* 2 vols. (1974).

Genovese, Elizabeth Fox, and Eugene D. Genovese. *Fruits of Merchant Capital: Slavery and Bourgeois Property in the Rise and Expansion of Capitalism* (1983).

Genovese, Eugene D. *The Political Economy of Slavery: Studies in the Economy and Society of the Slave South* (1967; 2d ed., 1989). Still the most influential overview of the slave South.

Hahn, Steven. *The Roots of Southern Populism: Yeomen Farmers and the Transformation of the Georgia Upcountry, 1850–1890* (1983). The fullest analysis of the southern yeomanry.

Harris, J. William. *Plain Folk and Gentry in a Slave Society: White Liberty and Black Slavery in Augusta's Hinterlands* (1985).

Joyner, Charles. *Down by the Riverside: A South Carolina Slave Community* (1984).

McWhiney, Grady. *Cracker Culture: Celtic Folkways in the Old South* (1988). Burdened with a questionable ethnic thesis, but includes valuable essays on southern farmers.

Oakes, James. *The Ruling Race: A History of American Slaveholders* (1982).

Wright, Gavin. *The Political Economy of the Cotton South: Households, Markets, and Wealth in the Nineteenth Century* (1978).

SEE ALSO **Technology and Social Change**; and various essays in the sections "**Periods of Social Change**," "**Processes of Social Change**," "**Regionalism and Regional Subcultures**," and "**Space and Place**."

URBANIZATION

Eric H. Monkkonen

CITIES HAVE FASCINATED thinkers and attracted scholarly attention for centuries. At the same time, most scholars have avoided becoming too engaged in defining exactly what they mean by "the city." In 1984, for instance, Jan DeVries commented that the challenge of defining "city" exactly was the "tar baby" of urban history. For American historians, the cautious avoidance of precise definitions has had a salutary effect, as the notion of what is urban and what is not is influenced by the changing city itself. And since the 1970s, settlement patterns in America have varied in such a way as to challenge most precise definitions of what a city is: flung out beyond the suburbs of older cities are dense areas of new residences, business parks, and shopping centers, many located in unincorporated areas. Are these cities? They certainly are not the country. For that matter, are the older suburbs that these places abut cities? In the spirit of American urban settlement patterns, this essay terms a city "any place which has legally incorporated itself," while the term "urban" denotes places with population concentration, even the unincorporated places. This means that incorporated suburban places are termed "cities" rather than "suburbs." Thus, for instance, Los Angeles County is an urban area which contains eighty-six cities.

In order to grasp the multistranded history of American cities, it is useful to think of them first in the broader context of urban growth, then to turn to their—broadly defined—political context, and to conclude with an overview of their changing social structures. The first part of the section on growth examines the precolonial and colonial antecedents of American cities, and the second traces in more detail the quantitative dimensions of urban growth in the two centuries since the creation of the United States. The second section describes the broad political context into which American cities have fitted. And the third section, divided into five parts, details the complex social structures of American cities.

GROWTH

Antecedents of American Cities Although historians usually date the urban revolution back to the growth of Ur, around 3000 B.C., probably less than 5 percent of the world's population lived in urban places until the seventeenth century. Then England and the Netherlands began to experience rapid urban growth, a growth which preceded that in North America by over a century. North America, like most of the world, had only had a small portion of its population living in places we would now identify as urban prior to the mid eighteenth century. The largest urban place until then had probably been what we call Cahokia, near present-day East Saint Louis, Illinois. Anthropologists estimate it to have had as many as twenty thousand people in the thirteenth century, which would have made it one of the world's larger cities. By the sixteenth century, Cahokia had been abandoned. But the lack of large urban places did not mean that the peoples of the North American continent were profoundly rural. It is more correct to think of the pre-European world as one of village settlements ranging in size from the tiny and seasonally occupied to permanently occupied places of perhaps a thousand people. Dispersed across the landscape, these villages were located at the natural crossing points and stops of transportation routes, both land and water.

One can imagine that well before Europeans began to come to the continent, nearly all of the modern American cities and towns had Indian predecessors—in the case of large cities spreading over many miles, multiple predecessors. Likely locations—bays, spots sheltered from prevailing winds, locations easily protected from attack, on river rapids, or on good land routes—attracted village dwellers prior to Europeans. Although much of their history is now lost to us, we can imagine that, like villages of the preindustrial world, they spanned the continent with a dense network of local relations and much thinner trade ties involving small items of high value which were exchanged over long distances (for example, pipestone from southern Minnesota appeared across the continent).

At first, European contact with North America caused only subtle shifts in established settlement patterns. The Spanish established urban sites (with very small populations) at Saint Augustine (1565), Tucson (ca. 1700), and Santa Fe (ca. 1609). The French made Pittsburgh (Fort Duquesne, 1754), Saint Louis (1764), Detroit (1701), and New Orleans (1718) major trading centers, and French fur traders became permanent dwellers in dozens of métis villages in the upper Midwest. At first, the urban centers established by northern Europeans seemed much less promising—whether it was the Dutch in New Amsterdam or the English in several scattered coastal sites—than those of the Spanish.

In fact, none of these places were cities as the Europeans thought of them. For the Europeans, a proper city had a charter from the monarch, significant defenses, a limited number of entry gates guarded with towers, and substantial masonry construction. What they built in North America were some temporary fortlike structures with wooden palisades, which were inexpensive but decayed and fell down within a few years. (Centuries earlier the inhabitants of Cahokia had constructed at least three palisades by means of similar techniques.) The French built slightly more substantial defenses in Montreal and Saint Louis. But on the whole, the early modern North American city looked casually constructed, highly temporary, and ramshackle to European eyes.

The early modern cities of the New World, laid out according to European urban standards, and even European laws in the case of the Spanish, reflected their varied national origins. In their plans can be seen traces of everything from new forts to English village patterns. The fantastic (and never realized) plan for a small nation-state, Azilia, Georgia (1717), near Savannah, a fortified square twenty miles on each side, tells us more about the European notions of its founder, Sir Robert Montgomery, concerning North America than about actual settlements. His plan makes concrete European urban values: the significance of the center, the idea of a geometrical order, and, of course, the need for permanent fortifications. James Oglethorpe's similar rectilinear plan for Savannah (1734) barely suggests the town's sparse population or modest prospects, for the city had grown to more than three thousand by the Revolution. On paper, Albany's plan of 1695, for instance, could be the classic fortified medieval town, with gates and strategically placed defensive positions, but its wooden palisade was never replaced with a rotproof masonry wall.

The Spanish plan for San Antonio (1722) outlines a similar European fantasy, but a visitor's comment some years later suggests a different reality:

> The town consists of fifty-nine houses of stone and mud and seventy-nine of wood, but all poorly built . . . so that the whole resembles more a poor village than a villa, capital of so pleasing a province. . . . (John W. Reps, *Town Planning in Frontier America* [1969], p. 54; cf. Fray J. A. Morfi, *History of Texas, 1673–1779,* translated by Carlos E. Castañeda (1935) p. 92)

The more realistic map of Boston (1640) indicates the shape of cities which were prosperous: it is that of an English village, its longer lots indicating garden plots, its meandering streets following natural paths. And in its boosters' descriptions the city made up for its failure to look European by what would become the characteristic American booster claim—its prospects for continued expansion and growth.

> The chiefe Edifice of this City-like Towne is crowded on the Seabankes, and wharfed out with great industry and coast, the buildings beautifull and large, some fairly set forth with Brick, Tile, Stone and Slate, and orderly placed with comely streets, whose continuall enlargement presages some sumptuous City. (Reps, *Town Planning,* pp. 173–174)

This passage hints at what the Europeans in North America looked for in a city: signs of economic activity in large warehouses and wharves, buildings of masonry (as opposed to cheap and plentiful timber), and a sense of order and compactness, even crowding. All of these values derive from the experience of living in medieval and Renaissance cities; the realization of these urban values in North America would prove to be difficult, if not impossible.

Thus, the urban United States has evolved out of complex geopolitical and multicultural origins—English, Spanish, Indian, and French. For even though pre-eighteenth-century North America may have had low levels of urbanization, small urban settlements dotted the landscape.

American Urban Population With the coming of constitutional government, we can begin to trace the urban transformation of America more systematically. Two background dimensions must be kept in mind. First, the total American population has expanded dramatically since 1790, when it was about 3.9 million, to about 230 million in 1990. Thus, when thinking about changing proportions, we must remember that they represent the movement of people within a larger pattern. Second, the territorial expansion of the continental United States took up much of the first half of the nineteenth century; not only did the population grow, but as it grew, it moved into newly established political regions. And this expansion, as shown by urban historian Richard Wade, was from its initiation an urban expansion, the new western cities and their transportation connections making possible the exploitation of the land by farmers, ranchers, and miners.

As the United States expanded its territory and increased its population, the nature of its society changed as well. Figure 1 shows the outlines of this change. In 1790, only 5 percent of Americans lived in villages, towns, and cities. Today, nearly 80 percent do. And this figure masks the large number of people living in areas neither city nor country, for only 2.5 percent of American families could be identified as living on farms by 1984, about half of the figure in 1970. In other words, in its first two hundred years, the United States went from a very rural farming nation to a highly urbanized nonfarming one.

In Figure 1 the upper line represents the percentage of people living in places with a population over 2,500, a traditional (and traditionally problematic) Census Bureau definition of "urban"; the lower line, the percent living in cities with a population over 100,000. A closer examination of the upper line shows the increased urbanization after 1840 and a temporary leveling in 1930. The 1840 acceleration can be attributed to several things: the population expansion from immigration, the increase in industrial production and productivity following the War of 1812, the bringing into production of rich new agricultural lands in the Midwest, and the exploitation of steam-powered vessels and of canals made possible by government subsidies. The 1930 leveling captures the severe im-

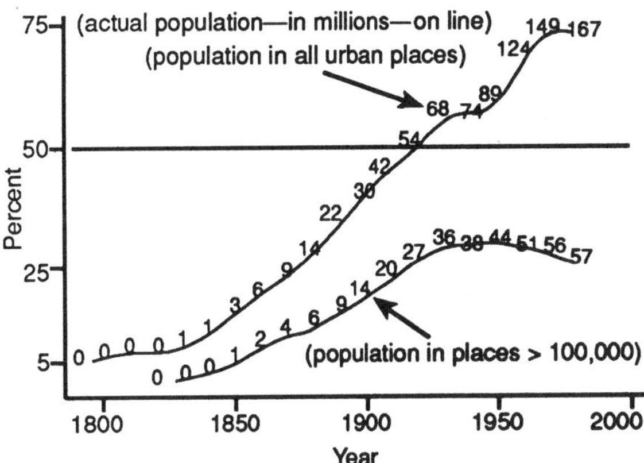

Fig. 1. Percent of total population in U.S. cities with a population greater than 2,500.

pact of the Great Depression, during which people returned to their farms (or, in the case of some Mexican Americans, were forcibly deported).

A closer look at the lower line is also merited. It, too, captures urban growth after 1840, and shows a steady increase in the percentage of the total population in large cities from 1840 to 1930. But something very important happened after 1930: the abrupt cessation of urban growth occurring in all cities had a more dramatic and apparently permanent impact on large cities—their proportion of the American population declined. We now know that this was the beginning of the suburban era in American history. This line also suggests the best way to think about suburbanization: continued urbanization in small cities. In the 1950s, urban commentators and critics often saw suburbanization as "anti-urban" and a deep cultural rejection of city life. But now suburbanization is being reconceptualized as, among other things, the continued growth of cities but rejection of the very large city.

This discussion of growth, which emphasizes city size, should serve to remind us that the medium-size city is the typical American city. Historians and other writers on urban affairs commonly focus on the biggest cities for reasons of rhetoric and communication. The many more people living in small cities each know something about the very large place, but very little about the many other smaller places. Thus the need for a common focus leads to writing and thinking about New York or Chicago or Los Angeles, rather than about smaller towns like the eight Romes. (In Georgia, Illinois, Indiana, Iowa, Mississippi, New York, Ohio, Pennsylvania, plus Rome City, Indiana. Of these, only three would appear in the count of places over 2,500—the Rome in New York with 40,000, in Georgia with 30,000, and in Illinois with 3,000 [1980 figures].)

Figure 2 shows the continued increase in the number of city units in America but mirrors only part of the continued absolute growth of the population. It also contains a hint of why the 1950s has been so associated with suburbanization, for we can see a sharp acceleration of the increase in places with populations over 2,500 in this decade. The number of local governments increased from four thousand to six thousand.

Figure 3 captures the consequence (and cause) of these changes. It displays the mean size of American cities and towns with a population over 2,500; it grew until the Civil War, was interrupted, and then resumed its growth until the Great Depression. It clearly shows the turnaround in urban size patterns and the continued shrinkage of the average city size in America since the 1930s. In fact, the mean city size has now declined to about that at the time of World War I—just under twenty thousand people. What the figure does not capture is location, for these many small cities are not isolated from other cities but are often adjacent to one another: they are the many new suburban cities which make up the mosaic of governments in metropolitan areas. Los Angeles County, for instance, in 1990 had eighty-six cities within its borders, some created since World War II and others nearly as old as the city of Los Angeles.

Although this shift of population away from very large cities has affected all cities, big and small, it became newsworthy only as it sporadically hit big cities in the mid 1970s. In part this large impact represented a misreading of statistics in the 1960s.

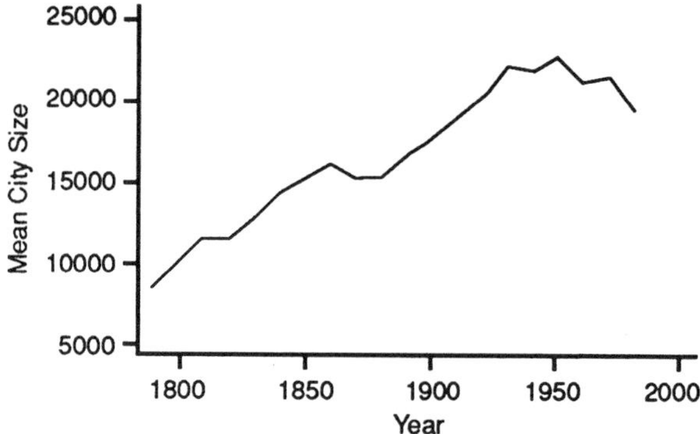

Fig. 3. Mean size of places with population greater than 2,500.

A careful look at Figure 4, which shows the mean size of cities with over one hundred thousand people, makes it clear that the downward curve in big city growth had begun in the earliest decades of the twentieth century. The shape of this curve amplifies a tendency visible in the previous figures and makes it apparent that the decline of the very large city has reversed the century of urban growth in a way which might have been hard to anticipate in, say, 1900. No wonder so many big-city leaders worry about their future, for this decline at least suggests that the future of an urban United States is in much smaller places.

As the urban population and the number of cities grew, the growth sites moved westward. If we examine the founding dates of the 148 largest American cities, we can see that the greatest number of eastern cities were founded in the 1830s, those of the Midwest in the 1840s, and those of the plains and the West in the 1880s. These figures may surprise some, for the popular image of the West is of a rural region. But in fact, California had reached an urban population concentration of 50 percent by

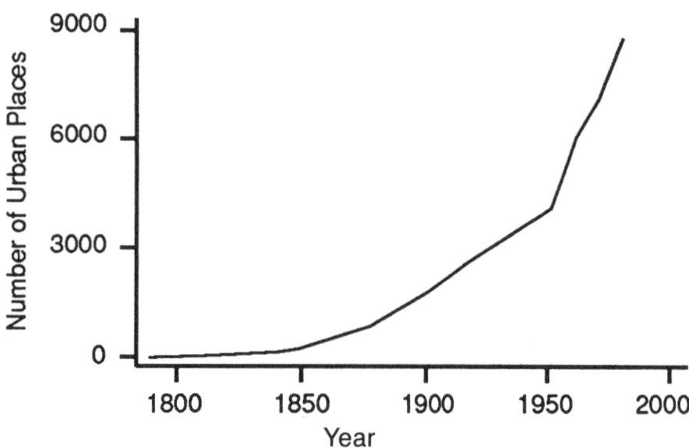

Fig. 2. Number of places with population greater than 2,500.

Fig. 4. Mean size of cities with population greater than 100,000.

about 1885, well ahead of the country in general, which did not reach this point until 1920.

In the nineteenth and early twentieth centuries, the people to fill these cities and towns came both from the countryside and from outside the borders of the United States. Later in the twentieth century they also came from natural increases, but urban family limitation practices (that is, the tendency of urban families to be smaller than rural ones) and high mortality kept cities from fueling their own growth. From the mid 1840s until World War I, immigration from Europe pushed population growth; by the end of the nineteenth century, many cities had a population more than 50 percent of which was foreign born. The differing reasons for leaving, the differing skills and economic resources, sorted out immigrants so that some cities took on an ethnic character which they still retain. By 1920, Saint Louis, Milwaukee, and Cincinnati, for instance, were heavily German. Providence and Boston were more Irish, while New Haven was more Italian and New York more Russian (Jewish).

Seaports and cities with large factories attracted more immigrants; consequently, in the South only New Orleans had a sizable immigrant population. With the formal restriction of immigration by Congress, the hostilities of World War I, and the Great Depression, immigration came to a near standstill until the 1980s. But migration to cities continued until 1929, the places of the transatlantic and transpacific immigrants now taken by blacks from the rural South and migrants from Mexico. The Great Depression put a ten-year stop to this flow, but the employment opportunities of World War II and the prosperity of the 1950s allowed it to resume. For African Americans, this "great migration" caused a remarkably abrupt demographic transition. In less than three generations their population changed from rural—only one person in twenty living in a city—to more urban than the country as a whole: now only one person in twenty lived in the countryside. While American cities have always had black communities within them, this enormous population surge was unprecedented.

Detroit, for instance, was the fourth largest American city in 1920 (with just over a million people), widely known for its automobile manufacturing and progressive politics under mayors like Hazen Pingree (mayor 1890–1897) and Frank Murphy (1930–1933). Thirty percent of its population was foreign born, but only 4 percent was black. Its population peaked in 1950 at nearly two million and then began to drop. By the mid 1970s, as the total population continued to decline, the city's population became over 50 percent black.

Thus the modern world of medium-sized cities (very often, if inaccurately, thought of as suburbs) was well established by the mid twentieth century. Big central-city growth peaked in the late 1920s. And the West, highly urban from the late nineteenth century on, continued its urban ascendancy. The peopling of these burgeoning cities has drawn on diverse ethnic and racial groups migrating from abroad and from the rural regions of the North American continent. The multiplicity of peoples and cities has made urban America quite different from other nations: more socially heterogeneous and less politically centralized.

POLITICS

Too often, the phrase "urban politics" conjures up a solitary image: the boss. The definition of politics should take on a broader scope than has been customary, for much of urban history includes the political—for instance, site selection, the federal system, the subsidization of technology, and the internal structure of city politics. As pointed out earlier, most American cities today have been sites of human habitation for millennia. The appearance of the United States is relatively recent, and it followed the regimes of various European nations in various places—England, Spain, France, the Netherlands, and, very briefly, Russia (at Fort Ross in California). These nations had been preceded by hundreds of different tribal groups. Thus, the political history of American cities under the Constitution can be seen as a very recent history, albeit a dramatically different and much bigger one (in terms of numbers of people affected).

Under the Constitution, cities have had two broadly distinct periods. During the first period, which lasted until about 1830, many cities continued their governance under forms inherited from the colonial era. Thus, at the beginning of the nineteenth century Boston had a town meeting; New York and Philadelphia, closed and self-perpetuating corporate councils; San Francisco was a Spanish military outpost; and New Orleans was part of New France. Some of these forms continued the traditions of medieval city governance. A corporate charter granted a city autonomy in social and economic matters as well as political; a freeman of the city belonged to the city corporation and could share freely in the privileges it extended. These included protection, the right to trade, and the obligation to pay for and defend the city. For example, in New York City and Philadelphia, only freemen could be council members or vote.

In England, the monarch had granted towns their corporate charters: "None but the King alone can create or make a corporation" (Sir Edward Coke, *Reports* [1612], vol. 10, p. 356). By the time of the Revolution, Parliament protected city corporations from royal interference. (In 1835, Parliament passed the Municipal Corporations Act, which sealed this transition of urban control from king to parliament. The act regularized all municipal charters and brought them into final conformance to the will of Parliament.) For the United States this is important, as the Constitution was silent on cities' status, by definition relegating their political creation and control to the states. And for social history, this political outcome, of little importance in the 1780s, has made profound differences.

First, the lack of any central regulation of city structure allowed for political diversity. In the colonial era, while New York City and Philadelphia had closed councils, Boston and Newport had town meetings in which any male property holder could participate. Yet overall, major offices went to the wealthy or to leaders of popular political factions. These colonial governments had the power to grant or sell the right to vend on streets (Boston); to set charges for carting (Philadelphia); to set the price of bread and ferry fees, and to grant monopoly franchises and the right to sell in the market (New York City). City councils regulated wages, maintained the wharves, and provided for the poor. Thus a strong tradition of local taxation and local welfare responsibility was passed on, and did not end until the New Deal's social legislation began federal supplementation of local responsibilities.

Second, lack of democratic representation forced ordinary people to turn to another means of political expression—rioting, which was frequent until the mid nineteenth century. Riots were typically directed, symbolic, political actions by men and apprentice boys who burned political or religious effigies, tore down houses, or broke windows. Elites sometimes participated in riots but almost always tolerated them. Some were regular events: in mid-eighteenth-century New York, for example, on both Pope Day and New Year's Eve, drummers led processions which smashed windows where candles were not lit. Pope Day, an anti-Catholic demonstration similar to Guy Fawkes Day, was officially sponsored by the governor in the 1740s. The procession hauled effigies of the pope and the devil; stopped in front of the homes of prominent Catholics, who sent out silver coins; and finished by burning effigies on bonfires.

Other public celebrations took on similar tones. For example, to celebrate repeal of the Stamp Act and the king's birthday in 1766, New York City's council supplied two roast oxen, twenty-five barrels of strong beer, and a hogshead of rum. There also were two poles, one of them topped with twelve tar and pitch barrels and surrounded by twenty cords of wood for a bonfire. The emergence of political parties in the 1790s began to foster public criticism of mobs; at the same time, mobs became wilder, less directed by elites.

And third, local politics and political culture were much more sensitive to local popular feelings and influence than was national politics. This took on great significance later in the mid nineteenth century. Between 1800 and 1820, property ownership as a requirement for the franchise had been dropped, except in a few towns where this restriction applied to local votes concerning property taxes. Consequently, white male suffrage became the rule by 1840, immediately prior to the transformation of the cities by mass immigration from Ireland and Germany. For instance, in the 1820s, 128,000 immigrants came to America; between 1845 and 1854, nearly 3,000,000. Of this latter flood, an enormous proportion came to cities where they exercised the franchise and quickly became a part of the urban political scene. Urban politics became the focus of intense ethnic activity, reflecting social change far more quickly than on the national level, a characteristic still present.

The second period of city governments, from 1830 until today, saw a new kind of charter. Granted almost automatically by state legislatures, it had widely standardized features allowing cities to raise revenues through property taxes and requiring them to have schools, courts, and such basic infrastructure as streets. They could borrow, sue, and be sued. Somewhat like the power of early business corporations being created at exactly the same time, urban corporate power was a legal tool which grew by accretion and amendment. The unforeseen political consequences of the American city's peculiar legal status were its relatively liberal suffrage history and its ultimate legal subservience to state government. This latter position, articulated by the judge and legal writer John Forrest Dillon in the nineteenth century, meant that local politicians often tried to get state governments to help structure and shape cities' legal conflicts. Surprisingly, much of the evidence so far is that state governments pretty much did as cities asked them, the most blatant partisan interference occurring when cities suffered fiscal stress.

From the point of view of our almost completely urbanized nation, there had been a tendency to think about the smaller villages and towns of the late eighteenth and early nineteenth centuries in terms of the oppositions of Gemeinschaft and Gesellschaft—the close, intimate community of then and the mass society of now. But the work of social historians has shown how in colonial cities, what Gemeinschaft there was, was achieved by racial, religious, and ethnic exclusion. For example, the town constable enforced the legal procedure of "warning out" any nonresident likely to become a pauper and, hence, dependent on the town's welfare. All residents were required to report such persons. Similarly, out-of-wedlock births threatened towns not because of the obvious violation of moral principles but because of the obligation to support all poor residents, including children (hence *The Scarlet Letter* misfocuses the reader's attention on moral rather than on welfare issues). Thus, the close communal support often came with the cost of aggressive hostility toward outsiders or the "wandering poor."

In contrast, port cities, though relatively small, were more vibrant; their racially diverse populations practiced a multiplicity of religions—African, Puritan, Anglican, Catholic, Quaker, Jewish, and pagan magic. And, especially in the early decades of the nineteenth century in the bigger cities, the changing economic structure opened up wage-paying jobs for young women, who seized the opportunity to live beyond immediate patriarchal control.

The cultural diversity of port cities and the growth of independent youth cultures could not escape the notice of any urban dweller, for city size and density were defined by transportation, usually walking. The "walking city," as it is known by historians, was usually limited in physical size to the distance a person could walk in half an hour. The economy of walking meant that the wealthier lived near the city's center, merchants near their warehouses, and people of different cultures and statuses very near one another. We should not conclude that in this heterogeneous environment, proximity implied understanding or friendliness; it may have meant that social distinctions of dress, accent, and cleanliness were all that much stronger.

In American cities until the 1830s, housing differences for the rich and the poor were as often on the inside of dwellings as on the exterior or in the location. Servants often slept on the floor; the poor jammed families into tiny dwellings located near those of the wealthy; merchants often lived in or over their warehouses. Most people (perhaps 80 percent) rented their houses, which has led historians to conclude that the wealthy used their capital for economic activities other than purchasing housing. Almost one-third of Philadelphians paid less than £10 per year for rent, which brought them a twelve-by-eighteen-foot, single-story dwelling. Thus no evidence for the importance of urban home ownership and its tie to property taxes has emerged for the nineteenth century.

Much of this began to change as early as 1830. Immigration continued, the employment of women for wages increased, and urban cultural diversity grew; at the same time residential, commercial, and industrial locations in cities changed. These structural changes, fostered by local governments, directly and indirectly subsidized a new transportation form: the railroad. The changes fostered by railroad transportation include what we now call suburbanization and allowed better-off urban dwellers to live in larger houses on larger plots of land. But these changes were intimately related to the larger change in the perception of the city and the country. In the seventeenth century, cities were places of freedom and safety: they had walls to keep out danger, whether invading armies or bandits. The countryside was a place of danger. By the 1850s, this notion and the corresponding reality had faded, and the visual image of the countryside as a paradise had begun to shape residential choice.

Urban transportation technology represented political choices: the building of ports, their dredging and maintenance by the Army Corps of Engineers, and the financing of canals and railroads all required political action. Typically, American cities participated by lending money to or investing in railroad companies which promised to build stations or repair shops in them or to construct feeder lines to them. These enormous sums were raised through voter-ratified bond issues; the voters, ordinarily quite stingy, supported such issues because expanded rail access ensured increases in property values. Similarly, the privilege to run a rail line or horse-drawn omnibus line was sold by city governments to private entrepreneurs. These entrepreneurs enjoyed monopoly privileges and the sure knowledge of where their lines would run (allowing them to invest in real estate holdings around the terminals they planned to build). The investments in real property often provided a greater return to urban street railroad companies than did the artificially low fares; and when the profits from this indirect subsidy were consumed in the early twentieth century, rail service usually declined. The clear political nature of the activity may be highlighted by contrast with England, where street railroad companies were not allowed to invest in (and augment their profits from) real estate; consequently, they served only middle-class areas and charged high fares.

INTERNAL SOCIAL STRUCTURE

Mobility From the colonial period through the end of World War II, American cities were characterized by high population turnover and transiency. Predictable career patterns and a life course of material security and health became reasonable expectations for ordinary people only after the welfare reforms of the New Deal and post–World War II prosperity. Young people attended school irregularly, were often apprenticed out or lived with relatives, and could not expect to follow anything like the orderly patterns of late-twentieth-century youth. Throughout the nineteenth century, urban families depended on their children's incomes; a typical working adult could not earn enough to support a family. Family budget studies have shown that mothers at home took in boarders, and the older children often delayed marriage so that they could contribute to the family income. For such families, high school was a luxury; universal high school attendance came only after World War I.

Those fortunate enough to stay able could expect to work until they died. Should they become unable to work in their old age and should their children be unable to care for them, they could only turn to the poorhouse. Poorhouses dotted the landscape; because they were usually run by the county government, they were located on farms on the edges of cities. They sheltered a variety of the poor, from tramps and pregnant destitute women to the elderly without means of support. As places of last resort, they were seldom occupied for long terms, the elderly coming to them to die. They were relieved of their grim task by New Deal social security and old age assistance legislation, which supplemented local welfare funds and stipulated that federal money not go to local government. Today's city- and county-run nursing homes are the direct institutional descendants of the poorhouse, and many occupy the original poorhouse buildings.

The unpredictability of individual lives was matched by the lack of residential stability. Even in the colonial period, about half of all urban families could not be found in the same place after a ten-year interval. While residential persistence varied from city to city, this figure characterizes the nineteenth and early twentieth centuries as well. But it masks in its averaging, for some families and individuals moved very often while others managed to stay put longer. The idea that in our past, cities had neighborhoods where generations of families lived has to be discarded except for the unusual family.

The most mobile people were tramps. In the colonial period and down to the end of the Civil War, tramps, or the "wandering poor," constituted the poorest part of the urban population. Many sought day work, went to rural areas for farm labor in the summer, and found seafaring jobs in ports. Young women had the most difficult time, for no community wanted single women who might become pregnant and be a burden on the local welfare. With the rise of factory employment, young women could find work in factory towns, a much better option than working as servants because of the independence which factory work offered. But in an unevenly expanding economy, any local downturn immediately sent people on the road, searching for work.

After the Civil War and the three-decade expansion of the railroad system, tramping became a mass phenomenon. Tramps rode in empty boxcars, providing the labor that filled the boxcars for their return trips. Typically, railroads tolerated the tramps when the companies knew that they were the labor source to load the paying cargo. While many tramps worked in rural locations—lumbering, harvesting, and mining—they returned to urban hubs to find job information, day labor, and lodging. In cities they shoveled snow and coal in the winter; year round they did construction, building the cities.

Tramps were incomprehensible to the middle class, who often talked about "wanderlust" as a psychological disease. One college professor devoted his life to the study of tramps: Dr. John J. McCook of Hartford, Connecticut, took tramp censuses and finally figured out in the 1890s that unemployment, not individual character flaws or affliction with "wanderlust," was the problem. When he began to deliver speeches announcing his conclusions, he was greeted with some skepticism, his middle-class auditors not quite ready to believe him. Tramping began to decrease after World War I, the automobile making tramps less visible and increased unemployment programs making tramping less a part of the average worker's life strategy. The Great Depression saw a startling but temporary return of tramping, especially of children and families. In the postwar era, migrant workers with their own cars have replaced the agricultural tramp, and changed industrial employment policies aimed at creating a stable work force have ended factory dependence on tramps.

Tramping never really resumed in mass form after World War II, and residential stability increased dramatically. Although the precise reasons for increased stability are hard to demonstrate, the best work so far suggests that the New Deal had a major impact. Both the increased income reliability provided by social security and the enormous federal subsidy to home mortgages fed this stability. Prior to the federal subsidization of the long-term mortgage, houses had to be purchased with short-term loans, the buyer paying only interest for, say, five years, with the entire principal coming due at the end. Thus buyers had to have a very stringent savings plan at the same time that they were paying interest. The stretching out of interest and principal payments for twenty or more years meant an easier burden but much greater interest payments; by subsidizing these and guaranteeing their payment, the federal government accelerated access to stable home ownership. Consequently, while home ownership had always been high in America relative to other nations, it became even higher. It also became of better quality, with water, electricity, and sewers the norm: one way the working poor had achieved home ownership was by building their own houses; in order to save, they often avoided sewer hookups and even electricity (only half of all urban dwellings had electricity in 1920).

Family and Ethnicity The high mobility, the slenderness of public welfare sources, the instability of employment and of the economy, and the intense linguistic and cultural fragmentation of American cities could be countered only by dependence on families. Thus the nuclear family had to stand as an economic resource and an emotional center. Such stress probably made family life difficult. The Victorian picture of the family sitting in a parlor should be shifted a bit: the family crowded into the kitchen, with the mother cooking for the family plus the boarders, the youngest child unsupervised on the floor, young girls doing piecework at the table, the older children out looking for work, the father either at work or at the tavern. For many men, socializing meant the tavern: both culturally and literally there was no other public meeting place. Identified by middle-class and working-class temperence reformers as a source of family stress and violence, the male drinking culture added one more stress upon nuclear family life. Like so many other sources of family stress, this, too, began to change in the twentieth century with the advent of national prohibition driving down liquor consumption and the measurable damage done by alcohol.

All of these family stresses impinged most on the poor, whether immigrants, rural migrants, or African Americans. In addition, for all but the native-born whites, racial, ethnic, and religious bigotry and violence made city life hard. Although as a political movement anti-Catholic nativism had ended prior to the Civil War, the Irish still faced discrimination in the job market. Conzen's study of nineteenth-century Milwaukee (1976) contrasts the Irish and the Germans, showing how their large and highly diverse community provided many political, religious, and economic opportunities for Germans, who as a consequence were able to choose whether to leave their ethnic world. The Irish, on the other hand, were limited by class to a much narrower range of economic opportunities, and by the end of the nineteenth century were more economically and residentially constrained than the Germans.

Zunz (1982) has found evidence that in Detroit in the early twentieth century, ethnicity became somewhat less significant in determining where people lived, class replacing it as a neighborhood-shaping factor. Its ethnic neighborhoods were most cohesive between 1880 and 1900, shifting in character to class neighborhoods in the 1920s (except for recent black migrants). In other words, ethnicity made a greater difference for neighborhood choice and restriction in the nineteenth century; economic access began to reshape neighborhood formation in the twentieth. The group exception to this generalization, African Americans, continued to suffer racial discrimination after ethnic discrimination had subsided.

In fact, the story of race and ethnicity in American cities must be traced very carefully. While in the early nineteenth century, Irish Protestants rioted against Irish Catholics, demonstrating a powerful and often violent interethnic hostility, by the twentieth century, only race riots remained. Radburn, New Jersey, the famous exemplar of the garden city concept popularized in America by Lewis Mumford, excluded blacks and Jews (presumably Asians and Mexican Americans would have been excluded had the development been on the West Coast). In other words, violent hostilities between Christian Europeans subsided prior to the Christian European hostility toward Jews, African Americans, Mexican Americans, and Asians. Housing discrimination was codified through the ostensibly private covenant between buyer and seller, the buyer promising not to resell the house to Jews, Mexican Americans, Asians, or blacks. In the postwar era, the Supreme Court (in *Shelley* v. *Kraemer,* 1948) made it illegal to enforce such discriminatory covenants, ending de jure, if not de facto, housing discrimination.

Within this complex set of histories, the common thread of African American urban history deserves a brief separate treatment. From the time Africans were brought to North America, there have been urban African communities, but until the third decade of the twentieth century these were proportionately small. Prior to this great migration, African American communities differed substantially from city to city and between the North and the South. Before the Civil War, southern urban blacks, both slave and free, held significant occupational niches, even though their political and religious freedom was highly restricted. In the antebellum North, on the other hand, black access to skilled occupations was blocked, so that economic distress tempered the freedom to worship and move about. After the war, northern cities developed different kinds of black communities: Washington, D.C., had a small black elite; Philadelphia's elite traced its roots to the eighteenth century while new migrants from the South constantly shifted the character of the city's black community; and cities in the Midwest had small communities of blacks who often had migrated from states directly south of them. Prior to the great migration after World War I, newspapers kept black communities in touch with activities in other cities of the region. Churches, schools, lodges, and small businesses provided a continuity and context for community life even as economic opportunity was continually blocked.

A brief contrast with the situation for Mexican Americans is instructive because southwestern cities were often Mexican. Santa Fe, for instance, had several hundred years of history prior to becoming a part of the United States. But after it did so, the takeover of political and economic power by Anglos altered the nature of the Mexican American city. In Santa Barbara, California, the transition took place in the two decades following the Civil War, as taxes, a numerical increase in Yankee voters, and outright discrimination eroded the power of the Mexican Americans. Only after the newcomers had secured their economic and political dominance did they and the city begin to romanticize old Mexico by the building of Spanish-style structures. Even the restoration of old adobes usually took place well after the power of the Mexican Americans had been usurped.

City and Industry All too often, the past of American cities is envisioned as being closely linked with industrialization. But the perceived close relationship of city and industry is somewhat more complex than used to be thought. Once the steam engine relieved the factory of dependence on water as a power source, industry could relocate nearer the other factors of production. But factory location and city economic base remained determined by a number of factors, including labor force, transportation, market location, and tradition. Heavy industry continued to evolve and change, so that a classic industrial city like Pittsburgh was actually in its smokestack period for only about a century. The era of the classic industrial city, from the 1870s to the 1930s, could be characterized by employment of large numbers of immigrant workers who lived near the factories. Factory owners and other large employers used black laborers as strikebreakers in time of union activity, then kept some on during less abrasive times. Workers usually lived near the factories, and ethnic clusters of housing usually matched ethnic sorting in jobs.

Factory locations quite often were suburban rather than purely urban, so that major clusters of immigrant residences were on the edges of big cities. In Pittsburgh, for instance, the famous steel mills of Homestead were a commuter train ride away from the city center, and workers lived in an adjacent suburban municipality. Pullman, Illinois, the center for the production of Pullman sleeping cars, was a southern suburb of Chicago where factory workers could live in the company-owned housing or in that of the nearby suburb called Roseland. Both were annexed by Chicago in 1889. The city of Los Angeles had industrial suburbs as early as 1890: in several cities in Orange County oil was extracted and processed.

Burgeoning urban and suburban factory employment meant good jobs for European immigrants until congressional immigration restriction,

World War I, and the Great Depression slowed immigration. In Congress, the Dillingham Commission (1907–1911) concluded that the "new" immigrants of the late nineteenth century, central and south Europeans, were a threat to cities. The commission helped to establish restrictions based on quotas established from the 1880 census. In itself, such restrictions would have meant good news for rural African Americans, with the opening up of factory employment in northern cities. But, caught in an unforeseeable twist of events, black migration began as city industries began to slow down and even to decline. The only upturn was the period of World War II, which reopened industrial employment to minorities and women. By the 1950s, the old trends had returned: employment opportunities were no longer in large factories, residence and work drifted apart, and suburban growth accelerated. Major federal policies exacerbated these conditions.

Suburbs The same New Deal reforms which enabled more Americans to buy homes functioned as a counter subsidy to the building of public housing. Consequently, far more money for housing went to the middle class than to the poor. And new housing, given the general preference for living in smaller cities and given the cost of land, was primarily in suburban locations. A series of federal acts to subsidize highways, which began in the early twentieth century, culminated in the 1956 Federal Aid Highway Act, which connected the nation's major cities with freeways and hastened the longer-term trend away from big cities. The actual plan for the interstate system had grown out of the War Plans Division of the Army General Staff, which during World War I had produced the "Pershing Map," showing all roads of prime war importance. Redrawn in 1935, it resulted in a 26,700-mile highway system.

These formal actions worked in concert with a major demographic trend: the baby boom. In the Great Depression, people had put off marrying and beginning families. Families had fewer children. The mobilization of World War II gave employment to millions and reinforced the New Deal's more direct federal responses to dearth. In the postwar era, a combination of economic optimism and catching up on postponed lives resulted in a temporary reversal of a 150-year demographic trend toward smaller families; the average family size doubled, from about two to about four children. This simple private decision, when spread across millions of families, and in the context of massive political policy shifts, resulted in the suburban era of American urban history.

This era permanently changed the shape of American cities. The shape had been latent since the mid nineteenth century, but found its full expression in the postwar years. And in the suddenly larger families, mainly white, now moving to new homes in residential suburbs, even the ideology of the era was affected. The Victorian notion that woman's place was in the home and her role was to be the emotional center of the family could finally, if temporarily, be realized in the new suburbs. Historians insist that this all be appropriately contextualized: "The suburban vision of the early 1950s was less a new expression of the domestic ideal than a feverish—and in the long run unsuccessful—attempt to erase the depression and the war and return to the 1920s" (Margaret Marsh, *Suburban Lives,* p. 185).

Urban Social Problems Seldom have policy, social preference, and private personal behavior smoothly meshed and reinforced one another in American cities. More typically, policy has had only a tiny impact, and social preference has been frustrated. The consequences have sometimes been tragic and the explanations thin. Race riots, for instance, have flared sporadically in American cities for centuries. Prior to World War II, almost all were directed against racial minorities, in particular African Americans. Most have been brutal and ugly. For instance, the burning of the New York Colored Orphan Asylum in the draft riots of 1863 can be accounted for, in part, by the racial hostility toward and economic competition with blacks felt by poor native whites and Irish immigrants. But how can racial hostility adequately explain the attack on an orphanage or the hanging of innocent blacks in response to the draft? Or how can the black riots of the mid 1960s be explained? We can note significant historical evolution—the recent riots focus on the destruction of property, for instance—but from a triggering incident, often a dispute over an arrest, to the enormous outpouring of anger and the equally enormous military or police response, one cannot provide a logical account, only a string of suppositions.

We can, however, note more systematically the consequences of urban riots. In the pre–Civil War era, riots could sometimes achieve specific objectives—the lowering of the price of bread, for instance, in the New York City flour riots of 1837; the control of Catholics by Protestants in the burning of the Ursuline convent in Boston in 1834; or the terrorizing and racial control of blacks in the Civil War draft riots. The destruction caused by the draft riots also ensured that city officials would never again rest easy about mobs. The post–Civil War building of armories, fueled by the particular spark of labor control, was also justified by the fear of a repeat of draft riots.

Race riots in the twentieth century have punctuated urban life at various points loosely related to wartime mobilization. From the antiblack riots during World War I—for instance, the Chicago race riots of 1919 over urban space (housing and jobs)—to the World War II race riots in Detroit and Los Angeles in 1943, fought in the context of competition over housing and federal pressure to integrate the work force, to the black riots of the 1960s, one can see the results in attempts to improve the riot control efforts of the police and the military, some efforts at human relations training and increased minority representation in the police, and a larger social concern with racism. On the other hand, the racial hostility and fear in the aftermath of riots, the physical destruction of poor neighborhoods, population flight, and a dramatic decline in businesses in the riot areas all point to long-lasting and negative impacts.

The scars of urban riots may seem impermanent and the riots sporadic, but the same cannot be said about the fear of crime, an urban issue of concern since the mid nineteenth century. The actual trajectory of crime trends may not have been of as much importance to people's perception as their more immediate impacts. Historians now think that crime dropped in per capita terms from the mid nineteenth century until as late as the 1950s, then reversed and began the climb to recent frightening heights.

This information is more important for what it disconfirms than for what it confirms. It disconfirms the notion that urban growth, in itself alone, has some sort of complex psychological consequences in turning people toward crime. It also suggests that any generalizations about crowding and crime or impoverishment and crime must be made with great caution, for in the late nineteenth century, at the point of greatest urban crowding and poverty, crime rates were declining. The American trends actually followed international trends, albeit at much higher levels, until the late 1950s, when very abrupt upturns sent America on its way toward its current situation.

One can conclude that crime rates are historically variable and are neither caused by some deeper aspect of the city itself nor inherent in any ethnic or racial group, but this conclusion does not alleviate the erosion of social confidence crime has caused. The most prominent indicator of feared crimes is homicide, and New York City is its bellwether. The city's rate of homicides per thousand fell from its historical high in the years between 1857 and 1864 to a low about 1950, then shot up. More worrisome is what appears to be the increasing proportion of killings by strangers: while murder is still largely a crime involving relatives and acquaintances, murders by strangers may be on the rise. The latter acts to prevent many people from using public space with a sense of safety.

Two major historical impacts on twentieth-century urban society have shown cities' sensitivity to larger economic and demographic changes: the Great Depression of the 1930s and the shifting participation of women in the paid work force. As indicated by the population shifts in Figure 1, the Depression caused a unique reversal of urbanization in America; people left cities to return to farms, even though the farm economy was also in crisis. Unemployment leaped from 3.2 percent in 1929 to 25 percent by 1933. Shantytowns called Hoovervilles dotted the urban landscape; thousands of working-class homeowners were unable to pay their property taxes and lost their homes to city governments, which in turn lost the revenues to pay their employees and fund their welfare programs.

Family size in America has been declining since the early nineteenth century, in part as a consequence of urbanization and the tendency of urban families to have fewer children. When families had an average of six children, the at-home mother was unable to seek wage labor for much of her adult life. As average family size declined to four

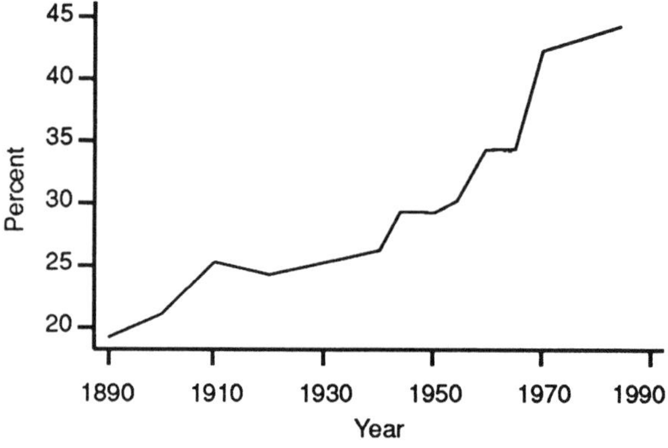

Fig. 5. Percent of adult women employed in wage labor force.

children by the late nineteenth century, married women were more able to seek wage work. Simultaneously, the opportunities for women outside the home increased, enabling more women to work and more women to remain single. World War II accelerated these long-run trends pulling more women into the labor force (see Fig. 5).

CONCLUSION

A series of watersheds occurred in the twentieth century which altered the nature of American cities: the 1920 turning point, when half of the American population lived in towns and cities, changed the character of a nation conceived as agricultural; the Depression of the 1930s interrupted urban growth and permanently destabilized the fiscal security of local government; and World War II and its aftermath, which accelerated the movement of women into the work force and, almost a cross-purpose, accelerated the movement of families out of large cities and into medium-sized ones.

The resulting urban world does not match classic visions of the city, sometimes leaving urban sociologists and geographers at a loss for the language with which to describe it. The low-rise housing, shopping malls, and business parks, the noncenteredness of what Kenneth T. Jackson has called the "Crabgrass Frontier," complicates our traditional wisdom about cities. The variety of the urban landscape does, however, show that the possibilities for urban complexity and diversity continue to expand far beyond the wildest expectations of an earlier generation of observers. The United States will continue to be a nation of cities of surprising, sometimes bewildering, multiplicity.

BIBLIOGRAPHY

General Works and Historiography

Chudacoff, Howard, and Judith E. Smith. *The Evolution of American Urban Society,* 3d ed. (1988).

Conzen, Kathleen, and Michael Ebner, eds. *Modes of City History* (1991).

Miller, Zane. *The Urbanization of Modern America. A Brief History.* 2d ed. (1987).

Monkkonen, Eric H. *America Becomes Urban: The Development of U.S. Cities and Towns* (1988).

Stave, Bruce, ed. *The Making of Urban History: Historiography Through Oral History* (1977).

Trotter, Joe W. "Afro-American Urban History: A Critique of the Literature." In his *Black Milwaukee: The Making of an Industrial Proletariat, 1915–45* (1985).

Weber, Adna F. *The Growth of Cities in the Nineteenth Century: A Study in Statistics* (1899; repr. 1963).

African Americans

Lane, Roger. *William Dorsey's Philadelphia and Ours* (1991).

Lewis, Earl. *In Their Own Interests: Blacks in Twentieth Century Norfolk* (1990).

Nash, Gary. *Forging Freedom: The Formation of Philadelphia's Black Community, 1720–1840* (1988).

Painter, Nell. *Exodusters: Black Migration to Kansas After Reconstruction* (1976).

Trotter, Joe W. *Black Milwaukee: The Making of an Industrial Proletariat, 1915–45* (1985).

Mexican Americans

Camarillo, Albert. *Chicanos in a Changing Society: From Mexican Pueblos to American Barrios in Santa Barbara and Southern California, 1848–1930* (1979).

Rios-Bustamante, Antonio, and Pedro Castillo. *An Illustrated History of Mexican Los Angeles, 1781–1985* (1986).

Suburbs

Binford, Henry. *The First Suburbs: Residential Communities on the Boston Periphery, 1815–1860* (1985).

Fishman, Robert. *Bourgeois Utopias: The Rise and Fall of Suburbia* (1987).

Jackson, Kenneth T. *Crabgrass Frontier: The Suburbanization of the United States* (1985).

Kling, Rob, Spencer Olin, and Mark Poster, eds. *Postsuburban California: The Transformation of Orange County Since World War II* (1990).

Marsh, Margaret. *Suburban Lives* (1990).

Warner, Sam Bass. *Streetcar Suburbs: The Process of Growth in Boston, 1870–1900* (1962).

Intellectual Life

Barth, Gunther. *City People: The Rise of Modern City Culture in Nineteenth-Century America* (1980).

Bender, Thomas. *New York Intellect: A History of Intellectual Life in New York City, from 1750 to the Beginnings of Our Own Time* (1987).

Sharpe, William, and Leonard Wallock, eds. *Visions of the Modern City: Essays in History, Art, and Literature* (1983, 2d ed. 1987).

White, Morton, and Lucia White. *The Intellectual Versus the City: From Thomas Jefferson to Frank Lloyd Wright* (1962).

Women

Berg, Barbara. *The Remembered Gate: Origins of American Feminism. The Woman and the City, 1800–1860* (1978).

Blackwelder, Julia K. *Women of the Depression: Caste and Culture in San Antonio, 1929–1939* (1984).

Stansell, Christine. *City of Women: Sex and Class in New York, 1789–1860* (1986).

Crime, Poverty

Gilje, Paul A. *The Road to Mobocracy: Popular Disorder in New York City, 1763–1834* (1987).

Katz, Michael. *In the Shadow of the Poorhouse: A Social History of Welfare in America* (1986).

Lane, Roger. *Violent Death in the City: Suicide, Accident, and Murder in Nineteenth-Century Philadelphia* (1979).

Monkkonen, Eric H. *Police in Urban America, 1860–1920* (1981).

———, ed. *Walking to Work: Tramps in America, 1790–1935* (1984).

Housing

Blackmar, Elizabeth. *Manhattan for Rent, 1785–1850* (1989).

Clark, Clifford E., Jr. *The American Family Home, 1800–1960* (1986).

Wright, Gwendolyn. *Building the Dream: A Social History of Housing in America* (1981, 1983).

URBANIZATION

Social Structure

Conzen, Kathleen N. *Immigrant Milwaukee, 1836–1860: Accommodation and Community in a Frontier City* (1976).

Doyle, Don. *The Social Order of a Frontier Community: Jacksonville, Illinois, 1825–1870* (1978).

Knights, Peter. *The Plain People of Boston, 1830–1860: A Study in City Growth* (1971).

Teaford, John. *The Unheralded Triumph: City Government in America, 1870–1900* (1984).

Thernstrom, Stephan. *Poverty and Progress: Economic Mobility in a Nineteenth Century City* (1964).

Zunz, Olivier. *The Changing Face of Inequality: Urbanization, Industrial Development, and Immigrants in Detroit, 1880–1920* (1982).

Other Works of Interest

Butler, Jon. *Awash in a Sea of Faith: Christianizing the American People* (1990).

Crouch, Dora P., Daniel J. Garr, and Axel I. Mundigo. *Spanish City Planning in North America* (1982).

Gordon, Linda. *Heroes of Their Own Lives: The Politics and History of Family Violence, 1880–1960* (1988).

Peterson, Jacqueline. "Prelude to Red River: A Social Portrait of the Great Lakes Métis." *Ethnohistory* 25, no. 1 (1978): 41–67.

Tobey, Ronald, Charles Wetherell, and Jay Brigham. "Moving Out and Settling In: Residential Mobility, Home Owning, and the Public Enframing of Citizenship, 1921–1950." *American Historical Review* (1990): 1395–1422.

Wade, Richard. *The Urban Frontier: The Rise of Western Cities, 1790–1930* (1959).

SEE ALSO **The City; Community Studies; The Suburbs.**

IMMIGRATION

David M. Reimers

BRITISH—MOSTLY ENGLISH—were the main settlers and contributors to the white population of colonial America. In the early seventeenth century English outreach included the Puritan experiment in Massachusetts, Roger Williams's Rhode Island (an involuntary offshoot of Massachusetts Bay), the Virginia Company's settlement at Jamestown, and Lord Baltimore's proprietary colony of Maryland. Later in the century English proprietorships were planted in the Carolinas, and English Quakers established the colonies of Pennsylvania, New Jersey, and Delaware.

COLONIAL AND EARLY FEDERAL IMMIGRATION

The Puritans who founded the Massachusetts Bay and Plymouth colonies were motivated by a desire to practice their Calvinist beliefs as they saw fit, but many other English settled in those colonies as well, especially after the end of the great Puritan migration of the 1630s. These later settlers, who came to better their economic position, soon outnumbered the Puritans. By 1700 only a minority belonged to the established Congregationalist churches of New England. In Rhode Island, where no established church existed, religious diversity flourished.

The Virginia Company's colony at Jamestown did not thrive initially as hundreds died during the "starving time." War with the Native Americans and, even more, disease took a toll on the early settlers. Finally, in the 1620s the British government took control of the colony. More efficient management and the development of tobacco culture enabled both Virginia and Maryland to grow and to attract more settlers.

A few of the early immigrants to Virginia, and to the other southern colonies as well, were younger sons of the gentry who came to the New World as soldiers, government officials, adventurers, or even settlers, to seek their fortunes. Yet fully half of seventeenth-century white immigrants to the South arrived as indentured servants. These men and women agreed to serve a term of labor, from four to seven years, in return for passage to the colonies. They had little choice if they wanted to migrate, for most were single and young, with no money to pay for the voyage. The indentured servants provided the labor for early Virginia and Maryland, and for the Carolinas as well.

George Calvert (Lord Baltimore), proprietary founder of Maryland, hoped to make that colony profitable and a haven for Roman Catholics, who were hated by Protestants in Great Britain and in the colonies. Yet Protestant settlers, some from England and some from Virginia, soon dominated there, and an uneasy truce existed between the two religious groups. Like Virginia, Maryland at first turned to English indentured servants for labor, then later to African slaves.

The Carolinas also began as proprietary colonies. The founders were eager for profit, and they, too, employed indentured servants; but slavery quickly became more important, especially in South Carolina. Since their colony was founded after 1660, white Carolinians had the example of slave codes and practices from neighboring and West Indian settlements to draw upon.

The middle colonies had a well-earned reputation for cultural diversity, and no colony or town was so racially and ethnically mixed as New Amsterdam, founded by the Dutch in 1625. The Netherlands permitted so many non-Dutch to settle because few of their own countrymen desired to leave Holland; only a few thousand went to America during the entire colonial era. Thus the Dutch West India Company recruited settlers from a number of European countries and transported African slaves. As early as 1643, a French Jesuit priest visiting New Amsterdam, then a town of only a few hundred inhabitants, claimed to have heard eighteen different languages spoken. While Father Isaac Jogues may have exaggerated, the city claimed Dutch, Sephardic Jews, French-speaking Walloons, English, Germans, Spanish, French, and African slaves, among others; thus, in spite of its Dutch appearance, it was truly diverse. In 1655 the Dutch added Swedish immigrants to their empire when they conquered the small New Sweden colony on the Delaware River. After the British seized New Amsterdam and renamed it New York in 1664, the city retained its remarkable mix of peoples.

The Quaker colonies in Pennsylvania and New Jersey attracted many non-English, largely because of religious toleration and the availability of cheap or free land. William Penn believed in religious toleration, and he was also eager for settlers to develop his colony economically. Of course the majority of the first settlers were Quakers, both English and Welsh, but members of the Society of Friends soon became a minority in their own colony.

Although a few Germans had emigrated in the early seventeenth century, their appearance in the New World is often traced to 1683, when thirteen religious dissenting Quaker and Mennonite families were lured by Penn to settle in Pennsylvania. Few Germans followed them at first, although Swiss Mennonites and Westphalian Dunkards—both radical, dissenting Protestant groups—also went to Pennsylvania. That colony proved to be a particularly congenial home to other dissenting German-speaking Protestants, but the great German migrations occurred in the eighteenth century.

Europeans were already bringing African slaves to the Western Hemisphere when the first boatload of Africans docked in British North America in 1619. These passengers were probably treated as indentured servants; and they, as well as other early African immigrants, received their freedom after a term of servitude. However, slavery had taken root even before Virginia and Maryland enacted the first slave codes in the 1660s. As health conditions improved, and as the plantation system for tobacco, rice, and indigo developed in the southern colonies, the economic value of slave labor was enhanced. Indentured servants supplied the bulk of workers until the end of the seventeenth century; then slavery became increasingly important, and the slave trade flourished.

The vast bulk of slaves were not brought into the southern American colonies but, rather, to the West Indies and Latin America. Yet imports of Africans to America increased after the 1680s, as slavery became important and slave codes became increasingly severe. About four hundred thousand slaves arrived in British North America during the seventeenth and eighteenth centuries, mostly in the southern colonies. With better health conditions, the slave population increased naturally, and by the time of the American Revolution, most African Americans had been born in the United States, not imported from Africa or the West Indies. Virginia had the largest number of slaves, followed by South Carolina and Maryland. African Americans, the vast majority of whom were slaves, constituted about 40 percent of the South's population, and 20 percent of the colonial total, by the 1770s.

At the end of the seventeenth century what became the United States claimed only two hundred thousand European and African settlers, plus an unknown number of Native Americans. The bulk of the colonists were English people who lived along the Atlantic coast. Yet important foundations for economic development had been laid by then, and immigrants were needed to achieve the goals that had been set. By 1700 the English were no longer so eager to seek economic opportunities abroad. Moreover, a change occurred in British government attitudes regarding migration. During the seventeenth century the British had feared overpopulation and had encouraged emigration to the New World, but by the end of the century British officials no longer believed that England had a surplus of people; hence they looked elsewhere for settlers to develop their North American colonies. Fortunately for the mother country, changes in the economies of northern Ireland and Germany prompted several hundred thousand persons to emigrate to America.

The largest group to enter the United States in the eighteenth century were people from northern Ireland (Ulster), later called Scotch-Irish (during the colonial period, they were usually called Irish). Originally from the Scottish Lowlands, they had settled in Ulster after 1600, encouraged by the English in order to plant a Protestant presence in Catholic Ireland. For several generations these Scots, who belonged to Presbyterian churches, farmed land obtained from the English. Conditions soured after 1717: periodic crop failures, rising rents, a failing linen industry, and religious conflict prompted a migration of over two hundred thousand Scotch-Irish over a sixty-year period.

The Scotch-Irish, who frequently came as indentured servants, mostly landed at Philadelphia, the colonies' main port for immigrants. From there they fanned out into the backcountry of Pennsylvania and down into Maryland, Virginia, and the Carolinas. They were known as devout Presbyterians, frontier farmers, and independent people. As English speakers and Protestants, they usually assimilated rapidly in the New World. Later generations often became Baptists or Methodists and lost much of their distinctive Ulster culture.

Next to the Scotch-Irish in numbers, and the largest non-British group to arrive in the eighteenth century, were immigrants from the western German states. Coming largely as families, they included dissenters such as the Mennonites, Schwenkfelders, and Moravians who settled in Pennsylvania and later became known as the "Pennsylvania Dutch." However, most eighteenth-century German immigrants were from establishment churches, Reformed or Lutheran. The initial German immigrants had sent word home of opportunities in America, and Pennsylvania's "newlanders," agents who scoured the German countryside for prospective migrants, provided additional—and exaggerated—information about the wonders of America.

One early German colony was located along the Hudson River around Newburgh and Rhinebeck, New York. Established as part of a scheme to develop naval stores, the project failed in 1712, and most of the Palatine Germans who had settled there moved on to Pennsylvania; only a few remained in New York. Because they lacked funds or were very poor, many Germans came as redemptioners, a form of indentured servitude. Like the Scotch-Irish, some Germans poured southward from Pennsylvania into the backcountry of the southern colonies.

Ulster Irish and Germans made up the largest groups to arrive in the eighteenth century, but they were by no means the only newcomers. Catholic Irish arrived, too, along with a few Jews who joined the first Jewish settlement that had been established at New Amsterdam in 1654. Other Jews settled in Charleston, Newport, and Philadelphia; they numbered between two thousand and three thousand by the time of the American Revolution.

Numerous, but considerably fewer than the Scotch-Irish and the Germans, were Scots and French Huguenots. Scots had arrived in the seventeenth century, some deported as religious dissenters and political radicals by the British government. Two Scottish groups tried to establish somewhat independent colonies in East New Jersey and southern Carolina; and although these attempts failed, many Scots still lived in those states. Those coming in the eighteenth century did so voluntarily (including some as indentured servants); the peak of their migration occurred after 1763, when about twenty-five thousand arrived in America. A good number of the Scots coming in the 1770s, as well as other British immigrants, were young, skilled male workers who had heard about labor shortages abroad. Scots included both Lowlanders and the more clannish Highlanders. These mostly Presbyterian immigrants located in New York and the Carolinas. A few of the Lowlanders became prominent merchants in colonial ports. During the American Revolution many Scots remained loyal to Great Britain; several thousand returned to England or went to Canada when the colonies won their independence.

French Huguenots, perhaps the last group to come in any numbers during the colonial era, totaled only a few thousand. These Protestants were escaping religious persecution in France and seeking religious toleration and economic opportunity. They settled in New York, South Carolina, and Massachusetts. A good many had skills that they plied in labor-short colonial America, and others became merchants. Although they founded French-speaking churches in cities like New York and Charleston, they assimilated rapidly as they prospered economically. They quickly lost much of their French heritage, spoke English, joined Anglican congregations, and married English colonists.

During the colonial era the voyage to America was particularly difficult. Crowded ships, poor quality of food, sickness, and long days and nights on sailing vessels made the immigrants eager to reach the New World. Trips could last six weeks or more and could be disastrous if an epidemic struck. There are cases on record in the eighteenth century when over half of the passengers died en route. Indeed, as many lives were lost on voyages of the immigrant trade as were lost on ships carrying slaves from Africa to the Western Hemisphere, and slave ships were notorious for their loss of lives.

By the end of the colonial era a distinctive ethnic mosaic had emerged. The New England colonies were overwhelmingly English with a few Scots, Scotch-Irish, and Huguenots. In the South the English also predominated among the Tidewater's white population; Scotch-Irish, Scots, and Germans were more noticeable in the backcountry. African slaves were concentrated in the Tidewater coastal areas. The middle colonies were the most diverse.

New York City especially contained many peoples; and significant numbers of Germans, Scotch-Irish, Welsh, Scots, and Dutch, and smaller numbers of blacks—along with the English—lived in Pennsylvania and New Jersey.

Immigrants were crucial for the economic development of colonial America, and colonial promoters actively recruited European and African laborers. However, the colonists were not happy when, in the eighteenth century, the British sent fifty thousand convicts to America for terms of seven to fourteen years. When colonial assemblies tried to halt this migration, the British government overruled them.

The arrival of so many different peoples led to social and religious conflict. Catholics were detested and feared nearly everywhere, and not until after the American Revolution did they win the right to worship as they pleased and receive full civil rights. The same was true for Jews, though in some states they did not obtain the ballot until well into the nineteenth century. As for Protestants, the established churches lost their privileges during and after the American Revolution and the nation moved toward a growing toleration of religious diversity, based on the principle that churches were voluntary and should not be supported by the state.

Not all conflict was religious. Some colonial Americans believed that Scots were too clannish, and when many remained loyal to England during the American Revolution, they earned further animosity. Of the non-English groups, Germans aroused the most anxiety, especially in Pennsylvania. Alarmed by growing German immigration, Benjamin Franklin, for example, asked, "Why should *Pennsylvania,* founded by the *English,* become a Colony of *Aliens,* who will shortly be so numerous as to Germanize us instead of our Anglifying them?" (Dinnerstein and Reimers, *Ethnic Americans,* p. 7). To "anglify" the Germans, English leaders set up a number of English-language schools in Pennsylvania, but they quickly foundered and the last one closed in 1763.

Despite such conflicts the new nation remained generally tolerant toward immigrants, and the Constitution contained no clauses restricting immigration. The United States did not even begin to count newcomers until 1819. During the first decade of the new nation's history, conflict developed over immigration and the relation of immigrants to foreign affairs, but it proved to be short-lived. Federalists did not like Irish and some French immigrants because they considered these newcomers too anti-English, while the Republicans believed that aristocrats fleeing the French Revolution harbored monarchist principles. As a result, Congress increased the naturalization period for aliens from five to fourteen years, and in 1798 passed, for a two-year period, the Alien and Sedition Acts, which curbed free speech and gave the president the right to deport allegedly dangerous foreigners. As the crisis in foreign affairs eased in 1800, these laws were not renewed and Congress again set the naturalization period (for whites only) at five years, where it has remained ever since.

Citizens of the new United States felt secure with their rising nationalism. Taking their cues from England, they modeled much in their government and laws after Great Britain, and English was clearly the dominant language among descendants of Europeans and Africans. Indeed, as immigration from Germany and the Netherlands amounted to only a trickle between 1789 and the 1820s, and the Dutch and German languages began to die among descendants of those two groups, Americans did not see the need for an official language. It was assumed that English was the nation's language and that much of American society would be Anglo in culture. The mass immigration after the 1830s began to change American culture and in turn to create new anxieties and conflict about the meaning of Americanism.

THE OLD IMMIGRATION

While immigration remained low during the Napoleonic Wars, it gradually increased between 1815 and 1830. Most of the newcomers were from Great Britain and did not seem particularly threatening. They included English, Scotch-Irish, and a growing number of Catholic Irish. After the 1830s immigration grew rapidly. In the 1830s almost six hundred thousand arrived in America, and between 1840 and the outbreak of the Civil War, over 4.5 million. The Civil War disrupted the flow; but, varying with economic conditions here and in Europe, the mass movement of Europeans began again after the end of the war. During the 1880s immigration exceeded 5 million, the highest total of any decade in American history until that time.

This mass immigration, often called the "old immigration," was dominated by Ireland and Germany. The largest group after the 1850s was the Germans, who were driven to the New World by poor economic conditions in their homeland and word of a better life in America. Like so many other old immigrants, Germans settled primarily in the Northeast and the Old Northwest (the present-day Midwest); the South (except Texas, New Orleans, and Baltimore) attracted only a few immigrants. In the Midwest, Ohio, Illinois, Wisconsin, Minnesota, Missouri, and Michigan became centers of German settlement. Germans were drawn to areas where other Germans had gone before them, where they could find employment and familiar institutions. The availability of free or cheap land was also an attraction.

Some Germans came as individuals, others as families. A few settled as groups and talked of building a New Germany in the United States. These efforts at state building failed, but nearly all-German-speaking towns, like Herman, Missouri, resulted from such planning.

In addition to dominating some rural regions and small towns, Germans quickly became the largest ethnic group in many American cities, sections of which became known as *Kleindeutschlands*. *Kleindeutschland* boasted German-speaking Lutheran churches, German newspapers, beer gardens, and a host of organizations appealing to the immigrants. German Catholics objected to the Irish control of the Roman Catholic church, and they insisted upon German-speaking priests in parishes where they predominated. Although the church officially frowned on such ethnic divisions, Germans were able to have their own priests in many cases.

The Irish were next to Germans in numbers and impact. Irish immigration to the United States was growing between 1820 and the 1840s, and no group was so destitute as the famine Irish, those refugees from the devastating failure of the all-important potato crop during the 1840s and 1850s. An estimated one million Irish starved when this vital crop, virtually the sole source of food, rotted in the ground; over one million Irish came to America. Although conditions improved after the "Great Hunger," Irish migration to America continued to be heavy until the early twentieth century.

Irish newcomers settled in the port cities of Boston, Philadelphia, and New York, then fanned out along the canal and railroad routes west, mostly to cities; few became farmers. The largely unskilled Irish faced considerable discrimination in finding employment as signs proclaiming "No Irish Need Apply" became common. Hence, they generally took the lowest-paying laboring jobs available; it took years and generations for Irish immigrants to move up the economic ladder. Of the major immigrant groups coming before the 1930s, only among the Irish were a majority women. Like the men, they were fleeing desperate poverty. In America single Irish women became domestic servants.

Like the Germans, Irish Americans had their own ethnic organizations and culture; in addition they dominated the Roman Catholic church. Because they knew English and arrived when universal white male suffrage was being adopted by most states, the Irish quickly moved into urban politics. By the late nineteenth century, Irish mayors and political machines were commonplace in cities like Boston and New York.

Others besides the Irish came to America from the British Isles in search of a better life. Because they knew English, were mostly Protestant, and often possessed skills needed in the growing industrial nation, the English, Scots, Welsh, Scotch-Irish, and Cornish had an easier time adjusting to a new country.

Scandinavians accounted for another large northwestern European group to arrive in the nineteenth century. A Norwegian community established in Kendall, New York, in 1825 is regarded as the first nineteenth-century Scandinavian settlement; it was followed by pioneering Swedish and Danish communities. The Scandinavian immigrants, not numerous before 1865, usually consisted of families and groups. In the late nineteenth century the number began to grow, and became a flood between 1880 and 1910. The center of Scandinavian settlement was in the upper Middle West: Minnesota, Illinois, Wisconsin, Iowa, and Michigan. When crops were good and land was available, Scandinavians stayed home; when otherwise, they left for America. Some Norwegian immigrants had been sailors who found better jobs in American ports. Although the bulk were farmers and many farmed in America, important Norwegian and Swedish communities also existed in cities like Chicago, which contained flourishing Scandinavian institutions.

A few of the first immigrants from Norway and Sweden were drawn by religious freedom and their distaste for the established Lutheran church at home, which they considered to be cold and indifferent to members' spiritual needs. A significant number of Scandinavians, principally Danes, had been converted by Mormon missionaries; they headed for the Mormon Zion in Utah. Scandinavians were often lured by an "American fever," triggered by letters of those who had already gone to the New World. These letters often contained tickets or money to purchase passage to the United States.

The first Asian immigrants appeared in the nineteenth century. Attracted by the discovery of gold in California in 1848, thousands of Chinese men crossed the Pacific on a miserable, weeks-long voyage to find their fortunes in American gold mines. Few did so, although many worked in the mining regions of the West before finding employment building the transcontinental railroads. Most eventually found their way to cities like San Francisco, and a few went east to found New York City's Chinatown.

Total Chinese immigration to the United States was not large, but in the early years Chinese workers were an important part of California's work force. Although some of the men were married, few brought their wives with them, and they lived in "bachelor societies" in the nation's Chinatowns. After the United States government banned virtually all Chinese immigration, including workers' wives, beginning in 1882, many returned to China. The Chinese population of the United States subsequently fell from over one hundred thousand in 1890 to under eighty thousand by 1940.

In the 1840s the United States acquired its first significant Mexican population when it annexed Texas (1845) and the Southwest (1848), including California, as part of the spoils of the Mexican War. Some seventy-five thousand Mexican citizens in the Southwest found themselves Americans. Most lived in what is now New Mexico and Arizona, where, because of their isolation and, later, new immigrants from Mexico, they maintained their Hispanic culture for generations. The early territorial legislatures of New Mexico conducted their business in Spanish but translated official documents into English. In 1892 a congressional committee counted 143 English-only schools in the territory, 92 bilingual ones, and 106 that held classes exclusively in Spanish. The state's schools and political affairs remained bilingual well into the twentieth century. Mexicans in California were overwhelmed by droves of fortune hunters searching for gold; as a result Mexican culture was less pervasive. Along the Rio Grande separating Texas and Mexico, isolated Mexican communities lived within their own culture, largely removed from the rest of the nation.

From its northern neighbor the United States also received immigrants. In the nineteenth century these were mostly French-Canadians. Facing poor economic conditions at home, French-Canadian farmers traveled south to find jobs in New England textile mills. They formed tightly knit French-speaking communities focused on family, mill, and church life. Like the German Roman Catholics, they resented Irish priests and battled to have French-speaking ones. Their communities received the constant reinforcement of new immigrants. In 1890 the census recorded 224,483 foreign-born French-Canadians, and in 1920, 545,643.

No matter where they settled, the immigrants had an enormous impact upon American society. Their labor was needed to build railroads, canals, and cities. It was also required for the mills, mines, farms, and factories. Yet as crucial as the economic impact was, no less was the social one. By the late nineteenth century, northern cities contained whole neighborhoods of immigrants in which their cultures flourished; in cities like New York, Chicago, and Boston, immigrants and their children were a majority. The foreign-language press, for example, boomed as thousands of monthly, weekly, and daily journals and papers were published. Some schools in Wisconsin and Ohio were conducted in foreign languages, particularly German. In the 1890s Wisconsin legislators enacted a law requiring all public and private schools to be conducted in English. So great was the public outcry that the law was quickly repealed and politicians linked to it were defeated in the next election. Not until World War I were German schools and German-language instruction suppressed. In local politics, the rise of ethnic politicians, chiefly among the urban Irish, helped to fashion a new style of political life.

The presence of so many newcomers alarmed native-born Americans who believed that they brought alien values, European poverty, and, above all, Roman Catholicism to the United States. Germans were considered too clannish, and their opposition to closing taverns on the Sabbath was criticized. The Chinese were regarded as racially inferior heathens who lowered the American standard of living and would never assimilate. Mexicans were seen as lazy and inferior. But of the Europeans, the Irish—because of their large numbers, their movement into politics, their poverty, and especially their Catholicism—were hated most. Conflicts between native Americans and Irish immigrants erupted into violence on more than one occasion and prompted calls to stem their immigration. To the nativists, those wanting restriction of immigration, Catholicism was un-American and a distinct threat to the future of the nation. The Know-Nothing movement of the 1840s and 1850s, politicized as the American party, expressed this hostility toward the Irish and vowed to lengthen the period required for aliens to become citizens.

Yet during the nineteenth century labor was in constant demand, and the immigrants supplied it. They also supplied the Union army with thousands of soldiers during the Civil War. Moreover, many old stock Americans considered their land to be a beacon of freedom. As a result, proposals to limit immigration failed in the nineteenth century, except for the Chinese, who fell victim to violent racism. The Chinese Exclusion Act, passed in 1882 and extended after that, barred virtually all future Chinese immigration. Other restricted persons included prostitutes, imbeciles, those likely to become a public charge, and those with contagious diseases. But these bans kept out few people, and immigration reached new heights after 1900. The federal government finally did assume responsibility for immigration and established Castle Garden, at the foot of Manhattan, as the main receiving station. In the 1890s a new center, Ellis Island, opened and became the gateway for almost three-fourths of all immigrants until it closed in 1954.

THE NEW IMMIGRATION

In the late nineteenth century a new pattern of immigration emerged. Although persons from eastern Europe and the Mediterranean had been coming to America before 1890, after that year their numbers grew substantially. By 1896 a majority of immigrants were from southern and eastern Europe, the so-called new immigrants, and they continued to dominate the statistics until Congress drastically limited immigration in the 1920s. In addition, although few Chinese entered after 1882, other Asians began to immigrate to the United States—most of them Japanese but also a few Asian Indians, Koreans, and, after 1910, Filipinos. Finally, Mexicans headed north in growing numbers after the Mexican Revolution of 1910.

The numbers of newcomers grew in the early twentieth century. In five different years between 1900 and World War I immigration topped one million, with 1907 being the peak year. Overall, about twenty-five million immigrants entered the United States between the late 1880s and the 1920s, making the era the greatest period of immigration in the nation's history.

This massive movement of people was largely the product of economic upheaval. The industrial changes that had begun in western Europe moved eastward from Germany into the Austro-Hungarian Empire and Russia. The changes included shifts in landholding, leaving millions of persons with smallholdings or without land. Many peasants had supplemented their incomes with home industries, but as those industries were taken over by factories, they found little alternative to migration. At first many headed for nearby cities in search of work, but ultimately they decided to go to America.

Industrial development was slow in coming to Italy, but in the southern part of that country, traditionally poor economic conditions were aggravated by tariff wars and economic slumps. As a result, millions of Italians left for the United States or Latin America.

For Jews, religious persecution in Russia triggered emigration. Pogroms, beginning in the 1880s, terrorized Jewish villages, and growing civil restrictions severely curtailed the opportunities available to Jews. To them America, with its tradition of religious toleration, beckoned. And Jews were not the only persecuted minorities. Armenians and Syrians also lived under foreign domination and looked to American toleration as salvation.

The millions of eastern and southern Europeans who migrated in search of a better life were aided by expanding railroad connections to port cities and by improved ocean transport. The coming of the steamship made possible transatlantic travel in a week or so at a low cost. Indeed, steamship lines in western Europe actively recruited immigrants; several even offered kosher food for their Jewish passengers. As before, the letters from those who had already gone frequently contained prepaid steamship tickets.

By the late nineteenth century, the voyage from European ports in France, the Netherlands, and Great Britain to America had vastly improved. The famine Irish, coming in the 1840s and 1850s, had suffered as much as many coming during the colonial era when sailing conditions were especially harsh. But as the century drew to an end, steam vessels replaced sailing craft, and they were not only much faster and cheaper, but they were also much healthier. Some immigrants still feared the trip itself, but more worried about whether they would get past American immigration officials, usually at Ellis Island, which became the main gateway to America in the 1890s.

While often not well educated, these newest immigrants were by no means the poorest citizens of their native lands. Most were young, single males. Among Italians 78 percent were male, and among Greeks the figure was 90 percent. Jews, however, usually came as families. Often the young men worked for a while, earned and saved some money, and then returned home to purchase land or go into business. Government statistics reveal that among immigrants arriving after 1908, about one-third returned home. The rates varied; some Balkan people returned home at a rate of almost 90 percent, but only 5 percent of the Jews did. Some immigrants made several trips to America before bringing their families and settling in the New World.

Italians, numbering almost five million between 1880 and 1930, were the most numerous nationality among the new immigrants. The first Italians to arrive were better educated than later arrivals and came from northern Italy; later, poverty drove a deluge of southern Italians, including many from Sicily, to seek transportation from Naples to America. At first they mostly congregated in the northeastern United States, locating in cities where Italian communities existed. Having few skills, little education, and no knowledge of English, they usually took unskilled laboring jobs, building subways, railroads, and urban buildings. They were also prominent in the New York garment industry.

Next to Italians in numbers were several million Jews who came from Russia, Poland, and Romania. The center of Jewish immigration was New York City, with its rapidly growing garment industry, the employer of both men and women.

Slavic groups from several lands outnumbered Jews. Among them were Russians, Ukrainians, Slovaks, Poles, Croatians, Serbs, Slovenes, and Bulgarians. They had distinct cultures and languages. In America they sought out their particular group or a Slavic enclave.

The great migration also included significant numbers of Greeks, Portuguese, Magyars (from Hungary), Czechs, and Armenians. Precise figures are lacking because groups like the Armenians, who were fleeing intense Turkish persecution, did not have their own countries. The first large numbers of people from the Middle East appeared after 1880, as Syrian Lebanese migrated from the Turkish Empire.

All of these people sought out their compatriots in American cities, where they could find help securing jobs and housing. The largest immigrant communities were found in the North and the West; the South attracted relatively few. In the case of Italians and Greeks, labor agents, the padrones, found employment for young men in return for a part of their wages. English-speaking padrones knew the American ways and could find jobs, write letters, and arrange for others to migrate. The padrones were considered exploiters who engaged in illegal labor contracting. By 1910 their influence had declined.

In the 1880s, Japan loosened emigration restrictions and Japanese immigrants, along with several thousand immigrants from Korea, came to work on Hawaiian plantations and on the West Coast. Again, these were mostly young, single men. In 1907–1908 the United States and Japan agreed to cooperate in curtailing further immigration of Japanese laborers. However, women were exempt until the 1920s, and Japanese men sent for their wives—often "picture brides" whom they had never seen or met. Between 1917 and 1924 Congress ended practically all Asian immigration. Because the Philippines was an American possession obtained as a result of the Spanish-American War, Filipinos were exempt; as a result thousands of Filipino men migrated to work as agricultural laborers. Legislation in the 1930s virtually ended this migration.

Revolutionary upheavals in Mexico beginning in 1910, along with intensive agricultural development in the American Southwest, prompted thousands of Mexicans to head north. And why not, with wages in the United States several times higher than in Mexico? The federal government did not keep statistics on Mexican immigration before 1908, and not until 1924 did it establish a patrol along the United States–Mexico border. Even then the patrol worried primarily about illegal liquor entering the United States or Asians trying to avoid immigration bans rather than about Mexicans. Thus during the 1920s, Mexicans, in order to avoid a literacy test and a head tax, slipped illegally into the United States. While over seven hundred thousand Mexicans were recorded as entering the United States between 1900 and 1930, the actual figure was probably twice that.

Most new immigrants, like the Italian laborers and Jewish garment workers, started at the bottom of the job ladder. By the time they arrived, many of the older immigrants had moved up to become foremen. Under them Slavs could be found in unskilled jobs in the steel mills, meat packing, and other heavy industry. The mines also beckoned to Slavs and Italians, who joined earlier waves of

Welsh, Irish, and English. Armenians and Portuguese worked in factories, and some Italians and Armenians went into agriculture.

Yet immigrants did cluster in particular industries. Young Greeks worked as bootblacks and opened small businesses. They peddled fruit and ran flower shops, candy stores, ice cream parlors, and restaurants. The center of settlement for the first immigrants from the Middle East, usually Eastern rite Christians, was New York City. From there they branched out and peddled goods across the United States. As a result Arab-speaking communities based on peddling and small stores could be found in Michigan, Illinois, and even on the West Coast.

As Southwest agriculturalists irrigated thousands of acres of land, they recruited Mexicans to pick the crops; these migratory laborers moved from farm to farm as the crops ripened. They also found work on the railroads, replacing European immigrants whose numbers fell as immigration restriction acts were passed in the 1920s. A few even moved to cities like Chicago and Kansas City to find industrial jobs.

Beginning with so little and facing a considerable amount of prejudice, many immigrants found life hard in the United States. They were jammed into foul-smelling tenements or apartments, sometimes sleeping four or five to a room. To help pay the rent, many immigrants took in boarders, usually their own countrymen and often relatives—thus making their living quarters even more crowded. Immigrants also worked at home, making paper flowers, wrapping cigars, or sewing garments. While cigar making at home might add to family incomes, this economic activity made apartments very unhealthy. Under such conditions, disease or poor health was common. Also common were industrial accidents that crippled many breadwinners and forced families into dire poverty. Before 1910 not all states offered workmen's compensation assistance; thus serious injury (as well as economic depression) was particularly hard on some immigrant families and workers.

Gradually many, but by no means all, immigrants improved their lot. Their progress was usually modest, with the worker moving from an unskilled job to a skilled one. Rags-to-riches sagas, such as that of Scot-born Andrew Carnegie, were rare. The goal of many was to own a home. By persistence on the job, or with help from children who went to work at an early age, immigrant families accumulated enough funds for a modest home. This success was hardly the gold in the streets that some had heard of before leaving for America, but compared with conditions at home, their lives seemed better.

Some new immigrants turned to trade unionism or politics to address their needs. Older craft unions, largely dominated by Germans and Irish, paid little attention to the problems of the unskilled laborers, and the mass industry employers managed to keep unions weak and ineffectual. A sharp increase in unionization during World War I raised hopes, but the loss of the U.S. Steel strike in 1919 set back unionization in steel. Not until the 1930s were the mass industries like steel, automobiles, and rubber successfully organized.

Yet in some industries immigrants won monetary gains, better working conditions, and even union recognition. The International Ladies' Garment Workers Union and the Amalgamated Clothing Workers represented Italian and Jewish garment workers, and in major strikes called in Chicago and New York City after 1910, they won the right to bargain with their employers.

Not satisfied with the opportunities provided by union activity, a few immigrants turned to politics. Of course, the urban machines solicited immigrants' votes, and in return helped them find jobs and housing. And for a few immigrants city jobs were possible. But government jobs were largely controlled by earlier immigrant groups and their descendants. The Irish, for example, furnished most of the police and firemen for many northern cities, and Irish women staffed the schools. By the 1920s, however, in New York City, Jews began to move into the school system, though not without conflicts with the Irish educators. After World War II, Jews, Italians, Greeks, Poles, and others really began to move up in American politics.

Many immigrants were not satisfied with the social and political agenda of mainline political parties, and they turned to radicalism. The Lower East Side of New York City was a center of Jewish socialism. Many Jews knew of socialist ideas before migrating to America. In New York, working conditions compelled them to look for radical solutions. They elected the first socialist sent to the United States Congress. Finnish socialists were no less active in the mining regions of Minnesota, where working conditions were poor, and Milwaukee Germans supported an active socialist party. Socialists did elect many local officials. Nevertheless, socialism, which peaked between 1910 and 1920, never attracted many Americans, native born or alien. Nor did the communists, who organized after the Russian Revolution. Radical groups published newspapers and handbills in many foreign languages, but they failed to attract the mass of the new immigrants.

Like the old immigrants, the newest Americans created and patronized their own ethnic institutions and organizations. Some, like the Polish National Alliance (founded 1880), were nationwide in scope, while others remained local. Some immigrants set up schools to instruct their children in their culture, instill pride in their homeland, or teach their native language. Literally hundreds of foreign-language newspapers and journals were sold on the streets of American cities, especially in the neighborhoods where the immigrants clustered. The foreign-language press informed readers of events at home and also instructed them on how to become Americans. Events at home were especially watched by those, like Armenians and Slavs, who lacked their own country. They followed World War I carefully, and many were pleased by the disintegration of the Austro-Hungarian Empire after the war.

Around 1915 German immigrants produced the largest number of foreign-language newspapers and magazines, but by then Jews had started over 150 newspapers, magazines, and yearbooks in Yiddish. The most famous Yiddish paper was Abraham Cahan's *The Forward,* which did not cease publishing daily in Yiddish until the 1980s. Immigrants also produced plays and pageants and wrote books, poetry, and novels about their experiences. The Yiddish theater of New York City's Lower East Side was famous for its actors and actresses. A generation of performers who later achieved fame on radio, on television, and in Hollywood got their start in vaudeville.

German Jews, who had arrived with little money between 1830 and the 1880s, had achieved middle-class status by the latter date, and some had become prominent bankers and department store owners. They looked with dismay at the incoming eastern European Jews with their Orthodox ways and foreign tongues. The *Hebrew Standard* put it thus in 1894: "The thoroughly acclimated American Jew . . . has no religious, social or intellectual sympathies with the Eastern European Jew. He is closer to the Christian sentiment around him than to the Judaism of these miserable darkened Hebrews" (Dinnerstein and Reimers, *Ethnic Americans,* p. 41). Yet the German Jews rallied to aid their eastern European co-religionists and established institutions to assist in their adjustment. They also founded the American Jewish Committee to fight anti-Semitism and prejudice generally.

Italians did not organize groups to fight the bigotry encountered by the new immigrants. But they did organize many local clubs based on their communities at home. Indeed, many did not think of themselves as Italians first but, rather, as coming from a particular province or town. The vast majority of Italians were Roman Catholics, but many, especially the men, did not attend church in Italy and brought an anticlerical tradition with them to America. The fact that the church in America was Irish-dominated did not help. For Italians, a *festa* (feast day) for a particular saint or the Madonna was important. An Italian *festa,* such as that of the Madonna of 115th Street in New York City, was a major community event.

Perhaps no organizations were as important as the many fraternal orders and the immigrant churches. Fraternal clubs flourished in the immigrant neighborhoods. They were a familiar place to gather for social life, and they sometimes helped needy immigrants by giving comfort to the sick and unemployed, and paying health and funeral benefits.

For many southern and eastern European immigrants the church was a central part of their life. For Greeks it was the Greek Orthodox church, and for Arabs it was Melchite, Maronite, and Orthodox churches, with masses conducted in either Arabic or Syriac. Poles, among others, were intensely devoted to the Roman Catholic church. Like other Catholic new immigrants, they preferred their own priests, not Irish ones. The controversy generated over nationality parishes plagued Catholic authorities for decades, and in some cases led to schisms; in 1904, for example, a group of Poles formed the Polish National Catholic church.

Americans wanted the labor of the new immigrants, but the growth of so many new ethnic neighborhoods, the spread of so many Catholic parishes and Jewish congregations, the violence and turmoil of clashes between capital and labor, and the corruption of some urban political machines made them uneasy. Some old-stock Americans founded settlement houses to help the newcomers adjust to American society and to learn about American culture. Jane Addams's Hull House in Chicago, along with hundreds of other settlement houses, reached out to many immigrants, but the numbers arriving seemed to be overwhelming.

Others urged that the schools Americanize the immigrants. For adults, this meant night classes in English and instruction about American history and government. For children, public schools were to teach them to speak English and to make good citizens out of them. Yet many immigrants, such as Italians and Poles, distrusted the public schools as cultural rivals. Moreover, families needed the income that their children brought in when they went to work. As a result, immigrant children usually dropped out at an early age; before World War I, only a small minority completed high school.

On the other hand, immigrants like Jews and Japanese favored education, and they urged their children to attend school and excel there. In California a high percentage of second generation (nisei) Japanese youth completed high school and attended college. In New York City, by 1915, Jews made up 85 percent of the city's free City College and a growing proportion of the students at New York and Columbia universities. However, most college-age Jews were not attending universities but were working.

Whether the children attended school for many years or few, they quickly learned English and took on American ways learned from books and the movies, and in the workplace. Only a minority of the second generation understood the language of their parents, and fewer still could speak it.

While some attempted to Americanize the immigrants and their children, others, fearful of what they perceived to be an alien influence on American values, turned to immigration restriction as a way to check the tide of foreigners. In the late nineteenth century, however, aside from the Chinese Exclusion Acts, only minor restrictions were enacted by Congress. From 1900 to 1917 further restrictions on Asians were put into effect along with a literacy test, a head tax, and the exclusion of anarchists.

These measures had little impact on the flow of Europeans to the United States, although World War I temporarily disrupted immigration (only 110,000 entered in 1918). The war also aroused fears about "hyphenated" Americans with double loyalties. Germans in particular were singled out for suspicion of possible divided allegiance, and German culture came under severe attack during and immediately after the war. German individuals were harassed, and the teaching of the German language was banned in many schools. German newspapers ceased publishing or began to publish in English.

Immigration grew to over eight hundred thousand right after the war, arousing new fears of a horde threatening America. Workers worried that immigrants might take their jobs, and businessmen feared that immigrants would bring radical ideas to America. Some old-stock Americans, who joined a revived Ku Klux Klan, believed that Roman Catholics were a menace. By the 1920s a consensus emerged in Congress to curtail immigration drastically. Moreover, the legislators decided to reserve the largest share of entry permits for northern and western Europeans.

After passing several stopgap measures, Congress passed the national origins system, which went into effect in 1929. Asians were practically barred, and approximately 150,000 persons were to be admitted annually from the rest of the Eastern Hemisphere. Each nation was to be given a share of this total based on its proportion of America's white population in 1920. A commission decided that Germans, Irish, and British represented about two-thirds of the American population; hence Great Britain, Germany, and Ireland were granted two-thirds of the total. Italy, which had sent as many as 250,000 annually in the first decade of the new century, now had a quota of fewer than 6,000. But this was exactly what Congress wanted: to radically reduce immigration from southern and eastern Europe. Largely because of labor needs in the Southwest and foreign policy considerations, Congress did not limit the Western Hemisphere to a fixed quota.

During the early years of the Great Depression, few Europeans wanted to come to America. With the rise of fascism in Europe during the 1930s, however, many Europeans, especially Jews, looked for a safe haven. But neither the Congress nor the president expressed willingness to take in many refugees; hence few were admitted then or during World War II. Hostility toward immigrants and fears about the economy were too great for the modification of the national origins quotas. Indeed, the United States deported several hundred thousand Mexican immigrants rather than allow them to go on relief during the Depression. And when Japan attacked the United States in December 1941, the federal government responded by interning more than 110,000 Japanese Americans, a majority of whom were native-born American citizens, in virtual concentration camps.

REVIVAL AFTER WORLD WAR II

After World War II, the racial and ethnic hostility responsible for such policies abated. Groups that had borne the brunt of discrimination now found increasing acceptance in American society. The United States government officially apologized to Japanese Americans for their internment, for example, and in 1990 began to pay a modest restitution to the camps' survivors. The improved economic situation also helped to create a more favorable climate for immigrants, and postwar presidents believed that a generous refugee policy was in the nation's interest.

As a result, Congress and the presidents modified the restrictions of the 1920s and made it possible once again for a growing number of immigrants to come to America. They amounted to four million in the 1970s and about six million during the 1980s. Immigration authorities recorded over one million new immigrants in 1989. The most important change occurred in 1965, when Congress scrapped the national origins quotas and introduced a system based mainly on family unification. For the Western Hemisphere, however, Congress imposed a ceiling for the first time. Other acts permitted European, Cuban, and Asian refugees to enter, some 2.8 million from 1945 to 1990; and in 1990 Congress passed a far-reaching act that increased immigration still further.

It was not the intent of the 1965 Immigration Act to open the door to large numbers of Latin Americans and Asians, but these peoples were able to take advantage of the new law to immigrate to America. By the 1980s only 10 percent of new immigrants were European; over 40 percent were Asian, and the most of the rest were from Mexico, the Caribbean, and Central and South America.

Refugees account for many of these newcomers. Right after the war special legislation permitted several hundred thousand survivors of the war and anticommunist refugees to circumvent the national origins quotas. For the most part these refugees had a relatively easy time adjusting to American society. In the 1950s the United States accepted thirty-eight thousand Hungarian refugees, and after a failed revolution in Czechoslovakia in 1968, several thousand Czechs. In the 1970s about one hundred thousand Soviet Jews entered, and again in the late 1980s Soviet Jews and Armenians were permitted by the Soviet Union to migrate to America.

After 1959, however, the bulk of refugees were Cubans and Indochinese. Cubans entered in several waves. The first, from 1959 to 1962, consisted of the elite of Cuban society; the second wave, from 1965 to 1972, of the middle class. These two groups amounted to over 600,000 people. The 120,000 Mariel Cubans, so called because they left from the Cuban port of Mariel in 1980, were largely male and working class.

The vast bulk of Cuban refugees settled in the Miami, Florida, area, with smaller communities in New York and New Jersey. Although the transition from Cubans to Cuban Americans was difficult at times, the first groups in particular made rapid strides in assimilating to and succeeding in American society. They helped transform Miami into a vital center of commerce and banking. The Mariel Cubans found the transition more difficult, although they did rather well on the whole.

Not many Indochinese lived in America before 1975. Few Americans would have guessed that 900,000 would be in the United States by 1990. But in 1975 the collapse of the American-backed government in Saigon, Vietnam, led to a mass exodus of people fearing Communist rule. About 130,000 came to America in the first wave. This group was an elite one, highly educated and skilled, many of whom knew English. Deteriorating conditions in Vietnam in 1978 led to another exodus, many of its members ethnic Chinese. Desperate to escape, a great number fled by boat. These "boat people" were joined by Cambodians fleeing the terror of their Communist government and by Laotians who had supported the Americans during the Vietnam War. Many of the later Indochinese endured terrifying conditions at sea and ended up in Southeastern Asian refugee camps before being cleared to come to the United States. With few years of formal education and lacking skills required for success in modern American society, many found the adjustment to life in the United States to be hard and required years of government assistance in order to survive.

Most Asians did not come as refugees but as regular immigrants under the immigration laws. Chinese and Filipinos migrated under special legislation until 1965, after which their numbers increased substantially. After 1981 Chinese were able to come from both Taiwan and the People's Republic of China. In addition, many Chinese entered from the British colony of Hong Kong, which had its quota increased.

These Asian immigrants had knowledge of the United States gained from American troops stationed overseas, the export of American products, and the advent of modern communications, such as the easy availability of American-produced television programs in Third World nations. A number of Asians knew of the United States because they had studied in American colleges and universities. And with the introduction of jet air travel, transportation to the United States became relatively cheap and very fast.

Unlike the early waves of Chinese, who were mostly males from the province of Canton, a majority of the newcomers were women and children, and they hailed from a variety of regions in China as well as from Taiwan. Some were well-educated professionals who found jobs in American hospitals, universities, and research centers. Many, however, were working-class families in which both men and women worked in order to make a living. The women frequently found employment in garment factories and the men in restaurants in the Chinatowns of New York, San Francisco, and Los Angeles.

Postwar Filipino immigration also was characterized by family migration. Filipinos were able to take advantage of a nursing and physician shortage to work in American medicine. Like many other Asians, they settled in Hawaii and California, and in large cities.

The first Korean immigrants were usually medical professionals or war brides from the Korean War (1950–1953). Not all of the educated Koreans found jobs in their specialties; instead they opened small businesses, including the green groceries of New York City and dry cleaning establishments. Their major communities were in the New York and Los Angeles areas.

Of the post-1945 immigrants no group was so well educated as Asian Indians. By 1990, eighteen thousand Indian physicians practiced medicine in the United States, and thousands of Indians were computer experts, scientists, or engineers connected with universities or research centers. Some also went into business, operating newsstands in New York City or owning motels and restaurants across the United States.

The East Asians were largely immigrating to the United States in search of better economic opportunities, or they were refugees. Much the same can be said for immigrants from the Middle East. Immigration from that region increased after 1945, and it was more diverse than the prior migration.

These immigrants included some Israelis, especially after the 1970s. Official figures do not indicate a large Israeli migration, but scholars believe that many came as visitors of one kind or another, then remained when their visas expired. The center of Israeli immigration was New York City.

Immigration from Iran was slight before the fundamentalist Islamic revolution of 1979. Then many Iranian students in the United States decided to remain. Some won status as refugees, but others entered under the regular immigration laws. Over all, immigration from Iran grew steadily in the 1980s, and by 1989 Iran was the tenth largest sending nation for immigrants to America. Iranians included a number of highly educated immigrants.

Arab immigrants after 1945 came from Jordan, Egypt, Iraq, Syria, and Lebanon. About 250,000 arrived between 1970 and 1990. In the 1980s Jordan supplied the largest number, but many entering with a Jordanian passport were Palestinians who had been displaced by several wars between Israel and her Arab neighbors. Their cultures differed; often the only thing identifying them as Arabs was that they spoke Arabic. While Arab immigration included some Christians, Muslims dominated the post-1960s migration.

Though always concerned about developments in the Middle East, some recent Arab immigrants and Arab Americans began to organize to fight prejudice in the United States after the 1967 war. The 1991 Persian Gulf War further heightened collective interest in projecting an improved image of Arab culture.

Like East Asian immigrants, Middle East Arabs included a substantial number of well-educated individuals who sought better opportunities in the United States or who were escaping the constant wars and civil wars in their countries.

Except for the Cubans, immigrants from Mexico, the Caribbean, and Central America were more apt to be of low socioeconomic status, and they immigrated to the United States largely for economic reasons. By the 1950s Mexico was the largest sending nation for American immigrants; and other than years when refugee flows were especially high, Mexico was annually the leading source country for American immigrants, averaging about sixty thousand annually. Unemployment and underemployment drove Mexicans north of the border, where wages were much higher. As in the past, most new Mexican immigrants settled in the Southwest, especially in Texas and California.

Because each nation was allotted only twenty thousand visas until 1990 (exclusive of immediate family members of American citizens; the number increased to about twenty-five thousand in 1990), not all Mexicans who wanted to immigrate to the United States could do so; hence, many crossed the Mexico–United States border without proper documents, living and working illegally in the United States. Mexicans were by no means the only illegal immigrants, but they were the largest single group. Many Americans worried about illegal immigration; as a result Congress passed the Immigration Reform and Control Act (IRCA) in 1986 to outlaw the employment of undocumented aliens. The legislators also granted an amnesty to some agricultural workers and those undocumented aliens who arrived before 1982. About three million persons applied for the IRCA amnesty to become regular immigrants; the majority were Mexicans.

Other Hispanics making the journey north were Guatemalans, Nicaraguans, and Salvadorans, many of whom were escaping the poverty and civil wars that ravaged their countries. A few were able to win political asylum, but most did not; and if they could not enter under the preference system, they crossed the border anyway. These Central Americans formed communities in Florida, Washington, D.C., San Francisco, and elsewhere in California.

Some Haitians entered illegally when their bids for political asylum were turned down. Until 1987, when the repressive government of Haiti was overthrown, Haitians had the misfortune to live not only under a cruel dictatorship but also in the poorest country in the Caribbean. English-speaking West Indian nations, such as Jamaica and Trinidad and Tobago, also sent growing numbers to the United States after 1965, as did the Spanish-speaking Dominican Republic.

Like the immigrants of old, the latest American newcomers frequently formed communities of their own, with three-quarters of them settling in New York, California, Florida, Texas, New Jersey, and Illinois. The well-educated immigrants frequently lived in suburban communities where no single ethnic group dominated. They listened to foreign-language television and radio programs and read ethnic newspapers and magazines. Muslims from Pakistan and the Middle East established mosques, and Korean Christians revitalized many Protestant churches. The Catholic church began to train Spanish-speaking priests to serve its many Hispanic parishioners. Many immigrants opened restaurants and shops catering not only to their fellow nationals but also to Americans generally. New immigrants revitalized many decaying neighborhoods.

These Third World nationals contributed to the United States's economic development after 1960, whether they were performing menial jobs in hotels, garment shops, or restaurants or cleaning office buildings. The skills of highly educated immigrants were important, too. Some American cities would have had to make drastic cuts in medical care if not for the availability of foreign medical professionals. And after 1970 a growing proportion of doctorates in mathematics, computer science, physics, chemistry, and engineering were awarded to immigrants.

Despite the economic contribution of these latest newcomers, many Americans worried that immigrants would not assimilate and would take jobs from Americans, or would end up on welfare. These charges were rehashes of earlier refrains about the social and economic impact of immigrants that had proved to be largely untrue. Uneasy Americans also worried about bilingual educational programs and about the fact that so many foreign languages were being spoken on the streets, or about the presence of foreign-language signs, television programs, and newspapers. While biculturalism was a feature of many of the cities where the new immigrants settled, the vast majority of new immigrants indicated that they were eager to learn English and become Americans.

Indeed, in the post-1945 era, immigrants appeared to be assimilating even faster than did earlier generations. The existence of a mass, compulsory public school system certainly fostered Americanization, and so did the development of a mass culture in music, television, the movies, and consumer products. It was very difficult to remain removed from the modern postwar society.

Nonetheless, a few Americans urged that immigration be restricted and others formed the U.S. English movement, insisting that states and the federal government should adopt constitutional amendments and laws declaring that English is the nation's official language. Some states did so, although the United States Constitution was not amended, as the proponents of U.S. English hoped. Moreover, it was not clear what these laws would really accomplish. By referendum California adopted such a provision for its constitution, but Los Angeles expanded its bilingual education programs the very next year. Violence against Asians was another sign of anxiety about immigration, as were conflicts between blacks and Hispanics in Miami.

Despite these manifestations of the nation's historical ambivalence about immigration, cries to restrict immigration got nowhere in the 1970s and 1980s. Indeed, the nation steadily liberalized immigration policy after World War II. For now, the United States remains a society open to many immigrants.

The millions of immigrants made an enormous contribution to American society. Young alien males served in the nation's many wars, including the Civil War. The newcomers also left a lasting impact upon American culture. In sports and high and popular culture, immigrant names figured prominently and they still do today. In the late nineteenth and early twentieth centuries, for example, Germans populated American orchestras. In the late twentieth century, no one could miss the great popularity in American society of music from the Caribbean and Latin America. American food, customs, and speech have all been changed and enriched by the constant stream of immigrants.

But perhaps no impact has been so profound as the economic one. The labor and technological knowledge that immigrants brought made it possible for the United States to develop into the modern industrial society that it is. Any number of American industries, such as steel, owed much of their rapid growth to immigrant muscle. A disproportionate number of American scientists are foreign-born. Without the input of those scientists who came to the United States between 1920 and 1940, the United States would not have been able to develop the atomic bomb, to name only one scientific achievement. In the 1990s immigrant doctors, nurses, and medical technicians were vital to many urban areas as were the thousands of ethnic enterprises that immigrants ran. Whatever the future of immigration in America, there can be little doubt that its economic impact will continue to be crucial.

BIBLIOGRAPHY

General Works

Archdeacon, Thomas. *Becoming American: An Ethnic History* (1983).

Borjas, George. *Friends or Strangers: The Impact of Immigrants on the U.S. Economy* (1990).

Daniels, Roger. *Coming to America: A History of Immigration and Ethnicity in American Life* (1990).

Dinnerstein, Leonard, and David Reimers. *Ethnic Americans: A History of Immigration and Assimilation* (1975; rev. ed. 1988).

Fuchs, Lawrence. *The American Kaleidoscope: Race, Ethnicity, and the Civic Culture* (1990).

Handlin, Oscar. *The Uprooted* (1951).

Jones, Maldwyn. *American Immigration* (1960).

Portes, Alejandro, and Ruben G. Rumbaut. *Immigrant America: A Portrait* (1990).

Thernstrom, Stephan, ed. *The Harvard Encyclopedia of American Ethnic Groups* (1980).

Specific Groups and Periods

Bailyn, Bernard. *Voyagers to the West* (1986).

Bodnar, John. *The Transplanted: A History of Immigrants in Urban America* (1985).

Butler, Jon. *The Huguenots in America* (1983).

Cinel, Dino. *From Italy to San Francisco: The Immigrant Experience* (1982).

Conzen, Kathleen Neils. *Immigrant Milwaukee, 1836–1860: Accommodation and Community in a Frontier City* (1976).

Diner, Hasia. *Erin's Daughters in America* (1983).

Dolan, Jay. *Immigrant Church: New York's Irish and German Catholics, 1815–1865* (1975).

Erie, Steven. *Rainbow's End: Irish-Americans and the Dilemmas of Urban Machine Politics, 1840–1985* (1988).

Fischer, David Hackett. *Albion's Seed: British Folkways in America* (1989).

Gjerde, Jon. *From Peasants to Farmers: The Migration from Balestrand, Norway, to the Upper Middle West* (1985).

Kitano, Harry, and Roger Daniels. *Asian Americans: Emerging Minorities* (1988).

Leyburn, James G. *The Scotch-Irish: A Social History* (1962).

Miller, Kerby. *Emigrants and Exiles: Ireland and the Irish Exodus to North America* (1985).

Moore, Deborah Dash. *At Home in America: Second Generation New York Jews* (1981).

Morawska, Ewa. *For Bread with Butter* (1985).

Mormino, Gary, and George Pozzetta. *The Immigrant World of Ybor City: Italians and Their Latin Neighbors in Tampa, 1885–1985* (1987).

Ostergren, Robert. *A Community Transplanted: The Trans-Atlantic Experience of a Swedish Immigrant Settlement in the Upper Middle West, 1835–1915* (1988).

Portes, Alejandro, and Robert Bach. *Latin Journey: Cuban and Mexican Immigrants in the United States* (1985).

Reimers, David. *Still the Golden Door: The Third World Comes to America* (1985).

Rischin, Moses. *The Promised City: New York's Jews, 1870–1914* (1962).

Saloutos, Theodore. *The Greeks in the United States* (1964).

Takaki, Ronald. *Strangers from a Different Shore: A History of Asian Americans* (1989).

Nativism and Restriction

Bennett, David. *The Party of Fear: From Nativist Movements to the New Right in American History* (1988).

Higham, John. *Strangers in the Land: Patterns of American Nativism, 1860–1925* (1955).

SEE ALSO **Community Studies; Ethnicity; Geographical Mobility; Nativism, Anti-Catholicism, and Anti-Semitism; Religion**; and various essays in the sections on "**Ethnic and Racial Subcultures**" and "**Regionalism and Regional Subcultures.**"

INDUSTRIALIZATION

Gary B. Kulik

WITH ELEGANT PRECISION, David Landes once defined the innovations that drove the British industrial revolution in the eighteenth century. Three principles were key: the "substitution of machines" for human skill; "the substitution of inanimate for animate sources of power," in particular through the advent of steam power; and the substitution of mineral for vegetable fuels, or coal for wood.

These innovations constituted the industrial revolution for Landes, creating unprecedented increases in productivity and in per capita wealth—the latter the economists' central measure of the industrial revolution. Moreover, they led to growth that was self-sustaining, allowing population to grow beyond Malthusian checks, and opened a new "age of promise" while altering the balance of power within and between nations and changing "man's way of thinking" as much as "his way of doing." The changes that Landes charted led inexorably, through the paths of rationality and efficiency, to the mass production economy.

Alfred Chandler's *The Visible Hand,* an ambitious account of the rise of the modern corporation in America, took a similar position. For Chandler, the American industrial revolution, and the managerial revolution that shaped it, awaited the widespread use of anthracite coal after the 1850s. Increasingly sophisticated and intensive uses of heat, combined with machinery, increased what Chandler labeled "throughput," which fostered mass production and the management structures needed to oversee it. He effectively emphasized the same substitution effects as Landes and came to interpret the years prior to 1850 as merely prelude to a mass production economy based on coal, steam, and iron.

In recent years this view of the industrial revolution has been challenged. Raphael Samuel, in an influential article, claimed that the role of machinery, factories, and steam power had been exaggerated. In some industries, notably cotton textiles, machines did replace the skill of hand workers. But in many other industries, especially the iron and steel industries and the railroads, the industrial revolution created jobs, such as railroad fireman and boilermaker, for which there were no precise preindustrial analogues. Moreover, the industrial revolution created new needs for the most strenuous forms of manual labor: iron puddlers and canal and railroad construction workers. Further, Samuel argued, concentration on machines, factories, and mass production ignores or slights the importance of other forms of production: workshops, cottage industry, and the sweated trades.

It is this latter point that several other scholars, notably Michael Piore, Charles Sabel, and Philip Scranton, have developed to further challenge what they regard as an exaggerated emphasis on mass production, and especially on the interpretation of its triumph as natural and inevitable. Responding in part to the crisis of the mass production economy (the decline of basic industries such as steel, textiles, and automobiles) in the late twentieth century, they have sought a new understanding of the past by looking for historical alternatives to mass production, specifically those manufacturing forms that emphasized craft skill, "flexible specialization," and batch, rather than bulk, production. Firms that practice flexible specialization have the capacity to shift production relatively quickly and inexpensively to meet new markets. Mass production firms, with their high fixed costs and inflexible technology, have no such capacity. Piore and Sabel have actually suggested that sustained industrial growth did not require mass production. Others have not gone so far, focusing instead on batch production as an industrial strategy far more pervasive historically than scholars have assumed and thus worthy of sustained close attention in its own right. But no scholar has yet authored a book-length historical investigation setting out the history of flexible specialization in America, nor has anyone constructed a counterfactual model imagining an industrial revolution without mass production in the manner of Robert Fogel's attempt to envision American economic development without the railroad.

If the Landes model of the industrial revolution has come to be seen as increasingly inapplicable to the British industrial revolution, it has long been of questionable utility in understanding American history. In the first place, early American industrial development did not depend on steam power. Waterpower was far more critical and far more pervasive, and it remained more important than steam power in American manufacturing until the 1880s. Second, the substitution of mineral for vegetable matter was of little consequence in the early years of American industry because charcoal was more important than coal to the early iron industry, and cordwood was more important than coal to steamboats and even to the railroad. Wood was the principal industrial fuel into the 1840s and was the constituent element of America's water-powered mills. Not only the mills but their gears, waterwheels, shafts, and machinery frames were composed of wood. Third, American factories, and thus machines, were important only in selected industries; cotton textiles most significantly. Just as Samuel has suggested for Britain, American development rested on the expansion of artisan workshops and cottage industry and centrally on the reorganization of the artisan trades under capitalist auspices.

American industrial development rested even more centrally on wood and waterpower. This argument has been made in two collections of essays edited by Brooke Hindle, but the full implications of the economic and cultural importance of wood and water in America have yet to be explored in sustained fashion. There is one older and richly suggestive treatment of these issues in Lewis Mumford's *Technics and Civilization,* first published in 1934. Extending the work of his mentor, the Scottish social theorist Patrick Geddes, Mumford defined three overlapping, interpenetrating, yet distinct technological regimes: the eotechnic, the paleotechnic, and the neotechnic. Each regime was based chiefly on the use of characteristic materials, modes of transport, and energy sources. Thus the eotechnic phase was an era of wood, sail, and waterpower and it stretched from roughly 1000 to 1750. Its successor, the paleotechnic era, was an age of iron, railroads, and steam and its dates varied by country but ran roughly from 1700 to 1900. The neotechnic age was marked by alloys and synthetics, the airplane, and by electricity and roughly coincided with the twentieth century.

The great virtue of Mumford's approach was that it dramatically extended the chronology of the industrial revolution, and thus recovered the long history of technological innovation in an era too quickly dismissed then and now as merely preindustrial. He was also among the first to write the history of machines as an aspect of cultural history, eschewing narrow economic or technological determinations. Yet his three-part schema, as he later admitted, never served to shape future scholarship. Mumford acknowledged some weaknesses of logic and chronology, though he never addressed the central weakness of his schema, the absence of a theory of historical change, or why societies passed from one epoch to the next.

Nevertheless, Mumford offered a grid with rich possibilities for the interpretation of America's industrial revolution. Prior to the widespread use of coal, iron, and steam power, Americans had established a thriving industrial economy. Most economic historians are now agreed that the key period of upward movement in the country's gross national product occurred between 1790 and 1840, that is, before the widespread introduction of paleotechnic methods. For historians seeking an "alternative" to the standard view of the industrial revolution represented by Landes and others, one is already available in the peculiarities of American development.

But was the United States "industrial" by 1840? By the standards of paleotechnic industry, it was not. But consider that Americans by 1840 had made extensive use of waterpower for grinding grain, sawing wood, fulling and carding wool, and spinning and weaving cotton. Mill owners had dammed rivers at the vast majority of mill sites in the Northeast. Other Americans had introduced key innovations in production technology and had gone a long distance toward the achievement of interchangeable parts, in clocks, whose movements were first made of wood, and principally in firearms. Merchants and master artisans had overseen a sweeping transformation of the urban trades, what one historian has referred to as "metropolitan industrialization," had also occurred. This was a transformation in the organization of work rather than in the tools necessary to the work, but it also was a result of technological transformations elsewhere in the economy. The great expansion of the needle trades depended on the mechanization of the cotton textile industry; the growth of cities depended on technological innovations in water supply. None of this was possible without a revolution in transportation that had been based on roads, canals, and the traditional power of wind to move the nation's fleet.

A WORLD OF WOOD AND WATERPOWER

Wood and water were central to America's industrial development, and they remained so well into the nineteenth century. This does not mean that iron was unimportant prior to mid century. It clearly was an essential component of edged tools, ship hardware, weaponry, and cookware, but it was far less important than it would become. Nor does it mean that wood and waterpower were unimportant after the 1840s. Wood remained a key building material and water continued to generate power, but both wood and waterpower clearly lost their centrality. Nor does it mean that America's abundant natural resources caused the American industrial revolution. People, acting on those resources, did that.

From the first years of settlement to the 1840s, America's vast forests formed the basis for its building technology, tools, agriculture, transportation, and fuel. The lumbermen, sawyers, carpenters, and wood shapers who turned America's forests into sawn lumber, houses and barns, charcoal for fuel, looms and spinning wheels, plows and farrows, barrels, wagon wheels and ships were at the center of an economy based centrally on wood. Wood provided Americans with their most mundane needs, shelter and warmth, and with some of their most highly specialized tools—clocks, sextants, and orrerries.

Much recent work in social history emphasizes regional and ethnic diversity. For example, the American landscape came to display vernacular building forms and techniques with their origins in West Africa, the Caribbean, Finland, and Germany, as well as England. Furniture styles, too, reveal regional and cultural differences. One American religious group, the Shakers, would come to be identified as the makers of especially elegant and graceful furniture. But local and ethnic variety tells only part of the story. In a labor-scarce, resource-rich environment, the reciprocal sawmill, balloon-frame construction, the Blanchard stocking lathe, the continuous-arm Windsor chair, and the clipper ship came to mark a special style of working wood. The cheapness and availability of wood seems to have promoted both a profligate and an innovative use.

The vast expanse of America's forests led to the extensive use of wood, and the relative scarcity of skilled labor led to the use of methods that required less skill. According to Dell Upton, Americans used more wood to build frame houses than did Europeans, but finished the wood minimally. In New England, for example, mill-sawed planks attached by pegs to the house frame replaced studs, which had to be joined to the frame by mortises and tenons. Log houses also used substantial amounts of wood and required no special joinery skills. Similarly, the widely adopted Virginia, or worm, fence used more wood than traditional post-hole fences but was self-supporting and required no joinery.

Colonists used wood with an intensity unknown to Native Americans, whose tree-felling practices were far different. Settlers tended to select large trees and simply fell them without regard for the many smaller trees destroyed in the process. In addition, Americans had very high standards for marketable wood, and the best wood was often used when the best was unnecessary. To speed their work, they developed a characteristic felling ax. The American ax, a classic example of anonymous invention as Brooke Hindle and Steven Lubar argue, had a short bit or cutting edge and a heavily weighted poll, or back edge. The ax was better balanced and was a more efficient tool than the unbalanced European ax. Extensive deforestation encouraged a wastefulness and a sense of exploitation that would linger well into the future.

Waterpower was America's principal source of energy. From the earliest settlement, water mills spread over the countryside. The small, custom grist mill for grinding grain was the most common, but the sawmill was the most distinctive. The reciprocating, or up-and-down sawmill, was introduced into America in the early seventeenth century, probably by the Dutch to New York, soon after by the English to Maine. Waterwheels provided power both for the horizontal movement of the carriage on which the log was fastened and the perpendicular movement of the saw, set in a rigid wooden frame. Before the end of the century there were hundreds of these sawmills in New England alone, many along the coast of Maine. The English had had experience with reciprocating sawmills since the early seventeenth century, but it would be two centuries before they were widely used in England;

most scholars believe that it was the opposition of hand sawyers that accounted for the long delay.

The reciprocating sawmill remained America's most distinctive technology for over a century. Its presence spoke to the needs of a society with a scarcity of labor and a plenitude of natural resources. By the mid 1700s vast stretches of the country had been deforested. The reciprocating saw and its more efficient successor, the circular saw, were ideal technologies for a society so intent, as the economic historian Nathan Rosenberg has suggested, on using its natural resources so prodigally.

The development of the American sawmill, and the absence of direct opposition to it, is representative of the American experience. There was no opposition because there were few hand sawyers. This was partly the result of labor scarcity and partly the result of the absence of an elaborate division of labor based on craft. No Americans rose up in opposition to mechanical sawmills because they had no reason to so rise up. The sawmill was the first, but not the last, "machine" introduced into America that failed to evoke a machine-breaking, or Luddite, opposition. Americans found other grounds for opposing the advance of industrial capitalism, but a deep-seated opposition to machinery was not among them.

There were many other types of water mills. Saw and grist mills could often be found in combination. Large merchant grist mills, located largely along the Mid-Atlantic coast, ground grain for international markets. After the grist and sawmill, the third most common water-powered mill was the bark mill that ground the oak or chestnut bark used in tanneries. Far less common were fulling mills, for the finishing of woolen cloth, and, after 1790, carding mills, for the processing of woolen fibers. There were also paper, powder, and linseed oil mills, and, in the South, cotton ginneries, rice mills, and sugar mills. By the 1790s, in Worcester County, Massachusetts, alone, there were 262 mills. The best estimates suggest a minimum of ten thousand, and perhaps as many as twenty thousand, in the entire country at that time.

Another specialized use of waterpower was for blast furnaces, forges, and rolling and slitting mills. First established in seventeenth-century Massachusetts, colonial ironworks were concentrated in the highlands of northern New Jersey and eastern Pennsylvania, western Massachusetts and Connecticut, and in tidewater Maryland. Producing both cast and wrought iron from local ores, these ironworks relied heavily on wood for fuel and for the wheels and gearing that transmitted power to the bellows. Isolated in the rural countryside, the largest of these works were self-contained communities of over one hundred workers run by a single ironmaster or his agents.

Colonial blast furnaces used waterpower more intensively than other mills. While in blast, for weeks or months at a time, they required the continuous use of water-powered bellows. They often began their work in spring when the weather was cool and supplies of water were abundant. Yet spring was the same season when great runs of salmon, shad, and alewives would ascend East Coast streams seeking to spawn. Dams blocked their passage, and farmers and furnace owners were in conflict. The common law was on the side of farmers; early statutes in Massachusetts and Rhode Island, for example, protected the rights of farmers to fish.

Some Americans used their rivers as extensively as their forests and with no more regard for the consequences. The extensive damming of streams in the Northeast effectively destroyed the North American Atlantic-salmon fishery. Dams also raised water levels, flooding upstream farmlands or rendering ineffective smaller upstream mills. Increasingly, as the legal historian Morton Horwitz has shown, American law came to favor mill owners over farmers and large mill owners over small. Such change provoked conflict, including some incidents of dam breaking, as farmers and fishermen defended their rights.

The most extensive users of waterpower were the cotton and woolen mills that stretched from northern New England through the middle states and into the South. Thus, by the end of the eighteenth century, furnace owners and cotton-mill owners had established their paramount authority over the nation's rivers.

The cotton mill was the first fully mechanized factory, its machines linked together and driven by a single power source. It made its first appearance in Pawtucket, Rhode Island, in 1790. In its earliest form, as a mill for spinning yarn, the American cotton mill was a wooden factory. Most mills built between 1790 and 1815 were framed in wood, employed wooden waterwheels and wooden shafts and gears. The machines, too, were largely made of wood. Iron-framed machines, iron gears and shafting, and iron waterwheels became increasingly widespread by the 1820s, when the spinning mill became an integrated cotton factory that combined both spinning and weaving. Productivity and machine speeds increased with the use of iron.

The cotton industry was long thought to be the key industry, the leading sector, of the industrial revolution and the model of mechanization that all other businesses would eventually follow. This is no longer a tenable argument. Mechanization, the replacement of hand labor by machines, is now properly seen as only one of several paths of self-sustaining growth. Adam Smith (1723–1790) recognized long ago the importance of division of labor, and it is clear that subdivided labor in gunmaking, in shoe production, and in the making of clocks, for example, was critical to early American economic growth. So, too, were the subtle patterns of "learning by doing" that economic historians have sought to discover, that is, improvements in production methods that require neither machines nor new divisions of labor. Also important were the complex patterns of what Sean Wilentz has labeled "metropolitan industrialization"—the mix of expanding capitalist authority, subdivided labor, and the emergence of the "sweated" (clothing, shoes, furniture) trades that eroded older forms of craft labor and came to characterize the economies of the eastern seaboard cities in the antebellum years. This new emphasis on the urban trades, especially on their importance to the first labor movement of the 1830s, has produced a substantially different history, one in which the roles of machinery and the textile industry have been marginalized.

Other historians have weighed in on this issue. In Alfred Chandler's *The Visible Hand,* the first textile mill owners bear closer resemblance to the doges of Venice and the burghers of Ghent than to the leaders of modern business corporations. In organizing their companies as simple partnerships or joint stock ventures and managing them through agents and superintendents, textile mill owners lagged behind the owners of railroads, whose use of the corporate form and middle-management hierarchies placed them on the high road to the modern corporation. The historian Thomas Cochran has taken this position to its farthest extreme, claiming that the textile industry did not possess the economic characteristics that would necessarily lead to further industrialization.

These and similar arguments have gone too far in marginalizing a key eotechnic industry and a major transitional link to the paleotechnic economy. Contrary to Cochran, the textile industry was an important locus of machine experimentation. Men who learned their skills in building and repairing textile machines, increasingly fashioned of iron, would later come to apply those skills to the production of railroad locomotives, to steam engines, and to the development of the machine tool industry. This was especially the case in cities such as Providence, Rhode Island, Lowell and Taunton, Massachusetts, and Philadelphia. Moreover, the textile factory was the place where working Americans first faced the special pressures of a workday defined not by the task but by time and dictated by the pace of machinery.

Cochran was right in one critical respect: the cotton industry did not lead to the immediate or thorough mechanization of the two "industries" that supplied it with raw material or bought much of its product. The mechanization of cotton cloth production led on the one side to the extension of plantation slavery in the South, and to the creation of a cotton culture that would have profound implications for the present. It led on the other side to the development of the clothing industry and its early reliance not on machines but on the hands of American needlewomen. In both respects it led, as Raphael Samuel has suggested, to an increased reliance on hard and onerous hand labor.

Understood in this way, the cotton mill was not simply a singular and unusual example of mechanization but it stood rather at the heart of a cotton economy that stretched from Alabama to the tenements of New York City, and whose economic importance was thus far greater than current accounts have it. The cotton industry rested centrally on the work of women. In the South, men and women equally shared the burdens of picking cotton; the cotton factories and the clothing shops depended overwhelmingly on women.

The emergence of the cotton industry was one aspect of the sweeping organizational and technical changes, which marked the years from 1790 to 1840, that were the result of the freeing of American entrepreneurial energy in the years following the Revolution. These changes were most noticeable in the cities where master craftsmen and merchants reorganized such trades as shoemaking, carpentry and furniture making, tailoring and the cooper's trade. Apprentices and journeymen became wage workers, which divided and subdivided the work of the traditional crafts. Technical changes within the eotechnic economy were also visible: Oliver

Evans's improvements to the gristmill, the development of the circular saw and the baloon-frame house, and the radical improvements in the design of waterpower systems, represented first by the works at Lowell, and in waterwheel design that would eventually lead to the replacement of the waterwheel by the turbine. The changes were visible in a third area, in the beginnings of what the British would later term the "American system" of manufacture, in innovations in clock making and in gun manufacture pointing toward an economy of mass production and interchangeable parts but resting centrally on an economy of wood. The first American clocks with interchangeable parts were clocks with wooden movements, and one of the key technologies in gunmaking was the Blanchard lathe, and its related machinery, for the fashioning of gunstocks.

Economic growth emerged out of the eotechnic economy and did so with critical legal and governmental support. The new nation erased internal trade barriers; created patent, postal, and banking systems; and eventually erected tariff barriers helpful to American manufactures. State governments provided extensive support for canal and turnpike projects, and the courts provided an increasingly favorable environment for entreprenurial energy.

This growth was largely confined to the North. The South remained a plantation society, in which manufacturing played only a limited role. Slavery inhibited the development of manufacturing by concentrating power in the hands of large landowners and by reducing the incentives customary to free labor. The initial success of southern planters in establishing strong staple economies for tobacco, cotton, indigo, and rice seems to have made them less able to respond creatively to the fresh opportunities of the antebellum era. Falling behind the North in this era, they would remain well behind it throughout the nineteenth century.

By 1840, Americans had taken their first steps toward self-sustained economic growth. Unlike the British, they had done so through the use of wood and waterpower. They used both with a special intensity and came to rely on technologies, such as the reciprocating sawmill, noted for their resource-intensity. And they shaped wood in unique ways. They also used wood and water in ways that were wasteful and heedless of social consequences, a pattern of practice that persists.

A WORLD OF IRON AND STEAMPOWER

Wood remained an important element of America's economy. Its use in housing construction and in furniture making increased as the population grew and moved west. The lumber industry moved west along with the population: to the upper Midwest by the mid nineteenth century, the far Northwest by the twentieth. Wood remained an important household fuel in rural areas into the twentieth century. Coal gradually replaced wood as a household fuel and wholly eclipsed it as an industrial fuel. By the 1850s, coal and coke had become the principal fuels of the second stage of the American industrial revolution.

Waterpower continued to be the principal source of manufacturing power until the 1880s and was given new and spectacular life in the large-scale western hydroelectric projects of the twentieth century. Steam power assumed increasingly greater importance in manufacturing and dominated land transportation through the railroad. Its impact on water transportation, despite the early and visible success of the river steamboat, was far more limited initially.

Steam power made its first appearance on the nation's waterways. Though the site of initial experimentation and first success was the eastern seaboard, the steamboat had its greatest impact on the western rivers. Through a series of innovations adaptive to the broad, relatively tranquil, and often shallow western waters, the American river steamboat took on its characteristic shape, broad and shallow in its hull, its wooden superstructure rising, as George Rogers Taylor wrote, like a "white, wooden castle." In truth, most were ungainly looking working boats stacked high with cotton or other goods. Soon outfitted with high-pressure steam engines and boilers, which derived from the innovations of Oliver Evans, the western steamboat proved to be both profligate of fuel and highly dangerous.

Evans's high-pressure engine was cheaper to build; it was lighter and smaller than its principal English rival, the Boulton & Watt condensing engine. But it used twice as much fuel, principally cordwood, and its boilers were prone to explode. Its relative fuel inefficiency seems characteristic of a society prone to use its natural resources prodigally. But its relative danger introduced a new note, one that would be increasingly, and disturbingly, visible in America's paleotechnic economy. In several key industries, Americans died or were injured at rates several multiples higher than in comparable British industries. No scholar has yet convincingly explained why. A society given to using its natural resources prodigally seems also to have used its labor in the same fashion.

Approximately seven thousand people lost their lives in steamboat accidents prior to 1853. The dangers of high-pressure boilers were widely known from an early date, yet some companies advertised that they could be operated by unskilled labor. Poorly trained and careless workers were part of the problem, but the basic trouble was that boilers could not stand the pressures to which they were subjected. Some were poorly made to begin with; many others were driven too hard by captains demanding "more steam" than their boilers could safely provide. Steamboat accidents resulted in demands for government intervention that led to federal regulation in 1838 and 1852. The latter act provided for the licensing of boats, pilots, and engineers, periodic inspection, and, according to Louis C. Hunter, "effective administration," which led to a reduction in the ratio of steamboat explosions to steamboat tonnage.

Though the steamboat has long captured the imaginations of historians and others, it represented one of the least important uses of steam power in the nineteenth century. The great age of the western steamboat was over by the end of the 1850s, as railroads began to carry an increasing amount of freight. Railroads also took freight away from eastern steamboats, though on some routes, such as the Long Island Sound route, steamships remained competitive throughout the nineteenth century. The deep-water boats of the Great Lakes, driven increasingly by screw propellers rather than paddle wheels, were less affected by railroad competition, but then they were slow to displace sailing vessels as well. The Great Lakes trade, the California and the Atlantic coastal trade, and ocean shipping remained the domain of sailing vessels until well into the late nineteenth century, even after the development of iron and steel hulls. The steam revolution in ocean shipping awaited the late-nineteenth-century development of twin screws and triple expansion engines.

The railroad represented a far more important use of steampower and of iron. From 2,800 miles of track in 1840, the rails would stretch more than 166,000 miles by the 1890s. Initially fueled by wood, American railroads began their conversion to coal in the 1850s and would complete it by the 1880s, when 90 percent of engines were coal-fueled. Wood-burning engines were prodigious users of wood. By one estimate, they turned four to five million cords to ash in the 1850s. Wood was also a dangerous fuel sending sparks that caused fires. Coal was more energy intensive, and was less prone to produce sparks, but it was also more corrosive of boiler and stack linings, to say nothing of the skin and lungs of engineers and firemen.

The railroad had an important, and not easily quantified, impact on America. In narrow economic terms alone, it bridged great distances bringing not only more speed than was possible previously but greater regularity. In 1857, it was possible to travel from New York to Pittsburgh by rail in one day; in 1800, it had taken more than a week. The railroad was a major user of iron and coal, which spurred the further development of those industries. Despite Robert Fogel's efforts to demonstrate that the railroad was not indispensable to late-nineteenth-century American economic development, that canals could have accomplished much the same, most historians now believe that his argument rested on too many questionable assumptions and failed to credit the secondary economic effects of the railroad, that is, in engineering and in fostering iron and steel production.

The railroad had a substantial cultural impact as well. It was, as Alfred Chandler has argued, the first of the great corporations, experimenting with forms of middle management never tried in industry before. The need for timely coordination of a rail transport system "required the creation of a sizable administrative organization" able to "monitor . . . day to day operations." It also played an important role, along with the telegraph, in standardizing and nationalizing time. And as John Stilgol has argued, the railroad became a powerful symbol of "metropolitan" elegance, order, and efficiency. But the railroad's "modernity" has evoked more negative images as well. Some of America's leading writers and artists, as Leo Marx has argued, saw the railroad as a threatening "machine in the garden." The German scholar Wolfgang Schivelbusch has argued that the railroad mechanized and denatured travel in a fashion similar to the ways in which the factory mechanized and denatured work, that trains produced forms of fatigue unknown to preindustrial peoples, and that train accidents caused unprecedented damage and injury.

Railroads were among the most dangerous of America's paleotechnic industries. Running fast over unfenced land, they were a danger to livestock. The "cowcatcher," a V-shaped device attached to the front of locomotives to prevent livestock from entangling the running gear, was one American response. Accidents that involved the death of passengers attracted substantial press attention, and line cuts depicting such accidents became a popular genre. According to Alfred Chandler such accidents prompted railroad companies to adopt new organizational structures with carefully defined management responsibilities. Carlene Stephans argues that they prompted the standardization of time. Yet accidents continued, and at rates well in advance of British practice. It was the railroad worker who paid the heaviest price. In 1889, according to labor historian Walter Licht, death rates among trainmen were more than twice as high in America as in Britain, injury rates four times as high. Brakemen were especially prone to injury, but all trainmen were at risk. In 1889, for every 117 trainmen employed, one was killed; for every 12 trainmen, one was injured.

The third form of steam power to shape America's paleotechnic age was the stationary steam engine. Introduced into the United States in the late eighteenth century for pumping water out of mines and later adopted for urban water supply, the steam engine was modified and improved by Oliver Evans and gradually was employed in manufactures. These engines were of the same high-pressure type that Evans developed for steamboats. After 1850, with improvements in fuel economy, efficiency, and speed associated with George Corliss and Charles Porter, the steam engine saw much greater use. In the 1880s it was the country's principal form of manufacturing power. The stationary steam engine helped to create a distinctive urban industrialism, shifting the locus of factory production away from rural waterpower sites and toward major urban areas and their immediate outskirts. The steam engine also helped to moderate, though not to erase, regional differences, which led to a more intense late-nineteenth-century industrialization in the South and the West. By 1899, there were over 8,000 stationary steam engines in use, compared with almost 21,000 locomotives and 1,500 steam vessels.

The high-pressure engine and boiler proved just as dangerous in manufacturing as it did on the rails and waters. Louis C. Hunter has calculated from insurance company records that there were 6,300 boiler explosions during the years 1867 to 1899, resulting in 8,400 deaths. Stationary boilers accounted for nearly three-quarters of the explosions and more than half the casualties. But such explosions did not attract the same congressional interest as steamboat explosions, perhaps because workers, not passengers, died. There was no federal effort to regulate steam power in manufacturing. Once again, death and injury were higher in the United States than in Britain; the number of boiler explosions per million inhabitants was three times higher in the United States.

By the end of the nineteenth century, steam power was inextricably linked to coal. The transition from cordwood fuel to coal was not rapid. The first locomotives, steamboats, and stationary engines were fueled by wood and their voracious appetites led to ever more intensive and extensive deforestation. But growing scarcity and higher prices for wood, combined with successful experimentation with anthracite coal, led to the increased use of coal. As late as 1850, 90 percent of the heat-energy needs of the country were met by cordwood; by 1900, over 70 percent were met by coal.

From the mid 1880s to the 1940s, coal was the principal fuel driving America's economy. It was not only the fuel of choice for steam boilers but also for iron and steel furnaces and houses and apartments. Anthracite coal from eastern Pennsylvania was the first coal to be widely used, and through the 1860s the state's anthracite fields produced more coal than the rest of the country combined. The coal industry became national with the discovery of high-quality coking coal in the Connellsville region near Pittsburgh and expansion of the coal industry into the southern Appalachians, Illinois, Iowa, and Missouri, and then west to the lignite fields of Montana and Wyoming.

Coal was a more efficient fuel than wood, allowing for cost savings on one eastern railroad of between 30 and 50 percent. It also allowed steamboats and locomotives to travel longer without having to stop and take on fuel and thus helped to accelerate the pace of America's industrial life. But arguably it had its most dramatic impact on the iron-and-steel industry. By 1880, 45 percent of all pig iron was being smelted with coke; by the early twentieth century, over 90 percent. The use of charcoal fuel limited the height of iron furnaces because charcoal was friable, too easily crushed by the weight of iron ore. Coal could maintain its shape under compression, and so furnace stacks grew taller; they were increasingly built of iron and steel rather than stone. With their increased size, and with coal, or more properly coke, providing a more intense heat, the volume and speed of production increased.

The increases in the volume and speed of production helped to spur the rise of big business and ultimately the rise of the new corporations. Consider first the changes entailed in shifting from wood to coal. During the nineteenth century, the cutting and sale of wood was an activity presided over by thousands of small producers who seemed to have required, as Arthur Cole argued many years ago, no distributive networks; money passed directly from consumer to producer. Production of coal required capital, mines, miners, and intricate distributive networks organized by rail and boat. The railroads themselves, as we have seen, demanded the kind of coordination and oversight typical of the modern corporation. The corporation—not the sole proprietor, the partnership, nor the joint stock company—became the characteristic business form of the paleotechnic era.

Coal mines and coal camps extended over a vast landscape, soon to be peopled by immigrants from Europe. The coal camps, or patches, with their characteristic tipples rising to the sky, the culm and waste piles abutting the small houses, and the adjacent lands scarred came to be the harshest of industrial landscapes. But the conditions above ground were better than those below. Coal mining was dangerous work and was made more dangerous, as Anthony Wallace has argued, by an aggressive and reckless disregard for safety on the part of mine owners and miners. The numbers of dead and injured in coal mining were not only large, but once again dwarfed comparable British rates. Wallace found that Pennsylvania anthracite miners were three to four times more likely to die in 1870 than their British counterparts.

The American iron and steel industry rested on coal. With its origins in the Appalachians, and especially in eastern Pennsylvania, the industry spread west to Pittsburgh and Gary, north to Buffalo, east to Baltimore, and south to Birmingham. The great furnaces and mills that rose up in the late nineteenth century were the largest industrial sites in the country. They stood at the center of a vast extractive economy that stretched from the newly opened ore fields of Michigan's Upper Peninsula to the coal fields of the Pittsburgh district and the Jones Valley of Alabama. Their products provided the rails that linked the country, the bridges that spanned rivers too large for wooden spans, and, after the development of the Bessemer and the open-hearth processes of steelmaking in the 1850s, the girders that would give American cities their distinctive verticality.

Iron and steel worked a revolution in other more subtle ways. Iron-framed machines with iron gears and shafts transmitted mechanical power more smoothly and with far greater speed than wood, and so the pace of work quickened. Well before Frederick Taylor (1856–1915) and "scientific management," American factory owners were known for driving their machines faster and their workers harder than the English. Iron and steel, with their greater dimensional stability, also gave effect to the experiments in interchangeable parts that had been under way prior to the 1840s and came to serve as the principal materials in America's mass production economy. From an economy dominated in the mid nineteenth century by consumer goods industries, most processing a form of agricultural harvest—grain, lumber, cotton, leather, and wool—the American economy had become by 1910 one in which the leading industries were manufacturers of producer's goods, and the first was machinery. Machines for making machines, for the shaping of metal, were at the heart of the growing mass production economy, and for what had come to be known as the American system of manufacture.

Two British engineers, Joseph Whitworth and George Wallis, were among the first to study what was distinctive about American technology. Both came to the United States to investigate how it had been possible for American technology, such as the Hobbs lock and the Colt revolver, to have so impressed Europeans at the 1851 Crystal Palace Exhibition. Whitworth and Wallis offered an explanation for America's technical proficiency, elements of which scholars have been working with ever since. They believed that labor was scarce in America and that unskilled labor commanded relatively high wage rates. They also argued that in the United States market forces were freer and that workers took more technical initiative because they were not as rigidly organized by craft and through master-apprentice relationships as Europeans.

Far more scholarly attention has been lavished on the quantifiable aspects of Whitworth's and Wallis's argument than on the cultural aspects. The economic historian H. J. Habakkuk authored a classic attempt to prove, through a combination of empirical history, economic theory, and comparative factor analysis, that American technological innovation was the result of the relative scarcity and dearness of labor. Most economic historians now regard the argument as plausible but overgeneralized and inadequately grounded in the available wage data. As yet no sustained research has been done on Anglo-American wage differentials over the full course of the early nineteenth century. Historians of technology have been more skeptical of the argument, preferring to assert that technical innovation arises more from technical enthusiasm than from self-conscious economic calculus and that much of what would become the American system, the development of interchangeable parts and special-purpose machine tools, emerged from government-subsidized "armory practice" where issues of military and national necessity, rather than issues of costs and profits, drove innovation. Historians of technology and economic historians are agreed, however, that whatever the causes of the American system, its effects were the result of the special-purpose machine tools that came to characterize the production of guns, typewriters, bicycles, and later, automobiles.

Nathan Rosenberg has sought to shift the focus of causal debate away from issues of labor and capital and toward issues of resources. His argument, yet to be fully tested or elaborated, is that American technology has been peculiarly resource-intensive, and the resource it most intensively used was wood. Wood was cheaper and more plentiful in the United States than in Britain and thus Americans came to develop a whole series of innovations for the cutting and shaping of wood, the Blanchard lathe among them, that served as the prototypes for the special-purpose machine tools that would ultimately shape metal and come to characterize the American system of production.

Two distinct but overlapping phases of America's industrial revolution are visible. The first was an age of wood and waterpower stretching into the 1840s. This was no epoch of bucolic charm, but an era capable of launching Americans into a period of self-sustaining economic growth. It was a period in which the key features of a later industrial landscape were developed—special-purpose machine tools and the factory—and in which American attitudes toward development first surfaced. It was in this era that Americans began to lay waste their forests and to dam their rivers with an energy unknown before. This was the other side of "economic growth." So, too, was the expansion of slavery that the cotton factory promoted and the enormous growth in women's industrial labor.

From 1840 to roughly 1900, Americans experienced an age of iron and steam. Building on the technical achievements of an earlier era, yet going far beyond them in scale, in speed, and in the uses of fire, America's inventors and entrepreneurs created an industrial economy that employed more than 38 million workers in 1910, over 8 million of them women. Where America's eotechnic workers were largely native born, British, or German, the workers of America's paleotechnic age were a broad mix of Europeans and an increasing number of African Americans, Chinese, Mexicans, Cubans, and Puerto Ricans. They would increasingly labor in factories and huge industrial works, and not craft shops; their work would be increasingly directed by corporations and not individual proprietors. While much production took place in the mass production industries, smaller works, owned by individual proprietors and producing in batches rather than in bulk, continued to function.

By the early twentieth century, the outlines of a new epoch were dimly visible, one in which alloys gradually became more important than iron and steel, in which fuel oil replaced coal, in which systems of energy distribution became as important as systems of energy production, in which automobiles and airplanes rivaled the railroad, in which white-collar workers gradually assumed numerical dominance. But even in this economy, what Mumford and Geddes once regarded hopefully as the "neotechnic," problems of depleted resources and reckless and injurious labor management practices continue, the legacy of two earlier epochs.

BIBLIOGRAPHY

Bauer, K. Jack. *A Maritime History of the United States: The Role of America's Seas and Waterways* (1988).

Bining, Arthur. *Pennsylvania Iron Manufacture in the Eighteenth Century* (1938; repr. 1970; 2d ed. 1973).

Bruchey, Stuart. *Enterprise: The Dynamic Economy of a Free People* (1990).

Chandler, Alfred D., Jr. *The Visible Hand: The Managerial Revolution in American Business* (1977).

Cochran, Thomas C. *Frontiers of Change: Early Industrialism in America* (1981).

Cole, Arthur H. "The Myth of Fuel Wood Marketing in the U.S." *Business History Review* 44 (1970): 339–359.

Cooper, Carolyn C. *Shaping Invention: Thomas Blanchard's Machinery and Patent Management in Nineteenth-Century America* (1991).

Cronon, William. *Changes in the Land: Indians, Colonists, and the Ecology of New England* (1983).

———. *Nature's Metropolis: Chicago and the Great West* (1991).

Dublin, Thomas. *Women at Work: The Transformation of Work and Community in Lowell, Massachusetts, 1826–1860* (1979).

Fogel, Robert. *Railroads and American Economic Growth: Essays in Econometric History* (1964).

Forman, Benno M. "Mill Sawing in Seventeenth-Century Massachusetts." *Old-Time New England* 60 (April–June 1970): 110–130.

Gordon, Robert B. "Hydrological Science and the Development of Waterpower for Manufacturing." *Technology and Culture* 16 (April 1985): 204–235.

Greenberg, Dolores. "Reassessing the Power Patterns of the Industrial Revolution: An Anglo-American Comparison." *American Historical Review* 87 (December 1982): 1237–1261.

Habakkuk, H. J. *American and British Technology in the Nineteenth Century* (1969).

Henretta, James A. "Wealth and Social Structure." In *Colonial British America: Essays in the New History of the Early Modern Era,* edited by Jack P. Greene and J. R. Pole (1984).

Hindle, Brooke, ed. *America's Wooden Age: Aspects of its Early Technology* (1975).

———, ed. *Material Culture of the Wooden Age* (1981).

Hindle, Brooke, and Steven Lubar. *Engines of Change: The American Industrial Revolution, 1790–1860* (1986).

Horwitz, Morton. *The Transformation of American Law, 1780–1860* (1977).

Hounshell, David. *From the American System to Mass Production, 1800–1932* (1984).

Hunter, Louis C. *Waterpower in the Century of the Steam Engine* (1979).

———. *Steam Power* (1985).

Kulik, Gary. "Dams, Fish, and Farmers." In *The Countryside in the Age of Capitalist Transformation: Essays in the Social History of Rural America,* edited by Steven Hahn and Jonathan Prude (1985).

———. "Representing the Railroad." *The Gettysburg Review* 2 (Summer 1989): 495–513.

Landes, David S. *The Unbound Prometheus: Technological Change and Industrial Development in Western Europe from 1750 to the Present* (1969).

Licht, Walter. *Working for the Railroad: The Organization of Work in the Nineteenth Century* (1983).

Marx, Leo. *The Machine in the Garden: Technology and the Pictorial Ideal in America* (1964).

Mayr, Otto, and Robert C. Post, eds. *Yankee Enterprise: The Rise of the American System of Manufactures* (1981).

Mercer, Henry C. *Ancient Carpenters' Tools* (1951; 3d ed. 1960).

Mumford, Lewis. *Technics and Civilization* (1934).

———. "An Appraisal of Lewis Mumford's 'Technics and Civilization'" (1934). *Daedalus* 88 (Summer 1959): 527–536.

O'Malley, Michael. *Keeping Watch: A History of American Time* (1990).

Piore, Michael J., and Charles F. Sabel. *The Second Industrial Divide: Possibilities for Prosperity* (1984).

Prude, Jonathan. *The Coming of Industrial Order: Town and Factory Life in Rural Massachusetts, 1810–1860* (1983).

Reynolds, Terry S. *Stronger Than a Hundred Men: A History of the Vertical Water Wheel* (1983).

Rosenberg, Nathan. *Perspectives on Technology* (1976).

Sabel, Charles, and Jonathan Zeitlin. "Historical Alternatives to Mass Production: Politics, Markets, and Technology in Nineteenth-Century Industrialization." *Past and Present* 108 (August 1985): 133–176.

Samuel, Raphael. "The Workshop of the World: Steam Power and Hand Technology in Mid-Victorian Britain." *History Workshop* 3 (Spring 1977): 6–72.

Saul, S. B., ed. *Technological Change: The United States and Britain in the Nineteenth Century* (1970).

Schivelbusch, Wolfgang. *The Railroad Journey: The Industrialization of Time and Space in the Nineteenth Century* (1986).

Scranton, Philip. *Proprietary Capitalism: The Textile Manufacture at Philadelphia, 1800–1885* (1983).

Smith, Merritt Roe. *Harpers Ferry Armory and the New Technology* (1977).

Stephans, Carlene. "'The Most Reliable Time': William Bond, New England Railroads, and Time Awareness in Nineteenth-Century America." *Technology and Culture* 30 (January 1989):1–24.

Stilgoe, John R. *Metropolitan Corridor: Railroads and the American Scene* (1983).

Taylor, George Rogers. *The Transportation Revolution, 1815–1860* (1951).

Wallace, Anthony F. C. *St. Clair: A Nineteenth-Century Coal Town's Experience with a Disaster-Prone Industry* (1987).

Wilentz, Sean. *Chants Democratic: New York City and the Rise of the American Working Class, 1788–1850* (1984).

Williams, Michael. *Americans and Their Forests: A Historical Geography* (1989).

SEE ALSO **Business Culture; Labor; The Natural Environment; Technology and Social Change.**

THE RISE AND CONSOLIDATION OF BOURGEOIS CULTURE

Mark C. Carnes

HISTORIOGRAPHY

NINETEENTH-CENTURY AMERICANS who worked with their heads rather than hands, who believed that the individual could rise through merit and effort, who proved their commitment to self-control by abstaining from sexual intercourse for long stretches of time, who attended or at least professed affiliation with Protestant churches, who lived in well-to-do sections of the expanding cities and suburbs—these were the people whom modern scholars have often identified as bourgeois or Victorian. Neither term is wholly satisfactory. It seems far-fetched to apply the label "bourgeois," which refers to the culture of the merchants and entrepreneurs of the walled towns of medieval France, to the middle-class people who transformed the United States into an urban, industrial nation. On the other hand, "Victorian," which has the benefit of contemporaneity (Queen Victoria reigned from 1837 to 1901), fails to give a sense of the dynamism of the economic and social transformations of the nineteenth-century United States. Moreover, both terms are unsuitable insofar as they were derived from foreign peoples: few nineteenth-century Americans regarded themselves as Victorian, and fewer still as bourgeois. Modern social historians have found it useful to employ either of these terms—and they are used almost interchangeably—chiefly to suggest the insufficiency of long-standing beliefs in the exceptional and unitary character of American culture and society.

That Americans had long conceived of their society as distinctive was apparent when the first Puritans vowed to establish their society as a "cittie upon a hill." In 1782 J. Hector St. John de Crèvecoeur defined "the American" as a "new man," someone who in "leaving behind all his ancient prejudices and manners, receives new ones." The French nobleman Alexis de Tocqueville in *Democracy in America* (1835) showed his acuity as a social historian by locating America's distinctive culture in the structure of American society. The long shadow of feudalism had not reached the New World, Tocqueville explained, and this allowed Americans to be born free and equal. In the absence of an aristocratic cultural elite and a benighted class of peasants, America emerged as a society of the middle class; though deficient in the cultivation of the finer arts, philosophies, and sensibilities that flowered in the palaces and salons of Europe, America throbbed with the acquisitive energy and democratic vitality of an egalitarian people. Nineteenth-century politicians, businessmen, ministers, literary figures, and historians generally followed Tocqueville's lead in identifying American society and culture with the middle class.

The great exception to Tocqueville's unitary paradigm was the plantation aristocracy of the South; but even this anomaly was dismissed as a foreign import, and one that was providentially removed by the North's victory in the Civil War. During the last third of the nineteenth century, however, the notion of a single "American way of life" was more seriously undermined by the simultaneous emergence of a fabulously wealthy class of financiers and industrialists, whose garish mansions and sprawling vacation resorts proved all too conspicuous, and of a miserably impoverished class of industrial workers and farmers, whose plight was highlighted by violent repression of a spate of strikes commencing in 1877. In 1893, historian Frederick Jackson Turner, who believed in the traditional uniqueness of the American character, asserted that with the disappearance of the frontier America would more closely resemble the highly stratified society that had long prevailed in Europe.

In the early twentieth century, progressive historians such as Charles A. Beard (1874–1948) and Vernon L. Parrington (1871–1929) went even further in challenging Tocqueville's rendering of America's egalitarianism: America was not a classless society but a social battlefield where the common people—farmers, mechanics, tradesmen, laborers—had long contested with powerful mercantile or landed elites. Beard argued that almost from the outset America had approximated the contentious class relationships of European society. In his view, the American Civil War constituted a social revolution marking the triumph of an emergent class of northern merchants and manufacturers over the quasi-feudal society of the South; in this way northern capitalists and industrialists had replicated the ascent of the middle classes over king and aristocracy during the seventeenth-century England, and the triumph of the bourgeoisie over the king, nobility, and clergy in eighteenth-century France.

Where Beard believed that reformers could engineer a truly democratic society in which the middle classes would ameliorate the plight of the poor, the subsequent generation of historians—many of whom had been radicalized by the Great Depression—looked upon the triumph of the American bourgeoisie with less sympathy and the prospects of meaningful reform with less hope. Perhaps the most famous was Matthew Josephson (1899–1978), a Marxist who portrayed with telling detail the inexhaustible greed, stupendous prodigality, spineless cupidity, and bare-faced thievery of the nineteenth-century industrial and financial "robber barons" and their paid lackeys in government. As if to ridicule Tocqueville's claim of America's exceptionalism, Josephson conferred upon his American subjects European costumes and labels: the tenant farmers of the American West became the "new Jacobins"; and the capitalists who defeated the South established a counterrevolutionary "Directory" that, as in the late stages of the French Revolution, managed to put down the "Mountain"—the radical Republicans.

Josephson's rendering of bourgeois culture verged on caricature. By magnifying the actions of the great malefactors, moreover, he left little space to consider the behavior of anyone else. That bourgeois capitalism might also encompass the lives of small manufacturers and shopowners, retail clerks and bookkeepers, and foremen and traveling salesmen (not to mention the wives and families of such men) was an assumption that never fit into Josephson's analytical framework, or that of other radical historians of his generation.

The "consensus" theorists of the 1940s and 1950s, exhilarated by America's prominent role in the defeat of Axis totalitarianism and basking in the postwar return to prosperity, resurrected Tocqueville's claim of American exceptionalism. America had indeed forged an essentially egalitarian, middle-class society whose broad base of agreement transcended divisions of region, ethnicity, class, and race. Political theorist Louis Hartz (1919–1986) echoed Tocqueville in noting that while bourgeois liberals in nineteenth-century Europe had necessarily resorted to violence to topple the king and aristocracy, the American middle class, confronting no such towering obstacles, developed a more equable and consensual means of resolving political disputes. In *People of Plenty* (1954) historian David M. Potter reworked Frederick Jackson Turner's "frontier thesis" so as to accord with an optimistic consensual perspective: the crucial factor in shaping the American character was not the frontier but the economic abundance it had generated through the availability of cheap land and plentiful resources. And though the frontier was long gone, the economic boom after World War II had demonstrated that Americans were far better off materially than their pioneering forebears; the American way of life had not perished, Potter noted, but had been reinvigorated by an economy of abundance.

By emphasizing the exceptionalism of American society and the continuity of its culture, consensus scholars tended to neglect social origins and cultural change. The American character had always been shaped by distinctive phenomena: by its unique environment, the absence of institutions and traditions with deep historical roots, and the experience of immigration. These forces converged in complex but seemingly inscrutable ways: historians might build a chain of plausible deductions on how the American character came to be, but these hypotheses could not be confirmed or disproved. For example, Turner offered little evidence that settlers embraced democratic institutions because they could buy cheap land on the frontier; nor did Potter convincingly show that economic abundance after World War II had effaced ethnic and class divisions. More troublesome still was the failure of consensus theory to explain how America could have erected a middle-class culture without the active and self-conscious agency of a middle class. This view culminated in Daniel Boorstin's monumental history of the American people, which, written over nearly a quarter century, celebrated the inventiveness and pragmatism of individual Americans, but failed to associate it with social classes. Thus his index includes "Borden Condensed Milk," "the Boston Red Sox," "bottling franchises," and "Bouquet, General Henry" but not "bourgeoisie"; and where one would look for "class," one would find that it jumps from "claimjumpers" to "cleaning powders" to "Gloria C. Cline."

The deep strata of cultural self-confidence upon which consensus theory had always rested eroded during the turbulent 1960s. Race riots, a counterculture that condoned drug use and advocated sexual self-expression, and the occasionally violent student protests against the Vietnam War all offered incontestable proof that American society had not been securely cemented by a unifying culture. Many historians—young ones especially—insisted that the consensus theorists' illusion of commonalty had merely patched the gaping holes in American society. These historians joined to create a "new social history" that looked beyond the ideology and culture of the dominant middle class to examine society "from the bottom up."

The agenda was invigorated by an egalitarian ethos: the new social history would give voice to peoples whom traditional historians had long neglected—ethnic and racial minorities, laborers and workers, and (somewhat later) women. Once the lives of these groups had been incorporated, the historical record would, it was thought, be complete. The new social historians' implicit and altogether unexamined assumption was that Tocqueville and those scholars who followed his lead had adequately chronicled the development of the middle class and its culture: where the consensus scholars had gone astray was in assuming that the middle class *was* American society.

Those new social historians who inclined to Marxism had additional reasons to neglect the middle class. Marx's conception of history as a struggle between classes presumed that contending classes would be conscious of their interests; but the American "bourgeoisie" did not have to overcome an entrenched aristocracy and thus evolved without developing a well-articulated sense of class consciousness. More important still because the middle class provided neither capital nor labor, it was irrelevant to the processes of production and to the unfolding of history itself. In Marx's view, the middle class is a transitory phenomenon whose existence obscures modern society's fundamental schism between the two producing classes; caught in a dialectical crush between capital and labor, it would eventually crumble. Marxian historians, then, had little reason to commit much effort to a subject that was at once anomalous, irrelevant, and moribund.

During the 1970s and 1980s, however, several social and intellectual trends converged to force a reconsideration of the role and meaning of the middle class. One was the graying of the counterculture and the apparent return of college students to a complacent normalcy; another was a rising tide of prosperity, especially during the spending boom of the Reagan years, which buoyed the middle classes. Marxists who had earlier foretold the imminent demise of the bourgeoisie were now reminded that Marx had asserted that history unfolds only gradually: the middle class, though ultimately doomed, might remain as an important social element for quite some time. And whatever its future prospects, no one could deny its significance to the nineteenth century. Finally, scholars intent on studying society "from the bottom up" began to recognize that the lives of their subjects were bound up with the people who paid their wages and supervised their labor, sold them goods and rented them housing, and sought to reform their family relations and to regulate their recreations. A social history of the working classes—at least for the nineteenth century—could not be written without a complementary understanding of bourgeois society and culture.

The attempts by the new social historians to recover the lives of peoples who had been missing from history, moreover, were often impeded by a lack of documentary sources. Statistics generated by government agencies, membership lists of church groups and labor unions, fragments of the material culture of working-class housing and homes—such information, however useful in addressing various scholarly debates, often failed to endow their subjects with a human voice. Social historians intent on interpreting these seemingly mute sources increasingly turned to methods derived from anthropology, semiotics and literary theory, folklore and mythology, and other fields of specialization in the social sciences.

The social sciences themselves were undergoing a transformation at this time. The functionalism pioneered by Talcott Parsons (1902–1979), which had for decades dominated American anthropology and sociology, was being challenged by social scientists who drew their inspiration from French structuralism. Functionalists had posited a tight fit between society's organization and culture, which enabled them to deduce the meaning and significance of cultural forms by determining the plausible social need it might address. Thus Parsons, for example, could claim that the emotional pressures of urban industrial life required that women perform specialized roles as helpmates and nurturers. But anthropologists such as Clifford Geertz and Victor Turner, who showed the complexity of human needs and the infinitely subtle ways that culture could address them, weakened the hold of functionalism on American social science. This breathed new life into all social history, especially the study of bourgeois culture and the middle classes. No longer could one accept at face value the assumption that Horatio Alger, Jr.'s "rags-to-riches" stories were popular because they accorded with the needs of an individualistic society; that voluntary associations proliferated throughout the nation to promote national identity and extend business networks; that the nuclear family was a product of urbanization and industrialization; or that modernity required the subjugation of women and the enervation of men. Every aspect of America's cultural record required reexamination through lenses formed by symbolic anthropology, semiotics, literary theory, and linguistic theory. Inasmuch as these new tools were chiefly employed in the interpretation of "words," they were ideally suited for examining a Victorian culture that had been consumed with the production and the preservation of written documents.

This overview is necessarily oversimplified. Historians do not usually undertake research with such conscious attention to prevailing sentiment and methodological trends: this is as true of the new social historians today as it was of conventional historians of the last century. No single methodological or political orthodoxy has ever settled over the discipline and suffocated dissent. Thus some scholars, especially those who cluster under the banner of American studies, continue to make a case for the exceptionalism of American culture. And some social historians continue to rely on functionalism to explain how social structures and cultural patterns are mutually reinforcing. What follows is a synopsis of at least some of the central issues and conclusions that have emerged during the 1970s and 1980s from these social historians. That so much remains unresolved is testimony to the richness of the sources and the vitality of the ensuing work on bourgeois culture.

ECONOMIC FACTORS IN THE MAKING OF MIDDLE CLASS

Although contemporary social historians have mostly moved away from the functionalist assumption that society and culture are so smoothly conjoined as to eliminate friction, they concur that society influences culture and vice versa. The task of modern social historians has been to outline the complex ways in which these phenomena have come together in particular instances. Thus this section is an organizational device, not an assertion that economic factors are primary social causes.

The economic forces that attended the rise of the American middle class—the revolution in transportation, the emergence of a nationwide market, the development of a mobile labor force; the spread of an entrepreneurial ethos—were themselves bound up with cultural changes. The construction of canals and railroads was achieved partly through the politics of the Whigs and their allies; the emergence of a nationwide market was closely related to the expansion of public education and the diffusion of literacy; the increasing mobility of the labor force was facilitated by the ascendancy of the nuclear family; and the rise of entrepreneurship was stimulated by the proliferation of self-help literature. To try to ascertain whether economic or cultural factors were primary is to misconstrue the nature of the problem; a more fruitful approach is to recognize that the cultural and economic factors were themselves linked to the emergence of a coherent and remarkably vibrant middle class. Exactly when this class originated, though, has been a source of dispute.

The colonization of North America was a byproduct of the commercial revolution that had been financed and organized by the European bourgeoisie. It has become an historical commonplace that many of the first settlers—even those in communities dominated by powerful religious elites—were keenly attuned to the economic prospects of the New World: in every colonial seaport there emerged an elite resembling the Old World mercantile bourgeoisie in Holland and England. By the time of the Revolution, most white Americans had improved their material conditions markedly. Historian Jackson Turner Main has estimated, for example, that nearly three-fourths of all white Americans had by then attained a middle-class standard of living, which he defined as owning at least one hundred pounds sterling in property (*The*

Social Structure of Revolutionary America [1965], pp. 112–113, 270–287). This group included self-sufficient farmers, artisans, mechanics, and, at the upper-middle rungs, professionals such as ministers, lawyers, and teachers.

Although Main's "middling" group was more comfortable than their counterparts in Europe, nearly half were self-sufficient farmers who possessed little more than the lands they cultivated, the animals they raised, and the requisite implements for these tasks. Colonial mechanics and artisans, moreover, were often perched precariously on the margins of bankruptcy. Probate records confirm that the material circumstances of most of these middling peoples were quite modest.

The middling peoples of the colonial era lacked access to the far-flung markets that had enriched the merchants of the coastal seaports and the planters of the tidewater South. The mercantile elite, which constituted no more than 5 percent of the population, owned more than half of the land, buildings, and taxable wealth of the largest cities (Stuart Blumin, *The Emergence of the Middle Class* [1989], p. 38). The plantation elite similarly attained a high standard of living through exports to Europe. The middling elements, by contrast, produced food and goods for their own consumption or for barter with nearby artisans and shopkeepers. On years when crop yields were high, they might trade for the iron kettles and silverware we know from probate records; but these occasional boons neither betoken a life of pleasurable consumption nor foretell the cultural transformation that would occur in the early decades of the nineteenth century. The avarice and shrewd dealings of the prototypical Yankee speak not of his farsighted business acumen but of the narrow range of his economic horizons.

During the late eighteenth and early nineteenth centuries, however, a momentous economic transformation was underway. The Napoleonic Wars thrust the European economy into chaos, driving peasants from their fields, disrupting traditional trading patterns, and destabilizing currency. Throughout Europe grain prices skyrocketed. American merchants involved in transatlantic trade, always keenly attuned to price fluctuations, eagerly transmitted word of the high prices to their forwarding agents in the hinterland. Shopkeepers and merchants who were situated along navigable rivers pooled their resources to construct turnpikes and plank roads into the interior; farmers in these regions began to cultivate exportable grain, haul it by wagons along the improved roads to the nearest forwarding agents, who then shipped it by sloop to the large coastal seaports. Substantial profits accrued at each stage of these transactions; many Americans were thus exposed for the first time to the financial rewards that could be gained through wide-ranging market forces.

The economic magnitude of this transformation, however, should not be overemphasized. Even in times of high prices, grain could not profitably be sent by wagon more than sixty or seventy miles (roughly one hundred kilometers) on even the best roads of that era; this effectively removed most New England farmers from access to this new market. Because everyone knew that grain prices would fall precipitously with the return of peace, moreover, even market-oriented farmers limited their risk by devoting only part of their land to cultivating exportable grains. A similar wariness curtailed the enthusiasm of the many urban tradesmen, artisans, and shopkeepers who tended to the needs of the farmers.

Nevertheless, in the early nineteenth century many people, having seen high profits, now craved more. But continuous profits depended on sustained demand; and this required creation of a broad market within the United States, which itself presumed both the growth of cities and the development of an effective system of transportation. The parsimonious Yankee of the colonial era detested taxation in nearly all its forms and was loath to spend public money on transportation improvements. But in the early nineteenth century a powerful constituency of market-oriented farmers and businessmen in favor of internal improvements goaded municipalities, states, and even the federal government into providing the requisite capital for the construction of thousands of miles of canals and railroads. This initiated a "transportation revolution," to use George Rogers Taylor's phrase, that webbed the nation with canals and railroads.

Farmers abandoned the rocky hills of New England and the exhausted soils of the coastal South, pushed over the Appalachian Mountains, and settled in the fertile valleys of the Ohio and Mississippi rivers and along the shores of the Great Lakes. Their grain and foodstuffs were collected at nearby towns and villages and then were shipped to cities along key points in the transportational grid. The large seaports of the Atlantic Coast, which initially functioned as commercial entrepôts, benefited from access to labor and materials, and so commenced factory production. With the expansion of the transportation network, though, new industrial cities arose nearer to the sources of raw materials. Most economic historians believe that sometime during the period from 1820 to 1845 the economy ascended from a relatively stagnant level onto a broad plateau of sustained growth that extended well into the twentieth century. By the time of the Civil War, certainly, there had evolved a tight matrix of rural, urban, and regional economies; indeed, the United States provided one of the best illustrations of Adam Smith's dictum that the broadening of the market results in specialization.

Historians disagree, however, on whether real wages increased during the early antebellum era: census statistics prior to 1840 are so incomplete that any estimate is problematic. What is clear is that economic specialization from 1830 to 1860 caused the price of many goods to plummet: clocks that had cost twenty dollars in the 1830s sold for three or four dollars thirty years later, and the price of factory-made, ready-to-wear clothing dropped by one-half to two-thirds in the same period. John Gurley and E. S. Shaw have concluded that the overall commodity price level fell nearly 50 percent from 1800 to 1860.

Aggregate data on wages and prices fail to indicate growing disparaties in income and wealth. The rising scale on which virtually all types of business operated—from people employed to the area served—enabled some entrepreneurs to amass fortunes. Edward Pessen has estimated that the wealthiest 4 percent of New York's population controlled about half the city's wealth in 1828; by 1845 they controlled two-thirds (*Riches, Class, and Power Before the Civil War* [1973], pp. 33–35). The number of New Yorkers worth over $100,000 or more tripled. Not only were the rich getting richer, but a middle class of nonmanual workers was advancing far more rapidly than were manual workers. Stuart Blumin has estimated that while the average antebellum worker earned about $500 to $600 annually, the white-collar worker earned upwards of twice as much. Perhaps more significant, nonmanual workers acquired skills that might lead to rapid advancement or to business ownership, while manual workers' prospects were far more limited (*The Emergence of the Middle Class* [1989], pp. 110–114). The comprehensive study of Poughkeepsie, New York, by historians Clyde Griffen and Sally Griffen have determined that 46 percent of the clerks in 1860 had moved into the ranks of the professionals or proprietors by the end of the decade; but fewer than one in four skilled workers and one in eight unskilled workers had advanced to a comparable degree (*Natives and Newcomers* [1978], p. 60). Antebellum white America was evolving into a three-tiered society characterized by an elite of merchants and southern planters; an increasingly broad middle class; and a wage-earning working class.

The widening gap between the workers and the emergent middle class was further reflected in a clear distinction in the nature of work. In the colonial period proprietors and master craftsmen had shared living quarters and often performed the same tasks. But the expanding scale of manufacturing and retailing operations entailed the creation of substantial bureaucracies, which in turned stimulated demand for clerks, bookkeepers, accountants, copyists, salesmen, and bill collectors. Proprietors now retreated to an office, and they hired a supervisor to watch over the production force and an office manager to superintend the growing army of nonmanual workers who processed orders, paid bills, settled accounts, and reckoned wages. When growth caused firms to expand beyond their walls in downtown business areas, new factories and warehouses were constructed on less expensive lands on the fringes of the city. This further separated the managerial from the working classes, the nonmanual from the manual workers.

Whether the increasing economic disparities caused manual and nonmanual workers to think of themselves as members of distinct classes is difficult to determine. Most scholarly effort has focused on the working classes, and social historians such as Sean Wilentz have chronicled the rise of a class consciousness and the evolution of a distinct working-class culture in antebellum America. Less attention, however, has been paid to the middle classes. Consensus historians, as has been noted, claimed that the boundaries between economic groups in America were so permeable as to render class identification all but meaningless. Some modern social historians have found evidence to support this view. For example, John S. Gilkeson, Jr., has concluded that leaders of mechanics' organizations in Providence, Rhode Island, endorsed middle-class values and explicitly identified with the middle class (*Middle-Class Providence* [1986]). Blumin, on the other hand, who insists that nonmanual and manual workers were becoming more conscious of their class affiliation, dismisses such pronouncements as reflecting the views not of most manual workers but of master craftsmen, who were in fact edging into the middle class. The issue of middle-class consciousness is further complicated by the entrepreneurial ethos that pervaded white-collar work: people who enshrined individual achievement and competition were perhaps unable or reluctant to articulate their class affiliations.

Consciousness, for social historians as well as for psychoanalysts, is by its nature elusive; an understanding of the *mentalité* of the American middle class requires an examination of its cultural productions.

THE RISE OF BOURGEOIS CULTURE (1800–1860)

"The whole state of man is a state of culture," Ralph Waldo Emerson wrote, anticipating modern anthropology; elsewhere, anticipating semiotics, Emerson defined culture as "all which gives the mind possession of its own powers" (quoted in Burton Bledstein, *The Culture of Professionalism* [1976], p. 29). The apostles of the mid-nineteenth-century middle classes spoke with prescient authority on the subject of culture not because of their intellectual sophistication (their uncritical enthusiasm for their own creations was, on the contrary, their most grating fault) but because they had witnessed in their lifetime a jumble of philosophies, religious beliefs, political ideologies, social customs, and gender roles coalesce into a vital cultural system.

Emerson's encompassing conception of culture contained a sharp political edge: his was the culture of the middle-class North, which when juxtaposed to the culture of the plantation South acquired special coherence and purpose—and, by 1865, a sense of invincibility. Middle-class culture combined the best aspects of romanticism—the enshrinement of human potential, the restless striving for personal betterment, the zeal for competition and conflict—and suffused it with a passion for self-control and a fetish for regularity. It achieved its finest embodiment, in Emerson's view, in the person of Abraham Lincoln: a self-made man, a striver consumed by ambition, and a fighter with keen competitive instincts who nevertheless supported temperance, was an ardent proponent of work, and believed in the law as the embodiment of rationality. When Lincoln became president in 1861, Emerson noted with satisfaction: "This middle-class country had got a middle-class president, at last" (quoted in Bledstein, p. 30).

The origins of this political culture were to be found in American Whiggery. Historian Daniel Walker Howe has determined that although both the Whigs and their Democratic opponents appealed to diverse constituencies, the Whigs chiefly derived support from businessmen and professionals (who favored self-control and individual betterment), from industrialists and often their employees (who sought to protect American manufactures), and from farmers (who favored internal improvements such as canals and railroads). The Whigs embraced industrialization and technology as means of bettering mankind, imagining that its message of personal reformation could be extended to all of American society; they endorsed the religious evangelism of the Second Great Awakening; and they despised the factionalism and political opportunism they associated with Andrew Jackson and his followers.

The Whig party collapsed during the 1850s. Whig counsels of moderation and statesmanship were lost amid the clash of passions over slavery that had been unleashed by repeal of the Missouri Compromise in 1854. But in *The Political Culture of the American Whigs,* Howe argues that the emergent Republican party was "an intensified version of northern middle-class whiggery, unashamedly sectional and freed from the impurities of compromise" (p. 277). The ideology of the Republican party, historian Eric Foner has shown, echoed the middle-class's advocacy of the self-reliant individual as well as its disparagement both of wage-earning as a form of dependency and of aristocratic wealth as an inducement to idleness. The Whig party may have been all but dead by 1854, but its political culture emerged from the war triumphant.

The emotional power of bourgeois culture was largely derived from its close association with evangelical religion. The Second Great Awakening, which raged across the nation in the 1820s and 1830s, had been the inspiration of lawyer turned itinerant preacher Charles Grandison Finney (1792–1875). He sought to humble human pride by depicting God's wrath, but he broke free from orthodoxy by asserting that everyone possessed the capacity to win God's grace: the truly penitent need only surrender to Him totally and without reservation. Finney's amalgam of ego-bashing and therapeutic redemption appealed to tens of thousands of people who flocked to revivals, camp meetings, and other ad hoc sessions.

Finney's message was powerful because it added emotional depth to a religious experience that, under the leadership of liberal theologians in Boston, had become nearly devoid of meaning. If, as the liberals contended, no God worthy of worship would consign His creatures to damnation, then the impetus for faith and the imperative to adhere to His laws were diminished. It might have been expected that the more relaxed tenets of liberalism would have appealed to the increasingly prosperous middle classes: as one's economic horizons expanded, it seemingly became easier to lower one's gaze from the Lord to the ledger. But the areas that were particularly scorched by this Great Awakening—the "burned-over" districts along the Mohawk Valley in upstate New York and the newly settled regions of Ohio—were regions of rapid economic growth and commercial development. That thousands of such peoples turned to God suggests that they had misgivings about their devotion to money-making and the material wealth they were beginning to acquire. The antebellum middle classes may have taken satisfaction in having a piano in the parlor, but it paled before the deeper emotional needs fulfilled by communion with God.

But as the German sociologist Max Weber pointed out long ago, religious fervor, especially of the Protestant variety, does not necessitate a repudiation of wealth. Indeed, social historians Paul E. Johnson (in *A Shopkeeper's Millennium* [1978]) and Anthony F. C. Wallace (in *Rockdale* [1978]) have argued that shopkeepers and manufacturers endorsed evangelical religion as a means of stimulating productivity among workers. Finney's insistence that each individual could and must reach out and grasp God's gift of salvation accorded with the needs of employers, who wanted their workers to become self-reliant and to eschew collective economic and political action. Moreover, Finney's denunciation of the tavern, the chief form of relaxation and socialization for many workers, also corresponded to employers' wishes. The Second Great Awakening, in Wallace's view, constituted an "evangelical counter-attack" against the workers, one that succeeded in establishing "Christian capitalism." "To put it simply," Johnson wrote in a similar vein, "the middle class became resolutely bourgeois between 1825 and 1835. And at every step, that transformation bore the stamp of evangelical Protestantism" (p. 8).

So capitalism needed to discipline workers, and society spewed forth the requisite ideology in the guise of a saving religion; workers went along with this seemingly transparent strategem in order to keep their jobs or to get better ones, much as some slaves prudently chose to feign docile loyalty to their masters. However, this bald sociological functionalism fails to explain why, if the revivals were play-acting, so many people broke down in fits of weeping and shaking. What accounted for the deeply imprinted emotional texture of the Great Awakening? Or why, for that matter, did women comprise a disproportionately large share of the converts?

Women's history, which shared somewhat belatedly in the resurgence of social history in the 1960s, advanced rapidly during the following decade. One of the signal achievements of women's history has been to delineate the profound changes in middle-class gender roles and domestic life during the early nineteenth century. Although the origins and timing of this transformation are still a source of debate, most scholars agree that it resulted from a complex interplay of economic, ideological, and religious factors. Roughly speaking, economic growth fostered a rigid division of labor by sex as middle-class women, no longer burdened with farm tasks—feeding animals, spinning and weaving, brewing, and so on—increasingly became purchasers of goods rather than producers of them. Women seized this break from the grinding labors of farm work to claim a more exalted role for themselves. Inverting earlier assumptions that women's minds were held captive to their reproductive systems, women such as Catharine Beecher (the eldest child of theologian Lyman Beecher), claimed that women are innately devoid of the baser drives that impell men to crave money and to indulge in sex. This idea dovetailed with Finney's belief that salvation was available to everyone willing to make the effort; inasmuch as women were closer to God, then, they were peculiarly well suited to effect the reformation of men and thereby of society itself. If this new ideology elevated women's status and advanced their claims of moral superiority, though, it also offered ideological justification for their confinement to a "domestic sphere" of home and family.

But because men were ensconced by day in a morally pestiferous atmosphere of money-grubbing and cutthroat competition, their reformation in the evenings was a dubious proposition; so it was to rearing Christian children that middle-class women devoted themselves. In this work they were aided by a new body of child-rearing literature, such as

J. S. C. Abbott, *The Child at Home* (1833), Lydia Maria Child, *The Mother's Book* (1831), Theodore Dwight, *The Father's Book* (1834), Heman Humphrey, *Domestic Education* (1840), and Lydia Sigourney's *Letters to Mothers* (1838). Where eighteenth-century ministers and authors counseled parents to "break the will" of refractory children, authors of the new advice books sought to induce piety and kindness. Children did not have to be purged of Satan, as Calvinism had maintained, but could be infused with God's grace much as a "mother fills a vessel with love." With the publication of Horace Bushnell's *Christian Nurture* (1847), this new doctrine received explicit theological sanction. Bushnell explained that the emotional pyrotechnics of the Bible-thumping evangelists had precipitated a false conversion; only through a gradual infusion of God's spirit, a task for which women were uniquely well suited, could human beings be led to grace.

By the mid nineteenth century the gender-bifurcated family, shaped by a conjunction of economic, ideological, and religious forces, had become one of the distinguishing features of Victorian society. In her *Cradle of the Middle Class* (1981) Mary Ryan has further shown how this new conception of family itself helped to perpetuate middle-class culture. Parents devised a "family strategy" that simultaneously advanced financial and moral goals in three major ways: by limiting how many children they had, so as to ensure that each child could be properly educated and his or her moral development monitored; by keeping children in school as long as possible, thus improving their chances for entering nonmanual occupations and sheltering them from the depradations of the adult world; and by encouraging sons to delay marriage until their late twenties or early thirties, thereby allowing them to save up enough capital to get started in business and to make an advantageous marriage. That each component of this strategy had become normative is reflected in three strands of evidence. First, fertility declined sharply: in 1800, a white woman of childbearing age would have on the average seven children, but a century later, this number had been halved. And while the decline in fertility affected nearly all social groups, it was most pronounced among native-born, middle-class women. Second, middle-class sons stayed in school longer than did boys of working-class parents. Stuart Blumin, for example, has found that in Philadelphia in 1860 more than three-fourths of the fifteen-year-old boys of professional or upper-middle-class fathers were still in school, while the same could be said of only one-fourth of the laborers' sons (p. 190). Third and finally, an increasing proportion of males remained at home well into their twenties: Richard Sennett's study of a middle-class suburb of Chicago has revealed that in 1880 a majority of thirty-year-old men were unmarried and still resided in the home of their parents (*Families Against the City* [1970], pp. 102–103).

Middle-class women derived moral authority from their role as mothers, but they soon acquired both the means and the rationale to influence a wider world. In *The Bonds of Womanhood* (1977) historian Nancy Cott has described how middle-class women, in coming together in prayer groups and reform societies, forged the bonds that provided the emotional resources and intellectual challenge necessary for a wider social role. Ryan has further documented how these women entered into a public role by championing various reforms. To protect the home from the brothel and tavern, women moved out of the domestic sphere to create and join temperance organizations and moral reform societies; and to ensure that young people would be exposed to these finer sensibilities, unmarried women, functioning rather like surrogate mothers, went into teaching with a missionary zeal. In the 1840s this movement was spearheaded by educational reformer Horace Mann (1796–1859), who, noting woman's inherent moral superiority, claimed that they should be charged with teaching the young. If school districts were not persuaded by this logic, they readily accepted its economics: women would work for about half as much as male teachers. By 1890 two out of three public school teachers were female.

Women's influences were so pervasive that Ann Douglas has written of the "feminization" of American Victorian culture—by which she means the replacement of an intellectually rigorous Calvinist patriarchal ethos by a vapid, liberal sentimentalism. This "feminized" culture originated in the alliance of ministers and middle-class women early in the nineteenth century but soon spread throughout American society largely through the printed word. Middle-class women and those who aspired to that status pored over religious tracts, magazines, and, increasingly, sentimental novels. James Fenimore Cooper's popular *The Last of the Mohicans* (1826) sold but 5,570 copies, and Herman Melville went almost unread, but books for women found an enormous audience: Fanny Fern's *Fern Leaves from Fanny's Port-folio* (1853) sold 80,000 copies, and Harriet Beecher Stowe's *Uncle Tom's Cabin*

(1851) sold over 300,000 copies in the year after it went to press.

A mawkish sentimentalism suffused many aspects of American culture. One example is the transformation in funeral customs: the death's heads and foreboding epitaphs of Calvinist tombstones were replaced in the nineteenth century by images of recumbent figures and inscriptions describing death as a gentle, even pleasant release from life. In 1831 Unitarian clergymen and literary figures established Mount Auburn Cemetery in Cambridge, Massachusetts; soon afterward, similarly inviting landscaped garden cemeteries appeared in New York, Philadelphia, Baltimore, and other American cities. Corpses, too, were doctored in response to the demands of a public that no longer cared to contemplate the grim physical realities of death.

There is much to Douglas's claim that Victorian culture foisted upon men and women alike a creed that tugged at their emotions rather than stimulating their minds, enshrined rigid gender role distinctions rather than calling for their reexamination, and gave rise to a consumerist culture and advertising clichés rather than examined lives and social criticism. If its forms seemed simplistic and superficial, though, its emotional depth should not be underestimated—for it was the same culture that, unable to abide slave culture, drew the North into a fateful collision with the South, and thereby helped to consolidate the middle class.

THE CONSOLIDATION OF BOURGEOIS CULTURE (1860–1900)

During the 1860s and 1870s the vital energy of bourgeois culture seemed to have been transmuted into greater mass. This was due in part to the Civil War, which sapped the nation's reformist impulses: people who had conceived of abolitionism as a humanitarian crusade were sobered that their efforts had summoned up the masculine demons of war. The Gilded Age was not without inspired religious revivalists or significant political and social reforms; but where the enthusiasts of the antebellum era had relied on moral sentiment and ardor, and had possessed a strong anti-institutional bias, late-Victorian Americans had grown distrustful of emotional displays and sought the solidity and lasting effect that could be achieved through the institutionalization of philanthropy and social reforms.

In part, the stolidity of the Gilded Age stemmed from the fact that the generation born in the 1820s and 1830s and shaped by the religious revivals and reformist enthusiasms of the era had themselves changed by the 1860s and 1870s. Husbands and wives whose parents had protected them as children from corrupting influences now built substantial homes in the new, quasi-rural suburbs. Businessmen and manufacturers, who as young clerks had scrambled to the top in a struggle with their peers, now managed substantial firms and commanded respect. Reformers and ideologues who had hoped to usher in a democratic millennium and to eradicate social injustice now constructed reform schools, asylums, penitentiaries, and hospitals, and they served as trustees of a host of philanthropic associations. Even the cultural critics—the would-be heirs to mavericks such as Henry David Thoreau and John Brown—now took a regular turn on the Chautauqua lecture circuit or found salaried positions as faculty in the burgeoning universities. Nearly all social movements were now supervised by salaried managers, securely trussed in constitutions, and regulated by Robert's rules of order.

Robert Wiebe has characterized the era as a "search for order," a time when middle-class Americans, bewildered by the changes wrought by rapid urbanization and industrialization, sought security and regularity by building elaborate bureaucracies. Alan Trachtenberg has employed a similar if somewhat more concrete metaphor: society and culture had undergone a process of "incorporation," as the predominant form of the modern business world seeped deep into American consciousness. Both Wiebe and Trachtenberg underscore those aspects of Victorian America that anticipated the twentieth century, but in so doing they neglected the continuity of middle-class culture and society throughout the nineteenth century. The decades after the Civil War are best understood as an era in which the values and initiatives of antebellum America were consolidated.

Economic consolidation was apparent everywhere: the years after 1870 saw the United States become an industrial colossus with an economic growth that was virtually unprecedented in history. Economists estimate that from 1874 to 1883, the gross national product increased by an astounding 44 percent. The railroads triggered the industrial boom, as the total track in the nation increased nearly sixfold. Iron output expanded nearly elevenfold. The growth of the nation's transportation system and producer's infrastructure resulted in increased output of consumer goods. A telling example is the telephone: invented in 1876 by Alexander Graham Bell, by 1900 it was found in 800,000 American businesses and homes (twice the total for all Europe). In 1860 less than 700,000 Americans had savings accounts, and total deposits totaled less than $150 million; by 1900 six million Americans had savings accounts with total deposits of $2.5 billion. One reason the Gilded Age was characterized by substantial homes and institutional edifices is that there was sufficient money to erect and furnish them.

The growth of business volume enabled the larger producers, wholesalers, and retailers to cut costs and operate more efficiently. This is expressed in the output of the average manufacturing plant, which increased over 300 percent from 1869 to 1899. With most wholesale and retail industries as well, the rise of the larger firm resulted in more salaried jobs for clerks, salesmen, and managers. From 1870 to 1910 the new middle class of clerical workers, salespersons, government employees, technicians, and salaried professionals rose from 756,000 to 5,609,000. If these ranks were increasing, though, the prospects of the small proprietors—shopkeepers, bakers, printers, and so on—were diminishing. The small general store found it increasingly difficult to compete with the Wanamaker's and Macy's, and the one-factory wire manufacturer with the great trust of Washburn and Moen. In balance, the center of gravity within the middle class was shifting to salaried work, where risks were greater but the prospects for spectacular advancement more limited. Boyhood dreams that had been inspired by the Horatio Alger tales were set aside, and the people who filled the new salaried ranks plodded along, hoping to advance incrementally, counting the years until their pensions would be payable, and settling increasingly for the trappings of middle-class comfort.

Religion, too, suffered from a "crisis of faith" during the postwar years. Charles Darwin was partly to blame. Though the impact of *Origin of the Species* (1859) on the United States was delayed by the Civil War, Darwin's rendering of nature as a chaotic arena in which all forms of life contended undermined the Victorian assumption that God had endowed human life with comprehensible purposes and meanings. Beliefs became indistinct, and the theological disputes that had promoted sectarianism in the past came to seem unimportant. Churchgoers cared more about the design of the hulking new cathedrals than the content of the liturgy, and about the fame of their preacher more than the force of his theological reasoning. Religion's chief purpose appeared to be the inculcation of the basic moral principles necessary for the smooth functioning of almost any society. In 1882 Henry Ward Beecher, the most conspicuous American theologian of the age, insisted that morality was "the indispensable ground of spiritual fervor," but his own life, as evidenced by his scandalous conduct ten years earlier with a married parishioner, suggest that neither morality nor spiritual fervor were what they had been.

As cities grew larger and larger and the range of personal contacts increased exponentially, Victorians anguished over how one could discern who indeed practiced what he or she preached. In the absence of the self-policing networks of gossip and accumulated face-to-face encounters that had characterized small-town American society, how could one determine whether an insurance agent could be trusted with a premium, or a traveling salesman with one's daughter? In *Confidence Men and Painted Women* (1982) cultural historian Karen Halttunen has demonstrated how Victorian Americans were bedeviled by the coquetry and artifice of those who trafficked on people's ignorance and betrayed their trust. Antebellum-era Americans had evaluated strangers on whether they manifested a "transparent sincerity"—unfrivolous clothes, a plain-speaking earnestness, simple but heartfelt mourning rituals, and so on; but a generation later Victorians scrutinized newcomers for elegance and mastery of social conventions, exemplified in a studied command of rules of etiquette and fashionable attire and hairstyles. By the 1860s and 1870s, Halttunen writes, "the sentimental demand for sincerity that had given rise to the complex code of genteel conduct had fallen away, leaving behind the social forms themselves" (p. 196). The rise of phrenology, which promised to unlock the secrets of the psyche by examining the bumps on a person's head, exemplifies this problematic search for the traces of "character" that were obscured by an elegant coiffure. The increasing reliance on higher education and professional degrees as protection against quackery and validation of educational attainments is indicated, as Bledstein has observed in *The Culture of Professionalism,* by the growth of graduate schools and professional associations during the late nineteenth century.

The new middle-class family, too, lost something of its moral fervor and gained in its place a new substantiality and self-conscious rectitude. The transition can be summarized by comparing the mid-Victorian March family of Louisa May Alcott's *Little Women* (1868–1869) with William Dean Howells's late-Victorian Laphams (*The Rise of Silas Lapham* [1885]) and his Basil Marches (*Hazard of New Fortunes* [1890]). Where piety is the cornerstone of Alcott's family (epitomized by Marmee's unceasing attempts to teach the girls to accept the will of God), it is pride that animates the newly rich Laphams (who seek to prove themselves middle-class by building a large suburban home and furnishing it and themselves ostentatiously) and governs the later, solidly respectable Basil Marches (who convey their middle-class standing with impeccable etiquette). In the latter cases, the criteria for assessing the late-Victorian family are increasingly defined in tangible terms: a well-appointed home in the suburbs, fashionable clothes, a uniformed maid, a nonmanual position with "prospects," a secure, four-digit income, and so on.

Whether relations between husbands and wives, and men and women more generally, also became increasingly formal and emotionally distant is a source of scholarly dispute. Many twentieth-century commentators, influenced by Sigmund Freud's insight that society places harmful constraints on human sexual drives, have depicted Victorian men as flinty, hard-hearted patriarchs, the women as docile, long-suffering victims, and their marriages as devoid of love and sexual fulfillment. This view is suggested by the title of Ronald G. Walter's anthology, *Primers for Prudery: Sexual Advice to Victorian America* (1974). Duncan Crow, in *The Victorian Woman* (1972), describes intercourse as taking place "in a dark bedroom into which the husband would creep to create his offspring in silence while the wife endured the connection in a coma" (p. 25).

In *Searching the Heart* (1989), on the other hand, Karen Lystra has maintained that intricate rituals of Victorian courtship subverted gender distinctions, and that the private disclosure of personal and sexual intimacies was all the more delicious for having been proscribed from public discourse. In *The Bourgeois Experience* (1984), Peter Gay has similarly chronicled the exuberant eroticism and sexual expression among many married Victorians. But these revisionists who have described Victorian marriages as companionate may have gone too far, for there is ample evidence to the contrary. The notion of separate spheres for men and women, initially advanced in the antebellum era as a reformist ideology, had by the 1870s and 1880s become frozen in human relations; and the intimate meeting of the minds became problematic once the minds of men and women were thought to be dissimilar.

The various emotional and psychological strains of Victorian life contributed to a variety of social malaises. In 1869 an American doctor, George M. Beard, told the New York Medical Journal Association that middle-class Americans were peculiarly susceptible to "neurasthenia," a type of "brain strain" caused by the hectic pace of modern life. Victorian social scientists such as T. S. Cooley and Ferdinand Tonnies, a German scholar, contrasted the close personal relationships of primitive societies with the more formal, impersonal, and contractual relationships of their own societies. These views culminated in Thorstein Veblen's *Theory of the Leisure Class* (1899), a trenchant attack on Victorian culture and its conspicuous consumption, which fueled economic growth but washed away a sense of self as well as aesthetic and moral principles.

The culture of consumption could be harmful in other ways, as Elaine Abelson has observed in her study of women shoplifters, *When Ladies Go A-Thieving* (1989). Abelson describes how women were enticed into brilliantly illuminated department stores, whose limitless panoply of goods were arrayed with seductive glitter in glass- and mirror-lined cases. For many, the compulsion to possess that which they could not afford was stronger than their fear of public exposure. That these women invested material objects with so much meaning conveys some sense of their own emptiness. Sociologist Richard Sennett has located the source of another form of emptiness in Victorian family life. Sennett concludes from his study of middle-class suburb of Chicago that the nuclear family was too closed and the gender roles too rigid to cope with the pressures of urban-industrial life; instead of providing the nurturance managers and businessmen needed, the middle-class family became a repository of unresolved tensions.

Victorians themselves complained of the artificiality and unreality of bourgeois existence. Many longed to share in the presumably deeper emotional experiences of premodern peoples and times. In *No Place for Grace* (1981) cultural historian T. J. Jackson Lears describes this antimodern sentiment as especially common among intellectuals, noting Henry Adams's preoccupation with medieval cathedrals, William Sturgis Bigelow's fascination with Japanese art and Buddhism, and Theodore Roosevelt's exaltation of a "strenuous life" of martial virtues. Lears's observation that Victorian culture contained this therapeutic antidote to its own materialism and superficiality is important; but this capacity of culture to redress the strains of social life was hardly unique to the Victorians, nor was it possessed solely among the intellectuals. One significant characteristic of bourgeois culture during the last third of the nineteenth century was the proliferation of a wide variety of "therapeutical" formal institutions.

Bourgeois women sought refuge from the constraints of the domestic sphere in a wide variety of clubs and voluntary associations. Middle-class men similarly flocked to fraternal orders, whose total membership approached six million by the end of the century. As I have documented in *Secret Ritual and Victorian Manhood in America* (1989), these all-male organizations featured successions of long initiation rituals that provided men with a secret theology antithetical to liberal theology and an alternative surrogate family of "brothers" far different from the one in which they had been raised. Professional sports, too, provided sustenance to city-dwellers bewildered by the new industrial order, ambivalent about the meaning of competition, and enervated by the pressures of the rigorous time schedules so central to industrial culture. An afternoon at the ballpark, Gunther Barth has shown in *City People* (1980), offered a drama that unfolded at a leisurely pace upon a grassy turf, as well as a resolution of competitive forces according to rules known to all and visibly enforced by uniformed umpires. Bicycling, leisurely strolls through well-manicured parks, band concerts—these and a thousand other diversions provided Americans with emotional release from the constraints of Victorian society. Though Freud rightly perceived that society inevitably places limits on self-fulfillment, he failed to recognize the extent to which all culture performs socially therapeutic functions. If civilization breeds discontents, it also spawns cultural forms to assuage them.

HEGEMONY AND DISSENT

Not all Americans shared in the delights or the dilemmas of Victorian culture, and many people within its orbit were unmoved by its attractions. For example, working-class parents knew that their inability to provide lengthy schooling would hinder their children's prospects for entering the ranks of the middle class; and the fact that the dream was unattainable caused many workers to reject it entirely. During the turbulent ten years that commenced with the bloody railroad strikes of 1877 and culminated in the Haymarket Square riot of 1886, many workers fought pitched battles against employers and the state. Forms of bourgeois cultural domination, such as middle-class reformers' attacks on the tavern, precipitated even more sustained opposition from industrial workers, as Roy Rosenzweig has documented for late-nineteenth-century Worcester, Massachusetts, in *Eight Hours for What We Will* (1983). Efforts by employers to combine industrial paternalism with bourgeois culture were similarly unsuccessful. The demise of the Pullman model town outside Chicago is one illustration. Built by George M. Pullman, developer of the sleeping car for railroads, Pullman, Illinois, was designed to instill middle-class work habits and a sense of identification with the company: workers' housing was well-built; tree-lined streets followed the contour of man-made lakes; and libraries, shopping arcades, and lyceums provided workers with access to the amenities of bourgeois culture. (By contrast, there were no taverns: alcohol was served only in the dining-room of the company hotel.) During the economic depression after 1893, however, smoldering resentments over company paternalism and its use of paid spies ignited an open rebellion when workers' pay was cut but their rents were not. The protracted strike that ensued led to the collapse of the Pullman experiment.

Bourgeois culture also failed to take hold in the deep South and Appalachia, where a strong tradition of hard drinking, bare-knuckle fighting, and other unchastened forms of self-expression were deeply rooted in male culture. At the other geographical extreme, many of the old Boston gentry, scorning the newly rich purveyors of Victorian culture and the mediocrity of its wares, remained steadfast in their cultivation of the genteel sensibilities of a preindustrial era. The delineaments of a distinct homosexual counterculture also began to appear in the larger cities; but because moral reformers labeled homosexuality a "crime against nature" and called for its suppression, most homosexuals kept a low profile; few other Victorians were even aware of this richly nuanced but hidden counterculture.

Overt racism prevented ethnic and racial minorities from gaining admission to Victorian society. Those few northern blacks who acquired enough money to approach the threshold of bourgeois culture were almost uniformly excluded from white fraternal orders, women's societies, recreational clubs, and sporting events. Native Americans were in a very limited sense given the prospect of citizenship by the Dawes Act of 1887, which empowered the president to grant 160 acres of reservation lands to each Indian family willing to abandon tribal life. The Dawes Act was conceived as a means of teaching Indians "the habits of civilized life" (that is, bourgeois culture): the possession of private property, the primacy of the nuclear family, and the benefits of sustained work. Only a few Native Americans accepted this offer to abandon their own way of life. Most tried to maintain their culture as best they could in the inhospitable environment of the reservations. Many of those who escaped were hunted down by the U.S. Army and slaughtered.

But if bourgeois culture was not quite hegemonic, its influence was pervasive. Some labor historians argue that notwithstanding the violent rebellions of the last third of the nineteenth century, most workers failed to think of themselves as an oppositional class. Rosenzweig has found that increasing numbers of industrial workers were indeed moving into white-collar jobs and joining middle-class organizations; the phrase "lace-curtain" Irish, connoting an identification with Victorian values, was becoming increasingly common (p. 81). The Knights of Labor even rewarded retiring officials with gifts of rural cottages and pianos, preeminent symbols of bourgeois domesticity.

Perhaps the best indicator of the potency of Victorian culture is how widely Victorian gender notions spread throughout American society. Women who helped to push wagons along the overland trail to the West imagined that they would eventually become proper Victorian mothers. This is further confirmed by Robert Griswold's analysis of some four hundred divorce petitions in his *Family and Divorce in California, 1850–1890* (1982). These documents reveal that even working-class men and women in the rough-and-tumble West expected their spouses to assume the roles "proper" for their sex. Suzanne Lebsock has documented in *The Free Women of Petersburg* (1989) how, on the eve of the Civil War, white women in that Virginia town similarly accepted the rigid gender distinctions that characterized Victorian society. By the 1880s and 1890s, the powerful solvent of bourgeois culture—in the form of evangelical revivals, temperance reform, and campaigns to chasten lewd behavior and smutty talk—had penetrated even the more remote recesses of the South. Even critics of Victorian culture had difficulty escaping its pull: thus the protagonist of Edward Bellamy's *Looking Backward, 2000–1887* (1888) awakens to discover a future utopia which, though purged of economic competition and monopoly capitalism, has retained Victorian gender conventions.

The extent to which bourgeois culture has survived the mighty political, social, and cultural upheavals of the twentieth century is a difficult issue, and one that extends beyond the scope of the present essay. Some claim that new and exuberant forms of entertainment, such as ragtime dancing, amusement parks, and movies shattered the decorous tone and moral authority of the family; others maintain that a pervasive skepticism and two world wars undermined faith in religious purpose and human progress; still others assert that the rise of the "organization man" and the huge corporations rendered the solitary striver obsolete.

Yet many aspects of Victorian culture have endured and others seem to be making a comeback. The agenda of the "Reagan Revolution"—strong family values and a reduced role of the federal government—would not have proved uncongenial to the middle classes of late-nineteenth-century America. Modern politicians routinely invoke bourgeois maxims on individual achievement; some even continue to cite Horatio Alger, Jr. Most, when pressed, profess a belief in God. Nearly all squirm, as did Henry Ward Beecher, when word of marital infidelities comes to the attention of the public. Moreover, "reformers" in ex-communist states in eastern Europe and in Russia speak of the merits of laissez-faire capitalism with a reverence that might have brought a smile to the face of a J. P. Morgan or an Andrew Carnegie. The world of the bourgeois America is not dead, but has instead been subjected to intense re-examination. What remains unchanged is the social historian's fascination for the subject. As Peter Gay observes, nineteenth-century bourgeois culture "has not lost its capacity to astound" (p. 9).

BIBLIOGRAPHY

Abelson, Elaine S. *When Ladies Go A-Thieving: Middle-Class Shoplifters in the Victorian Department Store* (1989).

BOURGEOIS CULTURE

Barth, Gunther P. *City People: The Rise of Modern City Culture in Nineteenth-Century America* (1980).

Beard, Charles A., and Mary R. Beard. *The Rise of American Civilization* (1927).

Bledstein, Burton J. *The Culture of Professionalism: The Middle Class and the Development of Higher Education in America* (1976).

Blumin, Stuart M. *The Emergence of the Middle Class: Social Experience in the American City, 1760–1900* (1989).

Boorstin, Daniel. *The Americans.* 3 vols. (1958–1973).

Carnes, Mark C. *Secret Ritual and Manhood in Victorian America* (1989).

Cott, Nancy F. *The Bonds of Womanhood: "Woman's Sphere" in New England, 1780–1835* (1977).

Douglas, Ann. *The Feminization of American Culture* (1977).

Foner, Eric. *Free Soil, Free Labor, Free Men: The Ideology of the Republican Party Before the Civil War* (1970).

Gay, Peter. *The Bourgeois Experience: Victoria to Freud* (1984).

Gilkeson, John S., Jr. *Middle-Class Providence, 1820–1940* (1986).

Griffen, Clyde, and Sally Griffen. *Natives and Newcomers: The Ordering of Opportunity in Mid-Nineteenth-Century Poughkeepsie* (1978).

Griswold, Robert L. *Family and Divorce in California, 1850–1890: Victorian Illusions and Everyday Realities* (1982).

Gurley, J. G., and E. S. Shaw. "Money." In *American Economic History,* edited by Seymour E. Harris (1961).

Halttunen, Karen. *Confidence Men and Painted Women: A Study of Middle-Class Culture in America, 1830–1870* (1982).

Hartz, Louis. *The Liberal Tradition in America: An Interpretation of American Political Thought Since the Revolution* (1955).

Howe, Daniel Walker, ed., *Victorian America* (1976).

———. *The Political Culture of the American Whigs* (1979).

Johnson, Paul E. *A Shopkeeper's Millennium: Society and Revivals in Rochester, New York, 1815–1837* (1978).

Josephson, Matthew. *The Robber Barons: The Great American Capitalists, 1861–1901* (1934).

———. *The Politicos, 1865–1896.* (1938).

Kasson, John F. *Rudeness and Civility: Manners in Nineteenth-Century Urban America* (1990).

Lears, T. J. Jackson. *No Place for Grace: Antimodernism and the Transformation of American Culture, 1880–1920* (1981).

Lebsock, Suzanne. *The Free Women of Petersburg: Status and Culture in a Southern Town, 1784–1860* (1984).

Lystra, Karen. *Searching the Heart: Women, Men, and Romantic Love in Nineteenth-Century America* (1989).

Main, Jackson Turner. *The Social Structure of Revolutionary America* (1965).

Ownby, Ted. *Subduing Satan: Religion, Recreation, and Manhood in the Rural South, 1865–1920* (1990).

Parrington, V. L. *Main Currents in American Thought* (1927–1930).

Persons, Stow. *The Decline of American Gentility* (1973).

Pessen, Edward. *Riches, Class, and Power Before the Civil War* (1973).

Potter, David M. *People of Plenty: Economic Abundance and the American Character* (1954).

Rodgers, Daniel T. *The Work Ethic in Industrial America, 1850–1920* (1974).

Rosenzweig, Roy. *Eight Hours for What We Will: Workers and Leisure in an Industrial City, 1870–1920* (1983).

Ryan, Mary P. *Cradle of the Middle Class: The Family in Oneida County, New York, 1790–1865* (1981).

Sennett, Richard. *Families Against the City: Middle-Class Homes of Industrial Chicago, 1872–1890* (1970).

Stansell, Christine. *City of Women: Sex and Class in New York, 1789–1860* (1987).

Taylor, George Rogers. *The Transportation Revolution: 1815–1860* (1951).

Tocqueville, Alexis de. *Democracy in America.* Translated by Henry Reeve (rev. ed. 1990).

Trachtenberg, Alan. *The Incorporation of America: Culture and Society in the Gilded Age* (1982).

Wallace, Anthony F. C. *Rockdale: The Growth of an American Village in the Early Industrial Revolution* (1978).

Wiebe, Robert H. *The Search for Order: 1877–1920* (1967).

Wilentz, Sean. *Chants Democratic: New York City and the Rise of the American Working Class, 1788–1850* (1984).

SEE ALSO **Business Culture; The Gilded Age, Populism, and the Era of Incorporation; Social Class; Wealth and Income Distribution.**

SOCIETY AND CORPORATE STATISM

Ellis W. Hawley

THE TERM "CORPORATE STATE" (or "corporative state") came into vogue in the 1920s when Benito Mussolini's regime in Italy began erecting a new governmental structure that was supposed to replace parliamentary institutions as the nation's lawmaking apparatus. As eventually completed, it consisted of employer, worker, and professional associations that embraced all Italians in their occupational capacities and formed the base for national corporations in each branch of production; the National Council of Corporations coordinated these groups from above. The regime portrayed this structure as the government best suited to the corporate order of a modern organizational society. It recognized that social policy must be based on occupation rather than location, that economic rather than political citizenship was what really mattered, and that modern production needed coordination that could not be met by unregulated markets, traditional community structures, or liberal parliamentary assemblies. It needed a "new state" to help it realize its potential for a harmonious efficiency beneficial to all.

In Italy the new structure never did much lawmaking. That remained the task of the fascist dictatorship. Nor were there many Americans who wanted to replicate the Italian structure as the answer to America's governmental needs. Yet some of the thinking behind the Italian action was part of a larger intellectual current in the capitalist world that did have American variants. More specifically, America has seen efforts to erect an "economic government" of associations and corporations grounded in the large-scale economic organizations of the private sector, of attempting to fill perceived organizational vacuums with hybrid mixtures of the public and the private, and of seeking to transform a liberal state of courts, parties, and assemblies into one more attuned to the world of corporate organization. These efforts have been of more than peripheral importance to American institutional development, and they deserve careful scrutiny by both political and social historians.

In what follows, I shall begin with the rise of corporate bureaucracy, its impact on economic and social organization, and the resulting calls for a new American state. I shall then look in turn at the proposals and actions of the pre–World War I era, the wartime arrangements and their subsequent influence, the period of the Great Depression and the New Deal, the fusions of business and government that became characteristic of the quarter-century following World War II, and the new ambiguity about state and society associated with developments in the 1970s and 1980s. As a whole, I hope to illuminate a process whereby America kept rejecting schemes to replace its liberal state with a corporate one, yet altered its polity and modes of governance in ways that allowed its new corporate elites to be among its most important political actors.

CORPORATE RECONSTRUCTION AND PROGRESSIVE REFORM

American governance appeared increasingly inadequate against the backdrop of a society being transformed not only by industrialization, urbanization, and immigration but also by what the historian Martin Sklar has called "corporate reconstruction." In 1875 large aggregations of income-producing property existed, and more and more Americans were becoming wage earners. But complex managerial hierarchies capable of coordinating specialized activities across and outside large business firms had only started to appear, primarily in the management of railroads. Half a century later such hierarchies were at the center of a new economy that featured massive accumulations of capital, innovative production techniques, mass consumer markets, and increasingly bureaucratized labor forces. They had become the means of enhancing the nation's productivity and in the process had generated intense debates over the fate of small entrepreneurs, community controls, worker welfare, and democratic governance.

Some historians have seen the development of this "visible hand" as part of a modernization process driven by market opportunities and technological imperatives. Others have seen it as an instrument of "monopoly capital," part of the process of capitalist evolution. But the extent to which the managerial hierarchies were created and defended by an expanding segment of the middle class has been largely ignored. Involved, to be sure, were "captains of industry" and "masters of finance," but an aspiring new salariat (the group of salaried workers, as distinct from the wage-earning proletariat), expanding as the corporations grew, provided much of the creativity, energy, and sense of social mission that drove the process of corporate reconstruction forward. In the words of Olivier Zunz, the lives of such people "exemplified the historically successful meeting of a large and ambitious project—the building of a continental economy—and an active social class" (*Making America Corporate,* p. 4). It was they who built a new kind of market-oriented bureaucracy that administered new kinds of marketing connections and workplaces, and they who reduced political and social obstacles by helping to divide and transform both the larger middle class and the growing class of industrial wage earners. Recruitment from an older middle class and its children became increasingly easy, and recruitment of workers and their children for the roles of clerical employee, semi-skilled machine tender, managerial foreman, and worker-consumer increased strikingly.

In the eyes of many commentators and protesters, however, the American polity was now seriously incongruent with the kind of economy that the nation was developing. Some called for a "people's state" that would mobilize the populace in defense of republican ideals and act to reverse the process of corporate reconstruction. Others demanded a new regulatory and welfare structure capable of ensuring that corporate power and productivity served the public good. A third group put forward designs for a government remade by the bureaucratizers of the private sector, grounded in the organizational revolution they were promoting, and therefore equipped to deal with the problems of modernity. America, many could agree, needed a new state. Many of America's social ills stemmed from the fact that its governmental machinery had been rendered obsolete. But about the shape and purpose of the new state and the extent to which it would displace traditional institutions, there was much disagreement.

Hence, the reformist impulses rippling through American political life in the late nineteenth and early twentieth centuries had their anticorporate and their corporate sides. In the creation of antitrust law, the defense of community controls, the attempts to preserve traditional workplaces, and the efforts to protect traditional artisans, farmers, and merchants, the polity embraced and tried to implement at least some of the designs associated with a "people's state." It also made limited room, typically in grudging fashion and with numerous constraints attached, for a diverse new array of regulatory and social agencies, grounded to some degree in critiques of corporate power. But driving the reform as well was an activism that emanated from the same captains of industry, masters of finance, salaried managers, and new technical professions that were fashioning the new economy. They sought not only a government better equipped to protect property rights and maintain social order but also one that could assist in the process of corporate reconstruction, provide helpful stabilizing and coordinative mechanisms, and govern through enlightened elites that understood economic development and the social adjustments it required.

Related to these corporate prescriptions was a political activism driven by the efforts of peripheral or threatened groups to organize themselves for more effective participation in a corporate world. Among such activists the answer was no longer the restoration of the old economy but the building of organizations and services that would enable the members of the groups involved to participate in and benefit from the new. In agriculture, such thinking gradually replaced the "agrarian democracy" championed by the Populist party and similar groups; this resulted, among other things, in increasing governmental intervention to promote scientific farming, cooperative action, and rural modernization. In labor the same sort of thinking was reflected in "business unionism" and in labor groups that sought supportive governmental reforms and services. In industries resistant to the creation of managerial hierarchies, workable substitutes were sought in associational structures linked to supportive government services, again with noticeably expansive effects on governmental activity. And in the professions, the search for new and rewarding corporate roles generated similar demands for organization building supported by governmental sanctions and services. Government, it was believed, could assist in bringing the benefits of modern organization and technology to backward areas; the result was a kind of governmental growth that influential segments of corporate America often supported.

The activism that produced such governmental expansion generally assumed that America's liberal state could be adapted to meet the needs of a corporate world. Its major innovation was the organized interest bloc that operated independent of party to secure and often to help administer benefits desired by members of the bloc. But also proposed and debated were schemes for entrusting broad societal responsibilities to a new regulatory and social service apparatus grounded in the new institutional affiliations and power structures of corporate America. The industrialist King C. Gillette (1855–1932), for example, proposed a union of polity and economy under one huge corporation. The Du Ponts talked of a corporate gentry that would do for modern America what the Founding Fathers had done for the early republic. The social worker Wilbur C. Phillips, founder of the corporative-minded National Social Unit Organization, suggested fusing democratic with technocratic action through a structure of interlocking popular and occupational councils. And Mary Parker Follett (1868–1933), a settlement worker moving toward a career as a managerial expert, proposed building a "new state" that featured efficiency-minded functional leaders working through a structure of occupational, factory, and neighborhood councils. Appearing in a variety of forms, moreover, was the notion that corporate America's new professional groups were the people best qualified to fill the perceived gap between liberal state and corporate institutions. Engineers, economists, social workers, and a variety of managerial specialists who were undergoing professionalization all had their visions of a new structure of authority that would arise outside the structures of the liberal state, entrusting their professions with larger roles in social management and thus providing the social machinery that a progressive society needed but could not secure through the workings of commercial markets or geographically based electoral politics.

A major organizational expression of "the corporate ideal in the liberal state," as the historian James Weinstein put it, was the National Civic Federation (NCF), founded in 1900 and especially active between 1903 and 1917. Its goal was a tripartite framework of business, labor, and public leaders that would operate outside the legally constituted state, would have its own industrial "statesmen," and would provide machinery to ensure that both public and private power were used "responsibly." In essence, national economic policy would emerge from tripartite councils and conferences informed by economic expertise; its implementation would come partly through governmental administration but mostly through trade agreements, corporate agencies, and associational action. In addition, NCF leaders saw their version of a new state as helping to contain the potential for social retrogression inherent in laborite socialism, agrarian populism, and individualistic "business anarchy." They inspired the Hepburn Bill (1908), which sought to entrust the interpretation and application of antitrust law to the friendly Bureau of Corporations. But opposition from what they called the "mercantile element," as opposed to the "corporation element," proved too strong. Even with President Theodore Roosevelt's support, the bill never came close to passage.

In some ways the designs of the NCF and similar groups resembled corporatist thinking in Europe. But in general they lacked the detail, rigor, and coherence of such thinking, tended to be more future-oriented, and were portrayed as extensions of America's traditional reliance on the associative or voluntarist sector rather than as rejections of liberal individualism. The established polity, moreover, was proving highly resistant to "corporatization." It could still empower executives who regarded themselves as "popular tribunes" rather than corporate organizers, and its legislative and judicial branches could be fiercely defensive of their prerogatives, not only against strong executives but also against "second governments" operating through corporatively structured councils, conferences, commissions, and committees. The extragovernmental framework built by the NCF never acquired the kind of power or machinery envisioned. Special business courts, like the Commerce Court for railroad cases established under the Mann-Elkins Act of 1910, proved incapable of sustaining themselves politically. And the scattered efforts of "community organizers" to engineer a "democracy" more compatible with the corporate vision of harmoniously interacting functional groups gave little promise of providing the building blocks of a new state.

Still, the decade preceding World War I did witness changes in government that made the established American polity less threatening to those engaged in corporate social reconstruction. At lower levels the trend was toward more policymaking by managerial hierarchies and more quasi-governmental roles for civic federations, chambers of commerce, and large corporate employers. Antitrust became less threatening after the Supreme Court's enunciation of a "rule of reason" in 1911 and the passage of the Clayton Antitrust Act and Federal Trade Commission Act in 1914; the latter offered at least some potential for the administrative agency envisioned in the Hepburn Bill. Public-private "partnerships" and "intersects" became the way to combine privatist efficiency with civil virtue, most notably in the new Federal Reserve System, the agricultural extension service, the promotional apparatus for foreign trade, and the beginnings of an employer-centered social insurance. Tripartism gained a foothold in the labor policy sphere, especially in the work of the Commission on Industrial Relations (1912–1915). And a potential "corporate veto" appeared in the post-1914 solicitude of many officials for maintaining "business confidence" as an essential ingredient in economic and political stability.

As war approached, moreover, the preparedness movement became another generator of proposals for a new state with corporative features. Engineers like Howard Coffin and Hollis Godfrey, scientists like George Ellery Hale, and physicians like Franklin Martin and Franklin F. Simpson promoted schemes under which professional societies would become part of a preparedness government potentially capable of serving as a war government. Preparedness enthusiasts from the business world, most notably the Wall Street operator and presidential adviser Bernard M. Baruch, were urging another joint business-government venture as the appropriate instrument for mobilization planning. And Secretary of Commerce William Redfield and Secretary of the Interior Franklin Lane were sympathetic to these preparedness designs. In need of new managerial capacities, America's liberal state was being urged to draw them from the private sector rather than to develop its own and, despite resistance from opponents of corporatism, this was in large measure the course that it would follow.

THE GREAT WAR AND ITS AFTERMATH

For some Progressives, World War I offered an opportunity to build the administrative state that America still lacked. But President Woodrow Wilson and Secretary of War Newton Baker hoped that emergency machinery could provide war-making capabilities without leaving a heritage of European-style "statism." They were receptive to schemes for drawing the needed machinery from the managerial resources of the private sector and then retiring it once the war was over; given business desires to contain threatening forms of statism, such schemes were quick to appear. A new group of organizational entrepreneurs with ties to both public and corporate life—exemplified by such individuals as Herbert Hoover, Arch Shaw, Harry Garfield, and Edward Hurley—proposed linking public-spirited forms of private and community organization to specially mobilized substitutes for governmental bureaucracy. Even this "minimal" bureaucratic statism, they argued, could be designed to be "destructible" when the need for a war government had passed. Set apart from the regular agencies of government and staffed by individuals on temporary leave from private pursuits, it could, in the words of Herbert Hoover, be made to "die overnight when peace was declared."

Foreshadowing and helping to facilitate this approach was the Council of National Defense (CND), established under the Army Appropriation Act of 1916. Here, as in much that would follow, governmental administrators were to work with and through public-spirited private leaders chosen not only for their wisdom and leadership qualities but also as representatives who in theory could speak for the various functional blocs of a modern organizational society, negotiate on their behalf, and commit them to common programs. Technically, these private commissioners were "advisers" and gatherers of "executive information," but they were also expected to play organizational roles. It was their job to help draw the necessary machinery from the private sector, and in practice the CND was soon producing organizational offspring, partly from the committee structures established by its commissioners and partly by bringing in new organizational developers with special commissions to act in particular areas. Although managerial power was eventually lodged elsewhere, the CND became the gateway through which the builders of the warfare state entered national service and undertook assignments that were supposed to maximize America's fighting strength while saving it from a statist future.

By 1918 the regular agencies of government were doing some war work. But as initially envisioned, most of the new managerial task had been entrusted to emergency agencies featuring structures in which business organizations, labor unions, professional societies, community councils, and other private-sector institutions had become functional units. In operation, moreover, such agencies as Herbert Hoover's Food Administration, Bernard Baruch's War Industries Board, and William G. McAdoo's war finance organization were able to develop relatively effective managerial capacities, partly by securing reserves of state power that they could invoke against noncooperators and partly through mechanisms for "engineering consent" to new forms of social authority. Some called it "war socialism," noting particularly the temporary nationalization of the railroads and the resort in other areas to governmental corporations. But to recent scholars, the term "war corporatism" has seemed more appropriate. America's warfare state had the integrative national elite, public-private interpenetration, functional representation, and harmonizing machinery of corporatist theory; and in its new structure of special councils, boards, administrations, committees, and tribunals, it had the kind of machinery commonly associated with a corporate state.

The question at war's end was whether the new managerial apparatus would be retired, as initially contemplated, or would become the nucleus of new exercises in peacetime state-building. The war, some analysts argued, had revealed even more clearly the incongruence between a modern economy and outdated political institutions, and from a number of these people came proposals for a Peace Industries Board, a Council of National Progress, and machinery that would adapt the wartime roles of labor unions and professional groups to peacetime purposes. The president, however, was basically unreceptive. So were Congress, the major political parties, the courts, the social critics of corporate power, and a variety of interest groups resentful of wartime constraints.

The proposals for retaining significant portions of the war government quickly foundered, as did less ambitious schemes for an industrial board in the Commerce Department and industrial relations agencies in the Department of Labor. And while structures resembling the war machinery did reappear in the postwar campaigns against "un-Americanism" and the high cost of living, their purposes and outlooks were different. Affiliated primarily with the Justice Department or with a Treasury Department that now embraced free market doctrines, they saw their mission not as filling organizational vacuums but as breaking up "conspiracies" and thereby restoring the effectiveness of America's traditional forms of social coordination.

By 1920 America had clearly rejected both the war-engendered socialist visions and the kind of corporate state advocated by some of the war managers. Its polity had reverted to an unruly pluralism, which some defended as a healthy expression of individual, local, and group liberty. Yet in the business and professional worlds the managerial ideals associated with corporate reconstruction and the war experience remained strong. They underlay a continuing critique that depicted much of America as uncoordinated, unstandardized, unscientific, inefficient, and hence unprogressive. They also underlay new designs for integration through economic, factory, and community councils, and they offered continuing support for informational and organizational projects that could allegedly turn conflict into teamwork and help to institutionalize the new forms of social authority essential to a progressive order. One response to postwar disorders had been the emergence of a support apparatus for such projects, primarily in a new array of foundation programs, research institutes, professional surveys, and private-sector think tanks. Of particular significance were the actions of the engineers, who in 1920 joined their societies in the Federated American Engineering Societies, elected Herbert Hoover its first president, and began a survey of waste in industry intended both to guide policy and to stimulate institutional formation.

Hoover quickly emerged as the leading figure in efforts to fill gaps in an emerging "organizational society" in order to contain "statism" on the one hand and impulses toward social disorder on the other. New institutional formations and greater social intelligence, he believed, could preserve initiative, inventiveness, and individuality, yet also enable Americans to "synchronize socially and economically" the "gigantic machine" they had built out of "applied science." In essence, he envisioned the creation of an "associative state" pulled from the associative sector of American life, infused with the "best thought" as brought together in think tanks like the National Bureau of Economic Research, and used to compensate for market and community failures. This became his goal as secretary of commerce, and from 1921 to 1928 he launched a wide array of projects intended to speed up the emergence of this associative machinery. Tackled in this way were the problems of industrial waste, cyclical and seasonal unemployment, ailing industries, social maladjustments, and industrial relations. And if the envisioned "synchronization" remained elusive, the projects did produce another complex of associations, councils, conferences, committees, institutes, and cooperation between public and private spheres that resembled those of the war years and that took on functions that anti-Hoover Progressives regarded as properly governmental. As Hoover saw it, the complex formed a "higher self-government" that constituted another step toward realizing American democratic ideals. But as critics saw it, they were structuring popular participation in ways that would lead not to government by the people but to government by trusts, technocrats, and corporate elites.

The idea of providing associational machinery through which an organizational society could correct its own malfunctions had its proponents in other administrative realms that had established a degree of independence from partisan politics. In such fields as education, health, social work, recreation, and conservation, administrative elites worked to implement managerial ideals through similar complexes of associations, councils, and intersects. In municipal and state government, a growing body of professional managers and planners engaged in the same kind of activity.

And within the Department of Agriculture still another version of the phenomenon could be found. There, to be sure, more administrative resources were being institutionalized within the state itself, primarily by harnessing bureau building to energies mobilized through interest-group politics. But like Hoover, the new Bureau of Agricultural Economics sought to combine individuality with synchronization through the marriage of applied expertise to associational activity. And in its schemes for a "better agriculture"—better both for farmers and for the nation as a whole—agribusiness associations, farm bureaus, coordinating councils, and professional societies were all to play important roles. For the bureau the period's farm problem was rooted less in exploitation than in the failure of agriculture to develop managerial and adjustment mechanisms comparable with those in corporate business. The bureau proposed to fill this gap not with a regulatory state, as some were proposing, but with an associative one.

In addition, the regulatory system established by prewar reformers now embraced managerial ideals and stressed "constructive" organization building rather than restrictive and "burdensome" prohibitions. Both the Federal Trade Commission and the Antitrust Division of the Justice Department were moving toward more emphasis on industrial self-regulation—not, so they said, to permit antisocial behavior but to achieve the social betterment that could come from fruitful forms of cooperation. The regulation of railroads and other public utilities was moving toward more cooperative modes with larger regulatory roles for private associations, despite considerable resistance from anticorporate groups that appealed to antitrust and populist ideals. And the establishment of new regulatory agencies, like the Federal Radio Commission and the Aeronautics Branch of the Commerce Department, followed corporate prescriptions for institutionalizing "business" values as opposed to "political" values, utilizing properly qualified administrative tribunals, and assigning major portions of the regulatory task to private organizations. Antitrust law and ideology retained some power, particularly in thwarting the movement to legalize cartels, shaping regulatory controls over the meat-packing industry, and blocking public-private collaboration in the electric power industry. But that they were losing power seemed evident.

In the eyes of some critics, the American liberal state was being penetrated, captured, and dominated by special interests. But as others saw it, the political economy had successfully adapted the "American system" to modern organizational needs. It had retained the traditional institutions of government (courts, parties, assemblies, administrators), partly by keeping them in spheres for which they were necessary and in which they were competent. It had accommodated a new organizational pluralism, expressed through organized interest groups (industrial, labor, farm, and special issue associations) that sought limited goals. And in its corporatively structured "cooperative system" (centering in the organizational networks and pools promoted by the Department of Commerce), it had provided the means by which corporate and technical elites could function as national planners and coordinators. As of 1928, moreover, these claims of success could be supported by pointing out the period's economic marvels, its relative freedom from political protest, and the mandate that Herbert Hoover had received in his election to the presidency. It was not until the economy collapsed following the stock market crash of 1929 that claims of success were overwhelmed by charges of failure, thus ushering in a renewed clash of competing schemes for establishing the "new state."

THE GREAT DEPRESSION AND THE NEW DEAL STATE

As president, Herbert Hoover tried to use his "cooperative system" of public-spirited associations both to alleviate suffering and to organize economic recovery. By 1932 he was also willing to expand the government's role, most notably by creating the Reconstruction Finance Corporation, modeled on the government finance corporation of World War I. But none of his recovery projects brought recovery, and as conditions worsened, other designs for altering economic behavior gained support. Populist and socialist prescriptions were again mobilizing sizable numbers, as were designs for a regulatory and welfare state. And emerging from both the business and the political systems was a new set of schemes for lodging the power to restore and maintain prosperity in corporative institutions modeled on those of the war years. Some proposed reviving a peacetime version of the Council of National Defense and allowing it to produce another set of organizational offspring. Some wanted to turn Hoover's public-spirited associations into coercive cartels capable of solving their "free rider" problems and forcing the noncooperative to do their part. Some, including Bernard Baruch and William G. McAdoo, would create a peacetime version of the War Industries Board, and some, including the 1931 version of the National Civic Federation, would remove antitrust constraints on business and labor organization and develop a tripartism with managerial and stabilizing capacities.

Two schemes receiving much publicity and indicating that corporate statism now had substantial business support were those associated with Gerard Swope of General Electric and Henry I. Harriman, chair of a special committee of the United States Chamber of Commerce. The Swope Plan, as set forth and debated in late 1931, would establish an "economic government," structured to include public supervision and labor representation, but operating basically through compulsory trade associations empowered by law to manage production, administer prices, and provide social insurance for industrial employees. Such "planning" institutions, Swope and his supporters argued, had become essential in a technologically advanced economy, and it was far better for industry to "evolve" them than to have them imposed by legislation. Harriman's Chamber of Commerce plan was less specific in its prescriptions and more inclined to fill the governmental gap with a "business commonwealth" than with tripartite structures. But it, too, would restore and maintain economic "balance" through trade associations that would function as economic councils, coordinate this associational activity through a national council of functional representatives, and provide an employer-centered form of unemployment insurance.

Hoover was not receptive. In his eyes such proposals were a perversion of associationalism that would lead to gigantic trusts, industrial decay, and fascist dictatorship. But in 1933, as the New Deal administration of Franklin D. Roosevelt searched for an industrial recovery program, the idea of a recovery planned and administered by government-backed cartels quickly moved to the fore. It was linked not only to war precedents but also to the kinds of administrative resources available; the conservative hopes for reviving business confidence; the liberal support for planning, pump priming, and welfare minima; and the belief among influential New Dealers that business administration was now evolving into a neutral technocracy. Dissenters were shunted aside, and the result was the National Industrial Recovery Act (1933), hailed by Roosevelt as "the most important and far-reaching legislation ever enacted by the American Congress." "I had part," he said, "in the great cooperation of 1917 and 1918 and it is my faith that we can count on our industry once more to join in our general purpose" (quoted in *Public Papers and Addresses,* vol. 2, pp. 252–253).

As finally passed, the National Industrial Recovery Act authorized a two-year experiment during which the antitrust laws would be suspended and officially recognized trade groups would formulate industrial codes that, when approved by the president, would have the force of law. Such codes were to regulate production, prices, and trade practices in ways that were supposed to end unfair competition, increase purchasing power, reduce unemployment, and conserve natural resources. They were also to contain provisions regulating hours, wages, child labor, and collective bargaining; and their capacity to plan was to be further enhanced by supportive tariff, tax, and public works policies.

The New Dealers played down the resemblance to corporatist formulations abroad, arguing that the goal of the new government-business partnership was the realization of liberal ideals. But Italian theoreticians saw striking parallels with their own state-building, and Hugh Johnson, the man in charge of the National Recovery Administration (NRA), found things to praise in Raffaello Viglione's *The Structure of the Corporate State* (English translation, 1933). Nor were the NRA codes the only corporative features of the early New Deal. Such agencies as the Agricultural Adjustment Administration, the Federal Coordinator of Transportation, and the Federal Grazing Service all had similar associational and committee structures, and under their charters law was being made and implemented through economic groups rather than through the political bodies traditionally entrusted with the task.

In operation, however, the new economic government could not re-create the "great cooperation of 1917 and 1918," at least not without resort to forms of repression and public spending unattainable in the political climate of 1933 and 1934. Its chief function became one of providing legal permits to agencies engaged in concerted market-sharing and restrictionism rather than concerted programs of market expansion and reemployment. And once branded an economic failure, it had little prospect of solving its political problems. It never found effective ways to neutralize small business and consumer protest, to give industrial labor and its associations a satisfactory role, to ground itself in a settled body of constitutional law, or to maintain the concordance and reputation of its central core of "wise men." Increasingly, the premises underlying America's closest approximation to a corporate state lost credibility and support; and by 1935, when the Supreme Court finally held the NRA codes to be unconstitutional, the New Deal was already moving toward alternative designs for a new American state. One tendency, as more administrative resources were institutionalized in the state itself, was toward an expansion of the regulatory and welfare apparatus begun during the Progressive period. The other was an emerging "broker state," acting not as a partner in capitalist planning but as the promoter of new checks and balances between competing interests and between dual structures of public and private governance.

Again the United States had rejected reforms that would replace its liberal state with a corporate one, and after 1935 it continued to reject schemes for the revival of NRA-style economic planning. The only exceptions were the "little NRAs" for the coal, petroleum, and trucking industries. Yet the trend toward administrative statism also fell well short of providing the envisioned capacities for national planning. By 1938 it had run into growing alarm about "bureaucratic despotism," expressed particularly in congressional rejection of the president's executive reorganization and regional planning bills. And while broker statism would give the nation a new collective bargaining system and the revival of antitrust as a regulatory tool, both of which aroused much alarm in the corporate world, it also left the managerial prerogatives and hierarchies of corporate America largely intact and accepted corporate power as a legitimate check and balance in its designs for a democratic pluralism. Nor was New Deal social legislation truly anticorporate, since it did, after all, link national social insurance to employment and occupational status, retain an important role for corporate welfare and philanthropy, and subsidize corporate designs for economic and urban development. In all these respects, the New Deal state developed along lines that corporate America would eventually find tolerable and would in time embrace as the kind of state required for continued economic and social progress.

Seen from the corporate perspective, the most frightening aspects of the later New Deal were its potentials for turning a regulatory antitrust policy into an organization-wrecking anticorporatism, for evolving statist bureaucracies imbued with hostility to corporate values, and for using the levers of compensatory spending, welfare entitlements, and labor empowerment to socialize ever larger sectors of the economy. As of 1939, however, these potentials seemed relatively well contained, and after 1939, in the context of a new preparedness movement and another world war, the containment became firmer and better established. The antitrust campaigns of Assistant Attorney General Thurman Arnold were shelved as obstacles to war mobilization and defense production. The vision of "cradle-to-grave" welfare, as embodied in the Wagner-Murray-Dingell bill of 1943, was effectively quashed. Labor's reach for a share in industrial management, most graphically manifest in a plan put forward by Philip Murray, president of the CIO, for a war government composed of tripartite industry councils, was likewise quashed.

In addition, spending prescriptions of the "capitalist stagnation" variety lost their power as a war-stimulated economy regained its capacity to provide full employment, and such expansions of statist power as were now occurring became less fearsome once it became clear that they were to be placed in relatively safe hands, were temporary in nature, and were narrowly confined to the specific task of war-making. Although Roosevelt's concern with preserving presidential power prevented the emergence of structures fully analogous to those of World War I, the war government did make use of business executives, industry committees, and arrangements in which governmental and business organization merged into larger structures of production management. Social progress, a number of the New Dealers seemed to believe, had to be won through fighting with businessmen, but this was not true of war-making capacity.

Indeed, by the time of Roosevelt's death in 1945, some business leaders were ready to incorporate most of the New Deal's state-building into a larger cooperative structure that would apply the lessons of war to the problems of peace. This was the view, for example, of the Committee for Economic Development, which claimed to link the "forward-looking" elements in business to those in government and academe. It was also the view of Chamber of Commerce president Eric Johnston, who thought it time for business and government to become friends "in search of solutions" rather than "enemies in search of lethal weapons." And it was the view of war administrators like Donald Nelson and Charles E. Wilson, who saw wartime successes as demonstrating the need for a continuing business-government partnership.

Roosevelt, moreover, had found these proposals "most heartening." He agreed that management, labor, agriculture, and the government must have "complete unity of purpose" if the nation was to take advantage of the "great opportunities ahead," and in March 1945 he endorsed a "New Charter for Labor and Management" as a major step in that direction. Under it, if the pledges of the business and labor signatories meant anything, business, labor, and government were to become postwar partners operating within a framework that recognized their joint interests in full employment, high wages, capitalist enterprise, and functional specialization. New Dealism, it appeared, could become more compatible with corporate ideals than had once been assumed.

FROM NEW DEALISM TO THE CORPORATE COMMONWEALTH

As peace returned in 1945, some economic analysts doubted that American corporate capitalism could work without the stimulus of war. But in the quarter-century that followed, it again became wonderfully productive and expansive, adapting its managerial hierarchies to new strategies of economic growth, and fulfilling, it seemed, the promises of a golden future that it had made in the 1920s. As some saw it, morever, the New Deal as modified by the post-1939 developments had provided a polity capable of working in harmony with the revitalized economy. It had, through its welfare, antitrust, and industrial relations measures, found ways to accommodate potentially hostile social groups. And it had, through its fiscal and monetary levers, its technical and educational services, and its legitimation of corporate property and power, found ways to solve the system's coordinative problems.

In both business and liberal political circles, however, the return to peace also brought new proposals for an additional governance, to be drawn from private-sector organizations and "statesmen," and to be entrusted with articulating national goals and maintaining national unity of purpose. Congressman Jacob Javits, for example, talked about a federal economic commission to marshal the "organic power" of the private economy. *Business Week* magazine advocated a "non-political" signaling agency able to steer investment and allocative decisions into constructive channels. And for Charles E. Wilson, back at General Electric following his war service, the ideal order was one in which industrial, professional, and labor associations would set up "expert advisory panels" in constant and continuous liaison with governmental decision makers. Admittedly, Wilson conceded, this sounded a bit like the fascist corporate state. But, as he saw it, the great difference would be real reliance upon trained expertise in the service of the public, not upon centralized imposition of some official political doctrine.

In the government that President Harry S. Truman inherited from Roosevelt, some strains of antibusiness liberalism persisted, notable particularly in denunciations of business-government cooperation as "fascistic" and in efforts to forge a "new antitrust" directed against undue concentrations of economic power. Truman favored postwar controls and reforms that most businessmen opposed, and in his campaign for reelection in 1948 he adopted a neo-Populist rhetoric in which corporate power and high finance appeared as unregenerate enemies of a virtuous people. Yet the dominant trend from 1945 to 1949 was toward greater business-government cooperation, renewed faith in the capacity of corporate power to serve democratic ends, and creation of an extragovernmental governance resembling that advocated by Wilson and Javits.

This trend was apparent in a new array of business councils established by agencies in the Interior, Commerce, State, and Defense departments. It was apparent in a cluster of governmental jobs largely reserved for businessmen on leave from the private sector, and it was especially apparent in the elaborate advisory and "partnership" structures attached to such agencies as the Council of Economic Advisers, the Economic Cooperation Administration, and the National Security Resources Board. In addition, it was reflected in Truman's extensive use of presidential commissions of private "statesmen" in order to mobilize the "best thought" on controversial issues. And attesting to its strength was the growing marginalization of those who charged that government was being captured or hamstrung for business purposes.

During Truman's second term, moreover, the trend toward business-government fusion and extragovernmental governance became still more pronounced. The response to a recession in 1949 was a Hoover-like effort to organize concerted business expansion of investment spending. In response to calls for a more "reasonable" antitrust policy, the Committee on Business and Government Relations began studying ways to put antitrust enforcement and federal regulation on a more "cooperative" basis. As cold war tensions fueled the creation of a "national security state" and "military-industrial complex," corporate power was enlisted as a partner in both. And as a new shooting war in Korea produced new economic disorders, Truman's response was to install Charles E. Wilson as head of another war government, which, as one might expect, featured the mobilization of private expertise and governance through another network of industry committees, conferences, and councils. At times, to be sure, administration officials were strongly critical of business actions, and in 1952 Truman's seizure of the steel industry was fiercely denounced in business circles. But the foundations for the business-government collaboration that would flourish under Truman's successor were clearly in place by 1953.

Some of those who helped to elect Dwight D. Eisenhower in 1952 hoped for a repeal of the New Deal and relegation of the "eggheads" to their ivory towers. But neither the new president himself nor the "corporate liberals" and "modern Republicans" with whom he staffed his administration shared such sentiments. Their vision was of a "corporate commonwealth" that would retain most of the New Deal state but would also curb "creeping socialism," keep mass and partisan politics within proper bounds, and realize further organizational benefits by building on the state's new linkages to private managerial capacities and responsible wielders of private power. The successes of World War II, Eisenhower believed, stemmed from action that created the kind of "cooperative unit" and state-society teamwork that he now had in mind. This was a "middle way" that should be the "American way," and in his mind, it seems, it was the coming to fruition of what he had started as president of Columbia University. There one of his proudest achievements had been the creation of an "American assembly" dedicated to teaching the leaders of business, government, labor, and the professions to plan cooperatively for their nation's future.

To a remarkable degree, this vision of a corporate commonwealth shaped federal policy during the Eisenhower years. It was resisted particularly by uncooperative labor, farm, small business, and minority groups, and by rejecters of the "middle way" on both the Left and the Right. But even as some concessions were made to these competing visions of the future, the corporate vision was being realized. It was reflected in measures that defined the proper role of the federal state, in the "stag dinners" through which Eisenhower sought to build and coordinate corporate "statesmanship," and most graphically in the new or expanded machinery for extra-governmental governance. In short order, the Interior, Labor, Agriculture, and Justice departments had adopted "cooperative" modes, which in practice meant larger regulatory and developmental roles for private associations, councils, and consortia. "Growth" programs in 1954 and 1958 and a "stabilization" program in the late 1950s were similarly dependent on private-sector partners, especially the Advertising Council and the Committee for Economic Development. And in the Commerce Department, where a Hooverian past was sometimes consciously invoked, the new

Business and Defense Services Administration took over the Korean War committees, linked them to industry divisions headed by volunteer experts and to a field service in which local business groups served as "cooperative offices," and used the resulting machinery to help administer departmental programs.

Meanwhile, a number of former New Dealers were embracing the notion of corporate statesmanship that underlay the ideal of the corporate commonwealth. Adolf Berle, David Lilienthal, and John K. Galbraith wrote books about a capitalist revolution that was supposed to be transforming corporate power into a force for the public good, and by the late 1950s a "new liberalism" was less concerned with power structures than with modernizing the "backward" and integrating the potentially irrational. By 1960, moreover, Berle was among those calling for the recognition and "constitutionalization" of the large corporation as a part of American government. In discussions at the Center for the Study of Democratic Institutions at Santa Barbara, he and other "neoliberals" were considering the need for giving corporate employees a constitutionally protected economic citizenship and for eventually establishing a formal "commonwealth of corporations" acting as a fourth branch of government. This amounted, so some of those involved admitted, to a form of the "corporative state." But it was what America needed if it were to avoid the triple perils of irresponsible private power, demagogic irrationality, and bureaucratic statism.

In the 1960s America continued to reject proposals for a formalized corporate state. It also returned the Democrats to power and made limited room for reformers who sought to end discriminatory practices and to empower the poor and neglected. But mainstream liberalism, as exemplified in John F. Kennedy's New Frontier and Lyndon B. Johnson's Great Society, still drew much of its inspiration from the idea of a corporate commonwealth. Its growth and stabilization programs rested not only on Keynesian economics but also on assumptions of a corporate "statesmanship" amenable to "national guidance." Its additions to the welfare and national security states were to come from a "growth dividend" rather than income redistribution, and its social improvement programs, like Eisenhower's, were to be implemented through a "creative federalism" that depended on private as well as local partners.

Writing in 1972, law professor Arthur Selwyn Miller noted that corporate states had four major characteristics: a merger of economic and political power, a legal nexus between the two, corporate bodies encompassing the two, and a conversion of individuals into "group-persons." And America, he thought, despite the incoherence of its national administrative apparatus, its failure to develop a European-style corporatism, and its professed commitments to freedom of contract and broker-state pluralism, was a land of legally encouraged "private governments" and public-private intersects that had all four of these attributes.

By the end of the 1960s, however, new critiques of the corporate world were gaining intellectual credibility and posing increasingly serious threats to the organizational loyalties, work ethics, managerial creativity, and careerist aspirations upon which its successes had long depended. One line of criticism, beginning in the 1950s but becoming much stronger in the 1960s, portrayed the malaise caused by the weight of bureaucratic structures and the resulting loss of individual autonomy. Seen from this perspective, a corporatized society must necessarily become an increasingly sick society. Other critics stressed the antisocial and antidemocratic aspects of a system that enabled a power elite to sustain itself through structures of domination, imperialism, environmental rape, and cultural impoverishment. Potential recruits to corporate roles were now becoming "counterculturalists," "new leftists," "neo-Populists," and "neoindividualists." And of greater importance for the American polity, a new wave of middle-class activism, focused particularly on environmental and consumer issues, was producing a new array of interest groups with their own experts and their own agendas for state-building. Corporate America was about to enter another time of troubles reminiscent of the 1930s.

UNSETTLEMENT AND AMBIGUITY

In the 1970s the economic policies that had seemed so successful in the 1960s no longer did so. The American economy entered a period of stagflation, weakening productivity, and waning competitiveness with the organized capitalisms evolving in Japan and western Europe; seen from the corporate perspective, a part of the problem could be attributed to a new incongruence between economy and polity.

Corporate "statesmanship," to be sure, continued to have a large role in President Richard Nixon's policies (1969–1974). Such agencies as the National Commission on Productivity, the Cost of Living Council, the Council on Environmental Quality, and the National Business Council for Consumer Affairs had features that led critics to characterize them as "creeping corporatism." But to the dismay of corporate leaders, a polity responsive to the new middle-class activism was not only threatening the stabilizing mechanisms worked out for particular industries but also was producing a new adversarial type of regulation, grounded in the notion of power over corporations rather than sharing power with them. Most graphically manifest in the areas of environmental protection, occupational health, and product safety, this new phenomenon was seen by some as amounting to a "second managerial revolution," shifting power from professional managers to anticorporate bureaucrats and in the process aggravating the nation's economic and social disorders.

The height of this anticorporate sentiment came in 1975 and 1976, when it became part of the anti-institutional backlash provoked by the Watergate scandal and other governmental and corporate misdeeds. In Congress support for the "regulatory revolution" was strong, and for the first time since the 1930s relatively serious consideration was given to proposals for legislating the breakup of some of the nation's largest corporations. As president, however, Gerald Ford encouraged only the most conservative aspects of regulatory reform—those, in other words, that had the backing of neoclassical economists as well as anticorporate critics. And by 1976 business mobilization to curb and roll back the regulatory threat was becoming a strong counterforce. Operating through the recently formed Business Roundtable, beefed-up versions of older business organizations, and a new array of political action committees and "pro-growth" groups, this business counteroffensive showed that it could block targeted proposals. It was also turning probusiness lobbying and public relations work into one of the few growth industries in the 1970s, and through support for a new conservatism in the intellectual community it was helping to make statist prescriptions and anticorporate critiques less respectable.

For most of those involved in the business counteroffensive, the goal was to contain and roll back governmental interference in business processes, and during the administration of President Jimmy Carter (1977–1981) this continued to be their goal. Yet once again, some corporate leaders saw the need for a greater governance that could cope effectively with the new economic problems and social demands, make the energies devoted to business-government conflict available for more productive purposes, and give American capitalism the kind of planning and coordinating capacities that its chief rivals were acquiring but that Carter's programs could not provide. In the early and mid 1970s, this group had linked itself not to conservative politics but to liberal advocates of an economic planning apparatus involving business, labor, and social science as well as government. And by the late 1970s they had become leaders and supporters of a "reindustrialization" movement that saw economic renewal coming through corporatist planning institutions utilizing a fruitful mix of both private and public resources.

In 1980 this solution became the subject of much publicity in academic and business journals, including a highly positive portrayal in a special issue of *Business Week*. It also gained adherents in the Carter administration, and in September 1980 the president announced a new economic program that seemed to accept the premises and prescriptions of the "reindustrializers." As *Newsweek* put it, the goal of "economic revitalization" was supposed to be achieved through "a smallish made-in-America version of the government-business partnership in productive Japan" (8 September 1980, p. 51).

Carter's subsequent defeat by Ronald Reagan ensured that the economic prescriptions followed would be those of "supply-side economics" rather than reindustrialization. Rejecting both Keynesian economic analysis and the neoinstitutionalism underlying the calls for capitalist planning, the new administration put its faith in permanent tax cuts intended both to provide the capital and incentives for economic renewal and to reduce the capacity of government for wasteful and destabilizing meddlesomeness. Yet for a time the agitation for corporatist planning institutions persisted, and in the context of the Reagan recession of 1982 and 1983 it took on new life. As the "industrial policy" movement, it again received widespread publicity, won the endorsement of a number of prominent Democratic politicians, and produced an array of industrial policy bills calling for such institutions as a National Council on Industrial Competitiveness, subcouncils in each of the major branches of production, and special banks to assist industrial restructuring and new industrial development.

Even as recovery undercut the agitation, moreover, elements of it persisted in consideration of special planning mechanisms for the defense and export sectors and in the notion that a national office of microeconomic management could greatly improve the policy output generated by existing industrial programs and forums. In addition, some observers saw persistence at the state level. There, despite the highly publicized defeat of Rhode Island's Greenhouse Compact bond issue (1984), new state economic development commissions were creating, often with federal support, the kind of planning bodies, consensus-building forums, lending instruments, and public-private partnerships envisioned in the national industrial policy bills.

America in the 1980s was not ready to embrace the kind of state-building envisioned in the industrial policy proposals. In some quarters, this tapped a persisting reservoir of hostility to state planning. In others it encountered a durable and still potent set of populist, republican, and entrepreneurial symbols, and in still others historical experience and the persisting fragmentation of American government, business, and labor were invoked as reasons why the schemes could never work. As it turned out, moreover, those seeking to give corporate elites a larger role in governance found other ways of doing so. This was the effect, in particular, of a conservatism that featured deregulation and de-unionization, reduced antitrust enforcement, enhanced corporate access to policy-making arenas, and the return of social tasks to philanthropic endeavor.

Yet the fact that the proposals were made and considered indicated a continuing state of unsettlement and ambiguity concerning the proper roles of government in the economy and private institutional power in governance. The mixture of pluralism, corporatism, and statism to be found in the American political economy of 1991 gave little promise of being a very stable one. And if history recorded persisting obstacles to the institutional realization of corporate statism in America, it also indicated a persisting capacity of the American political and business systems to produce designs for such institutions and make them part of the nation's political discourse.

CONCLUSION

In the twentieth century, the United States has repeatedly rejected the models for a corporate state that have come out of corporatist thinking about modern economic and social needs. It has produced its own variants of such thought and has made use of corporatist institutions for waging war and for achieving particular kinds of regulatory or promotional tasks. But peacetime movements toward a structure that would ultimately replace the liberal state with a corporate one have always encountered cultural and institutional obstacles strong enough to arrest them and produce countermovements. In practice, American governance of its new economy has taken place through what political scientist Charles Lindblom has called a "polyarchy," a system with one part of the governance grounded in economic institutions and the other part grounded in political institutions and processes. And even as these have provided checks and balances on each other, much as power is supposed to be checked and controlled in liberal theory, there have also been repeated efforts to connect the two, to make them partners in the attainment of national goals, and to construct intersects from which some analysts have expected a corporate state to emerge.

The problems, as seen by those who desire a more unitary system with greater managerial capacities, were that both areas of governance kept resisting full grants of power to managerial hierarchies and that the area of intersection remained unstable and vulnerable to questions about its legitimacy. Although some hailed it as a superior synthesis of privatist efficiency and civic virtue, others saw it as the source of such illiberal evils as the military-industrial complex, corporate subversion of popular sovereignty, and "arsenalization" of the entrepreneurial spirit.

Still, the system that emerged was one in which America's new corporate elites became and remained important participants in the governmental process. Corporate goals and ideals found a relatively secure place in the liberal state and clearly influenced its regulatory, diplomatic, and social policy. The system, moreover, acted as one of the barriers to close off alternative lines of social development and organization. As some of its architects intended, it helped to undermine and marginalize a socialist movement that seemed, in the early twentieth century, to be establishing a position from which it could offer an alternative vision of national progress. Similarly, it has helped to contain and marginalize a variety of populist impulses, in part by helping to destabilize and destroy the kinds of communities, associations, properties, identities, and technologies that might have provided a stronger base for personal independence and popular power.

And in the eyes of some, it has helped to demonstrate both the shortcomings of liberalism and the need for moving beyond it if the liberal goals of individual freedom and dignity were ever to be fully attained. In America, they say, the twentieth-century liberal state has shown only the capacity to produce a "balked corporatism," which, once produced, blocks much of the continuing quest for liberty and shores up structures of domination and inequality at odds with liberal values.

If America's peculiar and shifting mix of liberal with corporate statism has had its successes and deserves some of the acclaim once given it as a "middle way," it has also had its social costs.

BIBLIOGRAPHY

General Works

Benjamin, Roger, and Stephen L. Elkin, eds. *The Democratic State* (1985).

Fligstein, Neil. *The Transformation of Corporate Control* (1990).

Frese, Joseph R., and Jacob Judd, eds. *Business and Government: Essays in Twentieth-Century Cooperation and Confrontation* (1985).

Gerber, Larry G. *The Limits of Liberalism: Josephus Daniels, Henry Stimson, Bernard Baruch, Donald Richberg, Felix Frankfurter, and the Development of the Modern American Political Economy* (1983).

Gilbert, James. *Designing the Industrial State: The Intellectual Pursuit of Collectivism in America, 1880–1940* (1972).

Lindblom, Charles E. *Politics and Markets: The World's Political Economic Systems* (1977).

McConnell, Grant. *Private Power and American Democracy* (1966).

McCraw, Thomas K. *Prophets of Regulation: Charles Francis Adams, Louis D. Brandeis, James M. Landis, Alfred E. Kahn* (1984).

McCraw, Thomas K., ed. *Regulation in Perspective: Historical Essays* (1981).

Noble, David F. *American by Design: Science, Technology, and the Rise of Corporate Capitalism* (1977).

Tenenbaum, Susan. "The Progressive Legacy and the Public Corporation: Entrepreneurship and Public Virtue." *Journal of Policy History* 3, no. 3 (1991): 309–330.

Zunz, Olivier. *Making America Corporate, 1870–1920* (1990).

The Pre–World War I Period

Chandler, Alfred D., Jr. *The Visible Hand: The Managerial Revolution in American Business* (1977).

Dawley, Alan. *Struggles for Justice: Social Responsibility and the Liberal State* (1991).

Keller, Morton. *Regulating a New Economy: Public Policy and Economic Change in America, 1900–1933* (1990).

Kolko, Gabriel. *The Triumph of Conservatism: A Reinterpretation of American History, 1900–1916* (1963; rev. ed., 1977).

Lustig, R. Jeffrey. *Corporate Liberalism: The Origins of Modern Political Theory, 1890–1920* (1982).

McConnell, Grant. *The Decline of Agrarian Democracy* (1953).

Sklar, Martin J. *The Corporate Reconstruction of American Capitalism, 1890–1916: The Market, the Law, and Politics* (1988).

Skowonek, Stephen. *Building a New American State: The Expansion of National Administrative Capacities, 1877–1920* (1982).

Weinstein, James. *The Corporate Ideal in the Liberal State, 1900–1918* (1968).

Wiebe, Robert H. *The Search for Order, 1877–1920* (1967).

Between the World Wars

Alchon, Guy. *The Invisible Hand of Planning: Capitalism, Social Science, and the State in the 1920s* (1985).

Brand, Donald R. *Corporatism and the Rule of Law: A Study of the National Recovery Administration* (1988).

Burk, Robert F. *The Corporate State and the Broker State: The Du Ponts and American National Politics, 1925–1940* (1990).

Cuff, Robert D. *The War Industries Board: Business-Government Relations During World War I* (1973).

Fraser, Steve, and Gary Gerstle, eds. *The Rise and Fall of the New Deal Order, 1930–1980* (1989).

Hamilton, David E. "Building the Associative State: The Department of Agriculture and American State-Building." *Agricultural History* 64, no. 2 (Spring 1990): 207–218.

Hawley, Ellis W. *The New Deal and the Problem of Monopoly: A Study in Economic Ambivalence* (1966).

———. "Herbert Hoover, the Commerce Secretariat, and the Vision of an 'Associative State,' 1921–1928." *Journal of American History* 61, no. 1 (June 1974): 116–140.

———. *The Great War and the Search for a Modern Order: A History of the American People and Their Institutions, 1917–1933* (1979).

———. "The Corporate Ideal as Liberal Philosophy in the New Deal." In *The Roosevelt New Deal,* edited by Wilbur J. Cohen (1986).

Himmelberg, Robert F. *The Origins of the National Recovery Administration: Business, Government, and the Trade Association Issue, 1921–1933* (1976).

Since World War II

Barfield, Claude E., Jr., and William A. Schambra, eds. *The Politics of Industrial Policy* (1986).

Collins, Robert M. *The Business Response to Keynes, 1929–1964* (1981).

Draper, Hal. "Neo-Corporatists and Neo-Reformers." *New Politics* 1 (Autumn 1961): 87–106.

Galambos, Louis, ed. *The New American State: Bureaucracies and Policies Since World War II* (1987).

Griffith, Robert. "Dwight D. Eisenhower and the Corporate Commonwealth." *American Historical Review* 87, no. 1 (February 1982): 87–122.

Hawley, Ellis W. "Challenges to the Mixed Economy." In *American Choices: Social Dilemmas and Public Policy Since 1960,* edited by Robert Bremner, Gary W. Richard, and Richard J. Hopkins (1986).

Hays, Samuel P. *Beauty, Health, and Permanence: Environmental Politics in the United States, 1955–1985* (1987).

Hogan, Michael J. *The Marshall Plan: America, Britain, and the Reconstruction of Western Europe, 1947–1952* (1987).

Horwitz, Robert B. *The Irony of Regulatory Reform* (1989).

McQuaid, Kim. *Big Business and Presidential Power: From FDR to Reagan* (1982).

Miller, Arthur Selwyn. "Legal Foundations of the Corporate State." *Journal of Economic Issues* 6, no. 1 (March 1972): 59–79.

———. *The Modern Corporate State: Private Governments and the American Constitution* (1976).

Smith, Bruce L. R., ed. *The New Political Economy: The Public Use of the Private Sector* (1975).

Theoharis, Athan. "The Truman Presidency: Trial and Error." *Wisconsin Magazine of History* 55, no. 1 (Autumn 1971): 49–58.

Waring, Stephen P. *Taylorism Transformed: Scientific Management Theory Since 1945* (1991).

SEE ALSO various essays in the sections **"Periods of Social Change," "Regionalism and Regional Subcultures," "Science, Medicine, and Technology,"** and **"Work and Labor."**

WAR

Jeffrey Kimball

THE UNITED STATES' experience with war has been crucial to its development but relatively brief. War itself, however, is an ancient human invention, embedded in the interconnected social, economic, political, intellectual, and technological elements of culture. For most of their forty-thousand-year history, Homo sapiens has lived in primal hunter-gatherer societies, some of which waged rudimentary warfare against other hunter-gatherer societies, and some of which did not. Extensive military organization and more frequent warmaking accompanied the emergence of societies based on agriculture, which first appeared in the Near East about 7000 B.C. and in Central America about 2000 B.C. By the time modern nation-states began to form in Europe about the late fifteenth century, war appeared in four interrelated social forms: as a means of forming the nation-state, as international war between nation-states, as civil war, and as imperial war.

The United States, whose colonial and national history coincided with this modern period, practiced all four forms of warfare, each playing elemental roles in the country's development. Colonial America was a product of and participant in numerous wars and countless campaigns against Native Americans as well as several international wars between European states. The French and Indian War of 1754–1763 and its aftermath in Great Britain and America were contributing causes of the Revolutionary War (1775–1783), in which an independent nation was formed—although one imperfectly united and riven with sectionalism. The Civil War of 1861–1865 ended with one faction overcoming another, completing the process of nation formation begun with the Revolution, ensuring the continuance of the Union, and defining its political, economic, ideological, and social direction.

The United States has fought several international wars over trade, territory, politics, and principle against other, more or less militarily equivalent nations in the Americas, Europe, and Asia: the Quasi-War with France (1798–1800), the War of 1812 (1812–1815), the War with Mexico (1846–1848), the Spanish-American War (1898), World War I (1917–1918), and World War II (1941–1945). The cold war between the United States and the Soviet Union, which spanned the last half of the twentieth century, and which consumed more social and economic resources than any other American military endeavor, occupied an uncertain place between real war and imperfect peace.

The United States also waged many imperial wars—that is, campaigns, interventions, violent covert operations, and full-blown wars that pitted it, an expansive, technologically advanced, militantly commercial nation-state, against less technologically advanced, "traditional" peoples on their own territory. Several American wars—for example, the Korean War (1950–1953) and the anti-Iraq Persian Gulf War (1991)—combined elements of international, civil, and imperial war. By the second half of the twentieth century, the United States had evolved into a global hegemon, a development made possible by its economic strength, political strategy, and military might. In the process, war and war preparation had become a central element of American life.

TOWARD TOTAL WAR

From the late eighteenth through the twentieth centuries, Anglo-European-American wars tended to spiral toward "totality" and "absoluteness": governmental efforts at social, political, and economic mobilization were increasingly more comprehensive; political and military objectives were more consummate; and the consequences for people, societies, and economies were more costly. Not every war was "total" in every element of its conduct or "total" in its costs for all belligerents, but the period was frequently punctuated by ever larger and more lethal struggles.

Compared with those of the past, peacetime and wartime armed forces expanded dramatically during this period, both in actual numbers of men under arms and also in proportion to the population from which recruits were drawn. Mercenary armies in the sixteenth century seldom grew as large as twenty to thirty thousand troops; "regular," "professional" state armies of the seventeenth century often reached fifty to sixty thousand troops; and in the eighteenth century, Frederick the Great of Prussia commanded forces of up to two hundred thousand. By contrast, however, Napoleon Bonaparte's combined armies came to more than two hundred thousand troops in some campaigns of the early nineteenth century. In the American Civil War, Union forces at Gettysburg in 1863 numbered almost eighty-five thousand, while in 1865 the Union army totaled more than one million in all theaters. In the twentieth century, national armies and other forces under arms were measured in the millions, even in peacetime. Thus the proportion of uniformed western European personnel to the population increased from less than 3 per 1,000 in the seventeenth century to nearly 10 per 1,000 in the late twentieth. In 1987, the ratio for the United States was 9 per 1,000, and for the world 5.65 per 1,000.

When wars were waged between equivalent forces during the period from the American Revolutionary War to World War II, the battles fought tended increasingly to cover larger geographical territory, to involve more troops, to last longer, and to occur more frequently. Wars that began in one locality tended to metastasize nationally, continentally, and globally. Modern warring nations employed new military technologies, drew upon ever larger industrial and human resources, and often sought more absolute strategic and political aims.

The march toward total war was propelled by such profound cultural and historical developments as

- European colonial expansion into the Americas, Africa, and Asia beginning in the late fifteenth century;
- the democratization of politics and society, which began with the American and French revolutions in the late eighteenth century;
- the emergence of mass ideologies (republicanism, nationalism, capitalism, and socialism), which attended the revolutionary social changes in America and Europe before and after 1776;
- industrialization, which by the mid nineteenth century began to have a profound impact on war with its capacity to produce vast quantities of matériel and move and supply large and far-flung armed forces via steam-powered locomotion and internal-combustion engines;
- the professionalization of the military officer class by the mid nineteenth century, which in part was a response to the problems of managing modern, mass, mechanized military and naval forces, as well as a concomitance of managerial reforms in industrializing society;
- late-nineteenth-century imperialism, the second wave of Western, European American colonialism, which triggered revolutionary social forces in the Third World by the beginning of the twentieth century; and
- science, which with government direction by the twentieth century systematically applied the products of modern industry and technology to the making of weapons and machines of war.

NATIVE AMERICANS AND TOTAL WAR

In white-versus-white warfare, the absolute political and strategic goals of total war did not find full expression until the twentieth century. But these goals were presaged in the campaigns and wars Europeans and European Americans waged against Native Americans on both continents and other nonwhite peoples from the late fifteenth century onward. Imperial expansion in the Americas, Africa, and Asia involved Europeans in high-stakes struggles for territorial, economic, and political mastery of preindustrial societies. Deep cultural misunderstanding, racial prejudice, and technological disparity led to military skirmishes, campaigns, and wars resulting in the destruction of native armed forces, economies, and civilian populations. In fighting these wars, modern, technologically superior societies seldom if ever engaged in total mobilization, yet the impact on traditional societies was often absolute, for most premodern peoples were unprepared to withstand the onslaught. Not until the twentieth century would indigenous peoples mount unified, sustained, and effective opposition. This came with the peasant-based, revolutionary-war strategy, tactics, and political organization of Mao Tse-tung in China and Ho Chi Minh in Vietnam, and also with the development of the mass, nonviolent, direct-action tactics of Mohandas Gandhi in India.

Native American cultures at the time of European "discovery" and colonialism lacked the numbers, unity, political organization, economic base, technological infrastructure, and military strategy required for effective resistance. Among the gatherers, hunters, and incipient agriculturalists of North America were thousands of clans, tribes, and languages. These "Indians" possessed no sense of "nationality"; each tribe was "the people," and tribes made war against other tribes speaking different languages. Europeans encouraged such warfare and exacerbated it, as they played one tribe off against another with military, economic, political, or technological assistance. In battles against Europeans, Native Americans fought as they always had, as individual braves, not as cogs in a disciplined, social machine. They fought courageously, winning some battles but always losing the wars. European American conflict with Native Americans encouraged the emergence of modern racism and military practices that would contribute to the evolution of total war between white societies themselves. Many Native American tribes, meanwhile, were obliterated as people or cultures.

From the earliest colonial days, white strategy adapted to compensate for the problem that Native American warriors were difficult to find and fix in place for destruction in battle. Hence, instead of seeking out Indian warriors, white armies sought out Native American villages, fields, and herds in order to force warriors to fight. Even if braves persisted in avoiding pitched battle, European American forces could succeed in crushing tribal resistance by destroying village structures, animals, and crops and killing women and children or taking them into captivity and slavery. This ruthless approach continued through the nineteenth century, during the last third of which the U.S. Army on the Great Plains was aided by the deliberate and massive slaughter of bison by white civilians and by the army's ability to supply itself by railroad and to continue to fight during the winter months. Most surviving Native Americans were forced onto reservations and made to become officially dependent on government distributions of food, supplies, and education. Others were partially assimilated into the larger white culture.

RECRUITMENT AND DISCIPLINE IN REGULAR ARMIES

At the time of the Revolutionary War, the American military was heir to three centuries of colonial expansion in the Americas and several centuries of European military development, which peaked between the late seventeenth and mid eighteenth centuries.

The most salient feature of pre-revolutionary military systems, as compared with those of the postrevolutionary era, was their limited ability to tap national resources. The kings and queens of the dynastic, mercantilist states of Europe ruled with the cooperation of the hereditary aristocracy, who in turn enjoyed numerous privileges, including tax exemptions and the monopolization of military officerships. But the pool of potential officers was limited; the aristocracy barely comprised over 2 percent of the population of Europe. Command positions in military engineering, the artillery, and the navy requiring special skills were slowly made available to the bourgeoisie as the eighteenth century came to an end, but by and large the nobility continued to dominate these higher ranks well into the nineteenth century in many European countries.

Common soldiers and sailors were recruited from the rural and urban lumpen class—the landless, the unemployed, the very poor, and convicts. The relatively wealthy bourgeoisie and the producing peasantry, who were valued for their contributions to the economy, were virtually excluded from military service. In the British army, a large proportion of soldiers were drawn from the destitute classes of impoverished Ireland. In all armies, but particularly in the British army, a significant number of the rank and file were also foreign mercenaries. In the War of the Revolution, for example, the British hired thirty thousand mercenary troops from several German principalities, among them Hesse-Kassel (from which we get the term "Hessian").

The primary means by which the old regimes of Britain and Europe recruited the so-called dregs of society into the army and navy was impressment. Armed "press" gangs were able to cajole or force the poor into enlisting, because of their lower-class vulnerability and required allegiance to the divine-right sovereign. Ordinary soldiers might have felt loyalty to comrades or to the locality from which they were sometimes commonly raised, but in this prenationalistic age they were not nationalistic. Bureaucratic, administrative, and fiscal, the relationship between the government and the governed was external and mechanical. Ties to the government were not psychologically internalized as they would be after democratic and nationalistic revolutions produced citizens who would think of themselves as sovereign over the state or as organically one with the nation.

In colonial America, impressment became a divisive political and social issue. In 1747, for example, lower-class Bostonians rioted, assaulted sheriff's officers, took hostages, and destroyed property in protest against the Royal Navy's impressment of American seamen. A few years later, between 1755 and 1757, British army attempts to impress indentured servants caused disagreements with colonial servant masters over adequate compensation. The army's unscrupulous recruiting practices, along with its harsh discipline, moreover, eventually soured the indentured servants on enlistment. The incident became part of the growing list of simmering grievances that would ultimately lead to upper- and lower-class rebellion against British colonial authority. Most of these pre-Revolution complaints were directly related to British tax legislation, customs revisions, Admiralty Court measures, and troop-quartering acts that comprised British attempts to make the American colonies pay for the policing of the enlarged British empire after the French and Indian War, which included the stationing of regular troops in America.

The terms of service for common soldiers and sailors in the eighteenth century were usually twenty-five years, although death and desertion produced significant turnover in military units. They, as well as the officers, were "professionals," but only in the sense of having gained their military experience through prolonged service, not in the late-nineteenth- and twentieth-century sense of having received formal, specialized schooling in the theory and practice of a chosen career. They were also "regulars" in that theirs was the regular mode of fighting and the regular method of military organization and mobilization. In the War of the Revolution and the Napoleonic Wars (1796–1815), as farmers and peasants arose to resist regular, occupying forces by means of the unorthodox, harassing tactics of ambuscade and raid, they would be dubbed "irregulars" or "guerrillas."

Military service in regular armies did not grant the rank and file the honorable status it did the nobility. Moreover, in part because of the lower-class makeup of the common soldiery, the larger, civilian population of Europe and colonial America treated soldiers and sailors as social pariahs and parasites. In America, the Boston Massacre of 5 March 1770 was largely brought on by the uneasy relationship between the rank-and-file redcoats and the city's workingmen; public resentment at the presence of the British army in the city to enforce rigorous customs laws; the sexual taunts soldiers directed at Boston's young women; and the army's public displays of martial music, marching, and harsh discipline.

Within European armies and navies, rigid class differences between officers and soldiers combined with the latter's lack of adequate education and principled motivation, brought about the officers' rigorous and brutal disciplining of soldiers and sailors. For regular armed forces then, as now, military discipline had the primary social function of overcoming acculturated inhibitions against killing and of preparing soldiers and sailors to behave like the weapons they used, lethally and reliably. Discipline and training stripped inductees of their individuality and reconstituted them in the military ethos of subordination, physical strength and courage, and organized destruction. For regular soldiers in the eighteenth century, this was achieved through intensive parade-ground drills in shoulder-to-shoulder marching, maneuvering, and volley firing, combined with corporal punishment. Marching and chanting in unison, along with peer pressure, competition, fear of failure, fear of punishment, and military tradition, encouraged obedience, loyalty, regularity, duty, and esprit de corps—the fundamental motivations of postcivilized, regular military forces throughout history.

The immediate purpose of the parade drill was to prepare troops for the relatively rare but bloody, close-order, stand-up tactics of the land warfare of the day, which was largely dictated by the short-range, smooth-bore, inaccurate, bayonet-bearing, flintlock muskets carried by the rank and file. As late as the twentieth century, however, long after such drill was made obsolete by modern weaponry, it survived as a means of instilling precision and discipline.

Eighteenth-century corporal punishment included withdrawal of rations, head shaving, having to ride the wooden horse, gagging, spread-eagling, beating, having to run the gauntlet, and flogging. It had the primary coercive purpose of ensuring that the rank and file, lacking higher motivation, would fight at least from fear of their own officers rather than flee for fear of the enemy in battle. At sea, harsh discipline was intended to deter mutiny and weld ship and crew into a cohesive unit.

But cruel punishment, along with frail soldier-sailor motivation, ironically contributed to high rates of desertion in opportune circumstances. In the War of the Revolution, 17 percent of the thirty thousand Hessians in the British army deserted; like many before them who had fled Britain and

Europe to escape soldiering, most of these deserters eventually became American citizens. In another example, Britain's seizure, or impressment, of perhaps has many as six thousand sailors from American naval vessels at sea between 1803 and the start of the War of 1812—a war provoked in part by such impressment—was a response to the large-scale desertions from British ships while in American ports.

THE COLONIAL MILITIA

Colonial Americans' military experience before the French and Indian and Revolutionary wars was not, however, primarily with the regular army but with the militia. The American militia had its direct, social roots in Alfred the Great's (849–889) Saxon *fyrd* (the Anglo-Saxon word for army), when every English freeman was a part-time soldier. Revitalizing the institution, medieval and Elizabethan laws required every able-bodied freeman to provide himself with arms, undergo recurrent training, and respond to the crown's call for domestic service. Parliament's control of the London militia in 1642 initially served it well in its struggles with Charles I (r. 1625–1649), but the English militia fell into disuse with the creation of Oliver Cromwell's New Model Army in 1645 and the rise of the red-coated regular army after the English Civil War (1642–1649).

In America, the absence of large numbers of regular troops before 1755, the requirements of maintaining social and political order, and clashes with Native American, Dutch, French, and Spanish forces created suitable conditions for colonists in America to maintain a part-time soldiery drawn from freemen. Based on previous British militia practice, every colony except Quaker-influenced Pennsylvania passed laws of compulsory military obligation for able-bodied, free white males, who were required to possess arms, train periodically, and respond to government calls during emergencies. Colonial governors in most colonies appointed officers and called out the troops, but legislative assemblies, linking the constitutional issue of civilian control over the military to the political issue of legislative influence, affirmed their own right to vote funds, frame militia regulations, and oversee military administration.

The American yeomen and tenants obligated to be part of the militia viewed their obligation in a manner different from their Old World counterparts, whose service was seen as duty to one's sovereign, landlord, or hereditary superior. Part of a covenanted society in which the economics of labor and ownership produced numerous everyday contractual agreements, American freemen viewed their militia service, too, as a voluntary contractual agreement between actual or theoretical equals. Out of this cultural context came the militia mystique, encoded with images of the militiaman as an independent, self-reliant, part-time, soldier-citizen, free to make or break his military obligation.

The militia system was in many respects very unmilitary, especially as the frontier demarcation moved farther west. Militiamen from the older towns and counties nearer the Atlantic coast were usually more poorly trained, armed, clothed, organized, and disciplined than those nearer the frontier, where clashes with Native Americans or French and Spanish troops were more frequent. For them, the periodic muster on the village green was more of an occasion for socializing, rowdyism, and drinking than for hard drilling and instruction. Inferior to army regulars in military techniques and less steady in combat, militia units were employed as auxiliaries when regulars were available.

Law and custom distinguished between militia: the "ordinary" or "common" militia came to represent the general pool of manpower obligated to serve or from which lower-class men would be drafted when needed; the "enrolled militia" were those actually enrolled; and the "volunteer militia" were those who volunteered to serve during emergencies. Even though the militia system, unlike the regular military system, provided some opportunities for social mobility, and despite its special mystique, the militia reflected, perpetuated, and created class distinctions. Whether appointed by governors or legislators or elected by troops, officers were usually from the elite, propertied class, and as the danger from frontier warfare declined, exemptions from obligation could either be purchased by the affluent or were legislated for numerous groups: jailers, millers, gunsmiths, iron and lead workers, tutors and professors, public printers, judges, land office registrars, ministers, legislators, and certain government officials. In many colonies, and later in states, the volunteer militia were the elite cavalry and artillery, whose involvement sometimes reflected their higher socioeconomic positions and whose militia membership often conferred the additional status accruing from the fame and glory of war—as well as the personal contacts made during service.

DISCIPLINE, MOTIVATION, AND RECRUITMENT

The policy of George Washington and the Continental Congress during the War of the Revolution of raising and maintaining a regular Continental army augmented by state militia perpetuated the dual, regular/militia military tradition. Even though old punishments like flogging were still administered in Continental army units, this was a Revolutionary army recruited in the America of the militia mystique. Patriot officers and leaders placed greater emphasis than the old regime on inspiring individual motivation through educating troops about the purposes of training, discipline, and campaigning; awarding honorable status to rank-and-file soldiers by means of symbolic medals and service stripes; and, during these times that tried men's souls, disseminating propaganda about the cause of independence, service to country, and dedication to republicanism. Congressional militia brigades supported propaganda efforts by identifying Loyalists and fence sitters and then taxing, tar and feathering, expelling, or indoctrinating them.

The easing of coercive disciplinary severity would continue through the nineteenth and twentieth centuries as social norms of punishment evolved and also as warfare became more technically and managerially complex, for military authorities also needed to create tolerable conditions wherein skilled specialists would reenlist. Nevertheless, the relaxation of corporal discipline progressed slowly. When Continental troops deserted or mutinied because of poor pay, clothing, and rations, for example, General Washington resorted to flogging, running-the-gauntlet, and executions. A quarter of a century later, during the War of 1812, common soldiers charged with absence without leave were punished with hard labor, bread and water rations, riding-the-wooden-horse, and, for desertion, the firing squad. Flogging was abolished in 1861, but other severe punishments continued. In part reflecting the harshness of discipline and the unattractiveness of army life, one out of three soldiers deserted the U.S. Army in 1871. Executions by hanging were meted out through World War II and into the 1960s.

Although the 1950 Uniform Code of Military Justice, which applied to all the armed forces, moderated many punishments, draftees and enlistees continued to be beaten by some army drill instructors, and Marine Corps recruits periodically died at boot camp as a result of harsh training methods to the end of the twentieth century. In 1990–1991, as American troops were mobilized for the Persian Gulf War, soldiers stationed in Europe and America who conscientiously objected to fighting in the Gulf theater were manacled, brigged, confined to base, ridiculed, or forcibly shipped to Saudi Arabia, their protest and treatment censored from public view in the United States.

As motive forces of discipline and soldiering, nationalism and patriotism, which had their modern social and psychological origins in the American Revolution, would require time to develop fully. Victories and defeats in the War of 1812 and subsequent international wars, the trauma of the Civil War and Reconstruction, the transformation of a predominantly rural America into an urban industrial colossus, the gradual decline of local attachments through geographical mobility and mass communications, government propaganda during World Wars I and II encouraging nationalistic conformity, government purging of dissidence during the 1920s and the cold war, and other related developments would be required to bring about flag-waving nationalism and patriotism in the twentieth century.

Since the Revolution, only a small percentage of recruits enlisted primarily or entirely for reasons of patriotism, a motive that, in any case, was often accompanied by equally strong feelings of militarism and adventurism. Volunteering was and is mainly a function of socioeconomic conditions: enlistments and reenlistments are higher and desertions lower during times of recession and depression than during those of prosperity, as during the depression of the 1870s and the recessions of the 1980s and 1990s. Enlistment was and is also related to long-term regional income differentials in addition to current employment levels.

Ethnic cultural attitudes, immigrant status, religious and political preferences, localist loyalties, rural versus urban upbringing, father's occupation, and class status also affected enlistments, but personal economic welfare has always been a strong motivation. New England colonial soldiers were disproportionately the younger sons of farmers who had yet to inherit land, while Confederate guerrillas from Missouri and Kansas were disproportionately the eldest sons of slave owners who "rode with Quantrill" (guerrilla commander William Clarke Quantrill) to preserve their inheritance. Throughout the nineteenth century, the ranks of the regular army and navy were filled by the depressed and oppressed classes in American society. New European immigrants, African Americans, and social outcasts of varying nationalities and classes, unable to succeed in civilian society, often won personal pride, manly honor, income, and a home away from home in the regular armed forces.

Even during the post–Vietnam War era, after the U.S. Department of Defense changed its policy from partially conscripted to all-volunteer forces in 1973, enlistees overwhelmingly came from the poorer and lower middle classes of whites and minorities. In the army, the number of high school graduates declined along with Armed Forces Qualification Test scores. By the early 1980s, on account of recession and also perhaps because of the fading memory of the unpopular Vietnam War, the number and quality of recruits increased, but enlistment patterns reflected the age-old relationship with socioeconomic conditions and opportunities. Of male and female active-duty personnel in all branches of the military in 1989, for example, 34.8 percent were minorities.

Once in battle, men fought, then as now, primarily because of peer pressure, unit loyalty, responsibility to comrades in arms, fear of failure, fear of punishment, desire to survive, anger, self-pride, and sundry subconscious psychological impulses. But the ideologies of nationalism, patriotism, republicanism, and other "isms" operated to reinforce the ordinary motives for enlisting and, even if conscripted, serving and fighting. These ideologies ennobled military service for the masses, idealized baser motives, fulfilled or created a longing to be part of a larger entity, heightened the sense of obligation to society, encouraged enlistment, and strengthened ties of loyalty in conditions of less stern discipline.

Ideologies also served to justify the killing of fellow human beings by re-tribalizing social perspectives onto a national scale. Combining occasionally with racism and religious self-righteousness, political and nationalistic ideology functioned to dehumanized the "enemy," who did not belong to the same nation or subscribe to the same ideology, who were not really human but the evil "other." Patriotism in particular became intertwined with warfare and military service: it substantiated one's membership in the group and one's support of "us" against "them" through service in the armed forces, emotional encouragement of the troops, or advocacy of victory. Governments fostered patriotism for their own political purposes, and, by the late nineteenth century at least, corporations worked to identify themselves—and conservatism—with the symbols of patriotism for social and commercial purposes. Perhaps because Americans were of diverse origins and lacked a long history rooted in place, the flag after the Civil War became the icon around which most could rally in order to define their identity. By the time of the Progressive Era and World War I, war was seen by some nationalists as the one activity in which the greatest national cooperation and unity might be achieved in a most competitive and diverse country.

Inversely, service in the military has had the effect of socializing veterans in nationalism, patriotism, and militarism. The effectiveness of this socialization has varied, depending on many sociopsychological variables, including the attitudes veterans initially brought into military service. Nevertheless, Continental army officers who served outside their own colonies came to favor a stronger federal government; during and after World War I service in units drawn from national rather than strictly local pools of manpower encouraged the emergence of national perspectives; and veterans of World War II and the Korean War tended to be strongly supportive of militant cold war foreign policies.

With the eighteenth-century revolutions in America and Europe came other changes in military organization, recruitment, and mobilization. In America, enlistment terms were much shorter than those of eighteenth-century Anglo-European regular armies, varying from two or three years to the duration of the conflict, and they were encouraged by promises of land grants in the western wilderness, higher pay, and cash bounties—even though western lands had yet to be taken from Native Americans and the value of Continental paper money was inflated. While officers tended to be drawn from the upper classes and common soldiers from the lower classes, no formal hereditary restrictions existed to prevent free white males from enlisting and moving up in the ranks, and so the potential for social mobility was increased and the pool of potential recruits was enlarged compared to the past few centuries.

Even after these liberating developments of the American Revolution, there remained the problem of attracting enough recruits for the ever larger wars of America and Europe. One of the ironies of militant democracy and nationalism was that the right of national citizenship in the modern state, whether a republic or not, would now include the legal obligation to serve the state, while the government in turn came to possess enhanced legitimacy, which gave it additional power to compel such service. Through the first half of the nineteenth century, the other great powers of Europe turned to modified forms of conscription based on nationalism to build their armed forces.

PROFESSIONALISM, MANAGERIALISM, AND A NATION IN ARMS

Following German victory over the French in the Franco-Prussian War (1870–1871), the Austro-Hungarian Empire, Italy, Russia, and even France, the previous exemplar of military modernity, took steps to emulate the German model of the "nation in arms." It was an integrated system of mobilization, command, and logistics in which a mass army of active-duty soldiers was raised by conscription in both peacetime and wartime, backed up by a reserve force of former active-duty troops, transported to the front by rail locomotive, and led by a general staff composed of officers trained in military schools that commanded the army, planned war strategy for contingencies, and drafted and implemented manpower and economic mobilization plans. As the nineteenth century came to an end, the size of these armies and the supply of modern arms and equipment to them kept pace with growing populations, larger gross national products, modern taxation, and the industrial and technical capacities of each nation. Medical services were improved and professionalized; rations were manufactured in quantity, packaged, and stored for future use; electronic communications were gradually improved; and weaponry became more lethal with smokeless powder, repeating rifles, water-cooled machine guns, and long-range, accurate, high-explosive artillery.

Slow in adopting the German model of land warfare, Great Britain and the United States were unique among the industrial powers. Some prominent Americans had proposed state militia drafts during the War of the Revolution and the War of 1812, but it was not until the Civil War that first the Confederacy (1862) and then the Union (1863) resorted to "national" conscription. Both sides authorized exemptions, but in the North substitutes and commutation of service could be purchased, so that the effects of the draft fell more heavily on the poor. Discounting the Civil War experiment with conscription, which supplied only 6 percent of the Union forces, throughout the nineteenth century the United States continued to rely on the old dual system of volunteer regular forces augmented by volunteer militia. But the militia declined in fighting effectiveness and institutional significance as the century progressed, evolving into merely a reservoir of manpower from which volunteers for the regular army could be drawn. The volunteer militia became the National Guard and, especially during the last third of the century, was used, along with the regular army, to quell civil disorder and labor unrest.

Most Americans believed that a small regular army and navy were adequate for the nation's military requirements. Although at different periods during the nineteenth century, the United States had ambitions in Canada, Spanish and Mexican territory to conquer, and Native Americans to dispossess, it had no equivalently powerful, threatening enemies on its borders, as had the European states. Moreover, states'-rights advocacy, a laissez-faire political economy, and antimilitary concerns reinforced opposition to the creation of a large peacetime army. Between Reconstruction and the Spanish-American War, while Europe was turning to the nation-in-arms concept, the annual size of the U.S. Army averaged only twenty-five thousand men, who were occupied in the Reconstruction occupation of the South, fighting Native Americans on the plains, and breaking labor strikes.

With the reforms instituted under Secretary of War Elihu Root (1899–1904), the army began to move into the modern world of military organization. The Root reforms, which followed on the heels of the command and logistical failures of the Spanish-American War and which also represented a military version of Progressive centralization and administrative efficiency, increased the size of the peacetime regular army, created the Army War College in 1901, reorganized the army's system of staff and line schools, funneled federal aid to state National Guards, designated the National Guard as the country's organized reserve, and created a modern general staff. During last two decades of the nineteenth century and into the twentieth, naval command systems were also professionalized as huge steel-hulled, propeller-driven, steam-powered warships mounting large modern guns were sent to sea. Naval officers were generally more successful than army officers in lobbying for funds: fewer Americans feared a peacetime standing navy than a standing army; the steel industry benefited from shipbuilding; political allies were found among imperialists; and Alfred Thayer Mahan, Naval War College president (1886–1889, 1892–1893), articulated a persuasive and popular national-security rationale for naval and imperial expansion.

True national conscription came to the United States only with American participation in World Wars I and II. Although the Selective Service Act of 1917 permitted deferments for occupations deemed vital, it excluded substitutions, commutations, and bounties and was built not on the obligation of state militia but on the principle of the universal obligation of male citizens to the nation. America's first peacetime draft was instituted in September 1940, and extensions to the Selective Service Act were enacted after America entered the war in 1941 and continued through 1946. With the reinstatement of conscription in 1948 and its extensions to 1973, the United States experienced its first semipermanent peacetime draft, whose deferral policies, as with past recruitment policies, benefited the middle and upper classes.

Drawing on old American traditions of religious and secular opposition to war and compulsory military service, tens of thousands of conscientious objectors resisted the conscriptions of America's twentieth-century wars. During World War II, for example, the U.S. government classified 42,973 of the 10,022,367 inductees as conscientious objectors. Most were assigned alternative service in Civilian Public Service camps, where they were employed as laborers in forestry conservation and as test subjects in typhus, malaria, pneumonia, and nutrition experiments. Some did serve as attendants in mental hospitals and schools for the mentally deficient, thus fulfilling the broad humanitarian missions they had originally hoped for. But most were employed in rural conservation. They received no wages or benefits, and the system was largely run by the military. Through their protests against the types of service they had been given and the administration of the alternative system by the military, they developed nonviolent resistance tactics, which were to influence future protest movements.

During the unpopular Vietnam War, widespread conscientious objection, along with draft avoidance and evasion, desertions from the military, assassinations of officers in Vietnam, and mutinies at bases, in the field, and at sea, contributed to the government's decision to abandon conscription and adopt an all-volunteer policy in 1973. In 1980, however, the resumption of compulsory draft registration for eighteen-year-old men effectively created a standby conscription policy.

STRATEGY, TECHNOLOGY, AND SOCIETY

Democratization, nationalization, industrialization, professionalization, managerialization, and all the other socioeconomic forces transforming war in the nineteenth and twentieth centuries also transformed military strategy. With limited resources and logistical capability, sovereigns and generals of the seventeenth and eighteenth centuries were loathe to risk losing their expensively raised and maintained armed forces. They sought to avoid battle, preferring instead to seek out and hold territory against opposing combatants, who, like themselves, were bound to fixed lines of communication and fortification. The result was warfare with a "limited" impact on people and societies. Beginning, however, with the War of the American Revolution and continuing through the wars of the French Revolution, the Napoleonic Wars, and beyond, modern states often engaged in conflicts over ideology, nationality, and socioeconomic system, with each government capable of drawing more or less fully on its nation's resources to continue the struggle past merely rational calculations of cost effectiveness.

With so much at stake, or perceived to be at stake, it was not enough to outmaneuver an army along a line of communication to bring about its withdrawal or capitulation. As long as the enemy's armed forces remained and its people were willing, the enemy could resist. Government and military leaders therefore increasingly pursued ruthless strategies of mobility and combativeness, seeking battle with enemy forces to destroy their ability and will to fight. By the time of the American Civil War, the violent logic of total conflict had additionally identified as military targets the enemy economy and population that supported the armed forces. The Union's naval blockade of the Confederacy, General William T. Sherman's march through Georgia and the Carolinas (1864–1865), and General Philip H. Sheridan's campaign in the Shenandoah Valley (1864), for example, sought not only the destruction of the Southern economy but also the terrorization of the Southern people. By World War II the terrorization and direct destruction of the enemy population became high-priority strategic objectives—dramatically demonstrated by the Anglo-American naval blockades and aerial bombardment of German and Japanese civilians, as well as by Nazi massacres of captive populations.

Over 90 percent of the more than 100,000,000 war-related fatalities worldwide since 1700 occurred in the first nine decades of the twentieth century. Until about 1950, most of these were in Europe; since then most have been inflicted in the second and third worlds—almost always with American and first world involvement. Before 1960 civilians accounted for 50 percent of these deaths, but they made up 73 percent in the 1970s and 85 percent in the 1980s. Since its civil war, the United States' military losses have been considerably smaller than those of its co-belligerents, partly because it entered both world wars belatedly and partly because it has pursued strategies emphasizing its naval, air, and technological superiority. Because it has fought its wars on others' soils, it has also been spared the civilian slaughter.

The large-scale killing was made possible by industrial and scientific technology and by the transmutation of ethical standards. The revolution in military technology may be said to have begun with the introduction of gunpowder weapons to Europe in the fifteenth century. But it was not until the nineteenth century that improvements in the accuracy, range, rapidity of fire, and explosive force of firearms and artillery significantly exceeded the killing and destructive power of ancient weaponry.

Ethical standards mutated to accommodate total war. Many American and European citizens, who before World War II viewed the bombing of cities and civilians to be wholly immoral, for example, came to accept such behavior as morally legitimate by the time the war was in full swing. For scientists working on weapons of mass destruction, the ethical implications were troubling, especially when the U.S. government organized thousands of scientists and engineers in the Manhattan Project during World War II to develop nuclear weapons, which produced an exponential leap in military destructive capacity. Most scientists and engineers accepted the technical challenges of research and development and the national security rationales of war, overcoming whatever ethical doubts they may have had. Only a relative few articulated their concerns about the ethics of their research and the danger of a postwar nuclear arms race with the Soviet Union.

The nuclear-military age began on 16 July 1945, when the first atom bomb was exploded at the Trinity test site near Alamogordo, New Mexico, followed by the dropping of atom bombs on Hiroshima and Nagasaki, Japan, later that year. By the early 1950s, both the United States and the Soviet Union had tested thermonuclear weapons, which were immensely more powerful than Hiroshima-like nuclear weapons. By the mid 1950s and into the 1960s, both powers became capable of dropping tens of thousands of warheads on the other. From the 1950s through the 1980s, nuclear bombs proliferated geographically: several other countries, including Britain, France, China, and India developed nuclear weapons.

The very survival of the human species, whose cultural success had been so dependent on technology, now seemed threatened by nuclear technology. A 1983 World Health Organization study concluded that the combined effects of blast, fire, and radiation in a large-scale nuclear war (5,000–10,000 megatons) would result in the prompt deaths of 1.1 billion persons. An additional 1.1 billion would suffer injuries requiring medical attention. Scientists predicted that the fires from such a war would produce an atmospheric pall of smoke and soot over the earth, blotting out sunlight and triggering "nuclear winter" or "nuclear fall," which would mortally endanger the rest of the earth's population, along with its vegetation and animal life. Even non-nuclear, "conventional" weapons had grown by the end of the century to be ten to fourteen times more lethal than the conventional weapons of World War II.

Pervasive environmental degradation from military training and other activity, the devastation of war, the chemical- and nuclear-weapons–production emissions and waste also threatened humanity. The U.S. military, for example, was largely exempt from environmental regulation until 1986 and by 1991 was responsible for over fourteen thousand pollution sites. Its nuclear waste vastly exceeded that of civilian nuclear power plants, and the exhaust from its solid-fuel rockets was a prime cause of the erosion of the earth's atmospheric ozone layer. Thousands died from cancer: soldiers ordered to participate in post–World War II nuclear exercises, civilians affected by the atmospheric nuclear tests of the 1940s and 1950s, and civilians living near nuclear-production facilities.

Casualties of the nuclear-military age were not all physical, however. Most citizens were psychologically numbed from the overwhelming, incomprehensible nuclear sword of Damocles that hung over their lives. They were confused by nuclear euphemisms—for example, "countervalue target" for urban population target, "Peacemaker" for a multiple-warhead missile, and "nuclear exchange" for total nuclear war. And they came to feel politically impotent by their apparent inability to end the nuclear arms race.

The most visible psychological casualties of twentieth-century war were those who had experienced modern combat. Each battle produced psychological trauma, and if the fighting was more or less continuous, like most of the fighting between more or less equal foes in the twentieth century, "shell shock," "battle fatigue," or "traumatic stress syndrome" afflicted all of those in combat to one degree or another. The special conditions of the Vietnam War caused large numbers of American combat veterans to suffer from post-traumatic stress disorder after their tours of duty.

WAR AND THE ECONOMY

War has always profoundly affected economies. Wherever it occurs, fighting wreaks destruction on capital, resources, agriculture, farmers, workers, and consumers. War preparation and war waging strains economies as nations draw on their economic assets to support insatiable military machines. Military spending distorts economic development by diverting investment, research, and production into war technology and personnel and away from civilian production, social welfare, and medical care, and it undermines economic competitiveness by subsidizing wasteful managerial methods. It passes debt burdens onto future generations and encourages inflation by pumping money into unproductive military goods and increasing the demand for technical specialists and precious raw materials.

On the other hand, military spending has assisted some American businesses and occasionally stimulated the economy. In the American colonies, for example, some merchants benefited from British military spending during the 1754–1763 French and Indian War. Independence gained in the War of the Revolution freed American capitalists from British mercantile restrictions. The logistical fiascoes of the War of 1812 inspired postwar government subsidization of transportation development, while that war and the embargoes that preceded it rechanneled domestic investment into industrial production. Suppliers of army needs during the frontier wars of the nineteenth century profited, and the acquisition of vast Native American territories brought enormous resources to the nation as well as land and economic opportunities to corporations and individual citizens. The taking of Mexican-held territory during the War with Mexico (1846–1848) opened up trading opportunities in Asia. The Civil War stimulated the growth of Northern banking, iron, steel, railroad, clothing, agriculture, and other industries (although it also devastated the already industrially backward South, along with its agriculture). Spending and borrowing in America by World War I European belligerents vaulted America out of its prewar recession, and this, plus U.S. government war spending, meant that by the end of the war the United States had become the world's leading creditor and industrial producer. Colossal military deficit spending during World War II, which social conservatives found more politically acceptable than New Deal domestic deficit spending, took the United States out of its deep economic depression. Arms sales to the industrializing Second World and the preindustrial third world in the 1970s and 1980s helped to reduce the trade deficit.

Nevertheless, the economic advantages of government spending can be achieved through expenditures for either peace or war, and in fact spending for nonmilitary goods and services is more economic and generates more jobs than spending for military goods and services. The choice of whether to spend for peace or war is determined by those groups wielding political power. During the cold war, the policy-making elite, which sought to maintain American armed might in support of militant foreign policies, additionally seized upon military spending in the name of national defense and security as a politically acceptable means of stimulating the country's periodically sluggish economy through deficit spending—an approach that came to be known as "military Keynesianism."

Although successful during the Korean War era and the presidencies of John F. Kennedy and Ronald Reagan, this strategy had only short-term advantages. For fiscal year 1987, at the end of the Reagan military buildup, military spending totaled $367.3 billion, which amounted to 67 percent of the discretionary budget derived from taxes. Over 10 percent of this spending was hidden from public scrutiny in the secret "black" portion of the budget. Some, but by no means all, high-technology and aerospace industries benefited, but hundreds of billions of dollars for research, social services, medical care, education, transportation, and urban infrastructure were diverted to pay for the buildup. Even earlier, by the mid 1970s, perennially high levels of military spending had already brought about what some historians have called "imperial overstretch": an undermining of America's international economic competitiveness in the expensive effort to police its global hegemony.

America's participation in war and its enormous military expenditures since World War II also gave rise to what President Dwight D. Eisenhower referred to in his farewell presidential address as the "military-industrial complex," as he tried to warn the nation of its influence on the economy and on policy making. Most scholars agreed that this complex was an integrated military-governmental-corporate-labor-scientific-academic system that consisted of persons, groups, and institutions with vested psychological, social, and economic interests in high levels of spending for military forces and weaponry. Its twentieth-century social roots were in the centralized governmental agencies that sprang up during World War I to organize and administer the economic war effort; the military's planning for economic mobilization before World War II; the involvement of corporate and military leaders in the running of the "arsenal of democracy" of World War II and the cold war; and the various constituencies nationwide with a stake in war and military spending.

THE AFRICAN AMERICAN MILITARY EXPERIENCE

Beginning at least in the seventeenth century with the introduction of black slavery, whites were reluctant to include African Americans in the armed forces, fearing that armed slaves would rise in rebellion or that black military participation would lead to manumission or full rights of citizenship for the few blacks who were not slaves. In any case, slave owners were usually opposed to making their human capital available for military service. During the War of the Revolution and the War of 1812, whites additionally feared that recruitment of slaves and free blacks would provoke the British to encourage slave escapes, foment insurrections, and employ fugitive slaves as soldiers against their former owners—policies the British followed anyway. Until, if not beyond, the turn of the twentieth century, whites were also opposed to the recruitment of African Americans because of the enhanced status that military uniforms accorded their presumed racial inferiors.

Despite reluctance and opposition, however, colonies, states, and then the nation did turn to African Americans as a source of military manpower—first because they were, after all, men who could labor and fight, and, second, because of the general unwillingness of the comparatively prosperous white population to join the army and navy. There were, of course, additional reasons for the recruitment of African Americans. Conscription during the Civil War, for example, did bring forth hundreds of thousands of white soldiers, but high casualty rates, the demands of radicals and blacks, white working-class resentment toward the draft, and the adoption of emancipation as a Northern goal at the end of 1862 led the government to accept large numbers of African Americans into the Union army. Even in the South, military losses prompted the Confederacy in 1865 to enlist slaves in combat roles.

Forced to include African Americans in the military, white men of power ironically tried to exclude them from combat roles. Many African Americans, slave and free, who did participate in American wars were therefore employed in supporting roles only indirectly connected with martial exploits and combat—as trench diggers, road builders, garrison troops, teamsters, cooks, servants, and general laborers. Nevertheless, a significant number of African Americans did fight in the ranks of American combat forces in every major war since the seventeenth century as militiamen, regulars, sailors, privateers (seamen on armed private ships hired by the government to fight), pilots, and guerrillas. By the end of the Civil War, two hundred thousand African American volunteers had served in the Union infantry, artillery, cavalry, and navy, emancipating themselves and the nation from slavery. In the last half of the nineteenth century, four black cavalry and infantry regiments fought on the Great Plains and in the Spanish-American War. In twentieth-century wars blacks served in combat units in ever larger numbers. Nevertheless, as late as World War II, when over one million African Americans were inducted into the armed forces, as many as 75 percent of them were placed in the service branches. Reflecting the prejudice of the time, an army staff memorandum concluded: "There is a consensus that colored units are inferior to the performance of white troops, except for service duties."

Probably the only exceptions to black participation in U.S. government forces were the Seminole wars (1818; 1835–1842) and the Mexican War. But in the Seminole wars, fugitive slaves and slave descendants fought alongside Native Americans and were among the most militant of Seminole leaders. In Creek, *seminole* means "rebel" or "runaway," and in truth these wars can possibly be regarded as the most important of black rebellions in American history. Blacks also fought with the French against the British in the Revolutionary War and with the British against the Americans in both the War of the Revolution and the War of 1812. African Americans trained by the British for the Savannah campaign of 1778 persisted in fighting white Americans until 1786 in the Georgia swamps.

From colonial times to the War of 1812, black soldiers were, more often than not, placed in integrated units, and black sailors fought alongside white shipmates. But beginning in the War of 1812 and until the implementation of President Harry S. Truman's Executive Order 9981 of 1948, which outlawed discrimination in the armed services and federal government, black and white soldiers were usually segregated into separate units, while the navy, with such occasional exceptions as the Civil War, employed black sailors in menial labor.

Discrimination against African Americans in the armed forces assumed many forms: commissions were denied to qualified African Americans, white officers commanded black units, black soldiers received inadequate training and supplies, off-base housing available to whites was denied to African Americans with the consent of the War Department, and police and courts failed to provide equal protection and access to legal redress. Although Truman's desegregation order represented a turning point in military race relations, discrimination in some of these forms persisted long afterward.

Ironically, moreover, the removal of many of the barriers to full black participation in the armed forces by the mid twentieth century led to another kind of discrimination and exploitation: proportionally more blacks than whites were placed in dangerous combat roles. During the war in Vietnam, for example, blacks suffered 20.8 percent of combat deaths in 1966, a figure 7 percent higher than their percentage in the army and 9 percent higher than their percentage in the population. The reasons were complex and revealing. Combat units in these early years of fighting consisted primarily of regular enlistees—not draftees. Persistent racism and absence of opportunity at home had driven many African Americans—as well as Native Americans and Hispanics—to reenlist in the "prestige" and higher-paying combat battalions at rates twice as high as white rates. With growing black awareness of the ironies of discrimination in the armed services, their enlistments declined after 1967. Moreover, as draft inductions increased dramatically after 1965, the proportion of blacks and whites in the army came to more nearly approximate their proportions in the population at large. Still, Selective Service discriminated against the poor, whether black, red, brown, or white, because the poor won fewer deferments than the middle and upper classes. The poor were assigned to combat units in which educational achievement and technical skill were not as critical as they had become in the support units, and fewer promotional opportunities were available. Since more blacks were poor in proportion to their own numbers in the population, proportionally more of them ended up in combat units.

Except for the Civil War, African American participation in America's wars did not bring about an automatic advancement of black status. It did, however, cause African Americans to feel they had earned a greater claim on equality. Their participation in World War I, a war ostensibly for democracy; in World War II, a war against racism; and in the Korean War, another crusade for democracy, reinforced their sense of American social hypocrisy and injustice. World War II especially was a watershed in black history. Large numbers of African Americans served in the military, 1.2 million migrated from the South to the industrial cities of the North and West in search of defense-related jobs, and their experiences spurred renewed efforts for full civil rights by the 1950s. The nonviolent, direct-action tactics that would spearhead the massive civil rights struggle of the 1950s and 1960s were pioneered by white and black radical pacifists in the Fellowship of Reconciliation (1915), formed during World War I to assist conscientious objectors, and the Congress of Racial Equality (1942), both of which initiated desegregation actions during World War II and immediately thereafter.

The black military experience to the end of the twentieth century left an ambiguous legacy. On the one hand, it demonstrated that under more difficult circumstances African Americans were and are at least as courageous and intelligent as whites in combat situations and military leadership roles. In token fashion, the government acknowledged black military equality when General Colin Powell was appointed chair of the Joint Chiefs of Staff in 1989. But the results of black military service have been disappointing in achieving general social freedom and equality, for racial discrimination persisted at the end of the century, as demonstrated by the disproportionate numbers of black men and women who volunteered for military service.

WOMEN AND WAR

Male monopolization of military command and combat seems to have been originally rooted in the primal division of social labor between female childbearing and male hunting. Women's work, services, childbearing, child rearing and nurturing of men functioned to support the fighting of men against men, thereby legitimizing the "male" values of martial glory, bravado, violent courage, physical aggressiveness, and patronizing dominance while solidifying women's social subordination. In some early cultures, moreover, women were the booty of war: they were captured and made concubines, wives, and laborers.

In European and American armies up until the end of the Civil War, some lower-class women known as "camp followers" accompanied armies on the march and provided labor and services not otherwise supplied by the military. During the Revolution, for example, women who washed, mended, and cooked for the soldiers were officially provided half-rations by the army. When fighting erupted, these "Molly Pitchers" carried water and coffee to troops at the front, swabbed overheated cannon barrels with water, and nursed the wounded.

With the Civil War came more institutionalized military roles for women with their recruitment as frontline Union hospital nurses. Dorothea Dix, superintendent of army nurses, was integral in getting much-needed hospitals up and running; Mary Walker, an army surgeon, became the only woman to receive the Medal of Honor; and volunteer nurse Clara Barton went on to found the American Red Cross. In the South, some women took up arms in a militia fashion—not for "the cause," however, but for mere survival. These small, armed bands of poor, hungry women in Alabama, North Carolina, and Virginia raided mills and stores for food and other supplies.

Camp following came to an end when military forces began to be professionalized, industrialized, and institutionalized in the late eighteenth century, although civilian business and labor services continued to attend permanent and semipermanent American military bases at home and abroad. As for army nurses in antebellum society, gender prejudice in the medical bureaucracy kept women's proportionate numbers to 20 percent of nursing staffs, but by World War I they monopolized the profession.

By the mid twentieth century such revolutionary, peasant societies as China and Vietnam and such postindustrial societies as the United States recruited women into their armed forces for roles other than nursing or espionage. In World War II, for example, the army, navy, and marines employed women in clerical, administrative, and other occupations not associated with combat. Between 1942 and 1944 the Women's Airforce Service Pilots flew all types of aircraft from factory to air base, towed targets for aerial gunnery training, and made weather flights.

After 1973, with the shift to all-volunteer armed forces, the separate women's branches of the military were abolished, and the Department of Defense vigorously encouraged women to enlist in order to compensate for possible shortages in male enlistments and in response to altered perceptions of female roles in society. Promotional opportunities were opened, and in 1976 women also gained entry into the service academies. Between 1973 and 1989 the proportion of women in the military increased from 1.5 to 11 percent. Although excluded from occupational specialties involving direct combat, women were increasingly included in physically demanding, technically exacting, and dangerous roles. During the invasions of Panama (1989) and Iraq (1991), they were on the front lines of combat.

Even though proportionately more female high-school graduates enlisted and female recruits scored higher on intelligence and aptitude tests than males, many men continued to resist the employment of women in active duty, with the Marine Corps the most steadfast bastion of opposition. Reflecting ethnic discrimination and even worse employment opportunities for women than for men in civilian society, the proportion of minority female active-duty personnel in the armed forces exceeded minority males by 39.9 to 29.8 percent in 1989. African American women comprised 47.2 percent of female army personnel and 31.3 percent of all females in the active-duty military.

American wars also had a significant impact on women in civilian society. The departure of men to Europe in World War I, for example, created more job opportunities for women. Their home-front participation as factory, medical, and municipal workers, moreover, was the final and necessary catalyst in male legislators' support for the Nineteenth Amendment (1920) guaranteeing woman suffrage. Although returning veterans reclaimed many of the jobs women had filled during the war, women's work experience contributed to the postwar upswing in their participation in the job market compared to previous peacetime years.

With suffrage, women in twentieth-century industrial, parliamentary societies gained the political power to influence war and peace. In America they, along with minorities, have shown in polling responses and voting patterns statistically less of an inclination to support warlike policies than white males and males in general. This behavioral tendency probably reflects that part of female socialization and childrearing which stresses nurturing and nonviolent conflict resolution. Moreover, through their experience of discrimination, which they share with minorities, women in greater numbers than men generally view war as another instrument of domination, exploitation, and misery.

American women have played key roles in antiwar and peace movements from the pacifist religious sects of the early seventeenth century to the broad anti-interventionist and antinuclear movements of the late twentieth century, altering both Americans' perceptions of war and women's place in society. The Women's International League for Peace and Freedom (1915) and Women Strike for Peace (1961), for example, were early opponents of America's intervention in Vietnam. In turn, women's experiences in the anti–Vietnam War movement radicalized many of them by the late 1960s. The self-evolving consciousness of the women's movement, the feminist values women brought to war opposition, and the liberation motifs of the antiwar movement itself clashed head on with male chauvinism within antiwar (and civil rights) organizations. Both women and the peace movement were psychologically transformed by the experience.

SOCIAL DUALISM

American history is often written in the language of paradox. It is at once free but slave, progressive but tolerant of poverty, idealistic but materialistic, isolationist but imperial, antimilitary yet militaristic. The apparent paradox of these simplistic dualities evaporates when viewed as the product of differences between social groups within American society.

Antimilitarism, for example, originated with two groups of colonists: the religious sects who immigrated to America in the early seventeenth century to escape what they considered the moral evil of war, and those, mostly poor, who crossed the ocean to avoid military service and the devastation of war. The drafters of the antimilitary clauses of the Constitution were intellectual heirs of the militia tradition, the libertarian British "commonwealthmen" of the post–English Civil War era, the lessons drawn from the study of classical Greek and Roman militarism, and America's experience with militaristic British imperialism. The framers were worried about the threat to liberty that inordinate executive power backed up by military force posed, troubled by the financial and economic costs of supporting standing armies and navies in peacetime, and concerned that armed forces created a social impetus toward the fighting of wars. These themes were borne by later reformers, pacifists, anti-imperialists, and antimilitarists through the twentieth century. In this century of total war, Jane Addams, Lucia Ames Meade, A. J. Muste, Martin Luther King, Jr., and others viewed war as the breakdown of interstate politics, an impediment to civilized progress, and the ultimate expression of state miscalculation and social immorality.

The contrary, militaristic, tradition, however, was one celebrating the martial spirit. At the end of the nineteenth century, for example, Theodore Roosevelt, Brooks Adams, Alfred Thayer Mahan, and John Hay criticized what they considered to be the enervating, materialist, and complacent ethic of peaceful, commercial endeavor. In the ancient tradition of viewing warrior values as ennobling and invigorating, and accepting war as merely the continuation of state politics, they urged Americans to join Europe in its imperial questing.

The militaristic tradition was intertwined with American history, a history of constant warfare, with Native Americans, other nations, and other Americans. It was also a history of military interference in politics: from the threats of the Revolutionary War officers who wanted to be paid and pensioned, to the Reconstruction army that disobeyed its president, to General Douglas MacArthur's challenge to President Truman, to the powerful influence of the post–World War II military services and the military-industrial complex in the legislative and executive branches. The principle of civilian supremacy was always upheld, but military institutions and values nevertheless have had a tremendous influence on government and society since the seventeenth century. Even the militia tradition, for all of its unmilitary character, proved to be in essence militaristic. Militiamen, for example, were less disciplined and more ruthless than regulars in dealing with Native Americans. Volunteer militia units in the antebellum North and South were champions of martial enthusiasm and the militia mystique enabled Americans to view military heroes as citizen-soldiers who would beat swords into plowshares and serve the country as presidents and legislators.

During the second half of the twentieth century, both domestic and foreign policy was being fashioned by a coalition of government/corporate "ins-and-outers," national-security bureaucrats, military brass, and professional politicians with ties to the military and corporate worlds. Military expenditures absorbed a huge portion of the economy, redistributing wealth from some to other social classes and from the Rustbelt of the Northeast and Midwest to the Sunbelt of the Southwest and West, and then beyond America's borders via multinational corporate investment in and government arms transfers to other countries. In the 1990s the policy-making elite was divided on whether to emphasize the revitalization of America's declining economic competitiveness or to continue the policing of the second and third worlds with military power. Whichever policy Americans chose by the twenty-first century, it would involve decisions primarily having to do with the role of war and the military in their society.

BIBLIOGRAPHY

Anderson, Fred. *A People's Army: Massachusetts Soldiers and Society in the Seven Years' War* (1984).

Anderson, Karen. *Wartime Women: Sex Roles, Family Relations, and the Status of Women During World War II* (1981).

Berhahn, V. R. *Militarism: The History of an International Debate, 1861–1979* (1982).

Buchanan, A. Russell. *Black Americans in World War II* (1977).

Chambers, James W. *To Raise an Army: The Draft Comes to America* (1987).

Clifford, J. Garry, and Samuel R. Spencer, Jr. *The First Peacetime Draft* (1986).

Cunliffe, Marcus. *Soldiers and Civilians: The Martial Spirit in America, 1775–1865* (1968).

DeBenedetti, Charles. *The Peace Reform in American History* (1980).

Dyer, Gwynne. *War* (1985).

Figley, Charles, ed. *Stress Disorders Among Vietnam Veterans* (1978).

Fletcher, Marvin. *The Black Soldier and Officer in the United States Army, 1891–1917* (1974).

Geary, James W. *We Need Men: The Union Draft in the Civil War* (1991).

Gluck, Sherna B. *Rosie the Riveter Revisited: Women, the War, and Social Change* (1987).

Granatstein, J. L., and Robert D. Cuff, eds. *War and Society in North America* (1971).

Greenwald, Maurine W. *Women, War, and Work: The Impact of World War I on Women Workers in the United States* (1980).

Gross, Robert. *The Minutemen and Their World* (1976).

Harrod, Frederick S. *Manning the New Navy: The Development of a Modern Naval Enlisted Force, 1899–1940* (1978).

Higonnet, Margaret Randolph, et al., eds. *Behind the Lines: Gender and the Two World Wars* (1987).

Hoxie, Frederick E. *A Final Promise: The Campaign to Assimilate the Indians, 1880–1920* (1984).

Ingraham, Larry H. *The Boys in the Barracks: Observations on American Military Life* (1984).

Karsten, Peter. *Soldiers and Society: The Effects of Military Service and War on American Life* (1978).

Kennedy, David M. *Over Here: The First World War and American Society* (1980).

Koistinen, Paul A. C. *The Military-Industrial Complex: A Historical Perspective* (1980).

Linderman, Gerald F. *The Mirror of War: American Society and the Spanish-American War* (1974).

McCormick, Thomas J. *America's Half-Century: U.S. Foreign Policy in the Cold War* (1989).

MacPherson, Myra. *Long Time Passing: Vietnam and the Haunted Generation* (1984).

Martin, James K., and Mark E. Lender. *A Respectable Army: The Military Origins of the Republic, 1763–1789* (1982).

Melman, Seymour. *The Permanent War Economy* (1974).

Nalty, Bernard C. *Strength for the Fight: A History of Black Americans in the Military* (1986).

Nef, John Ulric. *War and Human Progress: An Essay on the Rise of Industrial Civilization* (1950).

Patton, Gerald W. *War and Race: The Black Officer in the American Military, 1915 to 1941* (1981).

Polenberg, Richard. *War and Society: The United States, 1941–1945* (1972).

Preston, Richard A., Alex Roland, and Sydney F. Wise. *Men in Arms: A History of Warfare and Its Interrelationships with Western Society* (1991).

Royster, Charles. *A Revolutionary People at War: The Continental Army and American Character, 1775–1783* (1980).

Sherry, Michael S. *The Rise of American Air Power: The Creation of Armageddon* (1987).

Sivard, Ruth L. *World Military and Social Expenditures, 1989* (1989).

Smith, George Winston, and Charles Burnet Judah, eds. *Life in the North During the Civil War: A Source History* (1966).

Strauss, William A., and Lawrence M. Baskir. *Chance and Circumstance: The Draft, the War, and the Vietnam Generation* (1978).

Valle, James E. *Rocks and Shoals: Order and Discipline in the Old Navy, 1800–1861* (1980).

Weeks, Philip, ed. *The American Indian Experience: A Profile, 1524 to Present* (1988).

Weigley, Russell F. *History of the United States Army* (1984).

SEE ALSO **The Military; Minorities and Work; The Nuclear Age; Peace Movements; Women and Work.**